THE

ENCYCLOPEDIA

OF

PROTESTANTISM

THE

ENCYCLOPEDIA

OF

PROTESTANTISM

VOLUME 1
A–C

HANS J. HILLERBRAND

EDITOR

Routledge
New York   London

Published in 2004 by

Routledge
29 West 35ᵗʰ Street
New York, NY 10001-2299
www.routledge-ny.com

Published in Great Britain by
Routledge
11 New Fetter Lane
London EC4P 4EE
www.routledge.co.uk

Routledge is an imprint of Taylor & Francis Books, Inc.

10   9   8   7   6   5   4   3   2   1

Printed on acid-free, 250-year-life paper
Manufactured in the United States of America

Library of Congress Cataloging-in-Publication Data

Encyclopedia of Protestantism / Hans J. Hillerbrand, editor.
   p. cm.
Includes bibliographical references and index.
  ISBN 0-415-92472-3 (set)
  1. Protestantism—Encyclopedias. I. Hillerbrand, Hans Joachim.
BX4811.3.E53 2003
280′.4′03—dc21

2003011582

Contents

Entry List A–Z

A

Abortion
Absolutism
Acts and Monuments
Adams, Hannah
Adiaphora
Advent Christian Church
Aesthetics
Africa
African American Protestantism
African Instituted Churches
African Methodist Episcopal Church
African Methodist Episcopal Zion Church
African Theology
Agricola, Michael
All-Union Council of Evangelical Christians-Baptists
Allen, Richard
Allen, Roland
Alline, Henry
Altars
Althusius, Johannes
Amana
American Baptist Churches
American Bible Society
American Bible Union
American Board of Commissioners for Foreign Missions
American Colonization Society
American Friends Service Committee
American Lutheran Church
American Missionary Association
American Society of Church History
American Unitarian Association
Americans United for the Separation of Church and State
Ames, William
Amish
Amissah, Samuel Hanson
Amsdorf, Nikolaus von
Anabaptism
Anderson, Rufus
Andrewes, Lancelot
Andrews, Charles Freer
Anglican Chant
Anglicanism
Anglo-Catholicism
Antichrist

Antinomianism
Anti-Semitism
Antitrinitarianism
Apocalypticism
Architecture, Church
Arminianism
Arminius, Jacobus
Arndt, Johann
Arnold, Eberhard
Arnold, Thomas
Art
Asbury, Francis
Asceticism
Asian Theology
Asian-American Protestantism
Assemblies of God
Atonement
Attoh-Ahuma, Samuel Richard Brew
Augsburg Confession
Augsburg Confession, Apology of the
Augsburg Interim
Augustana Evangelical Lutheran Church
Australia
Authority
Awakenings
Azariah, Vedayagam Samuel
Azusa Street Revival

B

Bach, Johann Sebastian
Backus, Isaac
Bacon, Francis
Baëta, Christian Goncalves Kwame
Baillie, John
Baltimore Conference
Baptism
Baptist Bible Union
Baptist Family of Churches
Baptist General Conference
Baptist Missions
Baptists
Baptists, Europe
Baptists, Global
Baptists, United States
Baptist World Alliance

ENTRY LIST A–Z

ENTRY LIST A–Z

Thematic List of Entries

Biographical

Adams, Hannah
Agricola, Michael
Allen, Richard
Allen, Roland
Alline, Henry
Althusius, Johannes
Ames, William
Amissah, Samuel Hanson
Amsdorf, Nikolaus von
Anderson, Rufus
Andrewes, Lancelot
Andrews, Charles Freer
Arminius, Jacobus
Arndt, Johann
Arnold, Eberhard
Arnold, Thomas
Asbury, Francis
Attoh-Ahuma, Samuel Richard Brew
Azariah, V. S.
Bach, Johann Sebastian
Backus, Isaac
Bacon, Francis
Baëta, Christian Goncalves Kwami
Baillie, John
Barnes, Robert
Barth, Heinrich
Barth, Karl
Bauer, Bruno
Baumgarten, Otto
Baumgarten, Siegmund Jakob
Baur, Ferdinand Christian
Baxter, Richard
Bayle, Pierre
Beecher, Henry Ward
Beecher, Lyman
Bell, George
Bengel, Johann Albrecht
Bennett, John
Bentham, Jeremy
Bentley, Richard
Berggrav, Eivind
Berkeley, George
Berkhof, Hendrikus
Beza, Theodore

Blair, James
Blake, Eugene Carson
Blake, William
Bliss, Philip P.
Blomfield, Charles
Blount, Charles
Blumhardt, Christoph Friedrich
Bodelschwingh, Friedrich C.C.
Boehme, Jakob
Boesak, Alan
Bonhoeffer, Dietrich
Booth, Catherine
Booth, Joseph
Booth, William
Bosch, David Jacobus
Boucher, Jonathan
Boudinot, Elias
Bourne, Hugh
Boyle, Robert
Bradstreet, Anne
Braght, Tieleman Jansz van
Brainerd, David
Bray, Thomas
Brent, Charles
Brenz, Johannes
Britten, Benjamin
Brooks, Phillips
Browne, Robert
Browning, Robert
Brownson, Orestes
Brunner, Emil
Bryan, William Jennings
Bucer, Martin
Bugenhagen, Johannes
Bullinger, Heinrich
Bultmann, Rudolf
Bunyan, John
Bushnell, Horace
Butler, Joseph
Butler, Josephine
Butterfield, Herbert
Buxtehude, Dietrich
Cadbury, George
Calixt, George
Calvert Family

THEMATIC LIST OF ENTRIES

THEMATIC LIST OF ENTRIES

Tyndale, William
Underhill, Evelyn
Van der Kemp, Johannes Theodorus
Van Dusen, Henry P.
Vaughan Williams, Ralph
Visser't Hooft, Willem Adolf
Walther, Carl Ferdinand Wilhelm
Walton, Isaac
Wang, Ming Dao (Wang Mingdao)
Watts, Isaac
Weatherhead, Leslie
Weber, Max
Weigel, Valentin
Weld, Theodore Dwight
Wesley, Charles
Wesley, John
Westcott, Brooke
Wheatley, Phillis
Whiston, William
White, Ellen Gould
White, William Hale
Whitefield, George
Whitgift, John
Wichern, Johann Heinrich
Wilberforce, Samuel
Wilberforce, William
Willard, Frances Elizabeth Caroline
Williams, Roger
Wilson, Woodrow
Winstanley, Gerrard
Witherspoon, John
Wolff, Christian
Wollaston, William
Woolman, John
Woolston, Thomas
Wordsworth, William
Wren, Christopher
Wu, Y. T. (Wu, Yaozong)
Wünsch, Georg
Young, Brigham
Zinzendorf, Nikolaus Ludwig von
Zöllner, Johann Friedrich
Zwingli, Huldrych

Creeds, Confessions, and Religious Works

Acts and Monuments
Augsburg Confession
Augsburg Confession, Apology of
Belgic Confession of 1561
Book of Common Prayer
Book of Concord
Cambridge Platform
Dort, Canons of
Gallican Confession
Geneva Catechism
Heidelberg Catechism of 1563
Helvetic Confession
Institutes of the Christian Religion

Schleitheim Confession
Tetrapolitan Confession
Thirty-Nine Articles
Westminster Catechism
Westminster Confession

Cultural and Social Issues

Abortion
Aesthetics
Anti-Semitism
Art
Best Sellers in America, Religious
Bible and Literature
Bill of Rights
Capital Punishment
Celibacy
Childhood
Christian Right
Church and State, Overview
Colonialism
Conscientious Objection
Creation Science
Cultural Protestantism
Culture
Darwinism
Democracy
Dissent
Divorce
Ecology
Economics
Education, Overview
Ethics
Ethics, Medical
Ethnicity
Euthanasia
Family
Freemasonry
Frontier Religion
Gender
Higher Education
Homeschooling
Homosexuality
Human Rights
Hymns and Hymnals
Individualism
Industrialization
Jungianism
Ku Klux Klan
Literature, Overview
Literature, German
Marriage
Masculinity
Mass Media
McGuffey Readers
Movies
Music
Music, American
Music, English Church

Institutions and Organizations

American Bible Society
American Bible Union
American Board of Commissioners for Foreign Missions
American Colonization Society
American Friends Service Committee
American Missionary Association
American Society of Church History
Americans United for the Separation of Church and State
Baptist Bible Union
Baptist General Conference
Baptist Missions
Baptist World Alliance
Bible Colleges and Institutes
Bible Societies
British and Foreign Bible Society
British Council of Churches
Cambridge University
China Inland Mission
Christian and Missionary Alliance
Christian Colleges
Church World Service
Consultation on Church Union (COCU)
Duke University
Friends General Conference
Friends World Committee
Halle
Lausanne Committee on World Evangelization
Lutheran World Federation
Mega-Churches
Moody Bible Institute
National Association of Evangelicals
National Council of Churches
Seminaries
World Council of Churches
World Methodist Council
World Vision

Movements

Absolutism
Amana
Arminianism
Awakenings
Basel Mission
Bible Camps and Conference Centers
Bible Conferences
Camp Meeting
Chaplaincy
Church Mission Society
Circuit Rider
Civil Rights Movement
Clapham Sect
Communism
Confessing Church
Dissent
Ecumenism
Enlightenment

Evangelism, Overview
Herrnhut
Higher Life Movement
Holiness Movement
House Churches
House Churches (Asia)
Interchurch World Movement
Intervarsity Christian Fellowship
Jesus Movement
Jews for Jesus
Keswick Movement
Kirchentag
Latitudinarianism
Levellers
Liberal Protestantism and Liberalism
Mass Movements (India)
Millenarians and Millennialism
Missiology
Missionary Organizations
Missions
Missions to Jews
Missions, British
Missions, German
Missions, North American
Modernism
Moral Majority
Moral Rearmament
New Age Movements
Oxford Movement
Pacifism
Parker Society
Pentecostal World Fellowship
Puritanism
Reformation
Restorationism
Réveil
Revivals
Sabbatarianism
Scientism
Scottish Common Sense Realism
Sectarianism
Seeker
Seeker churches
Sisterhoods, Anglican
Social Gospel
Society for Promoting Christian Knowledge
Society for the Propagation of the Gospel
Sudan Interior Mission
Sunday School
Temperance
Transcendentalism
Travels and Pilgrimages
Tribal Movements (India)
Voluntary Societies
Wesleyan Holiness Movement
World Missionary Conference
WWJD
Wycliffe Bible Translators
YMCA, YWCA
Youth for Christ

THEMATIC LIST OF ENTRIES

Theological

Synod
Theology
Theology Education: Asia
Theology, Twentieth-Century
Theology, Twentieth-Century, British
Theology, Twentieth-Century, Global
Theology, Twentieth-Century, North American
Toleration
Tongues, Speaking in
Tradition
Transubstantiation
Tribulationism
Vestments
Vocation
Westminster Assembly
Womanist Theology
Women Clergy
Worship

Traditions and Faith Groups

Advent Christian Church
African Instituted Churches
African Methodist Episcopal Church
African Methodist Episcopal Zion Church
All Union Council of Evangelical Christians-Baptists
Amana
American Baptist Churches
American Lutheran Church
American Unitarian Association
Amish
Anabaptism
Anglicanism
Anglo-Catholicism
Asian-American Protestantism
Assemblies of God
Baptist Family of Churches
Baptists
Baptists, Europe
Baptists, Global
Baptists, United States
Batak Protestant Christian Church of Indonesia
Black Methodists
Branch Davidians
Brethren, Church of the
Brethren in Christ
Broad Church
Calvinism
Christadelphians
Christian Churches, Churches of Christ
Christian Reformed Church in North America
Christian Science
Conservative Baptist Association
Church of England
Church of God, Anderson, Indiana
Church of God, Cleveland, Tennessee
Church of God in Christ
Church of God of Prophecy
Church of Scotland

Church of the Nazarene
Churches of Christ, Non-instrumental
Congregationalism
Deism
Disciples of Christ
Dutch Protestants in America
Dutch Reformed Church
Dutch Reformed Church in Africa
Episcopal Church, Scotland
Episcopal Church, United States
Evangelical and Reformed Church
Evangelical Free Church of America
Evangelical Lutheran Church in America
Evangelical United Brethren Church
Evangelicalism
Evangelicals, Germany
Evangelistic Organizations
Fellowship of Southern Churchmen
Free Church
Free Church Federal Council
Free Methodist Church of America
Free Will Baptists
Friends, Society of
Full Gospel Businessmen's Fellowship
General Association of Regular Baptist Churches
General Baptists
German Christians
German Groups in America
Gideons International
Gnesio-Lutherans
Gomarians
Huguenots
Hutterites
Independent Fundamental Churches
International Church of the Foursquare Gospel
International Pentecostal Holiness Church
Iona Community
Itineracy
Jehovah's Witnesses
Judaism
Lutheran Church—Missouri Synod, The
Lutheran Church in America
Lutheran Synodical Conference
Lutheranism
Lutheranism, Germany
Lutheranism, Global
Lutheranism, Scandinavia
Lutheranism, United States
Mennonites
Mennonites, General Conference of
Methodism
Methodism, England
Methodism, Europe
Methodism, Global
Methodism, North America
Methodist Episcopal Church Conference
Moravian Church
Mormonism
National Baptist Convention of America
National Baptist Convention, U.S.A.

THEMATIC LIST OF ENTRIES

Preface

Protestantism, alongside the Roman Catholic and Orthodox traditions, has been one of the three major manifestations of the Christian religion ever since the sixteenth century. Its total number of adherents is estimated to be roughly 391,000,000, to which should probably be added another 345,000,000 who are members of so-called independent traditions, most of which are distinctly Protestant. While statistics of this sort are not always reliable, one may well conclude that Protestants at present comprise some 40% of world Christianity, with Roman Catholicism and Orthodox churches comprising the rest. Protestantism is not confined to Europe and North America but has been, since the nineteenth century, a truly global phenomenon.

Unlike Roman Catholic and Orthodox Christianity, however, Protestant Christianity is divided not only geographically and culturally, but also theologically and ecclesiastically. There is no single Protestant Church as such the way there is, despite various diversities, a single Roman Catholic Church. Quite the contrary, there are dozens upon dozens of Protestant churches. Some of these, such as the Anglican Communion, are worldwide in scope and distribution of membership; others, such as the Church of the Prussian Union, are confined to a single country or are solitary church bodies or congregations, such as the independent snake-handling churches of the Appalachians in the United States. Despite such diversity, which Catholics in the past used to buttress their own truth claims (since truth, as Bishop Bossuet noted in the seventeenth century, must be one, not many), all of these traditions, however, have staked out the same truth claims as have the Roman Catholic and Orthodox churches. Until the modern era, all Protestant churches insisted on the exclusive prominence of Christian truth and, each in its own way, echoed the ancient Catholic notion that "extra ecclesiam nulla salus"— outside the church there is no salvation.

This diversity of Protestant traditions raises the question of their essential identity. The name "Protestant" itself comes, of course, from the "protest" which the supporters of the Reformation lodged in 1529 at Speyer against the decision of the Catholic estates and rulers to carry out the stipulations of the Edict of Worms against Martin Luther and his followers. The term is, therefore, a negative one, even though some interpreters of the action in 1529 have pointed to the root meaning of the Latin "protestari" as denoting "to bear witness." Still, while Protestantism may well be defined with a number of positives, it is also correct to call Protestant all those individuals and churches that repudiate the authority and office of the Roman pontiff of the Catholic Church.

This Protestant diversity finds its obvious explanation in the absence of a central authoritative entity— either person or structure—in Protestantism that would constitute normative authority (and power). The Protestant recourse to the Bible, or the Word of God, as ultimate authority has produced multiple divergent interpretations of the Bible. And ever new and different theological or biblical interpretations have frequently assumed structural concreteness. Yet, it is neither fair nor theologically accurate to contrast the relatively homogeneous Catholic and Orthodox churches with the bewildering diversity of Protestant denominations—and to find in this diversity proof positive for the non-viability of Protestant truth claims. The Roman Catholic tradition can sustain its theological homogeneity through the process of excommunication or inciting the voluntary separation of dissenting members. Thereby, the Roman Catholic Church is at once able to retain its relative homogeneity but also to become the source of the larger diversity within Christendom. The very existence of Orthodox and Protestant traditions suggests that the Roman Catholic Church has not been able to sustain its truth claims universally but has sloughed off dissent within its ranks. In Protestant churches, excommunication and dissent likewise have led to separation, but with a difference—the frequent result of the establishment of new groups and churches. The phenomenon of new ecclesial structures has been particularly prominent in places where the legal freedom to do so existed. The absence of "established" churches in North America and the non-European world has allowed dissent from the mainstream to express itself organizationally, sociologically in the form of new churches, each of which advances its own truth claims.

The diversity of Protestant groupings and churches, especially pronounced in the United States, has entailed two consequences. One is the difficulty of speaking of "the" Protestant understanding or view of almost any topic—be it worship, doctrine, ethics, etc. Even in regard to the traditional and hallowed and fundamental hallmark of Protestantism, namely, the priority of grace in salvation, there are diverse Protestant notions as to how exactly divine grace and human will and effort are to be related. Accordingly, while one might assume that a reference work on Protestantism would have definitive entries on the Protestant understanding of basic theological topics, grace, to cite one example, the reality is different and complicated.

Second, there is the increasingly popular (at least among scholars) tendency to use the plural and speak of "Reformations" of the sixteenth century, which is to denote the empirical reality of Protestant diversity in the sixteenth century. Analogously, the term suggests the use of the plural for "Protestantism" as well.

This *Encyclopedia of Protestantism* seeks to offer a comprehensive reference work for this diverse Protestant tradition, both historically and theologically. In so doing, we face the seemingly simple yet truly complex question as to what is and what is not Protestant, and, therefore, what is to be included in this reference work? To cite one example: Is the Unification Church a Protestant church? The answer is simple, if all non-Catholic traditions are considered Protestant. The Unification Church then is definably Protestant, and the definition of Protestantism is simply that Protestant is whatever is not Catholic (or Orthodox).

Historically, the question may be answered with relative ease. Protestant Christianity may be defined as those theologies, church structures, and polities that consciously separated themselves from the Roman Catholic Church. Therefore, Protestantism may indeed be defined negatively, that is, Protestantism is not Catholicism. This separation from Rome took place at first painfully and reluctantly. It is a truism that Martin Luther and the other early reformers did not want to separate themselves from the church. They were forced out of the Roman Church by excommunication rather than by their own decisions to leave it.

But it is an equal truism that, once the break had occurred, theological reflection made it clear to the Protestant reformers that their understanding of text and message differed categorically from that of the Catholic Church. There surely should be no doubt about that reality—the only exceptions seem to be systematic theologians who tend to view the past from the perspective of their understanding of the present. From a certain point onward, the reformers and their successors would not have returned to the Catholic Church even if they had been welcomed as a "sect."

Theologically, the argument leading to the emergence of the Protestant tradition was over authority. The radical newness of the Protestant assertion lay in the insistence that there were two dramatically different sources of authority—the church, in its various representations (council, bishop, pope), or Scripture. The reformers vigorously argued for Scripture and thereby against the Catholic notion that Scripture and tradition were in effective harmony. All Protestant groupings have been heirs to Martin Luther's insistence that the Word was not only the primary source of religious authority but also that it was self-affirming, clear, and self-evident in its message. The sixteenth century reformers tended to be arrogant in their strident polemic that the Catholic Church did not base its teachings on the Bible, but on what they called "human traditions." That, of course, was sheer polemic, but it did point to the fact that at issue was not so much the Word but whether or not that Word "alone" was the authority.

There were other pivotal Protestant affirmations. They focused on human salvation and argued that salvation was *sola gratia* and *sola fide*—solely by grace, solely by faith. Protestants also disagreed with Catholics on the number of sacraments. Contrary to the Roman Catholic affirmation of seven sacraments, Protestant churches affirmed only two, baptism and the Lord's Supper. Indeed, if it is the definition of a sacrament that it is a vehicle of divine grace, then many Protestant churches reject such a notion of a sacrament altogether, understanding the act of baptism or receiving bread and wine as symbolic. They speak instead of ordinances or memorial signs. Protestants have also emphasized the notion of the church as a community, rather than hierarchy, of believers, a notion found in Luther's concept of the priesthood of all believers, which made all Christians equal before God.

In this *Encyclopedia of Protestantism*, the historical dimension dominates. This is understandable inasmuch as Protestantism has had a rich and varied history, not the least because of the invigorating emergence of new Protestant groups and groupings ever since the sixteenth century. This rich history, much of which has not been thoroughly studied, deserves adequate and comprehensive treatment.

This *Encyclopedia* seeks to be an accurate and comprehensive reference work reflecting the best in current scholarship. At the same time, it strives to be neutral to the extent to which such is possible, since it is the responsibility of a reference work to present fairly the current understanding of a given topic. The *Encyclopedia* is also intended to be global in scope, thereby acknowledging that the twentieth century has truly turned Protestantism into a worldwide phenomenon that is no longer restricted to Europe and North America. Understandably, however, the *Encyclopedia* favors North American topics, though it is hoped not to the exclusion or marginalization of non-North American entries. One striking aspect of contemporary scholarship on Protestantism is that its European and North American component are far more thoroughly explored than Asian and African Protestantism. Arguably, it has been on the North American Continent that the rich diversity of Protestantism has come to bear its most meaningful fruit. Accordingly, North American Protestantism deserves special consideration in a reference work such as this.

A number of editorial policies are worth noting. The *Encyclopedia* includes a judicious number of entries that might be considered marginal in their relation to Protestantism. It includes literary and artistic figures as well as figures from public life, whose historical significance, however, does not lie in the realm of Protestant Christianity. The editorial decision was to be restrictive and only include those figures for whom it might be reasonably expected that prospective searchers will turn to a reference work on Protestantism to find the particulars.

A related policy had to do with the inclusion of figures still living. The vicissitudes of life might suggest that, given the longevity of reference works, any policy of this sort will quickly face the realities of life, but the editorial policy was to include living figures if the argument can be made that the individual has played a significant role in shaping and molding twentieth century Protestantism.

In these days of ecumenicity and post-Enlightenment understanding of the Christian faith, the Reformation of the sixteenth century and the ensuing Protestant traditions often seem terribly distant and without dynamic response to the issues and questions of the twenty-first century. Lutherans and Roman Catholics agreed, in the final years of the twentieth century that they possessed a common understanding of the doctrine of justification—over which the reformers of the sixteenth century had separated from the Roman Catholic Church. Other ecumenical agreements could be easily cited. Thus, some Protestants devoutly wish to find ways to be reunited with Rome.

Despite its four volumes, this *Encyclopedia* is by no means able to offer the kind of comprehensive coverage of much larger reference works. This reality allows mention of two recent reference works published in Germany—the *Theologische Realenzyklopädie*, with its 33 volumes to date, and the *Lexikon für Theologie und Kirche*, with 11 volumes to date. As regards biographies, the *Biographisch-Bibliographisches Wörterbuch zur Kirchengeschichte*, in over 20 volumes, also available on-line, may be commended.

As is invariably the case in a project that is the work of many hands, the four volumes do not necessarily represent what had been envisioned in the beginning. Thus, if the viewer of this Encyclopedia does not find the "obvious" author connected with a given entry, the reason will be quite complex, since it did not always prove possible to coordinate the schedules of prospective authors with the editorial schedules of a reference work of over 1000 entries.

It remains for me to offer a public word of appreciation to all who contributed significantly to this work. Kevin Ohe, now with the Encyclopedia Americana, proposed this project; Linda Hollick, formerly the publisher at Routledge New York, intervened at a crucial stage to set things right; and Sally Barhydt, who joined the editorial staff at Routledge late but sought to keep things on their right track with indefatigable determination. I also note with appreciation the help I received from the members of the editorial board as well as from Sheila Davaney, Linell Cady, and Mark Toulouse.

The preparation of this Encyclopedia proved to be a more formidable project than I had anticipated. I would be deeply amiss if the last sentence in this encomium were not an appreciation of my family, which once again supported my endeavor with grace. I hope that Bonnie, together with Susanna, Dylan, Johannes, Noah, Annika, Keenan, Maximilian, Addison, and Madeleine—who must have sensed that the last few years I was preoccupied with the "encyclopedia"—will derive insight and meaning from these volumes.

Hans J. Hillerbrand
Duke University

A

ABOLITIONISM

see Slavery, Abolition of

ABORTION

In ethical discussions the word *abortion* is used to describe the deliberate termination of the developing fetus in the mother's womb. Christian opinion from at least the time of the Didache has condemned "the slaying of the child by abortion" (Didache 2.2), although on the question of whether abortion is sometimes justifiable as the lesser of two evils, Protestant opinion is deeply divided. Roman Catholic and Evangelical leaders, working together, have led the ongoing opposition to abortion. Indeed, according to *The London Times,* "the Catholic and the fundamentalist Protestant religions form the backbone of the anti-abortion movement." However, the United Kingdom Abortion Act of 1967 closely followed the recommendations made by the Church of England in *Abortion: An Ethical Discussion of 1965,* a report issued by that group's Board for Social Responsibility. The act also enjoyed the support of the Presbyterian Church of Scotland, the Methodist and Baptist Churches, and the British Council of Churches. A comparable situation existed in the United States, where fundamentalist Protestant opinion was vehemently opposed to abortion on any grounds, whereas the leadership of many Protestant churches including the Episcopal, the Methodists, and the Society of Friends has consistently favored a more liberal position.

The Protestant case against abortion is rooted in the Sixth Commandment: "You shall not kill." This is linked to biblical passages that suggest that God's relationship with human beings predates their birth. Thus Jeremiah was told: "Before I formed you in the womb I chose you, and before you were born I con-secrated you" (Jeremiah 1:3). Likewise, we are told that immediately after the Annunciation, the fetus of John the Baptist "leaped for joy" in his mother's womb on discerning the presence of the newly conceived Christ in the womb of Mary (Luke 1:39, 44). Such texts imply that personhood goes back to conception and hence that the earliest dawn of life is entitled to an absolute protection.

Liberal scholars take a different position, noting that in biblical terms, life commences only when the breath enters the nostrils and the man or woman then becomes "a living being," and that this view has been consistently taught in the Jewish tradition since biblical times. Moreover, in the only biblical text to refer to a humanly caused miscarriage the passage does not regard the person whose violence caused the woman to lose her child as guilty of murder. Indeed the text does not even regard the loss of the fetus in itself as causing the woman "harm" because it goes on to specify what should happen "if any harm follows" (Exodus 21:23). In taking this view, the biblical law code embraced a far more liberal line than that of other ancient law codes such as the Sumerian, Assyrian, Babylonian, Hittite, or Persian, all of which equated the causing of a miscarriage with homicide. That the one biblical passage to discuss the issue takes a different line is potentially significant, especially because it immediately follows, and therefore qualifies, the teaching given in the Ten Commandments in the previous chapter.

Most Protestants today would not seek to resolve such issues by "proof-texting" in this way, given that abortion as we know it has only now become possible through the advance of modern medicine and is really quite different from the causing of miscarriage by violence or poison in earlier centuries. Likewise our understanding of fetal development is quite unlike the almost total ignorance with which the issue was surrounded in past ages. This change affects human attitudes toward the morality of abortion in wholly different ways.

For the opponent of abortion, modern medicine has shown that our biological identity goes back to the merging of our parental DNA to create a unique person. It has also shown us how very early sentience and pain awareness can be shown to be present, and from what an early date it is possible to obtain photographic evidence of manifestly human embodiment in, for example, a perfectly formed but tiny hand.

Other scholars highlight different issues such as the fact that 70 percent of fertilized ova spontaneously abort, in what a woman might experience only as a late period, or that a single fertilized ovum can sometimes develop into twins or a double ova merge back into a single entity. Such findings suggest that to date personhood from conception is barely intelligible, and they suggest instead that personhood develops imperceptibly slowly through the period of pregnancy and early infancy, and that no single borderline is of fundamental moral significance in an evolving and developing reality.

However, for almost all Protestant Christians (as indeed for Roman Catholics, too) abortion can never be regarded as good in itself. It is always an evil even if for some it can be a justified evil. In practice, through the doctrine of double effect, almost all Christians are able to persuade themselves that abortion is justified when the mother's life is in real peril. Most go much further and would allow abortion when the mother's health in general is at risk, when the pregnancy was the product of rape, or when the birth of a handicapped child was likely. A few go much further and embrace social considerations such as the well-being of the existing family or even the "woman's right to choose." These latter considerations are often felt to have changed the background against which abortion was initially legalized. Almost all countries introduced abortion for special cases, but by a process often referred to as "procedural deterioration," the situation has subsequently evolved so that "abortion on demand" is perceived by some to be the reality of the present position. This "sliding down a slippery slope" has caused some popular Christian opinion to wish to tighten the liberal abortion laws of the 1960s.

References and Further Reading

Badham, Paul. *Ethics on the Frontiers of Human Existence.* London: Paragon, 1992.
Board for Social Responsibility of the Church of England. *Abortion, an Ethical Discussion 1965: Personal Origins.* London: Church House Publishing, 1996.
Gardner, R. F. R. *Abortion, the Personal Dilemma.* Cumbria, UK: Paternoster, 1972.

PAUL BADHAM

ABSOLUTISM

Although applied by historians today to the period from the sixteenth to the eighteenth centuries, the term *absolutism* was not used then. The term "absolutism" was coined in France in the 1790s to describe the principle, or the exercise, of complete and unrestricted power in government; that is, a political system in which the prince as head of government acts free, or is believed to act free, of traditional laws and agreements, or *legibus absolutus*. As the theory of politics associated with the term was discredited, the term was used more and more widely as a way of characterizing the approach to politics, and the practice of politics, in the epoch that had just passed and had ended with the French Revolution. In the 1830s and 1840s, as the political tradition of absolutism also faded in central Europe, the term was translated from French into German and into English. A few decades later, historians began to discuss the scope and the legacy of political rule labeled absolutism, and in doing so they looked into the various periods or phases and into the various forms of absolutism.

In the late nineteenth century, historians distinguished a first or confessional phase of absolutism, the period dominated by the Hapsburg ruler Philip II in Spain and Ferdinand II in Austria, from the baroque variety best represented by Louis XIV in France, and from enlightened absolutism, or enlightened despotism, as exemplified by Maria Theresa and Joseph II in Austria, Frederick II in Prussia, and Catherine II in Russia. As German and Italian historians described the accomplishments of absolutist rulers, they replaced the older pejorative meaning of the term and elaborated the positive achievements of absolutism as a necessary phase of development in the formation of the modern state. By contrast, historians in Great Britain and France never praised the victory of absolutism over traditional laws and the victory of absolutist rulers over the estates and parliaments, as these representative bodies could be transformed into modern parliaments, as in eighteenth century Great Britain. In, for example, modern international historiography, the term absolutism possesses some significance only for the epoch between the Renaissance and REFORMATION on the one hand and the period of EN-LIGHTENMENT and Revolution on the other.

Within this limited chronological range, and only with regard to European history, several aspects of absolutist rule deserve special attention. In the area of economics, absolutist rulers believed in the strict application of the economic theory of mercantilism and in a policy of increasing the working population of their territories. In the field of culture they invested large sums of money to develop their courts into centers of cultural representation, in particular in the fields of architecture, the arts, and in music. The baroque style seems to have been congenial with their intentions.

In military matters they created well-trained professional armies with long-serving soldiers. In domestic politics, absolutist rulers not only pushed through modern forms of taxation, but they also attempted to discipline the population of their realms. For absolutist rulers, increasing the work ethic of their populations was a high priority. Especially in the period of enlightened despotism, absolutist rulers initiated social reforms. Recent research has shown, however, that many of the new laws and regulations pronounced by absolutist rulers were never followed or observed by any significant group of citizens under their control. Many of the edicts had to be repeated time and again. As a result, a marked discrepancy can be noted between the norms and intentions of absolutist rule and the realities of life for average citizens in the territories ruled according to this theory. Furthermore, there seems to be a particularly close correlation between the policies of absolutism and the crisis of the seventeenth century. On the one hand, the despotism of absolutist rulers and especially their aggressive foreign policy was one of the main causes for the deterioration of political, social, and economic conditions from the late sixteenth to the late seventeenth centuries, for which the term "crisis of the seventeenth century" is used by historians. On the other hand, absolutist rulers like Louis XIV of France claimed that they were better equipped to deal with this crisis than the representatives of estates and parliaments. Absolutism is, therefore, at least in part responsible for the severe consequences of the crisis of the seventeenth century. At the same time, absolutist rulers seem to have profited from this crisis because they promised a kind of crisis management and argued that only their absolute power would be able to bring back economic prosperity and restore political stability.

From the sixteenth to the eighteenth centuries, a close relationship can be observed between absolutism and the history of Christian churches in Europe. During the sixteenth century, rulers in all European countries considered the Christian churches a part of their exclusive regal domain. Because they based their power on the theory of the divine right of kings, they demanded complete obedience of the churches; in priests and pastors they saw the king's loyal servants. This approach caused severe difficulties both in Catholic and in Protestant countries. Whereas the French kings followed the concept of Gallicanism, that is, a

policy based on the assumption that they and not the pope in Rome had the ultimate right to rule over French Catholicism, kings in England relied on the concept of Anglicanism, which had been developed during the English Reformation. Within the Protestant and the Catholic territories of the Holy Roman empire, absolutism supported the policy of confessionalization of the churches. Religious reform movements such as PURITANISM in England and Jansenism in France opposed the divine right of kings. Within German LUTHERANISM, the movement of PIETISM was split over this issue. Although Pietists in Brandenburg–Prussia supported the absolutist rule of the Hohenzollern and were rewarded by the Berlin court with privileges for the Pietist institutions at HALLE, Württemberg Pietists took the side of the estates and defended traditional law. One of the lasting achievements of the religious opponents of absolutism is the fight for religious liberties, which, in due course, would become the cornerstone in the defense of all personal rights and liberties as spelled out in the American and in the French Revolutions. Even so, in the nineteenth and twentieth centuries in countries such as Sweden or Germany, remnants of the legacy of absolutism are found in the view of the church as a state institution.

References and Further Reading

Anderson, Perry. *Lineages of the Absolutist.* London: Verso, 1984.
Beik, William. *Absolutism and Society in Seventeenth-Century France: State Power and Provincial Aristocracy in Languedoc.* Cambridge, UK: Cambridge University Press, 1997.
Birn, Raymond. *Crisis, Absolutism, Revolution: Europe, 1648–1789.* Fort Worth, TX: Harcourt Brace Jovanovich College Publishers, 1992.
Brewer, John. *The Sinews of Power: War, Money and the English State, 1688–1783.* London: Routledge, 1994.
Elias, Norbert. *The Court Society.* Oxford, UK: Blackwell, 1983.
Gerhard, Dietrich, ed. *Ständische Vertretungen in Europa im 17. und im 18. Jh.* Göttingen, Germany: Vandenhoek & Ruprecht, 1974.
Henshall, Nicholas. *The Myth of Absolutism: Change and Continuity in Early Modern European Monarchy.* London: Longmann, 1996.
Lehmann, Hartmut. *Das Zeitalter des Absolutismus.* Stuttgart: Kohlhammer, 1980.
Miller, Stuart, ed. *Absolutism in Seventeenth-Century Europe.* Basingstoke, UK: Macmillan, 1993.
Oestreich, Gerhard. *Geist und Gestalt des frühmodernen Staates.* Berlin: Duncker & Humblot, 1969.
Rabb, Theodore. *The Struggle for Stability in Early Modern Europe.* New York: Oxford University Press, 1975.
Vierhaus, Rudolf. *Germany in the Age of Absolutism.* Cambridge, UK: Cambridge University Press, 1988.
Wilson, Peter Hamish. *Absolutism in Central Europe.* London: Routledge, 2000.

HARTMUT LEHMANN

ACTS AND MONUMENTS

Known as *The Acts and Monuments of the English Martyrs,* first published in 1563, this was the major work of the English scholar JOHN FOXE (1517–1587). The volume went through four editions in the author's lifetime (1563, 1570, 1576, 1583), and each edition had a slightly different title.

The Acts and Monuments was first conceived during the Protestant ascendancy of Edward VI as a general defense of the REFORMATION, demonstrating the antiquity of the Protestant interpretation of the faith. It was to be a rebuttal of the common Catholic gibe, "Where was your faith before Luther?" At first there was no intention to focus particularly on England, but for a number of reasons the first material that Foxe collected related to English Lollards. These were followers of the English reformer and theologian John Wycliffe (1330–1384), most of whom had suffered for their faith between 1410 and 1530. Martyrology was always going to be the basis of the history because martyrs were, for Foxe, the touchstone of the True Church. He saw the whole of ecclesiastical history in terms of the battle between the True Church (which suffered persecution) and the False Church (which inflicted it).

Before any of this could be written the circumstances in England changed. Edward VI died in July 1553 and was replaced by his Catholic half-sister, Mary. Foxe lost his position, and in the spring of 1554 fled first to the NETHERLANDS and then to Strasbourg, and later to Frankfurt and Basel. While Foxe remained in exile a dreadful saga of persecution unfolded in England. Starting in February 1555 nearly 300 English Protestants were burned at the stake; many others died in prison, and many more recanted. Foxe was both deeply distressed and intensely angry. To him this persecution, which was severe even by contemporary standards, demonstrated all the Satanic credentials of the Catholic Church (see CATHOLIC REACTIONS TO PROTESTANTISM; CATHOLICISM, PROTESTANT REACTIONS). What had been a somewhat academic exercise in church history became instead an intense personal crusade.

This did not happen at once. At first he was at a loss to know how to react to the horrifying news. He toyed with the idea of returning to ENGLAND but was persuaded that the cause would be better served if he wrote the history of what had occurred. He began to collect material, but not in any systematic way, and did not seem to know quite how to set about his task. He was well aware that he had only a small part of the story, and his first thought seems to have been to spread the news of the English persecution among the reformed churches of the continent. To that end he began to revise an earlier work, *Commentarii Rerum in Ecclesia Gestarum* (1554), mainly a history of the Lollards, to include some of the latest martyrs. However, before that project could come to fruition, Mary died in November 1558, and was succeeded by ELIZABETH I.

Elizabeth acted with careful deliberation. The persecution stopped at once, but it was over six months before her reformed settlement was in place, and longer still before a new team of bishops began to take over. It was December 1559 before Edmund Grindal was consecrated bishop of London. By that time he and William Cecil, the new and powerful principal secretary, had decided that Foxe's half-formed project was exactly the kind of propaganda statement that the new and fragile church needed. Above all, it was necessary to destroy the credentials of the Catholic clergy; to show them as cruel and lawless thugs. Foxe was soon working on the brief to produce a new martyrology (see MARTYRS AND MARTYROLOGIES) of the English church, in the vernacular, concentrating on the events of the last few years. A suitable printer was found in the person of the rich—and Protestant—John Day, and financial support was mobilized from the City of London. Foxe handed over his European material to his friend Henri Panteleon, and set to work. From then on he was a driven man, deeply committed to the task he had undertaken.

The first edition of the *Acts and Monuments* (eighteen hundred folio pages with fifty woodcuts) appeared in 1563, with a fulsome dedication to the Queen. This martyrology started with the Lollards and did not ignore the continental background, but it concentrated mainly on the events of Mary's reign. It was put together from registers, court records, letters, eyewitness accounts, and the testimonies of those involved. It was a massive undertaking, and only a portion of it was written in Foxe's own words, although his anger and total conviction are apparent on every page. It was enormously controversial, and enormously successful. The following year it was supported by publication of a volume of *The Letters of the Martyrs* from the same printer. This went under the name of MILES COVERDALE (1488–1569) but was actually the work of Foxe's friend Henry Bull. Foxe immediately joined the ranks of Europe's leading martyrologists, and at once set about correcting and revising his work. This was partly because he was genuinely sensitive to criticism and anxious to be accurate, but also because the agenda changed as Elizabeth's settlement took root. As the persecutors died out, it became less urgent to discredit them, and more urgent to build up the links between the Reformation and the early church.

In the second edition of *Acts and Monuments* in 1570 Foxe corrected some stories and incorporated new ones; he also went back to the persecutions of Diocletian, adding about 30 percent more text to its already great length. This edition was less triumphalist than the first and included more continental material, but it remained a firey and compelling piece of anti-Catholic propaganda. It was revised twice more in Foxe's lifetime, but much less drastically; and by the time he died it was an establishment classic, set up by order in all cathedrals, and spontaneously in many parish churches. The later editions had over 150 illustrations, many of them specially commissioned, and these added greatly to the impact of the text.

Foxe was not a nationalist in any modern sense, but shortly after his death Timothy Bright produced an abridgement of the *Acts* that placed much greater emphasis on the special providence of England, and that remained part of his legacy. In 1632 the seventh edition was converted by its editors into propaganda against the English prelate WILLIAM LAUD (1573–1645), and the later editions never recovered their early quasi-official status. The last of the old editions appeared in the fraught circumstances of 1684.

Revisions and new editions began again in the nineteenth century, fueled by the ecclesiastical struggles of that period and driven by partisan agendas. This prompted the British Academy in 1993 to authorize the production of a new scholarly variorum edition on CD-ROM.

References and Further Reading

Primary Sources:

Foxe, John. 1563, *Acts and Monuments of these latter and perilous dayes* (*Short Title Catalogue* 11222); 1570, *The First (Second–) Volume of the Ecclesiasticall History* (*STC* 11223); 1576, [the same] (*STC* 11224); 1583, *Actes and Monuments of matters most speciall and memorable* (*STC* 11225).

———. *Commentarii Rerum in Ecclesia Gestarum*. Argentorati: Vudenendelinus Rihelius, 1554.

———. *Rerum in Ecclesia Gestarum*. Basileae: per Nicolaum Brylingerum, et Ioannem Opporinum, 1559.

An Abridgement Of the Booke Of Acts and Monuments of the Church (London: J. Windet, 1589). *STC* 11229. Damian Nussbaum, "Whitgift's 'Book of Martyrs': Archbishop Whitgift, Timothy Bright and the Elizabethan Struggle over John Foxe's Legacy." In *John Foxe: An Historical Perspective*. 135–153.

Secondary Sources:

Collinson, Patrick. *Edmund Grindal, 1519–1583: The Struggle for a Reformed Church*. Berkeley: University of California Press, 1979.

Haller, William. *John Foxe's Book of Martyrs and the Elect Nation*. London: J. Cape, 1963.

Highley, Christopher, and John King, eds. *John Foxe and His World*. Aldershot, UK: Ashgate, 2002.

Loades, David. *The Oxford Martyrs*. London: Batsford, 1970.

———, ed. *John Foxe and the English Reformation*. Aldershot, UK: Ashgate, 1997.

———, ed. *John Foxe: An Historical Perspective*. Aldershot, UK: Ashgate, 1999.

Mozley, J. F. *John Foxe and His Book*. London: Society for Promoting Christian Knowledge, 1940. Reprinted 1970.

Norskov Olsen, V. *John Foxe and the Elizabethan Church*. Berkeley, CA: University of California Press, 1973.

Wabuda, Susan. "Henry Bull, Miles Coverdale and the Making of Foxe's Book of Martyrs." *Studies in Church History* 30 (1993) Suffolk, UK: Boydell & Brewer, 245–258.

Wooden, Warren. *John Foxe*. Boston: Twayne, 1983.

DAVID LOADES

ADAMS, HANNAH (1755–1831)

American author. Born on October 2, 1755, in Medfield, Massachusetts, Hannah Adams educated herself by reading books, learned Greek and Latin from divinity students lodging in her father's home, and became the first American female professional writer. Her *A Summary History of New-England* (1799), which presented an early account of the SHAKERS and was later abridged for school use (1805), provoked a controversy with conservative Calvinist Jedidiah Morse. Adams's more popular *Alphabetical Compendium of the Various Sects* saw four American editions between 1784 and 1817, when this lucid survey of world religions was marketed as *A Dictionary of All Religions and Religious Denominations*.

Although this work primarily featured Protestant sects, it included Deism, Paganism, Judaism, Islam, and (in later editions) various Asian religions. Adams sought to represent these diverse groups nonjudgmentally, but sometimes she intruded, as when reporting her personal distaste for the torments electively endured by Hindu yogis. *History of the Jews* (1812) is notable for its unusual early-American advocacy of the restoration of a Jewish homeland. Adams also published *The Truth and Excellence of the Christian Religion Exhibited* (1804); biographies and extracts from the writings of Christian apologists; and *Letters on the Gospels* (1824), spiritual instruction designed for young women. Adams's account of her difficulties in seeking an education and a literary career appeared in *A Memoir of Miss Hannah Adams* (1832), which was printed after her death on December 15, 1831 in Brookline, Massachusetts. The monument at her grave reads: "Hannah Adams, historian of the Jews and reviewer of the Christian sects."

References and Further Reading

Tweed, Thomas. "Introduction: Hannah Adams's Survey of the Religious Landscape." In *Dictionary of All Religions and Religious Denominations,* by Hannah Adams. New York: Oxford University Press, 2000.

WILLIAM J. SCHEICK

ADIAPHORA

Adiaphora is a Greek term meaning indifference. It was a concept originally used by the ancient Cynics and Stoics to designate actions that were understood as morally indifferent: neither good nor bad but neutral in themselves. In the Christian tradition this moral philosophy was adopted and appropriated to represent matters pertaining to actions, rituals, and doctrines that were deemed nonessential to the faith.

Although the word *adiaphora* is not found in the BIBLE, elements of its philosophical influence are inherent in New Testament writings. In the Gospel accounts Jesus is depicted as challenging several religious customs. For example, he considered Sabbath laws as adiaphora (Matthew 12:1–14; Mark 2:23–28; Luke 6:1–11). Paul had a similar approach toward various issues in his correspondence to other Christians. He perceived traditions concerning food (Romans 14:6; I Corinthians 8:8), observances of special days (Romans 14:5–6; Colossians 2:16), and circumcision (I Corinthians 7:19; Galatians 5:6) as matters of indifference.

Adiaphoristic ideas continued to develop throughout the early church. The first theologian to employ the term was plausibly Clement of Alexandria in *Stromata*. Numerous discussions discerning adiaphora also took place during the REFORMATION. One of the most significant debates during this time occurred between Erasmus of Rotterdam and MARTIN LUTHER. Erasmus's *De libero arbitrio* (1524) and Luther's response in *De servio arbitrio* (1525) debated the essentials of Christian faith and their applications. In the Reformation, LUTHERANISM was beset by an intense controversy over adiaphora, the Adiaphoristic Controversy. It dealt with issues such as ceremonies and the sacraments and was triggered by the imposition of the Leipzig Interim.

See also Catholic Reactions to Protestantism; Catholicism, Protestant Reactions

References and Further Reading

Hard, David C. "Doctrinal Adiaphora in the Debate Between Erasmus and Luther and its Impact on the Early English Reformation." http://www.ournet.md/~theology/adiaphora.htm (Accessed April 12, 2003).

Horn, Edward T. "Adiaphorism." In *Encyclopedia of Religion and Ethics*. vol. 1. Edited by James Hastings. New York: Charles Scribner's Sons, 1924.

Jaquette, James. *Discerning What Counts: The Function of the Adiaphora Topos in Paul's Letters*. Atlanta, Ga.: Scholars Press, 1995.

Verkamp, Bernard J. *The Indifferent Mean: Adiaphorism in the English Reformation to 1555*. Athens: Ohio University Press, 1977.

SHERRY PEMBER

ADVENT CHRISTIAN CHURCH

The Advent Christian Church is an evangelical denomination that arose in the United States during the mid-1800s. The church was formally established as the Advent Christian Association in 1860 by a group of former Millerites—followers of WILLIAM MILLER who had predicted Christ's literal return for October 22, 1844. Advent Christians were distinguished from most other adventist groups by their belief in conditional immortality, and from the conditionalist SEVENTH-DAY ADVENTISTS by the Advent Christian's Sunday observance and the decision not to recognize the prophetic ministry of ELLEN GOULD WHITE. Conditional immortality, the view that immortality is granted to the righteous only through the grace of God at the resurrection, is a belief the Advent Christian Church still holds and was originally advocated by George Storrs. Two related doctrines are that of "soul sleep," the view that death is a state of unconsciousness lasting until the resurrection; and annihilationism, the belief that the unrighteous are annihilated permanently rather than suffering eternally in hell.

The Advent Christian Church is congregational in nature, with regional conferences and institutions coordinated, although not controlled, by the Advent Christian General Conference of America. Missionary activity was begun in 1891 and remains an important focus, with the Advent Christian Church active in more than 30 countries. According to 2003 figures, the world membership of the Advent Christian Church is 61,000 with 26,000 members in the United States, 17,000 in India, and 5,000 in Nigeria. In 1964 the Life and Advent Union, another denomination with Millerite roots, merged with the Advent Christian Church.

See also Congregationalism; Millenarians and Millennialism; Missions

References and Further Reading

Hewitt, Clyde E. *Midnight and Morning*. Charlotte, NC: Venture Books, 1983.

———. *Devotion and Development*. Charlotte, NC: Venture Books, 1990.

Knight, George R. *Millennial Fever and the End of the World*. Boise, ID: Pacific Press, 1993.

JEFF CROCOMBE

AESTHETICS

Although the word *aesthetics* is based on ancient Greek, it is a modern invention, coined by German philosopher Alexander Baumgarten (1714–1762) to signify the "science of sensuous form of cognition and representation," *scientia sensitiva cognoscendi et proponendi est aesthetica,* as he defined the term in 1739. He composed the term "aesthetics" from *aisthesis,* the Greek noun meaning "perception," and intended by it the study of what is known as the "perfection" of human perception. The experience of beauty is a form of knowledge that is not abstract as are discursive propositions. Beauty is rather the formation of a unified, clear, and individual form in the field of sensation. This felt or sensuous apprehension of the beautiful constituted a form of knowledge in Baumgarten's view.

In the course of the eighteenth century, philosophers in Britain, France, and Germany investigated the operation of aesthetic judgment, widely understood in terms of the faculty of taste. The appreciation of art consisted of the pure exercise of enjoyment, which was considered important because it engaged what was variously defined as genius, imagination, spirit, intellect, soul, freedom, judgment, or taste. The form of experience enabled by the faculty to which these terms referred was widely characterized as "disinterested," that is, the experience was designed to satisfy no need other than the apprehension of beauty for its own sake. The work of art was not to fulfill such needs as hunger, sexual desire, or any other bodily requirement. Disinterestedness has remained the hallmark of aesthetic value and experience ever since.

Taste was often described as a *sensus communis,* a sense for what is right, fitting, or appropriate that was shared by many. The history of one tradition within Protestantism intersects importantly with the history of aesthetic thought on this point. PIETISM contributed significantly to German thought in the eighteenth century by stressing feeling as an intuitive discernment and an autonomous judgment. Baumgarten had been educated in a Pietist orphanage and university (HALLE), and one of the most important aesthetic theorists of the century, Karl Philipp Moritz (1756–1793), was raised in a devout Pietist home. Yet another Pietist, Friedrich Oetinger (1702–1782), likened the *sensus communis* to "heart," the nonrational sense for what is good and right on which the faithful rely in making moral judgments. The coupling of taste with common sense gave an important place to disinterestedness, because any moral judgment was not intended to benefit whoever made it but simply to exercise the inner light or sense shared by the community. Moral and aesthetic judgment suspended or subordinated personal interest to the common good. Each act of

judgment based on the *sensus communis* therefore reinforced the life of the community. This appealed to Pietists and Puritans (see PURITANISM) alike. JONATHAN EDWARDS (1703–1758) argued that true spiritual knowledge consisted of a "taste" for the "beauty of that which is truly good and holy." According to Edwards, contemplation of God's goodness entailed a forgetting of the self and is therefore properly described as disinterested.

If the Protestant Reformation trained a critical eye on virtually every liturgical, pictorial, musical, sculptural, poetic, and architectural form it inherited from Catholic Christianity, it is by no means accurate to consider Protestantism as inherently anti-aesthetic. Some, but hardly all, strains of Protestantism wasted little time in purging religious practice of such items as imagery, organs, architectural decoration, and highly formal liturgical programs. This purging, however, did not leave churches and devotional practice bereft of aesthetic features: it might be said to have exchanged one aesthetic sensibility for another. JOHN CALVIN (1509–1564) and his followers despised how readily the human desire for God invested itself in cultural forms that in turn were mistaken for God. "A perpetual forge of idols," as Calvin described it in the eleventh chapter of his *Institutes,* the human mind is strongly inclined to substitute its inventions for the real God to satisfy its needs by being able to control its own inventions. In Calvin's scheme, nothing could be more self-interested than idolatry.

However, this did not result in Calvinist churches shorn of aesthetic value. Calvinists in the NETHERLANDS, ENGLAND, and colonial America prized a plain style of architecture and adornment in dress and liturgics. This style encouraged worship to focus on a confession of faith for which human depravity and moral self-examination were paramount. In smooth, cleanly lit walls, rigorously organized grids of pews and sanctuaries, and spare architectural appointments, these acts of piety found a visual expression of the call to gather together and practice a "common sense" in which disinterestedness was a principal moral as well as aesthetic value. Indeed, it is impossible to distinguish aesthetic from moral judgment in much Protestant architecture, music, and liturgy. MENNONITES, Quakers, and many Evangelicals (see FRIENDS, SOCIETY OF; EVANGELICALISM) have regarded architecture as a shell to contain the human architecture of the assembled community of belief. Eschewing the sacramentalism of Catholic as well as Anglican, Lutheran, and some Calvinist worship, adherents of "radical" Protestantism have practiced a kind of aesthetic minimalism, but an aesthetic nonetheless (see ANGLICANISM; LUTHERANISM; CALVINISM).

Pietist, Lutheran, Episcopalian, Anglican, and, since the nineteenth century, Methodist and Presbyterian Protestants have found an important place for pictures (often mass-produced), stained glass, and elaborate church architecture in congregational life (see METHODISM; PRESBYTERIANISM). Architecture, instrumental music, and visual adornment accompany and artistically interpret highly developed sacramental and liturgical practices in many of these traditions. MARTIN LUTHER (1483–1546) had championed music and even wrote hymns, and he made a point of defending the visual arts against a politically threatening iconoclasm in Wittenberg in the early 1520s. Pentecostal, charismatic, and many BAPTIST communities depend significantly on vernacular music and dance. The incorporation of indigenous forms of dance, recitation, and song into liturgies of European origin over the past two centuries have produced new artistic forms that have helped fuel the global success of Protestant missions. Regardless of the confessional or nondenominational tradition, the choices that communities of belief make regarding the arts contribute fundamentally to the maintenance of shared identity. Implicit, if not explicit, in such choices are tastes that form and sustain Protestantism in its countless permutations around the world.

Yet taste as a feature of the religious community should not be defined solely in terms of disinterestedness. Believers very commonly practice a passionate rather than dispassionate engagement with art forms such as music, dance, prayer, devotional meditation, and visual art with the aim of procuring improved health, fertility, companionship, financial success, or peace of mind. In this way, an image of Jesus is deemed beautiful by virtue of its representing the power that is able to provide the desired benefit in an appealing or compelling manner. The image, the need it satisfies, the particular manner of visual representation, and the belief in God's power to provide satisfaction are all shared by the community. This collective sense informs judgments that are not disinterested but are nevertheless properly understood as aesthetic because they constitute an apprehension of beauty. If IMMANUEL KANT (1724–1804) and modern formalist critics would separate the experience of the image's style of representation from these other factors to delineate an autonomous mode of aesthetic judgment, this segregation does not necessarily occur in the context of religious belief, which remains deeply interested in the robust "life purposes" of sacred art.

References and Further Reading

Primary Sources:

Baumgarten, Alexander Gottlieb. *Texte zur Grundlegung der Aesthetik.* Translated by Hans Rudolf Schweizer. Hamburg: Felix Meiner Verlag, 1983.

Calvin, John. *Institutes ofthe Christian Religion.* Translated by Henry Beveridge. Grand Rapids, MI: Eerdmans, 1962.

Edwards, Jonathan. "Religious Affections." In *The Works of Jonathan Edwards,* edited by John E. Smith, vol. 2. New Haven: Yale University Press, 1959.

Kant, Immanuel. *The Critique of Judgment.* Translated by J. H. Bernard. New York: Hafner, 1951.

Luther, Martin. "Against the Heavenly Prophets in the Matter of Images and Sacraments." In *Luther's Works,* vol. 40. Philadelphia: Muhlenberg Press, 1958.

Secondary Sources:

Burch Brown, Frank. *Good Taste, Bad Taste, and Christian Taste: Aesthetics in Religious Life.* New York: Oxford University Press, 2000.

———. *Religious Aesthetics.* Princeton: Princeton University Press, 1989.

Eire, Carlos M. N. *War Againstthe Idols: The Reformation of Worship from Erasmus to Calvin.* New York: Cambridge University Press, 1989.

Gadamer, Hans-Georg. *Truth and Method.* New York: Crossroad, 1985.

Garside, Charles, Jr. *Zwingli and the Arts.* New Haven: Yale University Press, 1966.

Gregor, Mary J. "Baumgarten's Aesthetica." *Review of Metaphysics* 37 no. 2 (1983): 357–385.

Guyer, Paul. "Baumgarten, Alexander Gottlieb." In *Encyclopedia of Aesthetics,* edited by Michael Kelly, vol. 1, 227–228. Oxford, UK: Oxford University Press, 1998.

Morgan, David. *Visual Piety: A History and Theory of Popular Religious Images.* Berkeley: University of California Press, 1998.

Oetinger, Friedrich. *Inquisitio insensum communem et rationem.* Stuttgart: Friedrich Fromann Verlag, 1964.

Promey, Sally M. "Pictorial Ambivalence and American Protestantism." In *Crossroads of the Spirit: Religion and Art in American Life,* edited by Glenn Wallach and Alberta Arthur. New York: The New Press, 2000.

Wandel, Lee Palmer. *Voracious Idols and Violent Hands: Iconoclasm in Reformation Zurich, Strasbourg, and Basel.* New York: Cambridge University Press, 1995.

Woodmansee, Martha. "The Interests of Disinterestedness: Karl Philipp Moritz and the Emergence of the Theory of Aesthetic Autonomy in Eighteenth-Century Germany." *Modern Language Quarterly* 45 no. 1 (1984): 5–28.

DAVID MORGAN

AFRICA

The Protestant churches arrived in Africa together with the colonial administrators and explorers that followed the nineteenth-century partition of the African continent into bounded territories, particularly in those administered by Britain and GERMANY, that is Kenya, Uganda, and Tanganyika. In SOUTH AFRICA the Afrikaner communities had been present in Cape Town since the seventeenth century and were an expansive force of Dutch Protestantism. During the twentieth century, Anglican communities grew in British-controlled territories while there was an expansion of both ANGLICANISM and PENTECOSTALISM in South Africa. By the end of the British colonial period (1960s) the Anglican presence in Africa was strong, whereas Pentecostal and Evangelical churches were widely present in South Africa (see EVANGELICALISM). Today there are more than 200 million Protestants in Africa.

Nineteenth-Century Expansion

European powers began the exploration and occupation of African territories during the nineteenth century. As territories were "discovered" and explored, military forces, colonial officers, and missionaries began a process of colonization. Both the annexation of territories and the missionary enterprise required international treaties to set some rules. The Berlin Conference, which took place between November 15, 1884, and February 26, 1885, provided those rules.

Previously, explorers and missionaries had mapped territories unknown to Europeans while making contact with indigenous communities. DAVID LIVINGSTONE (d. 1873) had conducted sporadic explorations of the Zambezi River (southern Africa) and the Senegal and Gambia Rivers (West Africa) and had started some small Christian communities in South Africa, Tanzania, and Malawi. John Ludwig Kraft and John Rebmann, German missionaries of the London-based CHURCH MISSIONARY SOCIETY, had also explored the possible evangelization of East Africa as a region. Kraft arrived in Mombasa in 1844 after having served as a missionary in southern Ethiopia (among the Oromo). In June 1846 Rebmann joined Kraft in Mombasa and began contact with the Chagga peoples of the Tanganyika interior. Rebmann was the first European to see Mount Kilimanjaro in May 1848.

Throughout that period London remained the center of such missionary enterprise. The rise of African Protestantism started from a British outcry against SLAVERY and the foundation of the Committee for the Abolition of the Slave Trade in 1787 (see SLAVERY, ABOLITION OF). In 1795 the London Missionary Society was founded, an organization that was not solely dedicated to missionary work in Africa, but that together with a smaller organization, the Church Missionary Society, was to recruit European missionaries as well as freed African slaves willing to return to Africa as part of the colonial enterprise. It was through the West African forts that the missionaries saw the reality of slavery, the kingdom of Dahomey being a prominent center of slave trade.

The first Anglican missionary to Africa was Thomas Thompson, who was sent to Cape Coast Castle by the SOCIETY FOR THE PROPAGATION OF THE GOSPEL (SPG) in 1752. His successor, PHILIP QUAQUE, was himself an African who acted as chaplain to the boat crews. However, the first African to be ordained to the Protestant ministry was Jacobus Capitein, a West African Fante, who, after arriving in Holland as a boy, studied at the University of Leiden and in 1742 was sent back to West Africa as a missionary.

Between the years 1880 and 1900 the Protestant missionary enterprise came to depend on the colonial powers that supported Protestantism, mainly Britain and Germany. However, after the First World War African German territories such as Tanganyika and Cameroon became British. In Southern Africa the Dutch East India Company had already settled in Cape Town, South Africa, in 1652 and as a result Dutch missionaries had accompanied the Afrikaner communities involved in agriculture.

The Protestant missionary within the early colonial era, always associated with the reign of Queen Victoria, saw himself as a preacher and teacher of the biblical message of God. The Protestant preaching was done mainly through an interpreter and the missionary would move from one African village or settlement to another. For Protestants there was an immediacy of personal conversion that in most cases was associated with the colonial enterprise of education, which at that time included learning the biblical text. In the case of the Anglicans such life in Christ also included their involvement in hospital work, but for others, such as the Scottish Presbyterians, the strict observance of biblical law was at the center of the Christian life of all Protestants. The translation of the Bible into African languages played an important part of early missionary enterprises and fluency in an African language was made compulsory for most Protestant preachers. In the case of the Baptist Missionary Society in the Congo, for example, all missionaries were put on probation for three years until they proved that they could indeed learn an African language.

In most territories Protestant missionaries had to work within a general acceptance of Roman Catholic missionaries who competed for the conversion of African monarchs, tribal chiefs, and indigenous authorities. It was clearly understood that whoever converted the leaders would have their subjects converted as well. For example, in 1884 the Church of Scotland's Foreign Missions Committee wrote to the British Foreign Secretary, Lord Granville, appealing for a blockade of Portuguese advances in the Shire River area of Malawi that would eventually have an impact on the success of the missions at Blantyre and Livingstonia. After mass rallies in Glasgow, Edinburgh, and Aberdeen, a petition signed by eleven thousand ministers and elders of the CHURCH OF SCOTLAND was presented to Lord Salisbury. After an ultimatum to the Portuguese to withdraw their soldiers from the Shire a British Protectorate was established in 1889. Thus public opinion had supported the abolition of slavery against the Portuguese and missionaries had secured a territory where Catholics, Boers, and Arabs did not have much influence.

In the case of southern Africa, Protestant missionaries supported violent conflict and army occupation to break African systems of government that impeded the rapid conversion of Africans to Christianity. Although not widely supported, such practices helped the spread of Norwegian Lutherans in Zululand (1870s), and of the London Missionary Society in Matabeleland (1880s) and in Rhodesia after the Matabele war of 1893.

Within such Protestant expansion of the nineteenth century, the Scottish mission in Nyasaland (Malawi) and the Church Missionary Society efforts in Uganda were the most successful in creating a Protestant society that followed religious practices that were present in Britain while avoiding major confrontations with other missionary groups. Once again, reasons for such territorial success can be found in the fact that Britain was a clerical society where established churches had an enormous influence on people's lives, whereas in other European countries, such as Germany, the NETHERLANDS, and SWITZERLAND, anticlericalism had diminished the churches' influence within the colonial period.

Less-established Protestant groups, such as the BAPTISTS, had a smaller presence in Africa during the colonial period because their spheres of social and political influence were reduced. For example, the British Baptist mission at the Cameroon River had to be abandoned after the German takeover of the Cameroon in 1884 and the Baptists were not able to convince the British Government of the need of their presence within German territory. Shortly afterward, German missionaries from the BASEL MISSION replaced the British Baptist missionaries. German missionaries from the Bethel Mission, the Moravians (see MORAVIAN CHURCH), the Berlin Missionary Society, and the Leipzig Society also founded missions in Tanganyika (German East Africa), whereas missionaries from the Universities' Mission to central Africa, the Church Missionary Society, and the London Missionary Society moved into northern Rhodesia, Kenya, and Uganda.

Twentieth-Century Consolidation

By 1910, four thousand Protestant missionaries were present in Africa, with over fifteen hundred in South Africa and a handful in French West Africa. The largest meeting of Protestant missionaries took place that year in Edinburgh, with more than twelve hundred delegates, but with only one African from Liberia present (see WORLD MISSIONARY CONFERENCE). During the twentieth century Protestantism expanded throughout the continent

as the colonial territories were opened to all groups. Particularly after the period of independence, evangelical missionaries linked to Pentecostal groups and a variety of independent African churches made their presence felt within postcolonial Africa.

During the first half of the twentieth century the Anglican Church consolidated her presence in British East Africa, particularly in Uganda. After a brief confrontational religious war between Protestants (British) and Catholics (French) in 1892, Christianity grew with the support of the ruler of the largest kingdom, the kingdom of Buganda. The church missionary became very influential so that by the time of Ugandan independence most of the population were Christians and of those 50 percent were Protestants. The same happened in a smaller scale in Kenya where the central role played by the Anglican Church within the British colonial administration helped the rapid growth of indigenous African communities around Nairobi. Before the Mau Mau rebellion in the 1950s, Anglicans, Methodists, and the Church of Scotland also had a strong presence in rural Kenya. The exception on Protestant presence was the Northern Frontier District of the Kenya colony where expatriates in general and missionaries in particular were forbidden to live because of ethnic conflicts and the instability of the pastoral groups living in the area.

In South Africa the DUTCH REFORMED CHURCH had a complete monopoly until the nineteenth century; however, after the Boer Wars American Pentecostal missionaries started their preaching. Zionist and Pentecostal missionaries arrived in South Africa from the United States between 1904 and 1908. At the time of the establishment of the Union of South Africa in 1910, white Protestants or Pentecostals instructed and encouraged the participation of their laborers into the Pentecostal movement. Pentecostalism grew rapidly and today Pentecostals constitute 40 percent of the total population of South Africa. Of those, 10 percent are so-called classical Pentecostals, mainly members of the ASSEMBLIES OF GOD, the Apostolic Faith Mission, and the Full Gospel Church of God, with whites and blacks in every congregation. This group includes the formerly white-dominated International Fellowship of Christian Churches. The other 30 percent include groups that have a black membership such as the Zionist and Apostolic churches, including the Zion Christian Church, by far the largest denomination in South Africa. Others churches include the St. Engenas Zion Christian Church, the St. John Apostolic Faith Mission, and the Nazareth Baptist Church (*amaNazaretha*). There are also between four thousand and seven thousand smaller churches that gather membership at a local urbanized level. All those Pentecostal groups emphasize the power of the Holy Spirit in the church, manifested through healing, prophecy, exorcism, and speaking in TONGUES.

The South African situation is not unique. In countries such as Uganda and Kenya, where the Anglican tradition is well established, Protestants divide themselves between those with links to the colonial past and those who have broken ties with European-dominated traditions. There are those churches that are still related to centralized European reformed traditions (Anglicans, Methodists, Lutherans) and others that have stressed African traditions such as healing, dancing, spirit possession, and ancestral communication (Baptists, Pentecostals in general, African Independent Churches).

One important twentieth-century phenomenon has been the rise of the African Independent Churches (see AFRICAN-INSTITUTED CHURCHES). They have posed a challenge to ecclesiastical definitions and theologies that have otherwise divided Christianity in Africa between Roman Catholics and reformed Protestants. The African Independent Churches follow reformed traditions that use the BIBLE as the central marker of AUTHORITY and revelation. However, they also include African rituals and traditions that represent a departure from worship based on Bible readings, hymn chanting, and preaching. Within the preindependence period, prophets arose within the African colonies that combined new forms of reading the Bible and praying but also challenged the existence of colonial powers and therefore were part of resistance movements of an anticolonial nature (see AFRICAN THEOLOGY).

In the Belgian Congo (Zaire, now Democratic Republic of the Congo), for example, SIMON KIMBANGU started a movement in 1921 with the name of the Church of Jesus Christ, through which he challenged the reading of the colonial Bible. He was imprisoned and died in October 1951 after thirty years in prison. From 1954 Joseph Diangienda, Kimbangu's youngest son and a colonial civil servant, took over the leadership of the church, together with his two brothers. By 1956 a council of the Kimbanguist Church had been organized and by December 1957 the Belgians had recognized it as a church rather than as a rebel movement. In April 1960, just before independence, the body of Simon Kimbangu was brought from Elisabethville to a mausoleum in Nkamba, the Kimbanguist New Jerusalem. Kimbangu had been brought up in the Baptist tradition; however, by the time that his movement, then a church, was publicly recognized, his leader Simon Mpadi faced a church that endorsed polygamy and told the story of his fourteen resurrections.

Some of the most important African Independent Churches developed in Nigeria. The largest, the Aladura (the prayer-people) churches, began during the epidemic of 1918 in the context of Anglican communities. Joseph B. Shadare and other members of the Anglican parish of St. Saviour's at Ijebu-Obode sought help against an epidemic through prayer; in a dream he saw people divided between those who neglected prayer and those who used prayer constantly. Shadare began a prayer group supported by Sophia Odunlami, a young female schoolteacher, who began to have inspirations from the Holy Spirit. By 1921 the group had joined a Pentecostal group affiliated with the American Faith Tabernacle. On January 18, 1925, the Aladura group had its first independent meeting in Ibadan and groups affiliated with the ethnic Yoruba spread throughout Yorubaland. There are other Aladura congregations in Sierra Leone, Liberia, and Ghana. Vestments and gowns, rosaries, and crosses are used widely among Aladura congregations following symbolic theologies associated with the Anglican Church.

Since the 1970s Pentecostalism has provided a third response to the indigenization of African Protestant churches. The previous two, Ethiopian churches and Aladura, had provided a challenge to the colonial model of European Christianity. Most of these new congregations have their beginnings in groups of youth and women who challenged the reformed churches' European understanding of Christian life. Such congregations and fellowships relate themselves to the Assemblies of God and the Church of God but they also integrate elements of African society that they feel have enriched their understanding of the coming of the Holy Spirit and its role in the church today. Within such fellowships the emphasis is on the prosperity given by God and the blessings associated with the Old Testament. Such association of blessings/ richness and sin/poverty is close to the African model of traditional prosperity in which land or cattle were the signs of a fruitful life in community.

Despite being criticized by the reformed churches, these congregations have grown rapidly in the past twenty years, particularly in West Africa, a region otherwise dominated by Islam. However, what unites these "new churches" with the older reformed traditions is the democratic and egalitarian access to God and God's blessings, not mediated by ritual leaders but available through the Bible and through communal sessions of prayer and healing. For example, the Precious Stones fellowship, a group of women in Zimbabwe, originally related to the Families of God Pentecostal Group, began when the wife of the founder of the Families of God, Dr. R. Wutaunashe, had a vision from God in 1990. She saw a stream where stones were washed and in that vision she concentrated in a particular gem that was in the water. That group of women gathers in daily prayer to celebrate motherhood and the blessings of God on African women and girls. They perceive themselves as foundation stones for society and they challenge the patriarchal values given by traditional African societies. For some commentators they are part of a feminist discourse within Protestantism in Africa; for others they reiterate the patriarchal dominance within African society in general and African Protestantism in particular.

Geographical Distribution

There are pockets of Christians in the Northern African region; however, most of them belong to the Roman Catholic tradition within expatriate communities. Within sub-Saharan Africa the largest number of Protestants are located in East and southern Africa. Statistics per country (in percent, starting with Benin): Angola, 100,000; Benin, 10; Botswana, 30; Burkina Faso, 10; Burundi, 30; Cameroon, 10; Cape Verde, 2; Central African Republic, 25; Chad, 5; Democratic Republic of Congo, 5; Republic of the Congo, 5; Cote d'Ivoire, 6.6; Djibouti, 0.1; Equatorial Guinea, 2; Eritrea, 10; Ethiopia, 5; Gabon, 10; The Gambia, 5; Ghana, 30; Guinea, 1; Guinea-Bissau, 5; Kenya, 25; Lesotho, 50; Liberia, 50; Madagascar, 20; Malawi, 60; Mali, 1; Mauritania, 0; Mauritius, 15; Mozambique, 5; Namibia, 50; Niger, 0.1; Nigeria, 30; Reunion, 0.1; Rwanda, 5; São Tomé and Prîncipe, 10; Senegal, 1; Sierra Leone, 2; South Africa, 70; Swaziland, 50; Tanzania mainland, 25; Togo, 5; Uganda, 30; Zambia, 5; Zimbabwe, 5.

References and Further Reading

Campbell, James T. *Songs of Zion: The African Methodist Episcopal Church in the United States and South Africa.* Chapel Hill: University of North Carolina Press, 1998.

Corten, Andre, and Ruth Marshall-Fratani, eds. *Between Babel and Pentecost: Transnational Pentecostalism in Africa and Latin America.* Bloomington: Indiana University Press, 2001.

Hansen, Holger Bernt. *Modern African Spirituality: The Independent Holy Spirit Churches in East Africa 1902–1976.* London: I.B. Tauris, 1996.

Hastings, Adrian. *A History of African Christianity 1950–1975.* Cambridge, UK: Cambridge University Press, 1979.

———. *The Church in Africa 1450–1950.* Oxford, UK: Clarendon Press, 1994.

MacKenzie, J. M. *The Partition of Africa.* London and New York: Methuen, 1983.

Mate, Rekopantswe. "Wombs as God's Laboratories: Pentecostal Discourses of Femininity in Zimbabwe." *Africa: Journal of the International African Institute* 72 no. 4 (2002): 549–568.

Peel, J. D. Y. *Aladura: A Religious Movement among the Yoruba.* Oxford, UK: Oxford University Press for the International African Institute, 1968.

———. *Religious Encounter and the Making of the Yoruba.* Bloomington and Indianapolis: Indiana University Press, 2000.

MARIO I. AGUILAR

AFRICAN AMERICAN PROTESTANTISM

African American Protestants have been historically divided between two major streams of denominational adherents: those who have remained in predominantly white mainline denominations and those who have separated into predominantly black denominations. More than 80 percent of African American Protestants have chosen membership in the black denominations. The reasons for separation involved the legacy of slavery, acts of racism, issues of full ordination as clergy and election as bishops, and the desire for independence and autonomy from white control. Racial factors have also been involved for African Americans who belonged to predominantly black churches within white denominations.

The Legacy of Slavery and the Establishment of Black Churches

African American Christianity was a product of the fusion of elements from traditional African religions and Euro-American Protestantism during the several centuries of SLAVERY and the period of Jim Crow segregation that followed it. With the exception of the colony of Maryland, which came under Catholic influence, most of the thirteen colonies were founded by Protestant religious groups like the PURITANS who were seeking the freedom to practice their religion without persecution. Although Native Americans and Africans were viewed as subhuman by some, efforts toward conversion were pressed. COTTON MATHER wrote religious instructions for enslaved Africans in Boston. As early as 1667 the Commonwealth of Virginia passed laws, which other colonies followed, that permitted the BAPTISM and CONVERSION of African slaves without setting them free. In 1701 the Anglican SOCIETY FOR THE PROPAGATION OF THE GOSPEL IN FOREIGN PARTS began missionary efforts among slaves and Native Americans, but it was not until the early decades of the nineteenth century that many of the slaves became converted. In northern cities and places such as Charleston, South Carolina, some slaves were converted to Christianity during a national religious revival called the Great AWAKENING (1740–1760) by the itinerant evangelist GEORGE WHITEFIELD. However, it was the Second Awakening (1790–1830), which began in the frontier states of Kentucky and Tennessee in camp and tent meetings and swept through the plantations of the South, that affected many of the enslaved Africans. The REVIVAL brought with it an emotional, evangelical form of Protestant piety that became embodied among Baptists and Methodists. For many white slave owners and missionaries, however, Christianity was largely viewed as an instrument of social control, used to produce "obedient and docile" slaves.

Despite the many efforts to hinder or control their religious life, religion became the only institutional area where African slaves exercised a measure of freedom. Sometimes stealing off to the backwoods and bayous of southern plantations, or meeting clandestinely in the slave quarters, and at times even openly in services with whites present, they performed their own rituals, songs, and other cultural forms of religious worship. They also [developed] their own preachers and leaders so that the "invisible institution"—the underground slave religion—could effectively merge with the rise of institutional black churches in the latter half of the eighteenth and early nineteenth centuries. During several centuries of slavery, most political, economic, educational, and other cultural and social institutions were deemed illegal for blacks and remained relatively undeveloped. As the only significant social institution other than the family open to blacks, black churches took on multiple roles and burdens that differed from their white counterparts.

African American Baptist and Methodist Churches and Denominations

Emerging from the "invisible institution" of slave religion, the first known black churches arose before the American War of Independence with the establishment of the African Baptist or "Bluestone" Church on the William Byrd plantation near the Bluestone River in Mecklenberg, Virginia, in 1758, and the Silver Bluff Baptist Church on the South Carolina bank of the Savannah River sometime between 1750 and 1775. These first churches were of Baptist origin, which meant members believed that only adult baptism and baptism by total immersion in water were doctrinally correct. They also supported a congregational POLITY that asserted the autonomy of a congregation to choose its own pastor and to make decisions independent of any larger association. Early Baptist preachers George Liele, Andrew Bryan, and Jesse Peters (also called Jesse Galphin) were instrumental in founding the Springfield Baptist Church of Augusta, Georgia, and the First African Baptist and First Bryan Baptist churches of Savannah, Georgia. Liele became a missionary to Jamaica in 1783 and established the first Baptist churches there.

Whereas the Baptists founded the first black churches, it was the Methodists who organized the first black denominations, which also became the first national associations for African Americans. In 1787 former slaves RICHARD ALLEN (1760–1831) and Ab-

salom Jones established the Free African Society of Philadelphia, a mutual aid and benevolent society that assumed both secular and religious functions. Allen, Jones, and several black worshipers withdrew from the St. George's Methodist Episcopal Church in Philadelphia after being pulled from their knees during worship in a gallery they did not know was closed to black Christians. In protest, "All went out of the church in a body," according to Allen, "and they were no more plagued with [us] in that church." Two black churches arose out of the Free African Society. In 1790 Richard Allen founded the African Church that eventually was called the Mother Bethel African Methodist Episcopal Church, the mother church of African Methodism, whereas Absalom Jones became the rector of the St. Thomas African Episcopal Church in 1794. In New York City similar incidents of segregation during worship led to the withdrawal of the black members from the John Street Methodist Episcopal Church near Wall Street. Jealousy and competition for new members, however, resulted in the inability of both black Methodist movements on the East Coast to unite in one body.

The central questions of the full ordination of black preachers as clergy, the election of blacks as bishops (episcopacy), the desire for worship in their own cultural style, and issues of black independence and control of their own religious institutions finally led to the establishment of two black Methodist denominations. The "Allenites" of Philadelphia and Baltimore established the AFRICAN METHODIST EPISCOPAL (A.M.E.) CHURCH as a denomination in 1816 and elected Richard Allen as its first bishop. The Rev. Daniel Coker became the first A.M.E. missionary to Africa in 1820. In New York City Peter Williams and Francis Jacobs along with James Varick of Newburgh, New York, founded the AFRICAN METHODIST EPISCOPAL ZION CHURCH in 1821, led by Bishop James Varick. Both denominations became the institutional base of an incipient black middle class of free Negroes, and they adopted and adapted many of the organizational structures, worship rituals, and disciplinary rules of the Methodist Episcopal Church from which they withdrew. These included a connectional polity in which a bishop appointed pastors to churches, symbolic baptism by sprinkling water on the head rather than full immersion, and the system of itinerancy or circuit riding, which moved clergy to different churches after a designated number of years.

The A.M.E. Church distinguished itself in the field of education with the founding of Wilberforce University in 1857 by Bishop Daniel Payne, its first president. Although the A.M.E. church participated in the movement to abolish slavery, with Richard Allen using Mother Bethel as a hiding place for escaped slaves in the underground railroad (a system in which abolitionists helped blacks flee the slave states for safety in the North or Canada), Zionites became the leaders of abolitionism. Long known as the "Freedom Church," the A.M.E. Zion Church claimed such abolition luminaries as Sojourner Truth, Harriet Tubman, Rev. Jermain Louguen, Catherine Harris, Rev. Thomas James, and FREDERICK DOUGLASS, who was licensed as an A.M.E. Zion preacher in Rochester, New York. The A.M.E. Zion denomination was also the first of all Christian denominations, black or white, to extend the vote and full clerical ordination to women in 1898. Although both the A.M.E. Church and the A.M.E. Zion Church originated as northern black denominations, during the CIVIL WAR (1861–1865) they also sent missionaries to follow the Union Army's march through the South and recruit blacks and their churches to their fold. As a result, South Carolina has the largest number of A.M.E. churches in the United States, and North Carolina has emerged as the A.M.E. Zion stronghold.

The issue of slavery split the Methodist Episcopal Church in 1844 into northern and southern branches. The question of whether one could be a bishop in good standing in the denomination and a slave owner at the same time became the divisive issue. The split in Methodism foreshadowed the greater division of the country between the northern Union and the southern Confederacy during the Civil War. In 1866 the General Conference of the Methodist Episcopal Church, South—in response to the twin pressures of blacks who wanted autonomy and whites who wanted to dispense with the black membership—made arrangements for the eventual withdrawal of its black constituents at their petition. Thus the third black Methodist denomination, the Colored Methodist Episcopal Church in America, was founded in 1870 by Bishops William H. Miles and Richard H. Vanderhorst. Headquartered in Jackson, Tennessee, the denomination replaced the name "Colored" with "Christian" in 1954.

Although they had the earliest churches and the largest constituency of African American congregants, the black Baptists did not organize a national denomination until 1895 when the NATIONAL BAPTIST CONVENTION, USA (NBC, USA) was established. Its first president was the Rev. E. C. Morris. However, the principle of congregational autonomy plus the charismatic force of strong-willed pastors led to a number of denominational schisms. In 1897 the LOTT CARY FOREIGN MISSIONARY CONVENTION broke away. The NBC, USA experienced schism twice more in the twentieth century, once in 1915 with the formation of the NATIONAL BAPTIST CONVENTION OF AMERICA in a dispute over the control and ownership of a publishing house in Nashville, Tennessee, and again in 1961 with the organizing of the PROGRESSIVE NATIONAL

BAPTIST CONVENTION (PNBC). Led by the Rev. Dr. Gardner Taylor of New York's Concord Baptist Church, who became the first President of the PNBC, the supporters of DR. MARTIN LUTHER KING JR. (1929–1968) challenged the status quo of the NBC, USA and eventually withdrew to form the more politically progressive denomination.

African American Holiness and Pentecostal Churches and Denominations

In his memoirs JOHN WESLEY (1703–1791), the founder of Methodism, stated his belief that the attainment of "spiritual perfection" was possible in this life. This belief fueled the Holiness/Pentecostal movement among blacks and whites that arose in 1867 with the establishment of the National Camp Meeting Association for the Promotion of Holiness (see HOLINESS MOVEMENT). Members believed that a second blessing of the Holy Spirit or experience of "sanctification" was required beyond the act of individual SALVATION ("being saved" or "born again"). This blessing was manifested in a cathartic emotional experience that left some believers rolling in spasms on the floor ("falling out"), whereas others engaged in the uncontrollable movements of the "holy dance." These behaviors led to the popularized label of Holiness Christians as "holy rollers." In the quest to become more holy, a rigid and disciplined lifestyle evolved.

Among African Americans, the Holiness/Pentecostal movement became the major carrier of black folk cultural practices that middle-class black Baptists and Methodists attempted to discard in their desire to achieve the "order and decorum" of the worship services of their white counterparts. More foot stomping, handclapping, tambourine banging, and shouting occurred in the emotional cauldrons of the "sanctified people." Women members often wore modest white dresses and head coverings to symbolize their purity and quest for a more holy life. The massive black migrations to northern cities in the twentieth century gave rise to numerous sanctified "storefront" churches with names such as the "Fire Baptized Holiness Church." Because the sanctified churches also allowed horns, guitars, drums, and other musical instruments in their services, they also became the musical training ground for many African American blues and jazz musicians, and a dynamic interaction developed between the storefront church and the nightclub. For example, Thomas Dorsey, or Georgia Tom as he was known on the nightclub circuit, learned to play the piano in church and eventually brought the blues back to the churches in the form of "Gospel music" in the 1920s. His most famous song was "Precious Lord, Take My Hand."

The modern Pentecostal movement in the United States includes both black and white people and dates from the Azusa Street Revival held in Los Angeles, California, from 1906 to 1909 under the leadership of William J. Seymour, a black Holiness preacher. After attending the Azusa Street Revival in 1907, Elder Charles Harrison Mason, a black preacher from Memphis, Tennessee, led his Holiness group into PENTE- COSTALISM in that same year. Mason became the founding bishop of the largest black Pentecostal denomination, the CHURCH OF GOD IN CHRIST (COGIC). Originally, COGIC was interracial, and Bishop Mason ordained black and white Pentecostalists as Church of God in Christ ministers. However, the racial climate of the larger society affected this interracial stance, and the white clergy eventually withdrew from COGIC and established the predominantly white AS- SEMBLIES OF GOD denomination in 1914. By 1924 this brief interracial experiment had all but ended.

Pentecostalism has become the fastest growing sector of Christianity in the world, especially in the United States among Caucasians, African Americans, and Latinos, and in developing countries in Africa, Asia, and Latin America. From a few hundred members in 1907, the Church of God in Christ has increased to more than 5 million members.

African Americans in White Denominations

A smaller number of African Americans have always been members of churches in predominantly white denominations, such as the United Methodists, Presbyterians, Congregationalists, American Baptists, and Episcopalians. Blacks in the United Methodist Episcopal Church represented the largest number in any white denomination, about 400,000 members and 2,600 churches at the beginning of the twenty-first century. However, race continued to be a major factor, and the majority of black United Methodists were members of predominantly black congregations, often led by a black preacher.

In a segregated society, black preachers in white denominations endured much abuse and paternalistic treatment from their white colleagues. In the mid-nineteenth century, the Rev. James Pennington, a Presbyterian minister and an abolitionist, brought his own food and slept on the pews of the church when he attended denominational clergy conferences in New Jersey, while his white fellow clerics dined at the home of the host minister and stayed at inns. In 1939 when the UNITED METHODIST CHURCH was formed from a union of three largely white Methodist bod-ies—the Methodist Episcopal Church, the Methodist Episcopal Church, South, and the Methodist Protes-tant Church—the leaders created a separate black unit

in the new church. After dividing the country into five geographical units or episcopal jurisdictions, they added a sixth unit called the "Central Jurisdiction," which encompassed all black conferences, missions, and clergy. Although African Americans in the Central Jurisdiction could participate equally as other units in the national church, they were segregated at all other levels. Black bishops could have authority only over black Methodists, and they were not widely recognized nor respected by white members. The Central Jurisdiction of the United Methodist Church was not officially dissolved until 1966 when the EVANGEL-ICAL UNITED BRETHREN joined the denomination and a decade of civil rights upheavals had ended.

In spite of the incidents of racism, the factors of family tradition, local neighborhood church, educational opportunities, and the more abundant resources of white denominations have been appealing to the African American members and clergy that have remained with these denominations. The predominantly black denominations have had great difficulty in providing pension and health benefits to their clergy, whereas those in white denominations have greater access to these resources. Black clergy have also been attracted by the educational opportunities and greater financial support in white denominational seminaries.

Conclusion

The black churches and denominations of African American Protestants have yet to experience the steep decline in membership of the white mainline Protestant denominations over the past three decades. Part of the reason for the lack of decline is the greater loyalty of African Americans to their churches, and the roles and functions that churches have historically assumed in black communities. Although primarily focused on meeting the worship needs of their adherents, black churches and clergy have a long tradition of involvement in the political sphere. They have participated in civil rights protests and mobilized the vote to elect clergy-politicians and others who represent their interests. In economics, black churches have provided the financial resources and leadership for the formation of black-owned banks, insurance companies, shopping centers, and employment training programs. Since the civil rights movement, black churches have been extensively engaged in building housing for senior citizens, the working class, and poor people.

References and Further Readings

Allen, Richard. *The Life, Experience and Gospel Labors of the Rt. Rev. Richard Allen.* Edited by George A. Singleton. New York: Abingdon, 1960.

Austin, Allan D. *African Muslims in Antebellum America: A Sourcebook.* New York: Garland, 1984.

Du Bois, W. E. B. *Economic Cooperation Among Negro Americans.* Atlanta, GA: Atlanta University Press, 1907.

Frazier, E. Franklin. *The Negro Church in America.* New York: Schocken Books, 1964.

Herskovits, Melville J. *The Myth of the Negro Past.* Boston: Beacon Press, 1969 edition.

Lincoln, C. Eric, and Lawrence H. Mamiya. *The Black Church in the African American Experience.* Durham, NC: Duke University Press, 1990.

Mamiya, Lawrence H. "A Social History of the Bethel African Methodist Episcopal Church in Baltimore: The House of God and the Struggle for Freedom." In *American Congregations*, edited by James P. Wind and James W. Lewis. vol. 1. Chicago: University of Chicago Press, 1994.

Morris, Aldon. *The Origins of the Civil Rights Movement: Black Communities Organizing for Change.* New York: Free Press, 1984.

Thomas, Herman E. *James W. C. Pennington: African American Churchman and Abolitionist.* New York: Garland, 1995.

LAWRENCE H. MAMIYA

AFRICAN-INSTITUTED CHURCHES

In this essay we consider what, on the surface, is a simple question: what is the "Protestant-ness" of African-instituted churches? Rarely is the question posed so starkly in the literature on African-instituted churches. One reason why others may not have posed this question stems from the fact that the liturgies and theologies of African-instituted churches have hardly been the focus of scholarly analyses of a philosophical kind. What we have instead are historical discussions of their origins, sociological analyses, and descriptions of their worship patterns, organizational structures, schisms, and leadership (Webster; Peel; Turner; Omoyajowo). The situation has not been helped much by the fact that many founders of African-instituted churches and their successors in leadership seldom articulate, in anything that resembles scholarly work, their theologies or what might pass for philosophical or theoretical justification for their prophetic visions. Finally it is as though scholars take it for granted that their Protestantism is obvious in that generalized sense in which the definition of "Protestant" is identified with "non-Catholic."

Much has been written on African-instituted churches. To delineate the boundaries of the Protestantism of these churches, we must take seriously the genealogy of Protestantism itself in AFRICA. Although one must acknowledge Africa's long involvement with Christianity almost from its inception, the immediate impetus for the implantation of Protestantism on African soil must be traced to the second wave of evangelization that occurred in the nineteenth century, especially in West Africa. The earlier wave that witnessed the creation of Christian communities, including states, in the fifteenth and sixteenth centuries occurred before the Protestant REFORMATION. The fact that the second wave was post-Reformation and, for the most part, was dominated by Protestant groups—the CHURCH MISSIONARY SOCIETY (CMS), the Presbyterian Church, the Methodists, and the BAPTISTS—is the reason that this history is required for a proper accounting of the Protestantism of African-instituted churches.

The second wave of evangelization was characterized by a heterodoxy that saw several denominations jostling to win the souls of Africans for Christ. That there was such a plurality of denominations could not but affect the orientation of the people regarding the appropriateness of the standpoint of one faith, many interpretations. (More on this point shortly.) Additionally, the second wave of evangelization was directed less at the rulers of African societies and more at those who inhabited the margins and other ordinary folk. What this meant was that from the onset both congregations and ministers were characterized by a seeming equality that could countenance differentiation only at the level of merit, variously defined: the ability to read the BIBLE and, ultimately, with training, expound on its niceties and intricacies. Finally, seized of the underlying principles that had developed with the Protestant Reformation, the churches that took root in the continent, especially in the first half of the nineteenth century, were solicitous of the development of an African native agency instituted in the emergence of national churches. It is in the context of the foregoing that we can best situate the African-instituted churches and make sense of their Protestant pedigree. First, we present in a capsule the basic features of the Protestant faith.

Certainly any attempt to distill from its many variations an essential definition of Protestantism is sure to come to grief. Yet there are some common features that all share that we put under the rubric "Protestant." Although the importance of each feature will be differentially redeemed for each denomination, David A. Rausch and Carl Hermann Voss have proposed four organizing ideas identified as the basic tenets of Protestantism. According to the authors, "No religious faith can live by its denials. Thus, Protestantism affirms and testifies to certain principles and concepts—principles and concepts evident even within the Lutheran declaration of protest made by the minority princes at the Second Diet of Speyer (see SPEYER, DIETS OF). These may be summarized in part as (1) individual conscience and freedom of religion, (2) grace and faith, (3) the authority of the Bible, and (4) the PRIESTHOOD OF ALL BELIEVERS" (Rausch and Voss 1987:2). Individual conscience is the principle on which is founded the Protestant commitment to difference, heterodoxy, and TOLERATION. "Much of the complexity and diversity among Protestants and Protestant denominations stems from this concept" (Rausch and Voss 1987:2). We need not go into the details of the metaphysics of the self at the bottom of this commitment to heterodoxy, although it suffices to note that its acknowledgment of the radical insufficiency and fallibility of human nature, notwithstanding its capacity for moral discernment, underwrites Protestantism's insistence that only by the GRACE of God are we saved and only by FAITH might we "earn" that grace. Such is principle (2).

Given the provenance of Protestantism in the contradiction with the AUTHORITY of the original church, it is no accident that Protestant denominations insist on the authority of Scripture "as the absolute norm of the Christian faith. Protestantism has emphasized that the Bible's central message of grace and faith, can be as clear to the average man, woman, or child as to the highly educated and intellectually astute" (Rausch and Voss 1987:3). Finally the concept of the priesthood of all believers is probably the most important of the identifying features of Protestantism and it is one that is crucial to the protestant character of African-instituted churches. Although "community is essential in Protestantism" (Rausch and Voss 1987:4), the fact that Protestantism came to be in a radical break with the excesses of a church in which hierarchy laid waste to the imagination and energies of ordinary congregants made it imperative to deemphasize "church" and promote a community of self-directing believers each acting "as a 'priest' for other believers, that is, praying for one another, confessing to one another, helping one another" (Rausch and Voss 1987:4).

When the new wave of evangelization hit West African shores in the nineteenth century there were indeed among the ranks of the missionaries those who took seriously some of the principles just adumbrated. For that group, although they were convinced that the African converts had a long way to go before they could attain the level of civilization that Europeans had reached, there was no doubt in their minds that, as members of a common humanity, Africans were capable of reaching that pinnacle. Foremost among the ranks of this category of missionaries was the Reverend Henry Venn who for more than forty years was the secretary of the Church Missionary Society, the principal evangelizing arm of the Anglican Church in Africa and Asia. A capsule account of the core elements of his thinking on the aims, method, and scope of missions is crucial to understanding the Protestant character of African-instituted churches.

First, Venn believed and was able during his tenure to persuade the CMS of the cogency of his thought that the native church should be organized and developed as "a national institution" (Venn 1969:133).

> As soon as converts can be gathered into a Christian congregation, *let a native church be organized as a national institution*; avail yourself of national habits, of Christian headmen, of a church council similar to the Indian Panchayat; let every member feel himself doubly bound to his country by this social as well as religious society. Train up the native church to self-dependence and to self-government from the very first stage of a Christian movement. (Venn 1969:133)

Just so that no one would think that the reference to the creation of a native church as a national institution was gratuitous, Venn followed it with a further explication that "as the native church assumes a national character it will ultimately supersede the denominational distinctions which are now introduced by foreign Missionary Societies" (Venn 1969:133). By the latter injunction Venn meant to communicate the vision that the national church in, say, Nigeria would not be a pale imitation of the CHURCH OF ENGLAND by whose initial missionary efforts it was constituted. Rather, he said, the church in Nigeria would creatively adapt the rites and liturgies that the English church has given it and remake them after its own image, an exercise that would remain firmly anchored on "God's holy word."

> We of the Church of England are bound by our fundamental rules to train up every congregation gathered from the heathen according to the discipline and worship of the Church of England. But our own Prayer-book has laid down the principle that every national church is at liberty to change its ceremonies, and adapt itself to the national taste, and therefore we look forward to the time when the native church of India shall have attained that magnitude and maturity which will entitle them to modify and perfect themselves according to the standard of God's holy word. Then missionary efforts will cease; but inasmuch as we have infused Gospel truth, and supplied well-trained witnesses for the truth, our work will be found to praise and honour and glory through Jesus Christ. (Venn 1969:134)

It is significant that Venn spoke about a definite time that "missionary efforts will cease." In fact, he argued that the success of the mission was to be measured by how quickly it made itself irrelevant to the survival and thriving of the church it has helped to midwife. Such success would be seen as the capacity of the converts to take charge of not merely running their local church but, and this is more important, searching by their own light "for the hidden treasures of the [Bible], to bring them forth for the edification of others, to urge upon their countrymen its warnings, promises, and threatenings, as God's word written, to present in their own spirit and behaviour a living epistle of Christ, known and read of all men" (Venn 1969:134). Hence his conclusion:

> Regarding the ultimate object of a mission, viewed under its ecclesiastical aspect, to be the settlement of a native church, under native pastors, upon a self-supporting system, it should be borne in mind that the progress of a mission mainly depends upon the training up and the location of native pastors, and that as it has been happily expressed, the euthanasia of a mission takes place when a missionary, surrounded by well-trained native congregations, under native pastors, is able to resign all pastoral work into their hands, and gradually to relax his superintendence over the pastors themselves, till it insensibly ceases; and so the mission passes into a settled Christian community. (Venn 1969:137)

The model of church-making just described was that through which many Africans were introduced to Christianity in the early part of the nineteenth century. Lamentably, by the end of that century, a new breed of missionaries had taken over from the likes of Venn and the latter were less persuaded of either African agency or its capacities. Rather than a mission that was headed for euthanasia, the latter missions became somewhat "professionalized"; rather than native churches that were organized as national institutions, local churches became problematic parodies of the mother churches in the metropolis; rather than "self-governing, self-supporting, self-propagating" churches in native communities, local churches were substituted that depended on handouts from the mother churches and overseas congregations for their survival.

That Africans did not enthusiastically accept the new dispensation is evidenced in the proliferation of African-instituted churches. Perhaps one way to understand the Protestant character of African-instituted churches is to regard the denial of African agency and the thinly disguised attempts to hold the African church in extended, even permanent, pupilage, by the missionaries of the late nineteenth century and early twentieth, as the requisite "orthodoxy" against which the Africans were protesting. Needless to say, not all protesting Africans instituted new churches. Many chose to remain and work from within the established denominations. Their protest took a different path but their results have not been any less original and nationalistic as those who are familiar with the works of some of their members would attest. Of greater relevance to us are those who went ahead to found new African churches. As J. B. Webster puts it:

> The African churches were a revolt against changing mission practice in the twentieth century, but lightly veiled under proclamations of adherence to policy laid down in the nineteenth century. Broad and liberal theories aiming to create churches culturally identified with Africa were replaced by policies of stifling conformity which sought to produce in Africa an exact replica of the parent denomination. (Webster 1964:42)

Whether they originated from revolts within the Protestant mission societies or were independently founded, African-instituted churches, in their protest against the imposition of the ORTHODOXY of the established denominations or mother churches (as identified here) illustrate the first identifying tenet of Protestantism: individual conscience and freedom of religion. They were not prepared to accept the authority of the mother churches on matters regarding their capacity for church making or that of suiting *their* churches for *their* peculiar cultural terrain. Having been socialized into the idea that *their* church should speak in *their* respective national idioms, it was difficult for them to accept that, judged by the orthodoxies of the mother churches, they were heretics, apostates, or outlaws. There were divergences between the African founders of the churches and the established denominations on matters ranging from whether drumming and dancing were to be permitted in church ceremonies to the permissibility of polygamy (see PLURAL MARRIAGE) for clergy and laity alike. For the most part, African-instituted churches have been more tolerant of polygamy. As for other cultural elements, for example, naming ceremonies, funerals, and title-taking, so successful were they in Africanizing Christianity that the African replicas of the mother churches have been forced to incorporate similar elements into their rites and liturgies. Such practices will include drumming and dancing, the use of local names in BAPTISM, and even a benign approach to the occurrence of polygamy among the LAITY.

Principles (2) and (3) cited above will be dealt with more cursorily. The most problematic of the characteristic features of Protestantism is that of grace and faith. Given that many African churches are Spirit-based, it is difficult to claim that for them, we are saved by grace alone. A fundamental aspect of some of these churches turns on the centrality of pneumatology in their ECCLESIOLOGY. Such is the position of the Spirit that in Omoyajowo's view, "the [Cherubim and Seraphim] sees the Holy Spirit as almost a substitute for Jesus and it is this that markedly distinguishes it from other Churches" (Omoyajowo 1982:122). This is not surprising in light of the fact that many African churches did not emanate from a reaction to established churches but arose from "phenomena . . . which are considered a manifestation of the Holy Spirit—prophesying, interpreting dreams, seeing visions and interpreting them, speaking in tongues and healing by faith and praying" (Omoyajowo 1982:122).

The third of the features of Protestantism to consider is that regarding the authority of the BIBLE. In the first place it is hardly possible for any church to be regarded as such that does not evince a commitment to the authority of the Bible. Second, not only do African-instituted churches accept the authority of the Bible, in their deployment of it in their healing ministries, they underscore this acceptance. What may occasion controversy is whether one who seeks to make sense of the lineaments of scriptural authority requires specialized training or theological education of the sort that is rife in the mother churches. In disclaiming the necessity of specialized training and relying instead on the inspiration of the Holy Spirit in scriptural interpretation and understanding, the African churches incarnate the fourth characteristic feature of Protestantism: the priesthood of all believers. The discussion concludes with an exploration of this element.

Recall what was said above about the origins of the Protestant movement itself in revolt against the overreaching clericalism. Whether we speak of the African churches that originated from schisms within what are here called the Protestant mother churches or those that have their birth in variants of pneumatological inspiration, they all incarnate either explicitly or implicitly the principle of the "priesthood of all believers." Because access to the Holy Spirit does not require any specialized training of an intellectual kind, it is obvious that on this reckoning every believer, as a child of God, armed with faith, has the potential to be as anointed of the Spirit as everyone else. Although some may consider the tendency to fragmentation of African churches to be a problem, if not a defect, others have suggested that it could indeed be a positive aspect. Speaking of one of them, Omoyajowo has remarked: "The congregational structure of the Cherubim and Seraphim and its belief in the 'priesthood of all believers' are an orthodox and very effective evangelistic tool. The promotion of an indigenous ministry, however, is certainly not unchristian. On the contrary, it shows that Africans have the ability, with the endowment of the Holy Spirit, to shepherd the Flock of Christ; that leadership in the Church of God is not the prerogative of any one race" (Omoyajowo 1982:221). The adherence to the priesthood of all believers explains the subsequent evolution that we witnessed in the emergence of new Pentecostal churches in the closing decades of the last century. Thanks to the exertions and achievements of the earlier generation of African churches, no one now asks questions about the "Christianness" of the African churches or the "Africanness" of the Christianity authored by them.

This brings us back to the first identifying principle of Protestantism: the supremacy of individual conscience and freedom of religion. The discussion has turned full circle. In this piece, we have examined some principal themes of Protestantism with a view to establishing the criteria for adjudging African churches as Protestant. No doubt there are other aspects that need to be explored, including issues of DOCTRINE that are standard in discussions of Protestantism. On this score one must admit that there is more systematic theorizing and second-order explorations of such themes among the ranks of the African branches of the mother churches and the Catholic Church. Although there is an increasing body of literature about these issues on the part of scholars, there is a dearth of primary literature and philosophical reflections on them by the leading lights of the African churches themselves. One can only hope that the future brings about remedies for this lack.

See also African Theology; Baptist Missions; Evangelism, Overview; Missionary Organizations; Missions; Missions, British; Missions, German; Pentecostalism

References and Further Reading

Githieya, Francis Kimani. *The Freedom of the Spirit: African Indigenous Churches in Kenya.* Atlanta, GA: Scholars Press, 1997.

Isichei, Elizabeth. *A History of Christianity in Africa.* Grand Rapids, MI: Wm. B. Eerdmans, 1995.

Martey, Emmanuel. *African Theology: Inculturation and Liberation.* Maryknoll, NY: Orbis, 1993.

Omoyajowo, J. Akinyele. *Cherubim and Seraphim: The History of an African Independent Church.* New York: Nok Publishers International, 1982.

Peel, J. D. Y. *Aladura: A Religious Movement Among the Yoruba.* Oxford, UK: Oxford University Press, 1968.

Pero, Albert, and Ambrose Moyo, eds. *Theology and the Black Experience: The Lutheran Heritage Interpreted by African & African-American Theologians.* Minneapolis, MN: Augsburg Publishing House, 1988.

Rausch, David A., and Carl Hermann Voss. *Protestantism: Its Modern Meaning.* Philadelphia: Fortress Press, 1987.

Turner, H. W. *African Independent Church.* vols. I and II. Oxford, UK: Oxford University Press, 1967.

Venn, Henry. "On Nationality." In *Reverend William Knight, The Missionary Secretariat of Henry Venn* (1880). Reprinted in Henry S. Wilson, ed. *Origins of West African Nationalism.* London: Macmillan, 1969.

Webster, J. B. *The African Churches Among the Yoruba.* Oxford, UK: Oxford University Press, 1964.

OLÚFÉMI TÁÍWÒ

AFRICAN METHODIST EPISCOPAL CHURCH

The African Methodist Episcopal (often referred to as AME church) Church's origins date to the late eighteenth century when blacks in the Northeast of the United States became increasingly offended by racially discriminatory and segregationist policies of the mainly white Methodist Episcopal Church (see METHODIST EPISCOPAL CHURCH CONFERENCE). Forming a connection in 1816 under the leadership of RICHARD ALLEN, the AME Church included congregations from four states: New Jersey, Pennsylvania, Delaware, and Maryland. With only 1,000 members in 1816 the denomination now has over 3.5 million members in the UNITED STATES, CANADA, the CARIBBEAN and South America, and AFRICA. It has at least nineteen episcopal districts, one of them led by the first woman bishop in any black Methodist tradition.

The church organization, or POLITY, closely resembles that of other major American Methodist bodies. The AME has a General Conference that meets once every four years, a Council of Bishops, a General Board of Trustees, and a Judicial Council. Other boards and commissions typical of Protestant bodies are also evident, including those focused on pensions, Christian education, MISSIONS, and WOMEN. The AME supports a number of higher education institutions: Morris Brown College (Georgia), Allen College (South Carolina), Paul Quinn College (Texas), Shorter College (Arkansas), and Edward Waters College (Florida). Turner Theological Seminary, a constituent member of the Interdenominational Theological Center (Georgia) and Payne Theological Seminary, affiliated with Wilberforce University (Ohio), are the two graduate schools in theology. The AME publishes the *AME Christian Recorder,* the *AME Review,* the *Journal of Christian Education,* the *Voice of Missions,* the *Women's Missionary Magazine,* and the *Secret Chamber.* The AME Church has taken pride in its tradition of combining religious faith and social action.

The AME churches rose in a context of evangelical Protestant Christianity, racial discrimination and segregation, and the revolutionary and early national eras of human equality and freedom. Richard Allen, with the approval of a kind slaveholder, purchased his freedom from slavery. Having served as an itinerant preacher in the mid-Atlantic area for a number of years beginning in 1783 or 1784, Allen, as other African American Methodists, grew weary with racial restrictions and proscriptions in the Methodist Episcopal denomination. In particular, Allen, Absalom Jones, and a number of others decided to establish separate worship services in Philadelphia when they were forcefully ejected from an area of the church reserved for whites in the St. George Methodist Episcopal Church. Scholars differ on the precise date, but this group also during the late 1700s formed the Free African Society, a mutual aid society that was both religious and social service in nature. In 1794 Allen and others constructed the Bethel AME Church ("Mother Bethel") and over time gained independence of operations from the Methodist Episcopal Church. This process of withdrawing from white churches because of discriminatory treatment occurred in other

cities of the Northeast. In 1816 Allen, Daniel Coker of Maryland, Peter Spencer of Delaware, and others officially organized a new denomination. After Coker declined appointment as bishop, for reasons not absolutely clear, Allen assumed the bishopric and was instrumental in guiding the church's growth until his death in 1831.

Although most black Methodists remained with the Methodist Episcopal Church, the AME, for whatever reasons, considerably outgrew its counterpart, the AFRICAN METHODIST EPISCOPAL ZION (AMEZ) CHURCH, founded in the early 1820s. The AME's greatest geographical area of strength was the mid-Atlantic states, but it expanded as well into the Midwest, had a few churches in the South, and by 1850s had established a presence in California. The greatest AME membership growth, as with other black bodies formed before 1860, occurred as the denomination extended into the South during the CIVIL WAR. By 1860 the church had only about twenty thousand members, located mainly in the northeast; by 1876 it had increased tenfold to approximately two hundred thousand members. By 1890 clearly 75 percent of all AME members lived in the former Confederacy. The AME, furthermore, spread outside the United States into Canada, Haiti, and other parts of the Caribbean, and as early as the 1820s had established a presence in SIERRA LEONE, West Africa. Its presence in foreign lands would increase in the late 1800s and the twentieth century, especially in western and southern Africa and the Caribbean.

Like other independent black religious bodies, the AME Church represented the capacity of African Americans to survive and govern themselves apart from the system of SLAVERY. The AME was clearly among the most vigorous leaders in the fight against the slave system. Richard Allen organized the National Negro Convention movement, a group of black leaders discussing issues of pressing concern to the race, which held its first meeting in "Mother Bethel" Church in 1830. The Denmark Vesey Conspiracy to rebel violently against the slave system was planned in and with the support of members of the AME congregation in Charleston, South Carolina in 1822. Morris Brown, rumored to be among the conspirators, escaped to the north and became the second bishop in the AME Church. Members of the AME gave help and safe haven to those escaping slavery, publicly spoke against it, condemned it in print, and in other ways registered their moral disdain for the system (see SLAVERY, ABOLITION OF).

The AME Church has also been a strong advocate for civil rights for the African American population. Its clerical and lay members figured prominently in the Reconstruction and post-Reconstruction activities in the South. Henry M. Turner helped to found the

Republican Party in Georgia, served as postmaster, and was elected to, but later expelled from, the state senate. Richard Harvey Cain of South Carolina participated in the state reconstruction convention and held a U.S. congressional seat. Although some advocated emigration to Africa or other places in the late 1800s and early 1900s, most AME leaders and spokespersons insisted on claiming their American citizenship despite increasing segregation and disfranchisement. Reverdy C. Ransom called for a SOCIAL GOSPEL approach to solving society ills and was heavily involved in ecumenical activities to secure broad black religious support for tackling injustice. The modern CIVIL RIGHTS MOVEMENT also found strong support in the AME, represented by prominent individuals such as Oliver Brown, the lead plaintiff in the pivotal *Brown v. Topeka, Kansas Board of Education* case; Daisy Bates of the Little Rock school desegregation efforts; and Roy Wilkins of the National Association for the Advancement of Colored People.

As the nation entered the post–Civil Rights Era of the late 1960s, 1970s, and 1980s, the emergence of BLACK THEOLOGY sought to combine MARTIN LUTHER KING JR.'s conviction that the true understanding of Christianity included the commitment to freedom and justice with the by then deceased Malcolm X's views of black nationalism, self-help, and racial pride. JAMES H. CONE, a professor at Union Theological Seminary and an AME member, became the chief spokesperson for Black Theology in his many books and articles on race, religion, and human liberation. Jacquelyn Grant, another AME member, in her contributions to the rise of WOMANIST THEOLOGY, critiqued both FEMINIST THEOLOGY and Black Theology, ultimately prompting a considerable segment of the advocates of both schools of thought to incorporate more clearly and decisively the concerns of black and other women of color. Regarding issues of gender, the AME, as most Christian churches, has a mixed record. Sarah Ann Hughes was ordained deacon by an annual conference in the 1880s, but that ordination was later rescinded by the denomination. In the late 1940s the AME Church officially approved ordination at every rank of the ministry for women. In the 1990s the denomination elected its first woman bishop, itself a first among black Methodist denominations.

The AME Church at the dawn of the twenty-first century continued its membership growth and involvement in the quest of human justice.

References and Further Reading

Dictionary of Christianity in America. Edited by Daniel G. Reid, Robert Linder, et al., 30. Downers Grove, IL: Inter-Varsity Press, 1990.

Hill, Samuel S., ed. *Encyclopedia of Religion in the South.* 6–8. Macon, GA: Mercer University Press, 1984.

Lincoln, C. Eric, and Lawrence H. Mamiya. *The Black Church in the African American Experience.* Durham, NC: Duke University Press, 1990.

Morris, Calvin S. "African Americans and Methodism." In *Directory of African American Religious Bodies.* 2d edition. Edited by Wardell J. Payne, 32–40. Washington, D.C.: Howard University Press, 1995.

SANDY DWAYNE MARTIN

AFRICAN METHODIST EPISCOPAL ZION CHURCH

The African Methodist Episcopal Zion (AMEZ) Church, one of seven major groups in AFRICAN AMERICAN PROTESTANTISM, shares basic episcopal polity, church discipline, and Wesleyan theology with other American Methodists, although it has always shown greater openness than most Methodist counterparts to the role of laypeople and demonstrated a greater openness to women's leadership, including PREACHING. With roots traceable back to the 1790s, the AMEZ in the early 1820s broke from the Methodist Episcopal Church, and pursued EVANGELISM, civil freedom and justice, ECUMENISM, and MISSIONS, officially adding "Zion" to its title in 1848. By 2000 the AMEZ had about 1.3 million members, 6,000 ordained clergy, 12 active bishops, and 2,900 churches in the UNITED STATES, the CARIBBEAN, CANADA, South America, and west AFRICA. It also had thirteen general officers and heads of departments (including Publishing, Christian Education, and Public Affairs), a Judicial Council, Connectional Lay Council, and the Woman's Home and Overseas Missionary Society. It sponsors four colleges: Livingstone College (North Carolina), Lomax-Hannon Junior College (Alabama), Clinton Junior College (South Carolina), and the AME Zion Community College University (Liberia); one theological seminary: Hood Theological Seminary (North Carolina); and four major publications: *The Star of Zion* newspaper, the *AMEZ Quarterly Review,* the *Missionary Seer,* and the *Church School Herald.*

African Americans were found among the earliest Methodist churches, attracted to their EVANGELICALISM, and their frequent antislavery teachings and concern for others disadvantaged (see SLAVERY, ABOLITION OF). By the late 1780s the earlier antislavery tenor of white Methodists was diminishing, segregation in church services increasing, and the resistance to black ministerial rights remaining firm. Protesting racial prejudice, some black Methodists began worshipping separately from the John Street Methodist Episcopal Church in New York City in 1796, while still affiliated with the denomination. These earliest Zion leaders included Frances Jacobs, Peter Williams, William Miller, and William Brown. Shortly, members of the original African Chapel meeting place built the Mother Zion African Methodist Episcopal Zion Church, which was incorporated in 1801.

The Mother Zion, the Asbury Church, also in New York City, and congregations from Long Island, Pennsylvania, and Connecticut formed a society and by 1820 were requesting recognition as an annual conference of the Methodist Episcopal Church. Encountering opposition to their proposal from the New York Annual Conference, these churches held a conference in 1821 and elected James Varick superintendent. By 1824 the Zion Methodists had made a decisive, clear break with the mother denomination. Varick continued serving as bishop or superintendent until 1828 when he was replaced by the Southern-born Christopher Rush, who served for two decades.

With slower growth than its counterpart, the AFRICAN METHODIST EPISCOPAL (AME) CHURCH, the AMEZ expanded by 1860 into New York state, the New England states, and Canada and claimed affiliations in the District of Columbia, Maryland, Delaware, Pennsylvania, New Jersey, and Ohio. In the early 1820s the AMEZ had 6 churches and about 1,500 members, nearly 1,700 members in 1831, and less than 5,000 by 1860, although the CIVIL WAR era occasioned sharp membership growth for the AMEZ and other independent black religious groups. The AMEZ had 300,000 members in 1884, 450,000 in 1896, and 700,000 in 1916. During the 1880s and 1890s Zion came within 100,000 members of equaling the membership of the AME. Geographically, the center of Zion's membership shifted from the Northeast to the South, with North Carolina becoming Zion's greatest single area of strength. Like other postwar black religious groups, however, Zion continued its expansion westward into states such as Texas, Kansas, Oregon, California, and Nevada, and into the Caribbean, South America, and western Africa.

Zion's history is full of notable individuals. Denominational historians have included Christopher Rush, the second bishop, J. J. Moore, James W. Hood, and the twentieth-century David Bradley and William J. Walls. Antislavery forces included Zionites. The renowned abolitionist FREDERICK DOUGLASS started his public speaking career as an AMEZ exhorter. Harriet Tubman, the conductor on the Underground Railroad, became a lifelong member of the denomination. Bishop John J. Clinton was a great promoter, organizer, and agent of missions among the freedpeople. James Walker Hood was a church organizer, civil rights spokesperson, active in Reconstruction era politics, and an active bishop for forty-four years. Sarah Pettey during the 1890s was a strong advocate of equal rights for women in the church and society, TEMPERANCE, and women's suffrage. With clerical or-

dination denied most Protestant women during the late 1800s and early 1900s, Zion women secured this right in 1898 when Mary J. Small was ordained elder. Other prominent women ministers were Julia Foote, an author and Holiness advocate ordained in the 1890s as deacon and as elder in the early 1900s, and Florence Spearing Randolph, who enjoyed a long preaching and pastoral career in the twentieth century.

Historically the AMEZ has faced a number of crucial issues.

(1) A strong rivalry has existed between it and the larger and slightly older AME for membership and status as the oldest black denomination.

(2) Between 1852 and 1860 the AMEZ experienced a schism over the respective authority of bishops. The 1860 reconciliation recognized that all bishops held equal authority.

(3) After the Civil War the AMEZ defined its bishopric in line with other Methodists by dropping the term "superintendent" and electing bishops for life (or later retirement) without their having to stand for reelection quadrennially.

(4) From the Civil War period into the twenty-first century, the AMEZ discussed merger with the AME and the Christian Methodist Episcopal (CME) Church, and considered pan-Methodist consolidations with other American Methodists. During the early twenty-first century the AMEZ appeared near a successful union with the CME.

(5) Ecumenically Zion has participated in worldwide Methodist meetings, the NATIONAL COUNCIL OF CHURCHES, the WORLD COUNCIL OF CHURCHES, the 1960s CIVIL RIGHTS MOVEMENT, and joint activities with other black denominations.

Barring merger or some unseen calamity, the AMEZ promises to continue its strong presence well into the future.

See also Bishop and Episcopacy; Black Methodists; Methodism, North America

References and Further Reading

Edwards, L. J. "African Methodist Episcopal Zion Church." In *Dictionary of Christianity in America*. Edited by Daniel G. Reid, Robert Linder, et al., 30. Downers Grove, IL: InterVarsity Press, 1990.

Lincoln, C. Eric, and Lawrence H. Mamiya. *The Black Church in the African American Experience*. Durham, NC: Duke University Press, 1990.

Martin, Sandy Dwayne. *For God and Race: The Religious and Political Leadership of AMEZ Bishop James Walker Hood*. Columbia: The University of South Carolina Press, 1999.

Morris, Calvin S. "African Americans and Methodism." In *Directory of African American Religious Bodies*. 2d edition. Edited by Wardell J. Payne, 32–40. Washington, D.C.: Howard University Press, 1995.

Thomas, George O. "African Methodist Episcopal Zion Church." In *Encyclopedia of Religion in the South*. Edited by Samuel S. Hill, 6–8. Macon, GA: Mercer University Press, 1984.

Walls, William J. *The African Methodist Episcopal Zion Church: Reality of the Black Church*. Charlotte, NC: The AME Zion Publishing House, 1974.

SANDY DWAYNE MARTIN

AFRICAN THEOLOGY

African Theology Defined

African Christian theology is a discourse in which African theologians in different parts of the continent and representing different denominational and cultural traditions rearticulate the content and meaning of the Christian faith in and through the mediation of African culture to make it relevant to African people.

Insofar as it is Christian, African theology claims a legitimate place in the ecumenical history of the church. At least formally, it stands in continuity with, on one hand, the theologies of the early church fathers: Augustine, Cyprian, Athanasius, and Tertullian. On the other hand, African theology is also historically continuous with the Catholic theologies from the Middle Ages and the Council of Trent into the modern period, and with the theological perspectives of the Protestant Reformations of the sixteenth century and their modern offshoots. Insofar as it is African, African theology claims historical continuity with African traditional religious and cultural beliefs.

African Theology and the Reformation

If African Christian theology is marked by a profound pluralism both in its contemporary expression as well as in its historical derivation, then it follows that the variety, range, and complex relationships among the current and historical aspects of its identity make its depiction in terms of any one historical tradition (Catholic, Protestant, Orthodox) rather difficult. To be sure, African theology has a strong Protestant identity evidenced in some of its basic commitments, which include an emphasis on the BIBLE as the sole authority in matters of faith; the sinfulness of humanity; the belief that SALVATION is available only through FAITH in the GRACE and power of Christ and not primarily through human effort; the PRIESTHOOD OF ALL BELIEVERS; and other confessional claims generally associated with Protestant Christianity in its traditional forms. However, the Protestant identity of African theology is not necessarily traceable to the Protestant

REFORMATION of the sixteenth century in a straightforward way. First, African Protestantism was mediated through Protestant missionaries in the context of COLONIALISM. This meant that missionaries did not always distinguish between their own colonial cultures and the Eurocentric religious confessions they represented. Thus today Protestant African theology is often an odd mixture of aspects of European and American culture and some Reformation principles. Second, the reception of Protestant Christianity, indeed of all Christianity in Africa, was more or less in terms of prevailing African thought patterns and cultural frameworks despite missionary efforts. The result was a hybrid, heavily inflected African Protestantism that consisted of elements of African traditions, European culture, and Reformation theologies.

African Protestantism

The Protestant identity in African theology is most clearly evident in the African reception of Christianity, which in a fundamental sense was informed by a deep "protestant" thrust of its own. Africans vigorously protested against the colonialism that was so much an integral part of the missionary effort and also against missionary tutelage. Like the reformers of the sixteenth century, African Christians persistently and programmatically demanded religious and political freedom. When that protest was suppressed or ignored, as it often was, Africans broke away in large numbers not only from Catholicism but also from the mainline Protestant denominations and set up their own ecclesial institutions.

African Instituted Churches

Breakaway churches carried with them something of the teaching and beliefs of their parent denominations, albeit in modified form and often reinterpreted in the light of their own needs and new-found freedom. The rise of the so-called independent church movement throughout the continent was the result. AFRICAN-INSTITUTED CHURCHES (as they are sometimes called) are now regarded as the bona fide expression of a true African Protestant spirit. They have been compared both to the Donatists of the early church and also to the radical reformers of the sixteenth century. As with the latter, their theologies emphasize less the formal role of the Bible, the creeds, and the SACRAMENTS than the creative work of God's Spirit among believers. It is in the African-Instituted Churches that many theologians on the continent find inspiration for defining an African difference in theology, a difference marked by a multiple sense of Protestantism: in the historical sense inherited from missionary Christianity; in the sense of being a real protest against the theological as well as cultural shortcomings of that inheritance; and in the prophetic sense of being a protest against colonialism. In addition, African feminist theologies and the black theologies of SOUTH AFRICA have all exhibited the same spirit of religious and political protest (see FEMINIST THEOLOGY, BLACK THEOLOGY). In all these senses African theology, according to its Protestant advocates, embodies and in its own way perpetuates the legacy of protest initiated by MARTIN LUTHER and others in the sixteenth century.

Some of the leading Protestant African theologians are John Mbiti (Kenya), Kwame Bediako (Ghana), J. N. K. Mugambi, Gwinyai H. Muzorewa, John S. Pobee, Musa Dube, Kwesi Dickson, Itumeleng Mosala, and Mercy Oduyoye. Their major writings are cited below.

References and Further Reading

Bediako, Kwame. *Christianity in Africa: The Renewal of a Non-Western Religion*. Edinburgh: Edinburgh University Press, 1995.
———. *Theology and Identity: The Impact of Culture upon Christian Thought in the Second Century and in Modern Africa*. Carlisle, PA: Paternoster Press, 1999.
Dickson, Kwesi. *Theology in Africa*. London: Darton, Longman and Todd Ltd., 1984.
Dube, Musa. *Postcolonial Feminist Interpretations of the Bible*. St Louis, MO: Chalice Press, 2001.
Mbiti, John. *Bible and Theology in African Christianity*. Nairobi: Oxford University Press, 1986.
Mosala, Itumeleng. *Biblical Hermeneutics and Black Theology in South Africa*. Grand Rapids, MI: Wm. B. Eerdmans, 1989.
Mugambi, J. N. K. *African Theology: An Introduction*. Nairobi: Heinemann Kenya, 1989.
Muzorewa, Gwinyai H. *The Origins and Development of African Theology*. New York: Orbis Books, 1985.
Oduyoye, Mercy. *Hearing and Knowing*. New York: Orbis Books, 1993.
Parratt, John. *Reinventing Christianity: African Theology Today*. Grand Rapids, MI: Wm. B. Eerdmans, 1995.
Pobee, John S. *Towards an African Theology*. Nashville, TN: Abingdon, 1979.
Turner, H. W. *Religious Innovation in Africa: Collected Essays on New Religious Movements*. Boston: GK Hall, 1979.

EDWARD P. ANTONIO

AGRICOLA, MICHAEL (C. 1507–1557)

Finnish reformer. Agricola, reformer and father of Finnish literature, was born around 1507 in the parish of Pernaja (Swedish Pernå) in the province of Uusimaa (Swedish Nyland) about 70 kilometers east of Helsinki. His mother tongue was no doubt the Swedish common in the province, but very soon he acquired the masterly command of Finnish shown in his literary work.

Son of a well-established peasant and of bright intelligence, Michael was sent to school in Wiborg. There he acquainted himself with the ideas of humanism and the REFORMATION, which were already well known in the southern side of the Gulf of Finland in the Baltic countries. At school he took for himself the name "Agricola," common in humanist circles in GERMANY.

In 1528 Agricola was appointed as the secretary of Martin Skytte, the first bishop in Turku after the Reformation. Skytte was a devout Dominican friar, but an Erasmian reformist with respect for new ideas. In 1531, he sent the first Finnish students to Wittenberg. Agricola bought a Latin *postil*, or book of sermons, of the reformer MARTIN LUTHER, was ordained, and left for Wittenberg in October 1536. He attended the lectures of Luther and PHILIPP MELANCHTHON and translated the New Testament into Finnish with the help of a pair of fellow Finnish students.

Agricola received his doctorate in April 1539. Provided with letters of recommendation from Luther and Melanchthon, he was made the headmaster of the school in Turku and the canon of the cathedral chapter. The bishop was growing old and decrepit, and Agricola became the de facto leader of the diocese of Turku in the 1540s.

Martin Skytte died in 1550, but king Gustav Vasa left the see vacant, and when it was committed to Agricola in 1554, it was not the same as before. The king had divided it into two parts. The new diocese of Wiborg now composed the eastern part of Finland.

Agricola was a member of the Swedish peace delegation to Czar Ivan the Terrible in Moscow. He died on the return trip on April 9, 1557 and was buried in Wiborg.

Agricola wrote the *ABC book*, the first book in the Finnish language, printed in Stockholm in 1543. In addition to the alphabet, it contains the CATECHISM, based mainly on Luther's Small Catechism. Agricola's prayer book (1544) comprises more than eight hundred and more than six hundred prayers. Agricola used medieval sources, particularly the *Missale Aboense* of 1488, but also made use of evangelical prayer books. He took some prayers from Luther and Melanchthon, and also from Herzog Albrecht von Preussen and Kaspar von Schwenckfeld. He translated in extenso the *Precationes Biblicae* of Otto Brunfels and the *Precationes aliquot* of Erasmus.

The New Testament was published in 1548, a book of seven hundred pages in quarto and with one hundred woodcuts. The work contains two forewords, as well as prefaces for all the books of New Testament except the last. The Gospel forewords are from Jerome; Agricola translated them from Erasmus's New Testament. Other prefaces are from Luther's

BIBLE. More than five hundred marginal glosses come from Luther, too. In prefaces and glosses, Agricola revised his sources, making deletions and additions.

Agricola reported that he translated "partly from Greek and partly from Latin, German and Swedish books." He used the Greek Latin edition from Erasmus, the Vulgate, Luther's Bible, the Swedish New Testament published in 1526 and the so-called Gustaf Vasa's Bible of 1541. Agricola made use of all his basic texts. The influence of Greek and Latin is evident especially in the Gospels, whereas in translating the Epistles, Agricola mostly followed Luther.

It was Agricola's intention to translate the whole Bible, but the king refused to give a penny for the printing of the Finnish books, and the cathedral chapter of Turku was deprived of its resources. Nonetheless, Agricola published the Psalter and a selection of the Old Testament prophets and a Finnish manual and a missal, translated from the works of the Swedish reformer OLAUS PETRI.

References and Further Reading

Primary Sources:

Agricola, Mikael. *ABC—Kiria.* Stockholm, 1549.
Agricola, Mikael and Francis Peabody Magoun. *Mikael Agricola's Gospel According to St. Mark.* Helsinki: Suomalaisen Kirjallisuuden Seura, 1967.

Secondary Source:

Gummerus, Jaakko. *Michael Agricola, Der Reformator Finnlands.* Helsinki: Suomalaisen Kirjallisuuden Seura, 1941.

SIMO HEININEN

ALL-UNION COUNCIL OF EVANGELICAL CHRISTIANS-BAPTISTS

From 1944 to 1989 the largest Protestant denomination in the Soviet Union and, for this period, the only Protestant church with legal status in all Soviet republics was the All-Union Council of Evangelical Christians-Baptists (AUCECB).

Origins

Three indigenous Protestant movements emerged simultaneously in RUSSIA in the latter half of the nineteenth century that later would merge in the AUCECB. Factors contributing to the growth of Protestantism in tsarist Russia included: (1) the disillusionment of some with the Orthodox Church's social conservatism and subservience to the state (see ORTHODOXY, EASTERN); (2) the social ferment surrounding the reforms of Alexander II; (3) the mid-nineteenth century pietistic revival (see PIETISM) that spread through and beyond Russia's German Protestant colonies; (4) the publication of the Bible in the Russian vernacular (1876) and its widespread distribution; and (5) the peasantry's increased accessibility to Scripture through growth in literacy.

In the Caucasus beginning in 1867 BAPTIST believers emerged from the ranks of mostly middle-class *Molokani,* Orthodox schismatics who held beliefs similar to Protestants. Although German Baptists played a key role in the conversion of *Molokani,* Russia's German MENNONITE and LUTHERAN colonists, under pietistic influences, generated a following among Ukrainian and Russian peasants beginning in 1869. Detractors called these believers *Shtundists* because of their regular devotional hours (*stunden* in German). Finally, between the years of 1874 and 1878, Lord Radstock, a PLYMOUTH BRETHREN lay evangelist, won influential and wealthy St. Petersburg aristocrats to evangelical faith through compelling preaching in their palaces. Followers of the movement came to be called Pashkovites after their leader, Guards Colonel Vasilii A. Pashkov, who was banished from Russia in 1884, six years after Lord Radstock suffered the same fate.

From the 1880s to 1905 Oberprokurator of the Holy Synod Konstantin P. Pobedonostsev oversaw systematic repression of indigenous Slavic Protestants, including arrest, impressment, banishment, internal exile, confiscation of property, and the forcible separation of children from parents. The 1905 Revolution led Nicholas II to issue an Edict of Toleration that brought a brief respite to Russian Protestants, although the outbreak of World War I in 1914 brought new persecution stemming from government suspicions that Russian evangelicals held pro-German sympathies. In contrast, the Revolutions of 1917 ushered in a golden decade of evangelism for Evangelical Christians (successors of the St. Petersburg Pashkovites) and Baptists that spread across the country from Ukraine and the Caucasus.

The Soviet Era

Factors contributing to evangelical growth in the first decade of Soviet rule included: (1) the end of Orthodox state-church status; (2) Bolshevik fixation on ORTHODOXY as a serious ideological challenge and its assumption that Protestant growth would be at Orthodox expense; and (3) the influence of Lenin's secretary, Vladimir D. Bonch-Bruevich, a scholar of SECTARIANISM positively disposed toward Protestants. The relative freedom of the years between 1917 and 1927 led to energetic Protestant evangelism, publishing, missionary activity, promotion of Sunday schools, and leadership training. Whereas Evangelical Christians and Baptists totaled approximately 97,500 in 1912, by the end of 1928 their numbers exceeded two million members and adherents in some 7,000 churches.

Nevertheless, from 1926 forward, Soviet authorities increasingly pressured Evangelical Christians and Baptists to forsake their historic PACIFISM in favor of military service. In 1929, with the ascendancy of Joseph Stalin and a new draconian law on religion, Protestants, along with all religious believers, faced dire persecution: wholesale church closures, mass arrests, imprisonments, and executions. Baptist and Evangelical Christian central offices closed by 1935 and 1940, respectively, and at most a few hundred Protestant churches remained open on the eve of World War II.

In 1943 and 1944 Stalin granted modest concessions to Orthodox and Protestant believers, apparently to solidify the churches' support for the war effort and Soviet foreign policy. State authorities actually facilitated a meeting of the two major Protestant denominations on October 26, 1944, which formed the All-Union Council of Evangelical Christians and Baptists. Arminian theology (see ARMINIANISM) was an Evangelical Christian contribution that prevailed in the new union, whereas Russian Baptist features included stricter membership requirements enforced by excommunication, more precise doctrinal formulation, episcopal (centralized) church governance, and less involvement in compassionate ministries than was the Evangelical Christian custom. In fact, the state dictated AUCECB episcopal POLITY and disengagement from charitable outreach. In addition, Soviet preference for an amalgamation of Protestant groups led a portion of Pentecostals to join the AUCECB in 1945, as well as CHURCH OF CHRIST, Brethren, and MORAVIAN congregations in newly annexed territories. Mennonites entered the union in 1963.

By 1947 the AUCECB's *Bratsky Vestnik* [*Fraternal Herald*] was reporting 350,000 members in 3,000 congregations, with additional adherents numbering 3.5 million. However, the Khrushchev antireligious campaign (1959–1964) spelled another disaster for the denomination: authorities closed approximately half of all ECB churches and precipitated a painful denominational split over the issue of church–state collaboration. Dissidents, or *Initsiativniki*, who charged AUCECB had sold out to state demands to quell "unhealthy missionary tendencies," formed their own Council of Churches of Evangelical Christians-Baptists (CCECB), with a peak membership of perhaps 155,000 in 1965. The period 1964 to 1988 witnessed a state carrot-and-stick approach to ECB churches: permission in 1968 for an AUCECB correspondence course for pastoral training as opposed to numerous arrests of CCECB pastors and systematic harassment of unregistered congregations. Dissidents struck back with voluminous underground publishing and a remarkably effective Council of Prisoners' Relatives that regularly fed protests to the West.

Glasnost and *Perestroika*

Between 1987 and 1989 freedoms granted under Gorbachev's policy of *glasnost* (openness) spelled dramatic improvements for Evangelical Christians-Baptists and other believers: the release of all prisoners of conscience; an end to shortwave radio jamming; imports and in-country printings of Bibles in the millions; the revival of organized Christian charity, public evangelism, mission activity, and seminary education; the dismantling of the atheist establishment; and in 1990, the legal codification of the new religious liberty in national and republic-level legislation. The AUCECB itself underwent *perestroika* (restructuring) as its 1990 Congress (1) elected 44-year-old Ukrainian Grigori Komendant to succeed older leaders closely associated with Soviet church-state arrangements; and (2) changed its name to Union of Evangelical Christians-Baptists. Less-positive developments from an ECB perspective included the wholesale exodus from the denomination of Pentecostals and Mennonites; a shift from all-union to republic-level governance; and difficulties in overcoming a longstanding siege mentality, social separatism, legalism, and pastoral authoritarianism. The Euro-Asiatic Federation of Unions of Evangelical Christians-Baptists, formed in 1993, serves only as a consultative and coordinating body, in effect illustrating the transfer of denominational authority from the former AUCECB to the republic-level ECB unions. With the formation of many new Protestant denominations and substantial emigration of ECB faithful to the West, the denomination also faced a considerable challenge in disciplining and retaining new believers. Further troubles came in 1997 in the form of a restrictive Russian law on religion that spelled serious discrimination and harassment for non-Orthodox faiths.

Evangelical Christian-Baptist membership dropped from 550,000 in the mid-1980s to 208,705 in 1991, rebounding to 344,805 by 2001 for all post-Soviet republics combined.

See also Communism; Evangelicalism; Church; Pentecostalism

References and Further Reading

East-West Church & Ministry Report, 1993.
Rowe, Michael. *Russian Resurrection.* London: Marshall Pickering, 1994.

Savinskii, S. N. *Istoriia Evangel'skikh Khristian-Baptistov v SSSR* [*History of Evangelical Christians-Baptists in the U.S.S.R.*]. Moscow: AUCECB, 1989.

Sawatsky, Walter. *Soviet Evangelicals Since World War II*. Scottdale, PA: Herald Press, 1981.

Wieczynski, Joseph L., ed. *Modern Encyclopedia of Russian and Soviet History*. Gulf Breeze, FL: Academic International Press, 1976–1990. [Articles by M. V. Jones, Lawrence Klippenstein, and Paul Steeves.]

MARK R. ELLIOTT

ALLEN, RICHARD (1760–1831)

African American freedman, social leader, and first bishop of the AFRICAN METHODIST EPISCOPAL CHURCH. Born a slave in Pennsylvania, Allen grew up and matured in Delaware. As a teenager he attended prayer meetings with local Methodists (see METHODISM). Impressed with Allen's piety, his master allowed the slave to buy his freedom. Allen met leading white Methodist itinerants like Freeborn Garrettson and FRANCIS ASBURY, both critics of SLAVERY. In 1783 or 1784, Allen became a lay preacher, settling in Philadelphia in 1786 and preaching there at St. George's Methodist Episcopal Church. In 1787 he and other blacks left the church in protest over racism. Allen exercised leadership skills in Philadelphia's Free African Society (1787–1794) and in the Bethel African Methodist Church (established 1794), where he preached although still unordained. Bethel Church attracted the attention of notable Methodists like Asbury and Thomas Coke, and Allen was ordained a deacon by Asbury in 1799. Allen's public service was important to both black and white Philadelphians.

Continuing struggles with white Methodists led blacks to form the African Methodist Episcopal (A.M.E.) Church in 1816, and its conference chose Allen as bishop. Under his leadership the church gained members in several states, initiated MISSIONS in AFRICA and HAITI, and opposed the plans of the AMERICAN COLONIZATION SOCIETY to expatriate free blacks. Allen's publications are few: a *Narrative* (1794), co-authored with Absalom Jones, concerning a yellow fever epidemic in Philadelphia; a hymn book (1801); a *Life* (1833); and several addresses, letters, and sermons.

Modern views of Allen have been influenced by an explosion of interest in the man and the A.M.E. Church, beginning in the late nineteenth century and continuing to the mid-twentieth century. Allen emerged as a master organizer in African American society, providing leadership for a people seeking a group identity and collective progress. Thus the emphasis was on Allen's defense of blacks' actions in the yellow fever epidemic, his leadership of black Christians out of an unfair congregation and finally into an independent denomination, and his financial acumen, which allowed him to purchase land for church buildings in Philadelphia. This corporatist approach to Allen bypassed his theology. By the last third of the twentieth century and the beginning of the twenty-first century, conditions were right for a consideration of Allen's theological views despite the paucity of his texts. Both BLACK THEOLOGY and renewed attention paid to the originating acts of the United States in the 1770s and 1780s, in which Philadelphia was the center of activity, have encouraged a clearer view of Allen's theology. The difficulty posed by the shortage of extant documents is compounded by Allen's claim in his 1830 autobiography always to have preached a simple faith without doctrine. This claim is implausible because Allen joined the Methodists at a time when PREDESTINATION was being hotly debated and when the majority of Methodists were choosing the ARMINIANISM of JOHN WESLEY, although a minority remained committed to CALVINISM. Moreover, most articulate black Christians from 1760 to 1820 were Calvinists. Living in Philadelphia, the intellectual and religious crossroads of North America, Allen could scarcely have been unaware of these circumstances. It is possible that in 1830 he intended to avoid stirring up conflict over doctrine because he knew Arminianism had triumphed so thoroughly over Calvinism in North American religion.

The evidence, sketchy as it is, suggests that Allen preached an amalgamation of Calvinist and Arminian doctrines. The covenant between God and a chosen people, a staple of PURITANISM, appeared in his writings on the yellow fever epidemic. Blacks were a people in covenant with God and they were able to avoid the moral corruption attendant on the social disorder caused by the disease because they kept the terms of the covenant. The reformed heart, which was common to JONATHAN EDWARDS and free-will Christians, appeared prominently in his writings. Affection, benevolence, and virtue—all signs of a reformed heart—should lead to equality among the races. The freedom of the will in the matter of personal salvation, the centerpiece of Wesleyan Methodism, was implied throughout Allen's writings. Belief in the ability of ordinary people to turn to God without a long period of preparation was crucial to the success of the Methodists and the BAPTISTS, both black and white, in preaching to African Americans in the late eighteenth century and the nineteenth century. In preaching these doctrines, Allen would have had one foot in the world of his black peers and the other in the new African American religious sphere of the nineteenth century.

References and Further Reading

Primary Sources:

Allen, Richard. *A Collection of Hymns and Spiritual Songs.* Philadelphia: T. L. Plowman, 1801.

———. *The Life Experiences and Gospel Labors of the Rt. Reverend Richard Allen to Which Is Annexed the Rise and Progress of the African Methodist Episcopal Church in the United States of America, Containing a Narrative of the Yellow Fever in the Year of Our Lord 1793, with an Address to the People of Color in the United States, Written by Himself and Published by His Request.* New York: Abingdon Press, 1960.

Secondary Sources:

Payne, Daniel A. *History of the African Methodist Episcopal Church.* New York: Arno Press and the New York Times, 1969; reprint of 1891 edition.

Wesley, Charles H. *Richard Allen: Apostle of Freedom*, 2nd ed. Washington, D.C.: The Associated Publishers, 1969; first edition 1935.

JOHN SAILLANT

ALLEN, ROLAND (1868–1947)

English missionary. Roland Allen was born in Bristol, England. The youngest of five children, he was orphaned at an early age when his father, an Anglican priest, died in Belize City, British Honduras, now Belize. Allen was educated at St. John's College, Oxford, and at Leeds Clergy Training School for Anglo-Catholics. Ordained as a deacon in 1892, he went to north CHINA in 1895 as a missionary of the "High Church" SOCIETY FOR THE PROPAGATION OF THE GOSPEL (SPG). His assignment was to a small school in Peking, where he studied Mandarin, trained catechists, served as a district missionary, and acted as chaplain to the British Legation. When the Boxer Rebellion broke out in June 1900 he, along with the foreign community, remained under siege at the British compound until relief came two months later.

Returning to ENGLAND for furlough, he married Mary Beatrice Carlton in 1901 and they had two children, Priscilla and Iohn. He had no sooner returned to China with his new family when, after a few short months, his health broke and he was forced to return home in 1903. Allen then accepted the position as parish priest of Chalfont St. Peter in Buckinghamshire. Resigning in 1907 over an issue he called "baptismal rigorism," he never held another official Anglican position, but became a voluntary, nonpaid priest, the subject he proposed in his last major work, *The Case for Voluntary Clergy.* Many believed this was a turning point for him and the beginning of his "real" ministry. Until his death forty years later, he earned his living by writing or in other ways.

After this brief missionary and pastoral experience, he radically reassessed his THEOLOGY and VOCATION. Concerned about the paternalism practiced in China he published *Missionary Methods: St. Paul's or Ours?* in 1912 and *Missionary Principles* in 1913, which have become classics in the study of mission methodology and strategy. Often referred to as a radical proponent of the "Three-Selfs" indigenous church principles as espoused by Henry Venn, RUFUS ANDERSON, John Nevius, and others, he argued that they did not go far enough. Allen called for an additional spiritual dimension, the gift of the Holy Spirit in mission, and articulated this in *Pentecost and the World: The Revelation of the Holy Spirit in the "Acts of the Apostles."* In his understanding the Acts of the Apostles constitutes a missionary book and can be understood only in the context of the Holy Spirit in mission. He described the gift of the Holy Spirit of Acts 2 as enabling the recipients to preach Christ to people of every nation.

In 1914 Allen met Sidney J. W. Clark, a wealthy Congregationalist, who enlisted him to work for the envisioned Survey Application Trust (SAT) and its publishing arm, World Dominion Press. The Trust's deed of 1918 was laid down with the purpose of applying Clark's indigenous church principles asserted in his pamphlets and perpetuating Allen's MISSIOLOGY. The surveys advocated by Clark and Thomas Cochrane did not capture his interest; instead, Allen's attention was focused in the quality of work where mission activity was already established. His major contribution to the Trust came in his numerous writings. These writings greatly influenced the exposition of indigenous church principles that have become a major component in contemporary Protestant mission strategy, particularly among Evangelicals and Pentecostals.

Allen called for a mission strategy based on St. Paul's New Testament principles. Following this reasoning he insisted that they should be biblical and normative for all times and contexts. In 1927 he published *The Spontaneous Expansion of the Church and the Causes Which Hinder It,* in which he stated, "if the church is to be indigenous it must spring up in the soil from the very first seeds planted. . . . [I]f we want to see spontaneous expansion we must establish native churches free from our control" (pp. 4–5). However, his fellow clergymen did not understand or approve of this radical thinking. A mission theorist ahead of his time, he once remarked to his son that his works would not be appreciated until around 1960.

The Allens emigrated to Kenya in 1931 to live near their two children where he resided until his death in 1947. He resigned from public ministry and thereafter celebrated the sacraments only in his home. In his late years he became embittered and depressed over the fact that his ideas were all too often dismissed as impractical and unpalatable, resulting from his irritating and stinging criticisms of the mission policies of the Anglican Church. Allen's primary value lies in the area that most irritated the church leaders of his own day: the persistence of precisely those theological issues that are most easily evaded because current practice is called into question. Evangelicals continue to read his works and Ecumenists are now discovering those treasures. Not without his critics both then and now, Allen's influence has made a profound and lasting impact on missiology.

See also Anglicanism; Anglo-Catholicism; Deaconess, Deacon; Ecumenism; Missions

References and Further Reading

Primary Source:

Paton, David M., and Charles L. Long, eds. *The Compulsion of the Spirit: A Roland Allen Reader.* Grand Rapids, MI: Wm. B. Eerdmans, 1983.

Secondary Sources:

Allen, Hubert. *Roland Allen: Pioneer, Priest, and Prophet.* Grand Rapids, MI: Wm. B. Eerdmans, 1995.
Branner, John E. "Roland Allen, Donald McGavran and Church Growth." M.A. thesis, Fuller Theological Seminary, 1974.
———. "Roland Allen: Pioneer in a Spirit-Centered Theology of Mission." *Missiology: An International Review* V no. 2 (April 1977).
Long, Charles L., and Anne Rowthorn. "Roland Allen 1868–1947: Missionary Methods: St. Paul's or Ours?" In *Mission Legacies,* edited by Gerald Anderson, et al. Maryknoll, NY: Orbis Books, 1994.
Paton, David M., ed. *Reform of the Ministry: A Study in the Work of Roland Allen.* London: Lutterworth Press, 1968.

WARREN B. NEWBERRY

ALLINE, HENRY (1748–1784)

American evangelist. Born in Newport, Rhode Island, on June 14, 1748, Alline moved north with his family and other New England planters at age twelve to what would become Falmouth township, Nova Scotia. Because of the absence of educational and religious institutions in a frontier environment, Alline developed his innate intelligence and interest in religion and theology by immersing himself in devotional literature. After struggling for several years with a strong sense of sin and guilt, he experienced a full assurance of salvation on March 26, 1775, and shortly thereafter, a call to ministry. In keeping with the Congregationalist tradition of a learned ministry (see CONGREGATIONALISM), he proceeded to New England for theo-

logical training, only to be forced back by travel difficulties arising from the outbreak of the American rebellion. Deciding to defy convention, he began to preach and travel, organizing a number of New Light churches in the Annapolis Valley, two of which ordained him as an evangelist on April 6, 1779. Preaching the need for a "new birth," and with little interest in church finances and institutional organization, he was constantly on the move, covering most of Nova Scotia, and the settled parts of what became New Brunswick, before finally in 1783 heading south to New England. A few months later, on February 2, 1784, he died of consumption in North Hampton, New Hampshire.

During his short ministry he wrote many hymns, which were posthumously collected, reprinted several times in the United States, and used by Benjamin Randall (1749–1808) and the FREE WILL BAPTISTS. The churches Alline organized either collapsed after his death or joined the Regular Baptists, thereby breaking with his controversial anti-Calvinist theology (see CALVINISM). Expounded in his major works, *Two mites on some of the most important and much disputed points of divinity* (1781), and a pamphlet, *The anti-traditionalist* (c. 1783), Alline's thought was influenced by writer WILLIAM LAW (1686–1761) and religious mystic JACOB BOEHME (1575–1624). His antimaterialism, mysticism, egalitarianism, and his conviction that God's universal love enabled all humankind to be saved, appealed to Nova Scotia's frontier population disoriented by immigration and war. Historians have depicted Alline, therefore, as the apolitical leader of an early popular movement, who through religious language and experience offered hope and meaning during a time of political and social crisis.

References and Further Reading

Bumsted, J. M. *Henry Alline, 1748–1784.* Toronto: University of Toronto Press, 1971.
Rawlyk, George A. *Ravished by the Spirit: Religious Revivals, Baptists, and Henry Alline.* Kingston: McGill-Queen's University Press, 1984.
Stewart, Gordon T., and George A. Rawlyk. *A People Highly Favoured of God; the Nova Scotia Yankees and the American Revolution.* Toronto: Macmillan of Canada, 1971.

MARGUERITE VAN DIE

ALTARS

One of three liturgical centers in Christian churches, along with the pulpit and the baptismal font, the altar consists of a *mensa,* or single slab, placed horizontally atop a solid base or set of supporting columns and used during worship to support the elements of the Eucharist.

Pre-Reformation Altars

Christian altars derive from the stone altars upon which Roman and Jewish priests made animal sacrifices and placed offerings. The double meanings of sacrifice and offering, or gift, have variously informed Christian use of the altar throughout history, depending on changing understandings of the Eucharist. As the Eucharistic meal came to symbolize the sacrifice of Christ, the altar service or Mass was viewed as the reenactment of that sacrifice, and the altar was considered the holiest place within a church. With the doctrine of TRANSUBSTANTIATION, the significance of the altar and site of this miraculous transformation expanded exponentially, and Christians indicated the holiness of the altar with consecration rituals, placement in the chancel, and the use of veils to shield it from view. By the medieval period the altar's significance was indicated by a ciborium (a canopy placed above it), rood screens, elaborate sculptural programs ornamenting the base, retables, or structures rising from it and displaying scenes and figures, and reredos or large screens of niches filled with statuary that covered the wall behind it. Because altars were used to inter the bodies of saints or other relics, their sanctity was further enhanced. This practice lengthened the altar from its earlier near-square form to an oblong several feet longer than its width, a form that came to be known as the "coffin" style in later years. Christian altars have been constructed of either stone or wood since the early church.

Altar Controversy during the Reformation

The primacy of the altar as the holiest liturgical center and worship focus endured from the second century to the sixteenth, when it was challenged by the REFORMATION substitution of the Word for the sacrament as the focus of worship. MARTIN LUTHER, who slightly modified the mystical view of the Eucharistic transformation, substituting the presence for the body of Christ in the elements, relocated the celebrant behind the altar during the service and distributed both elements to the laity. These alterations significantly demystified the meanings associated with the altar, which Luther argued was not inherently sacred. Nevertheless, he did retain the altar and renamed the Eucharist service the "sacrament of the altar." JOHN CALVIN, who understood the meaning of the sacrament in terms of the elements' instrumentality in sealing God's covenant and in their signification of Christ's promise, also retained the altar and performed most of the service, except for the sermon, from behind it.

More radical reformers, however, attacked the altar as they condemned the doctrine of transubstantiation. The elaborate decoration of altars also enraged many who launched iconoclastic assaults on altar sculptures and reredos. HULDRYCH ZWINGLI, countering the real presence theology with one emphasizing Christ's gift of grace and the gathering of a spiritual community, attempted to re-create the setting of the primitive church by substituting a communion table for the altar. In the late sixteenth and early seventeenth centuries, the substitution of a table for the altar appealed strongly to Reformed groups, as did placing the table within the body of the gathered congregation. During the reign of ELIZABETH I, churchwardens in the CHURCH OF ENGLAND often moved the table, which normally stood altarlike in the chancel, to the center of the nave for communion services. This altar/table interchangeability corresponded to Anglican willingness to view the sacrament as both a sacrifice and a gift. In 1616, however, WILLIAM LAUD's directives relocated the table to the chancel and required that rails be placed around it, thus redefining it as a sacred altar despite cries of "popery" from Puritans.

Changing Significance of the Altar

After the Reformation, groups that viewed the Eucharist elements as containing some form of the mystical presence of Christ usually retained the altar, whereas those who argued that the essential spiritual nature of Christ could not be contained within material form tended to discard altars. Yet a brief historical survey demonstrates that a high church/altar and low church/table dichotomy never fully characterized Protestant use of these furnishings.

Humanistic philosophy and pursuit of reason in the eighteenth century fostered a classical aesthetic that downplayed the role of the mystical presence and shifted worship toward the Word. In Anglican churches designed by CHRISTOPHER WREN and James Gibb, highly decorated pulpits eclipsed altars as the most significant liturgical centers even though altars retained pride of place in the chancel. In Lutheran churches, pulpits similarly outshone altars.

The nineteenth century brought a renewed stature to the altar. Adherents of the German Reformed, Mercersberg theology produced ornamented altars in western Pennsylvania. Scandinavian Lutherans enhanced their altars with retables consisting of framed paintings of Christ. Anglican and Anglo-Catholic churches embraced the elaborate altars of the Gothic period, encouraging figural sculpture and reredos. Moreover, as Reformed denominations including Congregationalists, Presbyterians, BAPTISTS, and Methodists embraced the Gothic Revival, many congregations replaced their communion tables with ornamented altars to consistently apply the architectural style. No parallel shift in doctrine toward a sacrificial understanding of the sacrament accompanied this use, however. The application of what was perceived as an authentic historical style outweighed theological understandings of liturgical furnishings.

Renewed interest in formalist worship and altars also characterized the early twentieth century. Architect Ralph Adams Cram, propounding Gothic forms as most appropriate to Christian worship, significantly influenced not only Episcopalians and Lutherans but also liberal Protestant congregations seeking modern worship forms and unity among denominations. Many Unitarian, Congregationalist, Baptist, and Presbyterian congregations adopted the "split-chancel" liturgical arrangement that featured an altar placed in the center of the chancel and flanked by a lectern and pulpit on either side. Though made of wood, these altar-tables mimicked medieval "coffin" altars. Again, no transformation of doctrine accompanied this use.

These arrangements remained popular until the post–World War II ecumenical movement, which emphasized community over formalism and embraced the table as a symbol of community interaction with Christ. Reformed congregations abandoned altar-oriented arrangements, and Lutherans, Episcopalians, and even Catholics adopted tables as indicative of an accessible, community-oriented religious experience, sometimes placing the table in the center of the worship space and arranging seating around it. Altars, however, remain in wide use among congregations that embrace liturgical formalism or emphasize Christ's presence in the Eucharist.

See also Anglicanism; Congregationalism; Presbyterianism; Lutheranism; Methodism; Architecture, Church

References and Further Reading

Bishop, Edward. "On the History of the Christian Altar," *Downsider Review* (1905): 154–182.

Bond, Francis. *The Chancel of English Churches.* London: Humphrey Milford, Oxford University Press, 1916.

Pocknee, Cyril E. *The Christian Altar: In History and Today.* London: A. R. Mowbray, 1963.

Potter, G. R. *Zwingli.* Cambridge: Cambridge University Press, 1976.

Vajta, Vilmos. *Luther on Worship.* Philadelphia: Muhlenberg Press, 1958.

White, James F. *Protestant Worship and Church Architecture: Theological and Historical Considerations.* New York: Oxford University Press, 1964.

JEANNE HALGREN KILDE

ALTHUSIUS, JOHANNES (1563–1638)

German political theorist. Althusius was born in 1563 in the County of Wittgenstein-Berleburg and studied at the universities of Cologne and then Basel in SWIT-ZERLAND, where he received his doctoral degree in Roman law in 1586. In the same year, he was called to the Reformed Academy at Herborn (Hohe Schule) in the County of Nassau-Dillenburg as a member of the Faculty of Law. The academy had been founded two years before and immediately attracted students not only from GERMANY, but also from all over Europe. The first rector of the academy was Caspar Olevianus, co-author with Zacharias Ursinus of the HEIDELBERG CATECHISM.

In 1592, Althusius was called to the Reformed Academy of Steinfurt, located in Westphalia near the border with the NETHERLANDS. In 1596, the Count of Nassau-Dillenburg called him back to Herborn, which in the meantime had been transferred to the city of Siegen. Althusius was elected rector in 1599 and again in 1602, when the Academy was transferred back to Herborn.

Two years later, Althusius gave up his academic career to accept an appointment as syndic of the Reformed city of Emden in East Friesland. Emden was one of the first cities of Germany to adopt the Reformed faith and had become a veritable "Geneva of the North." Althusius remained in Emden for 34 years until his death in 1638. In 1617, he was elected elder of the Church of Emden. Combining the functions of syndic and elder, Althusius had a position that enabled him to coordinate civil and ecclesiastical jurisdiction and gave him enormous influence, which in a sense was comparable to that of JOHN CALVIN in Geneva. As a city syndic, Althusius defended the rights and liberties of the city of Emden and the Frisian estates against the Lutheran count. He tried to secure the northern Netherlands' support for his politics. In the end, however, he did not succeed in establishing a free Reformed Republic of Emden.

Althusius's major work is his *Politics* (*Politica methodice digesta*), first published in Herborn in 1603. This is one of the first books on early modern politics and makes him one of the founding fathers of political science. The central point of *Politics* is the problem of community building. Althusius saw the community not as a result of hierarchical power and rule concentration, but rather as a dynamic process of consensual and social, or, rather, consociational, institutionalizing, which starts with the formation of smaller communities and moves to the larger union of the whole. In many respects, Althusius's political theory represents an institutional alternative to the teachings of his older contemporary Jean Bodin: by viewing political authority as founded on smaller communities; by attributing sovereignty not to the ruler, but rather to the community; by limiting sovereign power not only by natural law, but also by positive, especially fundamental, law; and, finally, by conceding a right to resist tyrannical government, especially if religious freedom is involved. It is in this context that the beginning of constitutional thought must be sought and not in Bodin's absolutist concept of sovereignty. Moreover, the legal and political theoretical requirements for a subsidiary and federal concept are formulated here, enabling the structural accommodation of different community formations in a consociational commonwealth.

In *Politics*, Althusius follows the Ramist logic and emphasizes method and systematic reasoning. His argumentation relies heavily on the BIBLE and contains thousands of quotations, especially from the Old Testament. It is nevertheless a work of political theory, not of political theology. Althusius is highly interested in limiting each discipline to its own purpose; that is, in differentiating between theological and political reasoning or, in other words, between the Christian and the political communities. Notwithstanding, his political theory is deeply influenced by Christian Reformed thinking, especially the idea of COVENANT, yet without giving churchmen power over political matters.

The other main body of Althusius's work is devoted to Roman law and legal theory. He began his studies with a little book on Roman law in 1586 (*Iuris Romani libri duo*), which was constantly revised and enlarged over many years and, finally, in 1617, culminated in a comprehensive theory of justice (*Dicaeologica*).

After the second half of the seventeenth century and the end of the religious wars, the work of Althusius to a large extent fell into oblivion. In the last part of the nineteenth century, Otto von Gierke rediscovered *Politics* and gave a new impetus to the research of Althusius. Meanwhile, in Germany, a learned society had been founded (*Johannes Althusius Gesellschaft*) devoted to the research of the life and works of Althusius and his times. The impact of Althusius in recent decades seems to be based on the fact that his political theory has been vastly influential in the shaping of modern republican and federal governmental patterns, especially in the New World, and even more on his insights into the nature of the political order in general.

References and Further Reading

Primary Sources:

Althusius, Johannes. *Politica Methodice digesta et exemplis sacris et profanis illustrata. Cui in fine adjuncta est Oratio panegyrica de utilitate, necessitate et antiquitate scholarum.* Herborn, Germany: Corvinus, 1603; reprint, Aalen, Germany: Scientia, 1981.
———. *Politica Methodice digesta of Johannes Althusius (Althaus).* Reprinted from the Third Edition of 1614. Aug-
mented by the Preface of the First Edition of 1603 and by 21 hitherto unpublished letters of the author, with an introduction by Carl Joachim Friedrich. Cambridge, MA: Harvard University Press, 1932.
———. *The Politics of Johannes Althusius. An abridged translation of the Third Edition of Political Methodice digesta atque exemplis sacris et profanis illustrata and including the Prefaces to the First and Third Editions.* Translated, with an introduction by Frederick S. Carney. Preface by Carl J. Friedrich. Boston: Beacon Press, 1964.
———. *Dicaeologicae Libri Tres, Totum et universum Jus, quo utimur, methodicè complectentes: Cum parallelis hujus et Judaici Juris, tabulisque insertis, atque Indice triplici; uno, auctorum; altero, capitum singulorum; et tertio, rerum et verborum locupletiβimo et accuratiβimo. Opus tam theoriae quàm praxeos aliarumqué Facultatum studiosis utilissimum.* Herborn, Germany: Corvinus, 1617; reprint, Aalen, Germany: Scientia, 1967.

Secondary Sources:

Blickle, Peter, Thomas O. Hüglin, and Dieter Wyduckel, eds. *Subsidiarität als rechtliches und politisches Ordnungsproblem in Kirche, Staat und Gesellschaft.* Berlin: Duncker & Humblot, 2002.
Bonfatti, Emilio, Giuseppe Duso, and Merio Scattola, eds. *Politische Begriffe und historisches Umfeld in der Politica methodice digesta des Johannes Althusius.* Wiesbaden, Germany: Harassowitz-Verlag, 2002.
Dahm, Karl-Wilhelm, Werner Krawietz, and Dieter Wyduckel, eds. *Politische Theorie des Johannes Althusius.* Berlin: 1988.
Duso, Giuseppe, Werner Krawietz, and Dieter Wyduckel, eds. *Konsens und Konsoziation in der politischen Theorie des frühen Föderalismus.* Berlin: 1997.
Hueglin, Thomas O. *Early Modern Concepts for a Late Modern World. Althusius on Community and Federalism.* Waterloo, Ontario, Canada: Wilfrid Laurier University Press, 1999.
Scheuner, Ulrich, and Hans Ulrich Scupin, eds. *Althusius-Bibliographie: Bibliographie zur politischen Ideengeschichte und Staatslehre, zum Staatsrecht und zur Verfassungsgeschichte des 16. bis 18. Jahrhunderts.* Berlin 1973, 2 vols.

DIETER WYDUCKEL

AMANA

The Amana Church Society is the American descendant of the Community of True Inspiration, a mystically oriented pietist sect that formed in eighteenth-century GERMANY (see GERMAN GROUPS IN AMERICA). Because of economic pressures and religious harassment, the Inspirationists migrated to the United States in the 1840s, where they settled in western New York and adopted a communal economic system. Later, the Inspirationists migrated to Iowa, renaming themselves the "Amana Society" and eventually established seven geographically proximate villages. In 1932 the Society abandoned its economic communalism and reorganized itself as the "Amana Church Society," which continues to gather for worship in Amana's villages.

Origins

Amana's roots lay in German PIETISM, a late seventeenth-century reaction to mainstream German Protestantism. Inspired by the writing of PHILIPP JAKOB SPENER and August Herman Francke, the Pietists contended that state-sponsored LUTHERANISM had lost its evangelical fervor, substituting abstract theological disputes for true Christian piety. The more radical Pietists, called "Separatists," withdrew from their state churches, believing that independent assemblies for worship, or CONVENTICLES, provided better contexts for nurturing communion with God.

Two prominent Separatists, Eberhard Ludwig Gruber and Johann Friedrich Rock, became the founders of Amana's European precursor, the Community of True Inspiration. In 1714 Gruber and Rock were visited by like-minded (albeit more mystical) Pietists who believed that God spoke through divinely inspired human instruments. Encouraged by their visitors' words, Gruber and Rock threw their energies into forming the Community of True Inspiration. Rock himself became a *Werkzeug,* that is, an inspired minister through whom God spoke. Although Gruber never received this gift, he assumed the title "Overseer of the *Werkzeuge,*" organizing the association by recording its DOCTRINE and its behavioral guidelines, which stressed selflessness, sobriety, and separation from "worldly" activities.

Decline, Revival, and Migration

The Community of True Inspiration suffered decline during the second half of the eighteenth century. Gruber died in 1728 and Rock died in 1749, and although the Inspirationists had become well organized before their founders' deaths, the lack of charismatic leadership took its toll. Some Inspirationist congregations ceased to exist; others declined as their elderly members died off.

Between 1817 and 1823, however, the appearance of three new *Werkzeuge* brought revival to the flagging movement. The first of these prophets was Michael Krausert, who reported a divine inspiration shortly after encountering an Inspirationist congregation in 1817. Some members resisted granting Krausert status as a *Werkzeug,* but others affirmed his inspiration as a harbinger of revival. Soon, Krausert identified a second *Werkzeug,* Barbara Heinemann, who in turn prophesied that Christian Metz would also become inspired. By 1824 Metz was the community's only remaining *Werkzeug.* Krausert left the movement in 1819, doubting his own inspiration, and Heinemann lost the gift in 1823 upon her marriage, which was deemed inappropriate for a *Werkzeug.* Fortunately for

the group, Metz was a capable leader, fostering numerical growth and a renewed sense of purpose.

In response to harassment from German authorities, the Inspirationists migrated to the United States in 1843 and 1844, settling near Buffalo, New York. Here the Inspirationists formed a community separated from the world (see SECTARIANISM), retaining their German language and adopting a relatively strict form of economic communalism. Although the Inspirationists had experimented with some forms of economic collectivism before they emigrated, only now did they assign land ownership and the means of production to the entire community (see SOCIALISM). Some private ownership remained, and each community member was given a modest spending allowance, although members worked at community-owned industries without pay.

By the mid-1850s, the Inspirationists had constructed four small villages with over one thousand residents who worked together, shared community kitchens, and ate communal meals. However, the strains of numerical growth and concerns about the world's proximity soon compelled them to search for a more isolated region where they could prosper economically and spiritually. This search led them to eastern Iowa, where they relocated after 1855.

The Amana Society

The Inspirationists structured their Iowa communities after their New York communities. Eventually forming seven small villages, they incorporated under the name "Amana Society," a reference to Song of Solomon 4:8 (Amana means "remain faithful"). The membership of the Amana Society peaked in 1881 with some 1,813 members.

Werkzeug Christian Metz continued to exhibit inspired leadership until his death in 1867. At that point, Barbara Heinemann Landmann assumed Metz's role. Although Landmann had lost her inspired status in 1823, she remained with the movement, regained her *Werkzeug* status in 1849, and assumed added authority upon Metz's death. Even before Metz's death, however, formal leadership structures had developed that handled most community issues. A thirteen-member, all-male Great Council managed the society's temporal affairs and oversaw its spiritual life. Local councils in each village made additional decisions, operating within the Great Council's guidelines.

Each of Amana's seven villages contained one unadorned church building where the village's residents gathered for religious services eleven times per week. The congregants sat on unpainted, wooden pews, segregated by GENDER. The services, like the meetinghouses themselves, were characterized by simplicity and restraint: silent prayers, Bible Readings, recitations of inspired Amana pronouncements, and unaccompanied, chanted Hymns. According to one observer, the content of Amana's Sunday morning services has "not changed appreciably for 150 years" (Andelson 1997).

The Great Change

In many ways, the Amana Society comprised one of America's most successful communal experiments, lasting for almost ninety years. By the early twentieth century, however, member commitment to economic communalism had become tenuous. Younger members in particular found these ways restrictive, and growing financial strains intensified the desire for change. Finally, a special committee appointed by the Great Council polled the society's adult members about structural reorganization. With a majority of members in consent, the Amana Society reorganized itself in 1932. The society's economic enterprises were converted into a joint stock company, with each member becoming a shareholder. The society's religious functions were assigned to the autonomous Amana Church Society, which was governed by elected elders.

Presently, Amana Church Society members gather for worship only once a week, on Sunday mornings. Still, the society's religious rituals mirror earlier concerns about simplicity and Nonconformity to the world. Unadorned worship in simple meetinghouses, gender-segregated seating, remnants of plain dress—these practices continue to attract visitors to eastern Iowa, much as the Old-Order Amish attract tourists to regions of Pennsylvania, Ohio, and Indiana. Unlike the Amish, however, the reorganized Amana Church Society has not experienced numerical growth and entered the twenty-first century with a membership of 500, one-third of its historic membership high.

References and Further Reading

Andelson, Jonathan G. "The Community of True Inspiration from Germany to the Amana Colonies." In *America's Communal Utopias*, edited by Donald E. Pitzer. Chapel Hill: University of North Carolina Press, 1997.

Barthel, Diane L. *Amana: From Pietist Sect to American Community*. Lincoln: University of Nebraska Press, 1984.

Foerstner, Abigail. *Picturing Utopia: Bertha Shambaugh and the Amana Photographers*. Iowa City: University of Iowa Press, 2000.

DAVID L. WEAVER-ZERCHER

AMERICAN BAPTIST CHURCHES

The American Baptist Churches in the U.S.A. (ABC-USA) is a major Baptist denomination in the United States consisting of 5,786 churches with about 1.44 million members (2001 statistics). There are ABC-USA churches in all fifty states; about eight hundred of them are dually aligned with another, usually Baptist, denomination. The current name was adopted in 1972. From 1950 to 1972 the denomination was known as the American Baptist Convention. It was formally established in 1907 as the Northern Baptist Convention, but it had a long prehistory before its formal, national establishment as a denomination.

Background

The first Baptist church in America was established in 1638 in Providence, Rhode Island, with another church soon formed in Newport, Rhode Island in 1648. Although Baptists were, then as now, deeply committed to the autonomy of the local churches, they also believed deeply in the importance of associational cooperation. By 1670 the first regional association was founded (General Six Principle Baptists; see General Baptists). In 1707 the Philadelphia Baptist Association was established by five churches, which is the oldest continuing Baptist association in America. This Association was very influential and functioned as a virtual national body for its time. In 1742 it adopted the Philadelphia Confession of Faith, the first Baptist document of this type in America. It sponsored the establishment in Providence, Rhode Island of the first Baptist college in America in 1764 (later known as Brown University).

In the early nineteenth century many Baptist societies and organizations began to emerge. In 1800 the Boston Female Society for Missionary Purposes was founded, followed in 1802 by the establishment of the Massachusetts Baptist Missionary Society. This society first published in 1803 the *Massachusetts Baptist Missionary Magazine,* which remains today as the oldest Baptist periodical in continuous publication. Over the years, it had various names; today it is the official ABC-USA periodical, known since 1992 as *American Baptists in Mission.*

A major development was the formation in 1814 of the General Missionary Convention of the Baptist Denomination in the United States for Foreign Missions (known also as the Triennial Convention, which held its first meeting in 1817). The prime organizer of this Convention was Luther Rice (1783–1836), who had sailed for India with Adoniram and Ann Judson and others in 1812 (see Judson Family). The Judsons and Rice became Baptists on their voyage. The Judsons went to Burma and Rice returned to the United States to organize support for them and the budding Baptist overseas missionary enterprise. In 1846 the

Convention was renamed the American Baptist Missionary Union.

In 1924 the Baptist General Tract Society was organized in Washington, D.C. The name was changed in 1840 to the American Baptist Publication and Sunday School Society ("and Sunday School" was dropped in 1845). In the 1840s the Society relocated to Philadelphia. In 1832 the American Baptist Home Mission Society was begun in New York City, organized at the close of a Triennial Convention meeting. In 1833 the New Hampshire Baptist Convention approved the New Hampshire Confession of Faith, an expression of moderate Baptist CALVINISM, which became very influential in the life of Baptists.

On May 8, 1845 the SOUTHERN BAPTIST CONVENTION was founded in Atlanta, Georgia, representing a separation of southern Baptist churches from the Triennial Convention and the American Baptist Home Mission Society. The separation was prompted by issues related primarily to SLAVERY, the abolitionist movement (see SLAVERY, ABOLITION OF), and denominational structure.

In the 1850s and 1860s there also emerged separate conferences for various ethnic groups (e.g., the German Baptist Conference in 1851; the Swedish Baptist Conference in 1857; the Danish Baptist Conference in 1864), which used the languages of the immigrants forming these groups.

In 1853 the American Baptist Historical Society was established. In 1871 the Woman's American Baptist Foreign Missionary Society was organized, followed by separate women's home mission societies for the East and the West in 1877. Also significant for Baptists was the publication in 1876 of the first edition of Augustus Henry Strong's (1836–1921) *Systematic Theology*, which eventually saw eight editions and thirty printings.

Early History (to 1950)

The many strands of American Baptist life and organization came together on May 17, 1907 in a meeting in Calvary Baptist Church in Washington, D.C. to organize the Northern Baptist Convention (NBC). There were representatives from local churches, various associations, the American Baptist Missionary Union, the American Baptist Home Mission Society, and the American Baptist Publication Society. Thus, there emerged formally the national DENOMINATION now known as the ABC-USA, with the organizing groups maintaining their separate identities. Charles Evans Hughes, governor of New York, was elected as the first president of the Northern Baptist Convention.

In 1908 the NBC became a charter member of the Federal Council of Churches (now the NATIONAL COUNCIL OF CHURCHES). In 1910 the American Baptist Missionary Union was renamed the American Baptist Foreign Mission Society. In 1911 the Free Will Baptist General Conference (see FREE WILL BAPTISTS) merged with the NBC. That same year the NBC created its Ministers and Missionaries Benefit Board. The East and West women's home mission societies, formed in 1877, merged into one organization in 1913.

Early in the history of the NBC the tensions and controversy between FUNDAMENTALISM and MODERNISM were growing in the United States, especially in Northern Baptist Convention circles. In 1920 the Fundamentalist Fellowship was founded, which hoped to get the NBC to adopt the New Hampshire Confession of Faith. This failed in 1922, with the NBC voting instead that the New Testament was the "all sufficient ground of faith and practice." This led to the formation of the BAPTIST BIBLE UNION in 1923, which was transformed into the GENERAL ASSOCIATION OF REGULAR BAPTIST CHURCHES in 1932, a group that formally separated from the NBC. The controversy continued within the NBC, and in 1943 the Conservative Baptist Foreign Mission Society was formed. In the 1946 NBC annual meeting it became clear that this new Mission Society was viewed by the majority as inappropriate. Thus in 1947 the CONSERVATIVE BAPTIST ASSOCIATION of America was formed, also formally separating from the NBC.

Several other events of importance took place as well during these years. In 1921 Helen Barrett Montgomery (1861–1934) became the first woman to be president of the NBC. In 1924, in honor of the one hundredth anniversary of the American Baptist Publication Society, the Society published Montgomery's English translation of the Greek New Testament (the only other woman to have done this was Julia E. Smith in 1876). In that year also the publication arm of the Society became known as Judson Press. Also in 1921 the National Laymen's Movement was begun, which later became the American Baptist Men. In 1938 the first issue of *The Chronicle* appeared, which later became *Foundations,* which since 1982 has been known as the *American Baptist Quarterly,* the denomination's scholarly journal. In 1944 the NBC created a national conference center at Green Lake, Wisconsin, known at the American Baptist Assembly. In that year, too, the American Baptist Publication Society merged with the Northern Baptist Board of Education to form the American Baptist Board of Education and Publication.

History (1950 to the Present)

Growing out of the many developments of the recent decades and the post–World War II ethos, the NBC established a review commission, which led in 1950 to a new structure and name for the NBC. The denomination took the name of the American Baptist Convention (ABC) and created the top administrative office of general secretary. Reuben Nelson was the first person elected to this position. More recent general secretaries have been Robert C. Campbell, Daniel E. Weiss, and A. Roy Medley.

The American Baptist Women was established in 1951 (now known as American Baptist Women's Ministries). In 1955 both the home and the foreign women's mission societies were merged with the respective American Baptist Home and American Baptist Foreign Mission Societies. The ABC headquarters was relocated to a new facility in Valley Forge, Pennsylvania in 1962 (renamed in 1994 the American Baptist Churches Mission Center).

In 1965 the first of many churches in the African American tradition (see AFRICAN AMERICAN PROTESTANTISM) that belonged to various black Baptist denominations dually aligned with the ABC. Ethnic-racial sensitivities and issues led to the formation of the black caucus in 1968, the Hispanic and Indian caucuses in 1970, and the Asian caucus in 1972.

Another major denominational reorganization took place in 1972, which led to changing the name to the American Baptist Churches in the U.S.A. (ABC-USA). Beginning in 1973 the denomination moved from an annual to a biennial meeting. The Foreign Mission Society became known as the Board of International Ministries, the Home Mission Society as the Board of National Ministries, and the Board of Education and Publication as the Board of Educational Ministries. All three of these boards were known as the program boards. A general board was created, representative of CLERGY and LAITY, the range of geographical regions, and the ethnic-racial composition of the denomination. The general board became the policy-making agency of the ABC-USA, with interlocking relationships with the three program boards, whose meetings were held in common with the general board. Regional bodies also began to share more in the authority structures of the denomination.

In 1973 William T. McKee became the first African American to head a program Board (Educational Ministries). The Feminism and the Church Today project was organized in 1975, which became the Women and the Church project in 1985. In 1980 the Women in Ministry Project was established. In 1989 Jean B. Kim became the first woman to head a program board (Educational Ministries). In 1999 Trinette McCray was elected as the first female clergy president of the ABC-USA.

In 1992 various concerns and tensions within the ABC-USA led to the formation of two groups, the American Baptist Evangelicals and the Association of Welcoming and Affirming Baptists. Also, in 1992 the General Board approved a resolution stating that "We affirm that the practice of homosexuality is incompatible with Christian teaching."

Related Organizations and Denominational Data

The ABC-USA consists of thirty-four regions (related to cities, states, parts of states, and combinations of states; there is also a nongeographical Indian Ministries Region), each of which is led by an executive minister. There is an associate general secretary for Regional Ministries. There is also the Ministers and Missionaries Pension Board, led for many years by Gordan Smith. There are currently seven official caucuses: Asian, Black, Hispanic, Indian, Haitian, Women's, and Young Adult, which represent the interests of these groups within denominational life.

There are sixteen American Baptist–related colleges and universities (see CHRISTIAN COLLEGES; HIGHER EDUCATION) and ten American Baptist–related SEMINARIES and theological schools (American Baptist Seminary of the West, Andover Newton Theological School, Central Baptist Theological Seminary, Colgate Rochester Crozer Divinity School, Eastern Baptist Theological Seminary, Evangelical Seminary of Puerto Rico, Morehouse School of Religion, Northern Baptist Theological Seminary, Shaw University Divinity School, and The Samuel DeWitt Proctor School of Theology, Virginia Union University).

The American Baptist Homes and Hospitals Association, established in 1930, includes seventy-four retirement communities, twenty-six long-term care facilities, twenty children's homes and special services, and eight administrative facilities.

There are many other groups active in ABC-USA life, both within and outside of the official structures of the denomination. Mention has already been made of the American Baptist Evangelicals and the Association of Welcoming and Affirming Baptists. In 1968 the American Baptist Charismatic Fellowship (now known as the Holy Spirit Renewal Ministries in the ABC; Gary K. Clark, national chair since 1981) was organized, and since 1975 it has held a Holy Spirit Conference each summer at the American Baptist Assembly. Various other groups (e.g., the Fellowship of American Baptist Musicians, the Roger Williams Fellowship) serve particular interests within denominational life.

There are about four thousand ordained clergy within the ABC-USA, about 10 percent of whom are WOMEN. Free Will Baptists ordained women as early as 1876 (M. A. Brennan was the first). Although the evidence is difficult to assess, it appears that Susan Elizabeth Cilley Griffin was in 1893 the first woman ordained among what would become the Northern Baptists (see WOMEN CLERGY). By 1928 there were about fifty ordained women within the NBC.

In 2001 about 69 percent of ABC-USA churches were Euro-American, about 20 percent were African American, about 6 percent were Hispanic, with various Asian, American Native, and Haitian churches composing the rest. In that same year about 48 percent of ABC-USA church members were Euro-American, 46 percent were African American, a little over 3 percent were Hispanic, with the remaining 3 percent composing Asian Pacific, American Native, Haitian, and multiracial members.

The ABC-USA has extensive ecumenical connections. It is a member of the NATIONAL COUNCIL OF CHURCHES, the WORLD COUNCIL OF CHURCHES, and the BAPTIST WORLD ALLIANCE. It is an official observer at the NATIONAL ASSOCIATION OF EVANGELICALS and has an observer relationship with the Church of the Brethren (see BRETHREN, CHURCH OF THE).

Distinctives

The ABC-USA holds to classic Baptist principles, with emphasis on "the Lordship and atoning sacrifice of Jesus Christ, believers' baptism, the competency of all believers to be in direct relationship with God and to interpret Scripture, the importance of the local church, the assurance of freedom in worship and opinion, and the need to be Christ's witnesses within society" (from the 2003 ABC-USA web site). There is strong commitment to EVANGELISM, mission, justice, and ecumenical cooperation. The ABC-USA is an inclusive denomination. This is true in terms of its ethnic-racial composition and in terms of its theological spectrum.

In 2001 the General Board approved a new document, the Common Criteria for Cooperating Churches, which was subsequently accepted by at least 75 percent of the thirty-four Regions of the denomination and thus became effective in 2003. The Criteria include commitment to the statement "We Are American Baptists" (which is a short document that includes a fairly traditional statement of trinitarian faith, CHRISTOLOGY and ATONEMENT, and the AUTHORITY of the BIBLE) along with affirmation and participation in ABC-USA purposes and mission at the local, regional, and national levels.

See also Baptist Family; Baptist Missions; Baptists, United States

References and Further Reading

Barnes, Lemuel Call, Mary Clark Barnes, and Edward M. Stephenson. *Pioneers of Light: The First Century of The American Baptist Publication Society 1824–1924*. Philadelphia: The American Baptist Publication Society, 1924.

Brackney, William H. *Baptist Life and Thought: 1600–1980: A Source Book*. Valley Forge, PA: Judson, 1983.

———. *The Baptists*. Westport, CT: Greenwood, 1988.

Freeman, Curtis W., James William McClendon Jr., and C. Rosalee Velloso da Silva. *Baptist Roots: A Reader in the Theology of a Christian People*. Valley Forge, PA: Judson, 1999.

Leonard, Bill J. *Dictionary of Baptists in America*. Downers Grove, IL: InterVarsity Press, 1994.

McBeth, H. Leon. *The Baptist Heritage*. Nashville, TN: Broadman, 1987.

———. *A Sourcebook for Baptist Heritage*. Nashville, TN: Broadman, 1990.

Slaght, Lawrence T. *Multiplying the Witness: 150 Years of American Baptist Educational Ministries*. Valley Forge, PA: Judson, 1974.

Stevens, Daniel Gurden. *The First Hundred Years of the American Baptist Publication Society*. Philadelphia: The American Baptist Publication Society, 1925.

Torbet, Robert G. *A History of the Baptists*. 2d edition. Philadelphia: Judson, 1973.

Vedder, Henry C. *A Short History of Baptist Missions*. Philadelphia: Judson, 1927.

DAVID M. SCHOLER

AMERICAN BIBLE SOCIETY

The American Bible Society (ABS), established in New York City in 1816, rapidly evolved into one of the world's largest scripture production, distribution, and translation agencies. It worked tirelessly to promote pandenominational Protestant unity, served historically as a focal point for American missionary efforts, and developed innovative programs that sought to bring the Bible to a wider audience. By the dawn of the twenty-first century, the ABS constituted one of the most successful and longest-lived philanthropies in the United States. The society's modest beginnings and early struggles, however, offered little clue to its prosperous future.

International and local impulses both contributed to the society's founding. The ABS modeled its constitution and its administrative structure largely on the precedent of the BRITISH AND FOREIGN BIBLE SOCIETY (BFBS), which had been established in London in 1804. The BFBS carefully nurtured and financed the establishment of state and county BIBLE SOCIETIES throughout early nineteenth-century America. The leaders of these scattered organizations, concentrated disproportionately in New England and the middle Atlantic states, felt the need by 1816 for a national institution that would pool their financial resources and coordinate their distribution efforts. They adopted a constitution that stipulated their "sole object" as encouraging "a wider circulation of the Holy Scriptures without note or comment." They created a board of managers that included some of the most socially and politically prominent Protestant laymen of the young republic, and named their creation the American Bible Society.

The ABS's founders sought especially to overcome the denominational divisions and sectarian strife that appeared so pervasive on the antebellum American landscape. The broadly representative governing board appeared somewhat weighted toward Congregationalists and Presbyterians, but also included a respectable representation of Methodists, Baptists, Episcopalians, Quakers, and members of the Dutch Reformed Church. Still, denominational tensions always percolated just below the surface. The balance on the board shifted, for example, in response to demographic change and disagreements within the American Protestant polities. Methodists quickly achieved greater influence within the ABS and constituted a more powerful presence on the board as that denomination expanded rapidly in the 1820s and 1830s. They remained staunch ABS supporters throughout the nineteenth and twentieth centuries. Baptists, in contrast, withdrew from the Bible Society fellowship after a dispute over translation principles in 1836 and established a competing, denomination-based agency (see AMERICAN BIBLE UNION). The ABS quickly found that Christian unity proved difficult to achieve in practice, given that both theological wrangling and political contentiousness fragmented the movement.

Despite this apparent lack of unity, the ABS flourished as an institution. Several factors accounted for its remarkable growth. From its earliest days, the society remained a technological and organizational innovator. As a publisher, the institution rapidly incorporated such innovations as steam-powered presses, stereotype printing, and sophisticated binding equipment into its operations. By the mid-nineteenth century, the ABS's New York headquarters constituted one of the largest and most efficient manufacturing plants in America, and peers recognized the society as a leading force in the printing and publishing trades. Inexpensive mission editions, designed for mass distribution and heavy use, constituted the organization's stock-in-trade.

Other ABS innovations included the development of sophisticated distribution and promotional programs to accomplish its goals. The organization operated through a nationwide network of county and town auxiliaries that shared the ABS's mission, coordinated distribution within their local areas, and received a discount on scriptures purchased from the national office. The ABS thus linked together a national network of committed Christians who volunteered their money and expertise to the cause of circulating bibles and encouraging scripture reading. Gradually, over the course of the nineteenth century, the society relied more heavily on paid agents who handled distribution and fund-raising chores within specific geographical areas. These Bible agents, who reported to administrators in New York, monitored the activities of local auxiliaries, cultivated donors, and promoted the ABS among Protestant congregations. Special distribution programs, such as periodic efforts to supply every family in the United States with a Bible, also generated considerable excitement among the society's core constituency.

The most critical factor in the ABS's long-term success, however, involved the support services that it provided for Protestant denominations. The ABS offered financial backing and technical expertise for scripture translations in hundreds of languages during the nineteenth and twentieth centuries. The society established Bible houses throughout the Near East, Far East, South America, and Latin America, many of which constituted social and intellectual centers for American missionaries. Inexpensive Bibles proved instrumental in a broad range of Protestant missionary efforts, and denominations counted on the ABS for a steady and reliable supply of quality products. The society itself also remained on the lookout for new audiences. It printed special scripture portions for the freed slaves after the CIVIL WAR, pioneered in the production of brailled Bibles for the visually impaired, provided foreign language scriptures for distribution to immigrants arriving at Ellis Island, and even engaged in cooperative ventures with the Roman Catholic Church after the Second Vatican Council.

The society experimented with new products in the late twentieth century, such as a popular series of thematic scripture selections designed to help Christians understand and cope with various social and personal issues. Perhaps its best-known twentieth-century product, however, was the *Good News Bible* (1976). This common-language translation, based on the principle of dynamic equivalence and illustrated with strikingly effective line drawings, proved especially popular with new readers, younger audiences, and people who simply found the seventeenth-century language of the King James Version more baffling than enlightening. The ABS moved ahead with a variety of other innovative translations, even experimenting with multimedia scriptures.

Finally, the ABS also played a major role in cultivating the growth of Bible societies throughout the world. It proved instrumental in founding the United Bible Societies in 1946 and has remained a major financial and administrative supporter of that international consortium. The ABS helped train translators by sponsoring various institutes and funded worldwide distribution programs. It remains a dynamic, adaptable, and innovative organization that plays a significant global role while maintaining many traditional functions within American Protestantism.

See also Bible; Bible Translations

References and Further Reading

Dwight, Henry Otis. *The Centennial History of the American Bible Society.* New York: Macmillan, 1916.

Gutjahr, Paul C. *An American Bible: A History of the Good Book in the United States, 1777–1880.* Stanford: Stanford University Press, 1999.

Lacy, Creighton. *The Word Carrying Giant: The Growth of the American Bible Society.* South Pasadena, CA: William Carey Library, 1977.

Nord, David Paul. "Benevolent Capital: Financing Evangelical Book Publishing in Early Nineteenth-century America." In *God and Mammon: Protestants, Money, and the Market, 1790–1860,* edited by Mark A. Noll. New York: Oxford University Press, 2002.

Wosh, Peter J. *Spreading the Word: The Bible Business in Nineteenth-Century America.* Ithaca, NY: Cornell University Press, 1994.

PETER J. WOSH

AMERICAN BIBLE UNION

Established in 1850 in New York City, the American Bible Union (ABU) assumed a broad mandate to translate and circulate "the most faithful versions of the Sacred Scriptures *in all languages* throughout the world," according to its original 1850 constitution. However, the story of the ABU began with a translation controversy that created a schism within the AMERICAN BIBLE SOCIETY (ABS) during the 1830s. Baptist missionaries in Calcutta had applied to the ABS in 1835 for funding to publish a second edition of their revised New Testament in Bengali. Their request proved controversial because the missionaries elected to translate the Greek term *baptizo* as *immerse* rather than *baptize*. From the Baptist perspective, this choice reflected their desire to remain faithful to the original text and to favor biblical accuracy over mere transliteration. Other Protestants viewed their position as merely sectarian, and an attempt to sacrifice the purity of the biblical text in favor of a narrow theological perspective. The ABS's board of managers, which included a broad denominational representation, voted against sponsoring the translation. Most BAPTISTS on the ABS board, including such major figures within the denomination as William Colgate, Leonard Bleecker, and the Rev. Spencer Cone, resigned shortly thereafter. They established the American and Foreign Bible Society (AFBS) in 1836 as a competitor to the ABS, dedicated to financing biblical translations that supported their beliefs and, in their minds, to promoting scriptures that reflected accurate meanings found in the original Greek.

Controversy soon splintered the AFBS as well. The new organization supported and financed various "immersion" versions developed by overseas missionaries but adopted a fairly conservative approach toward English Bible translations. The AFBS essentially circulated a reprint of the 1611 King James Version, with some modernized spellings and a table that explained the proper meaning of various controversial words. Thus, for example, readers received instructions that Angel, Baptism, Baptize, Bishop, Charity, Church, and Easter should be read respectively as Messenger, Immersion, Immerse, Overseer, Love, Congregation, and Passover. The organization attempted to occupy a middle ground but managed to alienate two important constituencies. Non-Baptists largely viewed the AFBS's English Bible as an effort to cloak denominational principles within scripture, and they remained loyal to the more inclusive and broader-based ABS. Factions within the AFBS itself, including several powerful members who precipitated the initial withdrawal from the ABS, called for a more radical and thoroughgoing revision of the King James Bible.

This issue reached a critical stage in 1850 when the Rev. Cone and his colleague the Rev. William Wyckoff presented the AFBS with a more complete English revision. The organization balked at supporting this new translation, fearing that additional tinkering with the King James Version would irrevocably stamp them as sectarian and permanently cut off comity with other Christians. Cone, Wyckoff, Colgate, and numerous supporters viewed this as excessive timidity and a compromise of basic principles. They resigned from the AFBS, garnered significant financial and intellectual support within the Baptist denomination, and publicly announced their intention to form a rival bible society, vowing to correct over 24,000 documented errors that they had identified in the King James Version. They soon established the ABU with Cone as its first president.

The Union's organizational structure mirrored that of similar American antebellum voluntary institutions. Twenty-four managers met monthly to discharge institutional business, whereas standing committees set policies and supervised activities concerning publication and finance, agencies, versions, legacies, and the library. A small staff conducted affairs at the Union's headquarters on Chambers Street in New York City, and annual anniversary meetings rallied the faithful at prestigious urban churches. The managers established various membership categories for individual donors, and the monthly *Bible Union Reporter* informed the lay constituency. Preparing new translations constituted the highest priority. The ABU immediately announced its intention to support major English, French, and Spanish revisions, and appropriated additional money to circulate immersion versions in Burma, China, and India and to print an Armenian New Testament.

The ABU's reach, however, often exceeded its grasp. The English language project proved particularly problematic. Some of the initial translators lacked sufficient scholarly background and ability, and the committee on versions elected not to publish their New Testament in 1856. This, in part, precipitated an organizational crisis: Spencer Cone had died in 1855, several prominent officers and board members resigned, and some of the translators appeared embittered. Only a general reorganization and the addition of such recognized biblical scholars as Thomas Conant and Horatio Hackett to the translation team kept the project moving along. Still, progress was slow. A complete English New Testament appeared only in 1862–1863, at which time the ABU authorized the distribution of thousands of pocket-size Bibles for CIVIL WAR soldiers. Work on the Old Testament continued throughout the 1860s and 1870s, with individual parts often published serially in the *Bible Union Reporter*. In fact, the complete American Bible Union Version did not appear until after the ABU's dissolution. In 1883 the American Baptist Publication Society (ABPS) in Philadelphia assumed the work of both the AFBS and the ABU and established a new committee to review the Union's version. The ABPS finally issued an "improved edition" of the American Bible Union's New Testament in 1891 and a complete Bible in 1912, "based in part on the Bible Union Version."

Despite its relatively brief history and its overtly denominational roots, the American Bible Union illustrated some significant trends in late nineteenth-century biblical scholarship. It especially reflected the sectarian tensions, intellectual divisions, and personal controversies that severely fragmented the bible movement and strained ecumenical efforts throughout the nineteenth century. Perhaps most tellingly, it constituted part of a broader movement that called into question the authority and authenticity of the King James Version. By arguing that all translations excepting those of the original authors appeared fallible, that language needs to change in response to altered cultural circumstances, and that translators should focus on original meanings rather than words, the ABU placed itself within very modern theological currents.

See also Baptist Missions; Bible; Bible Societies; Bible Translations; Sectarianism

References and Further Reading

Gutjahr, Paul C. *An American Bible: A History of the Good Book in the United States, 1777–1880.* Stanford, CA: Stanford University Press, 1999.

Hills, Margaret T. *The English Bible in America.* New York: American Bible Society and The New York Public Library, 1962.

Winter, J. Gould, and John Winter. *The Claims of the American & Foreign Bible Society, Maintained and Vindicated.* Warren, OH: William J. Tait, 1845.

Wyckoff, William H., and C. A. Buckbee, eds. *Documentary History of the American Bible Union.* 4 vols. New York: American Bible Union, 1857–1867.

PETER J. WOSH

AMERICAN BOARD OF COMMISSIONERS FOR FOREIGN MISSIONS

Starting from a vision of global spiritual conquest shared by a gathering of students at Williams College in 1806, The American Board of Commissioners for Foreign Missions (ABCFM) became the flagship of American Protestant missionary outreach in the nineteenth century.

The Massachusetts General Association, a conservative Congregational conclave centered at Andover Theological Seminary, chartered the Board in 1810. As its controlling vision, the group adopted the Great Commission, Protestant terminology for Christ's New Testament charge to preach the Gospel in every land. New England Congregationalists (see CONGREGATIONALISM) provided most of the early funding and leadership to the formally independent missionary society. The United Foreign Missionary Society, a PRESBYTERIAN and DUTCH REFORMED group, joined the cause in 1826. Because the Board made no ecclesiastical claims, its missionaries maintained allegiance to their own denominations. The ABCFM expanded its geographic reach by deliberately seeking members outside New England and holding annual conferences in such places as Cincinnati and Detroit.

To facilitate fundraising, the Board regularly employed agents who promoted the formation of regional Foreign Mission Societies, as well as smaller local auxiliaries. Beginning in 1821, *The Missionary Herald* carried both news from the mission field and pleas for support to a national audience. Although the group raised just under $48,000 in its first five years, donations between 1855 and 1860 exceeded $2,000,000.

Early Missions

Outreach began in 1812, when four missionaries established outposts in India. Adoniram Judson stood at the forefront of this group, and although his theological convictions and missionary work soon turned in a

Baptist direction (see BAPTISTS; BAPTIST MISSIONS), his name became synonymous with foreign missions and his biography became an inspirational standard (see JUDSON FAMILY). Board missionaries reached Ceylon in 1816 and the Sandwich Islands (Hawaii) in 1820. Many island natives, including several key leaders, preferred missionary material aid and spiritual counsel to the exploitative edge of ongoing commercial contacts. By the 1830s, over 18,000 new believers testified to the efforts of more than ninety Americans and hundreds of native laborers. Hawaii became the Board's model of success, although critics such as American author Herman Melville (1819–1891) declared the mission an unwelcome assault on native culture.

Closer to home, Board missions among Indian tribes in the Old Southwest did not match Hawaiian successes. Mission schools and churches among the Cherokees, Choctaws, Chickasaws, and Creeks yielded some conversions and locally significant increases in literacy rates. However, they also fired resentment among Indian leaders who resisted Western ways, and angered Southerners eager to exploit tribal lands. Internally, Board members debated whether such "civilizing" efforts sullied their spiritual objectives. The Board was also involved in public controversy during the Removal Crisis, when such luminaries as Cherokee missionary Samuel A. Worcester and *Missionary Herald* editor Jeremiah Evarts forcefully defended tribal land claims in the South. Those efforts failed in the 1830s, but Board missionaries persevered in the trans-Mississippi West for most of the century, despite few long-term successes.

By 1850 the Board counted 157 ordained missionaries and 395 total personnel in ten countries. A dozen publication outlets distributed 37,000,000 pages of material annually in thirty languages. ABCFM free schools enrolled nearly 22,000 students. Eighty-five new churches had been established, with membership approaching 25,000.

Growth and Conflict

Growth complicated the Board's effort to maintain consistent mission policy. In the 1850s, Corresponding Secretary RUFUS ANDERSON pressed the society to reaffirm its spiritual purpose, encourage use of the vernacular in mission work, and support the timely transfer of new churches to native control. The Board's Prudential Committee generally concurred in an 1856 report, calling particularly for renewed emphasis on spiritual conversions and direct preaching rather than education, material aid, or other "auxiliary" purposes.

Board president Mark Hopkins also supported these commitments, but church leaders increasingly favored missions that strengthened their own denominational distinctiveness. When the Board's New-School Presbyterian allies reunited with their Old-School brethren in 1870, they also redirected their resources toward denominationally sponsored missions. The Board's Dutch and German Reformed contingents followed similar paths.

Later Developments

Doctrinal battles between Protestant liberals and conservatives in the late nineteenth century provided another source of conflict. The "Andover controversy," marked by debate over whether salvation was attainable in the afterlife, proved particularly divisive. Several conservative leaders departed when the Board affirmed its missionaries' theological freedom, although the society continued a liberal course. In the twentieth century, missions commonly emphasized education, material assistance, social services, and other "civilizing" efforts.

Lay persons accounted for 70 percent of mission personnel by 1910, with over half of them female. Women had long been active as supportive wives and "assistants," but public recognition rarely matched their contributions. In the twentieth century, they became the virtual backbone of the mission field. Many women carried the missionary title even though they lacked ordination. Although formally assigned to the care of indigenous females, they actually served widely in teaching, health care, and other social services.

Theological disputes, denominational resurgence, and the Board's departure from an aggressive spiritual agenda enabled more conservative evangelical groups committed to a "gospel first" strategy to gain mission-field prominence in the twentieth century. War and social upheaval in eastern Asia during the 1930s and 1940s reduced the Board's longstanding missionary presence in Asia.

The ABCFM's affiliation with the United Church Board for World Ministries in 1961 made it the missionary arm of the UNITED CHURCH OF CHRIST and ended 150 years of formal independence.

References and Further Reading

Anderson, Rufus. *Memorial Volume of the First Fifty Years of the American Board of Commissioners for Foreign Missions.* Boston: American Board of Commissioners for Foreign Missions, 1862.

Goodsell, Fred Field. *You Shall Be My Witnesses: An Interpretation of the History of the American Board, 1810–1860.* Boston: American Board of Commissioners for Foreign Missions, 1959.

Hanley, Mark Y. *Beyond a Christian Commonwealth: The Protestant Quarrel with the American Republic, 1830–1860.* Chapel Hill: University of North Carolina Press, 1994.

Hutchison, William R. *Errand to the World: American Protestant Thought and Foreign Missions.* Chicago: University of Chicago Press, 1987.

Strong, William Ellsworth. *The Story of the American Board: An Account of the First Hundred Years of the American Board of Commissioners for Foreign Missions.* 1910 Reprint ed. New York: Arno Press, 1969.

MARK Y. HANLEY

AMERICAN COLONIZATION SOCIETY

The American Colonization Society (ACS), officially the American Society for Colonizing the Free People of Color in the United States, was founded in the winter of 1816–1817 in Washington, D.C. by ROBERT FINLEY, a Presbyterian minister. Revolutionary-era America appeared for a time to be moving toward a slavery-free society. By the first decade of the nineteenth century, however, many church people, including some BAPTISTS, Methodists, and Presbyterians, had retreated from earlier, strong antislavery stances. Freeing enslaved blacks upon condition of their emigration to AFRICA seemed a perfect idea for some.

Supporters (e.g., James Monroe, John C. Calhoun, Bushrod Washington, and blacks including the Methodist Daniel Coker and the Baptists LOTT CARY, Collin Teague, and John Day) argued that colonization would end SLAVERY, bringing relief to the enslaved and removing a sinful taint from the country, thus solving the "problem" that many whites had with the presence of an unacceptable people. The ACS envisioned colonization as a vehicle for Christianizing and "civilizing" Africans and building a prosperous, truly free black nation.

ACS opponents (e.g., African-American leaders RICHARD ALLEN, FREDERICK DOUGLASS, and white abolitionist William Lloyd Garrison), with strong justification, regarded colonization as a scheme cementing slaveholding by removing free, antislavery black communities from support of enslaved siblings. Other concerns were the ACS's insufficient emphasis on the antislavery nature of the enterprise, the endeavor's impracticality, and the insistence that African Americans were already living in their rightful "home" while recognizing people's right to emigrate on their own terms to other lands.

The ACS thus contributed to the founding of the Liberian republic in 1847 and the transport of more than fifteen thousand blacks to LIBERIA by 1885. Nonetheless, the coming of emancipation and constitutional abolition of slavery and recognition of black citizenship crippled the ACS, which limped along until its final dissolution in 1963.

See also Black Methodists; Methodism, North America; Presbyterianism; Slavery, Abolition of

References and Further Reading

Reid, Daniel G., et al., eds. *Dictionary of Christianity in America.* Downers Grove, IL: InterVarsity Press, 1990. Salzman, Jack, et al., eds. *Encyclopedia of African-American Culture and History*, vol. 1. New York: Macmillan, 1996.

Martin, Sandy. *Black Baptists and African Missions: The Origins of A Movement, 1880–1915.* Macon, GA: Mercer University Press, 1989/1998.

Staudenraus, P. J. *The African Colonization Movement, 1816–1865.* New York: Columbia University Press, 1961.

SANDY DWAYNE MARTIN

AMERICAN FRIENDS SERVICE COMMITTEE

The American Friends Service Committee (AFSC) is one of the best known and most honored denominational humanitarian and social change organizations in the United States. Although founded and still governed by Quakers, it now is staffed largely by people who are not members of the Religious Society of Friends. While it still brings relief to victims of war and disaster all over the world, it has become equally committed to attempting to remove the root causes of violence and poverty by bringing about change in unjust social and political structures. This course has won it support in many quarters, but has also brought charges that the AFSC has become overly politicized and has lost touch with American Quakers.

Origins of the AFSC

The impetus for organization of the AFSC was U.S. entry into World War I. In May 1917, a small group of Philadelphia Friends, led by Haverford College professor Rufus M. Jones (1863–1948), met to organize what they called the Friends National Service Committee. Assuming that Quakers would be exempted from the draft, they wished to create a structure by which young Quaker men could render some sort of service, preferably aid to civilians in war-torn areas. Moving quickly, within two months this group had raised thousands of dollars, established a training unit at Haverford College, had made contacts with English Friends and Red Cross staff already engaged in relief work in France, and had changed the name of their organization to the American Friends Service Committee. Relations with the Wilson administration proved tricky, because while recognizing conscientious objection, it wished to keep those engaged in alternative service within the military. Not until February 1918 did the government accept the AFSC's work as an acceptable alternative to military service, by which time the first AFSC Reconstruction Units, as they became known, were already overseas.

In FRANCE, AFSC volunteers engaged in a variety of activities: nursing in hospitals, erecting new housing, farming lands for disabled owners, and otherwise attempting to restore normality to war-torn areas. Most of the members of the Reconstruction Unit, which included some women, were Friends deeply committed to pacifism and other Quaker beliefs, although a few caused concerns by drinking, smoking, refusing to attend religious worship, and even repudiating PACIFISM. The Red Cross was so impressed with the general quality of AFSC work, however, that they encouraged it to remain in France after the war, adding new responsibilities, including work with German prisoners of war.

After the Armistice in 1918, the AFSC made the critical decision to continue work in Europe. Its first major project outside France was in GERMANY, where it undertook a child-feeding program. By June 1920 it was feeding 615,000 children in 87 German cities; the number reached one million by the end of the year and continued to grow through 1924. It undertook similar work in Eastern Europe, particularly in RUSSIA. Its scrupulous neutrality allowed it to work effectively with both the American and Soviet governments. In 1922 it expanded work within the United States when it decided to offer food and clothing to the children of striking coal miners in Pennsylvania and Virginia. The success of such efforts led to the decision in 1924 to make the AFSC a permanent organization, with sections on foreign, interracial, home, and peace service.

Another critical point for the AFSC came in 1929 with the hiring of Clarence Pickett, an Earlham College professor and former Quaker pastor, as executive secretary. Pickett oversaw the expansion of AFSC work along the lines followed in the 1920s, which ranged from efforts to relieve the families of striking textile workers in North Carolina in 1929 to work among children and refugees during the Spanish Civil War. As conditions worsened in Germany in the 1930s, the AFSC set up offices in Berlin and Vienna to try to expedite the departure of Jewish refugees, aiding thousands in their escape before the outbreak of war. The AFSC also undertook new types of work in the United States, such as the attempted resettlement of hundreds of unemployed coal miners in Appalachia on subsistence homesteads. The deep friendship that developed between Pickett and Eleanor Roosevelt, who was especially interested in the Arthurdale Subsistence Homestead in West Virginia, brought the organization considerable positive publicity.

The 1930s also saw a new departure, what amounted to overt political activity by the AFSC. This was the Emergency Peace Campaign of 1936 through 1938, which enlisted hundreds of young Friends in peace caravans to try to arouse sentiment against U.S. involvement in already looming wars in eastern Asia and Europe. It worked in tandem with the political leanings of most American Friends, who tended to be isolationist Republicans in their sympathies.

When war did come, the committee once again engaged in relief work. Efforts in the Far East centered on China, with AFSC workers entering JAPAN after its surrender. The AFSC was generally excluded from Nazi-occupied Europe, although it did work in Vichy, France, before 1942, but after the war it again mounted major efforts, especially to feed children. In the United States its projects included aid to Japanese Americans in the internment camps and the administration of Civilian Public Service camps for conscientious objectors. The quality of AFSC work was so impressive that it won, along with its British counterpart, the Nobel prize for peace in 1947. By 1951, when Clarence Pickett retired, the committee had staff numbering in the hundreds engaged in diverse activities around the world.

Organizational Change

The 1950s also saw fundamental change in the organization. Since the late nineteenth century, American Quakers had been fractured into pastoral and unprogrammed bodies, the former often evangelical in sympathy and strong in the Midwest, the latter more politically and doctrinally liberal and largely on the east coast. In the AFSC's early years, it emphasized ties with the pastoral groups. For example, a 1933 study showed that the single institution that had produced the largest number of AFSC workers was Earlham College in Indiana. The first four executive secretaries—Vincent Nicholson, Wilbur K. Thomas, Clarence Pickett, and Lewis Hoskins—all came out of pastoral Friends.

After World War II, however, this more evangelical, pastoral Quaker strain would be notably less in evidence. On one hand, many of the Friends on the staff were convinced that too many Quakers had made dangerous compromises with the larger society, especially on matters of peace and nonviolence, and wanted to use the AFSC to bring Quakerism back to its radical roots. On the other hand, by 1960 a majority of AFSC staff were not Friends, and most of its donations and money came from non-Friends, impressed by the idealism and accomplishments of the organization. As non-Quakers became increasingly visible, some Quakers had a sense of loss of control, and resented it.

The new direction was also apparent in the programs and commitments of the committee. In the late

1940s, the AFSC made a critical decision to become outspoken in criticizing U.S. dependence on atomic weapons to counter Soviet expansionism, and became more prone to question Cold War orthodoxy. Between 1950 and 1960 several vital changes took place. One was a growing emphasis on domestic affairs in the United States. In 1950 a majority of AFSC funds were spent outside the United States. In 1960 a majority were being dispersed within the country. Much of that new domestic emphasis was focused on matters of race and support for the emerging civil rights movement. The AFSC, for example, was responsible for the first mass distribution of Martin Luther King, Jr.'s *Letter from the Birmingham Jail* (1968), and AFSC staffers like Jean Fairfax played important roles at critical times in places such as Little Rock and Mississippi.

Even more important was a shift in the nature of the AFSC's peace work. The turning point was the publication of *Speak Truth to Power* (1955), an articulate pacifist analysis of American military and foreign policy. As an internal summary put it, the report "challenged the assumption that under present circumstances power could be applied rationally, and a constructive program for peace carried on simultaneously with a program for military defense [and] . . . the assumption that force is the only realistic means of dealing with international problems." The authors concluded, "we would rather give up our military strength and accept the risks that this involves, than keep our guns and lose our democracy." A new vision of pacifism and the traditional Quaker peace testimony was emerging, one that did not simply resist participation in war, but sought fundamental social, political, and economic change in order to remove the sources of all kinds of violence. A 1957 reorganization of the Peace Education Department brought in a leading advocate of this vision, Norman Whitney, as the department's head. By 1960 almost half of AFSC expenditures were devoted to efforts to affect U.S. foreign policy. In the late 1950s and early 1960s, AFSC staff became increasingly visible in public protests, such as vigils at the White House and Fort Detrick, Maryland, to protest chemical weapons research and atmospheric testing of nuclear weapons.

Criticism of U.S. Foreign and Domestic Policies

From the 1950s to the 1970s, the AFSC expanded the range of its work to offer increasingly critical analyses of U.S. foreign and domestic policy. Typical was the 1965 call for a "New China Policy," which in many ways presaged Nixon administration policy in the early 1970s. In 1970 the AFSC called for greater attention to Palestinian rights in *Search for Peace in the Middle East*. In 1971 the AFSC published two important statements: *Who Shall Live*, on world population growth and control, and *Struggle for Justice*, a scathing critique of the American legal system. In 1968, for example, the AFSC annual report showed commitments ranging from support for the Poor People's Campaign in Washington to relief work in Biafra to attempts to mediate conflicts between India and Pakistan to experiments with corn productivity in Mexico to draft counseling all over the United States.

During the Vietnam War, the AFSC emerged as a major force in the antiwar movement. By 1964, staff were publicly expressing concern over U.S. policy, and in 1965, as President Lyndon B. Johnson substantially escalated American involvement, the AFSC offered a pointed response. It included meetings in Paris with a representative of the North Vietnamese government and statements urging a halt to hostilities by all sides with a negotiated settlement. The first mass demonstrations and teach-ins against the war also drew AFSC participation and support. In 1966 the AFSC, with the approval of the South Vietnamese government, began relief work in the south, most notably at Quang Ngai, where thousands of civilian victims of the war were fitted with artificial limbs and treated for other injuries.

Antiwar Activities

From 1966 the AFSC became more pointed and radical in its antiwar activities. In 1967 it began to send medical supplies to North Vietnam as well, arguing that it had a responsibility to relieve human suffering wherever it was found. One official, by 1967, was publicly comparing U.S. treatment of Vietnamese civilians to that of Hitler in Europe during World War II. Both staff and leadership found themselves involved in lengthy, tortuous debates over the conditions under which the AFSC could ally itself with other antiwar groups, especially those in the New Left that did not embrace nonviolence. In 1969 the AFSC joined with a wide range of antiwar groups in the New Mobilization to End the War or "New Mobe," and participated in the 1969 Moratorium Day demonstrations in Washington. Across the country it offered draft counseling and went to court to support staff who tried to withhold what they regarded as war taxes. By 1969 and 1970 antiwar activists with AFSC ties were engaged in radical direct action such as the destruction of draft records, albeit without AFSC endorsement.

This direction did not come without controversy. Many American Quakers, evangelical in religious views and politically conservative, were horrified by what they saw as disloyal, if not procommunist, activism. Even many AFSC staff, especially in the Baltimore, Chicago, and New York regional offices, privately expressed misgivings, arguing that the AFSC was compromising bedrock principles of nonviolence by allying itself with revolutionary leftist groups. Other Quakers, however, criticized the AFSC as too cautious and urged an even more searching critique of what they saw as the depredations of American militarism, capitalism, and imperialism. Many other Friends, especially those in the more doctrinally liberal, unprogrammed yearly meetings that made up Friends General Conference, remained largely supportive of AFSC activities.

These tensions burst into the open with the end of the Vietnam War. Senior staff and board members created considerable controversy with their uncritical view of the victorious communist regime in Vietnam and Cambodia; one was even charged with informing the Hanoi government that a leading Buddhist pacifist was a CIA agent. In a widely reported protest, Quaker economist Kenneth Boulding (1910–1993) staged a sit-in at AFSC headquarters in Philadelphia in March 1977. Today, many in the AFSC see this failure to apply the same standards to the communist regimes in Southeast Asia that AFSC applied to the U.S. government as one of the organization's worst failures.

AFSC Today

At the end of the twentieth century the AFSC continued many of the relief activities that brought it international acclaim in humanitarian circles. Local Quaker meetings still collected used clothing and put together emergency kits to be used in places hit by war or disaster. On the other hand, the AFSC has also felt it appropriate to take public stands on controversial social political issues that it saw as issues of peace, human rights, and justice. In 1979 it added gay men and lesbians to its affirmative action statement. It has embraced a pro-choice position on abortion. In the 1980s it endorsed the nuclear freeze movement and denounced the Star Wars missile defense program. It was outspokenly critical of Reagan administration policy in LATIN AMERICA and Israeli policy in the Middle East. In the 1990s it endorsed gay rights initiatives. These stands, and the relatively small number of Quakers on the AFSC staff (less than 20 percent in the year 2000) have brought charges that it is no longer an organization in which Friends offer service, but has instead become simply another leftist activist group, leading demands that it rename itself the American Service Committee. Some Quaker congregations and yearly meetings have cut ties for this reason. Other Friends, however, continue to see the AFSC as

the most powerful Quaker witness in the larger contemporary world.

References and Further Reading

Fager, Chuck. *Quaker Service at the Crossroads: American Friends, the American Friends Service Committee, and Peace and Revolution*. Falls Church, VA: Kimo Press, 1988.

Frost, J. William. "Our Deeds Carry Our Message: The Early History of the American Friends Service Committee." *Quaker History* 81 (1992): 1–51.

Lewy, Guenter. *Peace and Revolution: The Moral Crisis of American Pacifism*. Grand Rapids, MI: Eerdmans, 1988.

Pickett, Clarence E. *For More Than Bread: An Autobiographical Account of Twenty-Two Years' Service with the American Friends Service Committee*. Boston: Little, Brown & Co., 1953.

Smith, Allen. "The Renewal Movement: The Peace Testimony and Modern Quakerism" *Quaker History* 85 (1996): 1–23.

Weisbord, Marvin. *Some Form of Peace: True Stories of the American Friends Service Committee at Home and Abroad*. New York: Viking, 1968.

THOMAS D. HAMM

AMERICAN LUTHERAN CHURCH

Lutheranism was brought to North America by German and Scandinavian immigrants beginning in the 1620s, although well into the twentieth century, language, settlement patterns, theology, and piety tended to isolate Lutherans from other American Protestant groups. Moreover, theological debates, usually related to the interpretation of sixteenth-century Lutheran confessional documents, particularly the Augsburg Confession, and institutional mergers focused Lutheran attention internally. In 1988, with the formation of the Evangelical Lutheran Church in America (ELCA), most American Lutherans belonged to this body or to the Lutheran Church Missouri Synod (LCMS) and increasingly participated in ecumenical dialogues.

Before the arrival of Henry M. Muhlenberg (1711–1787) in North America from the pietist University of Halle, Germany, in the 1740s (see PIETISM, HALLE), colonial Lutherans were poorly organized and isolated not only from one another but also from the European churches they depended on for support and an educated clergy. The first North American Lutheran congregation was organized in 1649 in New Netherlands, whose boundaries extended from Manhattan to Albany, New York. The initially Dutch congregation was accustomed to being a religious minority, and it included a rich variety of nationalities among its membership. Its Reformed-influenced constitution provided the model for others in subsequent decades. Swedish immigrants brought their own Lutheran church to New Sweden with a royal mandate to evangelize among the natives; a second congregation formed in the Danish West Indies in the 1660s. However, the bulk of the Muhlenberg strand of Lutherans came from the Palatinate in the early 1700s and settled in New York and Pennsylvania. From his base near Philadelphia, Muhlenberg built up and gathered these congregations together. The Ministerium of Pennsylvania (1748) endeavored to unite Lutheran churches with a common order of worship and a means to ordain clergy.

Further migration spread Lutheranism into the western frontier and south into the Carolinas. By the early 1800s its leaders were increasingly Americanized. Samuel S. Schmucker, educated at Princeton, was the leader in organizing a seminary in Gettysburg and a General Lutheran Synod, a second effort to unite Lutherans of several backgrounds. His interest in reviving Lutheran confessional identity turned to revisionism, which prompted the American Lutheranism controversy in the 1850s which related to the question if distinctive Lutheran teachings should be sacrificed to accommodate the sentiment of American Protestantism. Schmucker's opponents included the southern Henkel family, which published an English translation of the *Book of Concord*, and the moderate founders of Philadelphia Seminary and the General Council (1867). Additional European immigration, mainly to the Midwest, provided the basis of a third, more strictly confessional body, the Synodical Council (1872), formed by groups such as the Missouri Synod and the Norwegian Synod.

Major theological disputes about ELECTION (PREDESTINATION), the proper basis for cooperation in SACRAMENT and PREACHING, CHILIASM, and membership in secret societies (The Four Points) consumed considerable energy late in the nineteenth century. Along with these debates came realignments among the synods according to their theological position (more or less strictly confessional) and their tradition of church practice (more or less pietistic). Relatively little official attention was given to issues such as abolition, woman's rights, or temperance, although many individuals were involved, particularly in the latter cause. Despite this doctrinal preoccupation, numerous Lutheran colleges were founded, seminaries established, and hospitals and other charitable institutions begun. William A. Passavant provided significant leadership both among the eastern churches and among the newcomers. The deaconess movement he introduced expanded with guidance from women such as Norwegian Elizabeth Fedde. Following the lead of other Protestants, Lutheran women such as Emmy Evald organized local and federated societies in support of the church's mission, both domestically and abroad, specifically in India, China, and Africa.

In the last two decades of the nineteenth century the trend toward institutional differentiation changed. Three bodies from the Muhlenberg tradition adopted The Common Service (1887), an order for worship that prepared the way for their reuniting as the United Lutheran Church in 1918. The United Norwegian Lutheran Church drew together three moderate groups in 1890. Throughout the twentieth century a series of mergers united bodies, first within ethnic groups and traditions of piety and then across them. Cooperation during World Wars I and II—providing chaplains to military personnel, relief efforts in Europe, and resettlement of refugees in the United States—facilitated the process of mergers. Student work on college campuses was another early arena of cooperation. In 1960 The American Evangelical Lutheran Church (ALC) joined the moderate German-based American Lutheran Church (founded in 1930) with most of the Norwegian-based synods and the commonly named "holy" or "sad" Danes, with headquarters in Minneapolis. This body was often characterized as more rural, more midwestern, and more pietist than the Lutheran Church in America (1963). The LCA included the United Lutheran Church, the Swedish Augustana Synod, and the "happy" Danes as well some others. It was characterized as more urban, more eastern, and more liberal theologically and socially. American Lutherans, led by such men as Franklin Clark Fry, assumed a greater role in world Lutheranism and the Lutheran World Federation.

As Lutherans moved beyond traditional ethnic enclaves, from the mid-twentieth century they increased efforts to expand their membership and to involve themselves more broadly in civic affairs. Caucuses were formed by African-American, Asian, Native American, and Hispanic Lutherans to promote their members' full participation in the life of the church. At its formation in 1988, the ELCA used a representational principle to ensure ethnic and racial diversity, gender balance, and lay participation in decision making. Women gained responsibility locally and in the larger church. In 1970 women's calls to ordained ministry were recognized. The Civil Rights Movement, the Vietnam War, and South African apartheid raised church members' consciousness of their role as citizens. National church bodies, cooperative agencies, and parachurch groups became bolder in making statements on political and social issues, intended more as advisories than as official requirements. Even so, some generated controversy, for example, the ELCA's social statement on human sexuality. In the mid-1970s heated disagreements about biblical interpretation and related issues divided the LCMS.

Having stood apart for decades, in the last half of the twentieth century Lutherans were energetic participants in ecumenical conversations, both official and informal. Cooperation grew between congregations and in local projects. Beginning in 1962 the churches engaged in formal dialogues with Reformed churches, Roman Catholics, and others in the United States and internationally. These dialogues and resulting agreements prompted debate among Lutherans about the essentials of their confessions and traditions. At issue were matters of doctrine such as justification relative to Roman Catholic theology and matters of governance such as the historic episcopate relative to Episcopalians. The LCMS continued its stricter standards of theological agreement, whereas the ELCA moved into full communion with churches in the Reformed tradition and the Episcopalians.

See also Lutheranism

References and Further Reading

Klein, Christa R. "Lutheranism." In *Encyclopedia of American Religious Experience: Studies of Traditions and Movements,* edited by Charles H. Lippy and Peter W. Williams, 3 vols., 431–450. New York: Charles Scribner's Sons, 1988.

Lagerquist, L. DeAne. *The Lutherans.* New York: Greenwood Press, 1999.

Nelson, E. Clifford, ed. *Lutherans in North America.* Philadelphia: Fortress Press, 1975.

Pelikan, Jaroslav. "Lutheran Heritage." In *Encyclopedia of American Religious Experience: Studies of Traditions and Movements.* Edited by Charles H. Lippy and Peter W. Williams. 3 vols., 419–430. New York: Charles Scribner's Sons, 1988.

Wiederanders, Robert C., and Walter G. Tillmans, *The Synods of American Lutheranism,* rev. ed. St. Louis: LHC, 1998.

L. DeAne Lagerquist

AMERICAN MISSIONARY ASSOCIATION

The American Missionary Association (AMA) was a nineteenth- and early twentieth-century missionary agency associated with New England Congregationalism. The AMA was formed in 1846 from the merging of the Union Missionary Society, the Committee for West Indian Missions, and the Western Evangelical Missionary Society.

As an evangelical mission agency (see Evangelicalism), the AMA continued the work of the parent organizations in Africa and Jamaica and initiated new work in Hawaii, Egypt, and Thailand. However, the primary distinction of the AMA was a strong antislavery agenda (see Slavery, Abolition of). The leadership protested against the silence of other mission agencies with regard to the "peculiar institution," and advocated both ecclesiastical reform and political action to end slavery. In 1847 the agency began to provide care and relief for slave refugees in Canada,

sending aid workers, teachers, and preachers to establish schools and churches. However, the primary field for the AMA was the United States. By the mid-1850s over one hundred missionaries had been sent to the West and to the slave states of Missouri, North Carolina, and Kentucky. These agents often suffered popular and political repression in their efforts to proclaim the gospel and establish religious schools on an avowedly antislavery basis.

By the outbreak of the Civil War, the AMA was functioning more as an antislavery society than as a conventional missionary agency. Throughout the war years, hundreds of teachers and missionaries provided relief, spiritual care, and education to the slaves escaping across the Confederate lines. Heroic efforts were given to the prevention of physical and sexual exploitation and abuse by the liberating Union Army. At the War's end, the agency refocused its efforts and energy toward meeting the multiple needs of the freedmen. By 1868 over five hundred missionaries were at work in the South, providing relief, aiding the former slaves in the acquisition of land and their civil and political rights, and establishing churches and schools. The Congregational Church movement was generally unsuccessful in the South, primarily because of the determination of black religious leaders to maintain their independence from white control. It is in the area of education that the AMA made a lasting contribution.

The leadership of the AMA viewed the development of educated, moral, and industrious African American citizens as essential to the survival of the black community and the nation. Hundreds of schools were founded and staffed throughout the South. As governments took responsibility for many of these elementary and secondary schools, the AMA shifted its focus to the development of normal schools and colleges. Some of these schools did not succeed nor survive, but among the successes were Hampton, Fisk, Atlanta, Dillard, and Howard universities.

Irrespective of the noble motives, tensions and difficulties soon emerged between AMA personnel and the African Americans they hoped to serve. AMA agents were not simply teachers or aid workers; they were deeply committed evangelical Christians of their time. They were particularly disturbed by card playing, drinking, dancing, and "worldly amusements" on the Sabbath. Their attempts to inculcate these mores into the community they served were not well received, particularly when these efforts turned to open and often stinging criticism of black religious leadership.

The more serious issue was that of control and paternalism. Although AMA agents had worked in partnership with black religious leaders and educational associations from the beginning, tensions soon arose over the control of educational institutions and the transition toward black faculty. AMA agents were not free of the paternalism and racial prejudice that marked the entire white society of the age. Whereas the AMA remained one of the more staunch defenders of education, moral reform, and political rights for African Americans, by the end of the century the realities of the "Reconstructed" South had greatly tempered the passion of the early years. However, the AMA continued to serve the black community of the South, and for over a century, AMA colleges and universities provided the best quality education available to southern blacks. The modern CIVIL RIGHTS MOVEMENT sprung directly from the faculties and graduates of those institutions.

By the end of the nineteenth century, the AMA had relinquished its international mission work to the AMERICAN BOARD OF COMMISSIONERS FOR FOREIGN MISSIONS and redirected much of its traditional missionary activity back toward NATIVE AMERICANS. In the twentieth century, the AMA was merged into the home mission department of the Congregational Christian Churches and in 1957 merged into the UNITED CHURCH OF CHRIST.

References and Further Reading

American Missionary Association. "The Constitution of the American Missionary Association." *The American Missionary* 34 no. 5 (1880): 157–179.

Beard, Augusts F. *A Crusade of Brotherhood: A History of the American Missionary Association.* Boston: The Pilgrim Press, 1909.

Richardson, Joe M. *Christian Reconstruction: The American Missionary Association and Southern Blacks, 1861–1890.* Athens: The University of Georgia Press, 1986.

Tinder, D. G. "American Missionary Association." In *Dictionary of Christianity in America*, edited by Robert D. Linder, Daniel G. Reid, Bruce L. Shelley, and Harry S. Stout, 47. Downers Grove, IL: InterVarsity Press, 1990.

JAMES D. CHANCELLOR

AMERICAN SOCIETY OF CHURCH HISTORY

The American Society of Church History (ASCH) was founded in March of 1888 through the efforts of PHILIP SCHAFF (1819–1893), a Swiss-American scholar whose energy and example greatly improved the level of critical historical scholarship in this country. Schaff, by then Washburn professor of church history at Union Theological Seminary in New York City, hosted seventeen academics at his mid-Manhattan home for the inaugural session. The small group there determined to form an association for personal interaction and mutual support, affirming their interest in pursuing "church history as a science in an unsectarian, catholic spirit." In December of that same year

ASCH convened for its first annual meeting. Schaff was named first president, and he served in that capacity for six years until his death in 1893. Meetings and membership were small, although annual fees were only $3. In its early years ASCH was largely an elite club for seminary professors who lived along the eastern seaboard.

The Society's first secretary was Samuel M. Jackson, bibliographer and lecturer at Columbia University, who corresponded at length with managers of the American Historical Association, a much larger professional organization founded four years earlier. Although relations between the two groups were cordial, they remained separate entities. Even though its resources were meager, the ASCH printed bound volumes of scholarly essays and papers, subsidizing as well the publication of a thirteen-volume collection known as *The American Church History Series.* During Schaff's presidency members apparently kept faith that their enterprises would succeed, but collapse seemed imminent between 1893 and 1895 when John F. Hurst was president. The following year George P. Fisher presided over a meeting that nullified ASCH independence and placed it within the AHA's larger aegis.

The existence of ASCH was rather vague and shadowy for the next ten years. Church historians continued to meet as a subsection of the larger group. Samuel Jackson sparred continuously with AHA administrators over the difficulty of publishing papers on ecclesiastical topics, although a modicum of Schaff's followers persisted in sharing their interest despite such problems. Finally, after nine years of indeterminate status, they reconstituted the society in 1906, and it has maintained vigorous activities ever since. Most of the administrative framework copied previous patterns, but one change in the renewed constitution, taking a lesson from either Schaff's longevity or Hurst's ineptitude, stipulated that no president could serve for more than one year or succeed himself. With that revised constitution and new bylaws ASCH was incorporated by the State of New York in March of 1916. Adding to Schaff's simple encouragement for students to pursue their work, the charter's statement of purpose mentioned support for publishing "papers, books, writings, reports, articles, and data." It also declared an intention to collect and preserve historical documents, create a depository library, and raise funds to facilitate scholarly endeavor.

Membership grew slowly during the first half of the twentieth century. There were approximately sixty adherents in the reorganized ASCH, and an average of one hundred more were added in ensuing decades. However, membership began to increase dramatically after World War II. In 1945 there were 444 people on the rolls, including a professor in JAPAN whose dues had been paid annually by an American friend. The list had grown to 618 in 1955; to 983 in 1965; and to 1,468 in 1975. Thereafter membership figures have fluctuated around an average of fourteen hundred people each year. Most of them reside in the UNITED STATES, but there are members in over twenty other countries as well, notably CANADA, ENGLAND, Japan, and the NETHERLANDS, even including one each in Cuba, Iran, and RUSSIA. Early in the twentieth century meetings were always held in New York, confirming an established profile of eastern parochialism. However, by 1925 Shirley J. Case, a church historian at the University of Chicago, prevailed in arguing for expansion. Thereafter a second annual meeting convened each springtime, mostly in midwestern cities at first to give ASCH more geographical balance. These patterns and this criterion have continued until the present.

One more structural evolution is worth noting. Early administrations were cliquish and self-perpetuating. They slowly expanded to include committees to supervise membership, research, and finances. By 1970, however, ASCH constituency had so increased in numbers, gender, geographical distribution, denominational variegation, and ethnic identity that control could no longer remain in the hands of a few. In that year restructuring allowed for more democratic participation. The new arrangement created a council, in addition to the usual president, president-elect, and secretary, the better to secure a wider range of advice and to distribute responsibility in formulating policy. A total of fifteen members now constitute three classes, each class serving for three years in a consultative body, and then adding a fourth year as members of a committee on nominations, which chooses succeeding personnel to the council.

Despite economic uncertainties and low membership, the Society inaugurated in 1932 what has turned out to be its most outstanding feature. That year it launched a journal, entitled simply *Church History,* with a circulation of 285. There had been previous attempts to support scholarly publication through ventures variously named "monographs" and "studies," but those efforts never exhibited much strength or elicited much support. By contrast the journal, which featured essays, book reviews, and roundtable discussions, proved a better outlet for professional expression. Original editorial offices were at the University of Chicago and, with rare and temporary exceptions, remained there until 1997. These continually vigorous editorial activities are now housed at Duke University, with the change of scene demarked symbolically by the addition of a subtitle to the masthead: Studies in Christianity and Culture. The new office functions with five editors, six associates, a board of fourteen advisors, and hundreds of willing consultants residing across the continent. Over the years the journal has become the touchstone and template of ASCH identity. With a current circulation of approximately three thousand in more than fifty countries, this crowning achievement demonstrates what church history stands for in this country. As an expression of the interests and activities of those who constitute ASCH, *Church History* embodies and exhibits the standards that define the state of the discipline in American thought and practice.

References and Further Reading

Bowden, Henry W., ed. *A Century of Church History: The Legacy of Philip Schaff.* Carbondale IL: Southern IL University Press, 1988.

HENRY W. BOWDEN

AMERICAN UNITARIAN ASSOCIATION

Until 1961 the American Unitarian Association (AUA) was the primary organizing body for Unitarianism in the UNITED STATES, an influential liberal Protestant denomination, which emerged from within Massachusetts CONGREGATIONALISM after the American Revolution. Unitarians have tended to stress inclusiveness and intellectual freedom throughout their history. This, at times, has produced a resistance to statements of principles, tests of membership, or denominational institutionalization. The history of the AUA reflects this tension, and can be told in terms of the internal debates and external challenges that forced Unitarians to assess their shared beliefs and perception of themselves as a group. Unitarians have not been mere reactionaries, however. They have also articulated a positive and coherent religious vision, one deeply committed to social responsibility, personal morality, intellectual freedom, and a good and just God.

Foundations

The American Unitarian Association arose in the context of debates between Arminian and Calvinist Congregationalists in eighteenth- and nineteenth-century New England. ARMINIANISM denies the doctrines of PREDESTINATION, vicarious ATONEMENT, and human depravity central to Puritan CALVINISM. Instead, Arminian liberals embrace the goodness and mercy of God and the possibility of universal SALVATION through Christ and human will. During the first Great Awakening (see AWAKENINGS), Arminian ministers Charles Chauncy (1705–1787) and JONATHAN MAYHEW (1733–

1804) pushed liberal, rationalistic Protestantism into the mainstream of New England religious discourse. Chauncy championed a "supernatural rationalism," maintaining the centrality of revelation and Scripture while claiming that the truths contained therein are open to analysis by "unassisted reason" (Wright 1975: xiv). He strenuously opposed what he considered to be the excessive emotionalism of the REVIVALS sweeping through New England mid-century because they neglected the role of the human intellect and will in religious life. Chauncy and fellow liberals did not completely deny the role of the affections in religion, but Chauncy's staid, literary PREACHING style reflected his rationalistic position and contributed considerably to liberal Protestantism's appeal to the educated, urban elite of New England.

Anti-Trinitarian theology is less important to understanding the founding of the American Unitarian Association than Arminianism, but it deserves to be mentioned. Most early Unitarians identified themselves as Arians, that is, they shared the views of the fourth-century theologian Arius who claimed that Christ was divine yet subordinate to God. Others, such as James Freeman (1759–1835), the minister of the first Unitarian church in America, subscribed to SOCINIANISM, based on the thought of radical REFORMATION theologian FAUSTO SOZZINI (SOCINUS) (1539–1604). Socinianism proclaimed Christ's humanity and special purpose as God's instrument and, by denying Christ's divine nature, was viewed by many Trinitarians as a greater HERESY than Arianism. Socinian movements took hold in POLAND, Transylvania, and ENGLAND before JOSEPH PRIESTLY popularized Socinian Unitarianism in Pennsylvania in 1794.

Unitarian Controversy and Unitarian Christianity

Despite their differences, liberal Arminians and orthodox Calvinists coexisted passably within the "Standing-Order" of Congregationalist churches until the nineteenth century. Then, in 1804, internal tensions turned to schism with the appointment of a liberal, Henry Ware (1764–1845), to replace popular, moderate Calvinist David Tappan (1752–1803) as the Hollis professor of divinity at Harvard College. The opposition to Ware from orthodox Calvinists was fierce and public, especially from Jedidiah Morse (1761–1826), a minister and an overseer for the college. Morse failed to block Ware's appointment in 1805, the 1806 election of liberal president Samuel Webber (1759–1810), or the appointments of three liberal faculty members over the next decade.

Morse retaliated by taking actions calculated to deepen the rift. One was to establish institutional separation by founding the Andover Theological Seminary in 1808 as a bastion of orthodox Calvinism. Second, in an 1812 pamphlet entitled "American Unitarianism," Morse insinuated that New England liberals such as James Freeman shared radical views with English Unitarian Theophilus Lindsey. A subsequent review by Jeremiah Evarts (1781–1831) in Morse's journal, the *Panoplist,* further alleged that liberals were in secret sympathy with Lindsey, a fact that they concealed deliberately and for which they should be denied Christian fellowship. Orthodox minister John Codman (1782–1847) quickly agreed and announced he would not exchange pulpits with liberal ministers. Codman's declaration was viewed by all as a serious rebuke to the Arminian clergy.

Deeply troubled, WILLIAM ELLERY CHANNING (1780–1842) responded for the liberals in 1815. He initiated an exchange of open letters with orthodox ministers refuting the charges made by Morse and Evarts and protesting their evident attempt to divide the Congregationalist Standing-Order. SECTARIANISM, not Unitarianism, was the real danger to Christianity. In 1819 Channing expanded on his arguments, delivering the first manifesto of American Unitarianism at the ordination of Jared Sparks (1789–1866) in Baltimore. In his address, "Unitarian Christianity," he articulated a positive statement of Unitarian beliefs, distinct from orthodox doctrine on the issues of God's unity and perfect moral nature, the lack of scriptural evidence for the Trinity, and the subordinate divinity of Jesus Christ. Channing went beyond supernatural rationalism to argue that the BIBLE could be analyzed like any other book using the techniques of HIGHER CRITICISM, and asserted that scriptural truth must always be harmonized with NATURAL LAW and the will of God.

"Unitarian Christianity" sparked what has been called "the Unitarian controversy," a period of around twenty years of public theological debate waged between such worthy opponents as Andover's Moses Stuart (1780–1852) and Leonard Woods (1774–1854) and Harvard's Henry Ware and Andrews Norton (1786–1853). Many Unitarian Christians rethought their resistance to denominational organization at this time and founded informal societies, such as the Anonymous Association and Channing's Berry Street Conference. Others published journals to facilitate communication between liberal congregations, a few of which would play prominent roles in the flourishing literary culture of the nineteenth century.

The American Unitarian Association

As part of this organizational trend, the American Unitarian Association was formed on May 26, 1825.

AUA founders were interested in addressing some of the structural needs of Unitarian Christians and in diffusing knowledge "of pure Christianity" throughout America. To this end the AUA published tracts and pamphlets, and sponsored missionary efforts in America for the purpose of organizing new churches (although a few missionaries also would go to INDIA in the antebellum period). Despite meager support from its members and little real power within Unitarian churches, the Association grew steadily over the next ten years, its membership made up of mostly well-educated, well-heeled, and urban parishioners from New England's oldest churches. By 1850 more than 90 percent of all Unitarian churches would be found in the northeast, while almost all of the Congregationalist churches within thirty-five miles of Boston would be Unitarian.

After debates with the orthodox Andover crowd abated in the early 1830s, Unitarians entered into a period of prolific creativity in literature, education, and social reform. Belief in progress and human perfectibility manifested in the promotion of "moral philosophy," education, and literature as important sources of moral influence and intellectual stimulation. Unitarian poets and authors include many of the literary lights of the age, including Oliver Wendell Holmes (1809–1894), Henry Wadsworth Longfellow (1807–1882), and Nathaniel Hawthorne (1804–1864). Education reformer Horace Mann (1796–1859) established the nation's first public school system and teaching college. Unitarian social reformers crusaded for the abolition of SLAVERY, prison reform, TEMPERANCE, women's rights, and ministry to the poor. Channing, Dorothea Dix (1802–1887), and ELIZABETH CADY STANTON (1815–1902) provided some of the most eloquent and impassioned defenses of human dignity and HUMAN RIGHTS during the nineteenth century.

The Challenge from Transcendentalism

Meanwhile, a new and bitter debate was fomenting that would force further denominational self-definition, this time from within the Unitarian fold. The Transcendentalist controversy, as it has come to be called, was a rebellion led by RALPH WALDO EMERSON (1803–1882), THEODORE PARKER (1810–1860), and MARGARET FULLER (1810–1850), among others, against the rationalism and Biblicism of the previous generation. "New School" Transcendentalists took the Unitarian principles of personal freedom, an ordered creation, and God's infinite moral goodness to new extremes, fusing them with European ROMANTICISM and Hindu mysticism. The result was a diverse constellation of beliefs shared by many Transcendentalists, including

that of an immanent, depersonalized God present in all of NATURE, a harmonious natural world, and the role of intuition in communing with God through nature. Some Transcendentalists declared the Bible, history, and much of Christian THEOLOGY irrelevant to religion and rejected revelation and the miracles of Christ. Emphasis on intuition and nature opened up access to religious truth for the unlettered masses, working against Unitarian elitism.

These views scandalized many Unitarians. From Emerson's "Divinity School Address" on July 15, 1838 until the CIVIL WAR, debates between Unitarians and Transcendentalists were frequent and acrimonious. Defenders of Unitarian Christianity Andrews Norton (1786–1853) and Francis Bowen (1811–1890) drew on their wide knowledge of higher criticism and philosophy to counter Transcendentalist pantheism and emphasis on intuition. Theodore Parker's sermons, "The Transient and Permanent in Christianity" and "The Relation of Jesus to His Age and the Ages," caused such furor among less-radical Unitarians that the Boston Association of Ministers took the unprecedented step of asking him to resign his ministry. Suddenly, Unitarians had to decide where the limits of their tolerance and inclusiveness lay. Parker refused to resign and continued to draw thousands to his antislavery lectures and sermons. His popularity with young Unitarian ministers prompted the American Unitarian Association to issue their first "declaration of opinion" in 1853, reaffirming their commitment to the authority of Christian Scripture, revelation, and personal freedom.

Transcendentalists were not only interested in provoking Unitarian wrath, however. Their contributions to literature, social reform, and education had far-reaching influence, disproportionate to their small numbers. A prime example of this was Thomas Starr King (1824–1864), minister to San Francisco's First Unitarian Church in the 1860s. A powerful orator and abolitionist like his mentor Parker, King is credited with persuading Californians to support the Union during the Civil War. King combined Transcendentalist love of nature with the so-called divine mandate of Manifest Destiny to produce a particularly Californian Unitarianism, as mystical as it was confident in California's special role in America's divine destiny.

Revitalization and Consensus

Many moderate Unitarians worked to keep the dispute from turning to a permanent rift. After the Civil War Henry W. Bellows (1814–1882) stepped forward to advocate a more unified Unitarianism with improved organization. Noticing the detrimental effect that the Transcendentalist controversy had on membership and morale, Bellows called for a national conference to bring churches together and revitalize the denomination. When the first national conference convened in 1865, Bellows was pleased to find that a "broad Church" group of moderate Unitarians made up the majority and were eager to work out a way for both conservative and radical Unitarians to be included in the new organization. Some Transcendentalists also expressed a conciliatory desire, notably Frederic Henry Hedge (1805–1890), whose understanding of Transcendentalist intuition contributed to his high valuation of Christianity rather than detracted from it, as was often the case. Bellows and many moderates saw Christianity as a "universal religion" that should not be so narrowly defined as to alienate free thinkers. He hoped to avoid doctrinal disputes and convince conference delegates to organize around common work rather than a common creed.

The first National Conference of Unitarian Churches was deemed a success, although dissent among radicals persisted. The next year at the National Conference, radical Francis Ellingwood Abbot (1836–1903) proposed a revision to the preamble of the conference's constitution that eliminated reference to the "Lordship of Jesus Christ" and gave a broader definition of Christianity as "Love, Righteousness, and Truth" (Wright 1975:79). When Abbot's proposal was rebuffed, several frustrated radicals formed the Free Religion Association (FRA), a small, diverse group of thinkers interested in "scientific religion," social reform, and humanism. Although the FRA never posed an institutional threat to Unitarianism, free religionists such as Octavius Brooks Frothingham (1822–1895) and Abbot exerted considerable influence on Unitarianism for years to come. Abbot was instrumental in bringing contemporary scientific concepts to bear on Unitarian thought, including the progressive evolutionary theories of Charles Darwin (see DARWINISM).

Under Bellow's influence Unitarians grappled with the issues of collective identity, consensus, and institutionalization for the next twenty-five years. In 1867 the NCUC adopted a clause to its constitution that made acceptance of its principles noncompulsory. Individuals drafted their own distillations of Unitarian belief, such as James Freeman Clarke's (1810–1888) *Ten Great Religions* and his 1886 answer to Calvin, "Five Points of New Theology." In 1887 the Western Unitarian Conference adopted William Channing Gannett's (1840–1923) statement of Unitarian principles, "Ten Things Most Commonly Believed To-Day Among Us," ending a long dispute between radical "Unity Men" and conservative Christian Unitarians that imperiled Western missionary efforts.

The Twentieth Century and the Universalist Renaissance

The twentieth century saw more organizational changes for the AUA and a general drift away from Christianity toward ethical humanism among Unitarians. The AUA was consolidated with the National Conference in 1884, and AUA president Samuel A. Eliot (1862–1950) did much to centralize and provide financial stability to the organization during his tenure (1900–1927). The Beacon Press was founded in 1902 to improve publishing efforts. Support for secular colleges and international service and missionary efforts expanded after World War I, whereas outreach to other liberal Christians was encouraged. "Logical theism" characterized early twentieth-century Unitarianism, a blend of natural theology, progressive evolution, and belief in experience as the key to knowledge. During the Depression this shifted toward a religious humanism, in which theism was downplayed for an ethics of human perfectibility, scientific reason, and service to humanity. These tendencies coalesced in the Humanist Manifesto of 1933, signed by several Unitarians, which defined religion as outmoded "doctrines and methods" and based morality on freedom and the "common good" rather than on supernatural sources.

The presidency of Frederick May Eliot (1889–1958), known as the "Unitarian Renaissance," was an optimistic period of community building with other liberal Protestants, a decentralization of AUA control, and increased lay involvement in AUA affairs. Unitarians of this period (1937–1958), both humanist and theist, debated the limits of freedom and organizational control, and participated on a large scale in national affairs and international service programs. Eliot's interest in promoting a universal liberal religion led him to begin the process of AUA merger with the Universalist Church of America, which his successor Dana McLean (1908–1986) completed in 1961.

See also Antitrinitarianism; Awakenings; Human Rights; Liberal Protestantism and Liberalism; Puritanism; Slavery, Abolition of; Transcendentalism; Universalism; Unitarian Universalist Association

References and Further Reading

Ahlstrom, Sydney E., and Jonathan S. Carey. *An American Reformation : A Documentary History of Unitarian Christianity*. San Francisco: International Scholars Publications, 1998.

Howe, Daniel Walker. *The Unitarian Conscience: Harvard Moral Philosophy, 1805–1861*. Scranton, PA: Wesleyan University Press, 1988.

Hutchison, William R. *The Transcendentalist Ministers; Church Reform in the New England Renaissance.* New Haven, CT: Yale University Press, 1959.

Robinson, David. "The Unitarians and the Universalists." In *Denominations in America,* no. 1. Westport, CT: Greenwood Press, 1985.

Wilbur, Earl Morse. *A History of Unitarianism.* Boston: Beacon Press, 1965.

Wright, Conrad. "American Unitarianism, 1805–1865." In *Massachusetts Historical Society Studies in American History and Culture,* no. 1. Boston: Massachusetts Historical Society and Northeastern University Press, 1989.

———, ed. *A Stream of Light: A Sesquicentennial History of American Unitarianism.* Boston: Unitarian Universalist Association, 1975.

ERIKA W. DYSON

AMERICANS UNITED FOR THE SEPARATION OF CHURCH AND STATE

Founded in 1947 in Washington, D.C. as Protestants and Other Americans United for Separation of Church and State (POAU), later changed to Americans United (AU), the organization represents a coalition of strict separationists. Support for religious freedom and separation of church and state as declared in the founding documents was favored originally by both rationalists and pietistic revivalists. However, the spectrum of interpretation of these two founding principles has ranged widely from "separationist" to "accommodationist," and the history of interaction among religious groups on these issues has been complex. For religious bodies to be separate from and yet enjoy interplay with the state and to act as a moral force on it has presented serious problems.

Wide-ranging anti-Catholicism has existed in the United States since the nineteenth century NATIVISM movement and the Know-Nothing Party. The founders of POAU denied that their organization was anti-Catholic, but it was definitely born in such a context. Fanned by Catholic agitation on behalf of public funding for parochial schools and President Franklin Roosevelt's (1882–1945) appointment of Myron C. Taylor as his personal representative to the Vatican in 1939, a number of Protestant leaders sensed a threat to the separation of church and state. An initial meeting held in September 1946 in Washington and others like it led to the organization of POAU on November 20, 1947. Among the leaders were such prominent figures as Edwin McNeill Poteat (Colgate–Rochester Divinity School president), Charles Clayton Morrison (*Christian Century* editor), John A. MacKay (Princeton Theological Seminary president), Methodist Bishop G. Bromley Oxnam, and Louise D. Newton (Southern Baptist Convention president). They issued a manifesto of eight points stating the objectives of the new organization.

Another immediate motivation for the founding of the group was the 1947 Supreme Court decision in the Everson bus case, which allowed the use of public transportation to take students to parochial schools (*Everson v. Board of Education,* 330 US 1). The manifesto called on "patriotic" citizens to "resist every attempt by law or the administration of law further to widen the breach in the wall of separation of church and state." In addition, it demanded the "immediate discontinuance of the ambassadorship to the papal head of the Roman Catholic Church." Denying any anti-Catholicism whatsoever, the manifesto correctly affirmed in its conclusion: "Profound differences separate us in the area of religious faith, but these differences have no relevancy in the pursuit of our objectives as clearly defined in this manifesto. The issue of separation of church and state has arisen in the political area and we propose to meet it there" (Pfeiffer, 1967).

Although AU in its beginnings appeared to be anti-Catholic, the initial anti-Catholic denial was certainly weakened by the publication of AU's early "bible," Paul Blanshard's *American Freedom and Catholic Power* in 1949. However, the AU experienced pilgrimage and change, and its separationist stance was far broader than matters involving the Catholic Church. AU established its headquarters in Washington, D.C., and local chapters in large cities across the nation. Already in 1948 the organization was publishing a single-sheet monthly newsletter, *Church and State Newsletter.* Expanding to sixteen and then twenty-four pages, the name was changed to *Church and State: A Monthly Review* (1952–1961) and finally to *Church and State.* The news organ called for "complete functional and financial separation." It provided reports and news analyses having to do with tax support for sectarian institutions and preferment for certain denominations, as well as profiling leaders and citizens who stood up in some way to defend separation of church and state. Reviewing literature in the field as well, the newsletter referred to itself as being "interfaith" and never accepted any commercial advertising, to avoid even the appearance of external pressure on the group's positions. Eventually AU also established the Americans United Research Foundation and the Americans United Fund.

In 1951 President Truman hoped to appoint Mark Clark as an Ambassador to the Vatican. AU, the National Council of Churches, and the National Association of Evangelicals combined forces in opposing the appointment and Truman was forced to withdraw the nomination. By 1984 times had changed; although opposed by AU and other strict separationists, President Ronald Reagan (1911–) appointed William Wilson as ambassador to the Vatican, and full diplomatic ties with the Vatican were established.

In 1960 religious fundamentalists campaigned against the presidential candidacy of Catholic John F. Kennedy. One of the ringleaders of the opposition, Southern Baptist W. A. Criswell, feared the "death of a free church and a free state." Because Kennedy repudiated aid to parochial schools as well as official ties with the Vatican, his presidential bid was actually supported by AU, which was more sensitive to the changing times. The liberal positions of the Second Vatican Council (1962–1965) also helped moderate anti-Catholic feelings in AU.

Since 1960 AU has given support to a wide range of issues. In 1962 it supported the *Engel v. Vitale* case and stated that the removal of school-sponsored prayer actually increased religious freedom (*Engel v. Vitale*, 370 US 421). In 1973 AU threw its support to *Roe v. Wade* in favor of women's freedom of choice. By the 1980s AU was opposing the political activities of the Moral Majority and Religious Right as being violations of separation. Many pamphlets were published by AU pointing out the mythical nature of views held by the Religious Right on the separation issue. More recently AU has opposed the use of tuition tax credits to assist any private schools. Its Research Foundation has also produced many materials, including videos, as aids to public school teachers in relation to teaching *about* religion. AU has also used its funds in support of lawsuits defending religious liberty. Its spokespersons have also given widespread testimony before Congress and state legislatures on separation issues.

See also Bill of Rights; Catholic Reactions to Protestants; Catholicism, Protestant Reactions; Christian Right; Church and State, Overview; Ecumenism

References and Further Reading

Americans United for Separation of Church and State. *Church and State*, vols. 1–55, Washington, D.C.: Americans United, 1948–2002.

Blanshard, Paul. *American Freedom and Catholic Power*. Boston: Beacon Press, 1949.

Boston, Robert. *Why the Religious Right Is Wrong About Separation of Church and State*. Buffalo: Prometheus Books, 1993.

Haynes, Charles C., ed. *Religious Freedom in America*. Washington, D.C.: Americans United Research Foundation, 1986.

Lowell, C. Stanley. *Embattled Wall*. Washington, D.C.: Protestants and Other Americans United, 1966.

Pfeiffer, Leo. *Church, State, and Freedom*, rev. ed. Boston: Beacon Press, 1967.

Wilson, John F., and Donald L. Drakeman, eds. *Church and State in American History*, 2nd ed. Boston: Beacon Press, 1987.

GEORGE H. SHRIVER

AMES, WILLIAM (1576–1633)

English Congregationalist and Calvinist theologian. Ames was born at Ipswich and educated at Christ's College, Cambridge. His tutor there was WILLIAM PERKINS, by whose preaching he was converted and whose Calvinist theology he adopted and developed (see CALVINISM). In 1601 he became a fellow of the college, but lost this position in 1610 for objecting, as many Puritans did, to wearing the surplice and for denouncing games of chance (see PURITANISM). He was briefly city lecturer in Colchester before departing for the NETHERLANDS, where conversations at Leiden with Henry Jacob and John Robinson led him to CONGREGATIONALISM, although he later wrote against Robinson's separatist tendencies, that is, the notion to separate from the established church. From 1611 to 1619 he served as chaplain to the English troops stationed at The Hague. In 1622 he became professor of theology at the Dutch University of Franeker, to which he drew pupils from all over Europe. In 1633 Ames left Franeker to become copastor with Hugh Peter of an English congregation at Rotterdam, but died soon after his arrival.

As a theologian, Ames developed a COVENANT THEOLOGY, held the supralapsarian version of PREDESTINATION, and refuted the Roman Catholic controversialist Robert Bellarmine. He wrote four books against the Dutch Arminian Nicholas Grevinchoven, and served as an official advisor to the Anti-Arminian majority at the Synod of Dort in 1618–1619 (see ARMINIANISM). Following Perkins, Ames described the goal of theology as the devout life, and was famed for skill in the analysis of moral and spiritual difficulties. Both as theologian and casuist he adopted the logical method of the anti-Aristotelian HUGUENOT martyr Petrus Ramus. Ames' best-known books, *The Marrow of Sacred Divinity* and *Cases of Conscience,* published in their original Latin versions in 1627 and 1630, respectively, were widely used and influential throughout Protestant Europe and in colonial New England.

Ames identified himself with the Puritan cause and name in *Puritanus Anglicanus* (1610), his Latin translation of an earlier Puritan work by William Bradshaw, to which he added a long introduction. In treatises of 1622, 1623, and 1633 he attacked the liturgy and episcopacy of the CHURCH OF ENGLAND. Congregationalist but not Separatist, Ames favored independent congregations formed by covenants that chose their own pastors. Thus he is considered a progenitor of the "congregational way" that was established temporarily in Cromwellian England and more lastingly in the Massachusetts Bay Colony. Indeed, the leaders of the Bay Colony had some hope that he might join them there, but this was prevented by his untimely death.

References and Further Reading

Primary Sources:

Ames, William. *The Marrow of Theology.* Translated from the 3d Latin ed., 1629, and edited by John D. Eusden. Boston: Pilgrim Press, 1968; reprint Durham, NC: The Labyrinth Press, 1983.

Eusden, John D., ed. and trans. *The Marrow of Theology.* 1968; reprint Durham, NC: The Labyrinth Press, 1983.

Secondary Sources:

Horton, Douglas, trans. *William Ames by Matthew Nethenus, Hugo Visscher, and Karl Reuter.* Cambridge, MA: Harvard Divinity School Library, 1965.

Sprunger, Keith L. *The Learned Doctor William Ames.* Urbana: University of IL Press, 1972.

DEWEY D. WALLACE, JR.

AMISH

Overview

The Amish reside in more than 200 settlements in twenty-six of the United States, mostly east of the Mississippi. The three most populous states are Ohio, Pennsylvania, and Indiana. New settlements form yearly, whereas others flounder and die. The largest settlement in Holmes County, Ohio, claims nearly 200 Amish congregations, also known as church districts. The Amish have more than 1,400 local church districts across the United States and about two dozen church districts in the Canadian province of Ontario. There are no church districts in other countries since the last Amish congregation in Europe became extinct in 1936.

The Amish population doubles about every twenty years. Counting adults and children, they number nearly 200,000 people. Typically, about eighty-five percent of their youth join the church, although in some communities more than ninety-five percent join. Although the Amish do not seek converts, outsiders, known as "English," may join if they comply with Amish guidelines. Four groups carry the Amish name: Beachy Amish, Amish Mennonites, New Order Amish, and Old Order Amish. The Beachy Amish and Amish Mennonites own automobiles and use public utility electricity. This essay focuses on the horse and buggy–driving Old Order and New Order

Amish. New Order groups make up less than ten percent of the Amish of North America. Compared to Old Order groups, New Order churches permit greater use of technology, encourage more personal BIBLE STUDY, and have stricter guidelines for their youth.

All Old and New Order Amish churches share several things in common wherever they live. They speak a German (Pennsylvania German) or Swiss dialect, end formal education at the eighth grade, wear distinctive clothing, reject the use of electricity from public utility lines, selectively adapt technology, and use horse and buggy transportation. At first glance, the Amish look alike, but there are more than a dozen different subgroups, each with its own practices. Some have black top buggies whereas other groups sport yellow, gray, or white tops. Even within subgroups, diversity abounds. Some districts permit the use of cell phones, but others do not. The farmers in one church district may milk their cows by hand whereas those in a neighboring district use automatic milkers. Some communities are wealthy and others are rather poor. Despite their differences, however, the Amish share a common history.

Protestant Origins and Beliefs

The Amish trace their history to the Anabaptist movement that emerged during the Protestant REFORMATION in Europe in the 1500s. Beginning in Switzerland in 1525 and spreading to other regions of Europe, the Anabaptists refused to baptize their babies. They argued that only adults who had made voluntary decisions to follow Christ should be baptized. Their defiant acts were a capital crime in a world that expected infant BAPTISM. The young radicals were soon nicknamed "Anabaptists," meaning rebaptizers, because they had previously been baptized as infants. The Anabaptists sought to practice the teachings of Jesus in daily life and gave greater allegiance to the Bible than to civil government. They were, in fact, some of the earliest proponents of the separation of church and state. The Anabaptist Movement is sometimes called the Radical Reformation because it sought to extend and expand aspects of the larger Protestant Reformation.

The Anabaptists outraged both civil and religious authorities who accepted the integration of church and state as a single social fabric. Anabaptists were considered heretics and many were executed. They were burned at the stake, drowned in lakes, tortured in public spectacles, and starved in dungeons. A 1,200-page book, the *Martyrs Mirror: The Bloody Theatre of the Defenseless Christians,* records many stories of their torture. Amish ministers often retell stories from the *Martyrs Mirror* in their sermons today.

The Amish emerged in 1693 as a distinctive group among the Anabaptists living in Switzerland and in the Alsace region of France. An Anabaptist leader named Jakob Ammann sought to renew church life by proposing certain changes. Ammann called for shunning wayward members of the church to maintain its purity. The differences led to a division in 1693, and Ammann's followers were soon called Amish. Many other Anabaptists eventually took the name Mennonite from a Dutch Anabaptist leader, MENNO SIMONS.

The Amish migrated to the Americas in several waves in the mid-1700s and again in the 1800s. They formed communities in Pennsylvania, Ohio, and Indiana and eventually spread to other states. They often settled near their spiritual cousins, the MENNONITES. Today some Old Order Mennonite groups use horse and buggy transportation, but the majority of Mennonites drive cars, wear contemporary clothing, support higher education, and use modern technology. The Amish and Mennonites are separate groups even though they share Anabaptist roots.

Religious Beliefs

The Amish subscribe to basic Christian and Protestant beliefs. However, they emphasize proper practice over doctrinal beliefs. They highlight the importance of community over INDIVIDUALISM. Although they have private property, they stress the importance of obedience to the authority of the church community. In addition to community, the Amish stress the importance of mutual aid, separation from the world, humility, PACIFISM, and the value of TRADITION.

Amish youth typically are baptized between the ages of sixteen and twenty two. Candidates are instructed in the *Dordrecht Confession of Faith,* an old Anabaptist confession written in 1632. At baptism, youth renounce the DEVIL and the world, confess their belief in Christ, and promise to submit to the church for the rest of their lives. Its lifelong consequences make baptism a pivotal turning point. A few youth elect not to join, but the vast majority pledge their lives to the church forever. Youth who have dabbled with cars, television, popular music, and in some cases alcohol and drugs, abruptly turn their backs on these worldly things at baptism.

The core value of Amish society involves self-denial and yielding to the church. The Amish speak of "giving themselves up" to the church. They emphasize self-surrender, submission, yielding to the will of God and to others, contentment, and a calm spirit. They detest individualism that promotes self-interest at every turn.

The Amish abhor pride and teach the importance of humility. Pride refers to attitudes and actions that clamor for personal attention and recognition. Showy clothing, wristwatches, fancy drapes, or ornaments on a harness, signal pride in Amish life. The prohibitions against cosmetics, jewelry, and personal photographs are designed to prevent pride.

Members are taught to obey those with authority over them: children their parents, students their teachers, wives their husbands, members their leaders, and younger ministers their bishop. Everyone is expected to obey the will of God as taught by the community. Despite the strong emphasis on humility and obedience, the Amish express great respect for the dignity of each person.

Rather than emphasizing emotional experiences and the assurance of SALVATION, Amish leaders speak of a "living hope," an abiding belief that God will grant faithful followers eternal life. They refrain from the individualistic, evangelical language of "personal" experience and "born again" CONVERSION. In a spirit of humility, they trust in God's providence for their salvation, believing that it flows from obedient living in the community of faith.

Finally, the Amish emphasize social separation from the world not only in belief, but also in their practices. The use of horse and buggy transportation, rejecting television and computers, wearing of distinctive clothing, refraining from membership in public organizations, and rejecting political offices all reflect their belief that the church should be a counterculture separate from the larger society.

Rules of Conduct

Amish values are translated into guidelines for daily living called the *Ordnung,* a German word that means rules and order. The Ordnung is a set of expectations for daily living. Usually unwritten, the rules are passed on by practice and oral tradition. They are updated as new issues arise. Members of each congregation affirm the Ordnung twice a year before the spring and fall communion service. The details of the Ordnung vary by subgroup, as well as by local congregation.

The Ordnung defines expectations and taboos for conduct ranging from personal dress to the use of technology. All Amish groups expect men and women to wear distinctive clothing. Married men are expected to grow a beard and wear an Amish-style hat and vest. Women wear a head covering and usually a three-piece dress that includes a cape and an apron. The details of color and style vary from group to group.

Unlike American culture, where dress is a tool of individual adornment, among the Amish it signals submission to the collective order and serves as a public symbol of group identity.

As part of their Ordnung most Amish groups forbid owning automobiles, tapping electricity from public utility lines, using self-propelled farm machinery, owning a television, radio, and computer, attending high school and college, joining the military, and initiating divorce.

Religious Services and Rituals

Twenty to thirty-five families who live near each other form a local congregation called a church district. Each district has geographical boundaries. The church district is the social and religious hub of Amish life. Members of each district meet for WORSHIP every other Sunday in one of their homes. The services, which rotate from home to home, often involve 150 or more children and adults. Following a three-hour worship service, members enjoy a light fellowship lunch followed by visiting. As districts grow, they divide.

Each district has three types of leaders: a bishop, two ministers, and a deacon. The leaders are selected by drawing lots among nominees in the congregation. Leaders serve for life without formal training or pay. The bishop is the spiritual head of the congregation. He officiates at baptisms, weddings, communions, confessions, funerals, and members' meetings. He also interprets and enforces the Ordnung. In addition to PREACHING, the ministers assist with other leadership responsibilities. The deacon helps the bishop and cares for special medical or economic needs of members.

The church district serves as church, club, precinct, and neighborhood all bundled together. Districts in fellowship with each other exchange ministers, support similar Ordnungs, and permit their members to intermarry. The Amish do not have church buildings, mission agencies, national religious conferences, or a central church office. Members are linked together through loose bonds of fellowship rather than by bureaucratic structures.

Their worship services have no altars, candles, organs, stained glass windows, choirs, or pulpits. Slow, unison singing in German, without rhythm or instruments, unites the community in worship. The ancient tunes are sung by memory. The words, many written by Anabaptist prisoners, are printed in a hymnbook called the *Ausbund.*

Fall and spring communion (see LORD'S SUPPER) services rejuvenate both personal faith and the bonds of community. In a self-examination service two weeks before communion, members confess their sins publicly and reaffirm their commitment to the Ordnung. If all is well, the congregation celebrates their renewed faith in a six-hour-long communion service that includes washing of feet as taught by Jesus. Unlike many Protestant services that focus on individual experience, Amish communion celebrates the unity of community. In fact, if dissension invades the church, communion may be delayed.

Like other humans, members sometime stray into sin and deviance. Those who violate a major teaching of the Ordnung—flying in an airplane, filing a lawsuit, plowing with a tractor—will be asked to make a public CONFESSION at a members' meeting. Those who defy the authority of the church may face excommunication.

Shunning typically follows excommunication. Based on Biblical teaching, shunning involves rituals that remind the wayward of their sin and seek to bring them back to fellowship. Expulsion is a heavy matter because it can lead to a lifetime of estrangement from family and friends. However, those who do fall from grace can always return to the fold if they are willing to confess their wrongs and mend their ways. Unbaptized persons who leave the community are not shunned. Although shunning may sound harsh to modern ears, the Amish faith has two key points of integrity: adult baptism by free choice and an open back door for wayward members who want to return with a contrite heart.

Youth and Education

Before 1950 the Amish youth attended small rural public schools. However, when small schools consolidated into large districts some Amish parents protested their loss of local control. Moreover, they considered "book learning" and study beyond the eighth grade unnecessary for farming. Some parents sat in prison for refusing to send their children to large public schools. Finally, in 1972, the United States Supreme Court, in *Wisconsin v. Yoder,* ruled that Amish children could end formal schooling after eighth grade.

A few Amish children still attend rural public schools, but the vast majority go to one- or two-room schools operated by Amish parents. Indeed, about 35,000 Amish youth attend some 1,300 private schools that end with eighth grade. Instruction is in English. The teachers are typically Amish women who have not gone to high school but are graduates of Amish schools themselves. A religious song and a Scripture reading may open the school day, but religion is not taught in a formal way. Reading, spelling, writing, and mathematics are the basic subjects. Science is not taught.

The quality of instruction varies considerably by group and region. The schools play an important role in passing on Amish values, developing friendships, and limiting exposure to the outside world. The schools contribute to the vigor and vitality of Amish life. After formal schooling Amish youth work in vocational apprenticeship programs on the farm or in small shops. Here they learn vocational skills that will serve them in adult life.

Youth eagerly await their sixteenth birthday, the traditional age when they begin *rumspringa,* a time of "running around." During this time, they spend more time with their peers on weekends and often begin dating. Rumspringa is a moment of freedom when youth are suspended between two worlds: the control of their parents and the supervision of the church. Because they have not been baptized, they technically are not under the Ordnung. Many youth adhere to traditional Amish behavior. However, others may experiment with worldly things—buying a car, going to movies, using alcohol, wearing English clothes, and buying a television or a DVD player.

Rumspringa gives Amish youth the impression that they have a choice regarding church membership, and indeed they do. However, all the forces of Amish life funnel them toward joining the church. Knowing they have a choice likely strengthens their willingness to obey church standards after they join.

Marriage and Family

Church and extended family are the primary social units of Amish society. Young people usually marry by the age of twenty-one. Daylong weddings are festive moments of celebration in Amish society. The ceremony follows a lengthy church service, held on a weekday at the home of the bride or a close relative. Several hundred guests join the festivities that often include a lunch and an evening meal. Once married, Amish couples on the average have six or seven children, but in some cases, twelve or more. Most families do not use artificial birth control unless advised by a physician for health reasons; however, some use natural methods of family planning. Some babies are born in local hospitals, but most greet the world at home or in a local birthing clinic.

Amish families reflect traditional gender roles in which the man serves as the spiritual head of the home. He is responsible for its religious welfare and matters related to the church and the outside world. As in most families, gender roles vary by personality. When husbands work at home, there is often considerable cross-sharing of roles—women assisting in the barn or shop, and men in the garden or around the house. Wives rarely hold full-time jobs outside the family when their children are young. The elderly typically live in an apartment or in a small house adjacent to the home of one of their children. Esteemed for their wisdom, the elderly pass on the wisdom, joys, and secrets of Amish life to typically dozens of grandchildren.

Occupations

Ever since religious persecution pushed them into rural areas in Europe, the Amish have been tillers of the soil—and good ones. Their ties to the land have served as a cradle for the nurture of their children. Church leaders have resisted large-scale mechanized farming for fear it would steal work from children and erode family solidarity. Using horse drawn equipment is one way of resisting large-scale, corporate style farming. With a few exceptions, most farms are small family operations that use horse-drawn machinery. For many years Amish farms were small, diversified operations with a dozen cows, some chickens, and a few beef cattle. Although many continue this tradition, other farms specialize in dairy, and in some cases, chickens or hogs. Some specialize in vegetables, herbs, greenhouse plants, and flowers. Despite popular myths, most Amish use insecticides, herbicides, and chemical fertilizers.

Economic pressures have encouraged many families to seek nonfarm employment. In some of the larger communities, the number of farmers dips below fifteen percent. More isolated areas still claim over seventy-five percent on the farm. The shift to nonfarm work is the biggest change in Amish society since 1975. Despite their growing involvement in business and commerce, the Amish remain a distinctly rural people, living along country roads and on the margins of small villages. Three types of nonfarm work flourish: small shops, construction work, and employment in English factories. Hundreds of small Amish-owned industries have sprung up in many communities. Most of these are small family businesses with less than ten employees. The bulk of them produce wood products—household and outdoor furniture, gazebos, small barns, lawn ornaments, doghouses, and mailboxes—to name but a few of the hundreds of products. Other shops specialize in fabricating metal. Annual sales in the larger businesses exceed five million dollars.

Many Amish do construction work—building homes and industrial structures for non-Amish people. In some communities the majority of Amish men work in English-owned factories located in rural areas. In Northern Indiana many Amish work in factories that build recreational vehicles. The growth of nonfarm employment has brought new wealth to many Amish communities.

Technology, Government, and Community

The Amish use technology selectively. Televisions, radios, and computers are rejected outright, but many other types of technology are used selectively or modified to fit Amish purposes. Amish mechanics often create new machines to fit their cultural needs. Moreover, much state-of-the-art technology, like gas grills, shop tools, camping equipment, and some farm equipment, is readily bought from non-Amish vendors. If left untamed, Amish worry that technology will harm their community by disrupting social traditions, family solidarity, and bringing foreign values through mass media. Technology is not considered evil in itself; "It's what it will do to the next generation," said one bishop. A car is not seen as immoral, but as a harmful tool that would pull the community apart. The Amish seek to master technology rather than becoming its slave. They try to tame technology—hoping to prevent it from harming family and community life.

The Amish pay state and federal income taxes, sales, real estate, and public school taxes. They also support their own private schools. They are exempt from Social Security taxes because they consider Social Security a form of insurance. The Amish believe that the Bible instructs them to care for the elderly and assist members who have special needs. To rely on commercial or government insurance would mock their faith that God cares for them through the church.

The Amish are taught to respect and pray for governing authorities according to Biblical admonitions. However, when caught in a conflict between their conscience and civic law, they recite the Scripture that they should "obey God rather than man." The intense persecution in Europe solidified their strong belief in the separation of church and state. The Amish are pacifists and refuse to enter the armed forces. They generally avoid politics, holding public office, and political activism. They are, however, permitted to vote in public elections. The Amish generally do not join public organizations or service clubs in the local community, but some of them do serve as members of local volunteer fire companies and emergency medical units. Although they do not develop intimate relationships with outsiders or marry them, they are typically good neighbors who enjoy many friendships with their English neighbors.

A strong sense of community regulates the rhythms of Amish life. Face to face conversation in homes, lawns, shops, and barns provides the social glue of Amish society. Without big organizations, Amish life thrives in a thicket of personal relationships that mix neighborhood, family, church, work, and leisure together. Despite many communal regulations, each individual is afforded respect and dignity.

See also Anabaptism; Baptism; Bible Study; Church and State; Confession; Conversion; Devil; Heresy; Individualism; Lord's Supper; Martyrs and Martyrologies; Pacifism; Preaching; Reformation; Salvation; Simons, Menno; Tradition; Worship

References and Further Reading

Hostetler, John A. *Amish Roots: A Treasury of History, Wisdom and Lore*. Baltimore: Johns Hopkins University Press, 1989.
Kraybill, Donald B. *The Riddle of Amish Culture*. 2nd ed. Baltimore: Johns Hopkins University Press, 2001.
———, ed. *The Amish and The State*. 2nd ed. Baltimore: Johns Hopkins University Press, 2003.
———, and Carl Desportes Bowman. *On the Backroad to Heaven: Old Order Hutterites, Mennonites, Amish and Brethren*. Baltimore: Johns Hopkins University Press, 2001.
———, and Steven M. Nolt. *Amish Enterprise: From Plows to Profits*. 2nd ed. Baltimore: Johns Hopkins University Press, 2003.
Nolt, Steven M. *A History of the Amish*. 2nd ed. Intercourse, PA: Good Books, 2003.
Scott, Stephen M. *Plain Buggies: Amish, Mennonite, and Brethren Horse drawn Transportation*. Rev. ed. Intercourse, PA: Good Books, 1998.
———. *Why Do They Dress That Way?* Rev. ed. Intercourse, PA: Good Books, 1997.
Stoltzfus, Louise. *Amish Women: Lives and Stories*. Intercourse, PA: Good Books, 1994.
Umble, Diane Zimmerman. *Holding the Line: The Telephone in Old Order Mennonite and Amish Life*. Baltimore: Johns Hopkins University Press, 1996.
Weaver-Zercher, David. *The Amish in the American Imagination*. Baltimore: Johns Hopkins University Press, 2001. [Sections of this essay are adapted by permission from Donald B. Kraybill, *The Amish: Why They Enchant Us*. Scottdale, PA: Herald Press, 2003.]

DONALD B. KRAYBILL

AMISSAH, SAMUEL HANSON (1907–1989)

African church leader. Amissah was one of the early Christian leaders in post-independence and post-missionary Africa. He was the first African and lay principal of Wesley College, Kumasi (1952–1963); the first general secretary of the All Africa Conference of Churches (AACC) in Zambia and later Kenya (1964–1971); and the first vice president of the Methodist Church, Ghana (1977–1979).

Born January 6, 1907, in Ghana, he enrolled in Wesley College in 1925. After graduation, he remained for twenty-eight years, first as a tutor, then vice principal, and finally as principal. He therefore spent more than half his career training teachers for Ghana's schools.

Because of his work in the Church Union Committee of Ghana, he became the first general secretary when the AACC began in Kampala, Uganda, in April 1963. Under his leadership AACC moved from Kitwe, Zambia to its new head office in Nairobi, Kenya. He made the AACC representative of the diversity of African men and women, young and old. He was involved in negotiations between the Muslim government of Sudan and their Christian neighbors, and the negotiations between Nigeria and Biafra.

In Ghana, Amissah chaired a commission in the Methodist Church that arbitrated between rival factions to ensure EVANGELISM would continue among the immigrant Fante community in Accra. He was also chair of the Songor Lagoon Committee of Inquiry.

In his final years he tried to prevent a Methodist leader from perpetuating himself in office. He died September 18, 1989 just before the final resolution of that crisis. Amissah's career exemplified the fact that Africans were able to take over positions of church leadership harmoniously in the post-colonial period.

See also Africa; Methodism, African Theology

References and Further Reading

Bartels, F. L. *The Roots of Ghana Methodism.* Cambridge: Cambridge University Press, 1965.
Beetham, T. A. *Christianity and the New Africa.* London: Pall Mall, 1967.
Hastings, Adrian. *The Church in Africa 1450–1950.* Oxford: Clarendon, 1994.

CASELY B. ESSAMUAH

AMSDORF, NIKOLAUS VON (1483–1565)

Protestant reformer. Born in Torgau on December 3, 1483, Amsdorf was educated at Leipzig and Wittenberg and became bishop of Naumburg-Zeitz. He was one of MARTIN LUTHER's earliest supporters and closest friends. Amsdorf, along with PHILIPP MELANCHTHON, helped lead Luther's movement when Luther was being hidden in the Wartburg Castle. Amsdorf is most remembered for his zealous defense of a conservative reading of Luther's teachings on the role of good works and the human will in SALVATION.

Involved in a number of heated polemical debates among the early Lutherans over the proper interpretation and application of Luther's reform, he helped initiate the GNESIO-LUTHERAN movement in the 1540s. Taking a radical interpretation of Luther's assertion that "good works are harmful to salvation," Amsdorf argued against Melanchthon in 1536 and George Major and Justus Menius in the 1550s over the role of good works in salvation. He also disagreed with Melanchthon over the matters of the role of the will in CONVERSION (rejecting Melanchthon's view that the will is a third factor in conversion), the relationship of the Lutheran churches to Rome, and the interpretation of the "real presence" of Christ in the Eucharist (see LORD'S SUPPER). Similarly, Amsdorf rejected the synergism of Johann Pfeffinger and Viktorin Strigel and wrote harsh critiques of the Leipzig and AUGSBURG INTERIMS, especially attacking the principle of concession in ADIAPHORA. Almost all of Amsdorf's writings are polemical treatises responding to immediate issues and debates of his day in an attempt to uphold and protect confessional purity.

See also Lutheranism; Catholicism, Protestant Reactions

References and Further Reading

Kolb, Robert. *Nikolaus von Amsdorf: Popular Polemics in the Preservation of Luther's Legacy.* Nieuwkoop, The Netherlands: B. De Graaf, 1978.
Steinmetz, David C. *Reformers in the Wings: From Geiler von Kaysersberg to Theodore Beza.* 2d. edition. Oxford, UK: Oxford University Press, 2001.

G. SUJIN PAK

ANABAPTISM

Historical Sketch of Anabaptism until 1600

Anabaptism formally began in SWITZERLAND in January 1525. It had been anticipated by the turbulence of the early REFORMATION, many critics of the state of the church, anticlericalism, and by those who felt that MARTIN LUTHER and HULDRYCH ZWINGLI did not consistently carry out the reforms called for by their own Bible study.

From 1525 to 1530 Anabaptism spread throughout Switzerland, South Germany, Moravia, and Austrian areas. Fearless evangelists and brilliant scholars, many of them touched by ANDREAS KARLSTADT, THOMAS MUNTZER, and Jakob Strauss and more than likely influenced by revolutionaries such as Michael Gaismair, led the movement. Three main streams emerged: Moravian/Hutterite, South/Central German Swiss, and finally the Northern German and Dutch. All had their peaceful branches and most also their revolutionaries.

The scholars, together with some Jewish scholars, produced a German translation of the Old Testament prophets (twelve editions) from Hebrew to German (1527) before Luther did. Luther said "my German followed (it) very closely" ["daran . . . meinem deustchen fast (sehr) nachgangn ist" (WA *Deutsche Bibel* II:2)].

These years brought publications, disputations, confessions of faith (Schleitheim, 1527), and repression. Intellectual foundations were laid in extensive disputations with Reformation leaders.

There also was bloody suppression because rebaptism (the charge by the rulers and the church) was punishable by death. During the years 1527 and 1535 in south and central GERMANY the increase in martyrs rose from 56 in 1527, to 200 in 1528; in 1529 the number declined to 152; and in 1530, to 89, making a total of 488. For the century from 1525 to 1618, of all the Anabaptist executions, 80 percent took place from 1527 to 1533 and 40 percent in 1527 and 1528. One result was the rise of APOCALYPTICISM, leading to MELCHIOR HOFMANN'S commentary on the Apocalypse (1530) and his commentary on Romans (1533). He was a gifted evangelist and bible expositor, although a furrier, and became the founder of Anabaptism in the NETHERLANDS. He exercised his leadership from prison from 1533 until his death in 1543. Obbe and Dirk Philips joined the movement in part through him. Others were attracted to the febrile apocalypticism, which led to the debacle of Münster, the bloody defeat of Anabaptists in that city.

During the decade of the 1530s the magisterial Reformation published booklets justifying the persecution of Anabaptists by Christian princes. That was partly in reply to eloquent pleas by PILGRAM MARPECK and Leupold Scharnschlager to Strasbourg authorities for tolerance. The Münsterite fiasco (1534) did little to support their claim that Anabaptists had no desire to force their views on others. This decade also brought the establishment of the Hutterite community by JACOB HUTTER in 1533 in Moravia that, after a complex geographic pilgrimage from Moravia to Transylvania to the Ukraine to North America, survives to this day.

Because of the spiritual and intellectual leadership of Scharnschlager and Marpeck, there was also an almost complete separation from SPIRITUALISM in its many forms. In Holland the movement was saved after the Münster debacle, by MENNO SIMONS who dedicated his considerable courage and skills to building communities in which nonviolent love was practiced within as well as to the outsider.

Menno Simons was actively sought to undo the damage of the Münster debacle and, although a fugitive, ministered effectively to his bruised flock. Some of his time had to be devoted to defending his CHRISTOLOGY and his severe church discipline. Notwithstanding, his leadership assured him the honor in later years of having the movement called Mennonites.

The last half of the sixteenth century saw a changed scene. Marpeck died in 1556 of natural causes; Menno followed five years later in 1561. Most important for the Anabaptists, in 1564 King Ferdinand died. None had been more persistent and effective in killing Anabaptists. He was proud that he had been able to keep Austria free of the Protestant and Anabaptist plague.

Although publications were the lifeline of the movement in the latter half of the century, the focus was on history, as exemplified by the *Martyrs Mirror,* although it was not published until 1660; the *Hutterian Chronicle* also began in the 1530s, circulating only in manuscript form until modern times. The oral tradition kept the community alive, and, once King Ferdinand died, even the Netherlands where he also reigned was free to develop culturally and institutionally.

Anabaptism has become a normative designation for the community of people who wished to go beyond the measures of reform taken by Luther, Zwingli, MARTIN BUCER, and JOHN CALVIN. Termed a child (though an "unsubmissive one") of the Protestant Reformation (Fritz Blanke), Anabaptism has been referred to by historians of the last century as "The Left Wing of the Reformation" (Roland Bainton), "The Radical Reformation" (George Huntston Williams), "the Free Church" (E. Payne, followed by most Baptists), and the "believers' church" (John Howard Yoder et al.).

The flood of new sources (court records but also Anabaptist writings, either recently discovered or newly identified and translated) has been a strong incentive to review the question of their faithfulness to New Testament teaching and their place within the Protestant Reformation and Western civilization. For those who wish to follow the early Anabaptists and test the contemporary relevance of their teaching for the postmodern age, the term "Anabaptism" has considerable meaning, always under review.

The Anabaptist Agenda

Modern Mennonites have been propelled forward in their quest for the abiding nature of the Anabaptist witness by energetic and gifted teachers and scholars. Historians such as Harold Bender, Robert Friedman, John Howard Yoder, Hans Hillerbrand, Walter Klaassen, Arnold Snyder, Werner Packull, James Stayer, Heinold Fast, and Hans Jürgen Goertz, and systematic theologians and ethicists such as Gordon Kaufman and Lawrence Burkholder have cheered these teachers and researchers on. Kaufman's contribution to the debate on the ethics of nuclear armament, his concern for the application of human imagination and reason to issues of Christology, put him in the best traditions of Anabaptism.

In trying to explain a new appreciation of their historic legacy to fellow church historians, Harold S. Bender in 1942 used the phrase "Anabaptist Vision." In spite of robust criticism, the phrase has remained in vogue (in particular as revised by Gordon Kaufman) and continues to put the Anabaptist position succinctly and accurately, even though the "Anabaptist Vision" betrayed a much greater debt to DIETRICH BONHOEFFER and Johannes Kühn than it did to Anabaptist sources. It inspired twentieth-century Mennonites to believe that their predecessors had lived and died for a cause still worthwhile.

Bender's portrait of the Anabaptist vision involved three central teachings or new conceptions:

1. The essence of Christianity as discipleship.
2. The church as a brotherhood [henceforth community].
3. A new ethic of love and nonresistance, or biblical pacifism.

Bender saw two foci in this vision: The essential nature of Christianity and of the CHURCH. He saw a community of love in which the fullness of the ideal of the Christian life is to be expressed. He distinguished between the Anabaptists and their contemporaries both in theory and practice. MARRIAGE was held in honor because it was normally a union of two believers who treated each other as brothers and sisters in Christ. The use of coercion or pressure in that relationship was considered a result of Adam's fall, which Christ had also undone. Stephen Boyd (1999) has suggested that whereas Luther saw emancipation from the fall's consequences for marriage as being in the future, the Anabaptists treated it as something already accomplished.

In modern times Anabaptist scholars gave critical attention to the way in which the first Anabaptists saw the state. How does one draw the limits of obedience to its demands? From the beginning this was a central issue in Anabaptist discussion of biblical categories. Because Jesus taught his disciples to love their enemies, members of this group renounced violence (see PACIFISM) and abjured the use of the sword, calling for holy living, justice, peace, and joy in accordance with the constitution of the church (= kingdom of God as defined by Paul, Romans 14:17). According to their interpretation of the New Testament, they upheld the separation of church and worldly government (see CHURCH AND STATE OVERVIEW), BAPTISM based on the faith of the recipient, and discipline within the fellowship of the believers. "Nonresistance" became an active search for justice and nonviolent reconciliation.

In recent decades victim-offender reconciliation programs have blossomed alongside disaster-relief programs. In Mennonite mental hospitals health professionals both developed their skills and applied the lessons they had learned in alternative service during World War II. They also answered the question: What do you do when a mad man threatens you or your loved ones? Like the sixteenth-century Anabaptists, modern Mennonites have tried to provide a haven of love for the mentally ill and the specially challenged, including the offenders against society.

The Response of the Reformers

The relation of Anabaptism to the Reformation is complicated. Although Anabaptists generally spoke with respect and appreciation of the work of Luther and reformers like Bucer, and acknowledged their debt to Erasmus and Zwingli, they were called "Schwärmer" ("fanatics" or "enthusiasts") because they placed religious values and spiritual obedience as vetted by their community of believers ahead of the social norms of their society. Generally speaking it is difficult for societies to treat dissenters with civility, especially when changes are rapid; during the Reformation much was in the process of change.

Leupold Scharnschlager, expelled from Strasbourg, in his farewell statement (1534) spoke appreciatively of the leadership of Martin Luther; he also voiced his disappointment that Luther did not carry through consistently with his earlier affirmations to finish the reformation. Seven times Scharnschlager appealed to Luther and affirmed at least two of Luther's early writings. Earlier he had appealed to Luther several times in a 1531 booklet on the limits of the state, lamenting the absence of "the obedience of faith" among the followers of the reformers.

The response of the reformers was swift and brutal. Both Urbanus Rhegius and PHILIPP MELANCHTHON, with the debacle of Münster in vivid memory, wrote booklets in 1536 urging Christian princes to suppress Anabaptists for being a threat to society. Anabaptists argued that among the reformers no baptismal vows were made (because infants were incapable of making such vows), lives were not being transformed, and true communities were not being built, all of which caused them to leave the state church. Repression only hardened their resolve to seek community wherever it could be found (Mattern 1998).

Modern Response

Some social historians have dismissed the Anabaptists' approach to community living and their social behavior as irresponsible and naive, charging that the peaceful brethren became a "threat to civilization" or were bent on "destroying civilization" (Claus Peter Clasen). Clasen breathes a sigh of relief that the Anabaptists had no "discernible impact" on the political, economic, or social institutions of their age. Therefore they cannot be called more than a "minor episode in the history of sixteenth century German society." After all, several "pious old women or journeymen" refusing to attend church can hardly be called a Reformation movement. Clasen's interest is whether, during the sixteenth century or even today, their political doctrines "could be considered a workable basis for the functioning of society." This question, he says, makes Anabaptism "appear in a new light." Two issues remain unaddressed. What constitutes a "workable basis"? How does one define the "functioning of society"?

Identity and Name Calling

It took some centuries for the epithets of the earliest critics ["Wiedertäufer" ("anabaptists," rebaptizers)] to become respectable. Anabaptists rejected this term as one of self-designation, claiming they were baptizing for the first time. The theology of baptism developed by BALTHASAR HUBMAIER and especially Christoph Freisleben, with its specific appeal to Romans 6 and the new life in Christ, was a formidable basis on which to build a religious reform movement. Zwingli was hard-pressed in his debate with Hubmaier to explain Romans 6 as a ground for infant baptism.

Because of the opprobrium attached to the term and its connotation of HERESY, condemnation, and execration, early Anabaptists preferred the term "Täufer" ("baptizers") or simply "Brüder und Schwestern" ("brothers and sisters"). In Holland and North Germany, as early as 1545, they were mostly called "Doopsgezinde" ("baptismally minded") and as "Mennisten" in a mandate by countess Anna of East Friesland. By the end of the sixteenth century, the term Mennisten was standard, based on Menno Simons, an ex-priest whose untiring work helped that community to purge itself of the tendency toward violence and thus to survive. Outsiders were likely responsible for the name. Menno carried out the mammoth task of drawing the disparate groups together after the peasant revolt involving Thomas Müntzer in 1525, and seeking to distance it from the Münsterites in 1535.

The Current Picture and Historical Models

Alongside its critics Anabaptism has had its admirers and followers, including the small group of Mennonites (less than one million worldwide) who with varying degrees of pride claim to be heirs of this legacy. With surprising diligence, ethnic groups are prone to cull praise from the larger world as if their legitimacy depends on it. Thus it is noted that ADOLF HARNACK, although denying the Anabaptists a place in the history of dogma (because they are "fundamentally untheological"), praised their place in ETHICS and their way of life, against the "heroic Luther and the iron Calvin." FRIEDRICH SCHLEIERMACHER called for

cancelling "the sentence of condemnation passed on the Anabaptists."

Faith and practice, which the Anabaptists tended to equate, involved the voluntary acceptance of baptism on confession of faith. The first baptisms they practiced brought with them a strong affirmation of reliance on God and a bonding between believers heightened by persecution—for soon their action was condemned as a capital crime. Only Strasbourg apparently was able to avoid killing people for being adherents to this "abhorrent sect." Under the reign of King Ferdinand, especially, there was a constant struggle to have princes and local rulers enforce the king's harsh decrees, which in turn brought continuing resistance and new converts.

In Tirol a decree ordered that the edict against the Anabaptists be enforced, especially against their leaders. Because there were an exceptional number of female leaders, a disproportionate number of women were executed. As Linda Huebert Hecht has shown, a number of women—even those of the nobility—were exiled, publicly humiliated, or forced to recant, an observation that has eluded countless male historians writing on Tirolian Anabaptism.

In some parts of Germany female Anabaptists were "chained" in their own homes, remanded to the custody of their husbands until they gave up their Anabaptist views and returned to the Reformed or Catholic church. By taking on the profession of midwifery, some Anabaptist women were able to circumvent infant baptism by claiming that the child had seemed sickly, then lying that it had been hastily baptized. They justified this act of civil disobedience by the precedent set by the Hebrew midwives of ancient Egypt (Exodus 1:15–22).

What was at stake was not only the practice of infant baptism but the issue of the authority of the state. Anabaptists agreed that the state was indeed ordained of God, but believed it could not coerce in matters of faith, or it would become the "whore of Babylon." This issue became a source of tension, especially for those who were employed by the state or other public bodies.

Many social factors played a role in their decisions, but in the last analysis, Anabaptism was sparked and continues to be inspired by a strong religious, spiritual drive. Without the continuing spiritual nurture provided by a community that practices binding and loosing, forgiveness and accountability, Anabaptism would not have survived.

References and Further Reading

Bender, H. S. "The Anabaptist Vision." *Church History* 13 (1944): 3–24.

Boyd, S. *Pilgram Marpeck, His Life and Social Theology.* Durham, NC: Duke University Press, 1992.

Dyck, C. J. *Spiritual Life in Anabaptism.* Scottdale, PA: Herald Press, 1995.

Goertz, Hans Juergen, ed. *Profiles of Radical Reformers.* Translated by Walter Klaassen. Kitchener, Canada: Herald Press, 1982.

Hecht, Linda Huebert, and C. Arnold Snyder. *Profiles of Anabaptist Women.* Waterloo, Canada: WLU Press, 1996.

Klaassen, Walter. *Anabaptism: Neither Catholic nor Protestant?* Kitchener, Canada: Pandora Press, 2001.

———, ed. *Sources in South German, Austrian Anabaptism.* Kitchener, Canada: Pandora Press, 2001.

Mattern, Marlies. *Leben im Abseits. Frauen und Mannem im Täufertum (1525–1550). Eine Studie zur Alltagsgeschichte.* Frankfurt, Germany: Peter Lang, 1988.

Piper, Otto A. *Protestantism in an Ecumenical Age: Its Root, Its Right, Its Task.* Philadelphia: Fortress Press, 1965.

Snyder, C. Arnold. *Anabaptist History and Theology, An Introduction.* Kitchener, Canada: Pandora Press, 1995.

Williams, George Huntston. *The Radical Reformation.* Philadelphia: Westminster, 1962. Kirksville, MO: 16th Century Journal Publishers, 1992.

WILLIAM KLASSEN

ANDERSON, RUFUS (1796–1880)

Congregational minister and foreign mission official. Anderson was born August 17, 1796, in North Yarmouth, Maine, the son of Rufus Anderson, a Congregational minister, and Hannah Parsons. Educated at Bowdoin College (1818) and Andover Theological Seminary (1822), he was ordained a Congregational minister in 1826. He started with the AMERICAN BOARD OF COMMISSIONERS FOR FOREIGN MISSIONS (ABCFM) as assistant secretary (1823–1832) and ended as a Prudential Committee member (1866–1875). While serving as foreign corresponding secretary (1832–1866) he supervised the Board's several hundred missionaries overseas and shaped, articulated, and implemented its policies. Afterward he published histories of the ABCFM missions in Hawaii, the Mediterranean, and India, and presented his understanding of missions in *Foreign Missions: Their Relations and Claims* (1869). He died in Roxbury, Massachusetts.

Anderson and Henry Venn of the CHURCH MISSIONARY SOCIETY articulated the "three-self" formulation of missions: the goal of missions was to create self-governing, self-supporting, and self-propagating indigenous churches. Anderson insisted that missionaries should take the gospel, not American culture, overseas. He warned against dependency on education as an evangelistic method. Despite some controversy, Board policies during his lifetime reflected his views.

EVANGELICALISM and CONGREGATIONALISM shaped Anderson's ideas. PREACHING and the CONVERSION of individuals were central. Independent mission churches would evolve in form but be Protestant in theology and polity. Anderson provided a theological rationale for the global expansion of American Protestantism and has widely influenced its mission thought.

See also Missions; Missionary Organizations; Missions, North American

References and Further Reading

Beaver, R. Pierce. *To Advance the Gospel: Selections from the Writings of Rufus Anderson.* Grand Rapids, MI: William B. Eerdmans, 1967.

Harris, Paul William. *Nothing but Christ: Rufus Anderson and the Ideology of Protestant Foreign Missions.* New York: Oxford University Press, 1999.

Hutchison, William R. *Errand to the World: American Protestant Thought and Foreign Missions.* Chicago: University of Chicago Press, 1987.

ROBERT A. SCHNEIDER

ANDREWES, LANCELOT (1555–1626)

English theologian. Andrewes was born in London in 1555 and educated at Pembroke College, Cambridge (B.A. 1571, M.A. 1578, appointed Master 1589). He was appointed to various ecclesiastical positions, serving successively as vicar of St. Giles, Cripplegate (1589), Bishop of Chichester (1605), Bishop of Ely (1609), and Bishop of Winchester (1618). At the Hampton Court Conference in January 1604, Andrewes was commissioned as a translator of the BIBLE. He died one year after James I, on September 26, 1626 in Winchester House, Southwark and was buried in Southwark Cathedral.

Andrewes was a diligent scholar, usually spending five hours a day in study and fluent in fifteen languages, and a skillful homilist. His well-known *Preces Privatae* (a collection of private devotions), for example, is entirely in Greek, Latin, and Hebrew. It was in the pulpit, however, that Andrewes gained most renown. He preached regularly to both ELIZABETH I and James, especially on the greater Church feasts and seasons (Christmas, Lent, Easter, and Pentecost). His 96 surviving sermons are stylistically elaborate [and admired by the poet and critic T. S. ELIOT (1888–1965)] and characterized by both wit and theological clarity.

In the company of fellow theologian RICHARD HOOKER (1554–1600) and divine and poet GEORGE HERBERT (1593–1633), Andrewes was a significant influence on the development of ANGLICAN theology. He wrote two long works of controversy against Robert Bellarmine, but was also a well-known opponent of PURITANISM. He argued, for example, for the centrality of the SACRAMENTS, without seeking specificity as to how grace is mediated through them. In all, he sought a middle ground, choosing to focus on central themes of Christian DOCTRINE: the Trinity and the Incarnation.

References and Further Reading

Primary Source:

Andrewes, Lancelot. *Sermons.* Edited by G. M. Story. Oxford: Clarendon Press, 1967.

Secondary Sources:

Lossky, Nicholas. *Lancelot Andrewes, The Preacher (1555–1626).* Translated by Andrew Louth. Oxford: Clarendon Press, 1991.

Owen, Trevor A. *Lancelot Andrewes.* Twayne's English Authors Series 325. Boston: Twayne Publishers, 1981.

GARY R. BROWER

ANDREWS, CHARLES FREER (1871–1940)

English missionary in India and friend of Mahatma Gandhi. Andrews was born in England in 1871. Brought up in the Catholic Apostolic Church, he joined the CHURCH OF ENGLAND as a young man and was ordained priest. After starting an academic career at Cambridge University, he went to India in 1904 with the Cambridge Mission to Delhi. He spent the rest of his life in India, initially teaching at St. Stephen's College, Delhi. During this period, he promoted the Indianization of the church, its leadership, mission, liturgy, and theology. He considered the disunity of the churches damaging to the mission, and, claiming to be a "High Church" Anglican, supported cooperation with Baptists and Presbyterians. His gift for friendship brought him close relationships with Hindus and Muslims. He increasingly identified with the Indian independence movement and its leaders, in particular forming deep friendships with the nationalist leader Gandhi (1869–1948) and poet Rabindranath Tagore (1861–1941). In 1914 he left formal missionary work, making his home at Tagore's ashram until his death in Calcutta in 1940. His principal work for Indian freedom included his dialogical relationship with Gandhi, promotion of nationalist thought through books and extensive journalism, and his successful campaign throughout the British empire for the abolition of the system of slavery known as indenture, for which he earned the title "Deenabandhu" (Friend of the Poor). Except for a brief period, his Christian motivation was strongly evident. He was most characteristically Protestant in his constant references in his speech and many writings to the scriptures, and in particular to the teaching and person of Christ.

See also Slavery, Abolition of

References and Further Reading

Primary Source:

Andrews, C. F. *What I Owe to Christ.* London: Hodder and Stoughton, 1932.

Secondary Sources:

Chaturvedi, Benarsidas, and Marjorie Sykes. *Charles Freer Andrews.* London: Allen and Unwin, 1949.

O'Connor, Daniel. *Gospel, Raj and Swaraj.* Frankfurt, Germany: Peter Lang, 1990.

Tinker, Hugh. *Ordeal of Love.* Delhi: Oxford University Press, 1979.

DANIEL O'CONNOR

ANGLICAN CHANT

Anglican chant developed as a means of singing the Psalms and biblical canticles that is neither specifically Anglican in origin nor restricted to Anglican in usage, but remains a distinctive element of Anglican worship. Its origin is found in the faburden technique, common throughout late medieval Europe, in which the traditional monophonic Psalm tones were sung in an improvised four-part harmony, with the basic tone in the tenor. The technique was not specifically English but widespread throughout Europe. For example, such faburdened Psalm tones appear in a number of sixteenth-century printed sources intended for German Lutheran use. In England faburden settings of the Psalm tones continued to be sung with the vernacular Psalms of the BOOK OF COMMON PRAYER in the Elizabethan period, as is witnessed in Thomas Morley's *A Plaine and Easie Introduction to Practicall Musicke* (London, 1597). By the early seventeenth century the connection with traditional Psalm tones disappeared and the four-part settings were through-composed, with the melody usually in the soprano.

The common types of Anglican chant are Single and Double, that is, chants that encompass either one or two verses of a psalm or canticle, respectively, although there are also Triple and Quadruple chants. Virtually every notable composer of the CHURCH OF ENGLAND, in every generation, has composed such chants, thus contributing to a significant element of Anglican choral evensong. Until the late eighteenth century such chanting was generally restricted to cathedrals and collegiate chapels, but under the influence of some Evangelicals, then later by Tractarians, Anglican chant took on a congregational aspect in parish churches. In the nineteenth century Anglican Chant spread to other denominations in the English-speaking world.

See also Book of Common Prayer; Church of England

References and Further Reading

Spink, Ian, *Restoration Cathedral Music, 1660–1714.* New York: Oxford University Press, 1995.

Temperley, Nicholas. *Jonathan Gray and Church Music in York, 1770–1840.* York, UK: St. Anthony's Press, 1977.

———. *The Music of the English Parish Church.* New York: Cambridge University Press, 1979.

Wilson, Ruth Mack. *Anglican Chant and Chanting in England, Scotland, and America, 1660 to 1820.* New York: Oxford University Press, 1996.

———. "Harmonized Chant." In *The Hymnal 1982 Companion,* edited by Raymond Glover, vol. 1, 215–237. New York: Church Hymnal Corporation, 1990.

ROBIN LEAVER

ANGLICANISM

Introduction

Anglicanism is a major strand of historical Christianity, deriving from the CHURCH OF ENGLAND. It currently exists in thirty-eight national or regional churches in more than 160 countries throughout the world. Together these churches (or provinces) constitute the Anglican Communion, a body of about seventy million Christians (about the same size as the LUTHERAN WORLD FEDERATION or the WORLD ALLIANCE OF REFORMED CHURCHES). Many of these churches are found in former colonies or dominions of the British Empire.

Anglicans are bound together by ties of history, THEOLOGY, a common POLITY, and a shared liturgical and spiritual tradition, although membership of the Anglican Communion is ultimately defined by being in communion with the archbishop of Canterbury, the bishop of the founding see of the Church of England. The archbishop of Canterbury exercises significant theological and pastoral leadership in the Communion, but he has little formal authority to intervene in the affairs of the autonomous provinces.

The term Anglicanism did not emerge until the 1830s. It is anachronistic when applied to the English REFORMATION, but it begins to be meaningful toward the end of the seventeenth century. Before the Reformation there was "the English Church" or "the Church in England" and after it "the Church of England." For several centuries "Anglican" was synonymous with the Church of England, but the description "Anglican" is now the prerogative of the whole Communion.

Authority in Anglicanism

It is arguable that the key to Anglican identity is its theory and practice of AUTHORITY in the church. Historically it has been open (though not without initial resistance) to fresh movements of ideas. At the Reformation it embraced (as did the continental reformers) the new learning derived from the rediscovered texts of the Greek New Testament and of the early Fathers. Anglican scholars responded to the critical impetus of the ENLIGHTENMENT and claimed that Christianity was eminently reasonable. Anglicans embraced the historicist movement and the historical (rather than the dogmatic) approach to disputed questions. This has been a feature of Anglicanism. Anglicans gradually came to terms with the scientific revolution and the theory of evolution (see DARWINISM) in the late nineteenth century. They also gradually responded to the emergence of the social sciences in the late nineteenth and early twentieth centuries, wrestling, for example, with the implications of social relativism and gender issues for Christian belief and practice. Within Anglicanism sound scholarship has the power eventually to call in question traditional positions.

As a result of a series of celebrated test cases in nineteenth-century England, Anglicanism is now characterized by comparatively unconstrained discussion and debate of theological issues, even among the CLERGY, and a relatively weak central teaching authority. In practice, no theological question is closed, although if a member of the clergy openly repudiated the doctrine of the Trinity or of the deity of Christ he or she could expect censure or discipline. At the same time Anglican liturgies affirm the ancient ecumenical creeds and the clergy are required to assent in fairly general terms to these and to the historic formularies, such as the sixteenth-century THIRTY-NINE ARTICLES of Religion, the Book OF COMMON PRAYER or its modern derivatives, and the forms for the ordination of the clergy. It could be said that Anglicanism combines official adherence to orthodox tradition with considerable latitude in practice.

Anglicanism upholds the unique authority of Holy Scripture (see BIBLE) as teaching the way of SALVATION. In dispute with Rome, the English reformers argued that nothing that was not expressly taught by Scripture or an evident inference from Scripture could be required as necessary for salvation. However, Anglican formularies do not give the same authority to Scripture in deciding the outward form of the church, its worship and structure. For this the guidance of the early church is needed, provided nothing is enforced that is "repugnant" to Scripture or oppressive to the Christian conscience. There is also recognition of the criterion of appropriateness to the circumstances. On the basis of primitive tradition, Anglicanism embraces the Canon of Scripture itself, the Creeds, the threefold ministry, and the structure of the Eucharist (see LORD'S SUPPER).

Anglicanism is both episcopal (see BISHOP AND EPISCOPACY) and synodical (see SYNOD) in its polity. It preserves the threefold ministry of deacons, priests, and bishops in historical continuity of ordinations. Many provinces of the Communion have women deacons and priests (see DEACONESSES, DEACONS); a few have women bishops. At every level of the church's life, bishops, other clergy, and lay people share in the government of the church. The episcopate has a special but not exclusive responsibility in matters of DOCTRINE, liturgy, and ministry. Bishops exercise oversight in their dioceses, in collegiality with clergy and lay people (see LAITY). As an episcopal college (or part of the universal episcopal college) they have corporate responsibility for leadership in their churches. The most visible expression of their communion is the ten-yearly LAMBETH CONFERENCE of Anglican bishops, which has significant moral and pastoral authority but no juridical power.

Although Anglicans are familiar with various expressions of primacy (particularly that of the archbishop of Canterbury), they do not accept the universal jurisdiction of the bishop of Rome, the pope. The repudiation of the Roman jurisdiction was a defining element in the English Reformation. The English reformers tended to see the Church of Rome as one "particular" or national church among others, moreover one that was singularly corrupt and in need of radical reform. Like several of the Protestant reformers, however, some Anglicans have been open to the idea of a reformed universal primacy, by human not divine right, without jurisdiction over particular churches and without potential infallibility, but nevertheless presiding among the churches in the cause of unity and charity.

Anglicans stand, therefore, with the Protestant churches in rejecting papal primacy in its current form, but deviate from them in not espousing equality of ministries. There is a certain ineradicable hierarchy in the Anglican understanding of holy order. Anglicanism has affinities to Eastern Orthodoxy (see ORTHODOXY, EASTERN) in its concept of national churches, especially where there is a special relationship to the state (most clearly as in England) and in its view of General or Ecumenical Councils as the highest authority in the church (rather than the pope).

It is seldom recognized that, in its view of authority, Anglicanism has inherited several aspects of the pre-Reformation Conciliar Movement. In the early fifteenth century this movement shaped several major Western councils. It attempted (and ultimately failed) to reform and control the papacy. The English reformers discuss the role of councils at length. Like MARTIN LUTHER, archbishop of Canterbury THOMAS CRANMER appealed to a free General Council. The conciliar principles of representation, constitutionality, and consent were reflected in the partnership between church and state in post-Reformation England. They are clearly embodied in modern Anglican synodical polity, without undermining the proper oversight of the episcopate.

However, unlike the conciliarists, Anglican formularies do not ascribe infallibility to General Councils. They teach that General Councils can err and have in fact erred. They also deny that it is the sole prerogative of the pope to call, preside at, and ratify the decisions of General Councils. Anglicans promote a conciliar way of working at various levels, from the very local to the provincial and beyond. They tend not to lose sleep over the hypothetical issue of a truly Ecumenical Council for today.

Anglican Spirituality

The spiritual and theological ethos of Anglicanism has been shaped by two theologians more than by any others: THOMAS CRANMER (1489–1556) and RICHARD HOOKER (1554–1600). The first was an archbishop of Canterbury and the compiler of the *Book of Common Prayer* (BCP) and of the first doctrinal formularies of the Church of England. The second was an obscure parish priest, but the author of the most seminal of all works of Anglican theology. The poems of GEORGE HERBERT (1593–1633) and the hymns of CHARLES WESLEY (1707–1788) are also among the peaks of Anglican spirituality.

Anglican LITURGY derives particularly from the BCP, which was drawn up by Cranmer in 1549 (revised by him in 1552) and reached its definitive form when the monarchy and the church's hierarchy were restored following the English CIVIL WAR and the Commonwealth period under OLIVER CROMWELL in 1662. In its central provision of Morning and Evening Prayer, the BCP combined a radical simplification of the monastic hours to suit lay piety with extensive use of ancient prayers. The medieval mass was reformed to eradicate the cult of the SAINTS, TRANSUBSTANTIATION, and the idea of a propitiatory sacrifice for the living and the departed. The emphasis was on the believing communicant's reception of the benefits of Christ's redemption in Holy Communion. Any hint of a human meritorious work in offering the Eucharist was avoided.

Cranmer's 1552 BCP represents the furthest point of revision of the Anglican liturgy in a Protestant direction. Since then there have been several attempts to recover the Anglican liturgical balance: first in 1662 with the triumph of High Church Anglicanism; then among the Nonjurors (who withdrew from the Established Church at the end of the seventeenth century); and again by the Tractarians of the OXFORD MOVEMENT in the mid-nineteenth century. Modern Anglican liturgy has been shaped by all these and by the liturgical renewal of the twentieth century. Eucharistic sacrifice (though not in a propitiatory sense) and the real presence (though not transubstantiation) are features of current Anglican liturgies worldwide.

Hooker is generally regarded as the greatest exponent of Anglicanism. Unlike JOHN JEWEL (1522–1571), the author of the *Apology of the Church of England*, Hooker's target was not Roman Catholic opposition to the English Reformation, but the contention of the Puritans within the Church of England (see PURITANISM) that the Reformation had not gone far enough. They demanded simplification of the liturgy in a less sacramental direction, abolition of such "popish" residues as the surplice, the sign of the cross in BAPTISM, and the ring in MARRIAGE. Above all, they called for the abolition of episcopacy and the setting up of church government by lay elders (see PRESBYTERIANISM). In his work *Of the Laws of Ecclesiastical Polity* (in eight books, not all of which were published in his lifetime), Hooker charted a different course from the polemical and *ad hominem* writings of archbishop JOHN WHITGIFT (1532–1604). Hooker reduced the issues at stake to the first principles of theology and law. He drew on the fathers, medieval schoolmen, lawyers, and the continental reformers themselves to mount a devastating counterattack on the Puritan platform. Hooker showed the scope and limits of the authority of Scripture, the role of reason, and the sovereignty of law in formulating the outward ordering of the church in worship and government. The profound incarnational and sacramental theology that is embedded in this work, ostensibly devoted to ecclesiastical polity, gives Hooker his importance in the Anglican theological tradition.

Anglicanism and Protestantism

The churches of the Anglican Communion regard themselves as both catholic and reformed and have sometimes spoken of themselves as a bridge communion between Protestantism on the one hand and Roman Catholicism and Eastern Orthodoxy on the other. The relationship between Anglicanism and Protestantism is not a simple one. There is a built-in tension and elements within Anglicanism pull both ways.

On the one hand, Anglicanism was decisively shaped by the Reformation and the Anglican reformers were strongly influenced (though not uncritically) by the Continental reformers, who generally were more creative than they were. From the mid-sixteenth century Anglicanism has been marked by the key features of the Protestant Reformation: JUSTIFICATION by GRACE, received through FAITH; an open BIBLE and the ministry of the word; liturgy in the vernacular with the participation of the laity; a married, pastoral ministry rooted in the community; communion in both kinds (the wine as well as the bread); the involvement of the laity in church government, whether in the form of the sovereign, parliament, local lay officers, or (for the past century) various forms of representative or synodical government; the abolition of religious orders (see MONASTICISM).

Until recently Anglicans were proud to style themselves Protestants (some, of course, still are). CALVINISM (its doctrines of grace, not its Presbyterian polity) was the prevailing theology during the reigns of ELIZABETH I and James I (the second half of the sixteenth and the first quarter of the seventeenth centuries). After the Civil War and Commonwealth periods in the mid-seventeenth century LUTHERANISM became the most favored Protestant communion for the next 150 years. Historically Anglicans saw the Church of England as a sister church of the Lutheran and Reformed Churches on the Continent.

On the other hand, Anglicans have always insisted on the catholicity of their church. The Anglican reformers were clear that they were not setting up a new church in Britain, but reforming the one church that went back to the Apostles, the fathers, the early martyrs, and the Celtic missionaries. Roman soldiers were probably the first Christians in Britain. It was known that the British church was represented at early councils. Anglicans become highly indignant at any suggestion that Anglicanism was founded in the sixteenth century by King HENRY VIII. The ancient structures of Catholicism survived the upheavals of the Reformation: the threefold ministry was maintained, with episcopal succession in the ancient sees; several medieval practices were reformed, not abolished; and traditional symbols including some vestments, the sign of the cross, and the ring in marriage were retained.

The High Church tradition within Anglicanism kept alive a sense of catholic continuity, although not—until the Oxford Movement—at the expense of a sense of affinity with the Reformation inheritance (see ANGLO-CATHOLICISM). A series of abortive private initiatives attempted to build bridges with the Roman Catholic Church abroad. Religious orders were restored in the second half of the nineteenth century. Although in very modern times Anglicans have become coy about the word Protestant, they have unequivocally affirmed that Anglicanism is not only catholic but also reformed.

It has sometimes been suggested (e.g., by the historian T. B. Macaulay) that the Church of England combines Calvinist Articles of Religion with a "popish" liturgy. This antithesis is highly questionable. The Thirty-nine Articles cover a wide range of contentious issues that are not specific to Calvinism and actually take a moderate position on the doctrine of PREDESTI-

NATION. Their clearest echo of a Reformation formulary is of the Lutheran AUGSBURG CONFESSION (on the marks of the visible church). On the other hand, as we have noted, the BCP is not untouched by Protestant sensitivities.

Unlike Lutheranism, Anglicanism does not have a strong sense of confessional identity (see CONFESSIONALIZATION). There is no comparable sense of it having been raised up by God to bear witness to vital truths. Anglicans, especially in England, tend to take their church for granted. For them it is just the ordinary way of being Christian. No one figure, not even Cranmer or Hooker, has the place in Anglicanism that Luther has in Lutheranism or JOHN CALVIN has in the Reformed tradition. However, in recent decades Anglicans have become more aware of their inheritance. ECUMENISM and cultural pluralism have prompted a modest revival of Anglican theology, and a critical reappropriation of the tradition.

Anglican Ecumenism

As a global communion, Anglicans have been engaged in ecumenical dialogue with other traditions. The Anglican–Roman Catholic International Commission (ARCIC) has produced a series of concise reports on ministry, the Eucharist, authority, justification, and ethics. The *Final Report* (1982) of ARCIC's first phase was endorsed in general terms by the Anglican Communion but received a cool response from the Vatican. Anglican–Orthodox dialogue continues to make significant advances.

The international Anglican–Reformed dialogue produced a notable report, *God's Reign and our Unity* (1984), which has not so far been properly received in the two communions. International dialogue between Anglicans and Lutherans produced the creative *Niagara Report* that majored on missiology and apostolicity and prepared the ground for regional agreements. A series of regional discussions between Anglicans and BAPTISTS will eventually feed into theological reflection on a global basis. Anglican–Methodist (see METHODISM, GLOBAL) international dialogue resulted in *Sharing in the Apostolic Communion* (1996).

In North America the EPISCOPAL CHURCH OF THE USA and the EVANGELICAL LUTHERAN CHURCH IN AMERICA have entered into an agreement (*Called to Common Mission,* 2001) for "full communion," involving mutual recognition of ministries and Lutheran acceptance of the historic episcopate. A similar agreement (*The Waterloo Declaration,* 2001) was reached between Anglicans and Lutherans in Canada. The British and Irish Anglican churches have entered into communion (in the Porvoo Agreement, 1996) with most of the episcopal Lutheran churches of Scandinavia and the Baltic. A lower level of agreement, not involving interchangeability of ministries, has been achieved between the Church of England and the Evangelical Church in GERMANY (EKD) in the Meissen Agreement (1991) and between the British and Irish Anglican churches and the French Lutheran and Reformed churches in the Reuilly Agreement (2000). Anglicans and Lutherans are moving closer together in several parts of the world, including AUSTRALIA, SOUTH AFRICA, and central southern Africa.

The Church of England and the (nonepiscopal) Methodist Church of Great Britain (see METHODISM, ENGLAND) are moving forward together on the basis of *An Anglican-Methodist Covenant* (2001).

References and Further Reading

Avis, P. *The Anglican Understanding of the Church.* London: SPCK, 2000.
———. *Anglicanism and the Christian Church: Theological Resources in Historical Perspective.* Revised and expanded edition. Edinburgh: T. & T. Clark, 2002.
Doe, N. *Canon Law in the Anglican Communion.* Oxford, UK: Clarendon Press, 1998.
Griffiss, J. E. *The Anglican Vision.* Cambridge, MA: Cowley Press, 1997.
Jacob, W. M. *The Making of the Anglican Church Worldwide.* London: SPCK, 1997.
McGrath, A., ed. *SPCK Handbook of Anglican Theologians.* London: SPCK, 1998.
Rowell, G., K. Stevenson, and R. Williams. *Love's Redeeming Work: the Anglican Quest for Holiness.* Oxford, UK: OUP, 2001.
Sykes, S. *Unashamed Anglicanism.* London: Darton, Longman & Todd, 1995.
———, Booty, J., and J. Knight, eds. *The Study of Anglicanism.* Revised edition. London: SPCK, 1998.

PAUL AVIS

ANGLO-CATHOLICISM

Anglo-Catholicism has been a major variety of Anglican churchmanship for almost two centuries. It began with the Oxford or Tractarian Movement of 1833, when some Oxford University dons, notably John Keble (1792–1866), John Henry Newman (1801–1890), and Edward Bouverie Pusey (1800–1882) proclaimed that the CHURCH OF ENGLAND was not merely a state-established faith, but an apostolic church bearing divine authority (see OXFORD MOVEMENT). They located its institutional and theological sources in the church of the first four Christian centuries, not in the sixteenth-century Protestant REFORMATION. They stressed the importance of the priesthood, corporate worship, and the SACRAMENTS as divinely ordained means of grace. Most startling was their assertion that ANGLICANISM is a variety of Catholicism, not of Protestantism. Their ideas gained national attention through the *Tracts for the Times* (1833–1841).

The movement reached beyond academia in the 1840s, as some parish priests expressed Tractarian theology by means of elaborate ritual. By the 1860s Ritualist priests staffed parishes in ENGLAND and SCOTLAND, and the movement had spread to the British settler colonies and the United States of America. Despite persecution, Anglo-Catholicism survived into the twentieth century, becoming the most vigorous and creative force within the Anglican Communion after 1918. It recovered the history of Christian liturgy, restored the Eucharist as the principal Sunday service, and popularized ceremonial and congregational singing. However, the 1960s saw a decline that left it fragmented, uncertain, and weak at the beginning of the twenty-first century.

Origins

Anglo-Catholicism's origins lie in both the early Evangelical movement and eighteenth-century High Churchmanship. Because many of its leaders grew up in Evangelical homes, they were transforming their own background rather than reacting against an outside threat. EVANGELICALISM, which stressed the necessity of a CONVERSION experience, is crucial to understanding their conversions to Anglo-Catholicism and (for some) to Roman Catholicism because those who convert once may convert again. Moreover, their doctrines were rooted in a vigorous High Church tradition that was more than mere Jacobite romanticism or anti-Jacobin reaction. Constitutional issues, especially Dissenters' rights, Roman Catholic Emancipation, and parliamentary reform, which undermined the British state's Anglican identity, were the movement's immediate spark. Cultural and pastoral issues, especially Victorian romantic medievalism and concerns over how industrialization and urbanization were changing the social order, shaped Anglo-Catholicism's development throughout the nineteenth century. Newman, a towering intellectual figure, is sometimes considered to have been Anglo-Catholicism's prime leader and most interesting man of ideas. His essay on "The Development of Doctrine," which argued that Christian beliefs were not immutable, but rather changed over time, and the *Apologia Pro Vita Sua* (1864), his spiritual autobiography, remain edifying reading. *Tract 90* (1841), which he wrote, interpreted the THIRTY-NINE ARTICLES to be congruent with nineteenth-century Roman Catholic teaching. Many bishops and most Oxford University authorities condemned the tract as dishonest and disloyal without giving Newman a chance to defend himself.

Some writers contend that Newman's conversion to Roman Catholicism in 1845 ended the Oxford Movement, or at least that it was a turning point in the movement's development. Before 1845, they argue, Tractarians had seen Evangelicalism as their main enemy, but for a decade thereafter their battle was with Roman Catholicism. However, other scholars argue that Newman's Anglican career illustrates Anglo-Catholicism's intellectual debts to the eighteenth century. His Evangelical background prepared him for Tractarianism and smoothed his way to Roman Catholicism. Although discarding distinctive Evangelical teachings, he remained intensely interested in prophecy and in the quest for personal holiness of life. Newman's activities show that much of the estrangement between Tractarians and their non-Tractarian Oxford colleagues was his own doing and that he left the Church of England because he chose to do so and not because Anglican leaders drove him out.

Ritualism and Anglo-Catholic Culture

Those historians who situate Newman as Tractarianism's central figure commonly argue that Anglo-Catholicism did not appear until the 1860s and 1870s, and that its emphasis on ritual marks it as a new development having little continuity with the Oxford Movement. They point to the fact that some Tractarian leaders opposed the introduction of elaborate ceremonial. They also stress the role of the Cambridge Camden Society, founded independently of the Oxford Movement, in uncovering the history of ritual and in contributing to the popularity of Victorian medievalism. They attribute the spread of ritual to a younger generation of parochial clergy, freed from the restraint of university-based leaders.

However, Tractarianism's Romantic, poetic, and aesthetic spirit certainly was consistent with the advance of ritual in public worship. Clergy, including High Churchmen and Anglo-Catholics, dominated the membership of the ecclesiological, antiquarian, and archaeological societies that proliferated in the nineteenth century. Evangelicals charged that the Cambridge Camden Society taught through art what Tractarianism taught through tracts. Some Tractarian leaders, notably Pusey, favored ceremonial advance. Pusey founded a church in Leeds, which introduced Ritualism to that Yorkshire industrial town. Hence, late twentieth-century historians argued that the development of ornate, Catholic ceremonial followed logically from Tractarian theology. Furthermore, Ritualism, including emphasis on the Eucharist rather than Matins as the principal Sunday service, surpliced choirs, altar crosses, lit candles, and wafer bread, can be found in the early 1840s in a few parishes throughout England. Their numbers grew as parishes in London's West End, southern English seaside resorts, and elsewhere adopted such customs. By the 1860s some priests wore eucharistic vestments, burnt incense, and chanted the service.

The Anglo-Catholic Movement's understanding of ceremonial changed over time. Men who were "advanced" in their own day found themselves old-fashioned twenty years later. A continuity of personalities, ideas, and practices can be traced from the Tractarians through the "ultrarubricians" (who wanted strict enforcement of the Ornaments Rubric) to the ultraceremonialists of the century's last quarter. Finally, some ritualizers used the third- and fourth-century church as their model, others called for a return to medieval practices, and a few imitated the practice of the nineteenth-century Roman Church.

Anglo-Catholicism was a countercultural movement that challenged Victorian society's dominant cultural values, that posed the challenge as much by creating an alternative lifestyle as through writing and preaching, and that appealed to groups disaffected from those values. Some women resisted the private, domestic role assigned them by patriarchal authority. Some men found "muscular Christianity" to be unfulfilling or even repelling. Some priests feared the decline in status of what they considered to be their sacred calling. Some laity and clergy doubted that the heterosexual, married state was the highest Christian ideal. Anglo-Catholicism attracted many of these people because it seemed to reject those values in favor of ones that answered their needs and desires.

The movement forged a subculture with its own language, dress, hairstyles, clothing, and mannerisms, all of which infuriated the traditional authority figures of bishops, politicians, parents, and husbands. Anglo-Catholics addressed clergy as "Father," not "Mister." They "heard Mass" as opposed to "going to Church." Their clergy were called "parish priests," not "vicars" or "rectors," lived in "presbyteries," not "rectories" or "vicarages," and wore cassock and clerical collar outdoors, not black suit and white stock. Most were clean-shaven, whereas Protestants favored side-whiskers or beards without moustaches. Their humor was especially childish in its sensibilities.

Anglo-Catholicism and Social Reform

Pusey kept the movement going after 1845, despite the spate of conversions that followed Newman's and attacks from Evangelicals and conventional churchmen. His published works demarcated Tractarian theology from that of Rome. His counsel helped maintain morale. Social reform was a major component of his theology, given that Tractarianism was an attempt to grapple with the problems of modern, industrial society, not to escape from those problems into Romantic medievalism. Pusey believed that corporate worship

alone could bridge the gap between social classes. When he put his social theology into action, he chose the industrial north of England as his sphere of action and he expressed his theology by means of Ritualism.

Other Anglo-Catholic clergy followed Pusey's lead, serving slum parishes in London's East End and in industrial towns. They devised revival services with rousing songs to convert the poor (see REVIVALS). They believed that ritual appealed to working-class sensibilities and that Anglo-Catholic theology challenged Victorian economic, political, and social values. Anglo-Catholic clergy were more likely than Evangelicals to favor the separation of church and state and to support trade unions and socialism (see CHURCH AND STATE OVERVIEW). By the end of the nineteenth century, it was customary for Anglo-Catholic clergy to serve a curacy in a slum parish as part of their training.

The Victorian working classes avoided church-going on the grounds that it was for the middle classes, and some also found middle-class values alien and repellent. However, Anglo-Catholic evangelism in slum parishes was no more successful than evangelism by other religious traditions. What mattered to working-class parishioners were priests who treated them with respect and sincere interest, not churchmanship or doctrine.

The Spread of Anglo-Catholicism around the Globe

Anglo-Catholicism, like Evangelicalism, had a global dimension. Early on in the movement's history, sympathizers appeared in Scotland and the United States. The Episcopal churches of both countries had an indigenous High Church tradition that facilitated the spread of Anglo-Catholicism. In Canada, New Zealand, and Australia, however, the small Anglo-Catholic presence was attributable exclusively to English influence.

Anglo-Catholics also engaged in the massive nineteenth-century Christian missionary project. Tractarians influenced the SOCIETY FOR THE PROPAGATION OF THE GOSPEL. Several religious orders, most notably the Society of the Sacred Mission, were founded specifically for overseas work. In the Pacific, the Anglo-Catholic bishops George Selwyn and John Patteson shaped New Zealand and Melanesian missions. The most unmistakably Anglo-Catholic endeavor was the Universities' Mission to Central Africa (1857), which sent missionaries to Zanzibar, Kenya, Uganda, Northern Rhodesia, Nyasaland, and SOUTH AFRICA (see AFRICA). In the twentieth century, Anglo-Catholics, most notably TREVOR HUDDLESTON and DESMOND TUTU, were in the forefront of opposition to South African apartheid. By and large, Anglo-Catholicism encountered much less opposition in the non-Western missionary field than it did in Great Britain, the United States, and the White Dominions.

Survival

The movement survived systematic attempts to put down Ritualism during the last third of the century. These attempts took the forms of cultural ostracism, popular intimidation, and political repression.

Cultural repression began in the 1830s. Thomas Arnold, headmaster of Rugby School, skewered the Tractarians in a widely read article in the *Edinburgh Review* entitled "The Oxford Malignants" (1836). *Punch* caricatured Ritualists as either simpering bumboys or sinister seducers of young women. Throughout the nineteenth century, Anglo-Catholics were depicted unsympathetically in novels (e.g., Margaret Oliphant's *The Perpetual Curate*), poetry (e.g., Martin Tupper's *The Ritualist Plan of Campaign*), and art (e.g., Holman Hunt's *The Hireling Shepherd*). Puseyite clergy were excoriated in the press, passed over for promotion, and insulted in the streets. The popular culture of the day thus branded Anglo-Catholics as dishonest, effeminate narcissists.

Violence began with the Exeter Surplice Riots in the mid-1840s, and continued throughout the century. Crowds disrupted Anglo-Catholic church services, barracked street missioners, smashed stained-glass windows, and burned books. Evangelical anti-Catholic voluntary societies, common in the period, sponsored, covertly or overtly, most of these popular disturbances. Notorious were the Manchester Protestant Operative Society in the 1840s and 1850s; the Church Association (1865), which intimidated clergy and worshippers with litigation and force; and the Protestant Truth Society (1890), which sold quasi-pornographic tracts and desecrated Ritualist churches.

Political repression began at mid-century, when prime minister Lord John Russell denounced Anglo-Catholics as "traitors within the gates" who aped Romish superstition. The movement was a target in parliamentary debates. The Church Association prosecuted Ritualist clergy for alleged violations of the statute law that enacted the Prayer Book rubrics. Hoping to bring order to the church by defining what was legal practice, Archbishop of Canterbury ARCHIBALD CAMPBELL TAIT persuaded Prime Minister Benjamin Disraeli to sponsor the Public Worship Regulation Act (1874). The law banned most Anglo-Catholic ceremonial and created special courts to hear cases. However, most Anglo-Catholic clergy refused to recognize the authority of secular courts to regulate religious worship, some refused to attend their trials, and several were imprisoned.

Whether prosecuted by law or persecuted by riot, Ritualist priests garnered the public sympathy accorded to martyrs and the support of conservative ceremonialists and traditional High Churchmen. Anglo-Catholics themselves organized the English Church Union (1860) to defend and spread their ideals. Finally, apologists shifted the defense for ceremonial from doctrinal uniformity to freedom of conscience. Thus, Anglo-Catholicism, which had begun as a movement to transform the Church of England, was a church party by 1914, enjoying respectability, but acknowledging the right of other church parties to exist.

The Twentieth Century

The First World War's most immediate effect on British religion was to legitimate the Anglo-Catholic practice of praying for the souls of the departed. Three quarters of a million men had died in combat, and their surviving mates and relations wanted comfort. War memorials were erected throughout Britain, Remembrance Day services commemorated the dead, and cathedrals enshrined books listing their names. A practice once condemned as popish offered survivors the comfort of doing something positive for the dead.

The interwar years also saw Anglo-Catholicism become triumphal. Five Anglo-Catholic congresses were held in London, beginning in 1923 with 13,000 delegates and culminating in celebrations of the movement's centenary in 1933 with 70,000 in attendance. Addresses by prominent clergy and colonial bishops (no English bishops participated) proclaimed Anglo-Catholic ideology and called for further ceremonial advance, especially for the adoration of the Blessed Sacrament. These congresses boosted Anglo-Catholic morale by displaying worship in all its splendor and projecting a sense of strength in numbers.

The movement's leadership decided to hold the sixth congress in 1940, but Hitler, appeasement, and the Second World War intervened. With few exceptions, Anglo-Catholics were silent about these tumultuous events, as was the church in general. Foreign secretary Lord Halifax was both a leading Anglo-Catholic layman and an Appeaser. The High Church Archbishop of Canterbury Cosmo Lang declared that "no praise could be too great" to give the government. During the conflict itself, Anglo-Catholics appeared more upset at proposals for church union in south India than at the devastation of war. Postwar congresses went into rapid decline. That of 1948 attracted 11,000 participants. Thereafter, attendance dropped (1,700 in 1958; 1,000 in 1978; 500 in 1988), the conferences grew shorter, and public attention to their doings waned.

Anglo-Catholic intellectual life also waned. Not a few distinguished figures wrote during the interwar years—among them J. V. Langmead Casserley, Gregory Dix, T. S. Eliot, Austin Farrer, C. S. Lewis, Eric Mascall, and Dorothy Sayers—and remained active after 1945. However, they were dead by the end of the 1960s, and no one of equal stature took their place.

It was at this point that the Second Vatican Council and the profound cultural changes in Western society associated with the decade of the 1960s transformed the religious world, including Anglo-Catholicism. Vatican II's modernizing spirit undercut Anglo-Catholicism by "Protestantizing" the Mass; liberalizing theological positions on Jews, "separated brethren," and non-Western religions; freeing secular clergy and religious orders from Counter-Reformation discipline; and encouraging (albeit unintentionally) theological speculation, liturgical innovation, and the charismatic movement. The cultural changes of the 1960s popularized practices (e.g., abortion, homosexuality, premarital sex, drug-taking) and beliefs (e.g., Eastern mysticism, feminism, human potentiality) that challenged traditional moral teaching and institutional authority. Anglo-Catholicism, once a counterculture, now seemed a fossil.

Anglo-Catholicism splintered over the issues of the Alternative Service Book (and the 1979 Prayer Book in the United States), the ordination of women, and the church's response to homosexuality. These issues cut across the traditional Catholic–Protestant divide, as conservative Anglo-Catholics now found that they had more in common with Evangelicalism than with liberal Anglo-Catholicism. The results were the movement's fragmentation and a revivified, triumphalist Evangelicalism at the beginning of the twenty-first century.

References and Further Reading

Chadwick, Owen. *The Spirit of the Oxford Movement: Tractarian Essays.* Cambridge: Cambridge University Press, 1990.
Hylson-Smith, Kenneth. *High Churchmanship in the Church of England From the Sixteenth Century to the Late Twentieth Century.* Edinburgh: T & T Clark, 1993.
Mumm, Susan. *Stolen Daughters, Virgin Mothers: Anglican Sisterhoods in Victorian Britain.* London and New York: Leicester University Press, 1999.
Newsome, David. *The Parting of Friends: A Study of the Wilberforces and Henry Manning.* London: John Murray, 1966.
Nockles, Peter B. *The Oxford Movement in Context: Anglican High Churchmanship, 1760–1857.* Cambridge: Cambridge University Press, 1994.
Paz, D. G. *Popular Anti-Catholicism in Mid-Victorian England.* Stanford, CA: Stanford University Press, 1992.
Pickering, W. S. *Anglo-Catholicism: A Study in Religious Ambiguity.* London and New York: Routledge, 1989.
Reed, John Shelton. *Glorious Battle: The Cultural Politics of Victorian Anglo-Catholicism.* Nashville and London: Vanderbilt University Press, 1996.
Reeves, Thomas C. "The Light that Failed: Reflections on Anglo-Catholicism in the Episcopal Church." *Anglican and Episcopal History* LXVIII (1999): 215–230.
Rowell, Geoffrey. *The Vision Glorious: Themes and Personalities of the Catholic Revival in Anglicanism.* Oxford: Oxford University Press, 1983.
Yates, Nigel. *Anglican Ritualism in Victorian Britain, 1830–1910.* Oxford: Oxford University Press, 1999.

D. G. PAZ

ANTICHRIST

The powerful image of an evil figure known as Antichrist has shadowed the Western imagination for two millennia. With the REFORMATION, Antichrist belief entered Protestant thought, where it proved remarkably tenacious. Whether "Antichrist" is identified as an individual, a demonic world system, or a propensity for wrongdoing embedded in the human heart, Antichrist belief has provided a means by which Christians, Protestants included, have thought about the nature of evil, sought to pinpoint hidden conspiracies, and visualized the end of history. To understand the role of Antichrist belief in Protestantism, one must trace its background in biblical literature and pre-Reformation Christianity. This historical perspective is particularly important because many twentieth-century notions about Antichrist were in fact simply variants of ancient ideas.

Origins of Antichrist Belief and Its Development to the Reformation

The belief in a supernatural being intent on fomenting chaos, corruption, and evil, in opposition to the principles of order, purity, and righteousness, emerged in the earliest cosmological writings of the Middle East. This being is personified in the Hebrew scriptures as "Satan," a fallen angel in rebellion against God. In Genesis, this evil figure, in the form of a serpent, tempts Eve, leading to the expulsion of Adam and Eve from the Garden. In the Book of Job, Satan instigates a series of trials designed to test Job's faith. In I Chronicles 21:1, Satan provokes David to defy God's wishes. In Daniel 7, the Evil One takes the form of four monstrous beasts from the sea.

Passing into Christian thought, this demonic enemy of God, variously called "Satan," "the DEVIL," "the adversary," "Beelzebub," and the "old serpent," frequently appears in the New Testament. During the first century A.D., there also appeared in Christian writings an evil figure who acts as Satan's surrogate, and does Satan's bidding, but is distinct from Satan.

This is Antichrist. The word itself occurs only three times in the New Testament, in I and II John. These passages contain ambiguities that helped give rise to different understandings of the term. In I John 2:18, the word appears in the plural, referring to individuals alive at the time: "Little children, it is the last time; and as ye have heard that antichrist shall come, even now are there many antichrists; whereby we know that it is the last time." I John 4:3 speaks of the "spirit of antichrist," rather than of a specific individual. Other New Testament terms, presumed to refer to the same figure, include "the man of sin"; "the son of perdition" (II Thessalonians 2:3); and "the Beast," the destroyer who hovers over the apocalyptic portion of the Book of Revelation until his own destruction at Armageddon. In II Thessalonians 2:8, this being is described as one "whose coming is after the working of Satan with all power and signs and lying wonders."

Some of these authors probably had identifiable historic personages in mind. The fourth beast's "little horn" in Daniel 7:8 likely refers to Antiochus IV of Syria, who brutally oppressed the Jews in the second century B.C., when Daniel was written. The Beast of Revelation is widely seen as a cryptic allusion to Nero, the persecutor of Christians who committed suicide in A.D. 68. Although Revelation was written after Nero's death, a belief widespread among the Christians of Asia Minor (to whom Revelation is addressed) held that Nero would be resurrected and resume his persecutions. Using the system of assigning numbers to letters that was prevalent in the ancient world, some scholars argue, the Beast's number, 666 (Revelation 13:18), points decisively to Nero. This association of specific individuals with Antichrist imagery would long influence Christian thought.

The Patristic writers offered differing interpretations of Antichrist. Origen (185–254) argued that the term did not refer to a present or future individual, but rather symbolized all forces opposed to the true faith. St. Augustine (354–430) similarly rejected literalist readings of the prophecies. The opposition of Christ and Antichrist, he argued, represents the ongoing struggle between righteousness and evil. Righteousness will ultimately triumph, Augustine believed, but the details of that victory remain hidden.

Although this view became orthodox Catholic doctrine, popular belief in Antichrist pervaded medieval Europe. Hildegard of Bingen, the twelfth-century German abbess and visionary, left vivid images of the Beast as a loathsome, demonic creature. The *Play of Antichrist,* a German religious drama dating from around 1160, enjoyed enduring popularity. The Calabrian monk Joachim of Fiore (c. 1135–1202), the best-known medieval prophecy interpreter, elaborated his system in his *Exposition on Revelation,* and in

intricate drawings collected in *The Book of Figures.* Joachim saw the Antichrist as a demonic figure who will arise in the last days and then be defeated by Christ, ushering in a third and final stage of human history, the Age of the Spirit. Joachim, in short, unlike Origen and Augustine, viewed Antichrist as a person, not merely a metaphor for evil.

With the rise of Islam in the seventh century and its spread through the Middle East, North Africa, and Spain, Antichrist was often identified with this new religion, its founder Muhammed, or specific Islamic rulers. In 1190, when Richard Coeur de Lion camped at Messina en route to the Third Crusade, he took the opportunity to confer with Joachim, who identified the Islamic emperor Saladin as the Antichrist and offered assurances that Richard would defeat Saladin and recover Jerusalem for Christ's millennial kingdom—a prophecy that failed.

In popular and scholarly Antichrist belief, Judaism and Islam were often linked as dual enemies of Christianity and the most likely spawning ground of Antichrist. Indeed, the belief that Antichrist would be a Jew (a conviction that survived into the late twentieth century among some American Fundamentalists) helped fuel medieval ANTI-SEMITISM and murderous assaults on the Jews, sometimes as the prelude to a Crusade (see FUNDAMENTALISM).

Antichrist Belief in Protestantism: From the Reformation to the Twentieth Century

As the Protestant Reformation convulsed Europe in the early sixteenth century, the leaders had to come to terms with Antichrist belief, which did, after all, have scriptural as well as folkloric roots. In practice, the leading reformers displayed considerable ambivalence about this belief, and indeed about millennialism itself, as presented in Revelation.

This ambivalence deepened with the rise of the Anabaptists and peasant radicalism in reformed regions of Germany. THOMAS MÜNTZER, the Protestant pastor who in 1525 attached himself to an ongoing peasants' uprising, was steeped in APOCALYPTICISM. Muntzer assured the peasants that the forces opposing them represented Antichrist, but that Christ would bring them victory. Müntzer was captured and beheaded in May 1525, after some 5,000 rebellious peasants had been slaughtered in a final battle near Frankenhausen. The Anabaptists who took over the city of Muenster in 1534 similarly interpreted their cause in apocalyptic terms and denounced their foes as agents of Antichrist. The Muenster rebels, too, were killed by beseiging armies when they tried to surrender in June 1535. All early Anabaptists, writes historian Walter Klaassen, "were united in their conviction that . . . Christ and Antichrist were locked in the final struggle."

Faced with these alarming developments, MARTIN LUTHER as early as 1522 lashed out at the Anabaptists and the turbulent peasantry, and dismissed the Book of Revelation, which seemed to be fueling their rebellion, as "neither apostolic nor prophetic." In preparing his German New Testament, Luther relegated Revelation to an appendix. The AUGSBURG CONFESSION (1530) denounced millennialism as "Jewish doctrine." The Geneva reformer JOHN CALVIN, although not explicitly rejecting Revelation, kept it at a distance, never including it in his Bible commentaries. In his commentary on Daniel, Calvin offered a historical rather than an eschatological interpretation. The beasts from the sea, for example, represent successive Roman rulers, not a demonic figure who will arise in the last days. A third leading reformer, HULDRYCH ZWINGLI of Zurich, went furthest in rejecting Revelation, which provided so much ammunition for millennialism and Antichrist belief. It was, he flatly proclaimed, "not a book of the Bible." Both the Lutheran and Reformed traditions, in short, began with a strong antimillennialist basis (which they still retain), and thus had little sympathy, at the doctrinal level, with Antichrist speculation.

At the same time, however, the potent Antichrist image proved highly attractive to the reformers in their polemical battles with Rome. Some medieval reformers had identified the Pope as the Beast, and this belief burgeoned after the Reformation. Luther in *Adversus exsecrabilem Antichristi bullam* (1520) insisted that Pope Leo X's bull denouncing Luther's views must emanate from Antichrist. In his 1530 German Bible, and often thereafter, Luther explicitly identified the Pope as Antichrist. Calvin's INSTITUTES OF THE CHRISTIAN RELIGION (1559) made the Pope/Antichrist connection, as did the 1560 Geneva Bible, prepared for English Protestant exiles in Geneva. Protestant woodcuts, including a particularly loathsome one by Melchior Lorch, portrayed the Pope as Antichrist. Taking root in Protestant thought, the Pope/Antichrist nexus would long endure.

The Reformation era also saw the expansion of the Ottoman Turks into Eastern Europe, and this, too, shaped the Reformers' ESCHATOLOGY. Luther's Bible links the Ottoman Empire with the mysterious kingdom of "Gog" mentioned in Ezekiel 38, widely believed in prophecy circles to be another foretelling of Antichrist. This connection, too, would survive into the early twentieth century, when the Ottoman era finally ended.

English Protestants readily embraced the Pope/Antichrist connection, and during the Puritan Revolution (c. 1560–1660), many dissenters denounced not only Rome, but also the established CHURCH OF ENGLAND, as Antichrist. One pamphleteer called unreformed Anglican priests "the excrement of Antichrist." New England Puritans carried this outlook to America, where it struck deep roots.

Antichrist belief figured in the pamphlet wars of the American Revolution. Some patriots identified the hated excise stamps required by the Stamp Act (1765) as the Mark of the Beast; others identified George III's minister Lord Bute, born on a Scottish island, as the "Beast from the Sea" foretold in Daniel. One pamphleteer demonstrated mathematically that the phrase "Royal Supremacy in Great Britain" added up to 666.

Early nineteenth-century prophecy expositors continued to identify Antichrist with contemporary figures. Although the pope remained a perennial favorite, some fingered Napoleon as a likely candidate. During the Crimean War (1853–1856), British prophecy writer John Cummings, in the best-selling work *The End* (1855), suggested that Russia was "Gog," the prophesied Antichrist power—an identification that would prove highly popular in Cold War America a century later.

Antichrist belief took a new turn in the mid-nineteenth century when the British churchman JOHN NELSON DARBY devised a system of prophecy interpretation called DISPENSATIONALISM. Assembling prophetic passages from various parts of the Bible, Darby offered a detailed end-time scenario. After a series of prophetic fulfillments closing out the present dispensation (the Church Age), Darby taught, will come the Rapture, when all true believers will join Christ in the air, followed by the Great Tribulation (Matthew 24:21), a terrible seven-year period of war and suffering. As the Tribulation ends, Christ will return with the raptured saints, defeat his foes at Armageddon (Revelation 16:16), and establish his thousand-year earthly reign—the Millennium—in Jerusalem. After the Millennium, Darby concluded, will come the Last Judgment and the new heaven and new earth foretold in Revelation. Dispensationalism won followers in England and America, where it was spread by Darby's preaching tours and writings, and by U.S. converts such as Cyrus Scofield, whose popular 1909 SCOFIELD REFERENCE BIBLE offered dispensationalist readings of Scripture.

Antichrist was central to Darby's system. According to this scheme, Antichrist will arise after the Rapture and win allegiance by posing as a man of peace. Midway through the Tribulation, however, Antichrist reveals his demonic nature, and unleashes a horrendous persecution of Jews—God's wayward but chosen people—and "Tribulation saints" who have accepted Christ after the Rapture. As the seven years end, Antichrist assembles his followers at Armageddon to meet a vast army approaching from the East (Revelation 9:16, 16:12). Defeated by Christ, who returns as the warrior king with his hosts, Antichrist is cast into a lake of fire during the Millennium. After mounting a final rebellion, he is once again defeated, this time to be tormented for all eternity with his followers.

As dispensationalism attracted increasing support among American evangelicals (see EVANGELICALISM) and fundamentalists, Antichrist belief flourished. As in the past, some sought to pinpoint his identity among contemporary figures. Benito Mussolini, the Italian fascist leader, was a particular favorite, especially because many dispensationalists held that the ten-toed statue in King Nebuchadnezzar's dream (Daniel 2:31–35) foretold Antichrist's rule over a ten-nation revived Roman Empire. Mussolini's 1929 Concordat with the Vatican further convinced many Protestants that he would soon reveal himself as Antichrist. Others, however, viewed Adolph Hitler as the Evil One. The death of both men in 1945 ended this line of speculation, but not interest in Antichrist, which not only survived but reached new heights, especially in America.

Antichrist Belief in Late Twentieth-Century American Protestantism

As the twentieth century wore on, Antichrist belief persisted. Echoing Luther, the Northern Ireland Protestant firebrand Ian Paisley, confronting Pope John Paul II in Strasbourg in 1988, denounced him as Antichrist. During the Communist rule of Nicolae Ceausescu in Romania, some suspected him of Antichrist tendencies. In the 1980s many Greeks viewed the European Common Market as a forerunner of Antichrist.

It was among North American fundamentalist and charismatic Protestants (and in parts of Latin America and Africa proselytized by missionaries from these groups), however, that late twentieth-century interest in Bible prophecy, and Antichrist belief specifically, flourished most vigorously. These beliefs were promulgated not only by the traditional methods—sermons, touring evangelists, prophecy conferences—but increasingly by Televangelists (see TELEVANGELISM), mass-market paperbacks, movies such as *The Rapture* (1991) and *The Omega Code* (1999), and even Internet websites and chat rooms. Hal Lindsey's *The Late Great Planet Earth* (1970), a popularization of dispensationalism, was *the* U.S. nonfiction bestseller of the 1970s, selling millions of copies worldwide. While refraining from naming Antichrist, Lindsey insisted that world conditions were ripe for his emergence. In a 1996 survey of U.S. and Canadian religious attitudes, 42 percent of the U.S. respondents agreed with the statement: "The world will end in a battle in Armageddon between Jesus and the Antichrist." (The comparable figure for Canada was 30 percent.)

As in the past, late twentieth-century Antichrist speculation reflected the political and social concerns of the day. With the postwar rise of the European Common Market and the move toward European unity, many popularizers revitalized the old belief that Antichrist would initially control a federation of European nations replicating the Roman Empire, before establishing a worldwide dictatorship. In *The Omega Code* film, the head of the European Union is unmasked as Antichrist.

With the rise of multinational corporations, worldwide communications satellites, myriad international organizations, and computer-based information systems and financial transfers, many prophecy popularizers focused not on the specific identity of Antichrist, but rather on the emerging political, economic, and technological systems that will enable Antichrist, when he does arise, to establish the global dictatorship foretold in Revelation. In his 1991 bestseller *The New World Order*, televangelist PAT ROBERTSON traced the history of an international money conspiracy beginning with the Bavarian Illuminati in the 1770s and pushed forward by the Rothschilds, Cecil Rhodes, the Federal Reserve Board, the Council of Foreign Relations, the Carnegie and Rockefeller foundations, and others in a closely connected web of internationalist individuals and organizations. All this, Robertson insisted, echoing Lindsey, was preparing the way for Antichrist, "a man totally energized by the power of Satan, raging in blasphemy against God and His angels, filled with hatred against the people who are made in God's image." Continued Robertson: "This world leader, who has come to be known as the Antichrist, will be more terrible than any human leader in history. . . . Despite his evil, the world will be so caught up in satanic deception and delusion that it will worship the Antichrist as a god."

The Persian Gulf War, the hostility of some Islamic nations to the United States, and violent incidents linked to Islamic terrorist groups also focused fresh attention on the ancient link between Islam and Antichrist. Iraqi ruler Saddam Hussein's rebuilding of ancient Babylon (whose destruction is foretold in Revelation 18) led some to focus on him as a possible candidate for the Antichrist role.

Tim LaHaye and Jerry B. Jenkins, the authors of a popular series of dispensationalist novels beginning with *Left Behind* (1995), wove together the internationalist and Islamic themes in popular Antichrist belief. As their story progresses, the Secretary General of the United Nations emerges as Antichrist, and moves the organization from New York to a rebuilt Babylon. By 2000 the LaHaye and Jenkins series had sold some 11 million copies, and scores of prophecy popularizers including Pat Robertson, James Hagee, Jack Van Impe, and the indefatigable Hal Lindsey were overseeing global television ministries and producing paperback books sold through Christian bookstores and mass-market outlets, all of which helped keep Antichrist speculation at a high pitch.

As the twentieth century ended, Antichrist belief, constantly evolving and adapting to current events as it had for centuries, retained a powerful grip on the imagination of many in the United States and other parts of the world. As a new century dawned, considerable evidence suggested that the continuing fascination with Antichrist was likely to remain an important factor in at least certain quarters of the Protestant world.

See also Mass Media; Millenarians and Millennialism; Publishing, Media

References and Further Reading

Boyer, Paul. *When Time Shall Be No More: Prophecy Belief in Modern American Culture*. Cambridge: Harvard University Press, 1992.

Cohn, Norman. *The Pursuit of the Millennium: Revolutionary Millenarians and Mystical Anarchists of the Middle Ages*, rev. ed. London: Temple Smith, 1970.

Emmerson, Richard K. *Antichrist in the Middle Ages: A Study of Medieval Apocalyptic Art and Literature*. Seattle: University of Washington Press, 1981.

Hill, Christopher. *Antichrist in Seventeenth Century England*. London: Oxford University Press, 1971.

Klaassen, Walter. *Living at the End of the Ages: Apocalyptic Expectation in the Radical Reformation*. Lanham, MD: University Press of America 1992.

McGinn, Bernard. *Antichrist: Two Thousand Years of the Human Fascination with Evil*. San Francisco: Harpers San Francisco, 1994.

Weber, Timothy P. *Living in the Shadow of the Second Coming: American Premillennialism, 1975–1925*. New York: Oxford University Press, 1979.

PAUL BOYER

ANTINOMIANISM

Antinomianism may be defined as the theological position that the Old Testament law is not binding on Christians. The Antinomian approach is so fundamental to Protestant theology, defining it and representing its edgy boundaries, that understanding it is critical to good theology. It has constantly been used as a term of abuse, sometimes without great precision. It was anticipated to some extent in the theology of the medieval Family of Love. Within MARTIN LUTHER's solafideist theology there was a certain antinomian potential. Luther did not merely assert that the Christian is forgiven, he asserted the doctrine of JUSTIFICATION by FAITH alone so that the sinner stood before God without claiming any works. Luther held the position of being a sinner (see SIN) and justified in a dialectical relationship. On occasion he argued that the law was not necessary for true Christians, but was necessary since even the justified remained sinners. Later in his life in the face of controversy he placed a greater emphasis on the role of the moral law.

Other REFORMATION theologians found his position uncomfortable. The issue exploded in a debate between Luther and Johannes Agricola at Wittenberg in 1537. The so-called antinomian controversy between the two grew out of Agricola's emphasis on the importance of denying the power of works-righteousness. Agricola retracted his views, but others maintained the position, among them NIKOLAUS VON AMSDORF. Luther accused many of the Anabaptists of antinomianism (see ANABAPTISM). The evidence of this was supposedly seen in the doctrines of the Anabaptist radicals at Muenster, although in fact eschatological interpretations of the BIBLE were critical in this case. JOHN CALVIN was careful to avoid any hint of antinomian views; he emphasized the need to maintain the moral aspect of the law because only the ceremonial law was abrogated by Christ's coming. He insisted that faith was confirmed by outward signs of conformity to the moral law.

Antinomianism remained during the next two centuries a tension within Protestant thought, and in the seventeenth century there was a revival of antinomian sentiment. It particularly flourished among the fringes of extremist Puritan and dissenting opinion (see DISSENT). ANNE HUTCHINSON, who arrived in Boston in 1634, privately taught that Puritan teaching was enforcing a covenant of works. A controversy erupted in the Massachusetts Bay settlement, and in 1638 she was exiled to Rhode Island, although her claim to direct revelation from God was a significant factor in her rejection.

In ENGLAND, too, antinomian views circulated among the sectarian groups that flourished with the introduction of religious liberty from 1647, occasioning a sharp denunciation by the formalist Calvinist theology of the WESTMINSTER CONFESSION. The Antinomians have been widely seen as a symbol of the radical edge of Protestantism, although recent scholarship has tended to challenge this emphasis. John Eaton was the founding father with his tract *The Honeycomb of Free Justification by Christ Alone* (1642); another favorite author was Tobias Crisp, and others included Walter Marshall, Samuel Richardson, and John Saltmarsh. All in various ways encouraged an intense spirituality that rose above "mere legality." Often interpreted in a Calvinist framework, they need to be seen as actually espousing a Lutheran theology, although they added to it a belief in eternal justification, a special kind of PREDESTINATION. For this and for alleged libertinism they were attacked by Calvinist Puritans like Samuel Rutherford and RICHARD BAXTER, who had moved to a more voluntarist understanding of faith. The ferocious debate was a reflection of how much Puritans wanted respectability.

Antinomian views survived in Particular Baptist groups in the eighteenth century. The sudden growth of the Moravian movement spread a Lutheran view of solafideism in England and America, and for some its implicit antinomianism became explicit in a libertine lifestyle (see MORAVIAN CHURCH). Some early Methodists rose up against the legalism of the law, but more typically Calvinist and Moravian Methodists were somewhat harshly tarred with the brush of antinomianism for their emphasis that the basis of assurance of salvation was an inner sense, not any outward evidence in life. Thus James Hervey's *Thereon and Aspasio,* a popular evangelical classic, was attacked as being antinomian. Such views were ferociously and insensitively attacked by JOHN WESLEY's associate, John Fletcher in his *Checks to Antinomianism.* A number of small but popular groups advocated the doctrine, including those associated with William Cudworth, James Relly, and William Huntingdon. Antinomian opinion fed into the origins of groups like the Universalists through James Relly, and the PLYMOUTH BRETHREN in their interpretation of Pauline theology.

Some scholars have suggested that antinomianism became a commonplace of popular religiosity, traced through a radical, albeit a shadowy, history of the Muggletonians, through to the antinomianism of WILLIAM BLAKE's poetry, although even here the antinomianism is conditioned by other exotic beliefs.

It should be emphasized that denial of the authority of the Old Testament law did not necessarily mean libertine lifestyles, despite the allegations of Burns's "Holy Willy's Prayer." The accusation of antinomianism seemed to carry with it an implication that blackened the reputation of a number of sectarian groups, often unjustifiably; they saw themselves as bound in Christ under a new ethical basis.

References and Further Reading

Cooper, Timothy. "The Antinomians Redeemed: Removing some of the 'Radical' from mid-Seventeenth-Century Religion." *Journal of Religious History* 24 no. 3 (2000): 247–262.

Gunter, W. Stephen. *The Limits of "Love Divine": John Wesley's Response to Antinomianism and Enthusiasm.* Nashville, TN: Abingdon Press, 1989.

Hall, David D. *The Antinomian Controversy, 1636–1638: A Documentary History.* Middletown, CT: Wesleyan University Press, 1968.

Hill, Christopher. "Antinomianism in English History." In *The Collected Essays of Christopher Hill.* vol. 2. Brighton, UK: Harvester Press, 1986.

Huehns, Gertrude. *The Antinomians in English History with Special Reference to the Period 1640–1660.* London: Cresset Press, 1951.

Rohr, John von. *The Covenant of Grace in Puritan Thought.* Decatur, GA: Scholars Press, 1986.

Stoever, William K. B. *"A Faire and Easie Way to Heaven": Covenant Theology and Antinomianism in Early Massachusetts.* Middletown, CT: Wesleyan University Press, 1978.

Wallace, Dewey D. *Puritans and Predestination: Grace in English Protestant Theology 1525–1695.* Chapel Hill: University of North Carolina Press, 1982.

PETER LINEHAM

ANTI-SEMITISM

The term "Anti-Semitism," first formulated in the late nineteenth century by the journalist Wilhelm Maar, refers to hostility toward Jews and the Jewish people on the basis of their race and ethnicity. Strictly speaking, therefore, the term points to a fairly recent phenomenon, one that made race the defining characteristic of Jews. The parallel term "anti-Judaism" has been used to designate and describe the lengthy historical phenomenon of hostility toward Jews because of their religion or of traits that are not racial.

Christianity has been severely implicated in the phenomenon of anti-Judaism for its longstanding—at times intense—expressions of support for such antagonism and hostility. There is disagreement in scholarship as to whether Christianity, given this history, is the essential ingredient in anti-Judaism. The Christian stance finds its explanation in the Christian conviction that Christianity—personified in Jesus of Nazareth—is the final and definitive revelation of God, a revelation that supersedes that of the Old Testament. Inasmuch as Christian reflection has derived essential insights from its interpretation of the Old Testament, it has argued that the Jewish interpretation of that text is erroneous. The inherent antagonism between the religions, each claiming to be the final revelation of God, becomes understandable.

The historical record of the relationship between Christianity and Judaism has been burdened by the reality that, ever since the fourth century and emperor Constantine, Christianity was—as the state religion—the formative societal force in Latin Europe. Christian society applied such terms as idolatry and blasphemy to other religions, notably Judaism, and derived from those terms the moral and theological justification for expulsion, suppression, and persecution of the Jewish people.

An argument can be made, however, that Christianity alone does not suffice as the full explanation for such anti-Judaic sentiment. Economic, social, psychological, and political forces were also operative in the repression and persecution of Jews. Often, Christian voices merely echoed, rather than caused, secular voices and action.

In many ways the Protestant tradition has been a reflection of this larger picture, and it is difficult to argue either that there has been a distinctly Protestant form of Anti-Semitism or anti-Judaism or that Protestantism has been more, or less, irenic than Catholicism. The Protestant emphasis on GRACE and the concomitant repudiation of the Law and what is called "works righteousness" has frequently deprived the Protestant tradition of the ability to understand the Old Testament–Jewish commitment to the Law and its mandate of righteous living. Indeed in REFORMATION polemic a parallel was often drawn between Catholics and Jews and their insistence on good works. The Protestant emphasis on grace harmoniously echoed the severe strictures the Apostle Paul made against the Law and those who observed it.

The Lutheran tradition in turn has been particularly burdened by the fact that MARTIN LUTHER took to the pen several times to publish about and against the Jews. Although his early writings were characterized by a great deal of sympathy—and in fact denounced the severe hostility toward Jews in the Middle Ages—a treatise of 1543, entitled *Von den Juden und Ihren Lügen* (Concerning the Jews and their Lies), was an emotional juxtaposition of traditional theological and social economic denunciations. This treatise gave Luther not only the reputation of being intensely anti-Semitic but also of being one of the very few Christian theologians of distinction who explicitly addressed the topic of the Christian relationship not only to the Jewish religion but also to the Jewish people.

A distinctive Protestant contribution to the phenomenon may be said to have been made in the late eighteenth century when—and under the impact of the ENLIGHTENMENT—traditional CHRISTOLOGY, which theologically had been the major stumbling block in Christian–Jewish relations, was abandoned by Christian theologians. This reversal of Christian self-understanding might well have heralded a new and more positive relationship with the Jews and the Jewish religion, although this was not the case. Thinkers such as GEORG WILHELM FREIDRICH HEGEL delineated a new understanding of religion that did not so much focus on doctrine, such as Christology, as on the "spirit" of a religion. This new scheme of interpreta-

tion saw the Jewish religion as marked by a servile spirit of obedience and subservience to the Law, inferior in all respects to Christianity, which particularly in its Protestant form heralded freedom. Traditional Christian sentiment about Jews was thereby allowed to continue despite a dramatically changed theological situation. In the early twentieth century German Protestants combined political conservatism and religion, prompting them to echo the increasingly intense Anti-Semitism of the time from a Protestant perspective.

The Nazi persecution of Jews and the HOLOCAUST saw both Catholics and Protestants largely silent. In the aftermath of that dreadful happening, however, Protestant churches both in GERMANY and elsewhere in Europe confessed their complicity in the crime by accepting—and enhancing—societal prejudices. More recently, Protestant church bodies of both Europe and North America have issued statements of theological reflection that have sought to put the Christian understanding of Judaism on a more positive basis. The foremost theological questions have been the continuation of the divine COVENANT with the Jews and thus the legitimacy of Christians proselytizing Jews.

See also Confessing Church

References and Further Reading

Cohn-Shebok, Dan. *The Crucified Jew: Twenty Centuries of Christian Anti-Semitism.* London: Harper Collins Religious, 1992.

Dinnerstein, Leonard. *Amtisemitism in America.* New York: Oxford University Press, 1994.

Eakin, Frank E. Jr. *What Price Prejudice? Christian Antisemitism in America.* New York: Paulist Press, 1998 [A Stimulus Book].

Evans, Craig A., and Donald A. Hagner, eds. *Anti-Semitism and Early Christianity: Issues of Polemic and Faith.* Minneapolis, MN: Fortress Press, 1993.

Farmer, William R. *Anti-Judaism and the Gospels.* Harrisburg, PA: Trinity Press International, 1999.

Gerlach, Wolfgang. *And the Witnesses Were Silent: The Confessing Church and the Persecution of the Jews.* Translated and edited by Victoria J. Barnett. Lincoln, NE: University of Nebraska Press, 2000.

Lindemann, Albert S. *The Jew Accused: Three Anti-Semitic Affairs: Dreyfus, Beilis, Frank, 1894–1915.* Cambridge, UK: Cambridge University Press, 1991.

Lipstadt, Deborah. *Denying the Holocaust: The Growing Assault on Truth and Memory.* New York: The Free Press, 1993.

Nicholls, William. *Christian Antisemitism: A History of Hate.* Northvale, NJ: Jason Aronson Inc., 1993.

HANS J. HILLERBRAND

ANTISLAVERY MOVEMENT

See Slavery, Abolition of

ANTITRINITARIANISM

The term "Antitrinitarianism" includes doctrines and conceptions formulated against the Trinitarian dogma as presented by the councils of Nicaea (325) and Constantinople (381). During the REFORMATION, Antitrinitarianism was sharply attacked both by Catholics—a constitution was issued by Pope Paul IV (August 7, 1555) and reaffirmed by Pius V (October 1, 1568)—and by Protestants (Lutherans, Zwinglians, Calvinists, Anglicans). Antitrinitarians were called by their opponents Zwinglians, Sabellians, and such after the names of ancient heretics including Arius, Paul of Samosata, Photinus, and Sabellius.

Beginnings of the Movement

In the first phase of the Reformation, Antitrinitarianism found adherents mainly in the circles close to ANABAPTISM. Oriented toward the realization of practical goals (the imitating of Christ in one's daily walk), Anabaptism rejected the ruminations as contradictory with the simplicity of the Scriptures. It had the tendency to attack the "philosophical"—not the "scriptural"—character of the trinitarian dogma.

Ludwig Haetzer (1529), a Swiss Anabaptist theologian who called into question the trinitarian dogma, claiming that Christ is not equal with the Father, belonged to the first Antitrinitarians in Anabaptist circles. Christian Entfelder (1536), who was active in Moravia, Strasbourg, and Königsberg, formulated his teaching about God as a threefold power under the influence of the German mysticism. The essence representing the foundations of the creation is the power of the Father; activism, as part of the world's creation is the power of the Son; the spirit of love present in all beings is the power of the Holy Spirit. Adam Pastor (1510–1552), active in the Mennonite Church but expelled in 1547, held that Christ had been created by the Father, who provided him with power, wisdom, and will, the Holy Spirit being only a "holy breath" inspiring virtuous life. Pastor's conceptions influenced German Antitrinitarianism at the end of the 1560s and at the beginning of the 1770s.

Antitrinitarianism found disciples among adherents of spiritualism. An important place was occupied by Johannes Campanus (1574), author of a popular work *Göttlicher und heiliger Schrift. . .* ("Restitution of Godly and Holy Scripture"), 1531, whose ideas were popular among revolutionary Anabaptists. In his work he argued that God the Father and Christ have the same essence and nature and represent two beings in one body similar to a man and his wife. The Son is subordinated to the Father as born from the Father before the world's creation. The Holy Spirit is not a being but a link between the Father and the Son.

The Apennine Peninsula and Switzerland

The Antitrinitarian sentiment in the Apennine Peninsula emerged at the end of the 1540s. Among the roots three catalysts deserve to be mentioned: the philological criticism of the Renaissance (Lorenzo Valla, Erasmus of Rotterdam); the religious thinking of the Spanish thinker Juan de Valdes, who was probably an Antitrinitarian himself but did not attach much importance to dogma and emphasized the ethical underpinnings of Christianity; and finally the social doctrine of German Anabaptism mainly through Anabaptist communities (HUTTERITES) in Moravia.

The first Italian Antitrinitarians were active in Naples and Padova. Girolamo Busale was the spiritual leader. Together with his followers he joined the Anabaptists in northern Italy toward the end of the 1540s. He managed to persuade many of them to accept his notions, even though they triggered protests among some Anabaptists. Busale rejected the trinitarian dogma and the eternity of Christ whom he defined as a human being—son of Mary and Joseph—although filled with divine power. He also claimed that immortality applied exclusively to moral persons, the souls of nonbelievers being annihilated. The division of the Italian Anabaptist conventicles during the Inquisition at the beginning of the 1550s accounts for the fact that SWITZERLAND became the new center of Italian Antitrinitarians' activities.

Discussions related to the problematic of the Trinity took place in Switzerland, mainly in territories occupied by Italians immigrants in the 1550s. They triggered irritation among orthodox Calvinists.

Notwithstanding internal theological conflict and tactical issues, Italian Antitrinitarians represented a dynamic and well-organized group. Among their outstanding members was Giorgio Biandrata (1515–1588), a physician with numerous contacts across central Europe where he practiced for a few years; Matteo Gribaldi Mofa (d. 1564), a famous lawyer who often resided in Switzerland where his family lived and professor at the University of Padova and later Tübingen; Giovanni Valentino Gentile (d. 1566), philologist and theologian; finally Lelio Sozzini (1525–1562), probably the outstanding theologian among them, born to a family of lawyers from Siena. He enjoyed warm relations with European intellectual elites.

The trinitarian dogma, criticized for its contradictions with the Holy Scripture and lack of rational justification, stood in the center of their meditation, inspired by others, the work of MICHAEL SERVETUS, *De Trinitatis erroribus libri septem* ("Seven Books about the Errors of the Trinity"), 1531. Servetus argued the positive notion of three distinguishable holy instances, linked through their unique nature and their holy origins from the same God and Father, a God begotten from Godself. Christ is eternal but not coexistent with God the Father; the Holy Spirit is treated as eternal divine power, even though its status is not fully explained. This theory, labeled by Calvinist and Catholic opponents as Tritheism, was to play an important role in the first phase of Antitrinitarianism in POLAND and Transylvania.

In his commentary to the prologue of the *Brevis explicatio in primum Iohannis caput* ("Short Explanation of the First Chapter of the St John's Gospel") of the early 1560s, Lelio Sozzini presented a radical reinterpretation of the traditional Christian doctrine. According to this interpretation Christ is not eternal God but a human elevated to divine dignity thanks to his merits; he is holy language (*sermo*) and the teacher of Holy Truth, who created a world of new spiritual values. The *Short Explanation,* first in manuscript, then printed and published in 1568 (along with commentary of an analogous subject by Lelio's cousin, FAUSTO SOZZINI), influenced the evolution of European Antitrinitarianism toward Unitarianism.

Doctrinal propositions of Italian Antitrinitarians faced an intense orthodox Calvinist reaction. Matteo Gribaldi was forced to retract his beliefs in Bern (1557); a similar fate struck Giovanni Gentile (1558) after his unsuccessful return in 1556. Giorgio Biandrata, who refused to sign an orthodox profession of faith, escaped in autumn 1558 to Poland.

All these repressions limited the scope of action of Italian Antitrinitarians and caused their emigration from Switzerland to central-eastern Europe (Moravia, Poland, Transylvania).

Polish–Lithuanian Commonwealth

The activities of Piotr from Goniadz constitute the prehistory of Polish and Lithuanian Antitrinitarianism. This student of Matteo Gribaldi, enthusiastic for Moravian Anabaptist doctrine, pursued underground activities after 1556 in the Polish–Lithuanian Calvinist Church. Those discussions were triggered by the thesis of Francesco Stancaro (1501–1574) who claimed that Christ was the mediator with the Father exclusively in his human nature. The opponents of the Trinity made use of the conflict around this idea to spread their theories.

Giorgio Biandrata was an important authority in the Polish Calvinist Church during this period despite Calvin's criticism of this thinker. Exploiting the fact that Stancaro was an admirer of his scholastic theory, Biandrata imposed his opinion against Stancaro's by rejecting all terms that were not in Holy Scripture, including "Trinity." Trinity was replaced by "the

Three," which designated God the Father, the Son, and the Holy Spirit, the two separate and subordinated to the Father. The adoption of the Tritheistic confession during the synod in Pinczow (April 2, 1562) led to a split within the Polish Lithuanian Calvinist church. The supporters of Reformed ORTHODOXY among Polish Calvinists founded a separate church (*ecclesia maior*) in 1563, distinct from the Antitrinitarian Church (*ecclesia minor*). These Calvinists tried to fight against Antitrinitarians with the help of secular authority. In 1564 King Sigmund August issued a decree against Antitrinitarians, which led to the temporary emigration of the minority. The Catholic COUNTER-REFORMATION efficiently paralyzed the actions of the Calvinists. As Cardinal Stanislaw Hosius pointed out "war between heretics means peace for the church," the persecution of one group was equal to the legalization of other groups.

The Antitrinitarian Church in Poland and Lithuania was a loose federation, formed by the adherents of three different doctrinal options. The first one—Tritheism—was the confession of a minority in the 1560s. In the aftermath of the discussions triggered by the "Prologue of Saint John's Gospel" by Lelio and Fausto Sozzini and Biandrata's letter to the Poles, the eternity of Christ was rejected. This was accepted by a majority of Antitrinitarians, later called Unitarians. The third movement regrouped supporters of the notion of Christ's eternity. Because of their unclear position regarding the Holy Spirit, they were called Ditheists. Piotr from Goniadz led the Lithuanian Ditheists. Polish Ditheists created a separate group under the leadership of the well-educated Stanislaw Farnkowski (1615/1617).

During the synods of early Antitrinitarianism, dogmatic problems were not the only topics to be discussed. The campaign against infant BAPTISM, inaugurated by Piotr from Goniadz led to a debate over rebaptism of adults in the mid-1560s, which eventually carried over into the field of Anabaptist sociopolitical doctrine. The latter became the subject of fierce discussions. The first to interpret the Anabaptist sociopolitical notions was Piotr from Goniadz in his *De primatutu ecclesiae Christianae* (1562–1564); later came two outstanding leaders and writers Grzegorz Pawel from Brzeziny (1526–1591) and Marcin Czechowicz (1532–1613). Consequently adult baptism by immersion was accepted in some communities, although widespread immersion practice in Antitrinitarian churches began only in the 1570s.

Most of the adherents of Antitrinitarianism enthusiastically greeted Anabaptist postulates of egalitarianism and social justice. During the synod of Pesznica (1568) ideas to make members of the gentry sell their property and distribute to the poor were proposed.

A Protestant religious community was founded in the town of Rakow, and Polish and Lithuanian Antitrinitarians joined it. The attempt to create a "New Jerusalem" did not succeed because of the lack of agreement with the Moravian Anabaptists. The spiritual orientation to oppose any organizational changes in Rakow prevailed until 1572 when Lublin became the dynamic center of the movement led by Marcin Czechowicz and his patron Jan Niemojewski (1598). The Unitarian communities of Jerzy Szoman (1591) and Szymon Ronemberg (1598–1604) also collaborated with Lublin.

This organizational recovery of Unitarianism is reflected in the publication of two catechisms. Jerzy Szoman wrote the first one in Latin (*Catechesis . . .*) in 1574. Marcin Czechowicz wrote the second, more extensive, one in Polish (*The Christian Talks*).

The religious doctrines of the Polish Unitarians after the Rakow episode retained many Calvinist elements, notably the conception of apology, predestination, and the LORD'S SUPPER. Unitarians rejected the entire clerical tradition on the basis of the primacy of the Scriptures, in particular, the New Testament as opposed to the Old Testament.

The scriptural approach led to the rejection of the trinitarian dogma and Christ's eternity, which sees Christ as designated to fulfill his mission by God the Father. Jesus sits on the right hand of the Father after his fulfilled mission. Unitarian CHRISTOLOGY is highly related to ETHICS and the moral imitation of Jesus Christ. It takes the path of peaceful Anabaptism as it claims the nonuse of violence and absolute PACIFISM. It advises neutrality toward the state and its institutions. A believer should neither hold any office of the "sword" nor any other position that would lead to the effusion of blood.

The social and political radicalism of Polish Unitarians raised concerns and protests not only in Catholic and Protestant circles but also within the movement itself. The center of the opposition was in Lithuania and Szymon Budny (c. 1530–1593). This philologist and biblical scholar rejected the Polish Brethren dogmatic conceptions and treated their radical social and political concepts with overt irritation and disregard. The Polish Brethren did not agree with Budny's conception that Joseph was the natural Father of Christ and had to be invoked in prayers. In his famous treatise *On the Magistrate using the Sword* (1583) Budny criticized the social and political concepts of the Polish Brethren. At the same time he supported the participation of gentry in wars and public life and defended its right to own property and have subjects. Budny was excommunicated in 1584, although his battle against sectarian tendencies was

taken over by FAUSTO SOZZINI (SOCINUS) (1539–1604), an Italian religious immigrant.

Sozzini arrived in Poland in 1579 to join the Unitarian Church but was refused because his religious positions shaped in Switzerland (1575–1578) diverged from the official confession of Polish Unitarians on many issues. In his work *De Iesu Christo Servatore* ("Concerning Jesus Christ the Savior") written in Switzerland and published in 1594, Sozzini revised traditional soteriology. According to Sozzini Christ's redemption did not occur on the cross but lay in the way Christ showed authentic living throughout his life. His resurrection confirmed the truth of his teaching. In *De Satu primi hominis ante lapsum* ("On the State of the First Human Before the Fall"), written in Switzerland and published in 1610, Sozzini rejected the concept of original sin. According to him Adam's descendants have not inherited original sin. Therefore any human is capable of moral excellence and deserves resurrection. Sozzini also rejected baptism of Christian families' descendants and treated the Lord's Supper as a purely symbolic rite.

Sozzini rapidly became an authority, despite his conflicts with the older generation of Polish Unitarians who treated him as a dangerous revisionist, largely because of his numerous works in which he defended his followers from the attacks of dogmatic radicals [*Ad Iacobi Paleologi liberum responsio* ("Response of Jacob Paleolog"), 1581], Jesuits [*Refutatio libelli, quem Iacobus Wujekus edidit* ("Refutation of the Work Published by Jacob Wujek"), 1594], and Calvinists [*De Jesu Christi Filiin Dei natura . . .* ("On the Nature of Jesus Christ, Son of God"), 1588].

Sozzini also fought against dogmatic radicalism in his own ranks. He had a dispute with the German ex-Jesuit Christian Franckener (1584) and Szymon Budny (1588). After this discussion Budny abjured his beliefs and rejoined the Unitarian Church a few years later.

Sozzini led discussions with Marcin Czechowicz and especially Jan Niemojewski, the leaders of the Unitarian Church in Lublin, who had both criticized his teaching. Sozzini did not manage to persuade them. Only in 1593 and with the help of his students he imposed his own notions regarding apology, redemption, and the Lord's Supper. During the next five years, Sozzini tempered his Anabaptist ethical rigor, allowing the gentry to hold governmental offices, participate in trials, and have serfs.

The bill passed by the synod of Lublin in 1598 enabled the gentry to carry weapons and dismissed Marcin Czechowicz from his position as minister of the city.

Transylvania and Hungary

Antitrinitarianism enjoyed better conditions to develop in Transylvania rather than in Poland and Lithuania, which remained Catholic. Transylvania turned Protestant in the second half of the seventeenth century. Only at the end of the century did real Catholic offensive take place.

The beginnings of Antitrinitarianism in Transylvania were related to doctrinal discussions in the Calvinist Church. Giorgio Biandrata played a key role in those discussions, similarly to what had happened in Poland. He knew the country well and had influence in King Jan Sigismund Zapolyi's (1540–1571) entourage. Together with FERENC DAVID (1510–1579), the superintendent of the Calvinist Church, Biandrata led the rejection of the scholastic terminology of the Trinity and the adoption of a confession drawing on the Gospels and early Christian traditions. This Subordinational Tritheism represented a temporary phase in the Transylvania Antitrinitarianism, the young Antitrinitarian Church accepting the christological doctrine of Lelio and Faust Sozzini and rejecting the eternity of Christ a few years later.

The beginnings of the Unitarian Church in Transylvania can be dated after the dispute in Gyulafehervar (Alba Julia) in 1568, which was won by the opponents of the Trinity concept. With the support of the Jan Sigismund Zapolyi, Unitarianism was officially recognized, along with Catholicism, Protestantism, and CALVINISM. It had many adherents in Turkish-dominated Southern Hungary.

As a sociopolitical doctrine and a ritual thesis (baptism of adults) anabaptism did not prompt great interest in Transylvania. The so-called Golden Age of Unitarianism in Transylvania (1540–1571) resulted in a rich production of works both in Hungarian and Latin. *De falsa et verus unius Dei . . . cognitione* ("About the False and Right Cognition of the Only God"), written by Biandrata and Dávid, published in 1568, is certainly the most notable work, which enjoyed important resonance in other European countries.

After the death of Jan Sigismund Zapoloyi (d. 1571), Stefan Batory—a fervent but tolerant Catholic—became Transylvanian palatine. Under his rule Unitarianism lost its privileged position. Batory introduced censorship, which limited the publication of Unitarian works.

The 1570s represent the most interesting and creative period of Unitarian theology in Transylvania, the latter going largely beyond the scope of strictly confessional issues. Johann Sommer (1574) rector of the Unitarian Collegium in Kolozsvar and Jacobus Palaeologus (1520–1585), an original Greco-Italian thinker and theologian, are among the most outstanding representatives of Transylvanian Unitarianism. Jacobus Palaeologus's manuscripts highly influenced the radical Unitarianism in Siebenbergen and Poland.

According to Palaeologus Christianity derived from JUDAISM and therefore there is harmony between the Old and the New Testaments, although there is no doubt about the primacy of the first. Christ—perceived as a human who had the gift of the divine power similar to that of other prophets—wanted Jews to do penance and accept him as King of Israel. Because this did not succeed, Christ commended his students to spread the Gospel to all people.

Palaeologus intended to prove that the disgrace of the Jews after Christ's death could be removed by an act of faith, Jesus being the Christ or the Lord's Anointed. Jews should respect the Old Testament rituals, however, even after their conversion.

Reducing the truths of salvation to faith in one God and Christ and rejecting traditional trinitarian theology, christology, and sacramentology, Palaeologus tried to build the foundations for a future union of the three monotheistic religions: Christianity, Judaism, and Islam. He believed that Muslims are Christian ancestors and also "sons of god." They also possess a holy law, the Koran being its imperfect form [*De tribus gentibus* ("About the Three People"), 1572]. In *Catechesis Christiana* ("Christian Catechism"), however, Palaeologus does not mention Islam, this subject being too controversial.

Ferenc Dávid was the champion of the new theology and spread it at synods. He also led numerous discussions, during which the issue of Christ's adoration and invocation in prayers had been raised. Dávid claimed that Christ is fully subordinated to his Father after his mission on Earth. Therefore Christ's adoration and invocation threaten monotheism because it makes Christ appear as equal to his Father. This issue triggered a conflict between Dávid and Biandrata, the latter accusing Dávid of doctrinal innovations forbidden by a resolution of the Sejm of 1572. In 1579 Dávid was sentenced to prison, where he died. Biandrata acknowledged the authority of the Unitarian Church. Demeter Hunyady (1592), a conservative theologian, became superintendent and the baptism of infants was restored.

Despite official prohibition and repression, radical Unitarian streams survived, for example, Unitarian communities in Southern Hungary, an area occupied by the Turks.

SABBATARIANISM lay on the edge of official Unitarianism. Matthias Vehe-Glirius (d. 1590), a German Hebraist and biblical researcher, played an important role in its development. Eastern Transylvania was the center of the movement and Andras Essi (d. 1599), a rich landlord, was its patron. The Sabbatarian doctrine had elements of Unitarianism (negation of the Trinity and of the divinity of Christ) and legalism of the Old Testament (respect of the Mosaic law, such as circumcision and the Sabbath). Sabbatarians, often accused of being Jewish and persecuted, were excluded from the Unitarian Church in 1616. In the 1920s and 1930s they turned into a Jewish sect. The Nazis killed its last members.

Relations between Unitarians from Transylvania and Polish Unitarians were resumed toward the end of the sixteenth century. *Explications locorum Veteris et Novi Testamenti ex quibus Trinitatis dogma stabiliri solet* ("Explanations Regarding the Trinitarian Dogma in the Old and New Testament"), 1598, by Gyorgy Enyedi (1554–1597) is a good example. Sozzini's influence is visible in this work.

Rhineland Palatinate

Antitrinitarianism in the Palatinate was not strong. It was muffled by both state and clerical authorities. This event had a large echo in Europe (not proportional to its intrinsic importance), which led to conflict in the relations between the Lutheran and the Calvinist churches.

At the end of the sixteenth century in Heidelberg, the capital of the Palatinate, sharp conflicts arose after Thomas Erastus's intervention regarding the superiority of the secular rule over the Reformed Church. Four members of the clergy—Johann Sylvan (1572), superintendent in Landenberg; Adam Neuser (1576), pastor in Heidelberg; Matthias Vehe-Glirius (1590), deacon in Kaiserslautern; and Jacob Suter, pastor in Feudenheim—were among Erastus's friends.

The origins of their Antitrinitarian interests have not been fully explained. Probably the reading of the works of Adam Pastor, but more likely, the works of Polish and Transylvanian Antitrinitarians, provided by Polish Calvinists, must have played a role.

The popularity of Antitrinitarian works, biblical studies, and the disillusion of the Reformed Church drew Sylvan, Neuser, Vehe-Glirius, and Suter to attend a session of the diet Parliament in Speyer and give to the Transylvanian deputy K. Bekes a letter addressed to Giorgio Biandrata. The letter expressed the wish to settle in Transylvania to start an activity in the local Unitarian Church. It was given to emperor Maximilian II who in turn gave it to Friedrich III, elector of the Rhineland Palatinate. Sylvan and Vehe-Glirius were immediately arrested (July 15, 1570). Neuser managed to escape but returned voluntarily to Germany in 1570 and was imprisoned. There was a great commotion related to the fact that compromising documents had been found in the homes of Neuser and Sylvan, in particular a letter in which Neuser declared

sympathy toward Mohammedanism. He also underlined the support Antitrinitarians would give to a Muslim conquest of Germany (doubts about the authenticity of this letter exist). Johann Sylvan was executed, although Neuser and Vehe-Girius worked in Poland and Siebenbergen among radical Antitrinitarians after numerous vicissitudes.

See also Socinianism; Unitarian Universalist Association

References and Further Reading

Balazs, Mihaly. "Early Transylvanian Antitrinitarianism (1566–1611)." In *From Servet to Palaeologus*. Baden-Baden, Germany and Bouxwiller, France: Editions Valentin Koerner, 1996.

———, and Keser Gizella, eds. *Gyorgy Emyedy and Central European Unitarianism in the 16–17th Centuries*. Budapest: Balassi Kiado, 2000.

Burchill, Christopher J. "The Heidelberg Antitrinitarians." In *Biblioteca dissidentum*. Edited by Andre Suegenny. vol. XI. Baden-Baden, Germany and Bouxwiller, France: Editions Valentin Koerner, 1989.

Cantimoro, Delio. *Eretici italiani del Cinquecento e altri scritti*. Edited by Adriano Prosperi. Torino, Italy: Enaudi, 1992.

Dan, Robert. *Matthias Vahe Glirius: Life and Work of a Radical Antitrinitarian with His Collected Writings*. Budapest/Leiden: Akademiai Kiado/E. J. Brill, 1983.

———, and Antal Pirnat, eds. *Antitrinitarianism in the Second Half of the 16th Century*. Budapest/Leiden: Akademiai Kiado/E. J. Brill, 1983.

Gorski, Konrad. "Grzegorz Pawel z Brzezin." In *Monografia z dziejow polskiej literatury arianskiej*. Cracow, Poland: Polska Akademia Umiejetnosci, 1929.

Kawecka-Gryczowa, Allodia. *Les imprimeurs des antitrinitaires polonais Rodecki et Sternacki*. Geneva: Droz, 1974.

Kot, Stanislas. *Socinianism in Poland. The Social and Political Ideas of the Polish Antitrinitarians in the Sixteenth and Seventeenth Centuries*. Translated by Earl Morse Wilbur. Boston: Starr King Press, 1957.

Pirnat, Antal. *Die Ideologie der siebenberger Antitrinitarier in den 1570er Jahren*. Budapest: Akademiai Kiado, 1961.

Rotondo, Antonio. *Studi e recerché di storia ereticale italiana*. Torino, Italy: Giappichelli, 1974.

Szczucki, Lech. "Marcin Czechowicz, 1532–1613." In *Studium z dziejow antytrynitaryzmu polskiego XVI wieku*. Warsaw: Panstwowe Wydawnictwo Naukowe, 1964.

———. *W kragu msylicieli heretyckich*. Wroclaw, Poland: Ossolineum, 1972.

Tazbir, Janusz. *A State without Stakes: Polish Religious Toleration in the Sixteenth and Seventeenth Centuries*. Translated by A. T. Jordan. New York and Warsaw: PIW, 1973.

Wilbur, Earl Morse. *A History of Unitarianism. Socinianism and its Antecedents*. Cambridge, MA: Harvard University Press, 1946.

———. *A History of Unitarianism. In Transylvania, England, and America*. Cambridge, MA: Harvard University Press, 1952.

Williams, George Huntston. *The Radical Reformation*. 3d edition. Kirksville, MO: Sixteenth Century Essays and Studies, 1992.

LECH SZCZUCKI

APOCALYPTICISM

In the Judeo-Christian tradition, this Greek term, referring to an unveiling of hidden truths, relates to beliefs rooted in ancient texts recounting cosmic struggles between good and evil, or revealing events that will unfold in the last days. In this latter sense, apocalypticism is closely related to ESCHATOLOGY, theological study concerned with final events in world history, such as the Second Coming and Last Judgment.

The Reformation Era

The intellectual world of the Protestant REFORMATION included canonical apocalyptic texts and long-standing traditions of apocalyptic speculation. As a literary genre, the apocalyptic form arose in ancient JUDAISM and passed into early Christian thought and writings. Of many Jewish and Christian apocalypses, some made their way into the BIBLE, including the Book of Daniel, the "Little Apocalypse" of Mark 13, and Revelation, the Apocalypse of John. Apocalyptic anticipations of Jesus' imminent return pervaded early Christianity.

As Christianity gained secular power, church fathers, including St. Augustine, discouraged end-time speculation and instead historicized the apocalyptic texts as allegories of the continuing struggle between the church and the world. In this struggle, righteousness will ultimately triumph, but the details of this final eschatological outcome remain unknowable. Apocalypticism continued to flourish in medieval Christianity, however, as evidenced in surviving cathedral sculptures, stained glass, tapestries, plays, accounts of wandering prophets, and the works of such mystics as Hildegard of Bingen and Joachim of Fiore. Apocalyptic desires to recapture Jerusalem from the Muslims helped fuel the Crusades.

The early Protestant reformers shared Rome's aversion to apocalypticism, even arguing for excluding Revelation from the canon or according it a lower status. JOHN CALVIN did not include this work in his Bible commentaries. This suspicion of apocalypticism deepened into horror during the Peasants' Revolt of the 1520s, when THOMAS MUNTZER inflamed his followers with tragically misguided apocalyptic assurances of their ultimate triumph over the armies marshaled against them. The early Anabaptists offered further alarming evidence of the dangers of unbridled apocalypticism (see ANABAPTISM). In 1534, proclaiming the advent of God's prophesied end-time kingdom, Anabaptists seized the Westphalian city of Munster and expelled the city's leaders. The inhabitants soon fell under the brutal and licentious rule of young Jan Bockelson ("John of Leyden"), endured starvation as armies rallied by the local bishop besieged the city, and faced indiscriminate slaughter in June 1535 when they tried to surrender. The bodies of Bockelson and his top lieutenants were suspended in a cage from a Munster church tower as a cautionary example.

For all their fear of apocalyptic excesses, however, the early Reformation leaders readily used apocalyptic themes when it suited their purposes. The GENEVA BIBLE (1560) identified the Pope as the Beast of Revelation, confirming a 1545 woodcut by Melchior Lorch portraying the Pope as a loathsome, fire-breathing beast with a long tail. The "Pope=Antichrist" link deeply infected Protestant thought, surfacing in the UNITED STATES, for example, during periods of heavy Catholic immigration and surviving for much longer in fundamentalist circles (see FUNDAMENTALISM).

Overall, however, the major Protestant bodies that emerged from the Reformation rejected apocalypticism. The Lutheran and Reformed churches were generally amillennial, rejecting the idea of a literal thousand-year millennial kingdom on Earth (Revelation 20:6), treating the apocalyptic scriptures as metaphorical expressions of the ongoing conflict between good and evil and avoiding undue speculation about the details of Christ's final triumph. Even the Anabaptists, repudiating the frenzies of the 1530s, turned decisively against apocalypticism.

Apocalyptic Movements in England and America

Protestant dissenters, however, often under the sway of self-taught laypersons, proved receptive to apocalypticism and to interpretations treating the prophecies as road maps to future events likely to unfold soon. Such interpretations have especially flourished at times of political or social upheaval, as in mid-seventeenth century ENGLAND, when Puritan reformers sought to purge English Protestantism of its papist remnants (see PURITANISM). As the purifying impulse spread, many observers eagerly concluded that biblical end-time prophecies were being fulfilled before their very eyes, and that Anglican leaders such as Archbishop WILLIAM LAUD fit descriptions of the Antichrist. So-called "Fifth Monarchy Men," interpreting apocalyptic imagery from the Book of Daniel as a prophecy that Christ's kingdom would emerge after four earthly empires had risen and fallen, proclaimed that the millennium would soon begin.

The Puritan clergy of New England shared this apocalyptic mindset. Some even viewed America as the chosen land where Christ's kingdom would arise. The enduring dream of American exceptionalism, viewing the United States as divinely favored and exempt from the fate of other nations, is rooted in this tradition. As religious revivals, the so-called "Great Awakening," swept America in the 1740s (see AWAKENINGS), some concluded that the millennium was at hand. REVIVALS, prayer circles, and transatlantic religious effort, JONATHAN EDWARDS speculated, could usher in the glorious age foretold in Revelation. Edwards was thus a postmillennialist, teaching that Christ's Kingdom can be attained in the present age. He and his followers were not shallow optimists, however. Espousing what historian James Davidson has called an "afflictive model" of spiritual progress, they also foresaw periodic setbacks and recrudescences of satanic influence. Nevertheless, their confidence that Christian effort could transform the present social order profoundly influenced the American worldview, inspiring periodic waves of revivalism and, in somewhat secularized form, reformist efforts to eradicate suffering, exploitation, and injustice.

Apocalypticism served political purposes during the American Revolution, as patriot preachers identified Great Britain, George III, and British officials with the ANTICHRIST. One imaginative writer, for example, fingered Lord Bute, born on a Scottish island, as the "beast from the sea" mentioned in Revelation. After the Revolution, Americans sought to create a society worthy of the struggle for independence, and the antebellum era was awash in reform efforts, including TEMPERANCE and antislavery campaigns (see SLAVERY, ABOLITION OF), crusades for more humane treatment of the insane and the rehabilitation of prisoners, and even cooperative utopian communities that arose as alternatives to the competitive market economy.

In such a climate, apocalypticism flourished with renewed intensity. Millennial expectations suffused the Campbellite (DISCIPLES OF CHRIST) church and other sects spawned by the frontier revivals of the Second Great Awakening, as well as early MORMONISM as preached by JOSEPH SMITH and his followers. In 1831, WILLIAM MILLER (1782–1849), a self-taught Bible scholar in upstate New York, after long study of chronological prophecies in the Book of Daniel, began to preach that Christ would return around 1843. Other Millerites, seeking greater specificity, finally settled on October 22, 1843. Despite criticism by established Protestant leaders, Millerite revivals attracted thousands, colorful charts elucidated Miller's calculations, and tracts and periodicals spread the word. When the 1843 date passed uneventfully, the leaders discovered their error (they had neglected to count 1 B.C. and 1 A.D. as two years) and announced a new date, October 22, 1844, laying the groundwork for a second and final "Great Disappointment." From the wreckage of Millerism, however, arose a new Protestant denomination, the SEVENTH-DAY ADVENTIST church. Although this denomination, which has more than 10 million members worldwide, avoids setting dates, it remains intensely interested in Bible prophecy.

Meanwhile, in early nineteenth-century Great Britain, apocalypticism stirred afresh on the margins of the established church. The Scottish minister EDWARD IRVING (1792–1834) drew crowds in London in the 1820s and 1830s with his predictions of Christ's Second Coming. He taught that the Battle of Armageddon would occur in 1868, and his emotional services featured glossolalia (speaking in TONGUES), which his followers viewed as one of the "signs and wonders" foretold by Jesus as a sign of the last days. In the same years, HENRY DRUMMOND, a member of Parliament with a layman's interest in apocalypticism, organized a series of annual prophecy conferences on his estate. Somewhat later, in *Signs of the Times* and *The End* (both 1855), both of which became bestsellers in England and America, the Scotsman John Cumming (1807–1881), following the lead of the German Hebraicist Wilhelm Gesenius, identified RUSSIA as the mysterious kingdom of Gog, whose destruction is foretold in Ezekiel 38.

The Rise of Premillennial Dispensationalism

Apocalypticism pervaded the PLYMOUTH BRETHREN, an English dissenting sect that arose in the 1830s. The movement's leader, JOHN DARBY (1800–1882), is best known for a system of prophetic interpretation, premillennial DISPENSATIONALISM, that proved remarkably long-lived and influential. Assembling prophetic texts from throughout the Bible, Darby constructed his system much as one assembles a picture puzzle until the full picture emerges. A premillennialist, he held that humanity will grow increasingly wicked, not gradually more righteous, as the end approaches.

Darby divided history into a series of epochs, or dispensations, each with its distinct means of salvation for the Jews (God's chosen people) and for the Gentiles. The present dispensation, the Church Age, he taught, represents a "great parenthesis" in the grand prophetic scheme. But it will soon end, as one can see from the fulfillment of the signs of the last days revealed by Christ to his disciples before his crucifixion: notably wars, wickedness, natural catastrophes, and the Jews' return to the Promised Land. (Dispensationalists after Darby found the rise of Zionism profoundly significant.)

Next on the prophetic calendar, according to Darby, will be the Rapture (I Thessalonians 4:16–17, and other texts), when all true believers will join Christ in the air. Then will come the Great Tribulation

(Matthew 24:21), when the Antichrist will establish his global dictatorship, forcing all to accept his rule and be branded with his name or his number, the dread 666 (Revelation 13:16–18). After seven years, the Antichrist's armies gather at Armageddon, an ancient battle site in Israel (Revelation 16:16), to battle a vast army marching from the East. At this moment, however, Christ returns, destroys the Antichrist and all earthly armies, and, from a rebuilt temple in Jerusalem, rules the Earth for a thousand years of peace and justice: the Millennium. All will now worship Christ as the promised Messiah, including a remnant of Jews who have survived the Antichrist's murderous persecution. After a final, unsuccessful uprising by the Antichrist comes the Last Judgment and the New Heaven and New Earth foretold in the soaring finale of Revelation.

While dispensationalism won some followers in Great Britain and elsewhere in Protestant Europe, its natural habitat proved to be North America and, ultimately, parts of LATIN AMERICA and AFRICA proselytized by U.S. missionaries preaching this doctrine. Darby made several evangelistic trips to America, and his teaching spread rapidly through his own writings and those of his followers. As historian Ernest Sandeen has argued, dispensationalism was crucial to the rise of the Fundamentalist movement, and Fundamentalists in turn helped spread dispensationalism. Highly important was the popular SCOFIELD REFERENCE BIBLE (1909), annotated by Cyrus Scofield (1843–1921), a Darbyite who wove dispensationalist doctrine throughout his notes. Prophecy magazines, annual prophecy conferences, and Darbyite institutions such as Chicago's MOODY BIBLE INSTITUTE (1886) and Dallas Theological Seminary (1924) spread the word as well.

Also contributing to the upsurge of apocalypticism in America was the rise of the JEHOVAH'S WITNESS and Pentecostal movements. The Jehovah's Witnesses, arising in the 1880s and growing to 14 million followers worldwide by 2000, espoused a particular version of apocalyptic belief based on the teachings of founder CHARLES TAZE RUSSELL (1852–1916). Modern PENTECOSTALISM is often dated from a 1906 revival in Los Angeles. Featuring ecstatic worship services, and appealing especially to poor whites and blacks, Pentecostalist denominations such as the ASSEMBLIES OF GOD and the CHURCH OF GOD (in many variant forms), supplemented by independent evangelistic and radio ministries, spread rapidly. Like the Irvingites before them, Pentecostalists preached that God's outpouring of supernatural gifts, such as glossolalia and divine healing, meant that the last days were at hand.

Not all U.S. Protestants embraced premillennialism. Lutheran, Reformed, and Anabaptist groups, such as the MENNONITES, remained amillennialist in their credal statements (despite defections to dispensationalism by the laity). Within late nineteenth- and early twentieth-century liberal Protestantism, a lingering postmillennialism, most fully developed in the SOCIAL GOSPEL theology of WALTER RAUSCHENBUSCH (1861–1918), found expression not only in church-building and missionary activity, but also in reform efforts to combat the evils of the urban-industrial age through legislation, housing codes, support for labor unions, crusades against alcohol and PROSTITUTION, and even CHRISTIAN SOCIALISM. President Woodrow Wilson's exalted vision of America's world role as he led the nation into war in 1917 had a distinctly postmillennialist tinge. This partially secularized postmillennialism would later influence liberal Protestantism's commitment to peace, nuclear disarmament, and civil rights. MARTIN LUTHER KING's celebrated "I Have a Dream" sermon of 1963, with its vision of righteousness flowing down like a river as Americans at last eradicated the sin of racism, is rich in apocalyptic imagery.

Apocalypticism in the Contemporary Age

Premillennial dispensationalism continued to pervade large tracts of U.S. Protestantism after World War II, as popularizers added the United Nations, the atomic bomb, the founding of Israel in 1948, and Israel's 1967 recapture of Jersualem's Old City to the catalog of end-time signs. Exploiting new communications technologies, they now spread their message via mass-market paperback books, audio cassettes, videotapes, television, global communication satellites, gospel music, comic books, Internet websites, and even automobile bumper stickers. (One warned: "If the Rapture Occurs, This Car Will Be Driverless.") According to a 1998 Gallup Poll, 39 percent of Americans believed it "very likely" or "somewhat likely" that the world would end by 2100 "because of Judgment Day or another religious event." Respected evangelical scholars criticized dispensationalism as a HERESY (see, e.g., Noll 1994), but its influence seemed if anything to be increasing as the twentieth century ended.

The pervasiveness of apocalypticism, and of dispensationalism in particular, in late twentieth-century global mass culture is illustrated by the phenomenal popularity of Hal Lindsey's *The Late Great Planet Earth* (1970), *the* nonfiction bestseller of the 1970s, and the *Left Behind* novels of Tim LaHaye and Jerry B. Jenkins beginning in 1995. In *The Late Great Planet Earth*, a slangy popularization of dispensationalism, Lindsey found nuclear war, the Soviet Union, Communist China, the United Nations, the NATIONAL

COUNCIL OF CHURCHES, computers, drug addiction, and much else foretold in prophecy.

In the *Left Behind* series, a fictionalized treatment of dispensationalism adapted to post-Cold War realities, the United Nations (UN) secretary-general emerges as the Antichrist. Controlling the global media, he wins over a gullible U.S. president and, in collaboration with Iraqi leaders, moves his headquarters to a rebuilt Babylon. In these novels, which sold multiple millions of copies and spawned a host of spin-off products including T-shirts, videocassettes, a juvenile version, and a popular movie, *all* secular institutions—the federal government, international agencies, multinational corporations, global media conglomerates—are preparing the way for the Antichrist. PAT ROBERTSON (1930–), head of the Christian Broadcasting Network and founder of the conservative political-action group the Christian Coalition, offered a similarly conspiratorial view of modern history as a prelude to the final satanic world system in his 1991 bestseller *The New World Order*. The prolific Hal Lindsey, in the 1996 prophecy novel *Blood Moon*, nimbly shifted from the Soviet threat to the menace of Islam and post-Cold War internationalism. In this novel, after a foiled nuclear assault on Israel by Muslim terrorists abetted by the Antichrist (once again, the UN secretary-general), Israel retaliates with an all-out nuclear attack that utterly annihilates the Islamic world.

As apocalyptic writers had done for centuries, these late twentieth-century prophecy popularizers won a large following by weaving into their scenarios contemporary trends that many people found deeply unsettling, and treating them as portents of the approaching end. As the twenty-first century dawned, apocalypticism—a central if sometimes muted theme in Protestantism from the beginning—remained very much alive.

See also Best Sellers in America, Religious; Christian Right; Lutheranism; Millenarians and Millennialism; Publishing, Media; Televangelism

References and Further Reading

Bak, Janos, ed. *The German Peasants War of 1525*. London: F. Cass, 1976.
Boyer, Paul S. *When Time Shall Be No More: Prophecy Belief in Modern American Culture*. Cambridge, MA: Harvard University Press, 1992.
Cohn, Norman. *The Pursuit of the Millennium: Revolutionary Millenarians and Mystical Anarchists of the Middle Ages*. Rev. ed. London: Temple Smith, 1970.
Davidson, James W. *The Logic of Millennial Thought: Eighteenth-Century New England*. New Haven, CT: Yale University Press, 1977.
Firth, Katharine R. *The Apocalyptic Tradition in Reformation Britain, 1530–1645*. Oxford, UK: Oxford University Press, 1979.
Hatch, Nathan O. *The Sacred Cause of Liberty: Republican Thought and the Millennium in Revolutionary New England*. New Haven, CT: Yale University Press, 1977.
Hill, Christopher. *Antichrist in Seventeenth Century England*. London, UK: Oxford University Press, 1971.
Moorhead, James H. *World Without End: Mainstream American Protestant Visions of the Last Things, 1880–1925*. Bloomington, IN: Indiana University Press, 1999.
Numbers, Ronald L., and Jonathan M. Butler, eds. *The Disappointed: Millerism and Millennarianism in the Nineteenth Century*. Bloomington, IN: Indiana University Press, 1987.
Patrides, C.A., and Joseph Wittreich, eds. *The Apocalypse in English Renaissance Thought and Literature*. Manchester, UK: Manchester University Press, 1984.
Sandeen, Ernest R. *The Roots of Fundamentalism: British and American Millennialism, 1800–1930*. Chicago: University of Chicago Press, 1970.
Tuveson, Ernest. *Redeemer Nation: The Idea of America's Millennial Role*. Chicago: University of Chicago Press, 1968.
Weber, Timothy P. *Living in the Shadow of the Second Coming: American Premillennialism, 1875–1925*. New York: Oxford University Press, 1979.

PAUL S. BOYER

ARCHITECTURE, CHURCH

Church architecture has been the most visible manifestation of the presence of Protestantism around the globe. In so being, it has also testified to the variety of forms of WORSHIP found in the various Protestant traditions as well as changing concepts about the functions of public worship. Protestant churches, in common with all Christian church architecture, are the reflection of what the community believes and practices in its life together in worship.

For the first century of the REFORMATION, the chief problem was adaptation of existing late medieval churches that dotted western Europe. Changing concepts of worship had made many of these buildings functionally obsolete for both Protestants and Catholics. The usual late medieval parish church was divided into two quite distinct spaces, a chancel for the worship of the clerical community and a nave for the laity. Both spaces were usually separated by a substantial roodscreen that obscured visibility of the high ALTAR. In Catholicism new concepts of space began to promote the visibility of the altar and the theater provided a model of such unobstructed space. New liturgical centers developed: the tabernacle on the high altar, communion rails, and confessionals. ICONOCLASM removed images no longer deemed appropriate such as those of the Trinity as three old men.

Changing concepts and practices of worship among Protestants also required alteration of existing buildings. Not until the second century of the Reformation were many new buildings for worship built. From this point on, as new traditions of worship evolved, new building types developed and the process continues today.

Basically most Protestant worship can be classified under nine traditions. We shall trace these in chronological order of development. It should be obvious that there has been much cross-fertilization over the past five centuries as various traditions borrowed from one another. Still, it is still possible to walk down a main street and guess the tradition of most church buildings before seeing the sign boards. So there is considerable consistency within traditions.

Lutheran

The Lutheran tradition turned out to be the most conservative. Many items remained in medieval churches in Germany and the Scandinavian countries that disappeared in other Protestant lands. MARTIN LUTHER had a high view of much of the existing culture but sought reform in frequent communion (see LORD'S SUPPER), an increase in PREACHING, and congregational song. None of these required wholesale iconoclasm and images were tolerated if not encouraged. Much medieval ceremonial remained. Luther was conservative in advocating BAPTISM of infants by immersion, which was currently disappearing in much of western Europe.

In October 1544 Luther presided over the dedication of the first building built deliberately for Protestant worship, the Castle Chapel in Torgau. It remains remarkably intact today with an impressive pulpit in the middle of one side of the nave and an altar at the end. As churches began to be built, especially after the massive destruction of the Thirty Years' War, Lutherans welcomed the baroque style emanating from Italy. Many of these buildings could be mistaken on the outside for Catholic churches. On the interior, a fondness developed for placing the principal liturgical centers together: pulpit, altar, and baptismal font. Both visibility and audibility became central, often calling for encircling balconies. A magnificent example was the Frauenkirche in Dresden (1726–1738), which, with multiple balconies, resembled an opera house. Theologian PAUL TILLICH once called it the ideal Protestant church.

The nineteenth century saw many romantic revivals of previous styles, exemplified in Germany by the architect Karl Friedrich Schinkel (1781–1841). Leaders in the first half of the twentieth century promoted a revival of gothic but this was superseded beginning in mid-century with the LUTHERAN CHURCH–MISSOURI SYNOD in the United States becoming the leading

champion of modern architecture. Indeed, the leading Protestant form maker in late twentieth century was Lutheran Edward Sövik (1918–).

Reformed

The Reformed tradition took much more radical steps in the sixteenth century. HULDRYCH ZWINGLI led a purge of the churches in Zurich in 1524, eliminating all images and (eventually) organs. The fear of idolatry loomed large in this iconoclasm. The focus of buildings shifted from altar to pulpit, from which the whole service was conducted. In JOHN CALVIN's Geneva, communion was served to people seated on movable benches placed around temporary tables in the aisles. This became the favorite practice for the Reformed churches in the NETHERLANDS and for Presbyterians in Scotland and America until about 1825.

Focus on the pulpit as the dominant liturgical center led to efforts to shape the building for maximum visibility and audibility. When building became common in the seventeenth century, this led to experimentation with a wide variety of shapes, most of them central in plan: Greek cross, square, circle, "T" or "L" shaped. Balconies became a standard hallmark of Reformed churches. A number of large churches were erected in France by the HUGUENOTS. All were destroyed in 1685 and a period of "wilderness," worshiping in barns with portable pulpits, ensued until the French Revolution.

America provided an opportunity for much experimentation. The Dutch built some octagons; all have now disappeared. The nineteenth century brought many changes (see below) expressed in current architectural styles. Communion in the pews prevailed among Presbyterians. Large central pulpits, high enough to allow eye contact with those seated in the balcony, dominated the interior. Currently, there seems to be an effort to restore a balance between word and sacrament, which is reflected in more prominent altar tables and fonts. The most spectacular Reformed church is the Crystal Cathedral (1977–1980) in Garden Grove, California, which is conceived of as largely a preaching space.

Anabaptist

The Anabaptist tradition has a quite different history. Here there were no buildings to inherit because these people were never an established church. Indeed, to this day, the AMISH prefer to worship in private homes with benches carted to each week's location. When buildings for worship became possible, MENNONITES and HUTTERITES turned to modest structures usually of wood. In more conservative groups these are distinguished by separate seating by sex, usually indicated on the exterior by twin entrances. The interiors often contain a long pulpit, capable of accommodating several people who will preside or preach. Most of these buildings have no pipe organs or other musical instruments. Usually towers and steeples are lacking and the buildings often have a domestic appearance even though used entirely for worship.

Anglican

Buildings in the Anglican tradition have gone through a long series of changes as Anglican worship itself has evolved. Medieval churches were adapted during the long Elizabethan era by the expedient of turning the chancels into eucharistic rooms where communicants gathered for increasingly infrequent celebrations of the eucharist (see LORD'S SUPPER). Altars became tables set parallel to the long sides and tablets of the Decalogue, Creed, and Lord's Prayer plus the royal arms were placed at the east end. Considerable iconoclasm had occurred under Edward VI. The seventeenth century saw a gradual return of the table to the east end, guarded now by communion rails.

The onset of extensive building of new churches came in the late seventeenth century after the destruction of eighty-seven churches in the great fire in the City of London. The dominating figure was Sir CHRISTOPHER WREN (1632–1723) who designed fifty-one city churches plus St. Paul's Cathedral (1675–1710), perhaps the most important Protestant church. Wren built mostly in classical styles, often with a staged tower. His "auditory" church was specifically designed for the Anglican liturgy with priority given to enabling "all to hear the Service . . . and see the Preacher." This often entailed a triple-decker pulpit and no chancel. Wren's work shaped much of Protestant church architecture in England and America for nearly two centuries. James Gibbs (1682–1754) married Wren's staged towers to a classical portico, creating a pattern still being imitated.

A major reversal came in the nineteenth century, however, largely attributed to the impetus of the CAMBRIDGE MOVEMENT with its efforts to return to the fourteenth-century English village parish church as the ideal. These buildings were built around the world as the Empire expanded and became the favored pattern for EPISCOPAL CHURCHES in America. These were altar-centered buildings with deep chancels now filled with surpliced choirs. A second gothic revival in the twentieth century, presided over by architect Ralph Adams Cram (1863–1942), continued this pattern until mid-twentieth century. Since then the liturgical movement has led to placing the altar closer to the people and to erecting new churches designed to enable maximum participation.

Puritan

The more radical groups within the CHURCH OF ENGLAND finally came to power in 1642 and started a fresh spate of iconoclasm and decoration of churches with scriptural passages. Only a few buildings were built by Puritans before 1689. The case in America was the opposite because new buildings were needed in each settlement. The typical seventeenth-century American Puritan building was square in plan with a pyramidal roof. Old Ship Church, Hingham, Massachusetts, 1681, is the sole surviving example. Eighteenth-century churches were oriented with pulpit in the midst of a long side opposite the main door. Pulpits, sounding boards, and pulpit windows were embellished with all the skills of the community's carpenters. In the nineteenth century, the orientation shifted to a short end with elegant pulpits, horseshoe balconies, beautiful entrance porticoes, and staged towers (clock, belfry, lantern, and spire). A major shift occurred with the burgeoning SUNDAY SCHOOL movement. Often the space for classes was created by raising the entire building or by flooring over the worship space at the balcony level. The rest of the nineteenth century saw a series of stylistic revivals and often assimilation of the Frontier tradition (see below).

Quaker (Society of Friends)

It is no surprise that Quaker worship, the most radical Protestant tradition, also demanded the most radical form of church architecture. These are buildings with no liturgical centers but with virtually all space devoted to congregational seating. Thus the Quaker meetinghouse puts everyone present, as it were, on stage with no distinctions among members. Because Quakers agreed that women should speak in worship but felt that their concerns were usually different from those of men, movable partitions might divide the space. By the nineteenth century these partitions were usually nailed permanently open and not replicated in new buildings. Twin entrances on the exterior denoted the division of sexes; otherwise these were plain simple buildings. If the community was large enough, balconies might be present; otherwise they are one-story buildings.

Even more radical was the small number of SHAKER buildings that made all space movement space to allow for dance as worship. The earliest of these were gambrel roofed and a standard color code of white and blue embellished the interiors.

Methodist

METHODISM has many of its origins in open-air preaching. The earliest chapels were intended as auxiliaries to the parish church so that preaching and special services could be held indoors. JOHN WESLEY early on decreed octagonal buildings with the intent of obtaining the largest accommodation as close to the pulpit as possible. The usual building eventually came to have a two-story facade with the interior balcony dictating the window locations. Double- or triple-decker pulpits were common, and the altar table was invariably surrounded by communion rails.

Nineteenth-century buildings went through a morass of styles from regency to romanesque. Late in the century the so-called Akron plan became a favorite with the interior oriented to a corner in which were wedged, in descending order, organ pipes, choir in concert stage arrangement, presiders' chairs, pulpit, altar table, and communion rail. In the mid-twentieth century Elbert E. Conover (1885–1952) led a campaign to persuade Methodists to build gothic or Georgian churches with a divided chancel similar to what Anglicans were then building. Until recently most Methodist churches were small town and rural; now most are suburban and modern architecture has been generally accepted.

Frontier

The Frontier tradition in worship, now the most widespread in America, is a product of the Second Great AWAKENING. Worship is planned for those on the frontier between faith and unfaith with the hope of producing new converts and solidifying the faith of those already converted. Like Methodism it owed much to outdoor camp meetings. More than anyone else, CHARLES G. FINNEY (1792–1875) brought the style indoors. In 1832 he leased the Chatham Garden Playhouse in New York City for purposes of worship and EVANGELISM. The stage freed him from the confines of the usual wineglass or tub pulpit. The pulpit became a desk from which the preacher could make fervent sorties in pleading for CONVERSIONS. In 1836 Finney built the Broadway Tabernacle, which provided an amphitheater for 2,500 and room for a choir, organ, and pulpit platform.

Many of the Frontier-tradition worship patterns became endemic in American Protestantism, drawing into itself Methodist, Reformed, Puritan, and even some Lutheran and Quaker congregations. It is not surprising that the pulpit platform arrangement with desk pulpit and chairs for preacher, visiting evangelist, and song leader became the dominant liturgical arrangement and probably still is in terms of the number of existing churches and those being built. The usual difference in Baptist churches is the presence of a baptismal pool.

The most recent development in the late twentieth century is the MEGA-CHURCH. Willow Creek Community Church in South Barrington, Illinois is the best known but they are legion in the Midwest United States. An effort is made to make these buildings as neutral as possible with no religious images and a platform occupied only by a tiny pulpit, actors, and musicians. At Community Church of Joy (nominally Lutheran) in Phoenix, Arizona an altar disappears after the old folks' "traditional" service. Worship and entertainment are treated as interchangeable commodities, and the building obliges by not making any faith statements.

Pentecostal

The twentieth century saw the rapid growth of the Pentecostal tradition with a premium on spontaneity and the present activity of the Holy Spirit. This tradition has not yet developed a distinct architectural style, although buildings of the Frontier type seem most congenial. In recent decades praise and worship services have used screens on which lyrics for congregational song can be projected. There are no inhibitions about using the latest electronic techniques or musical styles and space is often provided for small bands. Many of these groups began in humble storefront churches in big cities, but they are increasingly moving to architect-designed buildings in the suburbs.

Thus there is not a single Protestant architectural form or style but rather a vast variety, reflecting the infinite varieties of worshiping God within Protestantism.

See also Altar; Amish; Anabaptism; Anglicanism; Awakenings; Baptism; Calvin, John; Cambridge Movement; Church of England; Conversion; Dutch Reformed Church; Episcopal Church; Evangelism; Finney, Charles Grandison; Friends, Society of; Huguenots; Hutterites; Hymns and Hymnals; Iconoclasm; Lord's Supper; Lutheran Church–Missouri Synod; Lutheranism; Luther, Martin; Mega-Church; Mennonites; Methodism; Netherlands; Pentecostalism; Preaching; Presbyterianism; Puritanism; Reformation; Shakers; Sunday School; Tillich, Paul; Wesley, John; Worship; Wren, Christopher; Zwingli, Huldrych

References and Further Reading

Drummond, Andrew L. *The Church Architecture of Protestantism: An Historical and Constructive Study*. Edinburgh: T. & T. Clark, 1934.

Kilde, Jeanne Halgren. *When Church Became Theater*. New York: Oxford University Press, 2002.

Vereinigung Berliner Architekten. *Der Kirchenbau des Protestantismus von der Reformation bis zur Gegenwart*. Berlin: Kommissions-Verlag von Ernst Toeche, 1893.

White, James. F. *Protestant Worship and Church Architecture*. New York: Oxford University Press, 1964.

———. *The Cambridge Movement*. Cambridge: Cambridge University Press, 1962.

Williams, Peter. *Houses of God: Region, Religion, and Architecture in the United States*. Urbana: University of IL Press, 1997.

JAMES F. WHITE

ARMINIANISM

Used precisely, the term Arminianism applies to the Christian doctrine of ELECTION and PREDESTINATION developed by JACOBUS ARMINIUS (c. 1559–1609), Reformed pastor in Amsterdam and professor of theology at the University of Leiden. Used somewhat less precisely, the term refers to soteriologies, theological anthropologies, hamartiologies, and eccesiologies that are either implied by Arminius's thought or were developed more or less systematically by him. It also refers to those that, by their inner logic, connect coherently either with Arminius's doctrine of election/predestination or with others of his writings.

Arminius's Formal Education

Arminius was born in Oudewater, NETHERLANDS to a large immediate family of "middle-rank." Noteworthy in Arminius's education and career is the importance of the logic, rhetoric, and theological and philosophical method of Peter Ramus (1515–1572). Ramus's method was a product of the older Reformed theology and fit it well. In Dutch and English Reformed circles Ramus's logical method for a time rivaled that of Aristotle. As with Aristotle's method, one must first determine the category to which the idea to be investigated belongs. Ramus believed that every idea belonged to one or another of the liberal arts; each of the liberal arts had its proper sphere of ideas. Having properly identified the place of the idea, the investigator could proceed with a sharp division of each investigated idea into two parts (dichotomies), and then continue division of the resulting parts until one reached the investigated idea's most basic components. Ramus and his adherents believed this method of drawing dichotomies to be not only a way to truth, but also a way to determine the practical implications of an idea. It rests on two theological notions: all valid knowledge comes from the Trinitarian God and therefore must be related to God, and true knowledge has practical application or consequences. These postulates imply that all knowledge has a moral/ethical dimension.

Arminius's Earlier Theological Context

Even more deeply than by his superb theological education, the theological thought of Arminius, and of his Reformed opponents, was shaped by various reforming ideas that moved through the lower Rhine delta and valley and through the cities of the Hanse, especially from about the 1370s. Especially important was the spirituality of such persons as the Rhenish mystics and such movements as the Brethren of the Common Life. These called for renewed personal piety and social ethics defined in terms of fidelity to Scripture and the traditions of Augustinian and Benedictine spirituality and theology. They did not call for rebellion against the institutional church—only that its faith find personal and social expression beyond rituals and public pieties.

Except for his years at Geneva, Arminius's immediate theological context had been that of the first generation of the Reformed movement—the generation of which JOHN CALVIN was a younger member and a leader, but not the force that he was to become—even though, chronologically, Arminius and his peers belonged to the second or third generation of the movement.

The theological boundaries of that early Reformed generation in the Netherlands were not the boundaries developed in Geneva. Rather, they had been set by the Lutheran voice of PHILIPP MELANCHTHON and earlier Reformed voices, such as HULDRYCH ZWINGLI, HEINRICH BULLINGER, Zacharias Ursinus, Myconius, and Grynaeus. Their creedal bases were the BELGIC CONFESSION (Walloon edition, 1561; Dutch edition, 1562) and the HEIDELBERG CATECHISM (1563)—the earlier, not the later, editions.

Guy de Brès (de Bray) (d. 1567), a native of Bergen in Hainault, a southern province, had produced the *Belgic Confession* in 1561, precisely for the Protestant congregations in the Netherlands. Based on Calvin's GALLICAN CONFESSION (1559), the original *Belgic Confession* is nonetheless obviously of an independent spirit. Zacharias Ursinus (1534–1583) wrote the *Heidelberg Catechism* at the behest of elector Frederic III who wanted peace between Lutherans and Reformed in his territory. Ursinus, a student and disciple of Melanchthon and then a student of John Calvin, responded by developing a christocentric document, strictly Reformed only in several specific doctrines: the sacraments (especially regarding the issue of "real presence"), the authority of Scripture, the place of good works, and the CHURCH as the source of Christian discipline. Its doctrines of election and predestination say nothing of reprobation or of limited atonement, which gives them something of a Lutheran cast; but as a whole, the document is broadly Reformed.

The synods of Emden (1571) and Dordrecht (1574) declared these documents normative. Conceptually, both synods envisioned a national church, essentially and deliberately Reformed in theology and polity; but a church clearly aligned with historic Western Christianity and with broader Protestantism. Arguments concerning the authority of these synods did not arise until the late 1580s. Thus the theological context of Arminius's youth was indeed Reformed, but not bound to the thought of any one leader, although Calvin and Geneva did hold certain preeminence.

By the time Arminius had begun studies in the academy in Geneva, THEODORE BEZA, Calvin's son-in-law, had become the lodestar of the Genevan Reformed movement—not by self-appointment but by circumstance and consensus. He was faithful to Calvin but his emphases were far more affected by philosophy and more speculative than Calvin's, and he ventured into metaphysics, a territory little treated by Calvin (although Calvin certainly worked from metaphysical presuppositions). Beza's *Confession of the Christian Faith* and *On Predestination,* especially, reflect a much more scholastic, dialectic approach to theology than Calvin's. This approach, grounded in Aristotelian logic, tends to make one point methodologically as important as another to the validity of his theological system—not, perhaps, in terms of pastoral care and pastoral theology, but in terms of both the outer and inner logic of the system as a whole. So it was that ecclesiastical polity was believed to be logically and theologically as significant as, say, eschatology. The foundation and center of Beza's system was divine sovereignty; the doctrine of election/predestination, its linchpin.

Arminius began to sense the inelasticity of Bezan theology (which many took to be Calvin's theology) during his student days at Leiden. The theology faculty, with one exception, had developed positions that were certainly Reformed, but not as narrow as those in Geneva. Midway through his studies at Leiden, however, Arminius began to hear sharp reaction to that older, broader form of Reformed thinking, and demands for more meticulously stated doctrine.

Initially the debate focused on the relationship between the ecclesiastical and civil institutions. At the center of the debate, as Arminius experienced it, was Caspar Coolhaes (c. 1534–1609), Reformed pastor and sometime lecturer in theology in the University in Leiden from 1574 to 1578. He had come as pastor at the invitation of Leiden's burgomasters just as the "Erastian" polity that had been typical from the 1540s in the Reformed churches in the Netherlands had come under severe questioning. It continued to be typical, but decreasingly so, even after the Synod of Dordrecht (1574) had sought to impose the Genevan institutional pattern on all Reformed congregations in the northern provinces. "Erastian" polity and the broad theology of the early Reformed movement in the Netherlands had fit together with some success, but Geneva had now become the capital of Reformed theological thinking. Coolhaes, tolerant of views different from his, found little tolerance among the Genevans. For them, an erroneous ecclesiology was as serious a theological flaw as erroneous christology.

Further, to make his point, Coolhaes appealed to Scripture, the theologians of the early church, and then Protestant Reformation theology, beginning with its creeds and catechisms, although this practice, too, became an issue, given that Coolhaes was more likely to turn to the works of Zwingli, Melanchthon, Bullinger, and Ursinus than to those of Calvin, Luther, or Beza.

Although Coolhaes's original accuser was another Leiden pastor, it was not long before one of the five members of the University's theological faculty had taken up the cudgel. Lambertus Danaeus, who was in Leiden for only a year (1581–1582), became a powerful voice for the Genevan polity over against Coolhaes and the burgomasters of Leiden. Educated in law at Orleans, Paris, and Bourges (where he received a doctorate), Danaeus had converted to Protestantism under the influence of the martyrdom of Anne of Bourges in 1559. In 1560 he went to Geneva to study under Calvin. He returned to France in 1561 to serve as a Reformed pastor near Orleans until he was forced to flee at the time of the St. Bartholomew's Day massacre in 1572. He went back to the environs of Geneva, where he was assigned a pastorate. Here he formed a close friendship with Beza. In 1574 he was reassigned to a pastorate in Geneva and appointed to the faculty of the Academy. Beza, who probably knew exactly what he was doing, successfully urged and enabled Danaeus to receive a pastor call to Leiden and an appointment to the university faculty. We do not know Danaeus's views on predestination, but we do know that he viewed the ecclesiastical polity advocated by Coolhaes as theologically erroneous, even heretical.

Especially in questions of polity, the Netherlanders had generally feared more the ICONOCLASM of Reformed zealots than the authority of the burgomasters over the church. Now the Bezans were insisting that CONSISTORY must be a law unto itself. Arminius, following Ramus's method, and also drawing on earlier Reformed practice in the Netherlands, argued—as Coolhaes and his supporters did—that the burgomasters had the right to pass on Consistory's nominations to the offices of elder and deacon, although he was soon off to further studies in Geneva.

The growing influence of the Bezan point of view in the university and across the United Provinces prompted Coolhaes's exit from Leiden and his subsequent condemnation by a clergy-dominated national synod at Middelburg in 1581, and his deposition from the ministry and excommunication in 1582, by a clergy-dominated regional synod at Haarlem. These synods ignored his strong support from the burgomasters of Leiden. Dutch Calvinism was setting out on a new trail; but not all of the Reformed were to follow it.

Arminius went to Geneva to study just as Coolhaes was being ejected from Leiden and the Bezan point of view was coming to dominance in the United Provinces. He studied under Beza in Geneva intermittently between 1582 and 1586. In the interstices, he studied under Johannes Jacobus Grynaeus (1540–1617), who taught Scripture and was dean of the theological faculty at Basel. Grynaeus, a Lutheran except for his openness to a more nearly Calvinist, perhaps Zwinglian, understanding of the LORD'S SUPPER, apparently helped Arminius to a more critical appreciation of the logic of Peter Ramus (Arminius's earlier enthusiasm for Ramus had irritated Beza, among others) and to a refocusing on the christological character of earlier Reformed theology.

Arminius's attraction to Ramus's logic and theological method was probably taken very seriously by Beza. The fresh logic of Ramus's system seemed to Beza a source of theological error. In 1570 Ramus had applied for a professorial post under Beza. Beza turned him down, primarily because of this commitment. Somewhat later Ramus had sharply criticized the tendency of Beza's ecclesiology toward clerical control. He had also questioned Beza's persistence in using the term "substance" with reference to the Lord's Supper when it was precisely this term, however technically useful, that had been the focus of so much and such bitter debate within and between Christian traditions. Ramus's critiques and Beza's responses had built an obvious wall between them. Arminius's presence reminded Beza of these things.

Then, to make things worse, Arminius, back in Geneva in 1584, apparently studied considerably with Charles Perrot, a theologian shown by the evidence to have been an advocate of theological tolerance and a critic of Beza's emphasis on GRACE at the expense of "works." Arminius also seems to have cemented friendship with his fellow countrymen studying there, among whom there were some very significant dissenters from Beza's predestination-centered, Aristotelian approach. In fact, Dutch theologians who accounted themselves Reformed had fallen into trouble with Beza early on in Beza's career. Among them was Adrianus Saravia (1531–1613), who had helped Guy de Brès write the *Belgic Confession,* which was produced expressly for Reformed churches in Flanders and the Netherlands, and had taken it to Geneva for approval in 1561, only to have it rejected. Geneva did not really endorse it until 1581, when Beza included it, in edited form (Franciscus Junius, Arminius's predecessor on the Leiden faculty (1593–1602), had rewritten its article on civil magistracy), in his *Harmony of Confessions.* In the 1570s Saravia advocated Christian evangelization as a basic purpose in voyages of discovery and colonizing and ran afoul of Beza's insistence that the original Apostles had fulfilled Christ's command to evangelize and make disciples and the command therefore did not apply past the Apostolic Age. (Saravia joined the Leiden faculty in 1584. It is an irony that he served with Junius there.)

The data clearly indicate that, although he deeply appreciated the Christian character, the learning, the intellectual capacity, and the articulateness of Beza, Arminius had consistently appealed and adhered to pre-Bezan Reformed thought even in his studies in Geneva. The evidence shows that Beza knew of Arminius's DISSENT and that he believed it to be serious, but the evidence also shows that Beza actually supported Arminius's call to be a Reformed minister in the important town of Amsterdam. Later accusations that Arminius had betrayed both his friendship with Beza and his loyalty to Beza's theology simply are not true. He had not been personally very close to Beza, and he had never bought into Beza's theology—either its basic and central doctrine of election/predestination or its method, which was Aristotelian.

In October 1587 the Classis of Amsterdam, ministers and laity delegated from each of the parishes in and around the city, having read his letters of recommendation, including one from Beza, admitted Arminius to the ministry pending a call to be a Reformed pastor in Amsterdam and the passing of a theological exam. The Consistory of Amsterdam, the clergy of the city, met with Arminius and approved the action of the Classis. By February 1588 Arminius was conducting evening services—preaching and leading prayers—at the Old Church, although various complications delayed full ordination and pastoral assignment until August 1588.

However, the theological tangles arising out of the decisions at the synods at Emden (1571), Dordrecht (1574), and The Hague (under the direction of the Earl of Leicester), in 1586, had come to produce strong accusations and recriminations, especially on the matter of church–state relations. The synod at The Hague had ordered the Reformed churches in the United Provinces to follow the Genevan model. Then, just as Arminius took up his pastoral duties in 1587–1588, Leicester was forced out of office and the magistrates reversed the ruling of the earlier synod.

Arminius's marriage in 1590 to Lijsbet, the daughter of Laurens Reael, complicated the issues for both Arminius and those who would oppose him. Reael was a wealthy, well-connected grain merchant and polymath who, as his immediate forbears had done, played an important role in developing Dutch nationalism and the earlier form of Reformed tradition and in tying the two together. For Reael, as for many in the United Provinces' middle and upper classes, the Genevan model was theologically questionable and politically untenable.

Arminius's theological troubles began in 1591. Early in the year he represented Amsterdam on a commission charged by the States of Holland with drawing up a new church order. The commission recommended consistency in the practice developed earlier in the northern provinces—that the civil authorities take an active role in the nomination of pastors and in church discipline. Since the mid-1550s, Geneva, led by Calvin and Beza, had execrated such a position. In 1570 the Heidelberg Calvinists had excommunicated Thomas Erastus, accusing him of surrendering the authority of the church to the civil authority. Now Arminius found himself facing the same issue.

Arminius had until now faced increasing harassment from critics of his "Erastianism" where formerly he had enjoyed the support of the merchants and burgomasters. Now in the 1590s his theological opponents, who had generally responded to his critiques of the theology of the Reformed faith spreading from Geneva as source for intra-Reformed thought and debate, were now treating them as schismatic or worse. These reversals did not develop suddenly. An important cause lay in changes in the lifestyle and the loyalties of the merchants and burghers. Thinning were the ranks of merchants and burgomasters whose education had included the deep reading in theology and philosophy, not to mention the interest that capacitated them for subtle theological discussion. The new "breed" were not ignorant nor unintelligent nor indifferent to theological issues, although thanks to territorial discoveries, new maps, the political fluidity of the early modern political arrangements, and the increasing tendency of merchants, burghers, and burgomasters to think in terms of commercial law, profit, and loss, and vocational specialization, the theology and theological method of Beza and his adherents gained ascendancy. Helping this process along immensely was Petrus Plancius, a pastor in Amsterdam who, along with FRANZ GOMAR, took the lead among Arminius's theological opponents in 1592. They managed to have Arminius hauled before the consistory more than once. He was cleared of heresy, but the direction of the arguments brought up all of the unre-

solved questions about the appropriate relationship between the ecclesiastical and civil institutions and authorities. Also important was Plancius's production of a world map that was of great help to the merchants. The States General published it, and Plancius and several merchants laid the groundwork for the Dutch East India Company—all in 1592. Plancius's geographical work and business acumen helped him to weaken the strong feelings among some of the burghers that because he wanted the church to be independent of the state Plancius somehow would set church over against state.

In 1604 Arminius, now on the faculty of the University of Leiden, presented his customary public disputation, this time taking up the subject of predestination. He had already offended Franz Gomar (1563–1641), professor of New Testament in the university, by taking on some public duties in which he responded as a biblical scholar. Gomar officially objected that Arminius had crossed disciplinary lines, without sufficient expertise to do so. Gomar then held a public disputation of his own in which he took a very Bezan approach to the question of predestination. So Arminius had to fend off the attacks of both Plancius and Gomar, who soon decided to collaborate. For the remainder of his professorial career, he worked with the two issues: church–state relationships and predestination.

Arminius seems to have considered himself a faithful follower of the Reformed perspective on the Christian faith, and it would seem that he diligently sought to do his work as a theologian within its intellectual and ecclesial boundaries. What the evidence makes clear, however, is a sharp shift in what it meant to be Reformed that began to occur in the mid- to late-1550s as Calvin gained political control of Geneva, and accelerated as Theodore Beza began to assume Calvin's mantle.

Arminius's Theology

Arminius did not write a systematic theology. Rather, he left a collection of occasional works from which a systematic theology may be distilled, or at least inferred. These works include orations, lectures, poems, dissertations, disputations, exegetical pieces, and letters. Probably the most important of his works is his *Examination of Perkins' Pamphlet,* written in 1602, while he was still pastor in Amsterdam, but not published until 1612 after he died. Arminius admired WILLIAM PERKINS, a Cambridge scholar, and wrote what may be called a "review letter," of Perkins's *Concerning predestination . . .* (1598) as a base from which to discuss the doctrine of predestination. However, Perkins died in 1602 and the review letter, probably unfinished and unedited, went unsent. It was published after Arminius's own death, but it is probably the fundamental statement of Arminius's theology and of Arminianism, although in Arminius's later works some of its statements would find more nearly complete explication or be made more precise and would be better supported by Scripture and corroborated by citations of other literature.

Among those later works, the most important is probably Arminius's *Declaration of Sentiments*, which he read at The Hague in 1608, before the convened assembly of the States of Holland and West Friesland. Acrimony that threatened political unity as well as the peace of the Reformed churches had set in and the Synod of South Holland had demanded a written declaration from both Arminius and his nemesis and sometime colleague at Leiden, Franz Gomar.

In the *Declaration of Sentiments* Arminius presents his understanding of the DOCTRINE of election/predestination, making it clear that, although it clearly looms large in history and in the thinking of Dutch Protestantism, it is not systematically the foundational doctrine of the Christian faith (as the Bezans believe that it is). The doctrine, he says, must be discussed and understood within several constants set by primarily Scripture and confirmed by the historic teaching of the Christian Church: (1) it must be understood under the rubric of christology; (2) it must be evangelical; (3) it must not make God the author of sin; (4) it must not make the human being the author of salvation; (5) it must be scriptural, not speculative; and (6) it must not depart from the historic teaching of the Christian Church, especially the *consensus quinquaesaecularis* and the confessions of the Protestant Reformation, particularly the *Belgic Confession* and the *Heidelberg Catechism*.

Arminius then developed his doctrine of election/predestination in terms of four "decrees," retaining thereby the Reformed glossary.

> The first absolute decree of God concerning [i.e., for effecting] the salvation of sinful man, is that by which he decreed to appoint his Son, Jesus Christ, for a Mediator, Redeemer, Savior, Priest, and King, who might destroy sin by his own death, might by his obedience obtain the salvation which had been lost, and might communicate it by his own virtue.
>
> The second precise and absolute decree of God is that in which he decreed to receive into favor those who repent and believe, and, in Christ, for his sake and through him, to effect the salvation of such penitents and believers as persevered to the end; but to leave in sin and under wrath, all impenitent persons and unbelievers, and to damn them as aliens from Christ.
>
> The third divine decree is that by which God decreed to administer in a sufficient and efficacious manner the means which were necessary for repentance and faith;

and to have such administration instituted (1). according to the Divine wisdom, by which God knows what is proper and becoming both to his mercy and his severity, and (2). according to Divine justice, by which He is prepared to adopt whatever his wisdom may prescribe and put in execution.

> To these succeeds the fourth decree, by which God decreed to save and damn certain particular persons. This decree has its foundation in the foreknowledge of God, by which he knew from all eternity those individuals who would, through his preventing [i.e., prevenient] grace, believe, and, through his subsequent grace would persevere, according to the before described administration of those means which are suitable and proper for conversion and faith; and by which foreknowledge, he likewise knew those who would not believe and persevere. (Nichols tr. I:247–248)

Here, then, was a doctrine of absolute predestination, but one in which Jesus Christ is the object, and through him, the church—that is, those who are "in Christ." The person and work of Christ are not simply means to an end. All election is in and into Christ. Repentance and faith are required of those who would be in Christ; and these, far from being meritorious works, are gifts of divine grace enabled by the prior gift of prevenient grace. Prevenient grace is given to all and is a gift of divine grace, not an aspect of human nature. It enables choice in the matter of repentance and faith, and thus we may speak of "free will," but, says Arminius, it is better that we speak of free grace.

Arminius produced these four decrees in full confidence that they aligned well with Scripture and the soteriological intention of Scripture, with all "Christian teachers who held correct and orthodox sentiments," with Beza's *Harmonia confessionum* (Geneva, 1581) and with the *Belgic Confession* and the *Heidelberg Catechism* (in fact, clarifying them). He also claims that they are in accord with the nature of God, with human nature (whether before the Fall, after the Fall, or in the state of restoration), with the act of creation (understood theologically), with the nature of eternal life, with the nature of eternal death, and with the nature of grace. Further, it "states sin to be a real disobedience, and the meritorious cause of condemnation; and, on this account it is in the most perfect agreement with [the Reformed doctrines of] the fall and sin" (*Ibid.*, 251). It leads us to glorify God in his justice and mercy, and as the cause of all good and of our salvation; and the human being as the cause of SIN and "his own" damnation. It honors Jesus Christ by placing him for the foundation of predestination and the meritorious and communicative cause of SALVATION. It promotes salvation and is the power and means that lead to salvation because it creates within the human mind sorrow on account of sin, solicitude about CONVERSION, faith in Jesus Christ, a studious desire to do good works, and zeal in PRAYER. It confirms and establishes the order in which the gospel is to be preached: first, the requirement of repentance and faith, and then the promise of remission of sins, the grace of the Spirit, and life eternal. It strengthens the ministry of the gospel and makes it profitable in its proclamation, its sacraments, and its public prayers. It unites the twofold love of God—it reconciles God's love of righteousness and justice, and his love of human beings.

Early Arminianism

Arminius's death in 1609, probably before he had reached age fifty, removed the most learned and skilled of the advocates of the type of Reformed theology that was typical from Zwingli's day until Calvin's point of view and the belief that Geneva was the model for Christian society gained hegemony in the Netherlands in the late 1550s. From the late 1550s the older type began to give way, but it could still be found in those areas in which it had originally flourished, and it was in those areas that Arminianism arose.

Arminius had not intended to initiate a theological tradition. He died believing himself to be a faithful adherent to the Reformed faith. His followers, too, believed themselves to be genuinely Reformed. The States of Holland had, the year before Arminius's death, invited him and the ministers who believed as he did to meet with the States (parliament) and to present their understanding of the *Belgic Confession* and the *Heidelberg Catechism*. The meeting finally took place the year after Arminius's death. Forty-six of his supporters, several of them very close and longtime friends of his, presented what came to be called the Remonstrance of 1610.

The five articles of the Remonstrance declare:

1. That God, by an eternal, unchangeable purpose in Jesus Christ his Son, before the foundation of the world, has determined, out of the fallen, sinful race of men, to save in Christ, for Christ's sake, and through Christ, those who, through the grace of the Holy Ghost, shall believe on this his Son Jesus, and shall persevere in this faith and obedience of faith, through this grace, even to the end; and, on the other hand, to leave the incorrigible and unbelieving in sin and under wrath, and to condemn them as alienate from Christ, according to the word of the gospel in John iii.36. . . .

2. That, agreeably thereto, Jesus Christ, the Savior of the world, died for all men and for every man, so that he has obtained for them all, by his death

on the cross, redemption and the forgiveness of sins; yet that no one actually enjoys this forgiveness of sins except the believer, according to the word of the Gospel of John iii.16. . . .

3. That man has not saving grace of himself, nor of the energy of his free will, inasmuch as he, in the state of apostasy and sin, can of and by himself neither think, will, nor do any thing that is truly good (such as saving Faith eminently is); but that it is needful that he be born again of God in Christ, through his Holy Spirit, and renewed in understanding, inclination, or will, and all his powers, in order that he may rightly understand, think, will, and effect what is truly good, according to the Word of Christ, John xv.5. . . .

4. That this grace of God is the beginning, continuance, and accomplishment of all good, even to this extent, that the regenerate man himself, without prevenient or assisting, awakening, following and co-operative grace, can neither think, will, nor do good, nor withstand any temptations to do evil; so that all good deeds or movements, that can be conceived, must be ascribed to the grace of God in Christ. But as respects the mode of the operation of this grace, it is not irresistible, inasmuch as it is written concerning many, that they have resisted the Holy Ghost. Acts vii., and elsewhere in many places.

5. That those who are incorporated into Christ by a true faith, and have thereby become partakers of his life-giving Spirit, have thereby full power to strive against Satan, sin, the world, and their own flesh, and to win the victory; it being well understood that it is ever through the assisting grace of the Holy Ghost; and that Jesus Christ assists them through his Spirit in all temptations, extends to them his hand, and if only they are ready for the conflict, and desire his help, and are not inactive, keeps them from falling, so that they, by no craft or power of Satan, can be misled or plucked out of Christ's hands, according to the Word of Christ, John x.28. . . .

These Articles, thus set forth and taught, the Remonstrants deem agreeable to the Word of God, tending to edification, and as regards this argument, sufficient for salvation, so that it is not necessary or edifying to rise higher or to descend deeper.

This document's five articles generally satisfied the States General of Holland that its adherents were staying within the boundaries set by the *Belgic Confession* and the *Heidelberg Catechism* regarding election/predestination and its corollaries. However, they only aroused Gomar and others to greater effort in destroying the Arminians (who were now coming to be called "Remonstrants") and Arminianism. Gomar's most effective move was to enlist the active support of the *Stadtholder,* Maurice of Nassau, William the Silent's son and successor. Maurice, impatient with theological debate, yearning for the peace necessary for prosperity, and wanting a national church, saw that the REMONSTRANTS stood in his way because they held political and commercial power in many of the towns in the United Provinces and were theologically and pastorally astute—and they did not hesitate to fight back. Finally, in 1618, he sent armed forces to keep order in the troubled towns and he forcibly removed Remonstrant magistrates from office, replacing them with Contra-Remonstrants. When that task neared completion, he called for the national synod to meet at Dort (Dordrecht) in 1618–1619. Eleven of the leading Remonstrant ministers were there—in chains, as the accused.

On the basis of its revision of the *Belgic Confession* and its revision of the *Heidelberg Catechism,* the Synod of Dort condemned all Arminian doctrines, especially as they had been stated in the Remonstrance of 1610. Guided by Gomar, it adopted a Bezan interpretation of Calvin, of the confession and the catechism, and of the character of the Reformed movement. Remonstrants were prohibited from preaching, from worshiping together, and from printing or disseminating any of their literature—on pain of confiscation of goods and exile.

The Synod's own confession of faith, deliberately set in contradiction to the Remonstrance of 1610, is remembered in English by the acronym TULIP: T, total depravity; U, unconditional election/predestination; L, limited atonement; I, irresistible grace; P, perseverance of the saints. Only on the theological fact of total depravity did Remonstrants and Counter-Remonstrants agree; the Remonstrants also would agree that as long as one is a believer, that one cannot be lost, but the Counter-Remonstrants saw that as a simple tautology. It was not what they meant by perseverance.

In the backwash of the meeting of the Synod, many of the Remonstrant ministers fled the Republic. A strong contingent settled in Antwerp and there formed a congregation. Three of Arminius's closest friends—Johannes Uitenbogaert, Simon Episcopius, and Nicolas Grevinchovius—were among these. By 1625, however, many of the Arminians were back in what was now the Dutch Republic. Prince Maurice had died in 1625, and his brother Frederic Heinrich, who favored the Remonstrants, had followed him.

The Remonstrants now began to reorganize themselves in the Republic, and soon there were two Remonstrant "denominations." Through most of the seventeenth century the larger of the two drifted only very slowly away from the Protestant orthodoxy of its first generation. The smaller rather quickly translated Arminius's concern for toleration and freedom into LATITUDINARIANISM, and by the end of the century was deeply influenced by Unitarianism. Both tended to attract the more highly educated and well-to-do.

Early Arminianism outside The Netherlands

Arminianism, as an accepted theological stream within the Reformed movement, seems to have found its way to ENGLAND even before the Synod of Dort, but it seems to have come there and been received in bits and pieces. The only noteworthy representatives of a consistent Arminianism in England were Peter Baro and William Barrett. They were officially reprimanded, but were neither fined, jailed, nor silenced. It was a book by Baro that had irked William Perkins into writing his book on predestination, which in turn brought Arminius to write against Perkins (although Arminius's work was published posthumously). The CHURCH OF ENGLAND sent official observers to the Synod of Dort and these generally agreed with the Counter-Remonstrants. However, they had no authority to act either in the Republic or in England. Probably the earliest Christian group in England to align with Arminianism was the GENERAL BAPTISTS, who had connections with ANABAPTISM in Holland even before the Synod of Dort.

By the 1630s and 1640s Arminianism had gained an influential following in England, the most important Arminian being archbishop WILLIAM LAUD. RICHARD BAXTER, who titled one of his well-read books, *The Reformed Pastor,* deliberately sought to avoid partisanship and had some Arminian leanings.

In the eighteenth century JOHN and CHARLES WESLEY and their preachers promoted Arminianism in their preaching, teaching, and liturgy. Especially important was Arminius's concern that God's sovereignty and the workings of divine grace be understood christocentrically. John Wesley also published "The Arminian Magazine" to provide edifying reading for his Methodists and other interested persons. The Wesleyan movement has sometimes been called "Arminianism on fire." Some twenty million Christians would now account themselves classical Arminians. This would include several kinds of Methodists, including many United Methodists and the historic African American Methodist denominations; the theologically conservative WESLEYAN HOLINESS MOVEMENT, which includes the SALVATION ARMY, the CHURCH OF THE

NAZARENE, the CHURCH OF GOD (ANDERSON, INDIANA), and the WESLEYAN CHURCH; and Pentecostals with Wesleyan ties, such as the CHURCH OF GOD (Cleveland, Tennessee) and the Pentecostal Holiness Church.

Nineteenth-Century Arminianism

By the mid-nineteenth century, especially in the UNITED STATES and Great Britain, and in Britain's colonies, Arminianism appeared to have conquered all before it. Wesley's Methodists self-consciously presented themselves as Arminians. By the end of the century Wesleyans were claiming that even much of the Reformed tradition had become Arminian. Evidence abounded to substantiate the claim. Arminianism had early in the century found a home in revivalism, where "decision" loomed very large. Moderate Calvinists, especially those affected by the New School Theology and by such evangelists as CHARLES FINNEY, no longer testified to "having a hope of salvation." They now exclaimed, "Jesus saves me now." The Methodists, ever evangelistic, urged people to "decide now"—"The choice is yours." Formally the Methodists, and certainly even the New School Calvinists, warned against Pelagianism; and formally they retained Arminianism. The Methodist press, especially, was vigilant. In fact it fought a two-front battle: against the Calvinists and against flimsy notions of free will. In the local settings, however, theological precision was not usually a concern—at least not on the question of human freedom.

At the close of the century revivalism lay at the heart of the rise of the Wesleyan Holiness Movement and the later formation of new holiness denominations, and the still later Pentecostal revival and the formation of Pentecostal denominations. Here, too, "decision" was critical. To see it from another angle, the Arminianism preached among the poor was an antidote to the increasing mechanization and regimentation of life. It opened the door to hope.

Basic Ideas in Contemporary Arminianism

As the twentieth century has given way to the twenty-first, many have found in Arminianism at least a partial antidote to the omnipresence of practical applications of the social sciences, which are basically materialistic and deterministic, although what has been lost in the meantime is the inclination to think theologically. This has created some severe distortions in contemporary Arminianism.

As did classical Protestantism generally, Arminius and the classical Arminians committed themselves to the doctrines of salvation by unmerited grace alone, through faith, which had no merit, alone; Scripture alone as the authority for faith (doctrine) and practice; and the priesthood of all believers. They also committed themselves to confess that fallen humanity can exercise saving faith only through the operations of prevenient grace, and not through anything in human nature.

Arminius had developed a distinct kind of Protestant theology, however, and the Arminians were to develop it even more deeply and broadly. Most notably, Arminianism rejected (and rejects) the supralapsarian doctrine of unconditional predestination—the view held by Beza and Gomar and others that before Adam and Eve's fall, even before their creation, God had determined whether each of them would be saved or damned. It also rejected the sublapsarian (or infralapsarian) doctrine of unconditional predestination—the view held by Augustine and Luther and others that Adam and Eve freely chose sin; but ever since, all have been sinful from birth and that salvation comes only as a gracious gift from an absolutely sovereign God who predetermines that he will save some (although none merit anything but damnation). There were variations on both of these, and Arminians reject the variations, too.

Arminians are often said to hold a doctrine of conditional predestination. This is only partly true. Arminians hold that Christ is the object of predestination. He is the Predestined One. In Christ predestination is absolute—that is to say, one cannot be in Christ and be damned. This doctrine is rooted in the belief that God's sovereign will, expressed everywhere in Scripture, and made manifest in the person and work of Christ, is to save all who will receive God's way of saving. Predestination here is conditional in that the human being must make a choice for or against receiving and living out of God's way of saving (i.e., receive Christ and live "in Christ"), although the human being cannot make this choice out of its own resources. Rather, God provides to all prevenient grace, which enables them to repent and believe the gospel, the good news of Jesus Christ. In this sense, and in this sense alone, are we morally free. Otherwise we are always and ever "slaves to sin." Obviously some do not utilize that grace to believe, but abuse it. These will be damned so long as they continue their abuse of that grace.

Close to this doctrine is that of original sin. Here, Arminius and classical Arminians agree entirely with the long Christian tradition, including the Lutherans and the Reformed, that the human will is absolutely fallen and unable to do anything good out of its own resources. It is not simply tainted or partially disabled. Its horrid condition is not a consequence of creatureliness, of being "merely human." It is totally corrupt; it is actively evil. Nonetheless God gives to everyone that prevenient grace by means of which the will may turn to God and to God's saving grace in Jesus Christ. Arminians developed here a strong doctrine of human freedom, often called "free will," and this has led some of them into Pelagianism. As with Arminius, classical Arminians have been very careful to guard against any movement in the direction of Pelagianism. Contemporary classical Arminians have been reviving Arminius's understanding and avoiding Pelagianism by working in terms of "free grace" rather than "free will."

Probably the most contention between contemporary CALVINISM and Arminianism arises over the Arminian belief that believers may cease to believe, thereby losing their saving relationship to God and running the risk of being eternally lost. Many Calvinists hold to "eternal security" or "once saved, always saved." To Calvinists, Arminians finally have a fickle God—a blasphemy. To Arminians, Calvinists sound as if human moral behavior is finally of no account.

In his *Declaration of Sentiments* Arminius gave twenty arguments against both supralapsarianism and sublapsarianism and concluded that all twenty basically arrive at one point—they make God the author of sin. A corollary is that they make Jesus Christ simply a means to an end and not himself the alpha and omega, the beginning and the end. Arminius pointed out that this is "highly dishonorable to Jesus Christ" and "hurtful to [the proclamation of] salvation." Classical Arminians have retained these critiques of "Calvinism," often as accusations rather than as reasoned conclusions. Nonetheless they have usually preferred to resort to either a doctrine of divine "permissive" will or a reverent agnosticism about the origins of evil. Currently some Arminians have worked with the idea of the "openness" of God, but, to this point, that idea has proven to be too closely related to process theologies, with their (as classical Arminians see it) limited God, to offer "salvation to the uttermost," or salvation to all.

Arminius and Arminians reject Calvin and Beza's idea that the ATONEMENT is limited. Certainly not all avail themselves of its benefits, but Arminianism insists that must not be seen as a limitation on Christ's redeeming work in itself. Here, Arminius and his to-be-famous-student, Hugo Grotius, developed the governmental theory of atonement. What Christ did, he did for each and every person. That means that Christ's atonement, said Arminius, is not the payment of a penalty. If it were, all would be saved. Rather, Christ suffered for all in order that those who repent and believe could be forgiven. He suffered and died that awful public death so that everyone will see the sinfulness of sin and the costliness of forgiveness and will exercise the grace proffered them to turn to him

and forsake the selfishness, the egocentricity, which keeps the world that God governs in such a roil.

Where it has been influenced by revivalism or by Reformed EVANGELICALISM, Arminianism has sometimes favorably responded to the so-called ransom theory of the atonement, or the penal satisfaction theory, but these are generally incompatible with Arminianism's understanding of the workings of divine grace. Arminius's way of putting it was to say that we begin by understanding that God is kindly affectioned toward us and graciously moves us toward Godself by showing us our sinfulness and offering forgiveness.

A severe contemporary problem has arisen over the meaning of the term "evangelical" in the North American context. Are the Arminians evangelical? Conservative Reformed persons are inclined to see their tradition(s) as defining evangelicalism; consequently they deny that the Arminians are thoroughgoing evangelicals, although they do hold some beliefs in common with evangelicalism. Classical Arminians and Reformed would accept the *consensus quinquae-saecularis*: would agree that Jesus Christ was virgin-born; would agree on the realities of miracles and bodily resurrection, and that Christ died in our place for our sin; would agree that the Bible is divinely inspired and the sole infallible rule for faith and practice; and would agree that those who are in Christ will be saved and will dwell with him in heaven, and that those who are finally impenitent are lost and will suffer everlasting death in hell. Neither the Reformed nor the Arminian will press his/her definition of heaven or hell as an article of faith.

What's in a Name?

Across the four hundred years since the death of Arminius and the convening of the Synod of Dort, the term "Arminianism" has often been equivocated. Among many who would be Arminians, Pelagianism has run rampant and taken the name "Arminian." Many have come to believe that Arminianism is primarily disbelief in election/predestination. Others believe that it is about free will and not much else, and by free will, they mean something that is natural to us. This has only given good reason where there was no good reason for some, especially some more or less within the Reformed tradition, to label as "Arminianism" anything that seems out of plumb with their commitments to at least some of the petals of TULIP.

"Arminianism" here has been confined to the thought of James Arminius and to that which may be shown to be an evangelical development of that thought. This then has given the doctrine of election/predestination large place. In fact Arminianism, as

Arminius and classical Arminians such as John Wesley would have it, is an expression of the consensus of the first five centuries as that consensus was then interpreted and tempered in the atmosphere of the reformations of the sixteenth century, especially the Reformed reformation. This means that Arminianism is well within the boundaries of Christian orthodoxy.

References and Further Reading

Primary Sources:

The Writings of James Arminius, D. D. 3 vols. Grand Rapids, MI: Baker Book House, 1956 (reprint of 1853 edition).
Schaff, P., ed. *The Creeds of Christendom.* vol. 3. 1877.

Secondary Sources:

Bangs, Carl. *Arminius: A Study in the Dutch Reformation.* Nashville, TN: Abingdon Press, 1971.
DeJong, Peter Y., ed. *Crisis in the Reformed Churches: Essays in Commencement of the Great Synod of Dort, 1618–1619.* Grand Rapids, MI: Reformed Fellowship, Inc., 1968.
Harrison, A. H. W. *The Beginnings of Arminianism to the Synod of Dort.* London: University of London Press, 1926.
McNeill, J. T. *The History and Character of Calvinism.* Oxford, UK: Oxford University Press, 1954.

PAUL MERRITT BASSETT

ARMINIUS, JACOBUS (JACOB HARMENSZ) (1559–1609)

Dutch reformed theologian. Arminius is known for his formulation of a version of the doctrine of PREDESTINATION that Calvinists found unacceptably loose. His thought provided the theological basis for the REMONSTRANTS' movement in the NETHERLANDS and for ARMINIANISM.

Born in the Dutch town of Oudewater, Arminius lost his father at a very early age and was taken under the wing of the local pastor, Theodorus Aemilius. Suspected of Protestantism, Aemilius fled to Utrecht, taking his protégé with him to study at the Latin school there. After Aemilius's death in 1574 or early 1575, a new patron, the philosopher and mathematician Rudolph Snellius, took Arminius to study at the University of Marburg. There Snellius introduced him to the logic of Peter Ramus. Arminius returned to Holland soon after the death of his mother and siblings in the 1575 massacre of Oudewater's inhabitants by Spanish troops. In 1576 he matriculated at the newly founded University of Leiden, where he studied theology.

The Amsterdam merchants' guild provided him with a stipend to continue his studies at the University of Geneva under THEODORE BEZA, Charles Perrot, and other Calvinist luminaries in 1581. There he met Johannes Wtenbogaert, who would be his best friend for life and leader of the Remonstrants after his death. Arminius had to leave Geneva for a year (1583–1584) after his Ramism angered one professor. He returned, though, to complete his studies and received a very positive letter of recommendation from Beza. Before returning to the Netherlands, Arminius also spent a year at the University of Padua where he studied under the scholastic philosopher Jacobo Zabarella. In 1588 Arminius was appointed minister of the Reformed Church in Amsterdam, and in 1590 he married the daughter of a city council member. A favorite of the city's merchant oligarchs, Arminius served in Amsterdam for fifteen years, leaving his ministry with some reluctance in 1603 to become professor of theology at Leiden. The only native Hollander on the theological faculty, he filled this post until his death.

It was once thought that Arminius must have held a Calvinist view of predestination while a student in Geneva and later changed his view drastically. Carl Bangs, Arminius's foremost modern biographer, argues to the contrary, and his argument agrees with modern interpretations of the history of Reformed Protestantism. These emphasize the fluidity of the movement in its early years and the variety of views initially deemed acceptable, even in Geneva. Contrasting positions on such issues as the order of God's decrees were not even staked out until Reformed theologians began to apply the methods of scholastic philosophy to their subject. As Richard Muller emphasizes, Arminius himself played a crucial role in this development. In the debates over predestination that ensued, a narrower and more precise definition of Reformed orthodoxy—one that excluded Arminius's views—emerged. This definition was then encapsulated in the CANONS OF DORT and declared binding by the DUTCH REFORMED CHURCH.

Article 16 of the BELGIC CONFESSION OF 1561 declares that God delivers and preserves "all whom he, in his eternal and unchangeable council, of mere goodness hath elected in Jesus Christ our Lord." Arminius sometimes suggested that a national synod might do well to revise those words, but he always maintained that he taught nothing contrary to them. Controversy over his teachings first arose in 1591 after Arminius delivered a sermon on Romans 7:14 in which he held that the sinful man whom Paul describes was not the regenerate man justified by faith. Arminius's fellow minister Petrus Plancius accused him of Pelagianism and Socinianism. Amsterdam's burgomasters enjoined the ministers to "allow this whole matter to rest." In 1593 Plancius lodged accusations against Arminius after his interpretation of Romans 9 caused offense, and again Amsterdam's consistory ruled that Arminius's interpretation was acceptable. Although some continued to suspect Arminius's orthodoxy (an ambiguity facilitated by his lack of publications), no new controversy erupted until 1604, when Arminius laid out his views on predestination for his Leiden students. He explicitly rejected both supralapsarian and infralapsarian versions of the doctrine. FRANZ GOMAR, one of his colleagues, responded by publicly refuting his views, and the university was soon divided between Arminians and Gomarists. At issue was not only predestination but the status of confession and catechism as rules of faith and the authority of magistrates in religious affairs: Arminius and his supporters wished to minimize the first and enlarge the second. By 1608 the dispute was causing unrest in political as well as church circles. In May of that year the States of Holland summoned Arminius and Gomar to hold a disputation before it; later in the year the two appeared separately. On the latter occasion Arminius delivered his "Declaration of Sentiments," which Wtenbogaert drew on when drafting the Remonstrance of 1610 after the death of Arminius.

In brief, Arminius held that God first decreed to appoint his Son, Jesus Christ, as "Mediator, Redeemer, [and] Savior." God then "decreed to receive into favor [*those who repent and believe*]" in Christ, and to damn those who do not. God then "decreed to administer . . . the *means* which were necessary for repentance and faith." Finally God decreed to save certain individuals and damn others based on his "foreknowledge, by which he knew from all eternity those individuals who [*would,*] through his preventing grace, [*believe,*] and, through his subsequent grace [*would persevere,*]" and those individuals who would not (Arminius, *Writings,* 1:247–248). The crux of the difference between this formulation of predestination and Calvinist ones lies in the role of divine foreknowledge. Arminius's formulation of predestination is in fact only one part of a theology that also differed from Calvinist orthodoxy with respect to their doctrines of God, creation, and providence.

See also Calvinism

References and Further Reading

Primary Source:

Arminius, James [Jacobus]. *The Writings of James Arminius.* Translated by James Nichols and W. R. Bagnall. 3 vols. Grand Rapids, MI: Baker Book House, 1956.

Secondary Sources:

Bangs, Carl. *Arminius: A Study in the Dutch Reformation.* Nashville, TN: Abingdon Press, 1971.

Muller, Richard A. *God, Creation, and Providence in the Thought of Jacob Arminius: Sources and Directions of Scholastic Protestantism in the Era of Early Orthodoxy.* Grand Rapids, MI: Baker Book House, 1991.

BENJAMIN J. KAPLAN

ARNDT, JOHANN (1556–1621)

Lutheran divine and author. After initially intending to study the natural sciences and medicine, Arndt turned to the study of theology, which he pursued in Helmstedt, Wittenberg, Strasbourg, and Basel. He served various parishes, first in SWITZERLAND, then in north Central GERMANY, where he was involved in various controversies on account of his adamant Lutheran position. In 1611, Duke Christian von Braunschweig-Lüneburg appointed him General Superintendent, head of the church in his territory. This proved to be the most pleasant and productive time of Arndt's life.

Arndt's lasting reputation rests in his book *The Four Books of True Christianity* (Vier Bücher vom wahren Christentum) completed in 1606. Calling for personal piety and devotional life, Arndt's book came at a time when ORTHODOXY had incessantly emphasized THEOLOGY and DOCTRINE. Thus, *The Four Books* received both criticism and appropation and has been seen as a seminal forerunner of PIETISM.

In the last year of his life, he described the purpose of the book:

> Firstly, I wanted to draw the feelings of students and preachers back from the far too disputatious and polemical theology which has almost turned into a new Scholastic Theology. Secondly, my plan was to lead believers in Christ out of dead belief to fruitful faith. [In the original, "belief" and "faith" are the same word, *glauben.*] Thirdly, to bring them from mere knowledge and theory to the real practice of faith and blessedness in God, to show what genuine Christian life is, which is consistent with true faith, and what the Apostle means when he says, 'I live—but now it is not I, but Christ who lives in me'.

Arndt made generous use of medieval mystical authors, and based his counsel on humanity's essential, although still creaturely, kinship with God, on Christ as Savior and Healer and, therefore, model. The believer experiences all creation as encounter with God.

See also Spener, Philipp Jakob

References and Further Reading

Primary Sources:

Arndt, Johann. *True Christianity.* Translated and edited by Peter Erb, preface by Heiko A. Oberman. New York: Paulist Press, 1979.

Stout, John Joseph. *Devotions and Prayers of Johann Arndt.* Grand Rapids, MI: Baker Book House, 1958.

Secondary Source:

Braw, Christian. *Bücher im Staube: Die Theologie Johann Arndts in ihrem Verhältnis zur Mystik* ("Books in the Dust: The theology of Johann Arndt in its relation to Mysticism"). Leiden, Germany: Brill, 1986.

DAVID TRIPP

ARNOLD, EBERHARD (1883–1935)

German church reformer. Arnold was born near Königsberg (present-day Kaliningrad), East Prussia, on July 26, 1883. Before beginning his study of theology, philosophy, and education at the University of Breslau, Arnold experienced a religious conversion. Doubts about the legitimacy of infant baptism as well as the intimate connection between CHURCH AND STATE IN GERMANY prompted Arnold's decision not to seek ordination in the Lutheran church and to abandon his study of theology. He changed his studies to philosophy and received the doctorate from the University of Erlangen in 1909. During the next several years—also marked by severe illness—Arnold worked primarily as a journalist and writer until he became editor of the newsletter of the German Christian Student Association (with the German acronym DCSV) and the editorial director of a new publishing house, Furche Verlag, in 1915.

The years of World War I brought a shift from an earlier affirmation of the war to a rigorous PACIFISM. Later, Arnold began to focus on the meaning of Jesus' Sermon on the Mount and developed the notion of a radical discipleship. Subsequently Arnold was influenced by the German–Jewish philosopher Gustav Landauer's vision of a utopian socialism, which, together with what Arnold took to be the New Testament precedent, led to his establishment of a communitarian settlement in 1920. In 1926 the community, called Bruderhof by Arnold after the HUTTERITES in the sixteenth and seventeenth century, moved to a decrepit estate near Fulda in central Germany. In 1930 Arnold traveled to North America to establish contacts with the Hutterite communities there. In December 1930 he was ordained as a Hutterite minister and the Bruderhof near Fulda was recognized as a Hutterite congregation.

The coming of Nazi rule in Germany in January 1933 brought various tensions between Arnold and the new regime. A second Bruderhof was established in Liechtenstein to provide a home for the children of the Fulda Bruderhof, whom Arnold did not want to be exposed to Nazi indoctrination. Arnold died on November 21, 1935 from surgery. Two years later, when the Nazi government shut down the Fulda operation, all the members of that community migrated to England and were warmly received because Arnold's travels had prepared the ground.

References and Further Reading

Primary Sources:

Arnold, Eberhard. *Salt and Light. Living the Sermon on the Mount.* Farmington, PA: Plough Pub. House, 1998.
———. *Writings, Selected with an Introduction.* Farmington, PA: Plough Pub. House, 2000.

Secondary Source:

Baum, Markus. *Against the Wind: Eberhard Arnold and the Bruderhof.* Farmington, PA: Plough Pub. House, 1998.

HANS J. HILLERBRAND

ARNOLD, THOMAS (1795–1842)

English educator. The son of a customs collector, Arnold was born at Cowes on the Isle of Wight on June 13, 1795. He received his M.A. degree in 1817 from Oxford University and was ordained as a CHURCH OF ENGLAND deacon the following year. He was awarded a doctor of divinity in 1828 and just before he died was elected Regius professor of modern history at Oxford University. As headmaster of Rugby School (1828–1842), Thomas Arnold was known as an outstanding Christian educator in early nineteenth-century ENGLAND.

From 1819 to 1827 Arnold was a private tutor before assuming the post of headmaster of Rugby School, to which he added the duties of chaplain after 1831. Rugby, although fallen on difficult times in the 1820s, was an elite English public school for adolescent boys. Termed "public" in English terminology, these schools were private institutions of secondary education for the middle and upper classes.

Two aspects of his career are noteworthy: his headship at Rugby and his role as a public figure on religious issues. At Rugby in Warwickshire Arnold started out with a free hand from the school's trustees to make changes, improve staff conditions, and expel the most incorrigible of students. Using senior boys as prefects he instilled a more disciplined, moral regime to produce "Christian gentlemen" without excessive use of corporal punishments. His efforts restored confidence in Rugby in particular and "public" boarding schools in general, especially as two of his graduates later became archbishops of Canterbury, and others went on to distinguished university careers. His school was also memorialized in a famous novel *Tom Brown's School Days* (1857) by Thomas Hughes.

Arnold was not a strong educational innovator, although he did introduce some modern history and mathematics into an otherwise largely classical studies curriculum at Rugby. His charges did not study the physical sciences, and both distinctive school uniforms and organized sports were later developments to the public school ethos for which Arnold cannot be credited.

In public life Arnold was sometimes a controversial figure who wrote on social and religious questions. Typically he argued for a true national Christian Church in England, one that would encompass all who accepted the divinity of Jesus Christ, including Protestant dissenters and Roman Catholics. These views often collided with Protestant evangelical tendencies and also with English Catholic revivalism.

Less well remembered is Arnold's success at arguing for a separation between his roles as public controversialist and educator. He died one day before his forty-second birthday in 1842, a much admired role model for the Victorian era. His influence is attributed more to the sincerity of his Christian beliefs than his oratory, his scholarship, or his educational initiatives.

See also Catholicism, Protestant Reactions; Dissent; Nonconformity

References and Further Reading

Primary Sources:

Arnold, Thomas. *Fragment on the Church*. London: B. Fellowes, 1844.

———. *Principles of Church Reform*. London: S.P.C.K., 1962.

———. *Sermons Preached in the Chapel of Rugby School: With an Address Before Confirmation*. New York: D. Appleton, 1846.

———. *Christian Life and Doctrine; Sermons Preached Mostly in the Chapel of Rugby School, 1831–1834*. London: Longmans, 1878.

Secondary Source:

Stanley, Arthur Penrhyn. *The Life and Correspondence of Thomas Arnold*. Boston: Ticknor and Fields, 1860.

MICHAEL MCCRUM

ART

Protestant art has been both a villain and a hero in the history of Christianity. From the beginning the reformers displayed a great deal of discomfort with imaginative representations, and their posture toward images and relics shaped Protestant perspectives on art. ICONOCLASM in the early stages of the REFORMATION was poised to eliminate art from religion, and empty walls and ceilings of Protestant churches seemed to suggest that Protestant art was an oxymoron. Protestants other than Puritans and a few other extreme iconoclasts, however, were not opposed to art itself. Many Protestant traditions welcomed art as a means of illustration of their theological position. A tradition of religious art developed over centuries within Protestantism in its own right, and in doing so art found space in which visual expressions could be pursued apart from the shackles of the doctrinal control of the church in ways that had not been possible during the Middle Ages.

Art before the Reformation

Before the measures of reform set about deconstructing symbolic representations sponsored by church authorities, images of Jesus, Mary, and other saints, along with illustrations of religious experience of faith, had enjoyed widespread support throughout Western Christianity. These artistic forms of presentation had helped the believers to maintain their relationship with the sacred realm, and had served an important role in communicating the faith at a time when literacy was limited to a small group of people. The long tradition of spirituality that had developed around images and relics in the medieval times was an eloquent sign of the importance visual art had enjoyed for many centuries of church history.

The reformers of the sixteenth century took issue with what they perceived to be the practices of turning these images and relics into objects of worship and veneration under the aegis of the church, and condemned the religious use of art as idolatry. From the viewpoint of the reformers the symbolic forms of piety in the Roman Catholic tradition ceased to be a tool of facilitating the knowledge of the divine, but assumed a divine status of their own. Instead of bearing testimony to the holy and the sacred, the Reformers charged, art of the medieval times became religion. The disagreement over the meaning of religious art in the Reformation period signified the major fissure in the symbolic universe in Western Christianity, and the Reformers voiced the need to reassess the role of art in the life of the church.

Art in Service of the Word

After the Reformation art found itself in a world that privileged the written biblical text over symbolic representations of religion. Before the Reformation the BIBLE was regarded as part of the ecclesiastical tradition, and the AUTHORITY of the church had nearly absolute control over biblical interpretation. The Reformers objected that the Bible was the ultimate authority. MARTIN LUTHER first raised the banner of *sola scriptura* in defiance to the authority of papacy and councils, and gave the Bible the primary role in Christian life. In an effort to make the Bible accessible to people in its renewed role, Luther translated it into the German language. JOHN CALVIN, who led the Protestant movement in FRANCE and SWITZERLAND, focused on the exposition of the biblical text as well.

One could observe the transition from art to word in the works of the German Renaissance artist Albrecht Dürer. Although his earlier works of the woodcuts of the Apocalypse series of 1498 display Gothic emphatic emotions, Dürer's last painting commonly known as "The Four Apostles" (1526) foregrounds John who is reading the first part of his gospel, which introduces the incarnate word. Peter is standing next to him with a key that unlocks the gate of heaven, and the juxtaposition of the two apostles insinuates that the Bible is the key. In the adjacent panel Mark is holding a scroll, and Paul a copy of the Bible. The two biblical figures underscore the importance of the word, and along with the book Paul holds a sword that symbolizes his martyrdom. Paul dies for the sake of the word of God. An inscription attached to the paintings contains Revelation 22:18ff. in Luther's translation—the passage that warns against adding anything to or omitting anything from the word of God.

As the word took up the central place in Protestant religious life, art was given subsidiary function as a tool of illustrations of the biblical text. Luther's German Bible that opened a new era in the Reformation included illustrations of woodcuts for the biblical passages. The first translation of the New Testament in 1522 had twenty-one woodcuts, and the complete Bible in 1534 contained 118 of them. By the time of Luther's death in 1546 more than 500 drawings appeared in various versions of his translation. These woodcuts had only a secondary function as a visual aid, and any meaning they could generate was supposed to be already understood or spelled out in the text of the written word.

In the case of the New Testament, the majority of the drawings in Luther's Bible were about the book of Revelation, which contained graphic images amenable to visualization. New Testament books featured typical images of evangelists and apostles, whereas the Old Testament drawings were given more embellishments than those in the New Testament. Often, images from the Old Testament included scenes from the New Testament, particularly in the case of the prophetic books, so that one could look for the connection between the Hebrew prophets and the life and work of Jesus Christ and his apostles. Drawings appeared in Luther's prayer book, sermons, and hymns, as well. Because their setting was nonbiblical, these visual presentations were somewhat free in their approach in comparison with the other drawings featured in the Bible editions.

The emphasis on the word over art in the Reformation era determined the main contours of Protestant art for years to come, although visual symbolization in service of the word managed to find its way into the heart of Protestantism. Most remarkably, the open Bible on the pulpit in an empty liturgical space of the Protestant sanctuary was to make a lasting artistic impression. With the invention of movable type, the printed Bibles that facilitated PREACHING and teaching in Protestant churches offered a new artistic way of highlighting the central role of the word of God in the Protestant beliefs and practices.

Art That Survived the Reformation

Art succeeded in proving its usefulness as a means of illustration in the world of Protestantism; however, the catalog of arguments the Reformation raised against art was a long one. ANDREAS BODENSTEIN VON KARLSTADT called for the abolishment of art because he feared that people were considering artistic symbols equal to God. HULDRYCH ZWINGLI was adamantly opposed to the use of art in the church, even though he was willing to permit stained glass for private devotion. One could own any portraits, as long as they were not brought into the church for reverence. In later branches of Protestantism, art was banned altogether as a form of earthly pleasure that had no place in religion.

Artistic pursuits survived and eventually flourished with Protestant hues mainly because Luther saw the possibility of art as an effective, if not ideal, means of communicating the gospel. Unlike many other leaders of the Reformation including radical Reformers, Luther recognized that the weak-minded believers could benefit by religious objects, and welcomed the use of art in the making of a visual church designed to win over the Christians of the medieval iconic piety at a time of difficult transition of the Reformation.

Luther had an artist friend named Lucas Cranach the Elder, the court painter of the Saxony whose elector Frederick the Wise was friendly to the Reformer. Through Cranach's art, which included oil paintings, relief sculptures, and altarpieces, the theology of Luther enjoyed the benefit of visual expressions that widely disseminated Luther's teachings. Cranach's choice of the themes he chose to work on clearly showed the influence of his friend Reformer: "Allegory of Law and the Gospel," "The Law and the Gospel," "Christ and the Adulteress," and "Christ Blessing the Children." The work of Cranach and his shop in Wittenberg made the Saxony the seedbed of

Protestant art from the late sixteenth to the early seventeenth century.

Cranach's approach to painting over the years presented a telltale sign of the impact of the Reformation. An emotional piece of "Crucifixion" (c. 1500) would be representative of his earlier works, but after the Reformation was well under way, his paintings began portraying beautiful men and women and grand nature with exquisite, somewhat fanciful, details in contrast with the previous Gothic solemnity.

Cranach's later art was in consonance with the Protestant desire for realism, which was partially in reaction against the abstract representations of spiritual matters in Roman Catholicism. In the narrative presentation of the gospel account, Cranach sought the verisimilitude in the events he portrayed. His effort stood in contrast to the method of the earlier Catholic artists who included a series of events simultaneously in a single frame.

Other artists of the Reformation also sought realism and continued the artistic techniques of drawing that started with the Renaissance artists, who portrayed their conception of humanity as they were, sometimes all muscles and arms with no indication of emotion or thirst for spiritual liberation. Dürer, who studied the perspectival art of realistic rendering, sought to draw the world with a high degree of realism, as he gave every feather of a bird and every leaf of a wild flower a detailed treatment. In the next century the quest for realism sent Rembrandt van Rijn to search for his model of Christ in the Jewish community in Amsterdam.

In addition to realistic portrayals of biblical themes Cranach left a few portraits of Luther, which became the prototype for later artists, along with drawings of other Reformers and Protestant princes. Cranach's presentations undoubtedly helped the Reformers' message to be received favorably by many in the tumultuous times of the sixteenth century. The portraits of Luther presented him as a pious monk, even a saint, who honored the Bible, in contrast to the satirical caricature of the monks of the late medieval time that couched the Catholic Church leaders in images of beasts and even demons. Cranach's portrayals of the Reformers endowed them with the spiritual authority that pointed to the necessity of the breakup with Rome.

JOHN CALVIN of the second generation of the Reformation did not see much benefit in artistic endeavors. He instituted a word-oriented service, which left little room for the need of art in worship. Calvin acknowledged the work of paintings and sculptures as God's gifts—as long as they were not venerated. In general, art received a particularly cold shoulder in the areas governed by CALVINISM. More often than not,

Calvinists, who cared particularly for an open Bible in a bare sanctuary, made more ardent iconoclasts than other Protestant traditions. Presbyterian churches have refrained from placing any religious objects in the church, and have preserved the structure of brightly lit, undecorated low ceilings of the sanctuary. The only religious object Calvin was prepared to allow was a plain cross. Accordingly, the historic Lafayette Presbyterian Church of Brooklyn, New York did not even have a cross in the sanctuary, and the renowned Tiffany glass outside the sanctuary portrayed the creation of the world.

Calvin's theory of art was governed by ASCETICISM, following the Augustinian disdain of pleasures. The kind of pleasure Calvin delighted in discussing was God's pleasure, and any pleasure a human being may receive had to be through God's gift, whether it was music or art. Calvin added another limit to the artistic pursuits. Under all circumstances, the objects of visual representation were limited to the things that did not exist in the physical world. Making images of an animal or a stone was banned as an activity that could easily slip into idolatry.

From time to time the Reformers' suspicion toward art triggered violence. The absolute dependency on grace made the relics and the intercession of saints superfluous, and the Protestant aesthetic pursuit was from time to time overtaken by iconoclasm. The fate of art in the period of the Reformation was made precarious by the iconoclastic writing of Karlstadt and the call of Zwingli for the destruction of idols. Riots and destruction of images erupted in the second quarter of the sixteenth century, and religious images were being destroyed, and the interiors of church buildings whitewashed. Luther, whose excommunication forced him into hiding, was reportedly compelled to come out to stop the smashing of stained glass windows. The second half of the sixteenth century displayed the decline of religious art, and in an interesting contrast the court art gained the ascendancy.

Art managed to survive Protestantism because it proved to be of use for the cause of the Reformation, even though it never recovered the privileged place it had enjoyed before. Because art illustrated the notions close to the heart of the Reformation, and because the church buildings were designed and decorated in the light of the austere spirit of Protestantism, traditional themes were rendered in ways that showed the drastic change in theological thinking. For a remarkable example, whereas the medieval arts portrayed Christ as a man of sorrow marred and mutilated in the traditional type of the dead man in Pietà, Cranach's "Man of Sorrow" in the altarpiece in Meissen Cathedral presented Jesus on the cross as a figure who was up and alive with a hint of wound and with little blood showing.

Art as a Language of Theological Discourses

In Protestantism art was not always appreciated in its own right, as it was always a suspect for turning into something else the Protestant leaders dreaded. In the sixteenth century when the clarity of reality was being sought in the Word, art seemed to have too much ambiguity for comfort. Protestant art, however, proved itself as a keen observer of the teachings and practices of the Reformation.

While Protestant leaders were engaged in writing documents that would voice their new, or renewed, theology, Protestant art entered the foray by participating in theological discourses of the time through symbolic images. When the leaders of the Reformation underscored the SALVATION by God's grace alone—*sola gratia*—Protestant art offered a visual representation of God's grace. When the pulpit took up the central place in the house of worship, the paintings of the pulpit gave expression to the emerging identity of the *sola scriptura* of Protestantism. When Luther and Calvin retained BAPTISM and the LORD'S SUPPER as SACRAMENTS, because they are endorsed by the biblical text, the paintings of these liturgical events illustrated their importance in Protestant traditions.

The Reformers who called for the return to the Bible noted that the biblical literature recognized the sinful nature of humanity, while at the same time observing the persistence in God's gratuitous grace, which alone could redeem the sinful humanity from the hopeless fate of damnation. When the Reformers preached the teaching of the efficacy of God's grace alone to bring salvation to humanity, the Protestant paintings of the biblical themes on forgiveness drove home the point of God's gratuitous grace. It was the Reformation theology of forgiveness that permeated Cranach's "Christ and the Adulteress." The painting featured a gathering of religious leaders, who offered nothing but condemnation, and Cranach's brush added the tint of a demonic side to those who gathered to bring charge against the woman caught in the act of adultery in John 8. Cranach showcased Luther's theology of salvation by Christ's forgiving grace alone, without which there was no possibility of deliverance. In the subsequent seventeenth century the Protestant theology of *sola gratia* found its expression in the epic of JOHN MILTON's *Paradise Lost* and the paintings of Rembrandt. In "The Risen Christ Appearing to Mary Magdalene" the Dutch artist juxtaposed light and darkness in an effort to portray the grace that saved the world out of the shadow of death.

PURITANISM in New England did not show a penchant for art, and Puritans had only bare necessities for survival. They, too, demonstrated their theological stance with what they had to create for their religious life. Puritans designed meeting houses that had far too simple a structure to be called churches, and built them to look nearly identical from any direction because it was the place where worshippers gathered from all directions. Often the building had many windows so that it would have ample light inside because it was the beacon of the gospel.

When Protestant ORTHODOXY arose in the seventeenth century, the formulation of orthodox doctrine had its corollary with the emergence of the Baroque art, which appealed to senses and flourished among Catholics. Baroque art was partially in response to the Protestant lack of emphasis on art, as well as to the court art style that arose in the wake of the Renaissance and the Reformation and was not suitable for church art. In the silent debate with the emotional Baroque art, the Protestant-minded Dutch artists of the seventeenth century drew the daily life of serene homes. Johannes Vermeer's famous paintings of domestic life captured the moments of God's grace in the commonality of daily activities. The receding light in his paintings reproduced artistically the combination of the revelatory power of the transcendence with the immanent response of the human mind. His approach described the world as it was, rather than prescribing the world as it ought to be.

Protestant aesthetics surged in the sermons of JONATHAN EDWARDS of eighteenth-century America. Edwards underscored that one could experience the world by sense in all its wonder and horror, and elaborated his conviction passionately in "Sinners in the Hands of an Angry God." Whereas humans invited God's anger, God responded to the corrupt situations of humanity with benevolence. Edwards's writings created literary space that could provoke profound emotions, but Calvinism offered little provision for artistic rendering of the renewed religious feeling.

The Great Awakening (see AWAKENINGS), however, contributed to the opening of a window of imagination toward feeling and revelation that found their inroad into nineteenth-century ROMANTICISM. The Romantic artists believed that, as FRIEDRICH SCHLEIERMACHER expounded, a human being had the capacity of "feeling" God's presence and work. The Romanticist passion found its earlier expression in the works of PRE-RAPHAELITES who came together in 1848 to form the Pre-Raphaelite Brotherhood (PRB). The group included William Holman Hunt, John Everett Millais, and Dante Gabriel Rossetti. They rejected artificial academicism under the banner of truth to nature, and expressed religious feeling and ethical sincerity in a straightforward manner, rendering the pictures with detailed exactitude and bright colors.

Protestant art in the era of Romanticism found a moment of private visions rich in emotion in the paintings of Henry Fuseli and WILLIAM BLAKE. Although their paintings showed some distance from established religion, Blake's "Illustrations of the Book of Job" and "Ancient of Days" have been rated as a honest exploration for a profoundly individual experience of the divine being. In the twenty-two engravings for the book of Job he began with the portrayal of the satanic side of the deity and proceeded to declare the artistic triumph of redemption in Christ.

Blake, who preferred to deal with imaginative objects rather than with natural ones, believed that imagination was a means to perceive God. He drew rather than painted because he considered line drawing capable of giving expression to the infinite. He gave art a role in which it could redeem the world from arrogant rationalism and acquisitive materialism.

In America the Romantic quest for religious moments in art was palpable in the paintings of the Hudson River School of nineteenth-century America, which included Thomas Cole, Asher B. Durand, Jasper Cropsey, and Frederic Church. Whereas the textbook approach to drawing regarded the horizon or the vanishing point on the canvas as the place to start the work of imagination, the Hudson River School used the ending point to begin its referential posture to a world beyond. Light was shown to emanate from the point where it was presumed to disappear, and created ample bright space on the canvas. The light represented God's grace. As the light shone, salvation was offered as God's free gift.

Thomas Cole regarded art as an imitation of the Creator who brought into being peace out of chaos. In his "View from Mount Holyoke, Northampton, Massachusetts, after a Thunderstorm" (The Oxbow), Cole drew a picture of a wilderness after a storm. As a world of conflict was moving out after the storm, the artist on the border of the wilderness could see the mountain with a piece of writing in Hebrew, *Shaddai,* the oldest name of God in the Hebrew Bible, commonly, if erroneously, translated as the Almighty.

Durand's work was marked by its Calvinistic tone of *soli deo Gloria.* He refused to give the central role to humans because the sovereignty of God was the key. His exclusion of humans was so extensive that critics found him lacking social sensitivity.

In his painting of Cotopaxi, Church portrayed a mountain with a volcanic activity, which unmistakably pointed to Mount Sinai. He rendered a vision of a God whom one could sense in his paintings of "The Heart of the Andes" or "Above the Clouds at Sunrise." Church's pastor was HORACE BUSHNELL, who believed that human existence was filled with the mystery of the divine and the possibility of experiencing God. Undoubtedly, it was Bushnell's theology that showed up in Church's paintings.

The artworks of the Hudson River School contained a narrative, especially an allegorical narrative. Little wonder that the Hudson River artists took to the images in JOHN BUNYAN's *The Pilgrim's Progress.* Their approach to the striking beauty of nature in its glory was seen in Robin Williams's movie *What Dreams May Come,* which portrayed the devastation of tragedy along with the hope of the colorful celestial realm. The motion picture included credit to Church, Durand, and Cole.

Most of the Hudson River artists painted the American wilderness. The American icon of wilderness in their paintings represented both the harsh reality and the serene world. It was a place where human beings could be left to wander around, or a place where transcendence and immanence could come together. Sometimes the American wilderness in these paintings was called American Eden. The Hudson River artists indulged in the loss of paradise. At the same time they reached for the world of illumination, which could be found only as one abandoned the postures of self-reliance of human pride. In a profound way, if unwittingly, the paintings operated with the dynamics of a sermon in the Protestant churches, as they moved from despair to hope. They re-created the dreary reality, which made the need of salvation clear. They welcomed the gift of God's grace and drew it on the canvas.

Protestant art as a medium of theological formation continued to seek its authentic place in a world that emphasized literary clarity. Where beautiful words were valued, literature flourished, as one could observe in the world of Elizabethan and subsequent English literature. Emphasis on literature might offer partial explanation for the relative paucity of art in the English-speaking world, whereas Protestant art bloomed in the Dutch-speaking world, with an exception of the Hudson River School of nineteenth-century New York. Even there, interestingly enough, the area that witnessed the flowering of art had a historical connection with the Dutch culture.

Painting by Faith Alone

In Protestant theology, because salvation was through God's grace alone, the only proper response was FAITH. Typically Protestantism cited Romans 3:28 in support of this doctrine: "For we hold that a person is justified by faith apart from works prescribed by the law" (NRSV). In his translation Luther added the word "alone" to make it by faith *alone*; hence, *sola fide*. This theological posture of *sola fide* constituted the core of the Reformation faith along with *sola scriptura* and *sola gratia*.

From the very start the Reformation theology of *sola fide* made its appearance in art. As early as the sixteenth century, Cranach and his shop focused on the theme of Jesus welcoming children. Cranach's portrayal of "Christ Blessing the Children" featured little ones who offered nothing but trust and warmth toward Christ and other follow children. Most of the young ones in the painting displayed curious intensity to Christ holding one baby in his arms and tending another on a cushion, while other little ones were busy either playing with one another or adoring their mother. A response that required work on the pain of damnation was nowhere in sight on the painting. The theme based on Mark 10:14 had not received the attention Cranach gave to it. The theme was also in support of the infant baptism that Luther continued in contrast with the Anabaptists.

As Protestantism refused to grant any significance to works of faith for salvation, art lost a patron that used to turn to it for penance and devotion, although the freedom of grace also opened a new pathway for art, which now could pursue beauty apart from any ecclesiastical use. One could cite John Ruskin's intense pursuit of truth in the paintings. For Ruskin, a Calvinist, art had no independent value other than pointing to the spiritual meaning of nature. He was always skeptical of attempts to draw a face of Christ because he believed that the divine attributes could not be captured by a painting. Ruskin did not believe that the main function of religious art was to serve piety, but to point to the beauty of the world. God was in the beauty of the artistic form. His renderings of biblical stories did not agree with the text in the Bible, which did not seem to trouble him.

Art of Protest in Protestantism

In spite of the ambiguous relationship between THEOLOGY and aesthetics, art struck its root in Protestantism, given that it served as a persuasive means of illustration of the Scriptures and the theology of reform movement. Because the word "Protestant" originally meant those who stood for a cause, Protestant art also participated in the voicing of protesting spirit in church and society. The undecorated walls of the church buildings were not meant to be a sign of lack of artistic sensitivity, either; it was supposed to make a point that could not be made with traditional religious images that in the Reformers' estimation turned into objects of worship. Once the point of protest was made, Protestant art did not necessarily feel compelled to maintain the bare walls. Later in the nineteenth

century, Protestant churches began reclaiming the decorative interiors in places of worship, sometimes borrowing motifs from Catholic churches. One could find such a trace in the Lutheran Basilica in Berlin and St. John the Divine in New York, whose structure, left unfinished, displayed combination of Byzantine and Gothic elements. In a comparable fashion the churches in England saw the increased use of rituals and art in worship during the OXFORD MOVEMENT that brought the renewal of Catholic faith and practice in the nineteenth century.

The spirit of protest made its appearance in other works that represented social spirituality. These included the avant-garde expressionism of late nineteenth- and early twentieth-century Europe, the abolitionist drawings of nineteenth-century America, and the artworks that called for economic justice and global peace in the twentieth century. Although not limited to the Protestant camps, feminist artworks contributed to raising consciousness concerning the traditional role of genders, and transferring women to the foreground in art and society.

Protestant art, however, was not always critical of society. In the arena of popular culture in America, Protestant art reflected the ethos of INDIVIDUALISM and materialism as well. In the best-known example of Protestant art, Warner Sallman's portrayals of Christ—often referred to as icons of American Protestantism—communicated the intimacy of individual salvation and had a wide appeal to Evangelical taste, as well a type of marketable Christianity with a material Christ. His portrayal of Christ sought some distance from either Christ the mother of the medieval times or Christ the ruler of other times including the great nineteenth century of mission. For modern times Sallman's paintings of Christ offered fascination at a time when religious sensitivity was hungry for images of Christ away from the extremes of the emasculated feeble Christ and the sentimental superman Messiah, even though the multivalent religious sensitivity of the multicultural world might not so easily find peace with the icon of American Protestantism.

Art of Alternative Imagination

PAUL TILLICH argued that artistic symbols could open up a world in which the ultimate concern of human existence could be raised and pursued. He posited four levels in which art and religion could relate to each other: (1) art that did not deal with religion, but with general human existence: for example, impressionistic artists including Monet and Renoir; (2) art that did deal with ultimate concern, but stopped at showing human *unheimlich* finitude: for example, Van Gogh, Picasso, and Chagall; (3) religious art that posed no existential challenge, and therefore ended up being irreligious: for example, Sallman; (4) art religious both in style and in content that provided the correlation between existence and theology: for example, Grünewald's "Crucifixion," which Tillich called the greatest German picture ever painted. Art on the fourth level could communicate the ultimate to the churches—only if they knew what to look for.

In retrospect the Protestant religion may not have been a most welcoming home for art. Even where art was permitted, it was marginalized as a cultural activity that would never occupy the essential place in the life of the church. Nevertheless, Protestant art thrived in its own unique ways. Where the theological orientation of salvation by grace alone and by faith alone created suspicion toward art, Protestantism enabled artists to work on different objects of imagination and to identify alternative approaches to aesthetic representations. In the area of popular religious art Protestantism provided artistic space in which renderings of biblical and religious themes could be experimented within the light of cultural amalgamation, as one could observe in the *mestizaje* of religious art in Latin America and the portrayals of black Christ in African American communities.

In the final analysis Protestantism did not so much block artistic developments as it redirected the focus and the course of artistic pursuits in history. One could observe the impact of the release of the demands of doctrine in the paintings of Hans Holbein the Younger of sixteenth-century Basel. His paintings showed ambivalence toward the ideas of the Reformation. Like other artists of his era, he experimented with observation of physical reality, and drew a rotting body in "Dead Christ in the Tomb" (1521). Around 1530 he decided to abandon religious painting altogether.

GEORG WILHELM FRIEDRICH HEGEL has commonly been credited for defining the vocation of art as an expression of the spirit of its time (*Zeitgeist*). Protestant art has not only reflected the philosophical and aesthetic spirits of its historical times, but also facilitated the formation of the *Zeitgeist*. Art in Protestantism gave expression to the spirit of Protestantism, as it illustrated the biblical text on grace and faith, as it portrayed the pulpit and the table of communion at the center of the life of the church, and as it pursued the beauty of the world unhampered by the doctrines of the church.

See also Architecture, Church; Nature

References and Further Reading

Christensen, Carl C. "Art and the Reformation in Germany." In *Studies in the Reformation 2*. Athens: Ohio University Press, 1979.

Dillenberger, John. "Images and Relics: Theological Perceptions and Visual Images in Sixteenth Century Europe." In *Oxford Studies in Historical Theology.* New York: Oxford University Press, 1999.

Doss, Erika. "Making a 'Virile, Manly Christ': The Cultural Origins and Meanings of Warner Sallman's Religious Imagery." In *Icons of American Protestantism: The Art of Warner Sallman*, edited by David Morgan, 61–94. New Haven and London: Yale University Press, 1996.

Halewood, William H. *Six Subjects of Reformation Art: A Preface to Rembrandt.* Toronto and Buffalo, NY: University of Toronto Press, 1982.

Husch, Gale E. *Something Coming: Apocalyptic Expectation and Mid-Nineteenth-Century American Painting.* Hanover, NH: University Press of New England, 2000.

Jensen, Robin M. "The Arts in Protestant Worship." *Theology Today* 58 no. 3 (2001): 359–368.

Michalski, Serguisz. *The Reformation and the Visual Arts: The Protestant Image Question in Western and Eastern Europe.* London and New York: Routledge, 1993.

Morgan, David. *Protestant & Pictures: Religion, Visual Culture, and the Age of American Mass Production.* New York: Oxford University Press, 1999.

Moxey, Keith P. F. *Peasants, Warriors, and Wives: Popular Imagery in the Reformation.* Chicago: University of Chicago Press, 1989.

Promey, Sally M. *Painting Religion in Public: John Singer Sargent's Triumph of Religion at the Boston Public Library.* Princeton, NJ: Princeton University Press, 1999.

Smith, Jeffrey Chipps. *German Sculpture of the Later Renaissance, c. 1520–1580. Art in an Age of Uncertainty.* Princeton, NJ: Princeton University Press, 1994.

Tillich, Paul. *On Art and Architecture.* Edited by John Dillenberger. New York: Crossroad, 1987.

Veith, Gene Edward. *Painters of Faith: The Spiritual Landscape in Nineteenth-Century America.* Washington, DC: Regnery Publishers, 2001.

JIN HEE HAN

ASBURY, FRANCIS (1745–1816)

Methodist bishop. Francis Asbury was born to Joseph and Elizabeth Asbury on August 19 or 20 of 1745, about four miles north of Birmingham, England. Although both Elizabeth and Joseph were affectionately caring parents, providing a deeply religious home life for young Franky, it was Elizabeth who seemed to have taken the greatest care and time in nurturing him on Scripture and the deeper matters of God. At the age of six he was fluently reading the Scriptures. Later, Asbury would recall in his *Journal,* "I learned from my parents a certain form of words for prayer, and I well remember my mother strongly urged my father to family reading and prayer; the singing of psalms was much practiced by them both" (*Journal,* 1:720).

Many of Asbury's biographers have deemed that the earlier formative years, while he was at home, would prove to offer some of the most important education he would receive. Just exactly when Francis was sent to school is unknown, but it is known that his formal education abruptly ended before the age of ten.

Excessive beating by his tutor Arthur Taylor was not the kind of motivation to learning that would keep the young lad in school. Again, in his *Journal*, Asbury would recall his early childhood struggles at school:

My foible was the ordinary foible of children—fondness for play; but I abhorred mischief and wickedness, although my mates were amongst the vilest of the vile for lying, swearing, fighting, and whatever else boys of their age and evil habits were likely to be guilty of: from such society I very often returned home uneasy and melancholy; and although driven away by my better principles, still I would return hoping to find happiness where I never found it. Sometimes I was much ridiculed, and called Methodist Parson, because my mother invited any people who had the appearance of religion to her house. (*Journal*, 1:720)

Asbury's last traveling companion, John Wesley Bond, conveyed what may be one of the earliest known occurrences of God's indelible providence, on young Francis:

The Bishop's Father being a gardener by trade, used to put up his gardening tools, consisting of long shears, pruning saws, hoes, rakes, etc. in this place (a room attached to the house). One day Francis (the only son) was left in this upper room; nor was his danger thought of until his Father, called to his Mother said, "Where is the Lad; I heard him cry." His mother ran into the room and found he had crawled into a hole in the floor and fallen through. But by the kind providence of God the gardening tools had been recently removed, and a larger boiler nearly filled with ashes put in their place, into which he fell; this broke his fall, or the world most probably would have been forever deprived of the labours of Bishop Asbury. (Bull 1965:10)

The constant sense of God's providence in young Asbury's life would grow stronger with the years. After all, young Franky would grow up in a home where devotional meetings, Bible studies and prayer meetings were more the norm than the exception. Asbury's first recollection of religious awakening began around the age of seven, whereby he began to regularly read the Scripture. At the age of thirteen, a "traveling shoe maker who called himself a Baptist" (Bull 1965:25) was influential in another religious awakening. Bond records Asbury's recollections:

He held prayer meetings in our neighborhood, and my Mother who was a praying woman, and ready to encourage any one who appeared to wish to do good; invited him to hold a prayer-meeting at My Father's house. At that meeting I was convinced there was something more in religion than I had ever been acquainted with. And at one of these meetings, held by this man, I obtained that comfort I had been seeking. (Bull 1965:25)

Gradually, along with the influence of Alexander Mather, Asbury would find greater assurance in his spiritual awakening and full devotion to God.

I was then about fifteen; [says Asbury] and, young as I was, the word of God soon made deep impressions on my heart, which brought me to Jesus Christ, who graciously justified my guilty soul through faith in his precious blood; and soon showed me the excellency and necessity of holiness. About sixteen I experienced a marvelous display of the grace of God, which some might think was full sanctification, and was indeed very happy, ... At about seventeen I began to hold some public meetings; and between seventeen and eighteen began to exhort and preach. (*Journal*, 1:124–125)

Between the ages of seventeen and twenty, Asbury began his preaching venture at his mother's devotional meetings and in and around Birmingham, England. Eventually, after three or four years of routine preaching, Asbury traveled to London (August 1767) for admission, on a trial basis, to the Methodist Conference. The following summer, he was admitted into "full connection" of the Methodist Conference in Bristol. From this conference, he would be stationed at Colchester as a "circuit rider." Four years later, after having expressed a strong desire to visit America, the Methodist Conference, in Bristol, on Tuesday, August 6, 1771, granted that desire and appointed Asbury to America.

On Wednesday, September 4, 1771 Francis Asbury and Richard Wright, the two appointees of the Methodist Conference, set sail from the port of Pill near Bristol for America and landed on the shores of Philadelphia on Sunday, October 27, 1771. Upon arrival with a heart full of hope and vision, Asbury reflected on his first thoughts: "When I came near the American shore, my very heart melted within me, to think from whence I came, where I was going, and what I was going about" (*Journal*, 1:7). The very next day Asbury preached his first sermon in America.

At the end of Asbury's first full year on the circuit in America, he would be confronted to the core of his identity as an itinerant preacher with the very problems and issues that would eventually become the very making of his genius and legacy. The lack of adherence to the *General Rules*, poor organization, and lack of method for how to plant METHODISM in the colonies, as well as the omission of ordinances in the Methodist Societies, were just a few of the kinds of problems and issues that would show how capable Asbury was in bringing cohesion to the Methodist Societies.

Some of those problems would be resolved in 1784, when JOHN WESLEY appointed Asbury and THOMAS COKE as joint superintendents. Asbury, however, would insist that the Conference of Methodist preachers ratify his appointment. Against Wesley's wishes, Asbury assumed the title of bishop.

Asbury was indefatigable in his itinerancy and preaching. Despite his numerous ailments and ill health throughout a good portion of his life, Asbury relentlessly pushed on in his preaching and disciplined use of time for the spread of the Gospel through preaching. Undoubtedly Asbury more than Coke was the dominant shaping force in American Methodism.

Confidence in America's bishop should come as no surprise when one understands that of all Wesley's appointees, Asbury chose to remain in America during the Revolutionary War whereas most of the English itinerants returned home. After a long process of internal soul searching Asbury had begun to identify with the emerging birth of the American nation, although that would not mean that Asbury would always stand in agreement with the ethos of America, especially when it came to the issue of SLAVERY. Initially Asbury openly condemned slavery, but when confronted with the harshness of slavery in the deep South, and with what an inflexible stand against slavery might do to the conference, he acquiesced and made a distinction between saving souls and liberating bodies.

> We are defrauded of great numbers by the pains that are taken to keep the blacks from us; their masters are afraid of the influence of our principles. Would not an amelioration in the condition and treatment of slaves have produced more practical good to the poor Africans, than any attempt at their emancipation? (*Journal*, 2:591)

Francis Asbury died at George Arnold's farm in Spotsylvania (near Fredericksburg), Virginia on March 31, 1816 (Bull 1965:7). On October 15, 1924, president Calvin Coolidge, who considered Asbury as "one of the builders of our nation," unveiled an equestrian statue of Francis Asbury. The inscription on the statue reads: "His courageous journeying through each village and settlement from 1771 to 1816 greatly promoted patriotism, education, morality and religion in the American Republic."

See also Circuit Rider; Itineracy; Methodism, North America

References and Further Reading

Primary Sources:

Asbury, Francis. *The Causes, Evils and Cures of Heart and Church Divisions*. Salem, OH: Schmul Publishers, 1978.
———, Thomas Coke, eds. *Doctrines and Discipline of the Methodist Episcopal Church in America With Explanatory Notes*. Philadelphia: Henry Tuckniss, 1798.
———. *The Journal and Letters of Francis Asbury*. Edited by Elmer Clark, J. Manning Potts, and Jacob S. Payton. London: Epworth Press, 1958.

Secondary Sources:

Atkinson, John. *Centennial History of American Methodism, Inclusive of its Ecclesiastical Organization in 1784 and its Subsequent Development under the Superintendency of Francis Asbury*. New York; Phillips & Hunt; Cincinnati: Cranston & Stowe, 1884.
———. *Francis Asbury's Last Journey*. Greensboro, NC: Christian Advocate, 1955.
Bull, Robert J. "George Roberts' Reminiscences of Francis Asbury." *Methodist History* 5, no. 4 (July 1967): 25–35.
Ellis, Joseph J. *Founding Brothers*. New York: Alfred A. Knopf, 2000.
Feeman, Harlan. *Francis Asbury's Silver Trumpet*. Nashville, TN: Parthenon, 1950.
Lewis, James. *Francis Asbury: Bishop of the Methodist Episcopal Church*. London: The Epworth Press, 1927.
Salter, Darius. *America's Bishop: Life of Francis Asbury*. Nappanee, IN: Evangel Press, 2003.

K. STEVE MCCORMICK

ASCETICISM

When applied to religion, asceticism may be broadly defined as acts and attitudes of world-renunciation and self-discipline taken up for the sake of religious goals. The sociologist MAX WEBER famously argued for the existence of a particularly Protestant form of "inner-worldly" asceticism. Weber claimed that where most forms of asceticism involved flight from the world, the Protestant idea of the calling placed the world-renouncing impulse of asceticism within the roles and structures of ordinary life. Weber argued further that SECULARIZATION transformed Protestant asceticism into the driving spirit of modern capitalism. Subsequent arguments for and against Weber's theory highlight the importance of understanding varieties of ascetic behavior in their diverse historical contexts.

Origins and Definitions

Although any definition of asceticism will likely be controversial, the term when applied to religion has come to suggest a range of acts and attitudes of world-renunciation and self-discipline through which religious practitioners seek to approach certain transcendent goals. World-renunciation and self-discipline generally involve some degree of rejection of the world or worldly things and chastisement of the body or of the self more broadly understood. At the same time, the world and the body are the vehicles for the performance of asceticism.

The term *asceticism* is derived from the Greek *askesis*, a word that originally signified rigorous athletic or military "training." In ancient Greek philosophical discourse, the meaning of *askesis* broadened over time to indicate a training of mind and soul as well as body, with moral or spiritual goals. The origins of a particularly Christian ascetic theory and practice have been hotly contested. One strand of Protestant interpretation has denied the presence of asceticism in the BIBLE, especially the New Testament, arguing that ascetic currents entered the Christian tradition at a later date, perhaps through the influence of Greek culture. Some biblical scholars have questioned this assertion, however, arguing that both ascetic and antiascetic currents may be found in the earliest Christian literature.

By late antiquity ascetic ideas and practices such as fasting and CELIBACY were clearly visible within early Christianity, and the role of asceticism in the holy life was much debated. The development of MONASTICISM provided an institutional setting for the practice of Christian asceticism that flourished throughout the medieval period. At the same time, some Christian ascetics followed alternate paths, from the solitary anchorite to the wandering mendicant friar. Even though some forms of asceticism were condemned as heresy by Christian authorities, nevertheless a diversity of ascetic theories and practices remained.

A Reformation Debate

In the second decade of the sixteenth century, MARTIN LUTHER inaugurated what would become the Protestant rejection of certain ascetic traditions, arguing that Catholic ascetic theory and practice flew in the face of both human nature and divine will. Luther claimed that the Catholic theory that merit might be acquired through acts of ascetic renunciation wrongly credited human works, rather than God's GRACE, for bringing about the SALVATION of believers. Luther insisted further that traditional ascetic practices, most prominently celibacy and monastic vows, interposed human inventions in place of institutions ordained by God, such as MARRIAGE and the calling or VOCATION. Subsequent reformers, particularly JOHN CALVIN, expanded this conception of the calling and placed it at the center of the Christian life lived in fulfillment of God's will. Most Protestant theologians, however, still advocated world-renunciation and self-discipline as crucial parts of the Christian life. Luther and Calvin both promoted redefinitions of celibacy, chastity, self-mortification, and other fundamentals of the ascetic tradition even as they denounced asceticism's Catholic forms.

Protestant Asceticism

The concept of the vocation or calling, particularly its Calvinist variant, was crucial to Max Weber's account of ascetic Protestantism and its relation to modern capitalism. In *The Protestant Ethic and the Spirit of Capitalism*, first published in 1904–1905, Weber ar-

gued that the Calvinist conception of the calling demanded both rigor of work and austerity of life in fulfillment of God's will. An unintended consequence of this combination of rigor and austerity, which Weber called the "Protestant ethic," was the accumulation of capital. Gradually, Weber asserted, the Protestant ethic came unmoored from its religious goals, but the habits it had inculcated continued to be passed on in cultures formed by the Calvinist tradition. This secularized Protestant ethic became the "spirit" of modern capitalism, now promoting the accumulation of capital as a good in its own right rather than as a sign of God's approval, as Weber argued it had been for the later Calvinists.

Historians of Protestantism have offered diverse responses to Weber, arguing over whether and why it may be useful to speak of aspects of the Protestant tradition as ascetic. Proponents of the concept of Protestant asceticism suggest that it illumines continuities between Protestant ideology and practice and the medieval Christian tradition from which it grew. Opponents emphasize the sixteenth-century Protestant rejection of medieval Catholic ascetic theory and practice to argue that the foundations of Protestantism are profoundly antiascetic. The theological diversity of Protestantism (LUTHERANISM, CALVINISM, ANGLICANISM, Radical Reformation) also raises the question of the need for greater specificity. The concept of Protestant asceticism has provided a useful window into continuities with medieval Catholicism that polemic on both sides has tended to obscure. At the same time the ascetic theory and practice of the Protestant tradition did not originate apart from the sixteenth-century Protestant rejection of certain aspects of the Catholic tradition. Any theory of Protestant asceticism must therefore take this aspect of its origins into account.

References and Further Reading

Clark, Elizabeth. *Reading Renunciation: Asceticism and Scripture in Early Christianity*. Princeton, NJ: Princeton University Press, 1999.

Harrington, Joel. *Reordering Marriage and Society in Reformation Germany*. Cambridge, UK: Cambridge University Press, 1995.

Vaage, Lief E., and Vincent L. Wimbush. *Asceticism and the New Testament*. New York: Routledge, 1999.

Weber, Max. *The Protestant Ethic and the Spirit of Capitalism*. Translated by Talcott Parsons. London: George Allen & Unwin, 1930.

———. *The Sociology of Religion*. Translated by Ephraim Fischoff. Boston: Beacon Press, 1963.

Wimbush, Vincent L., and Richard Valantasis, eds. *Asceticism*. New York: Oxford University Press, 1995.

DEBORAH K. MARCUSE

ASIAN THEOLOGY

Christianity in Asia has a history as long as the history of Christianity that began in the land of Jesus's birth in the first century. It is, however, in the second half of the twentieth century that theology in Asia came to develop, first dutifully paying respect to Western church traditions and schools of theological thought, then boldly striking out on its own to manifest its originality and creativeness.

For Christian theology in Asia as well as for the world of Asia 1945 was a decisive year. In that year the World War II that devastated the Western civilization that had been shaped by Christianity came to an end. In the same year the Pacific War that rendered countless homes in ruins and millions of people dead in Asia came to a grinding halt. As the Western domination of Asia and the colonization of Asian peoples began to retreat, nation-building began in earnest in many Asian nations that had gained political independence. Women and men of Asia regained the sense of their own history. Their creative power for arts and literature was released from its captivity. Moreover, the resurgence of their centuries-old cultures and religions revitalized their cultural and religious activities; it also reclaimed the allegiance of the great majority of the people of Asia for their traditional faiths and morals.

While all this was happening, most Christians in Asia and their leaders watched as bystanders, aloof and bewildered. On the whole they were defensive, separating themselves from what was happening around them. Most of them, regardless of their Christian affiliations and backgrounds, drew a clear line between the church and the world around the church. They were taught to believe that the church had no business beyond its four walls. In what they believed and how they practiced their faith, they were very much a part of the Christian traditions they had inherited from the West, from church ARCHITECTURE to WORSHIP and of course to THEOLOGY. Christian theology in particular did not grow and develop beyond what had been imported from the West. It was uncritical adherence to the Western theological tenets only with varied emphases and nuances. In the process the Spirit was internalized and domesticated as the power bringing about personal SALVATION.

Since the year 1945 Christian theology has entered a new day. It has started a process of growth and development. It is a process bound not only to affect what Christians in Asia believe and how they practice Christian faith, but to reshape their experience of what God is doing in Asia. With different degrees of success Christian theology has crossed the line drawn between the church and the world of Asia in which

Christianity came to stay. It has begun to cast its eyes on vast resources available in Asia—historical, social, cultural, and religious—resources that are not related to the Christianity that had come from beyond Asian shores. Christian theology has awakened from its innocence and begun to grapple with what Christian faith means and what it stands for in its adopted lands. In this process of exploration and reorientation Christian theology will have to come face to face with Jesus, the very origin and heart of their faith, and wrestle with the meaning of his message and ministry in the world of Asia with many cultures and religions different from the culture and religion represented by Christianity in the West.

Just as the history of development in other fields of human activity and endeavor, Christian theology in Asia as a process of growth and development has had several stages. It has gone through the stages of adoption and imitation, accommodation and adaptation, contextualization and indigenization, deconstruction and reconstruction, culminating in the Christian theology grown out of the interactions between the stories of women and men in the BIBLE and the stories of women and men in Asia. It does not mean that these stages follow a chronological order, with one stage coming to an end to be succeeded by the next one. These stages in the process of growth and development often overlap one with the other, with the seed of the subsequent stage sown in the previous stage. A particular orientation can, however, be discerned in each stage in the process, the orientation that proves to be inadequate and thus gives way to the orientation in the next stage.

Adoption and Imitation

When children begin at an early age to practice Chinese calligraphy, they are instructed to copy Chinese characters written by master calligraphers over and over again until the characters they reproduce bear some resemblance to those of master calligraphers. With this painstaking ground work, some of the children will grow up to become master calligraphers themselves. Christian theology attempted in the nineteenth century and in the first half of the twentieth century was largely similar to the practice of Chinese calligraphy.

Christianity in those days was a foreign religion, a religion from the West. Very few original efforts were made to express Christian faith in a different way. As a matter of fact, deviation from the traditional formulations of faith, ways of worship, and HYMNS sung at the worship service was considered to be deviation from the Christian truth. What was taught at theological schools was the wholesale adoption of Christianity and adherence to it was considered to be a matter of primary importance. What dominated the theological discussion was different schools of Western theological thoughts and different theological emphases of diverse confessions and DENOMINATIONS. Christian mission, understood almost totally as efforts to evangelize people of Asia, had priority over theology. What concerned Christian theology in Asia in this adoption and imitation stage was not so much exploration of God's saving activity among people of Asia as the increase of the number of Christians and churches in Asia. Christian mission was the overriding preoccupation over and above all other interests.

Christian theology in Asia at this stage was an imitation theology. This was not only true of the fundamentalist Christianity that still exerts influence on many Christians and churches today, but also true of its more "liberal" counterparts. Names of prominent Western theologians were invoked, and their writings occupied bookshelves of the library and adorned the study of theological teachers. Theological debates at this stage were debates of Western theologians by proxy. It was very easy to identify theological centers in the West where most Asian theologians had done their advanced theological studies.

Accommodation and Adaptation

It became clear, however, that the "soil and water" of Asia proved to be not entirely hospitable to the Christianity that grew and developed in other "soil and water." It was discovered that unless Christianity acclimatized itself to the vastly different natural environments, it would remain a foreign religion in its adopted land: to this day Christianity in Asia still largely remains a foreign religion in the eyes of most people outside the Christian church. It was a matter of necessity that Christian theology had to set in motion the process of accommodation and adaptation.

Accommodation and adaptation were taking place almost unaware even to the firm believers in the "purity" of the Christian faith as the Bible was being rendered into the vernacular. Some Bible translators knew better. They knew that language is a universe of meaning rooted in the cultural tradition and religious faith of the people who speak it. When the Bible was rendered into the local language, the message it contains reached its hearers and readers not always the way it was intended by its translators. The message of the Bible heard was already adapted and accommodated to the world of meaning that had shaped the local community for ages. Theology, diverting from Western expressions of faith, was subtly in the making among Christian converts at the grass roots level,

largely unnoticed by many of those engaged in theological efforts in Asia.

Not so subtle were some theological efforts made, for example, in INDIA and CHINA, to express Christian faith in relation to local realities and idioms. Both India and China, among many Asian countries, have developed most sophisticated philosophical systems, elaborate religious traditions, and complex ethical codes. There was no lack of concepts, ideas, and idioms for Christian usage, and some theological efforts were made to express what Christianity believed and taught in those concepts and idioms. The concept of "heaven" in China, for instance, was adapted to Christian use as a personal God involved in human affairs. "Filial piety," the backbone of Confucian ethics, was stressed as essential for Christianity to gain the hearts of Chinese people. In India Hinduism was thought to be compatible with Christianity and terms such as *dharma* (cosmic law), *satyagraha* (truth force), or *bhakti* (devotion) found their way into Christianity. As Christian theology ventured out into the world outside Christianity in this way, it had to make it clear that even though form and language might change, the substance of the Christian truth would not change. It proved wrong, however. How it was wrong became the hotly debated issue in the ensuing years. The issue continues to be debated passionately in the churches and in theological schools in Asia today. Christian theology in Asia at this stage of accommodation and adaptation succeeded only in a kind of hybrid theology that did little justice either to Christian theology or to the other religions.

Contextualization and Indigenization

In retrospect there was a positive side to the attempts at accommodation and adaptation. These attempts taught many Christian theologians in Asia to take their Asian contexts seriously, and not just to use them as means and instruments of communicating the Christian faith. Unfortunately, this instrumental approach to cultures and religions still prevails among many Christian churches and theological circles in Asia today. Its chief concern is not to explore theological meanings embedded in those cultures and religions unrelated to Christianity, but to familiarize themselves with the religious idioms and cultural forms so that they can better communicate the Christian gospel they hold to be unique and absolute.

However, cracks were already made in the theological dams constructed by Christian theology in the previous times. With new awareness of the historical, cultural, and religious situations fundamentally different from those from which Christianity came, Christian theology in Asia began to take a course of its own, moving to another stage in the process of growth and development, even though it was still at an embryonic stage.

What dawned on Christian theological efforts in Asia at this stage is as follows: if the message of the Bible allowed itself to be planted in Western soil to give birth to what is known as Western theology, there is no reason why the same message of the Bible would not allow itself to be planted in Asian soil to give birth to Christian theology in Asia. In the midst of such theological effort, however, it was still assumed that the message of the Bible remained unchanged, even though the social-political and cultural-religious situations the gospel had entered were different from those of the Bible and of the West.

Christian theology developed in this way was thought to be indigenous to Asia. Because Asia consists of a great diversity of situations, Christian theology was bound to take diverse shapes, sizes, and colors, although the message was believed to remain unchanged—the message that Jesus was the only savior of the world and for the people of Asia. The awareness of Asia being different from the West paved the way for the growth and development of Christian theology in the next stage. Even though the central assertion of Christian faith was believed to remain the same, Christian theology in Asia came to have more and more local flavors and tastes, making itself more appealing to the theological appetite of Christians and more accessible to the local people unfamiliar with the history of Christianity in the West. What happened at this stage is that Christian theology came to be more contextualized and indigenized at least in form, although not always in contents.

Deconstruction and Reconstruction

It is to be expected, however, that when the form changes, the contents expressed through the changed and changing form cannot remain unchanged for ever. Christian theology in Asia thus entered the stage of deconstruction and reconstruction. It was the stage in which Christian theology finally began to grow and develop in the terms not dictated by others but informed by the historical realities people of Asia have to face in their daily lives. It has to learn to speak out of the world of Asia as well as out of the world of the Bible. What proved to be a matter of crucial importance was the fact that Christian theology in Asia found the key to unlock the barrier used to separate the two worlds—the world of the Bible and the world of Asia. That key was people both in the Bible and in Asia, both people in search of God and God in search of people. It was a theology grown out of interactions between God and people in the quest of the meaning

of life and history. The story of God looking for the first ancestors in the garden of Eden told in the third chapter of Genesis in Hebrew Scripture gained a deeper meaning in relation to the engagement of people and God within the spiritual universe of the people of Asia. Obviously the theological effort of deconstruction and reconstruction is an ongoing effort, constantly engaging Christian theology in its attempt to decipher how God is working out God's purpose in Asia.

Christian theology in Asia had to question time-honored theological concepts and find new ways to express theological realities it encountered. It was not as hard as it had been believed to be. What was required of it was simply to ask, for example, whether Asia had already been part of God's creation before its contact with Christianity, whether God's saving love included the great majority of the people of Asia who have remained outside Christianity, whether God acted in Asia only by way of Christianity from the West.

Questions such as these were of crucial importance because they challenged the theological assumption that Christians alone could claim birthright in God. This was a theological breakthrough. Once the breakthrough was made, Christian theology is now ready to develop and grow beyond the boundaries of the Christian church, believing that God is at work both outside the Christian church as well as inside it, in some cases more outside it than inside it.

In recent years Christian theology in Asia has learned to grow with people, both Christians and others, as they struggle for human rights and democracy, as they seek to be part of the spiritual forces in Asia to renew people and change society, as they work hand in hand with those who are exploited by the complicity of domestic and global economy and subjected to discrimination against women in male-dominated society. It is a theology inspired by Jesus's declaration when he first launched his mission and ministry of God's reign saying: "The Spirit of the Lord is upon me, because the Lord has anointed me to bring good news to the poor. The Lord has sent me to proclaim release to the captives and recovery of sight to the blind, to let the oppressed go free, to proclaim the year of the Lord's favor" (Luke 4:18–19). This "Mission Manifesto" of Jesus has come to be recognized not only as social activism but also revealing the spiritual depths of Jesus's engagement with people in the ministry of God's reign in the world.

Stories of God and Stories of People

Christian theology in Asia, varied in forms and idioms, has now developed into the story theology that gives account of how stories of God get embodied in stories of people of Asia and how stories of people of Asia respond to God's story embodied in their lives and histories. It has broken the boundaries set by the Christian theology constructed in the past. Its task is not to make systems of beliefs but to tell stories, not to come to people with a set of presuppositions of faith it learned by rote but to give accounts of God in the company of women and men in their daily lives, not to dictate what people should believe and confess but to learn to get closer to the heart of God by telling their stories.

Asia with its colossal land mass and exploding population, Asia abundant both in joys and sorrows, and Asia with inexhaustible sources of people's stories has to be the arena of Christian theology in Asia today. Engaging God and people in the rich soil and water of Asia, Christian theology has endless stories to tell. It has just begun its first chapter to be followed by many, many more chapters.

Christian theology in Asia has at last found what its main task should be. It has to find its way into the heart of millions upon millions of people in Asia, learning to tell their stories and fathom theological meanings hidden in the depths of these stories. This is a new start for Christian theology in Asia. In telling people's stories, Christian theology should be able to tell quite different stories about creation and its Creator, about God's love manifested in Jesus, about the Spirit as the power of God creating and recreating Asia through tribulations and celebrations of the life of the people of Asia. Out of such theological engagement with people and their stories, Christian theology will be able to help Christians and churches nurture self-understanding not derived from elsewhere outside Asia, but from God's saving activity in Asia. It will also enable Christians and churches in Asia to forge new relationships with their Asian neighbors and the world of Asia. A new stage for Christian theology is thus already set, and time will tell how Christian theology in Asia will play with a whole variety of actors on the stage, acting out a whole variety of scenarios in response to God's engagement with the people of Asia since the beginning of creation. It has found its theological home in Asia and in the teeming humanity who inhabit Asia.

See also Architecture, Church; Bible; China; Denominations; Fundamentalism; Hymns and Hymnals; India; Japan; Liberal Protestantism; Missions; Philippines; Salvation; Theology; Worship

References and Further Reading

Elwood, Douglas J. *What Asian Christians Are Thinking.* Quezon City, Philippines: New Day Publishers, 1976.

England, John, ed. *Living Theology in Asia.* Maryknoll, NY: Orbis Book, 1982.

Kim, Yong Bok, ed. *Minjung Theology.* People as the Subjects of History, Hong Kong: The Christian Conference of Asia, 1981.

Kosuke, Koyama. *Water Buffalo Theology.* Maryknoll, NY: Orbis Books, 1972; rev. ed., 1999.

Kwok, Pui-lan. *Discovering the Bible in the Non-Biblical World.* Maryknoll, NY: Orbis Books,1995.

Kyunq, Chung Hyun. *Struggle to Be The Sun Again. Introducing Asian Women's Theology.* Maryknoll, NY: Orbis Books, 1990.

Pierls, Aloycius. *An Asian Theology of Liberation.* Maryknoll, NY: Orbis, 1988.

Song, C. S. *The Believing Heart. An Invitation to Story Theology.* Minneapolis, MN; Fortress Press, 1999.

———. *Third Eve Theology, Theology in Formation in Asian Settings.* Maryknoll, NY: Orbis Books, 1979; rev. ed., 1990.

Sugirtharajah, R. S., ed. *Voices From the Margin. Interpreting the Bible in the Third World.* Maryknoll, NY: Orbis Books, 1991.

———, ed. *Asian Faces of Jesus.* Maryknoll, NY: Orbis Books, 1993.

———, ed. *Frontiers in Asian Christian Theology: Emerging Trends.* Maryknoll, NY: Orbis, 1994.

CHOAN-SENG SONG

ASIAN-AMERICAN PROTESTANTISM

The terms "Asian American" and/or "Asian and Pacific Islander American" have been convenient (and contested) means of classifying the nearly 13 million persons residing in the UNITED STATES who trace their roots to Asia and Oceania. But the Asian-American racial category belies the extraordinary ethnic and socioeconomic diversity of this population. The practice of lumping together Central Asians (Pakistani, Afghan, Burmese), South Asians (Indians), Southeast Asians (Thai, Vietnamese, Hmong, Filipinos, Malay), East Asians (Chinese, Japanese, Korean), and Pacific Islanders (Polynesian, Micronesian, Melanesian) is a disservice to each group's unique history and culture. It also does not alter the common perception that identifies Asian Americans with East Asians. The limitations of the term "Asian American" notwithstanding, this article attempts a historical overview of Asian-American Protestants.

According to the American Religious Identification Survey conducted by the City University of New York in 2001, 28% of the Asian-American population identified themselves as practitioners of "Asian" religions (Buddhism, Hinduism, Islam, etc), and 43% profess to be Christians. The majority of the Christians appear to be Protestants, although more precise figures are difficult to ascertain. Nevertheless, it is safe to say that Protestants represent a very significant presence among Asian Americans, past and present.

History of Asian-American Immigration

The patterns of Asian migration to the United States and the Americas are products of the increasing global socioeconomic and political strength of the United States since the mid-nineteenth century. American commercial ventures in CHINA and JAPAN, as well as its colonial experiment in the PHILIPPINES, created opportunities for persons from these countries to immigrate to the Americas. In the mid- to late nineteenth century, internal unrest and dramatic social changes in China and Japan, coupled with a high demand for cheap labor in the American West, created global "push-pull" factors for Chinese and Japanese immigration. After Chinese and Japanese immigration was banned, Filipinos were recruited to fill the labor demand in the 1920s and 30s. Before World War II, the Japanese and Chinese populations in the United States reached 150,000 and 107,000, respectively. Before World War II, the Filipino population reached 40,000. The Protestant presence among these three groups was rather small, but more is known about Chinese and Japanese Protestants than about Filipino Protestants.

Despite the factors that drew Chinese, Japanese, and Filipino immigrants to Hawaii and the United States, American public opinion grew increasingly hostile toward Asians and eventually led to the discriminatory Chinese Exclusion Act in 1882, the proscription of Japanese and Indian Asian immigration in 1924, and the banning of Filipinos (despite their status as American nationals) in 1934. Although the Chinese Exclusion Act was repealed in 1943, racially discriminatory restrictions were not ended until 1965. By then, the Chinese, Japanese, and Filipino population had become a small, but significant, presence in the United States (particularly in the Western states). Historians have often labeled this population the "first wave" of Asian immigrants.

After 1965, a large influx of immigrants from KOREA, INDIA, Southeast Asia, and other Asian and Pacific areas added to the Asian-American population. The Asian population in the United States has nearly doubled each decade since 1965. The Chinese and Filipino populations also experienced tremendous growth, making them the two largest Asian ethnic groups in the United States today. Only the Japanese population experienced decline, because of the near cessation of immigration from Japan. A significant presence of indigenous Protestants among this "second wave" of Asian immigration has recently drawn some attention among sociologists of religion, although much of this scholarship has focused on non-Christian Asian immigrants.

First Wave of Chinese and Japanese Protestants in America

Although the origins of Asian-American Protestantism can be traced to the American Protestant missionary enterprise in the nineteenth and early twentieth centuries, it is important to underscore the "indigenous" character of Asian conversions. Asian-American relationships with white Protestants and missionaries were complex, requiring sensitivity to the historical contexts in Asia as well as in the United States. Thus, the Diasporic Chinese subculture in Southeast Asia, the socioeconomic situation in Kwangtung Province from where the overwhelming majority of first-wave Chinese immigrants came, and a rapidly modernizing Meiji Japan provides a rich and necessary context for understanding Chinese and Japanese Protestantism in the United States during this period.

The first Asian-American Protestant congregation, Presbyterian Church in Chinatown, was organized in San Francisco in 1852 by a small group of Chinese Christian immigrants who had studied at the Morrison School in Macao. By the 1870s, Methodist, Congregational, and Baptist missions were formed in the San Francisco Bay area, Sacramento, and other urban centers with a significant Chinese presence. In these missions, the presence of white missionaries was vital to Chinese Christians' survival and ability to negotiate the increasingly hostile social climate.

Until the mid-twentieth century, the Chinese missions served an overwhelmingly male Chinese population. Immigration restrictions and cultural practices sharply limited the population of Chinese women. Because the Chinese American community was a "bachelor" society, the Chinese missions did not place a strong emphasis on family life. Family-oriented Chinese congregations would not appear until the 1940s, when the women and American-born children became a significant presence in the Chinese American community. The presence of missionary women in the congregations, schools, and rescue missions provided role models for Chinese Protestant women. Many of the American-born women would eventually assume public leadership roles,

Because male Japanese migrants were able to bring wives ("picture brides") from overseas until 1924, the Japanese congregations were composed of more stable and traditional families than the Chinese missions. Consequently, Japanese congregations were less dependent on Protestant denominations during this time. First-wave Chinese and Japanese American Protestant leaders exhibited strong nationalistic tendencies. As much, if not more, attention was given to developments in China and Japan than to American affairs. Furthermore, these leaders were as interested in Asian politics as they were in Asian evangelization. Indeed, nationalism was one of the strongest motives for Chinese and Japanese identification with Protestantism during this period. Many believed that Protestantism provided an effective critique of premodern Chinese and Japanese societies and had the potential to rebuild these nations into powerful, modern Christian democracies.

The pivotal turning points for the first-wave Japanese and Chinese Protestants were the Japanese American internment camp experience during World War II and the Communist victory in China in 1949. These events spurred a period of mainline Protestant emphasis on integration and assimilation. Ministry programs for Asian Americans were dismantled in the 1950s (e.g., the discontinuation of the Methodist Oriental Conference).

The relocation camps uprooted many Japanese families and resulted in a tremendous loss of monies and property. Afterward, some churches reorganized on the west coast, but the cessation of Japanese immigration and denominational pressures on the Nisei (second-generation Japanese Americans) to assimilate into mainstream American society challenged the viability of many congregations (although many became self-supporting). Nevertheless, some ecumenical organizations, such as the Japanese Christian Church Federation, survived.

As Communist China was drawn into the Korean conflict and the Cold War in the 1950s, pressures on Chinese Americans to demonstrate loyalty and assimilability, along with the loss of mainline engagement in missionary work in China, left many Chinese American Protestants relatively neglected. Despite an increasing Chinese immigration population and the call from Chinese American leaders for the support of ethnic ministries, mainline Protestants were in large part nonresponsive. The formation of the National Conference on Chinese Christians in America in 1955 in part represented an attempt to justify the necessity of ethnic-specific congregations.

In the late 1960s and early 1970s, Japanese and Chinese Protestants inspired by the CIVIL RIGHTS and ethnic consciousness movements began to advocate for greater Asian-American representation and ministry in their denominations. Repudiating the assimilationist policies of mainline denominations, caucuses were formed amidst a growing sense of Asian-American consciousness. Even as they noted the impact of a rapidly growing second-wave Asian immigration population, neither the caucus leaders nor the mainline Protestant denominations were prepared for the explosion of ethnic and theological diversity that occurred in the 1980s and 1990s.

Second-Wave Asian-American Immigrants

While Filipino, Korean, and other Asian Pacific American Protestants established missions and congregations before 1965, these entities became much more visible during the last quarter of the twentieth century. Although Roman Catholic affiliation was higher among Filipino and Vietnamese Americans, there was a growing Protestant (specifically, evangelical and Pentecostal-charismatic) presence in these communities. In fact, the 3,000 Korean, 1,000 Chinese, and hundreds of other second-wave Asian and Pacific American congregations today are predominantly evangelical and Pentecostal-charismatic in orientation. Unlike the first-wave Asian Americans, who preferred to maintain close ties to mainline Protestant denominations, the second-wave Asian-American Protestants exhibit stronger "separatist" tendencies. Although most Korean and many other Asian congregations are affiliated with a mainline denomination, their level of engagement and interest in these denominations is rather low compared to that of first-wave Asian-American Protestants.

The "separatist" evangelical-Pentecostal characteristics of most second-wave Asian-American Protestants can be traced to a number of sources. The continuing presence of fundamentalist and evangelical missionary work that continued throughout the mid-twentieth century influenced at least one generation of immigrants. Also, the "separatist" evangelical and Pentecostal identity provided stronger popular religious resources to weather the dramatic transformation of twentieth-century Asia. Finally, many second-wave Asian immigrants easily incorporated their indigenous expressions of faith with the evangelical revivalism to which they were exposed. In Asia, and subsequently, Asian America, a "separatist" evangelical-Pentecostal religious identity helped immigrants adjust to the trans-Pacific transposition of Asian societies in the twentieth century.

Some second-wave Asian-American Protestants, however, are offspring of the first wave. For example, the Japanese Evangelical Missionary Society (JEMS), the Chinese Bible Church movement, and other organizations were founded in the 1950s by English-speaking, American-born Asian-American fundamentalists and evangelicals. But most second-wave congregations and parachurch organizations were planted by post-1965 immigrants. For instance, such parachurch ministries as Ambassadors for Christ and the Chinese Christian Mission were created by recent Chinese immigrants.

The impact of the large group of second-wave Asian-American Protestants is inestimable. Congregations with traditional ties to mainline denominations have been pressured to adjust to the spirituality and ethos of the new immigrants. The divide between ecumenically oriented and evangelical Asian-American networks has increased. On the other hand, second-wave Asian-American Protestants are gaining ground within mainstream American EVANGELICALISM.

Contemporary Issues

Today, Asian-American Protestants face a number of critical issues. How they respond will determine their future directions.

1. *Asian-American consciousness.* Racial discrimination and Asian-American cooperation and empowerment have been significant concerns for first-wave Asian-American Protestants, but for second-wave Asian-American Protestant leaders these have not been perceived to be vital issues. Today, Asian-American diversity and religious and political climates combine to discourage race consciousness. Many second- or third-generation Asian Americans have abandoned racial identification in their congregational focus in favor of multiethnicity. Such decisions often come at the expense of relating to immigrant congregations that continue to speak their native languages.
2. *Intergenerational conflict and cooperation.* Related to the question of Asian-American consciousness is the issue of intergenerational conflict and cooperation. Will immigrants and their offspring maintain their congregations and ministries despite the diversity of age and cultural perspectives?
3. *Historic memory.* Will the second-wave Asian-American Protestants benefit from the experiences of first-wave Asian-American Protestants? Can a bridge be built between mainline and evangelical Asian-American Protestants? What can be retrieved from Asian-American history and Asian culture to form distinctively indigenous expressions of Asian-American Protestantism?

Asian-American Protestantism is a vibrant and growing presence within the Asian-American community today. Despite the challenges that it faces, it shall play an important role in an increasingly global Christianity of the future.

See also Asian Theology; Denomination; Pentecostalism

References and Further Reading

Guillermo, Artermio R., ed. *Churches Aflame: Asian Americans and United Methodism.* Nashville, TN: Abingdon, 1991.
Hayashi, Brian. *"For the Sake of Our Japanese Brethren": Assimilation, Nationalism, and Protestantism Among the Japanese of Los Angeles, 1895–1942.* Stanford, CA: Stanford University Press, 1995.
Ma, L. and Eve Armentrout. *Revolutionaries, Monarchists, and Chinatowns: Chinese Politics in the Americas and the 1911 Revolution.* Honolulu, HI: University of Hawaii Press, 1990.
Mark, Diane Mai Lin. *Seasons of Light: The History of Chinese Christian Churches in Hawaii.* Chinese Christian Association of Hawaii, 1989.
Min, Pyong Gap, and Jung Ha Kim, eds. *Religions in Asian America: Building Faith Communities.* Walnut Creek, CA: Altamira Press, 2002.
Pascoe, Peggy. *Relations of Rescue: The Search for Female Moral Authority in the American West, 1874–1939.* New York: Oxford University Press, 1990.
Yoo, David K. *Growing Up Nisei: Race, Generation, and Culture Among Japanese Americans of California, 1924–1949.* Urbana, IL: University of IL, 2000.
Yoo, David K., ed. *New Spiritual Homes: Religion and Asian Americans.* Honolulu, HI: University of Hawaii Press, 1999.

TIMOTHY TSENG

ASSEMBLIES OF GOD

The General Council of the Assemblies of God (USA) is the largest white and Hispanic Pentecostal denomination in the UNITED STATES. Organized to achieve the evangelization of the world, the loose-knit association of churches and ministers eventually became a full-fledged denomination, sponsoring various programs, a large overseas mission endeavor, and numerous institutions of higher education. The Assemblies of God (AG) became a founding member of the NATIONAL ASSOCIATION OF EVANGELICALS (NAE) to cooperate with other evangelical denominations, and later established the World Assemblies of God Fellowship to enhance its relationship to fraternally related church bodies around the world.

Origins

The roots of the Assemblies of God can be found largely in the nineteenth-century HIGHER LIFE MOVEMENT with its emphasis on Holy Spirit baptism as a work of GRACE subsequent to CONVERSION. They combined this experience of "full consecration" or empowerment for Christian witness with belief in the availability of physical healing through the atoning work of Jesus Christ and expectancy of the imminent premillennial return of Jesus Christ. Along with other radical evangelicals frustrated by the slow pace of conversions in the mission lands, they sought for the restoration of the spiritual power and dynamics of the

New Testament church to speedily accomplish the evangelization of the world. Hence, they anticipated that a supernatural outpouring of the Holy Spirit in the "last days," as predicted by the Old Testament prophet Joel (2:28–29), would bring about a great end-times harvest of souls (Matthew 24:14; Acts 1:8).

Believing that God would miraculously bestow unlearned languages on "Spirit-filled" believers to preach to non-Christians as happened on the Day of Pentecost (Acts 2:4), Kansas holiness preacher Charles F. Parham considered speaking in TONGUES to be the "Bible evidence" of Holy Spirit baptism (see HOLINESS MOVEMENT). When Parham and the students at his Bethel Bible School in Topeka, Kansas prayed to receive this experience on January 1, 1901, a revival followed with the participants professing to have received many languages. This event forged the chief distinctive of Classical Pentecostal theology and spirituality, that is, the belief that speaking in tongues (later viewed as functioning in prayer rather than for preaching) always accompanies Holy Spirit baptism. Later revivals followed in the wake of Topeka, notably in Houston, Texas; Zion, Illinois; Los Angeles, California; Indianapolis, Indiana; Memphis, Tennessee; Dunn, North Carolina; Nyack, New York; and elsewhere in North America and abroad.

Formation of the Assemblies of God

The founding fathers and mothers of the AG met at Hot Springs, Arkansas on April 2–12, 1914 to increase unity among themselves, encourage doctrinal stability, establish legal standing, bring order to the mission enterprise, and establish a ministerial training school. Like other early Pentecostals, they came from the ranks of the working classes and were ostracized from their former churches because of their newfound Pentecostal spirituality. The delegates represented a variety of independent churches and networks including the Association of Christian Assemblies in Indiana and, more important, the Churches of God in Christ (white) from Alabama, Arkansas, Mississippi, and Texas. Leaders among the latter had secured permission from bishop Charles Harrison Mason in 1911 to come under the umbrella of the largely African American CHURCH OF GOD IN CHRIST. This arrangement permitted them to issue credentials under the name "Church of God in Christ and in unity with the Apostolic Faith Movement." Whatever the circumstances, the relationship (never organic in nature) proved to be unsatisfactory. Acting for this group, Eudorus N. Bell, Archibald P. Collins, Howard Goss, Daniel C. O. Opperman, and Mack M. Pinson called for the meeting at Hot Springs to found a new organization; the predominantly white membership reflected the general racial divide of American Protestantism.

The delegates incorporated the General Council with a hybrid congregational and Presbyterian polity, offered limited ministerial privileges to women, and ruled that credentials would not be granted to divorced and remarried persons with a living former spouse. The first two officers elected were Bell as chairman (title later changed to general superintendent) and J. Roswell Flower as secretary. Fears of becoming a DENOMINATION, however, kept the Council in its early years from creating a statement of faith and a constitution and bylaws. After the inaugural meeting districts arose around the country, usually based on geographical areas, but also according to language and culture (e.g., Hispanic, German, Ukrainian).

Doctrine

The General Council has maintained fidelity to the historic doctrines of the Christian church, important teachings stemming from the Protestant and Radical Reformations of the sixteenth century, and later revivalist movements; these include belief in the Trinity, JUSTIFICATION by FAITH, the substitutionary ATONEMENT of Jesus Christ, believer's BAPTISM, progressive SANCTIFICATION, premillennial ESCHATOLOGY, and Christian PACIFISM (at the outset). The first doctrinal dispute, known as the "New Issue," centered on a proposed modal Monarchian view of the Godhead (God in one person with the redemptive Name of Jesus Christ) and led to a major schism. In response delegates to the council meeting at St. Louis, Missouri in 1916 approved the "Statement of Fundamental Truths" to preserve a Trinitarian and evangelical doctrinal witness. When questions arose in 1918 about the indispensability of tongues for Holy Spirit baptism, it declared the teaching of tongues as "initial physical evidence" to be its "Distinctive Testimony."

Early doctrinal manuals included *Bible Doctrines* (1934) by P. C. Nelson, *Knowing the Doctrines of the Bible* (1937) by Myer Pearlman, and a specialized discussion on Holy Spirit baptism, *What Meaneth This? A Pentecostal Answer to a Pentecostal Question* (1947) by Carl Brumback. Later publications included *Bible Doctrines: A Pentecostal Perspective* (1993) by William W. Menzies and Stanley M. Horton and the more extensive *Systematic Theology* (1994) edited by Horton. The General Council began to publish white papers known as "position papers" in 1970 to address doctrinal and practical issues troubling the churches; they were collectively published in *Where We Stand* (2001).

Organizational Development

The General Council located its headquarters and publishing wing, Gospel Publishing House, in Findlay, Ohio in 1914, and then moved them to St. Louis, Missouri in 1915, and permanently to Springfield, Missouri in 1918. To handle the increasingly complex responsibilities of its home and overseas mission efforts, it established the Missionary Department in 1919 and later the Home Missions and Education Department in 1937; other departments followed (e.g., youth, Sunday school, Missionettes, Royal Rangers). Two periodicals spoke for the new organization: the monthly *Word and Witness* and the weekly *Christian Evangel*. After their consolidation and with further name changes, the weekly *Pentecostal Evangel* became the official voice in 1919.

The final authority for DOCTRINE and practice resides in the General Council, a biennial gathering of all ordained ministers and lay representatives from the churches. Designated responsibilities have been given to two smaller bodies: The Executive Presbytery includes the General Council Board of Administration (General Superintendent, Assistant General Superintendent, General Secretary, and General Treasurer), Executive Directors of Home and World Missions, and Non-Resident Executive Presbyters from eight geographical regions, the language districts (e.g., Hispanic), and an ethnic fellowship (e.g., African American); it meets bimonthly. Made up of representatives from each of the districts, the General Presbytery constitutes the final court of appeal and handles business between the biennial meetings of the General Council.

Educational Institutions

Several small Bible institutes provided training in the early years. Often with little financial backing, some survived to become enduring institutions; others merged with these or ceased to operate altogether. Permanent institutions have included Glad Tidings Bible Institute (1919), later Bethany College of the Assemblies of God in Santa Cruz, California; Southern California Bible and Missionary Training Institute (1920), later Vanguard University of Southern California in Costa Mesa; Central Bible Institute (1922), later Central Bible College in Springfield, Missouri; Latin American Bible Institute (1926) in San Antonio, Texas; and Latin American Bible Institute (1926), now in La Puente, California. The General Council chartered Evangel University as the first national Pentecostal school of arts and sciences in 1955 and established the Assemblies of God Theological Seminary in 1973, with both institutions located in Springfield, Missouri. In the same city Global University provides distance education programs for those seeking training for various forms of Christian ministry. Nineteen endorsed schools of higher education, ranging from Bible institutes to colleges and universities, could be found across the United States by 2003. Hundreds of locally sponsored church-based Bible institutes also exist to serve congregations (see BIBLE COLLEGES AND INSTITUTES).

Missions

Within the first year of its existence approximately thirty missionaries gained membership in the General Council. Largely independent in their operation, they worked mainly in the traditional sites of Christian mission: Africa, India, China, Japan, and the Middle East; more would later serve in Europe, Latin America, and Oceania. In the early years the Missionary Department largely served to channel funds to missionaries. Beginning in 1943 it began to aggressively direct the strategy of the mission enterprise. Although committed to establishing self-governing, self-supporting, and self-sustaining churches in the mission lands, missionaries generally followed the paternalistic practices of their Protestant counterparts. Beginning in the 1950s they focused more emphasis on training indigenous leaders for the churches; the change from paternalism to partnership led to dramatic church growth in many places. Through the efforts of key leaders like Alice E. Luce, Ralph D. Williams, J. Philip Hogan, and Melvin L. Hodges, the General Council promoted the development of hundreds of ministerial training institutions around the world.

At the Council on Evangelism in St. Louis, Missouri in 1968, the General Council reaffirmed its mission as an agency for the evangelization of the world, a corporate body in which humanity may worship God, and a means for the discipleship of Christians. Despite the failure to address issues related to holistic mission (e.g., poverty, hunger), AG missions, already holistic in many quarters, increasingly moved in that direction without diminishing gospel proclamation. Such ministries include the Lillian Trasher Memorial Orphanage in Assiout, Egypt, the Assembly of God Hospital and Research Centre in Calcutta, India, HealthCare Ministries, and the AG-related Convoy of Hope.

Women in Ministry

As they had in the Holiness Movement, women played important roles in early PENTECOSTALISM and the Assemblies of God as evangelists, missionaries, and pastors. Originally offering them ordination only as evangelists and missionaries, the General Council belatedly began ordaining women as pastors in 1935. Before 1950 more than one thousand women evangelists traveled the country evangelizing and planting churches. Influential women included Marie Burgess Brown, Alice Reynolds Flower, Carrie Judd Montgomery, AIMEE SEMPLE MCPHERSON (in the AG from 1919 to 1922), Alice E. Luce, Chonita Howard, Hattie Hammond, and Florence Steidel. Nevertheless by midcentury, the number of women credential holders fell into a sharp decline. Early in the twenty-first century, church executives began to reemphasize the value of women serving in ministry positions.

Identification with Evangelicals

Conservative evangelicals laid plans for the NAE in 1942 and invited the participation of the AG and several other Pentecostal denominations to join in establishing a national evangelical voice, evangelizing the world, and working toward a Christian America. NAE membership subsequently identified Pentecostals as evangelicals and removed the cult status with which some observers had labeled them. The General Council also benefited from the cooperative programs that it offered such as National Religious Broadcasters, Accrediting Association of Bible Colleges, and Evangelical Fellowship of Mission Agencies. More than any other Pentecostal, Thomas F. Zimmerman, AG general superintendent (1959–1985), worked to build the alliance of evangelicals and Pentecostals. Along with the NAE, the General Council has worked with the Lausanne Committee on Evangelism, World Evangelical Alliance, and the PENTECOSTAL WORLD CONFERENCE. Because of these associations, it has refrained from involvement in conciliar bodies such as the WORLD COUNCIL OF CHURCHES.

The acceptance by evangelicals, calls for collegiate-level training for ministers, increasing denominational structures at the national and district levels, fear that the zeal and power of Pentecostal spirituality had declined, and growing affluence of Pentecostals triggered a reaction known as the "New Order of the Latter Rain." Beginning at the Sharon Schools and Orphanage in North Battleford, Saskatchewan, Canada in 1948, leaders claimed that a new outpouring of the Holy Spirit had begun. They sharply criticized organized Pentecostalism and called for the impartation of the gifts of the Holy Spirit through the laying on of hands in prayer, among other teachings. Although the General Council and its sister denomination, the Pentecostal Assemblies of Canada, condemned the movement, its influence continued in some quarters.

Progress and Challenges

The General Council showed strong signs of progress in certain areas as the twentieth century closed. When leaders of the exclusively white Pentecostal Fellowship of North America met with African American Pentecostal leaders at Memphis, Tennessee in 1994, AG representatives joined with others to dissolve that organization and form the racially inclusive PENTECOSTAL/CHARISMATIC CHURCHES of North America.

New revival movements, such as the "Pensacola Outpouring" at the Brownsville (Florida) Assembly of God that attracted more than 2.5 million visitors after it began in 1995, spiritually invigorated many AG people. However, the Pensacola Outpouring also brought division over certain revival phenomena that occurred, which had also characterized earlier Pentecostal spirituality.

A planned "Decade of Harvest" program to accelerate growth in the 1990s brought limited results, signaling new challenges for the future of the council: an aging clergy, misgivings about traditional church structures, and fears about the continued Pentecostal identity of the denomination. These have prompted leaders to explore the effectiveness of present church structures and programs. Statistics for 2002 show a church constituency in the United States of 2,627,029; 12,082 churches; and 32,374 ministers. The Council supported 1,841 foreign missionaries, working with fraternally related constituencies whose members and adherents numbered more than thirty-eight million people. Giving by the American churches totaled more than $346 million. To encourage the study of the Pentecostal Movement and the Assemblies of God in particular, the Council established the Flower Pentecostal Heritage Center in Springfield, Missouri; it publishes the archival quarterly *Assemblies of God Heritage*.

See also Conversion; Missions; Pentecostalism; Revivals

References and Further Reading

Blumhofer, Edith L. *Restoring the Faith: The Assemblies of God, Pentecostalism, and American Culture.* Urbana: The University of Illinois Press, 1993.
Cavaness, Barbara Liddle. "Factors Influencing the Decrease in the Number of Single Women in Assemblies of God World Missions." Ph.D. dissertation, Fuller Theological Seminary, 2002.
De Leon, Victor. *The Silent Pentecostals: A Biographical History of the Pentecostal Movement among Hispanics in the Twentieth Century.* Taylors, SC: Faith Printing Co., 1979.
General Council of the Assemblies of God. *Where We Stand.* Springfield, MO: Gospel Publishing House, 2001.

McGee, Gary B. *This Gospel Shall Be Preached: A History and Theology of Assemblies of God Foreign Missions to 1959.* Springfield, MO: Gospel Publishing House, 1986.

———. *This Gospel Shall Be Preached: A History and Theology of Assemblies of God Foreign Missions Since 1959.* Springfield, MO: Gospel Publishing House, 1989.

———. *People of the Spirit: The Assemblies of God.* Springfield, MO: Gospel Publishing House, 2003.

Poloma, Margaret M. *The Assemblies of God at the Crossroads: Charisma and Institutional Dilemmas.* Knoxville: University of Tennessee Press, 1989.

Robeck, Cecil M. Jr. "The Assemblies of God and Ecumenical Cooperation: 1920–1965." In *Pentecostalism in Context: Essays in Honor of William W. Menzies*, edited by Wonsuk Ma and Robert P. Menzies, 107–150. Sheffield, UK: Sheffield Academic Press, 1997.

Warner, Wayne E. "A Call for Love, Tolerance, and Cooperation." *Assemblies of God Heritage* 14 (Fall 1994): 3–4, 31.

Wilson, Everett A. *Strategy of the Spirit: J. Philip Hogan and the Growth of the Assemblies of God Worldwide, 1960–1990.* Irvine, CA: Regnum Books International, 1997.

GARY B. McGEE

ASSOCIATION OF AFRICAN INSTITUTED CHURCHES

See African Instituted Churches

ATONEMENT

The atonement refers to the divine act of reconciliation whereby God and the sinner are made to be "at one." Whatever its etymology, the word has gained a number of connotations that shape the way in which it has been understood, often containing the notion of recompense, as when it is said that someone seeks to atone for his offenses by some act of reparation. Central to the way the theology of atonement has developed is the notion of exchange, which derives from imagery that is at once monetary (the price or ransom for sin), judicial (the one punished in place of the many), and, above all, sacrificial (the perfect gift on the altar standing in for or being the vehicle of the offering of those otherwise unqualified to come before a holy God).

In taking its orientation largely from Anselm, archbishop of Canterbury's (1093–1109) *Why the God-Man*, Protestant theology aligned itself with a particular tradition of Western theology. Anselm rejected the mainstream Western view, which had itself derived from Augustine's adaptation of an Eastern conception. According to Augustine, Adam's sin brought him and the whole human race within the legal power of the devil by conquering Christ, who on the cross won freedom for the human race. Rejecting this on the grounds of its irrationality and theological unacceptability—for God is not obliged to negotiate with his creature, the devil—Anselm spoke of sin in terms of an unpayable debt owed to God's honor and of Christ's saving act as his free offering of his life to God the Father, a gift of infinite worth—not, however, as a punishment, but as an alternative to it. The atonement was thus an act of satisfaction that fulfilled the need for universal justice and the remission of sins without trivializing the moral law.

The Reformers

According to the mainstream of medieval piety, the means of appropriating the benefits of the atonement were the church's penitential system and sacraments. The Reformers' objections to this centered on the church's claim to control the means of salvation, by virtue of its possession of the "treasury of merits" won by Christ and the saints, and what they saw as the Pelagianism of the teaching that made salvation dependent on the efforts of the believer. Their objections were prepared for in the voluntarist theologies of Scotus and Ockham, which located the action of grace more in God's free action than in ecclesial processes. In the later Middle Ages, Wyclif and Hus prepared the way for the Reformation by a return to Anselmian themes, the former stressing the priority of the satisfaction won by Christ over human effort.

Two late medieval developments triggered the protests of MARTIN LUTHER (1483–1546): the offer of indulgences—by whose hearing or purchase a period in purgatory could be avoided—and the notion that salvation in Christ built upon the human agent's own preparatory achievement. Luther's twofold response was that salvation was won on the cross by Christ and was, therefore, absolutely free and unmerited; and that because of human sinfulness, which represents a bondage of the will (here he remained true to Augustine's position), salvation could be appropriated only by faith through divine grace. Luther was more concerned with the human appropriation of atonement than in a systematic account of its achievement on the cross, but like many theologians he drew on a range of biblical imagery in expressing its reality. He employed both the victory imagery of the tradition before Anselm and also insisted so strongly on the sole agency of Christ in bearing the sins of the world that he used language that some commentators have judged to be excessively punitive, in anticipation of the penal substitution theologies of some later Protestantism. His junior contemporary PHILLIP MELANCHTHON (1497–1560) more systematically linked justification with the atoning act of the cross, while still concentrating attention on the sinner's appropriation of salvation. Against the REFORMATION view of the complete forgiveness of sin through the atonement, the Roman Catholic Church at Trent combined a theology of the saving death of Christ with the teaching that sinners must continue to atone for their sins in this world and after death in purgatory; until recent times the two traditions have largely been in radical opposition to one another.

Later Protestant controversy on the atonement centered largely on JOHN CALVIN's (1509–1564) work, which was many-sided and provided the basis for later developments. Like Augustine and Anselm, he based the atonement on God's gracious response to human need, which takes shape in the death of his incarnate Son. Unlike some later theologians, Calvin never isolated the cross from the whole of Jesus' life and its outcome in resurrection and ascension. He was concerned with holding in tension the twofold claim that atonement is a divine act that is realized by the human action of his Son, both of them motivated by love. The interpretation of Calvin's thought is controversial in two respects. First, there is disagreement about the prominence and meaning of the punitive aspects of the cross. It is arguable that Calvin's prior concern was to show the atonement as a sacrifice, a gift of God's love, producing a generous picture of God as an "indulgent Father," but he does not evade the substitutionary aspects of the situation, that evil has been done and must be atoned for if it and its effects—death—are to be removed. For him, the death of Christ is essentially a sacrifice that expiates, appeases God, creates satisfaction, and pays the price for our redemption. As with Anselm, it is not a substitutionary punishment so much as a saving exchange, by God the Son before God the Father. Second, there is disagreement about whether Calvin taught the universality of the atonement, as appeared to be Anselm's position, or whether Christ died only for the elect, who were for him undoubtedly limited in number.

Orthodoxy and Its Aftermath

The relatively unsystematic thought of Melanchthon and Calvin was succeeded by Protestant ORTHODOXY, which represents a movement to systematically treat the doctrines of the Reformation, and tends to be rationalistic, often adopting Aristotelian logic and methodology. Sometimes traced to Melanchthon (Lutheran) and Théodore Beza (1519–1605) (Reformed), this tendency deeply marks the thought of later Reformed theologies in particular. The chief difference between Lutheran and Reformed is that the former concentrates on justification and the presence of Christ in the Lord's Supper, while the latter develops Calvin's teaching of the work of Christ especially in relation to predestination. There is, in LUTHERANISM, a tendency to narrow the theology of the cross to an Anselmian satisfaction, in a form stated by Melanch-

thon and later claimed by J. W. Baier to be one of the "fundamental articles" on the confession of which salvation depends.

For Reformed orthodoxy, Christ is the mediator who achieves reconciliation by bearing the enmity between man and God deriving from sin. Even in early Reformed confessions, however, a punitive note creeps in, leading eventually to doctrines of "penal substitution," which appear to suggest that God punishes the man Jesus in place of the elect. The origin of this penal emphasis is in the transformation of Calvin's doctrine of the old and new covenants, united in a single economy, to a contrast between the prelapsarian covenant of works, for whose breach by Adam Christ bears the punishment, and the covenant of grace he thus inaugurates. This "federal theology" has its roots in Ursinus, and spread throughout Europe and America, in Britain largely through WILLIAM PERKINS (1558–1602). His combination of a penal note with a rigid doctrine of limited atonement on the basis of double predestination was continued by John Owen, and, definitively for SCOTLAND, in the WESTMINSTER CONFESSION of 1647. Owen's apparently commercial and quantitative construction of satisfaction is often given as the reason for its later rejection.

Opposed to limited atonement were representatives of a more universal interpretation, influenced by the hypothetical UNIVERSALISM of French theologian Moise Amyraut (1596–1664), who taught that there were three covenants that were conditional in being contingent upon human response. The Synod of Dort ruled, against what it took to be the Pelagianism of this position, that Christ's death is sufficient for all, but efficient only for the elect. Those who tended to universalism were often also Arminian in tendency, stressing the efficacy of the free human will over divine determination, and included Baxter and Wesley. They were also influenced by Grotius, whose "rectorial" theory represented the cross as the expression of God's exemplary displeasure over sin. However, they had room for a broader interpretation of the cross than the governmental, Baxter stressing the qualitative sufficiency of Christ's satisfaction and Wesley freely using the language of juridical and sacrificial exchange. America's original contribution is best represented by American minister Jonathan Edwards (1703–1758), whose teaching is directed against the Arminian denial of justification by faith. In content, however, he later anticipated more liberal doctrines by assimilating atonement to Calvin's doctrine of Christ's intercession for sinners. The sacrifice is *God's* in coming into union in Christ with us, because of love.

Liberalism and Beyond

More radical reactions to penal theory are found in theologian Faustus Sozzini (Socinus) (1539–1604), who rejected traditional atonement theology on three main grounds. First, individualism generated the notion that because the penalty for sin was not transferable, Christ's death cannot be the cause of divine forgiveness. Second, libertarianism—that sin does not deprive one of freedom to do good unaided—led to an exemplarist theory of atonement, that Christ's self-giving to death is an example rather than a substitution. Third, a voluntarist theology claimed that God can, if he wishes, simply remit sin without requiring satisfaction for it. Socinianism, along with Deism and the Enlightenment, conquered much modern Protestant thought, so that nineteenth-century Protestantism was dominated by exemplarist conceptions of the atonement. Philosopher Immanuel Kant's (1724–1804) rejection of heteronomy (any salvation deriving "from without") and any determination by history, specifically by Jesus of Nazareth, is also influential. The critique was so radical that theologian Albrecht Ritschl (1822–1889) spoke of the "disintegration" of traditional conceptions during this period (Ritschl 1872: ch. 7).

In Germany, Friedrich Schleiermacher (1768–1834) took up the tradition of French theologian Peter Abelard (c.1079–1142), who taught that Christ's death is more an example than an exchange. His was a complex theology according to which the religious experience of Jesus, mediated through history, shaped that of the believer by removing the impediment to God-consciousness caused by sin. The cross, on which Jesus suffered but did not die, served as a demonstration of divine love rather than a sacrificial or substitutionary atonement. Ritschl took a more directly Kantian line, concentrating on a moral rather than experiential response to the Jesus of history, but again within a broadly Abelardian perspective. The period is also marked by a process of revulsion even among those more sympathetic to the tradition against soteriology shaped by dual predestination and a punitively or commercially conceived satisfaction.

G. W. F. Hegel's (1770–1831) concern to conceive reconciliation in terms of the relation between finite and infinite, within a broadly immanentist perspective, enabled later mediating theology to give more weight to the historical particularity. Dorner combined a development of the theology of the threefold office with a notion of the divine Christ's substitutionary bearing of the consequences of human sin. The Erlangen theology developed a theology of Jesus's active obedience, with Thomasius conceiving the cross, in the context of the incarnation, as expiation rather than satisfaction. It is where God's inner-trinitarian love and holiness are reconciled, a note similar to that later sounded in Britain by P. T. Forsyth (1848–1921).

In Britain, Samuel Taylor Coleridge (1772–1834) responded to Kant by developing a doctrine of the bondage of the will that required a more traditional Christian scheme of redemption, though largely in terms of divine regeneration of the will. The influence of Coleridge, along with the traditionalism and nationalism of the Tractarian movement, paved the way for a broad stream of Anglican theologies of the atonement, which made much of the doctrine of sacrifice. Scottish theology was marked by a strong reaction against quantitative notions of substitution—the notion that Christ's death was mathematically equal in value to the totality of human sins—by Irving and against limited atonement by McLeod Campbell. The latter's theology of Christ's vicarious sacrifice, stressing a filial rather than legal relation with God, shaped later notions of Jesus' vicarious penitence as the heart of the matter.

In America, as the influence of Edwards's Calvinism declined, so that of Unitarianism and exemplarism grew, with Horace Bushnell (1802–1876) influential in rejecting substitutionary theology. The movement, however, generated powerful reactions, especially in Princeton theologies, best represented by Charles Hodge (1797–1878). His is a philosophically sophisticated restatement of a federal, substitutionary, and expiatory scheme of salvation. Similarly, the English Congregationalist Dale defended a substitutionary scheme against Bushnell. P. T. Forsyth, a Scottish pupil of Ritschl, appears to have experienced an evangelical awakening that transformed him from being a "lover of love"—his characterization of the Abelardian, liberal tradition, which effectively denied the need for atonement—to "an object of grace." His theology centered on the cross, where human sin is both judged and atoned by the holy love of God, the combination of the two motifs indicating that atonement is both required by God's holiness and given by his love.

Twentieth Century

Forsyth continued to write during the first two decades of the twentieth century and represents, in his return to traditional forms, a leading strand of that century's highly various theologies. In Scotland, the influential James Denney stressed the vicarious and substitutionary nature of the cross of Christ. In continental Europe this strand is represented by Emil Brunner (1889–1966), stressing objective human guilt and divine wrath on the one hand, and their reconciliation through the love of God on the other. Like Forsyth, Brunner is sometimes likened to KARL BARTH (1886–1968), whose substitutionary doctrine of election, however, he rejected as containing too many penal overtones. Barth's mature doctrine, developed after the last war, is centered on a doctrine of reconciliation somewhat more broadly based than Forsyth's, giving a larger place to the doctrines of the incarnation and resurrection, and approaching universalism. A substitutionary theology of the cross combines with a liberalized doctrine of God—"the Judge judged in our place"—inverting, in the process, many of the categories of Protestant orthodoxy and stressing the representative suffering of the divine rather than the human Christ.

Abelardian critiques of all such doctrines have also flourished, in Britain taking their direction from the Anglican Rashdall (1919), with his strong rejection of substitutionary atonement. Such influences led to the neglect of the doctrine, although recent times have seen a revival of interest. In Scotland, the influence of McLeod Campbell is shown in the work of T. F. and James Torrance, who stress the love of God and the vicarious humanity, rather than substitutionary suffering, of Christ. Similar attempts to mediate traditional views while taking account of criticism are found in a replacement of substitution by representation, although on analysis, either the differences between the two conceptions disappear or the latter collapses into exemplarism. Exposition of atonement through metaphor is also prominent, stressing either its literary form and tending to exemplarism, or its capacity for realistic reference through appeal to traditional biblical imagery, as in Colin Gunton (1988).

References and Further Reading

Brunner, Emil. *The Mediator*. Translated by Olive Wyon. Philadelphia: Westminster, 1947.
Clifford, A. C. *Atonement and Justification: English Evangelical Theology 1640–1790—An Evaluation*. Oxford, UK: Oxford University Press, 1990.
Franks, R. S. *The Work of Christ*. New York: T. Nelson, 1962.
Gunton, Colin E. *The Actuality of Atonement*. Edinburgh: T & T Clark, 1988.
Heppe, Heinrich. *Reformed Dogmatics*. Translated by G. T. Thomson. Grand Rapids, MI: Baker, 1978. 281–409.
McCormack, Bruce. *For Us and Our Salvation: Incarnation and Atonement in the Reformed Tradition*. Princeton: Princeton Theological Seminary, 1993.
Rashdall, Hastings. *The Atonement in Christian Theology*. London: Macmillan, 1919.
Ritschl, Albrecht. *A Critical History of the Christian Doctrine of Justification and Reconciliation*. Translated by J. S. Black. London: Edmonston and Douglas, 1872.

COLIN GUNTON

ATTOH AHUMA, SAMUEL RICHARD BREW (1864–1922)

African reformer. Samuel Richard Brew Attoh Ahuma was a Wesleyan Methodist minister, journalist, nationalist campaigner, educator, and author. He was a son of the Rev. James Solomon, trained in Richmond College, England (1886–1888). He dropped his English names shortly after his return to Ghana in 1888 and was subsequently known as Attoh Ahuma. He became the principal of the grammar school in Accra and had a keen interest in local histories of his people as well as the development and use of his vernacular, Fante. He was a member of a nationalist group, the Aborigines' Rights Protection Society (ARPS).

In 1896 he became the editor of the newly formed local newspaper, *The Gold Coast Methodist Times,* which became the ecclesiastical mouthpiece of nationalist aspirations. The Colonial authorities in the Gold Coast (now Ghana) introduced a controversial land bill that the local people saw as an infringement on their right of ownership. The *Methodist Times* was the only forum that served as a vanguard of opposition, thus earning Attoh Ahuma the honor of being among the best journalists Ghana has produced. Attoh Ahuma was chided by European missionaries for the increasing political content of the *Methodist Times*. As a result he resigned as editor on January 1, 1898, the same day he became editor of the *Gold Coast Aborigines,* the new organ of the ARPS, which could no longer use the *Methodist Times* as its mouthpiece. He subsequently resigned from the Methodist ministry.

Attoh Ahuma set the pace for nationalist aspiration in Ghana in the 1890s because a number of Methodist ministers who were in line with the tradition that he set felt that there should be no dichotomy between religion and politics or between Christianity and nationalism. He was in the company of the earliest African nationalist leaders, trained in the Protestant tradition, who brought their education to bear on the struggle for political and cultural independence from colonial domination and also sought to combine African culture and forms with Christian content.

See also Africa; Methodism, Global; Nationalism

References and Further Reading

Primary Sources:

Attoh Ahuma, W. M. Cannel, and R. Hayfron. Fante translation of *Pilgrim's Progress*. 1886.
———. *The Gold Coast Nation and National Consciousness,* 2d edition. London: Frank Cass & Co., 1971.
———. *Memoirs of West African Celebrities*. Novel, 1905.
———. *The Gold Coast Nation and National Consciousness*. Novel, 1911.
———. *Cruel as the Grave*. Novel, 1913.

Secondary Sources:

Kimble, D. *A Political History of Ghana: The Rise of Gold Coast Nationalism, 1850–1928.* Oxford, UK: Oxford University Press, 1963.

Debrunner, H. W. *A History of Christianity in Ghana.* Accra, Ghana: Waterville, 1967.

CEPHAS N. OMENYO

AUGSBURG CONFESSION

The confession of Faith of the Lutheran estates submitted at the diet at Augsburg. The Augsburg Confession (1530) remains in many respects an accidental necessity that, in company with further historical accidents, became normative for Lutherans not only in Northern Europe but also around the world. The *volte face* came at Speyer in 1529 by the Catholic estates, which heretofore had agreed with their evangelical counterparts that individual temporal rulers owned the decision of whether to prosecute MARTIN LUTHER and his followers. Now the same clear majority—all faithful to Rome—declared that the temporal ban against Luther at the DIET OF WORMS (1521) must be executed by all.

The Evangelicals protested and became therewith (at least in England and North America) "Protestants." At about the same time, with the Battle of Pavia, the *Sacco da Roma,* and one more temporary peace with Francis I of France, emperor Charles V had acquired a relatively free hand within the Empire. Under the partial pretext of making joint preparations to defend the Empire against the advance of the Ottoman Turks up the Danube and to the gates of Vienna itself, he called the Diet of Augsburg to establish religious peace for consolidating these gains and meeting the new challenge.

At the same time Rome's opponents were in fact distancing themselves from the distinct majority in the Empire. Beginning in 1527 or 1528, those who were called "Lutheran" enacted and spread the *Saxon Visitation Articles* of 1527–1528, by which they took up diocesan visitations on their own to the extent that they began to examine and replace parish priests who taught contrary to the norms of Wittenberg. This sea change in the times was perhaps best encapsulated in the virtually simultaneous appearance of both the political reversal at Speyer and the publication of Luther's *Catechisms* (1529), by which even common people would be taught the new faith.

The politicians also stepped forward by sponsoring the abortive MARBURG COLLOQUY between the Swiss and the Wittenbergers (July 1529), the Marburg and Schwabach Articles (October 1529), and the Torgau Articles (March 1530). Thus, months before the Diet of Augsburg convened, there was an identifiable evangelical party that consisted not just of dissident theologians but also the likes of Elector John of Saxony, Margrave Georg of Brandenburg-Ansbach, Landgrave PHILIP OF HESSE, and the city of Nuremberg. By default they became the core group around which the "Protestants" gathered, once PHILIPP MELANCHTHON, with the counsel of others, had completed the Augsburg Confession.

The final document has three parts: an introduction and a conclusion, each written probably by the Saxon Chancellor Brück, with the Confession itself sandwiched between them. It in turn is divided into two sections: (1) "what is preached and taught among us" in which "there is nothing here that departs from the Scriptures or the catholic church, or from the Roman church," and (2) "Disputed articles, listing the abuses that have been corrected." Johannes Eck's quickly composed *Confutation of the Augsburg Confession* reveals in some detail how theologians of the old church perceived Melanchthon's work and even sheds light on its deeper meaning.

At first glance the product appears to have been of theological import almost solely. Its first twenty-one articles began by endorsing the three ecumenical creeds and continued his exposition with frequent appeals both to the Scriptures and the fathers, while, here and there, rejecting the teachings of the more radical groups that had sprung up in the evangelicals' wake. If, however, the *Augustana* is allowed to speak for itself, it appears not as a laundry list of doctrines but a systematically organized and theological whole that treated both practice and teaching and required adoption or rejection *in toto.*

Melanchthon did dress confessional reality in pleasing, inoffensive garb. The first article endorsed the broadest, the most fundamental, and most widely agreed on three ecumenical creeds, as confessed by both Lutherans and Catholics to this day. The second article moved easily from the Trinity to the fallen condition of humanity, according to which "from birth [humans] are full of evil lust and inclination." The third then introduced the solution to this tragic condition, namely "God the Son," who through the Holy Spirit "may make holy, purify, strengthen, and comfort all who believe in him. . . ." Of these three articles, even the eagle-eyed Eck could object only to the absence of any mention of the "spark of goodness" that much traditional Catholic teaching found as a remainder in humans after the Fall. What immediately followed these unobjectionable statements came in time to be the most hotly disputed article to this day, that is, number four on JUSTIFICATION by GRACE alone, although it did not do so immediately. Melanchthon presented it as little more than a smooth restatement of what he had written in the previous article, which in turn restated the confessional contents of article two.

In his *Confutation* Eck did point to what he called "Manicheean" tendencies on the grounds that it had no place for distinctly human merit in the divine economy of salvation. Hence, the contentious issue did not go unnoticed, but even the ardent author of the *Confutation* scarcely gave it high prominence. In fact Melanchthon built the entire remainder of the confession on article four.

From this point the *Augustana* moved to more practical and down-to-earth matters that impinged directly on the life of a Christian. His underlying intent showed through the smooth rhetorical character of how he ordered the materials. Thus, he began with points that were genuinely not subject to disagreement or were so central (e.g., article four on justification) and plausible that they could not be deferred, and then proceeded to allegedly ever more ancillary matters that made it appear as if the evangelicals had for the most part little new to propose. Moreover, he stated these teachings almost solely in positive terms, while ignoring any negative consequences that may have been lurking behind them, at least from Rome's point of view.

Article five may serve as an illustration. It confessed that the office of preacher/priest/pastor (Melanchthon left it vague) was instituted by God to provide Word and sacrament as "means" through which God "gives the Holy Spirit who produces faith, where and when he wills, in those who hear the Gospel." The author took an additional step when he condemned the Anabaptists (see ANABAPTISM) on the commonplace grounds that they taught "that we obtain the Gospel without the external Word." The only room remaining to opponents such as Eck was to caution that faith should have "love" added to it, as in the phrase *fides caritate formata*. Article six, "On the New Obedience," followed the same pattern. The *Augustana* affirmed that genuinely good works were the products of genuine faith, to which Eck could only reply that good works did not flow from faith so much as they formed it and made it acceptable to God.

Indeed the *Augustana*'s treatment of more general issues, such as the nature of the church, civic affairs, or even the SACRAMENTS, strongly suggested that the issues at least appeared to be discussible. In like manner Eck declared of the LORD'S SUPPER that the confession contained nothing "that could cause offense." For the most part, when he did object, it was only to aspects of subjects that a given article did not treat, such as the necessity that confession and absolution contained three elements, among which "satisfaction" was essential. Similarly, with respect to article fourteen that "those rightly called" referred only to "those called according to the laws and ecclesiastical ordinances that have been observed throughout Christ-

tendom." Eck even accepted the article on free will (eighteen) but roundly condemned the one (twenty) on FAITH and good works. He also strongly countered Melanchthon's rejection of the cult of the SAINTS (twenty-one) on the grounds that both of these articles condemned practices that the Church of Rome officially sanctioned and encouraged. At least on the surface it would appear that the Augsburg Confession became ever more contentious and divisive the farther it moved away from abstract doctrinal matters and the closer it came to common, recommended, and even mandated Roman practices.

A thoroughly misleading conclusion might well follow, that the evangelical–Catholic controversy had mostly to do with practice and little with theological substance. This misses the depth of the division between the two sides as it existed in 1530. The *Augustana* hinted at it with some frequency even in these articles about which there was supposedly nothing in dispute. Article seven may well amount to the lynchpin of Melanchthon's entire demonstration in these particular circumstances. The simple words appear to be—and have been so interpreted—open, inviting, and even accommodating: "It is enough for the true unity of the church that there be agreement on the preaching of the Word and the administration of the sacraments in accord with it. It is not necessary that human traditions, rites, or ceremonies instituted by human beings be alike everywhere." In reality, an entirely revolutionary understanding of "the church" lay beneath these words, and Eck saw it the moment Melanchthon, in the later articles, turned to the details of the issues between Rome and the evangelicals.

Once it is seen the point of the exercise is simplicity itself. Spelling it out in detail awaited the Formula of Concord (1577), but it was in the Augsburg Confession as well. When Melanchthon referred to ceremonies, procedures, modes of governance, and the like as ADIAPHORA or "things indifferent," he was not implying that they were of no account. Quite the contrary. Precisely because they were indifferent by their nature, no authority or tradition, not even that of Rome, had the right to draw up rules regarding how they should be observed. No "church" had that right. The only right that adhered to the true church was instead the obligation to proclaim the Word truthfully and to administer the sacraments faithfully in accord with it.

The *Confutation*'s specific objections to articles twenty-two to twenty-eight—the ones "under dispute"—help reveal the story of what was truly at stake. Clearly, Eck had already tipped his and Rome's hand with respect to article twenty-one. Taken together, they present something of a surprise, at least on the surface. In order, these articles treated receiving both the bread and the wine in the Lord's Supper or Mass, priestly marriage, the Mass as such, confession, proscriptions of certain foods at certain (before the Mass, during Lent) times, monastic vows, and episcopal authority. This is to say, every one of the articles "under dispute" had on the surface primarily to do with practices rather than teachings.

Nonetheless even while defending their use, the author of the *Confutation* virtually bypassed the practices themselves. Instead, for Eck, the nature and AUTHORITY of the church as such was at stake in any discussion of the right of churches to command and forbid. Here was the real issue that the *Augustana* posed. Thus Eck repeatedly defended these practices not only on the basis of their longevity and widely spread existence but also by reference to specifically Roman adoption of them, consensus regarding them, or (what is most telling) their conciliar and/or papal approval. Whenever even remotely possible he did seek biblical sanction. On the other hand a reasonably typical statement (here in defense of "The Cult of the Saints") declared that "we have not only the authority of the entire church but also the agreement of the holy church fathers, such as Augustine, Bernard, Jerome, Cyprian, Chrysostom, and the other doctors of the church." Thus the many particular "proofs" all defended one, central position, "the authority of the entire church."

Article twenty-eight on the authority of bishops illustrates the collision most vividly. At base, and with a digression into Roman episcopal behavior with respect to the evangelicals notwithstanding, Melanchthon was willing to grant a certain extended spiritual authority to bishops that was in reality identical to that held by any pastor, although he gave them no authority to coerce behavior or belief and, above all, disallowed any use of the weapons of whatever civil authority they might and did possess. This result made them little different from ordinary pastors, in that they were responsible for preaching and teaching the Word, administering the sacraments, and exercising modest oversight with respect to matters related to these duties. (Episcopal succession as such was not even an idea at this time; he would have nothing to do with episcopal succession.) Eck replied with the simple declaration that "everything that is asserted in this article against ecclesiastical and priestly immunity is without foundation." Luther's *Address to the Christian Nobility* conveyed that the Word of God created the church. For Eck and Rome, the church validated the Word.

Upon the public presentation of John Eck's *Confutation*, the emperor had declared Melanchthon's Confession to have been refuted. Melanchthon thereupon wrote a lengthy elaboration of the Augsburg Confes-

sion, the Apology, partially from notes he had made during the public reading of the Confutation. It was printed the following year.

Despite the public character of the Augsburg Confession, Melanchthon considered the Confession to be his own document and accordingly made minor changes in the 1530s, when new imprints were published. In preparation for religious colloquies of 1539 and 1540 Melanchthon prepared a new edition, published in 1540, later labeled the *Confession Augustana Variata*, the "altered" Augsburg Confession. At first generally accepted as yet another imprint of the original 1530 version, it was discovered to entail substantial changes in both article four (on justification) and article ten (on the Lord's Supper), the latter article embodying substantial changes in the direction of the Zwinglian-South German view of the sacrament.

As presented, received, and rebutted in 1530, the *Augustana* was therefore a theological confession with far-reaching practical consequences. After the events that led to the Peace of Augsburg (1555) it became ever more a theological document to be consulted as if it stood on its own and without practical context. To be sure, it became a part of the constitution of the Holy Roman Empire of the German Nation and adherence to it served thereby as a basis for a certain religious TOLERATION. Yet, even here, the document itself fell ever more securely into the hands of its theologians. At the meeting of the princes in Naumburg (1559), for example, the new, Reformed Elector Frederick of The Palatinate struggled mightily to include the wording of the *Variata* as an explanation of the unaltered confession, to find room under its politically protective umbrella. The theologians resisted, however, and their princes henceforth described themselves as being adherents to "the Augsburg Confession as it was presented to His Imperial Majesty at Augsburg in the Year 1530." They granted the *Variata* unspecified service as a further elaboration, but not necessarily with respect to a Reformed understanding of the Lord's Supper.

The meeting at Naumburg and ones that followed were discussions among the committed. In spite of theologians' penchant for doing so, the Confession should not, however, be studied as if it were a laundry list of doctrines and religious grievances. Instead proceeding from the foundation of article four on justification, its general subject was the extent and manner of ecclesiastical purview over daily religious life. To be sure, this unifying theme was not obvious to many—including Eck at first glance—nor did it become so in the subsequent *Formula of Concord*. Indeed this central question, at stake as Latin Christianity was breaking apart, has resurfaced only in the course of the twentieth century's ecumenical movement. The irony is that at the very heart of their ecumenical labors, many Protestants have in fact adopted the assumptions of Rome: they existed as "the church" even when Word and sacrament were nowhere in evidence.

See also Augsburg Confession, Apology of; Augsburg Interim

References and Further Reading

Grane, Leif. *The Augsburg Confession: A Commentary.* Minneapolis, MN: Augsburg, 1987.

Kolb, Robert, and Timothy J. Wengert, eds. *The Book of Concord. The Confessions of the Evangelical Lutheran Church.* Minneapolis, MN: Fortress Press, 2000.

Maurer, Wilhelm. *Historischer Kommentar zur Confessio Augustana.* 2 vols. Gütersloh, 1976–1978. Also available in English as *Historical Commentary on the Augsburg Confession,* translated by H. George Anderson. Philadelphia: Fortress Press, 1986.

Neuser, W. H. *Bibliographie der Confessio Augustana und Apologie, 1530–1580.* Nieuwkoop, Netherlands: DeGraaf, 1987.

Skarsten, Trygue R. "The Reception of the Augsburg Confession in Scandinavia," *Sixteenth Century Journal,* 11, no. 3, 1980, pp. 87–98.

JAMES M. KITTELSON

AUGSBURG CONFESSION, APOLOGY OF THE

Included in the BOOK OF CONCORD, PHILLIPP MELANCHTHON's *Apology of the Augsburg Confession* defends the central written statement of the EVANGELICAL FAITH AND REFORMS PREPARED FOR THE IMPERIAL DIET OF AUGSBURG IN 1530 at the time when the future of the Evangelicals was at stake: The Emperor of the Holy Roman Empire seemed inclined to enforce the 1521 EDICT OF WORMS and outlaw Evangelicals in German lands. Lack of conciliation could lead to war between the Catholics and Evangelicals, as did happen in 1547. Upon hearing the AUGSBURG CONFESSION on June 25, 1530, Emperor Charles sanctioned the Catholics' response, the *Confutatio Confessionis Augustanae.* The urgent task to craft an *apologia* of the document originally presented fell to MARTIN LUTHER's collaborator.

Melanchthon had a first draft of the *Apology* ready to be submitted to the Emperor on September 22. Because the emperor refused to accept the document and sided with the Catholics, the Diet ended. Melanchthon continued to revise the text, since October with a copy of the Confutation, and published the *quarto* version (named after its printing format) of the *Apology* in April/May 1531 with the first official print of the Augsburg Confession. The revised *quarto* version of September 1531 (augmented with feedback from Luther, MARTIN BUCER, JOHANNES BRENZ, and

Johann Agricola) was signed by Lutheran theologians in the 1537 meeting of the SCHMALKALDIC LEAGUE and was translated "freely" into German by Justus Jonas. The primary status of the *octavo* became unclear after the 1580 *Book of Concord* chose the *quarto* edition over the *octavo* that had been included in an unauthorized edition of the book.

The theological treatise, which extensively quoted the church fathers and the Scriptures, follows the structure of the Augsburg Confession, elaborating most on article 4 on JUSTIFICATION by faith. It explains the relation between forensic and effective righteousness, of being both declared and made righteous. The primacy of faith in one's salvation and holiness, upon which good works would necessarily follow (article 4, para. 72), is argued further in article 12 on repentance, the second longest article. The dynamics of law and gospel in Christian life and the nature of sanctified life of repentance are explained further with articles stressing the significance of institutional church, church offices, and SACRAMENTS as the external means of grace.

Despite efforts to preserve religious unity, the Emperor's Edict of April 15, 1531, ordered the Evangelicals to return to obedience to Rome. The Lutheran princes, ready to defend their faith in war, signed the *Apology* in 1537 with the Augsburg Confession. These two documents would shape Lutheran identity by becoming the norm for the forms of Protestantism approved in Germany in the Augsburg Peace of 1555.

See also Diet of Speyer; Evangelicalism; Lutheranism

References and Further Reading

Kolb, Robert, and Timothy J. Wengert, eds. *The Book of Concord. The Confessions of the Evangelical Lutheran Church.* Minneapolis, MN: Augsburg Press, 2000.

Lohse, Bernard. "Augsburger Bekenntnis, Confutatio and Apologie." In *Theologische Realenzyklopädie,* Band 4, 632–639. Berlin, New York: Walter de Gruyter, 1979.

KIRSI STJERNA

AUGSBURG INTERIM

In about the mid-sixteenth century Emperor Charles V attempted to resolve the disunity brought about by the Reformation controversy. After defeat of the SMALKALDIC LEAGUE in 1547, Charles V called an ecclesiastical commission at the Diet of Augsburg to draft a temporary document of imperial law—the Augsburg Interim. Adopted by the diet of the Empire on June 30, 1548, it provided a transitional religious agreement until the Council of Trent, which had convened in 1545, could include Protestant representatives in church reform discussions.

The Interim's twenty-six articles affirmed basic teachings and positions of the Roman church. Articles one through eight focused on the human condition, redemption, justification, faith and works, embracing the twofold justification—*duplex justificatio*—rejected after the 1541 REGENSBURG COLLOQUY. Such justification requires both the righteousness of Christ's merit and that infused by the Spirit. Other articles addressed SACRAMENTS and church practice. In concession to Protestants the Interim allowed LAITY to receive both bread and wine in the LORD'S SUPPER and permitted clerical marriage, both subject to papal dispensation (see CLERGY, MARRIAGE OF).

The Augsburg Interim was not to apply to Saxony, where the Lutheran ruler, Maurice, had sided with the emperor in the War of Smalkald. Accordingly the emperor promulgated a second document, the Leipzig Interim, which was slightly more irenic toward the Lutheran views.

The Pope denounced the Interim, preferring that discussions at Trent move more quickly. Charles V nevertheless enforced the Interim throughout most of his German empire until the 1552 Passau Treaty and the 1555 Peace of Augsburg superseded the Interim.

References and Further Reading

Mehlhausen, Joachim, ed. *Das Augsburger Interim von 1548: Deutsch und lateinisch*. Neukirchen-Vluyn, Germany: Neukirchener Verlag, 1970.

Peterson, Luther. "The Philippist Theologians and the Interims of 1548: Soteriological, Ecclesiastical, and Liturgical Compromises and Controversies within German Lutheranism." Ph.D. dissertation, University of Wisconsin, 1974.

Pfeilschifter, Georg, ed. *Acta Reformationis Catholicae Ecclesiam Germaniae Concernentia Saeculi XVI. Die Reformverhandlungen des Deutschen Episkopats von 1520 bis 1570*, vol. 6: 1538–1548, 255–348. Regensburg, Germany: Verlag Friedrich Pustet, 1974.

SUZANNE S. HEQUET

AUGUSTANA EVANGELICAL LUTHERAN CHURCH

Also known as the Augustana Synod, this group was the primary Lutheran denomination founded by immigrants to the UNITED STATES from SWEDEN. With the beginning of immigration in the 1840s and 1850s, pastors such as Lars Paul Esbjorn and T. N. Hasselquist formed ethnic Lutheran congregations in the Midwest. These congregations initially affiliated with an existing American Lutheran denomination, but withdrew and formed the Augustana Synod in June 1860, at Jefferson Prairie, Wisconsin. The Synod originally consisted of both Swedes and Norwegians, but the latter withdrew from Augustana in 1870. Synodical founders, influenced by PIETISM and critical of

State Church Lutheranism in Sweden, did not replicate the Swedish Episcopal structure in America. Strongly Lutheran in theology (the term "Augustana" refers to the AUGSBURG CONFESSION), synodical polity was essentially Presbyterian (see PRESBYTERIANISM), and its spirit reflected the moral and religious aspects of Scandinavian piety, and later, American Protestantism.

From 1860 to 1920, during the peak of Swedish immigration to the United States, the Synod grew and developed rapidly. Although it reached only a fraction of the immigrants, it was the largest single organization within Swedish America and founded numerous schools, colleges, social service agencies, and hospitals to serve immigrant needs. Besides congregations in thirty-five states and five Canadian provinces, the Augustana Synod had an active foreign MISSIONS program, especially in Tanzania, INDIA, CHINA, and JAPAN. As immigration ceased early in the twentieth century, the Synod made the difficult transition to the use of English and to being an American denomination. During the 1940s and 1950s, Augustana leaders were active in work to unite the various American Lutheran denominations, and in 1962 Augustana merged together with three other groups to form the LUTHERAN CHURCH IN AMERICA (1962–1988). By 1962 the Augustana Synod had grown to 625,000 members in more than 1,250 congregations in North America.

See also Lutheranism, Scandinavia; Lutheranism, United States

References and Further Reading

G. Everett Arden. *Augustana Heritage: A History of the Augustana Lutheran Church*. Rock Island, IL: Augustana Press, 1962.

Hugo Soderstrom. *Confession and Cooperation: The Policy of the Augustana Synod in Confessional Matters*. Lund, Sweden: CWK Gleerup Bokforlag, 1973.

MARK A. GRANQUIST

AUSTRALIA

Beginnings

Protestant Christianity in Australia was shaped by its origins in the British Isles; by the presence since the beginning of European settlement of a large minority of Roman Catholics, mainly of Irish background; and by the size and physical environment of the continent. In 1788 the British government established a penal colony in New South Wales on the eastern coast of Australia, from which grew the city of Sydney. A second settlement was made in Van Diemen's Land (Tasmania) in 1803. Although there were no apparent religious motives in the founding of these colonies, the British government appointed clergymen of the established CHURCH OF ENGLAND (Anglican Church) as chaplains, charged with the duty of providing a pastoral ministry to the whole population and inculcating order and morality. A third British colony was planted in isolated Western Australia in 1829. English Dissenters were prominent among the founders of South Australia in 1836 (see DISSENT; NONCONFORMITY). The flow of European settlement along the eastern seaboard led to the separation from New South Wales of the colonies of Victoria in 1851 and Queensland in 1859.

The dominant stream in Protestant Christianity in colonial Australia was shaped by the English evangelical movement of the eighteenth century (see EVANGELICALISM). The majority of the early Anglican clergy were evangelicals. Because of their close connection with the government they found it hard to minister effectively to the convicts, many of whom had long been estranged from organized religion. The clergy had more success with free settlers and the first generation of native-born Australians. From the early nineteenth century New South Wales became a center of missionary activity, both within Australia and in the islands of the South Pacific. The early attempts at missionary work among the Aboriginal people gained few converts, although some missionaries gained valuable knowledge of indigenous languages. From Sydney, missions were founded among the Maori of NEW ZEALAND by the (Anglican) CHURCH MISSIONARY SOCIETY in 1814 and the Wesleyan Methodists in 1822.

For the first thirty years, the Church of England was the only officially recognized religious body in the penal colonies and was therefore given land for churches and schools. Its hegemony was gradually eroded. From 1820 the government authorized the entry of Roman Catholic priests. Non-Anglican branches of Protestant Christianity established a separate existence, with their members often gathering to hold services and build chapels before the arrival of clergy. Their first ministers arrived: Wesleyan Methodist (1815), CHURCH OF SCOTLAND (1823), Congregational (1830), and Baptist (1834). During the following years almost every branch of British Protestantism was planted in the Australian colonies. Religious movements from the United States, such as Mormons (see MORMONISM) and SEVENTH-DAY ADVENTISTS, also started work. The only major religious body with a non-British background was the Lutherans, who first migrated from Germany to South Australia in 1838 and later spread elsewhere (see LUTHERANISM). The Australian colonies produced no new religious movements of significance.

A religiously mixed society, in which almost 30 percent of the population were Roman Catholics, pro-duced a strong feeling in favor of religious equality that led to a new relationship between CHURCH AND STATE. In 1836–1837 the Church Acts in New South Wales and Tasmania introduced a system of financial aid to religion, for the building of churches and the payment of clergy, in which Anglicans, Roman Catholics, Presbyterians, and Wesleyan Methodists stood on an equal footing. State aid to religion was opposed by liberals and by those Protestants who were committed to the voluntary principle, and between 1851 and 1895 it was abolished in all colonies.

Colonial Religion

During the mid-nineteenth century, each Protestant denomination established structures of self-government that were adapted to colonial conditions. In 1836 the Anglican Church founded a diocese of Australia, which was subdivided as settlement spread. Each diocese was governed democratically by a synod composed of a bishop, clergy, and lay representatives. The Wesleyan Methodists formed an autonomous Australasian Conference (embracing New Zealand and the Pacific Island missions) in 1854. Wesleyans, Primitive Methodists (see PRIMITIVE METHODIST CHURCH), and Bible Christians united nationally in 1902. The Presbyterians, who had imported a series of divisions from Scotland, achieved union in each colony in the second half of the century and formed a national church on a federal basis in 1901 (see PRESBYTERIANISM). The BAPTISTS, Congregationalists (see CONGREGATIONALISM), and Churches of Christ created unions or conferences of churches in each colony.

The religious demography of Australia that emerged during the nineteenth century was unlike any particular part of the British Isles, because in almost every region the population embraced significant proportions of Anglicans, Roman Catholics, Presbyterians, and Methodists. The level of nominal adherence was high: until the 1950s at least six in every ten Australians identified themselves with one of the three main Protestant denominations. Reflecting the influence of the Tractarian and Anglo-Catholic movements (see ANGLO-CATHOLICISM; OXFORD MOVEMENT), high church Anglican clergy disavowed the label "Protestant" and kept a distance from nonepiscopal churches. The Protestant denominations were most successful in large towns and middle-class suburbs, where they built many handsome churches. These were important centers of social life, surrounded by clusters of organizations and clubs that embraced every age group. On the other hand, Protestants had a smaller active following among the working class. They also found it hard to sustain a pastoral ministry in the outback, where European settlement was scattered over an immense area. New forms of ministry were devised, such as the (Anglican) bush brotherhoods and the (Presbyterian) Australian Inland Mission.

Between Protestants and Roman Catholics there were deep divisions, with occasional eruptions of sectarian strife. Religious separatism was reinforced by ethnic, class, and political differences. From the beginning of the twentieth century Irish-Australian Catholics, predominantly working class, tended to support the Australian Labor Party, whereas the majority of churchgoing Protestants identified themselves with conservative parties and doubted whether Catholics were truly loyal to the British Empire.

The colonial churches did not seek to be original, but sought to reproduce the patterns of church life they had known at "home." Developments in theology, church architecture, and styles of worship followed the British churches, usually a decade or so later. The debates over science and biblical criticism that began in the colonies in the 1870s largely echoed those in the British churches. It was also recognized, however, that Australian society was different, and that the churches needed to adjust overseas ideas and practices to meet local needs. Lay people assumed a more prominent role in church government than they had held in Britain. In every community, competition between denominations often stimulated activity and encouraged church building. In isolated and sparsely settled districts ("the bush"), denominational divisions counted for less, church buildings were shared, and clergy were expected to minister to all. To provide a ministry to the expanding population, all denominations relied heavily on recruits from Britain. Local candidates for the ministry were trained initially under the supervision of senior clergy and, from the second half of the nineteenth century, in denominational theological colleges. The colonial universities excluded the teaching of theology. By the beginning of the twentieth century, locally born clergy were becoming a majority.

During the final decades of the nineteenth century, the Protestant churches withdrew from the area of popular education. Initially they operated their own denominational schools and opposed a general system of schools when this was first proposed in the 1830s. However, from the 1870s, reflecting a shift in public opinion, Protestants generally accepted the introduction of a comprehensive system of state "secular" (nonsectarian) education in every colony. There were no further government grants to denominational schools until the 1960s. Whereas Roman Catholics developed a separate network of schools staffed by teaching orders, the Protestant churches relied on SUNDAY SCHOOLS and the family to impart Christian instruction to the young. They also maintained a small number of fee-paying secondary schools for boys and girls. These schools, modeled on the English public schools, were intended to educate the children of the upper middle classes. Through them the Anglican, Presbyterian, and Methodist churches established close connections with a large section of the political, business, and community leadership.

Australian Protestants in the nineteenth century were active in political and civic life. Protestant leaders sought to create a "Christian country." They regarded personal CONVERSION as primary, but they also gave a role to the government, to pass laws that would promote moral reform as the basis for prosperity and social stability. In the latter decades of the century the churches lobbied governments, with some success, for legislation to restrict the liquor trade and gambling and to preserve the sanctity of Sunday. Many of these laws survived until the 1960s. The Protestant moral reformers were given the locally coined epithet "wowser," meaning censorious and hypocritical in popular speech. During the 1890s, when depression and labor strikes brought an end to colonial prosperity, there was a shift in thinking within the churches toward "social Christianity" and the need for nonrevolutionary social reform. The Methodists, following a British model, founded the first Central Missions to reach the unresponsive urban working classes. All Protestant denominations began to establish their own welfare agencies and institutions to meet specific social needs.

Protestantism in Twentieth-Century Australia

Protestant Christians shared a dual patriotism toward Australia and the British Empire. Influential clergy wrote and spoke in support of the federation of the six colonies into the Commonwealth of Australia in 1901, and the churches campaigned successfully for the recognition of God in the preamble to the federal constitution. Because of their loyalty to Britain, Protestant leaders strongly supported World War I and conscription, although in each denomination there were some dissenting voices.

From the second half of the nineteenth century, non-Anglican Protestants worked together in Sunday School unions, charitable work, evangelistic missions, and councils of churches that were founded in each colony. A newly united nation in 1901 encouraged the idea of a national Protestant church. After federation, negotiations began for reunion of the main Protestant denominations. The Anglican and Baptist churches soon dropped out, but a scheme of union involving Methodists, Presbyterians, and Congregationalists, given up in the 1920s and revived in the 1950s, led to the formation of the UNITING CHURCH in Australia in

1977. However, a large minority of Presbyterians voted against union and remained as Presbyterians. Through their involvement in the Australian Student Christian Movement in universities, some prominent clergy became active in the ecumenical movement. An Australian council for the WORLD COUNCIL OF CHURCHES, founded in 1946, later became the Australian Council of Churches and, in 1994, the National Council of Churches in Australia. Relations with Roman Catholics were transformed during the 1960s largely as a result of the Second Vatican Council (see CATHOLICISM, PROTESTANT REACTIONS). Since the 1970s, all major denominations have cooperated to some extent in theological education, chaplaincies, the compilation of new hymn books, and joint statements on public issues. They have been influential in shaping public opinion in opposition to racism and in support of Aboriginal land rights.

Every Protestant denomination in Australia initiated and supported missionary work overseas. Their principal mission fields were in the adjacent region of the Pacific Islands and New Guinea, China, Korea, India, and East Africa. Missionary work among the Aboriginal people of Australia was given a lower priority. For a long period the Aborigines were widely seen as culturally inferior and doomed to extinction. Mission settlements tended to be separate from traditional life. From the 1960s, reflecting a greater understanding of Aboriginal culture and a change in government policy from assimilation to self-determination, the established mission institutions were handed over to local communities. An Aboriginal church with its own leadership began to emerge.

Since the colonial period, WOMEN outnumbered men in the congregations of Protestant churches. They played an important role in charitable work and fundraising, although they had few opportunities for public ministry. From the end of the nineteenth century, women were able to train for full-time church work as DEACONESSES and, in some places, represented local congregations in denominational assemblies and synods. In overseas mission fields, women of all denominations found an outlet for ministry and religious leadership that at home were open only to men. The first woman minister was ordained in a Congregational church in South Australia in 1927.

In the major denominations, after the spread of a moderate liberal theology through the theological colleges, the influence of evangelicalism waned (see LIBERAL PROTESTANTISM AND LIBERALISM). From the 1920s evangelicals, on the defensive, began to form a network of institutions and organizations, outside denominational structures, that were committed to a distinctly evangelical identity. These included Bible colleges, conventions, and nondenominational mis-

sionary societies. The Anglican diocese of Sydney remained a stronghold of conservative evangelicalism; its influence extended both nationally and beyond Australia.

During the interwar years the active membership of the Protestant churches diminished. The depression of the 1930s and World War II led to a heightened interest in social issues. In the 1950s there was a modest upsurge in church attendance and Sunday School enrollments as well as a wave of church building, comparable to the postwar religious boom in North America. Then, largely as a result of the cultural changes of the late 1960s and 1970s, the pace of growth slackened and the major denominations experienced a fall in both adherence and attendance. The influence of the Protestant churches on governments and in the wider society declined. At the same time, the immigration from Britain and northern Europe that once reinforced Protestant numbers fell away, so that during the 1980s Roman Catholics supplanted Anglicans as the largest religious denomination in the nation.

Since the 1970s there has been a shift in Australian religion toward secularization and religious pluralism, and also an expansion of evangelical and sectarian expressions of Christianity that make more stringent demands on their followers than did the old-established denominational traditions. The charismatic movement penetrated many Protestant congregations, and the various branches of PENTECOSTALISM grew in both numbers and influence, especially in Queensland. The largest of these bodies is the ASSEMBLIES OF GOD. By 2001 Pentecostals, although only one percent of the Australian population, constituted the largest group of weekly churchgoers outside the Roman Catholic Church.

Another significant movement in Australian Protestantism has been the growing visibility of women in religious leadership and the rising number of women engaged in the study and teaching of theology. Women were first admitted to the Methodist ministry in the 1960s and to the Presbyterian ministry in the 1970s. Since its formation in 1977, the Uniting Church has promoted gender equality. Among Anglicans, a long and divisive debate preceded the ordination of the first women priests in 1992, and some dioceses remained opposed.

Australian Protestantism—although the term Protestant is rarely used—is more diverse in its expressions than ever before. Every denomination embraces a range of opinion on many theological and social issues, and since the 1970s a discernible rift has emerged between liberals and conservatives. As the churches become more self-consciously Australian, there is a growing interest in the creation of an indigenous Christian spirituality that is related to the physical landscape and Aboriginal religious traditions.

See also Anglicanism; Congregationalism; Methodism; Presbyterianism

References and Further Reading

Breward, Ian. *A History of the Churches in Australasia.* Oxford, UK: Oxford University Press, 2001.

Carey, Hilary M. *Believing in Australia: A Cultural History of Religions.* Sydney: Allen & Unwin, 1996.

Emilsen, Susan, and William W. Emilsen, eds. *Mapping the Landscape: Essays in Australian and New Zealand Christianity: Festschrift in Honour of Professor Ian Breward.* New York: Peter Lang, 2000.

Harris, John. *One Blood: 200 Years of Aboriginal Encounter with Christianity. A Story of Hope.* Sydney: Albatross, 1990.

Jackson, H. R. *Churches and People in Australia and New Zealand, 1860–1930.* Wellington and Sydney: Allen & Unwin, 1987.

Kaye, Bruce, Tom Frame, Colin Holden, and Geoff Treloar, eds. *Anglicanism in Australia: A History.* Melbourne: Melbourne University Press, 2002.

Linder, Robert D. *The Long Tragedy: Australian Evangelical Christians and the Great War, 1914–1918.* Adelaide: Openbook, 2000.

Piggin, Stuart. *Evangelical Christianity in Australia: Spirit, Word and World.* Melbourne: Oxford University Press, 1996.

Thompson, Roger C. *Religion in Australia: A History.* 2nd ed. Melbourne: Oxford University Press, 2002.

West, Janet. *Daughters of Freedom: A History of Women in the Australian Church.* Sydney: Albatross, 1997.

DAVID HILLIARD

AUTHORITY

The concept of authority denotes the power and right to act with decisive effect in relation to particular circumstances and persons. The question of the reality and legitimacy of authority—the question of who or what may rightfully claim allegiance and enjoin obedience—is always a question raised with reference to particular configurations of human community.

This is evident in the varied traditions of Protestant thought concerning authority. From the time of the REFORMATION Protestant reflection on the nature and exercise of authority has focused on three mutually implicated relations: first, on the relation between Scripture and the proclamation, DOCTRINE, and discipline of the Christian community; second, on the relation between the congregation of Christian believers and those who lead in its ministry; and, third, on the relation between Christians—both individually and corporately—and the structures of civil governance. A fourth and fundamental relation cuts across all of these, that is, the relation between Jesus Christ and his gathered community. For this reason Protestant theology recognizes that the way in which the divine and salutary authority ascribed to Jesus by the Gospels is understood is basic to all other discussions of authority. This fact accounts for the intensity, promise, and peril that mark the varied treatments of scriptural, ecclesial, and civil authority in the history of Protestantism.

Authority in the Reformation Era

ADOLF VON HARNACK famously described the European Reformation of the sixteenth century as a reform of belief, but a *revolution* with regard to the authority of the CHURCH, its officers, and its traditions. MARTIN LUTHER's burning of the papal bull *Exsurge Domine* that condemned him in 1520, and HULDRYCH ZWINGLI's somewhat less dramatic act of defending the consumption of sausage in Zurich during the Lenten fast of 1522 can be taken to announce the breach as regards ecclesiastical authority that was opened up by Protestants in the early decades of the sixteenth century. Yet, any claim that, from its formative moment, Protestantism represents a repudiation of all authority would be profoundly misconceived. For the Protestant reformers discerned not only that authority was ingredient to the church's disease, but also that it was essential to its cure.

The reformers protested what they took to be improper dislocations and arrogations of authority within the corporate life and self-understanding of the Christian churches. Chief among these was a mitigation of the authority of Scripture in relation to the church, its cumulative traditions, and contemporary pastoral oversight, particularly as instantiated by the papacy. The divine authority of Christ, it was argued, was associated with and conferred on the reality and function of the Scriptures in an unparalleled way such that no church government could claim to enjoy comparable relation to Christ's own authority.

The reformers thus sought to curb pastoral abuses and to purify Christian proclamation and doctrine by ranging the entire life of the church clearly under the authority of Scripture. Sharp distinctions were drawn here: Zwingli opposed the manifold and contradictory "doctrines of men" to the "clear and certain doctrine of God" set forth in Scripture; Luther's earliest theses and tracts railed against claims to binding divine authority made on behalf of "merely human teachings." Protestants accounted for Scripture's authority by asserting its essential clarity or perspicacity, the sufficiency of its witness in matters of SALVATION, and its divine origin in the salutary activity of God. Clear, sufficient, and divine in origin, Scripture manifests, in JOHN CALVIN's words, "as clear evidence of its own truth as white and black things do of their colour, or sweet and bitter things do of their taste" (*Institutes*,

I.vii.2). Scripture, in short, was the unsubstitutable and effective means by which the Word of God addressed the church. Yet this "self-authenticating" (*autopistos*) character of Scripture needed to be adjoined, finally, by confession of the ever contemporary work of the Spirit of God. Scripture was therefore conceived in formative Protestantism as a living authority because peculiarly implicated in the activity of the living God. Recognition and trust in Scripture's authority flowed from its reception as inspired testimony to God's salutary coming to the world, now read and studied in a community of similarly inspired hearers.

It followed that the validity of any Christian doctrine rested solely on its conformity to the witness of the Scriptures in their grammatical, historical sense. This holds true for everything that has come down in the tradition, including the teachings of the fathers and councils of the early centuries. Scripture is logically antecedent to the church, being the womb from which the latter is born. As its source and basis, Scripture is also the ultimate standard and norm of the church's teaching, the "touchstone," "plumb line," and "master" of all its practice. Disputes are not decisively settled by appeals to the church teaching, ancient or modern—the authority of which, though not disregarded, is always secondary and subordinate—but solely and simply by appeal to Scripture. In dispute, a Protestant was one who desired to be and had to be defeated by Scripture, and not by appeal to the teaching and example of later generations of women and men, regardless of their personal sanctity or ecclesiastical standing.

Protestant confessional standards from this time ascribe a secondary functional authority to persons who exercise leadership in the church. In a manner formally similar to that of the tradition of Christian doctrine and practice, ministerial leaders exercise legitimate authority within the Christian community only insofar as their proclamation, teaching, and judgments evidence both dependency on and agreement with the scriptural testimony. Claims made for ministerial authority, far from being self-evident in the manner of Scripture, must be evidenced. Such authority derives its warrant from the scriptural record itself, that is, by the ordinances of Christ and the practice of the first apostles. Thus, despite drawing differing conclusions, Protestant advocates of episcopal, presbyterial, and congregationalist forms of church governance alike all concurred in principle that the POLITY of the church must comport with the biblical testimony. Similarly, moral and doctrinal discipline within and over the Christian community—for example, the practice of "the ban" in ANABAPTISM, or the exercise of presbyterial discipline in Reformed communities, and the exercise of the so-called power of the keys as-

cribed to Christian ministers to remit sin—have their positive and constraining warrants here.

The Challenge to Authority in Modern Protestant Thought

The magisterial reformers reserved some of their sharpest polemic for other Protestant "enthusiasts" and "spiritualists," for whom ecstatic experiences of the Spirit subordinated or even dissolved the binding authority of Scripture. Such emphasis on the authority of the inner testimony of the Spirit to the believer's spirit achieved enduring forms in later pietist and spiritualist movements during the seventeenth and eighteenth centuries (see PIETISM, SPIRITUALISM). So, for example, in his *Theses Theologicae* of 1675 the Quaker divine Robert Barclay confessed the personal inward experience of the Spirit to be the prime foundation of faith and life, in relation to which the Scriptures constitute a secondary and subordinate rule, they themselves being construed as but an archival record of the history of such inward testimony. Just over a century later FRIEDRICH SCHLEIERMACHER would echo these sentiments when, advocating for vibrant inward piety, he remarked that "every holy writing is merely a mausoleum of religion, a monument that a great spirit was there that no longer exists; for if it still lived and were active, why would it attach such great importance to the dead letter that can only be a weak reproduction of it?" (Schleiermacher 1988:134). On such views, the authority of inward spiritual experience is rooted in the proximate and present activity of the Spirit of God, showing how authority in Christian faith and practice is closely related to how the occurrence and reality of divine authority is grasped.

During the span of these same years the horrors of Europe's protracted "wars of religion" gave birth to widespread moral repugnance at the seeming impossibility of achieving stable social and political arrangements on the basis of an authoritative religious establishment. In this situation the idea of tolerance was embraced in wide swathes of Protestant thought as an important limiting concept to religious authority, especially when coordinated with civil power (see TOLERATION).

Further, these centuries also saw the emergence of rationalist and empiricist currents of thought in the European ENLIGHTENMENT, which challenged the validity and cogency of all traditional knowledges, including—indeed, first and foremost—that rooted in the Christian Scriptures. Taking the deductive surety of mathematics as the standard for all human knowing, rationalism repudiated the validity of authoritative teaching in the pursuit of knowledge. Rooted in observation and experiment, empiricism opened questions concerning the clarity, accuracy, and certainty of the scriptural record in unsettling ways. In both cases what was newly demanded was that traditional authorities must themselves be authorized by purportedly universal rational modes of inquiry: critical reason asks traditional ecclesial and biblical authority for their credentials and only those credentials deemed reasonable are admissible. In short, heteronomous authority and credulity were set against personal rational autonomy and criticism as the enemies of the pursuit of moral, religious, and political responsibility and maturity. In the name of the authority of the enlightened and autonomous subject, Protestant accounts of doctrinal and ecclesial authority then extant were subjected to relentless criticism.

Protestantism grappled with these challenges variously. Among those who acceded to modernity's terms of engagement was DEISM, which permitted only such beliefs as could be independently authorized by the arguments of "natural theoretical reason." In a more affective mode, NEOLOGY would exchange the authority of Scripture for the warrant provided by subjective certainty and inner peace, a view summarized under the slogan: "my experience is my proof." Translation of Protestant faith into the austere categories of autonomous moral reason represented another route of response, this one exemplified by IMMANUEL KANT, the "philosopher of Protestantism," particularly in his *Religion Within the Limits of Reason Alone.* Schleiermacher's subsequent epoch-making program to ground religion beyond the reach of rational and historical criticism in the universally demonstrable "feeling of absolute dependence" encouraged much subsequent Protestant thought to look to the deepest sentiments and pious conscience of the Christian as sites of authority.

HIGHER CRITICISM of the biblical materials participated in this contention with and for authority in modern Protestantism. Historical critics applied modernity's twin canons of universal rationality and empirical verifiability to the texts of Scripture in an effort to secure their clarity and sufficiency—that is, their truth—and in this way either to contest or to underwrite their authority. Thus, whether such readings aimed to vindicate or to repudiate the authority of the biblical record for the Christian community, they signaled a crisis of biblical authority and shared a common desire to warrant claims made for and from the authority of Scripture on other, independent grounds. Faced with this, certain streams of Protestantism made trenchant defense of the authority of Scripture by way of increasingly rigorous and thoroughgoing doctrines of its divine origin, inspiration, and infallibility. These doctrines frequently shared the cardinal assumption of the critics, that is, identification of a history "behind the text" as the decisive locus of the question of truth or falsity.

By the late nineteenth century there emerged attempts to revise the idea of authority by focusing on its perennial social and educational necessity. AUGUSTE SABATIER is representative here, acknowledging that the autonomy of conscience and action desired by moderns always "rests upon the authority of tradition and is its fruit." The authority of Bible and church are understood to be utterly transformed by rational criticism, yet they still properly persist, although now only as pedagogical and social "potencies of fact" (Sabatier 1904: preface). Such views at once echo and thoroughly revise the earlier reformers' concept of the living character of authority in the Christian community. Sabatier's contemporary ERNST TROELTSCH considered that contemporary Protestants fed on the biblical witness, but that this tradition was inert—even dead—apart from the productivity of those who tapped it. This, he argued, was what the doctrine of the inner testimony of the Holy Spirit was about. Notwithstanding the distance that separates Troeltsch's view from earlier versions of this doctrine, the question of authority in the church shows itself once more to be intimately related to convictions concerning the occurrence and locus of divine authority.

Recent decades have seen all received notions of authority in Protestant thought subjected to new challenges from a variety of quarters. The globalization of Protestant Christianity, together with the explosion of the discipline of critical hermeneutics has led to an awareness among many Protestants of the substantial difference the social and cultural location of the reader makes in the interpretation of Scripture. Claims regarding the authority of Scripture now must account for themselves in relation to other claims—not as previously, claims made by universal critical human reason, but now claims made by particular socially and culturally located forms of reasoning and experiences. These claims charge that what has hitherto represented itself as the "clear and sufficient witness of Scripture" has in fact been but one socially and culturally invested reading of these texts—largely Western, white, and male. On such views the reformers' contention that "scripture interprets itself," as well as modernity's desire to authorize only that reading of Scripture that survives disinterested rational scrutiny, have effectively, if unwittingly, handed Scripture over to all-too parochial interpreters and authorities. The hypertrophy of such views construes authority as an irredeemably ideological concept in Christian discourse that obscures the way in which all discourse and practice in the church is ultimately the self-interested application of power by its various members.

Conclusion

In its positive aspect the question of authority in Protestant theology concerns the warrants for Christian faith and life, what it is that gives rise to and permits the practices and discourses in which the Christian congregation enacts its freedom in ever changing circumstances: What authorizes such witness, such patterns of worship, such forms of service? In short, at issue is acknowledgment of the gospel's gracious provision of a definite orientation in the midst of life, God's authoring a concrete space—moral, social, and ontological—in which to speak and act.

Appreciation of this positive aspect is decisive for grasping its negative aspect. Only because the Christian community is concerned gratefully to acknowledge the divine provision of a hospitable sphere decisive for its life and witness does it concern itself with discerning the boundaries and limits of this sphere. In this sense the exercise of community discipline, doctrinal criticism, and social and political critique are in the first instance descriptive undertakings: clarification of instances when Christian practice or speech has abandoned that sphere wherein it may faithfully thrive, instances when it no longer comports with the gracious and salutary character of the power that has authored and continues to authorize it.

Thus variant understandings of authority within Protestantism can be seen to be rooted in variant convictions regarding the occurrence and reality of divine authority, convictions commonly articulated by doctrines of the Holy Spirit. A great deal trades on what is identified, for instance, as the chief site of the Spirit's work: the text of Scripture, the reading community, the conscience of the believer, the exercise of intellect on the order of things, or the unfolding of socio-historical processes. However, if attention to the loci of divine authority is an essential component, then all the more so is inquiry into the character of divine authority itself. The specific identity of the God of the gospel, and especially the enactment of this identity in the existence of Jesus Christ, will be a matter of decisive importance for a theological account of authority. For this reason, authority will not function as a strictly formal category, one whose meaning passes unchanged between Christian and other discourses. On the contrary, it is a concept whose substance will make manifest the difference made to speech and action by the effective advent of the gospel of God. This insight is expressed well at the outset of P. T. Forsyth's important study of authority when he observes: "All questions run up into moral questions; and all moral questions centre in the religious, in man's attitude to the supreme ethic, which is the action of the Holy One" (Forsyth 1952: 3).

See also Biblical Inerrancy; Modernism; Postmodernity

References and Further Reading

Achtermeier, Paul J. *Inspiration and Authority: Nature and Function of Christian Scripture*. Peabody, MA: Hendrickson Publishers, 1999.

Bauckham, Richard. *Scripture and Authority Today*. Cambridge, MA: Grove Books, 1999.

Calvin, John. *Institutes of the Christian Religion*. (1559 edition). Edited by J. T. McNeill. Translated by F. L. Battles, I: vi–x; IV: iii–xii, xx. Philadelphia: Westminster Press, 1960.

Evans, Gillian R. *Problems of Authority in the Reformation Debates*. Cambridge, UK: Cambridge University Press, 1992.

Forsyth, Peter T. *The Principle of Authority*. 2d edition. London: Independent Press, 1952.

Johnson, Robert C. *Authority in Protestant Theology*. Philadelphia: Westminster Press, 1959.

Kelsey, David H. *Proving Doctrine: The Uses of Scripture in Modern Theology*. Harrisburg, PA: Trinity Press International, 1999.

Osmer, Richard R. *A Teachable Spirit: Recovering the Teaching Office in the Church*. Louisville, KY: Westminster/John Knox Press, 1990.

Russel, Letty M. *Household of Freedom: Authority in Feminist Theology*. Philadelphia: Westminster Press, 1987.

Sabatier, Auguste. *The Religions of Authority and the Religion of the Spirit*. London: Williams & Norgate, 1904.

Schleiermacher, Friedrich. *On Religion: Speeches to its Cultured Despisers*. Translated by R. Crouter. Cambridge, UK: Cambridge University Press, 1988.

Zwingli, Huldrych. "Of the Clarity and Certainty of the Word of God." in *Zwingli and Bullinger*. Selected and Translated by G. W. Bromiley, 49–95. Philadelphia: Westminster Press, 1953.

PHILIP G. ZIEGLER

AWAKENINGS

Awakenings are complex religious movements of intense revivalism, ritual innovation, doctrinal controversy, denominational growth and conflict, and heightened public concern about the nature of true religion that have punctuated Protestant history since the eighteenth century, especially in the UNITED STATES and Britain. They are a prominent aspect of EVANGELICALISM and may be regarded as a defining feature of American religious history.

In America two such nationwide REVIVALS have been called "Great Awakenings," the first during the 1730s and 1740s and the second from the turn of the nineteenth century to 1844. Later periods of revivalism and charismatic religion have been identified that might qualify as awakenings, but none of them has yet gained that terminology. A related pattern of awakenings occurred in Britain, where they are known as

Evangelical Revivals. The first of these also took place during the 1730s and 1740s in ENGLAND, SCOTLAND, and WALES. A second and briefer Evangelical Revival appeared between 1859 and 1860 especially in Wales and Ulster. Awakenings have been controversial when they occur and they have remained so in contemporary historical and cultural interpretation.

The Great Awakening and the Evangelical Revival

The Great Awakening in America and the Evangelical Revival in Britain were a concurrent trans-Atlantic religious movement that emerged during the 1720s and 1730s out of a context of increasing popular concern with personal religion associated with PIETISM. On the European Continent, Pietism swept through GERMANY, the NETHERLANDS, and FRANCE during the late seventeenth century in reaction to the rationalistic doctrinal formulations of Protestant orthodoxy and the emerging secular philosophies of the ENLIGHTENMENT. Classically articulated by Lutheran pastor PHILIPP JAKOB SPENER in his 1674 book *Pia Desideria: or, Heartfeld Desires for a God-pleasing Improvement of the true Protestant Church,* Pietism promoted lay study of the BIBLE and community discussion of religious life. The movement also advocated educational and health reform, charitable institutions, and missions, exemplified by AUGUST HERMANN FRANCKE's orphanage and infirmary at HALLE, Germany and Count NIKOLAUS LUDWIG VON ZINZENDORF's communal group called the Moravian Brethren. Through the writings of JAKOB BOEHME, JOHANN ARNDT, Gottfried Arnold, and Gerhardt Tersteegen, Pietism also encouraged contemplation and mystical experience. Above all Pietism demanded a personal experience of spiritual regeneration and SANCTIFICATION, cultivating an intense emotional identification with the sacrificial sufferings of Christ and a childlike sense of spiritual dependency on the Risen Lord.

Pietism reached England in the early eighteenth century, where it resisted the ascendancy of ENLIGHTENMENT rationalism exemplified in JOHN LOCKE's 1695 treatise *The Reasonableness of Christianity.* The most important early English Pietists were the Congregationalist ISAAC WATTS and the Anglican WILLIAM LAW. Watts's two great poetical collections, *Hymns and Spiritual Songs* (1707) and *The Psalms of David Imitated in the Language of the New Testament* (1719), provided Dissenters with a new Pietistic hymnody that stressed the personal experience of regeneration and sanctification (see DISSENT; HYMNS AND HYMNALS). These emphases resonated with the Calvinist spirituality of seventeenth-century PURITANISM and PRESBYTERIANISM, thereby gaining adherents for Pietism among Congregationalists, BAPTISTS, and Presbyterians. The greatest early Anglican advocate for Pietism was William Law, whose widely read books, including *A Practical Treatise on Christian Perfection* (1726) and *A Serious Call to a Devout and Holy Life* (1728), emphasized the sanctified renovation of Christian life after regeneration rather than the New Birth itself.

By 1720 Pietism had crossed the Atlantic, influencing Lutheran, German Reformed, and Anabaptist churches in Pennsylvania and Dutch Reformed congregations in New York and New Jersey (see LUTHERANISM; ANABAPTISM; DUTCH REFORMED CHURCH; DUTCH PROTESTANTS IN AMERICA). In 1726 a young Dutch Reformed pastor named Theodore Frelinghuysen began preaching a conversionistic form of Pietism to his congregations in the Raritan Valley of New Jersey. Many received the New Birth, marking the first appearance of what would soon become the characteristic religious experience of the Great Awakening.

British Pietism gained a foothold during this period among Presbyterians in the Middle Colonies and New England Congregationalists (see CONGREGATIONALISM). In 1720 William Tennent, a Scots-Irish Presbyterian Pietist, took a pastorate at Neshaminy, Pennsylvania where he began training candidates for the ministry, among them his four sons. Six years later GILBERT TENNENT, one of those sons, accepted a call to a church in New Brunswick, New Jersey. The younger Tennent thus became a neighbor of Theodore Frelinghuysen and soon joined his Dutch Reformed colleague in preaching the necessity of the New Birth. As this interdenominational Pietist movement grew in the Middle Colonies, William Tennent expanded his educational efforts. In 1735 he opened the Log College in Neshaminy as a free-standing seminary for Presbyterian ministerial candidates of Pietist views.

In New England, meanwhile, a number of Congregationalist ministers had also absorbed Pietism. Among them was Solomon Stoddard, pastor at Northampton, Massachusetts from 1670 to 1730. Stoddard promoted Puritan/Pietist spirituality and presided over five different periods of intensified congregational concern for SALVATION during his sixty-year pastorate from 1660 to 1730. Stoddard's grandson JONATHAN EDWARDS joined the Northampton ministry in 1727 and in 1734, not long after Stoddard had died, the congregation experienced a massive 'revival of religion' under the preaching of its young pastor. Edwards wrote a compelling account of the events in Northampton called *A Faithful Narrative of the Surprising Work of God,* first published in 1736 by Watts in England. In *A Faithful Narrative* Edwards announced his hope that the Northampton revival presaged a much larger "season of grace" in which God would bring multitudes to true faith through the New Birth. The Northampton revival and Edwards's account of it marked another point of the Great Awakening's onset.

Back in England the writings of Law and the German Pietists inspired a group of students at Oxford to organize a religious society in 1729 that was derisively called "the Holy Club" and "the Methodists" for its ordered discipline of study, prayer, fasting, daily worship, almsgiving, and prison visitation. Led first by CHARLES WESLEY and then by JOHN WESLEY, his older brother and a fellow of Lincoln College, the Holy Club recruited a number of followers including GEORGE WHITEFIELD. In 1736 the Wesleys were ordained Anglican priests and immediately set off on a mission to America and the new British colony of Georgia, arriving there on March 9, 1736. Aboard ship was a group of Moravian missionaries who deeply impressed the Wesleys with their piety, dedication, and hymn singing. In Georgia, John created controversy by enforcing strict moral standards for admission to the LORD'S SUPPER, and the brothers returned to England early in 1738. Whitefield meanwhile had experienced the New Birth in 1737 after an extended period of fasting and ascetic discipline and embarked on February 1, 1738 for America, where he received a cordial but reserved reception in Savannah and Charleston before returning to England in the fall of that year. While Whitefield was in America the Wesleys gravitated to Peter Böhler's Aldersgate Street MORAVIAN CHURCH, where in the spring of 1738 Böhler helped guide both brothers to experiences of spiritual regeneration, famously described by John Wesley as having his heart "strangely warmed" by the infusion of the Holy Spirit.

Whitefield was ordained in late 1738 and immediately began to preach the necessity of the New Birth wherever he could find an invitation. When Anglican bishops refused to admit him to their dioceses, however, he took to the open air, preaching in cemeteries, commons, and town centers, a practice soon labeled "field preaching." Whitefield delivered his first field sermon to a crowd of coal miners at Hanham Mount in Bristol on February 17, 1739. His stentorian voice, powerful dramatization of the gospel, and charismatic emotional appeal to sinners to seek salvation converted many at Hanham, and Whitefield's vocation as "the Grand Itinerant" of the eighteenth century was sealed. The Wesleys soon joined Whitefield in field preaching and by the fall of 1739 the three young evangelists were itinerating in Bristol, London, and the Midlands with vast success, organizing converts into Methodist societies modeled on Pietist practice

and their Oxford Holy Club. The Evangelical Revival had begun.

While the Wesleys presided over the explosion of the Evangelical Revival in England, Whitefield returned to America where revivals had been gradually increasing since the publication of Edwards's *Faithful Narrative* in 1736. His controversial fifteen-month preaching tour brought the Great Awakening to its zenith. Landing at Cape Henlopen, Delaware, on October 30, he spent a month in the Middle Colonies, drawing crowds of ten thousand in Philadelphia while forging an interdenominational Evangelical alliance with Anglicans, German Pietists, Baptists, Dutch Reformed, and Presbyterians including Gilbert Tennent. Whitefield also began publishing a series of inflammatory *Journals,* in which he praised his clerical allies and criticized his opponents by name. He moved south in December through Annapolis, Williamsburg, New Bern, Charleston, and Beaufort to Savannah where he founded Bethesda, an orphan house on the model of August Hermann Francke's charitable institutions at HALLE. In the South, Whitefield's message included a moral witness against SLAVERY, for which Alexander Garden, Anglican Commissary at Charleston, banned him from preaching in Anglican parishes in the Carolinas. Undeterred, Whitefield spoke in Charleston's Congregational, Presbyterian, and Baptist meeting houses before sailing back to Philadelphia in April 1740.

Another tumultuous tour of the Middle Colonies ensued, featuring an entourage of up to forty ministers riding with Whitefield, most of them young Presbyterians from William Tennent's Log College. Then, after spending the summer of 1740 in Charleston and Savannah, Whitefield landed at Newport on September 14 to begin a New England tour that would mark the climax of the Great Awakening. Crowds of nearly twenty thousand people, the largest gatherings ever assembled in New England, greeted him on Boston Common as the city's Congregationalist ministers hailed his ministry. Whitefield traveled as far north as York, Maine, returned to Boston, then crossed Massachusetts to meet Jonathan Edwards at Northampton before sweeping south again through New Haven, New York, and Philadelphia. After celebrating Christmas at Bethesda, Whitefield sailed for England on January 16, 1741. In little more than a year he had traveled thousands of miles, preached hundreds of times, brought a charismatic experience of the New Birth to countless converts, and polarized the colonial churches around the beliefs and practices of a trans-Atlantic Evangelical movement he now led. He had just turned twenty-six years old.

The consummation of the trans-Atlantic awakenings between 1740 and 1741 did not produce much immediate conflict. In England John Wesley gathered converts into small Pietist "class meetings" bound together in local Methodist societies and served by resident elders and itinerant evangelists. Beginning in 1742 these leaders, many of them laymen, met at an annual conference presided over by Wesley himself, where the business of the Methodist "connexion" was conducted, to the consternation of Anglican authorities to whom it was technically subject. Whitefield, by contrast, relied on others to organize the Evangelical Revival beyond England. In Wales Howell Harris took the lead in assembling a cadre of Whitefieldian evangelists who drove the revival there to unprecedented heights. In Scotland local ministers like William McCulloch at Cambuslang organized the huge crowds that gathered there and elsewhere to hear Whitefield's revival preaching at massive Presbyterian public communions or "holy fairs." In America Whitefield's revival efforts were carried on by Anglican Devereux Jarratt and Presbyterian SAMUEL DAVIES in the South, Gilbert Tennent in the Middle Colonies, and Congregationalists Eleazar Wheelock and James Davenport in New England.

In both theaters of awakening, however, it was only a matter of time before the revival evoked more extreme forms of charismatic religion and schismatic conflict. In England the Wesleys' teachings produced a series of Methodist controversies during the early 1740s over the importance of "stillness" or mystical enlightenment, the extent of "Christian perfection" or freedom for consciously committed sin, and the ordination of lay preachers without university training. The most divisive dispute, however, concerned CALVINISM. In 1741 Whitefield openly embraced the Calvinist doctrines of original sin, PREDESTINATION, and ELECTION. The Wesleys answered with an Arminian position for free will, universal redemption, and the mutability of salvation. This fundamental disagreement among the Methodist leaders also divided their movement into rival institutional camps, with Whitefield's preachers, societies, and chapels withdrawing under the patronage of LADY SELINA SHIRLEY HASTINGS, countess of Huntington, while the Wesleys continued to perfect their own organization of classes, societies, circuits, and conferences.

These doctrinal and institutional tensions pervaded British METHODISM for the rest of the eighteenth century, and the Evangelical Revival also spread them to the Dissenters. Congregationalists, led by Philip Doddridge, took a moderate Calvinist view whereas Particular Baptists argued the merits of High Calvinism as propounded by London's John Gill. GENERAL BAPTISTS eventually embraced Unitarianism, forcing the sectarian separation of the New Connexion of General Baptists in 1770, who advocated ARMINIANISM. Yet out of this contested religious situation emerged a powerful interdenominational Evangelical movement, perhaps best gauged by the immense outpouring of hymns that flowed from the pens of Charles Wesley, William Cowper, Philip Doddridge, John Newton, Anne Steele, Samuel Stennett, Robert Robinson, and Edward Peronnet. The great *Selection of Hymns,* published by the Baptist John Rippon in1787, included contributions from virtually every major Revival constituency and established a canon of Evangelical sacred song that articulated the movement's spiritual consensus.

In America the Great Awakening's theological disputations and denominational conflicts primarily involved the major Reformed communions, the Presbyterians, Congregationalists, and Baptists. American Anglicans for the most part rejected all forms of Methodism, but their Reformed brethren gradually grew deeply divided over the Awakening and its implications. During the early 1740s the theological and institutional dimensions of the crisis grew increasingly intertwined. No matter how compelling the doctrine of the New Birth was to converts and revivalists, it stood in obvious tension with the Calvinist tenets of predestination and election and the American Puritan traditions of spiritual humility and perseverance. The New Birth also implied a grave challenge to church institutions. If true religion required a conscious experience of spiritual rebirth, then only the born-again should be members, and ministers, of the church.

Both of these issues exploded into the Awakening after Whitefield returned to England in 1741, fueled by the revival's continuing episodes of charismatic excess and schism. The most celebrated of these was the incendiary separatist ministry of James Davenport, Congregationalist minister at Southold on Long Island. Davenport itinerated in Connecticut after Whitefield had departed, haranguing his hearers for hours on end and obtaining from them extreme charismatic episodes of trance, glossolalia, and hysteria that he identified as signs of the New Birth. Davenport also denounced the Congregationalist establishment of Connecticut for resisting the Awakening and led his followers singing through the streets of New Haven in violation of the public peace. In response the Connecticut General Assembly exiled Davenport from the colony in May 1742 and passed "An Act for Regulating Abuses and Correcting Disorders in Ecclesiastical Affairs" that banned all unauthorized itinerancy. Davenport eventually recanted and published his *Confessions and Retractations* in 1744, but he had helped to unleash the separatist energies that attended the Awakening's advocacy of charismatic religion.

Elsewhere in New England some pro-revival ministers and lay exhorters joined Davenport's call for the regenerate to separate from a Congregationalist establishment that continued to admit members without requiring an account of their spiritual rebirth. Nearly one hundred such separations occurred during the 1740s and 1750s, afflicting one third of New England's parishes and bringing a new denomination, the Separate or Strict Congregationalists, into existence. By the mid-1740s some Separates in turn began to embrace believer's baptism as a sign of regeneration and formed yet another Great Awakening sect, the Separate Baptists, among whose early leaders were ISAAC BACKUS and Shubael Stearns. A similar schismatic pattern appeared in the Middle Colonies where Gilbert Tennent, leader of the pro-revival New Side Presbyterians, called for a born-again clergy in a combative 1741 sermon titled *The Dangers of an Unconverted Ministry*. The stark alternative, he proclaimed, was for the saved to "come out and be ye separate." Antirevival Old Side ministers, centered around Philadelphia, resisted Tennent's demand and forced the New Side to organize a schismatic Presbytery of New York and Philadelphia, which thrived from 1741 until reunion in 1757.

The Awakening brought theological controversy everywhere revivals occurred, but the most important and protracted debate took place in New England between two of the leading religious thinkers of their generation, Jonathan Edwards of Northampton and Charles Chauncy of Boston. Edwards had already emerged as the Awakening's prime defender by publishing *A Faithful Narrative* and preaching terrifying revival sermons during 1741 such as "Sinners in the Hands of an Angry God." Now he disclaimed the excesses of Davenport and the Separates while still defending the revival in a 1741 pamphlet *The Distinguishing Marks of a Work of the Spirit of God.* Edwards carefully differentiated phenomena that were not necessarily evidence of regeneration, including trance, speaking in tongues, and visions, from what he claimed was its true sign: a love of the excellency and beauty of God's plan of salvation through Christ. By refusing to condemn Separate extremism outright, however, he left the Awakening open to criticism as psychological or emotional delusion, an attack mounted vigorously by Chauncy in his 1742 sermon *Enthusiasm Described and Cautioned Against.* Arguing that the Awakening's internal and external effects were essentially mental illness, Chauncy asserted that the Bible, DOCTRINE, and reason were the best guides to true religion, not spiritual experience.

Edwards answered Chauncy's attack with *Thoughts Concerning the Revival of Religion in New England* (1742), to which the Boston minister replied with his massive *Seasonable Thoughts on the State of Religion in New England* (1743), launching an eighty-year contest for the soul of New England Congregationalism.

The two great combatants continued the controversy over the next fifteen years until Edwards's death in 1758. Their argument gradually evolved into a full-scale disputation between Calvinism and ARMINIANISM, with Edwards performing the crucial task of reconciling the Evangelical doctrine of the New Birth with Calvinism in treatises on the *Religious Affections* (1746), *Freedom of the Will* (1754), and *Original Sin* (1758). In response Chauncy elaborated an Enlightenment critique of the biblical narrative and Reformed doctrine that resulted in his embrace of Universalism in a treatise which, for the sake of church unity, he did not permit to be published until after his death as *Mystery Hid From the Ages* (1787). The New Light/Old Light controversy continued to be agitated by Edwardsean New Divinity ministers and Chauncyite Arminians through the beginning of the nineteenth century, eventually producing an Old Light separation in the Unitarian schism in 1824.

The Awakening continued to rage after 1741, but Whitefield's return in 1744 marked the reversal of its fortunes. Although vast crowds continued to attend his preaching everywhere, Old Side Presbyterians and Old Light Congregationalists actively opposed him both on the ground and in print. Whitefield returned their fire with characteristic vigor and recovered much credibility with his support for the successful 1745 American military campaign against the French stronghold at Louisbourg, Quebec, but the tide had turned. Despite important later revivals in Virginia and North Carolina among Presbyterians under Samuel Davies after 1748 and Separate Baptists under Shubael Stearns after 1755, the Great Awakening as an intercolonial religious movement was largely spent by the time Whitefield departed again for England in 1747. Although Whitefield would tour British North America four more times before his death in 1770 at Newburyport, Massachusetts, and regional revivals would flourish continually from 1750 through the mid-1790s, the extraordinary religious excitement of the Awakening's halcyon days did not stir American culture again during the eighteenth century.

The Second Great Awakening

One of the fundamental differentiations in modern Anglo-American Protestantism is the fact that massive awakenings of eighteenth-century scale continued to occur in America whereas they did not in the United Kingdom. Important Evangelical revivals happened in Wales and Ulster in 1859 and 1860 and in England and Scotland in 1870 through 1872, but they were regional movements largely limited to particular denominations, and they lacked the shaping power that the Second Great Awakening exercised in creating the religious culture of independent America.

The Second Awakening began in 1798 and 1799 at two different sites. One of these was Yale College, where TIMOTHY DWIGHT, a grandson of Jonathan Edwards, assumed the presidency in 1798. Rejecting the scholastic theological formulations and cautious evangelism of Edwards's students SAMUEL HOPKINS and Joseph Bellamy, Dwight began preaching a revival in 1799 to his students in New Haven. Among his converts were LYMAN BEECHER and Asahel Nettleton, who quickly spread the revival to Congregationalists in rural Connecticut and beyond. Their evangelism bore an unmistakably Edwardsean stamp as they urged their hearers to heed the danger of eternal damnation and contemplate the glory of God but to wait on the Spirit for an inward sign of regenerating grace and not trust in charismatic manifestations. The Second Awakening flourished in Connecticut from 1799 to about 1806 with a more contemplative and less demonstrative cast than the First, and it produced no major separations or schisms in "the land of steady habits."

Elsewhere in New England, however, Methodists and Baptists quickly capitalized on the nascent revival, bringing their unbridled evangelism to rapidly developing settlements on the northern and eastern frontiers. Methodism, which did not arrive in the region until 1789, exploded in the Upper Connecticut Valley of New Hampshire and Vermont and the Kennebec Valley of Maine. The Separate Baptists, however, benefited most from the Second Awakening in the region, expanding their already substantial base across the northern hill country from Blue Hill, Maine to Albany, New York. It was also among the Baptists that the only major schismatic movement of the early Second Awakening in New England occurred. Around 1800 two Vermont Baptist elders, Elias Smith and Abner Jones, began to oppose the denominational competition and doctrinal strife that grew especially intense in the Upper Connecticut Valley. Proclaiming a "restored gospel" based on the Bible alone and rejecting all creeds and church constitutions as profane human works, they gathered many converts into their Christian Connection.

The second site of the Second Great Awakening was the Cumberland region of central Kentucky and Tennessee on the trans-Appalachian frontier. Recently settled by Virginians and North Carolinians, the area possessed few towns or cultural institutions. Into this situation stepped James McGready, a veteran New Side Presbyterian minister who had led a revival in Guilford County, North Carolina in 1791 before moving to Logan County, Kentucky in late 1796. McGready immediately began preaching revival. In July 1798 the first conversions occurred at his Gaspar River congregation, and a year later trance and other charismatic manifestations began to appear. In June 1800 McGready's congregations gathered together at Red River for a sacramental meeting or public communion. When a woman began shouting and singing at the Monday revival sermon, John rushed through the meeting house exhorting. Soon the floor was littered with converts—men, women, and children—fallen in trance while others shouted, sang, and shook with physical manifestations of spirit possession. News of these events spread quickly, and next month at the Gaspar River sacrament meeting thousands encamped in the woods around McGready's meeting house to hear revival preaching. Baptist elders joined Methodist circuit riders and host Presbyterian ministers for an outdoor interdenominational season of charismatic revival, the first of what soon came to be called "CAMP MEETINGS."

Camp-meeting revivals spread like wild fire from Logan County through Kentucky and adjacent Tennessee. The largest and most famous of these was convened by BARTON W. STONE, another of McGready's students, at Cane Ridge in Bourbon County, Kentucky near Lexington in August 1801. A crowd estimated at between twelve and twenty-five thousand gathered on the gentle wooded slopes surrounding the meeting house, along with eighteen Presbyterian ministers and more than that number of Baptist and Methodist preachers. Religious pandemonium ensued, as preaching continued at multiple stations around the clock. An extraordinary range of charismatic "exercises" occurred in addition to the familiar trance, shouting, and speaking in tongues, including rolling, jerking of the head or limbs, dancing, laughing, singing, and barking. Sometimes these possessions continued for several hours before exhausting the converts. Cane Ridge became the symbol of the Second Awakening in the South and its general characteristics, if not its vast size and enormous spiritual intensity, were repeated countless times as the revival swept across the Appalachian Mountains first to the Carolinas and Georgia, then to Virginia and Pennsylvania.

By 1805 the primal phase of the Second Awakening in the South was over. Although revivals continued with real intensity, the Second Awakening, like the First, subsequently fell into doctrinal dispute and schism. Not surprisingly, Presbyterians in the most heated revival areas of Kentucky proved the most vulnerable to such conflict. Soon after the Cane Ridge camp meeting, Stone began preaching that the Scriptures themselves provided sufficient grace to trigger a regenerating conviction and efficacious faith in rational humans. His Presbyterian colleague Richard Mc-

Nemar, stationed nearby in southern Ohio, adopted similar teachings and added a powerful strand of millennial expectation that viewed the Awakening as a sign of Christ's imminent return. In 1803 they and three other ministers withdrew from the Synod of Kentucky to form the independent Presbytery of Springfield. A year later they dissolved that institution in favor of pursuing a Restorationist faith based in the Bible alone, much as Elias Smith and Abner Jones were doing in New England at the same moment. McNemar joined the SHAKERS, a New England sect also from the Revolutionary period, whose missionaries arrived in the Ohio Valley in early 1805 and converted many erstwhile Springfield Presbyterians to their celibate, communal, and millennial gospel. Stone, on the other hand, gathered his followers into a Restorationist church they simply called "Christian." RESTORATIONISM also flourished elsewhere in the South, where it was embraced in 1808 by Presbyterian schismatic Thomas Campbell's Christian Association in western Virginia and Pennsylvania. Campbell's son Alexander extended the vision of a nondenominational apostolic community, organizing the DISCIPLES OF CHRIST, the largest Restorationist sect of the Second Awakening, in 1827. East of the Appalachians the Restorationist movement also flourished, with James O'Kelly's Republican Methodists, an egalitarian sect from the Upper South, merging with Elias Smith's Christian Connection in 1809.

Meanwhile in the Cumberland region the Old Side Presbyterians had protested against what they regarded as the Arminian teachings of New Side revivalists and contested their authorization of lay exhorters to preach in the revival. In 1810 their agitation finally provoked Finis Ewing and Samuel McAdow to lead a group of New Side churches to form the Cumberland Presbyterian Church. In German-speaking areas of the Upper South and Pennsylvania two new Pietist sects appeared in 1800 and flourished in the Second Awakening, the BRETHREN IN CHRIST gathered by German Reformed pastor William Otterbein and the Evangelical Association founded by Lutheran Jacob Albright and Mennonite Martin Boehm.

Whereas the early Second Awakening thus produced a significant amount of sectarian dispute and schism, it also united vast regions of the new nation in a common evangelical religious culture. In just a few years scattered Presbyterian, Baptist, and Methodist enclaves expanded across the length and breadth of the land. Just as important, they created an evangelical religious style of born-again spirituality and moral discipline, lived out in gathered congregations of the regenerate and punctuated by the rituals of the camp meeting, that penetrated all levels of American society. In denominational terms the Methodists emerged from the Second Awakening as the largest religious body in the new nation. Much of the credit for this success belonged to their indefatigable leader bishop FRANCIS ASBURY, whose tight administrative control of the far-flung network of Methodist circuit riders honed it into the most effective medium of religious change in American history. The Baptists, more divided and less well organized than the Methodists, nonetheless made great strides behind their farmer-preachers to stand just behind their principal rival. Ironically, the Presbyterians, who played such a major role in the Awakening's onset, were handicapped by a shortage of trained ministers and deeply divided by Restorationism and other dissenting movements, and despite regional gains in New England and a Plan of Union they signed with the Presbyterians in 1801, the Congregationalists continued to fall behind their evangelical competitors.

The War of 1812 brought the residual revivals of the early Awakening to a halt, but the remarkable vitality of popular EVANGELICALISM quickly reasserted itself by the end of the decade. The center of this second wave of revivalism was Upstate New York, a region originally settled mainly by New England Evangelicals from the Upper Connecticut Valley, then opened to intensely rapid development by the completion of the Erie Canal in 1825. The leading evangelist of this later phase of the Second Awakening was CHARLES GRANDISON FINNEY, a country lawyer from Adams, New York who was converted at the age of twenty-nine and ordained a Presbyterian minister three years later.

Finney developed a unique and powerful style of preaching that brought revivals between 1825 and 1827 to the booming Mohawk Valley towns of Rome, Utica, and Troy. Finney's theology was decidedly Arminian—he argued that sinners were "bound to change their own hearts"—his wrenching sermons often provoked emotional outbursts from his listeners, and he encouraged women to pray publicly at prayer meetings. Despite protests against these practices from Lyman Beecher and Asahel Nettleton, Finney brought the revival to northeastern cities including Philadelphia, New York, and Boston before enjoying his greatest success in the 1830–1831 revival at Rochester, New York. Over the next few years Finney developed a set of controversial "new measures" that professionalized urban revivalism. They including week-long "protracted meetings" in hired halls as well as churches, employment of a minister of music to prepare worship music appropriate to revivals, and "the anxious seat," a front-row bench designated solely for those who publicly expressed their need of salvation. Finney defended these "new measures" to great acclaim in his 1835 *Lectures on Revivals of*

Religion, the Second Awakening's most important book about revivalism. At the end of the Awakening Finney embraced perfectionism and abolitionism (see SLAVERY, ABOLITION OF), two causes he continued to advocate later as professor of theology and president of Oberlin College.

If Finney proclaimed an irenic and centrist vision of Evangelicalism, his colleagues in Upstate New York did not follow it. During the 1820s and 1830s the region experienced revivals of such intensity and rancorous competition that it became known as "the BURNED-OVER DISTRICT." Out of this epicenter of discord came radical new restorationist, perfectionist, and eschatological sects, the most important of which were JOSEPH SMITH's Church of Jesus Christ of Latter-day Saints (see MORMONISM), John Humphrey Noyes's Oneida Community, and WILLIAM MILLER's Adventist movement (see SEVENTH-DAY ADVENTISTS). In 1826 Smith experienced an angelic vision describing ancient engraved records buried near his home in Palmyra, New York. He claimed to have found and translated these records, which told the epic story of an extinct Israelite tribe that had fled the Babylonian Captivity, sailed to America, built a civilization, received the gospel directly from the risen Christ, and was destroyed in a fratricidal war. Published in 1830 as *The Book of Mormon,* Smith's text was embraced by thousands as a new Scripture that solved the roiling doctrinal disputes of the day and provided a blueprint for rebuilding Zion in America. Smith, hailed as the true prophet of God by his followers, organized the Mormons according to the patriarchal and communal model of *The Book of Mormon,* eventually including polygamy, and led them on a much-persecuted pilgrimage that ended with his murder by a mob in Carthage, Illinois in 1844. His successor BRIGHAM YOUNG shortly thereafter led the Mormons to Salt Lake City, Utah where they finally built their communal religious regime.

John Humphrey Noyes, a theology student at Yale and Andover Seminary during the 1830s, formed communal societies at Putney, Vermont in 1840 and Oneida, New York in 1848. Like Smith, Noyes proclaimed a set of radical restorationist and eschatological beliefs and exercised absolute authority over his community. He announced that Christ had returned at the destruction of the Second Temple in Jerusalem in 70 A.D. and had appointed Noyes to rule the millennial kingdom on earth in the Last Days. Although never large, the Oneida Community gained fame and no little scandal from its eccentric sexual practices including the sharing of partners, initiation of virgins by Noyes and other leaders, and selective breeding of community children.

Perhaps the most radical of all the Second Awakening's sectarian movements, however, were the Millerites or Adventists. New York Baptist William Miller's 1835 book *Evidences from Scripture and History of the Second Coming of Christ about the Year 1843* tapped a deep reservoir of eschatological expectation and speculation that had attended the Awakenings since Jonathan Edwards. Miller offered proofs for Christ's imminent return based on complex calculations from biblical prophecies, especially the Book of Daniel and the Book of Revelation. These apparent demonstrations from an unassailable text convinced many that the end was nigh. Early convert Joshua Hines publicized Miller's predictions and organized the Adventists as a religious movement. When the promised Second Coming did not occur, Miller recalculated the date for October 22, 1844. His movement survived "the Great Disappointment," however, when two younger leaders, Hiram Edson and ELLEN WHITE, reported seeing in vision Christ entering God's temple in heaven on that date to begin preparations for the Last Judgment.

Events like Joseph Smith's murder and "the Great Disappointment" marked the exhaustion of the Second Great Awakening, but an even more fundamental source of evangelical disarray was its internecine dispute over slavery. Ever since Whitefield, moral and social reform had been part of the evangelical cultural agenda. During the Second Awakening Lyman Beecher took the lead in organizing voluntary associations to introduce greater moral discipline in American public life, including the American Society for the Promotion of Temperance (1826). By the 1830s an "Evangelical empire" of interlocking moral reform societies addressed public issues from education and literacy to international peace. The most intractable social problem Evangelicals faced, however, was slavery. After independence most evangelical denominations condemned slavery and threatened to excommunicate slaveholding members. In the South, however, this public religious imperative gradually privatized, with slaveholding becoming a matter of individual conscience and masters urged to make the gospel available to their slaves as a Christian duty. At the same time many Evangelicals supported the AMERICAN COLONIZATION SOCIETY (1816), an effort to relocate free blacks and manumitted slaves in Africa. By 1820, however, the resurgence of the cotton economy induced southern Evangelicals to mount a biblical defense of slavery based on Israelite precedent in the Old Testament.

Among African Americans the Second Awakening had an enormous impact. In the North, free blacks formed their first independent denominations under Methodist influence: RICHARD ALLEN's AFRICAN

METHODIST EPISCOPAL CHURCH (1816) and James Varrick's AFRICAN METHODIST EPISCOPAL ZION CHURCH (1822). In the South many Evangelical masters had indeed supported Christianization of their slaves, albeit with a version of the gospel heavily skewed toward obedience on earth and joy in heaven. Although slaves attended formal services provided by their masters, they also created their own religious culture that blended together evangelical elements of charismatic experience and biblical imagery with surviving West African religious practices including spirit possession and an extended ritual dance called the ring shout. Slave religion also produced its own Afro-Evangelical mode of preaching, called the chanted sermon, that along with the ring shout centered worship in furtive "brush arbor" meetings away from the eyes of masters and overseers. The revolutionary potential of evangelical teachings was not lost on the slave community as the leaders of the three major slave rebellions of the period, Gabriel Prosser, Denmark Vesey, and Nat Turner, were all Methodists who received the call to rebel through religious visions.

With Nat Turner's Rebellion in 1831 and the South Carolina Nullification Crisis in 1833, the slavery issue became increasingly agitated by evangelical abolitionists in the North who gravitated to the American Anti-Slavery Society (1832). In 1837 the Presbyterians divided in the New School/Old School schism, which broke along regional lines without specifically raising the slavery problem, whereas the Disciples of Christ maintained neutrality, arguing that it was a strictly political matter. The ecclesiastical crisis came to a climax, however, between 1843 and 1844 when both the Methodists and the Baptists divided North and South explicitly over the question of whether a Christian minister could own slaves. These denominational fractures extinguished what remained of the Second Awakening and fatefully engaged Evangelicals as rival partisans in the conflict that would eventually lead to civil war.

Interpretive Issues

Awakenings are complex and controversial events, and it should come as no surprise that they continue to raise difficult and hotly debated definitional and interpretive questions today. The term "Great Awakening" first appeared as a historical concept in 1841 in Joseph Tracy's book of the same name. In an 1880 study John Henry Overton coined the term "the Evangelical Revival" for its British counterpart. By the 1940s historians had begun writing about a "Second Great Awakening" in early nineteenth-century America and a "Second Evangelical Revival" in mid-nineteenth century Wales and Ulster. Are there other such episodes that should also be regarded as "great awakenings?" To answer that question in turn requires a definition of such movements, their causes, qualities, and consequences. Scholars have not closely addressed the problem of additional awakenings, but the definitional and interpretive issues surrounding the First and Second Great Awakenings and the Evangelical Revival have generated some of the most important recent critical discourse about modern Protestantism.

There are many candidates for "great awakening" designation in British and American history since 1844. Some of these later revivals even took place concurrently in both nations, as the Great Awakening and Evangelical Revival had. In Britain intense revival episodes occurred in Wales and Ulster in 1859 and 1860, in Scotland during the 1870s by the evangelism of American revivalists DWIGHT L. MOODY and IRA B. SANKEY, and in Wales during 1905 and 1906, although these revivals were of limited regional and denominational extent and they did not make a transformational impact on British religious culture, where Evangelicals remain a limited minority. In America, however, awakening-like movements have continued to appear regularly since the Second Great Awakening. The Businessmen's Revival of 1858–1859 was cut short by the CIVIL WAR, but the case could be made that it resumed with the Moody–Sankey urban revivals of the 1870s in northern cities. Those powerful evangelistic crusades, combined with the resurgence of southern Evangelicalism after Reconstruction and the Holiness Revival in the Midwest, could readily be construed as a nationwide postbellum great awakening, complete with a new doctrinal emphasis on SANCTIFICATION, new schismatic movements, and a new style of revival song called the gospel hymn.

An even stronger argument can be mounted that the Fundamentalist–Pentecostal revivals of 1901 through 1914 and 1919 through 1925 were a great awakening. The decades before and after World War I witnessed powerful revivals across the United States from which emerged FUNDAMENTALISM and PENTECOSTALISM, the two most important shaping forces in twentieth-century American Protestantism. As in the certified Great Awakenings, controversies over religious experience and doctrine raged among Evangelicals during this period, especially claims about speaking in tongues and the inerrancy of Scripture, bringing schismatic divisions in almost every denominational family.

Two more great awakenings might be claimed since World War II. The first of these is the immediate post-War renewal of Fundamentalism and Pentecostalism led by the evangelism of BILLY GRAHAM and

ORAL ROBERTS and consolidated by the organization of the NATIONAL ASSOCIATION OF EVANGELICALS in 1943. Although not as extensive as other episodes, the post-War revival marked the renewal of these movements and their outfitting for further success in the third Fundamentalist–Pentecostal revival of 1974 through 1990, sometimes called the Bicentennial Revival. For size, extent, intensity, and impact, this most recent nationwide revival measures up well against either of the first two Great Awakenings. It also produced new mass-media evangelistic techniques, a distinctive form of worship music called the praise song, powerful new religiopolitical movements like JERRY FALWELL's MORAL MAJORITY and Ralph Reed's Christian Coalition, and a seismic shift in denominational fortunes toward the SOUTHERN BAPTIST CONVENTION, the ASSEMBLIES OF GOD, the CHURCH OF GOD IN CHRIST, and the Church of Jesus Christ of Latter-day Saints. From this evidence it seems clear that great awakenings have continued since the Civil War as a distinguishing aspect of American Protestantism and that at least two or three have fair claim to that appellation.

Critical interpretation has focused on the two canonical Great Awakenings in America. The problems are legion, and of the most basic kind: Why did they begin? How are they to be defined? When and why did they end? The interpretive debate began in the 1950s with the fundamental problem of the Great Awakening's origins. European historians and social scientists had been arguing the relationship of the English Evangelical Revival to the Industrial Revolution since Elie Halevy's *The Birth of Methodism* (1903). At mid-century the Marxist view prevailed that it was a class response to economic alienation, a case presented most persuasively in E. P. Thompson's *The Making of the English Working Class* (1963). In America the Second Awakening offered a promising case for such social causation interpretations. A number of studies, led by Whitney R. Cross's 1950 book *The Burned-over District; the Social and Intellectual History of Enthusiastic Religion in Western New York, 1800–1850,* argued that the Second Awakening arose from the impact of rapid socioeconomic change on the individualistic American character classically described in Frederick Jackson Turner's *The Frontier in American History* (1920). This view found its most sophisticated expression in Donald G. Mathews's influential 1969 essay "The Second Great Awakening as an Organizing Process, 1780–1830: An Hypothesis," which focused on the social control created by revivalist networks and denominational institutions.

There appeared to be no comparable origin for the First Awakening, however. Occurring in a stable agrarian colonial society, the Great Awakening did not seem to be a response to social or political crisis. What, then, could explain it? In a series of essays and books including a biography of Jonathan Edwards, literary critic and historian Perry Miller answered by locating the sources of the Awakening in the rhetoric of the JEREMIAD, a genre of seventeenth-century New England Puritan sermons. The jeremiad depicted events such as famine, earthquake, and military defeat as divine judgments brought on the people by their sinfulness and lack of faith, the only remedy for which is repentance and renewal of true religion. According to Miller, this literary strategy was based on myth rather than historical reality. There was no real decline in religiousness, nor of course was it a cause of divine punishment. The jeremiad did serve, Miller concluded, as an ideal vehicle to renew religious commitment, which function it performed again during the Great Awakening when revivalists precipitated a cultural crisis by turning its focus from public religion to private belief and assurance of salvation.

This literary interpretation, with its emphasis on religious rhetoric and Calvinist doctrinal formulation, held sway into the mid-1960s, when a new generation of feminist and liberationist historians began to interpret both Awakenings through the social categories of race, class, and gender. Eugene G. Genovese and Albert Raboteau highlighted the role of the evangelical movement in transforming southern plantation culture and slave religion, whereas Mary Beth Norton and Nancy F. Cott emphasized the Awakenings' valorization of women and children as its ideal converts and sanctified Christians. Ann Douglas pressed the gender case so far as to read "the feminization of American culture" in the Second Awakening's cultivation of a female audience and women's sensibilities. Rhys Isaac's influential 1982 book *The Transformation of Virginia, 1740–1790* outlined a "dramatistic anthropology" in which the First Awakening provided marginal Baptists and Presbyterians with new ideological and ritual resources that they deployed to improve their social status.

Although these sociocultural investigations yielded rich new evidence and crucial interpretive insights, none of them fully addressed the problem of causation. In 1982, however, an influential essay by Jon Butler introduced a new Postmodern view of the First Awakening by returning to Miller's emphasis on religious rhetoric. Moving far beyond Miller's claims, Butler insisted not only that the Awakening was expressed in rhetorical forms but that it was itself a fictional construction of what he called "interpretive literature." Applying Postmodern literary criticism to newspaper accounts and controversial literature written by revivalists and their opponents, Butler argued that the Great Awakening was more a dramatic cultural image than a religious reality.

Subsequent studies of both Awakenings have followed this line of literary analysis. In 1986 Harry S. Stout provided a detailed reader response interpretation of the Great Awakening's revival sermons in *The New England Soul: Preaching and Religious Culture in Colonial New England*. Three years later Nathan O. Hatch's book, *The Democratization of American Christianity,* extended this perspective to the Second Awakening, arguing that its crucial feature was the emergence of a "sovereign audience" for popular religion through the Evangelicals' creation of democratic public media including camp meetings and Finneyite urban revivalism, religious magazines, printed sermon collections, and spiritual autobiographies, and hymnody. In the 1990s Stout and Frank Lambert both published biographies of George Whitefield that emphasized the First Awakening's ideological agenda, entertainment value, and media presentation. The title of Lambert's 1999 book, *Inventing the "Great Awakening,"* neatly summarizes the current claim of this interpretive view that in America's primal religious movement, the medium was the message.

The Awakenings have thus become a centerpiece of Postmodern American historical interpretation. Butler, Stout, Lambert, and Hatch have made an undeniably important contribution to the understanding of American Evangelical Protestantism. Their central claim that the Awakenings were media-driven, however, leaves questions of religious experience, belief, and institutions in suspension. If conversion experiences and sanctified lifestyles were essentially induced by an evangelical media barrage, what exactly is their status as religious phenomena? What is to be made of changing denominational fortunes among competing evangelical communions, beyond the differential popular appeal of their various media outlets? What accounts for termination of Awakenings—did they stop simply because religious media lost their appeal, or did they actually continue on below the surface of public culture after the media spotlight turned off? Most important, in what sense can the "sovereign audience" of the Awakenings be said to have been religious at all, if the classical confessions and denominational institutions of American Protestantism were relativized and subsumed under the more fundamental agency of media consumerism? These are weighty questions about the past, and the future, of American Protestantism and indeed of American culture at large. Their salience, and the continuing debate about them, is tribute to the fundamental importance of the Awakenings in understanding the history and cultural legacy of Evangelical Protestantism.

References and Further Reading

Boles, John B. *The Great Revival: Beginnings of the Bible Belt.* Lexington, KY: University Press of Kentucky, 1996.

Butler, Jon. "Enthusiasm Described and Decried: The Great Awakening as Interpretive Fiction." *Journal of American History* 69 no. 2 (September 1982): 305–325.

Carwardine, Richard. *Transatlantic Revivalism: Popular Evangelicalism in Britain and America, 1790–1865.* Westport, CT: Greenwood Press, 1978.

Cott, Nancy F. *The Bonds of Womanhood: "Woman's Sphere" in New England, 1780–1835.* New Haven, CT: Yale University Press, 1977.

Crawford, Michael J. *Seasons of Grace: Colonial New England's Revival Tradition in its British Context.* New York: Oxford University Press, 1991.

Cross, Whitney R. *The Burned-Over District; the Social and Intellectual History of Enthusiastic Religion in Western New York, 1800–1850.* Ithaca, NY: Cornell University Press, 1950.

Douglas, Ann. *The Feminization of American Culture.* New York: Knopf, 1977.

Goen, C. C. *Revivalism and Separatism in New England, 1740–1800: Strict Congregationalists and Separate Baptists in the Great Awakening.* Middletown, CT: Wesleyan University Press, 1987.

Hambrick-Stowe, Charles E. *Charles G. Finney and the Spirit of American Evangelicalism.* Grand Rapids, MI: Wm. B. Eerdmans, 1996.

Heyrman, Christine Leigh. *Southern Cross: the Beginnings of the Bible Belt.* New York: A.A. Knopf, 1997.

Isaac, Rhys. *The Transformation of Virginia, 1740–1790.* Chapel Hill: University of North Carolina Press, 1982.

Johnson, Paul E. *A Shopkeeper's Millennium: Society and Revivals in Rochester, New York, 1815–1837.* New York: Hill and Wang, 1978.

Lambert, Frank. *Inventing the "Great Awakening."* Princeton, NJ: Princeton University Press, 1999.

Miller, Perry. *Nature's Nation.* Cambridge, MA: Harvard University Press, 1967.

————, and Alan Heimert, eds. *The Great Awakening: Documents Illustrating the Crisis and its Consequences.* Indianapolis, IN: Bobbs-Merrill, 1967.

Norton, Mary Beth. *Liberty's Daughters: the Revolutionary Experience of American Women, 1750–1800.* Boston: Little, Brown, 1980.

Numbers, Ronald L., and Jonathan M. Butler, eds. *The Disappointed: Millerism and Millenarianism in the Nineteenth Century.* Bloomington: Indiana University Press, 1987.

Raboteau, Albert J. *Slave Religion: the "Invisible Institution" in the Antebellum South.* New York: Oxford University Press, 1978.

Schmidt, Leigh Eric. *Holy Fairs: Scottish Communions and American Revivals in the Early Modern Period.* Princeton, NJ: Princeton University Press, 1989.

Semmel, Bernard. *The Methodist Revolution.* New York: Basic Books, 1973.

Shipps, Jan. *Mormonism: The Story of a New Religious Tradition.* Urbana: University of Illinois Press, 1985.

Stout, Harry S. *The Divine Dramatist: George Whitefield and the Rise of Modern Evangelicalism* (Imprint). Grand Rapids, MI: Wm. B. Eerdmans, ca. 1991.

———. *The New England Soul: Preaching and Religious Culture in Colonial New England.* New York: Oxford University Press, 1986.

Watts, Michael R. *The Dissenters from the Reformation to the French Revolution.* Oxford: Oxford University Press, 1978.

STEPHEN MARINI

AZARIAH, VEDAYAGAM SAMUEL (1874–1945)

Indian church leader. Azariah was born near Tinnevelly (Tirunelveli), South India on August 17, 1874, and died at Dornakal, South India on January 19, 1945. He was the son of a Tamil Nadar convert who became an Anglican pastor, and who died during his son's infancy. Azariah attended Madras Christian College, although without graduating, and in 1895 was appointed traveling secretary for South India of the YMCA.

Impressed by the evangelistic zeal of Christians in Ceylon he developed a vision that Indian Christians should take responsibility for their church and for spreading Christian faith. In 1903 he and some friends founded the Indian Missionary Society (IMS) for the Tinnevelly area; in 1905, with K. T. Paul and others, he founded a more broadly based National Missionary Society. Azariah joined the earliest IMS mission, working from a disused brewery in the neglected Telugu-speaking area of Dornakal in Madras diocese. Ordained (although without seminary training) in 1909, he attended the WORLD MISSIONARY CONFERENCE in Edinburgh the following year. His speech on the relations of Western missionaries and national Christian workers made a deep impression.

In 1912 he became the first Indian Anglican bishop, with Dornakal as his diocese and (at first) an entirely Indian clergy. His period of office saw rapid church growth; thousands from the depressed Mala and Madiga communities became Christians. Although a supporter of the Indian national movement, Azariah clashed with Gandhi, who believed the mass movements to the church were politically damaging. Azariah urged Indian Christians to show initiative, self-support, and generosity. Newly baptized converts pledged themselves to evangelism, and the magnificent Dornakal Cathedral was built entirely with local resources. Azariah also incorporated aspects of Indian cultures into church worship. He lamented the effects of Western denominationalism on India, and he was one of the leaders of the movement that resulted in the CHURCH OF SOUTH INDIA, although he died before its inauguration.

See also Anglicanism; Denomination; India; Mass Movements, India; Missions; Missions, British; South India, Church of; YMCA, YWCA

References and Further Reading

Primary Source:

Azariah, V. S. *Christian Giving.* London: Lutterworth Press, 1954.

Secondary Sources:

Graham, Carol. *Azariah of Dornakal.* London: SCM, 1946.
Harper, Susan Billington. *In the Shadow of the Mahatma: Bishop VS Azariah and the Travails of Christianity in British India.* London: Curzon Press and Grand Rapids, MI: Wm. B. Eerdmans, 2000.

ANDREW F. WALLS

AZUSA STREET REVIVAL

Although, like most Protestants, modern Pentecostals trace their origins to beliefs and practices from the New Testament church, they also recognize more recent precursors. Among the most important of these was the series of events known as the Azusa Street Revival, whose principal instigator was William Seymour, an African-American preacher who had attended Charles Parham's Bible school in Houston, Texas. Following the teachings of his mentor, founder of the Apostolic Faith Movement, Seymour held that glossolalia (see TONGUES, SPEAKING IN) was the necessary sign of the baptism of the Holy Spirit and the third stage in Christian maturation, following CONVERSION and SANCTIFICATION. Although already so regarded by some in the HOLINESS MOVEMENT, Parham's (and Seymour's) innovation was insistence on the necessity of glossolalic evidence for this third level of experience.

Seymour introduced Parham's ideas when he became pastor of a Nazarene church in Los Angeles. But his belief that only those who had spoken in tongues had actually received the baptism of the Holy Spirit offended church members who had claimed the experience for much of their lives without glossolalic evidence. Seymour argued that they had only experienced sanctification and that another stage in Christian maturity awaited them. Expelled from his pastorate, he began to hold meetings in the homes of sympathetic supporters. A breakthrough occurred on April 9, 1906, when an 8-year-old boy became probably the first of Seymour's followers to experience the baptism of the Holy Spirit evidenced by speaking in tongues. Seymour rented an abandoned Methodist church at 312 Azusa Street in Los Angeles and began three years of meetings characterized by such charismatic gifts as speaking and singing in tongues.

Crowds flocked to Azusa Street. By late summer, some twelve hundred people attended a prayer meeting there. The San Francisco earthquake of April 1906 contributed to the Revival's success; supportive evangelists argued that the disaster signaled the imminence of doomsday and urged people to join the Revival while time allowed.

By year's end, nine Pentecostal congregations were meeting in Los Angeles. Although Seymour was affiliated with the Apostolic Faith Movement, William Parham did not capitalize on his protege's successes. Parham was disturbed by the interracial character of the Azusa Street Revival, fearing that some of the glossolalia going on there was illegitimate. Parham held that after the glossolalia signaling the baptism of the Holy Spirit, believers would use their spiritual gift to spread the gospel using earthly languages spoken through divine grace. By dismissing some of the Azusa Street glossolalia as babbling and attempting to assert his influence, Parham created openings for Pentecostal groups to rival his own movement. Seymour's meetings led directly to the development of African-American Pentecostal denominations, such as the CHURCH OF GOD IN CHRIST, and influenced the emergence of primarily white groups, including the ASSEMBLIES OF GOD and the United Pentecostal Church.

See also Pentecostalism

References and Further Reading

Goff, James R., Jr. *Fields White Unto Harvest: Charles F. Parham and the Missionary Origins of Pentecostalism.* Fayetteville, AK: University of Arkansas Press, 1988.

Hollenweger, W. J. *The Pentecostals: The Charismatic Movement in the Churches.* Minneapolis, MN: Augsburg, 1972.

WILLIAM M. CLEMENTS

B

BACH, JOHANN SEBASTIAN (1685–1750)

German organist and composer. Chronologically, the music of Bach coincides with a peak point in European humanism, in that he was born in 1685 and died in 1750, just as the "modern world" was taking shape. He is less decisively, or at least less straightforwardly, representative of the era than his contemporary Handel who, born in the same year as Bach, died nine years later: for Handel's favorite métier was heroic opera, the most patent and potent manifestation of the High Baroque's self-glorification, so that most of his music was directed toward human gratification, rather than to the worship of God. Handel, born in staunchly Teutonic HALLE, spent his apprentice years in Italy, where in his early twenties he produced dazzling ceremonial works as well as heroic operas; and was then established in ENGLAND, to become an icon of the rising middle class, with its ethical rather than religious morality. Handel was thus a European figure, if not yet fully international, whereas Bach was content to remain parochially a servant of the Lutheran church, fulfilling a series of ecclesiastical appointments. True, he made two arduous pilgrimages, on foot, to visit the ancient organist Reinken and the brilliant Scandinavian organist DIETRICH BUXTE-HUDE—but that was in the interests of music, and of God, not of self-advancement.

It is often said that Bach was born "out of his time," a statement that conflicts with the view that genius always knows the right time and place to be born. In fact there was no such conflict, and the rightness of time and place was, if in a sense negative, positive in that the Bach family, the longest and most distinguished musical dynasty known to European history, came from the province of Thuringia, where the countryside was of considerably physical beauty, whereas

the human community was small, self-subsistent, and culturally energetic. The Thuringians were sturdy, devout folk, dedicated to music both for worship and pastime; yet they could not afford to be cozily self-indulgent. GERMANY was a network of petty princedoms, distracted throughout the fifteenth and sixteenth centuries by religious and political dissension that attained a horrifying climax when, in the seventeenth century, Catholic emperors strove ruthlessly to extirpate the Lutheran HERESY. The Thirty Years' War was possibly more appalling in devastation than any European war before the presumptively enlightened twentieth century. Catholics and Protestants (the latter originally Lutherans and Calvinists) both called themselves Christians yet were driven to extravagancies of cruelty and hatred in their pursuit of what they deemed to be truth. J. S. Bach became the greatest—the most profound, but also the most exalting—of Christian composers; and his preeminence depended on the degree to which his music was bifurcated between Catholic and Protestant values, in a way that suggests that a *conjunctio oppositorum* (in the Jungian sense) was fundamental to Christianity's triumph.

The life and work of Bach's greatest German predecessor, HEINRICH SCHÜTZ (1585–1642), who survived through the Thirty Years' War, to a degree anticipated this. It would seem that if a man is strong enough, belief may batten on distress—he may even feel the psychic realities of his nature the more deeply when the world seems to be passing him by. Certainly for Schütz the bifurcations entailed by the war were not all loss; it was to its enrichment that Schütz's music could fuse the Italian flamboyance of the Catholic and autocratic south with the Teutonic abnegatory flavor of the Protestant incipiently proletarian north. In musical terms, the Italiante elements brought operatic lyricism and figurative opulence, whereas the

Germanic elements fused old-fashioned contrapuntal "science" with a harmonic acerbity learned from the Italians, but rendered darker and gloomier. Schütz himself went to Italy to study with "the sagacious Monteverdi," whose sun-baked brilliance irradiated his early works, and through them the chapels of German princelings. Yet Schütz's music preserved, and progressively intensified, a mystical quality that concentrates on Christ as a Man who became God, equating his suffering with ours; and "our" anguish was in Schütz's day undeniable because after the war Teutonic oases of humanism precariously prospered over an abyss. This was sometimes literally true. Esterházy, later the home of Haydn's benevolent patron, was a fairy-tale Versailles built by woefully oppressed serfs over a marshy morass, with the intent to prove that whatever a *Roi Soleil* could do a German princeling could do, if not better, at least in the teeth of more inimical circumstances.

By Bach's day the vainglory of a decadent humanism was to some degree in abeyance. The decline of central government and the warring multiplicity of petty tyrannies led to an idealistic if unfulfilled desire for order, reflected in the attempt of Karl Ludwig's Peace Church to reconcile Catholics, Lutherans, and Calvinists—a task then not feasible, and apparently still beyond our capabilities 300 years later. Of course these dissensions were never merely doctrinal: they also involved tensions between the old-fashioned medieval Chain of Being and the Harmonic Cosmology of seventeenth-century mathematician-philosophers such as GOTTFRIED LEIBNIZ and Spinoza, who may even be said to anticipate aspects of the ENLIGHTEN-MENT, and of whose work Bach had some knowledge. This affected religious teaching itself—for instance in CHRISTIAN WOLFF's attempt at a compromise between Lutheran JUSTIFICATION by FAITH alone and Leibnizian rational comprehension. Throughout his career Bach came intermittently into conflict with church dignitaries who were more theologically "progressive" than he; we are apt to forget that ISAAC NEWTON died a year before Bach's St. Matthew Passion was completed, and that Enlightened Voltaire was Bach's contemporary.

Eisenbach, where several generations of Bachs lived and worked, epitomizes the cultural ambivalence into which Bach was born. It was a small walled town guarded by watchtowers, with a few thousand working-class Protestants of almost medieval outlook serving an elaborately bureaucratic court. This court nurtured art, architecture, and culture that were French and Italian rather than German, and in part aristocratic and Catholic, in part intellectually Enlightened and Deist (see DEISM). Given these conditions, it is not surprising that the Lutheran Church cultivated a con-

servatism born of desperation. At the same time it had the courage of passionate conviction, especially in educational matters. Centuries earlier, MARTIN LUTHER himself had maintained that "if theology is not the beginning, middle, and end of life we cease being men and return to the animal state." The basis of Lutheran education, to which Bach still adhered, remained theology, supported by the medieval trivium of grammar, rhetoric, and dialectic. They were considered exemplars of divine law. Everything was taught in the universal tongue of Latin. Greek was fostered as the language of the New Testament, and later in the curriculum Hebrew was studied, as the Old Testament's tongue. However, for Lutherans in the sixteenth century, as for Bach in the eighteenth, the chief succor to theology was music, in that "those who have mastered this art are made of good stuff." Luther pointed out that St. Paul had encouraged the use of music in preaching Christian doctrine—"the whole purpose of harmony is the Glory of God; all other use is but idle juggling of Satan."

Because Bach was orphaned when he was ten, it was fortunate that his musical precocity was such that he was able to embark on some kind of career at the age of fifteen, when he sang professionally in the Mettenchor at the Ritterakademie, a boarding school for the sons of the nobility at St. Michael's convent in Lüneberg. From this modest start he proceeded through a series of church appointments in townships such as Arnstadt, Ohrdruf, and Mülhausen—the last named especially important because there he met his first wife Barbara, "settling down" with her, hoping to be a cantor whose duties embraced not only singing, but also organ and violin playing, and choir training and the composition of music for use over the church year. Gradually he took on his first real job as household musician to Duke Wilhelm Ernst of Weimar. Bach was twenty-three, and we think of his years at Weimar as the first "period" of his creative maturity. He made music for a band of talented musicians, covering every phase of church ceremonial, and borrowing conventions of recitative, arioso, and aria from Italian *opera seria,* now directed not toward Very Important Persons of the social world, but toward a presumptively historical man who had the inestimable advantage of also being God! Bach stayed at Weimar for nine years, during which he created some of his greatest music, mostly for soloists, chorus, and the small baroque opera orchestra.

Equally important, however, was his music for solo organ; at this time he was more renowned as a keyboard player than as a composer. During the Weimar years Bach's organ music was often cast in fairly large forms such as a Prelude (or Fantasia, or Toccata), which tended to be free and sometimes improvisational in structure, linked to a fully developed Fugue; there is a latent "program" in the form in that the preludial section seems to be associated, in its relative freedom, with mankind's "ongoing" state, whereas the unity and "many-in-oneness" of the fugue aspires toward the completion, and perfection, of God. Alternatively, and more modestly, Bach composed chorale preludes for organ that were "settings" of Lutheran popular hymns, with the tune played on a solo stop, garlanded by other parts that might be derived from fragments of the tune, or might independently weave a tapestry that illustrated, or commented on, the meaning of the hymn's words that, although not audibly uttered, would have been familiar to Bach's congregation. This was an essentially Lutheran form to which Bach remained constant throughout his life.

When he left Weimar, Bach was thirty-two. It has sometimes been considered odd that so devout a Lutheran should have moved to the court of prince Leopold of Coethen. His duties at Weimar, involving oppressive and sometimes stupid clerics and a gaggle of recalcitrant and rascally schoolboys, were not all a bed of roses; and that Leopold offered Bach twice the salary he received at Weimar must have been an inducement to a young man with a wife and a quiver of small children. The demands of music, as well as economics, may also have encouraged Bach to spread his wings; despite his conservative approach to religion, he was fascinated by the burgeoning technical possibilities of music, especially in the area of tonality, and must have welcomed the opportunity his new appointment offered to explore composition for well-tempered keyboards, for solo violin and solo cello, and for melody instruments with keyboard continuo. The Twenty Four Preludes and Fugues in all keys of the chromatic scale, written in 1722, were innovative works so enthusiastically received that Bach added a second set in 1740; and of course these works are now a basic bible of instrumental music. Although Bach seems to have written surprisingly little concerted "entertainment" music for the prince's delectation he did, during these years, visit Carlsbad with Leopold. There he met Christian Ludwig of Brandenburg, who commissioned the set of six concertos that are now among Bach's most frequently performed works.

The few cantatas that Bach wrote at Coethen are dedicated to aristocrats among Leopold's friends rather than to God, although their idiom is barely distinguishable from that of Bach's church cantatas—perhaps unsurprisingly because monarchs were supposed to be God's emissaries on earth. It is also significant that among the instrumental virtuoso pieces, the most famous—the *Chaconne* for solo violin of 1720—has recently been proven to be laden with "secret" Christian symbolism. For Bach sacred and profane were never far separated—which is why he could courageously face catastrophes before which most of us would quail. When he returned to Coethen after the Carlsbad expedition, he was appalled to discover that his beloved wife had, in his absence, sickened and died, leaving him with four children to care for. Could this Act of God (as Bach must have considered it) have generated in him a need to return to the Christian fold? Bach soon remarried. His new wife was the devoted and deeply musical Anna Magdalena who, in between giving birth to more children, proved an even more loving mate than Barbara, and one who was, moreover, helpful as copyist in Bach's professional career.

Perhaps seeking a new start with his new wife Bach applied for the vacant post of cantor at St. Thomas's, Leipzig. The city burghers tended to favor the proficient and fashionable GEORG PHILIPP TELEMANN (1687–1767) at the expense of Bach, and have been roundly if unfairly abused for their impercipience. Bach got the job because Telemann rejected it; and the inhabitants of Leipzig have complacently purred ever since. Bach stayed there for the rest of his life, during which, returning to the liturgical cycle of the church year, he produced his greatest works, not only in the shape of church cantatas, but also in the form of (at least two) Passion settings, according to the Gospels of St. John and St. Matthew.

These supreme works tell Christ's story in narrative, quasi-operatic terms, in the process demonstrating why Bach, the greatest of Christian composers, had to be a protesting Protestant who stressed the miracle of a specific Man who was also God, rather than the complementary miracle of a God who assumed human identity.

At this point we must inquire more deeply into what Lutheranism meant to Bach in the full flowering of his musical glory. Let us consider the sublime passage in the *St. John Passion* of 1724 that opens with the crowd's murderously homophonic yelling for the blood of Christ—here the *turba* are unredeemed and, as crowds tend to be, more bestial than human. The Evangelist then depicts the scourging of Christ in arioso that rhythmically enacts the gestures, and even the sounds, of lashing, and in sharp dissonance makes manifest Christ's (and vicariously our) pain. With scarcely a pause the music sinks, with magically assuaging effect, from "tragic" G minor to its flat submedient, E flat major—a key later to be associated (especially by Mozart and Beethoven) with human and humane compassion. Solo bass chants an arioso harmonically "earthed" on long pedal points and slowly dropping chromatics, yet generating from upward-arching arpeggios a radiant release. Despite fierce incidental dissonances the lines, floated across the beat of Time, dispense balm as the words tell of the redemptive import of Christ's pain. For this movement only, Bach introduces an obbligato lute, revering to the medieval identification of Christ Man-God with lute- or lyre-playing Orpheus, who hoped to conquer sin and death through the power of music. Christ being Very God as well as Man succeeds where Orpheus failed. His triumph is aurally incarnate in the aria into which the arioso leads.

During his last years at Leipzig Bach seems to have wearied somewhat of the rigor of ecclesiastical duties, perhaps because of the disparity between God's presumed perfection and humanity's inevitable imperfection. However this may be, the major religious work of these years is not Lutheran but a Roman High Mass made up of pieces he had written over the past twenty-five years, compiled, recomposed (with different texts), and added to over the years 1747 to 1748. Bach copied out the score in his noble calligraphy, with help from Anna Magdalena, and the work stands as an "ideal" *demonstratio* of the heart of the Christian mystery that Bach can hardly have expected to be performed, in Germany, as a totality. Certainly he did not hear it so performed. It stands as an "absolute" statement of faith parallel to the dramatic testaments of his Passions; they tell a story in operatic terms, revealing that that history is transhistorical, whereas the Mass enacts in the ceremonial terms of the High Baroque, a rite that incorporates—gives body to—a human tale that is also divine.

The sublime work uses all the then-basic techniques of European music, ranging from five-part counterpoint (five being traditionally a holy number), to operatic arioso and aria, to the court dances of mundane lords and masters who for a moment are allowed to deputize for God (it may be a typically wry Bachian joke that in these vaingloriously "mundane" sections the number of parts is briefly increased to six or even eight!). At the end, after the ultimately tragic G minor Agnus Dei, in which the melodic line is tense with "difficult" intervals like diminished fourths and diminished sevenths, has achieved peace for the individual spirit by way of an extremity of suffering, the Mass concludes with a return to its public function, with a Dona nobis pacem that reduplicates the music employed for the "Gratias agimus." This has occasioned surprise, even dismay, as though Bach were skimping of effort. The idea of a giving that is also a receiving is ratified by Bach's use of the same music, given that the two different texts symbolize the hypostatic union of Christ with his church. Because Jesus gave thanks when he broke bread, Christians call it the Holy Eucharist and believe, or are supposed to believe, that in the act of communion God becomes incarnate in his communicants, effecting a (momen-

tary) identity between God and Man. The idea that the "Dona nobis pacem" is a prayer for peace negates this efficacy; rather it may be considered a laudation of the peace(ful union) that passes understanding, not because sacrifice consists of praise and thanksgiving, but because it is offered with those ends in view. The use of the same music for the "Gratias agimus" and the "Dona nobis pacem" thus rounds off the Mass both musically and theologically. After those tragically purgatorial arias, the Benedictus and the Agnus Dei, there could be no further process, let along progress; we leave the church to resume our lives, renewed certainly in spiritual, possibly also in physical, strength. In this Bach's Lutheran muse becomes one with the Voice of God that speaks in his High and Solemn Roman Mass because to compose for the good of the (ideal) work is to compose—to put together—his work, well done, *perfectum ex perfecto,* to make people "better." And it does.

Bach's High Mass was an idealized act of devotion that is now, so many years on, a practiced act over much of the world. The three major works that he composed subsequent to the mass were abstract testaments that did not call for communal "realization" but sought the perfection of mathematics, especially in the mystical union of canon. These works were the Goldberg Variations for harpsichord (1741), the Musical Offering presented to Frederick the Great in 1747, and the unfinished Art of Fugue, composed between 1745 and 1750, when death intervened. Each of these works retreated deeper into the musical magic of Number, and into "pure" forms that are independent of "material" media: indeed the *Art of Fugue* specifies no definitive medium, although it can mostly be performed on a keyboard, which is probably how it was played, to himself, by the blind and ailing Bach.

Even so, it is significant that Bach's final composition seems to have been not an abstract work like *The Art of Fugue* but a return to the basic Lutheran concept of a chorale prelude setting of a popular hymn tune, the unheard words of which refer autobiographically to the composer's impending death: *Vor deinem Thron tret 'ich.* Yet if this prelude—said to have been dictated by Bach from his sickbed, if not at death's door—reflects a return to a "people's music" and the wellsprings of Lutheran tradition, it is at the same time of extraordinary contrapuntal and mathematical ingenuity, thereby betraying its "late" provenance.

Musically, the hymn tune, fragmented into its clauses, is in the top line, on a solo stop. It is introduced by a prelude in diminished note values, incorporates interludes, and is rounded off by a postlude. Throughout, all the melodic lines are totally thematic, appearing both *rectus* and *inversus,* and in diminution and augmentation. There is not space here to chart the mathematical dovetailing of the lines, but we must comment on the last interlude and subsequent coda, in which the tenor part is *rectus* in crotchets, answered by the alto, *inversus* in quavers, and then by the bass part (pedal), initially in crotchets, then in quavers. In the coda a chain of ornamentally resolving suspensions modulates from benedictory G major through the "suffering" key of E minor toward an aspirational A major; but the end is in surrender and resignation when the pedal has the theme in inversion, answered by the *cantus firmus* (the hymn) *rectus* in the soprano, with the two inner parts in canon at the diminished speed. Undulating six–three chords, with the F sharp and E natural both flattened, remain strictly thematic, although melodic identity and metrical definition dissolve, in the counterpoint's hierarchy of speeds, into a seemingly endless, modally plagal AMEN. The music runs down—like a clock, or a failing heart—as the pulse flags, beneath the immobile, sustained inverted pedal on which the hymn tune itself comes to rest. There could be no more precise musical synonym for the acceptance of death, identified with the will of God.

In this last choral prelude we do not need the gloss of the unspoken text to tell us that the Intellectual Love of God transcends, but does not efface, human suffering as well as joy. Dictating this music, Bach was dying into beatitude, as is inherent in the purely musical events that tell us, in Spinoza's words, that "death becomes less hurtful in proportion as the mind's clear and distinct knowledge is greater and, consequently, in proportion as the mind loves God more." The parts of us that "perish with the body are of little importance when compared with the part that endures." Even if one thinks that only oblivion succeeds death, one has to admit that miraculous "perfection" of this last chorale prelude seems to defeat time (and death?) in being "beyond" it. The music *persists*, at once an epiphany and an epitome of Bach's lifework. In listening to this piece—even more than in listening to the mathematically abstract words referred to above—it is "as though" we are entering the state called Paradise: a condition that is independent of the Roman Catholic, the Lutheran, or any other church.

References and Further Reading

Primary Sources:

Cantata *Christ leg in Todesbanden.* 1708.
St. John Passion. 1724.
St. Matthew Passion. 1727?.
Fantasia and Fugue in G Minor for organ.
Chorale Prelude for organ: *Vor deinen Thron tret 'ich.* 1750?.
High and Solemn Mass in B Minor: assembled 1747–1748.
The Well-Tempered Klavier: 48 Preludes and Fugues for keyboard. 1722 and 1740.
Goldberg Variations for harpsichord. 1741.
The Musical Offering. 1747.
The Art of Fugue. 1745–1750.

Secondary Sources:

Bosman, Leonard. *The Meaning and Philosophy of Numbers.* London: Rider and Co., 1932.
Chiapusso, Jan. *Bach's World.* Bloomington: Indiana University Press, 1968.
Geiringer, Karl. *Johann Sebastian Bach.* New York: Oxford University Press, 1966.
Kaufmann, Walter. *Critique of Religion and Philosophy.* London: Faber and Faber, 1958.
Luther, Martin. "Table Talk." In *Selected Writings.* Edited by John Dillenberger. Chicago: University of Chicago Press, 1961.
Mellers, Wilfrid. *Bach and the Dance of God.* London: Faber and Faber, 1980.
Scherchen, Hermann. *The Nature of Music.* Trans. William Mann. London: Dennis Dobson Ltd., 1950.
Spinoza, Benedictus de. *Ethics.* Translated by R. H. Elwes. New York, 1936.
Watts, Alan. *Myth and Ritual in Christianity.* London: Thames and Hudson, 1954.

WILFRID MELLERS

BACKUS, ISAAC (1724–1806)

Baptist minister and historian noted for his advocacy of the separation of church and state. Backus was born in January 1724 near Norwich, Connecticut, and the fervor of the Great Awakening resulted in his experience of conversion in 1741. Backus joined the Congregational church in Norwich but, unhappy with its opposition to a religion of experience, he withdrew in 1746 to help form a New Light/Separatist congregation and became an itinerant lay preacher.

In 1748 Backus was ordained as the pastor of a New Light/Separatist congregation in Titicut, Massachusetts. There he began to struggle over the issue of infant baptism, finally affirming believer's baptism in 1751 and refusing to baptize infants. He himself was baptized by immersion in August 1751. Backus left the Titicut church in 1756 to become pastor of a congregation in nearby Middleboro, Massachusetts that restricted communion to those who had been baptized as believers. Backus's congregation ultimately united with nearby Baptist churches, among which he was to made his most lasting contributions.

Without formal education, Backus was a self-taught apologist and historian who helped transform the status of New England Baptists from a sectarian denomination to a respectable part of the religious community. In his *History of New England,* first published in 1777, Backus cites John Robinson and other Puritan theologians to demonstrate that Baptists, rather than the established Congregationalist Church of New England, are the logical heirs to the Puritan tradition, seen in its purest form in the Plymouth colony.

Backus was influential in the formation in 1767 of the Warren Baptist Association, a cooperative organization of New England Baptists that played a significant role in the struggle for religious liberty in New England as well as in the newly formed United States of America. In 1772 Backus became an agent of the Warren Association in the cause of religious liberty, even representing Baptists before the Massachusetts delegation to the Continental Congress, where he argued (unsuccessfully) that the same principles that supported political freedom also supported religious freedom.

Most of all, therefore, Backus is remembered for his efforts toward separation of church and state in New England. He opposed any submission to state control of religion, including the obtaining of licenses to exempt individuals from paying church taxes. Even using the system to one's advantage, he said, is still granting the state the right to rule in matters of faith. Backus died in 1806. Although he did not live to witness the end of CONGREGATIONALISM as the state church of New England, he did see his crusade enshrined in the First Amendment to the U.S. Constitution.

References and Further Reading

Primary Sources:

Backus, Isaac. *A History of New England with Particular Attention to the Denomination of Christians Called Baptists*, 2nd ed. 2 vols. With notes by David Weston. 1871.
Backus, Isaac. *Isaac Backus on Church, State and Calvinism: Pamphlets, 1754–1789.* Edited by William G. McLoughlin. Cambridge, MA: Belknap Press, 1968.

Secondary Sources:

Hoovey, Alvah. *Memoir of the Life and Times of the Rev. Isaac Backus.* 1850.
McLoughlin, William G. *Isaac Backus and the American Pietistic Tradition.* Boston: Little, Brown, 1967.

T. FURMAN HEWITT

BACON, FRANCIS (1561–1626)

English philosopher. Bacon was born in London on January 22, 1561, to Sir Nicholas Bacon, a distinguished lawyer, and his wife. Bacon followed his father's footsteps into the legal profession and was knighted after the accession of James I. He progressed in office and became Lord High Chancellor in 1618. Bacon entered the peerage as Baron Verulam in 1618 and three years later became Viscount St. Albans. His career was ended ignominiously in 1621 by a charge of bribery and corruption, which he admitted, impris-

onment for a few days in the Tower of London, and deprivation of Parliamentary rights. He died on April 9, 1626. Bacon's public career was paralleled by a quite separate activity as an essayist. Of greatest influence were his *Advancement of Learning* (1605), the *New Atlantis* (1618), and the *Novum Organum* (1620). In these he argued for a comprehensive scheme of human knowledge, called his "grand instauration," in which scientific knowledge was derived by a method of induction from facts to theories. This "Baconian" method had a great influence on the subsequent philosophy of science. His vision of a new institution for scientific discourse culminated in the founding of the Royal Society in 1660.

Bacon's philosophy of science was a clear reflection of his Protestant faith. The priority of facts and the experimental method, the revolt against established tradition, and the desirability of cooperating with nature for the good of man and the glory of God were all expressions of a thoroughly biblical perspective, in contrast to the heritage of scholasticism and Greek science. For Bacon "conflict" between science and religion was not possible because God had given us "two books," the book of Scripture and the book of nature, each of which was necessary for our well-being and neither of which could contradict the other. The laws of science and the moral law came from the same Creator.

References and Further Reading

Johnston, A., ed. *Francis Bacon.* London: Batsford, 1965.
Webster, Charles. *The Great Instauration: Science, Medicine and Reform 1626–1660,* 2nd ed. London: Peter Lang, 2002.

COLIN A. RUSSELL

BAËTA, CHRISTIAN GONCALVES KWAME (1908–1994)

Ghanaian church leader. Baëta was a committed Protestant churchman, ecumenist, academic, and statesman. He was born at Keta in Gold Coast (Ghana) into a Presbyterian family. He studied at the Scottish Mission Teacher Training College in Akropong, Ghana at the Evangelische Missionsseminar in Basel, SWITZERLAND and at King's College, London. He was ordained into the ministry of the Evangelical Presbyterian Church in 1936 and later became the Synod clerk (chief executive) of his church (1945–1949) and a Presbyterian chaplain at the University of Ghana. He chaired both the Christian Council of Ghana (the main ecumenical Protestant organization in Ghana) and the Ghana Church Union negotiating Committee.

Baëta was present at the ecumenical gathering at Tambaram, INDIA, which discussed the mission of the church. Later, he became the vice-chair and chair of the International Missionary Council (IMC) and superintended the process of integration of the IMC into the WORLD COUNCIL OF CHURCHES (WCC) in 1961. He served on the Commission of the Churches on International Affairs and the Central and Executive Committees of the World Council of Churches.

As a scholar and a first-generation African theologian he served the University College of Gold Coast (now University of Ghana) from 1949 to 1971, rising from senior lecturer to professor and head of the department of theology, which he helped to transform into an inclusive department for the study of religions. He held several visiting professorships, including Union Theological Seminary in New York, Selly Oak Colleges in Birmingham, UK, and the Ruhr-Universität in Bochum, Germany. He was a fellow of the Ghana Academy of Sciences from 1961 until his death and was its president for two consecutive terms. He was awarded five honorary doctorate degrees in JAPAN, the UNITED STATES, GERMANY, Hungary, and Ghana. He was committed to BIBLE TRANSLATION particularly into Ewe, his mother tongue.

Baëta was a member of the Legislative Council of the Gold Coast, 1946–1950, member of the Coussey Committee on Constitutional Reform for the Gold Coast, and later served on the Constitutional Assembly of Ghana in 1969. As early as the 1940s Baëta saw that THEOLOGY and politics are inseparable.

See also Africa; African Theology; Ecumenism

References and Further Reading

Primary Sources

Baëta, Christian Goncalves Kwame. *Prophetism in Ghana.* London: SCM, 1963.
———. *The Relationship of Christians with Men of Other Living Faiths.* Accra: Ghana Universities Press, 1971.

Secondary Source:

Pobee, J. S., ed. *Religion in a Pluralist Society: Essays in Honor of C.G. Baëta.* Leiden: Brill, 1976.

CEPHAS N. OMENYO

BAILLIE, JOHN (1886–1960)

Scottish Theologian. A Free Church minister's son from the remote Highlands of Scotland, John Baillie was born in 1886. After studying philosophy at the University of Edinburgh and theology at New College, he spent two years as an assistant minister and four (1915–1919) with the YMCA in FRANCE. Between 1919 and 1934 he taught in North America, latterly at Union Seminary, New York. From 1934 until his retirement in 1956, Baillie occupied the Chair of Divinity at Edinburgh, exerting considerable influence as moderator of the general assembly of the CHURCH OF SCOTLAND (1943), convener of the Kirk's special commission for the Interpretation of God's Will in the Present Crisis (1942–1946), one of the presidents of the WORLD COUNCIL OF CHURCHES (1952), dean of the university's faculty of divinity and Principal of New College (1950–1956), and participant in the Anglican-Presbyterian conversations that produced the "Bishop's Report" in 1957. He was awarded several honorary degrees and made Companion of Honour by the queen.

Despite early indebtedness to IMMANUEL KANT (1724–1804) and ALBRECHT RITSCHL (1822–1889), for most of his life Baillie could not be identified with any philosophical or theological school. As a schoolboy, he learned to reconcile the insights of Highland Calvinism with the humanism of the Renaissance and ENLIGHTENMENT. As a student he rejected the extremes of fashionable Hegelianism. As a young professor, he was neither a fundamentalist nor a modernist. In later years, while welcoming the Barthian movement as a salutary corrective to contemporary theology, he always—and increasingly—kept his distance from it. Though uneasy with some of the traditional formulations of historic Christianity, he demonstrated his essential fidelity to their substance in the eloquent apologetics of *Invitation to Pilgrimage* (1942) and the disciplined piety of *A Diary of Private Prayer* (1936), a devotional classic subsequently translated into many languages. His sermons, lectures, and numerous publications, all marked by exceptional lucidity and grace of style, gained him recognition as one of the foremost theologians of his generation.

He died at Edinburgh in 1960, and his portrait hangs in the New College Senate Room.

References and Further Reading

Primary Source:

Baillie, J. "Confessions of a Transplanted Scot." In *Contemporary American Theology: Theological Autobiographies.* Edited by V. Ferm. 2nd series (1933): 31–39.

Secondary Sources:

Fergusson, D., ed. *Bibliography in Christ, Church and Society: Essays on John Baillie and Donald Baillie.* 1992.
"John Baillie." In *Dictionary of Scottish Church History and Theology,* edited by N. Cameron. 1993.

ALEXANDER C. CHEYNE

BALTIMORE CONFERENCE

The Baltimore Conference, also known as the Christmas Conference, marked the formation of the first independent Wesleyan Methodist church and the official beginning of the Methodist Church in America. Meeting from December 24, 1784 through January 2, 1785 at Lovely Lane Chapel in Baltimore, Maryland, the approximately sixty Methodist preachers in attendance created a church and set the precedent for future Methodist polity in America.

The Methodist movement originated as a reform movement within the CHURCH OF ENGLAND; however, in America after the Revolution a lack of Anglican clergy left the Methodists without access to the sacraments. Demands for ordination grew over the final years of Revolution as American Methodists pled with JOHN WESLEY for action.

In 1784 the demands had become strident enough for Wesley to act. He ordained Thomas Vasey and Richard Whatcoat and then set THOMAS COKE apart as a superintendent for the Methodists in America. Wesley provided Coke with a book of worship called *The Sunday Service of the Methodists in America,* an abridged version of the Church of England's Articles of Religion, and a letter of instruction for the American Methodists.

The group arrived in America in November and met FRANCIS ASBURY in Delaware. Asbury refused Wesley's plan without a vote of the preachers in America, and Freeborn Garrettson was sent out to gather all of the preachers for a conference in Baltimore.

The Baltimore Conference commenced on Friday, December 24 and met continuously for the next ten days. Garrettson was successful in his effort to alert the itinerating Methodist preachers about the conference. Sixty of eighty-three American Methodist preachers attended at least some part of the conference. Although the Methodist movement in America was primarily a lay movement, only the licensed traveling preachers were invited to the conference. The omitting of the LAITY from the conference set a precedent for Methodist conferences that would last for most of the next century.

At the conference opening Coke read Wesley's letter of instructions to the gathered preachers. Then, in an important change from Wesley's wishes, Asbury requested to be elected superintendent, not appointed by Wesley. The assembled preachers elected Asbury unanimously. Through the election Asbury altered the authority relationships between himself, Coke, and Wesley. The move also created an important precedent for American Methodism because, unlike British Methodism under Wesley, the final power now rested with the preachers voting in conference. By taking this step the Conference declared itself competent to make ecclesiastical decisions. Methodist conferences would henceforth involve themselves in all matters regarding the care and regulation of the ministry, a pattern that still exists today. A Methodist bishop (see BISHOPS AND EPISCOPACY) ordains individuals, but the conference of the clergy decides who receives ordination. Drawing from this antecedent, elections would decide all issues in the future of Methodism. The democratization of the decision-making process marked an important step in Americanizing the Methodist system.

After the decision by the Conference, Asbury accepted the vicarious ordination from Wesley, and the actual ordination was carried out by Coke, Whatcoat, Vasey, and William Otterbein, a German Presbyterian minister. Asbury was ordained deacon, elder, and then set apart as superintendent on three consecutive days. Asbury took his place as the acknowledged elected leader of American Methodism along with Coke who was an appointed superintendent.

Most of the nine days of the Conference were spent creating the *Doctrines and Disciplines of the Methodist Church in America,* the basic rule book of American Methodism. The conference defined Methodist faith by adopting the Articles of Religion as amended by Wesley and by taking several stands on social issues. One of the more significant issues addressed by the Conference was the relationship between the American Methodist Church and Wesley. The conference resolved this issue with the adoption, over the opposition of Asbury, of the Binding Minute, which committed the American Methodists to Wesley's commands and pledged themselves to be his sons in the Gospel. Although the Conference had declared itself competent to make its own decisions, the membership of the Conference did not want to sever all ties with Wesley. The Binding Minute was mostly symbolic and would be rescinded during a controversy a few years later only to be readopted when Wesley was on his death bed. The Conference also took several strong ethical stands against SLAVERY and alcohol (see TEMPERANCE), setting a precedent for strong social stands by the Methodist movement in America.

Attendees at the Conference also took it on themselves to create programs for the new church. The Conference created a new college, Cokesbury College, and authorized MISSIONS to the Indians (see also MISSIONS, NORTH AMERICAN). As a final act the Conference named the new church the Methodist Episcopal Church, reflecting both its Wesleyan heritage and its Episcopal polity.

The Baltimore Conference set several important precedents for future conferences: the conference spent most of its time on matters of polity and theology, writing the discipline, regulating the ministry, and defining the faith; the conference followed its Wesleyan heritage and took strong ethical stands; the conference selected the Episcopal leadership; and finally created programs for the church.

The Baltimore Conference was also a time for PREACHING and REVIVAL, a feature of Conferences that would blossom over the next few decades into the CAMP MEETING movement. Although the Conference served as a time of fellowship among the preachers, by prohibiting the attendance of laity it excluded nonwhites, women, and local preachers from the decision-making process.

Although the Conference yielded a new church, the actual participants displayed little sense of the historical importance of their actions. No minutes were kept and no attendance records survive from the Conference. Asbury himself devoted only a short description of the conference in his journal. This Conference was not the first General Conference; it was an irregularly called Constitutional Conference. It made no provision for its own continuity or succession and gave itself no place in Methodist POLITY. Nevertheless this conference did set a pattern for the general work to be done at annual conferences to come.

See also Slavery, Abolition of; Methodism; Methodism, North America; Methodist Episcopal Church Conference

References and Further Reading

Andrews, Dee E. *The Methodists and Revolutionary America, 1760–1800: The Shaping of an Evangelical Culture*. Princeton, NJ: Princeton University Press, 2000.

Baker, Frank. *From Wesley to Asbury: Studies in Early American Methodism*. Durham, NC: Duke University Press, 1976.

Heitzenrater, Richard P. *Wesley and the People Called Methodists*. Nashville, TN: Abingdon Press, 1995.

Williams, William H. *The Garden of Methodism: The Delmarva Peninsula, 1769–1820*. Wilmington, DE: Scholarly Resources, 1984.

ADAM ZELE

BAPTISM

Broadly speaking, magisterial Protestantism—Lutheran, Reformed, Anglican—maintained, and still continues to practice, the central ritual act of baptism grounded in Holy Scripture, that is, the application of water to the candidate in the name of the Father, the Son, and the Holy Spirit. Marked by the common desire to correct what they viewed as distortions in the DOCTRINE and subsidiary rites surrounding baptism in the existing Western church, the varying baptismal theologies of these three Protestant families came to expression in the prayers and exhortations accompanying the water rite in their new liturgical books. Once they had reached a stable form by the middle of the

sixteenth century, the orders for baptism went without further fundamental change until well into the twentieth century. Such changes as took place in Protestant THEOLOGY in this area during the intervening period were reflected rather in the understanding and practice of confirmation (or lack thereof), which cast a retrospective light on what was believed to happen at baptism. In the twentieth century, the classic Protestant churches participated, together with Roman Catholicism, in an ecumenical Liturgical Movement that recaptured, in a new situation, many of the ritual patterns and doctrinal views of the early centuries of Christianity. Throughout their history, these Protestant churches—all of which retained the baptism of infants as indeed the predominant practice—have also been challenged by the more drastic "reforms" of the "radicals" in the sixteenth century and the continuing "anabaptist" bodies, whereby baptism is administered only to those able personally to profess their faith in Christ. At stake in baptism, of course, are entire soteriologies and ecclesiologies.

Accordingly, most of this article is devoted to the theology and rites of baptism in sixteenth-century Protestantism. Then some attention is given to confirmation. After a description of the liturgical revisions that affected "Christian initiation" in the latter half of the twentieth century, an attempt will be made to characterize the current situation in its trends and desiderata.

Baptism in the Protestant Reformation

Luther

In his attack on the prevalent sacramental system, *The Babylonian Captivity of the Church* (1520), MARTIN LUTHER fundamentally exempted baptism: "Blessed be the God and Father of our Lord Jesus Christ, who of his rich mercy has preserved at least this one sacrament in his church unspoiled and unspotted by man-made ordinances, and made it free to all races and classes of men; nor has he allowed it to be suppressed by foul money-grubbing and ungodly monsters of superstition" [*Weimarer Ausgabe* (the Weimar edition of Luther's Works; hereafter *WA*) 6:526f.]. Luther's insistence on the continuity of baptism indicates that his desire was to reform the church, not to create a new one. Nor, clearly, was he too concerned about the subsidiary ceremonies, although by stages, in the two German *Taufbüchlein* of 1523 and 1526, he cut from the ritual most of the secondary items that he had earlier, for all their unimportance, retained: breathing under the eyes of the baptizand, placing salt in the mouth, touching the ears and nose with spittle [the *effeta*; cf. Mark 7:33], anointing the breast and between the shoulders before baptism, signing the top of the head with chrism after baptism, giving a lighted candle into the hand. The order of 1526 kept an initial consignation of the forehead and breast, a much simplified exorcism, and the vesting in a white robe after the water. Luther's most significant ritual innovation was the composition of the "Flood Prayer (*Sintflutgebet*)" to be said over the water, a theologically rich text using biblical typology in a patristic manner (cf. I Peter 3:20f.; I Corinthians 10: 1–4; Romans 5:12–21). After recalling the justice and mercy of God displayed at the Deluge and at the Red Sea, the text declares that the baptism of Jesus "sanctified and set apart the Jordan and all water for a saving flood, and an ample washing away of sins" and goes on to pray that

> through thy same fathomless mercy thou wouldst look graciously upon this [*Name*], and bless him with a right faith in the spirit, so that through this healing flood all that was born in him from Adam and all that he himself has added thereto may be drowned and submerged; and that he may be separated from the unfaithful, and preserved in the holy ark of Christendom dry and safe, and ever fervent in spirit and joyful in hope serve thy name, so that he with all the faithful may be worthy to inherit thy promise of eternal life, through Christ our Lord. (*WA* 12:43f.; 19:539f.)

This prayer, with various adaptations, made its way into several Protestant orders for baptism, especially those that also show otherwise a strong sense of the sacramental efficacy of the water rite.

It may be wondered how Luther squared the continuing baptism of infants with his doctrine of JUSTIFICATION: how was the *sola fide* ("by faith alone") to avoid sinking into a *sine fide* ("without faith")? In the first place, in both *Taufbüchlein* the minister's questions about the renunciation of Satan, belief in the Triune God, and the desire for baptism continue to be addressed to the infant, who responds "through the godparents." Here Luther may be drawing on the notion of "vicarious faith (*fides aliena*)" known at least since St. Augustine, whereby the sponsors, the congregation, and even the whole church may supply what is lacking in the infant. In the second place, however, Luther can combine the notion of vicarious faith with the idea that an infant may actually have, or be given, faith:

> Infants are helped by vicarious faith: the faith of those who present them for baptism. For as the word of God, whenever uttered, is powerful enough to change the heart even of the ungodly, and these are not less deaf or incapable than any infant, so all things are possible through the prayers of a believing church when it presents the infant, and he is changed, cleansed, and renewed by the faith infused. (*WA* 6:538)

Luther could cite the leaping of John in Elizabeth's womb at the presence of Jesus in Mary's as an embryonic instance of faith at the encounter with the Word (*On Rebaptism*, 1528; *WA* 26:156, 169). Third, however, Luther could also, in the *Large Catechism*, so emphasize the priority of God's grace and command as to deny any constitutive role at all to faith on the part of the subject of baptism:

> We do not set the greatest store by whether the baptizand believes or not, for baptism will not thereby become wrong, but rather everything depends on the Word and commandment of God. . . . My faith does not make baptism but receives it. . . . We bring the child with the purpose and hope that he may believe, and we pray God to grant him faith, but we do not baptize him on that account, but solely because God has commanded it. [*Bekenntnisschriften der Evangelisch-Lutherischen Kirche* (*BSELK*), p. 701f.]

How deeply this latter sense is written into the Lutheran tradition is shown by the disquiet in the responses of Lutheran churches to the statement in the ecumenical Lima text, *Baptism, Eucharist and Ministry*, that "Baptism is both God's gift and our human response to that gift."

Where faith upon personal responsibility makes a comeback in Luther is precisely in his provision of two CATECHISMS for household and parochial use—presaged, of course, by the very translation of the baptismal rite into the vernacular in the *Taufbüchlein*. Those who had been baptized in infancy needed instruction later in faith, morals, PRAYER, and the rites of the church, including baptism, CONFESSION, and the LORD'S SUPPER. As a literary and pedagogical genre, the catechism spread throughout magisterial Protestantism and even into Roman Catholicism.

The Swiss

After Leo Jud had in August 1523 introduced at Zurich a simplified form of the medieval baptismal rite in the vernacular, along the lines of Luther's first *Taufbüchlein*, HULDRYCH ZWINGLI in May 1525 produced a much more drastic revision that excised all the secondary ceremonies except the vesting with the white robe. It omitted the traditional interrogations about renouncing Satan and professing the faith and, in a very significant move, addressed to the godparents the question "Do you wish this child to be baptized into the baptism of our Lord Jesus Christ?" Luther's Flood-Prayer was included in reduced form, omitting reference to the sanctification of water and changing the petition so as to read

> that thou wouldst look graciously upon this thy servant, [*Name*], and kindle the light of faith in his heart whereby he may be incorporated into thy Son, and with him be buried in death, and in him be raised to newness of life; that so, following him daily, he may joyfully bear his

cross, and hold fast to him with true faith, firm hope, and fervent love; and that for thy sake he may so manfully quit this life, which is nothing but a death, that at the last day he may appear fearless at the general judgment of thy Son. [*Corpus Reformatorum* (hereafter *CR*) 91:334f.]

According to his treatise *On Baptism, Rebaptism and Infant Baptism* of May 1525, Zwingli was reluctant to affirm the spiritual efficacy of "an external ceremony" but viewed baptism as "an initiatory sign" by which we are "pledged" to God, "an outward sign that we are introduced and engrafted into the Lord Jesus Christ and pledged to live to him and to follow him" (*CR* 91:238, 252). For a couple of years Zwingli had had doubts—expressed in 1523 and 1524 to local Anabaptists—about the baptism of infants, but he returned to defend it on covenantal terms, by analogy with circumcision of the Old Testament.

For JOHN CALVIN in Geneva also, the baptism of infants is a mark, in the wake of circumcision in the Old Testament, of the inclusion of the offspring of Christian parents into the now extended COVENANT of salvation, although his language in the question of sacramental efficacy oscillates between "conferral" and "testimony." By far the greater part of his independently composed French baptismal order in *The Form of Prayers . . . According to the Custom of the Ancient Church* (1542) consists in a baptismal instruction addressed to the parents and the congregation, who are both to witness the present act and also to be reminded of the use and fruit of their own baptism. After a description of the wretchedness of humankind in its fallen condition, Calvin recalls the divine promise of regeneration by the Holy Spirit through participation in the death and resurrection of Christ, beginning with the pardon of all our faults. Moreover

all these graces are conferred on us, when it pleases God to incorporate us into his church by baptism. For in his sacrament he testifies to us the remission of our sins. And for this cause he has appointed the sign of water, to show us that, as by this element the body is cleansed of dirt, so he wishes to wash and purify our souls, so that no stain may any more appear in them. Then also he there represents to us our renewal, which consists in the mortification of our flesh, and the spiritual life which he excites and engenders in us. . . . As he imparts to us his riches and blessings by his word, so he distributes them to us by his sacraments. (*CR* 34:186f.)

The prayer for the baptizand then runs thus:

Lord God, Father eternal and almighty, since it has pleased thee by thine infinite mercy to promise us that thou wilt be our God and the God of our children, we pray thee that it may please thee to confirm this grace in this present infant, born of a father and mother whom thou hast called into thy church, and, as he is offered and consecrated to thee by us, that thou wouldst receive

him into thy holy protection, declaring thyself to be his God and Saviour, remitting to him the original sin of which the whole lineage of Adam is guilty, and then afterwards sanctifying him by thy Spirit, so that when he comes to the age of understanding, he may know and adore thee as his only God, glorifying thee all through his life, so as to obtain evermore from thee remission of his sins. And so that he may obtain such graces, may it please thee to incorporate him into the communion of our Lord Jesus Christ, so that as a member of his body he may share in all his benefits. Hear us, Father of mercy, that the baptism which we administer to him according to thine ordinance may bring forth its fruit and virtue, such as has been declared to us by thy gospel. (*CR* 34:188f.)

The parents must promise that when the child reaches "the age of discretion" they will instruct him in the doctrine of the creed and in the Scriptures (Calvin will provide *Le catéchisme de l'église de Genève*) and exhort him to obey the divine law of love toward God and neighbor for God's glory and the neighbors' edification. Only then does the minister baptize the child.

England

A chief channel of liturgical influence between continental Protestantism and the English reformation was MARTIN BUCER, who not only shaped the baptismal rites of Strasbourg (with rationale in the *Grund und Ursach* of Christmas 1524) but also wrote the sacramental parts of the *Einfaltigs Bedencken* or *Pia Deliberatio* for Archbishop Hermann of Cologne (1543), on which THOMAS CRANMER and his men drew for the first *Prayer Book* of 1549, and then by his criticisms of that book, the *Censura*, affected the second *Prayer Book* of 1552. Bucer's characteristic view of baptism was both instrumental and pneumatological, as seen in the Strasbourg rite: "Let us pray that the Lord will baptize [this infant] with water and the Holy Spirit, so that the outward washing which he will perform through me may be inwardly fulfilled in deed and in truth by the Holy Spirit; for that second birth which is signified by baptism takes place in water and in the Holy Spirit, as the Lord says in John 3" (cf. Fisher, 34–37).

The baptismal rite in the first English BOOK OF COMMON PRAYER began with an appeal to John 3, followed by an adaptation of Luther's Flood-Prayer, which Bucer had included in his text for Hermann. From the medieval rite the book retained a prebaptismal signing with the cross on forehead and breast, a single exorcism, the postbaptismal vesting in white, and an anointing of the head, with the sense now specified thus: "Almighty God, the Father of our Lord Jesus Christ, who hath regenerated thee by water and the Holy Ghost, and hath given unto thee remission of all thy sins, he vouchsafe to anoint thee with the unction of his Holy Spirit, and bring thee to the inheritance of everlasting life." The prebaptismal renunciation of Satan and profession of the creed are made by the godparents who, having been reminded of the saving promises of Christ, are told that "these infants must also faithfully for their part promise by you that be their sureties, that they will forsake the devil and all his works, and constantly believe God's holy word and obediently keep his commandments." After the baptism, the godparents are charged in their

> duty to see that these infants be taught, so soon as they are able to learn, what a solemn vow, promise and profession they have made by you. And that they may know these things the better, ye shall call upon them to hear sermons, and chiefly you shall provide that they may learn the creed, the Lord's prayer and the ten commandments in the English tongue, and all other things which a Christian ought to know and believe to his soul's health, and that these children may be virtuously brought up to lead a godly and Christian life, remembering always that baptism doth represent unto us our profession which is to follow the example of our Saviour Christ, and to be made like unto him, that as he died and rose again for us, so should we which are baptized die from sin, and rise again unto righteousness, continually mortifying all our evil and corrupt affections, and daily proceeding in all godliness of living.

A catechism was provided to aid ministers and parents in their instruction of the children.

In line with Bucer's *Censura* concerning several "dramatic signs" that, for all their antiquity, did not come from Scripture and were indeed subject to misunderstanding as "profane sport," the second English *Prayer Book* dropped the exorcism, the white robe, and the postbaptismal chrismation of the head. The prebaptismal consignation, by which the infant was associated with "Christ crucified," was shifted to a place immediately after the water rite and was now administered to the forehead without oil. In one highly significant matter, Bucer's advice was rejected: he had wanted to transform the postbaptismal exhortation of the godparents into questions concerning their willingness to raise the child in the Christian faith in such a way as to replace the interrogations by which they renounced Satan and professed the faith "on behalf of the infants" and "in their place." On the contrary, the sponsors' speaking for the child was retained. The *Book of Common Prayer* of 1662 included the precision that the child's promises were made "by you that are his sureties, *until he come of age to take it upon himself.*"

The Anabaptists

It may be debated whether ANABAPTISM is better viewed as a radicalization of the magisterial Reforma-

tion or rather as principally indebted to the Millenarians and mystics of the middle ages (see MILLENARIANS AND MILLENNIALISTS). Some scholars have argued that there may in fact be a greater affinity between Luther and the *Schwärmer*, as outcomes of medieval movements, than either party was willing to recognize.

In the case of THOMAS MÜNTZER, the concern of the Zwickau prophets for social change was joined with a concern for the spiritual renewal of the individual. In his "Protestation" concerning "real Christian faith and baptism" (1524), he attacked the practice of infant baptism, and the associated loss of a preparatory catechumenate, for encouraging a "fictive faith (*gedichtiter glaube*)": "by the making of infants into Christians, Christians became infants." Real faith and baptism consist in an "imitation of Christ," bearing the cross through the troubled waters of trial and suffering. In Zürich a group of revolutionaries, impatient with Zwingli's plans for a constitutional reform of the church, took up Müntzer's views, and, in a later letter to Müntzer of September 5, 1524, CONRAD GREBEL set forth his own understanding of believer's baptism: "As Scripture describes it for us, baptism signifies that, by faith and the blood of Christ, sins have been washed away for him who has been baptized, having repented and believed, and continuing to believe; it signifies that a man is dead and ought to be dead to sin and to walk in newness of life and spirit, and that he shall certainly attain salvation if by inner baptism he lives the faith here signified" (see L. von Muralt and W. Schmidt, *Quellen zur Geschichte der Täufer in der Schweiz*, vol. 1 [Zürich: Hirzel, 1952], p. 17f.). Meanwhile Grebel had, on January 21, 1523, acceded to George Blaurock's request to baptize him, and with further (re)baptisms at Zollikon the new church of the Zürich BRETHREN IN CHRIST had been founded. What for them was baptism appeared to other eyes as rebaptism, and so the epithet "Anabaptist" came into use.

The most learned and competent Anabaptist theologian was BALTHASAR HUBMAIER, who had been a student of the scholastic John Eck. In reply to Zwingli's *On Baptism, Rebaptism and Infant Baptism* Hubmaier wrote a treatise *On the Christian Baptism of Believers* (1525). From his clear reading of simple Scripture he saw a constant baptismal pattern of hearing the preached word, repentance, faith in Christ, baptism, and following Christ in good works [*Quellen zur Geschichte der Täufer* (hereafter *QGT*) 9, 146–151]. In *A Form for Baptism* (1526–1527) Hubmaier set forth the order used "at Nicolsburg and elsewhere." The candidate was first to be tested on faith and morals by the bishop/elder, who would then present him to the congregation and ask for prayer that God would "graciously grant to the candidate the grace and power of his Holy Spirit and complete what he had, by his Holy Spirit and divine word, begun in him." The candidate professed faith in reply to questions substantially close to the Apostles' Creed, renounced the DEVIL, declared his willingness to accept the fraternal discipline of the church ("the keys"), and voiced his desire "to be baptized in water according to the institution of Christ, and thus to be incorporated and enrolled into the external Christian church for the forgiveness of sins." After the baptism of the candidate in water in an unspecified mode, the congregation were to pray, on his behalf and their own, for increase in faith and for perseverance. Finally the bishop laid his hand on the head of the newly baptized, declaring his right henceforth "to be reckoned among the Christian community, sharing as a member in its keys, and in the breaking of bread and prayers with the other Christian sisters and brothers" (*QGT* 9, 349f.). In addition to the baptism "of the Spirit, given internally in faith," and that "of water, given externally through the oral confession of faith before the church," Hubmaier characteristically spoke of a third baptism, that "of blood in martyrdom or on the deathbed," whereby the latter could be understood as "a daily mortification of the flesh until death" (*QGT* 9, 275; 313f.).

Pedobaptist critics have constantly charged BAPTISTS with "voluntarism," but although it is true that the exercise of the will excludes infants from baptism, it by no means excludes, as the critics often assume, the prevenience of grace. In the twentieth century the most astounding advocate of believer's baptism was in fact KARL BARTH, whose first unease with pedobaptism related to its inappropriateness even within the Calvinist tradition of baptism as divine testimony— "cognitive" not "causative"—because the infant was not capable of receiving that "visible word" (*Die kirchliche Lehre von der Taufe*, 1943). In a section of the fragmentary part IV/4 of his *Church Dogmatics* ("Baptism as the Foundation of the Christian Life," 1967), Barth put forward the positive view of the believing reception of baptism as the first act of obedience following upon the divine baptism with the Holy Spirit.

Confirmation

The test of the completeness of baptism as entrance into the church is whether the baptized receive the holy communion (communion being the instance of continuing participation in the body of Christ). In the Eastern churches, following what was apparently patristic practice, all the baptized, including infants, are admitted to communion immediately after the baptism in water and the chrismation that is viewed as the pneumatological focus of the total rite. This has not been regularly the case in Western Christianity for almost a millennium, where an interval of years typically ensues between baptism in infancy and the reception of holy communion. What J. D. C. Fisher called the "disintegration" of Christian initiation in the West came about gradually in the second half of the first millennium as baptisms were administered soon after birth by the parish priest, whereas "confirmation"—the postbaptismal imposition of hands and anointing of the brow with chrism—was reserved to the bishop, who might not become available until much later; baptized but unconfirmed children at first continued to receive communion, but then a time came when children were no longer seen as fit subjects of communion because of the dangers their clumsy ingestion posed to the sacramental body and blood. This double delay allowed confirmation and communion to become reassociated, at least in a loose way, by virtue of their common postponement until a child's having reached the years of reason or age of discretion, when also the first sacramental confession took place. On the Roman Catholic side, the council of Trent deduced from the temporal gap—though with some embarrassment—that neither confirmation nor communion, unlike baptism, was necessary to SALVATION.

With some medieval and renaissance precedents for the instruction of children in the creed, the commandments and the virtues, and prayer, the magisterial reformers developed the question-and-answer catechism as a means for inculcating faith, morals, and ecclesial practices. Provided the actions were not considered a sacrament or "observed as the bishops desire it," Luther in a sermon for Laetare Sunday 1523 found no fault "if every pastor examines the faith of the children to see whether it is good and sincere, lays hands on them, and confirms them" (*WA* 11:66); but although providing the two Catechisms (1529), Luther composed no German order for "confirmation." The want was supplied in some places by such as JOHANNES BUGENHAGEN and PHILIPP MELANCHTHON, and "confirmation"—with varying emphases and under various names—became in LUTHERANISM an established way of concluding catechesis and admitting to communion for the first time. Thus an instructed faith, personally professed, was seen as appropriate, and perhaps requisite, to participation in the Lord's Supper, even while it was characteristically insisted that regenerative faith had in some sense been given in infant baptism.

Calvin expressed a visceral dislike of papist confirmation and its "filthy oil" whereby the baptismal "water sanctified by the word of God" was robbed of half its efficacy, as though baptism were only for the forgiveness of sins whereas the gift of the Spirit for newness of life depended on the anointing in confirmation. Like Zwingli before him (*CR* 89:122f.) Calvin mistakenly imagined an "ancient custom" whereby "the children of Christians," having been brought to baptism in infancy, were then, "at the close of childhood or the start of adolescence, again presented by their parents and examined by the bishop according to the form of the catechism then in common use" and, on "having their faith approved," were "dismissed with a solemn blessing" (*Institutes* IV.19.4). Calvin himself provided the Genevan church with a catechism but no rite for confirmation. Although the children of Christian parents belonged to the church by virtue of the covenant promise signified in their baptism as infants, they were not admitted to the Lord's table before being able to deliver a catechetical account of their faith in the presence of the church. As a rationale for the delay in communion, some later Reformed theology has distinguished between an appropriately passive reception of baptism and the capacity for action entailed in the eucharistic command to "do this" (I Corinthians 11:24f.).

In Reformation ENGLAND children were required to be able to say in the mother tongue the creed, the Lord's prayer, and the Ten Commandments, as well as to answer questions from the provided Catechism, before being brought by a godparent to the bishop for "confirmation." Having reached "the years of discretion" and "learned what their godfathers and godmothers promised for them in baptism," the children might now "themselves with their own mouth, and with their own consent, openly before the church ratify and confess the same, and also promise that by the grace of God they will evermore endeavour themselves faithfully to observe and keep such things as they by their own mouth and confession have assented unto." The confirmation service in the *Prayer Book* of 1549, recognizing that in baptism the candidates had been regenerated and had received forgiveness of sin, now asked God to "send down from heaven . . . upon them thy Holy Ghost" with his sevenfold gifts and, in a second prayer, to "confirm and strengthen them with the inward unction of thy Holy Ghost . . . unto everlasting life," the bishop laying his hand on their heads and signing their forehead with the cross. By the book of 1552 the punctual epiclesis of the first prayer ("Send down") was softened to a prayer for "strengthening" with the Holy Spirit and a "daily increase" in his gifts; the consignation disappeared, and the prayer at the simple imposition of the episcopal hand was reformulated as one for the "defense" afforded by "heavenly grace." It had been recognized from the start that confirmation is "most meet to be ministered when children come to that age, that partly by the frailty of their own flesh, partly by the assaults of the world and the devil, they begin to be in danger to fall into sin." A concluding rubric declared that none shall "be admitted to the holy communion, until such time as he [can say the catechism and] be confirmed."

In German PIETISM of the seventeenth century, catechesis became for PHILIPP JAKOB SPENER (1635–1705) an opportunity to "bring the head into the heart," and confirmation the occasion for the catechumen to ratify or "renew" his baptismal covenant, testify to his experienced "conversion," and vow to lead a Christian life (see Repp, 68–71). For FRIEDRICH SCHLEIERMACHER (1768–1834) confirmation was "the offering and acceptance of a personal confession of faith," the "supplying of what was lacking in infant baptism" and thereby its "true and worthy completion" (*Der christliche Glaube*, §138, 2). In the eighteenth and nineteenth centuries, confirmation—by now as widespread among the Reformed as among the Lutherans—became seen as specification of membership in a particular congregation or DENOMINATION (where baptism had simply been into "the Christian church"), but it also acquired an independent weight through associations with the end of schooling, a "great festival of youth," and entry upon civic and economic privileges. Among humanistically inclined pastoral theologians of the twentieth century, under the influence of psychology and sociology, confirmation became a "rite de passage," the sacrament of puberty, following upon baptism understood as the sacrament of infancy.

The Ecumenical and Liturgical Movements

The Liturgical and Ecumenical Movements of the twentieth century, whose currents often flowed together, looked to the early church as a source for both the renewal of WORSHIP and the reconciliation of divided Christianity. Baptism became an important feature in both. Revisions of service books, both in the Roman Catholic Church and in magisterial Protestantism, found models for the practice of "Christian initiation" in the rites described and expounded in the extant catechetical lectures of some of the great bishops of the fourth and fifth centuries. This inevitably privileged the process as undergone by adult converts. In the work of revision and in the printing of the new books, pride of place was frequently given to orders for baptism on personal profession of faith, with a preceding catechumenate, an immediately succeeding "Spirit" gesture (often), and the expectation of first communion (always). In relation to this adult pattern the procedures for baptizing infants were "adaptations," although many resisted seeing "believer baptism" as the "theological norm." From the responses made by the churches to its "convergence document" on *Baptism, Eucharist and Ministry* (1982), the Faith and Order Commission of the WORLD COUNCIL OF CHURCHES was able to discern "an increasing awareness that originally there was one complex rite of Christian initiation" and to conclude that "all are agreed that the first sign in the process of initiation into the body of Christ is the rite of water baptism. Whichever emphasis is made in the understanding of confirmation [whether as 'the special sign of the gift of the Spirit' or as 'the occasion for a personal profession of faith by those baptized at an earlier age'], each is related to baptism and to holy communion. This may be taken as a hopeful sign that the churches are coming to an understanding of initiation as a unitary and comprehensive process, even if its different elements are spread over a period of time. The total process vividly embodies the coherence of God's gracious initiative in eliciting our faith" [*Baptism, Eucharist and Ministry 1982–1990* (*BEM*), Geneva: WCC, 1990, p. 112].

This convergence, however, did not yet fully settle the ecumenical question of reconciliation among the existing churches. Roman Catholics, Lutherans, Anglicans, and to a lesser degree the Reformed, have considered a presumed "common baptism" as the very basis of ECUMENISM; but, as the churches' responses to *BEM* showed, the matter is more complicated, both from the Baptist side, where the inclusion by other churches of infants in baptism offends against the Baptist judgment that such are not proper subjects of the rite, and also from the Orthodox side, where some question the authority and capacity of non-Orthodox bodies to administer baptism at all (see further Best and Heller).

Baptismal Policies in the Current Situation

In "overseas missions" Protestants have historically known both a "blood and soil" approach, rather like the early CONVERSION of the Germanic nations, in which entire tribes or peoples have adopted Christianity (and received baptism) at a swoop, as in parts of AFRICA and the Pacific, but also a slower advancement by hard-won individual conversions and baptisms, as in parts of Asia. In the historic Protestant heartlands, amid social and cultural changes, public Christianity has declined more sharply than in some other parts of Europe. Opinions have varied between a generous policy of infant baptism, seeking to fan the embers of a residual faith among the folk, and a stricter baptismal discipline, attempting to give the church a sharper profile amid an increasingly secular or religiously plural populace. In any case the CHURCH OF ENGLAND'S statistics are striking: between 1950 and 2000, the rate of infant baptisms for every thousand live births in the

nation fell steadily and steeply from 670 to 210, whereas the absolute number of baptisms of "other persons" rose from about 10,000 to about 50,000 a year (of whom some 40,000 were children aged between one and twelve years, and some 10,000 were by that standard "adults").

Even in the United States, where the public practice of Christianity among Protestants remains much more prominent than in Europe (and where Baptist denominations also find their strongest representation), proposals for the creation or restoration of an "adult catechumenate," whether initiatory or remedial, find favor among "mainline" churches. There are ecumenical calls for a "baptismal spirituality," whereby the whole of the Christian life would be treated as living from, or into, one's baptism in the midst of a baptismally aware community, sustained by the preached word and the Lord's meal.

References and Further Reading

Armour, Rollin S. *Anabaptist Baptism: A Representative Study.* Scottdale, PA: Herald Press, 1966.

Beasley-Murray, George R. *Baptism in the New Testament.* New York: St. Martin's Press, 1962.

Best, Thomas F., and Dagmar Heller, eds. *Becoming a Christian: The Ecumenical Implications of our Common Baptism.* Geneva: World Council of Churches, 1999.

Bromiley, Geoffrey W. *Baptism and the Anglican Reformers.* London: Lutterworth, 1953.

Fisher, John D. C. *Christian Initiation: The Reformation Period.* London: SPCK, 1970.

Flemington, William F. *The New Testament Doctrine of Baptism.* London: SPCK, 1948.

Hubmaier, Balthasar. *Schriften = Quellen zur Geschichte der Täufer 9.* Edited by Gunnar Westin and Torsten Bergsten. Gütersloh, Germany: Mohn, 1962.

Johnson, Maxwell E. *The Rites of Christian Initiation: Their Evolution and Interpretation.* Collegeville, MN: Liturgical Press, 1999.

Jordahn, Bruno. "Der Taufgottesdienst im Mittelalter bis zur Gegenwart." In *Leiturgia 5: Der Taufgottesdienst,* edited by K. F. Müller and W. Blankenburg, 349–640. Kassel, Germany: Stauda, 1970.

Moody, Dale. *Baptism: Foundation for Christian Unity.* Philadelphia: Westminster, 1967.

Old, Hughes O. *The Shaping of the Reformed Baptismal Rite in the Sixteenth Century.* Grand Rapids, MI: Wm. B. Eerdmans, 1992.

Repp, Arthur C. *Confirmation in the Lutheran Church.* St. Louis, MO: Concordia, 1964.

Schlink, Edmund. "Die Lehre von der Taufe." In *Leiturgia 5: Der Taufgottesdienst,* edited by K. F. Müller and W. Blankenburg, 641–808. Kassel, Germany: Stauda, 1970.

Schmidt-Lauber, H. C., and K. H. Bieritz, eds. *Handbuch der Liturgik,* 294–332. Göttingen: Vandenhoeck & Ruprecht, 1995. [August Jilek, "Die Taufe," 333–353; Günther Kehnscherper, "Die Konfirmation."]

Spinks, Bryan. " 'Freely by His Grace': Baptismal Doctrine and the Reform of the Baptismal Liturgy in the Church of Scotland, 1953–1994." In *Rule of Prayer, Rule of Faith,* edited by Nathan Mitchell and John Baldovin, 218–242. Collegeville, MN: Liturgical Press, 1996.

Stevenson, Kenneth. *The Mystery of Baptism in the Anglican Tradition.* Norwich, U.K.: Canterbury Press, 1998.

Stookey, Laurence. *Baptism: Christ's Act in the Church.* Nashville, TN: Abingdon, 1982.

Wainwright, Geoffrey. *Christian Initiation.* London: Lutterworth, 1969; reprint 2002.

GEOFFREY WAINWRIGHT

BAPTIST BIBLE UNION

As the twentieth century began, Northern Baptists in the UNITED STATES were optimistic about the future and eager to expand their denominational structure. Yet the historic conviction of congregational independence caused many to be suspicious about growing centralization and ECUMENISM. More disturbing was the fear that theological liberalism, biblical criticism, evolutionary science, empirical psychology, and the SOCIAL GOSPEL were becoming accepted in Baptist schools and churches. Noted liberals like William Newton Clarke, George Burman Foster, SHAILER MATHEWS, WALTER RAUSCHENBUSH, and HARRY EMERSON FOSDICK drew increasing attention and criticism from conservatives in the denomination. To good old-fashioned Baptists MODERNISM seemed to compromise the reliability of the Scriptures, the possibility of supernatural intervention, the deity of Christ, the validity of evangelical CONVERSION, and the expectancy of Christ's imminent return.

The leader of the conservative critics was William Bell Riley, pastor of the First Baptist Church of Minneapolis, Minnesota. An ardent defender of premillennialism and an arch opponent of evolution, Riley was the principal organizer of the World's Christian Fundamentals Association. Beginning in May of 1919 the WCFA sponsored a series of BIBLE conferences throughout the country warning that "the Great Apostasy" foretold in Scripture "was spreading like a plague throughout Christendom." Over 6,000 people reportedly attended the Philadelphia meeting. Sensing an opportunity to capitalize on the antimodernist sentiment among Baptists, Riley and a group of concerned conservatives called for a "General Conference on the Fundamentals" to precede the meeting of the 1920 Northern Baptist Convention (NBC). Amid a chorus of "Amens," J. C. Massee compared modernist teachers to Philistines who use their Delilah-like seductions to weaken and blind God's people. He pronounced any Baptist institution that harbored liberalism to be unsafe until it had been purged of the source of "pernicious percolating poison."

The well-attended event lasted for two days. Curtis Lee Laws, the editor of the Baptist periodical the *Watchman Examiner,* described the participants as followers of Christ "who still cling to the great fundamentals and who mean to do battle royal" for "the faith once delivered to the saints." When the official convention meeting began, fundamentalists were organized and ready. They passed votes forcing the denomination to pull out of the Interchurch Movement and approved an investigation to determine the ORTHODOXY of Baptist schools. The aim of the "fundamentalist fellowship" was to cleanse the DENOMINATION of liberalism. Before the 1922 meeting of the NBC, Massee challenged fundamentalists to "keep the fight going," but this time denominational loyalists were not surprised. Riley offered a motion that recommended the New Hampshire Confession be adopted by congregations. Prominent liberal pastor Cornelius Woelfkin of the Park Avenue Baptist Church in New York City countered with a substitute proposal that affirmed the New Testament as a sufficient basis of faith and practice. Woelfkin's alternative passed by a margin of two to one.

The fundamentalists were divided into two groups: moderates who wanted to remain as a "loyal opposition" within the NBC, and militants who pushed for "strict separation." A meeting was called in 1923 and the Baptist Bible Union (BBU) was formed. T. T. Shields, pastor of Jarvis Street Baptist Church in Toronto, was elected president, a position he held until 1930. The BBU adopted The New Hampshire Confession with a premillennial gloss as its faith statement, although Shields was an amillennialist. Shields stated that the aim of the BBU was to be broader than just the NBC. He vowed "to mobilize the conservative Baptist forces of the continent, for the express purpose of declaring and waging relentless and uncompromising war on modernism on all fronts." One of the fronts on which the fundamentalist BBU waged its war was against evolution, attacking it as "unscientific, unscriptural, anti-Christian, atheistic, and man-degrading." They appealed to professors in Baptist schools "who have been inoculated with this virus, not to spread the unholy contagion among students committed by godly parents to their care" and appealed to governing boards to discover those that adopt "this anti-Christian philosophy and remove every such professor from his chair."

The BBU's most infamous fundamentalist crusader among Southern Baptists was J. Frank Norris, also known as the "Texas Tornado." For forty-three years he held forth as pastor of the First Baptist Church of Fort Worth, Texas. Norris was the master of outrageous and acrimonious agitation. He attacked Baptist leaders as "lick-the-skillet, two-by-four, aping, asinine preachers" and charged denominational schools with being full of "simian-headed, sawdust-brained" professors teaching "evolution and infidelity." He referred to one prominent pastor as "the Infallible Baptist Pope" and "the Holy Father." In a 1926 sermon series entitled "Rum and Romanism," Norris accused the mayor of Fort Worth of misappropriating city funds for Catholic causes. One of the mayor's associates came to see Norris at his office. The two exchanged heated words. When it was over the complainant lay dead on the floor, the victim of Norris's gun, earning him a reputation as the "pistol packin' preacher." The trial was media circus, and Norris was acquitted on the grounds of self-defense.

In 1927 the BBU acquired the title to Des Moines University, which proved to be the undoing of both the school and the union. Conflict quickly emerged between BBU president Shields and school president H. C. Wayman. The result was chaos. Trustees fired the faculty and administration. Students rioted. The school went bankrupt. Shields returned to CANADA under the cloud of scandal, and participation in the BBU fell off sharply. In response to calls for a more strictly separated association the BBU met one last time in 1932. The thirty-four delegates voted to disband and reorganize as the GENERAL ASSOCIATION OF REGULAR BAPTISTS. Led by their chief controversialist, Robert T. "Fighting Bob" Ketcham, the GARB continued to wage a publicity campaign against Northern Baptist liberalism. Riley and other moderate fundamentalists remained in the NBC until 1947 (the year of his death) when they formed the CONSERVATIVE BAPTIST ASSOCIATION of America. Norris founded the Premillennial Baptist Missionary Fellowship in 1931 that later became the World Fundamental Baptist Missionary Fellowship and again split in 1950 giving rise to the Baptist Bible Fellowship.

The lifespan of the BBU was brief but potent. Most fundamentalist Baptist groups in America trace their origins either directly or indirectly to it, and prominent Baptists from John Birch, to BILLY GRAHAM, to JERRY FALWELL have historical connections in it. The fundamentalist triumvirate of Riley, Shields, and Norris did much to shape the public image of FUNDAMENTALISM as fussy and fissiparous, prompting E. J. Carnell to describe old-style fundamentalism as "orthodoxy gone cultic" (Carnell 1959:113). Yet given that reformed fundamentalism has become the new orthodoxy of the largest Baptist group in the world suggests its legacy may be far greater than the founders of the BBU ever imagined.

See also Baptists, United States; Darwinism; Liberal Protestantism and Liberalism; Southern Baptist Convention

References and Further Reading

Ammerman, Nancy Tatom. "North American Protestant Fundamentalism." In *Fundamentalisms Observed,* edited by M. E. Marty and R. Scott Appleby. vol. 1, 1–65. Chicago: University of Chicago Press, 1991.

Carnell, E. J. *The Case for Orthodox Theology.* Philadelphia: Westminster Press, 1959.

Carpenter, Joel A. *Revive Us Again: The Reawakening of American Fundamentalism.* New York: Oxford University Press, 1997.

Hankins, Barry. *God's Rascal: J. Frank Norris and the Beginnings of Southern Fundamentalism.* Lexington: University of Kentucky Press, 1996.

Marsden, George M. *Fundamentalism and American Culture.* New York: Oxford University Press, 1980.

Sandeen, Ernest R. *The Roots of Fundamentalism and American Culture.* New York: Oxford University Press, 1980.

Tarr, Leslie K. *Shields of Canada.* Grand Rapids, MI: Baker Book House, 1967.

Weber, Timothy P. *Living in the Shadow of the Second Coming: American Premillennialism 1875–1982.* Chicago: University of Chicago Press, 1983.

CURTIS W. FREEMAN

BAPTIST FAMILY OF CHURCHES

The growth of the Baptist "family" of churches began in the early seventeenth century with a few individuals prepared to state their beliefs: JUSTIFICATION by FAITH; the Lordship of Jesus Christ; the autonomy of the local church; the AUTHORITY of Scripture; the separation of CHURCH AND STATE; the PRIESTHOOD OF ALL BELIEVERS; soul liberty; regenerate church membership; and the ordinances of BAPTISM and communion (LORD'S SUPPER) as symbols of spiritual realities. Since that time the BAPTISTS have grown into a worldwide DENOMINATION and are now recognized as the largest evangelical affiliation of churches in the world.

Origins

In 1608 JOHN SMYTH, a graduate from Cambridge, England and pastor of a Separatist congregation in the town of Gainsborough, Lincolnshire sought freedom from continuing persecution by James I, the ruler of ENGLAND. Smyth and his congregation, along with his associate Thomas Helwys, fled to Amsterdam, where they reestablished their church. Rejecting infant BAPTISM in favor of adult baptism, John Smyth baptized himself and then members of his congregation. Modeled scripturally after the New Testament church, the church consisted of autonomous congregations of believers. Adult baptism in the church was carried out by the washing of water, the baptism of the Spirit, and a confession of faith as the scriptural basis for a Christian CONVERSION. In 1612 Helwys left with a portion of the Amsterdam congregation to move back to the British Isles and as a result a number of Baptist churches were founded in England.

Baptist Churches in Britain

Two groups of Baptist churches in England had separate origins. The GENERAL BAPTISTS (Arminians) believe in a *general* ATONEMENT and taught that Christ's death applies to the freedom of the individual who would believe and accept it (see ARMINIANISM). General Baptists separated themselves from the CHURCH OF ENGLAND and followed the Puritan belief that the church should consist of men and women who confess their faith in Christ as Savior (see PURITANISM). Baptism was limited to those old enough to make a confession of faith.

Particular Baptists (Calvinists) hold to *particular* atonement. Their theological convictions are based on ELECTION: those who have been predestined to salvation by God (see CALVINISM; PREDESTINATION). They hold similar views to those of the General Baptists with regard to baptism and a confession of faith. The earliest Particular Baptist church was established in London, England in the year 1638, moving to a more radical position of baptism by immersion.

Helwys promoted the Christian principle of religious liberty, advocating separation between church and state. The royal government of England imprisoned Helwys, where he died as a martyr for his cause of freedom. It was this vision of freedom that inspired many Baptists to migrate to North America on September 6, 1620 on the legendary ship Mayflower. Despite differences between the General and Particular Baptists, their churches merged to form a united denomination in 1891, as the Baptist Union of Great Britain and Ireland.

John Howard Shakespeare, general secretary of the Baptist Union from 1898 to 1924, contributed to the structure and shape of the Baptist denomination in England: he organized major fund drives; initiated ecumenical dialogue with other denominations; assisted in the organization of the BAPTIST WORLD ALLIANCE in 1905; planned the construction of the Baptist Church House; and restructured the Baptist denomination under the leadership of superintendents. Ecclesiastical unity and efficiency were predominant characteristics of the Baptist Union as they encouraged superintendents to keep close ties on local churches and pastors, dividing England and Wales into ten districts under the Ministerial Settlement and Sustentation Scheme. English Baptist colleges are conducted as independent centers of study: Bristol College founded in 1679; Regent's Park in Oxford (1810); Spurgeon's College in London (1856); and Manchester (1866).

Baptist Beginnings in Colonial America

During the colonization of America many immigrants from England and WALES adopted Baptist views after their arrival in the New World. ROGER WILLIAMS, an English Puritan clergyman, immigrated to America, arriving at Boston in 1631. Separatist tendencies were contrary to prevalent views held by the established Congregational Church of early New England (also known as the Church of Standing Order). Legal action was taken against those people who disagreed with their self-governing policy. Sentiments of opposition toward the government expressed by Williams included endorsement of: separation of church and state, Indian land claims, and religious tolerance (see TOLERATION). Roger Williams was banished from the Massachusetts Bay Colony for preaching such new and dangerous opinions, and established the first official Baptist church in America at Providence, Rhode Island around 1638 (Brackney 1988:129). Williams remained a Baptist for only a few months but his influence was significant in political and religious history as he promoted religious liberty for all. He also served as missionary to American Indians, and wrote *The Bloody Tenent*, published in England while seeking a charter for the Providence colony.

Dr. John Clarke established the first congregation with Baptist convictions at Newport, Rhode Island in 1648. Because of bitter persecution Baptist churches grew slowly during the seventeenth century. In 1670 the first regional association of churches was established in New England named the General Six Principle Baptists. In Rhode Island Sabbatarians established their first church by 1671 (see SABBATARIANISM). These Seventh-Day Baptists continued to fellowship with other Baptists only when numbers were insufficient to establish their own churches. In 1707 five churches in New Jersey, Delaware, and Pennsylvania formed the first association in America, enabling missionary efforts to begin. By 1760 the Philadelphia Association extended from Connecticut in the north to Virginia in the south. The Charleston Association was formed in 1751 and soon others were initiated as a revival (called the Great Awakening) spread the Christian faith (see REVIVALS, AWAKENINGS). The results of revival made a deep impact on Baptist growth in North America.

The New Light Congregationalists, emphasizing a *new light* experience through the Holy Spirit, joined the Baptist churches and became known as Separate Baptists. They held theological views similar to General Baptists, stressing the individual's freedom to choose salvation, a general atonement, and the Christian state of apostasy (the possibility of falling from GRACE). The Regular or Particular Baptists placed an emphasis on Calvinist views such as Predestination, God's sovereignty, and irresistible grace given to those people chosen by God for salvation.

Under the leadership of Benjamin Randall in New Hampshire, FREE WILL BAPTISTS challenged the Calvinist views of this time period. As a result, the Free Will position nudged Separate Baptists toward a Regular Position, softening the extremes of Calvinism among Regular Baptists. By 1790 there was a total of 979 Baptist churches with a membership of 67,490, representing a sudden increase of Baptists in the country since the initial report of sixty churches in 1740. Congregations were predominantly Separate Baptists who maintained a distance from Regular Baptists, criticizing them for negligence in principles of church membership.

Toward the end of the colonial period Separate and Regular Baptists joined together in missionary endeavors to the South and in CANADA. A notable element of Baptist history during the colonial period in America was the missionary work of WILLIAM CAREY (1761–1834) in Bengal, INDIA, which began in 1792 and left a lasting legacy of established Baptist Missions and churches in that country. Carey, a cobbler from Moulton, England, was the first missionary appointed by the Baptist Missionary Society (BMS) of England, and he baptized his first convert at Serampore, Bengal in 1800. Carey first promoted the idea of ecumenical dialogue among the diversity of denominations found on the mission field in India. As VOLUNTARY SOCIETIES were organized for foreign missions, Baptists both in England and America were spurred onward to evangelistic efforts at home and in overseas missions. American missionaries ADONIRAM JUDSON and Luther Rice were instrumental in the mission work of Burma (now Myanmar), arriving at Rangoon (now Yangon) on July 13, 1813. Judson served as a missionary in India and Rice returned to America to enlist support for missions among American Baptists.

Baptist Churches in North America

From the 1800s onward American Baptist churches continued to escalate numerically as they perfected their organizational structures, promoted missionary endeavors in other countries, and entered into divisive controversies, which contributed to their formation as a major evangelical Christian denomination in North America. The four largest Baptist denominations in the United States are the SOUTHERN BAPTIST CONVENTION, the AMERICAN BAPTIST CHURCHES, the NATIONAL BAPTIST CONVENTION U.S.A., and the NATIONAL BAPTIST CONVENTION OF AMERICA.

Division between North and South

In 1795 ISAAC BACKUS estimated that Baptist churches numbered 1,152 and were in a strong position to make major contributions to American life. In 1802 Baptists in New England started to initiate benevolent societies to advance the interests of the denomination, leading to the organization of congregations in the North and West. The principle of organization is based on voluntary individual membership within independent charters. This is in contrast to the more centralized method used by Baptists in the southern states.

On May 18, 1814 the General Convention of the Baptist Denomination was formed, also known as the Triennial Convention. In 1826 disagreements between the North and South over methods of organization led to the formation of societies unconnected to churches in the North, whereas in the South the formation of an association or convention plan was based on adopted churches. An influential Baptist from Boston, Massachusetts named Francis Wayland convinced the Convention to limit its operation to an independent society for foreign missions. The Triennial Convention moved its headquarters from Philadelphia, Pennsylvania to Boston, Massachusetts, cutting back further participation by Southern Baptists. In 1844 Francis Wayland engaged in literary debates with Richard Fuller of Charleston, South Carolina over the moral imperative of the North against SLAVERY in the South.

Between 1826 and 1845 relations between Northern and Southern Baptists continued to deteriorate. Factors related to this division include (1) the slavery controversy between proslavery and antislavery parties; (2) the antimissionary movement promoted by the South in opposition to those in the North who devised programs to encourage conversions; (3) the Campbellism controversy: a rational faith employing an ecumenical view to move beyond denominationalism, known as "Christians only"; and (4) disagreement over methods of organization pushing Southern Baptists to a more unified convention method rather than the many society meetings held by the North.

Two factors led to schism in 1845: (1) the Home Mission Society declined approval of the nomination of Rev. James E. Reeve, a slave owner from Georgia, to serve as a home missionary; (2) an inquiry from the Baptist State Convention of Alabama to the Board of the Triennial Convention, requesting whether slaveholders could act as foreign missionaries, was turned down by the Home Mission Society. These events, known as the *Georgia Test Case* and the *Alabama Resolutions,* hastened the schism between North and South leading to the Augusta, Georgia meeting of Southern Baptists on May 8, 1845 to form the Southern Baptist Convention. Francis Wayland was a support to the Southern states during this dilemma, but held that the division represented just one more formulation of a mission society in the Baptist denomination. Southerners regarded the split as an opportunity to develop their own denominational views separate from the North.

American Baptist Churches in the USA

Known at first as the Northern Baptist Convention, it was organized in 1907 and created for the purpose of coordinating the many Baptist mission agencies that were in existence at that time. In 1950 the name changed to the American Baptist Convention, and then again in 1973 to its present name of American Baptist Churches in the USA. The headquarters is at Valley Forge, Pennsylvania, also the site of a publishing branch called the *Judson Press*. Membership is about 1.5 million in 4,800 congregations distributed among thirty-four regional jurisdictions.

In 1911 the Convention became a charter member of the Federal Council of Churches of Christ and the International Faith and Order Movement. The first president was Charles Evans Hughes, governor of New York, who was an advocate of social activism. During the year 1911 a merger occurred between the Northern Baptist Convention and the Free Will Baptist General Conference, becoming the Freewill Baptists in America. With the rapid development of boards, educational programs, commissions for stewardship, missions, and social service, the Northern Baptists ultimately became embroiled in what is known as the modernist/fundamentalist controversy, a bitter conflict between internal liberalism and conservative elements in the early 1920s. The main body of Northern Baptists assumed a mediating position in 1922, centering on the sufficiency of scripture as foundation of faith and practice.

In 1950, with the change in name to the American Baptist Convention, an open invitation was given to other Conventions to unite together and form a national body of Baptists.

Congregations from the Baptist African American traditions achieved a dual-alignment status with the Convention and attitudes of religious tolerance became a predominant factor in the future shaping of Baptist affiliations. With the second name revision to the American Baptist Churches in the USA, more authority was given to the regional bodies and local churches.

Theologically, American Baptist beliefs include conservative, neoorthodox, liberal, and charismatic renewal traditions. With an emphasis on the autonomy of each church, some congregations have joined the Association of Welcoming and Affirming Baptists, an association formed during the 1991 biennial meeting of the denomination at Charleston, West Virginia. Their purpose is to support those who are needy, weak, and oppressed; to promote justice for all people; to express unity in diversity and diversity in unity; and to embrace pluralism while respecting individual theological differences.

Fundamentalist Baptist Churches

The Northern Baptist Convention met in Denver, Colorado in 1919 and made four decisions that ultimately alienated conservatives in their ranks: (1) authorizing funding projects to raise money; (2) organizing denominational boards to oversee Northern Baptist Convention work; (3) initiating a denomination newspaper called *The Baptist*; and (4) voting to join the INTERCHURCH WORLD MOVEMENT. In response to what were considered moves to entrench liberal leadership in the denomination, conservatives moved to organize a group called the Fundamentalist Fellowship. They met annually before the Convention to plan strategic moves in the voting process, so those influenced by liberalism might be purged out of the denomination. When this process failed, the BAPTIST BIBLE UNION was formed in 1923 at Kansas City, Missouri consisting of two groups: moderate conservatives who wanted to remain in the convention and militant separatists who wanted to split off. As an outgrowth of this organization the GENERAL ASSOCIATION OF REGULAR BAPTIST CHURCHES was formed in 1932. Major leaders include W. B. Riley, A. C. Dixon, J. Frank Norris, and T. T. Shields of Canada. Moderate Fundamentalists remained in the Northern Convention for another twenty years with influential leaders such as Frank M. Goodchild, J. C. Massee, and Curtis Lee Laws.

In 1943 the Conservative Baptist Foreign Mission Society was formed and the general body of the CONSERVATIVE BAPTIST ASSOCIATION of America in 1947. The World Baptist Fellowship (WBF) led by John Franklyn Norris (1877–1952), a militant fundamentalist known as the *Texas Cyclone*, was founded in 1950. Norris was a notorious leader, having been indicted and tried for murder, perjury, and arson during his ministry. The WBF suffered two splits as a consequence of the personality and methods of Norris: the Baptist Bible Fellowship of Springfield, Missouri in 1952 and the Baptist Bible Fellowship (BBF) in 1950. The Southwide Baptist Fellowship (SBF) consisted of independents and numerous disgruntled Baptists who were avid evangelists from the Northern Baptist Convention, known for their fundamentalist beliefs and behaviors. Fundamentalist churches in America number around 10,000 and are gathered into a number of separate general bodies.

Free Will Baptists

There are two streams of Free Will Baptists: Paul Palmer formed the General Baptist churches in North Carolina in the 1720s and Benjamin Randall led another group in 1780 in New England. In 1911 many Free Wills joined the Northern Baptist Convention and in 1935 the Palmer and Randall lines merged to form the National Association of Free Will Baptists (NAFWB). Free Wills are known for their intense conservatism, central organizational structure, and the practice of foot washing.

The Southern Baptist Convention (SBC) is the largest conservative, evangelical Baptist organization in the United States, consisting of 17.4 million baptized believers. Approximately one half of all Baptists in the United States belong to the Southern Baptist Convention. There are around 47,000 churches spread throughout all fifty states in the United States, making it the largest Protestant denomination. The Southern Baptist Convention, organized on May 8, 1845 in Augusta, Georgia, separated from the General Missionary Conference of the Baptist Denomination (Triennial Convention) and the American Baptist Home Mission Society. The Home Mission Board (HMB) and the Foreign Mission Board (FMB) were formed in 1845 and the Sunday School Board in 1891. Women like Charlotte "Lottie" Diggs Moon (1840–1912), a famous missionary to CHINA, and Annie Armstrong of Baltimore, a leader in home missions, encouraged women to become involved in missionary work in Asia and AFRICA.

The SBC experienced remarkable growth as membership increased 250% between 1940 and 1980. Reasons for dynamic growth include a fervent evangelistic and missionary emphasis; a strong denominational consciousness; resistance to prevalent liberalism in the modernity of the twentieth century; unified leadership in boards and state conventions in relationship to local congregations; an emphasis upon theological education in SEMINARIES; and the publication of SUNDAY SCHOOL materials for churches. Southern Baptists have refused involvement with the NATIONAL COUNCIL OF CHURCHES and the WORLD COUNCIL OF CHURCHES, although their agencies cooperate with a diversity of programs offered by the National Council of Churches.

Theologically most Southern Baptists are conservative evangelicals and adhere to the scriptural authority of the BIBLE in the determination of their ecclesiology and social action in the community. Southern Baptists baptize by immersion accompanied by a public confession of faith; do not believe in the conveyance of sacramental grace in baptism or communion; and hold to both Calvinist and Arminian viewpoints.

Although they do not adhere to a universal confessional creed, they use a faith statement called *The Baptist Faith and Message* (BFM), first adopted in 1925 and revised in 1963, that is based on the *New Hampshire Confession*.

The Southern Baptist Convention leadership has become increasingly conservative; a revision of the BFM in 2000 insists that women submit to their husbands and be banned from ordination as church pastors. In a decision to strengthen the traditional Baptist position and in reaction to liberal attempts to modernize the denomination, the SBC requested that more than 5,400 appointed missionaries from the Southern Baptist International Mission Board sign the amended faith statement by May, 2003 or face termination in their positions. As a result missionaries faced the doctrinal dilemma of agreeing to the terms of the faith statement or leaving their ministries in the countries they served. A number of congregations have left the SBC and joined the moderate Cooperative Baptist Fellowship (CBF) formed in 1991, with headquarters situated in Atlanta, Georgia.

American Baptist Association (Landmarkers)

In the early 1900s Landmark groups located primarily in Texas, Oklahoma, and Arkansas protested the *convention* system used by the Southern Baptist Convention. Led by James R. Graves of Tennessee, a preacher in the Southern Baptist Convention, they opposed the use of *executive boards* implemented by Baptist churches from the North. The United States General Association drew the Landmark groups together in March, 1905 to support the *Old Landmarks* teaching of the church as local and visible. Landmark teachings require: a properly authorized administrator to validate Ordinances; belief in a direct succession of Baptist churches from the time of Christ; rejection of baptism in other churches; no pulpit affiliation with other denominations; exclusive observance of the Lord's Supper in the local church; and missionary work carried out by the local church rather than through a Convention.

Named the American Baptist Association (ABA) in 1924, the groups membership grew to 200,000 by 1950. Ben M. Bogard, a leader and defender of the faith and work of the ABA, wrote a well-known book called the *Baptist Way-Book* advocating views held by J. R. Graves. Landmark Baptists in the U.S.A. number about 500,000 and are primarily located in the states of Arkansas, Oklahoma, Texas, Louisiana, Mississippi, and California. On May 25–26, 1950 a number of churches from the American Baptist Association met in Lakehead, Florida and voted to split in protest over the issue of accepting messengers who were not members of the churches they represented. From this schism the North American Baptist Association formed a new denomination, which later changed its name to the Baptist Missionary Association of America in 1969. The ABA claims about 250,000 members in 1,700 churches predominantly found in the southern states.

National Baptist Conventions

There are currently four predominantly African American Baptist denominations in the United States: the National Baptist Convention of the United States of America, Inc.; the National Baptist Convention of America; the National Baptist Evangelical Life and Soul-Saving Assembly of the USA; and the PROGRESSIVE NATIONAL BAPTIST CONVENTION, Incorporated.

During the middle of the nineteenth century an emergence of black Baptist churches and organizations took place. Despite laws preventing the organization of black churches, many came into existence as early as 1778 in Georgia, Boston, New York, and Philadelphia. The first black association of eight churches occurred in Ohio in 1834. In 1886 the first national Black Convention was organized, composed of 600 church delegates from seventeen states. On September 28, 1895 the National Baptist Convention, the largest African American denomination in America and the world, was established in Atlanta, Georgia.

In 1915 the Convention separated into two distinct organizations in a dispute over the ownership of the National Baptist Publishing Board. In an attempt to claim rights to the publishing house, the Convention adopted a new charter and was incorporated under the title National Baptist Convention of the United States of America, Incorporated. This new charter was rejected by others, however, and the National Baptist Convention of the U.S.A., Inc. was established under the leadership of the Rev. R. H. Boyd, claiming over 2.5 million members and over 11,000 congregations by 1956. Both denominations adhere to similar theological positions on: scriptural authority; the Lordship of Jesus; baptism of believers; separation of church and state; autonomy of the local church; and state associations.

The National Baptist Evangelical Life and Soul-Saving Assembly was founded in 1920 in Kansas City, Missouri under the auspices of the National Baptist Convention of America, Unincorporated. In 1936 they declared independence from the Convention, dedicating their work to evangelism, relief work, and the support of charities. In 1951 the Assembly consisted of 264 churches and 58,000 members.

The Progressive National Baptist Convention emerged in 1961 after a schism within the National Baptist Convention of the United States of America, Incorporated. Factors leading to division include: dissatisfaction with the leadership of J. H. Jackson; the structure of convention and controversy concerning the CIVIL RIGHTS MOVEMENT of the 1960s; and methods used by MARTIN LUTHER KING JR. in opposition to racism. The PNBC headquarters are found in Washington, D.C. and are in formal alignment with the American Baptist Churches. By 1984 they had approximately one million members.

Baptist Churches in Canada

British Empire Loyalists emigrated to what is now known as Atlantic Canada, that is, the Provinces of Nova Scotia, New Brunswick, and Prince Edward Island, as well as to Quebec and Ontario in the late eighteenth century. This movement of emigrants opened a gateway to Baptist growth in the Maritimes and spread westward to the rest of Canada over the next century. Ebenezer Moulton, the first Baptist minister in Canada, established a church in the Annapolis Valley, Nova Scotia in 1760. Factors leading to the growth of the Baptist organization in Canada include the Revivals of the Great Awakening; missionary endeavors by HENRY ALLINE, who was a Congregationalist, a fervent evangelist, and preacher; and the emergence of Freewill Baptist churches in New Brunswick and Nova Scotia. Pioneer leaders include Ebenezer Moulton, Nathan Mason, Shubael and Daniel Dimock, Benjamin Randall, and Avery Moulton. Baptists from the Arminian (Free Baptists) and Calvinistic (Regular Baptists) branches united to form the United Baptist Convention of the Maritime Provinces in 1905.

Missionary work was a prevalent feature of Canadian Baptists. Reverend Samuel S. Day, a native of Ontario, was the first Baptist missionary in the country of Telugus, in India, and founder of the American Baptist Telugu Mission. As American citizens he and his wife sailed from Boston on September 22, 1835, arriving at Calcutta on February 5, 1836. Richard E. Burpee and his wife Laleah were the first Canadian Baptist missionaries who left from Nova Scotia and arrived in Burma on April 20, 1845. Support for the Burpees came from two Maritime associations as they worked under the auspices of the American Baptist Missionary Union.

On August 26, 1849 the Grande Ligne Mission of Quebec became a driving force in missions and merged with the Canada Baptist Missionary Society to become the Baptist Evangelical Church of Grande Ligne. In 1888 the Regular Baptist Missionary Convention of Ontario merged with the Canada Baptist Missionary Convention East and the Baptist Foreign Missionary Society of Ontario and Quebec. The combined mergers of the Church Edifice Society for Ontario and Quebec and the Superannuated Ministers' Society culminated in the formation of the Baptist Convention of Ontario and Quebec.

The Baptist Union of Western Canada (for two years called a Convention) developed in 1907 from Baptist associations in the British Columbia Convention, the Convention of Manitoba and the Convention of the North-West. Their first meeting as the Baptist Convention of Western Canada was held in November 1907. Obstacles hindering the unity of Baptists across Canada included the fundamentalist/modernist controversy of the 1920s, which produced schisms from the Baptist Convention of Ontario and Quebec and the Baptist Union of Western Canada. Because of antimodernism sentiments T. T. Shields founded the Union of Regular Baptist Churches of Ontario and Quebec in 1927. This second indigenous Baptist denomination of Canada is presently known as the Canada-wide Fellowship of Evangelical Baptist Churches.

The Baptist Federation of Canada was organized in 1944 (later renamed the Canadian Baptist Federation), which merged with the Canadian Baptist International Ministries to form the Canadian Baptist Ministries in 1995, as a national agency consisting of four autonomous Baptist Conventions: The Convention of Atlantic Baptist Churches (538 churches, 62,000 members); the Baptist Convention of Ontario and Quebec (372 churches and 43,000 members); the Baptist Union of Western Canada (167 churches, 22,000 members); and the Union d'Eglises baptistes francaises au Canada (the Union of French Baptist Churches in Canada) (32 churches, 1,733 members). There are four seminaries: McMaster Divinity College in Ontario, Acadia University in Nova Scotia, Carey Hall linked with Regent College in British Columbia, Faculte Theologie Evangelique in Quebec, and one lay training institute named Atlantic Baptist University in New Brunswick. The headquarters of the Canadian Baptist Ministries is in Mississauga, Ontario from which is published the *Canadian Baptist Magazine* on a quarterly basis.

Baptist World Alliance

The Southern Baptists, Northern Baptists, and British Baptists were instrumental in gathering Baptist unions and conventions together into the Baptist World Alliance. The BWA was first established in London in 1905 as an international organization and serves as a beacon light to the nations of the world. BWA conferences are held every three years with representatives of over 125 countries in attendance. Its purpose is to promote world peace and religious liberty, provide relief funds in emergency situations, and provide

a neutral environment for Baptists to discuss cultural and theological issues.

Worldwide Family of Baptists

Baptists have grown to encompass a worldwide fellowship of churches consisting of almost forty-six million baptized believers in 206 Baptist conventions and unions. This includes ethnic Baptist groups in North America that primarily come from European, Hispanic, Asian, and other cultural backgrounds as well as in countries where missionaries from representative mission boards in North America and Europe have established Baptist churches. Albert W. Wardin has compiled a helpful book called *Baptists around the World: A Comprehensive Handbook,* designed to classify Baptists worldwide, emphasizing the history of Baptists in each particular area or country. The Baptist World Alliance continues to list up-to-date statistics in an annual directory, providing information on recent changes in memberships and churches, as well as on the additions of any new Baptist conventions.

See also Baptist Missions; Baptists, Europe; Baptists, Global; Baptists, United States; Biblical Inerrancy; Congregationalism; Liberal Protestantism and Liberalism; Women Clergy

References and Further Reading

Armstrong, O. K., and Marjorie M. Armstrong. *The Indomitable Baptists: A Narrative of Their Role in Shaping American History.* Garden City, NY: Doubleday Press, 1967.
Baker, Robert A. *The Southern Baptist Convention and Its People: 1607–1972.* Nashville, TN: Broadman Press, 1974.
Barnes, William Wright. *The Southern Baptist Convention, 1845–1953.* Nashville, TN: Broadman Press, ca. 1954.
Brackney, William H. *The Baptists.* New York: Greenwood Press, 1988.
Craig, John. *Forty Years Among the Telugus.* Toronto: Department of Agriculture, 1908.
Daniel, Orville E. *Moving with the Times.* Toronto: Canadian Baptist Overseas Mission Board, 1973.
Jones, William H. *What Canadian Baptists Believe.* Canada: Chi-Rho Communications, 1989.
Lumpkin, William L. *Baptist Confessions of Faith.* Valley Forge, PA: Judson Press, 1959.
McBeth, Leon. *Women in Baptist Life.* Nashville, TN: Broadman Press, 1979.
———. *The Baptist Heritage.* Nashville, TN: Broadman Press, 1987.
———. *A Sourcebook for Baptist Heritage.* Nashville, TN: Broadman Press, 1990.
Payne, Ernest A. *The Baptist Union: A Short History.* London: Carey Kingsgate Press, 1959.
Renfree, Harry A. *Heritage and Horizon: The Baptist Story in Canada.* Mississauga Canada: Canadian Baptist Federation, 1988.
Torbet, Robert G. *A History of the Baptists.* Valley Forge, PA: Judson Press, 1965.

Tull, James E. *Shapers of Baptist Thought*. Valley Forge, PA: Judson Press, 1972.

Walker, Ken. "A Time to Decide." *Christianity Today* (April 2003): 36–37.

Wardin, Albert W. *Baptists Around the World*. Nashville, TN: Broadman & Holman, 1995.

DONNA J. KERFOOT

BAPTIST GENERAL CONFERENCE

With a growing dissatisfaction in the cold formality of the Swedish established Lutheran Church, a Pietistic revival spread throughout SWEDEN in the early nineteenth century. Small groups called *läsare* (or "Bible" readers) met in homes for study, prayer, and mutual support. From these groups came the Swedish Baptists, founded when seaman Fredrick O. Nilsson (b. 1809) arranged the first believer's baptism in 1848, having been baptized himself the year before.

Nilsson's act was seen as a public DISSENT from the state, and after being tried, he was banished from the country in 1850. Eventually coming to the UNITED STATES in 1853, Nilsson founded several congregations in Minnesota. During this time a number of Swedish Baptist congregations were also being established in Illinois by a former Lutheran lay-preacher and school teacher, Gustaf Palmquist (1812–1867). Palmquist, impressed by the *läsare* and the AMERICAN BAPTIST CHURCHES, was baptized and ordained in August 1852, establishing the first American-Swedish Baptist congregation a month later. Nilsson and Palmquist, who had met in Sweden, worked together to organize Swedish Baptist congregations into what later became the Swedish Baptist General Conference of America in 1879.

Although slow in the beginning, the last two decades of the nineteenth century saw a relative explosion in growth. Large numbers of Swedish immigrants, some Baptists already, founded numerous new congregations in the Midwest, increasing membership from 3,000 in 1879 to 22,000 in 1902. After the turn of the century, however, immigration slowed and church ministry became more English centered, culminating with the drop of "Swedish" from the name in 1945.

With this sluggish growth came the impetus for stronger organization. Previously aided by other American Baptists, and despite the financial crisis it created, the Baptist General Conference (BGC) separated from other Baptist groups and became self-supporting. This included moving their seminary from Chicago to St. Paul, Minnesota in 1914 and renaming it Bethel Seminary; forming a denominational periodical, a merging of preexisting Swedish and English Baptist periodicals; developing social services, particularly orphanages, homes for the aging, and hospitals; and forming their own Baptist Missions board in 1944.

Conservative in THEOLOGY, and with a strong Baptist TRADITION, the denomination is congregational in government, where independent congregations form a fellowship of like-minded churches. The Baptist General Conference once again experienced an increase in membership in the last half of the twentieth century. As missionary programs expanded, the ethnicity of the denomination also diversified. Although still predominantly in the Midwestern, Northern, and Pacific United States, with the International Ministry Center in Arlington Heights, Illinois, housing the executive ministry team and the national ministries, the denomination includes more than seventeen ethnic groups from nineteen nations (notably in Asia, AFRICA, and LATIN AMERICA). Membership numbers now are close to 200,000 found in more than 950 congregations worldwide.

See also Baptist Family; Baptists; Baptists, United States; Lutheranism, Scandinavia

References and Further Reading

Communications, Baptist General Conference. "BGC History." Video. 2002. www.bgcworld.org/media/media.htm (Accessed April 24, 2003).

Magnuson, Norris. *How We Grew*. Arlington Heights, IL: Communications, Baptist General Conference, 2002.

———. *Missionsskolan: The History of an Immigrant Theological School, Bethel Theological Seminary, 1871–1981*. St. Paul, MN: Bethel Theological Seminary, 1982.

Olson, Adof. *A Centenary History*. New York: Arno Press, 1980.

H. CHAD HILLIER

BAPTIST MISSIONS

Baptists have been a missionary people. First they sought to win their neighbors to the faith, although Calvinistic tendencies among the English Baptists hindered the process of missionary work, whereas Baptists in America were more outreach oriented. The major Baptist denominations in America had their roots in world MISSIONS, and today several Baptist bodies elsewhere sponsor missionary agencies. Missions are the integrating center of their corporate life.

The first Baptist congregations formed in ENGLAND at the beginning of the seventeenth century bore the imprint of continental ANABAPTISM, as seen in an emphasis on believers' BAPTISM and the CHURCH as a voluntary fellowship of the regenerate. As dissenting separatists they suffered persecution, and discrimination continued after the passage of the Toleration Act in 1689. In the face of eighteenth-century DEISM, skepticism, and rationalism, those in the "Particular" or Calvinistic wing of the movement took a defensive position (see CALVINISM; PREDESTINATION). Not wishing to usurp God's prerogative to save those whom he elected, they saw themselves as ministers to the chosen few rather than evangelists to the many. In America the Baptists were more missionary minded, and the Philadelphia Baptist Association (founded 1707) sent evangelists as far south as Charleston to form new churches. Similar outreach efforts occurred among Massachusetts and Virginia Baptists, and by the early nineteenth century organized work occurred among blacks in Maryland, white settlers on the frontier (Massachusetts Baptist Missionary Society, 1802), and the native population (New York [City] Baptist Missionary Society, 1800).

The Work of the British Baptists

An evangelical stream entered into English Particular Baptist circles through continental PIETISM, METHODISM, and Anglican EVANGELICALISM. JONATHAN EDWARDS's 1747 tract, *An Humble Attempt to Promote Explicit Agreement and Visible Union of God's People in Extraordinary Prayer,* which the Baptists began reading in 1784, also had an impact. Edwards argued that the Great Awakening in New England signified the last days of history were about to begin (see AWAKENINGS). The spread of the gospel throughout the world would occur, but this expansion of the church required united prayer. Andrew Fuller of Kettering used Edwards's emphasis on the balance between divine sovereignty and human responsibility to counter the hyper-Calvinist belief in total depravity that precluded unconverted sinners from repenting and believing the gospel. This attitudinal shift along with the knowledge of other missionary efforts paved the way for WILLIAM CAREY (1761–1834), a young bivocational pastor in Moulton, Northamptonshire, to develop his missionary vision. He raised the idea of missionary outreach in 1789 and soon won the backing of Fuller and other prominent figures. At his installation into a regular pastorate at Leicester in 1791, Carey read a manifesto for the new venture, *An Enquiry into the Obligation of Christians to Use Means for the Conversion of the Heathens,* and it was published a year later. At the Northamptonshire Association meeting on May 30, 1792 Carey appealed for action with the memorable line, "Expect great things; attempt great things." Four months later the group voted to form "The Particular-Baptist Society, for propagating the gospel amongst the heathen." It soon was renamed the Baptist Missionary Society.

On June 13, 1793 the BMS sent its first missionaries to INDIA, Carey and John Thomas, a medical doctor. Arriving in Bengal in November Carey chose to be self-supporting and found a job as manager of an indigo plantation. He quickly learned the language, established a church, engaged in agricultural research, set up a school, and fought against social injustices like *sati,* the immolation of a widow on her husband's funeral pyre. In 1799 he was joined by the printer William Ward (1769–1823) and educator Joshua Marshman (1768–1837), and they settled in the Danish enclave of Serampore. Functioning as a team (the "Serampore Trio"), they carried out educational, translation, and publication work. Among their achievements were publishing the BIBLE in Bengali and other languages, establishing the first newspaper in India, founding Serampore College (1818), engaging in dialogue with Hindu intellectuals, and opening new stations in Bengal, Orissa, North India, and Ceylon as additional missionaries from Britain arrived.

An important BMS endeavor was in Jamaica, where two former American slaves, George Liele and Moses Baker, had launched an indigenous Baptist work in 1783. They asked for assistance from the BMS when the planters opposed evangelizing the slave population, and the first workers arrived in 1814. The trio of Thomas Burchell (1799–1846), James Philippo (1798–1879), and William Knibb (1803–1845) founded churches among the blacks and plunged wholeheartedly into the struggle against SLAVERY. The Baptists contributed significantly to passage in 1834 of the Emancipation Act abolishing slavery throughout the Empire, and securing an end to the apprenticeship system that kept the former slaves in de facto bondage (see SLAVERY ABOLITION OF). Missionary work also took place in Trinidad and other West Indian islands.

In 1842 the Jamaican Baptist Association obtained independence, founded Calabar College to train clergy, and formed the Jamaica Baptist Missionary Society that worked in AFRICA with the BMS mission on Fernando Po island and in Cameroon. Founded in 1841 by John Clarke (1802–1879), the mission drew heavily on Jamaicans such as Joseph Merrick (1818–1849) who did important work in BIBLE TRANSLATION. Although deeply motivated by missionary zeal and welcomed by whites who wrongly assumed that the "repatriated" Jamaicans would thrive in the difficult African climate, the mission lacked sufficient support and ended by 1853. However, the main BMS work in Cameroon, led by Joseph Jackson Fuller (1825–1908), born in slavery in Jamaica, and Alfred Saker (1814–1880) from England, was more successful. They translated the Bible and developed a Christian community among the Douala people.

When the Germans placed Cameroon under colonial rule, the BMS left and in 1891 German Baptists began working there. They formed a board in 1898 and operated it as their major field. When the Allies in

World War I expelled the German missionaries, Carl Bender (1869–1935), an American citizen, was allowed to stay and preserved the work from complete destruction. German missionaries eventually returned, and with their ethnic counterparts in the North American Baptist Conference, labored in British West Cameroon. The Paris Evangelical Mission administered the Baptist field in French-ruled Cameroon. By the end of colonial rule in 1961 three separate Baptist denominations had emerged.

In 1877 a wealthy Baptist businessman, Robert Arthington (1823–1900), who had the vision of a chain of mission stations across Africa, gave the BMS committee funds for a reconnaissance of the Congo basin. He also supported the efforts of the BMS and other societies in Africa and India that engaged in pioneer work, and was the leading missionary philanthropist in the nineteenth century. Two missionaries who had served in Cameroon, Thomas Comber (1852–1887) and George Grenfell (1849–1906), in the early 1880s transported a steamer overland to the navigable stretch of the river and established a new mission there. The missionaries soon were drawn into the international controversy over the brutal atrocities perpetrated in King Leopold's Congo Free State and only belatedly embraced the cause of reform. In the twentieth century the Belgian Congo was a major BMS field and continued so after independence.

BMS activity in CHINA began in 1859–1860. Its most noted missionary was the Welshman Timothy Richard (1845–1919), a landmark figure in Chinese Christian history, who began work at the Shandong mission in 1870. Convinced of the need for the church to be self-supporting, he urged that itinerant EVANGELISM should be left to Chinese Christians and missionaries should focus on reaching the leaders of society with a message that linked Christianity with the benefits of Western civilization. He was prominent in relief work during the famines of 1876–1879 in north China and argued that Western scientific expertise was needed to avert similar disasters. Because of differences with colleagues over THEOLOGY and strategy, the BMS allowed him to work independently in literacy and educational ministry and he played an important role in the Chinese national reform movement. A dozen BMS missionaries were killed in the Boxer Uprising of 1900 and the mission came close to extinction, but after the revolution in 1911–1912 its educational and medical programs prospered. A decline set in during the 1930s and World War II, and two years after the Communist victory in 1949 the BMS mission was closed.

The New Connexion General Baptists also had a missionary society that began a work in Orissa, India in 1821. It merged with the BMS in 1891. The Ladies' Association for the Support of Zenana Work and Bible Women in India, formed in 1867, was linked with the BMS. In the twentieth century the BMS opened fields in Brazil and several other countries.

Missions of North American Baptists

Baptists in the UNITED STATES followed Carey's work with interest. Various pastors corresponded with him, denominational papers published his letters, local groups prayed and gave money to the Serampore mission, and BMS workers often visited New England on their travels. However, the first body to appoint missionaries was the AMERICAN BOARD OF COMMISSIONERS FOR FOREIGN MISSIONS, founded by Congregationalists in 1810. In the first group that sailed to India in 1812 were Adoniram (1788–1850) and Ann Hasseltine (1789–1826) Judson (see JUDSON FAMILY) and Luther Rice (1783–1836). On the outward journey they intensely studied the New Testament to prepare for expected controversies with the Baptists and instead became convinced of the correctness of believer's BAPTISM. After arriving in Calcutta, they declared themselves Baptists, were rebaptized, and resigned from the American Board. The Judsons were forced to leave and go to Rangoon, Burma in 1813 while Rice returned home to raise support for their work.

His efforts resulted in the creation in May 1814 of "The General Missionary Convention of the Baptist Denomination in the United States of America for Foreign Missions," popularly known as the Triennial Convention because it met every three years, or simply the General Convention. Based on the already existing state conventions and organized on the society model, it was the first national association of Baptists in the country. It appointed Judson as its first overseas missionary and for a brief time sponsored mission activity among settlers and Indians on the frontier with the appointment of John Mason Peck (1789–1857) and Isaac McCoy (1784–1846). Peck's efforts led to the formation of the American Baptist Home Mission Society in 1832, which took responsibility for efforts in the West, later in MEXICO and the CARIBBEAN, and after the CIVIL WAR, among the former slaves in the South. Joanna P. Moore (1832–1916) was renowned for her educational work among the freedmen.

Rather than return to India, Rice served as the agent of the Triennial Convention and became engrossed in a futile effort to found a missionary training school, Columbian College, in Washington, D.C. (now George Washington University). Judson, on the other hand, preached and did translation work, founded a church, was imprisoned during a local war in 1824–1826, and suffered his wife's death soon after. He was joined by George Dana Boardman (1801–1831), who began working among the Karen people, the most successful of the Burmese mission operations. After Boardman's death, Judson married his widow Sarah (1803–1845) who had played a major role in the Karen mission. He finished the Burmese Bible translation in 1834 and a large Burmese dictionary in 1849. He intended to take his invalid wife home in 1845 but she died on the journey. While on his only furlough, where he was feted as a hero throughout the Protestant community, he married a noted author, Emily Chubbock (1817–1854). He died in Burma four years later, and Emily took the surviving children back to America and helped popularize his labors.

The General Convention opened new works in India—the Telegu mission in 1835 (known as the "Lone State Mission" because the only station for many years was at Nellore) and in 1836 the one in Assam—and entered Thailand in 1833 and China in 1842. In the 1830s it sent missionaries to FRANCE, DENMARK, and Greece, and also supported the indigenous German Baptist work led by Johann G. Oncken (1800–1884). Also noteworthy was the LIBERIA mission initiated under the leadership of LOTT CARY (c. 1780–1828) and Collin Teague (c. 1780–1839), African Americans from Virginia. The FREE WILL BAPTISTS in New England founded a mission society in 1832, and under the direction of Jeremiah Phillips (1812–1879) they inaugurated a work among the Santal people in Orissa, India. In 1847 the Seventh Day Baptists launched a mission in China.

However, abolitionist sentiments in the General Convention and Home Mission Society and a decision not to appoint missionaries who were slave owners led the southern members in May 1845 to break with the national society and form a separate SOUTHERN BAPTIST CONVENTION. This was a centralized denominational body that represented churches and functioned through boards. The northerners continued the society approach, that is, bodies composed of individual members that linked the efforts of the individual Baptist associations and statewide organizations. The foreign mission society was renamed the American Baptist Union.

After the Civil War both the northern ABMU and the SBC Foreign Mission Board expanded their operations. The ABMU's Karen mission flourished and was extended to the Kachins and other Burmese hill peoples, while in Assam a mass movement occurred among the tribal (non-Hindu) Garo and Naga, the various enterprises in China rapidly grew, struggling Baptist works in Europe were assisted, the acquisition of the Livingstone Inland Mission's stations in the Congo basin in 1884 added a major new field, a work was initiated in Japan in 1873, and the Philippine

Islands were entered in 1901. The Southern board began with a mission in China led by Lewis Shuck (1814–1863) who transferred from the ABMU, and a Yoruba work in Africa. The "Landmark" movement (which stressed missions supported only by local churches) and the trauma of the Civil War almost ruined the SBC, although the Foreign Mission Board revived in the 1870s and soon had thriving undertakings in BRAZIL, JAPAN, NIGERIA, and China. The most noteworthy manifestation of Landmarkism was the Gospel Mission of T. P. Crawford (1821–1902) in China.

A vital aspect of Baptist missions was the women's societies. In 1871 the Woman's Baptist Foreign Missionary Society (East) was formed in Boston and the WBFMS (West) in Chicago. These boards, which merged in 1914, recruited young women for service under the ABMU and provided their support. Their leading lights were Lucy W. Peabody (1861–1949) and Helen Barrett Montgomery (1861–1934). The SBC counterpart was the Woman's Missionary Union, founded in 1888. It engaged in fund-raising and educational work for missions, but did not administer funds or appoint missionaries. Its major effort was the annual Christmas offering, named for Charlotte "Lottie" Moon (1840–1912), a teacher and evangelist who served in China. Over time it brought in 2.5 billion dollars for SBC missions. The Free Baptist Woman's Missionary Society (1873–1916) raised funds and supported female Free Will Baptist workers.

Canadians first became involved under the American Baptists. Samuel S. Day (1808–1871) of Ontario pioneered the Telugu Mission in 1835, others served after him, and a Canadian auxiliary to the ABMU was formed in 1866. The Maritime Baptists formed a mission board in 1865 and began sending workers to ABMU fields in Burma and Thailand. Then in 1873 the Baptists in Ontario-Quebec established a board and opened a field of their own in the Telugu area, and also sent workers to Bolivia. Under pressure from those in the western provinces, a nationwide Canadian Baptist Foreign Mission Board in 1911 was formed (now the "overseas" board), which was also supported by women's societies. In the twentieth century it extended its work to Africa.

American Baptist Missions in the Twentieth Century

When the Northern Baptist Convention was formed in 1907 the ABMU remained an autonomous agency but in 1910 changed its name to American Baptist Foreign Mission Society. In 1911 it absorbed the Free Will Baptist Society when the parent merged with the NBC. World War I had a devastating impact on missionary enthusiasm, although the ABFMS still had 833 missionaries in 1921. The New World Movement fund-raising effort in the early 1920s to support denominational activities achieved only half of its hundred million dollar goal, thus forcing retrenchment. Allegations of "modernism" in the missionary force resulted in incessant controversy, and separatist fundamentalists founded independent "faith" missions—Baptist Mid-Missions (1920) and the Association of Baptists for World Evangelism (1927) (see MODERNISM, FUNDAMENTALISM). Many NBC fundamentalists left in 1932 to form the GENERAL ASSOCIATION OF REGULAR BAPTIST CHURCHES (GARBC), and this new body embraced the independent societies.

The Depression, unhappiness with the Laymen's Missionary Inquiry report redefining mission work, and threat of a new World War led to further declines in funding, while long-smoldering dissatisfaction with the so-called "inclusive" policy of the ABFMS and growing denominational connectionalism led to a further schism. In 1943 the Conservative Baptist Foreign Mission Society was formed (Now CBInternational), which the NBC refused to recognize and by 1947 another denomination had formed. Both the GARBC and CONSERVATIVE BAPTIST ASSOCIATION soon had many more missionaries than the parent NBC serving in dozens of countries around the world. The Swedish immigrant BAPTIST GENERAL CONFERENCE placed most of its missionaries with the ABFMS, but grew dissatisfied with the inclusive policy and in 1944 set up its own board. In 1950 the NBC was renamed the American Baptist Convention and in 1972 the AMERICAN BAPTIST CHURCHES USA, and the mission society, which by then had taken over the woman's board, became the Board of International Ministries. By 1982 the number of missionaries had fallen to 203.

The SBC-FMB also suffered economic difficulties, and the Seventy-five Million Campaign in 1920–1925 fell short of its goal. The Cooperative Program (1925) put mission funding on a firmer basis, but the steep drop in receipts during the depression seriously threatened the enterprise. From separatist fundamentalism in the 1930s emerged the World Baptist Fellowship and later the Baptist Bible Fellowship and other groups, all of which supported foreign missionaries. The FMB launched an aggressive program of evangelism in Europe, and after World War II founded the International Baptist Theological Seminary in Zurich-Rüschlikon, Switzerland to train indigenous workers. While the mainline Northern Baptist mission fragmented and sharply declined, the Southern Baptist effort in the postwar years experienced spectacular growth. Its force of 711 career missionaries in 1950 rose to nearly 4,000 by 1995, with works in over 100 countries, thus making it the largest Protestant mis-

sionary agency in the world. Although the American Baptist missions participated actively in ecumenical activities, the Southern Baptists generally remained aloof from these.

Quite important was the work of African American Baptist groups. In 1879 black churches sent missionaries to Nigeria and Liberia, and in 1880 William W. Colley (1847–1909), who had served with the FMB in Liberia, brought about the formation of the Baptist Foreign Missionary Convention of the USA, and returned to Africa under its auspices. This marked the beginning of cooperative work by black Baptists. In 1895 several groups united to form the main denominational body, the NATIONAL BAPTIST CONVENTION, USA, and it became its mission board. Its long-time corresponding secretary, Lewis G. Jordan (1854–1939), recruited several outstanding missionaries for its fields in Malawi and Liberia like Emma B. Delany (1871–1922) and Landon N. Cheek (1871–1964). An independent society, the Lott Cary Baptist Foreign Missions Convention, solicited support from the black denominations for its mission enterprises.

A Global Advance

Other national churches sent out missionaries under the British or American board or formed missionary societies of their own—for example, NEW ZEALAND (1885), AUSTRALIA (1913), SOUTH AFRICA (1892), SWEDEN (1889), GERMANY (1898), and NORWAY (1915)—and sent workers to many countries. Missions sponsored by the smaller Baptist bodies in the United States also expanded, so that at the end of the twentieth century, at least twenty-nine denominational boards were in existence. The British BMS ministries flourished as well. At the same time, more and more mission churches gained independence from the Western boards, and now a majority of the unions and conventions that belong to the Baptist World Alliance are in Africa, Asia, and LATIN AMERICA. Several of these younger churches engage in "foreign" missions themselves, the most notable being the ones in Brazil and South Korea.

Baptist advance continues in spite of wars, political crises, denial of visas to expatriate missionaries, and strong opposition from rival religions like Islam, Hinduism, and Buddhism. The one uncertain element in this otherwise optimistic picture is the theological controversy that rocked the Southern Baptist Convention in the 1980s and 1990s. Those dissatisfied with the new direction of the SBC formed the Cooperative Baptist Fellowship, which began sending missionaries itself when the FMB refused to appoint candidates or accept money from churches identified with the CBF. It also cut off all support to the International Baptist

Seminary in Rüschlikon, forcing the European Baptist Federation to assume control. It was moved to Prague in 1995, where it now provides advanced training to European and Third World theological students. In a denominational restructuring, the FMB became the International Mission Board and missionaries were directed to shift their emphasis from institutional ministry to that of evangelism and church planting. All personnel were also required to sign the Baptist Faith and Message creedal statement, which included controversial clauses restricting the ordained ministry only to males and requiring wives to submit to their husbands. Whether these changes will have a negative effect on the mission effort remains to be seen.

See also Methodism; Missions; Slavery; Slavery, Abolition of

References and Further Reading

Anderson, Gerald H., ed. *Biographical Dictionary of Christian Missions.* New York: Macmillan, 1998.

Daniel, Orville E. *Moving with the Times.* Toronto: Canadian Baptist Overseas Mission Board, 1973.

Estep, William R. *Whole Gospel—Whole World: The Foreign Mission Board of the Southern Baptist Convention, 1845–1995.* Nashville, TN: Broadman & Holman, 1994.

Hunt, Alma. *History of Woman's Missionary Union.* Nashville, TN: Convention Press, 1976.

Martin, Sandy D. *Black Baptists and African Missions: The Origins of a Movement, 1880–1915.* Macon, GA: Mercer University Press, 1989.

McBeth, H. Leon. *The Baptist Heritage: Four Centuries of Baptist Witness.* Nashville, TN: Broadman, 1987.

Neely, Alan. *A New Call to Mission.* Macon, GA: Smith & Helwys, 2000.

Pierard, Richard V. "The Globalization of Baptist History." *American Baptist Quarterly* 18 (June 2000): 164–176.

Russell, Horace O. *The Missionary Outreach of the West Indian Church: Jamaican Baptist Missions to West Africa in the Nineteenth Century.* New York: Peter Lang, 2000.

Stanley, Brian. *The History of the Baptist Missionary Society 1792–1992.* Edinburgh: T & T Clark, 1992.

Torbet, Robert G. *A History of the Baptists,* 3rd ed. Valley Forge, PA: Judson Press, 1963.

———. *Venture of Faith: The Story of the American Baptist Foreign Mission Society and the Woman's American Baptist Foreign Mission Society, 1814–1954.* Philadelphia: Judson Press, 1954.

Wardin, Albert W., ed. *Baptists around the World: A Comprehensive Handbook.* Nashville, TN: Broadman & Holman, 1995.

RICHARD V. PIERARD

BAPTISTS

Baptists, sharply divided between Calvinists and Arminians, originated among early seventeenth-century English separatists and soon spread to America. After 1660 they were persecuted by the English authorities, but emerged into the safety of toleration in 1689. Their numbers were hugely augmented by revivalism from the eighteenth century, and the majority began to support overseas missions. In the nineteenth century they spread to continental Europe, but their main impact was as part of the Evangelical consensus of Britain and America. Divisions over theological liberalism generated the Fundamentalist controversy of the 1920s. Although the Baptists had by then become a global community, their strength still lay overwhelmingly in North America.

Origins

The Baptists were Protestants who, like the Congregationalists, believed that the church consists of a gathered community of believers, but who also held that baptism should be administered only to those making a personal profession of faith. The first Baptist, JOHN SMYTH (1554–1612), led his separatist church from Gainsborough, Lincolnshire, to Amsterdam in 1608. There, probably in the following year, he baptized first himself and then the others "out of a bason" (and therefore not by immersion, later the almost universal Baptist practice). Whether he had been influenced by the Anabaptists of the NETHERLANDS is uncertain, but he was definitely swayed by its Arminian theology to accept the doctrine of general redemption, so that his followers subsequently became known as General Baptists. The lay leader of the party, Thomas Helwys (1550–1616), returned in 1612 to found the first Baptist church in England at Spitalfields. His book, *The Mystery of Iniquity* (1615), was a plea for full liberty of conscience, thus inaugurating an enduring Baptist concern. By 1626 there were at least five General Baptist churches in England.

The other main strand of Baptist church life consisted of those who accepted the Calvinist doctrine of particular redemption and so were called Particular Baptists. The conviction that baptism should be administered only to believers emerged among the separatists of London during the 1630s, and by 1644 representatives of seven churches signed a confession of faith designed to distinguish its adherents from General Baptists. Already, in 1639, ROGER WILLIAMS (1603–1683) had established the first Baptist church in America at Providence, Rhode Island. Although within a year Williams had rejected all forms of baptism, there were soon other Baptists in America. In 1654 the first president of Harvard College, Henry Dunster (1612–1659), was forced to resign after he had reached Baptist convictions. Meanwhile, in the convulsions of the CIVIL WAR and interregnum, Baptist views spread, especially in the Cromwellian army, which carried them to SCOTLAND and IRELAND. John Miles founded the first congregation in Wales, at

Ilston near Swansea, in 1649. Although the Particulars were careful to guard the independence of each local church, the churches of ENGLAND and WALES began to group themselves in regional associations for mutual advice, financial support, and evangelistic outreach. By 1660 there were about 130 Particular Baptist and roughly 110 General Baptist churches. Two smaller groups existed independently: the Seventh-Day Baptists (first attested in 1653), holding that Saturday was to be observed as the sabbath; and the open membership churches, such as the one in Bedford in which John Bunyan (1628–1688) served as elder, where the question of baptism was not regarded as a barrier to church fellowship.

Persecution and Toleration

The restoration of the monarchy in 1660 heralded a period of persecution for religious dissent. Excluded from public office, Dissenters were prohibited in 1664 from meeting in groups of more than five. At Broadmead Baptist Church in Bristol, the preacher would speak from behind a curtain to avoid identification by informers. Thomas Hardcastle, its pastor, was imprisoned seven times. Some Baptists were given a measure of protection because one of their leaders, William Kiffin, was also a prosperous London merchant whom the king valued as a source of loans. In a period when the pressure slackened, both main Baptist groups issued a confession of faith. The Particular Baptist version, issued in 1677 (reissued in 1689), was modeled on the Savoy Declaration of the Independents (1658) and ultimately on the WESTMINSTER CONFESSION, revealing the closeness of the denomination to other Calvinistic Dissenters. The Orthodox Creed of the General Baptists (1679) includes their distinctive ecclesiology. Apart from the elders (or ministers) and deacons (responsible for finances) of the individual churches that they possessed in common with the Particulars, the General Baptists maintained "bishops or messengers" who enjoyed translocal authority and ordained elders. Furthermore they invested a general assembly with the power to superintend local churches.

From 1689, with the passing of the Toleration Act, all Dissenters could worship without fear. Baptists settled into a quieter life and began to build permanent meeting houses. They were, nevertheless, racked by controversy in the 1690s over whether it was proper to sing only Psalms or also, as Benjamin Keach successfully urged, hymns of human composition. There were to be several Baptist hymnwriters in the eighteenth century, perhaps the most distinguished being Anne Steele. In 1719, at a meeting of dissenting ministers at Salters' Hall in London, a majority of Particular Baptists reaffirmed their Trinitarian convictions, but a majority of General Baptists, preferring to express their faith in only biblical language, declined to do so. Thereafter, most General Baptists moved steadily toward an Arian theology and eventually, in the nineteenth century, converged with the Unitarians. The Particular Baptists maintained their orthodoxy, often adopting a high version of Calvinism, as in John Gill's major work *The Cause of God and Truth* (1735–1738).

Revival

In 1707 five Particular, or Regular, Baptist churches in America formed the Philadelphia Association, which gradually gathered support from the whole of the English colonies. In 1742 it issued the Philadelphia Confession, identical to the English 1689 confession except that it added a vindication of hymn singing and the laying on of hands after baptism. There were also a number of General Baptists, often called Six-Principle Baptists because of their appeal to the six principles of Hebrews 6:1, 2, which included the laying on of hands. The Great Awakening gave rise from the 1740s to another stream, the Separates, who began as revival converts wishing to worship outside the established CONGREGATIONALISM of New England and then embraced believer's baptism. Their outstanding leader, ISAAC BACKUS (1724–1806), guided them toward merger with the Regular Baptists. Together with John Leland (1754–1841), Backus also championed religious freedom and ultimately helped secure the First Amendment of the federal constitution. Commitment to the separation of church and state became normal among Baptists. By 1795 Backus estimated that there were 1,152 Baptist churches in the United States. African Americans were already beginning to organize separate churches in 1758. In Nova Scotia an indigenous revival led by Henry Alline (1748–1784) turned, after his death in 1784, into a strong Baptist movement, and American Baptists carried their convictions into Ontario.

In Britain the teaching of the Bristol Baptist Academy, reinforced from the 1770s by the thought of the American Congregationalist Jonathan Edwards (1703–1758), encouraged a combination of evangelistic enthusiasm with firm but moderate Calvinism. The Evangelical theology of Andrew Fuller (1754–1815) inspired an upsurge of home missionary activity and the foundation, in 1792, of the Baptist Missionary Society, which began its work by sponsoring WILLIAM CAREY (1761–1834) at Serampore in India. Meanwhile, Dan Taylor established (1770) a New Connexion of General Baptists, devoted to expansion and less punctilious than earlier General Baptists about questions of church order. The small Scotch Baptist denomination, upholding the views of Archibald McLean, who insisted that churches must have a plurality of elders, spread from Scotland, where the brothers James and Robert Haldane led a vigorous evangelistic thrust. In Wales revivalism spilled over into Baptist life, producing able preachers, among whom Christmas Evans was the most celebrated.

The Nineteenth Century

The earliest American missionaries supported by the denomination were Adoniram (1788–1850) and Ann JUDSON (1789–1826), who reached Baptist convictions in 1812 while sailing to the east. Their example led to the creation, in 1814, of a triennial convention to promote the cause of missions and coordinate the work of the various Baptist associations. Anti-mission Baptists, who upheld high Calvinism and often clung to traditional customs such as foot washing, refused to cooperate and gradually organized separate associations. Likewise in England, the Strict and Particular Baptists formed their own associations from the 1830s in order to preserve their high Calvinism and to maintain the traditional Baptist practice of close communion, that is the restriction of the Lord's Supper to baptized believers. Most Baptists in England, however, were persuaded by the arguments of Robert Hall that communion should be open to all believers, and that principle became a hallmark, in Canada for example, of English as opposed to American influence. The Baptist Union of Great Britain and Ireland, formed as a ministers' gathering in 1812 but more formally organized from 1833, increasingly became a nationally representative body, eventually absorbing the New Connexion in 1891. That was a sign of the supersession during the nineteenth century of the old Calvinist/Arminian divide by awareness of common Evangelical convictions. In America the widely used New Hampshire Confession (1833) likewise ignored the points of difference between the two traditional doctrinal positions. Growing sectionalism in the United States encouraged the establishment of a SOUTHERN BAPTIST CONVENTION in 1845, the dividing point being a Southern refusal to support non-Baptist agencies. In its ranks from the 1850s there developed a Landmark movement that insisted, initially against the Churches of Christ, that baptism must always be administered by an officer of a properly organized Baptist church.

Baptist work in continental Europe began with the formation of a church in Hamburg in 1834. Its leader, J. G. Oncken, seized every opportunity for the planting of Baptist churches in other countries, especially among German speakers. In Sweden a similar orga-

nizing genius was Anders Wiberg, a former Lutheran minister. In the Russian Empire, indigenous movements of spiritual reform laid foundations for Baptist life, a Russian Baptist Union being formed in 1884. Transylvania, at first Hungarian but later Romanian, became the other strongest area of Baptist work in Europe. In all these countries opposition from state churches was perennial. Meanwhile missions were establishing particularly successful Baptist communities in INDIA, Burma, the Congo, and CHINA, where the American Lottie Moon (1840–1912) and the Welsh Timothy Richard earned fame as pioneers.

Baptists played a full part in the permeation of British and American society by Evangelical religion during the nineteenth century. They produced influential academic writings such as Francis Wayland's (1796–1865) *Elements of Moral Science* (1835) and John L. Dagg's *Manual of Theology* (1857); they supported educational efforts and campaigns of moral reform, especially the temperance cause; and in Britain they pressed politically for full civil equality and disestablishment. CHARLES SPURGEON (1834–1892) was undoubtedly the century's greatest preacher in the English-speaking world. Theology, however, began to be a divisive force in the Baptist mainstream. In 1879 C. H. Toy resigned from the Southern Baptist Seminary because he had accepted German biblical criticism. Eight years later, in the Down Grade Controversy, Spurgeon retired from the Baptist Union because it harbored those who had embraced liberal doctrinal views. The social gospel, championed in England by John Clifford and in America by WALTER RAUSCHENBUSCH (1861–1918), added another bone of contention. Despite the efforts of mediating theologians such as Augustus H. Strong and Edgar Y. Mullins, polarization grew ominously.

The Twentieth Century

The century opened with the creation of the Northern Baptist Convention (1907; from 1950 the American Baptist Convention; from 1972 the American Baptist Churches in the United States) and the steady consolidation of the British Baptist Union by J. H. Shakespeare. Splits, however, were imminent in North America. The denomination representing African Americans in the United States, the National Baptist Convention (1895), divided in 1915 into two, the original body adding "Inc." to its title. The culmination of the earlier theological polarization came in a crisis after the First World War, when Fundamentalists led by W. B. Riley in the North, J. Frank Norris (1877–1952) in the South, and T. T. Shields in Canada denounced the views of Modernists such as SHAILER MATHEWS (1863–1941) of Chicago and HARRY EMERson Fosdick (1878–1969) of New York. Although in Britain the controversy was much more muted, its ultimate result was the establishment in America of the General Association of Regular Baptist Churches (1932) and the Conservative Baptist Association of America (1947), and in Canada of the Fellowship of Evangelical Baptist Churches (1953; a merger of two earlier organizations). The bodies representing German and Swedish immigrants, the North American Baptist Conference (1865) and the Baptist General Conference (1879), did not unite with other Baptists despite gradually dropping German and Swedish as their language of worship. The fragmentation of Baptist life in the United States meant that by 1984, apart from innumerable independent congregations, there were supposed to be at least fifty-two distinct denominations in the country.

In the twentieth century Baptists were, for the first time, a global movement, a development symbolized by the establishment in 1905 of the Baptist World Alliance. Russian Baptists suffered persecution under the Soviet state, but nevertheless continued to grow. The denomination mushroomed in several lands of sub-Saharan Africa such as Nigeria. Parts of northeastern India, such as Nagaland, became almost solidly Baptist. Unusually, the Church of North India (1970) incorporated Baptists in a reunion scheme. Despite the involvement of a few figures, such as the English historian E. A. Payne, many Baptists feared that the ecumenical movement would lead to heresy or Rome. Women rose to greater prominence in Baptist affairs, with influential figures such as Helen Barrett Montgomery (1861–1934) of the Northern Baptists chairing their denominations and women becoming ministers in most Baptist groupings. Their role was one of the lesser issues debated among Southern Baptists, at over 15 million members by far the largest Baptist body in the world, in their fierce and sustained controversy over biblical inerrancy from 1979 onward. Two outstanding Baptists were Billy Graham (1918–) the leading evangelist of his day, and Martin Luther King Jr. (1929–1968), the assassinated civil rights leader. By 1995 both India and Brazil had more than one million Baptist church members, but it was nevertheless predicted that in 2010, 63 percent of the world's Baptists would still live in North America.

References and Further Reading

Brackney, William H. *The Baptists*. New York: Greenwood Press, 1988.
Briggs, J. H. Y. *The English Baptists of the Nineteenth Century*. London: Baptist Historical Society, 1994.
Brown, Raymond. *The English Baptists of the Eighteenth Century*. London: Baptist Historical Society, 1986.
George, Timothy, and David S. Dockery, eds. *Baptist Theologians*. Nashville, TN: Broadman Press, 1990.
Lumpkin, William L. *Baptist Confessions of Faith*. Valley Forge, PA: Judson Press, 1959.
McBeth, H. Leon. *The Baptist Heritage*. Nashville, TN: Broadman Press, 1987.
McLoughlin, William G. *New England Dissent, 1630–1833: The Baptists and the Separation of Church and State*. 2 vols. Cambridge, MA: Harvard University Press, 1971.
Sobel, Mechal. *Trabelin' On: The Slave Journey to an Afro-Baptist Faith*. Westport, CT: Greenwood Press, 1979.
Stanley, Brian. *The History of the Baptist Missionary Society, 1792–1992*. Edinburgh: T. & T. Clark, 1992.
Starr, Edward C. *A Baptist Bibliography*. 25 vols. Rochester, NY: American Baptist Historical Society, 1947–1976.
Wardin, Albert W. *Baptists around the World*. Nashville, TN: Broadman & Holman, 1995.
Zanders, Jane. *Baptists and Others*. Nashville, TN: Broadman and Holman, 1997.

D. W. Bebbington

BAPTISTS, EUROPE

Baptists are a denomination of Protestant Christians whose origins lie in post-Reformation England. They are dissenters on the landscape of English Christianity and hold to the authority of Scripture, the centrality of Christ in their doctrines, a commitment to share the gospel in faithfulness to the Great Commission (Matthew 28:19–20), and the practice of believer's Baptism to signify a professing believer's church. In most countries Baptists are considered part of the Free Church Tradition, also called the "believer's churches." Theologically Baptists in Europe are confessional, following a Confession of faith that Julius Koebner wrote in 1848, which contains mildly Calvinist articles (see Confessionalization). Most of the Baptist conventions/unions have adopted unique modern confessions similar in theological tone. Baptist Polity is rigorously congregational, and their organizational and institutional life beyond their congregations is entirely voluntary. Baptists are found in every nation in Europe, stretching from Ireland to Russia and Turkey.

There are two principal theories of Baptist origins in Europe. First there are those who hold to an Anabaptist evolution toward modern Baptist principles (see Anabaptism). If validated, this would mean that Anabaptist ideas or groups, likely from the Dutch Mennonite community, led to the appearance of Baptists in late sixteenth and early seventeenth-century England. This view was widely advanced in the nineteenth century by historians in England and the United States who believed that there was at least an ideological connection. Much research went into this and other theories, eventually producing a more plausible second hypothesis that Baptists are direct descendents of English Puritan Separatists (see Puritan-

ISM). In due course there were contacts between early Baptists and MENNONITES in Amsterdam and Rhynsburg, but Baptists pursued their own separate identity in returning to England in 1612. The first congregation was established that year at Spitalfields near London. Thus it can be said with historical certainty that the people called Baptists emerged in seventeenth-century Britain and the European history of Baptists begins at that point. It should be noted that a minority of Eastern European Baptists hold that they are related to Anabaptist groups of the sixteenth century, largely because of their espousal of religious liberty that they hold in common with Anabaptists.

In the native soils of England, WALES, SCOTLAND, and Ireland the Baptist family of Europe began to grow in the seventeenth century. During that period English Puritan Separatists evolved to Baptist principles of believers' congregations signified by believer's baptism and religious liberty. An informal association among English General Baptists in London may be seen as early as 1626. By the 1660s in England three major branches of Baptists had clearly emerged: General Baptists holding to a general understanding of Christ's atonement, Particular Baptists believing that Christ died for the Elect, and Seventh Day Baptists who continued to recognize the Sabbath. Baptist principles and practices, especially in the Calvinistic branch, spread into Wales and Scotland, and created church associations and national unions by the nineteenth century. Similarly in Ireland, beginning in 1813, English Baptists working as the "Baptist Irish Society" sent missionary pastors to establish a Baptist presence there. The first church dates from the 1650s in Dublin and a union was formed in 1895. Baptists in Britain grew to a major category of NONCONFORMITY and started theological colleges, a missionary society for overseas (1792) and domestic (1797) work, and various benevolent organizations. The Baptist Union of Great Britain, started in earnest in 1831, was greatly enhanced in 1891 with the merger of the General and Particular branches of historic Baptist development. There has been a modest amount of schism among Baptists in Britain, producing in 1829 the Strict Baptists who are High Calvinists, and in Scotland the Scotch Baptists (1766) who held a primitivist understanding of the church, and the Haldanites (1808), a revivalistic movement. Irish Baptists, whose Union dates from 1895, have declined participation in the Baptist Union of Great Britain and followed a theologically conservative path under the influence of disciples of CHARLES H. SPURGEON. In Wales, where Baptist preaching began in the Olchon Valley in 1633, the Baptist Union has a separate identity from the British Union but supports missionaries of the Baptist Missionary Society. A similar cooperation exists between the Baptist Union in Scotland (oldest church at Leith, 1652) and the British Union. Representatives of the Baptist Union of Great Britain and that of Scotland are active in the work of the European Baptist Federation (EBF) and in the BAPTIST WORLD ALLIANCE.

Baptist origins on the continent of Europe can be dated with certainty from 1815 when baptisms occurred at Nomain in Flanders, after which the first congregation was started in FRANCE by Haldanite Baptists from Scotland. American Baptist missionaries began a work at Douai and Paris from which the French Baptist Federation eventually sprang in 1919. French Baptists, although small in number, sent missionaries to Belgium and SWITZERLAND, as well as to AFRICA and the CARIBBEAN. The first Belgian church was started at Ougree and the Union of Baptists in Belgium was founded in 1922.

European Baptist expansion in significant numbers traces from 1834. That year Johann G. Oncken (1800–1884) was traveling as a colporteur for the British Continental Society, and upon meeting the Rev. Barnas Sears, a professor from Hamilton, New York, he received believer's baptism from Sears. Shortly thereafter Sears personally ordained Oncken (an unusual circumstance) and the German Baptist pioneer gathered a church in Hamburg. From his base in Hamburg, Oncken was the driving force behind the establishment of a theological school, a Union, and a publishing house, Oncken Verlag. For many years Oncken and his disciples (particularly Julius Koebner and G. W. Lehmann, together with Oncken known as the "Kleeblat") conducted missionary tours of northern, eastern, and central Europe, starting congregations and advocating religious liberty before civil authorities. This gave the German Baptist community a premier role in the development of Baptists in Europe. Oncken's response to a magistrate in Oldenburg—"Every Baptist a missionary"—became a motto for Baptists in Europe.

Typically Baptist growth in various nations of Europe has followed a pattern of planting individual congregations, then establishing near-regional associations or clusters of churches, and finally forming a union or convention of the affiliated churches in a given country. In Western Europe the epicenter of Baptist life is in GERMANY. Ministerial students have been trained at Hamburg Seminary (now Elstal) for work in Austria, HUNGARY, POLAND, and the Balkan states and Baltic republics. Baptist churches and organizations in this area with German origins date from the mid to later nineteenth century: Lithuania (1841); Romania and Bulgaria (1845); Austria and Switzerland (1847); Poland (1858); Russia (1864); Ukraine (1869); Hungary (1874). Baptists in the heart of Europe surrounding German borders have grown steadily over a century and a half. In Switzerland, for instance, from a church in Zurich in 1849 came congregations in most cantons and in 1923 the Swiss Union. In 1845 Julius Koebner, Oncken's colleague, baptized the first Dutch convert and started a church at Gasselternijveen. A Dutch Union was formed in 1881. Polish Baptist work began at Adamow near Warsaw in 1858 under German auspices and later a Slavic mission emerged there. The Polish Union came together in 1942, involving both groups. In Bohemia the first Baptist congregation appeared in 1885 at Hledsebe among the Czechs. German missionaries founded a church at Brandys in Slovakia in 1877. From these roots came connections with Hungarian and German unions, and eventually the Czechoslovak Baptist Union in 1919. Since dissolution of that nation into two republics in 1992, separate organizations of Baptists exist in the Czech Republic and Slovakia. Among the Iberian peoples a Baptist church was gathered at Madrid in 1870 by American Baptists; later Swedish and Southern Baptists established missions in Spain. In Portugal the first church was at Oporto in 1888 with a union developed by 1946. Numerous Baptist mission organizations have opened missions in Portugal since 1950.

In Scandinavia the strongest Baptist family is in SWEDEN, followed by smaller unions in NORWAY and DENMARK. The Swedish work dates from 1864, with a major schism in 1892 over Pentecostal influences in the Union that led to a separate association founded at Orebro, which continues. In 1860 the first congregations were founded in Norway at Porsgrunn and Larvik and a union in 1877. Danish Baptists reckon their development from 1839 in Copenhagen with a union since 1865. Swedish Baptists conducted missionary work in FINLAND beginning in 1854 at Fogo Island, leading to a Swedish-speaking union in 1883 and a separate Finnish Union in 1903.

Eastern European Baptists have evolved against stiff odds inherent in "established church" Christianity, and in the twentieth century Marxist opposition to Christian expansion. There are large numbers of Baptists in Ukraine, Belarus, and Russia, with a strong Baptist presence in the Baltic republics. Baptist life in Russia commenced with Oncken's visit in 1864, with the first baptism in 1867 among the Molokans. In the 1870s Baptist congregations were formed in the Caucasus and near Moscow. The first Russian Baptist Union was formed at Novo Vasil'evka in 1884, eventually becoming under Marxist government the ALL UNION COUNCIL OF EVANGELICAL CHRISTIAN BAPTISTS (AUCEB) that included Pentecostals (see PENTECOSTALISM) and Mennonite Brethren congregations from the 1940s and 1960s, respectively. In Ukraine Oncken was again the initial catalyst, a church being planted at Kosiakovko in 1875. Baptist development in the region was stunning, reaching 2,000 congregations by 1920. A Ukrainian Union was formed in 1918, becoming part of the Russian Union in 1925 and the AUCEB in 1944. Separate organized Baptist life in Ukraine reemerged in 1993, with a second group of formerly underground Baptist congregations also surfacing in a second national organization. Baptisms occurred in Belarus beginning in the 1880s, with a church formed at Kha'ch in 1907. Under freedom in the early Communist era, a union formed at Minsk in 1927, later assimilated into the AUCEB. In 1993 again a separate Baptist organization appeared in Belarus. Among the Baltic republics, Baptist missionary work commenced in Latvia in 1861 near Libau and this grew to a union of churches in 1885. German missions started a congregation in Lithuania at Memel in 1841 and a separate union was formed in 1933. Likewise evangelical work sponsored by Germans began a congregation in Estonia in 1884. Strong Baptist unions in the southeast date from 1908 in Bulgaria and Romania (1919).

Baptist development in southeastern Europe is small but tenacious in several difficult historical contexts. Hungarian, German, and Romanian Baptists all evangelized Serbia in the period 1875–1925. These ethnic groups combined to create in 1926 the Baptist Union of Yugoslavia. Serbian Baptists in turn started congregations in Macedonia in 1936; from this beginning a union took shape in 1991. A similar history may be written for Baptists in Bosnia. The first churches there were gathered separately by Serbian, Romanian, and German missionaries. In 1992 with the dissolution of Yugoslavia, Bosnian Baptists built an association of churches unique to the nation. In Croatia missions commenced from Hungarian work in 1883 at Zagreb and a Croatian conference was organized in 1921. American Baptists attempted church planting in Albania as early as 1840 but efforts were forbidden in the country. The civil wars in the former Yugoslavia created a new opportunity for Protestant missions in Albania in the 1990s and church development moves ahead under the separate auspices of Southern Baptists, Canadian Baptists, and smaller U.S. Baptist organizations. A similar circumstance ensued in Slovenia, where Baptist churches were part of the Baptist Union of Yugoslavia until 1993 when a separate Baptist Union for Slovenia was formed with several hundred members.

American Baptist missions in Greece date from 1836, followed by subsequent attempts to plant churches in 1851 and 1871, with American support withdrawn in 1886. Southern Baptists attempted another mission in the 1960s with only a handful of congregations designated "The Evangelical Church of

Greece" as a result. Similarly in neighboring Islamic Turkey there are a few congregations sponsored by Southern Baptists and Canadian Baptists, with no associational union. Perhaps the sturdiest Baptist work in the region is in Romania and Bulgaria. Romanian Baptist life stems from Germans in 1845 at Bucharest and Ukrainian missionary efforts in 1862 at Cataloi. A Hungarian Baptist church opened in the Transylvanian region in 1871, providing a third beginning. All Romanian Baptists came together in the union of 1940. In Bulgaria the first church was formed at Kazanlik in 1876 by Germans, with a second start at Ruse in 1888 by Romanians. A Bulgarian union was begun in 1908.

After World War I, and with encouragement from the Baptist World Alliance, Baptist leaders from the Northern Baptist and Southern Baptist Conventions in the United States, plus the Baptist Union of Great Britain and Ireland, in 1920 met in London to discuss refugee issues and development of Baptist missions. Southern Baptists assumed sponsorship of missions in Spain, Italy, Yugoslavia, Hungary, Ukraine, and Romania. Northern Baptists likewise were responsible for supporting work in France, Belgium, Switzerland, Czechoslovakia, Finland, Poland, Norway, Denmark, and Russia. The British agreed to assist France, Italy, Czechoslovakia, Finland, and the Baltic states. Finally German Baptists, including German Baptists from the United States and CANADA, were given oversight of Bulgaria, Poland, and Austria. As a codicil to the London Conference, Portugal took responsibility for missionary work in Brazil. This arrangement had a profound impact on Baptist development in Europe from 1925 to the 1960s. Respective unions took the shape and polity of the sponsoring bodies: thus, Italy had a definite Southern Baptist connection, Germany was close to American Baptists and the BMS gradually withdrew its influence, except as a participant in the European Baptist Federation as a partner. Following maturing unions in western Europe, the removal of the domination of the USSR, and theological changes in the Southern Baptist Convention in the United States, most of the Baptist unions have charted independent courses, training their own leaders and cooperating in the European Baptist Federation (EBF). All of the Baptist unions maintain offices in central cities and publish a magazine or newspaper to inform their constituencies.

The European Baptist Federation has its roots in the London Conference of 1920 and is an outgrowth directly of the work of the BAPTIST WORLD ALLIANCE (BWA) in Europe. In 1949 the Baptist World Alliance formed regional fellowships around the world to coordinate its work and the result in Europe was the European Baptist Federation. The European Federation is the most highly organized of the six regional

fellowships of the BWA and is manifested in congresses held every five years, and in mission and education projects. Its divisions include Theology and Education, Mission and Evangelism, Communications, and External Relations. There is a Lay Academy operated in Budapest, Hungary, an overseas mission that sponsors workers in Africa, the European Baptist Press Service (EBPS), and a Baptist Women's Union administered from a central office in Bad-Hamburg, Germany. There are about fifty conventions/unions in forty-six countries affiliated with the EBF.

Mention must also be made of the European Baptist Convention. As the Foreign Mission Board of the U.S. Southern Baptist Convention increased its efforts in Europe and the Middle East after World War II, Southern Baptists moved to unite the churches and associations they supported under a single administration. The result was the founding in 1958 of the Association of Baptists in Continental Europe and later in 1964 this became the European Baptist Convention (EBC). Over fifty congregations across Europe are members of this English-speaking body that has also been geographically identified with the presence of United States Armed Forces in Europe under the North Atlantic Treaty Organization (NATO).

Institutional life among Baptists in Europe has been slow but steady since the late nineteenth century. In 1949 the Southern Baptist Foreign Mission Board instituted a theological school in Rueschlikon, Switzerland largely to train pastoral leadership for churches and unions in postwar Europe. In 1993 the Southern Baptists withdrew their support for the school and it was relocated the following year to Prague, Czech Republic where it continues under European Baptist auspices. Similar theological schools exist in Sweden, Denmark, Norway, Finland, Poland, Spain, the Netherlands, Hungary, and Serbia under auspices of individual Baptist unions. Theological schools abound in the east as well, in Latvia, Russia, Ukraine, Belarus, and Russia. Missionary activity also continues from external Baptist sources, notably from the United States. The principal smaller mission organizations that have personnel or institutions in Europe are the Association of Baptists for World Evangelism, Baptist Mid-Missions, Conservative Baptists, Evangelical Baptists, and the Baptist Bible Fellowship.

European Baptists have influenced Baptists in many regions beyond Europe. German Baptists started churches in the northeastern United States beginning in the 1830s and this led to the formation of a German Baptist Conference in America (later the North American Baptist Conference). In the 1850s Swedish Baptists planted churches in the upper Midwestern United States and this evolved to the BAPTIST GENERAL CON-

FERENCE. Similarly, Danish, Norwegian, Italian, Polish, Slavic, and Hispanic missions in the United States, supported by European counterparts, became the beginnings of ethnic Baptist associations across North America. Through missionary efforts, British Baptists have fostered work in INDIA, Bangladesh, Africa, the Caribbean, LATIN AMERICA, AUSTRALIA and NEW ZEALAND, CHINA, and Southeast Asia.

At present, European Baptists are a multiethnic, multiracial, multilingual Protestant minority scattered across the continent. They number in excess of 800,000 members in 12,000 congregations. The largest Baptist organizations within a given nation number 150,000 in Great Britain and 120,000 in Ukraine.

References and Further Reading

Balders, Günter. *Theurer Bruder Oncken: Das Leben Johann Gerhard Oncken in Bildern und Dokumenten.* Kassel, Germany: Oncken, 1978.

Brackney, William H. *Historical Dictionary of the Baptists.* Lanham, MD: Scarecrow Press, 1999.

Kirkwood, R. Dean. *European Baptists: A Magnificent Minority.* Valley Forge, PA: International Ministries, 1981.

Parker, G. Keith. *Baptists in Europe: History and Confessions of Faith.* Nashville, TN: Broadman Press, 1982.

Payne, Ernest A. *The Baptist Union: A Short History.* London: Carey Kingsgate Press, 1959.

Rushbrooke, J. H. *The Baptist Movement in the Continent of Europe.* London: Carey Kingsgate Press, 1923.

Torbet, Robert G. *Venture of Faith: The Story of the American Baptist Foreign Mission Society and the Woman's American Baptist Foreign Mission Society 1814–1954.* Philadelphia: The Judson Press, 1955.

Wardin, Albert. *Baptists Around the World: A Comprehensive Handbook.* Nashville, TN: Broadman and Holman, 1995.

White, Barrington R. *The English Separatist Tradition.* London: Oxford University Press, 1971.

WILLIAM H. BRACKNEY

BAPTISTS, GLOBAL

According to the BAPTIST WORLD ALLIANCE (BWA), Baptists today number over forty million baptized believers found in more than 200 countries under the leadership of 206 different organizations identified as Baptist. BWA is organized into six regional fellowships in North America, Asia, AFRICA, CARIBBEAN, LATIN AMERICA, and Europe, which give evidence of the worldwide presence of Baptists. In addition there are Baptist organizations throughout the world that are not members of BWA. Baptists may have begun in the Northern hemisphere, but today the largest growth is in the Southern hemisphere as Baptists increasingly become multiethnic and multinational.

This global presence is a recent phenomenon in Baptist history. Baptists began in isolated communities in ENGLAND and the English colonies that would be known as the United States of America. Their

global identity did not emerge until the nineteenth century when Baptists developed missionary organizations seeking to reach the world. In modernity, Baptists' global understanding was of the world as the MISSIONS field "ripe unto harvest" and they organized themselves accordingly. Part of the postmodern challenge for Baptists today is that in many places once known as the mission fields there now exist developed Baptist organizations demanding recognition as partners in the task of presenting the Christian gospel. These leaders are contesting both the decision-making process and the identity of the decision makers of established mission organizations. The Baptist global identity founded on missionaries is now being challenged by the global perspective of a BAPTIST FAMILY seeking to provide resources to meet needs around the world.

Such a widespread presence around the globe was not a feature in Baptist beginnings where Baptists were concerned with organizing what they believed would be the "true" church on the basis of believer's BAPTISM. Neither the seventeenth-century beginnings in England nor those in America included a worldwide focus for Baptists. Baptists reacted against the corruption they perceived in established churches both in England and the colonies. In the earliest confessions of faith from seventeenth-century England, Baptists focused their identity on being the church gathered voluntarily by God, with Christ as the head, composed of believers who had been baptized upon their profession of faith. In their occasional references to PREACHING the gospel to others, the reference was to the area in which the signers of the confession were located. Early Baptists believed in sharing their faith, but they did not have a global perspective.

Diversity was a hallmark of Baptist identity from the beginning. The diversity of small groups struggling to survive contributed to the lack of a global perspective among Baptists. Once Baptists became visible enough in the English Independent/Separatists milieu to be identified, there were two groups, General and Particular, so called for their different understandings of ATONEMENT. The General Baptists believed salvation was for everyone who responded to God's call through Christ. The Particular Baptists believed salvation was only for the elect (see CALVINISM; PREDESTINATION). Even in beginning the practice of believer's baptism by immersion there was diversity. One group believed the practice could be done on the basis of the New Testament whereas the other group believed that there needed to be some succession so they sent a representative to Holland who then returned and baptized the other believers by immersion.

As the Baptist movement grew, the desire for a common identity led to conflict. The theological view that eventually dominated, sometimes called hyper-Calvinism, emphasized that God had already decided from the beginning of time who was saved and who was damned. The consequence of this theology was Baptists turning in on themselves and not reaching out even to those around them because they believed God had already made the eternal decision. This theological understanding also contributed to the lack of development of a global identity.

The modern vision that launched Baptists on their first understanding of a global perspective was articulated at the end of the eighteenth century. The earliest record of a Baptist leaving one country to minister in another was of George Lisle (Leile), freed slave and preacher in the Silver Bluff Church in Georgia, who went to Jamaica in 1782 where he established a church and vibrant ministry. Lisle was not sponsored by any mission organization and apparently never succeeded in his attempts to solicit help from British Baptists, but in his correspondence with them he did articulate a vision of Baptists in one country being concerned about the souls of people in another country.

British Baptists began to glimpse this new vision about a decade later. In 1787 the English shoe cobbler and pastor WILLIAM CAREY proposed that his local ministerial association should discuss whether the command of Jesus to "teach all nations" was binding on all ministers for all time. Those who believed God had already decided SALVATION for all people and needed no human assistance defeated his proposal. Supposedly Carey reached a different understanding from this dominant theological view through his study of languages, geography, and scripture. It took five years, one book, *An Enquiry into the Obligations of Christians to use means for the Conversion of the Heathen*, and one sermon on Isaiah 54:2 in which Carey urged his fellow ministers to expect great things from God and attempt great things for God, before Carey could get a hearing. In 1792 the organization that would be known as the British Missionary Society was formed, and Carey was sent to INDIA as their first missionary. These humble beginnings opened Baptists to a different understanding of the world and their place in it.

Baptists in the United States did not organize for mission until 1814. In 1812 Ann and Adoniram Judson sailed to India as Congregationalist missionaries from Massachusetts, but through study sought believer's baptism and became Baptists (see JUDSON FAMILY). They were not allowed to stay in India and found the place to begin their mission service in Burma. Their colleague, Luther Rice, reached the same conclusion about baptism and returned to the United States to raise money for the new Baptist missionaries who were already on the field with no visible means of support. Baptists in the United States were already inspired by William Carey and seized the opportunity offered by the Judsons to organize in May of 1814 in Philadelphia what would be known as the Triennial Convention to support mission endeavors in the United States and around the world. Many Baptist missionary organizations would come from this humble beginning, sending missionaries throughout the world. Again, it was a revolution for Baptists to begin to identify themselves globally instead of only locally or nationally.

Under the leadership of Johann Gerhard Oncken, who founded a Baptist church in Hamburg, GERMANY in 1834, and his fellow evangelists, Julius Wilhelm Köbner and Gottfried Wilhelm Lehmann, German Baptists were mission oriented from the beginning. Oncken's motto, every Baptist a missionary, reflected the significance of mission to Baptist identity by the middle of the nineteenth century. Although influenced by British and American Baptists, Oncken had reached his views through his own study and was an independent leader and organizer of Baptists in Europe. Oncken, his colleagues, and German settlers in other countries contributed to the spread of Baptists throughout Europe, including Russia and Ukraine.

Of the 400 years of Baptist history, only in the last 200 years has global mission work been a significant factor in Baptist identity. Although supporting mission work is the dominant view, it still is not characteristic of all groups called Baptist as can be seen in the groups called PRIMITIVE BAPTISTS or Old Baptists who do not engage in missionary work. Nevertheless the practice of sending missionaries from Baptists in the Northern hemisphere appeared to explode after World War II, with peace and prosperity increasing the Baptist ability to organize and fund mission enterprises. However, by the end of the twentieth century challenges to mission sending being the whole of Baptist global perspective appeared. Many Baptist bodies formed in the nineteenth century in Latin America, Asia, and Europe were over 100 years old. They no longer saw themselves as "mission fields" but as viable, developed religious organizations with national leaders. Conflicts emerged around the world between missionary-sending organizations and indigenous leadership over theology, leadership, organizational structure, and financial control.

A new global perspective of partnership between worldwide Baptist bodies is emerging. Partnership is a relationship involving close cooperation between parties having specified and joint rights and responsibilities (Webster's New Collegiate Dictionary, 1973). For Baptists this would mean sharing the responsibility and redistributing the resources to meet specific needs. Leadership would be exercised by those in the area where ministry would occur rather than by an organization somewhere else. This perspective is not fully formed and Baptists can still become conflicted over the issues of THEOLOGY, leadership, organization, and control of the resources. The conflicts arise when it appears the partners are unequally yoked, that one partner has more leverage than the other, and that they are not partners in the enterprise of sharing the Gospel, but still operating under a command-control operational model.

The shift in perspective from the Baptist world being divided between givers who dominated the leadership, theology, and control of resources for supplicant receivers to a worldwide Baptist family in partnership sharing resources to meet needs is exhibited in a variety of ways. This shift can be seen in the Baptist World Alliance that defines itself as a fellowship of believers around the world. Through its Congresses, research, its advocacy for justice, HUMAN RIGHTS and religious liberty, and its work to redistribute resources from the countries that have to those that are in need, BWA brings Baptists together in partnership. BWA still struggles with domination by those Baptists with the greatest resources, but it is one reflection of the shift in global perspective.

Another arena of evidence of Baptist groups insisting on being viewed as equal partners can be found in the European Baptist Federation (EBF) since the collapse of communism. For decades Baptists in the West prayed for and sought to provide political and financial aid for Baptists under communist control. Now freed from that control, Baptists in the former communist countries view themselves as equal partners in the European Baptist Federation.

Granted, Baptist unions in former communist countries are not financially independent because of the economic upheaval in their countries. Many of these unions are defining their identity anew, now that they are no longer forced into union with other groups who are not Baptist as they were under communism. Another aspect of emerging identity for Baptist unions in these countries is the conflict over who collaborated with the communists and whether the collaboration was necessary for the survival of the Christians or for personal power. Nevertheless these Baptists remind other Baptists that they kept the Baptist expression of Christianity alive under conditions Christians in the West have not faced. Because of the differences in their experience European Baptists do not always understand or appreciate each other. However, as early as 1981 Dean Kirkwood noted that Baptists in the communist countries had much to teach their fellow believers in the West—that they were not only recipients of aid, but authoritative leaders in their own right. A relationship between Baptists in Europe char-

acterized by mutual respect and sharing of resources instead of control by Western Europeans is still emerging. Partnership between European Baptists and Baptists in North America is also emerging and includes struggles over the same issues.

Albert W. Wardin in *Baptists Around the World: A Comprehensive Handbook* (1995:8) illustrates the multinational and multiracial composition of Baptists. For example, his data demonstrated that 42 percent of Baptists are from the southern hemisphere and 58 percent from the northern hemisphere. He also showed how Baptists outside of Britain and North America had increased from 4.5 percent in 1852 to 25 percent today. Wardin's data are necessary to understand the identity issues within the Baptist family between former imperial powers and their former colonies or territories.

In Africa, for example, Baptist mission-sending agencies had a history of cooperating with the colonial powers in whatever country they operated, and perpetuating the social stratification of the colonial system. The association of Baptists with COLONIALISM has led to many conflicts over theology, leadership, organizational structure, and the control of economic resources. African leaders argue that the financial power of the foreign mission agencies has hampered the development of African leaders, theology, and organizations that are authentically African (see AFRICAN-INSTITUTED CHURCHES; AFRICAN THEOLOGY). Instead what has developed mirrors the groups that fund them and weakens the impact of Baptists in Africa.

Statistics from the All Africa Baptist Fellowship indicate that in Africa there are over three million baptized believers in more than 17,000 Baptist churches composing forty-four Baptist conventions and unions in twenty-five countries. Each of these countries has its own socioeconomic, political context in which Baptists are seeking to minister. Such diversity means there is no one African perspective, but rather many perspectives as Africans minister to their own situation and develop theologies for communicating the Gospel. Partnership with wealthier Baptists that would contribute to redistribution of economic resources under the leadership of African Baptists could make a momentous difference not only for the Baptists, but also for the circumstances in which they minister.

Even in Asia and Latin America the issues of developing authentic leadership, theology, organizational structure, and economic resources exist. The struggle in these areas is not so much tied to colonialism as the need to be free from foreign influence. In Latin America, for example, the church tied to colonial power was the Catholic Church, not the Baptists or any other expression of evangelical Christianity.

However, Baptist unwillingness to get involved in political or economic issues has hindered Baptist influence throughout Latin America as it has in Africa. Baptists are perceived as supporting the status quo and indigenous leaders are emerging who clearly see this behavior as inappropriate and ineffective in their contexts.

In both Asian and Latin American countries Baptists have developed to the point that there are conflicts between the national leaders and mission-sending agencies. The issues of developing national leadership, theology that communicates in the ministry context rather than mirroring the theology of the missionary from another context, and control of economic resources provided by partnership agencies are being worked out. In Asia and Latin America, as in Africa, there is tremendous national diversity and the need is critical for Baptists to develop leadership and theology in those distinct situations instead of imposing this structure from outside.

Further evidence of the shift in global perspective is found in the view of historians that Baptist history needs a different focus. Historical surveys of the entire Baptist family need to be written from the perspectives of those to whom the missionaries were sent. Through the twentieth century Baptist historical surveys generally were written from the perspective of British and North American Baptists and the missionaries they sent around the world. Telling the Baptist story in a more inclusive way that recognizes the contributions of all Baptist groups could broaden our understanding of what it means to be Baptist in vastly diverse contexts. Such a retelling could also point out why churches in some areas are growing whereas others appear to be stagnant or dying as Baptists around the world seek to shape a global identity.

Baptists have not always had a global identity. Through a shift in understanding of themselves as local churches to an identity as cooperating mission-sending people, Baptists emerged around the world. Once again Baptists are in a time of identity transition. The ideal of partnership is one aspect of the emerging global Baptist identity. The ideal is not yet made concrete globally, although there are different groups seeking to practice this ideal. Later historians will be able to look back and analyze the identity that emerged from this shift. At this time Baptists know they are participating in a shift of identity from dividing the world into mission senders and mission receivers to a partnership of worldwide Baptist organizations working together to minister in diverse contexts.

See also Africa; Baptism; Baptists; Baptists, Europe; Baptist Missions; Baptists, United States

References and Further Reading

Cupit, L. A. (Tony), ed. *Baptist Faith and Witness*. Book 2. McLean, VA: Baptist World Alliance, 1999.

Enyoba, B. Uche. "Baptist Presence in Africa." Paper presented at the All Africa Theological Educators' Conference, November 2000, Ibadan, Nigeria.

Kirkwood, Dean R. *European Baptists: a Magnificent Minority*. Valley Forge, PA: International Ministries/American Baptist Churches in the USA, 1981.

Kretzschmar, Louise. "Baptist Theological Education in Africa, Particularly in South Africa." *Baptist History and Heritage* 36 no. 1/2 (2001): 190–212.

McBeth, H. Leon. *The Baptist Heritage: Four Centuries of Baptist Witness*. Nashville, TN: Broadman Press, 1987.

Moreno, Pablo P. "Baptists in Latin America and their Theological Contributions at the End of the Twentieth Century." *Baptist History and Heritage* 36 no. 1/2 (2001): 273–296.

Obaje, Yusuf Ameh. "Theological Education in the 21st Century: An Agenda for Baptists in Africa." Paper presented at the All Africa Theological Educators' Conference, November 2000, Ibadan, Nigeria.

Pilli, Toivo. "Union of Evangelical Christians-Baptists of Estonia, 1945–1989: Survival Techniques, Outreach Efforts, Search for Identity." *Baptist History and Heritage* 36 no. 1/2 (2001): 113–135.

Shurden, Walter B. *The Life of Baptists in the Life of the World*. Nashville, TN: Broadman Press, 1985.

Wardin, Albert W. *Baptists Around the World: A Comprehensive Handbook*. Nashville, TN: Broadman & Holman Publishers, 1995.

Waruta, Douglas W. "Celebrating Christ: The Hope of Africa" and "Biblical Interpretation and African Traditional Thought." Papers presented at the All Africa Theological Educators' Conference, November 2000, Ibadan, Nigeria.

Websites Offering Examples of Baptist Partnership:

Alliance of Baptists. http://www.allianceofbaptists.org

American Baptist Churches USA. http://www.abc-usa.org

Baptist World Alliance. http://www.bwanet.org

Cooperative Baptist Fellowship. http://www.cbfonline.org

Lott Carey Foreign Mission Convention. http://www.lottcarey.org

Virginia Baptists. http://www.vbmb.org

PHYLLIS RODGERSON PLEASANTS

BAPTISTS, UNITED STATES

Baptists are the second largest religious denomination in the UNITED STATES. In Revolutionary-era America Baptists were a scattered and insignificant sect numbering less than 70,000. By the CIVIL WAR they had grown twelve times that large, and after World War I their rolls swelled to over seven million. By some estimates there are as many as 35 million Baptists currently in the United States, which accounts for three-quarters of all Baptists worldwide. There are more than fifty distinct Baptist bodies in the United States, but over 90 percent of them belong to congregations associated with the SOUTHERN BAPTIST CONVENTION (16 million), NATIONAL BAPTIST CONVENTION USA (5 million), NATIONAL BAPTIST CONVENTION OF AMERICA (3.5 million), National Missionary Baptist Convention of America (2.5 million), PROGRESSIVE NATIONAL BAPTIST CONVENTION (2.5 million), AMERICAN BAPTIST CHURCHES USA (1.4 million), or Baptist Bible Fellowship International (1.2 million). Although Baptists are known to be contentious and fissiparous, they nevertheless share an amazing consensus around a set of convictions and practices that includes simple biblicism, conversional faith, believer's BAPTISM, regenerate membership, gathered ECCLESIOLOGY, congregational POLITY, evangelical MISSIONS, soul liberty, and separation of CHURCH AND STATE.

English Puritanism

Baptist roots in America grew in the soil of colonial separatism. The "Pilgrim Church" that migrated from ENGLAND to Holland and eventually to America in 1620 was one prominent example. Before immigrating to Amsterdam they were part of the congregation led by JOHN SMYTH, the original Baptist, before his "re-baptism." Transplanted PURITANISM provided a favorable theological climate for Baptist growth in the new world. Some that joined the movement came as convinced Baptists to America. These English Baptists were of two sorts: Particular Baptists who were oriented more toward Westminster CALVINISM and General Baptists who were somewhat inclined toward free-will ARMINIANISM.

One of the early Puritan immigrants was ROGER WILLIAMS who arrived in 1631. Williams refused to officiate to "an unseparated people" who thought that they could walk a middle path not entirely in or out of the CHURCH OF ENGLAND. He consequently left Boston, Massachusetts and served as a minister for the more independent congregations in Salem and Plymouth. His radical views soon caught the attention of the Massachusetts authorities. Williams was brought to trial before the General Court where he contended that their congregations were impure, their claim to the land was unclear, and their civil enforcement of religion was unfounded. He declared that civil magistrates have no business meddling "in matters of conscience and religion." When Williams was banished from Massachusetts in 1635 he fled "in the bitter winter season" to Narragansett Bay where he purchased land from the Indians. He organized and secured a charter for the colony of Rhode Island that guaranteed religious liberty for all people, including "Papists, Turks, Jews, and Atheists," and that established a "wall of separation between the garden of the church and the wilderness of the world."

In 1639 Williams became converted to the Baptist persuasion and was believer-baptized by Ezekiel Holliman who had been a member of the congregation in Salem. Williams helped to found the First Baptist Church at Providence, but within a few months he lost confidence in his new community and became a Seeker. Nevertheless his conviction of soul liberty became prototypical, not only of Baptist identity, but of American spirituality, and the colonial experiment of Rhode Island gestured in the direction that was followed by American DEMOCRACY.

Early Baptists met with much opposition from the established churches of New England because anyone that opposed infant baptism was regarded as an incendiary of the commonwealth. In 1651 John Clarke, the pastor of the Baptist congregation of Newport, Rhode Island, and two associates were arrested for preaching at the home of a fellow Baptist in Massachusetts. Clarke and another paid fines, but their companion Obadiah Holmes refused and was given thirty lashes on Market Street in Boston. Holmes accepted his punishment as identification with Jesus, declaring: "[I] am not ashamed of His sufferings, for by His stripes am I healed." Likewise, Henry Dunster was forced to resign as president of Harvard in 1654 because of his open declaration that infant baptism was without biblical warrant. Still Baptist growth continued in New England. The First Baptist Church of Boston was established in 1665, although Baptist services were not legally permitted in Boston until 1682. The Boston Church spread the message and provided visionary leadership for fellow strugglers throughout the region.

The center of Baptist strength during the colonial period was in the mid-Atlantic region where, unlike New England, there was no established church, attributed largely to the peaceable influence of the Quakers (see FRIENDS, SOCIETY OF) who settled there. In 1688 a Baptist congregation was planted in Pennepek, just outside Philadelphia. Its pastor was Elias Keach, son of the English Baptist leader, Benjamin Keach. Baptist congregations soon began to spring up throughout Pennsylvania and New Jersey. In 1707 five churches joined together to form the Philadelphia Baptist Association, and in 1742 the Association adopted as its statement of faith the Second London Confession of Particular Baptists. The addition of two articles that described the practices of hymn singing and the laying on of hands after baptism as ordinances of Christ brought General and Particular Baptists closer together.

Baptists first appeared in the South in 1696, when a church from Kittery, Maine relocated to Charleston, South Carolina. By 1736 four new congregations were established in the colony. General Baptists came from England to southern Virginia by 1700, but the congregations that survived were the result of missionary work in northern Virginia by Particular Baptists from Maryland between 1743 and 1756. Baptists spread to North Carolina through the preaching of Paul Palmer, a General Baptist, who between 1727 and 1735 constituted three churches in Chowan, Camden, and Onslow counties. Although Particulars were more prominent in the New England and mid-Atlantic regions and Generals tended to be concentrated in the frontier of the South, colonial Baptists gradually became theological hybrids as congregations accommodated both types.

American Evangelicalism

The evangelical REVIVALS known as the Great Awakening (see AWAKENINGS) swept through the American colonies, bringing new life and increased membership to Baptists. In 1700 there were less than twenty-five churches with fewer than 1,000 members. By 1740 the number increased to sixty churches with a membership of just over 3,000, and before the turn of the century that grew to almost 1,000 churches with just under 70,000 members. Baptists in New England were the initial beneficiaries of the revivals, although the evangelical movement eventually spread to the middle and southern colonies (see EVANGELICALISM). Congregationalists who were receptive to CONVERSION theology were called "New Lights." These churches were fertile soil for Baptist growth because many of them broke with the Congregationalists and became known as "Separate Baptists." Yet not all Baptists were enthusiastic about the revivals. Regular Baptists were cautiously suspicious about evangelical emotionalism, whereas Separate Baptists embraced revival as "the surprising work of God."

One of the key leaders of Separate Baptists in New England was ISAAC BACKUS, who began his ministry in 1748 as pastor of a New Light Congregational church in Middleborough, Massachusetts. In 1756 Backus and the Middleborough congregation reached the conviction "that truth limits church communion to believers, baptized upon profession of their own faith." They reorganized as a Baptist congregation, and Backus continued as the minister for fifty more years. Another important Separate Baptist leader was Hezekiah Smith, who like Backus led a group of New Light Congregationalists in Haverhill, Massachusetts to become Baptists. Although Smith continued as pastor of the church in Haverhill for over forty years, he spent much of his time in itinerate preaching, founding over thirteen congregations and earning himself the title of "the Baptist [GEORGE] WHITEFIELD." Smith was one of only a few educated Baptist pastors in America. As New England Baptists grew in number and status, they recognized that their churches would not be well served by "a common illiterate minister" and founded Rhode Island College (later Brown University) in 1764 with the hope of providing "a new succession of scholar ministers."

The evangelical revivals had less of an effect on Baptists in the mid-Atlantic colonies, in part because of the influence of the preexisting evangelical Calvinism of the Philadelphia Association and the insusceptibility of New Light Presbyterians to the Baptist vision. Yet Baptists in the region enjoyed gradual growth. A well-educated and esteemed leader of the period was Morgan Edwards who served briefly as pastor of the First Baptist Church of Philadelphia but spent most of his ministry organizing Baptists for education and home mission work. Edwards became the first historian of American Baptists, compiling a comprehensive collection of Baptist sources. One of the most influential Baptist leaders of the region was John Gano whose twenty-six-year pastorate built the first Regular Baptist Church of New York City into a thriving congregation of over 200 members. Gano's theological moderation and denominational cooperation made it possible for General, Six Principle, Regular, and Separate Baptists to work together.

George Whitefield made three tours through South Carolina in 1740, preaching on seventy-nine occasions, yet his reception among the Regular Baptists in the Charleston area was mixed. Isaac Chanler, pastor of the strict Calvinistic congregation at Ashley River, welcomed Whitefield to his pulpit as did other area Baptists, but Thomas Simmons, pastor of the First Baptist Church of Charleston, was cool to revival dramatics. Simmons's young successor, Oliver Hart, led the Charleston church and three others to form the Charleston Association in 1751 after the pattern of the Philadelphia Association. The Charleston Association provided organizational stability and educational support for Baptists in the South. Hart's thirty-year pastorate ended with the British occupation of 1780, beginning a period of decline for Charleston-area Baptists.

The most significant increases for Baptists in the South resulted from the work of the Separate Baptists led by Shubal Stearns and Daniel Marshall, who in the wake of the Whitefield revivals came from Connecticut to North Carolina in 1755. Stearns and Marshall settled in the fast-growing area of Sandy Creek, which was located at the convergence of three busy southern trade routes. The meetings of the Sandy Creek Baptists were "noisy," characterized by emotionally charged preaching and worship. They represented the conversion-oriented theology that was typical of the evangelical revivals. Separate Baptists popularized the practice of the "evangelistic invitation," which occurred at the end of the sermon and called on sinners that "were anxiously inquiring the way of salvation, to come forward and kneel." Although earlier Baptists observed "two ordinances" (baptism and LORD'S SUPPER) or followed "six principles" (repentance, FAITH, baptism, laying on of hands, resurrection, and eternal judgment), Separates practiced "nine rites" (baptism, Lord's Supper, love feast, laying on of hands, foot washing, anointing the sick, the right hand of fellowship, the kiss of charity, and dedicating children).

The evangelical zeal of the Sandy Creek Church led to an increase in membership that rose to over 600. This rapid growth was attributed in no small measure to an Arminianized Calvinism, which stressed that saving GRACE depended as much on "preaching it up" as on "praying it down." Although some Baptists were "like mules that can't reproduce," the Sandy Creek Church was prolific. In just forty-two years they started seventeen congregations and called out 125 ministers. Because the call of God did not depend on—or even need to wait for—education, Separate preachers were quick to enter the fields that were "white unto harvest." Unlike the Regulars, Separate Baptists allowed WOMEN to participate in leadership roles including PREACHING and exhorting, serving as deaconesses and eldresses (see DEACONESSES AND DEACONS), as well as assisting in baptizing and administering the Lord's Supper. The Sandy Creek Association was established in 1758, but friction soon led to fraction as it split into three bodies for North Carolina, Virginia, and South Carolina, thus demonstrating the Baptist principle of church growth: "divide and multiply." By the end of the eighteenth century tensions gradually subsided as Regulars and Separates moved toward reconciliation. The result was the formation of what in some places came to be called the "United Baptists" and anticipated the denominational unity that was to come.

African Diaspora

The slave trade brought those who had been believers "in the black gods of an old land" and "in the white gods of a new land" to a place where they became believers "in the new Jerusalem" (Walker 1989). Black Baptist identity is not rooted in a European consciousness but in an African one. It would be a mistake to explain the development of African American Baptists simply as an extension of Anglo Puritanism and American Evangelicalism. The African diaspora provided a context for what can only be described as a transformation of slave religion into a distinctively Africanized Christianity. European slave traders and colonial American slave owners initially resisted the conversion of Africans to Christianity. Only a few names of black members appear in the records of Baptist churches before 1750. As slaves were allowed by their masters to attend revival meetings, many embraced the faith among the Baptists. In the second half of the eighteenth century black converts were regularly received into predominantly white congregations. By some estimates in 1790 enslaved Africans may have constituted as much as 40 percent of the membership among Baptist churches in the South. In colonial South Carolina where slaves were a majority of the general population, blacks outnumbered whites in some churches. The First Baptist Church of Charleston, for example, reported in 1796 that most of its 248 members were black.

Before 1800 there were at least ten independent black Baptist congregations in the South. The earliest of these "chattel churches" was organized near Savannah, Georgia between 1773 and 1778. The pastor was George Leile, a slave who was converted in the predominately white Buckhead Creek Baptist Church in Burke County, Georgia and ordained for missionary work on the surrounding plantations. After the British withdrew from Savannah in 1782, the church disbanded. Leile and a few of the freed slaves decided to go to Jamaica. Some of the congregation followed DAVID GEORGE, another leader, first to Nova Scotia and then to SIERRA LEONE. A third group went with Jesse Galphin to Augusta, Georgia, where they established an independent Baptist congregation. The remnant formed the First African Church of Savannah in 1788 led by one of Liele's converts, Andrew Bryan. In 1802 when the membership had grown to over 700, the Second African Baptist Church of Savannah was formed. During the same time independent black Baptist congregations were established throughout Virginia, in Williamsburg, Petersburg, Norfolk, and Charles City. The first independent black Baptist congregation in the North was Joy Baptist Church in Boston, Massachusetts, organized in 1805, and was soon followed by churches in New York, Pennsylvania, New Jersey, and Illinois.

That blacks and whites came to share a social and spiritual ethos united by a common evangelical faith and practice is clear, as are the reasons African slaves were attracted to the Baptist movement. Conversion theology conveyed the welcome theme of equality for each and all. The liberating news of salvation tapped into the deep longing for freedom. Congregational polity afforded black churches self-determination in a white culture that controlled all other social institutions. Evangelical theology was accessible to educated and uneducated alike. The lack of formal requirements for ordination allowed congregations to meet leadership needs by calling and ordaining their own ministers. Yet the appeal was more existential than doctrinal. For many the gospel became a revolutionary manifesto. Enslaved Africans living as wayfaring strangers resonated with the biblical story of redemption and deliverance. Their suffering and oppression were transformed by the apocalyptic vision of God's inexorable justice, calling into question the enlistment of Scripture to underwrite the institutions of SLAVERY and oppression. Not all followed the example of the militant Baptist preacher Nat Turner who led the slave revolt of 1831 "with the words of the prophets ringing in his ears," but for black preachers the gospel was as a subversive story. Judgment day was coming when the world would be turned upside down and everyone would answer for his or her deeds (see SLAVERY, ABOLITION OF).

Slave religion among black Baptists resulted in a transformation of the Christian story in light of the history and experience of enslaved Africans in America. What is more, it became the means for a transmigration of the spirituality that African slaves brought with them to America. The emotional enthusiasm fostered in the praise gatherings allowed for a fragmentary expression of their ancestral faith. Worship for black Baptists was a free and spontaneous celebration involving the whole person—body and soul. This distinctive spirituality found expression in the music of the black church: spirituals, gospel, and soul. Preaching depended not only on a simple biblicism but on a prophetic imagination. As promised, in the last days God was pouring out the Spirit, inspiring the young to see visions and the old to dream. The confluence of these streams coming from American evangelicalism and the African diaspora gave birth to a Baptist identity that is uniquely African American.

Democratic Populism

It has been suggested that if historians were to ask who was responsible for religious liberty in America, their answer would be "JAMES MADISON," but if the question could be put to Madison he might very likely reply "John Leland and the Baptists." It is widely recognized that from their beginnings Baptists were tireless advocates of soul liberty and a disestablished church. What is less well known is how these Baptist convictions became instantiated in the constitutional guarantees of religious freedom and the separation of church and state. New England Baptists resisted the taxation system that supported the Congregational churches, by forming a "grievance committee"

chaired by Isaac Backus to voice their protest. They even lobbied delegates to the First Continental Congress in 1774, calling for the separation of church and state. The Massachusetts delegation agreed to look into the matter more fully; however, John Adams remarked that it would be more realistic to expect a change in the solar system than for Massachusetts to give up an established church. The planets continued to run their courses, but Massachusetts disestablished its church in 1833.

Baptists in Virginia began a petition campaign in 1770 to the House of Burgesses (the colonial legislature of Virginia), calling for relief from harassment and restrictions on Baptists and other dissenters. It was not uncommon for their ministers to be imprisoned, fined, or beaten with legal sanction as purveyors of "vile, pernicious, abhorrible, detestable, abominable, diabolical doctrines." By 1775 Baptists were demanding complete religious liberty. Their efforts gained a positive hearing from governor THOMAS JEFFERSON, who in 1777 wrote and proposed a bill to the Virginia legislature that would have disestablished the Protestant Episcopal Church and provided religious freedom for all. The legislation was viewed as too radical and failed to gain approval, but it paved the way for future gains. The leader in the Baptist battle for religious freedom in Virginia was John Leland, a fierce advocate for the disestablishment of the church from the state. Leland fused the conviction of religious liberty with the theory of natural rights thus enabling Baptists and deists (see DEISM) to join forces in abolishing the vestiges of an established church and instituting the guarantees of religious liberty. With Baptist backing, Jefferson's bill for religious freedom became Virginia law in 1786.

When a new federal constitution was drafted by Congress and sent to the states for approval, Virginia Baptists under Leland's leadership voiced their apprehension that the document failed to sufficiently secure the liberty of conscience. They planned to work against its ratification and to support Madison's opponent for election to the Virginia constitutional convention of 1788. Concerned that the new constitution was in jeopardy and that he might not be elected, Madison sought out a conversation with "the Baptist preacher." The meeting according to one account took place under "the swinging limbs of a lonely oak" in Orange County, Virginia. After some time, reassured that further protections of religious liberty would be forthcoming, Leland reportedly declared, "Mr. Madison, I will vote for you." With the support of the Baptists firmly behind him Madison was elected, and the constitution was ratified in Virginia by a narrow margin of only ten votes. In 1789 Madison introduced the BILL OF RIGHTS, which contained the promised provision that "Congress shall make no law respecting an establishment of religion, or prohibiting the free exercise thereof."

After fourteen years in Virginia, Leland returned in 1791 to his native Massachusetts where he continued to preach and for two terms served in the state legislature. He gained national notoriety when on New Year's Day in 1802 he presented a 1,235-pound "Mammoth Cheese" to President Jefferson as a gift from the citizens of Cheshire, Massachusetts. That same day Jefferson sent a letter to the Danbury Baptist Association of Connecticut in which he described the first amendment as "building a wall of separation between church and state." Two days later Leland preached a sermon with overtones of political messianism at the Sunday service in Congress. His text was "Behold, a greater than Solomon is here," which Leland applied to Jefferson, who sat in the congregation, rather than to Jesus. Leland was not one to withhold extravagant rhetoric, describing the presidency as America's "greatest orbit" occupied by Jefferson who is its "brightest orb."

With the passing of the eighteenth century a milieu of homogeneous ecclesiastical authority was replaced by a context of pluralistic popular religion, but the democratization of Christianity in America was less a matter of religion exercising influence over politics and more about the church becoming the embodiment of popular culture. America was on the verge of becoming "a Christian nation." No group epitomized this newly democratized Christianity better than the Baptists, who opposed government establishment of religion but enjoyed the privileges of grassroots support, and populist religion had no greater champion than "the cheesemonger" preacher John Leland.

Denominational Unification

Baptists first organized at a national level on May 18, 1814. Thirty-three delegates assembled at the First Baptist Church of Philadelphia to form the General Missionary Convention of the Baptist Denomination in the United States for Foreign Missions. The vision of Baptists united in missions began with Luther Rice who pledged to Ann and Adoniram Judson that he would enlist support for their mission work in Burma (see JUDSON FAMILY). The Triennial Convention (as it came to be called) adopted foreign missions as their cause. By the second meeting in 1817 the convention expanded its commitment to include home missions for the growing American West (see MISSIONS, NORTH AMERICAN) and theological education with the founding of Columbian College (later George Washington University).

The vision in the early years favored a convention pattern in which membership would consist of churches that sent contributions and delegates to a central organization that in turn carried out the ministries of the convention. Francis Wayland, however, the president of Brown University and a key Baptist leader, changed his mind and began to advocate for a society organization in which membership would be based on the voluntary financial contribution of individuals. At the 1826 meeting of the Triennial Convention delegates voted to return to a society method with foreign missions as the single benevolence. By so doing, Wayland argued, they were preserving "the absolute independence of the churches" and "the inviolability of the individual conscience."

As Wayland exemplifies, some of the resistance to denominational unity had its source in American INDIVIDUALISM. Others branded these "new fangled" ideas as unbiblical and called for the reliance on God's sovereignty in communicating the gospel. "Jonah wasn't sent to Nineveh by a society," argued Daniel Parker. Still others questioned the motives of missionaries. John Taylor called Luther Rice "a modern Tetzel" and said that missionaries "love money like a horse leech loves blood." In the end missionary theology prevailed, and the antimissionary movement that became known as the PRIMITIVE BAPTISTS diminished. The Baptist General Tract Society (later the American Baptist Publication Society) was formed in 1824, and the American Baptist Home Mission Society was established in 1832, thus providing support for Baptist work in foreign missions, home missions, and Christian education.

In the beginning the Triennial Convention managed to avoid the issue of slavery, even electing Richard Furman, an ardent proslavery advocate from South Carolina, as the first president. Many southerners agreed with Furman that "the right of holding slaves is clearly established in the Holy Scriptures," although there was a strong antislavery movement in Kentucky led by David Barrow. Among Baptists in the North abolitionist sentiments grew as the American Baptist Anti-Slavery Convention gained support. In an effort to avert a conflict the Triennial Convention adopted a neutrality statement at the 1841 meeting, but in 1844, when it became clear that no slaveholders would be appointed as missionaries, a call was issued for "a consultative gathering" of Baptists in the South. The Southern Baptist Convention was formed the next year in Augusta, Georgia as a multipurpose convention that initially included Foreign and Home Mission Boards with the addition of a Sunday School Board in 1891. Long after the CIVIL WAR was over, Southern Baptists remained deeply committed to its "noble cause," clinging to the belief that what the Confederacy had failed to establish with its armies would ultimately triumph through the Christianized culture of the South.

African American Baptists were frustrated by the racism that excluded them from the two predominantly white denominations. The racism of Southern Baptists was overt. The racism of Northern Baptists was more subtle. Yet neither fellowship welcomed them as equals. Numerous state and regional black Baptist bodies were formed after the Civil War, but three anticipated the dream of a national denomination. W. W. Colley, who for a time served as a missionary in Africa, prepared the way by forming the Foreign Mission Baptist Convention in 1880. The American National Baptist Convention was organized six years later for the purpose of home missions, and in 1893 the Baptist National Education Convention was established. With the consolidation of these three groups in 1895 and the formation of the National Baptist Convention in Atlanta, Georgia the dream of denominational unity became a reality.

Contentious Fragmentation

In 1850 there were fewer than one million Baptists in the United States. By 1922 Baptists grew to over eight million. Denominationalism provided structure for that growth. Yet at the same time Baptists became increasingly fragmented. In the mid-nineteenth century the shrill voices of Landmarkism began asserting that Baptist churches were the only true churches and had existed in unbroken succession since the days of the Apostles. Landmarkers argued that only believer's baptism by immersion in a Baptist church was valid and that participation in the Lord's Supper was to be limited to members of the local congregation that administered it. Landmarkism had little effect on Northern Baptists, but it remained a divisive force and an irruptive threat to the unity of the Southern Baptist Convention even after the splintering off of several Landmark groups at the turn of the century. The most prominent of these offshoots are the American Baptist Association and the Baptist Missionary Association. The influence of Landmarkism among Southern Baptists is evident in their strong emphasis on local church autonomy (often to the exclusion of the church universal) and their ecumenical suspicion that kept them from joining either the WORLD COUNCIL OF CHURCHES or the NATIONAL COUNCIL OF CHURCHES (unlike American and National Baptists who are participating members in the ecumenical movement).

The hard-won unity of National Baptists was short lived. The first split came in 1897 when a group expressing a desire to retain ties with white Baptists withdrew and organized the Lott Carey Foreign Mission Convention. Disagreements over the denominational publishing house and the adoption of a charter resulted in another schism that led to the formation of the National Baptist Convention of America in 1915. A third major division arose in the midst of the CIVIL RIGHTS MOVEMENT. Those that favored social activism and denominational reform joined New York pastor Gardner C. Taylor in establishing the Progressive National Baptist Convention in 1961. The National Missionary Baptist Convention of America is the result of a separation in 1988 from the National Baptist Convention of America, ironically by those that supported the independence of the denominational publishing board.

Perhaps the most fractious and factious controversy is "the Battle for the Bible." Among Northern Baptists it lasted for three decades. Before the 1920 meeting of the Northern Baptists there was a large preconvention rally. Curtis Lee Laws described the assembly as true believers "who still cling to the great fundamentals and mean to do battle royal" for the faith. The "fundamentalists" went on the attack against MODERNISM and liberalism in the SEMINARIES and on the mission field (see LIBERAL PROTESTANTISM AND LIBERALISM). A militant fundamentalist group separated in 1932 to form the GENERAL ASSOCIATION OF REGULAR BAPTISTS. A more moderate group remained in the Northern Baptist Convention until 1947 when they organized the Conservative Baptists of America.

The Battle over the BIBLE was more protracted among Southern Baptists. They averted schism in the 1920s by affirming a confession of faith. Under the leadership of J. Frank Norris, in 1932 frustrated fundamentalists organized what became the World Baptist Fellowship. In 1950 a breakaway group separated from Norris's autocratic control and founded the Baptist Bible Fellowship, which fifty years later counted over a million members. Controversy among Southern Baptists again erupted with the publication of *The Message of Genesis* in 1961 by Ralph Elliot, a professor at Midwestern Baptist Theological Seminary. K. Owen White, a fundamentalist pastor from Houston, Texas pronounced biblical criticism to be poisonous and warned of "death in the pot" being cooked up in the seminaries. Elliot was dismissed from his teaching position, and the Convention revised The Baptist Faith and Message in 1963, but the controversy raged on. It broke out again when G. Henton Davies suggested in the *Broadman Bible Commentary* that God might not have commanded Abraham to kill Isaac. The Convention voted in 1970 to have the Genesis commentary rewritten.

The final Battle for the Bible was fought in the 1980s when messengers elected a succession of presidents who reformed the Southern Baptist Convention according to the theology of BIBLICAL INERRANCY. Moderates were forced out or left. The Cooperative Baptist Fellowship was organized in 1991 as an alternative mission society and leadership network. With the issue of the Bible settled, more Baptist Battles loom on the horizon: GENDER roles, ministerial AUTHORITY, WORSHIP styles, ABORTION, HOMOSEXUALITY, resurgent Calvinism, insurgent PENTECOSTALISM, and both ecumenical and intradenominational relations. As JOHN BUNYAN once observed, Baptists are "a turbulent, seditious, and factious people," which suggests that when it comes to Baptist life, "the more things change, the more they seem to stay the same."

References and Further Reading

Armstrong, O. K., and Marjorie M. Armstrong. *The Baptists in America.* Garden City, NY: Doubleday, 1979.

Brackney, William H., ed. *Baptist Life and Thought: 1600–1980.* Valley Forge, PA: Judson Press, 1983.

Freeman, Curtis, James McClendon, and C. Rosalee Velloso Ewell. *Baptist Roots: A Reader in the Theology of a Christian People.* Valley Forge, PA: Judson Press, 1999.

Hudson, Winthrop S. *Baptists in Transition: Individualism and Christian Responsibility.* Valley Forge, PA: Judson Press, 1979.

Leonard, Bill J. *Baptist Ways: A History.* Valley Forge, PA: Judson Press, 2003.

McBeth, H. Leon. *The Baptist Heritage: Four Centuries of Baptist Witness.* Nashville, TN: Broadman Press, 1987.

Newman, Albert Henry. *A History of the Baptist Churches in the United States*, 6th ed. Philadelphia: The American Baptist Publication Society, 1915.

Sobel, Mechal. *Trabelin' On: The Slave Journey to an Afro-Baptist Faith.* Westport, CT: Greenwood Press, 1979.

Torbet, Robert G. *A History of the Baptists.* Valley Forge, PA: Judson Press, 1973.

Walker, Margaret. "We Have Been Believers." In *This is My Country: New and Collected Poems.* Athens: University of Georgia Press, 1989.

Wardin, Albert W., ed. *Baptists Around the World.* Nashville, TN: Broadman Press, 1995.

Washington, James Melvin. *Frustrated Fellowship: The Black Baptist Quest for Social Power.* Macon, GA: Mercer University Press, 1986.

CURTIS W. FREEMAN

BAPTIST WORLD ALLIANCE

Formed in London in 1905, the Baptist World Alliance (BWA) is the world confessional body that links BAPTISTS from around the world. It is a fellowship of Baptist unions and conventions in over 200 countries with a membership of more than 44 million baptized believers and a community of approximately 110 million people. Its main aims are to enable international fellowship between Baptists; to support their work and witness, especially in those parts of the world where they experience particular difficulties; and to represent their concerns, especially in the areas of mission, humanitarian aid, and human rights.

Baptist ecclesiology sees the local congregation as the primary manifestation of the church of Jesus Christ, with regional and national unions resulting from fellowship and joint action between such local churches. Similarly, the BWA provides an international means whereby national unions, and individuals and churches within them, are able to enjoy Christian fellowship, support and encourage one another in Baptist witness, and engage in strategic reflection and cooperation.

The work of the alliance is advanced through:

1. a quinquennial congress, which draws thousands of representatives and individual participants and meets for WORSHIP, fellowship, and the presentation of Baptist life and concerns from different continents and contexts.
2. the annual general council composed of representatives of the member unions and conventions, which conducts the regular business of the alliance.
3. a general secretary and a small executive staff based at the alliance's headquarters in the United States, together with the regional executive secretaries who support the work of the six regional (continental) Baptist bodies.
4. a president and a number of honorary vice presidents from the regions who represent the alliance both within its constituent churches and before other churches, secular agencies, and governments.
5. the many volunteer participants who participate in the work of the alliance and represent it.

Although three quarters of the membership of BWA is to be found in the UNITED STATES, the meetings and focus of the alliance have a clear international identity. Although expressing a considerable diversity of cultural and theological outlook, the alliance represents the core concerns of Baptists, especially in the areas of fellowship, EVANGELISM, and religious freedom.

See also Baptist Family; Baptists, United States; Baptists, Global

References and Further Reading

Lord, F. Townley. *Baptist World Fellowship: A Short History of the Baptist World Alliance.* Nashville, TN: Broadman Press, 1955.

See also the reports of the various congresses, councils and study commissions, the BWA website http://www.bwa-baptist-heritage.org and a new history of the alliance to be published in 2005.

CHRISTOPHER J. ELLIS

THE BARMEN DECLARATION

In May of 1934, in Barmen, GERMANY, a new synod of evangelical (Protestant) churches was formed, uniting Lutheran, Reformed, and United Churches that, on the basis of the traditional confessions of Protestantism, were in opposition to the State (Reich) Church that supported and was supported by the Nazi regime. This Synod of the Confessing German Evangelical Churches adopted a Theological Declaration (Erklärung), which set forth theological notions that would be the basis of their unity and their opposition. It proved to be one of the most significant church documents of the twentieth century.

The Situation

After the rise to power of National Socialism in Germany, a struggle for the control of the evangelical church began and in July 1933 reached a critical juncture. As head of the Nazi party, Adolph Hitler (1889–1945) called for a nationwide church election to establish a new National (Reich) Evangelical Church, uniting all Evangelical churches under a single Reich bishop subject to state control. A movement within the church, "The Faith Movement of German Christians," supported Hitler's efforts, and with the help of the Nazi party won the election and gained control of the new church. The goal of the GERMAN CHRISTIANS was to effect a coordination (Gleichschaltung) of the new church with the new Nazi state. Along with most Germans, the German Christians realized that the Führer was leading Germany out of the depths and despair of the postwar 1920s into a new world of promise and national fulfillment. They found in this present "German hour," and especially in the leadership of the Führer, a providential blessing of the Creator, and a corresponding call to the church, in obedience to the command and law of God, to support and unite with the new Germany. According to the seventh guideline of the Faith Movement of German Christians, Christians should "see in race, in the people (Volkstum) and nation a divine ordering for our lives which, according to God's law, the church must be concerned to uphold." A leading theologian, Paul Althaus, wrote that "the church lives by the grace of Jesus Christ, but as a Christian community of its German people, it also lives by the grace of history, by virtue of which God calls his people, raises them up, and awakens its heroes to deliver them from their distress."

The Barmen Synod

These events and this thinking led to the rise of a confessional movement in the Evangelical Church, which claimed that the Reich church was in fact both unconstitutional and heretical because it did not recognize the sole authority of the Gospel of Christ as interpreted by the confessions of the churches. In October 1933 the government applied the infamous "Aryan paragraph" to the church, preventing Christian Jews from serving as pastors or holding any church office. This interference in church affairs led resisting pastors to form the "Pastors' Emergency Defense League," under the leadership of Pastor MARTIN NIE-MÖLLER, to defend and support pastors who were victims of this edict. In November 1933 the German Christians held a meeting in the huge Berlin Sport Palace to enlist open support for the Aryan clause by calling for the liberating of the church from all things Jewish, including the Old Testament and the "Rabbi Paul." This action, along with the increasing co-option of the state church by the Nazis and the intensification of punitive measures against the pastors of the Defense League, made it necessary for resisting churches, which sought to be guided by their confessions rather than edicts of the state, to unite, to become a truly "confessing" church. Thus on May 29–31, in an exceptional show of unity that brought together Lutheran, Reformed, and United Protestant churches, a national synod, The Confessing Synod of the German Evangelical Church, was convened in Barmen. A Theological Commission composed of Lutherans Thomas Breit as moderator and Hans Asmussen as secretary, and the Reformed Bonn professor KARL BARTH, was formed to present to the synod a theological declaration that would address the issues the churches were facing and around which they could unite.

The Preparation and Presentation of the Declaration

The meeting concluded when Asmussen presented and the synod adopted a "Theological Declaration" (Theologische Erklärung), drafted chiefly by Barth. As a theological document it was intended to counter German Christian theology and to establish the CONFESSING CHURCH as the authentic Evangelical Church of Germany, not to bring about the dissolution of the Reich church but to restore it to its constitutional basis. The statement was received by the delegates "with thanks to God" and with certainty "in their belief that a common word had been put in their mouth." However, before it was finally accepted, the declaration was seriously debated and went through a number of drafts. The result was a successful compromise between Lutheran and Reformed concerns. Lutherans, concerned to maintain their confessional integrity, insisted that the declaration not be received as a new confession establishing a new church. On the other hand, the declaration, or the Barmen "Confession" as it came to be known, did have the effect of establishing the Confessing Church as the authentic Evangelical Church of Germany vis-à-vis what was judged to be the unconstitutional and heretical Reich Church. In addition, Lutherans were committed to the two kingdoms doctrine, which had the effect of separating the word of God as revealed in the gospel of Christ from the law of the creator as manifest in the present-day political reality of Germany. This perspective was reflected especially in the fact that the declaration makes no reference to the Jewish question, which was judged to be a political matter of the law, and not an ecclesial issue of the gospel. On the other hand, the Reformed emphasis on the kingship of Christ over both church and state is reflected especially in the first thesis, which states that Jesus Christ is the only Word that the church must hear, as well as in the fifth thesis, which speaks of the "power of the Word by which God upholds all things."

The first thesis, the key to the entire declaration, makes it evident that the controversy with the German Christians is primarily theological, and only indirectly political, when it states that Jesus Christ, not present-day powers, people, or ideologies, is the only Word that the Church has to hear. Subsequent theses set forth the important implications of this first thesis. The second concerns the Christian life, insisting that Christians must know themselves not only to be forgiven by Christ, but also as totally claimed by him for "free and grateful service." The third and fourth theses, on the form and calling of the church, reject the proposition that its external form might be determined by something or someone other than its head, Jesus Christ. In particular, the fourth thesis rejects the notion that leadership in the church could be determined by the prevailing political model, that is, the "leadership principle" (*Füehrerprinzip*). To the contrary, in the last analysis leadership in the church belongs to the congregation.

The fifth thesis has to do with the relationship of the church to the political order, recognizing the particular calling of both church and state, rejecting any confusion of the two realms, but also insisting that the church is called by God to remind the state of its responsibility to God's kingdom and justice.

The sixth thesis provoked little discussion. Summarizing the message of the declaration as a call to the church "to deliver to all people the message of the free grace of God through sermon and sacrament," it claims to be nothing more or less than a faithful exposition of the confessions on which the churches stand, particularly the Lutheran.

For Lutherans the purpose of the declaration was to help the churches maintain their confessional integrity and freedom from state control; for Barth and many in the Reformed tradition, its purpose was to facilitate a reformation of the church by bringing it back to that one Word it has to hear. Consequently, with the end of the war and the reestablishment of the church, Lutherans had no more need for the Barmen Declaration, whereas primarily for churches in the Reformed tradition in Germany and throughout the world it continues to function as a new confession. In 1967 it was added to the Book of Confessions of the Presbyterian Church in the United States; it also served as a "Symbol of Contemporary Liberation" in the South African struggle against apartheid. For some, notably the Lutheran church, it belongs to history; for others it is a living document, on the one hand calling the church to be its orthodox self, or on the other hand, calling the church to promising and prophetic service of the world.

The Text of the Barmen Declaration

In view of the "German Christians" and of the present Reich Church Administration, which are ravaging the Church and at the same time also shattering the unity of the German Evangelical Church, we confess the following evangelical truths:

1. Jesus Christ, as he is attested to us in Holy Scripture, is the one Word of God whom we have to hear, and whom we have to trust and obey in life and in death.
   We reject the false doctrine that the Church could and should recognize as a source of its proclamation, beyond and besides this one Word of God, yet other events, powers, historic figures and truths as God's revelation.
2. As Jesus Christ is God's comforting pronouncement of the forgiveness of all our sins, so, with equal seriousness, he is also God's vigorous announcement of his claim upon our whole life. Through him there comes to us joyful liberation from the godless ties of this world for free, grateful service to his creatures.
   We reject the false doctrine that there could be areas of our life in which we would not belong to Jesus Christ but to other lords, areas in which we would not need justification and sanctification through him.
3. The Christian Church is the community of brethren in which, in Word and sacrament, through the Holy Spirit, Jesus Christ acts in the present as Lord. With both its faith and its obedience, with both its message and its order, it

has to testify in the midst of the sinful world, as the Church of pardoned sinners, that it belongs to him alone and lives and may live by his comfort and under his direction alone, in expectation of his appearing.

We reject the false doctrine that the Church could have permission to hand over the form of its message and of its order to whatever it itself might wish or to the vicissitudes of the prevailing ideological and political convictions of the day.

4. The various offices in the Church do not provide a basis for some to exercise authority over others but for the ministry [lit., "service"] with which the whole community has been entrusted and charged to be carried out.

We reject the false doctrine that, apart from this ministry, the Church could, and could have permission to, give itself or allow itself to be given special leaders [Führer] vested with ruling authority.

5. Scripture tells us that by divine appointment the State, in this still unredeemed world in which also the Church is situated, has the task of maintaining justice and peace, as far as human discernment and human ability make this possible, by means of the threat and use of force. The Church acknowledges with gratitude and reverence toward God the benefit of this, his appointment. It calls to mind the Dominion [Reich] of God, God's commandment and justice, and thereby the responsibility of those who rule and those who are ruled. It trusts and obeys the power of the Word, by which God upholds all things.

We reject the false doctrine that beyond its special commission the State should and could become the sole and total order of human life and so fulfill the vocation of the Church as well.

We reject the false doctrine that beyond its special commission the Church should and could take on the nature, tasks and dignity which belong to the State and thus become itself an organ of the State.

6. The Church's commission, which is the foundation of its freedom, consists in this: in Christ's stead, and so in the service of his own word and work, to deliver all people, through preaching and sacrament, the message of the free grace of God.

We reject the false doctrine that with human vainglory the Church could place the word and work of the Lord in the service of self-chosen desires, purposes and plans.

The Confessing Synod of the German Evangelical Church declares that it sees in the acknowledgment of these truths and in the rejection of these errors the indispensable theological basis of the German Evangelical Church as a confederation of Confessing Churches. It calls upon all who can stand in solidarity with its Declaration to be mindful of these theological findings in all their decisions concerning Church and State. It appeals to all concerned to return to unity in faith, hope, and love.

References and Further Reading

Barmer Symposium (Arnoldshain, 1983). *Barmer Theologische Erklaerung, 1934–1984.* Bielefeld: Luther Verlag, 1984.

Burgsmueller, A., and R. Weth. *Die Barmer Theologische Erklaerung: Einfuehrung und Dokumentation.* Neukirchen-Vluyn: Neukirchener Verlag, c. 1983.

Cochrane, A. C. *The Church's Confession Under Hitler.* Pittsburgh: Pickwick, 1976.

Locke, Hubert G., ed. "The Barmen Confession: Papers From the Seattle Assembly." In *Toronto Studies in Theology,* vol. 2. Lewiston: The Edwin Mellen Press, 1986.

Scholder, Klaus. *The Churches and The Third Reich, I and II.* Philadelphia: Fortress Press, 1988.

Wolf, Ernst. *Barmen. Kirche zwischen Versuchung und Gnade.* Munich: C. Kaiser Verlag, 1957, 1980.

ROBERT T. OSBORN

BARNES, ROBERT (c. 1495–1540)

English theologian. Barnes was born at Lynne, and studied at the Austin Friars, Cambridge, and the University of Louvain, receiving his D. D. from Cambridge. Named prior of his house, he was converted by Thomas Bilney to reformed German beliefs. Barnes discussed German THEOLOGY at the White Horse Inn, and on Christmas Eve 1525 he preached against ecclesiastical abuses in a heterodox sermon mixing gospel reverence with criticism of episcopal worldliness. Charged by Cardinal Thomas Wolsey and four bishops with twenty-five heresies, Barnes refused recantation initially, but finally abjured on the advice of Stephen Gardiner, Wolsey's secretary, to avoid being burned. Imprisoned for six months, he was caught distributing a copy of WILLIAM TYNDALE's Bible while under house arrest. Wolsey ordered him burned. Forewarned, Barnes staged his "suicide" before fleeing ENGLAND.

Befriended at Wittenberg, he published a summary of the AUGSBURG CONFESSION, *Sentenciae* (1530), and a *Supplication to King Henry VIII* (1531), an antiepiscopal work urging a national CHURCH in which FAITH alone justified. He later accommodated the importance of works in a covenanted society, a Bucerian principle (see MARTIN BUCER) reflected in English PURITANISM.

In 1531 Barnes carried MARTIN LUTHER's disapproving letter on HENRY VIII's divorce to England. Henry, contemplating an alliance with the League of Schmalkald (see SCHMALKALDIC LEAGUE), let THOMAS CROMWELL appoint Barnes a representative to Lutheran courts. He matriculated at Wittenberg (June 1533). Appointed royal chaplain (summer 1535), Barnes promoted Lutheran theology, hoping to accommodate royal policy where possible. After 1538, when religious negotiations between GERMANY and England failed, Barnes's influence at court crumbled. Cromwell's fall, Henry VIII's divorce from Anne of Cleves, and a new non-German foreign policy led to his attainder by Parliament and burning at Smithfield in the summer of 1540.

Barnes helped prepare England for the adoption of a LITURGY and DOCTRINE under archbishop THOMAS CRANMER, still reflected in the BOOK OF COMMON PRAYER (1549), that had many Lutheran elements.

See also Bible; Bible Translation; Lutheranism; Tyndale, William

References and Further Reading

Clebsch, William A. *England's Earliest Protestants*. New Haven, CT: Yale University Press, 1964.
McGoldrick, James Edward. *Luther's English Connection*. Milwaukee, WI: Northwestern Publishing House, 1979.
Tjernagel, Neelak S. *Lutheran Martyr*. Milwaukee, WI: Northwestern Publishing House, 1982.

BARBARA SHER TINSLEY

BARTH, HEINRICH (1890–1965)

Swiss philosopher and theologian. Barth was born on February 3, 1890 in Berne, younger brother of the Protestant theologian KARL BARTH. He obtained his Ph.D. in 1913 with a dissertation on Descartes, and from 1918 he taught at the *Höhere Töchterschule* (high school for girls) in Basel. In 1920 Barth qualified as a lecturer at the faculty of philosophy at the University of Basel with his study *Die Seele in der Philosophie Platons* (Tübingen 1921), from then working first as an outside lecturer and from 1928 as a professor in Basel. There he died on May 22, 1965.

The work of Heinrich Barth lent great momentum to the early "dialectic theology." Beginning with Marburg New Kantianism, Barth moved toward Christian existential philosophy and on this basis sought to mediate between the philosophies of Plato and IMMANUEL KANT. His studies "Gotteserkenntnis" ("Knowledge of God") (Basel 1919) and *Das Problem des Ursprungs in der platonischen Philosophie* (Munich 1921) are exemplary for this mediation attempt. It was from Marburg New Kantianism that Barth took the concept of "origin" (*Ursprung*). The meaning of "origin" is determined as the ability to think, in that thinking is declared the sole creative principle of being. Barth identifies this term "origin" with the highest Platonic concept, the concept of good. Because the origin of all existence cannot be located in

the created world, this origin must be transcendental and separated from the visible world. Thus the New Kantian understanding of "origin" is identified in the works of Heinrich Barth with the Platonic concept as a creative principle. This mediation attempt had a significant influence on Karl Barth. The identification based on ideas of Heinrich Barth is apparent in Karl Barth's interpretation of God as the "origin," which in transcendence contrasts to the created world, in the second edition of his commentary on the Epistle to the Romans.

The proximity of Heinrich Barth's works to early dialectic theology in terms of content was lost over the years. However, throughout his life, Barth remained a critical observer of the theological works of his brother Karl and also extensively criticized existential philosophy and its influence.

See also Neo-Orthodoxy; Theology; Theology, Twentieth-Century

References and Further Reading

Primary Sources:

Barth, Heinrich. *Philosophie der praktischen Vernunft*. Tübingen, Germany: J. C. B. Mohr, 1927.
———. *Das Sein in der Zeit*. Tübingen, Germany: J. C. B. Mohr, 1933.
———. *Philosophie der Erscheinung*. Stuttgart, Germany: Klett, 1959–1966.
———. *Erkenntnis der Existenz*. Basel, Switzerland: Schwabe, 1965.

Secondary Sources:

Grund, Dorothea. *Erscheinung und Existenz*. Amsterdam: Rodopi, 1999.
Gürtler, Paul. *Der philosophische Weg Heinrich Barths*. Basel, Switzerland: Schwabe, 1976.
Huber, Gerhard, ed. *Philosophie und christliche Existenz*. Basel, Switzerland: Helbing & Lichtenhahn, 1960.

ANDREAS MÜHLING

BARTH, KARL (1886–1968)

Swiss theologian. Barth came from a long line of clergy on both his mother's and father's sides; he seemed destined to be a theologian. His father Fritz was a Reformed pastor of a moderate, evangelical cast; his mother Anna was a pastor's wife of some influence and descended from distinguished pastors. Karl Barth himself became one of the dominant Protestant theologians since the REFORMATION.

Personal Characteristics and Early Liberalism

Karl Barth was at heart a Basler. He was born in Basel, SWITZERLAND, the eldest of five children, and he relished his time there, free from the conventionalism and stuffiness he saw embedded in much Swiss society. This was something of a lifelong theme with Barth: although a deeply devout, orthodox theologian, Barth was no conventional churchman. He favored the playful, sometimes bohemian face of the Swiss character. He was the enemy of all pretension.

Barth was also a serious theologian and a serious and courageous pastor. A second theme of his life was the search for a calling worthy of the dedication of a whole life. Beginning in his university days Barth longed to join the avant-garde movement of German theological faculties: academic Liberalism (see LIBERAL PROTESTANTISM AND LIBERALISM). Later, in Berlin, Barth was captivated by the great historian of Christian DOCTRINE, ADOLF VON HARNACK. Barth soon moved to the theology faculty at Marburg and became a ready disciple of the leading theological liberal, Wilhelm Herrmann. From him he learned a Christian piety stripped of all metaphysics and utterly dependent on the miracle of faith. Although Barth's views shifted later in his life, his tutelage under Harnack and Herrmann remained a major influence.

Like many intellectuals in prewar GERMANY, Barth participated in the IMMANUEL KANT revival, which was especially vigorous at Marburg. Certain elements of Kant's critical philosophy would survive all revolutions in Barth's theology. So too, Barth would never lose his love of history, awakened by Harnack. The major work of Barth's maturity, the *Church Dogmatics* (four volumes in twelve parts, 1932–1968) is studded with historical examples, and the central ontological category of his anthropology is "the historical." More important, Barth absorbed from Herrmann a serious devotion for FRIEDRICH SCHLEIERMACHER, the architect of modern academic Protestant theology, and adopted an utterly single-minded CHRISTOLOGY, in which Christ was both the content of and the means to theology. Although both lessons would undergo radical transformations, neither would be left behind in Barth's maturity. This has led some students of Barth to claim that Barth's theological revolution was an internal correction, rather than a repudiation, of academic liberalism.

Finally Barth's appreciation of music, a lifelong pleasure, should not be overlooked. His love of Mozart was well known; it may be that Mozart combined these life themes of play and seriousness with an unrivaled artistry that Barth always admired.

Barth had a deep longing for intimacy and enjoyed a rich and vibrant circle of friends. So strong was this pull in his life that it became a theme in his *Dogmatics*. In volume 3.2, he argued that the creation narratives showed that the *Imago Dei* (image of God) in human beings was a relationship or COVENANT with

one another: the *analogia relationis*. Because human beings were made for relation, hell and hellishness were isolation and loneliness. Barth dreaded such punishment all his life, and his intimacies were not untroubled.

Barth's professional friendships were stormy; his marriage seems not to have fared much better. Barth married Nelly Hoffmann in 1913, when Nelly was only nineteen and Barth was a well-established pastor of twenty-seven. They shared a love of music, and together they raised five children. They remained married their whole lives and had by many standards a successful marriage, yet their letters testify to the pain and seasons of estrangement in their life together.

One source of that conflict was the presence of Charlotte von Kirschbaum in Barth's life and household. From 1929 on Kirschbaum was Barth's live-in secretary, undertaking research for the *Church Dogmatics*, preparing manuscripts for publication, traveling with Barth to professional lectures, and welcoming guests to the Bergli, a mountain retreat, where the two spent their summers. Barth and Kirschbaum's friendship was a true intimacy—although probably not sexual—and appears to be the one unblemished, though costly, success amid Barth's troubled relationships.

The Break with Liberalism

Barth began his academic career as a graduate assistant to the Ritschlian theologian, MARTIN RADE, and his liberal journal *Christliche Welt* (*Christian World*). A few years later, at the cusp of INDUSTRIALIZATION, he became pastor of the small rural parish of Safenwil, Switzerland. Barth plunged into the "labor question" and became a democratic socialist. He visited the healing mission of CHRISTOPH FRIEDRICH BLUMHARDT, Bad Boll, and came under the influence of Blumhardt's eschatological realism: Christ is Victor! Yet Safenwil did not strike Barth as a success. He could not translate his academic liberalism into the pulpit and could not hold together or integrate his socialism, soteriological realism, and strict Kantian theological method. It appears Barth held all three at once, with equal seriousness, but without resolution. Barth was never a systematizer—he opposed that kind of Cartesianism all his life—but he *was* a thinker of rigorous consistency. The decades from World War I to the launching of the *Church Dogmatics* in the early 1930s were marked by a relentless, vigorous, and polemical quest to find just this consistency.

Indeed we may see Barth's animus toward Schleiermacher, particularly vivid in the 1920s, as a counterweight, launched in desperation against the massive architectonic of the *Christian Faith,* a work Barth could only admire all his life. The first step away from Schleiermacher-inspired liberalism was the first edition of Barth's *Epistle to the Romans,* but it was the explosive and expressionistic second edition in 1922 that marked Barth as a theological revolutionary, and the term "Dialectic Theology" was born. In Barth's eyes dialectical theology cast a broad net: it repudiated a starting point in theology, championed by Schleiermacher, in which God and the world were given together in pious awareness; more positively, it replaced such "coinherence" by an external encounter of God and creature; and it signaled that theology must be in constant movement, resting in neither denial nor affirmation of theological claims.

Academic Theologian and Leader of the Confessing Church

Shortly after the first edition of the *Epistle to the Romans* was published Barth joined the faculty at the University of Göttingen, Germany. Although Barth continued to give lectures at a breathless pace—he had the productivity of a nineteenth-century novelist—Barth knew better than anyone how much he had to learn. It is a window into the influence and scope of theological liberalism to read what Barth, as a young professor, had not read: none of the "older Protestants," little of JOHN CALVIN, even less of the medieval scholastics. He set to remedying his blind spots at a feverish pace. Through his publications of the 1920s, from the *Göttingen Dogmatics,* his first stab at systematic work, to his lectures on Anselm, *Fides quaerens Intellectum* (1931), we see Barth reading the past with a real air of discovery. One way to understand Barth's revolution in theology is to see it as a movement from a Protestant margin to a Catholic center. By 1932, the year of the first volume of the *Church Dogmatics,* Barth stood squarely within the broad tradition of the Latin West, and his remarkable innovations in dogma were cast into high relief by the tradition that formed the backdrop.

Barth is often called the theologian of Basel, but in fact he had a mobile early career: Göttingen to 1925; Münster to 1930; and Bonn until his expulsion from Germany in 1935. By 1934 Barth was caught up in the thicket of Nazi bureaucracy and jurisprudence because he had refused to sign the Hitler loyalty oath or give the Nazi salute to begin his classes. His public reasons for refusal were rather tame—he claimed he would sign were he allowed to acknowledge God's law as supreme—but Barth's real views were already well known. In 1933 he had issued his condemnation of Nazism, "Theological Existence Today!" Some 37,000 copies were printed within the year. In 1935 Barth was removed from his professorship and exiled to Switzerland. Yet Barth remained a partisan of Ger-

many and the German people, and after Germany's defeat, he eagerly accepted an invitation to return to the rubble of Bonn to deliver lectures in theology: *Dogmatics in Outline.* Although lacking the technical depth of the *Church Dogmatics,* these lectures, with their wit, humanity, and quiet tenderness for the German people, may be the best introduction to Barth's mature work.

During World War II Barth supported the churches' resistance to Hitler through the CONFESSING CHURCH movement. The BARMEN DECLARATION, a confession of opposition to the Nazification of Christianity by the GERMAN CHRISTIANS, was forged largely by Barth and reflected his governing maxim in theology. The first commandment—Thou shalt have no other gods before me—demands complete loyalty to the God of Israel and forbids any effort to find the divine through "lesser gods," the forces of history, NATURE, or ideology. The Barmen Declaration, like the Confessing Church it announced, was an ambiguous achievement. It clearly opposed the attempt to make the church an arm of the Nazi state, but, as Barth later regretted, it did not expose or repudiate directly the "Aryan paragraph" (a prohibition even of baptized Jews in church orders) or the Nuremburg racial laws. Barth continued to advise from exile and exhorted the Swiss to oppose Nazism openly; he joined the Swiss army and stood sentry on its borders. Above all, however, Barth worked on the *Church Dogmatics,* already a theology of some thousand pages in the late 1930s.

The *Church Dogmatics*

The *Church Dogmatics,* massive as it is, was never completed, although Barth worked on it until his death. By any measure it must be considered one of the masterworks of Protestantism, indeed of Latin Christianity. A measure of its greatness is its resistance to summary or redescription. We might compare the *Dogmatics,* in this respect, to Euclid's *Elements:* the answers are not nearly as interesting or important as the work that leads one there. The first volume, *The Doctrine of the Word of God,* lays out a kind of post-Kantian theological method—the Word of God is the condition for the very possibility of theology. After that Barth settles down to a straightforward dogmatic work. Volume two, *The Doctrine of God,* embraces both the doctrine of Divine attributes or perfections and, like the Protestant scholastics, the doctrine of ELECTION. Perhaps surprising for one known for his opposition to all natural theology, Barth devotes volume three to the doctrine of creation. The *Dogmatics* breaks off with volume four, the *Doctrine of Reconciliation,* where Barth develops with magisterial completeness the doctrine of Christ's person and work. The fifth volume, never begun, promised a doctrine of Redemption and Last Things.

Common to the whole work is the conviction that Christ alone is the center of theology. It is not enough to say that Christ is the founder or teacher or even savior of the religion; it is not even sufficient to affirm that he is the Incarnate Son of God. Rather, Barth asserts that Christ, as Incarnate Word, is the *only* point of indwelling of God with creature—there is no *analogia entis* (analogy of being) or point of contact—and that Christ as eternal Son of the Father is the only proper object of divine election and foreordination. As the "Judge, judged in our place" Christ is the only victor over evil, a force Barth called "nothingness." Alternatively, we might express this Christological concentration under the category of covenant: In Reformed style Barth saw the divine pact with Israel—I shall be your God; you shall be my people—as the heart of God's work *ad extra* (toward the world), and all creation and providence constitute the stage setting for this pact, brought to its final and eternal fullness in Jesus Christ. In this way the people of Israel are the centerpiece of and key to all human history and the church is the "environment" or community of this one Jew, Jesus of Nazareth.

Barth's governing categories are thus historical and actualist in character: God is the triune event of Jesus Christ, whose person is the act of calling, judging, and saving. Barth made quiet use, throughout the *Dogmatics,* of current historical criticism of the Bible and modern philosophy and social sciences, although the explicit character of the *Dogmatics* is an unstudied openness to the Bible's narrative, figural, and dynamic unity. Although no inerrantist, Barth saw in Holy Scripture the unique revelation of God, whose Authority rested on its true center and content, Jesus Christ. Some of the most powerful and innovative exegeses in modern theology can be found in the *Church Dogmatics,* especially in volumes two and four.

Finally Barth exemplified his Reformed heritage in his conviction, expressed throughout the *Dogmatics,* that the Church and its Liturgy and Sacraments are not central to the Christian life, but are rather servants of its mission, to stand in solidarity with the world and announce its redemption. The church witnesses to Christ who is the only true means of Grace. From beginning to end the *Church Dogmatics* is an unfolding of the Augustinian and Reformation themes: *sola Scriptura, sola gratia, sola Christus.* Although some have identified the hallmark of the *Church Dogmatics* in its leisurely pace, its innovative Calvinism, or—for some critics—its "Neo-Orthodoxy," it may be better to find that hallmark in the work's joyful confidence.

Barth described himself as the "joyful partisan of the good God," and it is this exuberance that unites the great expanse of the *Church Dogmatics* and drives it on.

Conclusion

Karl Barth died in Basel in 1968. He did not found a theological school as such—indeed it would be hard to know how such a massive dogmatic work could be followed—but his legacy can be measured against two scales. First is the steady scholarship dedicated to assessing and developing themes in his dogmatic theology. Second and even more important is the widespread Protestant conviction, even by theological liberals, that theology is a discipline that must be carried out, not in blind allegiance to the past, but rather in lively conversation with Tradition, the past that is alive.

See also Theology; Theology, Twentieth Century

References and Further Reading

Primary Sources:

Barth, Karl. *Gesamtausgabe.* Zürich, Switzerland: TVZ, 1973.
——. *Church Dogmatics.* Edited and translated by G. W. Bromiley and T. F. Torrance. Edinburgh: T & T Clark, 1936–1969.
——. *Antwort* (*Answer,* a Festschrift with complete bibliography). Zürich, Switzerland: EVZ, 1956.
Busch, Eberhard. *Karl Barth: His Life from Letters and Autobiographical Texts.* Translated by J. Bowden. Philadelphia: Fortress, 1976.

Secondary Sources:

Hunsinger, George. *How to Read Karl Barth.* New York: Oxford University Press, 1991.
Jungel, Eberhard. *God's Being is Becoming.* Translated by J. Webster. Grand Rapids, MI: Wm. B. Eerdmans, 2001.
McCormack, Bruce. *Karl Barth's Critically Realistic Dialectical Theology.* New York: Oxford University Press, 1995.
Von Balthasar, H. U. *The Theology of Karl Barth.* Translated by E. Oakes, S.J. San Francisco: Ignatius Press, 1992.

Katherine Sonderegger

BASEL MISSION

The Evangelische Missionsgesellschaft Basel, otherwise known as the Basel Mission (BM), was founded in 1815 as an ecumenical and international Protestant mission to train candidates as missionaries to work overseas for various European missionary societies. The very early leaders were Rev. Nicolaus von Brunn and C. G. Blumhardt who served as president and inspector/director, respectively.

The Basel Mission had two major influences. First, a strong German Protestant Pietist influence (see PIETISM), particularly from the state of Württemberg, South Germany, spearheaded its founding at Basel, SWITZERLAND and provided the bulk of its leaders. Second, there was a strong trade influence, mainly because Basel was a strong trade center; the key sponsors of the mission were committed Christian businessmen.

The Basel Mission adopted the Pietistic theology with a strong biblical commitment; a strong emphasis on the importance of "personal CONVERSION" to Christ and individual piety; a strong Christian fellowship; a keen sense of PRAYER; and a deep commitment for mission and EVANGELISM. The Basel Mission avoided theological controversies and concentrated on the church's task of expanding the Kingdom of God on earth. It consequently became a major Protestant institution in Europe that trained men for organizations such as the CHURCH MISSIONARY SOCIETY of England and the Netherlands Missionary Society, that in turn sent these men overseas as missionaries.

After thirteen years of training missionaries the Basel Mission itself set out to send out missionaries. Its first attempt was in the Caucasus region of Southern RUSSIA, but the missionaries were expelled by the Russian dictatorship. The next attempt was in West AFRICA, first an unsuccessful one in LIBERIA in the 1820s and later a successful one in the Gold Coast (now Ghana) in 1828. After suffering initial setbacks because of illness that resulted in the death of fourteen missionaries between 1828 and 1913, the Basel Mission's mission in Ghana gained roots in the 1840s. Their success is mainly attributed to the involvement of a group of black Christian ex-slaves who were recruited from the West Indies to Ghana. Therefore the church they planted, the Presbyterian Church of Ghana, is the oldest Basel Mission partner church.

South INDIA was the second oldest and most concentrated field of the Basel Mission. They started work there in 1834. CHINA was the third Basel Mission field. Because China was neither a British nor a German colony, the Basel Mission faced a lot of opposition by the local people and authorities. Cameroon was added to the Basel Mission's fields when in 1886 the German colonial authorities invited the Mission to operate there. After the First World War, INDONESIA became part of Basel Mission's mission fields.

Generally the Basel Mission missionaries built a culture of Christian village life, developing agriculture, vernacular education, industry and trade, and providing social amenities in most of their mission fields. Altogether, by 1914, the Basel Mission had sent out more than 400 missionaries abroad. The two World Wars that brought in their trail economic poverty and the expulsion of the missionaries from most of their mission fields severely disrupted the work of the Basel Mission.

Today, the Basel Mission (now incorporated into Mission 21) continues to send short-term professionals known as fraternal workers who are invited by indigenous churches to collaborate with local agents of their respective fields. Mission 21 has a policy of promoting contextualization of the Gospel in the fields where they work. Mission 21 also joins other ecumenical institutions that promote missions including Pentecostals and Congregationalists (see PENTECOSTALISM; CONGREGATIONALISM).

See also Missionary Organizations; Missions

References and Further Reading

Jenkings, Paul. *A Short History of the Basel Mission.* Basel, Switzerland, 1989.

S. N. OMENYO

BATAK PROTESTANT CHRISTIAN CHURCH OF INDONESIA

With a membership of about 3.5 million in nearly 3,000 congregations, the Batak Protestant Christian Church (Huria Kristen Batak Protestan, HKBP) is the largest Protestant Church in Southeast Asia. Christian MISSIONS to the Batak lands in Tapanuli, Northern Sumatra were begun by the Dutch in 1857; in 1861 the first BAPTISM took place; in the same year the German Rhenish Mission (RMG), of a mixed Reformed-Lutheran character, entered the field. Ludwig Ingwer Nommensen (1834–1918), one of the great missionaries of that era, integrated Batak social structures into the incipient church, and so created a strong "people's church." Until the present day the encounter of the Christian faith with Batak culture and religious beliefs (ancestor worship) constitutes a theological and practical challenge.

In 1930 the HKBP became an autonomous body, but until World War II the Rhenish missionaries still occupied the leading positions. Justinus Sihombing, *Ephorus* (presiding bishop) 1942–1962, led it into the LUTHERAN WORLD FEDERATION (LWF) in 1952, although the HKBP church order and its confession of faith (1951; new confession 1996) contain Calvinist elements. This confession is also a splendid illustration of how a confession of faith reflects pertinent cultural issues (see CONFESSIONALIZATION). The church also joined the CCA and the WORLD COUNCIL OF CHURCHES in 1962 and was cofounder of the Council of Churches in Indonesia. The HKBP Nommensen University at Pematang Siantar and Medan was founded in 1954; in 1978 its theological faculty was transformed into a separate institute. The church produced Christian leaders at the national level, including Dr. T. S. G. Mulia (1896–1966); Amir Sjarifuddin (1907–1948), the only Christian who became prime minister of the Indonesian Republic; and the outstanding lay theologian General T. B. Simatupang (1920–1990).

Initially the HKBP included most ethnic subdivisions of the Batak people. In the course of time, however, these subdivisions formed independent church bodies. In the early twenty-first century the HKBP is mainly the church of the Toba Batak. Other separations were motivated by the opposition against foreign leadership (1927) or against alleged abuses (1964). Bataks also constitute the majority within the Indonesian Methodist Church. During the 1990s the church was deeply troubled by a long-term quarrel, fanned by the Soharto government; in the end the schism was healed.

Tapanuli is still the heartland of the HKBP, but as the Bataks migrated to other parts of INDONESIA, they took their churches along with them, even abroad. There are 170 congregations in Greater Jakarta alone, and four in the UNITED STATES.

See also Baptists; Dutch Reformed Church; Lutheranism; Methodism; Missionary Organizations; Missions

References and Further Reading

Aritonang, Jan S. *Mission Schools in Batakland (Indonesia) 1861–1940.* Leiden/New York/Cologne: Brill, 1994.
Hutauruk, J. Raplan. "Batak Churches" and "Batak Protestant Christian Church." In *A Dictionary of Asian Christianity,* edited by Scott Sunquist, 67–69. Grand Rapids, MI: Wm. B. Eerdmans, 2001.
Nyhus, Edward O. V. "An Indonesian Church in the midst of Social Change: The Batak Protestant Christian Church, 1942–1957." Ph.D. dissertation, University of Wisconsin–Madison, 1987.
Pedersen, Paul B. *Batak Blood and Protestant Soul: The Development of National Batak Churches in North Sumatra.* Grand Rapids, MI: Wm. B. Eerdmans, 1970.

THOMAS VAN DEN END

BAUMGARTEN, OTTO (1858–1934)

German theologian. Born January 29, 1858, in Munich, Baumgarten comes from the Protestant *Bildungsbürgertum.* His father was the liberal historian Hermann Baumgarten, and his cousin was MAX WEBER. After his university studies (Strasbourg, Göttingen, Heidelberg, and Zürich) and a brief pastorate, he received his doctorate in HALLE in 1887 and his university teaching license in 1889 in Berlin. Baumgarten was married in 1883, although his wife died in childbirth in the same year and he never remarried. From 1890 to 1894 he was a professor of practical theology at Jena, and from 1894 to 1926 he taught at Kiel. He died there on March 21, 1934.

The liberal Baumgarten influenced many areas of science, church, and politics. As a theologian Baumgarten, along with Paul Drews and Friedrich Niebergall, took part in a reorientation of the practical theology at the beginning of the twentieth century. Instead of a one-sided orientation on systematic theological questions, they successfully promoted the importance of other sciences (empirical sciences, social sciences, psychology, etc.). As a coeditor of the dictionary *Die Religion in Geschichte und Gegenwart* as well as publisher of the *Monatsschrift für Kirchliche Praxis* (since 1907 *Evangelische Freiheit*) he participated actively in the academic discussions of his time. In the *Evangelische Freiheit* Baumgarten regularly published a chronicle (*Kirchliche Chronik*), which showed him as a critical observer of the church and political events of his time.

Baumgarten participated in the work of the *Evangelisch-sozialen Kongress,* from 1911 to 1921 and was its chairman as a successor to ADOLF VON HARNACK. Despite differences in specific questions, Baumgarten stood with MARTIN RADE, FRIEDRICH NAUMANN, Paul Goehre, and Weber as an important representative of Protestant social liberalism. Baumgarten opted early for a social and democratic constitutional state, and he supported the demands of the civil social reformers who wanted to overcome the class society of the Empire with social welfare programs. Like other liberal Protestants, Baumgarten supported a separation of state and church. In 1896 he supported striking dock laborers in Hamburg; in 1911 and 1912 he defended the ministers Carl Jatho and Gottfried Traub, in so-called *Lehrbeanstandungsprozessen,* because of their religious opinions.

Politically Baumgarten was a follower of the national liberals. He supported a militarily strong position for GERMANY in Europe and was, for example, a member of the *Deutscher Flottenverein.* At the same time Baumgarten, who had close connections to English culture and politics, engaged in attempts to come to an agreement with Britain. In the First World War, Baumgarten fought against a politics of annexation. He represented the politics of reform and was for a democratization of Germany. Thus during the Weimar Republic he was among the most important supporters of democracy and republic within German Protestantism, and for several years he was a prominent member of the German Democratic Party (*Deutsche Demokratische Partei*). His public fight against anti-Semitism (among other things as a member of the *Verein zur Abwehr des Antisemitimus*) and his early argument against national socialism in the publication *Kreuz und Hakenkreuz* (1926) led to public conflicts with the Nationalsozialistische Deutsche Arbeiterpartei (NSDAP) Nazi party in the last years of his life.

See also Anti-Semitism; Church and State Overview; Confessing Church; German Christians; Liberal Protestantism and Liberalism; Socialism, Christian

References and Further Reading

Primary Source:

Baumgarten, Otto. *Meine Lebensgeschichte.* Tübingen, Germany: J.C.B. Mohr, 1929.

Secondary Sources:

Bassi, Hasko von. *Otto Baumgarten. Ein "moderner" Theologe im Kaiserreich und in der Weimarer Republik.* Frankfurt, Germany: Peter Lang, 1988.
Brakelmann, Günter. *Krieg und Gewissen. Otto Baumgarten als Politiker und Theologe im Ersten Weltkrieg.* Göttingen, Germany: Vandenhoeck & Ruprecht, 1991.

NORBERT FRIEDRICH

BAUMGARTEN, SIEGMUND JAKOB (1706–1757)

German theologian. Siegmund Jakob Baumgarten, praised by Voltaire as "the crown of German scholars," was born in Saxony March 14, 1706 the son of Pietist minister Jakob Baumgarten. He studied at the Halle Orphan Asylum (where his father was inspector general) and then went on to the University of Halle. He became inspector of the Halle Latin School in 1726 where he preached with G. A. Franke and later went on to join the theology faculty. He was appointed to a professorship in 1743. Baumgarten produced a vast body of work on a wide range of subjects before passing away July 4, 1757 in HALLE.

Baumgarten fused the Pietist tradition with the rigorous, logical, and systematic philosophy of his elder contemporary CHRISTIAN WOLFF (1679–1754), another famous citizen of Halle. In doing so, he sought to preserve the experiential and ethical PIETISM of PHILIPP JAKOB SPENER while embracing the scientific rationalism of his day. The result was an earnest ORTHODOXY that addressed almost every sphere of the Christian life, including history, dogmatics, exegesis, morals, and hermeneutics. It was Baumgarten's hope that fusing Pietism with rationalism would establish the validity of Pietistic faith in the world by demonstrating the compatibility of profound Christian devotion with ascendant human reason. His success is questionable.

Baumgarten's greatest student, admirer, and biographer, JOHANN SALOMO SEMLER, is sometimes referred to as "the father of rationalism," and he came to propagate a theological rationalism that eventually,

purposefully or not, displaced devout Pietism in nineteenth-century Prussia. For this reason Baumgarten is often viewed as a transitional figure from Pietism to rationalism, rather than a preserver of the former.

References and Further Reading

Primary Sources:

Baumgarten, S. J. *Auszug der Kirchengeschichte.* 4 vols. Halle: 1743–1762.
———. *Evangelische Glaubenslehre.* 3 vols. 1759–1760.
———. *Geschichte der Religionsparteien.* 1760.

Secondary Source:

Schloemann, Martin. *Siegmund Jacob Baumgarten: System und Geschichte in der Theologie des Übergangs zum Neuprotestantismus.* Göttingen, Germany: Vandenhoeck & Ruprecht, 1974.

JON PAUL SYDNOR

BAUR, FERDINAND CHRISTIAN (1792–1860)

German theologian. Baur was born in Schmiden near Stuttgart, Germany, on June 21, 1792, and died on February 12, 1860, in Tübingen. He was the founder of the new "Tübingen School" and was one of the most important Protestant theologians of the nineteenth century. Son of a pastor, he attended the Protestant schools of Blaubeuren and Maulbronn (1805–1809) and studied Protestant THEOLOGY at Tübingen (1809–1814). After successfully completing his university exam in 1814 at the head of his class, and then serving as a vicar, he started teaching as a "Repetent" (Tutor) in the renowned Evangelische Stift in Tübingen (also home to GEORG W. F. HEGEL in his student days). In 1817 Baur returned to the school of Blaubeuren as a professor, teaching classics and history, where DAVID F. STRAUSS and Friedrich Th. Vischer were among his pupils. It was in Blaubeuren that Baur developed his major thoughts. In 1826 Baur returned to Tübingen University as professor of ecclesiastical history, where he remained until his death.

In his 1828/29 lecture on "Christliche Symbolik" Baur described Protestantism and Roman Catholicism as necessary historic phases in the development of the Christian faith. As much as Baur emphasized the differences between the two, he also stated that they both carry certain aspects of truth. Protest arose from Baur's Roman Catholic colleague at Tübingen, JOHANN A. MÖHLER, who saw the subsuming of Protestantism back into the Roman Catholic church as the inevitable outcome of this dialectical approach. Baur responded with "Gegensatz des Katholizismus und Protestantismus nach den Prinzipien und Hauptdogmen der beiden Lehrbegriffe. [. . .]" (1833; in the second edition of 1836 he makes use of Hegelian concepts). Against Möhler, Baur emphasized the freedom of research and criticism against false, even Protestant, authorities. The classic term "historic-critical" derives from the subtitle of Baur's article "Über Zweck und Veranlassung des Römerbriefs [. . .]. Eine historisch-kritische Untersuchung" (1836).

See also Neo-orthodoxy

References and Further Reading

Primary Source:

Baur, F. C. *Ausgewählte Werke in Einzelausgaben,* edited by Klaus Scholder. Stuttgart/Bad Cannstatt: Frommann-Holzboog, 1963–1975.

Secondary Source:

Hodgson, Peter C. *The Formation of Historical Theology. A Study of F. C. Baur, New York 1966.* Oxford, UK: Horton Harris, The Tübingen School, 1975.

JOHANNES SCHWANKE

BAXTER, RICHARD (1615–1691)

Puritan divine. Baxter was a leading English Puritan (see PURITANISM) minister during the tumultuous decades of the seventeenth century. In his own mind a champion of church unity, Baxter nevertheless found himself embroiled in all of the religious and political controversies that beset ENGLAND from the onset of its CIVIL WAR through the Restoration of Charles II and the GLORIOUS REVOLUTION. He hoped for an inclusive national church that could embrace moderate Puritans like him but would also welcome a wide range of other Protestant believers into a body held together through common belief in what he called "mere Christianity."

Born in Rowton, Shropshire, November 12, 1615, Baxter received a spotty education before being ordained a deacon in the CHURCH OF ENGLAND in 1638. After brief stints in Dudley and Bridgnorth, he was called as curate to Kidderminster, Worcestershire in 1641, shortly before the outbreak of civil war. By that point, Baxter was already at odds with the Church of England's episcopal hierarchy in principle and practice; he specifically refused to swear the so-called "et cetera" oath that gave approval to the national church's DOCTRINE and discipline. When fighting commenced, he sided with Parliament, believing it offered the best chance for change toward political and religious moderation. He soon fled to Coventry, ostensibly for safety reasons, where he remained until he accepted a chaplaincy in OLIVER CROMWELL's army in 1645. To his dismay, he found that Parliament's cause had fallen into the hands of religious sectarians and political extremists, and that no amount of preaching or arguing on his part could change that.

Baxter returned to his Kidderminster parish in 1647 and began a successful ministry that continued until the Restoration. He poured his energies into being a preacher of "evangelical passion" and a pastor of gracious sensitivity to his flock of mostly weavers and other artisans. They responded favorably to his promotion of a Christian spirituality that celebrated humanity's rationality and physicality. He professed that the things of both the mind and the senses (perhaps especially natural beauty, music, and poetry) could aid in deepening one's devotion. Baxter communicated such sentiments to a wider audience in *The Saints Everlasting Rest* (1650), one of many devotional, pastoral, and theological works he wrote and published during the interregnum. Few if any of his writings generated more complaints than his first book, *Aphorisms of Justification* (1649), a controversial doctrinal treatise. Conversely, *The Reformed Pastor* (1656) garnered wide praise for the pastoral instruction it provided and the exemplary minister it showed Baxter to be. By that point, area clergy of various Protestant stripes had already welcomed Baxter's proposal to form a Worcestershire Association of Ministers, a sign of his growing prominence and a reflection of his broader concern for church unity on a national scale.

After Oliver Cromwell's death and his son Richard's short-lived rule (1658–1660), Baxter joined hosts of other Englishmen in endorsing and aiding the return of Charles II and the restoration of the monarchy. A believer in limited monarchy, Baxter wanted the English state to avoid any pro-Catholic or pro-French policy and to limit any further religious fragmentation among English Protestants. To that end, he resumed efforts to build a political consensus in favor of a comprehensive church settlement, one that would allow most of the country's Protestants to feel at home in the national church. The outlook seemed bright when Baxter was offered a royal chaplaincy, which he accepted, and the bishopric of Hereford, which he declined. The latter proved an omen of things to come. Baxter could not in good conscience embrace episcopal church governance, at least not in the form in which it existed before the Civil War. His efforts and those of his Puritan allies at the Savoy Conference of 1661, however, proved fruitless. Parliament's Act of Uniformity (1662) not only reestablished episcopacy, it demanded rigid compliance with the liturgical forms set out in the BOOK OF COMMON PRAYER. In the face of this exclusive religious settlement, Baxter reluctantly left the established church and joined the ranks of nonconformists (see NONCONFORMITY).

During the last thirty years of his life, Baxter remained committed to the same causes that had animated him earlier. He emerged as the leader of the moderate or "presbyterian" branch of nonconformists (see PRESBYTERIANISM), and continued to work for sufficient concessions to allow them to rejoin a modified Church of England. Although he had no parish or pulpit of his own, he managed to preach often and well, adding to his national reputation. With no pastoral duties, he devoted even more of his time to writing, publishing more than 100 additional works, including *Richard Baxter's Catholick Theologie* (1675), and maintaining a voluminous correspondence. He exchanged letters with English notables including JOHN TILLOTSON, ROBERT BOYLE, WILLIAM PENN, JOHN ELIOT, and INCREASE MATHER, but also with many ordinary folk. More often than not, his books or someone else's were the main topic of discussion. Baxter's views were eclectic enough to prompt attacks from all sides and dangerous enough in the minds of some state officials to warrant his arrest. He was tried for sedition in 1685 and imprisoned for 18 months. Baxter lived long enough to witness the Glorious Revolution (1688) and the Act of Toleration (1689), a measure that granted most Protestant nonconformists civil liberty and freedom of worship but did not re-create England's national church along the comprehensive lines Richard Baxter had always wanted. Baxter died December 8, 1691.

References and Further Reading

Primary Source:

Baxter, Richard. *The Practical Works of the Rev. Richard Baxter.* 4 vols. London, 1707.

Secondary Sources:

Keeble, Neil H. *Richard Baxter: Puritan Man of Letters.* Oxford: Oxford University Press, 1982.
Keeble, Neil H. and Geoffrey F. Nuttall, eds. *Calendar of the Correspondence of Richard Baxter.* 2 vols. Oxford: Clarendon Press, 1991.
Lamont, William M. *Richard Baxter and the Millennium.* Totowa, NJ: Rowman and Littlefield, 1979.
Nuttall, Geoffrey F. *Richard Baxter.* London: Thomas Nelson, 1965.
Trueman, Carl. "Richard Baxter on Christian Unity: A Chapter in the Enlightening of English Reformed Orthodoxy." *Westminster Theological Journal* 61 (1999): 53–71.

RICHARD W. POINTER

BAYLE, PIERRE (1647–1706)

French philosopher. Born in Carla (Languedoc), FRANCE in 1647 Bayle was known as a skeptical philosopher and critic who advocated TOLERATION for atheists, Jews, and Muslims in *Miscellaneous Thoughts on the Comet* (1682–1683); *What A Wholly Catholic France Under Louis the Great is Like* (1685) and the *Philosophical Commentary* (1686–1687). He defended the right of conscience to err, without state interference, laying the foundation for separation of CHURCH AND STATE before and after the FRENCH REVOLUTION. Bayle's *Historical and Critical Dictionary* (1697) influenced Diderot's *Encyclopedia* and Voltaire's critique of Roman Catholicism.

Bayle attended the College of Puy-Laurens, and for eighteen months, the Jesuit University of Toulouse, where he excelled at debate and converted to Rome. Relapsed, he fled to Geneva, returning to France to teach philosophy at the Protestant Academy of Sedan. When Louis XIV closed it (1681), Bayle took a similar position in Rotterdam.

As editor and main contributor to the monthly *News From the Republic of Letters* (1684–1687), Bayle influenced francophone Europe. His *General Criticism* (1685) of the Jesuit Louis Maimbourg's *History of Calvinism* put PIERRE JURIEU's own in the shade. Their animosity manifested itself in controversies over Calvinist ORTHODOXY, repatriation, PACIFISM, citizenship, and other political and confessional issues.

Although Bayle maintained membership in the Reformed Church of Rotterdam, where he was buried, and admired MARTIN LUTHER's courage and JOHN CALVIN's *Institutes,* he felt the REFORMATION had tyrannized over conscience. Influenced by Augustinian predestinarianism, Bayle denied that dogma or God's mysteries could ever be certainly understood. His writing, misjudged as irreligious until the later twentieth century, gradually cast doubt on dogmatism, but was consistent with the Hebraic notion of an inscrutable God.

References and Further Reading

Labrousse, Elisabeth. *Pierre Bayle.* 2 vols. The Hague: Martinus Nijhoff, 1963.
Robinson, Howard. *Bayle the Sceptic.* New York: Columbia University Press, 1931.
Tinsley, Barbara Sher. *Pierre Bayle's Reformation, Conscience and Criticism on the Eve of the Enlightenment.* Selinsgrove, PA: Susquehanna University Press, 2001.

BARBARA SHER TINSLEY

BEECHER, HENRY WARD (1813–1887)

American clergy. Considered the greatest preacher of his era, Henry Ward Beecher was a charismatic orator whose powers of persuasion helped popularize and advance the cause of the abolition of slavery in mid-nineteenth-century America and promoted a liberal social agenda from his pulpit late into the century. Beecher's advocacy for HUMAN RIGHTS and justice earned both him and his congregation, Plymouth Congregational Church of Brooklyn, a place in history. Plymouth came to be known as the "Grand Central Depot" of the Underground Railroad, Beecher "one of [its] most prominent Directors," and its congregation "large stockholders in that line."

Born on June 24, 1813 in Litchfield, Connecticut, he was the son of LYMAN BEECHER, a leader of the Congregational Church who was himself a gifted preacher, and Roxana Beecher. Henry was one of the couple's eleven children, who also included Catherine (b. 1800), Edward (b. 1803), HARRIET BEECHER STOWE (b. 1811), and Isabella Beecher Hooker (b. 1822). Henry Ward Beecher married Eunice Bullard in 1837 and the couple had ten children.

From 1826 to 1830 Beecher attended Mount Pleasant Classical Institute in Amherst, Massachusetts. In 1834 he graduated from Amherst College, and in 1837 received a divinity degree from Lane Theological Seminary. During his years in seminary Beecher first went public with his antislavery message, writing editorials supporting abolition in the *Cincinnati Journal,* a Presbyterian publication. Ordained in the "New School" Presbytery of Cincinnati, Ohio in 1838, he served first as a pastor of the First Presbyterian Church in Lawrenceburg, Indiana in 1837, following which he served from 1839 to 1847 as pastor of the Second Presbyterian Church of Indianapolis, Indiana.

For the rest of his career, from 1847 to 1887, he served as pastor of Plymouth Church (now Plymouth Church of the Pilgrims) in Brooklyn, New York, a parish gathered and built for him by five dedicated admirers. From this church he profoundly influenced public discourse on the issues of mid-nineteenth-century America. From his earliest days of preaching, Beecher stood in opposition to the prevailing Calvinist theology (which his father propounded) of humankind's utter depravity, stressing instead God's love in Jesus. Beecher shared with his siblings "the conviction that all human beings exhibited nothing intrinsically flawed that might prevent them from achieving their full potential through the exercise of their freedom" (Brauer).

His message was uplifting and strikingly different from what American parishioners were accustomed to hearing in the mid-nineteenth century—as he spread "the good news about salvation" for all believers instead of "the bad news about damnation" (Ryan). So popular was this message and the powerful delivery of his sermons that he regularly drew a crowd of 2,500 on Sundays. His Brooklyn church became a necessary stop for visitors to New York. Beecher's preaching was a precursor by more than a century of a similarly affirmative good news about God and the gospel that was delivered from many mainstream Protestant pulpits in the late twentieth and early twenty-first centuries.

Rather than emphasizing dogma or creeds in his sermons, Beecher addressed social issues from the pulpit—beginning by advocating for the abolition of slavery and continuing with leadership in other causes including WOMEN's rights, TEMPERANCE, and the need to wipe out civil corruption. In 1854 Beecher led his congregation in strong opposition to the passage of the Kansas–Nebraska Act. Through their successful efforts to raise funds to buy rifles for northern settlers who sought to move to Kansas and establish it as a free (rather than slaveholding) territory, his name entered the popular vernacular when these rifles became known as "Beecher (or Beecher's) Bibles." At the start of the CIVIL WAR, Beecher raised money to support a volunteer Union regiment. In 1863 he conducted a lecture tour of ENGLAND to popularize the Union cause to sometimes skeptical audiences, who were often won over thanks to Beecher's oratorical gifts. After the end of the war Beecher characteristically advocated reconciliation, affirming his optimistic view of human potential. Beecher's lifetime of active involvement in politics and direct advocacy allied him first with the Free Soil Party, which he joined in 1852, and then the Republican Party, to which he belonged from 1860 onward.

Despite his forward thinking on many issues of the day, Beecher was influenced by the values of the Victorian Era in which he came of age, a period that historian Carl E. Schorske has described as "morally secure, righteous, and repressive . . . intellectually committed to the rule of the mind over the body and to a latter-day Voltairism [of] . . . social progress through science, education, and hard work." In this climate, Beecher promoted a THEOLOGY that drew heavily on the most forward-leading secular thought of the time, "synthesizing prevalent ideas from outside the world of religion and articulating them in terms the common man could understand." Beecher gave theological substance to the idealistic philosophy of the romantic poets and philosophers like WILLIAM WORDSWORTH, Thomas Carlyle, and SAMUEL TAYLOR COLERIDGE, showing that God's spirit was to be found not outside the world but within it—both in the beauty of the natural world and in the inherent goodness of humanity (Abbott:xxi). In this way Beecher synthesized the elements of what has been described as a "new democratic faith" for midcentury America, incorporating "Emerson's self-reliance, Webster's constitutionalism, CHARLES GRANDISON FINNEY's pietistic-perfectionism, and Francis Wayland's laissez-faire capitalism" (Abbott:xvi). As the century progressed Beecher also embraced DARWINISM. It can be argued that, even more than ABRAHAM LINCOLN or RALPH WALDO EMERSON, Beecher stands as the "preeminent spokesman for his age," with his version of "romantic evangelical Christianity [that both] carried the nation into the [Civil] War and [subsequently] reunited it through liberal Protestant evolutionism after Lincoln's death" (Abbott:xix).

Beecher extended his influence beyond the pulpit and lecture circuit through a lifetime of publication. From 1861 to 1863, he served as editor of *The Independent,* a Congregational publication, and from 1870 to 1881 was editor of his own journal, the *Christian Union.* He wrote and published extensively, including publishing his weekly sermons from Plymouth Church for several decades. In 1844 he wrote a popular pamphlet, *Seven Lectures to Young Men.* Among his many well-known and widely read books were *The Life of Jesus, the Christ* (1871) and *Evolution and Religion* (1885).

In 1874 Beecher's life was marked by controversy and his reputation seriously damaged. He was sued for damages totaling one hundred thousand dollars by Theodore Tilton, a former coworker, friend, and member of Beecher's Brooklyn congregation, for allegedly committing adultery with Tilton's wife, Elizabeth M. Richards Tilton, four years earlier. This was considered one of the great scandals of the post–Civil War era. The trial in 1875 lasted six months and ended in a hung jury. Beecher later was cleared of all charges by a panel of his own Plymouth Church. Although the tarnish of scandal clung to Beecher, he remained in his pulpit and continued to be widely popular and influential for the rest of his life as a preacher, writer, and public speaker. Beecher died in Brooklyn of a cerebral hemorrhage in March 1887, and his funeral was attended by thousands.

See also Congregationalism; Liberal Protestantism and Liberalism; Slavery, Abolition of

References and Further Reading

Primary Sources:

Beecher, Henry Ward. *Bible Studies: Readings in the Early Books of the Old Testament, with Familiar Comment, Given in 1878–79 by Henry Ward Beecher.* Edited from stenographic notes of T. J. Ellinwood by John R. Howard. New York: Fords, Howard, and Hulbert, 1893.
———. *Evolution and Religion.* New York: Fords, 1885.
———. *God Unknowable, and How to Know Him.* London: James Clarke, 1876.
———. *Lectures to Young Men: On Various Important Subjects.* Pamphlet, 1844.
———. *The Life of Jesus, the Christ.* New York: J. B. Ford, 1871.
———. *Morning and Evening Exercises: Selected from the Published and Unpublished Writings of the Rev. Henry Ward Beecher.* Edited by Lyman Abbott. New York: Harper, 1874.
———. *New Star Papers, or Views and Experiences of Religious Subjects.* New York: Derby and Jackson, 1859.
———. *The Overture of Angels.* New York: J. B. Ford, 1870, c. 1869.
———. *Proverbs from Plymouth Pulpit.* New York: D. Appleton, 1887.
———. *Twelve Lectures to Young Men.* New York: Ford, Howard, and Hulbert, 1884.
———. "War and Emancipation." A Thanksgiving sermon preached in the Plymouth Church, Brooklyn, NY, November 21, 1861.
———. *Yale Lectures on Preaching.* New York: J. B. Ford, 1872.

Secondary Sources:

Abbott, Lyman. *Henry Ward Beecher.* Introduction by William McLoughlin. Reprint of 1903 edition published by Houghton-Mifflin, Boston. New York: Chelsea House, 1980.
Brauer, Jerald C. "Introduction." In Stephen H. Snyder, *Lyman Beecher and His Children.* xv. Brooklyn, NY: Carlson Publishing, 1991.
Clark, Clifford Edward, Jr. *Henry Ward Beecher: Spokesman for Middle-Class America.* Urbana: University of Illinois Press, 1978.
Fox, Richard Wrightman. *Trials of Intimacy: Love and Loss in the Beecher-Tilton Scandal.* Chicago: University of Chicago Press, 1999.
Glenn, Myra C. *Thomas K. Beecher: Minister to a Changing America, 1824–1900.* Westport, CT: Greenwood Press, 1996.
Goodell, John. "The Triumph of Moralism in New England Piety: A Study of Lyman Beecher, Harriet Beecher Stowe, and Henry Ward Beecher." Ph.D. thesis, Pennsylvania State University. Ann Arbor, MI: Xerox University Microfilms, 1976.
Plymouth Church of the Pilgrims, Brooklyn, NY website: www.plymouthchurch.org
Rourke, Constance. *Trumpets of Jubilee: Henry Ward Beecher, Harriet Beecher Stowe, Lyman Beecher, Horace Greeley, P.T. Barnum.* New York: Harcourt, Brace and World, 1963.
Ryan, Halford R. *Henry Ward Beecher: Peripatetic Preacher.* Westport, CT: Greenwood Press, 1990.
Schorske, Carl E. *Fin-de-Siecle Vienna: Politics and Culture.* New York: Vintage Books, 1981.
Shaplen, R. *Free Love and Heavenly Sinners.* New York: Knopf, 1954.
Snyder, Stephen H. *Lyman Beecher and His Children: The Transformation of a Religious Tradition.* Brooklyn, NY: Carlson Publishing, 1991.
Theodore Tilton vs. Henry Ward Beecher: Action for Criminal Conspiracy tried in the City Court of Brooklyn, Chief Justice Joseph Nielson, presiding, verbatim report by the official stenographer. 1875. Microfiche. New York: Burke Library, Union Theological Seminary.

PAUL WILLIAM BRADLEY

BEECHER, LYMAN (1775–1863)

American theologian. A Congregationalist and Presbyterian pastor, revivalist, reformer, and theological educator, Lyman Beecher was one of the best-known

American clergymen of the first half of the nineteenth century. Born in New Haven, Connecticut, Beecher became a preacher of the Second Great Awakening (see AWAKENINGS) under the influence of TIMOTHY DWIGHT, who became president of Yale College during Beecher's student years there. As a revivalist Beecher preached a modified CALVINISM similar to that of his theologian friend, NATHANIEL WILLIAM TAYLOR, that also provided theological content for an ongoing battle with Unitarianism. He was also active in promoting social reforms, especially TEMPERANCE and SABBATARIANISM, which he understood as harbingers of a coming millennium.

After pastorates in East Hampton, New York; Litchfield, Connecticut; and Boston, Beecher in 1832 accepted the presidency of Lane Seminary in Cincinnati. There he became embroiled in controversies over abolitionism, in which his chief opponent was THEODORE DWIGHT WELD, over his anti-Catholicism, as evidenced in his 1835 *A Plea for the West,* and over his "New School" theology. Although acquitted of HERESY by the Presbyterian General Assembly in 1835, Beecher's views were nonetheless a precipitating cause of the Old School–New School schism of 1837.

Retired after 1850 Beecher died in Brooklyn, New York. Later generations have often forgotten his contemporary significance, perhaps in part because of the fame of his several children, especially HARRIET BEECHER STOWE and HENRY WARD BEECHER.

See also Millenarians and Millennialism; Slavery, Abolition of; Unitarian-Universalist Association

References and Further Reading

Primary Source:

Cross, Barbara M., ed. *The Autobiography of Lyman Beecher.* 2 vols. Cambridge, MA: Belknap Press of Harvard University Press, 1961.

Secondary Sources:

Harding, Vincent. *A Certain Magnificence: Lyman Beecher and the Transformation of American Protestantism, 1775–1863.* Brooklyn, NY: Carlson Publishing, 1991.
Henry, Stuart C. *Unvanquished Puritan: A Portrait of Lyman Beecher.* Grand Rapids, MI: Wm. B. Eerdmans, 1973.

DONALD L. HUBER

BELGIC CONFESSION OF 1561

The Belgic Confession is the first general formulation of Reformed faith for the NETHERLANDS. Its title, sometimes given in Latin as *Confessio Belgica,* refers to the whole of the Low Countries, both north and south, given that the confession was written before the division into

what eventually became the Netherlands and Belgium. Guy de Brès, a Reformed pastor from the southern town of Mons, drafted the text, perhaps as early as 1559. A French version was published in 1561; a Dutch translation appeared the next year. Reformed leaders sent a copy to King Philip II of Spain, the Habsburg ruler of the Netherlands. They accompanied the text with a petition declaring obedience to the civil magistrate, even as the supplicants offered what they regarded as a true declaration of Christian belief. The governing authorities firmly rejected this plea for acceptance and TOLERATION. Indeed, several years later, in 1567, de Brès himself suffered martyrdom.

The text contains thirty-seven articles that draw on JOHN CALVIN's grand design and are closely modeled on the GALLICAN CONFESSION of 1559. The first eleven articles address knowledge of God, Holy Scripture, and the nature of the Trinity. Articles 12 through 15 concentrate on humanity and the fall. The next half dozen possess a Christological orientation with explanations of the Incarnation and Christ's dual nature. Human redemption through Jesus Christ, the next logical subject, is discussed in articles 22 through 26. A sequence of eight articles then touches upon the church, ecclesiastical polity, and the SACRAMENTS. Article 36 considers issues surrounding civil government, whereas the final article, appropriately enough, speaks to the Last Judgment.

See also Martyrs and Martyrologies

References and Further Reading

"The Belgic Confession" (French text with English translation). In *The Creeds of Christendom,* edited by Philip Schaff, vol. 3, 383–436. Sixth edition. Grand Rapids, MI: Baker, 1990.

RAYMOND A. MENTZER

BELL, GEORGE KENNEDY ALLEN (1883–1958)

Bishop of Chichester. After his studies at Oxford University, George Bell was ordained in 1907 to an assistant curacy at Leeds, in northeastern ENGLAND, where he gave special attention to the intellectual life of underprivileged young men. He taught at Oxford 1910–1914, and was then called to be chaplain (secretary) to Archbishop RANDALL THOMAS DAVIDSON of CANTERBURY. This gave him insight into the national and international responsibilities of his church, as well as its need for self-government. As Dean of Canterbury Cathedral from 1924 to 1929, Bell began his active support of the arts and artists, most conspicuously, the dramatists John Masefield, T. S. ELIOT, and Dorothy L. Sayers.

It was a government-sponsored cultural mission to SWEDEN in 1942 that brought Bell into contact with DIETRICH BONHOEFFER and allowed him to act as an intermediary between German church leaders in opposition to Hitler and the British government. As Bishop of Chichester (1929–1958), Bell led the Anglican church into the Life and Work Movement and into the WORLD COUNCIL OF CHURCHES. Bell supported the formation of the united Churches of South India and of North India and helped begin unity talks with METHODISM. He advocated for the unemployed and for refugees from Nazi oppression, as well as in support for the persecuted CONFESSING CHURCH in Germany. During the Second World War, he protested publicly against bombing of civilians.

On his memorial plaque in Chichester Cathedral, Bell is described as "A True Pastor, Poet and Patron of the Arts, Champion of the Oppressed, and Tireless Worker for Christian Unity."

See also North India, Church of; South India, Church of

References and Further Reading

Primary Source:

Bell, George K. A. "The Church and The Resistance Movement" (1957), in, *I Knew Dietrich Bonhoeffer*. Edited by Wolf-Dieter Zimmermann and Ronald Gregor Smith; translated by Käthe Gregor Smith. London: Collins/Fontana, 1967, pp. 196–211.

Secondary Source:

Jasper, Ronald C. D. *George Bell, Bishop of Chichester*, London: Oxford University Press, 1967.

DAVID TRIPP

BENGEL, JOHANN ALBRECHT
(1687–1752)

Lutheran theologian. Born June 24, 1687, near Stuttgart, GERMANY, Bengel studied THEOLOGY in Tübingen between 1703 and 1709. He was appointed tutor at the university there and became teacher at a monastery school in Denkendorf near Esslingen (Württemberg) in 1713. In preparation for assuming that office, Bengel was granted an extensive leave to visit other schools. This took him to HALLE, where AUGUST HERMANN FRANCKE had established a number of institutions, most of which were educational in nature. The encounter with Francke and the PIETISM he represented left a lasting impression on Bengel, particularly the emphasis on CONVERSION, which he embraced. Back in Denkendorf, Bengel focused for many years on his teaching responsibilities, and it was not until the early 1740s that his career

took a more public turn. Beginning in 1741 he was promoted to increasingly more prestigious ecclesiastical positions in Württemberg; in 1749 he was made a member of the Consistory.

Aware of the inaccessibility of useful and reliable editions of ancient Christian texts, Bengel began a prolific editing career, which eventually focused on preparing an edition of the Greek New Testament. This edition appeared in two version in 1734, a large edition with a critical apparatus, which summarized the editorial principles and listed variant readings, and a "pocket edition" that essentially included only the Greek text with brief annotations.

Nine years later Bengel published a two-volume *Gnomen Novi Testamenti,* a thorough commentary on the New Testament. Alongside these textual efforts, Bengel also published other works, such as a commentary on the Book of Revelation, which he saw as a handbook of church history. His studies suggested to him the date of June 18, 1836, as the date of the Second Coming.

Bengel died November 2, 1752, in Stuttgart.

References and Further Reading

Burk, Johann Chr. Fr. *Dr. Johann Albrecht Bengels Leben und Wirken.* Stuttgart, 1831.

HANS J. HILLERBRAND

BENNETT, JOHN COLEMAN
(1902–1995)

American ethicist. Bennett is perhaps most known for his contributions to social ethics. A self-proclaimed liberal theologian, Bennett produced a vast literature of books and journal articles that dealt with ETHICS, ECUMENISM, international affairs, COMMUNISM, and church relations. He also was cofounder of the influential journal *Christianity and Crisis*. He was a social activist who participated in the CIVIL RIGHTS MOVEMENT and openly opposed U.S. involvement in the Vietnam War. To help voice opposition to this war, Bennett cofounded, with Rabbi Abraham J. Heschel, the organization Clergy and Laymen Concerned About Vietnam.

Bennett was born in Kingston, Ontario, CANADA, the son of a Presbyterian minister. He was educated at Williams College, Oxford University, and Union Theological Seminary and was an ordained minister for the Congregational Church. Bennett began his career as a professor of Christian THEOLOGY and the philosophy of religion. His teaching positions included Auburn Seminary (1931–1938), the Pacific School of Religion (1938–1943), and Union Theological Seminary where he was dean (1955) and then president (1963).

Throughout his career Bennett was involved in a variety of ecumenical activities. He promoted ecumenism in the college classroom, he served on the Second Assembly of the WORLD COUNCIL OF CHURCHES (1954), the World Council of Churches Department of Church and Society, and other ecumenical councils and conferences. His ethics focused on the social engagement of Christianity. John C. Bennett ended his career as president of Union Theological Seminary in 1970 and died in 1995 at the age of 92.

See also Liberal Protestantism and Liberalism

References and Further Reading

Primary Sources:

Bennett, John Coleman. *Social Salvation: A Religious Approach to the Problems of Social Change.* New York: Scribner, 1935.
———. *Christianity and Communism.* New York: Association, 1952.
———. *Christians and the State.* New York: Scribner, 1958.

Secondary Source:

Long, Edward Leroy Jr., and Robert T. Handy, eds. *Theology and Church in Times of Change: Essays in Honor of John Coleman Bennett.* Philadelphia: Westminster, 1970.

JAY LAUGHLIN

BENTHAM, JEREMY (1748–1832)

English philosopher. Bentham was born in London on February 15, 1748 and began his studies at the Westminster School in 1755 at the age of seven. By fifteen Bentham completed his bachelor's degree at Queen's College Oxford. He left the legal profession soon after his admission to the Bar in 1769 and began a lifelong study of philosophy. In founding Utilitarianism, Bentham developed an influential ethical philosophy that sought to maximize pleasure in life and minimize pain. He died June 6, 1832, and an effigy of his body containing his bones and clothing resides at the University College, London.

In the preface of *A Fragment on Government* (1776), Bentham introduced the concise thesis of Utilitarianism: "the greatest happiness of the greatest number." In *Introduction to the Principals of Morals and Legislation* (1789), Bentham posited that good and evil could best be determined by calculating the amount of pleasure against the amount of pain. He applied this "principle of utility" to many practical topics such as prison reform, jurisprudence, and animal welfare. Bentham funded *The Westminster Review* (est. 1823), a journal devoted to circulating Utilitarian positions on social issues. He remained decidedly hostile toward religion. A strident atheist, Bentham considered the ideal society to be completely secular. In *Church of Englandism* (1818) he argued for disestablishment. The Anglican Church, Bentham said, encouraged rational laxity on the part of believers. Bentham's *Analysis of the Influence of Natural Religion* (1822) faulted religiously based moral systems for their lack of scientific reasoning.

See also Anglicanism; Empirical Theology; Ethics

References and Further Reading

Crimmins, James E. "Bentham on Religion: Atheism and the Secular Society." *Journal of the History of Ideas* 47 no. 1 (January–March 1986): 95–110.
Dinwiddy, John Rowland. *Bentham.* Oxford and New York: Oxford University Press, 1989.

ARTHUR J. REMILLARD

BENTLEY, RICHARD (1662–1742)

English theologian. Bentley was born in Oundle, Yorkshire, England, in 1662 and died in Cambridge in 1742. He was a noted CHURCH OF ENGLAND clergyman, Master of Trinity College, Cambridge, Regius professor of divinity, archdeacon of Ely, and classical and New Testament textual critic. After graduation in St. John's College, Oxford, and a short time as a schoolteacher, Bentley first became a private tutor and then librarian to the king. In 1691 he contributed an appendix to Dr. John Mill's edition of the history of John of Antioch, or "Malelas," in which his analysis of the text proved that this chronicle was written centuries later than it claimed to be. Bentley also made important critical observations on the fifth-century New Testament manuscript, the Codex Alexandrinus.

In 1692–1693 Bentley gave the first series of the Boyle Lectures, endowed to defend Christian belief against atheism and DEISM (effectively, against THOMAS HOBBES). This series, finally published as *A Confutation of Atheism,* leaned heavily on the findings of ISAAC NEWTON, with Newton's general approval. In 1700, after his crushing acumen had proved that the *Epistles of Phalaris* and other works were spurious, he was appointed Master of Trinity.

Next to the Boyle Lectures and his orthodox apology, *Remarks upon a Late Discourse of Free Thinking* (1713), his chief theological work was his *Proposals for Printing a New Edition of the Greek Testament and St. Hierom's Latin Version* (1721), pointing to the oldest Greek manuscripts and the Vulgate for recovering the text as it had been in the early fourth century. Although not carried out, his project helped to establish the need, possibility, and methods of such an edition.

References and Further Reading

Primary Source:

Dyce, Alexander, ed. *The Works of Richard Bentley, D.D.* 3 vols. London: 1836–1838; reprinted New York: AMS Press, 1966.

Secondary Source:

Jebb, R. C. "Bentley, Richard." In *Dictionary of National Biography,* vol. II, 306–314. London: Oxford University Press, 1921–1922.

DAVID TRIPP

BERGGRAV, EIVIND (1884–1959)

Norwegian lutheran bishop. The son of a bishop, Berggrav studied at the University of Oslo with the intention of becoming a pastor, but a crisis of faith postponed his decision to seek ordination for many years. He pursued further study in GERMANY, edited a periodical called *Church and Culture,* and taught in high schools for ten years, before finally accepting a pastorate in 1919. From 1925 to 1929 he served as chaplain at a prison in Oslo, during which time he also wrote a doctoral dissertation in the psychology of religion.

In 1929 he was appointed bishop of Hålogaland, NORWAY's most northern diocese, and in 1937 he was called to be bishop of Oslo and primate of the Church of Norway. Because of his reputation as a liberal thinker, this appointment was strongly opposed by Ole Hallesby, leader of the Pietists within the church. In time, however, Berggrav gained widespread support because of his efforts to improve relations between liberals and conservatives. After the German invasion of Norway in 1940 he created the Joint Christian Council to facilitate cooperation between all church factions in opposition to the Nazis. In 1942 Berggrav and the other Lutheran bishops all resigned in protest against government interference in the churches. After the Joint Christian Council issued "The Foundation of the Church," a confessional document stressing the Christian obligation to take a stand against tyrannical and unjust state authorities, Berggrav was arrested. As a leader of the Norwegian struggle against Nazism, he spent the duration of World War II imprisoned in a rural cottage.

After the liberation of Norway he was both admired and attacked for his efforts to restrain vengeance against Nazi collaborators. In the postwar period he was active in the formation of the WORLD COUNCIL OF CHURCHES until his retirement in 1950.

See also Liberal Protestantism and Liberalism; Lutheranism, Germany; Lutheranism, Scandinavia; Pietism

References and Further Reading

Heling, Arnd. *Die Theologie Eivind Berggravs im norwegischen Kirchenkampf.* Neukirchem-Vluyn: Neukirchener, 1992.
Robertson, Edwin. *Bishop of the Resistance: a Life of Eivind Berggrav.* St. Louis, MO: Concordia Publishing House, 2000.

ERIC LUND

BERKELEY, GEORGE (1685–1753)

Anglo-Irish clergyman and philosopher. Berkeley was born in or near Kilkenny, Ireland, on March 12, 1685. After a preparatory education in Kilkenny, he entered Trinity College in Dublin, receiving his B. A. in 1704 and his M. A. in 1707. Three years later he accepted ordination in the Church of Ireland, the Irish counterpart of the CHURCH OF ENGLAND. At this point, only twenty-five years of age, Berkeley had also written two of the major philosophical treatises upon which his reputation as an original and provocative thinker depends (*A New Theory of Vision,* 1709, and *A Treatise Concerning the Principles of Human Knowledge,* 1710). A third work, published in 1713, polished that reputation to an even greater brightness (*Three Dialogues between Hylas and Philonous*).

Although Berkeley seemed destined to pursue an academic career of some distinction, probably at his alma mater, he left Ireland in 1713 for England, where he found much stimulation and intellectual excitement in the company of poet Alexander Pope (1688–1744), politician Joseph Addison (1672–1719), writer Richard Steele (1672–1729), and his own countryman, satirist JONATHAN SWIFT (1667–1745). He then completed two tours of the European continent, the second one lasting five years, from 1716 to 1720. When he returned to England and Ireland, he found what he perceived to be a society in serious moral decline. Speaking of England in particular, he wrote in 1721 that "other nations have been wicked, but we are the first who have been wicked on principle."

Though Berkeley had been appointed senior lecturer (*in absentia*) at Trinity College in 1717, he saw greater financial security in obtaining a post in the Church of Ireland that carried with it a guaranteed annual income. This came in 1724 with his appointment as dean of Derry, a position that suggested his clerical side would now dominate the philosophical one. Even more surprising, perhaps, was Berkeley's determination to become a missionary, with the stipend from Derry to serve as a kind of launching pad that would propel him all the way to the New World.

Berkeley believed that the old world was in decline and that the New World now offered the greatest promise for a resurgence of religion and virtue. Athens and Rome were no more, and soon Paris and London, too, would fall into ruin.

Berkeley wrote:

Westward the Course of Empire takes it Way;
    The first four Acts already past,
A fifth shall close the Drama with the Day;
    Time's noblest Offspring is the last.

Berkeley traveled to the Island of Bermuda, with the dream of erecting a college that would attract both blacks and Indians, but more important, would be a kind of seminary to train ministers "for the better supplying of churches in our Foreign Plantations." By 1725 Berkeley had published the details of his plan, won a royal charter for it, and even begun to gather donations from all over England and Ireland. Moreover, he obtained from Parliament a promise of major funding to come. Among other things, Berkeley saw this outpost of empire as a bulwark against Catholicism, and a valuable boost to "the protestant religion [that] hath of late years considerably lost ground."

Berkeley as Missionary

In September 1728 Berkeley, now recognizing Bermuda as a poor choice, set sail for Rhode Island. Unlike Massachusetts and Connecticut, Rhode Island had no college and Berkeley believed it might be a fertile ground for his utopian dream. In his nearly three years in Rhode Island, he aided the Protestant cause by preaching in Newport's Anglican church, encouraging the missionaries sent out by the Society for the Propagation of the Gospel, and writing a powerful apologia (*Alciphron,* 1732) on behalf of traditioned Christianity and against the freethinkers then enjoying great popularity in England. He also waited for the promised grant from Parliament that never came. In September 1731 Berkeley returned to England, then to Ireland.

Back in England, Berkeley was welcomed into the membership of the Society for the Propagation of the Gospel. In a sermon preached to that society, Berkeley made clear how much missions were still on his mind, though he acknowledged that "it is hardly to be expected, that so long as Infidelity prevails at home, the Christian religion should thrive and flourish in our Colonies abroad." With Queen Caroline in his corner, Berkeley won appointment as Bishop of Cloyne in southern Ireland. There he labored for nearly twenty years on behalf of his church, his country, and his people. In 1752 he retired from his bishopric, returning once more to England to be near his son at Oxford. In January of 1753 he died there and is buried in Christ Church Cathedral.

Long remembered in Ireland, England, and around the world, the philosopher-churchman also left an indelible mark in America: at Berkeley College of Yale University and at the University of California's site in Berkeley, named in his honor.

References and Further Reading

Gaustad, Edwin S. *George Berkeley in America.* New Haven: Yale University Press, 1979.

Keynes, Geoffrey L. *A Bibliography of George Berkeley, Bishop of Cloyne: His Works and His Critics in the Eighteeenth Century.* Oxford: Oxford University Press, 1976.

Luce, A. A., and T. E. Jessop, eds. *The Works of George Berkeley, Bishop of Cloyne.* London: 1948–1957; reprinted, 1964.

EDWIN S. GAUSTAD

BERKHOF, HENDRIKUS (1914–1995)

Dutch reformed theologian of the Hervormde Kerke. Berkhof studied in Amsterdam, Leiden, and Berlin and served as a pastor and part-time teacher before becoming the first director of the Reformed Church seminary in Driebergen. In 1960 he became professor of dogmatics and biblical theology at the University of Leiden from which he retired in 1981.

Berkhof was active in ecumenical endeavors. He was chair of the Council of Churches in the NETHERLANDS (1974–1983) while also participating in the WORLD ALLIANCE OF REFORMED CHURCHES and the WORLD COUNCIL OF CHURCHES where he served on the Central Committee (1954–1975).

Berkhof wrote approximately twenty books, some of which were translated into other languages. His *Christian Faith* (1979; rev. ed. 1986) was a one-volume survey of the whole of THEOLOGY in fifty-nine chapters. This work is marked by the influence of KARL BARTH, although it moves away from Barth in some areas, particularly in CHRISTOLOGY. Berkhof begins Christology "from below," to ascertain what Jesus looks like "in the light of a careful investigation of the sources and within the framework of his own time" (*Christian Faith* [1986]:271). Although he pursued the study of theology with academic rigor, Berkhof's perspective was also that theology was "not something to learn so much as something to do and practice" (xii).

Berkhof attempted to "present a restatement of the gospel which is as up-to-date and lucid as possible" and to strike a path "between rigid traditionalism on the one side and rudderless modernism on the other" (xi).

References and Further Reading

Berkhof, Hendrikus. *Christian Faith.* Rev. edition. Grand Rapids, MI: Wm. B. Eerdmans, 1986.

———. *The Doctrine of the Holy Spirit*. Atlanta: John Knox Press, 1976.

———. *Two Hundred Years of Theology*. Grand Rapids, MI: Wm. B. Eerdmans, 1989.

DONALD K. McKIM

BEST-SELLERS IN AMERICA, RELIGIOUS

Considering the recent popularity of apocalyptic books such as the *Left Behind* series by Tim LaHaye and Jerry B. Jenkins, colonial America does not seem so long ago. Contemporary readers of this best-selling series get a multivolume dose of eschatological thrill, not unlike the experience colonists got from *The Day of Doom,* the Rev. Michael Wigglesworth's 1662 poem about the final judgment. To be sure, colonists devoured other religious books—*The Practice of Piety* by Lewis Bayly (1665) and *The Pilgrim's Progress* by JOHN BUNYAN (1681) were also popular—but *The Day of Doom* earned a place in the history of religious best-sellers for being the first to sell to at least one out of every one hundred Americans, and for summarizing Calvinistic doctrines so memorably that schoolchildren for a century were required to recite its rhymes:

> They wring their hands, their caitiff-hands
> and gnash their teeth for terrour;
> They cry, they roar for anguish sore,
> and gnaw their tongues for horrour.
> But get away without delay, Christ pitties not your cry:
> Depart to Hell, there may you yell, and roar Eternally.

Americans no long longer snap up copies of doctrinal doggerel, but they buy tales of the apocalypse by the millions. Only the form has changed.

Because what Americans read is directly connected to what they think, scholars study religious best-sellers to help understand the character of American popular religion. Best-selling religious books articulate the ideas and values by which people live or imagine themselves living. Not only do religious best-sellers say what readers want to hear, but readers urge them on their friends and family because they say what readers want others to hear, too. Thus they provide clues to the character of popular religious belief. As former Simon & Schuster editor Michael Korda said, "Like stepping on the scales, [the best-seller list] tells us the truth, however unflattering, and is therefore, taken over the long haul, a pretty good way of assessing our culture and of judging how, if any, we have changed."

Constructing a definitive list of American religious best-sellers can be tricky. Although religious books have sold voluminously in America since the early colonial period, best-sellers were not tracked until 1895, when the literary magazine *The Bookman* instituted its monthly list of best-sellers. Lists have proliferated ever since, but none without limitations. Newspapers such as the *New York Times* survey secular bookstores, which carry only a fraction of the religious books sold in the United States. Similarly the Christian Marketplace Top 50 List names titles that are sold only by the constituents of CBA and the Evangelical Christian Publishers Association. Furthermore contemporary lists favor short-term sellers over long-term favorites because they are based on periodic rather than cumulative sales. Determining which religious books have sold in the greatest quantities relative to the era in which they were published requires careful use of both historical sources and diverse contemporary lists, a task that is rewarded with illuminating evidence of constancy and change in American popular religion.

Bible

The single best-selling book in the United States has always been the BIBLE. Until the middle of the twentieth century that meant the King James Version, introduced in 1611, four years after English settlers first arrived at Jamestown, Virginia. The King James Version monopolized sales until 1952, when the Revised Standard Version was issued to satisfy the groundswell for a more reader-friendly Bible. Other best-selling Bibles have followed. Zondervan published the New International Version in 1978 and Thomas Nelson published the New King James Version four years later. Despite the immense popularity of these twentieth-century translations, their sales were far outpaced by a paraphrase, *The Living Bible* (1971), which has sold by the tens of millions and inspired the production of *The Message,* the paraphrase NavPress published in 2002. Whatever the version, nine out of ten households in America own at least one Bible, with the typical count being three copies per household.

Eighteenth and Nineteenth Centuries

In the first decade of the eighteenth century, all the books that met media historian Frank Luther Mott's criterion for best-sellers—sales equal to at least one percent of the U.S. population when the book was first published—were religious. There were three: Robert Russell's *Seven Sermons* (1701), a collection of the English minister's homilies on eternal damnation; John Williams's *The Redeemed Captive Returning to Zion* (1707), a grisly first-person account of a Puritan minister who returned from a forced march from Massachusetts to CANADA after witnessing the slaughter of family and neighbors by Native Americans and enduring relentless proselytizing from Jesuits; and John Flavel's *Husbandry Spiritualized* (1709), meditations from another English minister using farmwork to illustrate Christian DOCTRINE. Besides being religious, all the best-sellers from this decade were nonfiction and all were written by ministers, two out of three of whom were English, not American.

The situation was much different a century later. In the first decade of the nineteenth century, the books that sold to one percent of Americans were not expressly religious. Americans instead were buying biography (Mason L. Weems's *Life of Washington*), historic social criticism (Joseph Addison and Richard Steele's *The Spectator*), romance (Jane Porter's *Thaddeus of Warsaw*), poetry (Lord Byron's *Poems*), and history (Washington Irving's *History of New York*). No doubt they were also buying religious titles, just not in blockbuster quantities. Best-sellers at the beginning of the nineteenth century were not only more secular than their predecessors, but they also included an increasing presence of fiction as well as domestic authors, sometimes women. These attributes would also become true for religious best-sellers.

Religion may have less and less been the primary subject of nineteenth-century best-sellers, but it was hardly absent from them. Mott found that about a third of all best-sellers published before 1915 had "a strong religious element." The perspective was predominantly Protestant, sometimes blatantly anti-Catholic as in *The Wandering Jew* by Eugene Sue (1845). Practical guides to Christian living were popular, as evidenced in the sales of *The Young Christian* by Jacob Abbott (1832), *The Mother at Home* by John S. C. Abbott (1833), and *The Christian's Secret of a Happy Life* by HANNAH WHITALL SMITH (1883). Novels became a mainstay, including *Barriers Burned Away* (1872) and *Opening a Chestnut Burr* (1874) by E. P. Roe, stories that ended with a religious CONVERSION after a calamity such as a fire or a shipwreck. Biblical novels by J. H. Ingraham (*The Prince of the House of David*, 1855) and Lew Wallace (*Ben-Hur*, 1870) captured the imaginations of the nation's readers. So did novels by women. Susan Warner's *The Wide, Wide World* (1850) told the story of the Christian perseverance of Little Eva, who is sent away from home at the age of ten; Augusta J. Evans's *Beulah* (1859) chronicled a woman struggling with religious doubt; and Mrs. Humphry Ward's *Robert Elsmere* (1888) explored the work of a minister who rejects biblical supernaturalism in favor of the SOCIAL GOSPEL. Although an increasing proportion of American religious best-sellers were written by Americans, many still were imports, including *L'Abbé Constantin* by Ludovic Halévey (1882), a story of devout Americans

who move to a French estate and become local benefactors, and *Quo Vadis* by Henryk Sienkiewicz (1896), a novel about the life and suffering of the Christians during the decadent reign of Nero.

Twentieth Century

Five kinds of religious best-sellers predominated in the twentieth century. The first was biblical and inspirational fiction. Far and away the biggest phenomenon in this category is *In His Steps* by CHARLES SHELDON, a novel originally serially read in vespers services and published to great fanfare in 1897. *In His Steps* has never gone out of print, and its message that discipleship can be reduced to one question, "What would Jesus do?" had so much appeal that it spawned WWJD clothing and jewelry in the 1990s as well as the twenty-first century's ecofriendly critique of American consumption, "What Would Jesus Drive?" Other twentieth-century inspirational best-sellers include *The Shepherd of the Hills* (1907) and *The Calling of Dan Matthews* (1909) by Harold Bell Wright, novels that championed rural Christian INDIVIDUALISM against the encroachment of faithless urbanism; *The Nazarene* (1939) by Sholem Asch, the story of Jesus told from three different perspectives; *The Robe* (1942), by Lloyd C. Douglas, a novel about the crucifixion of Jesus; *The Silver Chalice* (1948) by Thomas B. Costain, a novel about a Greek artisan who makes the chalice used in the Last Supper; and *The Day Christ Died* (1957) by Jim Bishop, a journalistic account of Jesus's last day, beginning at Gethsemane and ending on Golgotha. Most of these novels became feature films.

Devotional and inspirational nonfiction together constitute another category of twentieth-century religious best-sellers. Some are contemplative. *The Song of Our Syrian Guest* (1903) by William Allen Knight put Psalm 23 in the context of ancient shepherds to give a mystical rendering of this favorite biblical passage, and *Streams in the Desert* (1925) by Mrs. Charles E. Cowman is a daily devotional that uses poetry, scripture passages, anecdotes, and meditations to consider the will of God. In *Peace with God* (1954), evangelist BILLY GRAHAM used passages from the Bible to explain that four simple steps led to certainty of SALVATION. Other books in this category are autobiographical. *The Cross and the Switchblade* (1963) by David Wilkerson tells about his early ministry to gangs in New York City, culminating in the conversion of gang leader Nicky Cruz. *Joni* (1976) is the inspirational story of Joni Earekson's struggles to adjust after a diving accident left her paralyzed below the neck.

Scripture supplements comprise a third category of religious best-sellers in the twentieth century. This category includes Bible story books for children. *The Story of the Bible* (1904) by Jesse Lyman Hurlbut, a Methodist Episcopal minister who was active in the Sunday School Union and Tract Society, has been in print for a century. Another children's best-seller, *Egermeier's Bible Story Book* (1922) by Elsie E. Egermeier, is likewise still in print. A third scripture supplement, this one for adults, has sold nearly as long. It is *Halley's Bible Handbook* (1927), which the Rev. Henry H. Halley published two years after the Scopes trial. The purpose of this book was to show the inerrancy of the Bible as well as its contemporary relevance. Using history, geography, and archaeology, Halley proceeded to defend creationism and attack historical criticism of the Bible. He also claimed that Catholicism and Islam were curses foretold in the Book of Revelation and that white Christians were meant to rule over blacks and Jews.

A fourth type of religious best-sellers of the twentieth century is apocalyptic literature. The nonfiction book that championed this theme was Hal Lindsey's *The Late Great Planet Earth* (1970). Lindsey popularized premillenial ESCHATOLOGY, claiming that contemporary events were fulfillments of prophecies from the books of Daniel, Matthew, and Revelation, and that true believers would soon be "raptured," leaving the world in hellish tribulation that would end only when Jesus returns for the final judgment. This perspective inspired the best-selling *Left Behind* series, which deals with the lives of persons converted to Christian faith after the RAPTURE who must endure the Tribulation. The apocalyptic vision of Lindsey and LaHaye perceives Satan and his vast assembly of demons doing battle with angels for the hearts and minds of human beings. Lindsey's second best-seller, *Satan is Alive and Well on Planet Earth* (1972), advanced this belief, as did *Angels: God's Secret Agents* (1975) by Billy Graham. This view was politicized in the best-selling novel by Frank Peretti, *This Present Darkness* (1986), a thriller that portrayed demonic forces at work in churches that preach unity and universities that question TRADITION.

In contrast to the beleaguered suspiciousness of apocalyptic best-sellers are books that promote positive thinking, the final category of religious best-sellers in the twentieth century. In these books God is the ultimate friend in a high place, someone who can be called on to help believers reach their goals. The first positive thinking best-seller was Lloyd Douglas's 1929 novel, *The Magnificent Obsession*, in which the protagonist discovers the biblical formula that guarantees success. In *The Power of Positive Thinking* (1952), NORMAN VINCENT PEALE assured millions of readers that they would never be defeated if they followed his ten rules for success. In *Prison to Praise* (1970) and *Power in Praise* (1972), Merlin Carothers explained that thanking God for everything, including adversity, was the key to the happy life. More recently, *The Prayer of Jabez: Breaking Through to the Blessed Life* (2000) by Bruce Wilkinson claimed that God will give a storehouse of material and spiritual blessings to everybody who asks, so we should ask and ask often for health and wealth, praying the New King James Version of I Chronicles 4:10: "Oh, that You would bless me indeed, and enlarge my territory, that Your hand would be with me, and that You would keep me from evil, that I may not cause pain."

Significance

Just as Christianity is one of the religions of the book, the UNITED STATES can be called a nation of the religious best-seller—meaning, of course, the Bible and other books that readers believe put biblical truths into plain language and a contemporary context. There is both constancy and change in these best-sellers. *The Day of Doom* of the seventeenth-century is stylistically and theologically distant from *The Late Great Planet Earth* of the twentieth century, but both use terrifying visions of the final judgment to prompt readers to choose the side of the elect (see ELECTION). Similarly *The Practice of Piety* bears little resemblance to *The Power of Positive Thinking,* but both offer practical advice to acting the way God would have us act. The similarities show the religious concerns that have preoccupied Americans through the centuries; the differences show what has characterized Americans at particular historical times. More generally the history of religious best-sellers shows the longstanding preoccupation in America with Christian faith in terms of both belief and behavior. The Christianity of American religious best-sellers has been more individual than social, more pragmatic than mystical, more concrete than abstract, and mostly but not exclusively Protestant. America is, of course, far more diverse than the religion of its best-sellers; nevertheless the faith that Americans by the million want to read is a significant indication not only that America is religious but also how America is religious.

See also Apocalypticism; Bible and Literature; Bible Translation; Biblical Inerrancy; Bunyan, John; Culture; Eschatology; Mass Media; Publishing, Media; Tribulationism

References and Further Reading

Fisher, Allan. "Evangelical-Christian Publishing: Where It's Been and Where It's Going." *Publishing Research Quarterly* 14 (Fall 1998): 3–11.

Goss, Leonard George, and Don M. Aycock, eds. *Inside Religious Publishing: A Look Behind the Scenes.* Grand Rapids, MI: Zondervan, 1991.

Korda, Michael. *Making the List: A Cultural History of the American Bestseller, 1900–1999.* New York: Barnes & Noble, 2001.

Mott, Frank Luther. *Golden Multitudes: The Story of Best Sellers in the United States.* New York: Macmillan, 1947.

JOHN P. FERRÉ

BEZA, THEODORE (1519–1605)

Calvinist reformer. Beza was a French humanist, reformed theologian, and the handpicked successor of JOHN CALVIN in Geneva. For nearly four decades after Calvin's death in 1564, Beza served as chief minister of the Genevan church, taught theology at the Academy of Geneva, and was a recognized leader in exile of the reformed churches in FRANCE. Beza played a crucial role in preserving Calvin's theological legacy and promoting international CALVINISM.

Theodore Beza was born at Vézelay in Burgundy on June 24, 1519 to parents of France's lower nobility. At age nine Beza was placed under the tutelage of the renowned Hellenist (and secret Lutheran) Melchior Wolmar, who over the next five years imparted to his pupil a love for classical philology and literature. Beza received his license in law from the University of Orleans in 1539, but his passion for humanistic studies overshadowed any legal ambitions. For the next decade he participated in a sodality of gifted French humanists in Paris, studying Greek and Latin classics and writing poetry. Beza's *Poemata* (1548), a collection of witty and sometimes erotic poems, situates him as a Christian humanist critical of the Catholic hierarchy.

In October 1548, as he recovered from serious illness, Beza converted to Protestantism and together with his (clandestine) wife Claudine Denosse fled to Geneva. At the recommendation of Calvin and Pierre Viret, Beza was installed as professor of Greek at the Academy of Lausanne in November 1549. Beza's pen was active during his ten-year sojourn in Lausanne. His humanistic training is evident in the play *Abraham sacrifiant* (1550), in his exegetical notes and Latin translation of the New Testament (*Annotationes,* 1556; revised until 1598), and in his contribution to the French *Psalter* (begun by Clement Marot; completed by Beza in 1562). Beza's polemical writings in this period reveal a maturing theologian, committed to Calvin's reform program. In *De haereticis* (1554), he attacked SEBASTIAN CASTELLIO and his defense of religious TOLERATION, justifying instead the right of magistrates to punish heretics (see HERESY). The *Tabula praedestinationes* (1555) offered a schematized defense of Calvin's doctrine of double PREDESTINATION (with Beza's own supralapsarian accent). A more comprehensive statement of Beza's theology appeared in the *Confession de la foi chrétienne* (1559), written for his aged Catholic father.

Theodore Beza's tenure in Lausanne ended in October 1558, hastened when the magistrates proscribed sermons on predestination. At the invitation of Geneva's ministers Beza was elected city preacher in Geneva in December and, the following spring, was named rector of the newly established Genevan Academy. The growing religious crisis in France, however, soon captured Beza's attention. In 1560 the Genevan clergy sent him to Nérac to "teach the Word of God" to the noble house of Bourbon. The following year the reformer led the Protestant delegation at the COLLOQUY OF POISSY in September 1561, where Beza defended the Protestant religion and the legitimacy of the French reformed churches in the presence of the Catholic royal family. Poissy proved to be a final, failed attempt to procure religious concord. When the First War of Religion began in April 1562, Beza marched with the Huguenot armies as chaplain to Louis de Condé (see HUGENOTS).

Beza provided strategic leadership for the reformed churches of France during the decades of civil war and confessional violence preceding the EDICT OF NANTES (1598). He secretly raised money and mercenaries for the Huguenot war effort; he provided theological and political counsel to the beleaguered churches; he served as confidant and advisor to Protestant notables such as GASPARD COLIGNY, Jeanne d'Albret, and her son Henry of Navarre (the future Henry IV); and he presided over the National Synod of La Rochelle (1571). In the aftermath of the Saint Bartholomew's Day Massacre (August 24, 1572), Beza defended the right of Protestant magistrates in France to revolt against the Valois monarchy. His *Du droit des magistrats* (1574) remains a classic in the history of resistance literature. Likewise, historians now recognize Beza as the chief editor and compiler of the massive history of the reformed churches in France, the *Histoire ecclésiastique* (1580).

Beza remained to the end of his life a prominent minister and professor in Geneva. He preached more than three thousand sermons from the pulpit of St. Pierre's (only eighty-seven sermons are extant). As a member of the Genevan CONSISTORY, he defended the practice of CHURCH DISCIPLINE to reprove sinners and preserve the purity of the Christian CHURCH. (Beza went further than Calvin in regarding discipline the "third mark" of a true church.) As professor of theology Beza taught many future leaders of the reformed movement (among them Kasper Olevianus, Antoine de La Faye, Franciscus Junius, ANDREW MELVILLE, and JACOBUS ARMINIUS) and wrote several dozen treatises against Catholic and GNESIO-LUTHERAN opponents. Scholars continue to debate Beza's fidelity to Calvin's theology and his role in emerging Protestant ORTHO-DOXY. His theological writings, collected in the three-volume *Tractationes theologicae* (1570–1582), evince a theological system more formal in definition and more scholastic in method than that employed by Calvin. Beza was also more explicit than his predecessor in affirming the doctrine of limited ATONEMENT and fiercer in his opposition to episcopal government (see BISHOPS AND EPISCOPACY), although these discontinuities appear to be more a matter of method than substance. Theodore Beza died on October 13, 1605, still committed to the theological legacy and pastoral priorities of his "spiritual father" John Calvin.

See also Confessionalization; Conversion; Puritanism; Reformation

References and Further Reading

Primary Sources:

Beza, Theodore. *Du droit des magistrats.* Edited by Robert Kingdon. Geneva: Droz, 1971.
———. *Histoire ecclésiastique des églises réformées au royaume de France.* Edited by Baume and Cunitz. 3 vols. Nieuwkoop, The Netherlands: B. de Graaf, 1974.

Secondary Sources:

Baird, Henry Martyn. *Theodore Beza, the Counsellor of the French Reformation, 1519–1605.* New York: Putnam's Sons, 1899.
Geisendorf, Paul. *Théodore de Bèze.* 2nd edition. Geneva: Alexandre Jullien, 1967.
Kingdon, Robert M. *Geneva and the Consolidation of the French Protestant Movement, 1564–1572.* Geneva: Droz, 1967.
Manetsch, Scott M. *Theodore Beza and the Quest for Peace in France, 1572–1598.* Leiden: Brill, 2000.

SCOTT M. MANETSCH

BIBLE

The Bible is the centerpiece of the Protestant faith. Since Martin Luther, Protestants have called the Bible the Word of God and have reserved a central place in their worship services for PREACHING from this Word and the hearing of the Word. The Bible provides Protestants with their primary AUTHORITY for faith and practice, and many look to it to provide guidance on matters of daily living. Although important translations of the Bible existed long before the birth of Protestantism, Protestantism gave rise to several of the most enduring examples, most notably the King James translation of the Bible, known in Britain as the Authorized Version. These translations altered the course of religious history in many ways. Because they were in the languages of the people, rather than in the official church language of Latin, individuals had greater access to them. Because of the advent of printing, people could own their own copies of the Bible and read the translations for themselves. Moreover, this accessibility encouraged individuals to interpret the Bible for themselves.

Translation

The Bible is the most translated book in history. The process of translation requires decisions on the part of the translators about vocabulary, grammar, syntax, and style, both in the original language and in the receptor language. Translation often turns into interpretation. Sometimes translators have slanted the meanings of passages to support their own theological doctrines, and at other times they have transmitted the words of Scripture without change but supplied notes in the margins to indicate their differences with the text. From the beginning of BIBLE TRANSLATION, translators have faced the challenge of maintaining faithfulness to the language and style of the original languages while rendering those languages in a manner that is understandable and meaningful to their contemporaries.

Written originally in Hebrew, Greek, and probably some Aramaic, the books of the Bible underwent a long history of translation before their Protestant translations into German, English, and other (North) European languages in the sixteenth and seventeenth centuries. Even before the New Testament was canonized, Jews living in Greek cities who no longer spoke or read Hebrew needed a Greek version of the Hebrew Bible, or Old Testament. Thus, Ptolemy Philadelphus commissioned a Greek translation of the Hebrew scriptures that has become known as the Septuagint, or LXX. The legend surrounding this text is that seventy-two translators labored for seventy-two days to produce this translation. The Septuagint arranges the books of the Hebrew Bible differently, and the LXX contains some books that are not in the Hebrew Bible. These books would later be called Apocrypha; they are included in most Catholic translations of the Bible but are absent from Protestant translations—with the exceptions of modern study Bibles.

The earliest church considered the Septuagint as its Bible, and many New Testament writers quoted from it rather than from the Hebrew version of the Old Testament. Many early Latin versions depend on the

Septuagint, but in the fourth century Jerome (342–420) produced the Vulgate, the most important Bible translation before the Protestant translations of WILLIAM TYNDALE (1494–1536) and MARTIN LUTHER (1483–1546). In 382 Pope Damasus commissioned Jerome to produce a new translation based on the Old Latin versions and the available Greek and Hebrew manuscripts of the Old and New Testaments. Although he worked from the Septuagint initially, he soon began to work directly from the Hebrew text in his translation of the Old Testament. Jerome's Vulgate appeared in installments, issuing the complete text in 405. Although the Vulgate's early reception was unfavorable, it eventually replaced the Old Latin versions of the Bible, and it influenced greatly the early Protestant versions of the Bible. It served as the basis for the first English Bible translation, which John Wycliffe produced in 1382.

The Vulgate served as the major Bible translation of the church through the Middle Ages because Latin was the official language of the church. By the twelfth and thirteenth centuries, however, tremendous changes were taking place across Europe that would challenge the church's authority and would require new Bible translations. The rise of the nation and the division of Europe into various discrete political regions, each operating politically and economically in its own languages, provided the first blow to the predominance of Latin as the official language of a unified political sphere—Christendom—over which the Roman Church claimed ultimate rule. Another factor in the move away from Latin as an official language was the breakup of the social hierarchy of the Middle Ages, which meant that individuals increasingly used their vernacular language rather than Latin to communicate in their everyday affairs. In addition the rise of literacy and the invention of the printing press meant that for the first time people could read the Bible, and other publications, themselves in their own houses rather than having the Bible read to them in church by a priest. Finally the flowering of the Renaissance across Europe renewed a significant interest in ancient languages, and scholars offered new translations of Homer's *Odyssey,* Virgil's *Aeneid,* and other major works of antiquity. These factors all contributed to the rise of new translations of the Bible.

The Protestant REFORMATION introduced many important changes to the religious landscape of Europe, chief among them new translations of the Bible. In GERMANY Luther challenged the Catholic Church in many ways regarding doctrine and practice, but one of his most enduring contributions to the Protestant faith was his translation of the Bible into German. Rather than basing his translation on the Vulgate, he returned to the original languages of Greek and Hebrew and produced a German vernacular Bible that incorporated many of Germany's regional dialects. Luther's translation was the first vernacular translation of the Bible in Protestantism, and it became the model for English translations.

Although Wycliffe's pre-Reformation version was the first English translation, it was overtaken in the sixteenth century by the translation of William Tyndale. A linguist and scholar, Tyndale translated the New Testament from the Greek and the Old Testament from the Hebrew. When his bishop refused to support the translation he moved to Germany where he produced the first printed New Testament in 1525 and the Old Testament in 1534. Tyndale used his Bible as a means of protest, questioning in marginal notes many of the liturgical practices of the CHURCH OF ENGLAND. His elegant translations captured not only the meaning and style of the original languages but also provided a base from which a vernacular version of the English Bible could be produced.

In 1611 the most famous and most enduring English translation of the Bible appeared. When James I took the throne in England in 1603, he found himself embroiled in a religious controversy over the nature of church authority and the nature of church organization. Groups of reformers, calling themselves Puritans, challenged the episcopal structure of the Church of England as too like the Catholic Church (see BISHOPS AND EPISCOPACY). James convened the Hampton Court Conference (1604) between the Anglicans and the Puritans to settle some of their differences. Thinking that James would be sympathetic to their cause because of his support of Scottish Protestant groups, the Puritans hoped that the new king would favor their reforms. Instead James sided with the Anglicans, but as a means of placating the Puritans, he commissioned a new translation of the Bible. Several translation teams, consisting of fifty-four scholars from several British universities, completed this translation of the Bible. Their translation was based on the original Greek and Hebrew rather than on the Vulgate, although they used many of Tyndale's translations as the basis of their own. The King James Version influenced numerous writers from William Shakespeare and JOHN MILTON to contemporary novelists such as Reynolds Price and John Updike. Its language and ornate style remain unsurpassed, and it continues to be one of the world's best-selling Bibles (see BIBLE, KING JAMES VERSION).

Protestants, however, are by nature reformers, and the language and style of the King James Bible were eventually found in need of reform and revision. In the twentieth century a flood of translations inundated Protestant Christians as scholars and translation committees updated the Bible for new generations. From 1946 to 1952, an American group of translators produced the Revised Standard Version (RSV) of the Bible. This translation took into account new manuscript discoveries and was the most faithful to the Greek and Hebrew manuscripts of the New and Old Testaments. Not everyone approved of the translation, however, and some churches held Bible burnings of this new translation for what they believed to be its challenge to the authority of the King James Version. The RSV did provide modern English-speaking Protestants with a faithful translation in a meaningful and understandable language.

In the late twentieth century a number of translations appeared, each trying to improve on the previous translation and each touting its faithfulness to the original languages. The most popular of these was the New International Version (NIV), which a group of conservative biblical scholars produced. It was produced between 1973 and 1978, and its goal was to provide the beauty of the King James Version while offering a new generation of readers a Bible in accessible language. Of all the modern translations, the NIV became the best-selling Bible.

The significance of Bible translation has been a crucial part of the Protestant use and understanding of the Bible. Since Luther all translators or translation committees have tried to produce a version of the Bible that can be read and interpreted by individual believers and that is faithful to the original languages. Because Protestants have encouraged the reading authority of the individual believer, Bible versions have been challenged and the work of translators has been questioned. At stake for such readers is the Bible's inspiration and its infallibility (see BIBLICAL INERRANCY). Does translation tamper with the inspiration of the Bible? Do translations tamper with the Bible's infallibility? Is the Bible infallible if it can be translated in so many different ways? Can translations be trusted if one uses the word "virgin" to describe Mary, the mother of Jesus, and another uses the word "young woman"?

Inspiration and Infallibility

Although various translations seek to transmit the Bible to new generations of readers, Protestants often raise questions about whether these translations are inspired by God. In the view of most Protestants, the Bible is God-inspired; that is, the Bible's words are breathed forth by God. Difficulties arise, however, when the mechanics of such inspiration are discussed. Did God breathe forth all the words of Scripture so that the human writers of the biblical books had no control over their writing tasks? Were the human authors of Scripture simply receiving God's dictation with an angel sitting on their shoulders to guide their pens? Were the translators of the Bible inspired by God? Since Luther there have been a variety of Protestant views of biblical inspiration.

Luther himself believed that biblical writings must "preach and bear Christ." Because of his view, he called the book of James a "right strawy epistle." His questions about James, Jude, Hebrews, and Revelation led him to question their inspiration and to give them apocryphal status in his canon.

JOHN CALVIN believed that God dictated the Scriptures. If God dictated the Scriptures, God must have had some role in selecting the writers of the biblical texts. Calvin believed that the diverse styles of the writers of Scripture could be attributed to the work of the Holy Spirit.

In the twentieth century a number of different views of inspiration have been developed. Most prominent among conservative Protestants is the theory of verbal inspiration. Adherents of this theory hold that God breathed every verse of Scripture, even though they admit that human writers played a significant role in the transmission of the Scriptures. According to the proponents of verbal inspiration, the biblical writers possessed their own personalities and were products of their own times. However, God prepared them to be God's instruments in writing Scripture. Such early twentieth-century verbal inspirationists as A. A. Hodge and B. B. Warfield contended that the Scriptures had not been dictated, but the biblical books appeared as if they had been dictated. Some verbal inspirationists, notably Charles Augustus Briggs (1841–1913), argued that verbal inspiration could be restricted to matters of faith and morals.

A more liberal theory of inspiration argued that not the words but the religious experiences that the Bible records are inspired. HARRY EMERSON FOSDICK (1878–1969), pastor of Riverside Church in New York City, believed that these experiences provide glimpses of God's progressive revelation. English New Testament scholar C. H. Dodd (1884–1973) contended that the Bible's inspiration is to be found in the quality of the "religious genius" that its writers brought to it. Nineteenth-century theologian FRIEDRICH SCHLEIERMACHER (1768–1834) asserted that the "Spirit of the Christian community" inspired the Bible.

A third group of theologians and Protestant scholars, who have become known as neoorthodox theologians, returned to Luther's view of inspiration. KARL BARTH (1886–1968) believed that the Bible contains the Word of God and that it becomes the word of God as it is preached to individuals and congregations in their own existential settings.

Out of this doctrine of inspiration has developed the notion of the Bible's infallibility. This doctrine, which is peculiar to Protestants, teaches that the Bible contains no mistakes or errors in its teachings of revealed truths. Most Protestants, especially in the formal declarations of their denominations, uphold the idea that the Bible is infallible. However, Protestants tend to divide along the lines laid down by their doctrine of inspiration. For the verbal inspirationists, the Bible contains no errors because words dictated by God cannot contain error. For the liberals like Schleiermacher, the message of the Bible is infallible but the words are not. Thus, historical criticism of the Bible may have convinced believers that Moses did not cross the Red Sea, but the infallible message of God's power and providential love remains the same. For the neoorthodox, the words are less important than the message preached from the Word of God. The truth of the Bible is infallible, but it addresses hearers in their own situations and has the power to change them.

These various views of inspiration and infallibility govern the ways in which Protestants reserve a special place for the Bible in their faith and practice. For some a view of the Bible's infallibility has verged on bibliolatry, that is, the Bible becomes an idol that is worshipped in and of itself for its inerrant truth. For others, the infallibility of the Bible's message has helped them use the Bible to enhance their public worship and guide their private religious life.

Biblical Criticism and Interpretation

Although Luther and other reformers tended to read the Bible literally in the sense that readers should focus on the word of Scripture itself and not its historical setting or allegorical quality, the Protestant Reformation's emphasis on the individual interpreter contributed to a revolution in biblical studies in the eighteenth and nineteenth centuries. During that time, the Bible, like any other literary text, became the subject of intense philological, textual, historical, and literary scrutiny. Biblical scholars applied the tools of reason and science to their readings of the Bible to establish the historical contexts of certain units of Scripture or to determine the best manuscript evidence for certain readings of particular texts. Such critical readings of the Biblical texts paved the way for numerous new interpretations of Scripture, thereby providing believers with various methods with which they could read the Bible on their own.

Textual criticism seeks to establish the most reliable text of any part of Scripture. Because no extant copies of the original manuscripts for the Old or New Testament exist, textual critics perform a crucial service. They aim to establish or restore the original wording of the biblical texts where such words have been lost in the process of copying or recopying the texts. New Testament textual critics compare existing manuscripts to determine which reading of a particular passage is the best one. Although the practice of textual criticism is far beyond the expertise of most individual readers, textual critics provide translators with tools they need to do their work. In their never-ending work, textual critics lay the groundwork for translators, who must choose which of the many alternative readings of various passages they should translate. Textual critics work in the background to make the study of the Bible more fruitful and accurate.

Historical criticism aims to provide a picture of the historical setting of the biblical events as accurately as possible. Historical critics provide information about the political, social, economic, and cultural settings of the biblical stories and often use archaeology to achieve its purposes. These critics have questioned whether a certain event could have happened at a particular time and place. For example, the Bible describes Joshua's conquest of the city of Jericho, but historical critics have found through archaeological evidence that Jericho was not a city of great magnitude at the time of Joshua's conquest. Such evidence offers individual readers choices about the way in which they read the Joshua story.

Even more far-reaching than historical criticism is literary criticism. Literary criticism, in its oldest meaning for biblical studies, examines literary sources and literary forms as ways of exploring the meaning and understanding of the texts. Perhaps the most famous source theory has been applied to the Pentateuch, the first five books of the Bible. Luther and other precritical thinkers believed that Moses wrote these books, and that they were a single unit. By the late eighteenth century and early nineteenth century, a number of scholars had noticed that many of the books in the Pentateuch contained more than one account of the same event. Thus, in the Joseph story in Genesis 38–50 there are two sets of names for the brothers and father and two accounts of Joseph's capture. Would one author have written these different accounts? Literary source critics theorized that at least four sources lay behind this story, and others like it, and that the sources were all written at different times in Israel's history to reflect religious concerns of that time. The Jahwist (J) source was the earliest and the Priestly (P) account was the latest. According to this theory, these sources were pulled together by a later editor into a form close to their present one. Literary source criticism of the Old Testament has evolved over the past two hundred years so that various versions of this theory have come to dominate various readings of the Old Testament narratives.

New Testament literary source critics tend to focus primarily on the Synoptic Gospels—Matthew, Mark, and Luke. These critics argue that these Gospels hold several sources partially in common, from which they draw their stories. Not all New Testament source critics can agree on the number or the nature of the sources. The most common theory holds that a hypothetical sayings source, Q, and Mark provide the sources for Matthew and Luke.

Form criticism is another kind of literary criticism of the Bible. Form critics examine the ways that certain literary forms function in expressing meaning. These critics analyze the forms that arise out of certain settings and the ways that those forms are used in those settings. Form critics—beginning with the Old Testament—originally focused their attention on oral forms and the ways that a community passed those along in particular settings, like the use of the psalm of lament at mourning services for the individual or the community. New Testament form critics have tended to focus on literary rather than oral forms, so that many examine the ways that pronouncement stories or miracle stories function in a community's setting.

Another form of literary criticism is redaction criticism. These critics examine the ways in which various editors (redactors) have reworked the traditions or sources. In the late twentieth century, a number of other literary critical methods focused on the audience, the readers, the literary structure of the text, the social setting of the stories, the political meaning of the story's context, and the rhetorical devices used by the biblical culture.

Biblical criticism plays an important role in defining the function of the Bible in modern CULTURE. These critics elevate the Bible to a place of respect in the canon of Western literature. Using these various tools, the critics open the books of the Bible to critical examination in the ways that they would examine Dante's *The Divine Comedy,* John Milton's *Paradise Lost,* William Faulkner's *The Sound and the Fury,* or Margaret Atwood's *The Handmaid's Tale.* Protestants have reacted to biblical criticism in mixed ways over the years, with some embracing the freedom it provides to explore the biblical texts and others rejecting it for its challenges to the truths of the Bible.

Out of this encounter with biblical criticism, Protestants have established three methods of interpreting the Bible. Although each method is discrete, elements of one method are carried over into other methods. These methods do not represent a hierarchy, and Protestants often move between one or the other. The first method is the literal. Protestants who interpret the Bible literally usually believe that the Bible contains no errors, the Bible is verbally inspired, and that truth resides within the text itself. From this perspective, any passage to which an individual reader turns already contains truth that will speak to him or her. Because the truth already resides in the text, no critical tools are necessary to bring that truth to the surface.

Another interpretive method is the devotional, and it sometimes involves a literal approach to the text but allows the text to have a broader meaning. This method involves two components: the private and the public. On a private devotional level, individuals read and interpret the text as a guide to their personal lives and faith. They may use devotional handbooks to lead them in their study of the Bible, but this private devotional approach involves a close daily reading of a selected passage. This method often involves PRAYER as a tool for guidance in the selection and application of the biblical passage. This private devotional method epitomizes the Protestant tendency to individual understanding and judgment.

The second component of the devotional method is the public reading of Scripture. This occurs in the context of a Christian community where a pastor or worship leader reads a selected passage of Scripture—sometimes regulated by a lectionary—and leads the congregation to reflect on it. The Scripture passage may have little to do with an individual reader's spiritual life but more with the life of the individual as it relates to the larger community. The passage may also lead to reflection on the responsibilities of the community to the world at large. Often the public and private forms of devotional interpretation intersect so that a private devotional reading leads to greater understanding of the public devotional reading. The devotional method is closest to the neoorthodox idea that the Bible addresses people in their existential situations (see NEO-ORTHODOXY).

The third form of Protestant biblical interpretation is the critical. The readers who practice this method of interpretation embrace the fruits of biblical criticism and apply them to their readings of Scripture. Practitioners of this method might compare different versions of the same story as it appears in the same biblical book or in a different biblical book. Critical readers are alert to parallels between stories in the Old and New Testaments. They often seek out books on history, literary criticism, or archaeology that supplement their readings of the Bible. Critical readers of the Bible have difficulty reading the Bible literally, but they can often read the Bible devotionally, incorporating their critical insights into their devotional readings. Individuals who practice the critical method embrace the freedom that the Protestant notion of the Bible's accessibility gives them, and they assert along with the liberal view of biblical inspiration that the truth of the Bible rather than its structure is the most significant aspect of studying and understanding the Bible.

See also Bible, King James Version

References and Further Reading

Alter, Robert, and Frank Kermode. *The Literary Guide to the Bible*. Cambridge, MA: Harvard University Press, 1987.

Bobrick, Benson. *Wide as the Waters: The Story of the English Bible and the Revolution It Inspired*. New York: Simon & Schuster, 2001.

Campenhausen, Hans von. *The Formation of the Christian Bible*. Philadelphia: Fortress, 1972.

Chase, Mary Ellen. *The Bible and the Common Reader*. New York: Macmillan, 1962.

Frei, Hans. *The Eclipse of Biblical Narrative: A Study in Eighteenth and Nineteenth Century Hermeneutics*. New Haven, CT: Yale University Press, 1974.

Greenslade, S. L. *The Cambridge History of the Bible*. Cambridge: Cambridge University Press, 1963.

Jeffrey, David Lyle. *A Dictionary of Biblical Tradition in English Literature*. Grand Rapids, MI: Wm. B. Eerdmans, 1992.

Lewis, J. P. *The English Bible from KJV to NIV*. Grand Rapids, MI: Wm. B. Eerdmans, 1981.

McGrath, Alister. *In the Beginning: The Story of the King James Bible and How It Changed a Nation, a Language, and a Culture*. New York: Doubleday, 2001.

Metzger, Bruce M. *The Text of the New Testament*, 2nd ed. Oxford: Oxford University Press, 1968.

Myers, Allen C., ed. *The Eerdmans Bible Dictionary*. Grand Rapids, MI: Wm. B. Eerdmans, 2001.

Pelikan, Jaroslav. *The Reformation of the Bible and the Bible of the Reformation*. New Haven, CT: Yale University Press, 1996.

HENRY L. CARRIGAN JR.

BIBLE AND LITERATURE

It would hardly be too much to say that literary culture in much of the world is inseparable from the culturally transformative power of Christianity. In particular, since the REFORMATION and the wide dissemination of printed vernacular BIBLES that resulted, Protestant Christianity has been the predominant channel for scriptural influence upon literature in Europe, AFRICA, Asia, and throughout the English-speaking world. It must be acknowledged that this influence has often been more by way of achieved biblical literacy than by theological persuasion; much of the most evident obligation is among writers avowedly secularist, even anti-Christian, whatever their religious roots. Moreover, explicitly Christian novelists, poets, and playwrights in the modern period are at least as likely to be Catholics—though it might be argued that for many of them, at least implicitly, the Reformation tradition has shaped the process and occasionally the content of their relationship to the Bible as a foundational text. All of this means that the story of the relationship of the Bible to literature remains, as it was through late antiquity and the Middle Ages, inextricably connected to the history of biblical translation and vernacular literacy.

Introduction

Two thousand years ago, textually preserved literacy and literature were substantially unknown beyond certain Mediterranean and Oriental cultures. Chinese textual culture of the first century B.C. was largely devoted to matters of bureaucracy and the strategic use of ancestral legend. Only a tiny elite, the *chu-tzu*, mastered and recapitulated fragments of pertinent oral tradition in textual form. In the Mediterranean and contiguous Middle East this pattern was varied and enriched by the appearance of epic narrative (Homer), philosophical reflection (Plato, Aristotle), and religious drama (e.g., Euripedes, Aeschylus, Sophocles) of the Greeks. The Romans were scions of the Greek stock, but under the administrative demands of empire, literacy more directly served political purposes.

What marks the emergence of Christian influence in literature is the appearance and remarkably swift dissemination of the Gospels themselves—not as an elite but as a popular and vernacular body of texts. In the eventful *koiné* reportage of the Gospels, the nearly breathless countercultural story in Acts and the multicultural apostolic letters of the New Testament there emerges a contraliterature—neither elite nor ethnocentric, concerned neither with statecraft nor the provisions of aristocratic entertainment.

It is thus to the Great Commission itself that we owe the myriad cultural transformations affected by the Bible. As in Africa, SOUTH AMERICA, and many other parts of the world, so in most of Europe the birth of literacy and literature was essentially, not accidentally, coincident with the arrival of Christian missionaries. In these cultures there had not been, before their arrival, effective means of writing. Literature, as we think of it, was the province of oral culture only. Biblical translation and paraphrase were typically undertaken in the first or second missionary generation, providing for hundreds of languages in the first instance of their written form. The second generation of texts, as in Anglo-Saxon ENGLAND, are usually creative works of Christian reflection and scriptural formation. King Alfred the Great (d. 851), alone called "great" among the kings of England, earned his reputation not by his military exploits but by translating and introducing Christian classics to his people. Subsequently, in a barbarous Germanic culture where all power came from the spilling of blood, it became increasingly possible to say, as later Lord Lytton would, that "the pen is mightier than the sword."

Reformation and Renaissance in English Literature

The profusion of English translations in the sixteenth century (Tyndale, Coverdale, Rogers and Taverner, Geneva Bible, Bishops Bible), culminating in the King James Version (KJV) of 1611, allowed the Bible itself to be read, often with freshness and power, as a rich anthology of primary literature. It is not insignificant that sixteenth-century poets such as Sir Philip Sydney and his cousin the Countess of Pembroke attempted their own poetic translations of Scripture. The Psalms in particular had many early Protestant translators who engaged their work as much in pursuit of poetry as piety (e.g., Thomas Wyatt [1503–1542], Henry Howard [1517–1574], Earl of Surrey). This intimate relationship of English texts with the Psalms continued on through to the twentieth century, engaging on the way such eminent poets as Sandys, Poet Thomas Carew (1595–1640), Herbert, John Milton (1608–1674), Vaughan, Addison, Watts, Preacher Charles Wesley (1707–1788), Smart, Robert Burns (1759–1796), Henry Wadsworth Longfellow (1807–1882), Hardy, Rudyard Kipling (1865–1936), and Ezra Pound (1885–1972).

Of the seventeenth-century "Golden Age" in English literature it may be said that in no other period has the effect of the Bible upon literary English been so pervasive. When William Shakespeare (1564–1616), in *Measure for Measure,* could critique Puritan theology by setting his own title text (from Matthew 7:2) in a rich context of the Puritans' favorite quotations from Romans—precisely so as to undermine their doctrinal emphasis—more was in evidence than a vigorous hermeneutical dispute among differing branches of Protantism. Clearly, Shakespeare could depend upon an impressive degree of biblical literacy among theatergoers as well as their informed interest in divergent views on the matter of grace.

One of the most evident literary effects of the Reformation in sixteenth-century English literature is the emergence into prominence of biblical narratives that had not had a significant literary presence because they were not previously part of the Catholic liturgical cycle or canonical lectionary (i.e., not directly connected to the established *historia salvationis humanae*). Calvinist covenant theology, Protestant typology, and sheer dramatic narrative interest all contribute to the rise of poems and plays on figures from the book of Judges (e.g., Jephthah and his daughter, Deborah; Samson) and the book of Ruth.

Between 1480 and 1660 more than half of all books printed in England were devoted to theological or religious subjects; nearly all of these were part of a flourishing Protestant debate and pedagogy and, accordingly, copiously indebted to biblical proof-text and discourse. No other period in any European culture has witnessed such a pervasive influence of the Bible on all other types of literature. Only in America, and then for a briefer period during the colonial years, was this intensity of biblically indebted publication even remotely approached.

Shakespeare's own scriptural text was most often the Geneva Bible, with its extensive annotations so strongly reflective of Reformed doctrine. Yet his views seem often at variance with these doctrines, inclining to a more Catholic position. English clergyman John Bunyan's (1628–1688) Bible was almost certainly the KJV, though his own prose reflects this far less than we might expect. John Milton was fond of the KJV, but was so learned a Bible reader and lay-theologian that his sophistication in matters both textual and doctrinal go far beyond the simple free-churchman's evangelical homilizing that made Bunyan the favorite author of the masses well into the nineteenth century. If Bunyan's allegories *Pilgrim's Progress* (1678, 1684) and *The Holy War* (1682) are dependent upon a thoroughgoing biblical literacy in simple readers, Milton's overtly biblical poems *Paradise Lost, Paradise Regained,* and *Samson Agonistes* are as much dependent upon a high degree of literacy in classical literature and biblical commentary. It is also clear that the success of works as diverse as *Pilgrim's Progress* and *Paradise Lost* helped ensure a self-perpetuating character for biblical influence, even as they shaped and in distinctive ways characterized that influence. The "gospel according to Milton," so to speak, became in itself a dominant influence upon subsequent English literature (even among writers like William Blake, who abhorred Milton's theology), and Bunyan continued to be an "interpreter" to biblical literature for writers through the nineteenth century (e.g., Charlotte Bronte [1816–1855]), so compelling a voice as occasionally to displace in authority the texts he interpreted.

In many instances it has been the free-church or evangelical tradition that, in England, has proven to be the strongest conveyance for biblical formation among writers. Even an ex-Puritan such as John Locke (1792–1856) became a legitimating conduit for biblical undersanding of self-consciousness and the imagination among poets like Blake and William Wordsworth (1770–1850) (Brantley 1984), and their evangelical past, though rejected in principle, did not prevent Percy Shelley (1792–1822) and his wife Mary Wollstonecroft Shelley (1797–1851) from reading the Bible to each other as after-dinner entertainment. In many such cases, however—writers such as Thomas Hardy (1840–1928), Somerset Maugham (1874–1965), Joyce Cary (1888–1957), and the laureate poet John

Betjeman (1906–1984) all come to mind—the vital influence of the KJV text read in their youth long outlived their participation in any active form of Christian worship. Thus, however counterintuitively, even the prose of D. H. Lawrence (1885–1930) is heavily salted with KJV phrases (e.g., *The Man Who Died, Apocalypse, The Rainbow*), and he was highly self-aware in his employment of biblical parallelism (*The Boy in the Bush*) in his attacks upon Christianity.

North American Literature

In its earliest chapters, American literature was a literature of religious polemic and spiritual exhortation. This is not surprising: it branched off from English literature just at that point in the seventeenth century when the power of the Bible as a literary source was at its zenith. The Puritans who settled in America were, moreover, some of the most biblically literate of Englishmen. Yet there were differences. Early American literature is not typically characterized by Miltonic or quasi-medieval retellings of biblical narrative. Rather, given the established typological hermeneutics of Puritan theology, the American tendency was to draw the stuff of literary narrative from frontier experience and then to shape and structure its claim to enduring, even eternal, significance by encoding recorded events with explicit reference to biblical typology. From the early triumphalist chronicles and journals of the settlers [e.g., Thomas Shepherd's *The Covenant of Grace* (1651); COTTON MATHER'S (1663–1728) *Magnalia Christi Americana* (1702), on to modern American mythography in such texts as Walker Percy's (1916–1990) *Love in the Ruins* (1971)], there is a tendency to privilege for purposes of plot the "here and now," even while charging its elements with a transvaluing typology drawn on biblical prototypes. In the early period, as Sacvan Bercovitch and others have shown, biblical typology provided a means whereby wilderness life in the colonies could become the literal realization of central scriptural metaphors: fall, exile, exodus, pilgrim history, promised land, and even millennial kingdom are woven almost seamlessly into the narratives of William Bradford, John Winthrop, Roger Williams, poet Michael Wigglesworth (1631–1705; *The Day of Doom*, 1662), Cotton Mather, Jurist Samuel Sewall (1652–1730), and Jonathan Edwards. Writers like Edward Johnson, in his *Wonder-Working Providence of Sion's Saviour* (1654) see America as the literal Promised Land, and American experience as a biblically foreshadowed "text" about God's unfolding plan for human redemption. Indeed, both the APOCALYPTICISM and MILLENNIALISM characteristic of much American literature can seem to assume, as writer Giles Gunn

(1938–) puts it, that "the Bible was proleptically American" (Gunn 1983:XX).

By the 1700s this style of writing had begun to grow wearisome: clergyman Timothy Dwight's (1752–1817) Miltonic allegorical epic, *The Conquest of Canaan* (1775), populated with eighteenth-century Americans bearing Hebrew names, was unsuccessfully "biblical," a relic of his grandfather Jonathan Edwards's day. This echoing of Puritan style was to persevere for the time being only in emergent black American literature, such as poet Phyllis Wheatley's (1753–1784) "Thoughts on the Works of Providence" (1770). Yet it reemerged in mainstream American literature of the nineteenth century as a subversive use of biblical codes, typology, and language to call Puritan theology itself into question. Herman Melville's (1819–1891) *Moby-Dick* (1851), *Pierre* (1852), *The Confidence Man* (1857), and *Billy Budd* exhibit a fierce resistance to Calvinist readings of Scripture, even as they display in their antagonism a rich synthesis of biblical narrative and typology that few European writers could match. Nathaniel Hawthorne's (1804–1864) use of biblical allusion is likewise parodic and antagonistic, and Ralph Waldo Emerson's (1803–1882) triumphant self-actualism and antinomian pursuit of the "God within" simply inverts or redefines the biblical material it borrows. These writers came to discover, as Emerson puts it, that "out from the heart of nature rolled/The burdens of the Bible old" ("The Problem"), whether they chose to have it so or not. As with Melville, Poe, Hawthorne, and others, Emerson is obliged in his own jeremiad essay "On Self-Reliance" (1841) to use biblical rhetoric to oppose biblical values, anticipating in this way unintentionally ironic notes in poet Walt Whitman's (1819–1892) famous "Song of Myself." The latter poem, the thirty-third second of Whitman's *Leaves of Grass* (1855), is a protest of the triumphant self or "old Adam"—curiously grounded, Whitman later admits, in the language of both testaments ("A Backward Glance O'er Travelled Road").

Subsequently, the "American jeremiad," a political sermon in which social criticism is joined to calls for a spiritual renewal, has come to be recognized as a foundational and mythopoeic American literary genre indebted to biblical modeling. Frontier outpost sermons such as those of Peter Bulkeley (1583–1659) in the seventeenth century take their place on a continuum with those of apocalyptic televangelists and the speeches of Martin Luther King, Jr. (1929–1968) in tending to read contemporary events as though they were written down in an unfolding text to which the Bible is the master code. Characterized not only by biblical rhetoric and diction, but formed upon biblical narrative and dependent for its wide appeal on extensive popular knowledge of the Bible, the jeremiad has in turn had a powerful influence on other American literary genres. Included here must be the novel of protest, of which not only nominally Christian writers such as Sinclair Lewis (1885–1951; *Elmer Gantry* [1927]) but also Jewish writers have written many in the United States. *Portnoy's Complaint* (1969) by Philip Roth (1933–), *Herzog* (1964) by Saul Bellow (1915–), *Joshua Then and Now* (1980) by Canadian novelist Mordecai Richler (1931–2001), and, though less paradigmatically, *My Name is Asher Lev* and *The Chosen* by Chaim Potok (1929–) all share elements of the Protestant jeremiad tradition in America, taking their place alongside novels such as John Steinbeck's (1902–1968) *The Grapes of Wrath* (1934), James Baldwin's (1924–1987) *The Fire Next Time* (1963), and William Faulkner's (1897–1962) *Go Down, Moses* (1942) as well as plays like Archibald Mac-Leish's (1892–1982) *J.B.* (1958), a modernization of the Job story, and Robinson Jeffers's (1887–1962) dramatic poem *Dear Judas* (1929). But the force of biblical influence has, in these works, largely shifted away from biblical narrative and diction to vestigial religious or cultural tradition in which the Bible itself is an archaism, and where the biblical narrative more directly informs plot and action, as in Gore Vidal's (1925–) *Messiah* (1954) or John Barth's (1930–) *Giles Goat Boy* (1966), it can well be in a form that Theodore Ziolkowski calls a "demonic parody of the life of Christ" (Ziolkowski 1972:XX).

By the end of the twentieth century, American and Canadian fiction within a recognizably biblical tradition, with a few notable exceptions (e.g., Walker Percy's [1916–1990] *The Second Coming* [1980], Rudy Wiebe's *The Blue Mountains of China* [1970]), typically treats its scriptural heritage in an overtly antagonistic fashion. Sometimes there is a double-edged character to the antagonism, such as in Margaret Atwood's (1939–) *The Handmaid's Tale* (1985), a horrific dystopia in which American arch-conservatives have erected a society based on a rigid implementation of perverted but recognizably Puritan "Old Testament" laws and social customs. Atwood's is an antijeremiad expressing fears of a right-wing and "biblicist" America declaring itself the only "chosen" nation, but it carries a clear recognition that the religious tyranny is a perversion of biblical and specifically Protestant values, not an outworking of them. In North American literature generally, the age of "soft" allusion to the Bible—so comfortable for genteel nineteenth-century writers like Longfellow, Emily Dickinson (1830–1886), John Greenleaf Whittier (1807–1892), Stephen Leacock (1869–1944), or Robert Frost (1874–1963)—is apparently over. As in Barbara Kingsolver's (1955–) *The Poisonwood Bible* (1999),

engaging the Bible as a foundational text now more clearly than ever addresses the question of its authority—not merely in its literary but in its religious sense.

Postenlightenment European Literature

The period of the Great Evangelical Revival in England produced a flurry of biblically influenced lyricism (e.g., Elizabeth Rowe, Hannah More, Charles Wesley, William Cowper, Christopher Smart). The novels of Henry Fielding (e.g., *Joseph Andrews* [1742], *Tom Jones* [1749]) offer, however, an atypical measure of residual biblical influence in this increasingly popular romance/epic genre. By the time of William Blake (1757–1827; *The Marriage of Heaven and Hell* [1793], *Jerusalem* [1820]) and the Romantic poets of Germany and England, the Bible was still of great literary and philosophical interest (e.g., JOHANN WOLFGANG VON GOETHE [1749–1832], SAMUEL TAYLOR COLERIDGE [1772–1834]) but it was being subjected to a process of often radical reconstitution by the poets who used it (see Leo Damrosch, *Symbol and Truth in Blakes's Myth*, and Stephen Prickett, *Words and the Word*). This period witnessed, effectively, the commencement of modernist hermeneutics in both biblical and literary criticism (see Prickett, *Words and the Word;* and Hans Frei, *The Eclipse of Biblical Narrative*).

In France the influence of Calvinist tradition is evident more in the breach than in the observance, as the literary careers of the two most prominent French ex-Calvinist writers, JEAN-JACQUES ROUSSEAU (1712–1778) and André Gide (1869–1951), may serve to illustrate. The direct influence of the Bible upon French literature is by far more evident in twentieth-century Catholic writers such as François Mauriac (1885–1970; *La Pharisienne; L'Agneau*) and Raymond Abellio (*La Fosse Babel; Les Yeux d'Ezechiel sont ouverts*), just as in the nineteenth century it infused most visibly the poetry of Alfred de Vigny (1797–1863; *La Colère de Samson; Le Mont des Oliviers*).

In Germany, the nineteenth-century lyric poetry of Friedrich Rückert (1788–1866), drawing heavily on biblical wisdom literature and Lutheran New Testament typology, is complemented by the poetry of J. C. Friedrich von Schiller (1759–1805). Both writers are indebted to the "mystical" biblicism of seventeenth-century Silesian lyricist Johannes Scheffler (1624–1677). This vein of Germanic biblical lyricism, drawing heavily on the Passion narratives and their themes of atonement and resurrection, flows powerfully into the modern period, for example, in the poetry of Austrian Georg Trakl (1887–1914). Goethe's extensive familiarity with both the Bible and its traditions of commentary are evident in both his *Faust* (1790; 1808; 1832) and his romantic hymns (e.g., "Christ ist erstanden"). Eminent nineteenth-century poets living in Germany also made significant contributions that depart from the mystical and romantic coloration of their countrymen: Heinrich Heine (1797–1856) in "Belshazzar" and "Die Passion Blume" shows biblical influence vigorously contesting with Hellenic tradition and holding its own. Heine's work may be seen as heralding a revival of biblical character and subject, which was to parallel historical interest in biblical narrative among German theologians in the early twentieth century. Mennonite Herman Suderman's novel *Das hohe Lied* (1908) and play *Sodoms Ende* (1891) were later to enjoy considerable popularity, though as his play *Magda* suggests, Suderman's emphasis is often upon rebellion against the authority of biblical mores. A teenage James Joyce (1882–1941) accompanied his parents to see a Dublin performance of *Magda;* to their consternation, they found the Protestant play an apologue for the author's rejection of both family and faith.

Russian fiction likewise exhibits a strong thread of biblical influence, though the stitching is not of Protestant but of Russian Orthodox making. There are, however, points of close contact. Fyodor Dostoyevsky's (1821–1881) *Idiot* is a type of fictional transfiguration of Jesus, and the catalyst for transformation of his protagonist Raskolnikov in *Crime and Punishment* comes when the murderer reads from the New Testament of one of his victims about the resurrection of Lazarus. Biblical language and biblical worldview are everywhere in the religiously eclectic Tolstoy (1828–1910). In Mikhail Solokhov's novel of protest *The Master and Margarita* it is the devil himself who confirms to a distraught protagonist (by historical flashback) that Jesus really was tried before Pontius Pilate, Soviet propaganda notwithstanding. And the Siberian Gulag prisoner protagonist in Aleksandr Solzhenitsyn's (1918–) *One Day in the Life of Ivan Denisovich* is brought to hope through the biblical witness of a fellow prisoner, a Baptist.

The success of Solokhov's type of historical fictionalizing of biblical narrative is seen in the wide number of examples that have appeared in northern Europe especially. Selma Lagerlof's (1858–1940) *Kristuslegender*, offering legendary adaptations of apocryphal gospel narrative, and her fellow Swede Par Lagerkvist's (1891–1974) novel *Barrabas* (1953), a look at the Passion of Christ from the perspective of the released brigand, are part of a rich genre of modern biblical fiction. Included are works such as Thomas Mann's (1875–1955) landmark four-part novelization *Joseph und seine Bruder* (1930–1943) and his novella on the giving of the law, *Das Gesetz* (1944), Polish

novelist Henryk Sienkiewicz's (1846–1916) *Quo Vadis?* (1896) concerning the life and ministry of St. Peter, Oscar Wilde's (1854–1900) provocative fictionalization of the life and death of John the Baptist in his play *Salomé* (1893), and, more recently, Polish-born Yiddish novelist Scholem Asch's (1880–1957) *The Nazarene* (1939) and *The Apostle* (1943). *The Last Temptation of Christ* by Greek novelist Nikos Kazantzakis (1885–1957) is a revisionist presentation of Jesus in the tradition of Lagerkvist.

The power of biblical mythos to generate the patterns of personal and community life is persistent in all Western literatures. The Bible's central tropes, themes, and symbols continue to provide, as Northrop Frye has suggested (following Blake), the "great code" of Western art and literature. In the modern period this is perhaps most especially true in regional literatures. Norwegian expatriate O. E. Rolvag offers a powerful American example in *Giants in the Earth* (1927), aspects of which are mirrored in Icelandic novelist Gunnar Gunnarson's *Kirken paa Bjerget* (1924–1928) and Mennonite Canadian Rudy Wiebe's *A Peace Shall Destroy Many* (1962). In this genre one would also want to place Moravian Gerhart Hauptman's *Der Narr in Christo, Emmanuel Quint* (1910). But biblical encoding as an aspect of ethnic identity has become a major theme in African literature in the later twentieth century, not only among European Africans such as South African Alan Payton (*Cry, the Beloved Country* [1949]) but in postcolonial African writing as well. For Chinua Achebe (1930– , *The Arrow of God* [1964]), the Bible was instrumental to an education in English; this point of purchase allows him to rewrite European novels of Africa (e.g., Graham Greene's [1904–1991] *Heart of the Matter*) from an African point of view, a viewpoint often more biblically acute in its articulation than European counterparts.

It would be difficult to find a contribution of Christianity to world civilization more foundational than this, that Bible translation and paraphrase should have become midwife to so many great vernacular literatures. But there is more: traditions of textual commentary and exposition, as well as of theological reflection, have had an effect almost as prodigious. Communities formed by a common text quickly develop cadres of trained readers. The relationship of biblical hermeneutics, exegesis, and theological reflection to literary theory and practical literary criticism in Western culture, for example, is essentially parental. This parenting is evident in both Jewish and Christian traditions: highly visible proponents of agnosticism such as Harold Bloom (1930–) and Jacques Derrida (1930–) represent a mere secularization of the talmudic and midrashic commentary on which

231

they were raised; so also the American new critics, in their antimetaphysical austerity, represent a stringent secularizing of Protestant textual method and, in their goal of the intelligently independent reader, the ideal Bible reader of their own more frankly Reformation roots is clearly visible. Matthew Arnold's notion of the literary critic as a kind of secular priest (*God and the Bible*) or Northrop Frye's sense that what we now think of as "literature" is effectively a "secular Scripture" (*The Secular Scripture; The Great Code*) likewise bear consistent witness to an enormous and, as George Steiner has properly observed, largely unrepaid cultural debt to the Bible and biblical tradition.

See also Biblical Translation.

References and Further Reading

Bercovitch, Sacvan. *The American Jeremiad.* Madison: University of Wisconsin Press, 1978.

Brantley, Richard E. *Locke, Wesley and the Method of English Romanticism.* Gainesville, FL: University of Florida Press, 1984.

Damrosch, Leopold. *God's Plot and Man's Stories: Studies in the Fictional Imagination from Milton to Fielding.* Chicago: University of Chicago Press, 1985.

———. *Symbol and Truth in Blake's Myth.* Princeton, NJ: Princeton University Press, 1980.

Fisch, Harold. *The Biblical Presence in Shakespeare, Milton, and Blake.* Oxford: Clarendon, 1999.

Frei, Hans. *The Eclipse of Biblical Narrative: A Study in Eighteenth and Nineteenth-Century Hermeneutics.* New Haven, CT: Yale University Press, 1974.

Frye, Northrop. *The Great Code: The Bible and Literature.* London: Routledge, 1982.

Gunn, Giles, ed. *The Bible and American Arts and Letters.* Philadelphia: Fortress Press, 1983.

Jeffrey, David Lyle, ed. *A Dictionary of Biblical Tradition in English Literature.* Grand Rapids, MI: Eerdmans, 1992.

———. *People of the Book: Christian Identity and Literary Culture.* Grand Rapids, MI: Eerdmans, 1996.

Prickett, Stephen. *Words and the Word: Language, Poetics and Biblical Interpretation.* Cambridge: Cambridge University Press, 1986.

Steiner, George. *Real Presences.* Chicago: University of Chicago Press, 1989.

Ziolkowski, Theodore. *Fictional Transfigurations of Jesus.* Princeton, NJ: Princeton University Press, 1972.

DAVID LYLE JEFFREY

BIBLE CAMPS AND CONFERENCE CENTERS

During the twentieth century, Bible camps and conferences became extremely popular among English-speaking Protestants worldwide. Although no unified organization or single pattern emerged, camps and conferences typically offered programs of lectures, music, and recreational activities during summer months and sometimes during the off-season. *Camps* were oriented toward children or adolescents; *conference centers* or *retreat centers* toward families or groups of adults. Many were located in scenic spots in the mountains or near oceans or lakes. Christian Camping International/USA, one umbrella association, claimed 1,000 member organizations that hosted 5.5 million guests annually in the late 1990s. Outside the United States, another 1,000 organizations are affiliated with various national chapters of Christian Camping International, but many camps and conferences did not join this or any association. Thus their total number, in the United States and worldwide, is uncertain.

Camps for youth had a significant influence on twentieth-century Protestantism. Most mainline Protestant churches organized camps along denominational lines, and they tended to see such camps as the continuation of church-based religious education. Evangelical, fundamentalist, and Pentecostal churches established their own camps, but even more widespread and influential were independent camps founded by influential religious leaders like evangelist Jack Wyrtzen (1913–1966), who established Word of Life Camp in Schroon Lake, New York, in 1947. Conservative leaders like Wyrtzen usually saw camp as a place for young people to seek conversion, to reconsecrate themselves, and to receive callings to missionary service and ordained ministry. As women entered the workforce in increasing numbers in the 1980s and 1990s, two-income families relied on camps to serve as caretakers for school-age children during the summer months and camp attendance boomed. As a result, specialty youth camps emerged that focused, for example, on wilderness experiences, weight loss, honing special skills such as music, or aiding children with various handicaps.

Bible conference centers for adults generally emphasized education, inspiration, wholesome fellowship, and social recreation. Some scheduled their own summer or year-round programs anchored by notable preachers, musicians, or entertainers. This type of conference generally hired a large staff to serve as program directors, waiters, and housekeepers. On the other hand, retreat centers did not generally provide recreation or conference speakers, but they often did offer pastoral counseling or spiritual direction as well as simple meals to small groups and individuals.

Scholars generally trace the origins of Bible camps and conference centers to camp meetings, which institutionalized revivalism during the nineteenth century. Camp meetings began in the late eighteenth century among southern Methodists in the United States; after the 1800 camp meeting revival at Cane Ridge, Kentucky, their popularity increased dramatically and spread to the Baptists, Presbyterians, and others. By the end of the nineteenth century, many camp meetings had established grounds with permanent structures; some, such as the Methodist assemblies on Martha's Vineyard (established 1835) and at Ocean Grove, New Jersey (1869), and Chautauqua, New York (1870), had transformed themselves into summer resorts for middle-class and wealthy families. At these upscale sites, camp meeting sermons gradually became inspirational or educational lectures; hymn-sings were transformed into concerts by choral societies and professional musicians; rude family tents were replaced with charming wood cottages; and the original emphasis on conversion was forsaken in favor of a genteel desire for moral uplift and wholesome recreation. Chautauqua especially became a popular center for adult education after the Chautauqua Institution was established in 1874, and by 1876 the first of scores of copycat associations had been established at Wellesley Island, New York; Petosky, Michigan; and Clear Lake, Iowa. Later, dozens of traveling chautauquas circulated throughout small-town America offering lectures and concerts under large tents. In 1921 the nearly one hundred traveling chautauquas visited 9,597 American towns.

Another precursor to Bible camps and conferences was the annual convention begun in 1875 in Keswick, a village in the English Lake District. American and British participants in the Holiness movement began the conference, which stressed practical Bible teaching that helped believers to live the "higher life in the fullness of the Spirit." In the 1880s evangelist Dwight L. Moody (1837–1899) organized a similar annual conference in Northfield, Massachusetts. Like the Keswick meetings, to which they were often compared, the Northfield conferences featured speakers from various denominations who focused their lectures on Bible exposition and practical Christian living rather than on systematic theology or denominational distinctives.

Of the other conferences held during the last quarter of the nineteenth century, the best known was the Niagara Bible Conference. Known at first as the Believers' Meeting for Bible Study, the conference met annually from 1876 until 1900, most often at a resort hotel in Niagara-on-the-Lake, Ontario. Though ostensibly an occasion for simple study of Scripture, the conference became the foremost vehicle for the dissemination of premillennialist teaching in North America. The meetings were marked by an interdenominational flavor, and conference organizers welcomed anyone who would subscribe to the fourteen-point Niagara creed, which espoused biblical inerrancy and other conservative doctrines that were later embraced by fundamentalists.

In the twentieth century new conferences combined various elements from camp meetings, Chautauqua,

Keswick, Northfield, and Niagara. The best known of these was the Winona Lake Bible Conference, founded in 1895 near Warsaw, Indiana, which included a six-week chautauqua program with local and national secular talent—musicians, magicians, actors, and even silent movies—followed by a one- or two-week Bible conference program of speakers who addressed Keswickian higher life, Northfield-style preparation for Christian service, and Niagara-inspired prophecy teaching. The conference was held adjacent to a large lake on a spacious and beautiful campus, and many recreation opportunities were available, such as swimming, boating, golf, and roller-skating. Winona Lake, like other camp and conference grounds, became a tourist destination for Protestant families who wanted to enjoy a respectable summer vacation.

Winona Lake's secular chautauqua program declined after World War I even as the Bible conference continued to prosper. Not surprisingly, other conferences founded in the twentieth century generally rejected professional secular entertainment but otherwise embraced the Winona model, interspersing wholesome outdoor recreation with preaching and lectures on a variety of religious topics. Some of these included Montreat near Black Mountain, North Carolina (established 1897); Mount Hermon near Santa Cruz, California (1906); and Camp-of-the-Woods in Speculator, New York (1916).

Nondenominational Bible conferences typically drew participants from many Protestant traditions by avoiding points of doctrinal disagreement—especially about BAPTISM, PREDESTINATION, and church POLITY. Indeed, the conferences generally claimed to wish to avoid all controversial topics, but nevertheless most organizers and attendees operated with important presuppositions—that the Bible was entirely reliable, that Christians should seek ways to apply its teachings to their own daily lives, and that each person should experience a personal conversion to vibrant faith, followed by noticeable spiritual growth. Some conferences also assumed certain doctrinal points such as dispensational premillennialism; only in rare cases might leaders permit a speaker to disagree publicly with a cardinal doctrine of a conference.

Youth camping began in the second half of the nineteenth century as part of the Muscular Christian movement; it grew dramatically after the establishment of the Boy Scouts in England (1908) and the United States (1910). In the early twentieth century, denominational and nondenominational conferences began to schedule youth events. At first most ran concurrently with adult offerings so that families could continue to stay together in family tents or cottages; later many conferences also offered separate youth camps. For example, Ridgecrest Baptist Assembly near Black Mountain, North Carolina, was established in 1909, but a separate camp for boys was started in 1929 adjacent to the assembly, and a camp for girls began in 1955.

By the middle of the century a more vigorous outdoors ethos began to emphasize remoteness, resulting in the establishment of such youth camps as Hume Lake (1946), near King's Canyon National Park in California, and Honey Rock (1951) in northern Wisconsin, owned by Wheaton College. In 1966 Honey Rock established an Outward Bound–style program for college students, becoming the first Christian camp to adopt a wilderness/adventure curriculum. Young Life, an interdenominational outreach to high school students active in 550 U.S. communities, operated a network of seventeen camps by the end of the century; three of them emphasized wilderness camping.

At the outset of the twenty-first century, the vitality of Bible camps and conferences was evident not only in the number of sites around the world, but in the variety of conference types. Primitive camp meeting grounds, used once per year, still dotted the rural United States. Virtually all denominations operated their own campgrounds or conference centers—some with extensive programming, others available for rental by individual congregations. Prophecy seminars and Bible exposition were still available at many independently owned conference sites. Youth camping was popular among all groups from fundamentalist to liberal. Indeed, camps and conference centers had become a part of the Protestant mainstream both in North America and, increasingly, around the world.

See also Moody, Dwight Lyman.

References and Further Reading

Brown, Kenneth O. *Holy Ground, Too: The Camp Meeting Family Tree.* Hazelton, PA: Holiness Archives, 1997.

Mattson, Lloyd, *Christian Camping Today.* Wheaton, IL: Harold Shaw, 1998.

Sandeen, Ernest R. *The Roots of Fundamentalism.* Chicago: University of Chicago Press, 1970.

JAY BLOSSOM

BIBLE COLLEGES AND INSTITUTES

The Bible College or Institute is an essential element in the training of ministers for many Evangelical/Fundamentalist denominations and independent churches. Tracing their origin to certain European schools formed in the 1800s to train church workers and missionaries who lacked high school or college training, Bible institutes began in America in 1882 with the founding of A. B. Simpson's Missionary Training Institute in New York City. Other prominent pastors and evangelists followed suit, and over time the Bible Institute became the preferred means of preparing pastors for many churches. These early institutions were dedicated to the integration of English Bible instruction, spiritual formation, and practical ministry participation and training, usually in urban settings. Their purpose, in the words of DWIGHT L. MOODY, was to train "gap men [and women], who are trained to fill the gap between the common people and the ministers" (Witmer 1962:36).

The original stated purpose of Bible institutes in America was not to replace colleges and SEMINARIES. Rather, as traditional seminaries and colleges adopted theological positions that were unacceptable to conservatives, they began to form their own institutions that would represent their conservative perspective. This tendency intensified in the 1920s with the theological struggle known as the Fundamentalist–Modernist Controversy. Consequently, Bible institute curricula represented a particular conservative theological position, usually tied to DISPENSATIONALISM. As Bible institutes began to replace colleges and seminaries as the preferred form of pastoral training, the majority of them entered a path of educational upward mobility that transformed them into Bible colleges, liberal arts colleges, and even universities and graduate-level seminaries. In the process the original emphasis on a high degree of integration between BIBLE instruction and practical ministry training has almost always suffered.

The mission drift that has historically turned Bible institutes gradually into colleges and, in some cases, universities should not be seen as detrimental to the Bible institute movement. The original need for practical church workers that gave rise to the Bible institutes is perennial in Christianity, and as Bible institutes have become primarily dedicated to postsecondary training, new institutes (usually church-based, but often virtually identical to the earliest examples) spring up by the hundreds to replace them. Furthermore American missionaries trained in the Bible schools have founded thousands of schools in other countries that are virtually identical to the schools their founders graduated from in the UNITED STATES.

Historical Development

The earliest schools for the training of ministers in America were the colonial-era colleges such as Harvard (1636), Yale (1701), and Princeton (1754). Whereas Harvard and Yale were founded from the beginning as colleges on the model of British colleges, Princeton is usually seen to trace its origin to the Log College, founded in Neshaminy, Pennsylvania in 1746. This school, with perhaps some thirty other "log colleges" that were patterned after it, gave instruction at a level somewhere between grammar school and college. (There were no high schools at the time.) Their purpose was to train ministers as quickly as possible for the expanding Western frontier of the American colonies. Because of this similarity of instructional level and purpose, Bible colleges often claim to have descended from the Log College.

The direct line of descent, however, is traced from European religious training schools such as the Pastor's College founded by CHARLES HADDON SPURGEON in the 1850s and the Kaiserswerth school founded in 1836 by German Lutherans (which was founded to train DEACONESSES). Other important European schools were the Mildmay schools and the East London Bible Institute in London. Evangelical leaders such as Simpson, Moody, and A. J. Gordon visited these and other schools on their European tours and admired them in subsequent writings. Within a short time of visiting such European schools all three of these leaders were to found American Bible institutes modeled after them.

What impressed the American evangelists about the schools was the fact that they drew their students from working-class backgrounds, trained them in very practical skills for immediate ministry, gave women the opportunity to be trained for Christian service, and quickly produced thousands of religious workers (from pastors to deacons to SUNDAY SCHOOL teachers to missionaries and street evangelists). The missionary enthusiasm of the time to reach the teeming masses both overseas and in the newly burgeoning American urban centers created a great sense of urgency for training workers in much larger numbers and social diversity than traditional colleges and seminaries could produce.

The most influential of the early American Bible institutes was MOODY BIBLE INSTITUTE, founded in Chicago in 1886. Moody, a shoe salesman with no higher education, had become a renowned evangelist after his highly successful campaign in Great Britain in 1873 and gained a position of leadership among American Evangelicals through a series of mass evangelistic meetings in the United States. During the 1880s, however, the enthusiasm for mass meetings in America began to wane, and Moody began to explore other means of evangelistic outreach. Earlier he had adopted the pattern of the Mildmay schools he had visited in England, appointing a normal school principal, Emma Dryer, to begin a "Bible Work" to train women as Bible teachers and Christian workers in short classes (Brereton 1990:53). In 1886 Moody launched an effort to raise $250,000 from the citizens of Chicago to expand that work into what became, in 1889, a "Bible Institute for Home and Foreign Missions." Moody's aggressive promotion of the school soon turned the Moody Bible Institute into the largest, wealthiest, and most prestigious of the American Bible schools and made it a popular model for many other schools in terms of organization, curriculum, and even doctrine.

The newly founded Bible schools were successful in training large numbers of men and women for practical Christian work, and thus became very popular among fundamentalist Christians who were deeply concerned about evangelizing the American working class, with its millions of recent immigrants, as well as reaching the millions of people overseas who had not heard the Gospel. Mainline Protestants of the time were also concerned about the same people, and they also founded training schools to train church workers and missionaries, especially through such agencies as the YMCA. They were often more focused on social and physical needs than were the conservatives, but because all such schools were concerned with practical work among the poorer classes, the distinction between mainline missionary training schools and the conservative Bible schools was slight for many years. Nevertheless the theological rift between the two emphases would increase over time.

As the divide between conservative and liberal Protestants widened because of the Fundamentalist–Modernist controversy of the 1920s, fundamentalist churches abandoned the mainline Protestant denominations and their colleges and seminaries and either founded new denominations or remained independent. As a result they began to lean more on Bible institutes and colleges for the training of pastors. This tendency was strong especially in Reformed revivalist and WESLEYAN HOLINESS churches, as well as the new Pentecostal churches, which were popular among the working classes and strongly rejected LIBERAL PROTESTANTISM. Although it is clear that the original Bible school founders were very serious about training a massive army of lay workers, the Bible schools had been producing pastors from the beginning. It is likely that some of the earliest founders intended this result, given the fact that Moody lacked formal theological training himself and Spurgeon's college in ENGLAND had always had the intention of training pastors who lacked higher levels of previous formal education. Many founders would have shared Spurgeon's opinion that "the fervor of the generality of the [university-trained] students . . . lagged far behind their literary training" (Ringenberg 1984:160).

In addition to training ministers, the Bible schools served a larger role for many independent churches. Because they often developed periodicals, radio programming, and broadcast networks, and hosted national conferences, the Bible schools provided many of the functions of a DENOMINATION. Some of them, especially Moody and the Bible Institute of Los Angeles (Biola), became de facto interdenominational headquarters for many independent churches. Denominational schools were usually tied intimately to their denominational headquarters, serving as the educational arm of the denomination and as an invaluable tool for socializing ministers into the denominational culture.

Curricular Structure

The curriculum of the early Bible schools was focused on the training of relatively uneducated lay people to serve as pastor's helpers, Sunday school officers, Bible teachers, door-to-door evangelists, missionaries, gospel musicians, urban mission workers, YMCA and youth club workers, and visitors for jails, hospitals, and senior citizen facilities (Brereton 1990:viii). Consequently the Bible schools focused on practical training rather than the classical learning favored by colleges and universities. The Bible was seen to be the primary textbook for every class. Rather than teaching Hebrew and Greek, which in some schools were offered as electives, the schools focused on studying the English Bible and using it for particular tasks of Christian work.

By the 1920s the Bible was usually studied in Bible schools by what was called the "inductive" method. Rather than leaning on commentaries or exegesis of the original languages, students would read the biblical text several times, and then go to it with questions that they would either formulate for themselves or receive from their professors in lists. The 1922 catalog from Biola described its approach to Bible study as being that which is "pursued in all other branches of scientific study, the INDUCTIVE METHOD. Every passage of scripture bearing upon [a] doctrine is examined and its exact meaning in the light of the context determined . . ." (Brereton 1990:89). It is very important to note that they sought to establish a *scientific* rationale for their method of scripture study. Although conservatives of the time often scorned their opponents as "Modernists," they were themselves thoroughgoing modernists in their approach to knowledge. Science, which they perceived in the Baconian sense to be a body of proven facts established through the scientific method, had been hijacked by theorists, they maintained, who based their science on unproven hypotheses such as Darwinian evolution in biology or the Graf–Wellhausen Documentary Hypothesis in biblical studies. Conservatives saw the Bible as a book of facts guaranteed by divine verbal revelation and discoverable through observation. By basing their biblical studies methods on what they perceived to be the scientific method rather than theories, they sought to

maintain an intellectual high ground vis-à-vis their opponents.

Bible study often involved reading through the entire Bible multiple times to get a sense of the whole. The unity of Old and New Testaments was stressed, and a "scarlet thread of redemption" was seen as the unifying theme of biblical revelation. In many schools, dispensational THEOLOGY was an important organizing theme for understanding the Bible. After getting a sense of the whole, students took courses in Old or New Testament survey, getting a panoramic view of the testaments as well as sections within them such as Pentateuch, Historical Books, Poetic Books, Major Prophets, the Gospels, Pauline Epistles, and the like.

A very popular method of biblical study was the "synthetic method," which was used by James Gray, dean at Moody for many years beginning in the 1890s. Gray required students to read a particular book of the Bible through in one sitting several times to get a sense of the sweep of the book's content. Afterward students made and memorized content outlines for the book. Often students were required to do this for each book of the Bible. Gray included definitions of biblical terms, cross-references from other books and from both Testaments, and typology to increase the students' appreciation for the unity of the Bible's message. In addition to study of each book of the Bible, curricula usually included courses in Bible Geography, Bible Introduction (usually with an apologetic function), and courses on how to teach the Bible, such as "Blackboard Drawing."

The Bible was not just examined to learn facts. Rather, students sought out practical questions related to ministry and the spiritual life. The Pentecostal movement was born in 1901 when students at Charles Parham's Bethel Bible School were left with an assignment to answer the question, "What is the biblical evidence for the Baptism in the Holy Spirit." Inductive study of the book of Acts led students to the conclusion that the only consistently mentioned evidence was speaking in tongues. Upon reaching this conclusion the students moved immediately to practice and prayed to receive the same evidence for themselves. Because PENTECOSTALISM went on to become what was perhaps the most successful religious and social movement of the twentieth century, the role of this method of Bible study in Bible colleges should not be underestimated (Jenkins 2003:8).

In addition to courses aimed directly at the study of the Bible, the Bible schools stressed preparation for "personal work." Each student was expected to be able to engage in personal EVANGELISM or "soul-winning" during and after his or her Bible school training. At Moody students learned over the course of four terms of study how to deal with "the uninterested, the interested but ignorant . . . the interested with difficulties, the self-righteous, the backslider, the fearful and despairing . . . those with erroneous views of the truth (such as Catholics, Jews, and Christian Scientists) . . . the procrastinator, the obstinate, and the skeptic" (Brereton 1990:101). A classic text used in personal evangelism classes was REUBEN ARCHER TORREY's *How to Bring Men to Christ*.

Schools often referred to this work as a "clinic" or "laboratory" component that would give a practical outlet to the "how to" knowledge gained in the classroom. Not only did this allow students to "learn by doing" but it also helped them retain the "fire for souls" that usually motivated them to study in the first place. Activities included personal evangelism on urban streets and from house-to-house, but also evangelism and manual labor in institutions such as jails, poorhouses, rescue missions, hospitals, and convalescent homes. Many students engaged in such activities as leading church choirs and teaching Sunday school or Bible classes. They also organized impromptu street services, served in large evangelistic campaigns, passed out tracts, and engaged in other such activities that often resulted in the founding of new churches.

Beyond the courses on the Bible itself and personal evangelism, students usually took a few courses on nonbiblical subjects. Those with little previous education could take courses such as reading, writing, and arithmetic. English literature and history made their way into Bible school curricula from early times. Whereas liberal arts courses were generally minimized to make more room for studying the Bible, courses in the social sciences (psychology, sociology, anthropology, economics, and political science) were sometimes taught, usually having the Bible as a primary textbook. Such subjects were seen as adding nothing to biblical revelation, and were approached for whatever practical content they might have that would be useful for ministry. At some schools students were able to choose specialties in areas such as foreign MISSIONS, church music, Christian education, and pastoral ministry.

Although time brought changes in the Bible school curriculum, including stronger general education requirements and usually lessened practical ministry requirements, the basic philosophy and structure of the Bible school curriculum generally persisted for at least a hundred years.

Accreditation and Upward Mobility

The emphasis on practical training for lay workers meant that the first programs of study in the Bible institutes were usually one or two years in length and not limited to those who had a high school education. When the first were established, high school graduates were few in number, and less than 5 percent of Americans attended college. Nevertheless there was pressure on Bible schools to copy the prestigious methods and standards of traditional colleges. There was considerable determination among the first and even second generation of leaders to resist what was seen as a worldly temptation, but by the 1920s and 1930s many programs expanded to a third and even fourth year. Many schools changed the name from Bible Institute to Bible College when they began to offer a four-year degree.

Rising educational standards in the United States, especially after World War II, dramatically increased the number of high school graduates in the country, even as the G.I. Bill was increasing the percentage of Americans attending college. The opportunity to enroll students at the government's expense was a powerful inducement to higher standards and accreditation. The rise of the Neo-Evangelical movement and the decline of FUNDAMENTALISM created significant inducement to higher academic levels as well. In 1947 the Accrediting Association of Bible Colleges (AABC) was founded under the auspices of the NATIONAL ASSOCIATION OF EVANGELICALS to help Bible colleges and institutes upgrade their offerings. This move was a self-conscious effort to counter the tendency for Bible Colleges to convert themselves into liberal arts colleges to gain regional accreditation.

The establishment of an accrediting agency for Bible Colleges helped stem the tide of Bible colleges turning into liberal arts colleges, but by 1960 approximately half of all Bible Institutes had followed the upward path to becoming Bible Colleges, and in the 1980s and 1990s a new wave of upward mobility broke out. As regional accrediting agencies began to look more favorably on single-purpose institutions, Bible Colleges began to seek dual accreditation by both the AABC and their appropriate regional accrediting association. Many Bible colleges continued to turn into liberal arts colleges and even universities offering graduate programs. Examples of such upward mobility include the first American Bible Institute, A. B. Simpson's Missionary Training Institute (1882), which became Nyack College; the Boston Missionary Training School (1889), which quickly became Gordon College; the Bible Institute of Los Angeles (1913), which became Biola University (1981); the Training School for Christian Workers in Los Angeles (1899), which became Azusa Pacific University (1981); Philadelphia School of the Bible (1914) and the Bible Institute of Pennsylvania (1913), which merged to become a Bible college before it became Philadelphia Biblical University (2001); Southern

California Bible School (1920), which became Vanguard University (1997); and Southwestern Bible School (1927), which became Southwestern Assemblies of God University (1994).

Renewal Movements

This path of upward mobility that converts Bible schools into colleges and universities is tied closely to the sociological tendency of betterment among Evangelical churches that has been exhaustively documented by social scientists such as H. RICHARD NIEBUHR, Liston Pope, Milton Yinger, and others. As young churches and religious movements mature and prosper, they often tend to join the middle classes enthusiastically, leaving ministry to the poor and working classes behind. As they do so, their colleges seek the same upward mobility that their members are experiencing. In the process new churches tend to rise up to fill the gap at the lower end of the social spectrum. In response to the need to train workers quickly these churches usually repeat the process of institutional formation that gave rise to the first Bible Colleges.

During the 1980s and 1990s hundreds of new Bible institutes sprang up in the United States to fill the churches' needs for lay workers with practical ministry training. Some of them became accredited Bible Colleges. Many of these schools were extensions and distance education efforts of accredited Bible Colleges, although many were freestanding as well. Schools related to popular television or radio evangelists were also founded, along with some related to revival movements such as the Brownsville School of Revival in Pensacola, Florida. Additionally, programs like Master's Commission rose up to give young people a chance to spend a year or more of their life in Christian service training. During the same period a number of unrecognized accrediting agencies also sprang up to give the new schools an appearance of credibility.

As long as churches exist among the urban poor, there will likely be a need for the kind of "gap" ministers that Moody envisioned, and Bible institutes and colleges will continue to rise up to meet their needs.

References and Further Reading

Brereton, Virginia Lieson. *Training God's Army: The American Bible School 1880–1940*. Bloomington and Indianapolis: Indiana University Press, 1990.
Carpenter, Joel A., and Kenneth W. Shipps, eds. *Making Higher Education Christian: The History and Mission of Evangelical Colleges in America*. Grand Rapids, MI: Wm. B. Eerdmans, 1987.
Findley, James J. Jr. *Dwight L. Moody, American Evangelist, 1837–1899*. Chicago: University of Chicago Press, 1969.
Jenkins, Philip. *The New Christendom: The Coming of Global Christianity*. New York: Oxford University Press, 2002.
Marsden, George M. *Fundamentalism and American Culture: The Shaping of Twentieth Century Evangelicalism, 1870–1925*. New York: Oxford University Press, 1980.
Niebuhr, H. Richard. *The Social Sources of Denominationalism*. New York: Henry Holt & Company, 1929.
Pope, Liston. *Millhands and Preachers*. New York: Yale University Press, 1942.
Ringenberg, William C. *The Christian College: A History of Protestant Higher Education in America*. Grand Rapids, MI: Wm. B. Eerdmans, 1984.
Witmer, S. A. *The Bible College Story: Education with Dimension*. Manhasset, NY: Channel Press, 1962.

JOSEPH L. CASTLEBERRY

BIBLE CONFERENCES

From the late nineteenth century to the mid-twentieth century, the Bible conference was a prominent institution among conservative evangelical Protestants in the UNITED STATES. Large interdenominational conferences served as both centers for spreading evangelical and fundamentalist teaching and as venues for "safe" and "spiritual" vacations.

Several British conferences were the forerunners of the BIBLE conference movement in North America. The Keswick conventions begun in 1875 in ENGLAND became popular centers for Bible teaching with a stress on Christian holiness expressed in surrender of one's will to God to achieve victory over conscious sin. Also influential was the Mildmay Conference founded by Anglican clergyman William Pennefather in 1864, one of the first conferences to display prominently the vacation element.

The most important American Bible conference, the Niagara Bible Conference, held annual meetings in Niagara-on-the-Lake, Ontario, CANADA, from 1883 to 1897. Under the leadership of Presbyterian clergyman James H. Brookes of St. Louis, Missouri, Niagara became a major center of teaching the premillennial return of Christ to earth, one of the major doctrinal emphases of the conferences.

Arising about the same time as Niagara was the Northfield Bible Conference begun by American evangelist DWIGHT L. MOODY in Massachusetts. Moody followed the pattern of the Mildmay Conference of Pennefather, whom he had met in Britain. Holding his first meetings in 1880 and 1881 and then continuously from 1885, Moody established his Northfield Conference as a center for conservative Bible teaching.

The THEOLOGY expounded at the Bible conferences was generally evangelical Protestant, with three characteristic emphases. In addition to premillennialism, Bible conference speakers usually avowed an unswerving commitment to the inerrancy of the Bible and many advocated Keswick Holiness piety. These three emphases later played a large role in the development of fundamentalist theology.

The first half of the twentieth century saw a remarkable growth in Bible conferences. After the demise of Niagara, A. C. Gaebelein founded the Sea Cliff Bible Conference in New York, one of the fruits of which was C. I. Scofield's influential SCOFIELD REFERENCE BIBLE. Typical of these conferences, and perhaps the most influential, was the Winona Lake Bible Conference in northern Indiana, founded in 1895. Patterned on Northfield, Winona also stressed cultural elements, including the establishment of a successful chautauqua program. Winona attracted some of the leading lights of conservative EVANGELICALISM, such as WILLIAM JENNINGS BRYAN, who served as the organization's president, and renowned evangelist BILLY SUNDAY, who made his summer home in Winona Lake.

After the middle of the twentieth century, Bible conferences declined in popularity. Aging facilities, theological dissension, and changing tastes in both leisure and worship among evangelicals combined to end the heyday of the conference movement. The patterns of the Bible conferences, however, remain evident in the youth camps, seminars, and retreats still popular among fundamentalist and evangelical audiences, as shown by the continued popularity of youth camps such as Word of Life in New York and the Wilds in North Carolina.

See also Biblical Inerrancy; Fundamentalism; Holiness Movement; Keswick Movement

References and Further Reading

Aron, Cindy. *Working at Play: A History of Vacations in the United States.* New York: Oxford University Press, 1999.

Beale, David O. *In Pursuit of Purity: American Fundamentalism Since 1850.* Greenville, SC: Unusual Publications, 1986.

Sandeen, Ernest. *The Roots of Fundamentalism: British and American Millenarianism, 1800–1930.* Chicago: University of Chicago Press, 1970.

MARK SIDWELL

BIBLE, KING JAMES VERSION

The translation of the Bible into English, authorized by King James I of ENGLAND, or, as the official title page of the translation rendered the matter, "translated out of the original tongues, and with the former translations diligently compared and revised, by his majesty's command." The translators of the "authorized" version drew heavily on the translations of WILLIAM TYNDALE (c. 1494–1536) as well as on other existing translations, such as the Bishops' Bible, used mainly in churches, and the Geneva Bible, with its heavy Puritan notes (see PURITANISM).

James authorized this translation at the beginning of his rule. He appointed some fifty-four divines who worked in six committees, with a final review by a committee of twelve members. The scholars began their work in 1607; the new version was published in 1611 and proved more of a revision of existing earlier translations than a new work. The term "authorized" must be understood as meaning (given that no record of a formal authorization of the translation exists) that King James "authorized" the work of translation by appointing a committee to undertake the task.

The King James Version has had a dramatic impact not only on the English language but also on English religion. This influence continues to the present, especially among conservative Protestant circles. Corrected versions of the Authorized (King James) Version were published in 1762 and in 1769. A major revision occurred in 1881 and 1885, the revision of the Old Testament and the New Testament, respectively. The foremost challenge to the traditional prominence of the King James Version was the Revised Standard Version of the Bible, published in 1952.

See also Bible and Literature; Bible Translations

References and Further Reading

The Cambridge History of the Bible. 3 vols. Cambridge: Cambridge Univ. Press, 1963–1970.

Stine, R. C. *Bible Translation and the Spread of the Church. The Last Two Hundred Years.* Leiden, New York: E. J. Brill, 1990.

HANS J. HILLERBRAND

BIBLE SOCIETIES

Pandenominational Protestant institutions dedicated to publishing and distributing the scriptures without doctrinal note or commentary began forming and coalescing into a coherent movement during the early nineteenth century. The BRITISH AND FOREIGN BIBLE SOCIETY (BFBS) and the AMERICAN BIBLE SOCIETY (ABS) quickly emerged as the most influential, well-funded, and broadly based national organizations. From the outset, denominational, political, and territorial tensions proved difficult for these organizations to overcome, and a series of schisms developed within the bible movement. Still, the bible societies proved remarkably successful at publishing and circulating unprecedented numbers of inexpensive scriptures. They incorporated cutting-edge technological innovations in their printing and binding operations, experimented with new forms of corporate organization to advance their mission, and initiated a broad range of bible translation programs. Bible society work aggressively supported and undergirded Protestant missionary activity throughout the world during the nineteenth century (see MISSIONS, MISSIONARY ORGANIZATIONS). National rivalries and doctrinal disagreements persisted, however, and increasingly fragmented the movement during the early twentieth century. Eventually, the established organizations attempted to pursue a more cooperative course, and they created an international fellowship known as the United Bible Societies in 1946. This federation soon underwrote its own extensive translation program. It also encouraged indigenous bible societies in historically non-Protestant countries, thus signaling a marked shift away from the movement's Anglo-American roots. Since the Second Vatican Council in the early 1960s, bible societies have enjoyed a more cordial relationship with the Roman Catholic Church and participated in numerous interconfessional translation projects. By the late twentieth century, bible society publications often emphasized common language versions, incorporated helps for new readers, featured thematic selections and scripture portions, and experimented with multimedia translations.

Basic Principles and Early History

Organized scripture distribution efforts were occasional and sporadic before the nineteenth century with a few exceptions. The Canstein Bible Institution (1710), established at HALLE, Germany, produced low-cost editions of German, Polish, Bohemian, and Ancient and Modern Greek bibles, and remained active at the turn of the twenty-first century. The French Bible Society (1792) proved more typical, achieving only marginal status and dissolving within a decade of its creation. Others pursued very limited aims, such as one London-based bible society that confined its efforts to naval and military personnel. Some denomination-based organizations, including the SOCIETY FOR PROMOTING CHRISTIAN KNOWLEDGE (1698) and the SOCIETY FOR THE PROPAGATION OF THE GOSPEL IN FOREIGN PARTS (1701), incorporated scripture distribution within their larger missionary purposes. For the most part, however, bible production and dissemination remained largely a haphazard and generally commercial affair until the formation of the British and Foreign Bible Society in 1804. Shortly thereafter, the bible movement exploded as the BFBS fostered the formation of independent bible societies throughout the European continent and North America. The following active, long-lived, and influential societies began operations in the early nineteenth century, largely modeling their constitutions on the BFBS: Hibernian Bible Society (1806), Finnish Bible Society (1812),

Danish Bible Society (1814), Netherlands Bible Society (1814), Icelandic Bible Society (1815), Swedish Bible Society (1815), Norwegian Bible Society (1816), and American Bible Society (1816). By 1816 scripture distribution organizations dotted the globe and carried out their activities from Philadelphia, Pennsylvania, to St. Petersburg, RUSSIA.

Several historical impulses and early nineteenth-century trends contributed to the founding of the BFBS and its contemporary institutional partners. Considered together, these factors illuminate the bible movement's fundamentally radical and transformative qualities. First, bible societies reflected complex social and economic changes that appeared to be altering life and work within European and North American cultures. The BFBS, for example, grew from a committee of the Religious Tract Society, which had been established in 1799 to produce attractive and morally acceptable literature for an increasingly literate and urbane British working class. An evolving technological revolution in the print trades made all sorts of popular pamphlets and newspapers broadly accessible across the social spectrum, and religious folk strove to include their perspectives in the rapidly expanding literary marketplace. Bible society founders and early nineteenth-century managers constituted a newly emerging, articulate, socially prominent, and prosperous urban middle class with a finely honed humanitarian sensibility. Philanthropic and charitable work provided them with a means of personal salvation, as well as a method for bridging the growing class gulf that accompanied industrialization.

Second, bible societies attempted to negotiate the theological and social divisions that seemed to be fragmenting Christianity. The BFBS defined its core mission in deceptively simple terms as encouraging "the wider circulation of the Holy Scriptures without note or comment," thereby hoping to avoid doctrinal disputes and interpretive disagreements. Indeed, "without note or comment" soon became the movement's definitive phrase and oft-repeated mantra, etched in the constitution of bible societies throughout the world. Organizations hoped to unite their frequently contentious constituencies behind the notion that scriptural truth transcended denominational bickering. Separating the biblical text from prefatory material, explanatory notes, and interpretive marginalia seemed to hold out the elusive promise of Christian, or at least Protestant, consensus.

All societies strove for wide-ranging denominational cooperation, although the specific composition of boards and supporters varied according to national and local circumstances. The BFBS's constitution explicitly mandated that the thirty-six member governing committee must include fifteen Anglicans, fifteen

Dissenters, and six foreigners resident in or near London. Methodists, Quakers, and CHURCH OF ENGLAND adherents (see METHODISM; FRIENDS, SOCIETY OF) mingled at board meetings, lending a remarkably unsectarian quality to the proceedings. Denominational composition differed considerably in the more heterogeneous American environment. Congregationalists and Presbyterians initially dominated the ABS governing board (see CONGREGATIONALISM, PRESBYTERIANISM), reflecting their prestige and status within the national Protestant polity, but Methodists occupied an increasingly prominent position in the movement by the 1830s, underscoring their remarkable growth. Pandenominationalism proved definitive, regardless of national context.

Third, the movement articulated a global missionary outlook that characterized nineteenth-century Anglo-American Protestant endeavors. "Foreign" remained a key word in the BFBS's lexicon, given that the second article of its constitution pledged the organization to "according to its ability, extend its influence to other countries, whether Christian, Mahometan, or Pagan." Concerns over a scripture shortage in WALES initially convinced the founders to split their organization off from the Religious Tract Society. Within two years the BFBS produced thousands of Welsh New Testaments, shipped substantial numbers of Gaelic scriptures to SCOTLAND, encouraged the formation of a Hibernian Bible Society in IRELAND, published a Gospel of John in Mohawk for distribution in Upper CANADA, and began funding William Carey's translations efforts in Serampore in INDIA. English language scriptures soon reached ports ranging from Sierra Leone to the West Indies, translation work began in CHINA and western AFRICA, and consignments of Spanish New Testaments arrived at Buenos Aires. The ABS entered the foreign field in the mid-1830s, placing a bible agent in the Near East and supporting missionary translators throughout the world. Such commitments would increase significantly as the nineteenth century wore on.

Finally, the bible movement reflected the symbiotic relationship and uneasy tensions between nationalizing forces and particularistic local cultures that often collided in the nineteenth century. On the surface, the ABS, the BFBS, and such other large organizations as the Netherlands Bible Society appeared highly centralized, capitalized, and institutionalized by the mid-nineteenth century (see NETHERLANDS). By the time the American Bible Society opened its landmark Bible House building in New York City in 1853, for example, it had emerged as one of the largest and most technologically sophisticated publishing houses in the United States with its own state-of-the-art printing department, bindery, manufacturing division, and

workforce that numbered in the hundreds. Further, thirty-seven paid bible agents, each responsible for a specific geographical territory and each employing a network of distributors and colporteurs (salesmen), coordinated distribution and fund-raising activities throughout the nation and reported to the home office in New York. Philanthropic religious institutions like the bible societies operated on a scale virtually unknown to most early nineteenth-century businesses. Their boards of directors, drawn from the ranks of railroads, insurance companies, and other corporate concerns, played a very influential role in systematizing and bureaucratizing nineteenth-century organizational culture.

Yet, bible societies also remained oriented toward towns, localities, and small communities in important ways. Both the BFBS and the ABS initially relied almost exclusively on local auxiliaries and associations, usually coincident with small geographical territories, to carry out fund-raising and distribution. These county, town, and borough-based organizations could affiliate with the national bodies by drafting acceptable constitutions that embraced the principle of "without note or comment," and by pledging to contribute all funds not needed for local purposes to the national organizations. Auxiliaries received discounts on scripture purchases from the national institutions, organized their own annual meetings that brought together local Protestant religious leaders, and voluntarily canvassed their neighborhoods door-to-door in an effort to determine scripture needs. Middle-class women played an especially critical role at the local level. They often assumed major responsibility for managing these benevolent organizations by keeping accounts, coordinating scripture supply and demand, soliciting subscriptions from poor and working-class Christians, and participating in broader networks of female philanthropy. Although excluded from the governing boards and management of the national organizations, they carved out new social roles for themselves on the local level and stretched the permeable boundaries of acceptable women's activities in Victorian Christian culture (see WOMEN). Centralization and lingering localism thus reinforced and mutually influenced each other in the bible movement, creating a dynamic and subtly changing relationship.

Controversial Aspects

Christian unity proved difficult to achieve in practice. Beginning in the 1820s, a series of denominational and territorial schisms fragmented the bible movement and posed serious problems for the national bible societies. Competitors emerged, tensions simmered, and political controversies remained remarkably long-lived. The national societies attempted to minimize conflict and stress their catholicity, but questions surrounding the biblical text itself, the boundaries of "without note or comment," and rivalries on the mission field strained relationships. As a result, the movement never fully avoided the controversy nor achieved the Christian unity that its supporters coveted.

The Apocrypha affair generated the most intense difficulties for the BFBS during the 1820s. Roman Catholics considered the Apocryphal books part of the Old Testament, and Lutherans wanted them included within their versions (see LUTHERANISM). Initially, the BFBS hoped to pursue a flexible policy by incorporating the books as requested, thus underscoring its international and broadly inclusive ambitions. Dissenting churches, especially the very vocal Scottish Presbyterians, vehemently disagreed and insisted that these books did not belong within the inspired canon (see DISSENT). After several years of debate, the BFBS in 1826 forbade any monetary allocations for printing books that contained the Apocrypha, and also agreed that its own publications should be issued fully bound so that distributors could not insert the Apocryphal books before binding. These strictures did not fully satisfy dissenters because the BFBS also chose to remain in fellowship with other European bible societies that circulated the Apocryphal books. The two largest Scottish auxiliaries in Glasgow and Edinburgh quickly seceded from the BFBS, along with thirty-eight of the forty-eight remaining societies in Scotland and several in England. Subscriptions and donations dropped substantially and relations between the British and Scottish bible societies worsened throughout the century, even as the society's stance also alienated supporters in the more liturgical traditions.

The American Bible Society followed the BFBS's lead in the Apocrypha affair, but another denominational controversy involving Baptists proved even more damaging to Christian unity within the United States. Beginning in the early 1830s, the ABS's board of managers contributed monetary support to missionaries in an effort to encourage translations that conformed in substance and style to the authorized King James Version. Baptist missionaries in Calcutta petitioned the ABS board in 1835 to publish a second edition of a revised Bengali New Testament. The BFBS previously rejected this same remonstrance, primarily because the missionaries insisted on translating *baptizo* as *immersion*. The British society believed that the Baptists had sacrificed basic translation principles in an effort to promote their own denominational agenda, and that the bible society could not place its imprimatur on a version that many Christians could not support. The ABS agonized long and hard over this issue, given that Baptists constituted the

fastest-growing denomination in the United States and formed an influential minority voice on the board. Ultimately, the American society took the same position as its British partner, rejecting the missionaries' request and stipulating that all future versions must prove acceptable to all denominations within the ABS family. Baptists viewed this position as a retreat from nonsectarianism, withdrew from the ABS fellowship, and established a rival organization called the American and Foreign Bible Society in 1837. This schism essentially severed relations between the ABS and Baptists for the remainder of the nineteenth century, and positioned the American Bible Society as an unflagging supporter of the King James Version. A subsequent translation controversy within the American and Foreign Bible Society resulted in the formation of the Baptist-based AMERICAN BIBLE UNION in 1850, which began circulating its own English language immersion version of the scriptures.

Denominational tensions often challenged the bible movement's efforts to forge a broad Christian coalition, but political and territorial conflicts also threatened comity throughout the nineteenth century. Within the American context, SLAVERY proved an especially intractable issue. Christian abolitionists began petitioning the ABS in the 1830s to distribute scriptures to slaves, a position that slaveholders and many southern supporters considered anathema (see SLAVERY, ABOLITION OF). The organization elected to take a conservative position in the interest of perpetuating institutional harmony, leaving the question of bibles for slaves in the hands of local southern auxiliaries, where it usually remained dormant. The ABS even hoped to remain friendly with its powerful southern friends after the outbreak of the CIVIL WAR, although hostilities caused the secession of rebel auxiliaries and resulted in the founding of a short-lived Confederate States Bible Society in 1861. After the resumption of peace in 1865, the ABS quickly moved to reconstruct its southern auxiliaries and hire a new corps of southern-based bible agents, although scripture distribution to the newly freed slaves languished for some time thereafter.

Territorial disputes reflected other tensions within the movement as well. The Philadelphia Bible Society (1808) refused to participate in the founding of the ABS because of an unwillingness to surrender its own autonomy, an intense urban rivalry with New York City, and a suspicion of vast national combinations. It did not formally affiliate with the national society until 1840. The Connecticut Bible Society, alleging institutional mismanagement and questionable fundraising practices, terminated its affiliation with the ABS in 1900. The most significant, troublesome, and long-lived controversy of this sort within the ABS, however, occurred within New York City. The New York Bible Society had been founded in 1807 and reorganized numerous times over the course of the next century. It proved especially active in distributing scriptures at humane and criminal institutions, naval and military stations, hotels, and to immigrants arriving at Ellis Island. Acrimonious conflict emerged with the ABS, also based in New York, over fund-raising practices, distribution boundaries, and the auxiliary's own increasingly evangelical focus (see EVANGELICALISM). The local organization initially declared its independence from the ABS in 1913, and continuing tension resulted in a final rupture in 1971. The New York Bible Society supported the English translation known as the New International Version (1978), which solidified its standing among evangelicals, and eventually reincorporated as the International Bible Society (IBS) (1983) and relocated to Colorado Springs (1989). For many years, the IBS prevented the American Bible Society from carrying the New International Version as part of its product line, thus damaging the latter society's standing with the increasingly significant evangelical constituency within American Protestantism. Deep-rooted historical tensions within the movement thus continued to influence bible society affairs well into the twentieth century.

Competitive pressures and nationalistic urges also fostered international disagreements between the societies. The BFBS, ABS, and National Bible Society of Scotland (NBSS) all moved more aggressively into the mission field during the late nineteenth century. They established large agencies in which several provinces or countries were grouped together under the supervision of an agent directly responsible to one of the national societies. Public relations material and fund-raising appeals especially emphasized the global nature of bible work and the foreign mission component of bible society activities. Each society found it increasingly critical to maintain its own institutional presence throughout the world to satisfy the expectations of donors and supporters. Duplication of effort and bureaucratic wrangling often resulted as several society offices functioned within individual countries. Conflict between the societies usually focused on such issues as distribution practices and principles, competing translations that often varied in quality and content, relations with denomination-based missionaries in the field, and differing interpretations of the "without note or comment" clause in bible society constitutions. Tensions proved most severe in the Near East, China, JAPAN, KOREA, and Central America, where the ABS and BFBS both maintained strong agencies. Less competition occurred in Africa and India, which remained dominated by the BFBS and where American missionaries constituted a much smaller presence.

International Cooperation

Efforts to overcome divisiveness within the movement produced a variety of compromises and solutions. In some instances, the societies agreed to carve up territory according to mutually agreed upon boundaries. BRAZIL was divided between the ABS and BFBS in 1903, and the societies agreed to split Japan that same year. In other instances, voluntary withdrawal resolved the issue: the ABS withdrew from Persia and the BFBS agreed to abandon Central America, excepting British Honduras, in 1913. Five years later, the ABS ceased working in Korea and the BFBS closed its agency in the PHILIPPINES. Agreements proved difficult to negotiate, however, until a new generation of bible society administrators more committed to international cooperation and interested in streamlining institutional resources began influencing the movement in the late 1920s and early 1930s.

Developments in China became the immediate catalyst for the competing societies to articulate a new approach to bible work. The BFBS, ABS, and NBSS maintained a long and significant presence there, each agency primarily serving its own national missionaries and employing its own colporteurs. The growth of indigenous churches with strong local leadership forced the societies to recognize that they needed to play a more circumscribed role in China, and caused them to question the nature of missionary enterprises. At a joint meeting held in London in 1932 the BFBS, ABS, and NBSS agreed to encourage the formation of a self-governing and locally administered China Bible Society, and to step back into a joint advisory role. This important departure proved to be the new model for encouraging bible work in areas formerly considered the "mission field." The conferees at the 1932 meeting also attempted to resolve other points of conflict by agreeing to jointly administer agencies where they worked in common territories, to codify a common body of translation principles, to respect national boundaries, and to encourage cooperative planning.

Over the course of the next fifteen years, these collaborative efforts began to bear fruit. Jointly administered agencies, usually established by the ABS and BFBS but also including some NBSS participation, became the norm throughout South America and the Near East. Christians established independent bible societies in Japan (1938), India (1944), and Brazil (1948). Although war with Japan prevented the establishment of a full-fledged China Bible Society, Chinese Christians gradually assumed control over the China Bible House, which operated out of Hong Kong and coordinated scripture distribution work after the Communist takeover. In 1939 the Netherlands Bible

Society hosted an international conclave at Woud-schoten, attended by representatives from the United States, Britain, Scotland, NORWAY, and FRANCE, as well as the host country. Delegates supported a resolution to form a federation known as the "Council of Bible Societies," with the goal of coordinating international scripture distribution and encouraging the formation of indigenous bible societies throughout the world. World War II soon intervened and this specific plan never achieved fruition, but the growing emphasis on cooperation laid the groundwork for a more successful and long-lasting endeavor after the conclusion of hostilities.

Bible society representatives from twelve European countries and the ABS met at the Elfinsward Conference Center in Haywards Heath, England, in May 1946 to assess the status of the movement and attempt to fashion a cooperative global effort to address the spiritual needs of churches, refugees, and believers throughout the world. They agreed on the need for a new international organization, the United Bible Societies (UBS), to serve as a central clearinghouse, coordinator, and support mechanism for the bible movement. Membership remained open to national bible societies and committees that agreed on the core principle of circulating the scriptures without doctrinal note or commentary. A requisite six societies quickly agreed on the need for the new organization, and within one year sixteen national institutions joined the fellowship. New bible society federations, often formed through the merger of long-established local organizations, were established in GERMANY, SWITZERLAND, Czechoslovakia, France, Belgium, and Austria. The founders encouraged national movements in historically non-Christian countries as well, and by the end of the 1940s welcomed national representatives from India and Ceylon, Japan, Korea, China, and Brazil into the fellowship. The UBS also cultivated close ties with the newly formed WORLD COUNCIL OF CHURCHES, and soon emerged as the ecumenical voice of the bible movement in international affairs.

The creation of the UBS did not, of course, resolve all tensions within the world bible movement. Disagreements persisted over the extent to which bible societies should promote biblical understanding as well as merely distribute scripture. More venerable institutions such as the BFBS often proved reluctant to abandon their agency operations and turn bible work over to relatively small and, in their view, inexperienced Christian communities. Large national organizations such as the ABS often felt that international concerns distracted from real needs within their own countries and that a disproportionate share of institutional funds and resources was absorbed by the UBS through its burgeoning world service budget. Disputes arose over allocations within the UBS budget, and smaller societies sometimes resented the degree of oversight and the controls over expenditures demanded by the international agency. Translation policies also proved controversial on occasion because a developing body of international standards and techniques could conflict with the work of missionaries and linguists at the grassroots level.

Clearly, however, the establishment and rapid growth of the UBS fundamentally altered the bible society movement. International issues now assumed a much more prominent posture within each individual society. The UBS stimulated the founding of dozens of national organizations in Asia, Africa, South America, and the Middle East. Support for new translations skyrocketed, and a much more scholarly and sophisticated program developed for training translators, disseminating scholarly texts, and producing printed helps and aids. The historical dynamics that defined relations between the older European and North American societies had been irrevocably altered. Perhaps most significantly, UBS meetings provided an important ecumenical venue that gave participating Christians and church leaders a much more complex view of postwar global realities.

Late Twentieth-Century Trends

The United Bible Societies stimulated all participating organizations to move in new directions during the latter half of the twentieth century. Broader social developments, rapid technological changes, and extraordinary political events also exerted a tremendous impact on the bible movement during this period. Less obvious shifts within global Christianity further affected the societies in unanticipated ways. Perhaps most surprisingly and least predictable in some respects, bible societies no longer functioned as purely Protestant affairs.

A biblical revival movement occurred within the Roman Catholic Church during the late 1940s and 1950s, stimulated at least in part by Pope Pius XII's desire to encourage daily bible reading and scripture distribution among all Catholics, as well as his efforts to support serious scholarly work in the seminaries. The Second Vatican Council's *Dei Verbum* document, promulgated in 1965, opened up new possibilities for ecumenical cooperation by encouraging widespread access to the scriptures and acknowledging that translation work might satisfactorily be carried out with non-Catholic individuals and institutions. Liturgical changes within Catholicism further emphasized the importance of greater biblical literacy among lay people. United Bible Societies leaders quickly opened negotiations with the Vatican's Secretariat for Promoting Christian Unity. Before long Roman Catholic priests began attending UBS Council meetings, bible society translators met regularly with Roman Catholic biblical scholars, and the ABS reserved a place for Roman Catholic representatives on its denominational advisory council. In 1968 the UBS and the Roman Catholic Church adopted a series of guiding principles for interconfessional translations that endured for nearly two decades. The UBS cautiously encouraged member societies to consider translating and publishing the Apocrypha when requested by the churches, and many complied. Dozens of interconfessional translation projects that involved collaboration between Roman Catholic, Protestant, and occasionally Orthodox scholars began almost immediately after the signing of the 1967 agreement. The ABS, for example, published a special edition of its English-language *Good News Bible,* including the Apocrypha and bearing the imprimatur of a Roman Catholic bishop, thereby breaking with the precedent established during the Apocrypha controversy in the 1820s. By 1987 fully 161 Interconfessional Bibles and New Testaments had been published as a result of joint initiatives between bible societies and the Vatican.

As bible societies found other new audiences throughout the world, pressures built to expand their product line and redefine the boundaries of "without note or comment." Newly literate readers required contextual helps, illustrations, and background information to understand biblical text, and translators struggled with the problem of providing adequate marginal notes while avoiding doctrinal interpretation and theological advocacy. During the 1950s and 1960s, bible societies increasingly experimented with thematic selections, aids for readers developed in cooperation with local churches, and special imprints with customized covers that promoted specific ministries. Major societies altered their charters to reflect the new realities. The BFBS's bylaws noted in 1968 that authorized publications could include aids to readers, and the ABS inserted the word "doctrinal" before "note and comment" in a 1971 constitutional revision. By the 1990s the UBS moved even further along in this direction by approving comprehensive guidelines for full-fledged study bibles. Individual societies now considered producing publications that included reflective questions, thematic indices, articles on the nature of the bible, and suggested readings.

Similarly, societies in the late twentieth century increasingly sought to produce and distribute common language scripture versions, directed both at new readers and at individuals who found traditional translations frustrating and baffling. A major effort to produce a completely new Spanish bible, which began in 1950 and ultimately became known as the *Version Popular,* proved extraordinarily successful as an evangelization tool in Latin America and provided particular inspiration for this movement. Bible society translators soon began producing readable modern versions in indigenous languages throughout Latin America. A common language version of Mark in Aymara, initially published as a diglot with Spanish by the Bible Society of Bolivia, constituted the initial endeavor in 1966. The ABS took perhaps the boldest step in this direction by publishing the *Good News for Modern Man* English New Testament in 1966. This radical departure from more literal approaches to translation rested on the principle of dynamic equivalence, whereby translators sought to capture the meaning and sense of biblical concepts by using contemporary language and imagery. The translation featured attractively simple line drawings by the Swiss artist Annie Valloton, a memorable cover composed of mastheads from English-language newspapers throughout the world, and an appealing prose that infuriated some traditionalists but brought many readers to a newer understanding of the biblical message. It also underscored the distance that the ABS had traveled from its early embrace of the King James Version as a basis for all translation work. Indeed, by the 1990s societies even began experimenting with the concept of multimedia translations that blended sound, visuals, and text for new generations of Christians who absorbed the gospel message in fundamentally distinct ways.

Ultimately, these changes in bible society policies reflected radical shifts within Protestant Christianity during the late twentieth century. Older societies such as the ABS and BFBS remained influential and major financial supporters of the global bible movement, but the emphasis had shifted toward reaching new readers, cultivating diverse audiences, and empowering indigenous national societies throughout the world. UBS scripture distribution statistics in the 1990s illustrate a dramatic expansion of new reader portions and selections produced for South Americas, Asians, and Pacific Islanders. Over one hundred member societies composed the UBS fellowship by the end of the twentieth century, as the collapse of the Soviet Union in 1989 stimulated the formation of numerous revitalized organizations throughout Eastern Europe. Bible societies themselves also constituted a smaller voice within the world bible cause. The remarkable expansion of evangelicalism meant that such organizations as Wycliffe Bible Translators, the International Bible Society, Open Doors, and many similar agencies carried out very successful scripture distribution and translation programs with a more overt doctrinal focus, and necessarily remained outside the bible society movement. Finally, societies found themselves questioning their commitment to print as new communication technologies offered important opportunities and challenges for bringing God's word to a new age in the twenty-first century.

See also Bible, Bible Translation

References and Further Reading

Canton, William. *A History of the British and Foreign Bible Society. With Portraits and Illustrations.* 5 vols. London: John Murray, 1904.

Dwight, Henry Otis. *The Centennial History of the American Bible Society (1816–1916).* New York: Macmillan, 1916.

Foster, Charles I. *An Errand of Mercy: The Evangelical United Front, 1790–1837.* Chapel Hill: University of North Carolina Press, 1960.

Gutjahr, Paul. *An American Bible: A History of the Good Book in the United States, 1777–1880.* Stanford: Stanford University Press, 1999.

Howsam, Leslie. *Cheap Bibles: Nineteenth-Century Publishing and the British and Foreign Bible Society.* New York: Cambridge University Press, 1991.

Lacy, Creighton. *The Word-Carrying Giant: The Growth of the American Bible Society (1816–1966).* South Pasadena, CA: William Carey Library, 1977.

Moulton, James. *A History of the British and Foreign Bible Society, 1905–1954.* London: British and Foreign Bible Society, 1965.

Robertson, Edwin H. *Taking the Word to the World: 50 Years of the United Bible Societies.* Nashville, TN: Thomas Nelson Publishers, 1996.

Strickland, William P. *History of the American Bible Society from Its Organization to the Present Time.* New York: Harper and Brothers, 1849.

Wosh, Peter J. *Spreading the Word: The Bible Business in Nineteenth-Century America.* Ithaca, NY: Cornell University Press, 1994.

PETER J. WOSH

BIBLE TRANSLATION

Translation of the BIBLE flows from Christian belief in Jesus as the incarnate Word of God, as well as from Jewish precedent in the production of the Septuagint (a Greek translation of Hebrew language Jewish Scripture) in the second and third centuries BCE. For the early Christian community the imperative of Jesus to take the gospel to all nations (Matthew 28), alongside the experience of Pentecost, made translation fundamental to Christian identity. All people were to hear the good news and praise of God in their own language. Throughout Christian history the translation of the Bible has been associated with MISSIONS to people of different languages and cultures, the determination of authoritative Scriptures, and the challenge of reform.

Early Translations

By the end of the second century, translations of the different portions and versions of the New Testament appeared in Latin and Syriac. In the next century it was translated into Sahidic (Coptic), and in the fourth century into Ethiopic and Georgian. Ulfilas translated the Bible into Gothic in the fourth century, inventing for this purpose the Gothic alphabet. Cyril and Methodius invented the Glagothic alphabet (which evolved into modern Cyrillic) in the ninth century to translate the Bible into Slavic. These translations set in motion a process in which literacy went hand in hand with Christianization. Translations in the fifth through seventh centuries into Nubian, Armenian, and Arabic made the Bible available to the peoples on the southern and eastern fringes of Christian lands. Translations in the eighth and ninth centuries marked the spread of Christianity to the Anglo-Saxons, Germans, and Franks. In the twelfth to fourteenth centuries translations into Spanish, Italian, Dutch, Polish, Icelandic, middle-English, Persian, Bohemian, and Danish continued the process of preparing vernacular Bibles for groups in which Christianity was being established.

These translations, the first virtually in tandem with the formation of the New Testament canon and motivated by a similar need for an authoritative source of Christian teaching and WORSHIP, drew new peoples and languages into the sphere of influence and authority of an increasingly institutionalized church. In the West this institution also spread a universal religious culture through the use of Latin. During the last decades of the fourth century, at the instigation of Pope Damascus, Jerome (345–420) completed a translation of the Bible into Latin from original Hebrew and Greek sources. This translation, known as the *Vulgate Bible,* became the standard authorized text for Latin Christendom. Along with the formation of standard creeds and definitions (Nicean in 325 and Chalcedonian in 451), and liturgies (fifth century onward), it gradually became a symbol of universal ORTHODOXY with the power of the Roman church to enforce it. By the fourteenth century the universality of the Latin Bible rather than the universal availability of the Scripture in indigenous languages had become the basis of scriptural authority in the Catholic Church, and the supremacy of the *Vulgate* was affirmed by the Council of Trent in 1546 as a direct answer to the creation of vernacular Bibles by Protestant reformers.

Reformation Turn to The Vernacular

John Wycliffe (1329–1384) first challenged the hegemony of the *Vulgate Bible,* and the ecclesial power it represented, by preparing a translation into vernacular English and stressing its accessibility to laypersons. The reformer MARTIN LUTHER (1483–1546) translated the New Testament into German in 1522. With this the Protestant movement became defined in part by its assertion that the Bible should be available to all Christians in the vernacular, given that the AUTHORITY of the Bible was manifest in the Christian tradition, the believing community, and the inspired reading of individual Christians. In 1534 Luther's complete translation of the Bible was published, and its final revision in 1545 before his death helped shape German prose style for centuries to come. SWEDEN and DENMARK also adopted standard translations of the scriptures in the mid-fifteenth century. The *Uppsala Bible* was printed in 1541 and the *Christian III Bible* was printed in Copenhagen in 1550, and revised in 1589 and again in 1633. The first widely accepted Dutch Bible was printed in 1558 and called the *Mennonite Bible*. Later it was more widely known as the *Biestkens Bible* after the printer of its 1560 edition. Dutch Calvinists used a translation based on Luther's Bible and first printed in 1561–1562. The 1637 *Staten-vertling* produced by the governments of the Netherlands became the standard Dutch version for both Calvinists and MENNONITES until the twentieth century. These state-sponsored translations are reminders of the link between Biblical authority, uniformity, and the interests of Christian governments in both.

The Bible was translated from the *Vulgate* into vernacular French by the reformer Jacque Lefèvre, with a New Testament published in 1523 and the Old Testament and Apocrypha in 1528. In 1530 they were published together as the *Antwerp Bible*. The *Neuchâtel Bible* published in 1535 by Robert Olivetan drew on Lefèvre's work, as did subsequent revisions culminating in the French GENEVA BIBLE of 1588. In both Italy and Spain the ecclesial climate was unfriendly to Protestant translations. Antonio Brucioli began a translation into Italian in the 1530s, but the first full translation was published in Geneva in 1562. Giovanni Diodati produced a translation in 1607. The revised version of 1641 remained in use until modern times. A complete Spanish Bible was published in Basel in 1569, the work of Cassiodoro de Reyna. New Testaments were published earlier by Francisco de Enzina in Antwerp in 1543 and Juan Pérez de Pineda in Geneva in 1556. In addition to these widely read translations, portions of the Bible were translated in a number of minor European languages and dialects in the seventeenth century, including Irish, Latvian, Saami, Estonian, and Nogay. This process of translation into the languages of groups on the periphery of Europe, usually as part of Protestant missions to these cultures, has continued into the twentieth century, even as some of these languages have become extinct.

The Renaissance fascination with the original language texts of classical literature and philosophy led

scholars in Italy and then across Europe to seek out and examine Greek and Hebrew manuscripts of the Biblical texts. Lorenzo Valla (1405–1457) published a comparison of the *Vulgate* with a Greek text in 1444. This first critical examination of a work of assumed authority (Valla also showed the *Donation of Constantine* to be a fake) would both spur the reformers and lead to a revised edition of the *Vulgate* in 1590 and again in 1592.

The *Complutensian Polyglot Bible,* with the Greek and Hebrew Old Testament, Greek New Testament, and Latin Vulgate was printed in Alcalá, Spain between 1514 and 1517. A delay in papal authorization allowed the Basle printer Froben to publish a hastily prepared Greek New Testament and new Latin translation by Desiderius Erasmus (1467–1536) before the *Polyglot* could be widely circulated. Simon Collines printed a critical edition of the Greek New Testament in 1534. Revision of this edition continued under Robert Estienne (who fled to Geneva because of his Protestant leanings), and finally THEODORE BEZA in Geneva. Beza's 1565 edition of the Greek New Testament eventually became known as the *Textus Receptus* and became the basis of the King James' New Testament. From 1488, when Jews in Soncino, Italy published a Hebrew Old Testament through the middle of the sixteenth century, Hebrew Old Testaments of increasing critical value were printed. The *Textus Receptus* was not so daring as Erasmus's first edition in attempting to reconstruct the original text, but alongside the use of Hebrew Old Testaments its advent marked a period in which the norm for biblical scholarship, and Bible translation, would be the use of original language texts critically examined.

WILLIAM TYNDALE pioneered translation of the Bible into English from Greek and Hebrew. It earned him the enmity of the English bishops and forced him to flee to Protestant territories on the continent. His New Testament was published in 1525, but his Old Testament was not completed because he was arrested near Brussels in 1535 and martyred in 1536 (see MARTYRS AND MARTYROLOGY). MILES COVERDALE'S complete English Bible appeared in 1535, followed by the *Matthew Bible* in 1537. Coverdale's revision of the latter was the 1539 *Great Bible*. English reformers living in exile in Geneva produced the English *Geneva Bible* in 1560. The first period of English-language Bible translation would culminate in the translation sponsored by King James I, published in 1611. Its New Testament was based largely on Tyndale's translation work. Like the Luther Bible it set not only theological but literary standards for centuries. Its basis in the widely published Greek *Textus Receptus* and its ubiquitous force in English-speaking Protestant circles eventually gave it an authority independent of the beauty of its prose or its scholarly merit.

Despite some scholarly efforts Catholics responded in a limited way to the vernacular translations of Protestants. The French *Rheims-Douai* Bible was published from 1582 to 1610, and a Dutch Catholic Bible was printed in 1548. However, both were based on a *Vulgate* text already shown to be flawed. After the council of Trent, authority was seen by the Catholic church to rest more in the traditional dogma realized through the church hierarchy than in publicly accessible Scripture. By the opening of the seventeenth century authority in the Catholic Church had lost the initiative in producing either critical editions of Biblical texts or new translations.

The significance of new Bibles, in translation or in the original languages, was greatly enhanced by the development of the movable type press by Johannes Gutenberg from 1445 onward. His Bible (1456) was the first complete book printed in the Christian world, and signified a new era in which identical copies of the same book would be available both to the masses and scholars. By the time of the REFORMATION, presses could be found across Europe. Their output, whether in the form of vernacular Bibles, critical editions of original language texts, or reformation manifestos and theologies, spurred the breakdown in the authority of the Catholic church, and the variegated development of Christian churches from the sixteenth century onward.

Missions and Translation

The Renaissance and the Reformation continued to spur vernacular and critical translations of the Bible in Europe. In the same period the spread of Christianity beyond Europe inaugurated an era in which Bible translation was closely associated with the missionary enterprise, and the European "discovery" of non-Christian languages, religions, and cultures. Roman Catholic missionaries were working in both the New World and Asia in the sixteenth century, and at least for liturgical purposes were translating portions of Scriptures and the Psalms into indigenous languages. It was the arrival of the Dutch in the Indonesian archipelago, however, that marked the first systematic effort to translate the Bible into a non-European language. Corneius Ruyl completed a translation of Matthew's Gospel into Malay in 1612, and it was printed in diglot form with Dutch in 1629. An entire Bible, largely completed by Melchior Leydekker before his death in 1701, was published in 1733. Rivalries and disagreements between translators working with different dialects of Malay led to the delay, as did questions about whether to use the special language of the royal courts and proper terminology for God in a Muslim environment. The early Dutch translations went hand in hand with the development of linguistic and cultural studies that refined the Dutch understanding of the languages of the Malay Archipelago and their relationship to its various cultures. The problems of defining the vernacular when translators worked in isolation with unfamiliar languages, deciding when translations in each of several dialects were necessary, and fixing religious terminology in a non-Christian religious environment have become central problems for the modern era of missionary translation of the Bible. Missionary efforts to overcome these problems helped spur the scholarly study of non-European languages and cultures, as well as the preservation of both their literary and oral traditions.

JOHN ELIOT was a pioneer of missions among NATIVE AMERICANS, and his translation of the Bible into the language of the Pequot tribe of Massachusetts in 1663 was the first in North America. In the nineteenth century missionaries would add translations in dozens of languages, developing unique alphabets in the process and preserving cultures under threat from Anglo-European settlement. In INDIA the translation work was pioneered by Henry Martyn (1781–1812) and WILLIAM CAREY (1761–1834). Martyn translated the New Testament into Urdu, as well as Persian, Arabic, and Hindustani. Carey translated the Bible into Bengali, as well as a number of related dialects. Both Martyn and Carey also pioneered the study and translation of indigenous literature. Portions of the New Testament had been translated into Chinese by Roman Catholics before 1800; however, it was Robert Morrison who first completed a translation of the Bible in 1819. With the opening of CHINA to greater foreign influence after the Anglo-Chinese war, both revisions of Morrison's Bible and translations and transliterations into the many different Chinese dialects were written. A controversy over the appropriate term for God ("Shang Ti" vs. "Shen") divided the missionary community. Up to the present Chinese Bibles using either term are available. Translations into the languages of sub-Saharan Africa began in 1816 with a translation into Bullom (SIERRA LEONE), translations into Swahili, the dominant language of East Africa, and various South African dialects followed in the nineteenth century (see SOUTH AFRICA).

The process of Bible translation, which Protestant missionaries initially related to the reformed mandate to make God's authoritative word available to all, gradually influenced missionary assessments of non-European culture. Each controversy over terminology brought more sharply into focus the issue of how non-Christian cultures, and even religions, could be a medium through which God's Word was revealed.

The question of whether a religion could prepare people to hear the Gospel was inextricably linked to the question of whether a language and culture had been prepared by God to receive God's Word. Just as vernacular Bibles in an increasingly literate culture had helped spur the Reformation by creating an independent source of authority, so missionary translations and growing literacy undermined a missionary monopoly on authority in newly emerging Christian communities. Since the middle of the twentieth century independent churches and church leaders have sprung up across the Christian world. Idiosyncratic interpretations of vernacular Bibles have been combined with indigenous worldviews and religious practices in a logical extension of the principle that all languages, and hence cultures, can be bearers of the good news.

Bible Societies

The rapid expansion of Bible translation and publication was facilitated by the formation of the BIBLE SOCIETIES. The BRITISH AND FOREIGN BIBLE SOCIETY (BFBS) was founded in 1804 with an ecumenical leadership and a mandate to produce and distribute Bible translations without notes or commentary. The model quickly spread through British territories, as well as in RUSSIA (1810) and most of Protestant Europe. Throughout the nineteenth and twentieth centuries the Bible Societies played a key role in directly or indirectly funding and distributing new translations of the Bible. At its centenary the BFBS reported having published more than 200 million Bibles or portions of the Bible.

In 1946 the United Bible Societies was formed to foster cooperation among the thousands of independent Bible Societies. Earlier in 1934 the WYCLIFFE BIBLE TRANSLATORS was founded by Cameron Townsend. Its translators focus on languages of small, often isolated, groups whose languages have not been studied or reduced to written form. In the 1990s Wycliffe Translators had worked on over 1,200 languages. They are closely associated with the Summer Institute of Linguistics, whose anthropological and linguistic work often provides the basis for translation efforts. By the year 2002, largely through the Bible Societies and Wycliffe, complete Bibles had been translated into more than 400 languages, and portions into over 2,300 languages. In addition to the Wycliffe Translators and the work of UBS consultants there are a number of smaller Bible translation organizations, many formed out of dissatisfaction with the methodologies of the dominant translation agencies.

Up until the twentieth century most Bible translations aimed at literal translations based on either the original languages of the Bible or a standard translation into English or another European language. The translations were undertaken by Europeans or Americans who learned indigenous languages from local informants or available literature. Since World War II both the Bible Societies and the Wycliffe translators have focused on using native language speakers as the primary translators, assisted by linguists and scholars with expertise in Biblical languages. Translations are team efforts with translators, exegetes, editors, and experts on style working together to create accurate and readable translations. This work is based on a theory of translation called the "functional" or "dynamic equivalence" method. It was pioneered by Eugene Nida. Early translations were of the "formal equivalence" type, trying to establish a one-to-one correspondence between terms in the source and receptor languages. The dynamic equivalence model assumes that meaning is found in larger language structures, and that the closest natural equivalent to the source language in the receptor language may not have a word-for-word, or even sentence-for-sentence, correspondence. Bible Societies have sponsored dynamic equivalence translations in both European and other major languages, with the *Today's English Version* (*Good News for Modern Man*) being the best known in English.

Scholarly Commentary

Controversy over both the method and basis for new Bible translations has arisen since the nineteenth-century development of Biblical criticism and the discovery of dozens, then hundreds, of Bible manuscripts earlier than those used for the major European translations. By the late nineteenth century critical editions of the New Testament varied from the *Textus Receptus* in numerous details, as did the best Hebrew texts of the Old Testament. Translations based on these editions were caught up in larger conflicts over the authority of Scripture and its basis in a literal reading of the text. The result was a profusion of twentieth-century translations, particularly in English, that seek in differing ways to provide Christians with an authoritative basis for their own belief and practice.

A succession of scholarly formal translations *Revised Version* (1885), *American Standard Version* (1901), *Revised Standard Version* (1952), *New English Bible* (1971), *New International Bible* (1978), and *New Revised Standard Version* (*NRSV*, 1989) sought to keep up with the discovery of more ancient manuscripts and advances in textual criticism. Underlying their authority is the assumption that critical, scientific analysis of both text and literary content carried out by an ecumenical team of scholars yields a universally authoritative translation. The *NRSV* also recognizes the changing influence of cultural norms on language by making a consistent effort to use inclusive language. The *Today's English Version (1976)*, using the dynamic equivalence method underpinned by extensive critical commentaries on the original language texts, makes the Bible accessible to the growing number of English speakers unfamiliar with religious terminology. Paraphrases by J. B. Philips and Kenneth Taylor (*The Living Bible,* 1971) have enjoyed popularity, and the latter has been so widely distributed under so many different titles to Christians unfamiliar with formal translations that it has a wide degree of influence despite its scholarly shortcomings.

The *New American Standard Bible* (1971) was published as a strictly literal translation for those whose concept of Biblical authority is rooted in formal correspondence with the original texts. The *New King James Version* (1982) was produced to meet the needs of Christians committed to the *Textus Receptus* and style of the *King James Bible,* but who can no longer fathom the meaning of sixteenth-century English. Its authority lies less in text or scholarship than in its impeccable Protestant pedigree, long association with fundamentalist dogma (see FUNDAMENTALISM), and the extent to which its language permeates traditional English language worship in many traditions. The *New Jerusalem Bible* (1966) is based on a French Catholic translation (*La Bible de Jérusalem,* 1956). It is distinctive in following the sequence of the most recently discovered Old Testament texts in distinction from the common Hebrew Bible, retaining *yhwh* instead of the conventional translation "Lord," and its early use of inclusive language.

The diversity of translations of the Bible is more than matched by the diversity of special editions of all translations with notes from different theological perspectives, addressed to different age groups, genders, social classes, and even focused on particular uses of the Bible in daily Christian life. Particularly in the UNITED STATES, exploitation of specialized markets has been influential in motivating new translations and new editions of older translations. The JEHOVAH'S WITNESSES have produced their own *New World Translation of the Holy Scriptures* in English and over 100 other languages—making significant changes from other versions to bolster their particular doctrines. The Church of Jesus Christ of Latter Day Saints (see MORMONISM) has supplemented the Bible with translations of its own unique Scripture, *The Book of Mormon.*

Although few Christian cultures can match the resources of the English-speaking world, a similar range of translations is appearing wherever the Christian community is varied enough to support them. Just as the first Christians translated their Scriptures to address the varied cultures of the ancient world, modern Christians appear to be determined to make translations available that meet the needs of a diverse society and its variety of linguistic subcultures. It remains to be seen whether the enormous diversity of translations, and their diffusion throughout society, will serve as a unifying force in Christianity or reflect its process of fragmentation into competing sectarian groups.

References and Further Reading

Canton, William, and John Murray. *The Cambridge History of the Bible. A History of the British and Foreign Bible Society.* London: Cambridge University Press, 1910.

Orlinsky, Harry M., and Robert G. Bratcher. A *History of Bible Translation and the North American Contribution* (Biblical Scholarship in North America, no. 17). Atlanta: Scholars Press, 1991.

Sanneh, Lamin. *Translating the Message, the Missionary Impact on Culture.* Macon, GA: Orbis Books, 1989.

Smalley, William A. *Translation As Mission: Bible Translation in the Modern Missionary Movement* (The Modern Mission Era, 1792–1992, an Appraisal). Macon, GA: Mercer University Press, 1991.

Stine, Phillip C., ed. *Bible Translation and the Spread of the Church.* New York: E.J. Brill, 1990.

ROBERT HUNT

BIBLICAL INERRANCY

Inerrancy is a theory about the authority of the Christian BIBLE. It holds that the original writings—the "autographs"—are free of error in all about which they speak: matters scientific and historical as well as theological and moral. Their errorless status is based on the work of the Holy Spirit who superintended the words used as well as the events described and the teachings entailed.

The language of "inerrancy" regarding scriptural AUTHORITY emerged in the late eighteenth and early nineteenth centuries, given prominence by orthodox Protestant theologians. Its concern for exactitude and the treatment of the Bible as a reliable source of information about all aspects of the world reflected the growing influence of science. Inerrantists sought to counter the incursion of the ENLIGHTENMENT with its own form of empirical and rational argument.

The concept of inerrancy today is regularly confused with the view of oracularity. The latter asserts that the words of the original Scripture were dictated by the Holy Spirit, becoming the literal oracles of God. The former takes account of the human factor in the process of inspiration. Adducing the varying vocabulary pools and styles of authorship in the books of the Bible, God protected the authors for erroneous use of their words. While allowing for authorial creativity in the writing process, therefore, inerrantists assert that such takes place under a pneumatological supervision that precludes mistakes on any and every topic considered.

While sharing the common conviction of Scripture's plenary inspiration, inerrantists divide into conservative, moderate, and liberal parties. Conservative inerrantists trust the transmissive power of the Holy Spirit to ensure that certain received translations carry the authority of the inaccessible autographs themselves. This perspective is noted for its practice of harmonizing apparently conflicting reports of events, arguing for the historical veracity of accounts of the world's beginnings and endings, and attacking critical scholarship as the tool of "secular humanism." Moderate inerrantists allow for a more influential role of human factors in the creation of the originals, noting individual differences in authorial style and substance, and the impact of culture. Historical and literary criticism that discloses oriental hyperbole in reportage of events, the function of other genres such as narrative in biblical writing, and the limitations in ancient cosmology are not rejected, although a sharp eye is kept out for the intrusion of an antisupernaturalist bias in biblical scholarship. Textual criticism that seeks for the closest approximation to the yet inaccessible originals is actively pursued. Although the autographs are sacrosanct in all respects, subsequent editions and translations bear the marks of the human hand that make possible small errors in historical and scientific details. The salvific heart of Scripture in matters of faith and morals, however, is secured, for the trajectory of the Spirit's power that produced the originals ensures the absolute trustworthiness of today's approved texts.

Liberal inerrantists acknowledge a greater role for the human factor in the creation of the errorless autographs, as well in the transmission process, granting a larger place for the legitimacy of historical, literary, and textual criticism. Its most notable feature is the insistence on the recognition of varying genres in biblical writings. It looks for authorial intention, reading, for example, accounts of the world's creation and consummation as theological in genre and housed in primitive cosmology, and therefore not to be treated as "informational," that is, accurate history in the modern sense.

Inerrancy, particularly in its "conservative" form, has often been used as a litmus test for ORTHODOXY among some evangelical circles within Protestantism.

See also Bible Interpretation; Evangelicalism; Fundamentalism; Pentecostalism

References and Further Reading

Fackre, Gabriel. *The Christian Story*. vol. 2. Grand Rapids, MI: Wm. B. Eerdmans, 1987.
Geisler, Norman L., ed. *Inerrancy*. Grand Rapids, MI: Zondervan Publishing, 1979.
Henry, Carl F. H. "God, Revelation and Authority." In *God Who Speaks and Shows*, vol. IV. Waco, TX: Word, 1979.
Youngblood, Ronald, ed. *Evangelicals and Inerrancy*. Nashville, TN: Thomas Nelson, 1984.

GABRIEL FACKRE

BILL OF RIGHTS

The term "bill of rights" commonly refers to a written enumeration of the fundamental rights and liberties of citizens protected from infringement by civil government and a specification of the limitations on the arbitrary or capricious exercise of government powers. The phrase "bill of rights" is not found in the U.S. Constitution; however, it is a common designation for the first ten amendments adopted in 1791.

British statutory and common law sources, along with natural rights theory, influenced colonial and early states bills of rights. The Virginia Declaration of Rights (1776) was also a model for not only the first amendments to the U.S. Constitution but also the bills of rights in other states and around the world.

The U.S. Constitution drafted in 1787 did not contain a bill of rights. George Mason's proposal that the Constitution be "prefaced with a Bill of Rights" was rejected unanimously by the state delegations. Few delegates opposed a bill of rights in principle; rather, they believed that one was unnecessary given the limited, enumerated powers of the proposed national government. Some of the most influential states, however, ratified the Constitution with a strong recommendation that it be amended to safeguard liberties. James Madison took the initiative in the First Federal Congress, convened in 1789, to propose provisions that were shaped into the amendments sent to the states for ratification.

These amendments, known as the American Bill of Rights, set forth fundamental freedoms and procedural safeguards that the civil government may not deny individuals. The first amendment protects the freedoms of religion, speech, press, assembly, and petition. Its provisions respecting the nonestablishment and free exercise of religion are among the most innovative features of the Bill of Rights. The fourth amendment prohibits unreasonable searches and seizures by the state. The fifth amendment disallows compelled self-incrimination; the deprivation of life, liberty, or property without due process of law; and the taking of private property without fair compensation. The sixth amendment affords criminal defendants the rights to a speedy and public trial, to an impartial jury, to confront accusers, and to a lawyer. The eighth amendment prohibits cruel and unusual punishments. The Bill of Rights originally restricted the national government only. The fourteenth amendment (1868), however, has been interpreted by the U.S. Supreme Court to apply selected portions of the Bill of Rights against state governments.

References and Further Reading

Amar, Akhil Reed. *The Bill of Rights: Creation and Reconstruction.* New Haven, CT: Yale University Press, 1998.

Rutland, Robert Allen. *The Birth of the Bill of Rights, 1776–1791.* Chapel Hill: University of North Carolina Press, 1955.

Schwartz, Bernard. *The Great Rights of Mankind: A History of the American Bill of Rights.* New York: Oxford University Press, 1977.

DANIEL DREISBACH

BISHOP AND EPISCOPACY

The term "bishop" derives, by way of Anglo-Saxon usage, from the Greek *episcopos,* for overseer, referring to one who oversees the life of the ecclesial community as its chief pastor, usually in a region referred to as a diocese. In the New Testament the office is not certainly identifiable as a distinct order of ministry, but in the second century the role of bishop emerged as a separate office, distinguished from the ministries of presbyters and deacons (see DEACONESS, DEACON) with which it developed, over time, into a threefold pattern of ministry. During this period the bishop's oversight was tied closely to liturgical presidency, although the office eventually developed sacramental significance in itself and the succession by which AUTHORITY was passed from one bishop to the next became an important symbol of the church's unity, of the connection between the local community to the wider CHURCH, and of continuity in the apostolic faith.

After Constantine's legitimation of Christianity, the responsibilities of bishops increased, as did their political significance, as they became responsible for wider regions of a growing church. By the eve of the REFORMATION bishops were the highest order in a hierarchy of some seven orders of ministry, often exercising considerable secular as well as ecclesial influence, despite the general distinction between the church's spiritual authority and the temporal authority of monarchs. The sixteenth-century reformers held various opinions about the value and legitimacy of the episcopal office: some retained the office; some retained it but eliminated the historic succession that attached to it; others eliminated the office altogether, believing that the importance of bishops could not be substantiated by a reading of the plain sense of the New Testament. Nevertheless the ministry of oversight has continued in some form in all the churches of the Reformation regardless of whether they distinguish the office or use the title. The ECUMENISM of the last half-century has seen a return of appreciation for the symbolic significance of the office within the threefold pattern of ordained ministry and discussions of the role of bishops have yielded fruitful insights into ecclesiology, apostolicity, and the question of church order.

The Bishop in the New Testament

Although the New Testament contains a varied ecclesiology, two ideas arguably predominate. One is the notion of the church as a royal priesthood whose identity is rooted in Christ, the great high priest. Alternatively, the church is the body whose head is Christ and whose members are given a variety of gifts for the work of Christ in the world. Along the lines of the second model, leadership in this body was first focused in those appointed directly by Christ (apostles), but others who had the gift of leadership emerged within this period. These leaders were not seen strictly as successors to the apostles at this time and the difference between those designated elders and those designated overseers is not entirely clear. A representative example of this indistinctness is found in Acts 20, when Paul sends for the elders (*presbuterous*) of the Church in Ephesus and charges them to be overseers (*episcopous*) of the flock. A similar lack of clarity pertains in Acts 6 to the appointment of seven to the service (*diakonia*) of the word in care of the widows: whether this task amounts to an office is not certain, although the formality of the laying on of hands by the apostles certainly suggests a trajectory toward a more formal pattern of ordination. Hints of such a pattern can be found in the Pastoral Epistles, although the distinction between bishops and presbyters is, even there, not yet clear. By the close of the first century, however, the first letter of Clement of Rome identifies bishops and deacons as distinct roles appointed by the Apostles to lead "the future believers" and implies that presbyters were assisting in the work of the bishops in their local communities (*I Clement* 42,43). Some scholars now see possible parallels of this first-century pattern to the orders of ministry at Qumran, although the precise status of the relationships between Qumran and the early Christian communities has not been established.

The Development of the Monarchical Episcopate

The turn of the second century brought increasing concern about schism and so-called gnostic heresies that threatened the church. In this context, the monarchical, or single bishop, distinguished from presbyters or elders, became the norm: the bishop was the symbol of the church's unity in the apostolic faith. Ignatius of Antioch, writing probably early in the second century, grounded the unifying power of the bishop not in his lineage in a historic succession—an idea whose time was yet to come—but in a symbolic pattern in which the bishop is the "type" of God, the divine father. In turn the presbyters, a kind of college of ministers around the bishop, are "types" of the apostles, and the deacon a "type" of Christ. The semi-platonic connection here, particularly between the ministerial organization of bishops and deacons and the divine reality, can be seen as an indication, if not the source, of the sacramental interpretation of ministerial orders. Under the continuing pressure to distinguish the apostolic faith from "gnostic" HERESY, the notion arose of a line of succession from one bishop to the next, particularly near the end of the second century in Irenaeus's writing, but the point of succession was not so much the maintenance of a historic line of persons as it was the continuity of the apostolic faith.

Throughout this period, the bishop was the chief presider at the Eucharist and in this capacity, the bishop's role was thought of as "priestly." Thus the emerging pattern of episcopacy rejoined the biblical ecclesiology of the church as a royal priesthood, mentioned above: the bishop, prayerfully chosen by the people, is a symbol of Christ, and is therefore the high priest of a priestly people and shares in the "princely spirit" of Christ. This THEOLOGY of episcopacy, as well as the bishop's prerogative to ordain other ministers, is reflected in the prayer for the ordination of a bishop found in Hippolytus's *Apostolic Tradition,* customarily dated to the third century.

Episcopacy after Constantine

Upon the occasion of the CONVERSION of the Roman emperor Constantine in the fourth century, the churches in the West grew rapidly and the bishops began to expand their responsibilities over wider regions of the church. As a result, presbyters began to carry more responsibility for local ecclesial communities and to preside at their eucharists in the absence of the bishop. As a result of this development, presbyters were increasingly referred to as priests because they now extended the liturgical presidency of the bishop. Deacons continued to be associated with service to those in need and, ritually, with the service of the eucharistic table. This core pattern continued unchanged into the Middle Ages, but with some development in three main areas: structure, ritual practice, and theology. Structurally the three orders—bishops, priests, and deacons—became by the high middle ages the crown of a scheme of "minor orders" with various responsibilities for the administration of the church's mission and LITURGY. Ritually bishops were distinguished especially by their power to confer orders and to administer CONFIRMATION. (The latter originated as a postbaptismal rite over which, until the fourth century, the bishop normally presided, but which became separated from the baptismal rite as the bishop's presence to the local community was not always possible.) Theologically the bishop's power to ordain was increasingly seen as the result of a substantial change in the ontological character of the bishop (a change that pertains, in forms appropriate to their offices, to priests and deacons as well). This is reflected in the ordination rites of the time in which, by contrast to earlier ritual patterns, the bishop ordained priests and deacons not by laying on hands within the context of the community's prayer, but with a verbal formula that conferred ordination by the power resident in the bishop.

Episcopacy in the Reformation Traditions

Consistent with their wider theological concerns, the reformers were generally troubled by two aspects of the medieval episcopacy: its hierarchical ascendancy over what they interpreted as a sacrificial priesthood, and the notion of a power inherent in the person of the bishop. Both of these militated, in their view, against the sufficiency of Christ and the direct communion of the whole church with him. Nevertheless the reformers and the churches that followed them took these concerns in many different directions.

MARTIN LUTHER himself did not see evidence in the New Testament for an episcopal office distinct from the work of presbyters and emphasized the priestly character of the whole church, over which certain members functioned as presiders and pastors. Although the German Lutheran churches ultimately eliminated the position of bishop, Swedish Lutherans retained the office and its historic succession but downplayed an emphasis on powers peculiar to the office. Danish Lutherans took a middle position, retaining the office but eliminating the element of historic succession in its ordination process. Other reformers identified pastors, teachers, elders, and deacons as the orders of ministry that could be found in the New Testament, and saw no evidence for an indelible change in the character of the bishop or other ordinands as a function of their ordination.

Concern to avoid any intimation of such power in the bishop led JOHN CALVIN, JOHN KNOX, and others to eliminate the office and replace the laying on of hands in ordination to the extension of the "right hand of fellowship" by the ordaining ministers. Knox used the term "superintendent" for a time to refer to an episcopal role that was not a permanent office but that was responsible for organizing ordinations and seeing to the care of vacant cures. The CHURCH OF ENGLAND adapted the Sarum usage of the medieval church in ways strongly influenced by MARTIN BUCER, retaining the office of bishop and the notion of historic succession, but challenging the excessive hierarchical emphasis of the episcopacy. JOHN WESLEY initially adapted the Anglican position, but eventually ordained leaders for the churches in the UNITED STATES, SCOTLAND, and ENGLAND, substituting as Knox did the term "superintendent" for "bishop" (and "elder" for "presbyter"). Wesley felt empowered to perform such ordinations because he understood the biblical evidence to suggest the difference between bishops and presbyters to be a difference of degree, not of kind, and understood himself to be exercising episcopal oversight of the Methodist societies. Other reformed traditions that descend from the Reformation, particularly churches of congregational POLITY and those that are independent, sometimes retain the use of "bishop" as the title of their chief local pastor and a few of these bishops occupy an earned preeminence in a network with other local congregations of similar lineage. The MORAVIAN CHURCH retains the bishop and a claim to succession in the apostolic tradition, yet self-governs on a presbyterian model.

What is important to underline, amid the various directions in which the episcopacy was taken by churches of the Reformation, is the *de facto* reality of the ministry of oversight in many different forms that is exercised in all churches as a matter of institutional necessity and, except in the most insistently congregationalist communities, of the symbolic expression of connection between local congregations and the wider church.

Modern Developments in the Theology of Episcopacy

The persistence of a ministry of *episcope* in all churches, whatever its form, has made possible a degree of theological convergence on orders in the modern period. Multilateral dialogue through the Faith and Order Commission of the WORLD COUNCIL OF CHURCHES led ultimately in 1982 to the issuance of *Baptism, Eucharist and Ministry* (*BEM*), which rep-

resents this convergence not only on orders but on the outlines of shared Theology of the SACRAMENTS. Although noting the ambivalence of the New Testament evidence for the early Christian communities' patterns of ministry, *BEM* acknowledges the historic usefulness of the threefold pattern of ministry (bishops, presbyters, deacons) while recognizing that its practice has sometimes been diminished or corrupted. *BEM* also acknowledges the need for orders to serve the permanent, collegial, and communal aspects of the whole church's ministry, whatever form those orders take, and in relation makes distinctions between apostolic succession, apostolic tradition, and the historic episcopate. Apostolic succession is the manifestation in ordered ministry of the whole church's commitment to the apostolic tradition, defined by *BEM* as "continuity in the permanent characteristics of the church of the apostles." The historic episcopate is one important way of preserving an orderly transition in ministry that serves the apostolic tradition of the church. Churches that have no historic succession of bishops are urged to consider whether this traditional symbol might better serve their grounding in the apostolic tradition; at the same time churches that do maintain a historic succession of bishops are urged to recognize the ministry of oversight that exists in churches without bishops and to measure the adequacy of their own episcopal practice by the apostolic tradition to which the whole church is called. The bishop in succession is, in sum, acknowledged as an important "sign, though not a guarantee, of the continuity and unity of the church."

Since the publication of *Baptism, Eucharist and Ministry* bilateral dialogues among churches descending from the Reformation have focused from time to time on the place of episcopacy in the life of the church. A productive example is that between the EVANGELICAL LUTHERAN CHURCH IN AMERICA and the EPISCOPAL CHURCH in the United States. Their INTERCONFESSIONAL DIALOGUE has produced a "Concordat of Agreement" signaling a mutual recognition of ordained ministries. This agreement hinges in important ways on some of the distinctions that appeared in *Baptism, Eucharist and Ministry* as applied to episcopacy: among other things, Lutherans agree to the joint ordinations of all bishops in the future for the sake of the mission and in recognition of the importance of the sign of historic succession; Episcopalians, on their part, acknowledge in Lutheran orders the apostolicity that must characterize the church in faithful execution of its mission and submit the efficacy of the historic episcopate under the judgment of that apostolicity. The legitimacy of the liturgical and canonical provisions required for this agreement to be enacted remains a subject of some debate in both churches, yet the agreement signals the enduring importance of the episcopal ministry in contemporary discussion among Reformation churches.

See also Congregationalism; Lutheranism; Methodism; Presbyterianism

References and Further Reading

Ainslie, James L. *The Doctrines of Ministerial Order in the Reformed Churches of the Sixteenth and Seventeenth Centuries*. Edinburgh: Clarke, 1940.
Barrett, C. K. *Church, Ministry and Sacraments in the New Testament*. Grand Rapids, MI: Wm. B. Eerdmans, 1985.
Bradshaw, P. F. *Ordination Rites of the Ancient Churches of East and West*. New York: Pueblo, 1990.
———. *The Anglican Ordinal*. London: SPCK, 1971.
Haendler, G. *Luther on Ministerial Office and Congregational Function*. Philadelphia: Fortress, 1981.
Mitchell, Nathan. *History and Theology in the Sacrament of Order*. Dublin: Gill and MacMillan, 1983.
Moede, G. F. *The Office of Bishop in Methodism*. New York: Abingdon, 1964.
von Campenhausen, Hans. *Ecclesiastical Authority and Spiritual Power in the Church of the First Three Centuries*. London: A. and C. Black, 1969.
World Council of Churches. *Baptism, Eucharist, and Ministry*. Geneva: World Council of Churches, 1982.

JAMES W. FARWELL

BLACK METHODISTS

Black Methodism first emerged in America as Wesleyan Methodist itinerants reached out to enslaved populations with a message that resonated with them. Soon separate denominations arose as blacks wanted political and economic independence from the segregationist patriarchal structures of white METHODISM. Black Methodism offered members of the black community leadership opportunities to speak out on social and political issues. Issues of education and MISSIONS to AFRICA dominated black Methodism in the nineteenth century. During the twentieth century Methodism continued as a central force in the black community as it asserted itself toward the achievement of Civil Rights.

Early Black Methodism

Blacks occupied a prominent position in the Methodist movement from the very earliest days in America. Methodists were among the first churches to begin the widespread Christianization of blacks in America. At the first Methodist class meeting in America one of the five attendees was a young black servant named Betty. JOHN WESLEY's emissaries commented on the large numbers of blacks who responded to the Methodist message.

Blacks were attracted to Methodism for two reasons. The Methodist message appealed to an enslaved population and the messengers were appealing to the hearers. The key attraction for blacks to Methodism was the Arminian theology. Unlike GEORGE WHITEFIELD and the Calvinist Methodists who supported SLAVERY and made a strong distinction between the body and soul, Wesleyan Methodists had a holistic understanding of the body and soul. A person needed to be bodily free to exercise the freedom of will granted by God. If someone was under the yoke of another, she or he was not free to respond to the call of God as God intended.

The Methodists brought a message that condemned slavery and racism in uncompromising terms and they lived out that message. Wesley spoke out vehemently against slavery. A newly converted slave owner's first act was frequently to free his slaves and thereafter preach abolition. The Methodist faith was also accessible. The Methodist class meeting allowed blacks to experience Christianity in an emotional manner that emphasized hymn singing and testifying. Methodists preached in the vernacular, not in highly theological language.

Possibly the most important aspect for black acceptance of the Methodist message was the messengers themselves. Because the Methodist movement was a lay movement, preachers did not need ordinations or educational credentials. Methodism offered opportunities for blacks to participate in the movement as class leaders, exhorters, and preachers. One early black preacher was Harry Hosier (1750–1806). He was a small man who preached with such fervor that all who heard him remarked on his power. He traveled and preached with FRANCIS ASBURY and THOMAS COKE throughout the 1780s and 1790s. Although uneducated, he was immensely popular and drew mixed audiences that outnumbered the audiences that gathered to hear the white preachers accompanying him. Coke claimed Hoosier was one of the best preachers in the world.

Although Methodism in America began with egalitarian ideals, the reality quickly began to change. The initially strong antislavery platform was suspended after only six months, setting off a rapid process of capitulation to slavery interests. The changes forced blacks into secondary and subservient roles, leading to schism and the creation of separate black Methodist denominations.

Creation of the African Methodist Episcopal Church

The first black Methodist denomination was the AFRICAN METHODIST EPISCOPAL (AME) CHURCH. RICHARD ALLEN founded the AME Church in Philadelphia, Pennsylvania in 1816. Born a slave, Allen converted to Methodism after hearing the preaching of a Methodist itinerant. His owner, at the urging of a Methodist itinerant, agreed to sell Allen his freedom. Five years later Allen had raised $2,000 and purchased his freedom. Allen, like Hoosier, attended the CHRISTMAS CONFERENCE and traveled with Asbury, who was impressed with Allen and ordained him deacon in 1799.

In 1787 Allen moved to Philadelphia and joined St. George's Methodist Episcopal Church (MEC). One Sunday in late 1787 an overzealous sexton requested that Allen and several others move to make room for whites to sit. The men requested that the sexton allow them to finish their prayers and then they would move. The sexton demanded that they leave immediately and pulled Absalom Jones out of his seat. Allen, Jones, and several others then walked out. The walkout led to a realization by the black membership that they needed to act to ensure their freedoms.

In 1794 Allen raised money to build Bethel Church. Bethel functioned as a meeting and worship space for blacks. The leadership of St. George's MEC wanted to control Bethel or have it turned over to the Pennsylvania Annual Conference of the MEC. The presiding elder of the Philadelphia District demanded that Bethel's founders turn the church over to the conference, but Allen and his supporters refused. Eventually they were forced to place the church under the supervision of the conference, once again returning the membership of Bethel under the authority of whites. Black ministers could be ordained only as deacons, not elders. Thus, the membership of Bethel remained dependent on the whites of St. George's for the SACRAMENTS.

James Smith White, an elder at St. George's, in 1805 examined Bethel's charter and decided to demand payment for ministerial services to Bethel. This sparked a desire on the part of the Bethel membership to change their charter. They added the Black Supplement giving Bethel unique status among MEC churches. The supplement along with a refusal to pay for ministerial services resulted in the withdrawal of white minister services in 1807.

The situation came to a head in 1816 when Robert Burch of St. George's attempted to preach at Bethel Church. Burch went to the Pennsylvania Supreme Court to force Bethel to open its pulpit. Bethel won the court fight, but decided that more decisive action was needed to prevent further problems. To get out from under the social political control of the MEC, on April 9, 1816 Allen called a meeting in Philadelphia with delegates from several disaffected black Methodist churches in Baltimore and Philadelphia. The meeting created the African Methodist Episcopal Church with a polity and theology based on the MEC. Richard Allen was elected as the first bishop of the

new church. Initially the AME church was made up of five churches with 1,067 members.

Creation of the African Methodist Episcopal Zion Church

The second major black Methodist denomination was the AFRICAN METHODIST EPISCOPAL ZION (AMEZ) CHURCH. Peter Williams, the child of slaves, became a Methodist in the 1760s. After the Revolutionary War Williams was sold to a trustee of Wesley Chapel in New York who allowed him to purchase his freedom. After purchasing his freedom Williams joined John Street Methodist Episcopal Church in New York.

During the late 1790s the black members of John Street decided to hold their own meetings and in 1796 built the African Chapel. The new church grew well, but suffered from constant financial problems because of the poor economic condition of the congregates. Eventually the church grew and split into two churches, Asbury and Zion.

Richard Allen, after separating from the MEC and forming the AME Church, attempted to reach out to Williams and the black Methodists of New York, but they accused Allen of encroachment, stealing members from their churches, and of taking advantage of their financial problems. They refused to join the AMEs. In 1820 the future AMEZ churches began to move toward separation. Initially they were not interested in separation, only in protecting black Methodist property during the Stillwell Property controversy of 1820. Separation came in three steps, beginning in 1820 when the future members of the AMEZ Church separated from the New York Conference and appointed James Varrick as Superintendent. The following year Williams and his supporters claimed that they were still within the MEC, but were a separate, special conference. Then in 1822 they effectively broke with the MEC over ordination, although they continued to profess loyalty to the MEC despite operating as a separate church. The group appealed to the 1824 General Conference for recognition as a special conference. After being rebuffed at the General Conference Williams and his supporters founded the Black Methodist Episcopal Zion Church based on the same POLITY and THEOLOGY as the MEC and named James Varrick as its first bishop.

Black Methodism in the Nineteenth Century

Nineteenth-century black Methodist churches were similar to white Methodist churches except they tended to emphasize lay involvement, a strong lay stand against slavery, and autonomy over church affairs (particularly property). Black Methodist churches were organized around a series of conferences: General, Annual, and Quarterly. The General Conference was the main legislative body, the Annual Conferences handled annual matters such as placing and ordaining clergy, and the Quarterly Conferences dealt with the running of a local church. Black Methodism operated in a top-down structure with strong bishops. Illiteracy was a problem in the early black church, forcing bishops into authoritarian roles.

Black Methodism focused on education as a means to lift the social status of the black race. SUNDAY SCHOOLS occupied a prominent place in the structure of most individual churches. Daniel Payne, an AME bishop, fought in the 1840s to establish a ministerial reading course and higher educational standards for clergy. In 1866 Bishop Payne served as the first president of Wilberforce University. He was the first black man to serve as the president of an American university. The AME denomination went on to found two more colleges, Allen College in South Carolina and Morris Brown College in Georgia. The AMEZ Church founded its only college, Livingstone College in North Carolina, in 1885. The smallest of the three major black Methodist denominations, the Christian Methodist Episcopal Church founded four schools, the first of which was Paine College in Georgia.

Within black Methodist churches during the nineteenth century there was an emphasis on lay involvement attributed partly to Methodism's background as a lay movement. Black churches tended to form out of laity-led black classes or choirs. A lack of ordained clergy also forced the LAITY to assume greater roles. Black Methodist churches, because of the larger lay involvement, retained the love feast as a central rite far longer than did the white churches; many black Methodist churches still celebrate a regular love feast.

Among the laity, women made up the majority of the churches' membership. However, women rarely held official leadership positions outside of the Sunday School program. Two notable exceptions were Jarena Lee and Amanda Berry Smith. Lee attended Bethel Church in Philadelphia in the 1810s when she first received the call to preach. She approached Richard Allen, but he discouraged her. Several years later when she could no longer resist the call, she preached an impromptu sermon in front of Allen and received his blessing to continue preaching. In 1836 she published her autobiography, a remarkable glimpse into a black woman's spiritual journey as she confronted racism and sexism. Several women followed in Lee's steps, preaching in AME churches until a motion at the 1852 General Conference to allow licensing of female preachers was resoundingly defeated. The other black Methodist denominations all had similar rules. Several years later Amanda Berry Smith re-

ceived the call to preach. Smith preached primarily to holiness groups and traveled to Britain, Africa, and INDIA before returning to the UNITED STATES to work for the TEMPERANCE movement.

Although the laity of the major black Methodist churches were strongly against slavery, the leadership of both the AME and AMEZ churches did not take a strong abolition stand until just before the outbreak of the CIVIL WAR. Richard Allen favored gradual emancipation over more radical approaches. Not until 1856 when the AME church discovered some members were purchasing slaves and then owning them while they purchased their freedom did the issue became a central debate in a General Conference. In 1856 the AME Church came out publicly as strongly against all forms of slavery. The AMEZ church issued a similar resolution later that same year. Individuals, however, took a strong stand much earlier: in 1810 Daniel Coker published the first antislavery pamphlet written by a black individual.

After the Civil War both the AME and AMEZ churches focused their missionary efforts on the Southern states. Black churches had been banned throughout most of the South, so it proved a fertile mission field. The AME and AMEZ made inroads among freed slaves in the South, creating fear among white southerners. The white leadership of the METHODIST EPISCOPAL CONFERENCE decided the best way to counter the Northerners was to create a new denomination for Southern blacks. In December of 1870 a conference of the black members of the MEC was held in Jackson, Tennessee and the Colored Methodist Episcopal Church was created. The first two elected bishops were Henry Miles and Richard Vanderherst. The CME Church changed it name in 1954 to the Christian Methodist Episcopal Church.

After Reconstruction black Methodist Churches turned their attention to Africa. Although Daniel Coker of the AME church went to Africa in 1820, the three major black Methodist churches did not launch official missions to Africa until the 1890s. The AME church went into West Africa in 1891 and SOUTH AFRICA in 1896. The AMEZ Church went into Ghana and LIBERIA in the twentieth century.

Black Methodism in the Twentieth Century

In the twentieth century the three major black Methodist denominations repeatedly tried and failed at an organic union. The initial attempts resulted in the formation of the Tri-Federation Council. The Council led to the closer working relationship the three denominations enjoy today.

When American black Methodists began to evangelize Africa, they found that Africa already had a form of Methodism. British Methodism was active in Africa for over seventy-five years before the American denominations arrived. Today most African countries have national Methodist Churches as a result of the British Methodist Missionary Society. Although theologically they resemble Black Methodism in America, they differ in several significant factors. Most national churches have term bishops who return to the local parish when their term is over. Most African Methodist churches adapted local customs into a participatory form of worship. Like Black Methodism in America, education has tended to be the major focus of the African Churches. The largest of the African Churches are in ZIMBABWE, Kenya, Ghana, Ivory Coast, and South Africa. Each of these churches, founded by British Methodism, became independent churches in the 1960s, and today their combined membership is almost 1.5 million.

Black Methodist theology in the twentieth century has drawn heavily from Latin American LIBERATION THEOLOGY. JAMES HAL CONE, an AME minister and a professor of systematic theology at Union Theological Seminary in New York, is the most important theologian in twentieth-century black Methodism. Cone draws from liberation theology to relate Christian theology to the black experience (see BLACK THEOLOGY). For Cone, God is a dynamic deity involved in human affairs with liberating power battling oppressors and standing in unity with the oppressed.

Black Methodist churches in the twentieth century retained their tradition of strong episcopal leadership. In 1928 the AME church attempted to check the ecclesial autocracy by passing a rule that required bishops to be moved after two quadrennia. That same General Conference began to allow lay delegates to attend General Conference. The other major black Methodist denominations also passed legislation limiting episcopal stays in an annual conference and allowing lay delegates to attend their General Conferences. One of the founders of the National Association for the Advancement of Colored People (NAACP) was an AMEZ bishop, Alexander Walters. In 1984 Leontine Kelly became the first black woman bishop in a Methodist church, the UNITED METHODIST CHURCH.

When compared to white Methodist WORSHIP, modern black Methodism features an emotional style that draws the congregation into the worship experience; however, compared to black Holiness or Baptist worship practices, Methodist worship seems sedate. Flowing from their CHURCH OF ENGLAND roots the Methodists have a more liturgical worship style. Singing is prominent and the preached word is the center of the service. Music has been an important carrier of the Methodist theology and black experience ever since Richard Allen published the first volume of black

hymnody in 1801, *A Collection of Spiritual Songs and Hymns.* At the beginning of the twenty-first century, black Methodism is alive and well. In 2002 the AME church was the fastest growing church in North America.

See also Arminianism; Baltimore Conference; Bishop and Episcopacy; Calvinism; Civil Rights Movement; Hymns and Hymnals; Itinerancy; Methodism, England; Methodism, North America; Slavery, Abolition of; Wesleyanism; Women Clergy

References and Further Reading

Baer, Hans A., and Merrill Singer. *African American Religion, Varieties of Protest and Accommodation,* 2nd ed. Knoxville: University of Tennessee Press, 2002.

Baldwin, Lewis. *"Invisible" Strands in African Methodism: A History of the African Union Methodists Protestant and Union American Methodist Episcopal Churches, 1805–1980.* Metuchen, NJ: Scarecrow Press, 1983.

George, Carol V. R. *Segregated Sabbaths: Richard Allen and the Rise of the Independent Black Churches, 1760–1840.* New York: Oxford University Press, 1973.

Gregg, Howard. *History of the African Methodist Episcopal Church: the Black Church in Action.* Nashville, TN: A.M.E. Church Sunday School Union, 1980.

McClain, William B. *Black People in the Methodist Church: Whither Thou Goest?* Nashville, TN: Abingdon Press, 1984.

Richardson, Harry V. *Dark Salvation, The Story of Methodism as It Developed Among Blacks in America.* Garden City, NY: Anchor Press, 1976.

Shockley, Grant S. *Heritage and Hope, The African American Presence in United Methodism.* Nashville, TN: Abingdon Press, 1991.

Walls, William J. *The African Methodist Episcopal Church.* Charlotte, NC: A.M.E. Zion Publishing House, 1974.

ADAM ZELE

BLACK THEOLOGY

Black theology was launched with JAMES HAL CONE'S landmark volume, *Black Theology and Black Power* (1968). However, several other works were foundational to the beginning of black theology as an option in constructive THEOLOGY, including Joseph Washington's *Black Religion;* Albert Cleage, Jr.'s *Black Messiah;* Gayraud S. Wilmore's *Black Religion and Black Radicalism;* and James Deotis Roberts's (with co-editor Fr. James Gardiner) *Quest for a Black Theology.*

Black theology did not spring up as a totally new phenomenon. The CIVIL RIGHTS MOVEMENT, the non-violent movement of Dr. MARTIN LUTHER KING, Jr., the black nationalism of Malcolm X and others, and the black power and black consciousness movements were among the forces that gave birth to black theology.

The most direct and immediate basis for black theology was found in the rise of black power. However, to understand the movement that erupted in the late 1960s, one needs to revisit black history for at least 200 years. The religious roots were manifested in the ministry of RICHARD ALLEN in the late seventeenth century. Wilmore's volume, mentioned above, is an invaluable resource in revisiting the history that gave birth to black theology.

In both youth and temperament, Cone was the proper person to develop a black theology. Cone was in his late twenties when he completed his doctoral studies in theology. He belonged to the same generation as members of the Student Nonviolent Coordinating Committee, who were moving away from Dr. King's nonviolent program to embrace black power as an option. The message of a nationalist leader, Malcolm X of the Nation of Islam, was also being heard. Cone adopted much of the spirit and language of this youthful, more militant group of leaders, of which Stokely Carmichael was a leader. Cone had studied KARL BARTH well. He captured the anger of the Black Power advocates and the dogmatic theological temperament of Barth. This combination radiated in his passion for racial justice. This led him as a black church theologian to reread the BIBLE and reconceive the Christian faith as a basis for black liberation from oppression. Cone's temperament, genius, and commitment to freedom for his people laid the groundwork for a new departure in theological discourse.

The Black Church and Black Theology

Black theology would have been stillborn if it had not been for the readiness of black church leaders, clergy, and lay to receive and act on its message. As early as 1966, black church leaders had begun to consider "black power" as a clear option to King's nonviolent-only approach to black freedom. A statement published in the *New York Times,* July 31, 1966 set the stage for a new outlook for the witness of the black church in the area of race relations. Leading church persons represented by the National Committee of Negro Churchmen declared: "Powerlessness breeds a race of beggars. We are faced with a situation where conscienceless power meets powerless conscience, threatening the very foundations of our nation."

This statement, drafted by a group of black scholars in religion and church leaders, goes on to relate a positive view of "power" to freedom, love, justice, and truth. This initiative by church leaders set the stage for the flowering of a theology of Black Power that surfaced later. The tragic and untimely death of King left a void, which needed a new ideological shift to be filled. Black power was already being considered as a way to move forward. This period of black church history was characterized by an outburst of ECUMENISM. All Protestant denominations were involved,

and black Catholics were represented. There were caucus units in all white denominations with black members. This strong ecumenical consensus was in support of racial justice. It was the National Committee of Black Christians that summoned black theologians to draft statements on black theology for mission and ministry.

The Development of Black Theology through Dialogue

Along with Cone's *Black Theology and Black Power,* there was the powerful influence of Cleage's *Black Messiah,* as well as his Detroit ministry at the Shrine of the Black Madonna. These two volumes, together with the changing climate in the black churches and communities, set off a tide of publications among black theologians and religious scholars.

Roberts's *Liberation and Reconciliation* (1971) was not a direct response to Cone's liberation-only emphasis, although it was perceived by some to be just that. However, Roberts's career as a theologian preceded Cone by at least a decade. Based at Howard University's Divinity School, Roberts was moved to get involved. As a contemporary of King, Roberts brought his mediating message forward and blended it with the new liberation motif. Other colleagues helped broaden and deepen the black Theology conversation. Major Jones took up the theme of the "black awareness" in his *Black Awareness: A Theology of Hope* (1971), focusing on this dimension of the new movements. The new awareness expressed in the phrase "black is beautiful" had a vital message for theological reflection. It had much to say about self-respect and appreciation of heritage. Jones was also influenced by the emergence of the "theology of hope," and attempted to bring theology and ETHICS together in his writings.

An unusual challenge to James Cone's theology came from an unlikely source. His brother, Cecil Wayne, a theologian and pastor, questioned the undue emphasis on "black power" by all black theologians. His book *The Identity Crisis in Black Theology* (1975) devotes a chapter to the critique of Washington, Cone, and Roberts. Cecil observes a lack of attention to African traditional religion, the CONVERSION experience of African slaves, and black people's belief in an Almighty Sovereign God.

During the first decade of black theology, there was little criticism by black WOMEN religious scholars. However, a woman theologian, Jacquelyn Grant, a doctoral student of James H. Cone, wrote an important book titled *The White Woman's Christ and the Black Woman's Jesus* (1989). In this work she states clearly the different Christological concerns of black women and white women. She also describes the differences between the concerns of black male theologians and those of black women theologians. Her work is very important, because she was a somewhat isolated voice at that time. She lays the groundwork for a more powerful critique of black women theologians in womanish theology. The work of black women theologians has expanded the horizon of the black theology enterprise.

Along the way, we must consider the input of religious philosopher Cornel West. West, who earned a doctoral degree with emphasis on Marxist ideology and religion, insists that all black theologians have omitted social analysis in their interpretation of theology. Later womanist theologians adopted a multidimensional attack against oppression, including GENDER, race, and class, and thus have embraced West's critique.

It is obvious that James H. Cone's vision has broadened and deepened through the years. He has reached out to the black church. This is evident in his book *For My People: Black Theology and the Black Church* (1984). Roberts's writings reveal a similar outreach. This is true of his *Roots of a Black Future: Family and Church* (1980) and *The Prophethood of Black Believers: A Theology for Ministers* (1994). There has been an increasing awareness that vital black theology is church theology with a focus on witness and ministry. The important book by James Evans, *We Have Been Believers*, illustrates this point.

Black theologians were in conversation with African and Afro-Caribbean theologians almost from the beginning of the movement. These discussions appeared to be an attractive and mutually rewarding exchange; however, they had to be encouraged by some theologians within black theology circles. This was especially true of Gayraud S. Wilmore and Charles Long. When the theological discussion became interdisciplinary, this dialogue intensified. The founding of the Society for the Study of Black Religion, which included female and male religious scholars from several fields, greatly enhanced this African/African American conversation.

Latin American and black theologians found common ground around the theme of liberation from oppression. Asian theologians engaged the religiocultural and sociopolitical outlook of theology. Thus black theologians, under the leadership of Cone, held conversations on several continents through the Ecumenical Association of Third World Theologians. In this way, the provincial early approach of black theology was given a universal vision. In these same conversations, the importance of social analysis, as refined by Latin American liberation theologians, was expressed in the doing of theology. At the same time,

the struggles of women were beginning to be noted and addressed.

The Future of Black Theology

In surveying the essentials of the black theology movement, we have closely followed the career of James H. Cone, who more than anyone else has personified the spirit of this vital movement. At the dawn of the twenty-first century, the growth, development, and outreach of black theology have become universal. The liberating and reconciling aspects of black theology have influenced the mission and ministry of black churches. We now have not only a second and third generation of black theologians and religious scholars, but also evidence that church leaders are being influenced by their research, teaching, and publications. In this process, the vital legacy of black theology is secure.

See also African Theology; Asian Theology; Christology; Liberation Theology; Womanist Theology

References and Further Reading

Chapman, Mark L. *Christianity on Trial: African-American Religious Thought Before and After Black Power*. Maryknoll, NY: Orbis Books, 1996.

Douglas, Kelly Brown. *The Black Christ*. Maryknoll, NY: Orbis Books, 1994.

Hopkins, Dwight M. *Black Theology of Liberation*. Maryknoll, NY: Orbis Books, 1999.

Roberts, James Deotis. *Black Theology Today: Liberation and Contextualization*. Toronto Studies in Theology, vol. 12. Toronto: Edwin Mellon Press, 1983.

Sawyer, Mary R. *Black Ecumenism: Implementing the Demands of Justice*. Valley Forge, PA: Trinity Press International, 1994.

Traynham, Warner R. *Christian Faith in Black and White: A Primer in Theology from the Black Perspective*. Wakefield, MA: Parameter Press, 1973.

Witvliet, Theo. *The Way of the Black Messiah: The Hermeneutical Challenge of Black Theology as a Theology of Liberation*. Translated from the Dutch by John Bowden. Oak Park, IL: Meyer Stone, 1987.

JAMES DEOTIS ROBERTS

BLAIR, JAMES (1656–1743)

Scottish-American churchman. Blair was born in SCOTLAND in 1656 and died at Williamsburg, Virginia, April 18, 1743. He was ordained to the ministry of the CHURCH OF SCOTLAND in 1679 and placed in charge of the Presbytery of Dalkeith. He was dismissed from this parish when he refused to sign a test oath to the heir apparent to the British throne, James II, and he moved to London. In 1685 he went to Virginia to be the rector of the parish at Varina, later called Henrico.

On December 15, 1689, the bishop of London named Blair the first commissary to Virginia. A commissary represented the bishop of London in a colony, but could not ordain or confirm. He then served the parish at Jamestown until 1710, when he became the rector of Bruton parish in Williamsburg, where he remained until his death. One of Blair's major accomplishments was the founding of the College of William and Mary. The charter for the college was granted on February 8, 1693, and Blair served as president from then until his death. For a brief period in 1740–1741, Blair was acting governor of Virginia. As commissary, he called meetings of the CHURCH OF ENGLAND clergy, disciplined clergy, and sat in the Council of the Colonial Government.

References and Further Reading

Primary Sources:

Blair, James, Henry Hartwell, and Edward Chilton. *The Present State of Virginia, and the College.* Edited (with an introduction) by Hunter Dickinson Farish. Williamsburg, VA: Colonial Williamsburg, Inc., 1940. [Originally written 1697 and first published London: John Wyatt, 1727.]
———. *Our Saviour's Divine Sermon on the Mount.* 5 vols. London: J. Brotherton, 1722.

Secondary Source:

Rouse, Parke E. *James Blair of Virginia.* Chapel Hill: University of North Carolina Press, 1971.

DONALD S. ARMENTROUT

BLAKE, EUGENE CARSON (1906–1985)

American presbyterian minister and ecumenical leader. Born of Presbyterian parents in Missouri, Eugene Blake was theologically educated at the University of Edinburgh and Princeton Theological Seminary, where, dissatisfied with the prevailing liberal and fundamentalist theologies of the 1920s, he chose NEO-ORTHODOXY instead. Ordained by the PRESBYTERIAN CHURCH IN THE UNITED STATES, Blake pastored large congregations in New York and California for 20 years, building a reputation for prophetic PREACHING, skilled administration, and social justice activism. In 1951, Blake became Stated Clerk of the Presbyterian Church. During his tenure, he spurred the denomination to take open stands on social issues. A supporter of the CIVIL RIGHTS MOVEMENT, Blake attended the 1963 March on Washington, where he apologized for white Protestants, stating, "We come, and late we come, but we come."

More notable was Blake's active role in ECUMENISM. From 1954 to 1957, Blake served as president of the NATIONAL COUNCIL OF CHURCHES, augmenting the activism and influence of that body. In his denomination,

he supervised the 1958 merger with the United Presbyterian Church of North America. In 1960, Blake preached, "A Proposal Toward the Reunion of Christ's Churches," which outlined his plan for organic union of mainline Protestants on a basis, "both catholic and reformed." Subsequently, representatives of several Protestant denominations participated in the ongoing CONSULTATION ON CHURCH UNION (COCU) seeking to enact unification. He furthered his ecumenical consensus theology as General Secretary of the WORLD COUNCIL OF CHURCHES (1966–1972). Increased involvement of Roman Catholic and Eastern Orthodox clergy characterized his administration, as did greater leadership from Third World and nonwestern Christians, particularly at the 1968 Uppsala Assembly.

See also Orthodoxy, Eastern; Presbyterianism

References and Further Reading

Primary Source:

Blake, Eugene Carson. *The Church in the Next Decade.* New York: Macmillan, 1966.

Secondary Sources:

Brackenridge, R. Douglas. *Eugene Carson Blake: Prophet with Portfolio.* New York: Seabury Press, 1978.
Moorhead, James H., ed. "The Legacy of Eugene Carson Blake." *Journal of Presbyterian History.* 76 no. 4 (1998): 251–316.

STEPHEN R. BERRY

BLAKE, WILLIAM (1757–1827)

English poet. Little appreciated in his own lifetime, William Blake is now seen as a visionary and one of the greatest poets in English literature. He enjoyed little commercial success, his brilliant works were often misunderstood, and, indeed, some contemporaries thought him mad.

Born November 28, 1757, the son of a London hosier, Blake spent almost his entire life in the British capital city. Apprenticed to an engraver, Blake grew up in a vibrant urban artisan culture influenced by traditions of religious DISSENT and political radicalism. He studied art at the Royal Academy Schools and around 1787 devised a method of illuminated printing in which writing and illustrations appeared on the same page to be later colored in brilliant shades. Through this highly original artistic medium Blake set out his vision of the universe.

His work ranges over historical, classical, and literary themes, but latterly turned more to biblical ones. Blake was an English enthusiast for the French Revolution and a critic of his own country's "dark Satanic

Mills" or the harshness of early industrialization. Likewise he opposed the rational, Newtonian philosophies and sciences of his day in favor of a more mystical vision of man and creation.

His later illuminated books give the impression of conventional Christian images and themes, dealing as they do with such topics as creation, the death of Abel, Christ, and so on. Blake's visionary interpretation of such subjects is both highly original and religiously unorthodox, even heretical. His images juxtapose an old, tyrannical father-god against a young, liberating son-god. His view of the creation, for example, indicates that evil is present in the nature of man from the beginning, contrary to the conventional Christian view.

Blake's artistic output was both vast and difficult to interpret, as he devised his own mythology by a reinterpretation of biblical themes. To appreciate the work of this most unusual genius requires considerable effort on the part of the student as well as the help of his many subsequent interpreters.

William Blake died August 12, 1827, and was buried without a headstone in the Protestant dissenters' burial ground in London. Today he is a much-commemorated literary giant, the object of a large number of critical studies, and seen as a prophet whose alternative visions of both humanity and deity command great respect.

References and Further Reading

Ackroyd, Peter. *Blake*. London: Sinclair-Stevenson, 1995.
Erdman, David V. *Blake: Prophet Against Empire*. Princeton: Princeton University Press, 1954.
Thompson, E. P. *Witness Against the Beast: William Blake and the Moral Law*. New York: The New Press, 1993.

FRED DONNELLY

BLISS, PHILIP PAUL (1838–1876)

American hymnwriter. Bliss was born in 1838 and grew up in a Methodist home. He made his profession of faith in a Baptist revival service, was baptized by a minister of the Christian Church, joined the Presbyterian community of his spouse, served as a choir director and SUNDAY SCHOOL superintendent with the Congregationalists, and led music for evangelical meetings of all types. He began his career as a music teacher, and in 1864 he and his wife relocated to Chicago where he worked with the music publishers Root and Cady.

Bliss was a friend of the evangelist DWIGHT L. MOODY and was arguably the most popular gospel singer-songwriter of the nineteenth century. In many respects his contemporary IRA SANKEY, who outlived him by over thirty years, overshadowed Bliss. Yet in

a brief span of twelve years between 1864 and 1876 Bliss wrote words and music that have endured for generations. Along with W. B. Bradbury's "Just as I Am," his hymn "Almost Persuaded" was a standard invitation in evangelical REVIVALS. "Hold the Fort" became a theme song for the prohibition, suffrage, and labor movements. His hymns "Jesus Loves Even Me," "Let the Lower Lights Be Burning," "I Will Sing of My Redeemer," "Hallelujah, What a Saviour!," and "Wonderful Words of Life" are classics of gospel hymnody. His music gave voice to the romantic EVANGELICALISM and evangelical ethos of the popular democratized Christianity in America. Bliss compiled his first book of hymns entitled *The Charm* in 1871 and continued to produce one book a year until his death. With Sankey, Bliss published the popular hymnal *Gospel Hymns and Sacred Songs* in 1875, which contained many of his songs and increased his influence. In all he composed over 400 hymns and sacred pieces, giving rise to his reputation as "the Charles Wesley of the nineteenth century."

Moody invited Bliss to accompany him in 1873 as the music director for a series of revival meetings throughout ENGLAND that were to bring Moody to international attention. When Bliss declined, Sankey accepted. A year later Bliss entered full-time into the ministry as a music evangelist, joining the popular evangelical preacher D. W. Whittle in twenty-five revival meetings. Bliss and his wife died in a train wreck on December 29, 1876 while traveling to meet Whittle for a singing engagement at Moody's Tabernacle in Chicago.

See also Hymns and Hymnals; Music, American

References and Further Reading

Primary Source:

Bliss, P. P., and Ira Sankey. *Gospel Hymns and Sacred Songs*. New York: Biglow and Main, 1875.

Secondary Sources:

Corts, Thomas E. "Blessed Bliss." In Christian History Institute (www.gospelcom.net/chi/BRICABRF/ppbliss.shtml).
Hall, Jacob. *Biography of Gospel Song and Hymn Writers*. New York: Fleming Revell, 1914.
Nason, Elias. "Life of P. P. Bliss." In *The Lives of The Eminent American Evangelists Dwight Lyman Moody and Ira David Sankey*. Boston: B. B. Russell, 1877.
Scheips, Paul J. *Hold the Fort! The Story of a Song from the Sawdust Trail to the Picket Line*. Smithsonian Studies in History and Technology, no. 9. Washington, DC: Smithsonian Institution Press, 1971.
Simons, M. Laird. *Holding the Fort*. Norwich, CT: Henry Bill Publishing Co., 1897.
Smucker, David. "Philip Paul Bliss and the Musical, Cultural and Religious Sources of the Gospel Music Tradition in the

United States, 1850–1876." Ph.D. dissertation, Boston University, 1981.

Whittle, Daniel Webster. *Memoirs of P. P. Bliss*. New York: Barnes and Co., 1877.

CURTIS W. FREEMAN

BLOMFIELD, CHARLES (1786–1857)

Bishop of London. Bloomfield was born at Bury St. Edmund, ENGLAND, where his father was a schoolmaster. He was educated at the grammar school of Bury and at Trinity College, Cambridge, where he excelled as a student. He took his B.A. in 1808 with high honors, and was elected fellow of Trinity College, Cambridge shortly thereafter. Ordained in 1810, he was appointed to a number of benefices in rapid succession, and in 1820 was appointed to the benefice of St. Botolph, Bishopsgate.

Early in his career he demonstrated an aptitude for classical scholarship and published several works, including editions of the *Prometheus Vinctus* (1810), Callimachus (1815), and Euripides (1821). He also wrote several pieces of classical scholarship for the Edinburgh and Quarterly reviews. In 1822 he was made archdeacon of Colchester and in 1824 he was appointed to the see of Chester. Four years on, in 1828, he was made bishop of London.

As bishop of London he dedicated a considerable amount of energy to performing his duties, and proved himself to be something of a reformer. He successfully rallied for a significant amount of money, providing much needed aid to churches and schools and to clergymen, and managed to build many churches in the London area. He also did much to eliminate abuses of plurality and nonresidence (holding several parishes concurrently and, therefore, being generally "non-resident" in several) still extant among clergy in the early nineteenth century. He resisted the tractarian OXFORD MOVEMENT, although he did express sympathy with some of the calls for reform in the CHURCH OF ENGLAND, and resisted Catholic emancipation as well. He was forced to resign in 1856 because of ill health and died a year later in 1857.

See also Anglicanism

References and Further Reading

Biber, George. *Bishop Blomfield and His Times*. London: Harrison, 1857.

Blomfield, Alfred. *A Memoir of Charles James Blomfield*. 2 vols. London: John Murray, 1864.

ALEC JARVIS

BLOUNT, CHARLES (1654–1693)

English philosopher. Blount was born on April 27, 1654 in London and died of suicide in August 1693.

Educated by his free-thinking father, Sir Henry Blount, he embraced Stoicism and the ideas of EDWARD LORD HERBERT OF CHERBURY; Benedict Spinoza; and THOMAS HOBBES, whose ideas and works he borrowed from, translated, and publicized. He adapted and translated Herbert's *De religione laici*; Spinoza's *Tractatus theologico-politcus*, which appeared in his *Miracles no violations of the laws of nature* (1683); and popularized Hobbes in his *Last Sayings and Dying Testimony of Thomas Hobbes* (1680). A free thinker and radical Whig, Blount was a persistent critic of the CHURCH OF ENGLAND.

In *Anima Mundi* (1679) he defended the primacy of a rational natural religion. In works such as *Great is Diana* (1680) and *Two First Books of Philostratus* (1680) he offered veiled attacks on the clericalism of the Church of England in critiques of pagan idolatry and Islam. In a series of manuscripts, including "A Summary Account of the Deist's Religion," which appeared in his collection *Oracles of Reason* (1693), he attacked ecclesiastical corruption and orthodox Protestant understandings of miracles and divine revelation, while championing the primacy of human reason, religious TOLERATION, and freedom of the press. As a radical Whig accused of being a Deist and an atheist himself, Blount's works helped stimulate the development of anticlericalism and DEISM in ENGLAND. By passing on and popularizing the ideas of earlier free thinkers such as Herbert, Spinoza, and Hobbes and through his own critiques of Christian ORTHODOXY, he influenced later Deist writers such as JOHN TOLAND and MATTHEW TINDAL.

References and Further Reading

Primary Sources:

Blount, Charles, Thomas Burnet, Charles Gildon, and others. *The oracles of reason consisting of 1. A vindication of Dr. Burnet's Archiologiae. 2. The seventh and eighth chapters of the same. 3. Of Moses's description of the original state of man, &c. 4. Dr. Burnet's appendix of the Brachmin's religion. 5. An account of the deist's religion. 6. Of the immortality of the soul. 7. Concerning the Arrians, Trinitarians and councils. 8. That felicity consists in pleasure. 9. Of fate and fortune. 10. Of the original of the Jews. 11. The lawfulness of marrying two sisters successively. 12. A political account of the subversion of Jewdaism, and original of the millenium. 13. Of the auguries of the ancients. 14. Natural religion as oppos'd to divine revelation. 15. That the soul is matter. 16. That the world is eternal, &c. in several letters to Mr. Hobbs and other persons of eminent quality and learning*. London, 1693.

Blount, Charles. *Miscellaneous works*. New York: Garland, 1979, 1695.

Secondary Sources:

Berman, David. "Disclaimers as Offence Mechanisms in Charles Blount and John Toland." In *Atheism from the Reformation to the Enlightenment.* Edited by Michael Hunter and David Wootton. Oxford: Clarendon Press, 1992.

Champion, J. A. I. *The Pillars of Priestcraft Shaken: The Church of England and its Enemies 1160–1730.* Cambridge: Cambridge University Press, 1992.

Redwood, J. "Charles Blount (1654–93), Deism and English Free Thought." *Journal of the History of Ideas* 35 (1974): 490–498.

ROBERT D. CORNWALL

BLUMHARDT, CHRISTOPH FRIEDRICH (1842–1919)

German theologian. The younger Blumhardt (son of Johann Christoph Blumhardt, 1805–1880) was the successor of his father as pastor in Bad Boll-Württemberg. He anticipated what came to be known as "Religious Socialism" *(Religioeser Sozialismus)* and had influence on dialectical theology. Blumhardt joined the Social Democratic Party and became its parliamentarian. This was incomprehensible for his church, and brought him into conflict with many of his contemporaries.

He was born in Möttlingen near Calw-Württemberg. He studied theology in Tübingen, and was vicar in several parishes before he became the assistant to his father in Bad Boll in 1869 and his successor in 1880. In 1894 he withdrew from the parish, criticizing the official church of his time. In 1899 he joined the Social Democratic Party out of a sense of solidarity and social responsibility, and between 1901 and 1906 he was a member of Württemberg parliament. During World War I he was one of the few who avoided a national pathos and who saw the war as the judgment of God. In his last years he withdrew from politics but remained the spiritual head of Bad Boll, supporting the worker's movement, the peace movement, and the emancipation of people in mission countries.

Blumhardt represents a down-to-earth and secular Christianity: the kingdom of God develops its healing and serving power already in this world because Jesus is victor and is changing the world in this age. The Christian lives within the political and social situations. The Christian's walk through life becomes the visible gospel, which is expressed not only in preaching but also in living. The socialist vision of a coming society without classes—and without class struggle—means the temporal salvation by God. The kingdom of God, however, means the eternal liberation, which is awaited in hope.

References and Further Reading

Bittner, Wolfgang J., ed. "Gedanken aus dem Reich Gottes." In *Damit Gott kommt.* 1992.

Harder, Johannes, ed. *Ansprachen, Predigten, Reden, Briefe. Neue Texte aus dem Nachlass.* 3 vols. NeuKirchen Vluyn, 1978.

Lejeune, Robert, ed. *Eine Auswahl aus seinen Predigten, Andachten und Schriften.* 4 vols. Erlenbach: Zurich, 1925.

Lim, Hee-Kuk. "Jesus ist Sieger bei Chr. Fr. Blumhardt. Keim einer kosmischen Christologie." Ph.D. dissertation, University of Basel, 1994.

Macchia, Frank D. "Spirituality and Social Liberation. The Message of the Blumhardts in the Light of Wuerttemberg Pietism, with Implications for Pentecostal Theology." Ph.D. dissertation, University of Basel, 1989.

Meier, Klaus-Juergen. "Christoph Blumhardt. Christ, Sozialist, Theologe." Ph.D. dissertation, University of Bern, 1977.

Sauter, Gerhard. "Die Theologie des Reiches Gottes beim älteren und jüngeren Blumhardt." Ph.D. dissertation, University of Göttingen, 1962.

Specker, Louis, ed. *Politik aus der Nachfolge. Der Briefwechsel zwischen H. Eugster-Zuest u. C.B.* Theologische Einführung. Zürich: Arthur Rich, 1984.

Stober, Martin. "Chr. Fr. Blumhardt d.J. zwischen Pietismus und Sozialismus." Ph.D. dissertation, University of Tübingen, 1995.

Thurneysen, Eduard. *Christoph Blumhardt.* München: Chr. Kaiser, 1926. 1926, 1962.

GERHARD SCHWINGE

BODELSCHWINGH, FRIEDRICH CHRISTIAN CARL VON (1831–1910)

Lutheran church leader. Pastor and leading representative of the deaconry in GERMANY in the second half of the nineteenth century, Bodelschwingh was born on March 6, 1831 in Haus Mark near Tecklenburg, a descendant of the ancient nobility in Westphalia. His father Ernst was the president of the Prussian Province on the Rhine, and later, for a short time, served as finance secretary and secretary of the interior in Berlin. In 1848, in the aftermath of the Revolution, he lost his position and returned with his family to Westphalia. For his son Friedrich the years in Berlin brought connections to the court and to the Hohenzollerns as well as the acquaintance with high-ranking representatives of revivalism, a movement that also proved to be of importance for his parents.

After graduation from grammar school in 1849, Bodelschwingh finished an apprenticeship in Lower Pomerania and worked as the manager of an estate, although his occupation did not satisfy him. The question of a goal to his studies was constantly on his mind, and he decided to study THEOLOGY. He began his studies in 1854 in Basle. Here he was influenced especially by the revivalist BIBLE lectures of Carl August Auberlen, and by the spirit of the Basle Missionary House. He made connections with theologians in SWITZERLAND and in Württemberg, and he became acquainted with leading characters of the deaconry. After a few semesters in Erlangen and in Berlin, Bodelschwingh passed the first theological exam in 1858 and went as an assistant preacher to Paris. The German congregation there encompassed mostly common and poor people.

Bodelschwingh was in charge of the education of children, built a school, and collected money in Germany for the construction of a small church. Because of health problems, he had to leave Paris and, in 1864, took over the second pastorate in Dellwig in Westphalia. There he concentrated on the Christian design of the farmers' lives. To that end and toward the formation of a congregation in general, starting in 1865 he put out the Sunday "Westphalian *Haufreund.*" What was important for Bodelschwingh was outlined in the preamble to the second volume: "Against the storm of the times, to hold on to the sanctuaries of faith, to preserve on that basis the Christian German customs and discipline, Christian German faithfulness and innocence, the heritage of tradition-bound ancestry, to preserve and to conserve, and, where such virtues have been eradicated, to plant the seeds for them again." With this attitude in mind Bodelschwingh became a voluntary chaplain in the Prussian war against Austria (1866) and against FRANCE (1870/71).

The sudden death of the Bodelschwinghs' four children, within a period of fourteen days, triggered a deep and long-lasting crisis in the parents. Bodelschwingh tried to make a new beginning. In 1871 he took charge of Bethel near Bielefeld, a small shelter for young epileptics. Founded in 1867, a small deaconess training center named "Sarepta" was added in 1869. Systematically and piece by piece, Bodelschwingh began to expand the institution. New houses were added, where, consistent with the Wichern teachings on family life, the parents lived alongside the sick and the handicapped. Hence, Bethal became a whole community for the sick.

In addition to the expansion, new plans were made. In 1877 "Nazareth," the training post for young deacons, was founded. Increasingly Bodelschwingh concentrated on the problem of the "wandering poor,"—migrant workers, the unemployed, or those without a home—people who were literally on the street. To keep them in place, in 1882 Bodelschwingh built the worker's colony "Wilhelmsdorf," and in 1899 the upland colony "Freistatt." For the homeless in Berlin "Hoffnungstal" outside the city was founded. In all of these institutions, there was not only a strict prohibition of alcohol, but the daily routine in general revolved around decidedly Christian rules. The motto that Bodelschwingh outlined was: "Work instead of pittance."

To finance all of these activities, Bodelschwingh used his personal and family connections. However, the expansion of the work opportunities required public financing as well as political measures and legal regulation. Bodelschwingh was elected to the Prussian Assembly in 1903, and there he fought hard and successfully for a law that mandated the building of workplaces for migrant workers. He also sought public support for the construction for housing for workers. Because he saw the growing influence of political and especially theological liberalism as a primary danger, he set up the "Bethel Theological School" for the "positive" education of future pastors. In addition to the Theological Week, held throughout the year by conservative revivalist professors from different German universities, there was also an educational track for education of missionaries, an interest since the days of his studies in Basle. At the end of his life Bethel was not only the largest institution of the Internal Mission, but also a symbol for evangelical deaconry in Germany. Bodelschwingh died in Bethel on April 2, 1910.

After his death in 1910 his son, Friedrich Jr. (1877–1946), nicknamed "Pastor Fritz," took over the leadership of the institution. He was driven by the same conservative revivalist mentality as his father. Yet, he was more reclusive. Bethel was expanded further, but young Bodelschwingh was conscious of a more medical and sociopedagogic professionalism. In May of 1933, because of his integrity and capacity to mediate, Bodelschwingh Jr. was nominated to the position of presiding bishop in Germany. However, worn down by the infighting of the GERMAN CHRISTIANS as well as by the attitudes of the Confessional Lutheran bishops, he stepped down a few weeks later. In the following years, in letters and in dialogue, he was an intermediary in the best sense between the diverse groups of the Confessional Churches. After tough negotiations, he succeeded for the most part in saving the majority of "his" patients from the "euthanasia" murders of the Nazi years. He also strongly supported the "Church Unity Project" of Bishop Wurm in Württemberg, and, in 1945, he was a significant figure in the rebuilding of the Evangelical Church in Germany.

See also Confessing Church; Evangelicals, Germany; Lutheranism, Germany

References and Further Reading

Primary Sources:

Bodelschwingh. Friedrich von *Ausgewählte Schriften* (*Selected Writings*). 2 vols. Bethel: Alfred Adam, 1958–1964.
———. *Briefwechsel* (*Letters*). Edited by Alfred Adam. 2 vols. Bethel: Alfred Adam, 1966–1974.

Secondary Sources:

Gerhardt, Martin, and Alfred Adam. *Friedrich von Bodelschwingh. Ein Lebensbild aus der deutschen Kirchengeschichte (Friedrich von Bodelschwingh. An Image of Life in German Church History)*. 2 vols. Bethel: Bethel Verlag, 1950–1958.

Kaiser, Jochen-Christoph. *Sozialer Protestantismus im 20 Jahrhundert (Social Protestantism in the 20th Century)*. Munich: Oldenbourg Verlag, 1989.

Pergande, Kurt. *Der Einsame von Bethel (The Lonely One From Bethel)*. Bethel: Bethel Verlag, 1953.

MARTIN GRESCHAT

BOEHME, JAKOB (ALSO BOEHM, BÖHM, BEHME, BEHMEN) (1575–1624)

German mystic. Boehme's THEOLOGY drew upon Christian, Hermetic, astrological, alchemical, and Kabalistic traditions combined with the notion of a passionate God seeking expression in material form. His influence on subsequent theologians and philosophers was considerable. Born in the village of Altseidenberg, near Görlitz, Silesia (now Zgorzelec, Poland), Boehme was apprenticed as a shoemaker, married, and established himself in this trade in Görlitz, then a Lutheran community coming under the indirect influence of Calvinist ideas (see CALVINISM). At the age of twenty-five he underwent a mystical experience when a ray of sunlight reflected in a pewter dish revealed to him the nature of a Godhead that penetrates and suffuses all existence, including suffering and pain. This epiphany, elaborated and articulated in numerous publications during the next two decades, forms the core of Boehme's spiritual legacy.

Boehme's development as a religious writer was gradual, retarded perhaps in part by his continuing employment as a shoemaker and later as a merchant for several years after his revelation. His first important treatise, an obscure work filled with baroque allusions and entitled *Die Morgenröte im Aufgang* (*Red Rays of the Dawn's Light*) (1612), attracted a small circle of followers, while also prompting both religious and civil authorities to censor him. Boehme agreed to cease writing, a promise he kept for five years. Secretly resuming his writing, Boehme produced tracts and longer works that circulated privately. When in 1623 a friend published a portion of Boehme's *Weg zu Christo* (*The Way to Christ*) the mystic once again experienced persecution and had to leave Görlitz for Dresden, where he survived on the largesse of wealthy friends and continued to gather followers about himself. In 1624 he returned to Görlitz where he died later that year.

Boehme, an autodidact, cannot be considered to have approached his topic in a rigorous fashion, and his works reveal both the limits and the strong points (e.g., Paracelsian alchemy) of his own learning. Yet some of the ideas he put forth were startlingly innovative, and presented a direct challenge to the biblical literalists and systematic theologians of his day. Boehme conceived of God as infinite and indescribable, but also as an entity that seeks to become "thing" and to be able to know itself. It is God's creation that makes God whole, and vice versa. God emerges, by choice, out of pure Oneness and Completeness into what might be called a differentiated actuality that can be perceived and loved. Boehme combined this idea with ones more in agreement with orthodox LUTHERANISM, such as the assertion that the SACRAMENTS do not take away sin.

Boehme writes of the Godhead (Gottheit) possessing a "will, that is also called God, which is also called the one God, who wants nothing more than except to find and grasp himself. . . ." Taken in isolation, Boehme's description of God's desire to manifest himself was not necessarily in conflict with the Lutheranism of his day, although Boehme's emphasis on the "longing" or "hunger" for self-knowledge of God's undifferentiated nonbeing (das Nichts) placed the writer outside the pale of ORTHODOXY, as did his insistence that matter—and its corollary, Evil—were absolutely necessary for the continued existence of the Divine Spirit. Finally Boehme asserted that God's longing could never be entirely satisfied, thus turning into a bitter and self-destructive fire that caused great pain to the Godhead itself. This claim placed him far outside any acceptable seventeenth-century Protestant theology, and yet has been one of the elements of Boehme's theology, along with his interweaving of Kabalistic ideas, that has most intrigued later readers. Likewise, Boehme's claim that God could not have foreseen the rebellion of Lucifer put the mystic in opposition to Calvinists and any others who stressed PREDESTINATION and the omniscience of God.

Boehme conceived of reality as multifaceted, at times described in Trinitarian terms, elsewhere as a sevenfold unity. His revelation unveiled the "Being of Beings," the Byss (roughly, reason), and the Abyss (absurdity). The Abyss possesses the hunger for self-knowledge, but exists only as a ideal in a sense close to Plato's meaning, until it can manifest itself in a living being. Before this manifestation, God has "no tendency towards anything," but the vacuum of the Abyss is not total because it has the potential to become something real. Evil is the rebellion of self-centered, spiritually blind activity that rejects the undifferentiated power of God; yet this God does not desire to remain in this state, and the struggles and suffering of God to escape nothingness bear some resemblance to human suffering brought on by evil. At the same time Boehme advocated the "sinking of the mind into the mercy of God." Critics such as the Danish Lutheran bishop Hans Martensen have argued that Boehme poses an impossibility when he describes God emerging from nothingness, yet able to radiate good and love.

Boehme regarded himself as a Christian and frequently protested his own orthodoxy, yet he reserved some of his most severe attacks for the narrow and "crude" interpretations of God and heaven put forth by many Protestant churches, the institutional manifestations of which Boehme regarded as the "whore of Babylon." For him, the divine order with its ineffable truth and the fatherhood of God over all human beings stood far above the achievements of any ecclesiastical institutions. Living as he did in a time of combative confessional politics (the first years of the Thirty Years' War coincide with Boehme's last period of productivity), where loyalty and conformity to an established church were among the most prized virtues, it is little wonder that his works were widely condemned in his own lifetime. At the same time his conception of the passion and longing of God undoubtedly spoke to many whose own experience of the Protestant REFORMATION was intensely subjective and emotional.

Boehme left no organized school of theological thought, but his works remained part of the intellectual landscape of the Baroque era and beyond. PAUL TILLICH saw Boehme influencing at least indirectly GEORG W. F. HEGEL, Arthur Schopenhauer, FRIEDRICH NIETZSCHE, Henri Bergson, and Martin Heidegger. Boehme's dialectic, although limited in scope and expressed in a frequently difficult style, unquestionably provided Hegel with a model, and had an even greater influence on FRIEDRICH SCHELLING. More recently Carl G. Jung cited Boehme in the development of the former's theory of alchemical individuation process (see JUNGIANISM). Boehme's interest in the will and in intuition has obvious echoes in Schopenhauer, although one must be careful not to equate Boehme's understanding of the will of the as yet undifferentiated Godhead with the term as used in debates over human free will. Both Boehme's metaphor of light and his exploration of the mystical nature of the encounter with the personal God influenced the writings of GEORGE FOX. The Rosicrucians claim inspiration from Boehme, and the mystic had a considerable following in ENGLAND as well. Boehme's greatest contribution may be in his attempts to show the relations among the seemingly contradictory elements present in the "Being of Beings": dispassionate passivity and passionate longing, matter and nothingness, balance and opposition, love and anger.

References and Further Reading

Primary Sources:

Boehme, Jakob. *Confessions,* compiled and edited by Scott Palmer. New York: Harper & Brothers, 1954.

Law, John, ed. *The Works of Jacob Behman.* London: Richardson, 1764.

Peukert, W.-E., ed. *Sämtliche Schriften.* Stuttgart: F. Frommanns Verlag, 1955–1961. [A reprint of Boehme's collected works, including his letters, published in 1730.]

Zeller, W., trans. *Weg zu Christo.* New York: Paulist Press, 1978.

Secondary Sources:

Stoudt, J. J. *Sunrise to Eternity: A Study in Jacob Boehme's Life and Thought.* Philadelphia: University of Pennsylvania Press, 1957.

Walsh, David. *The Mysticism of Innerworldly Fulfilment: A Study of Jacob Boehme.* Gainesville, FL: University Press of Florida, 1983.

Weeks, Andrew. *Boehme: An Intellectual Biography of the Seventeenth-Century Philosopher and Mystic.* Albany: State University of New York Press, 1991.

PAUL SHORE

BOESAK, ALAN AUBREY (1945–)

South african leader. Boesak was a key South African Reformed antiapartheid activist during the 1980s, president of the WORLD ALLIANCE OF REFORMED CHURCHES from 1982 to 1991, president of the South African Council of Churches in 1984, and South African ambassador to the United Nations in Geneva, SWITZERLAND in 1995.

Alan Boesak grew up in the Dutch Reformed Mission Church (Nederduits Gereformeerde Sendingkerk or NGSK), the main Reformed church within the South African mixed-race "Colored" community. He attended Bellville Theological School, the NGSK training college associated with the University of the Western Cape.

In 1964, as a second-year student at Bellville, Boesak met BEYERS NAUDE, an antiapartheid white Reformed minister who had been forced out of his office as moderator of the (white) Dutch Reformed Church (Nederduitse Gereformeerde Kerk) for his views. Naudé encouraged Boesak's activism and political interests, and persuaded him to seek ordination in the NGSK as an effective platform from which to work for the ending of apartheid in SOUTH AFRICA.

Boesak was ordained in 1968. For two and a half years he pastored a local congregation, which lost its church building when the neighborhood in which it was located was declared "whites-only." He left the parish ministry to pursue a doctoral degree at the Reformed Theological Seminary at Kampen in the NETHERLANDS, where he was introduced to the international Reformed community. At Kampen he published a number of books and articles on BLACK THEOLOGY, collaborating with the American black theologians JAMES HAL CONE, James A. Joseph, and J. Deotis Roberts, Sr. He also published his doctoral dissertation, *Farewell to Innocence, a Social-ethical Study on Black Theology and Black Power,* in which he argued that "liberation is not only 'part of' the gospel, or 'consistent with' the gospel. It is the content and framework of the gospel of Jesus Christ" (p. 14).

Upon his return to South Africa in 1976, Boesak joined the "Broederkring" ("Brothers' Circle") of South African Reformed Clergy dedicated to opposing apartheid, becoming its chair in 1977. He was also appointed the "student minister" for NGSK students and faculty who study or lecture at the University of the Western Cape, the Peninsula Technikon, or Bellville Training College.

He spent the academic year 1980–1981 teaching at Calvin College, Grand Rapids, Michigan. Returning to South Africa, he was elected the first president of the Alliance of Black Reformed Christians, a group of political activists within the South African Reformed Churches in 1981. The following year he was sent as a delegate to the World Alliance of Reformed Churches, where he was elected its president. At the WARC meeting in Ottawa, CANADA, he led the delegates to condemn the theological defense of apartheid as HERESY. This led the WARC to expel the two white Reformed South African Churches from membership.

In 1983 Boesak formed the United Democratic Front, a legal umbrella organization, which united more than 700, many otherwise illegal, organizations to become the focus of opposition to apartheid at a time when the South African government banned all political organizations. In his opening address Boesak argued that "apartheid is a cancer in the body politic of the world, a scourge on our society, and an everlasting shame to the church of Jesus Christ in the world and in this country. It exists only because of economic greed, cultural chauvinism, and political oppression, attained by both systemic and physical violence and a false sense of racial superiority. And . . . therefore we must resist it" (*If This Is Treason, I Am Guilty,* pp. 39–40).

Boesak's rise in stature and influence in South Africa was recognized in 1984 when he was elected president of the South African Council of Churches. Two years later he was selected moderator of the NGSK church. Boesak used these offices as a platform from which he traveled the world, garnering support for the antiapartheid crusade.

In 1988 the UDF was banned by the South African government, which led in 1989 to a massive campaign of defiance against the government. Boesak's campaign against apartheid, however, was overtaken by political events. In 1989 F. W. De Klerk was elected president of South Africa and, to everyone's shock and surprise, unbanned the African National Congress and other radical political groups. The following year he released Nelson Mandela from prison and within a few years, legally dismantled apartheid. The elections of 1994 led to the election of Nelson Mandela as president. Boesak led the ANC efforts in the Western Cape in the election of 1994, and was appointed South Africa's ambassador to the United Nations in Geneva Switzerland in 1995.

Boesak's meteoric rise did not survive South Africa's stunning reversal of political fortunes. In 1990, just after DeKlerk was elected, Boesak's extramarital affair with Elena Botha, a prominent white television producer and niece of Stoffel Botha, a hard-line pro-apartheid cabinet officer, became public. He resigned all his church positions, divorced his wife, briefly married Elena, and turned his attention entirely to politics.

A second and greater scandal swirled around Boesak while he was ambassador to the United Nations, forcing him to resign within the year. This time he was accused of misappropriating international development funds. He was tried in 1999, convicted, and sentenced to a six-year jail term. Boesak has maintained that he was innocent of intentional wrongdoing, although he has admitted his failure to exercise appropriate control over his financial managers.

See also Dutch Reformed Church in Africa

References and Further Reading

Primary Sources:

Boesak, Alan. *Farewell to Innocence: A Socio-ethical Study on Black Theology and Black Power.* Maryknoll, NY: Orbis Books, 1977.

———. *Black Theology, Black Power,* London: Mowbrays, 1978.

———. *The Finger of God: Sermons on Faith and Sociopolitical Responsibility.* Maryknoll, NY: Orbis Books, 1982.

———. *Black and Reformed: Apartheid, Liberation, and the Calvinist Tradition.* Maryknoll, NY: Orbis Books, 1984.

———. *Walking on Thorns: The Call to Christian Obedience.* Grand Rapids, MI: Wm. B. Eerdmans, 1984.

———. *If This Is Treason, I Am Guilty.* Grand Rapids, MI: Wm. B. Eerdmans, 1987.

———. *Comfort and Protest: Reflections on the Apocalypse of John of Patmos.* Philadelphia: Westminster Press, 1987.

———. *God's Wrathful Children: Political Oppression and Christian Ethics.* Grand Rapids, MI: Wm. B. Eerdmans, 1995.

———. *Shadows of Light : Biblical Meditations in a Time of Trial.* Pretoria, South Africa: J. L. van Schaik Religious Books, 1996.

Boesak, Alan and Charles Villa-Vicencio. *A Call for an End to Unjust Rule.* Edinburgh: Saint Andrew Press, 1986.

CORNELIS H. LETTINGA

BONHOEFFER, DIETRICH (1906–1945)

German theologian. Bonhoeffer was born in Breslau, GERMANY (present-day Wrocław, POLAND), on February 4, 1906. He studied Protestant THEOLOGY in Berlin under ADOLF VON HARNACK, KARL HOLL, and Reinhold Seeberg. He became a pastor and then a lecturer (*Privatdozent*) in theology and served as one of the leading figures in the CONFESSING CHURCH. He published several important theological works, joined in the resistance movement against Adolf Hitler and the Nazi regime, and suffered imprisonment followed by execution on April 9, 1945, just weeks before Hitler's suicide and the end of World War II. Bonhoeffer is famous for books such as *The Cost of Discipleship, Life Together, Ethics,* and *Letters and Papers from Prison,* the latter two published posthumously. Many other editions of his writings appeared, especially in the postwar era, culminating in a sixteen-volume edition of his complete works available in both German and English.

Bonhoeffer may be the most important Protestant pastor and theologian to have lived and worked within the crucible of Adolf Hitler's Germany. His importance derives from theological writings developed in response to the Nazi state, writings that have made a significant impact on theology since the middle of the twentieth century. He is also known for his political role and his martyrdom in opposition to the Hitler regime. Bonhoeffer sparred with the regime from the beginning, first within the German Church Struggle, in which he helped lead Confessing Church forces in their opposition to the enthusiastically Nazi *Deutsche Christen* ("GERMAN CHRISTIANS"), and then in political opposition to the regime itself. Imprisoned in April 1943 for his involvement in the resistance, Bonhoeffer suffered execution as one of a handful of specific enemies of the regime sought out for punishment in the chaos of the war's closing days. Other German theologians of his era made significant contributions to Protestant thought, and other Christians suffered and died because of their opposition to Nazi rule. No one, however, combined theological impact with clarity of political response and subsequent martyrdom as did Bonhoeffer. Thus his life as well as his theological writings must be considered to measure his impact as a Christian and a theologian.

Bonhoeffer's Life

Dietrich and his twin sister Sabine were the sixth and seventh of eight children born between 1899 and 1909 to Karl and Paula (von Hase) Bonhoeffer. The father, a prominent professor of psychiatry and neurology, moved in 1912 from Breslau to the University of Berlin, which meant that the Bonhoeffer children grew up near the center of German intellectual and political life. They benefited from this association, but also suffered mightily in the turbulence of that German era. The second son, Walter, died on the western front in 1918. Klaus and Dietrich were executed in 1945 for their opposition to the Nazi state, as were two sons-in-law, Hans von Dohnanyi (married to Christine) and Rüdiger Schleicher (married to Ursula). A third son-in-law, Gerhard Leibholz, fled with Sabine to England because of his Jewish mother, so that five of the eight children suffered death, the death of a spouse, or emigration during the Third Reich.

As Dietrich grew up in this fated but high-achieving family, he decided early that he would study theology, a surprising choice, given that the family was not particularly active in its church attendance or piety. He excelled, however, earning his doctorate at the young age of twenty-one. He served as a curate for one year in a German congregation in Barcelona, before completing his *Habilitation* (a second dissertation that grants one the right to teach at a German university) by the age of twenty-four. Bonhoeffer then spent 1930–1931 as a Sloane fellow at Union Theological Seminary in New York, making the acquaintance of REINHOLD NIEBUHR, among other theologians. He also met and worked with Frank Fisher, a black student at Union who gave him access to Harlem, its religious practice and its music. Bonhoeffer returned to Germany in 1931 to begin offering lectures in theology at Berlin. Active in ECUMENISM, he was appointed that year to the position of youth secretary at the World Alliance for Promoting International Friendship through the Churches conference in Cambridge.

When Hitler came to power in January 1933, Bonhoeffer was among that minority of Protestant pastors and church leaders who felt no trace of temptation to endorse the new regime. This decision may have grown out of his theology, but other aspects also contributed: his extensive experience abroad, which counteracted the insular nationalism of many colleagues; his friendship with Christians of Jewish descent, including his brother-in-law Gerhard Leibholz; and the politics of the Bonhoeffer family. His family did not indulge in that combination of enthusiastic nationalism and rigid conservatism that prompted Protestant theologians such as Paul Althaus and Emanuel Hirsch to greet Hitler as a gift from God. Conservative antisemitic and nationalist views among Protestants led to the formation of a group, the *Deutsche Christen,* or German Christians (DC), who wanted an Aryan Christianity and thus had no problem merging their commitment to Nazi ideology with Christianity. They joined the Nazi Party, often becoming Stormtroopers as well; they wore their brown uniforms to church; they displayed the swastika alongside the flag of MARTIN LUTHER in their sanctuaries; and they expected in 1933 to fall heir quite naturally to church leadership in Hitler's new Germany.

Bonhoeffer opposed the German Christians from the beginning, although with great frustration. In 1933 their candidate for national bishop, Ludwig Müller, prevailed and his program dominated Protestant church affairs for the rest of the Nazi era. Already in September 1933 the "Brown Synod" (so called for the preponderance of "brown" shirts, i.e. Nazis, at the synod) in Berlin voted in favor of imposing the "Aryan Paragraph" on clergy and other employees of the church, an unsolicited act of solidarity with Hitler's state. This paragraph, part of a new Nazi law dealing with the German civil service, allowed only "Aryans" to be in the civil service. MARTIN NIEMOLLER and Bonhoeffer led those who saw this both as an unwarranted interference in church affairs and a denial of the efficacy of BAPTISM. German Christians then celebrated the REFORMATION that fall by calling for the removal of the Old Testament from the Bible. In response to these outrages, Niemöller's Pastors' Emergency League (*Pfarrernotbund*) grew into an organization representing more than a third of all Protestant clergy.

In the midst of this fray Bonhoeffer chose to remove himself by accepting an October appointment to serve two German-speaking parishes in London. He followed events closely, however, participating in preparation for and noting with approval the creation of the BARMEN DECLARATION in May 1934. This document, composed primarily by Swiss theologian KARL BARTH, formed the basis for the Confessing Church (*Bekennende Kirche*), and Bonhoeffer spent the balance of the decade as a leading figure in that group, always pushing it toward a more radical stance. He also continued working in the ecumenical movement, cultivating his friendship with GEORGE BELL, bishop of Chichester in England. In 1935, in opposition to Deutsche Christen control of theological education in universities, the Confessing Church asked Bonhoeffer to lead an alternative preachers' seminary, first at Zingst and then at Finkenwalde. By September 1937 this activity was closed by the Gestapo, and Bonhoeffer began suffering a series of travel and speaking restrictions. He sailed to New York in June 1939 at the invitation of American friends, although he decided almost immediately that the impulse to take safe haven abroad had been wrong, as he explained to Niebuhr:

I have made a mistake in coming to America. I must live through this difficult period of our national history with the Christian people of Germany. I will have no right to participate in the reconstruction of Christian life in Germany after the war if I do not share the trials of this time with my people . . . [ellipses in Bethge]. Christians in Germany will face the terrible alternative of either willing the defeat of their nation in order that Christian civilization may survive, or willing the victory of their nation and thereby destroying our civilization. I know which of these alternatives I must choose; but I cannot make that choice in security. (Bethge 1970:559)

Bonhoeffer returned to Berlin in July and the next month accepted an invitation from his brother-in-law Dohnanyi to become an agent for the Abwehr, Germany's military organization for counterintelligence.

Dohnanyi served as advisor to Colonel Hans Oster, second in command of the Abwehr, and also to Admiral Wilhelm Canaris. This made him a major figure in the so-called Canaris conspiracy in which Canaris tried to use this spy apparatus as a cover for the resistance movement. Bonhoeffer's primary role in the Abwehr was to act as a link to the outside world, taking advantage of his international contacts. For example, he met with Bishop Bell in SWEDEN in 1942, giving him names and details about the conspiracy. The conspirators hoped for explicit Allied support and even the promise of a negotiated settlement, rather than the demand for unconditional surrender, in the event the conspiracy proved successful in removing Hitler. Bell brought this message to the British government, but could not overcome its suspicions. Bonhoeffer was speaking for the German Abwehr after all, the spy service, and might be involved in some sort of double game. Work as a spy and a conspirator also posed a problem for Bonhoeffer himself. Much of the fruitfulness of his wartime writing stems from the hard questions of Christian ETHICS in the face of tyranny. As a Christian could he be traitor to his own government? Could he oppose the AUTHORITY of his state? Could he even participate in a plot to assassinate the head of state? Bonhoeffer took his faith as a Christian and his responsibility as a pastor very seriously. He decided, however, that Christian ethics required him to act boldly in contradiction to the traditional norms.

Bonhoeffer and Dohnanyi were both arrested in April 1943. For many months they were interrogated, separately, as the Gestapo unsuccessfully tried to ferret out information to incriminate them and their Abwehr colleagues. Gestapo efforts redoubled after the assassination attempt on Hitler on July 20, 1944, and in September they found incriminating documents. This led to Bonhoeffer's transfer in October from Tegel prison to a Gestapo cell on Prinz-Albrecht-Strasse, and then to the Buchenwald concentration camp in February 1945. Two months later Bonhoeffer and a handful of others were transferred by a circuitous route to Flossenbürg, the camp where he was executed on April 9.

Bonhoeffer's Theology

Bonhoeffer began his theological studies in 1923 in Tübingen, where he came under the influence of Adolf Schlatter. This exposed him to the theological emphasis on history and reason as advocated by the giant among liberal theologians, von Harnack, who also happened to be a neighbor and family friend (see LIBERAL PROTESTANTISM AND LIBERALISM). Back in Berlin in 1924 Bonhoeffer also found the "Luther Renaissance" of the church historian Karl Holl and Reinhold Seeberg. He remained marked by the intellectual rigor encouraged by Harnack and the focus on Luther found in Holl and Seeberg, but these emphases did not encompass his thought. Although Berlin in the 1920s may have represented the best of the past in the German theological tradition, the future had begun to take shape to the west of Berlin in Göttingen and then Bonn.

There Barth attracted attention in the 1920s by his vigorous "no" to the ENLIGHTENMENT idea that theological inquiry meant studying history and studying Christianity as one religion among many. Emphasizing the otherness of God, the inadequacy of religion to reach God, and the inability of human reason to find God's truth through historical study, Barth developed a dialectical method that insisted on the gap between God and humankind. He coupled this with a neo-orthodox insistence that the basic truths of Christian doctrine should be taken at face value, not given up in the face of historical and rational uncertainties. Bonhoeffer did not meet Barth until 1931 and he never was a student of Barth as such, but he tempered the rigor of his theological training in Berlin and his strong commitment to Martin Luther with the methods and the Christocentric focus insisted on by Barth. For both of them the primary goal of theology was to seek out God's message to humans as revealed in Jesus Christ.

Bonhoeffer first came to widespread postwar attention with two books that emphasized his spiritual intensity. In *The Cost of Discipleship* he criticized the state of contemporary Protestant Christianity:

Cheap grace is the mortal enemy of our church. . . . Cheap grace means grace as bargain-basement goods, cut-rate forgiveness, cut-rate comfort, cut-rate sacrament; grace as the church's inexhaustible pantry, from which it is doled out by careless hands without hesitation or limit. It is grace without a price, without costs. (DBW/English, vol. 4:43)

Protestants had always emphasized SALVATION as a free gift from God, not to be earned by good works. Bonhoeffer, whose Christian faith had proved very costly indeed, insists that such a casual acceptance of grace is too easy, too readily allows a life completely uninfluenced by real discipleship to Christ, a discipleship that costs one's entire life. Bonhoeffer also became known through *Life Together,* a book describing the virtually monastic regimen practiced by Bonhoeffer and a small group of seminarians at Finkenwalde in the mid-1930s. His goal was to create a group of brothers living together in Christian community, following a path of discipline, BIBLE reading, and PRAYER.

In both of these books Bonhoeffer seemed to call Christians to a religious intensity consistent with his own biography, ultimately including a willingness to die for Christ. However, postwar readers also got to know Bonhoeffer through *Letters and Papers from Prison,* a very different book representing documents he had written and smuggled out of Tegel prison in 1943 and 1944. Here Bonhoeffer seemed to emphasize not religious intensity but a less traditionally religious life, a church ready for a "world come of age." As he wrote on July 16, 1944 to Eberhard Bethge, "God would have us know that we live as men who manage our lives without him. The God who is with us is the God who forsakes us (Mark 15:34). The God who lets us live in the world without the working hypothesis of God is the God before whom we stand continually" (Bonhoeffer 1972:360). Bishop JOHN A. T. ROBINSON accentuated this radical side of Bonhoeffer with his *Honest to God,* published in 1963. The idea of a "world come of age" led to concepts such as "religionless Christianity," the complete acceptance by Christians of secularization, and even enthusiasm for the theology that says "God is dead."

Theologians still argue about the extent to which Bonhoeffer's experience of political conspiracy, arrest, and imprisonment changed his theology. There also remain students of Bonhoeffer who range from traditionalists to revolutionaries in their understanding of his message. However, increasing exposure to the full range of his writings—from his doctoral dissertation in 1927 to his theological letters, love letters, poems, and scraps of fiction written in prison—suggests important threads of continuity. Bonhoeffer recognized from the beginning that the modern age places a challenge before the church (see MODERNISM). Enlightenment theology had tried to find a respectable place for Christian ideas within the university, alongside history, philosophy, and the physical sciences. This was a diminished place, carrying the risk that Christianity could be discarded entirely. Modern society had tried to find a niche for the CHURCH, a place where religion would be tolerated in the busy secular life of nation states and corporations, but without the natural dominant place of the church experienced in earlier times. Bonhoeffer recognized these tendencies and struggled to find and defend a place for the church. This can be found in his doctoral dissertation, *Sanctorum Communio,* and his *Habilitation, Act and Being,* as well as in *The Cost of Discipleship* and *Life Together.* Along with Barth, Bonhoeffer rejected "religion" as an attempt by humans to reach up to God, and he struggled to understand Christian faith as the response of individuals to God's call through Jesus Christ.

Bonhoeffer expected his *Ethics* to be his *magnum opus.* He began this work in 1939, in the crucible of his intense response to the Hitler state, and he left it unfinished on his desk at the time of his arrest in 1943. This work has drawn increasing attention. Viewed together with his biography, it has appealed to individuals struggling to find Christian responses to a difficult world, whether in the opposition to apartheid in SOUTH AFRICA or in the safe material comfort of the postmodern West. Bonhoeffer's legacy has not diminished, but it is increasingly nurtured by an active International Bonhoeffer Society and by the major effort in the last years of the twentieth century to make available in both German and English virtually every word he ever wrote.

Bonhoeffer and the Jews

Among the crimes of the Nazi regime, the brutal ideology of ANTI-SEMITISM and the systematic murder of six million Jews have elicited the most thorough condemnation and may represent the most troubling question for Christians. Without doubt, Hitler's hatred of Jews followed upon a long Christian tradition. It also included a specifically German component in Martin Luther's vitriolic *On the Jews and their Lies* (1543). In contrast to most Christians in Germany, Bonhoeffer showed a great deal of public sympathy for and defense of Jews, beginning with a bold lecture and article in April 1933, "The Church and the Jewish Question." Here he advised not only questioning the state and giving aid to victims, but he wrote these famous words, "The third possibility is not just to bandage the victims under the wheel, but to put a spoke in the wheel itself" (*No Rusty Swords,* 221). Bonhoeffer also helped lead the fight against application of the Aryan Paragraph within the church, as noted above, and he gave comfort to Christians of

Jewish descent in his own circle. Finally, he participated in Operation 7, an effort by the Abwehr to bring a small number of individuals designated Jewish by Nazi law to safety in Switzerland.

To the surprise of his friends, these philosemitic credentials did not entirely withstand scrutiny. Friendship toward "Jews" often had meant friendship toward Christians of Jewish descent. Furthermore, even in his supportive lecture in April 1933, Bonhoeffer suggested that Jews had brought suffering on themselves by their failure to please God, and he recommended CONVERSION as the best solution to the problem. Eberhard Bethge responded in the 1970s and 1980s to critics of Bonhoeffer. As part of his extraordinary role in Bonhoeffer studies—student at Finkenwalde, closest friend, recipient of most of the letters from prison, relative by marriage, editor of all the major works, and author of the definitive biography—Bethge acknowledged Bonhoeffer's early willingness to denigrate Jews, but he argued that Bonhoeffer became increasingly sympathetic to Jews as fellow human beings and to their special relationship with God. Bethge also became a leader in the development of postwar Jewish–Christian dialogue and the increasing willingness of Christians to respect the Jewish faith. As the person closest to Bonhoeffer's life and career, both before and after 1945, Bethge arguably represents the truest expression of Bonhoeffer's legacy on the relationship between Christians and Jews.

See also Neo-orthodoxy; Theology, Twentieth Century

References and Further Reading

Primary Sources:

Bonhoeffer, Dietrich. *The Cost of Discipleship.* Translated from the German by R. H. Fuller. New York: Macmillan, 1948.
———. *Letters and Papers from Prison.* Enlarged edition, edited by Eberhard Bethge and translated from the German by Reginald Fuller et al. New York: Macmillan, 1972.
———. *Dietrich Bonhoeffer Werke.* Edited by Eberhard Bethge et al. 16 vols. Munich: Christian Kaiser Verlag, 1986ff.
———. *Dietrich Bonhoeffer Works.* Translated from the German edition and under the general editorship of Wayne Whitson Floyd Jr. and Clifford J. Green. 16 vols. Minneapolis, MN: Fortress Press. 1996ff.

Secondary Sources:

Bethge, Eberhard. *Dietrich Bonhoeffer: Man of Vision, Man of Courage.* Translated from the German by Eric Mosbacher et al. New York: Harper & Row, 1970.
De Gruchy, John W. *Bonhoeffer and South Africa: Theology in Dialogue.* Grand Rapids, MI: Wm. B. Eerdmans, 1984.

———, ed. *The Cambridge Companion to Dietrich Bonhoeffer*. Cambridge: Cambridge University Press, 1999.
Robinson, John A. T. *Honest to God*. London: SCM, 1963.

ROBERT P. ERICKSEN

THE BOOK OF COMMON PRAYER

Preparation of the service book for the Anglican Church, known as the Book of Common Prayer, was the work of THOMAS CRANMER, appointed Archbishop of Canterbury by HENRY VIII in 1533. Cranmer exploited the widest range of strictly liturgical material to achieve, by translation and composition, the English rites first used in Tudor churches on Whitsunday 1549.

The great crisis in Christendom that constituted the Protestant Reformation was primarily a pastoral undertaking. Once Henry VIII had repudiated papal headship of two provinces of the medieval Western Church, it was not long before the royal whim wished "general rogations and processions to be made," if only to petition divine intervention for a good harvest and successful campaigning in France. Always anxious to serve his "godly prince," the archbishop produced the English Litany in the spring of 1544, and although showing the first fruits of real liturgical genius, it cannot compare with the early vernacular Services of MARTIN LUTHER and other continental divines. Nevertheless, it does afford the earliest evidence of work from Cranmer's liturgical library. Intercessory prayers giving clear priority to the persons of the "holy, blessed, and glorious Trinity" would have surprised many who were accustomed to venerating a full range of the church's saints. At the same time, in the context of rites recognized by, and used in the worship of, the late medieval Western Church, much would have to change before real liturgical reform was a remote possibility. [If the second Tudor was happy enough to be depicted in his Psalter as the penitent David, his subjects might well regard him as a Catholic King David who, despite repudiation of the "bishop of Rome," went regularly to Mass because he prized traditional rites and observances.] Accordingly, Cranmer used those lingering years of Henry's reign to best advantage, researching a remarkable range of service books in a study that fast became a workshop for worship.

The best introduction to the stunning achievement of the English Prayer Book is thus a realization of the complex range of liturgical forms used by a hierarchy of medieval priests and prelates. In the *Missal* they treasured the ordinary and Canon of the Mass; in the *Breviary* they found eight Offices for use by day and night, together with the Kalendar and Psalter. For priests the *Manual* or *Sacerdotal* (paralleled by the *Pontifical* for bishops) set out the six remaining sacraments; and a weighty tome of a *Processional* carried musical settings for the choreography of many a major festival and holy day. To extract enduring excellence from such traditional diversity, and to do so in one service book, itself convenient and affordable, is an attainment way beyond creative evolution in liturgical language and a sure measure of Cranmer's success.

The Order of the Communion, 1548

With the death of Henry in 1547, the uncertainties of a new reign obliged a man of Cranmer's temperament to take no risks lest he fail to carry his clergy with him and offend conservative parishioners content with traditional religious observance. Despite undoubted vision and a genuine determination to transform what was essentially the priest's Mass into a communion of all the people, Cranmer's initial progress was in a way rapid. The first Prayer Book was far from complete, and the coup that enabled Edward Seymour to dominate the Council as Lord Protector of the nine-year-old Edward VI (1537–1553) hardly made for stability in the early days of the reign. Even so, by proclamation in March 1548, Edward praised God that he knew "what by his word is meet to be redressed" as his uncle's Council enacted an "Order" for the use of the "holy Sacrament and most blessed Communion."

What followed was an English form for communion of the people, which followed the Latin Mass but was opposed to notions of sacrifice. All "unseemly and ungodly diversity" was eschewed and a promise extended "further to travail for the reformation."

The interim rite presented a "general Confession" after which the priest, who at that moment had to be "turning him to the people" to pronounce absolution, was to offer scriptural words of reassurance (the origin of the so-called "Comfortable Words"), a prayer for worthy reception (to be known as the "Prayer of Humble Access"), and words of administration for both bread and wine that emphasized those elements as gifts of Christ. The theme was forgiveness, not offering. Protestant sources drafted by MARTIN BUCER for a *Church Order* proposed for Köln by Archbishop Herman von Wied in 1543 were adapted by Thomas Cranmer from a later Latin translation. The English archbishop also seemed to value the way Services used in Zürich and Strasburg were focused on simple scriptural sentences in the Lord's Supper. Although caution remained a measured ingredient of his "Order," Cranmer's success in providing the Council with a stopgap but acceptable vernacular for the distributing of both bread and wine to worshippers at Communion signaled real progress to observers of the English situation. The royal proclamation clearly favored moderation and a commitment to advance step by step until the "setting forth of such Godly orders . . . to God's glory" would be achieved as the ultimate goal.

The Book of Common Prayer, 1549

Its composition was largely complete in a draft in September 1548 that was debated in the House of Lords in mid-December. The symbolism of the publication of the Prayer Book in time for compulsory use by Whitsunday (June 9, 1549) provided unique imagery. A truly enduring achievement, Cranmer's work and subsequent 1552 revision compressed to the convenient compass of a single service book the full spectrum of liturgy used by bishops and priests conducting the worship of the medieval Western Church. In the *Missal* the ordinary and Canon of the Mass were contained, whereas the *Breviary* set out the Divine Offices, Kalendar, and Psalter. The *Sacerdotal* (or *Manual*) set out sacraments (the eucharist excepted) ministered by priests, just as the *Pontifical* served bishops; and musical settings for major festivals were to be found in the *Processional*. Even then, as Cranmer's Preface was at pains to explain, such complexity was further confounded by "great diversity in saying and singing" as regional use often abused what little system existed. Some followed "Salisbury use, some Hereford . . . some Bangor, some of York and some . . . Lincoln." No wonder a cost-effective bonus was claimed when "henceforth, all the realm shall have but one use."

If, at first sight, the Book of Common Prayer's most radical departure concerned its use of the vernacular or "such language as [the people] might understand" instead of "Latin . . . which they understand not," close scrutiny soon called in question various traditionalist claims. For however hallowed prose might dignify Prayer Book worship, new doctrinal emphases had begun to reject Rome's teaching on the Mass and on Penance, likewise removing references to purgatory, the cult of the Blessed Virgin, and the Saints. In short, and in marked contrast to the liturgies this service book replaced, a principled "Preface" placed the sharpest focus on the need for scriptural worship. Cranmer was determined to reestablish his grasp of a valued patristic emphasis—namely, that "all the whole Bible . . . be read over once in the year," to ensure that parish clergy "be stirred up to godliness themselves, and be more able to exhort others by wholesome doctrine." The Primate certainly made much of "The Table and Kalendar" to explain with due care and clarity how "the very pure word of God, the holy scriptures" were set out to provide the core of the new liturgy, his clergy thus needing "none other books for their public service, but this book and the Bible." Accordingly, in 1549 the Book of Common

Prayer retained the principal Services of the medieval English Church and also rejected collects, prayers, and rites that Cranmer and his colleagues believed to be in conflict with the new stress on the supremacy of scripture all Protestant reformers revered.

With lay folk particularly in mind, the eight canonical "Hours" were reduced to two truly congregational Services—"Matins" and "Evensong"—Orders largely given over to the saying and chanting of canticles, an advancing cycle and selection of psalms, and collects and lections from both the Old and New Testaments as directed by the Kalendar. Concerning the sacraments, the Book of Common Prayer scrupulously reworked divine Service with regard to both baptism and the eucharist. "The Supper of the Lord" and "Holy Communion," if still "commonly called the Mass" (in this respect the title followed Luther's liturgy of 1523), were given priority. Yet it was also denied the traditional sacrificial emphasis that had long made it the sacred climax of liturgy. Instead, Cranmer focused his Communion full-square on Christ—the "Pascal lamb offered up . . . once for all," on the "sacrifice of praise and thanksgiving," and on members of the congregation offering their own "souls and bodies" as "a reasonable, holy, and lively sacrifice." Even so, in these early days of reformation Cranmerian caution saw fit to preserve traditional structures that, language and the distribution of wine as well as wafer apart, the English Mass retained a recognizable profile. In the "Administration of Public Baptism," the priest "looking upon the children" still had a form of exorcism to command "unclean" and "cursed" spirits not "to exercise any tyranny toward . . . infants . . . called to be of [Christ's] flock." If the salt and spittle of Sarum no longer obtained, once baptized, the candidates were still to be clothed with the "white vesture, commonly called the Chrisom," and duly anointed.

The Book of Common Prayer, 1552

Invited to "assess the contents of the book of sacred rites" and indicate whether he considered "anything" in Cranmer's first liturgy "which might be more fully explained, in a manner consistent with the word of God and suitable for edification in faith," Martin Bucer's *Censura* raised "a few small points which if . . . not fairly interpreted might seem . . . insufficiently consistent" with holy writ. Such urbanity contrasted favorably with the offense felt by JOHN HOOPER, who wrote to inform HEINRICH BULLINGER of a service book so "manifestly impious" and "doubtful" in construction that, "if it be not corrected," he could not bring himself to "communicate with the church in the administration of the Supper." Long accustomed to their medieval heritage, both clergy and people might be expected to criticize any change in a timeless and valued round of divine worship. As evangelicals committed to advance their cause little by little, Cranmer and his colleagues had clearly retained in the 1549 Services many conservative features to veil radical reformation. However, West Country folk were not so easily deceived, and although the protest embraced a far wider range of discontent, the so-called "Prayer Book riots" registered their opposition. In no way deterred by such "ignorant men," Cranmer's revised liturgy went ahead to unveil many obscurities and at last afforded English worship the language of unambiguous Protestant commitment. Somerset had fallen; and when Warwick warmed to the quickening pace of reformation, the updated Prayer Book was duly authorized by the Act of Uniformity in April 1552. The Book of Common Prayer now consisted of evangelical Services to treat of sin, repentance, faith, and Christ's forgiveness. Although all forms and Orders were couched in biblical terms, the emphasis was especially pronounced in sacramental matters. Accordingly, infant baptism was meaningful only in a context of repentance and faith. With the old *Canon missae* dismantled, a communion service prefaced by challenge in the Ten Commandments so laid down the law that the unfolding message of the Lord's Supper powerfully upheld the forgiveness achieved by Christ and made available by faith. In a clever redistribution of the various components of the late medieval Latin Mass, Cranmer had successfully removed all sacrificial emphases. His "Order for the Administration of the Lord's Supper or Holy Communion" mentioned Christ's offering only as a past event, whether explained in the quaint language of the Exhortation how "the Son of God did vouchsafe to yield up his soul by death upon the Cross for your health," or in the better known and unmistakable institution narrative itself, the memorable proclamation that Christ suffered death upon the cross and "made there (by his one oblation of himself once offered) a full, perfect and sufficient sacrifice, oblation, and satisfaction for the sins of the whole world. . . ."

A startling reference to the new Communion found its way into the *Greyfriars' Chronicle*—namely, that "on Allhallow day beganne the boke of the new servis of bred and wyne in Powlles" (St Paul's Cathedral), so dramatic was the contrast with the "Mass" of 1549. The Decalogue, and no longer the *Gloria,* provided the prelude to set readings of scripture in Epistle and Gospel. After the Nicene creed and sermon (the rubric requiring a sermon is itself significant for the evangelical emphasis that Word and Sacrament properly stand in parallel), the Prayer for the Church, Confession, and Absolution all precede the *Sursum Corda* (ancient introit to the

Canon). The so-called "Prayer of Humble Access" followed, its new position, with that of the Prayer for the Church, evidently opposed to all notion of either propitiatory sacrifice or adoration of the elements of bread and wine. Moreover, the old "consecration prayer" became a straightforward rehearsal of Christ's own institution of the Supper recited from the gospel narrative. Another rubric then instructed "the minister" to communicate himself "in both kinds" and, after he had given the sacrament to his assistants, to "deliver it . . . after to the people in their hands kneeling." After Communion, all were to recite the Lord's Prayer aloud. The Prayer of Oblation (now made an alternative to a prayer of thanksgiving) followed to afford a sacred opportunity of congregational self-offering and what Cranmer made a moment of spiritual oblation to Almighty God. Recited in such a heightened context, too, the *Gloria* was superbly placed to afford a liturgical climax of real insight to the whole Service. In short, and to his evident satisfaction, the Tudor Primate had transformed the old priestly Mass into a Communion of all the people.

No overall review of Cranmer's liturgy can omit reference to the remarkable way his service books reset gems of ancient worship to perfect them for posterity. A true man of common prayer, Cranmer had the ability and understanding to couple a translator's sensitivity with genuine feeling for primitive petitions that as often as not themselves respected both scripture and the best patristic tradition. Where they did not, Cranmer worked conscientiously to transform collects from earlier sources by addition and substitution. Precisely defined, a collect is a short prayer peculiar to the worship of the Western Church that preceded the reading of the Epistle at the Eucharist. Such collects aimed to invoke the Almighty, make a specific petition, and conclude with an ascription honoring the Christ by whose merits the faithful can expect an answer to prayer. Used in worship since the fifth and sixth centuries, many collects were the more familiar by hallowed placing in the *Sarum Missal,* a presence Cranmer so revered that he translated them directly or skillfully paraphrased and augmented the originals when crude medieval Latin cramped his style. Likewise, when his reforming purpose was thwarted by any hint of lingering superstition in worship, Cranmer penned new collects as outstanding for succinct theological argument, for directing devotion, and for literary expression. Most of these compositions related to pastoral planning and the fundamental teaching of the church in seasons such as Advent, Christmas, and Lent. The "Collect for Ash Wednesday" thus gave repentance priority over fasting, just as the collect for Advent II lauded the supremacy of scripture, a biblical theology nowhere better conceived than in Cranmer's "Collect for Christmas Day." With clarity, the Primate's "Preface" explained what he intended the Prayer Book to achieve in the worship of the Tudor Church, just as in the matter "Of Ceremonies" an attempt was made to reason "why some be abolished, and some retained."

The Elizabethan Prayer Book

Catholic succession in the person of Mary (1516–1558), daughter of Catherine of Aragon, followed the early demise of the evangelical Edward VI. But for that queen's lack of progeny, the Book of Common Prayer might never have resurfaced. As it was, with the accession of ELIZABETH I (1533–1603) to the Tudor throne in 1558, the church secured a "supreme Governor" of protestant conviction whose Council and High Court of Parliament reintroduced the Prayer Book. An Act of Uniformity (January 1559) made clear that this was still "religion by law established," a tricky diplomatic situation for the shrewd woman who had declined the hand of Spain's Philip II, dictating careful qualification of reformation faith and practice to parry risks of papal displeasure and, in consequence, the risk of renewed Catholic threats from the European mainland. Although a virtual reissue of Cranmer's 1552 liturgy, the Elizabethan Prayer Book differed in a number of subtle details. Principally, in the matter of the Lord's Supper, the "ornaments rubric" of 1549 reappeared with at least a permissive allowance that enabled priests to wear vestments. It was a notion sustained by the removal of a lengthy "black rubric," which, in 1552, had disputed any idea that kneeling to take communion implied "any adoration is done, or ought to be done, either unto the sacramental bread and wine there bodily received, or to any real and essential presence there being of Christ's natural flesh and blood." When taken together with words of administration that now prescribed both the old 1549 formula and a new memorialist emphasis for the new 1552 rite ["Take and eat this, in remembrance that Christ died for thee.... Drink this in remembrance that Christ's blood was shed for thee ..."], the holy supper seemed to offer the faithful a choice between "real" and "spiritual" presence. Finally, the inclusion of the Articles of Religion provided a dramatic appendix to the Book of Common Prayer. Yet here too various omissions and qualifications made that formulary less forthright in its Protestantism to frustrate and displease a growing opposition soon to be called "Puritan" (see PURITANISM).

It should be stressed that the Bible was the most discussed book of Elizabethan times, just as the celebrated "Authorized" or "King James' Version" became the most influential volume published in Stuart England. Because Cranmer had founded his liturgy firmly in holy scripture, it was hardly surprising to find in William Shakespeare's plays, whether comedy or tragedy, numerous allusions audiences at the Globe would have recognized. The Bard made at least forty-two references to the work of Cranmer and his use of the Bible in the Book of Common Prayer—eighteen relate to the Old Testament, a further eighteen to the New Testament, and six to the Apocrypha. In short, granted the fact that Shakespeare belonged to only the second generation of English people able to hear and read scripture in their own tongue, the impact of the Bible refracted through the Elizabethan Prayer Book is profound by any standards.

The Book of Common Prayer, 1662

In Book Five *Of the Laws of Ecclesiastical Polity* (1597), RICHARD HOOKER's well-chosen words waxed eloquent on "the form of Common Prayer." However, prolonged his defense of the liturgy observed by the establishment, critics of reformed conviction—Baptist, Independent, Presbyterian, Separatist, members of the Society of Friends, with others of a general "Puritan" persuasion—increased their opposition to set forms of worship. When the Puritan cause triumphed in the English CIVIL WAR and Archbishop WILLIAM LAUD was beheaded in January 1645, the abolition of episcopacy itself (October 1646) and the withdrawal of the Book of Common Prayer inevitably followed. By 1650 a man's compulsory attendance at his parish church was no longer required, always provided that he worshipped elsewhere. So if the English liturgy certainly lived on, it was because truly memorable language resonated in many a mind, and did so until the Prayer Book itself was brought back shortly after the Restoration of Charles II (1630–1685) in 1660.

Although the king himself showed a readiness to embrace a degree of comprehension within any restored national church (his Declaration at Breda had, after all, promised "liberty to tender consciences"), Presbyterian failure to keep the Convention Parliament in session after agreement on the immediate political settlement allowed old-style Anglicans to steal a march and gain an initiative ultimately used against those who longed for toleration. The so-called "Cavalier Parliament" accordingly took charge, and even if the erstwhile assumption that English people were by definition members of the CHURCH OF ENGLAND no longer applied, a Book of Common Prayer was once again restored by the Act of Uniformity (May 1662), and ordered to be in use by the middle of August (St. Bartholomew's Day). In March the bishops in Convocation had made the archbishop responsible for printing and publishing the new Book. This was a liturgy based on the 1559 and Jacobean texts, albeit one revised (between December 13 and 18) by a committee dominated by Bishop Matthew Wren of Ely, and served as secretary by William Sancroft, at that time canon chaplain to Bishop John Cosin of Durham, himself of no mean influence in the deliberations. Widely respected for his grasp of liturgy, Wren argued that "whatsoever is not very perfect and right, be it never so small, should now be set right, to prevent all after quarrels." He was also convinced that every care had to be taken to ensure that "in setting it right, it be done with as little alteration as well may be." A new "Preface" explained the revision in succinct terms: rubrics for "the better direction" of officiating clergy; clarification by removal of archaisms, ambiguities, together with positive "more perfect rendring [sic] of . . . holy scripture" (namely, the use of the 1611 A.V. for Epistles, Gospels, and Scripture Lessons); and the insertion of some "convenient" additions.

By any standards, the inclusion of the Psalter constituted the principal addition to a service book that also contained a number of new Collects (F. E. Brightman noted them to be "admirable of their kind") and occasional prayers. A political climate of deference to the faithful North of the Border arguably prompted parallels with the Scottish Liturgy. At Communion, for example, a rubric of 1662 referred to the scriptural narrative as "The Prayer of Consecration"; and at "Morning" and "Evening Prayer," after the Anthem ("In Quires and Places where they sing . . .") prayers for the reigning monarch, the royal family, for "Clergy and People," with "A Prayer of Saint Chrysostom" and Pauline text (II Corinthians 13) were offered to conclude both Orders "daily throughout the year." Of particular moment, too, in the prayer for "the whole state of Christ's Church *militant here in earth*" was a sentence praising the Almighty for those "servants departed . . . in . . . faith and fear" and seeking "grace so to follow their good examples." Likewise, the Litany, which had hitherto provided formal liturgical scope for intercession beyond the daily "Orders" (the title given by the Reformers to the contracted medieval "Offices"), was no longer isolated. From 1662 new sections of "Prayers" and "Thanksgivings" for use before the two concluding prayers (those of St. Chrysostom and the Pauline "grace") were introduced to prove of real value to the worship of pastoral ministry. A "General Thanksgiving" provided a fitting place in the liturgy "to those who desire . . . to offer up . . . praises and thanksgivings for . . . mercies vouchsafed." From this time, the prayer (perhaps a composition of Bishop Reynolds of Norwich) proved a popular addition, and one widely used not only in the Church of England but in the eighteenth century by the Protestant Episcopal Church of the United States and throughout what later became the worldwide Anglican Communion. Overall, however, the revision was limited in the extreme, and advocates of real liturgical change—whether High Church Laudians or long-suffering Presbyterians—were frustrated by a service book little different from that of 1552.

Revisions and Controversies

From the start, and with each and every subsequent revision, those who proved best able to read the religious pulse of the nation enabled compromise to succeed. At the Restoration, that was the invidious role of Gilbert Sheldon. Any attempt to understand the many controversies surrounding the Book of Common Prayer must take account of the way successive administrations have invariably used the myth of "uniformity" as a tool of polity in both church and state. Granted such a checkered history, its conspicuous triumph as an inspirational service book fashioning the humanity of all sorts and conditions in meaningful worship is no mean achievement. That it has served so many for so long can also be attributed to the fundamental principles of Cranmer, whose compositions compared and contrasted the liturgical heritage of the Western Church with scriptural and patristic standards. By reason of its timeless appeal to Holy Scripture, the Prayer Book has thus ensured a biblical quality that has molded not only the literature but also the very fabric of the nation. That the 1662 revision has been perceived as the Book of Common Prayer in classic form can readily be appreciated from the vociferous clamor of Prayer Book Societies in both England and America to resist its replacement. The 1928 book—arguably a "High Church" attempt to qualify Protestantism some four hundred years on!—was thwarted by Parliament's refusal to grant it uniformity before the law. After fifty years (in which time the church establishment maneuvered to change a system that embarrassed free-thinking Members of Parliament as much as committed prelates), a much-vaunted *Alternative Service Book* (ASB, 1980), itself approached by over a decade punctuated with numerous trial ventures known to church historians as *The Series*, was intended to provide new lamps for old. That it failed had much to do with a banality of language unable to sustain for contemporaries Coleridge's "willing suspension of disbelief for a season"—words surely as applicable to religious as to poetic faith. Whether further advance in the "one good new service-book" promised for *Common Worship* (2000) will prove any more acceptable than the ASB is a moot point. That liturgy, subtitled "Services and Prayers for the Church of England," was duly authorized for new millennium use on Advent Sunday (December 3, 2000). Clear that "forms of worship . . . express . . . faith and help to create . . . identity," the "Preface" sets out the Church's "responsibility to proclaim the faith 'afresh in each generation'." Yet the most cursory survey will perplex those truly concerned (in the words of that self-same "Preface") to "affirm their loyalty to the Church of England's inheritance of faith." For even the fascination of diversity in an age of ECUMENISM must balk at a calendar of "Holy Days" affording "commemoration" to those, such as "Ignatius Loyola, Founder of the Society of Jesus, 1556" (July 31) and "John Henry Newman, Priest, Tractarian, 1890" (August 11), in their lifetime good Christian men, but both of them decidedly opposed to that tradition.

Protestant worthies are well enough represented—"John Calvin, Reformer, 1564" (May 26); "Richard Baxter, Puritan Divine, 1691" (June 14); "William Tyndale, Translator of the Scriptures, Reformation Martyr, 1536" (who like Thomas Cranmer is given bold print); and "Martin Luther, Reformer, 1546" (October 31). However, if "Jerome, Translator of the Scriptures, Teacher of the Faith, 420" (September 30) is included, where is ERASMUS, without whose urbane genius and philological expertise the Bible of the REFORMATION and the reformation of the Bible would have been long delayed? In the matter of the sacrament, too, it seems unlikely that so vast and varied an "Order for the Celebration of Holy Communion also called The Eucharist and The Lord's Supper"—no fewer than eight "Eucharistic Prayers" are offered, or four more than the overindicted ASB—can either confirm or create Anglican identity. Moreover, if "Traditional Language" is to be found, an alphabetical arrangement of consecration prayers ("Prayer A" up to "Prayer H") provides no inspiration and little acceptable advance from the late 1960s and the so-called "Series" days. Baptism, "the beginning of a journey with God" when the "wider community of the local church and friends welcome the new Christian" is made to paint "many vivid pictures." This is done in a mere twenty-five pages, itself an interesting contrast to Communion that, when "Supplementary Texts" are taken into account, runs to well over three hundred. As for the key occasional Services of 1662—"The Order of Confirmation"; "The Form of Solemnization of Matrimony"; "The Order for the Visitation of the Sick"; and "The Order for the Burial of the Dead"—they have no place in *Common Worship*. In short, for such, and Services for the "Ordering of Bishops, Priests and Deacons," the Book of Common Prayer lives on. And so it surely must if words from the "Preface" of *Common Worship* are to make any sense

of its claim that "when the framework . . . is clear and familiar and the texts are known by heart . . . the poetry of praise and the passion of prayer can transcend the printed word." The very idea that such "worship can take wing and become the living sacrifice of ourselves to the God whose majesty is beyond compare and whose truth is everlasting" demands searching theological analysis. In days of delusion and dwindling congregations, it prompts a full measure of speculation. New rites set out in language unsympathetic to their traditional beliefs rarely reassure congregations. Choice, flexibility, and novelty have never been Anglican criteria. In Book of Common Prayer terms, to be sure, quite the reverse has long been the case. For the historic faith of England's Protestants came into being because of a principled opposition to innovation, and the long-sustained classic revisions of Cranmer's essentially biblical liturgy owe their staying power to gradual, but never the dramatic, change so foreign to true Anglican identity.

References and Further Reading

Brightman, F. E. *The English Rite: Being a Synopsis of the Sources and Revisions of the Book of Common Prayer*, 2nd rev. ed. 2 vols. London: Amersham, 1983–1984.
Brooks, P. N. *Cranmer in Context*. Philadelphia: Fortress and Cambridge, UK: Lutterworth, 1989 [Joint publication].
Cuming, G. J. *A History of Anglican Liturgy*, 2nd ed. London: Macmillan, 1982.
Dickens, A. G. *The English Reformation*, 2nd ed. London: Batsford, 1989.
Elton, G. R. *The Tudor Constitution*, 2nd ed. Cambridge: Cambridge University Press, 1982.
Ketley, J., ed. *The Two Liturgies of Edward VI*. Parker Society. Cambridge: Cambridge University Press, 1844.
MacCulloch, D., ed. *The Book of Common Prayer (as Revised and Settled at the Savoy Conference, 1662)*. London: Everyman, 1999.
MacCulloch, D. *Thomas Cranmer: A Life*. New Haven, CT: Yale University Press, 1996.
Whitaker, E. C., ed. "Martin Bucer and the Book of Common Prayer." In *Alcuin Club Collections* No. 55. Great Wakering, UK: Mayhew-McCrimmon, 1974.

PETER NEWMAN BROOKS

THE BOOK OF CONCORD

The collection of ten documents that constitutes the formal definition of public teaching for many Lutheran churches, published in 1580 for a majority of Lutheran churches in Germany (from 1580), Sweden, and Finland (from 1663), and subsequently for Lutheran churches founded throughout the world by European immigrants or by missionaries.

This collection of the three ancient ecumenical creeds of Western Christendom and seven documents defining doctrine in the midst of the controversies of the sixteenth century became the secondary authority (under and subject to Scripture) because of specific conditions within the development of MARTIN LUTHER's (1483–1546) reform movement. The concept of defining public teaching in a "confession of faith" as a document emanated from the decision of Philip Melanchthon (1497–1560), Luther's Wittenberg colleague, to answer the demand of Emperor Charles V for an explanation of reform measures taken by princely and municipal governments to reform their churches according to Luther's model with a "confession." Melanchthon's AUGSBURG CONFESSION (*Confessio Augustana*) included not only a defense of reforms but also a definition of public teaching, which established that the Lutherans adhered to the teaching of the Catholic tradition. His orientation as a biblical humanist led Melanchthon to believe that effective communication was a critical part of public teaching; Luther's view of the divine power of the spoken delivery of the biblical message ("the living voice of the Gospel") convinced him that such a public confession conveyed God's Word effectively to its hearers and readers.

The Ecumenical Creeds

The Book of Concord contains the Apostles, Nicene, and Athanasian Creeds because the Lutheran churches wished to anchor their teaching firmly in the universal tradition of the church, particularly in its understanding of the Trinity and the person and work of Christ.

The Augsburg Confession and the Apology of the Augsburg Confession

Melanchthon composed the Augsburg Confession in 1530 as an explanation of how Lutheran teaching corresponded to that ancient tradition on a series of twenty-one doctrinal topics, presented in the humanist form of commonplaces (*loci communes*), called in the case of a confessional document "articles of faith" from the ancient understanding of individual doctrines as "articulations" (members) of the "body of doctrine" (the analogy of faith). This section of the confession was a reaction to Roman Catholic charges that the Wittenberg Reformation departed from the church's tradition. It affirmed fundamental points of that tradition and condemned ancient heresies opposed by the church (especially antitrinitarian and anabaptist errors). The twenty-one doctrinal articles affirmed Lutheran belief in the Trinity and Christ as one person, truly God and truly human. It explained the Lutheran understanding of original sin (since Adam all people "cannot by nature possess true fear of God and true trust in God"; Augsburg Confession II), and the justification of the sinner ("we cannot obtain forgiveness of sin and righteousness before God by our merit,

work, or satisfaction, but . . . receive forgiveness of sin and become righteous before God out of grace, for Christ's sake, through faith when we believe that Christ suffered for us and that for his sake our sin is forgiven . . . "; Augsburg Confession IV). From this central affirmation, the confession describes the delivery of that righteousness through proclamation of the Gospel and use of the sacraments, which, as forms of God's Word, convey this forgiveness. In two articles the confession taught that good works of new obedience flow from faith in Christ. It also treats the church ("the assembly of all believers among whom the Gospel is preached in its purity and the sacraments are administered according to the Gospel"; Augsburg Confession VII), the sacraments of baptism, confession and absolution, and the Lord's Supper, order and human traditions in the church, the Christian calling to serve in and to obey secular government, the Last Day, freedom of the will, the cause of evil, and the invocation of the saints.

In addition, the Augsburg Confession addresses seven issues of reform (communion in both kinds, clerical marriage, the mass, penance, rules for fasting and other practices, monasticism, episcopal power). Some scholars suggest that the confession above all aimed at a proper definition of episcopal power that would permit integration of the preaching and practice of Luther's theology into the medieval system of church governance. It is clear from Melanchthon's adaptation of the material contained in the confession for use in FRANCE (1534) and ENGLAND (1536), and from the extent of his treatment of the doctrine of justification in his Apology of the Augsburg Confession, that he regarded this doctrine as the hermeneutical center of the biblical message and the heart of its proper proclamation.

Melanchthon developed the confession's doctrinal articles from Luther's summary of his theology in his *Confession on Christ's Supper* (1528), the "Schwabach Articles" prepared in 1529 as Lutheran princes organized a defensive league, and the "Marburg Articles" (1529) formulated in a dialog between Swiss theologians under Huldruch Zwingli's (1484–1531) leadership and a group around Luther. In addition, Melanchthon employed drafts prepared by Wittenberg theologians for the explanation of their reform measures (called, since the eighteenth century, the Torgau Articles, although which drafts actually were used is unclear).

After the formal presentation of the Augsburg Confession to the imperial diet on June 25, 1530 by the princely and municipal governments for whom Melanchthon had composed it, Emperor Charles appointed a commission of Roman Catholic theologians to prepare a refutation. Their "confutation" was submitted to the diet on August 3. Although Charles refused to give the Lutheran estates a copy of the "confutation," Melanchthon prepared a defense of his position from notes taken during its reading. Charles spurned Melanchthon's defense (September 3), so he continued to revise it, publishing it with the first printing of the confession itself in April 1531.

This Apology of the Augsburg Confession, revised in September at Luther's suggestion, met the objections of the confutation, particularly in its extensive explanation of the Lutheran teaching of the justification of the sinner before God. The apology develops its argument with extensive biblical and patristic materials and with impressive rhetorical skill. Its treatment of justification was based upon Luther's and Melanchthon's understanding of the power of God's Word to effect the forgiveness of sins and a new life for believers. Melanchthon contrasted God's word of "law," which "always accuses" the sinner, with his word of "promise," the gospel, which is God's power to save the fallen. Only faith in Christ as mediator and propitiator can accept the promise, and therefore salvation comes through faith alone. The apology also emphasizes that this faith produces good works.

Luther's Schmalkald Articles and Melanchthon's Treatise on the Power and Primacy of the Pope

From the early 1540s, many Lutherans also regarded three documents by Luther as key definitions of their faith. His Schmalkald Articles, composed with the help of colleagues in late 1536 at the request of Elector John Frederick of Saxony (1370–1428), were designed to provide an agenda for presentation of the faith at the papally called Council of Mantua, although scholars also view them as the reformer's response to John Frederick's request for a clear assertion of his belief, as a doctrinal "last will and testament." The articles are divided into three sections. The first confesses the doctrines of the Trinity and the person of Christ, on which, Luther stated, both sides publicly agreed. The second section treats the "teaching of Christ and faith," with a few positive statements from Scripture (Romans 4:25, John 1:29, Isaiah 53:5-6, Romans 3:23-8, Acts 4:12) and an extensive critique of those elements of late medieval theology and piety the reformer believed obscured and contradicted biblical teaching regarding salvation through Christ: the mass, monasticism, papal authority, and a long list of abuses—indulgences, devotions to relics and the saints, pilgrimages, and so forth. The third section briefly affirmed Luther's teaching regarding critical topics on which he thought it possible to reach agreement with Roman Catholic theologians of good will:

sin, the law, repentance, the means of grace, and a series of topics regarding order in the church, as well as justification and good works. In these articles Luther sharply demarcated his teaching from that of Rome in order to make clear discussion possible at the papal council. At a meeting of princes and theologians of the Schmalkald League (of Evangelical princes and cities) in February 1537, it was decided to use the Augsburg Confession instead of Luther's articles for the agenda of discussion at the council. Though the council was delayed and Lutherans appeared only once in the three sessions of the subsequent Council of Trent, without successfully engaging Catholic opponents in dialogue, the Schmalkald Articles came into use in the 1540s and 1550s as a confessional standard for some Lutheran churches.

At this meeting the princes requested a supplement for the Augsburg Confession on the topic of the papacy. Melanchthon composed a "Treatise on the Power and Primacy of the Pope." It employed biblical and patristic arguments to reject the pope's claim that by divine right he is the superior of all bishops and pastors, that by divine right he has the authority to bestow and transfer political power, and that all who wish to be saved must obey him as the Vicar of Christ on earth.

Luther's Catechisms

Luther's Large and Small Catechisms were also included among the "confessions" of the Lutheran churches, for they quickly had become a kind of "bible of the laity" in congregation and family use, and Lutheran leaders regarded a clear understanding and confession of the faith a necessity for all Christians. Luther himself undertook the task he had first urged upon colleagues, the preparation of an instruction handbook for basic Christian instruction, in 1529. This enchiridion followed a general plan for such instruction current in the Middle Ages, dropping the Ave Maria but anchoring teaching of the young in the Decalog, the Apostles Creed, and the Lord's Prayer. By changing the order of these three parts, Luther followed his conviction that the crushing of the sinner through the law (Decalog) must precede the apprehension of the gospel (Creed), which produces the life of faith (expressed first of all in the Lord's Prayer). To these three parts Luther added instruction on baptism and the Lord's Supper and later private confession and absolution, along with sections on the believer's daily devotional life of morning, mealtime, and evening meditation and prayer, and on Christian service in the world, developed in a household chart as a delineation of Christian callings in daily life. Through citation of relevant Bible verses, this chart sketched Luther's concept of God's calling believers to serve the neighbor in the family circle (including economic life), the political community, and the church. Luther's brief explanations of the parts of this handbook for Christian living employed biblical material extensively. It centered on his belief that Christ "my lord, . . . has redeemed me, a lost and condemned human being, purchased and freed me from all sins, death, and the power of the devil, . . . with his holy precious blood and his innocent suffering and death, . . . in order that I may belong to him, live under him in his kingdom, and serve him . . . " (explanation of the second article of the Creed).

At the same time Luther issued his small handbook for daily life, he published a digest of sermons he had preached in 1528 and 1529 on the Decalog, Creed, Lord's Prayer, baptism, and the Lord's Supper, along with instructions for receiving private absolution. This Large Catechism (1529) provided help for pastors and parents in understanding the teachings they were to convey to parishioners, children, and servants.

The Formula of Concord

The Formula of Concord (1577) was composed to resolve a quarter century of controversy over the proper interpretation of Luther's and Melanchthon's theologies. Occasioned by disagreement over the best way to defend Lutheranism against the military and ideological assault threatened by Charles V after his victory over Lutheran princes in the Schmalkald War (1547), several of these disputes began when Melanchthon and his Wittenberg colleagues were involved in working out concessions to the emperor for the new elector of Saxony, Moritz, who had sided with Charles in the war and thus won the electorate of Saxony and lands, including the University of Wittenberg, from his cousin, John Frederick. The emperor demanded that all Protestants in Germany submit to a new religious policy his advisors formulated "the Augsburg Interim" (1548), which essentially returned Protestants to the Roman obedience and medieval dogma, expressed in the manner of Erasmian reformers. It elicited a compromise policy from Moritz's government, labeled by its foes "the Leipzig Interim." Though never officially adopted by the electoral Saxon estates, partial introduction of its program and the willingness of its authors to seek peace by public compromise disturbed some of Melanchthon's students. Sensitive to nonverbal (i.e., ritual) elements of communication, they insisted that the Leipzig Interim approach of concession in "adiaphora" (neutral matters neither commanded nor forbidden by Scripture) would convince the laity that Lutheran leaders had

abandoned their confession of faith embodied in changes previously made in medieval practices.

These radical defenders of the Wittenberg heritage, later called "GNESIO-LUTHERANS" by scholars, differed from their Philippist opponents—relatively more conservative from a medieval perspective—in four ways. The Gnesio-Lutherans were more decisive in public confession, the Philippists more prepared to paper over differences for the sake of public peace. The former rejected governmental interference in the spiritual life of the church; the latter were more willing to accept governmental dictates in ecclesiastical practices. Gnesio-Lutherans were more eager than their opponents to separate themselves from medieval church polity and liturgical practices, and their expression of Luther's views on justification, good works, and sin tended to emphasize more sharply the reformer's departure from scholastic doctrines.

A series of controversies developed from the dispute over adiaphora, particularly over good works, the role of the law in Christian life, and the bondage or freedom of the will. In a separate dispute, the reformer of Nuremberg, ANDREAS OSIANDER (1498–1552), was criticized by Gnesio-Lutherans and Philippists alike for departing from Luther's understanding of justification. Osiander attempted to place Luther's understanding of grace and faith within the Platonic conceptual framework he learned in his study of the Kabbala; he taught that the indwelling divine righteousness of Christ saves the believer.

Parallel to contention over these issues, the dispute between Luther and Zwingli over the presence of Christ's body and blood in the Lord's Supper was revived through Lutheran criticism of John Calvin (1509–1564) and Johann Bullinger (1504–1575) (after 1552). In the 1560s some of Melanchthon's disciples, chiefly at the University of Wittenberg, fell under increasing censure from others among Luther's and Melanchthon's students, who believed that these Wittenbergers were "crypto-Calvinists," teaching Calvin's spiritualizing views of the Lord's Supper while pretending to be Lutheran. In fact, they were less influenced by Calvin than by certain elements in Melanchthon's thought, which they developed in a different direction than did, for instance, one of their leading critics, Martin Chemnitz (1522–1586), superintendent of the church in the city of Braunschweig, a disciple of Melanchthon who had distanced himself from Melanchthon's successors in Wittenberg, particularly on the Lord's Supper and Christology. Their attempt to propagate their views out of the public eye justifies their being labeled secretive, but they may best be called "crypto-Philippist."

Repeated attempts to resolve this range of controversies failed between 1552 and 1569, when a colloquy at Altenburg produced yet more distance between Gnesio-Lutheran and Philippist theologians. As a result, the Philippists added their own charges of heresy against their opponents to those the Gnesio-Lutherans had lodged against them, enlarging the agenda of controversy for German LUTHERANISM. The campaign for Lutheran concord began again in the efforts to address the agenda of controversy by a leading churchman from Württemberg, Jakob Andreae (1528–1590). His original approach in 1569 and 1570, based upon his "Five Articles," brief statements on five controverted issues, followed Philippist proposals for ending concord. After a definitive break with the Wittenberg theological faculty (1570), however, he issued another call for unity in his *Six Christian Sermons* (1573), which dealt with the controversies in a manner designed to win broad adherence through support for the main group of Gnesio-Lutherans without alienating moderate Philippists (1573). He revised his argument into the "Swabian Concord" (1574). Refined in its theological argumentation to take Philippist concerns into consideration by two leading north German theologians, Chemnitz and David Chytraeus (1530–1600) of Rostock, (the "Swabian-Saxon Concord" [1575]) and supplemented by another south German attempt at formulating concord, the Maulbronn Formula (1576) Andreae's proposal was reworked into the Solid Declaration of the Formula of Concord, which contains also an epitome of this longer statement of settlement. A preliminary draft of the Solid Declaration, the Torgau Book, was circulated among Evangelical ministeria throughout Germany in 1576, and their criticisms were incorporated into the final version. Rejected by the crypto-Philippists because of its teaching on the Lord's Supper and the person of Christ and by radical Gnesio-Lutheran followers of Matthias Flacius Illyricus (1520–1575), a leading Gnesio-Lutheran thinker, because of its doctrine of original sin, the Formula of Concord nonetheless won wide acceptance among German Lutherans after its appearance in the Book of Concord.

The Formula of Concord was intended to reiterate the teaching of the Augsburg Confession in regard to the controverted issues of the quarter century after Luther's death. It rejected Flacius's definition of original sin (in Aristotelian categories) as the essence of the sinner and designated it instead as a deep corruption of the spiritual powers of the sinner, resulting in a total breach in the relationship with God. Sinners have no freedom of will to turn themselves to God but must depend on the power of the Holy Spirit. In response to Philippist concerns, however, the formula teaches that the Holy Spirit does move the hearts and minds of sinners to trust in God and, with all Gnesio-Lutheran thinkers of the period as well, repudiates the idea that the "purely passive" situation of the fallen human creature in conversion excludes such a Spirit-caused turning of the will and the mind. The will has a passive capacity to be moved to faith.

The formula repeats the Evangelical rejection of Roman Catholic concepts of human merit in the creation of human righteousness in God's sight, providing a summary of Chemnitz's critique of Tridentine teaching on that topic. It also rejects the ideas of Osiander, insisting with Luther that the Word of God in the means of grace creates a new reality in the new creature and does so because of the obedience of Christ to the Father in sacrificing himself for human sins and in his resurrection from death.

From God's gift of righteousness in his sight flows the practice of good works, which the formula defines as necessary, not for salvation but for the Christian life. It emphasizes the proper distinction of law and gospel as "an especially glorious light," required for proper interpretation of Scripture. Following Melanchthon and meeting Philippist concerns about ANTINOMIANISM, it affirms a third use of the law, in addition to its use for the ordering of society and for the accusation of sinners and the crushing of their pretensions. This third use repeats the first two in the lives of Christians, calling them to repentance, but also provides guidance for ethical decisions to those motivated by the Gospel.

The Formula of Concord affirmed Luther's teaching that Christ's body and blood are truly present in the bread and wine of the Lord's Supper, received through the mouth, also by unbelievers, and that they convey comfort and strength to believers, especially to those weak in faith. This teaching was based upon the presupposition that God's almighty Word establishes reality and should be interpreted literally in the words of the institution of the Lord's Supper. It was supported in the formula through Chemnitz's adaptation of Luther's teaching regarding the sharing of the characteristics of Christ's divine and human natures (*communicatio idiomatum,* or communication of attributes). Chemnitz argued that Christ's human nature, because it is united with the divine nature in the one person of Jesus Christ, can be present wherever and in whatever form God wills. The formula insists that the two natures never possess the characteristics of the other nature but share them within the unity of Christ's person. The characteristics of the divine nature are specifically communicated to the human nature, according to the argument of the formula. In a supplemental article implicitly aimed against Calvinist teaching, the unity of Christ's person is indirectly affirmed by the confession that he descended into hell.

The Formula of Concord addresses the adiaphoristic controversy by positing the freedom of churches in external and neutral matters and the necessity of a clear confession of faith, also through the maintenance of liturgical and other ecclesiastical customs, when the clarity of public teaching is under threat. The document also places Luther's understanding of the election of the children of God, predestination, clearly within the proper distinction of law and gospel, affirming God's unconditional choice of those who are saved and human responsibility for the rejection of God and faith in him. It insists that the knowledge of election to God's kingdom can be known only through the means of grace. The formula concludes with a rejection of anabaptistic, spiritualistic, and antitrinitarian doctrines.

The Book of Concord has exercised varying roles in the public life of Lutheran churches through the past four centuries. It remains the official definition of doctrine for the majority of Lutheran churches.

References and Further Reading

Primary Sources

Kolb, Robert, and Timothy J. Wengert, eds. *The Book of Concord, The Confessions of the Evangelical Lutheran Church.* Minneapolis, MN: Fortress, 2000.
Kolb, Robert, and James A. Nestingen, eds: *Sources and Contexts of the Book of Concord.* Minneapolis, MN: Fortress, 2001.

Secondary Sources

Dingel, Irene. *Concordia controversa, Die öffentiche Diskussionen um das lutherische Konkordienwerk am Ende des 16. Jahrhunderts.* Gütersloh: Gütersloher Verlagshaus, 1996.
Kolb, Robert. *Confessing the Faith, Reformers Define the Church, 1530–1580.* Saint Louis, MO: Concordia, 1991.
Maurer, Wilhelm. *Historical Commentary on the Augsburg Confession.* 2 vols. Translated by H. George Anderson. Philadelphia: Fortress, 1986.
Peters, Albrecht. *Kommentar zu Luthers Katechismen.* 5 vols. Edited by Gottfried Seebass. Göttingen: Vandenhoeck & Ruprecht, 1990–1994.
Spitz, Lewis W., and Wenzel Lohff, eds. *Discord, Dialog, and Concord: Studies in the Lutheran Reformation's Formula of Concord.* Philadelphia: Fortress, 1977.
Wenz, Gunther. *Theologie der Bekenntnisschriften der evangelisch-lutherischen Kirche.* 2 vols. Berlin: de Gruyter, 1996, 1998.

ROBERT KOLB

BOOK OF MARTYRS

See Acts and Monuments

BOOTH, CATHERINE (1829–1890)

"Mother of the Salvation Army," preacher, and writer. Catherine Booth was called the "the most famous and influential Christian woman of the generation" by the *Bible Christian Magazine* at the time of her death. Her theological writing proclaimed "women's right" to preach the gospel and her own career as an independent preacher and the cofounder of the SALVATION ARMY made her a prominent and influential public figure.

Early Years

Catherine Mumford was born on January 17, 1829 at Ashbourne, Derbyshire. Her parents were Methodists and her father was a wheelwright and coach builder. The Mumfords moved in 1845 to London, where Catherine met WILLIAM BOOTH (1829–1912), a pawnbroker's assistant and lay preacher, who was later ordained by the Methodist New Connexion. On June 16, 1855, Catherine and William Booth were married. They had eight children: Bramwell (b. 1856), who succeeded his father as General of the Salvation Army; Ballington (b. 1857); Catherine (b. 1858); Emma (b. 1860); Herbert (b. 1862); Marion (b. 1864); Evangeline (b. 1865), General of the Salvation Army from 1934 to 1939; and Lucy (b. 1868).

The three major influences on Catherine Booth's preaching and theology were METHODISM, revivalism, and holiness. The writing and examples of Americans James Caughey, CHARLES GRANDISON FINNEY (1792–1875), and PHOEBE WORRALL PALMER (1807–1874) were particularly important. These mid-century revivalists encouraged individuals to seek salvation actively and preachers to devise means to encourage them. Their work was widely criticized in Britain because many believed this theology overemphasized the role of individual will at the expense of the Holy Spirit, and others deplored the dramatic, emotional revivalist services. The Booths believed these techniques could win souls and adopted a revivalist style that included the penitent form, a seat set aside for those seeking conversion, and vivid, energetic preaching.

John Wesley (1703–1791) and other early Methodists taught that holiness, or entire sanctification, was possible but not required of Christians. By mid-century, holiness theologians insisted that all believers renounce sin and when infused with the Holy Spirit, their hearts, minds, and wills would become the very likeness of God. It was, Mrs. Booth wrote in her pamphlet *Holiness,* "an inward transformation into the very likeness of Christ." This theology was particularly important to Mrs. Booth because it allowed for a new approach to female ministry. Christians had long claimed that Eve's sin disqualified women from religious authority, but when women and men could equally attain holiness, it lessened the weight of Eve's sin and diminished the significance of other differences between men and women. Holiness theology also emphasized that the presence of the Holy Spirit in a convert's heart could justify unconventional behavior if the Spirit prompted it.

Many American holiness advocates supported female ministry, including Phoebe Palmer, whose 1859 speaking tour of England occasioned Mrs. Booth's first public writing on the subject of female preaching. During Palmer's tour, the Reverend A. A. Rees, minister of the Bethesda Free Church in Sunderland, wrote a pamphlet called *Reasons for Not Cooperating in the Alleged 'Sunderland Revivals,'* to encourage others to shun Palmer's meetings. Mrs. Booth's response, *Female Teaching: or the Rev. A. A. Rees versus Mrs. Palmer, Being a Reply to the Above Gentleman on the Sunderland Revival,* was published in December 1859. Her pamphlet demonstrated her familiarity with Scripture and the writing of a number of prominent theologians. Her argument rested on what she termed a common sense reading of Scripture. Passages were considered in light of the particular verse as well as within the context of the chapter and the whole Bible. The historical context was also considered. She argued, for example, that Paul's command "let your women keep silence in the church" was a charge to the women of Corinth, not to women in all times and places. It should be read with an earlier passage in which Paul directed women to cover their heads when they prayed or prophesied. She also pointed to the women preachers and prophets in the Old and New Testaments and the passage in Joel, "your sons and daughters shall prophecy."

Her pamphlet drew heavily on the writing of other Methodists and holiness advocates. Her work was nevertheless distinctive. She argued that any woman called to preach had the "right to preach" without any "man-made restrictions." She did not believe women's preaching heralded the last days, like nineteenth-century prophetic figures, nor did she claim women to be the weak, the foolish, or the low, like many female preachers before her. Rather, she asserted that the church must be committed to vigorous soul-saving, and women were essential to that mission. This argument distinguished her even from those contemporaries who thought women might preach but only with an extraordinary call and when their authority did not extend to other areas of church life. Her pamphlet was widely read and a second edition was printed in 1861. It was substantially revised and reprinted in 1870 for the Christian Mission, later the Salvation Army.

In 1857 Mrs. Booth began to speak in public, addressing women and children's temperance audiences. In 1860 she took her husband's place in the pulpit when he was ill. The local and Methodist press expressed surprise at this unusual arrangement and one newspaper claimed she wore her husband's clothes when she preached. But the Methodist New Connexion approved her work and she continued to preach with her husband. For the next thirty years she continued to preach by invitation, alone, with her husband, and with other preachers, male and female.

In 1861 the Booths left the Methodist New Connexion when they were not permitted to work as itinerant evangelists but were instead obliged to accept a regular circuit. The Booths commenced a series of independent revivals in England and Wales over the following four years. Their work met with resistance from Methodists and other Nonconformists because of prohibitions on female ministry and revivalism.

In 1865 the Booths settled in London. She continued to work as an independent revivalist, speaking in chapels and halls in London and elsewhere. Mr. Booth established the East London Christian Mission, a mission based in London's most populated working-class district.

The mission adopted a structure of class meetings, circuits, and annual conferences loosely based on the Methodists. Mrs. Booth served on several committees, attended the annual conferences, and preached frequently at mission meetings. In 1879 the Christian Mission adopted a military-style structure and a new name, the Salvation Army. Catherine Booth never held an official title but came to be known as the Army Mother. Her influence was felt in the army's theology and practice, particularly in relation to women. The Salvation Army institutionalized women's right to preach the gospel, and thousands of women were local corps officers, divisional officers, and leaders in the Salvation Army's social services. Mrs. Booth was the most important force in establishing women's position in the army and a powerful example to the army's new converts.

In addition to preaching, Mrs. Booth was the author of many books including *Practical Religion* (1878), *Aggressive Christianity* (1880), *Holiness* (1881), *Mrs. Booth on Recent Criticisms of the Salvation Army* (1882), *The Salvation Army in Relation to Church and State* (1883), and *Popular Christianity* (1887), all published by the Salvation Army. She was active in the social purity campaigns of the 1880s. Along with other leading salvationists, she was involved in W. T. Stead's 1885 crusade to raise the age of consent for girls.

Mrs. Booth was diagnosed with breast cancer in 1888 and in that year she ceased all public activity. She died October 4, 1890 in Clacton. She was buried in Abney Park Cemetery, London.

References and Further Reading

Green, Roger. *Catherine Booth: A Biography of the Co-founder of the Salvation Army.* Grand Rapids, MI: Baker Books, 1996.

Walker, Pamela J. "'A Chaste and Fervid Eloquence': Catherine Booth and the Ministry of Women in the Salvation Army." In *Women Preachers and Prophets Through Two Millennia of Christianity.* Beverly Mayne Kienzle and Pamela J. Walker, eds. Berkeley, CA: The University of California Press, 1998.

PAMELA J. WALKER

BOOTH, JOSEPH (1851–1932)

English missionary to Malawi. Joseph Booth was born on February 26, 1851 in Derby, ENGLAND. He later emigrated to AUSTRALIA, where in 1891 he was called to missionary service. Arriving in MALAWI in 1892 as a proponent of the self-supporting industrial mission, he established the Zambezi Industrial Mission (1892) and the Nyassa Industrial Mission (1893).

A restless spirit, Booth changed his ecclesiastical allegiance several times and was responsible for the establishment of seven separate churches in Malawi, notably the Churches of Christ, the Seventh-Day Baptists, and the SEVENTH-DAY ADVENTISTS. He was often regarded as a maverick, and the radicalism of his evangelical faith drove him to adopt such causes as the seventh day, PACIFISM, and anti-COLONIALISM. Opposing colonial rule on principle, he held out a vision of "Africa for the African" that led him, in his petition to Queen Victoria of 1899, to demand independence for Malawi by 1920.

Booth's legacy is found in the ministry of such Malawians as John Chilembwe, Elliot Kenan Kamwana, and Charles Domingo, the forerunners both of an African expression of Christian faith and of political independence. The Nyasaland (Malawi) government declared Booth a prohibited immigrant in 1907, and, when he was mistakenly implicated in the Chilembwe Uprising of 1915, he was deported from SOUTH AFRICA to Britain, where he died on November 4, 1932. Although frustrated by frequent failures, Booth proved to be a catalyst in the making of modern Malawi.

See also Africa; African Theology; Missionary Organizations; Missions

References and Further Reading

Primary Source:

Booth, Joseph. *Africa for the African*, Baltimore, MD: Morgan College Press, 1897.

Secondary Sources:

Kavaloh, Brighton G. M. "Joseph Booth: An Evaluation of His Life, Thought and Influence" Ph.D. dissertation, University of Edinburgh, 1991.

Langworthy, Harry. *"Africa for the African": The Life of Joseph Booth.* Blantyre, Malawi: CLAIM, 1996.

Shepperson, George, and Thomas Price. *Independent African: John Chilembwe and the Origins, Setting and Significance of the Nyasaland Native Rising of 1915.* Edinburgh, UK: Edinburgh University Press, 1958.

KENNETH R. ROSS

BOOTH, WILLIAM (1829–1912)

Founder and first general of the SALVATION ARMY, innovative preacher, evangelist, and organizer. Booth founded a small home mission in 1865 to save the souls of London's working class. In 1879, he reorganized the mission into the Salvation Army, which quickly grew into a dynamic organization with members across Great Britain, North America, Europe, and the British Empire. In 1890 the Salvation Army began an extensive social service program. Booth was deeply influenced by mid-century revivalism, holiness theology, and Methodism, and these theologies shaped both his preaching style and his conviction that countless numbers of people were lost in sin and must be saved. His achievements, in turn, convinced many Protestants to borrow the army's dramatic techniques and to develop social service programs that would offer a new way to reach the destitute.

Booth was born April 10, 1829 at Snenton, a suburb of Nottingham. His father, Samuel Booth, was a laborer who worked at a variety of trades. His mother, Mary Moss Booth, was a domestic servant before her marriage. Little is known about his family's religious background. Booth joined a Wesleyan chapel at age fifteen and began to preach in the streets of Nottingham soon after. In 1843 he was apprenticed to a pawnbroker in Nottingham, moving to London in 1849, where he worked for a pawnbroker and continued as a lay preacher with the Wesleyans.

In 1849 a controversy divided the Wesleyan Methodists. Several ministers published a series of anonymous pamphlets denouncing the connexion's lack of democracy, excessive centralization, and indifference to EVANGELISM. One example they cited was the response to James Caughey (1810–1891), an American revivalist much admired by Booth, who was touring England as an itinerant evangelist. The Wesleyans' governing body disliked his irregular methods and barred him from their pulpits despite his acclaimed ability to win souls. Some clergy believed this decision meant that the desire for rules and order had surpassed the hunger for souls. Clergy and laypeople associated with the dispute were expelled from the

Wesleyan Methodists. They formed the Wesleyan Reform Union. William Booth, already noticed for his preaching skills, was engaged as a full-time preacher by the Reformers. He met Catherine Mumford (1829–1890) at a Reform meeting and they were married in June 1855. The couple had eight children, all of whom served in the Salvation Army: Bramwell (b. 1856), who succeeded his father as General of the Salvation Army; Ballington (b. 1857); Catherine (b. 1858); Emma (b. 1860); Herbert (b. 1862); Marion (b. 1864); Evangeline (b. 1865), General of the Salvation Army from 1934 to 1939; and Lucy (b. 1868).

From the beginning of his career, William Booth had little interest in following a conventional path to ministry. He wanted to prepare for ordination but he was convinced he also ought to work as an itinerant evangelist, saving lost souls and restoring those who had fallen away from their faith. From 1852 through 1855, he sought a way to achieve these two goals. He took several positions as a circuit preacher with the Reformers and studied briefly with an independent minister, but these proved unsatisfactory. In 1854 he began to study for ordination in the Methodist New Connexion under the Reverend Dr. Cooke. He was also permitted by the connexional authorities to accept invitations to preach in London and elsewhere. During these years his reputation as an effective, energetic revivalist was established.

Some leaders in the connexion, however, did not sanction the itinerant REVIVALS Booth wished to pursue, and the governing body insisted that he work as a regular circuit preacher from 1857 to 1861. Revivalism was regarded by some Methodists as an effective way to save souls, but others deplored the sensational preaching and emotional conversions associated with revivals. This debate divided Methodists for decades. Impatient with the restrictions placed on him, Booth quit his position with the Methodist New Connexion in 1861 and spent the following three years as an itinerant revivalist in Cornwall, Wales, the midlands, and the north. During these years, he further developed his reputation as a revivalist and met many evangelicals whose support would be important to the Salvation Army.

His wife, Catherine, preached with him. In 1859 she published a pamphlet in support of women's preaching that proclaimed "women's right to preach the gospel." In 1860, when he was too ill to preach, she took his place in the pulpit and preached for the first time. Although Methodists did not sanction female ministry, this unusual arrangement was permitted and the local and Methodist press commented favorably on her sermons. Still, her preaching violated rules and conventions accepted by most mid-nineteenth-century Christians. As a result, many churches and chapels barred the Booths during their evangelistic tours, and some clergy discouraged their congregations from attending. The Booths' revivalist style was also viewed with grave suspicion. They were believed by many of their contemporaries to rely too heavily on dramatic preaching, dire warnings, and the heightened emotional state of the listeners. Revivals disrupted the orderly conduct expected of congregations.

Founding the Christian Mission

In 1865, William and Catherine Booth both received invitations from evangelical organizations to preach in London. The potential scope for evangelical work in ENGLAND's largest city convinced them to settle there permanently. Since mid-century, Anglicans and Nonconformists had sought innovative means to reach the urban working class, the social group least likely to attend religious worship services. London's working class was considered particularly challenging because the population had grown so rapidly and lived in densely packed neighborhoods filled with Irish and Jewish immigrants and English-born people seeking work in the burgeoning industries located there. It seemed to require special means because it was so vast and uniformly poor.

William Booth was an important innovator and organizer of methods designed to reach this population. He began the East London Christian Mission, soon renamed the Christian Mission, in 1865 with funds from several evangelical organizations and individual philanthropists. He began preaching in rented halls and in the streets. By 1868, a London newspaper reported that the mission's 140 services drew 14,000 people weekly. By 1872 it had established twelve London mission stations and eight outside London. William Booth, a small group of salaried workers, and many lay evangelists preached at open air services followed by indoor services at rented halls, did house-to-house visitations, organized mother's meetings and tea meetings, and carried out administrative duties. The Christian Mission was modeled on the Methodist system of governance with mission stations, circuits, committees, and annual conferences. William Booth served as the general superintendent and was responsible for the establishment of new stations, hiring preachers, and policy decisions. In 1868 he began a monthly magazine devoted to the mission's work, *The East London Evangelist,* renamed *The Christian Mission Magazine* in 1870.

Theology

The doctrines adopted at the first annual conference in 1870 were essentially Methodist but the emphasis on holiness, or entire sanctification, was unusual. JOHN

WESLEY (1763–1791) argued that holiness might be attained in this life but was not required for salvation. In the 1820s and 1830s, American theologians reinterpreted this doctrine, asserting that it was the duty and privilege of all Christians to attain holiness. They taught that all believers must renounce sin and when infused with the Holy Spirit, their hearts, minds, and wills would become the very likeness of God. Their ideas reached England through the published work and preaching tours of evangelists James Caughey (1810–1891), CHARLES FINNEY (1792–1875), Phoebe Palmer (1807–1874), and others. William Booth was deeply influenced by all these evangelists, both in his theology and enthusiasm for revivalism. He wrote in 1889 that seeing Caughey preach had a "powerful effect on my young heart . . . filling me with confidence in the power and willingness of God to save all those who come unto Him but with an assurance of the absolute certainty with which soul-saving results can be calculated upon when proper means are used for their accomplishment." William Booth believed that holiness was an absolute necessity for Christian life and the only assurance of heaven. His preaching was calculated to bring sinners, even those who attended religious services regularly, to understand that holiness was required of them. In 1865 the evangelical weekly the *Revival* reported that "searching questions, loud warnings, hearty exhortations, Jesus the Saviour from all guilt, the penalty and power of sin, Mr. Booth is this sort of preacher." This combination of revivalist preaching and holiness theology shaped all aspects of William's Booth work and set him apart from many other evangelists and home missionaries.

To his critics, Booth's theology overemphasized individual will and allowed anyone, even someone with no religious education and a previously wicked life, to be the judge of his or her own spiritual state. It resulted in men and women without the usual clerical education or theological training assuming positions of spiritual authority. This offended the established denominations and Booth was widely criticized.

In 1872 William Booth wrote *How to Reach the Masses with the Gospel* to detail how he proposed to "bring in the thousands who at present seem to be outside the pale of all religious influence and operation." This was to be achieved, first and foremost, by working-class people. Booth was convinced that working-class evangelists could succeed where others could not because they knew and appreciated their own communities. Christian Mission converts addressed their own workmates and friends when they preached on street corners and their language and style were familiar to their audiences. Booth argued that working-class preachers could achieve greater results in their own communities than the educated, middle-class clergy had done.

The Christian Mission, and later the Salvation Army, allowed women to preach and assume the same religious and practical authority as men. The unusual authority allowed women distinguished it from its contemporaries, earning it considerable criticism from clergy, the national press, and religious publications. William Booth argued that not only was female preaching justified in Scripture, but an absolute necessity if all the lost souls were to be saved.

The Salvation Army

In 1879 William Booth reorganized the Christian Mission into the Salvation Army with a strict hierarchical chain of command, military titles and uniforms, and strict discipline. William Booth was the Salvation Army's general. This new position gave him extensive powers, including control over all the army's property and the right to name his successor. The army's newspaper reported that Booth told those assembled at the annual conference, "Now this is a war. We are sent to war. We are not sent to minister to a congregation and be content if we keep things going. We are sent to make war against the bulk of people, against any number, and stop short of nothing but the subjugation of the world to the sway of the Lord Jesus." These changes caused some to quit the army but the organization continued to grow. By 1884, 1,644 officers ran 637 corps across Great Britain, and another 688 officers ran 273 corps in North America, Europe, and in the British empire.

The Salvation Army was regulated by rules and a clear chain of command put into place by William Booth. In 1878 he published the *Orders and Regulations* followed by *Doctrines and Disciplines* in 1881. These books were regularly updated and modified as the army grew. Booth also began a weekly newspaper chronicling the Salvation Army's activities, *The War Cry* (1879–). The newspaper borrowed its style from the new mass circulation dailies and, particularly when compared to other religious publications, it was an innovative newspaper that attracted readers with the latest techniques.

William Booth was a revivalist. He used emotional appeals, stirring music, and drama to induce his audience to seek conversion. Booth encouraged his soldiers and officers to create spectacles to attract audiences. They wrote new words to popular music hall tunes, marched through the streets with brass bands, and borrowed techniques from the theaters and circuses. They drew thousands into the London halls and received extensive coverage in the press. By the early 1880s, William Booth was a stock figure of fun. The famed music hall performer Marie Lloyd sang about him, and *Punch* cartoons ridiculed his uniform and title.

William Booth's enhanced power and the growth of the Salvation Army caused many clergy, journalists, and social critics to comment on the organization. Some critics claimed his power over the Salvation Army exceeded even that of the pope's power over the church. Others accused Booth of using the army's money for his own benefit. A number of clergy, both Anglican and Nonconformist, published pamphlets expressing horror that the army permitted uneducated men and women to preach and many noted that William Booth's humble background did not merit his power over such a large, growing organization.

In Darkest England and the Way Out

In 1890 William Booth published *In Darkest England and the Way Out.* Booth proposed a solution to the problem of poverty and misery in England. He would establish a city colony where the destitute would meet their immediate need for food and shelter and begin the process of spiritual rejuvenation. They would proceed to a farm colony, where their health would be recovered and their character reformed. They would then be ready to find employment at home or in an overseas colony. Booth's book was not original. It borrowed ideas from the social-imperialist and social gospel movements and used information gathered by a number of Victorian social investigators. The book was widely and favorably reviewed. William Booth was an excellent fund raiser and within a year, he had raised over ten thousand pounds through donations and book sales. The publication of the book marked the beginning of a social service wing of the Salvation Army. It offered a range of programs, including industrial training for the unemployed, shelters for the homeless, and homes for unmarried mothers. This wing of the army became increasingly prominent and earned considerable respect. This newfound respect also gained William Booth the admiration of many who had once criticized him and the army. In 1904 he was received by the king and was granted an honorary doctorate from Oxford University in 1907.

During the last decade of his life, much of the actual administration of the Salvation Army passed to Booth's eldest son and a small group of senior officers, although William Booth continued as general. He traveled across Great Britain, Europe, North America, Australia, and Palestine. He preached at Salvation Army meetings and at large, public gatherings and was received by leaders including President Roosevelt. He died October 20, 1912 and was buried at Abney Park in London.

See also Salvation Army; Booth, Catherine; methodism; Palmer, Phoebe Worrall; Finnay, Charles' Grandson.

References and Further Reading

Ervine, St. John. *God's Soldier: General William Booth,* 2 vols. London: William Heinemann, 1934.

Sandall, Robert, et al. *The History of the Salvation Army,* 6 vols. London: The Salvation Army, 1979 reprint.

Walker, Pamela J. *Pulling the Devil's Kingdom Down: The Salvation Army in Victorian Britain.* Berkeley: University of California Press, 2001.

PAMELA J. WALKER

BOSCH, DAVID JACOBUS (1929–1992)

African theologian. Bosch was born near Kuruman, SOUTH AFRICA, December 13, 1929. He was educated at the universities of Pretoria and Basel. In his dissertation from Basel, Bosch addressed the link between the mission of Jesus and ESCHATOLOGY.

Bosch worked as a missionary among the Xhosa people in the Eastern Cape Province of South Africa from 1957 to 1966. The Theological School of Decoligny, of the DUTCH REFORMED CHURCH, appointed Bosch to be senior lecturer of church history and MISSIOLOGY in 1967. While at the school, he helped found the ecumenical Transkei Council of Churches, later known as the Eastern Cape Provincial Council of Churches.

David Bosch's missiological writings included twelve books, more than 160 journal articles, seven pamphlets, and four University of South Africa study guides. His most significant writing was *Transforming Mission* (1982), in which Bosch detailed missiological paradigm shifts throughout church history. Bosch served as the general secretary of the multiracial and ecumenical Southern African Missiological Society (1968–1992), editing its journal, the *Missionalia*.

In 1972 Bosch was appointed to chair of the Department of Missiology at the University of South Africa. There he edited the journal *Theologia Evangelica*. His missiological contributions were marked by their biblical foundation and evangelistic emphasis.

Bosch participated in the WORLD COUNCIL OF CHURCHES, the LAUSANNE COMMITTEE ON WORLD EVANGELIZATION in Manila, and the World Evangelical Fellowship. He died April 15, 1992.

See also Africa; African Theology; Ecumenism; Missions

References and Further Reading

Primary Sources:

Bosch, David Jacobus. *Witness to the World: The Christian Mission in Theological Perspective.* Atlanta, GA: John Knox Press, 1980.

————. *Transforming Mission: Paradigm Shifts in Theology of Mission.* Maryknoll, NY: Orbis Books, 1991.

Secondary Sources:

Kritzinger, J. N. J., and W. A. Saayman, eds. *Mission in Creative Tension: A Dialogue with David Bosch.* 1st edition. Pretoria, South Africa: S.A. Missiological Society, 1990.

Saayman, Willem, and Klippies Kritzinger, eds. *Mission in Bold Humility: David Bosch's Work Considered.* Maryknoll, NY: Orbis Books, 1996.

CHRISTOPHER M. COOK

BOUCHER, JONATHAN (1738–1804)

English clergyman. Clergyman, scholar, and philologist, Boucher was born in Blencogo, Cumberland (now Cumbria), ENGLAND on March 12, 1738, and was educated at the nearby Wigton grammar school. When he was sixteen Boucher traveled to Virginia to offer private tutoring to families of Virginian planters. Among his students was George Washington's stepson, John Parke Custis, with whom he began a long friendship.

In March 1762 Boucher returned to England where he was ordained by the bishop of London. Soon after ordination Boucher returned to America to assume the role of rector in parishes throughout Virginia and in Annapolis, Maryland. During his residence in Maryland he became an outspoken opponent of the "vestry act," which sought to diminish pastoral authority. Despite his reputation for eloquence, Boucher's Royalist sympathies and denunciation of colonial resistance to the Stamp Act at the outset of revolutionary hostilities alienated him from his parish. Boucher perceived the climate had become so menacing that he would eventually preach from his pulpit only with the security of a loaded pistol in easy reach.

Forced ultimately to vacate his office, Boucher returned to England where his loyalism was finally repaid by the offer of a government pension. In 1784 he was appointed vicar of Epsom in Surrey, where, until his death in 1804, he continued to develop a reputation as a compelling orator. Throughout his life Boucher maintained scholarly interests. He made important contributions to William Hutchinson's two-volume *History of the County of Cumberland* (1794), and in 1797 published *A View of the Causes and Consequences of the American Revolution,* consisting of thirteen sermons he had delivered in America between 1763 and 1775. As evidence of his continued fondness for the friends he had made in America, irrespective of their political disagreements, he dedicated his work to George Washington, a gesture for which he received a cordial response. In later life Boucher cultivated his passion for philological study, devoting fourteen years to compiling "A Glossary of Provincial and Archaic Words," which he envisioned as a supplement to Dr. Johnson's Dictionary. Only extracts of Boucher's Glossary were ever published, although it eventually helped form the basis of Noah Webster's Dictionary after 1831.

References and Further Reading

Primary Sources:

Boucher, Jonathan. *A View of the Causes and Consequences of the American Revolution, with an Historical Preface.* London: G. G. and J. Robinson, 1797.

————. *Boucher's glossary of archaic and provincial words.* London: Black, Young and Young, 1852.

Secondary Source:

Zimmer, Anne Y. *Jonathan Boucher, Loyalist in Exile.* Detroit: Wayne State University Press, 1978.

KELLY GROVIER

BOUDINOT, ELIAS (c. 1740–1821)

American Christian activist. Boudinot was born in Philadelphia, Pennsylvania on May 2, and died in Burlington, New Jersey, October 24, 1821. He was a notable lawyer, statesman, and lay Christian activist in colonial and Revolutionary America. During the War for Independence, he served as George Washington's commissary of prisoners and in 1783 presided over the Continental Congress. In the United States Congress under the new Constitution, he represented New Jersey for three terms, after which he directed the National Mint. While filling these public positions, Boudinot also pursued a wide array of philanthropic efforts. He opposed SLAVERY in principle and, as a lawyer, defended free African Americans from threats of reenslavement (see SLAVERY, ABOLITION OF). He was also eager to assist projects aimed at the betterment of NATIVE AMERICANS, a cause he supported by publishing in 1816 *A Star in the West,* which argued that Native Americans were descended from the Jewish Diaspora. As a Presbyterian, Boudinot also offered considerable service to his church. He was a long-time trustee of the Presbyterian General Assembly and served as an influential trustee at the largely Presbyterian College of New Jersey (later Princeton University) from 1772 until his death. His selection in 1816 as the first president of the AMERICAN BIBLE SOCIETY testified to the esteem in which he was held as one of the nation's leading lay activists.

In his religious as well as political activities, Boudinot was firmly evangelical, solidly Federalist, and determinedly Whig. His concern for education, at the College of New Jersey and elsewhere, was part of an extensive effort to stem the tide of DEISM and solidify the place of orthodox Christianity. In his eyes, deistic tracts like Thomas Paine's *Age of Reason* (1794) threatened readers with eternal perdition and society with immoral dissolution. After Thomas Jefferson's election as president in 1800, Boudinot became increasingly alarmed about the state of religion in the United States, where he saw dueling, Sabbath breaking, excessive drinking, and the frantic scramble for wealth as sure signs of social decay. In response to these crises, Boudinot published two works, *The Age of Revelation* (1801), which provided a mass of argument against the "irreligion" of Paine, and *The Second Advent of Christ* (1815), which presented a traditional Christian view of the End as a check to the uncertainties of the age.

After a destructive rebellion at Princeton in 1807 his fellow trustees chose Boudinot to address the students on their duties and privileges. As an antidote to what the college authorities considered unprincipled resistance to discipline, Boudinot delivered a memorable prescription of republican, deferential virtue as a cure for the disorder, the immorality, and the impertinence he perceived in Jeffersonian America. In this effort, as in most of his lengthier writings, Boudinot drew on principles of Newtonian science and Scottish moral philosophy, as well as traditional PRESBYTERIANISM. At the end of his life he continued the quest for a truly Christian America by donating most of his considerable estate to religious organizations, including the American Bible Society, the AMERICAN BOARD OF COMMISSIONERS FOR FOREIGN MISSIONS, and the new seminary of the Presbyterian Church at Princeton.

See also Enlightenment

References and Further Reading

Primary Source:

The Life, Public Services, Addresses, and Letters of Elias Boudinot. Edited by J. J. Boudinot. Boston: Houghton Mifflin, 1896.

Secondary Sources:

Boyd, George Adam. *Elias Boudinot: Patriot and Statesman, 1740–1821.* Princeton, NJ: Princeton University Press, 1971.

Noll, Mark A. "The Response of Elias Boudinot to the Student Rebellion of 1807." *Princeton University Library Chronicle* 43 (Autumn 1981): 1–22.

MARK A. NOLL

BOURNE, HUGH (1772–1852)

British theologian. Born April 3, 1772 at Ford Heys Farm, Stoke-on-Trent, Staffordshire, England, he was cofounder with William Clowes of the PRIMITIVE METHODIST CHURCH, the second largest Methodist group after the Wesleyans. A carpenter, he was converted in 1799 as a result of reading the works of JOHN WESLEY and Fletcher of Maddeley and the preaching of a Methodist local preacher. Attendance at a love feast led to the decision to join the Methodist society.

He was persuaded, despite his shyness, to become a preacher and became involved in the revivalism that swept the northwest of England in the early 1800s. Through the influence of "crazy" Lorenzo Dow the evangelist and his CAMP MEETINGS in 1808, his neglect of Wesleyan Methodist class meetings led to his expulsion. He and Clowesites joined together to form a society called the Primitive Methodists. Bourne gave administrative shape to the growing movement, acting as its general superintendent and secretary of conference at various times and editor of its *Primitive Methodist Magazine* until late in his life.

Bourne was also historian and hymnologist to the movement, publishing from its Bemersley headquarters and assisted by his brother James its history in 1823 (based mainly on his journals), subsequently revised in 1835. He also compiled its hymnbooks in 1809, 1821, and 1824 (which drew from his own writings and much revivalist hymnody from the States).

He traveled widely, acting as superintendent for circuits in the Trent valley. The success of Primitive Methodism owed much to his administrative abilities and creative writing skills as well as his insistence on strict discipline, stemming from his teetotalism. Bourne went on a mission to British North America (Canada) and spent some time in the United States in the years 1844 to 1846. He continued to preach until the year of his death in 1852. He died at his home in Bemersley on October 11 and was buried at his request at the Englesea Brook chapel where there is a Museum of Primitive Methodism.

See also Evangelism; Hymns and Hymnals; Methodism; Revivals

References and Further Reading

Milburn, Geoffrey. *Primitive Methodism.* London: Epworth Press, 2002.
Wilkinson, J. T. *Hugh Bourne.* London: Epworth Press, 1952.

TIM MACQUIBAN

BOYLE, ROBERT (1627–1691)

English theologian and scientist. Boyle was born January 25, 1627, at Lismore Castle, IRELAND, the penultimate of fifteen children of the Earl of Cork and his second wife. His father was a powerful but pious man who counted James Ussher among his closest friends. After three years at Eton College, Boyle spent nearly five years on the Continent under the tutelage of a Huguenot living in Geneva, Isaac Marcombes, related by marriage to Jean Diodati, whose church Boyle attended. While in Geneva, Boyle read daily from JOHN CALVIN'S INSTITUTES OF THE CHRISTIAN RELIGION. On one memorable occasion, he was terrified by a violent thunderstorm; his prayer for deliverance having been answered, he later dated his CONVERSION and his vow to live piously from this experience.

After returning to ENGLAND in 1644, Boyle lived briefly with his elder sister, Katherine Lady Ranelagh, a brilliant and pious woman whose social circle included poet JOHN MILTON, Samuel Hartlib, and leading Parliamentarians. Soon afterward Boyle took up residence at the Dorset estate he had inherited upon his father's death, Stalbridge Manor. In that bucolic environment, largely apart from the English CIVIL WAR, Boyle began writing the intensely religious works, none published until many years later, that mark his origins as a writer. His interest in science actually came shortly after this and grew out of his desire to use the new science to advance what he often called "the Empire of Man over the Creatures." Indeed, throughout his life Boyle maintained parallel research programs in natural philosophy and THEOLOGY, often using insights from one to inform the other. The English tradition of natural theology derives substantially from his works, which were frequently reprinted, translated into Latin and various European languages, and epitomized. At his death he endowed a lectureship "proving the Christian Religion against notorious Infidels," including not only "atheists" but also adherents of Judaism and Islam, both of which Boyle had studied more extensively than most of his fellow Christians. A highly interesting unpublished treatise on the diversity of religions survives in Latin translation among the Boyle Papers. He died December 31, 1691.

See also Huguenots

References and Further Reading

Primary Sources:

The Works of Robert Boyle, 14 vols. Michael Hunter and Edward B. Davis, eds. London: Pickering & Chatto, 1999–2000.

Secondary Sources:

Hunter, Michael, ed. *Robert Boyle Reconsidered.* Cambridge, UK: Cambridge University Press, 1994.

Maddison, R. E. W. *The Life of the Honourable Robert Boyle F.R.S.* London: Taylor & Francis, 1969.

Wojcik, Jan W. *Robert Boyle and the Limits of Reason.* Cambridge, UK: Cambridge University Press, 1997.

EDWARD B. DAVIS

BRADSTREET, ANNE (c. 1612–1672)

English-American poet. Born in 1612 or 1613 in Northamptonshire, England, Anne Dudley was related to Sir Philip Sidney, married Simon Bradstreet (c. 1628), immigrated to Massachusetts Bay (1630), raised eight children, and authored the first book of published colonial poetry, *The Tenth Muse Lately Sprung Up in America* (1650). After her death on September 16, 1672, in Andover, Massachusetts, Bradstreet's more personal verse, together with her revision of her published work, appeared in *Several Poems* (1678). Her poetry, influenced by an informal education and PURITANISM, is especially notable for its record of personal feelings sometimes at odds with the social and religious conventions of her colonial milieu.

In "The Prologue" Bradstreet objects to standard claims that women are unable to write creatively, and asks for a modest acknowledgment of female literary capability. Queen ELIZABETH I is celebrated in a long poem as a model of wisdom whose Protestant reign confutes notions of female ineptitude. Still more personal is the poet's muted anger in "Upon the Burning of Our House," which abruptly retreats into formulaic cant to contain her irritation with God for depriving her of cherished possessions. A similar threat of insubordination is evaded in a short poem on the pending transatlantic trip of her son Samuel. On such occasions Bradstreet typically reminds herself of the sinful pride that informs such rebellious sentiments.

Bradstreet's best poem is "Contemplations," in which the memory of paradise lost and the experience of time becomes every Christian's cross. This theme informs the poem's structural division into several crosslike fragments, a Protestant design indicative of the poet's humble disavowal of constructing vain earthly monuments to herself.

References and Further Reading

Dole, Raymond F. *Anne Bradstreet: A Reference Guide.* Boston: G. K. Hall, 1990.

White, Elizabeth Wade. *Anne Bradstreet: "The Tenth Muse."* New York: Oxford University Press, 1971.

WILLIAM J. SCHEICK

BRAGHT, TIELEMAN JANSZ VAN (1625–1664)

Mennonite martyrologist. Van Braght was born in Dordrecht on January 29, 1625 into a Mennonite cloth merchant family, which trade he also pursued. He was ordained to the ministry in 1648 in Dordrecht. Toward the end of his life he became embroiled in the intra-Mennonite controversy about how much MENNONITES should accommodate themselves to their surrounding culture. Staunchly on the conservative side, which argued for as much separation from society as possible, van Braght published in 1657 his *School of Moral Virtue* (*School der zedelijke deugd*), which had some 18 editions.

Van Braght's historical legacy lies in his publication of *The Bloody Theatre or the Martyrs' Mirror of the Defenseless Christians . . . who suffered and died for the Testimony of Jesus their Savior* (*Het Bloedig Tooneel of Martelaerspiegel der Doopsgesinde, of weereloose Christenen*), which first appeared in 1660, with a second edition published in 1680. It was a collection of the stories of Anabaptist martyrs from the sixteenth century, written for the purpose, expressed in the illustration of the title page, of depicting a suffering Jesus and his followers as they were crucified, beheaded, or drowned. Van Braght's purpose was stated in his foreword, which pointed to the worldly involvements of his fellow Mennonites in Holland who in his judgment had become affluent and complacent.

Van Braght used several sources on which he drew extensively, such as Adriaen Cornelis van Haemstede (1525–1562), a Reformed pastor who collected martyr stories from the days of the early Christian church to the sixteenth century, including some Anabaptist martyrs.

See also Anabaptism; Martyrs and Martyrologies

References and Further Reading

Braght, Thieleman J. van (Thieleman Janszoon). The bloody theater, or, Martyrs' Mirror, compiled from various authentic chronicles, memorials, and testimonies; translated from the original Dutch or Holland language from the edition of 1660 by Joseph F. Sohm. 15th ed. Scottdale, PA: Herald Press, 1987.

Gregory, Brad S., *Salvation at Stake: Christian Martyrdom in Early Modern Europe*. Cambridge.

Lowry, James W., *The Martyr's Mirror Made Plain: a study guide and further studies*. Aylmer, Ont.; Lagrange, IN: Pathway Publishers, 1997.

Oyer, John S., *Mirror of the Martyrs: stories of courage, inspiringly retold, of 16th century Anabaptists who gave their lives for their faith*. Intercourse, PA: Good Books, 1990.

HANS J. HILLERBRAND

BRAINERD, DAVID (1718–1747)

New England missionary. Brainerd was born in Haddam, Connecticut, on April 20, 1718. Orphaned at the age of 14 and tubercular, he experienced periods of morbid depression while still in his early years. By 1739, when entering Yale College, he had a conversion experience and thereafter supported REVIVALS known collectively as the First Great AWAKENING. While at Yale he continued attending such services, although college officials frowned on them. In 1742 he compared campus clergy unfavorably with the more spiritually alive preachers of the Awakening. Thomas Clap, president of Yale, demanded an apology, but Brainerd refused and was expelled as a consequence. A year later he offered to apologize, but by then it was too late. Yale never granted him a degree.

After studying theology for several months with Jedediah Mills of Ripton, Connecticut, Brainerd was licensed to preach on July 20, 1742, by the Congregationalist Association of Ministers, then meeting at Danbury. Later that same year he received a commission from the Society in Scotland for the Propagation of Christian Knowledge, one of the few corporations established to subsidize Protestant missionary efforts in the American colonies. Brainerd's first native American charges were Housatonics, an Algonquin group residing at Kaunaumeek, midway between Albany, New York, and Stockbridge, Massachusetts. His work there from April 1743 to November 1744 was not a marked success. Brainerd then moved to another mission field, whereas the natives relocated to Stockbridge under the tutelage of John Sergeant.

Subsequent work along the Delaware River continued to be sporadic and ineffective. With principal sites at Crossweeksung and Cranberry in New Jersey, Brainerd made several futile expeditions into Pennsylvania's Susquehanna Valley as well. He never stayed at one place long enough to learn a native language or to become familiar with local customs. He filled a gloomy journal with musings about sinfulness and failures, but his records point to approximately 100 baptisms and a promising future. Always dogged by poor health, Brainerd died on October 9, 1747, at the home of his fiancee, Jerusha Edwards. Her father, the renowned preacher JONATHAN EDWARDS (1703–1758), was impressed with the young man's diary and published it as an example of Puritan virtue. It became a classic devotional handbook, and many later volunteers for missions invoked Brainerd's work as a determinative factor in their decision.

See also Missions, North America; Puritanism

References and Further Reading

Day, Richard E. *Flagellant on Horseback*. Philadelphia: Judson Press, 1950.

Edwards, Jonathan. *An Account of the Life of the Late Reverend Mr. David Brainerd*. Boston: D. Henchman, 1749. Subsequent editions, Boston: Samuel T. Armstrong, 1812; St. Clair Shores, MI: Scholarly Press, 1970.

Wynbeek, David. *David Brainerd: Beloved Yankee*. Grand Rapids: Eerdmans, 1961.

HENRY W. BOWDEN

BRANCH DAVIDIANS

The vast majority of Americans had never heard of the Branch Davidians before 1993, when the phrase entered the American public lexicon to describe a sinister "doomsday cult" founded by a "charlatan" named Vernon Howell. In fact, however, although press accounts routinely characterized Howell (a.k.a. David Koresh) and his followers as renegades or upstarts, the Davidian sect had been in existence since the 1920s as an offshoot of the SEVENTH-DAY ADVENTISTS. Indeed, the apocalyptic worldview that united the community at Mount Carmel, Koresh's role in that community, and the content of his preaching are all incomprehensible without some understanding of Adventist theology. The failure of federal law enforcement authorities to gain such understanding was, arguably, the primary cause of the trail of events that left a total of ninety people dead outside of Waco, Texas, by April 19, 1993.

Davidian Adventism began with Victor Houteff (1886–1955), an immigrant to the UNITED STATES from Bulgaria. Adventist founder Ellen White had identified the church itself with Revelation's 144,000 "servants of God," but by the time Houteff converted to Adventism, its ranks had swelled to nearly a half-million. Reasoning that this indicated a falling away from the original message, Houteff declared in 1929 that God had appointed him the "angel from the east" and set him the prophetic task of purifying the community. Reading Scripture far more literally than White and her successors had, Houteff further declared that the KINGDOM OF GOD would be an earthly place in Palestine, to which he would, upon Christ's Second Coming, take the 144,000 purified Adventists. Houteff dubbed his group "Davidian," in reference to their intention of reestablishing the "Davidic" messianic kingdom. In 1935, awaiting Judgment Day, he and his small group of followers settled on land outside of Waco. Houteff named the place Mount Carmel.

Houteff's Davidians tirelessly engaged in efforts to convey their message to the entire membership of the Seventh-Day Adventist Church, dispatching missionaries nationwide and internationally, and mailing tens of thousands of tracts. Houteff's death in 1955 was a cruel blow to his, by then, roughly 1,500 followers. His widow, Florence, assuming leadership of the community, declared that the end was indeed near and would occur during Passover 1959. She summoned all Davidians to gather at New Mount Carmel (a second settlement, which Koresh and his followers would later occupy), and approximately 900 faithful answered her call. When nothing of an apocalyptic nature happened, the group dispersed, and a disillusioned Florence Houteff moved to California.

Subsequent years saw a series of court battles among the Davidian diaspora over who controlled the Mount Carmel property. In the early 1960s Ben and Lois Roden and a small band of followers won access to the property. Under the leadership of Ben Roden, who saw himself as one among many "Branches" of the Rod of Jesse, this new "Branch Davidian" community thrived through the 1970s. To such Adventist practices as the Saturday Sabbath and a very fluid style of scriptural interpretation, the Rodens added the celebration of such festivals as Passover and the feast of Tabernacles. They also continued Houteff's prophecy of the literal kingdom. Moreover Lois Roden claimed a prophetic vision of the Holy Spirit as female.

In 1981 Vernon Howell (1959–1993) arrived at Mount Carmel under Lois Roden's leadership, Ben having died in 1978. A recent convert to Adventism, Howell had a remarkable facility for scriptural interpretation and was a spellbinding preacher. He quickly bonded with Lois Roden, antagonizing her son George, who saw himself as the heir apparent of Mount Carmel's leadership. Whether or not allegations of a sexual liaison between Howell and Roden were true, she favored him over her son, and by 1983 Howell was claiming to be a new "angel of the east." When Howell traveled to Israel in 1985 George Roden took control of Mount Carmel, renamed it Rodenville, and ousted Howell's followers. Returning from Israel, Howell, who had now taken the name David Koresh (pointing to his prophetic role as a "Cyrus" figure), settled with forty followers in Palestine, Texas.

The next three years saw a period of rapid expansion among the ranks of Branch Davidians, following Koresh whom they recognized as a Messiah (a Son of God, though not divine). During this period Koresh also revealed that his messianic role would entail taking several wives, for the purpose of bringing into the world the generation of elders who would rule in the Kingdom. In 1988, after a bizarre challenge from George Roden over who had the power to raise a woman from the dead ended in a gun fight, Koresh and his followers regained possession of Mount Carmel.

In accord with Adventist tradition dating back to the Millerites, Koresh's branch Davidians believed they were living in the end times, and they believed the Second Coming would involve pitched battle against the forces of darkness and depravity. The Bureau of Alcohol, Tobacco, and Firearms unwittingly stepped into that latter apocalyptic role on February 28, 1993, with an ill-conceived and never fully justified attack against Mount Carmel that left four federal agents and six Davidians dead, and many more—including Koresh—wounded. During the fifty-day siege that ensued, FBI agents, treating the standoff as a "hostage situation," refused to acknowledge that Koresh's theological discourse regarding the Seven Seals of Revelation was anything other than "Bible babble." They also refused to heed the advice of religious studies scholars who urged restraint, opting instead for the analyses of anticultists who diagnosed Koresh as psychotic and his followers as brainwashed. On April 19, eighty Davidians, sixteen of them under five years old, died in a fire following the violent insertion of CS gas into the buildings.

A chapel now occupies the Mount Carmel site, along with eighty-six trees memorializing Mount Carmel's dead.

See also Apocalypticism; Millenarians and Millennialism

References and Further Reading

Jenkins, Philip. *Mystics and Messiahs: Cults and New Religions in American History.* New York: Oxford University Press, 2000.
Tabor, James, and Eugene Gallagher. *Why Waco? Cults and the Battle for Religious Freedom in America.* Berkeley: University of California Press, 1995.

MARY ZEISS STANGE

BRAY, THOMAS (1656–1730)

English clergyman. Thomas Bray was born at Marton, Shropshire, ENGLAND in 1656 and died in London on February 15, 1730. In 1696, to assist clergy in teaching the catechism effectively, he published the first volume of his *Catechetical Lectures,* which became very popular and made him rather famous. In the *Lectures,* Bray presented his COVENANT theology, which stressed that apostolic succession was a necessary part of the covenant. This meant that God authorized only ministers ordained in apostolic succession to preach the covenant and administer the SACRAMENTS. Also in 1696, the Bishop of London named Bray the first commissary to the colony of Maryland. As commissary, Bray represented the Bishop of London but could not ordain or confirm. He soon learned that CHURCH OF ENGLAND clergy in the colonies had no books, so he decided to help establish parochial libraries in the American colonies. This led to the estab-

lishment of the SOCIETY FOR PROMOTING CHRISTIAN KNOWLEDGE in 1699. Bray arrived in Maryland on March 12, 1700, but returned to England early in 1701, where he participated in the founding of the SOCIETY FOR THE PROPAGATION OF THE GOSPEL IN FOREIGN PARTS, which was chartered in 1701. In 1723 an organization was established to convert and educate Negroes, and it was made official in 1730 with the title "Doctor Bray's Associates."

References and Further Reading

Primary Source:

Bray, Thomas. *Catechetical Discourses on the Whole Doctrine of the Covenant of Grace, Delivered in 32 Lectures, on the Preliminary Questions and Answers of the Church-Catechism.* 4 vols. London: W. Haws, 1701.

Secondary Sources:

Laugher, Charles T. *Thomas Bray's Grand Design: Libraries of the Church of England in America, 1695–1785.* Chicago: American Library Association, 1973.
Lydekker, John Wolfe. *Thomas Bray, 1658–1730: Founder of Missionary Enterprise.* Philadelphia: Church Historical Society, 1943.
Steiner, Bernard C., ed. *Rev. Thomas Bray, His Life and Select Works Relating to Maryland.* Baltimore: Maryland Historical Society, 1901.

DONALD S. ARMENTROUT

BRAZIL

Brazil is often known as the largest Catholic country in the world and as the main center of spiritism, although now it also probably has the second largest community of practicing Protestants in the world. In the 2000 census 15.5 percent (26 million people) proclaimed themselves to be Protestant, of whom over three quarters claim weekly practice. Implanted in the nineteenth century, Protestantism grew slowly until the 1950s. Growth rates spiraled in the 1990s and continued in the early twenty-first century. All Protestants are usually known as *evangélicos,* and the vast majority would be evangelical in the Anglophone sense.

Protestantism was officially excluded by the Portuguese from colonial Brazil, but there were two attempts to introduce it linked to foreign interests. French HUGUENOTS with assistance from JOHN CALVIN's Geneva had a colony in Guanabara Bay near Rio de Janeiro from 1555 to 1567. They organized a reformed church and a confession of faith, but were weakened by the actions of their own Catholic governor and eventually wiped out by the Portuguese. The Dutch held parts of the sugar-growing area of northeastern Brazil between 1624 and 1654; two reformed presbyteries were founded and mission work was carried out among the Indians in indigenous languages. After the Dutch were driven out, however, no traces remained of Protestantism.

Soon after independence in 1822, the first lasting Protestant presence was established, through German Lutheran immigrants who came not for religious but for economic reasons (see LUTHERANISM). This resulted eventually in the Evangelical Church of the Lutheran Confession in Brazil, the major form of what is usually referred to as "immigrant Protestantism." Using the German language, it did not attempt to convert native-born Brazilians. Even today, over ninety percent of members have German surnames. Strong identification with pan-Germanic sentiment in the 1930s worried the Brazilian government, which closed the network of German-language parochial schools.

After the Second World War faith and Germanness gradually separated and the church identified more with its Brazilian context. In the 1970s it was the only Protestant denomination officially to criticize the military regime, even though a nonpracticing Lutheran (Ernesto Geisel) was one of the military presidents. LIBERATION THEOLOGY became influential in the church and attempts were made at Lutheran Base Communities in the rural south. In recent decades the church has lost members through migration, urbanization, and secularization, leading to the rise of evangelical and charismatic currents that seek to make it more competitive.

The second major type of Protestantism in Brazil is represented by the historical mission churches. Congregationalists from 1855, Presbyterians from 1859, Methodists from 1867, and Baptists from 1882 all sought to convert Brazilians using Portuguese. Most missionaries were American, with some Europeans. (The first Portuguese-language church, Congregationalist, was opened by Robert Reid Kalley, a Scottish doctor who cultivated his relationship with the emperor.) The uncertain legal status of such churches was slowly clarified, and was definitively resolved with the separation of state and the Catholic Church in 1890 (see CHURCH AND STATE, OVERVIEW). Early Protestants were aided in this battle for legal acceptance by liberals and freemasons.

Although historical Protestantism provided autonomy and advancement for some sections of the middle class, it came with the ethos of the expanding capitalist countries and failed to touch most of the illiterate masses. Foreign denominations were transplanted. By the early twentieth century most were under Brazilian leadership but the style remained equally remote from the masses and the elites. Despite heavy investment in

schools to reach the elite, the result in conversions was negligible and historical Protestantism struggled to produce an intelligentsia, a difficulty compounded by the tendency for democratic denominations to become more authoritarian, in line with Brazilian political culture.

Nevertheless the historical churches (led by the Brazilian Baptist Convention and the Presbyterian Church of Brazil) remained dominant within Protestantism until the 1970s. By 2000 they represented less than a third of Protestants, but still enjoyed some intellectual and transdenominational leadership and moderate numerical growth, largely through their more charismatic sectors. In 2002 a career politician converted to PRESBYTERIANISM came a close third in the presidential election. The Brazilian Baptist Convention, meanwhile, is still probably the second largest denomination, especially strong in Rio de Janeiro.

The third major type of Protestantism in Brazil is PENTECOSTALISM, which has grown so much it now represents two-thirds of the Protestant field (some eighteen million people), making Brazil the world center of Pentecostalism. Brazilian Pentecostalism has had three waves of institutional creation. The first occurred in the 1910s with the arrival of the Christian Congregation (1910) and the ASSEMBLIES OF GOD (AG, 1911). The former was introduced among Italian immigrants in São Paulo by an Italian who had become Pentecostal in Chicago; and the latter began in the north with two Swedish Baptists who had also become Pentecostal in Chicago. The AG is now the major Protestant denomination, but initial fortunes were modest. Faster growth dates only from the 1950s, coinciding with rapid urbanization and the beginnings of other important denominations: the Four-Square (brought by Americans in 1951); Brazil for Christ (1955, founded by Manoel de Mello, a working-class man); and God is Love (1962, founded by David Miranda). The third wave started in the late 1970s and gained strength in the 1980s; its main representatives are the Universal Church of the Kingdom of God (UCKG, founded in 1977 by Edir Macedo) and the International Church of the Grace of God (1980, R. R. Soares). By 2000 the UCKG was an immensely powerful and controversial organization, owning a major television network (TV Record) and electing a large caucus to congress. With its prosperity, teaching, and strong hierarchical leadership, it was very wealthy and was building major cathedrals.

Of the seven major Pentecostal denominations mentioned, one (the Four-Square) was founded by Americans, one was founded by an Italian, one by Swedes (Swedish missionaries were important in the AG until the 1950s), and four (the most recent ones) by Brazilians from the lower or lower-middle classes.

Each "wave" of new churches has updated Pentecostalism's relationship to Brazilian society, innovating in methods, THEOLOGY, and ETHICS, although all these are basically lower-class churches. The middle class has been increasingly reached from the 1960s by charismatic breakaways from the historical churches, and from the 1980s by independent communities with innovative and sometimes controversial methods (such as Reborn in Christ, and Heal Our Land). These have placed Pentecostal phenomena in less tabooridden formats and mirror "postmodern" cultural trends. The founders are often upper-middle-class people with entrepreneurial experience.

In 2000 the largest denomination was the Assemblies of God, divided into two main branches that function separately (the General Convention and Madureira). Between them, they represent a community of about eight million. BAPTISTS come next, mainly in the Brazilian Baptist Convention. After that come two Pentecostal groups with very different characteristics. The Christian Congregation, the first Pentecostal church in Brazil, rejects contact with all other churches and scorns the mass media, public preaching, and politics. It spreads through family and neighborhood networks, and is very strong in the interior of the state of São Paulo. The Universal Church of the Kingdom of God is a church of the big cities and has grown rapidly through heavy investment in the media.

By 2000 the social characteristics of the Brazilian Protestant community gave it an importance beyond its percentage in the population. In Greater Rio de Janeiro by the early 1990s a new Protestant church was being opened per day. Of the fifty-two largest denominations, thirty-seven were of Brazilian origin. Protestantism (and especially Pentecostalism) is disproportionately of the poor, the less-educated, and darker-skinned. It is thus a national, popular, and fast-growing phenomenon. The more traditional northeast region lags far behind all other regions in percentage of Protestants. Nationally, *evangélicos* are stronger in the cities than in the countryside and the Catholic Church is disproportionately rural, and women are heavily overrepresented. However, recent decades have also been marked by an expansion of Protestantism into social sectors where it was previously almost unrepresented: entrepreneurs and executives; the military and the police; showbusiness people and sportsmen (seven of the twenty-two players in the Brazilian soccer squad that won the 1994 World Cup were *evangélicos*). In the Rio shanties, where the state is absent, Protestant churches are often the only organizations apart from organized crime. Their role as a vibrant part of civil society is increasingly spoken of.

Unlike some parts of Latin America in Brazil, Protestantism has long enjoyed total freedom of religion and legal equality. Socially, discrimination and even persecution persisted until the second half of the twentieth century in some parts of the northeast. By the end of the century there was virtually no social ceiling on Protestantism, although increasing fusion of Pentecostalism with elements of Brazilian popular religiosity was contributing to negative media representations. As the percentage of declared adherents to Catholicism declined sharply in the late twentieth century, post-Vatican II ecumenical initiatives sometimes gave way to denunciations of "sects" by Catholic hierarchs. There is very little ecumenical dialogue between Catholics and Pentecostals, and the latter also have tense relations with the Afro-Brazilian religions, which they generally characterize as demonic.

Even within the Protestant world, representative transdenominational bodies have struggled. The National Council of Christian Churches (which includes the Catholic Church) has only a very limited number of historical Protestant churches. An influential Brazilian Evangelical Confederation, consisting of most historical churches, existed from the 1930s, but was effectively allowed to die after the 1964 military coup. It was resurrected by some Pentecostal congressmen after redemocratization in the 1980s and used for dubious financial purposes, leading to its closure. A Brazilian Evangelical Association was then founded in 1991 and for a time was fairly broad, although by the end of the century there was no truly representative organ of Brazilian Protestantism, a lack that diminished its political clout in key moments of national life.

Nevertheless Protestantism achieved great political visibility in the last fifteen years of the twentieth century. The first Protestant in congress was a Methodist minister elected in 1933, immediately after the secret ballot was introduced. From the 1950s until the end of the military regime in 1985, there were always about a dozen Protestant congressmen, distributed across many parties, with a discreet presence and no official support from their denominations. They were nearly all from the historical churches. Pentecostals became politically involved in large numbers only with the 1986 election for a constituent assembly. Since then several major Pentecostal denominations (AG, UCKG, Four-Square) have organized official candidacies and won congressional seats. In 2002 sixty Protestants were elected to congress, two-thirds being members of Pentecostal churches, most of them official church candidates. Although Protestant politicians have gained a reputation for conservatism, timeserving, and even corruption, there is also a growing Protestant left wing (including Pentecostals). In 2003 the left-wing Lula government contained two Protestant cabinet ministers and several parliamentarians.

The expansion of Protestantism to new social spheres has included the CONVERSION of career politicians and political militants from all points on the ideological spectrum, who then continue their political activity as *evangélicos*.

Protestant political involvement has been especially great in the state of Rio de Janeiro, where four out of five state governors between 1994 and 2003 were Protestants. It was there that the UCKG also elected its first senator, a bishop of the church who was well known for being a singer and director of a large social project. Social work is an area in which the historical churches were heavily involved from the late nineteenth century, especially with schools and hospitals. Advanced institutions at the time, they often later declined or became more secularized; fast-growing Pentecostalism concentrated on EVANGELISM. However, from the 1980s the social thrust of Protestantism was renewed, especially by the newer Pentecostal and charismatic churches. The Brazilian branches of foreign Protestant social agencies such as WORLD VISION have also been important. In 2002 a national network of Protestant social institutions was established.

About half of all Protestant politicians have had links with the religious media. In fact, with the exception of the United States, Brazil produces the largest number of Protestant television programs in the world, and most are Pentecostal. Protestant radio programs in Brazil date from the 1940s and became very common in the 1950s. Today hundreds of radio stations are owned by churches. Television programs began timidly in the 1970s, and there was some importing of American material for a short time, but by the early 1990s scores of Protestant programs were all nationally produced. Media evangelism may be somewhat more efficacious evangelistically than in the United States, but its main importance is in fortifying the self-image of an expanding minority.

Brazilian Protestantism has been exported heavily since the 1980s. This has happened first through the emigration of Brazilians and the creation of Brazilian churches in the diaspora. The United States and Japan have been the main destinations, but in 2000 there were also thirty Brazilian churches in London. Second, Brazilian Protestantism has been exported through missionaries, making it one of the "emerging countries" of Protestant mission. Although there are still about two thousand foreign missionaries in Brazil (mostly in smaller denominations and in work with the few indigenous Indians, making their presence almost invisible), the country also has more than two thousand missionaries abroad. Baptists and Presbyterians have sent missionaries since 1911, but it was only in the 1970s that mission sending really took off. In 1982 the Association of Brazilian Transcultural Missions was formed. Comibam (Congresso Missionário Ibero-Americano) took place in 1987, followed by a great expansion in the number of autochthonous Brazilian mission agencies and number of missionaries. By 2000 ninety percent of all Brazilian missionaries abroad were working under the auspices of Brazilian agencies. The countries with the largest contingents were Paraguay, Bolivia, and the United States, followed by Portugal, Spain, Mozambique, Guinea-Bissau, Uruguay, and Argentina. Four-fifths were working amongst Portuguese- or Spanish-speaking people. However, there were also missionaries in countries such as Albania, Mongolia, and India. From the 1990s there was an effort to direct more missionaries to North Africa and Asia. In 2000 there were some one hundred Brazilian missionaries in the United Kingdom, a significant inversion of historic flows.

Many sending agencies are transdenominational, although the major denominations also have their own agencies. The Pentecostal churches usually follow the traditional model of denominational transplant. Thus the UCKG, founded in a poor suburb of Rio de Janeiro in 1977, began work abroad in 1985 and by 2000 had branches in over seventy countries covering all continents. God is Love and the Christian Congregation also invest heavily in international expansion, although currency devaluation after 1999 slowed the Brazilian missionary effort.

By the end of the twentieth century many Brazilian Protestants were convinced they would soon be a majority in their country. While Catholicism was losing members, however, by no means were all turning to Protestantism. The religious future of Brazil is likely to include a revitalized Catholicism retaining a large percentage of the population, with a vast and extremely fragmented Protestant field, and a considerable sector of non-Christian religions and nonbelievers.

See also Congregationalism; Conversion; Ecumenism; Evangelicalism; Methodism; Missions; Televangelism

References and Further Reading

Burdick, John. *Looking for God in Brazil.* Berkeley: University of California Press, 1993.
Chesnut, Andrew. *Born Again in Brazil.* Piscataway, NJ: Rutgers University Press, 1997.
Cox, Harvey. *Fire From Heaven,* chapter 9. London: Cassell, 1996.
Freston, Paul. *Evangelicals and Politics in Asia, Africa and Latin America,* Chapter 1. Cambridge, UK: Cambridge University Press, 2001.

———. "Pentecostalism in Brazil: A Brief History." *Religion* 25 (1995): 119–133.

———. "The Transnationalisation of Brazilian Pentecostalism: the Universal Church of the Kingdom of God." In *Between Babel and Pentecost: Transnational Pentecostalism in Africa and Latin America,* edited by André Corten and Ruth Fratani, 196–215. London: Hurst/Bloomington: Indiana University Press, 2000.

Ireland, Rowan. *Kingdoms Come: Religion and Politics in Brazil.* Pittsburgh: University of Pittsburgh Press, 1991.

Lehmann, David. *Struggle for the Spirit.* Cambridge, UK: Polity, 1996.

Martin, David. *Tongues of Fire.* Oxford: Blackwell, 1990.

Willems, Emilio. *Followers of the New Faith.* Nashville, TN: Vanderbilt University Press, 1967.

PAUL FRESTON

BREECHES BIBLE

The term "Breeches Bible" was a popular reference to the GENEVA BIBLE of 1560 because of the use of the word "breeches" instead of "aprons" or "loincloths" in Genesis 3:7. In this translation Adam and Eve "sewed fig leaves together and made themselves breeches."

During the reestablishment of Catholicism in ENGLAND and the religious persecution of Queen Mary's reign (1553–1558), many English Protestants sought exile in Geneva, SWITZERLAND. Living in a city under the religious influence of JOHN CALVIN and THEODORE BEZA, and bustling with biblical scholarship and translation activity, the English exiles desired a new version of the BIBLE. In 1557 the New Testament and the Psalms resulted largely from the work of William Wittingham, who relied on WILLIAM TYNDALE's translation but included revisions from the Greek and Hebrew texts and Beza's Latin version. Wittingham, aided by Anthony Gilby and Thomas Sampson, then proceeded to translate the entire Old Testament using MILES COVERDALE's Great Bible along with various Hebrew and Latin texts. With further revision of the New Testament, the complete text of the Geneva Bible was published in 1560.

With the ascension of Queen ELIZABETH I in 1559, and the reestablishment of Protestantism in England, the Great Bible was restored to every parish church as King HENRY VIII had earlier decreed, but the Geneva Bible became the family Bible of England and SCOTLAND and the Bible of the early Puritans in America (see PURITANISM). Its popularity was attributed in part to its innovations of using Roman type, verse divisions that made the use of concordances possible, the manageable quarto size, and textual notes that promoted a Protestant, and to a lesser degree Calvinist, interpretation of scripture (see CALVINISM). The Geneva Bible went through more than 140 editions until it was eclipsed by the Authorized Version (King James) Bible a generation after the latter appeared in 1611.

See also Bible Translation; Bible, King James Version

References and Further Reading

Ackroyd, P. R., C. F. Evans, G. W. H. Lampe, and S. L. Greenslade, eds. *The Cambridge History of the Bible.* vol. 3, 155–159. Cambridge: Cambridge University Press, 1963.

Pelikan, Jaroslav. *The Reformation of the Bible: The Bible of the Reformation.* New Haven, CT: Yale University Press, 1996.

TIMOTHY E. FULOP

BRENT, CHARLES HENRY (1862–1929)

American Episcopal bishop. Born in 1862 in Toronto, CANADA and raised there, Brent was ordained to the Episcopal priesthood in Buffalo, New York in 1887. The next year he went to work in Boston, Massachusetts with the Cowley Fathers, becoming deeply immersed in the Anglo-Catholic movement of the EPISCOPAL CHURCH. In 1901 he was elected bishop of the PHILIPPINES, a position he held until 1917 when he became senior chaplain of the American Expeditionary Forces in Europe.

In the Philippines he oversaw the mission work of the Episcopal Church, attended to the needs of Americans in Manila, and energetically combated the opium trade in the Far East. After the War he took up his position as bishop of Western New York, and from 1926 to 1928 was in charge of the Episcopal churches in Europe. He was a major figure in the Ecumenical Movement, attending the WORLD MISSIONARY CONFERENCE in Edinburgh 1910, participating in the Life and Work movement, and spearheading the Faith and Order movement, presiding at its first meeting in Lausanne, SWITZERLAND in 1927.

Brent's many interests grew out of a coherent THEOLOGY, one that was rooted in the Anglo-Catholic movement of his time. This theology fused the SOCIAL GOSPEL with an "establishmentarian ideal" in which the CHURCH was responsible for all of society, and society would be regenerated by its participation in the life of the church. "It is God's will that the Church should be coterminous with society, and that the unity of life thus produced should make the 'communion of saints' a reality on earth and not a mere theory," he wrote in *With God in the World.* The purpose of Christian mission was to regenerate the spiritual, social, and economic life of a people. There were two corollaries to this view. One was that mission would be ineffective if the church were not united in its basic approach to the world, and thus Brent worked hard in the ecumenical movement to bring the branches of Christianity together in thought and action. A second was that the church needed to be indigenous, living out its mission differently among various nations and peoples. The shape of the church universal was cruciform: it was both catholic and indigenous, and the purpose of this cruciform church was to regenerate the totality of society according to the will of God.

See also Anglo-Catholicism; Ecumenism

References and Further Reading

Primary Sources:

Brent, Charles Henry. *The Spirit and Work of the Early Christian Socialists.* New York: Longmans, Green, 1896.
———. *With God in the World.* New York: Longmans, Green, 1899.
———. *Adventure for God.* New York: Longmans, Green, 1905.
———. *The Sixth Sense.* New York: Longmans, Green, 1911.
———. *A Master Builder, being the Life and Letters of Henry Yates Satterlee, the first Bishop of Washington.* New York: Longmans, Green, 1916.
———. *The Mount of Vision.* New York: Longmans, Green, 1918.

Secondary Sources:

Douglas, Ian T. *Fling Out the Banner! The National Church Ideal and the Foreign Mission of the Episcopal Church.* New York: The Church Hymnal Corporation, 1996.
Norbeck, Mark. "The Legacy of Charles Henry Brent." *International Bulletin of Missionary Research* 20 (October 1996): 163–168.
Zabriskie, Alexander C. *Bishop Brent, Crusader for Christian Unity.* Philadelphia: Westminster Press, 1948.

ARUN W. JONES

BRENZ, JOHANNES (1499–1570)

Lutheran theologian and church organizer. Brenz was influential in the development of orthodox Lutheran THEOLOGY. Born in Weil, Brenz began his studies in Heidelberg in 1514 where he subsequently met JOHANNES OECOLAMPADIUS, MARTIN BUCER, and PHILIPP MELANCHTHON, and where he witnessed MARTIN LUTHER's participation in the Heidelberg disputation of the German Augustinians in 1518. Converted to the new REFORMATION Theology, Brenz became a city pastor in Schwäbisch-Hall in 1522 and gradually introduced ecclesiastical reforms.

In the mid-1520s he defended Luther's doctrine of the real presence of Christ in the LORD'S SUPPER against Oecolampadius and was a driving force in the establishment of LUTHERANISM throughout northern Swabia. In 1527 and 1528 Brenz wrote an early Lutheran CATECHISM, in 1529 he supported Luther against HULDRYCH ZWINGLI at Marburg, and in 1530 he was present at the Diet of Augsburg. At the request of Duke Ulrich, Brenz participated in the writing of a church order for the duchy of Württemberg and was instrumental in the reorganization of the University of Tübingen. After the Catholic victory in the War of Schmalkald had forced Brenz to flee from Schwäbisch-Hall in 1548, he took refuge in Basel before finally going to Stuttgart where he became provost of the collegiate church in 1553. He died in Stuttgart in 1570.

Developing a theme in Luther's CHRISTOLOGY Brenz argued in his 1561 *De personali unione duarum naturarum in Christo* that omnipotence and omnipresence are properties properly communicated to the human nature of Christ while on earth, and that it is by way of this power of ubiquity that Christ is present in the sacrament. (This account differs from Chemnitz's *multivolipresence* view that claims Christ's body is present only where He so wills.) Brenz's staunch defense of central Lutheran teachings helped to preserve the distinctiveness of Lutheranism.

See also Sacraments

References and Further Reading

Primary Source:

Brenz, Johannes. *Werke: Eine Studienausgabe.* Edited by Martin Brecht, et al. Tübingen: Mohr, 1970ff.

Secondary Sources:

Brandy, Hans Christian. *Die späte Christologie des Johannes Brenz.* Tübingen: Mohr, 1991.
Brecht, Martin. *Die frühe Theologie des Johannes Brenz.* Tübingen: Mohr, 1966.
Estes, James Martin. *Christian Magistrate and the State Church: The Reforming Career of Johannes Brenz.* Toronto: University of Toronto Press, 1982.

DENNIS BIELFELDT

BRETHREN IN CHRIST

The Brethren in Christ originated in Lancaster County, Pennsylvania, around 1780. Throughout their history, they have been characterized by a synthesis of evangelical PIETISM and ANABAPTISM. The late nineteenth century brought numerous changes to the church, including the introduction of WESLEYANISM. Since 1950, the denomination has shed various aspects of its sectarian past, including plain dress. At the twentieth century's close, the Brethren in Christ Church consisted of over 80,000 members in twenty-three countries.

Origins

The beginnings of the Brethren in Christ can be traced to Revolutionary-era Pennsylvania. In the latter half of the eighteenth century, a significant number of Pennsylvania's German-speaking residents embraced the teaching of ministers who advocated heartfelt CONVERSION (the "new birth") and a pietistic approach to the Christian faith. One of these ministers, Martin Boehm (1725–1812), was particularly influential among Lancaster County's MENNONITES. Boehm ultimately left the Mennonites for more ecumenical pursuits, but his preaching resonated with a small group of Mennonites who sought to meld his Pietism with their Anabaptist convictions. This group, which emerged around 1780, soon took the name River Brethren, most likely because of its proximity to the Susquehanna River. For reasons unknown, this same group changed its name to Brethren in Christ at the time of the CIVIL WAR.

The most prominent early leader of the River Brethren was Jacob Engel, the son of Swiss Mennonite immigrants. When and how Engel and his fellow founders broke from their Mennonite churches is not clear. Most scholars posit a gradual emergence of the movement, beginning as occasional prayer meetings before becoming a more distinct church body around 1780. In 1788 two River Brethren families migrated to CANADA, where the brethren became known as "Tunkers" (a reference to the church's mode of BAPTISM, which was trine immersion). Until 1870 southern Ontario and southeastern Pennsylvania constituted the movement's geographical centers.

A confession of faith, written near the eighteenth century's close, outlines the River Brethren's early theological convictions. In addition to emphasizing the new birth, the confession reveals distinct Anabaptist-Mennonite emphases, including believers' baptism, renunciation of the world, CHURCH DISCIPLINE according to Matthew 18, footwashing, and the rejection of the sword (see PACIFISM). As a whole, the confession indicates that the early River Brethren remained committed to Anabaptist-Mennonite ecclesiology, ethics, and practices even as they embraced a more ecumenical, pietistic spirituality.

Expansion, Conflict, and Transitions

Despite relatively slow numerical growth during their first century, the River Brethren extended their geographical reach, starting churches in Maryland, New York, several midwestern states, and eventually California. Two schisms in the 1850s reduced the church's membership by spawning two new church bodies: the "Yorkers," now known as the Old Order River Brethren, and the "Brinsers," who became the United Zion Church. Both schisms can be traced to a dispute over the use of meetinghouses. When the Brinsers constructed a meetinghouse, thus challenging the traditional River Brethren practice of worshiping in homes, they were excommunicated. Shortly thereafter, the conservative Yorkers broke ties, dissatisfied that the Brinsers had not been disciplined severely enough. Meetinghouses would soon become common among the remaining River Brethren.

Further progressive steps reshaped the late nineteenth-century Brethren in Christ. With the initiation of protracted revival meetings, SUNDAY SCHOOLS, and TEMPERANCE advocacy, the church mirrored other late nineteenth-century American Protestant movements. Gospel songs and choruses replaced slow, metered hymnody, the conversion experience was made more immediate, and child conversions became commonplace. To some church members, these developments represented a creeping worldliness that threatened the church's traditional values. Most, however, embraced them as strategies that would help the church in the work of EVANGELISM.

In addition to adopting new outreach strategies, some Brethren in Christ churches embraced the holiness doctrine of entire sanctification. Drawing on the work of JOHN WESLEY (1703–1791) (see Wesleyanism), holiness advocates urged Christians to seek a "second work of grace" that would eradicate the sinful nature. The Brethren in Christ in Kansas became the church's strongest holiness advocates, and by 1910 the Brethren in Christ General Conference had officially adopted this theological perspective, incorporating the phrase "grace of cleansing completed" into its doctrinal statements. Although some Brethren in Christ churches rejected this view of sanctification, it remained the denomination's official position, promulgated by emotional preaching at the church's holiness-oriented CAMP MEETINGS.

Twentieth-Century Developments

Energized by the Protestant call to evangelize the world, the Brethren in Christ commissioned its first overseas missionaries in 1897. Beginning with MISSION outposts in AFRICA and INDIA, the Brethren in Christ established churches in over twenty countries during the twentieth century. By the century's end, only thirty percent of the denomination's 80,000 members lived in North America.

In the meantime, two world wars challenged the historic Brethren in Christ commitment to nonresistance. During World War I, some church members, including future Canadian bishop E. J. Swalm, were imprisoned for their refusal to perform military service. Even as these imprisonments strengthened some members' nonresistant resolve, others abandoned the church's pacifist stand. During World War II, only fifty percent of Brethren in Christ young men in the United States became conscientious objectors (see CONSCIENTIOUS OBJECTION). The church's effort to discipline those who joined the military was largely unsuccessful. Some military participants simply left the church; in other cases, local churches refused to enact disciplinary measures.

Between the two wars, the denomination wrestled with dress-related issues. As some members challenged the church's long-standing practice of plain dress (a practice rooted in its Anabaptist past and reinvigorated by holiness teaching), the church adopted a formal dress code. These prescriptions, adopted in 1937, remained on the books until 1952. Denominational historians would later recall these years as a regrettable era of legalism.

By 1950 most Brethren in Christ leaders had determined to move their church toward the evangelical Protestant mainstream. In 1949 the church joined the NATIONAL ASSOCIATION OF EVANGELICALS, a decision that epitomized its desire to associate more fully with other evangelical denominations. The history of Messiah College, founded by the Brethren in Christ in 1909, paralleled this trajectory, increasingly drawing students and faculty from an array of mostly evangelical Protestant churches. Even so, the Brethren in Christ Church continued its association with the Mennonite World Conference and the Mennonite Central Committee, and its late twentieth-century doctrinal statements continued to espouse Anabaptist principles, including pacifism. While some church leaders found this continuing connection to Anabaptism burdensome (especially in the area of church growth), others found the dialectic between evangelical piety and Anabaptist obedience both true to the church's past and meaningful for the church's future (Wittlinger 1978:ix).

See also Conscientious Objection; Mennonites; Pacifism; Wesleyanism.

References and Further Reading

Sider, E. Morris, ed. *Reflections on a Heritage: Defining the Brethren in Christ.* Nappanee, IN: Brethren in Christ Historical Society and Evangel Publishing House, 1999.

Wittlinger, Carlton O. *Quest for Piety and Obedience.* Nappanee, IN: Evangel Press, 1978.

DAVID L. WEAVER-ZERCHER

BRETHREN, CHURCH OF THE

Three women and five men started the movement later known as Brethren or Dunkers on an early August morning in 1708. One of them immersed their leader, Alexander Mack Sr., in the Eder River at Schwarzenau, in Wittgenstein, three times in the names of the Trinity upon his confession of faith in Jesus Christ. Having received this "threefold" BAPTISM, Mack then baptized the rest. Their movement sought to renew Christianity through a close reading and practice of the New Testament and the pattern of ancient Christianity, primarily as portrayed by the seventeenth-century historian, Gottfried Arnold. Intentionally choosing no name for themselves, they wished to be known only as sisters and brothers in Christ. In mid-nineteenth century in America the group adopted the name German Baptist Brethren, which they changed to Church of the Brethren in 1908. In Germany their opponents called them *Neu-Täufer* (New Anabaptists). Other nicknames included Tunkers, or in English, Dunkers or Dunkards (in Dutch, Dompelaars), all referring to the baptismal practice of immersion.

The eight originators of the Dunker, or Brethren movement (using the archaic English word "Brethren" to refer to women and men) were religious separatists mostly of poor artisan economic background who fled to Schwarzenau. Alexander and Anna Maragretha (Kling) Mack came from wealthy, prominent families near Heidelberg. Radical Pietism, the more separatist wing of the renewal movement known as PIETISM, and Anabaptist literature and contacts (see ANABAPTISM) influenced the Brethren, who organized around immersion baptism upon adult confession of faith and the practice of mutual church discipline. They adopted a fuller Eucharistic ritual called the love feast, consisting of feetwashing, a simple meal (the agape of ancient Christianity), and the bread and cup of the Eucharist, all preceded by a lengthy period of self-examination and repentance (see LORD'S SUPPER). At the love feast and other times, the Dunkers greeted each other with a holy kiss exchanged among men, or among women, but never across gender lines. The kiss and the address of "sister" and "brother" intended to show spiritual love. They also practiced anointing for healing (not to the exclusion of medical arts, however). They refused to swear oaths and fight in war (see PACIFISM), and avoided the use of courts. They lived austerely to share material resources with the needy, often themselves.

Their evangelistic, eschatalogical preaching gathered a second congregation in Marienborn (Isenburg-Büdingen). They were expelled in 1715 and moved to Krefeld. The Schwarzenau congregation migrated to Surhuisterveen, Friesland (Netherlands) in 1720. A group from Krefeld, led by Peter Becker, emigrated to Germantown, Pennsylvania, in 1719, perhaps in part over dissension about church discipline in Krefeld. They worshiped together for the first time in America on Christmas Day 1723, when Becker baptized new converts and held a love feast. Mack's group immigrated in 1729, and by 1735, most of the European Brethren had come to America, numbering a few hundred. The few members in Europe assimilated into other groups or remained separatists.

The Brethren suffered a division in 1728, led by Conrad Beissel, minister of the third Brethren congregation (Conestoga), who taught speculative concepts from JACOB BOEHME. Beissel upheld CELIBACY above marriage, and worship on the seventh day of the week. His community, eventually named Ephrata, built several large monastic houses and chapels. Slowly the Brethren recovered and spread. By 1770 they had reached New Jersey, Maryland, southern Virginia, the Carolinas, and perhaps formed a congregation in Georgia, with the largest concentration in Pennsylvania. According to Morgan Edwards, they numbered more than 1,500 members, with many more participants because of large families. The Revolutionary War brought some repressive consequences, most notably the arrest of the Germantown printer, Christopher Sauer II, whose press and wealth were seized because of his objection to war. In the last decade of the eighteenth century, some Brethren spread into eastern Tennessee, Kentucky, southwestern Ohio, and into southern Missouri near Cape Girardeau.

In the 1790s the Brethren suffered a doctrinal dispute when a minister in North Carolina, John H. (probably John Hendricks from Pennsylvania), preached UNIVERSALISM, meaning no punishment for sinners and no heaven or hell. The Annual Meeting, a yearly gathering that slowly emerged after 1742 to resolve difficulties, sent ministers to counsel with John H. When he refused to abandon universalism, the Annual Meeting expelled him and his supporters from membership in 1798. The few Brethren in eastern Tennessee were not "disfellowshiped," probably because of closer ties to the ministers in southern Virginia. Most of the Brethren in the Carolinas, Kentucky, and Missouri were lost in this decision, perhaps a thousand people. Many of them remained affiliated together, and were known as the Far Western Brethren. Some of them moved north and joined Brethren congregations, as Brethren from Virginia and the Carolinas moved into Ohio, Indiana, and Illinois in the first decade of the nineteenth century.

The first half of the nineteenth century brought both standardization and new tensions. Revivalism (see REVIVALS) swept through Kentucky. Some of the Far Western Brethren in Kentucky and some Brethren in southern Indiana followed ministers Peter Hon (Hahn) and Adam Hostetler into the Restoration movement of Alexander Campbell (see CAMPBELL FAMILY) and BARTON STONE in the 1820s. Meanwhile, one of the Far Western Brethren ministers, George Wolfe II of Illinois, continued to promote Brethren teachings and the importance of Annual Meeting. Wolfe led the remaining Far Western Brethren to reconciliation with the rest of the Brethren between 1840 and 1860. However, Peter Eyman led a small division in Indiana, forming in 1848 the New Dunkards, or CHURCH OF GOD (not the CHURCH OF GOD, ANDERSON, INDIANA).

Annual Meeting increasingly took on a standardizing role, establishing wording for the anointing ritual (1827) and baptism (1848). By this time Brethren prohibited WOMEN from speaking in worship. Sarah Righter Major, from the Philadelphia congregation, felt divinely called to preach, and did so upon invitation (see WOMEN CLERGY). Annual Meeting sent a committee to investigate in 1834, but the men declined to silence a woman who could preach better than they. As Brethren spread, shared patterns of daily worship in homes, congregational worship held in homes or plain meetinghouses, and the Annual Meeting held them together. Congregations often had multiple meeting points and a team of several self-supporting ministers without formal education. The yearly love feast, typically attended by all local members and many from nearby, allowed for communication and circulation of members and ministers that promoted consensus of faith and practice. In 1851 Henry Kurtz started a paper, *The Gospel Visitor,* to aid communication.

Around the mid-nineteenth century, Brethren founded their first congregation in Iowa (Libertyville, 1844, the oldest one continuing west of the Mississippi), in Oregon (Lebanon, in Willamette Valley, 1854), and in California (near Monterey, 1856). All had a core of Far Western Brethren associated in some way with George Wolfe II. The Oregon group struggled with internal controversies over universalism. The California group gradually drifted toward congregational polity, eventually joining the Progressive branch in the division of the 1880s.

Brethren stayed united in their opposition to SLAVERY and war as the nation divided (see SLAVERY, ABOLITION OF). Rarely active in abolition, some Brethren helped freed slaves reach safety in the North. One of them, Samuel Weir, was freed in 1843 when the family that held him joined the Brethren in Botetourt County, Virginia. Elder B. F. Moomaw helped Weir move to Ohio. There, Sarah Righter Major and her husband, Thomas, who had moved to Ohio, encouraged him to preach. Late in life Weir became the first African American minister and elder among the Brethren.

During the CIVIL WAR, Brethren in the South suffered more from conscription laws and war than Brethren in the North. Elder John Kline, from Virginia, labored extensively on both sides to promote unity in the church. He was killed by local irregulars near his home in 1864. Elder Peter Wrightsman from

Tennessee negotiated exemptions from military service. The few Brethren in Missouri and Kansas suffered losses of property and sometimes life from guerilla raids.

Although war did not divide the church, tensions with modernism did. By the 1870s a young generation of ministers challenged some of the marks of distinction from the world upheld by the elders who had led during the Civil War. Interest in foreign MISSIONS led congregations in northern Illinois to send Christian and Mary Hope to DENMARK as the first Brethren foreign missionaries, despite opposition from older ministers at Annual Meeting. Meanwhile, various Brethren entrepreneurs attempted to start Brethren schools (high schools and normal schools). A firebrand for progress from central Pennsylvania, Henry Holsinger, agitated throughout the 1870s for a formally educated, salaried ministry along with allowing church colleges, Revivals, and SUNDAY SCHOOLS. He insulted the older ministers for their lack of education and what he saw as excessive reliance on TRADITION rather than scripture. The conflicts culminated in a three-way division in the early 1880s. Several older ministers in southern Ohio withdrew in 1880, creating the Old German Baptist Brethren, when Annual Meeting refused their petition to halt creeping innovations such as higher education; revivals; paid, educated ministry; and Sunday Schools. In 1882 Annual Meeting disfellowshiped Henry Holsinger for his disregard of Annual Meeting's authority and abrasive comments. Holsinger's supporters organized the Brethren Church (known informally as Progressive Brethren) in 1883. A key factor in the divisions was the role and power of Annual Meeting to interpret scripture and to set standards for the whole church.

The most numerous group, the German Baptist Brethren, attempted to be both conservative and progressive, seeking primarily to avoid further division. The lack of a specific agenda bestowed a mixed legacy for this group's future. Within a generation, they adopted much of the progressives' agenda. In 1895 they launched an aggressive, funded foreign mission program, sending Wilbur and Mary Stover and Bertha Ryan to INDIA, also precipitating an institutional denominational structure. In 1908, when the church's name changed to Church of the Brethren, they launched a mission to CHINA. Numerous Brethren colleges were founded in the second half of the nineteenth century, of which survive six related to the Church of the Brethren, and one to the Brethren Church. Both denominations have theological seminaries, started in the twentieth century.

In the early twentieth century, the Church of the Brethren cautiously adopted progressive currents, gradually relaxing symbolic patterns of separation from the general culture. Two issues illustrate this change. In 1911, after years of debate, Annual Meeting made the required plain dress, which became fixed in the mid-nineteenth century, no longer grounds for disfellowshiping. When the United States entered World War I, the Church of the Brethren convened a special national conference in Goshen, Indiana, in January 1919. The conference counseled Brethren men not to train for war or wear the uniform. Upon government threats of prosecution for treason, church officials retracted the statement and recalled printed copies of it. With the church uncertain, many Brethren men fought as soldiers or served as noncombatants in uniform, whereas some maintained the peace teaching. These changes weakened the role of the church as interpreter of scripture and guide in faith and practice, endorsing new appeals to individual conscience as the arbiter of faithful life.

American optimism about progress in the early twentieth century combined with Brethren interests in holy living and mission to give birth to new urban congregations, homes for orphans and the elderly, and church camps for youth. Women's participation in foreign and home missions raised questions about women in ministry. In 1911 Martha Cunningham Dolby, an African American Brethren woman, became the first woman to be listed officially as a licensed minister, although full ordination for women was not accepted until 1958. Ironically, the Ohio congregation she attended told her to join an African American denomination around 1924, two years after the Brethren launched their last major foreign mission, in NIGERIA.

At the end of the nineteenth century, Brethren followed newly opened railroad routes in agricultural colonization. New congregations, some short-lived, emerged in the Dakotas, Montana, Idaho, and CANADA's prairie provinces, where an Annual Conference was held in 1923, the only time outside the United States. Other areas of migration included Washington, Oregon, and California, Michigan, Alabama, and Louisiana, as well as Oklahoma, Texas, and Arizona.

After World War I, leaders such as M. R. Ziegler and Dan West sought to reinforce the church's peace teaching. However, during World War II only about ten percent of eligible Brethren men served as conscientious objectors in Civilian Public Service (CPS), newly created by the MENNONITES, Quakers (see FRIENDS, SOCIETY OF), and Brethren. In China, thirteen Chinese Brethren and three missionaries were killed during the Japanese invasion. After World War II, Brethren launched a massive relief ministry in Europe, creating several service organizations, including the Heifer Project. Immensely popular, the Brethren service programs blended Christian values with postwar American idealism, and replaced the church's missionary emphasis. The focus on service and peace shaped Brethren leaders such as Andrew Cordier, who served in the United Nations, and Gladdys Muir, who started the first college-level peace studies major at Manchester College in 1948.

Many Church of the Brethren leaders accepted new theological currents after World War I, especially Protestant liberalism, diminishing the emphasis on the church's distinctive New Testament teachings and practices. Some resisted, such as the Dunkard Brethren, who withdrew in 1926 over the loss of plain dress. In the Brethren Church (Progressives), controversy over fundamentalism led to a division in 1937–1939, creating the more fundamentalist Fellowship of Grace Brethren Churches, with college and seminary in Winona Lake, Indiana. In the 1990s the Grace Brethren divided when a group insisted on requiring threefold immersion baptism for those transferring membership. The new group is the Conservative Grace Brethren Church.

The Church of the Brethren Annual Conference in 1958 allowed for the first time the transfer of membership from other denominations without requiring threefold immersion baptism, and bread and cup communion without the full love feast. In reaction, several conservative Brethren formed the Brethren Revival Fellowship (BRF), to promote the distinctive teachings and practices of the church. Social changes in the United States since the 1960s have affected the Church of the Brethren. Despite continued peace teaching, a small percentage of Brethren men were conscientious objectors to the wars in KOREA and Vietnam (see CONSCIENTIOUS OBJECTION). During the Vietnam war, two Brethren alternative service workers in Vietnam were killed. In 1973 the Women's Caucus was formed to advance equality for women in the church.

The Brethren in the early twenty-first century reflect many results of the acculturation to mainline Protestantism. Attendance at love feast is much smaller and those holding the peace witness are a minority, even though it is still the church's teaching. Congregations with strong BRF ties maintain high rates of observing distinctive Brethren teachings and practices. Brethren in Nigeria outnumber the membership of the Church of the Brethren, which has declined significantly since 1963 to about 135,000 in 2000. In 2002 the Michigan district ordained an openly homosexual person one month before Annual Conference voted to prohibit such ordinations. Renewed interest in the heritage of the Brethren in the late twentieth century culminated in the *Brethren Encyclopedia* in 1983, a cooperative production of all the Brethren bodies. James McClendon completed a systematic theology from an Anabaptist perspective in 2001. The future of the Brethren remains open.

References and Further Reading

Bowman, Carl F. *Brethren Society: The Cultural Transformation of a "Peculiar People."* Baltimore: Johns Hopkins University Press, 1995.

Brubaker, Pamela. *She Hath Done What She Could: A History of Women's Participation in the Church of the Brethren.* Elgin, IL: Brethren Press, 1988.

Durnbaugh, Donald F. *Brethren Beginnings: The Origin of the Church of the Brethren in Early Eighteenth-Century Europe.* Philadelphia: Brethren Encyclopedia, Inc., 1992.

———, ed. *The Brethren Encyclopedia.* Oak Brook, IL and Philadelphia: The Brethren Encyclopedia, Inc., 1983.

———. *The Brethren in Colonial America.* Elgin, IL: Brethren Press, 1967.

———. *European Origins of the Brethren.* Elgin, IL: Brethren Press, 1958.

———. *Fruit of the Vine: A History of the Brethren, 1708–1995.* Elgin, IL: Brethren Press, 1997.

Eller, Vernard. *War and Peace from Genesis to Revelation.* Scottdale, PA: Herald Press, 1973, 1981.

Lehman, James H. *The Old Brethren.* Elgin, IL: Brethren Press, 1976.

Sappington, Roger E. *The Brethren in the New Nation.* Elgin, IL: Brethren Press, 1976.

———. *The Brethren in Industrial America.* Elgin, IL: Brethren Press, 1985.

Stoffer, Dale R. *Background and Development of Brethren Doctrines, 1650–1987.* Philadelphia: Brethren Encyclopedia, Inc., 1989.

JEFF BACH

BRITISH AND FOREIGN BIBLE SOCIETY

The British and Foreign Bible Society (BFBS) began as a cross-denominational (though predominantly Evangelical) society in 1804 in London, with the aim of translating and distributing the BIBLE in as many languages as possible. It established numerous overseas territories and agencies, and increased the number of languages in which the Bible is available from 67 in 1804 to more than 2000 by 2000. It quickly became a model for other national BIBLE SOCIETIES to follow. BFBS overcame many difficulties of cross-cultural translation and project viability, but its exclusion of the Apocrypha from translations led to secessions of European and Scottish Societies in the 1820s. With the proliferation of national Bible societies, the 1946 formation of the United Bible Societies (UBS) saw the BFBS reduce its overseas operations, to operate more as one national society among many. While the BFBS's primary objective has been the production and distribution of printed Bibles, its impact has gone further, with contributions to education and literacy, expansion into other media of Bible production, and the development of a research facility in its library at Cambridge University.

Foundation and Purpose

Late eighteenth-century British EVANGELICALISM produced many benevolent societies for the advancement of Christianity. When the Religious Tract Society decided not to distribute Bibles in Welsh, a new society was formed for that purpose. On March 7, 1804, The British and Foreign Bible Society was established in London. It immediately attracted a wide range of cross-denominational support, especially from the Evangelical wing of the CHURCH OF ENGLAND and Nonconformist Churches (see NONCONFORMITY). Its patron was WILLIAM WILBERFORCE, and its foundation membership included such luminaries as GRANVILLE SHARP, Zachary Macauley, and the bishops of London and Salisbury. The Society's aim was to encourage and promote a wider circulation of the Holy Scriptures without note or comment, on a world-wide basis. The 300 people at its first meeting raised a subscription to begin the Society's work of providing Bibles in any language for which there was a readership. This has remained its objective, although the statement of aim has been expanded to embrace more modern situations as "to provide Bibles and Bible-related resources using print and other media; to offer training, information, and advice; to link congregations and individual Christians into the world-wide Church; and to supply specialist back-up services wherever appropriate."

Development

The BFBS organized itself on a committee basis with auxiliaries and agencies throughout the world. The territorial agencies established permanent depots and traveling sales agents, called "colporteurs." By the time of its centenary in 1904, the BFBS employed more than 1,000 overseas staff members and had some 2,000 affiliated societies in the British Dominions. In cooperation with local churches and missionary societies, its main activity has been the translation, printing, and distribution of Bibles or Scripture portions in as many languages as possible. Problems arose regarding cross-cultural communication in translations (including the vexed issue of whether to include explanatory notes) and the practical viability of small readership in many languages. However, the first 20 years of the Society's work progressed smoothly, and its organization and methods became a model for many similar societies in other countries, many of which were supported actively and financially by the BFBS. In 1825–1826, the first significant problem arose, when the German Bible Societies withdrew from the London Committee because the BFBS refused to include the Apocrypha in its translations.

Dissatisfaction with the BFBS's treatment of this issue also saw the secession of the Scottish Societies. The proliferation of Bible societies generated both by the BFBS's auxiliary system and the inevitable tensions within such a broadly based group, as well as independent developments in other countries, led to the formation in 1946 of the United Bible Societies (UBS), a coordinating body set up to achieve greater efficiency in the task of Bible production. Since then, the BFBS has effectively scaled down its overseas role, seeing itself as one among many national Bible societies. It maintains an active role in the UBS, exemplified by the 2002 appointment of BFBS Chief Executive Neil Crosbie to the office of General Secretary of the UBS.

Scope and Influence

The BFBS's work expanded quickly and continuously. This is clearest in the large numbers of translations and distributions of Bibles throughout the world, its formative influence on many national Bible Societies, and its continuing involvement in the UBS. However, the BFBS's influence has exceeded this. It has also contributed to the growth of education and nationalism, as its provision of cheap texts in the vernacular has promoted literacy in developing countries as a byproduct of its primary objective. To embrace the needs of the modern world, the BFBS has branched into various media of biblical production, including audio cassettes, television series, and academic teaching materials. The BFBS has also developed a research culture, particularly with its establishment of a library to acquire and preserve copies of the Bible in all standard editions. Since 1804, it has systematically added all its own editions and acquired numerous private collections of printed Bibles and manuscripts. In 1985, the library was relocated to Cambridge University. The collection of more than 35,000 volumes in more than 2500 languages represented contains all of the historical documents of the BFBS as well as various secondary works and catalogues of biblical production, and as such it constitutes a significant research facility.

See also American Bible Society; Bible Translation; Wycliff Bible Translators

References and Further Reading

Browne, George. *The History of the British and Foreign Bible Society, From Its Institution in 1804, to the Close of its Jubilee in 1854.* 2 vols. London: British and Foreign Bible Society, 1859.

Canton, William. *A History of the British and Foreign Bible Society.* 5 vols. London: John Murray, 1904–1910.

Howsam, Leslie. *Cheap Bibles: Nineteenth Century Publishing and the British and Foreign Bible Society.* Cambridge, UK: Cambridge University Press, 1991.
Roe, James Moulton. *A History of the British and Foreign Bible Society, 1905–1954.* London: The Society, 1965.

LES J. BALL

BRITISH COUNCIL OF CHURCHES

The British Council of Churches (BCC) was formed in 1942 by the merger of the Council on the Christian Faith and the Common Life, the Commission of the Churches for International Friendship, and the British Section of the World Conference on Faith and Order. Its objects were common action in EVANGELISM, youth work, social responsibility, and the promotion of international friendship. It also became the main link between the British churches and the WORLD COUNCIL OF CHURCHES. Sixteen churches and interdenominational agencies such as the YMCA, YWCA, and SCM (Student Christian Movement) became members. The first President was Archbishop WILLIAM TEMPLE.

The BCC's response to the postwar world was shown in two early reports, *The Era of Atomic Power* and *Christian Witness in the Post-War World* (1946). A new department for interchurch aid and refugees illustrated its practical concerns. In 1957 Christian Aid week in May was initiated to support this; local Christian Aid committees were often the nuclei of support for local councils of churches, which numbered 300 by 1960.

In September 1964 the BCC held a British Faith and Order Conference at Nottingham. The proposal that the churches should covenant together "in appropriate groupings such as nations" to work and pray for unity by an agreed date (suggested as Easter Day 1980) led to different developments in ENGLAND, WALES, and SCOTLAND. More significant was the idea of Areas of Ecumenical Experiment, subsequently termed Local Ecumenical Projects (more recently Partnerships), in which congregations of different traditions could come together. The Sharing of Church Buildings Act (1969) facilitated this process, which rapidly became the main way of establishing churches in new housing areas.

After the Second Vatican Council the Roman Catholic Church was invited to appoint consultants (1968) and Roman Catholics joined many local councils of churches, the number of which doubled in the 1960s. Pope John Paul II's visit to Great Britain in 1983 encouraged Roman Catholics to consider membership in the Council. A major conference in 1987, "Not Strangers but Pilgrims," led to the dissolution of the BCC in 1990 and its replacement by a Council of Churches for Britain and Ireland, with the Roman Catholic Churches in England, Wales, and Scotland as full members. A new council (Churches Together in England) was set up, and the Welsh, Scottish, and Irish Councils were reshaped. The separate departments were abolished; and Christian Aid, whose annual turnover and staff were much larger than any other part of the Council, became a separate agency.

See also Ecumenism; Evangelism;

References and Further Reading

Churches Together in Pilgrimage. London: BCC/CTS, 1989.
Palmer, Derek. *Strangers No Longer.* London: Hodder & Stoughton, 1990.
Payne, E. A. *Thirty Years of the British Council of Churches, 1942–1972.* London: BCC, 1972.
Templeton, Elizabeth. *God's February: A Life of Archie Craig 1888–1985.* London: BCC/CCBI, 1991.

DAVID M. THOMPSON

BRITTEN, EDWARD BENJAMIN (1913–1976)

British composer. Britten, born at Lowestoft, England, on November 22, 1913, was demonstrably the most influential English composer of the mid-twentieth century. Culturally a member of the CHURCH OF ENGLAND, his attitude toward the established church was ambivalent. Instead, his musical life was dominated by his public PACIFISM, his concern with musical education, and his private, complex, and intentionally hidden love for men and boys. Britten wrote few pieces specifically for the liturgy: for Anglican Morning Prayer, two settings of Psalm 100 (1934 and 1961), and two settings of the hymn *Te Deum Laudamus* (1935 and 1943); for Roman Catholic use, a setting of Psalm 95 (1961) and a *Missa Brevis* (1959); and for occasional use, six short anthems. However, he wrote sacred music (often for church performance) throughout his career, notably five cantatas (*A Ceremony of Carols,* 1942; *Hymn to St. Cecilia,* 1942; *Rejoice in the Lamb,* 1943; *St. Nicholas,* 1948; and *Cantata misericordium,* 1964); a church opera (*Noye's Fludde,* 1958); and three "church parables" (*Curlew River,* 1964; *The Burning Fiery Furnace,* 1966; and *The Prodigal Son,* 1968). Furthermore, his music for solo voices includes settings of religious poetry of JOHN DONNE, T. S. ELIOT, and W.H. AUDEN, among others. Britten's best-known sacred work (*A War Requiem,* written in 1962 for the newly rebuilt Coventry Cathedral) juxtaposes the traditional *missa pro defunctis* with Wilfred Owen's bitter poems condemning the follies of war. Like Britten's operas (especially *Peter Grimes,* 1945; *Billy Budd,* 1954; *The Turn of the Screw,* 1954; *Owen Wingrave,* 1970; and *Death in Venice,* 1973), his larger sacred works display his incisive social and political critique (often of the church), which is characterized by a passionate appeal for justice for victimized adults and innocent victims.

Britten died December 4, 1976, at Aldeburgh, England.

Reference and Further Reading

Brett, Philip. "Britten, (Edward) Benjamin." In *The New Grove Dictionary of Music Online,* edited by L. Macy. http://www.grovemusic.com (Jan. 14, 2003).

WILLIAM FLYNN

BROAD CHURCH

The term "Broad Church" was used to describe those members of the CHURCH OF ENGLAND (and to a lesser extent other parts of the Anglican world) who emphasize the broad, liberal, and inclusive nature of ANGLICANISM. The term has tended to function within the Church of England in a way similar to the use of the term "Liberal" among other religious bodies. The Broad Church position stands against the "High Church" emphasis on the Catholic and sacramental nature of the Anglican system with its elevated view of episcopal and priestly ministry, and the "Low Church" emphasis on the Protestant nature of the Anglican system.

Although there have been individuals throughout the history of ANGLICANISM who have emphasized the rational and inclusive nature of their tradition, the term Broad Church came in vogue in the middle of the nineteenth century during the height of the High Church/Low Church conflicts stirred by the Catholic revival of the OXFORD MOVEMENT. The Broad Church agenda was twofold. The first was to argue that the church should be comprehensive and tolerant concerning points of theological and doctrinal controversies and to admit varieties of opinion. They opposed any idea of subscription to specific statements of belief. The second (often only implicit) was that this broadness and inclusivity should be used to help address the new intellectual challenges to inherited belief, by rethinking traditional formularies in light of modern intellectual advances. Broad Church spokespersons argued in particular for an openness to the new science represented by Charles Darwin (see DARWINISM) and the new historical approach to the study of the BIBLE. *Essays and Reviews* (1860), the first work in English to incorporate elements of the new biblical criticism, is considered one of the most noteworthy of the Broad Church productions. Although the impulse has continued to mark an important strain of Anglicanism, by the twentieth century the term began to be less used, being replaced by the category Modernist.

See also Liberal Protestantism and Liberalism; Modernism

References and Further Reading

Chadwick, Owen. *The Victorian Church.* 2 vols. New York: Oxford, 1966–1970.
Reardon, Bernard M. G. *Religious Thought in the Victoria Age: A Survey from Coleridge to Gore.* New York: Longman, 1995.
Warre Cornish, F. *The English Church in the Nineteenth Century.* 2 vols. London: Macmillan, 1910.

ROBERT BRUCE MULLIN

BROOKS, PHILLIPS (1835–1893)

Popular American preacher and briefly Episcopal bishop of Massachusetts. Brooks was born in Boston on December 13, 1835, into an old, well-established New England family. He attended Boston Latin School and Harvard College, graduating from the latter in 1855. At Harvard and thereafter, Brooks read widely in Romantic literature, which would prove to have a significant influence on him. Brooks chose to pursue seminary training for the ministry of the Protestant Episcopal Church and enrolled in Virginia Theological Seminary at Alexandria. The seminary had spearheaded evangelical renewal within the Episcopal Church, although Brooks found it disappointing academically. Upon graduation in 1859, he served two Episcopal churches in Philadelphia. During and immediately after the CIVIL WAR, Brooks, who was an outspoken supporter of President ABRAHAM LINCOLN, won a reputation for pulpit eloquence. In 1869 he accepted a call to pastor Trinity Church in Boston, and it was here that his fame as a powerful preacher blossomed. He died January 23, 1893.

Although Brooks had moved in evangelical circles since his boyhood at St. Paul's, by the 1870s he had identified himself with the emerging liberal BROAD CHURCH party. Among his more important theological influences were SAMUEL TAYLOR COLERIDGE, FREDERICK DENISON MAURICE, and HORACE BUSHNELL. Brooks's *Lectures on Preaching* (1877), delivered at Yale Divinity School and later published, also proved to be popular among a wide spectrum of Protestants, both conservatives and theological liberals. Brooks's revealing definition of preaching as "the bringing of truth through personality" appealed to Romantic sensibilities and fed the pulpit celebritism of his day. Brooks continues to be known for the words of the popular Christmas carol "O Little Town of Bethlehem."

Brooks was elected bishop of Massachusetts in 1891 over the opposition of conservative High Church clergy; he served as bishop until his untimely death in 1893. Several volumes of Brooks's sermons were published in his lifetime.

References and Further Reading

Primary Source:

Brooks, Phillips. *The Yale Lectures on Preaching*. New York: E. P. Dutton, 1907.

Secondary Sources:

Albright, Raymond. *Focus on Infinity: A Life of Phillips Brooks*. New York: Macmillan, 1961.
Allen, A. V. G., ed. *The Life and Letters of Phillips Brooks*. 3 vols. New York: E. P. Dutton, 1901.
Lawrence, William. *Life of Phillips Brooks*. New York: Harper, 1930.
Woolverton, John F. *The Education of Phillips Brooks*. Urbana: University of Illinois Press, 1995.

GILLIS J. HARP

BROWNE, ROBERT (1550–1633)

English separatist. Born in 1550 at Tolethorpe, in Lincolnshire, Robert Browne is considered by many to have been the founder of the English Puritan Separatist tradition. Browne's pilgrimage into radical religion began in the early 1570s during student days at Cambridge University. There he fell under the influence of THOMAS CARTWRIGHT, a university lecturer who denounced episcopacy in favor of PRESBYTERIANISM. While preaching in and around Cambridge without episcopal authorization, Browne clashed with authorities about his views that only congregations—not a bishop—had the right to appoint pastors. Convinced that a true church could not exist within the unreformed English parish system, Browne formed a congregationally oriented church of his own at Norwich in the spring of 1581.

Browne expressed his ecclesial vision in his best known publication, *A Treatise of Reformation without Tarrying for Any,* in 1582. He said that a true CHURCH was composed of visible believers, separated from the world and voluntarily joined together by a covenant made with God and one another. Imprisoned at Norwich for his Separatist activities, Browne was freed through the intervention of an influential relative, William Cecil, Lord Burghley. Along with his coreligionist, Robert Harrison, and members of the Norwich congregation, Browne then fled to Middelburg in the NETHERLANDS. Once there Browne and Harrison quarreled over several issues, including whether the children of congregants should be regarded as members. Disillusioned and embittered by controversy, Browne moved in 1583 to SCOTLAND, then back to ENGLAND. After further trouble and another imprisonment, Browne recanted Separatism in 1586 and made peace with the church he had rejected five years earlier.

In 1591 he received Episcopal ordination and became rector of Thorpe Achurch, where he remained until his death in 1633. Browne's writings formed the mainstream of future Separatist ecclesiology, out of which would come both Baptist and Congregational forms of Protestantism in seventeenth-century England and New England.

See also Baptists; Bishop and Episcopacy; Congregationalism; Dissent; Puritanism

References and Further Reading

Primary Source:

Peel, Albert, and Leland H. Carlson, eds. *The Writings of Robert Harrison and Robert Browne*. London: Allen & Unwin, 1951.

Secondary Sources:

Brachlow, Stephen. *The Communion of Saints: Radical Puritan and Separatist Ecclesiology*. Oxford: Oxford University Press, 1988.
Burrage, Champlin. *The True Story of Robert Browne*. London: Frowde, 1906.
White, B. R. *The English Separatist Tradition*. London: Oxford University Press, 1971.

STEPHEN BRACHLOW

BROWNING, ROBERT (1812–1889)

English poet. Browning's life did not merely span the transformation of Britain from an aristocratic and agrarian into a modern industrial society but also saw the displacement of poetry as the dominant art form. When we think of ROMANTICISM, we think of poetry; when we think of Victorian literature, we think primarily of its prose. In this changing aesthetic climate Browning's creation of the dramatic monologue (beginning with the chillingly psychopathic *Porphyria's Lover* [1836]) was to give a new psychological and interpretative role to poetry, opening the way to the modernistic experiments of Thomas Hardy and T. S. ELIOT.

Although his robust Protestantism is obvious in its skeptical mockery of Renaissance Italian Catholicism (*The Bishop Orders his Tomb*) and even more so of its modern counterpart (*Bishop Blougram's Apology*), at a much more profound level his originality of poetic form is matched by originality of theological thought. The interior space and interpretative freedom of the individual begun by the REFORMATION had created in the Romantics a new kind of interiority. For Browning, who openly declared that a poet's business was with man's soul, that was to lead directly to a new psychological interest in both the characters of his own society, and of past figures whose roles had hitherto been symbolic and typological. With people like Karshish—an imaginary doctor investigating the raising of Lazarus—or St. John, in *A Death in the Desert*—he attempted to understand the states of mind of those who had actually witnessed the events of the New Testament. Opposed equally to evangelicals who stressed God's punishments over his love, and evolutionists who stressed protoplasmic origins over what he saw as humanity's divine destiny, Browning sometimes preaches too much, and sometimes misreads current debates, although his humor and realism rarely permitted facile optimism, and never allowed despair.

See also Darwinism; Evangelicalism; Individualism; Modernism

References and Further Reading

Halliday, F. E. *Robert Browning: His Life and Work.* London: Jupiter Books, 1975.
Hawlin, Stefan. *The Complete Critical Guide to Robert Browning.* London and New York: Routledge, 2002.

STEPHEN PRICKETT

BROWNSON, ORESTES AUGUSTUS (1803–1876)

Brownson was a Universalist, Unitarian, and Transcendentalist minister, religious thinker, and editor until 1844, when he converted to Roman Catholicism. He was born in Stockbridge, Vermont on September 16, 1803.

Brownson was a restless religious pilgrim whose life and thought for the first half of his career reflected the plasticity of American religious identification during the early nineteenth century. He identified himself first with the Presbyterian tradition (see PRESBYTERIANISM), and then he moved in turn to Universalism, to social radicalism, to Unitarianism, and to Transcendentalism. As a young Universalist minister, Brownson fostered through the pulpit and the press three fundamental affirmations of the emerging liberal Protestant tradition in America: the dignity of humanity, religious liberty, and free religious inquiry. He struggled, however, to reconcile these affirmations with the conceptions of the sovereignty and benevolent fatherhood of God that he had also received from his Reformed religious heritage. By his early thirties, under the influence of the French social and Romantic-idealist philosophical tradition, he reacted against the excessive rationalism of his early years and began to emphasize the religious humanism of clergyman WILLIAM ELLERY CHANNING (1780–1842) and the Transcendentalism of essayist and poet RALPH WALDO EMERSON (1803–1882). By his early forties, under the influence of the French St. Simonian Pierre Leroux, he moved away from the liberal Christian tradition and the Romantic individualism of Transcendentalism, emphasizing instead ecclesial communion and tradition, and the necessity of the church in the process of SALVATION, SANCTIFICATION, and reform. This theolog-

ical change led him into the Catholic Church in 1844. He died in Detroit, Michigan on April 17, 1876.

References and Further Reading

Primary Source:

Brownson, Henry F., ed. *The Works of Orestes A. Brownson.* 20 vols. Detroit: H. F. Brownson, Publisher, 1898.

Secondary Sources:

Patrick W., comp. *Orestes A. Brownson: A Bibliography, 1826–1876.* Milwaukee: Carey, 1997.
Ryan, Thomas R. *Orestes A. Brownson: A Definitive Biography.* Huntington, IN: Our Sunday Visitor. 1976.
Schlesinger, Arthur M., Jr. *Orestes A. Brownson: A Pilgrim's Progress.* Boston: Little Brown, 1939.

PATRICK W. CAREY

BRUDERHOF

See Society of Brothers

BRUNNER, EMIL (1889–1966)

Swiss theologian. Emil Brunner was born in Winterthur, SWITZERLAND, on December 23, 1889. He was educated in Zurich, Berlin, and New York (Union Theological Seminary), before becoming professor of theology in Zurich (1924–1966). His career included periods as visiting professor at Princeton Theological Seminary (1938–1939) and the Christian University of Japan (1953–1955). Brunner died in Zurich on April 6, 1966.

Brunner was one of the central thinkers of modern European Protestantism, and a key figure in the emergence of dialectical theology (see NEO-ORTHODOXY) in the 1920s and 1930s. During that period of significant change and development Brunner's work made an important contribution to the rejection of theological liberalism and the reassertion of God's essential Otherness. Unlike his near-contemporaries KARL BARTH (1886–1968) and RUDOLF BULTMANN (1884–1976), however, Brunner did not remain at the forefront of theological inquiry. The advent of political theologies in the 1960s was inimitable to Brunner's more abstract work, and his books are now little studied. The reasons for this situation, and the cause of Brunner's initial impact, are contained within the basic structures of his philosophical theology.

Central to any understanding of Brunner's thought is *Wahrheit als Begegnung* (1938), published in English in 1943 as *The Divine-Human Encounter*. In this study in theological epistemology Brunner asked the question, "How do we know God?" and answered that knowledge of God arises from an encounter between the individual and the Risen Lord, in the power of the

Holy Spirit. This encounter is conditioned by Christianity's eschatological character, by which the experience of today's believer is qualitatively the same as that of the first Christians. Christian truth therefore confronts the individual with the moment of decision, in which God encounters them and they are saved.

From this methodological insight Brunner recognized two substantive questions: "Who is the Risen Lord?" and "Who is the individual?" Brunner's Reformed Protestant upbringing had conditioned him to give a straightforward answer to the first question. The Risen Lord is the crucified Jesus of Nazareth, the Word of God. The Word is entirely other than the world, yet comes to the world (John 1:14) to save those who believe. This dialectical event is good news, the Gospel of redemption in which Christ is revealed as the medium by which God and humanity are joined, thereby paradoxically binding together and yet separating God and humanity. In doing so, this same Gospel both fulfils and annuls the Law, bringing to the world the possibility of new creation in Christ (II Corinthians 5:17).

A significant corollary of Brunner's understanding of revelation is that humanity needs reason to understand the possibility of SALVATION, which is why Brunner argued that although human reason can never reach God, it can approach Him (an argument that provoked Barth's infamous "Nein!" in 1934). Brunner's use of reason at this point in his theological system is entirely plausible, an acknowledgment that God's order remains inherent to creation and that although he rejects any notion of natural theology, nevertheless it is possible to perceive that creation is knowable because it is ordered. Brunner reasons that if one does not hold that this is the case, then one has no basis on which to argue that people can recognize the Word as the Word of salvation.

This conviction about the relationship of revelation to reason underpins Brunner's theological anthropology, in which his work was heavily influenced by such religious thinkers as JOHANN HAMANN, SØREN KIERKEGAARD, Johann J. Griesbach, Ferdinand Ebner, and Martin Buber. Much has been made of Brunner's apparent religious EXISTENTIALISM, yet it can be reduced to a conviction that the personal God encounters human persons as another person, Jesus of Nazareth. This is possible, argues Brunner, because humanity's essence is God-relatedness, a quality that one must understand existentially and therefore historically (not theoretically). Brunner finds this religious personalism in the BIBLE, most explicitly in the Pauline epistles, where he also finds an understanding of FAITH as a particular form of human existence in which the individual acknowledges that he/she does not belong to him/herself, but belongs to the Risen Lord. This biblical personalism emphasizes both

the transforming GRACE of encountering Jesus Christ and the need to understand humanity's fallen nature as the immediate context for that encounter, and lies at the heart of Brunner's theology.

Although Brunner was a key figure in the development of dialectical theology, his well-known arguments with Barth cast light on any evaluation of Brunner's abiding significance. Like Barth, Brunner wanted to address the kerygmatic necessity of encountering God the Other, and he shared Barth's belief that this was the only way in which the individual could be saved. Unlike Barth, however, Brunner was also convinced that the task of THEOLOGY was to service the church with the deepest possible understanding of human nature, particularly its existential predicament and its yearning for salvation, so that the church might help people to understand, and thereby turn back toward God. Barth condemned this endeavor, although that condemnation should not influence judgment of Brunner's motivation.

The more significant intellectual weakness of Brunner's position is that it presents too reified an understanding of human existence: what appeared in the 1930s and 1940s to be a bold appreciation of the central characteristics of life now appears naïve and obsolete. In this respect Brunner, to some extent like Bultmann, was himself an important mediation between the theological and philosophical concerns of his era. If his program no longer finds favor, it is as much for the now deeply unfashionable philosophical questions that Brunner asked as for the theological answers he gave.

See also Eschatology; Individualism; Liberal Protestantism and Liberalism; Theology, Twentieth Century

References and Further Reading

Primary Sources:

Brunner, Emil. *The Divine-Human Encounter.* Translated by Amandus W. Loos. London: SCM Press, 1944.
———. *Revelation and Reason.* Translated by Olive Wyon. London: SCM Press, 1946.
———. *The Divine Imperative.* Translated by Olive Wyon. London: Lutterworth Press, 1937.
———. *The Mediator.* Translated by Olive Wyon. London: Lutterworth Press, 1934.
———. *Dogmatics.* 3 vols. Translated by Olive Wyon (I and II) and David Cairns (III). London: Lutterworth Press, 1949; 1952; 1962.

Secondary Sources:

Hart, John W. *Karl Barth Vs. Emil Brunner: The Formation and Dissolution of a Theological Alliance 1916–1936.* New York: Peter Lang, 2001.
McKim, Mark G., ed. *Emil Brunner: A Bibliography.* Lanham, MD: Scarecrow Press, 1997.

Schuurman, Douglas James. *Creation, Eschaton, and Ethics: The Ethical Significance of the Creation-Eschaton Relation in the Thought of Emil Brunner and Jürgen Moltmann.* New York: Peter Lang, 1991.

GARETH JONES

BRYAN, WILLIAM JENNINGS (1860–1925)

American statesman and lay theologian. A vigorous exponent of both the SOCIAL GOSPEL and biblical FUNDAMENTALISM, William Jennings Bryan was a unique figure in the Progressive Era of the United States. He ran three times unsuccessfully as the Democratic candidate for president (1896, 1900, and 1908). His stirring oratory and massive following made him the leading figure in his party until the election of Woodrow Wilson in 1912, and he did much to transform the Democrats into advocates of modern liberalism (using the power of the state to aid farmers, small businessmen, and wage earners). He also served as Secretary of State from 1913 to 1915, resigning his post to protest the Wilson administration's tilt against GERMANY after the sinking of the Lusitania.

Bryan, one of the most popular speakers of his day, alternated speeches defending Christianity with ones boosting such reforms as corporate regulation and the popular election of senators. During the final decade of his life, the "Great Commoner" campaigned energetically in the service of moralist causes, particularly for prohibition and against the growing influence of DARWINISM. He died on July 26, 1925 in Dayton, Tennessee, several days after leading the prosecution in the Scopes trial.

Politics and Beliefs

Bryan was born in Salem, Illinois on March 19, 1860, heir to the populist tradition of the Democratic Party and to evangelical piety. His parents attended separate churches, his father Baptist and his mother Methodist, but the family prayed together three times a day, and each child was expected to hew to spiritual discipline. At the age of fourteen, William attended a Presbyterian revival with some friends and then helped form a congregation within that church. He would remain a Presbyterian for the rest of his life. In the 1920s he battled against "modernists" in the church who sought to revise the stern dicta of the WESTMINSTER CONFESSION, but he always refused to engage in interdenominational conflicts. He often attended other Protestant churches and sternly denounced anti-Catholic prejudice.

More than any other politician of his day, Bryan routinely drew on Scripture to underline the righteousness of his own views. "If my party has given me the basis of my political beliefs," he concluded in 1924, speaking at his last Democratic convention, "my Bible has given me the foundations of a faith that has enabled me to stand for the right as I saw it."

Bryan brought this vision of democracy as expressed in the Good Book to bear on every major issue he cared about. In 1899, to press the case that employers should pay higher wages, he declared, "God made all men, and he did not make some to crawl on hands and knees and others to ride upon their backs." A year later, while opposing, on anticolonialist grounds, the U.S. war against Filipinos fighting for their independence, he asked, "If true Christianity consists in carrying out in our daily lives the teachings of Christ, who will say that we are commanded to civilize with dynamite and proselyte [sic] with the sword?" In 1908, to underline the urgency of breaking up trusts, he told a Carnegie Hall audience, "I insist that the commandment, 'Thou shalt not steal' applies as much to the monopolist as to the highwayman."

Bryan's Theology

Although Bryan's theology was fundamentalist, he endorsed the practical remedies to society's ills proposed by such liberal Social Gospelers as WASHINGTON GLADDEN (1836–1918) and WALTER RAUSCHENBUSCH (1861–1918). He also cooperated with the Federal Council of Churches, the bastion of Protestant reform activism founded in 1908.

Neither did Bryan take a stand in the clash between premillennial and postmillenial visions of the Second Coming. He once quipped "that there were too many people who didn't believe in the first coming of Christ to worry about those who didn't believe in the second." An optimistic Democrat, he was convinced that ordinary people could steadily improve the social and the spiritual condition of the world, yet he also believed that evil forces would suffer retribution and grew alarmed, after the cataclysm of World War I, about what he perceived as the growing influence of amoral secularism in American culture.

In the 1920s Bryan became involved in a series of clashes with Protestant modernists like HARRY EMERSON FOSDICK (1878–1969). Bryan insisted that the fundamentalist creed of the majority ought to prevail in the public sphere. His positions generated the scorn of H. L. Mencken (1880–1956) and numerous other secular and liberal critics. Bryan was firmly convinced that any nation that allowed destructive, unchristian practices to flourish was a nation on the road to ruin. Few theistic modernists objected when he applied this view to attacks on the liquor "trust." The demand for prohibition enjoyed support from nearly every Protestant denomination. Far more controversial was

Bryan's decision to throw his declining energies into the crusade against Darwinism.

Bryan objected to evolutionary theory on the grounds of what might be called sentimental democracy as well as on his faith in the literal truth of the Bible. He feared that agnostic intellectuals were seeking to substitute a cruel belief in "the struggle of the fittest" for faith in a loving God—the only basis for moral and altruistic conduct for most ordinary people. Bryan, like many other Americans at the time, collapsed Darwinism into social Darwinism, particularly the variety articulated by influential scientists in the early twentieth century who, for example, promoted eugenics as the surest way to improve the human race. The consequence, the evangelical populist predicted, in a speech he did not live to deliver, would be "a system under which a few supposedly superior intellects, self-appointed, would direct the mating and the movements of the mass of mankind—an impossible system!" Hitler's grisly embrace of eugenics, both in theory and practice, suggests that Bryan's fear was not entirely misplaced.

Bryan's lasting historical significance is as a prophetic layman who eloquently and tirelessly warned of threats to the interests and beliefs of white Christians from the working and middle classes. His sincerity, warmth, and messianic ardor won him the hearts of many Americans who cared deeply for no other politician in the 1890s and first quarter of the twentieth century.

References and Further Reading

Bryan, Mary Baird, and William Jennings Bryan. *The Memoirs of William Jennings Bryan*. Chicago: John C. Winston, 1925.

Bryan, William Jennings. *In His Image*. New York: Fleming H. Revell, 1922.

Coletta, Paolo, *William Jennings Bryan*. 3 vols. Lincoln: University of Nebraska Press, 1964, 1969, 1969.

Larson, Edward J. *Summer for the Gods: The Scopes Trial and America's Continuing Debate over Science and Religion*. New York: Basic Books, 1997.

Russell, C. Allyn, "William Jennings Bryan: Statesman-Fundamentalist." In *Voices of American Fundamentalism: Seven Biographical Studies*. Philadelphia: The Westminster Press, 1976. 162–189.

MICHAEL KAZIN

BUCER, MARTIN (1491–1551)

(Original surname Butzer. Pseudonyms: Aretius Felinus, Conrad Trew von Fridesleven, Waremund Luithold)

German reformer. Bucer, the reformer, shaper of ecclesiastical policy, and irenic theologian, was born on November 11, 1491, in Sélestat, a city in the Alsace region of GERMANY. He grew up in a modest home, but he did attend the reputable Latin School in his hometown. He entered the Dominican order in 1507, which committed him to an academic career, and he was sent to Heidelberg in 1517 to complete his general studies. There, in April 1518 he met MARTIN LUTHER, who had come to attend a meeting of the Augustinian order. The disputation, which Luther conducted, won Bucer over to Luther's theology. This did not mean, however, that he abandoned his own theological views. Indeed ideas from Thomas Aquinas, Erasmus of Rotterdam, and Luther merged in Bucer's THEOLOGY. These sources formed his understanding of JUSTIFICATION according to which the sinner was justified on the basis of FAITH in Jesus Christ. The justified individual became a new person whose faith in the Holy Spirit enabled him/her to live not for him/herself but to serve all humankind. By emphasizing the social-ethical dimension of REFORMATION teachings, Bucer sought to initiate a comprehensive transformation of society.

Bucer's embracing Luther's ideas placed him into a difficult situation. After some effort he obtained a dispensation from his monastic vows and served for a while as a secular priest in the service of the imperial knight Franz von Sickingen. In the summer of 1522 Bucer married Elisabeth Silbereisen, a former nun, and in November he attempted to bring the city of Weissenburg (Wissembourg) over to the side of the Reformation. He was, however, unsuccessful. In May 1523 he fled with his wife as an excommunicated priest to Strasbourg.

In this Alsatian metropolis he placed himself in the service of Luther's followers, including Matthäus Zell, WOLFGANG FABRICIUS CAPITO, and Kaspar Hedio. He worked with enormous energy as a minister, BIBLE interpreter, translator of the writings of other reformers, especially Luther, and versatile popular writer on theology. When the city council prohibited the celebration of Mass in 1529, Strasbourg moved officially to the side of the Reformation. At this time Bucer was also vigorously engaged with HULDRYCH ZWINGLI's notion that questioned the bodily presence of Christ in the bread and wine of the LORD'S SUPPER.

After 1529 Bucer saw the necessity of changing the theological and political position taken by him and the city of Strasbourg, particularly when the Diet of Augsburg in 1530 made clear the city's theological and political isolation. The Lutheran princes and theologians refused to allow Strasbourg to sign on to the AUGSBURG CONFESSION (Confessio Augustana). Zwingli's death in 1531 worsened Strasbourg's difficulties. Bucer tried every way to reconcile with Luther and Wittenberg without giving up his own point of view and his connection to the Swiss position held by Zwingli. For Bucer, Luther's concept of the unity of the Sacrament (*unio sacramentalis*) seemed best suited to formulate the question of how Christ is present at the LORD'S SUPPER—a mystery that one can approach from various sides and a question one can formulate in various ways. Bucer never tired of proposing new methods, and his reputation unmistakably suffered. Not all adversaries were prepared to see him as an honest broker who wanted to unify the position of reform. However, in May 1536 Bucer succeeded in unifying the Protestants' position on the LORD'S SUPPER. Most German cities in the south agreed to the concord, but the Swiss did not.

In his effort to secure a unified position, Bucer greatly broadened his theological views, and his reputation grew in Strasbourg and southern Germany. He was enlisted by the cities of Ulm (1531), Frankfurt (1533), and Augsburg (1534/1537) to serve as counsel and organizer of ecclesiastical policy. Bucer established good relations with foreign rulers such as HENRY VIII OF ENGLAND (1531) and the King of FRANCE (1534–1535). He also developed a close relationship with PHILIPP OF HESSE. Bucer reorganized ecclesiastical life in Hesse, introduced CONFIRMATION as a part of the CHURCH, and succeeded in returning a considerable number of Anabaptists to the Hessian church.

In 1533, while he was working to consolidate the Reformation in Strasbourg, an agreement was reached concerning a confession of faith. In 1534 an ecclesiastical order was established and Bucer published his first CATECHISM. In 1538 the Latin grammar schools in the city were reorganized, and the humanist Johannes Sturm became their director. Other important figures taught there, most notably JOHN CALVIN.

After 1539 Bucer's activities in theological and ecclesiastical matters widened and changed in emphasis. All of his skills had been employed to reconcile the people to shared theological positions. He now came into conflict with orthodox believers, and this caused renewed criticism and mistrust among his own ranks. However, so long as the preaching of the Gospel was allowed, Bucer was convinced that the crucial elements for implementing the Reformation were in place. With great vigor he attempted to establish a national council not led by the pope. As spokesperson for this new understanding, he wrote reports, pamphlets, and (anonymous) dialogues. In 1540 during the Colloquy of Worms, at the bidding of the emperor, he secretly worked on a document with the Catholic theologian Johannes Gropper. This was to provide the basis for comprehensive unification of the church. Early in 1541 an agreement was reached in Regensburg on the DOCTRINE of justification, but the question of ecclesiastical offices and the celebration of the Mass prevented full agreement. Bucer was not demor-

alized, however, and sought, together with the archbishop of Cologne, Hermann of Wied, to effect a program of church reform in his jurisdiction. Military pressure from the emperor, however, destroyed the political agreements required for such wide-ranging plans to succeed. The decisions made at the Council of Trent regarding the doctrine of justification (1545) concluded the era of theological colloquies.

The defeat of the Protestants in the Smalkaldic War (1546–1547) resulted in a call for self-criticism and penitence in Strasbourg. Bucer supported the "Christian community" that arose in this setting in certain church parishes. People agreed to live virtuous lives. At the same time Bucer was passionately fighting against accepting the Interim of the victorious emperor. When Strasbourg surrendered, Bucer fled to England in April 1549. He was received with great honors and was appointed a professor at Cambridge University. Bucer died during the night between February 28 and March 1, 1551, in Cambridge.

Bucer dedicated his final energies to composing *De regno Christi,* a massive theological and political treatise on reform. Again he outlined the objective that had defined his life: that devout Christians in vigorous communities will comprehensively transform both the church and the world.

Bucer's theology was principally a theology of dialogue. The full life requires the individual and the community to hear the demands and receive the support of others. This made Bucer an advocate of religious and political tolerance. His sensibility for both the powerful and the possible worked toward the same goal. Bucer belongs among the reformers who included all of Europe in their vision of reform, not just the church and political policies within the German empire. Accordingly his impact on other theologians, among them Calvin, was wide-ranging.

See also Anabaptism; Dialogue, Interconfessional; Lutheranism; Orthodoxy; Toleration

References and Further Reading

Primary Source:

Bucer, Martin. *Opera omnia.* Series 1: *Deutsche Schriften,* 13 vols. Gütersloh: Mohn, 1960–; series 2: *Opera Latina.* 5 vols. Paris and Leiden: Brill, 1955–; series 3: *Korrespondenz.* 4 vols. Leiden: Brill, 1979–.

Secondary Sources:

Greschat, Martin. *Martin Bucer.* Munich: Beck, 1990.
Krieger, Christian, and Marc Lienhard, eds. *Martin Bucer and Sixteenth Century Europe.* 2 vols. Leiden: Brill, 1993.

MARTIN GRESCHAT

BUGENHAGEN, JOHANNES
(1485–1558)

Protestant theologian and reformer. Born in 1485 at Wollin in the Dukedom of Pomerania, and hence called *Pomeranus* ("the Pomerian"), Bugenhagen was one of the founding fathers of the Lutheran church and influenced large parts of Protestantism (see LUTHERANISM). His endeavors came into effect predominantly in northern GERMANY, Scandinavia, and the Baltic States; he even influenced the south of Germany and southern Europe with his numerous biblical commentaries and tracts. As a teacher at the city school at Treptow on the Rega from 1505 (and a vicar at St. Mary's Church from 1517), and a lecturer at the monastery of Belbuck, he came to embrace humanist ideas, which called for a sound knowledge of philology as the basic means for the interpretation of the BIBLE. Additionally he embraced the Erasmian notion of the *Philosophia Christi*. This is how he found his way to the REFORMATION.

Influenced by MARTIN LUTHER's and PHILLIPP MELANCHTHON's teachings, he started shaping the structures of the Protestant church in 1523 as the first protestant rector at Wittenberg in accordance with the ministry of an evangelical bishop. His organizational gifts were made obvious in the church orders he composed, which in the sixteenth century had an enormous impact on the cities of Braunschweig, Hamburg, and Lübeck (in 1528, 1529, and 1531, respectively) and the territories of Pomerania, DENMARK, Schleswig-Holstein, and Braunschweig-Wolfenbüttel (in 1535, 1537–1539, 1542, and 1544, respectively).

His academically based religious attitude had been demonstrated in his *Harmony of the Accounts of the Four Gospels of the Passion and Resurrection of Jesus Christ,* which was printed several times after 1524 to 1526 and was widely accepted as a popular book of devotion until the seventeenth century. In his instructions for sermons he offered substantial help concerning theological clarity to the new protestant preachers. As his exegesis was oriented toward pastoral practice, his early commentaries on Psalms, St. Paul's letters, and the books of the Old Testament (1524–1527) met with widespread response. Bugenhagen not only was a philologist and pastor, but he also proved to be a skillful administrator in the Reformation reorganization of church and society after 1528. He mediated the conflict between the Duke of Pomerania and the Elector of Saxony. Mayors and princes often asked him for advice; in particular, he was on cordial terms with the King of Denmark, Christian III, who was interested in theology. His fundamental opponents were the papacy and Roman Catholicism. All in all, he contributed to the formation of a protestant identity.

Bugenhagen was a professor of biblical exegesis at the University of Wittenberg until his death in 1558.

References and Further Reading

Hauschild, Wolf-Dieter. "Bugenhagen, Johannes." In *Oxford Encyclopedia of the Reformation,* edited by Hans J. Hillerbrand, vol. 1. New York: Oxford University Press, 1996.

Holfelder, Hans Hermann. "Bugenhagen, Johannes." *Theologische Realenzyklopädie* 7 (1981): 354–363.

Vogt, Karl August Traugott. *Johannes Bugenhagen Pomeranus: Leben und ausgewählte Schriften, Elberfeld 1867.* Bibliography of the printed works, published in the sixteenth century: *Bibliotheca Bugenhagiana. Bibliographie der Druckschriften des Johannes Bugenhagen.* Leipzig: 1908. Reprint: Nieuwkoop, 1963.

WOLF-DIETER HAUSCHILD

BULLINGER, HEINRICH (1504–1575)

Swiss reformer. The chief pastor (*Antistes*) of the Reformed church of Zurich from 1531 to 1575, Heinrich Bullinger's influence on the Reformed tradition was ensured by his many publications, his voluminous correspondence, his ministrations to refugees from many parts of Europe and ENGLAND, and his Second HELVETIC CONFESSION.

Early Life

Born on July 18, 1504 in Bremgarten, about ten miles west of Zurich, Bullinger was the youngest of the five sons of his father Heinrich, the parish priest, and his mother Anna, who were not formally married until 1529. While at the University of Cologne, where he became Bachelor of Arts in 1520 and Master in 1522, Bullinger became interested in reform through a study of the church fathers and the New Testament. When he returned home Bullinger already had embraced an evangelical position. From 1523 until 1529 Bullinger lectured on the BIBLE to the monks at the nearby Cistercian monastery at Kappel. In 1527 he spent several months in Zurich attending lectures by HULDRYCH ZWINGLI and studying Greek and Hebrew, and in January 1528 he, along with Zwingli, attended the disputation that brought Bern into the Reformed fold. In 1529 he replaced his father as pastor of the church in Bremgarten, which had just embraced the Reformed teaching. In December 1531, after Zwingli's death in the battle of Kappel, Bullinger was invited to Zurich.

The Covenant and the Anabaptists

Throughout his career Bullinger condemned the teachings of ANABAPTISM. He was present at the three disputations with Anabaptists at Zurich in 1525, and he wrote two books against them, one in 1531 and the other in 1561. However, Bullinger's opposition to the radicals is best understood within the context of his COVENANT thought, which he developed between 1525 and 1527 along with Zwingli. In 1534 Bullinger published *The One and Eternal Testament or Covenant of God,* his definitive work on the topic, at a time when he thought that the Anabaptists were an especially dangerous threat. Bullinger taught that the Jews before Christ and Christians in New Testament times lived under the single covenant that God first made with Adam and renewed with Abraham and Moses (see JUDAISM). When Christ fulfilled the covenant, the SACRAMENTS of circumcision and the Passover were replaced by BAPTISM and the Eucharist (see LORD'S SUPPER), but the conditions of the covenant—FAITH and love of the neighbor—were never altered. Just as circumcision brought the Jews into the covenant, so does baptism enroll the individual into the covenant and into the single Christian community that is ruled by the civil magistrate, whose laws enforce the conditions of the covenant. The source of the errors of the Anabaptists was their rejection of the AUTHORITY of the Old Testament, where Bullinger found both the origins of the covenant and the norms for the Christian community. The Anabaptists rejected not only infant baptism, but also Bullinger's concept of the single sphere, a united covenanted community ruled by the Christian magistrate.

Bullinger and Calvin

Although Bullinger and JOHN CALVIN were two of the architects of the early Reformed tradition, they disagreed on three important issues. First, they were never able to agree on the matter of CHURCH DISCIPLINE. Bullinger's doctrine of the single sphere, where the civil magistrate controlled all discipline, clashed with Calvin's system, where the civil magistrate punished crime whereas the separate ecclesiastical tribunal, the CONSISTORY, dealt with discipline. Nor did they ever concur on PREDESTINATION; Bullinger clung to his carefully stated doctrine of single predestination and never accepted Calvin's concept of a double decree. They were, however, finally able to agree on the Eucharist in the *Consensus Tigurinus* (Zurich Consensus) of 1549, in which Calvin muted his concept of the Eucharist as an instrument of GRACE and Bullinger abandoned Zwingli's strict separation between the internal and external, accepting the idea that the Lord's Supper is more than a remembrance, that it also functions as the external seal of an inner work.

The Second Helvetic Confession

In 1536 Bullinger was a principal contributor to the earliest common creed of the Reformed churches, the First Helvetic Confession. Then, in 1561, he crafted a personal CONFESSION of faith, which became the widely accepted Second Helvetic Confession (1562), a comprehensive declaration of the Reformed faith. Perhaps his most important bequest to the Reformed churches, it had a pervasive influence, not only in SWITZERLAND but also elsewhere in western and eastern Europe as well as in England and SCOTLAND.

Conclusion

Bullinger greatly influenced the Reformed churches during the sixteenth century. He published 119 works in Latin and German—including commentaries on all the books of the New Testament and his *Decades,* a summary of his theology—which, translated into several other languages, found their way into every part of Europe. He was a prolific correspondent; his extant letters, to and from individuals all over Europe, number over twelve thousand pieces. In the 1540s and 1550s he ministered to exiles from Italy, GERMANY, and England. He wrote the first treatise dedicated to the covenant (a topic that also permeates his other works) and his Second Helvetic Confession was widely accepted. Along with Zwingli and Calvin, Bullinger was a principal architect of Reformed Protestantism.

References and Further Reading

Primary Sources:

Büsser, Fritz, and Joachim Staedtke, eds. *Heinrich Bullinger Werke.* Zurich: Theologischer Verlag, 1972.

Gäbler, Ulrich, and Erland Herkenrath, eds. *Heinrich Bullinger 1504–1575: Gesammelte Aufsätze zum 400. Todestag* (Heinrich Bullinger 1504–1575: Collected Papers for the 400th Anniversary of His Death). 2 vols. Zürich: Theologisher Verlag, 1975.

Secondary Sources:

Baker, J. Wayne. *Heinrich Bullinger and the Covenant: The Other Reformed Tradition.* Athens: Ohio University Press, 1980.

Biel, Pamela. *Doorkeepers at the House of Righteousness: Heinrich Bullinger and the Zurich Clergy, 1535–1575.* Bern: Peter Lang, 1991.

Gordon, Bruce. *Clerical Discipline and the Rural Reformation: The Synod in Zurich, 1532–1580.* Bern: Peter Lang, 1992.

McCoy, Charles, and J. Wayne Baker. *Fountainhead of Federalism: Heinrich Bullinger and the Covenantal Tradition. With a Translation of De testamento seu foedere Dei unico et aeterno (1534) by Heinrich Bullinger.* Louisville, KY: Westminster/John Knox Press, 1991.

Rorem, Paul. *Calvin and Bullinger on the Lord's Supper.* Bramcote, Nottingham, UK: Grove Books, 1989.

J. WAYNE BAKER

BULTMANN, RUDOLF KARL (1884–1976)

German biblical scholar. Bultmann was born into a clergy family in Wiefelstede, near Oldenburg in Protestant North GERMANY, on August 20, 1884. From 1903 to 1907 he studied theology in Tübingen, Berlin, and Marburg, and from 1908 pursued his academic specialty in Marburg as assistant to Wilhelm Heitmüller. In 1910 he published in the Göttingen history of religion school monograph series, FRLANT, his Ph.D. equivalent, the *Liceutiat in theology*, a monograph on rhetorical criticism of the New Testament. His advisor was Johannes Weiss, and he compared it to "the style of Paul's preaching and the cynic-stoic diatribe." His qualification for university teaching, on the exegesis of Theodore of Mopsuestia, was submitted in 1912 (and published in 1984). A physical disability prevented military service, and after World War I Bultmann was the new generation's leading continuator of his biblical teachers' history of religion(s) school. In addition to J. Weiss this group included H. Gunkel (who taught Bultmann in Berlin), W. Wrede (whose work on the messianic secret Bultmann extended in 1920), W. Bousset (who with Reitzenstein looked for parallels in non-Jewish religions and was followed along this track by Bultmann), and W. Heitmüller (who had also contributed to the "school's" work on hellenistic parallels to the New Testament). After brief stops in Breslau (beginning in 1916) and Giessen (1920) Bultmann succeeded Heitmüller to his Marburg chair in 1921. He retired in 1951 and died in Marburg on July 30, 1976.

Bultmann's biblical scholarship is rooted in the more radical wing of LIBERAL PROTESTANTISM, but his theology was shaped by the more conservative Ritschlian Wilhelm Herrmann (1846–1922). Unlike KARL BARTH he did not repudiate his liberal Protestant past, but as a New Testament theologian aimed to preserve its critical heritage and relate it to the new THEOLOGY required by the dramatically changed cultural situation after the War. His generally positive review article in the Ritschlian journal *Die Christliche Welt* (1922) on the second edition of Barth's *Epistle to the Romans* associated him with the so-called dialectical theology of 1921–1933, and he published six of his important hermeneutical articles in its journal *Zwischen den Zeiten* [Eng. tr. *The Beginnings of Dialectic Theology* (1968)] and *Faith and Understanding* (1969). Despite this shift it is striking how closely his theology still reflected the existential emphasis of

Herrmann and remained in the mold of the anthropologically oriented theology of FRIEDRICH SCHLEIERMACHER, now translated into the neo-Reformation idiom of revelation, Word, and faith, avoiding Herrmann's terms "religion" and "experience." His existential understanding of "history" (Geschichte) was learned from Herrmann and clarified with the help of Wilhelm Dilthey and (from 1926) Martin Heidegger.

The work that established Bultmann's professional reputation was *The History of the Synoptic Tradition* (1921, second edition 1931; Eng. tr. 1963, revised 1968). This classic contribution to the form criticism pioneered by Gunkel for the Old Testament and J. Weiss among others for the New, classified the literary forms to be found in the synoptic gospels. Bultmann's own interest in *Formgeschichte,* expressed in the title of his book, lay in understanding the *history* of the transmission of the traditions contained in the synoptic gospels. This continuation of historical-critical scholarship was only indirectly theological, and Protestant only in the sense that radical biblical criticism was then still a mainly Protestant preserve. However, focusing attention on the activity of the early CHURCH between Jesus and the gospels contributed to the Protestant rediscovery of "the church" much heralded in that period between the wars. Even though Bultmann did not emphasize the early church's activity of proclamation, as Dibelius did, the history of traditions approach to the gospels dovetailed with the kerygmatic theology that he developed in the 1920s and did not much modify over the following fifty years. Relatedly, there is no reason to suppose that his skepticism about how much could be known about Jesus was theologically motivated, but it fit this Pauline and Reformation theology of the Word, especially the Word proclaimed, and caused him no discomfort.

Liberal Protestant life-of-Jesus research had already been criticized from a Lutheran perspective by Martin Kähler in *The so-called historical Jesus and the historic biblical Christ* (1892, second edition 1896; Eng. tr. 1964). Kähler's subsidiary argument that the gospels do not provide the kind of biographical information that the liberals found in them gained further support in the history-of-traditions analysis of the gospels pioneered by William Wrede and Julius Wellhausen and developed in Bultmann's form criticism. However, Bultmann was not helped by Kähler's "biblical Christ" and the "picture" of Jesus derived from the gospel narratives. His own reaction against the quest of the historical Jesus moved away from the narrative quality of the gospels (and of human experience and identity) to a Pauline-Lutheran Kierkegaardian-dialectical theology (see NEO-ORTHODOXY) emphasis on God's Word of judgment and grace, and the decision and obedience of faith. This postwar re-

316

sponse to the destruction of liberal idealism had some of its roots in a dissatisfaction with his teacher Herrmann's appeal to the "inner life of Jesus." Bultmann denied that knowledge of Jesus's "personality" was available, or that it could ever lead to a knowledge of God, and it was this problem of how to speak of God in the modern world that attracted him in 1921 to the Reformers' Pauline interpretations of God and faith being debated in the "Luther renaissance" and advocated by Barth and FRIEDRICH GOGARTEN. In 1929 he disputed "the significance of the historical Jesus for the theology of Paul," and *Existence and Faith* (Eng. tr. 1930) contained his own sketch of the apostle's theology.

Bultmann's skepticism about liberal life-of-Jesus research did not mean that nothing could be known about Jesus as a historical figure. His book on *Jesus* (1926, Eng. tr. *Jesus and the Word*, 1934) claimed only to present the earliest (Palestinian) strata of the synoptic tradition, but he was confident that the Jesus found here was the historical figure who stood behind early Christianity as its founder. He later summarized his conclusions about Jesus's proclamation at the outset (as a presupposition) of his *Theology of the New Testament* (Vol. 1, 1948; Eng. tr. 1951) and in the section on Judaism in his *Primitive Christianity* (1949, Eng. tr. 1956), arguing that Christianity emerges only after the cross and resurrection.

The account of historical work provided in the introduction to *Jesus and the Word* illustrates Bultmann's consistent concern to speak of God through his New Testament scholarship. He claims to be aiming at an "encounter with history," and says his book provides information about *his* dialogue with history in the hope it might lead its readers to make their own highly personal encounter with history (p. 13). He did not deny that historians establish historical facts, but with Dilthey claimed far more for history as a humanistic discipline than that. It should provide self-knowledge, and in this self-knowledge Bultmann (following MARTIN LUTHER and JOHN CALVIN) found knowledge of God. He later explained this account of history and self-understanding at greater length and in debate also with R. G. Collingwood in his 1955 Gifford Lectures, *History and Eschatology: the Presence of Eternity* (1957). In contrast to a positivistic historiography concerned only to get the record straight, Bultmann was interested in the effect of this work on the historian as a human being.

Bultmann's "encounter with history" was mediated through the interpretation of texts, the historical records handed down from the past, and this required the "theological exegesis" and New Testament theology for which he is justly most renowned. Whereas nineteenth-century idealist historiography reckoned to "view" the past, and perceive God's Spirit moving in the events behind the texts, Bultmann's focus was on the texts themselves, and this brought him back to the Reformers' (and Barth's) attention to scripture. Unlike Protestant scholasticism their concern was not to extract doctrinal information from infallible texts but to hear their witness to the revelation of God in Christ and respond to it. History for Bultmann therefore involved hermeneutics, the theory of the interpretation of texts pioneered in the modern period by Schleiermacher and Dilthey. Before 1921 Bultmann had studied the "religion" of the New Testament and had looked for a theory of religion that would enable him to interpret it theologically now that German idealism was fading. Although recognizing the MODERNISM of Barth's *Romans* (2nd edition) he also saw it standing in line with Schleiermacher's *Speeches* (1799) and Rudolph Otto's *Idea of the Holy* (1917). Its most important term for Bultmann was "faith," a word that implied theological "understanding" and was (as in the New Testament) defined by reference to its object. He appreciated Barth's emphasis on the Christ preached in the present but was disconcerted that Barth also insisted on the historical life of Jesus as "a time of revelation." He was also critical of the trace of biblicism present in Barth's theory of revelation, although not (he argued) in his exegetical practice. Against any hint of "objectifying" the revelation of God in Christ in the historical life of Jesus or the written text of scripture, the neo-Kantian Bultmann restricted it to the "event" of contemporary proclamation, responded to in faith.

Although agreeing with Barth's call for *Sachexegese* (theological exegesis) Bultmann insisted also on the necessity of *Sachkritik,* that is, theological criticism of the text of scripture in the light of its *Sache,* content, or essential (theological) subject matter, the gospel. A biblical author, even Paul, might not always live up to his own best insights. What was "said" must be clarified and if necessary corrected in the light of what was "meant"—that is, what the modern interpreter thinks he meant. This immanent criticism of a text (e.g., I Corinthians 15) could be supported by what the author said elsewhere, but is inevitably a risky subjective judgment based on the interpreter's own understanding of the gospel, as in Luther's 1523 criticism of the canon. Bultmann's later program of "demythologizing" the New Testament exposed the dangers of *Sachkritik,* which had led to Barth's protest back in 1922.

The theological aims and orientation of Bultmann's critical scholarship are visible in his essay on "The Problem of a Theological Exegesis of the New Testament" (1925, Eng. tr. *The Beginnings of Dialectic Theology,* 1968). He argues that textual interpretation involves self-interpretation, and that this occurs in the interpretation of history. Systematic theology and historical theology or exegesis fundamentally coincide, the former engaging in conceptual explication of human existence as determined by God, the latter in the interpretation of human being found in the texts—which it must articulate in the concepts of the modern interpreter's own day. Around this time he discovered in his colleague Heidegger's phenomenological analysis of human existence (*Being and Time* was published in 1927), a formal description of the structure of human existence that itself owed much to Christian theology (especially St. Paul, Augustine, Luther, and SØREN KIERKEGAARD). It did not anticipate theology by explicating faith's understanding of itself—that is, the human being confronted by God—but its account of human being provided theology, and so theological interpretation of the New Testament, with the conceptuality it needed.

More important than the use of Heidegger's terms to articulate Paul's theology was Bultmann's prior conviction that all theological statements must be understood to refer to human existence in relation to God. Paul had used a variety of anthropological and soteriological terms and Bultmann mapped out the apostle's theology in 1930 and 1948 by analyzing these, describing first "man prior to the revelation of faith" and second "man under faith." Cosmological, salvation-historical, ecclesiological, and futuristic aspects of Paul's thought received inadequate attention, but this powerful individualistic interpretation made sense of Paul's talk of God without recourse to the kind of objectifying metaphysics that Bultmann thought was finished. It remained a theology of the word, not a philosophical anthropology because what it explicated was the self-understanding of faith that occurred in obedient response to the kerygma or "word of the cross" (I Corinthians 1:18). Like Paul in Romans and Galatians, and like Luther, this theology centered on the doctrine of JUSTIFICATION by FAITH, which Bultmann insisted was Paul's real CHRISTOLOGY.

The second volume of Bultmann's *Theology of the New Testament* (1951, Eng. tr. 1955) summarized his interpretation of John, which had been adumbrated in earlier essays and in several word studies prepared for Kittel's *Theological Dictionary of the New Testament* (1933–), and had received its full expression in the magisterial Meyer commentary (1941, Eng. tr. 1971), perhaps the greatest theological biblical commentary of the century. This gospel lent itself to Bultmann's existential interpretation more readily than Paul on account of antecedent similarities between John's INDIVIDUALISM, moral dualism, present ESCHATOLOGY, focus on revelation and faith, and Bultmann's own ex-

istentialist Lutheran theology. It is also arguable that Bultmann's view of New Testament theology as theological interpretation of New Testament texts is better articulated in a commentary or account of each literary text separately, than by all seven epistles of Paul being homogenized into a theology of the historical Paul behind the texts. Other New Testament writings were not regarded by Bultmann as truly theological. His classic *Theology of the New Testament* is therefore defective in its failure to interpret these other writings (especially the Synoptic Gospels) theologically. They receive some consideration within the work's historical framework, which describes the development of early Christian thought, including both precanonical stages and some noncanonical writings (Apostolic Fathers). This landmark "New Testament theology" thus remains a combination of the historical paradigm that still dominates New Testament scholarship and the more literary-theological paradigm (always informed by historical exegesis and context) suggested by his focus on the interpretation of key texts.

In 1941 Bultmann also published a provocative article on "The New Testament and Mythology," which unleashed the "demythologizing" controversy of the 1940s and 1950s (see *Kerygma and Myth*, vols. 1 and 2, edited by H.-W. Bartsch, 1953, 1962). Motivated by an evangelistic concern to communicate the gospel, it nevertheless disturbed conservative church authorities and earned a shameful synodical condemnation. It was a matter of critical theological interpretation that Bultmann claimed had already been undertaken by the Johannine evangelist in rejecting the tradition's mythological pictures of the future and interpreting early Christian eschatology existentially as "present eschatology." He also thought he was applying in the epistemological realm the Reformers' principle of justification by faith alone. To demand a belief in the incredible was to make faith into a "work." Critics argued that important dimensions of the gospel, notably the cosmological, went away without leave in this reductionist interpretation, overdetermined by a contemporary scientistic worldview. The new religious studies of the 1960s were more positive about "myth" than a member of the CONFESSING CHURCH resisting Nazi ideology under the banner of a theology of the cross had been. A new generation of critical New Testament scholarship took up again the tasks of the history of religion school in which Bultmann was educated, but showed less interest in the theological and philosophical problems that made the 1920s such an important period for German Protestant thought. Since his death Bultmann's hermeneutical heritage has accordingly been taken up by a more conservative theological scholarship and by Roman Catholic scholars who have also recognized in him the towering theological figure in twentieth-century New Testament studies.

See also Jesus, Lives of; Neo-Orthodoxy

References and Further Reading

Primary Sources:

In addition to works mentioned in this article, see *New Testament and Mythology and other Basic Writings,* edited by S. Ogden. Minneapolis, MN: Fortress Press, 1984.
Bultmann, Rudolf. *Jesus Christ and Mythology.* New York: Charles Scribner's Sons, 1958.

Secondary Sources:

Cahill, P. Joseph. "Theological Significances of Rudolf Bultmann." *Theological Studies* 38 (1997): 231–274.
Morgan, Robert. *Rudolph Bultmann.* Oxford: Blackwell, 1989.
Wilder, Amos N. "New Testament Studies 1920–1950: Reminiscences of a Changing Discipline." *Journal of Religion* 64 no. 4 (1984): 432–451.

ROBERT MORGAN

BUNYAN, JOHN (1628–1688)

English writer and preacher. The author of *Pilgrims' Progress* (1678, 1684), Bunyan was born in the parish of Elstow in Bedfordshire in November 1628, educated locally, and served in the civil war Parliamentarian army between 1644 and 1647. Following a deep spiritual crisis in the early 1650s, Bunyan was converted to an *evangelical* Christian faith and emerged as a leading preacher within the Particular Baptist church based in Bedford. He was imprisoned for his beliefs in 1660 and remained a prisoner for most of the time until his release in 1672, when he became a pastor in his church. Bunyan's intense activity as an author continued in the 1670s through the production of the first part of *Pilgrim's Progress* in 1678, and he developed as a nationally known Nonconformist leader. There is some evidence that toward the end of his life, Bunyan supported collusion with the Catholic King James II in his attempts to secure religious toleration for England's non-Anglican Nonconformist and Catholic minorities. Bunyan died in London on August 31, 1688.

Bunyan's Development

Bunyan was the son of a tinker or brazier, Thomas Bunyan (1603–1676) and his wife Margaret, née Bentley (1603–1644). Young Bunyan may have attended a school at Houghton Conquest, Bedfordshire, an establishment closely connected with the University of Cambridge and its strong Puritan influences. From the time he came to the age of military service (at sixteen;

November 1644 until July 1647), Bunyan served in the Parliamentarian army fighting in the English civil war, his service being centered on the garrison at Newport Pagnell in Buckinghamshire. This period undoubtedly exposed Bunyan to the strongly Protestant currents circulating in the Parliamentarian forces. Following his discharge, Bunyan returned to Elstow, took up work as a tinker, and married in either 1648 or 1649. His wife brought to their marriage the influences of a "godly" Puritan home background, along with Protestant devotional books that strongly influenced John Bunyan's spiritual development, including Arthur Dent's *The Plaine Mans Path-way to Heaven* (1601) and Lewis Bayly's *The Practice of Piety* (pre-1613). The couple had four children. His wife died in 1658 and Bunyan married again in 1659. With his second wife Elizabeth (d. 1692) he had three children.

In the course of his first marriage, Bunyan underwent a protracted spiritual crisis and depression, the details of which he recounted with unflinching candor in his autobiography, *Grace Abounding to the Chief of Sinners* (1666). This traumatic state was engendered by his failure to pursue righteousness. He underwent extreme despair and came to see himself, as he recalled in *Grace Abounding,* as one among those "poor creatures . . . that though not much guilt attended the Soul, yet they continually have a secret conclusion within them, that there is no hopes for them." Bunyan was gradually rescued from his agonized spiritual and psychological condition by a separate or "gathered" church that met in Bedford under the ministry of John Gifford, which was a Particular Baptist Church. Bunyan also studied MARTIN LUTHER's (1483–1546) *Commentary on St. Paul's Epistle to the Galatians,* where he found the comforting Protestant doctrine of the Reformation, that men and women were solely made acceptable—"justified"—in God's eyes, not through their own efforts, good works, or obedience to God's law, but by faith in Christ's redeeming action. Bunyan felt he could be the sinner he recognized himself to be and yet not be condemned, because Christ had died for him. Therefore, Bunyan derived from Luther the notion of personal salvation grounded in Christ, which was also conveyed to him in the religious discourse he heard among the members of the Bedford church: " . . . they talked how God had visited their souls with his love in the Lord Jesus." Bunyan joined that church in about 1655, when he and his family moved from Elstow into Bedford, and he rapidly emerged as one of its leading preachers, evangelizing in Bedford and the villages of Bedfordshire. His undoubted effectiveness as a preacher came from the authenticity of his testimony grounded in personal experience: he recalled that he "carried that fire in my own conscience that I perswaded them to [his hearers] to beware of . . . ."

The central core of his preaching iterated the essentials of the Protestant Reformation doctrine of salvation, "the Doctrine of Life by Christ, without Works." However, Bunyan came to believe this vital doctrine was under threat from the new Quaker movement, which, he believed, stood for justification by means of good works and deeds of the law. In his first book, *Some Gospel-Truths Opened* (1656), he insisted that men and women were "not profited by the works of the law . . . salvation was . . . fully, and completely wrought out for poor sinners by the man Christ Jesus." He continued to publish in defense of classic Protestant doctrines of salvation in works such as *The Doctrine of the Law and Grace Unfolded* (1659).

By this time Bunyan had become known as the prominent religious radical who, in *A Few Sighs from Hell* (1658), excoriated the abuses of the wealthy and promised an apocalyptic revenge against them. In 1660, the year of the restoration of the monarchy and of the CHURCH OF ENGLAND, he was targeted for prosecution for refusing to abandon his worship in Bedford's separate congregation and to conform to the national church. Bunyan provided an account of his arrest (at the hands of the restored Bedfordshire royalist authorities, in October 1660), investigation, indictment, and incarceration (and attempts to circumvent it) in the manuscript *A Relation of the Imprisonment of Mr. John Bunyan,* first published in 1765. He was specifically charged under an act of Parliament of 1593 forbidding attendance at worshiping meetings outside the established church, and was sentenced in 1661 despite a passionate appeal by his wife. However, his subsequent twelve-year imprisonment in Bedford was a far less severe penalty than those provided for in the 1593 statute—banishment and execution. Perhaps because of reluctance on the part of the Bedfordshire authorities to make a martyr out of a popular preacher, Bunyan, jailed rather than exiled or hanged, was treated more kindly than the law required.

That is not to say that his spell in prison was a pleasant prospect. He was agonizingly concerned about his family's welfare during his imprisonment, especially that of his blind daughter, Mary. There was, clearly, a need to justify his refusal to conform to the church that had resulted in his detention. Having already resumed in prison the writing career he had begun before his arrest, Bunyan published in 1662, from prison, *I Will Pray with the Spirit,* a defense of his Protestantism and his rejection of the Book of Common Prayer, which he described as "taken out of the Papisticall Mass-Book; being the Scraps and Fragments of the devices of some Popes, some Friars . . . ." Released from prison under a pardon issued by King Charles II in May of that year, Bunyan took up the pastorate of the church in Bedfordshire openly and threw himself into the missionary and administrative work of his church. He also delivered an authoritative rendition of Protestant doctrine, *A Confession of My Faith, and a Reason of My Practice in Worship* (1672), in which he set out the Reformation teaching that the righteousness of Christ was credited to the sinner as an outer garment, but was received by the faith implanted by the Almighty in the elect.

Bunyan's Later Career

In the 1670s Bunyan dealt with issues of particular concern to his church. In 1673 his *Differences in Judgment About Water-Baptism, No Bar to Communion* argued that believer's baptism should not be a source of discord in the church. While in the 1673 work *A Defence of the Doctrine of Justification, by Faith in Jesus Christ,* Bunyan again upheld fundamental Protestant doctrines of salvation, in the 1674 book *Peaceable Principles and True,* he focused on the more internal issue of baptism that divided the Baptist churches. He returned to Protestant dogmatics, on an elementary explanatory level, in his 1675 *Instruction for the Ignorant,* which contains classic Reformation formulations. This work can be seen, alongside *Saved by Grace* and *The Strait Gate,* as preceding Bunyan's best-known work, *Pilgrim's Progress* (in two parts, 1678, 1684), as a literary popularization of Protestantism.

Indeed, working through allegory, *Pilgrim's Progress* was a supreme achievement in providing a popular understanding of Protestant doctrine. This is rendered negatively and satirically as well as positively, for among the allegorical types in the *Pilgrim's Progress,* part I, is the derisory figure of the giant pope, "grown . . . crazy and stiff in his joynts." Here, in the year 1678, when Protestant England was terrified with allegations of a popish plot against the nation's religion, freedom, and laws, Bunyan delivered a comic version of a Reformation overview of history according to which the demise of the papacy was, literally, only a matter of time. *Pilgrim's Progress* also provided Bunyan with a further avenue for proclaiming the central doctrines of the Protestant Reformation concerning the means of salvation.

During the decade of the 1670s, when Bunyan's volume of published work and leadership in his church expanded, he also faced serious personal problems. First, he was the target of allegations of impropriety with a young woman, Agnes Beaumont. Then the Bedfordshire magistrates arrested him in 1675 under an Anglican clerical initiative, and he spent six months in jail. The Popish Plot of 1678 fed demands, mounted by the newly formed pro-Nonconformist and anti-Catholic Whig party, for the exclusion from the succession to Charles II, of the king's Catholic brother, James, Duke of York (later King James II). In that political crisis Bunyan almost certainly sympathized with Whig politics, living, as he did, in a Whig-dominated borough and county. Nevertheless, Bunyan's politics were far from extreme, for he preserved a strong English Protestant sense of the importance of the crown for the realization of an apocalyptic anti-papal vision. In a work of the early 1680s, *Of Antichrist, and His Ruine,* Bunyan urged his readers to "let the King have verily a place in your Hearts, and with Heart and Mouth give God Thanks for him . . . ."

This same period of the early 1680s was one of phenomenal authorial productivity for Bunyan. In *The Life and Death of Mr Badman* (1680) he presented a vivid extended sermon, in protonovel form, on the implications for an archetypal moral reprobate of the Protestant doctrines of predestination, arising from the datum of justification by faith. In *The Holy War,* Bunyan provided a complex extended metaphor of Protestantism's insistence on God's free grace and pardon. The second part of *Pilgrim's Progress* (1684) reiterated the theme, set out in the first installment, of the Christian's journey into eternal life, though with a stronger appreciation of feminine themes. Bunyan was now at the height of his powers and fame as an author. Sixteen of his works were published during the 1680s. In *Seasonable Counsel* (1684) he advised his fellow Nonconformists to adopt a patient stance during a renewed period of persecution. He reaffirmed the Protestant doctrine of Christ's all-sufficing work as redeemer in *The Advocateship of Jesus Christ* (1688) and, in the same year, dealt further with Christ's redeeming work in *Good News for the Vilest of Men.* In 1687 he was reported to be at one with those Protestant Nonconformists who supported the attempts of the Catholic King James II to give civil rights to that community and to the English Catholics by repealing discriminatory laws. Bunyan was an active minister of his church and died of a sudden illness he contracted in the course of his pastoral work. His wife Elizabeth survived him along with five of his children; he is buried in London's major Nonconformist cemetery, Bunhill Fields. John Bunyan stands out as the most effective popularizer of Protestant dogmatics in the English language.

References and Further Reading

Primary Sources:

Bunyan, John. *The Pilgrim's Progress from This World to That Which Is to Come, Parts I and II.* Edited by James Blanton Wharey, 2nd edition revised by Roger Sharrock. Oxford: Clarendon, 1960.

———. *Grace Abounding with Other Spiritual Autobiographies.* Edited by John Stachniewski and Anita Pacheco. Oxford, New York: Oxford University Press, 1998.

Secondary Sources:

Brown, John. *John Bunyan: His Life, Times and Work.* 2nd ed. London: Wm. Isbister, 1886.
Collmer, Robert G., ed. *Bunyan in Our Time.* Kent, OH, and London: Kent State University Press, 1989.
Greaves, Richard L. *John Bunyan and English Nonconformity.* London and Rio Grande, OH: Hambledon Press, 1992.
Hill, Christopher. *A Turbulent, Seditious and Factious People: John Bunyan and his Church.* Oxford: Clarendon, 1988.
Keeble, N. H., ed. *John Bunyan: Conventicle and Parnassus.* Oxford: Clarendon, 1988.
Laurence, Anne, W. R. Owens, and Stuart Sim, eds. *John Bunyan and His England 1628–1688.* London and Ronceverte, WV: Hambledon Press, 1990.
Mullett, Michael A. *John Bunyan in Context.* Keele, Staffs.: Keele University Press, 1996.

MICHAEL A. MULLETT

BURIAL TRADITIONS

See Funerary Rites

BURNED-OVER DISTRICT

The term "Burned-Over District" has been used to characterize the religious practices of western New York State from 1800 to 1850. Successive waves of REVIVALS, religious "ultraism," and new religious movements have been likened to the wildfires that periodically swept portions of the primeval forests surrounding early settlers. The religious uniqueness of the area is said to be demonstrated by the frequency of its revivals, by the number of religious innovators who were natives of, or resident in, the area (especially CHARLES GRANDISON FINNEY and JOSEPH SMITH), by the unusually high level of support enjoyed by social reform movements (including TEMPERANCE and antislavery), and by the fact that several new religious movements (such as MORMONISM, Oneida perfectionism, and the adventism of WILLIAM MILLER) either originated or found a congenial home there.

The intensity of religious expression in western New York in the first half of the nineteenth century is indisputable. What is less certain is that such expression was unique. Recent scholarship has suggested that there was a band of "burned-over districts" stretching from western New England through western New York and northern Ohio to Michigan and beyond—even as far as Utah. Yankee origins and latter-day variations of PURITANISM connected these far-flung regions. Further study of the Yankee/Puritan culture of these places should continue to yield valuable insights into the history of American Protestantism.

See also Slavery, Abolition of

References and Further Reading

Cross, Whitney R. *The Burned-Over District: The Social and Intellectual History of Enthusiastic Religion in Western New York, 1800–1850.* Ithaca, NY: Cornell University Press, 1950.
Potash, P. Jeffrey. *Vermont's Burned-Over District: Patterns of Community Development and Religious Activity, 1761–1850.* Brooklyn, NY: Carlson Publishing, 1991.
Rowe, David L. *Thunder and Trumpets: Millerites and Dissenting Religion in Upstate New York, 1800–1850.* Chico, CA: Scholars Press, 1985.

DONALD L. HUBER

BUSHNELL, HORACE (1802–1876)

American theologian. Born in Bantam, Connecticut, in 1802, Bushnell was minister of North Congregational Church, Hartford, Connecticut, from 1833 to 1859. He continued to preach, lecture, and write until his death in 1876. From 1849 to 1854, Bushnell's critics among Congregational clergy in Connecticut sought to try him for HERESY, largely because of two books: *God in Christ* (1849) and *Christ in Theology* (1851). His views expressed in these books and others marked an abrupt change from the CALVINISM of JONATHAN EDWARDS and his successors that had dominated Trinitarian New England for a century.

Bushnell opposed the literalistic interpretations of and prosaic reasonings from biblical texts practiced by his peers and emphasized the pervasive presence of symbol, image, analogy, parable, and story in the Bible. He developed a theory of language in which the role of metaphor was given a fundamental place and used this theory as a theological method. Bushnell's most famous book, *Christian Nurture*, appeared in its final form in 1861. Here he countered the view, prevalent in his time, that every true Christian must experience a sudden radical CONVERSION experience. He argued that conversion could take place over a long period of nurture by and within the Christian community.

Bushnell was influenced by such European thinkers as SAMUEL TAYLOR COLERIDGE (an interpreter of IMMANUEL KANT) and FRIEDRICH SCHLEIERMACHER. He contributed powerfully to the emergence of a new liberalism among Protestant theologians in the United States.

References and Further Reading

Cheney, Mary Bushnell. *Life and Letters of Horace Bushnell.* New York: Arno Press, 1969; orig. publ. 1880.
Duke, James O. *Horace Bushnell on the Vitality of Biblical Language.* Chico, CA: Scholars Press, 1994.
Edwards, Robert L. *Of Singular Genius: of Singular Grace: A Biography of Horace Bushnell.* Cleveland, OH: Pilgrim Press, 1992.
Smith, H. Shelton, ed. *Horace Bushnell.* New York: Oxford University Press, 1965.

DONALD A. CROSBY

BUTLER, JOSEPH (1692–1752)

English bishop and apologist. Butler was born on May 18, 1692 in Wantage, Berkshire, ENGLAND. His father, a local linen-draper and devout Presbyterian, expected Joseph to pursue a ministry in that church. Butler was educated under Rev. Philip Barton, master of the grammar school at Wantage, before being sent to dissenting academies in Gloucester and then Tewkesbury. At the academy in Tewkesbury Butler formed a profound and lasting friendship with Thomas Seeker (eventually archbishop of Canterbury), and began questioning his allegiance to the precepts of PRESBYTERIANISM. After considerable anguish, Butler joined the CHURCH OF ENGLAND. By this time he had begun reading widely and was especially captivated by Samuel Clarke's treatise, *Demonstration of the Being and Attributes of God.* At the age of twenty-two, Butler initiated a correspondence with Clarke concerning proofs of God's unity. Clarke regarded his exchange with the precocious Butler as significant enough to append to subsequent editions of his work.

After taking his degree from Oriel College, Oxford in 1718 Butler was ordained deacon and priest and was appointed preacher at the Chapel of the Rolls, where he remained until he was thirty-four. In this office Butler delivered his influential *Fifteen Sermons* (1726), including a celebrated discourse on human nature—emphasizing practical aspects of Christian life. Butler subsequently served nearly ten years in virtual seclusion as a parish priest in Stanhope before being appointed in 1736 as head chaplain to Queen Caroline, wife of King George II. In the same year he also published his most important philosophical work, *Analogy of Religion, Natural and Revealed, to the Constitution and Nature.* After the queen's death in 1737 Butler accepted the position of bishop of Bristol. After a short return to royal service in 1746, and his subsequent refusal to accept appointment as Archbishop of Canterbury, Butler finally accepted the bishopric of Durham in 1750, where he died two years later.

Butler is esteemed as among the foremost British moral philosophers. His characteristically melancholic temperament was shaped in part by what he believed was the irredeemably irreligious condition of his age. Resolutely distrustful of "enthusiasm," Butler was singularly unmoved by the methods of Evangelical Revivalism as a means of addressing contemporary complacence, so much so that he implored JOHN WESLEY to desist from preaching in his diocese. Butler's most important theological treatise, *Analogy of Religion, Natural and Revealed,* can be understood only within the context of the crucial theological debate then raging between adherents to Natural religion, on the one hand, and to Revealed religion on the other. His work constitutes a robust defence of Revealed Religion against Deist attack, which argued that God can be known only through the rational study of NATURE rather than through supernatural conviction.

Beginning with the contention that nothing can be known completely through experience, Butler sought to demonstrate that the seemingly separate spheres of analyzing Nature and analyzing Religion were in fact analogous, and that the inexplicabilities and obscurities that one meets with in examining Nature one may reasonably expect to find likewise in the scheme of Religion. If difficulties are thus admitted by Deists in the course of their contemplation of the constitution of Nature—whose author they accept to be God—then, Butler argued, the existence of comparable difficulties and conundrums in the sphere of religion cannot constitute a fair objection against its truth and divine origin. In the light of the inherent limitations on what human beings can know, Butler insisted that adherence either to Natural or to Revealed religion relies not on evidence, but only on "probability" because, as he put it, "we cannot have a thorough knowledge of any part without knowing the whole," and "to us probability is the very guide of life"—a line of argument that had a tremendous impact on DAVID HUME. Having situated probability at the center of both reason and belief, Butler endeavors to justify an acceptance of such doctrines as a future state and the immortality of the soul. Although the Scottish philosopher James Mill would later allege that Butler's argument "furnished . . . one of the most terrible persuasives to atheism ever produced," it is also said that so formidable was Butler's rebuke to Deist refutations of Revealed Religion that no compelling answer to his Analogy has ever been offered.

Although Butler's contribution to the Deist controversy was crucial, his greatest legacy is his enduring influence on Christian ethics. Although he is at pains throughout his treatise to explain why, philosophically, it is illogical to dismiss as incredible the supernatural over the natural, his real interest is in practical, not speculative, observance. Butler believed that the moral nature of man, his conduct throughout life, is that on account of which alone an inquiry into religion is meaningful. The fullest surviving account of his ETHICS is to be found in the fifteen sermons delivered at the Chapel of the Rolls culminating in 1726. Like other eighteenth-century thinkers, Butler sought to answer THOMAS HOBBES's contention that human nature was motivated primarily by self-interestedness. Aligning himself with the moral position of the Third Earl of Shaftesbury, Butler rejected such basic human egotism, and like Ralph Cudworth before him, sought more dignified footing for human ethics. He conceived of human nature as composed of aspects, with appetites, affections, and passions constituting one group, and the principles of self-love, benevolence, and conscience constituting another. Butler's ethical speculation consists in analyzing the interrelation of these parts, and concludes that "our nature, i.e. constitution, is adapted to virtue, as from the idea of a watch it appears that its nature, i.e. constitution or system, is adapted to measure time." Butler's writings had a formative influence on Cardinal JOHN HENRY NEWMAN's thought and it has been said that nothing superior in value to Butler's sermons has been added to ethical science during the interval between Aristotle and IMMANUEL KANT.

See also Deism; Evangelicalism; Revivals

References and Further Reading

Primary Sources:

Butler, Joseph. *Fifteen Sermons Preached at the Rolls Chapel.* London: 2nd edition, 1729. [Six sermons added in the 1749 edition.]
———. *Analogy of Religion, Natural and Revealed, to the Constitution and Nature.* London: Knapton, 1736.

Secondary Sources:

Bartlett, Thomas. *Memoirs of the Life, Character and Writings of Joseph Butler.* London: John W. Parker, 1839.
Cunliffe, Christopher, ed. *Joseph Butler's Moral and Religious Thought: Tercentenary Essays.* Oxford: Clarendon Press, 1992.
Mossner, E. C. *Bishop Butler and the Age of Reason.* New York: Macmillan, 1936.
Penelhum, Terence. *Butler.* London: Routledge & Kegan Paul, 1985.

KELLY GROVIER

BUTLER, JOSEPHINE ELIZABETH (1828–1906)

British feminist and campaigner for the civil rights of prostitutes. Life-long member of the CHURCH OF ENGLAND, Josephine Butler was of such devout Evangelical piety that her name appears in the Anglican Calendar of Saints on December 30, the anniversary of her death. Born on April 13, 1828, in Millfield, Northumberland, Josephine was the seventh of nine surviving children of John Grey and his wife Hannah Annett. The Greys were members of the Church of England, almost certainly of the Evangelical wing (see EVANGELICALISM), and strong supporters of the antislavery campaign (see SLAVERY; SLAVERY, ABOLITION OF). Their children learned early about the horrors of slavery and were familiar with contemporary social issues, although in other respects Josephine's education was sporadic. Her childhood home in Dilston, Northumberland, was extremely happy and the siblings remained close, even when marriage took them abroad.

In 1852 Josephine married George Butler and moved to Oxford, where he held the post of public examiner. While living in Oxford, the Butlers "rescued" the first of many prostitutes to be housed and individually cared for by them (see PROSTITUTION). Three sons were born and then a daughter, Eva, who was tragically killed in 1864, at the age of five, in a fall from the first floor landing of their Cheltenham home. In 1866, while still grieving, they moved to Liverpool, where Josephine began a ministry among the imprisoned women of the "Bridewell" in Liverpool Workhouse to "find some pain keener than my own."

In 1866 she became President of the North of England Council for the Higher Education of Women, but in 1869 her commitment to this cause was displaced by the demands of the campaign to repeal the Contagious Diseases Acts. These Acts of 1864, 1866, and 1869 allowed the police to detain any woman suspected of prostitution in fourteen naval and military towns, to examine her for venereal disease on pain of imprisonment if she refused, and to detain her in a certified hospital if found to be diseased. This infringement of the civil rights of women (any woman might legally be detained under the Act) was regarded by Josephine Butler as a shocking example of the double standard. She agreed to become the Secretary of the Ladies National Association for repeal of the Contagious Diseases Acts, even though she anticipated the cost to her family life, her health, and even to her social status because convention decreed that it was unacceptable for a respectable woman to speak publicly on such a taboo subject. She began a courageous campaign of pamphlet and letter-writing, Parliamentary lobbying, petition gathering, and nationwide speaking, which lasted until 1886. Although she had a devoted group of followers, notably among radical Nonconformists (see NONCONFORMITY), the campaign aroused hostility to the extent of putting her in physical danger at times. She spoke to audiences of working men, exhorting them to reject the Acts, and was the only woman to give evidence before a Royal Commission in 1871. Members of Parliament were exceptionally slow to commit themselves in support of her arguments, even Prime Minister William E. Gladstone proving equivocal, but in 1886 the Acts were finally repealed, attributed particularly to the Parliamentary efforts of James Stansfeld MP. *Personal Reminiscences of a Great Crusade* (1896) is Josephine Butler's account of the campaign.

The treatment of poor women and prostitutes on the European continent, especially in Paris, Geneva, and Brussels, became an abiding concern from 1874 onward, and she traveled there regularly, demanding to inspect state brothels and challenging the activities of the police charged with regulatory authority. The British and Continental Federation for the Abolition of Government Regulation of Prostitution was formed in 1875, with Butler as joint secretary. This campaign had some success, including the exposure of the traffic in young girls from England to Belgium (1880).

In 1885 Butler became involved in W. T. Stead's hard-hitting campaign against child prostitution in London, conducted through his newspaper, the *Pall Mall Gazette*. Sensational headlines in the course of this campaign ensured that the facts of child prostitution became public knowledge, as Butler and Stead had intended.

Her campaigns for "purity" began in the early 1870s and included speeches to audiences of young men about the dangers and disadvantages of uncontrolled sexuality. In 1886 she joined the newly formed National Vigilance Association for the Repression of Criminal Vice and Immorality, but soon found that its methods, repressive action against "immoral" individuals, clashed with her own favored approach of inculcating personal morality. She spoke of "the necessity of purity of life in all who would join us" (*Sursum Corda*, 1871).

Josephine Butler's religion has been inadequately defined until the recent discovery of a spiritual diary that, according to Helen Mathers, contains convincing evidence of Evangelical conviction. David Bebbington, in *Evangelicalism in Modern Britain: a History from the 1730s to the 1980s* (1989), identifies four defining characteristics: Biblicism, Crucicentrism, Activism, and Conversionism. All are readily apparent in her writings, both published and unpublished, and the Spiritual Diary provides evidence of a deep commitment to personal prayer and Bible study. No man or woman, she argued, could move her from truths learned directly from God. Her conviction of her right *as a woman* to stand up for her beliefs made her theology explicitly feminist (see FEMINIST THEOLOGY). It is most clearly stated in her Introduction to *Woman's Work and Woman's Culture* (1869), which contains a radical account of the attitudes of both Jesus and St. Paul toward women and highlights the role of Mary Magdalene, a witness of the Resurrection.

She sought models of the Christian woman she hoped to be and found her greatest example in a fourteenth-century Italian Catholic saint, Catharine of Siena. Her 1878 biography of Catharine depicts a woman who was, like herself, both a practical reformer and a contemplative mystic, called by God to be a leader of both men and women.

Butler believed herself to be called to undertake a mission to destroy the sin of regulated prostitution and even the institution of prostitution itself. She proclaimed her right, as a woman, to preach and teach her beliefs openly, quoting the prophet Joel "your sons *and your daughters* will prophesy." In these respects she was a radical, anticipating the Christian feminism of the twentieth century; in others she was a true Victorian, campaigning with the zeal of a Wilberforce against the sin of "white slavery" (see WILLIAM WILBERFORCE). Butler died on December 30, 1906, at the home of her son George in Northumberland and is buried at Kirknewton.

References and Further Reading

Primary Sources:

Johnson, George W. and Lucy A. Johnson, eds. *Josephine Butler: An Autobiographical Memoir.* Extracts from Butler's major autobiographical writings. London: Simpkin, Marshall, Hamilton, Kent & Co., 1909.

Smaller collections held by Northumberland County Record Office, Newcastle, Liverpool University Library, and St. Andrews University Library.

The Women's Library (formerly Fawcett Library). Extensive collection of correspondence and pamphlets. London: Guildhall University.

Secondary Sources:

Bell, E. Moberley. *Josephine Butler: Flame of Fire.* London: Constable, 1962.

Boyd, Nancy. *Three Victorian Women Who Changed Their World. Josephine Butler, Octavia Hill, Florence Nightingale.* New York and Oxford: Oxford University Press, 1982.

Caine, Barbara. *Victorian Feminists.* Oxford: Oxford University Press, 1992.

Mathers, Helen. "The Evangelical Spirituality of a Victorian Feminist. Josephine Butler 1828–1906." *Journal of Ecclesiastical History* 52, no. 2 (2001): 282–312.

McHugh, Paul. *Prostitution and Victorian Social Reform.* London: St. Martin's Press, 1980.

Petrie, Glen. *A Singular Iniquity: The Campaigns of Josephine Butler.* London: Viking Press, 1971.

Walkowitz, Judith. *Prostitution and Victorian Society: Women, Class and the State.* Cambridge: Cambridge University Press, 1980.

HELEN MATHERS

BUTTERFIELD, HERBERT (1900–1979)

English historian and religious thinker. Born October 7, 1900, at Oxenhope, Yorkshire, Butterfield was a lifelong Methodist and sometime lay preacher. For sixty years he was a member of Peterhouse, Cambridge, and served in Cambridge University as a lecturer (1929), then professor of modern history (1944), and finally Regius professor of modern history (1963) until he retired (1968). He died at Sawston, Cambridgeshire July 20, 1979.

Butterfield was, arguably, the most influential Protestant historian in the English language in the twentieth century. His influence derived not from any particular work of Protestant church history, but from the historical and religious ideas he developed within his general historical studies and that others adopted for their own studies in many fields. It gradually became clear that his insights were dependent on his Methodist spirituality and his practice of DISSENT from the reigning powers and orthodoxies in any field.

His fame rested on a modest book, *Whig Interpretation of History* (1931), in which he exposed the fallacy of reading history backwards from something desirable in the present to something desirable in the past, and then drawing a straight line of causation forward again from the earlier to the later. The products of such thinking came to be called "Whig history." Among his examples of the fallacy was the tradition of crediting the REFORMATION and PROTESTANT WHIGS for religious liberty in England. By contrast he explained the relative liberty experienced in contemporary England as an unintended consequence of continuously complex and changing interactions among people, including Catholics, Anglicans, and Nonconformists, involving economic, political, social, and religious factors over a long period of time.

His writings dealt with a wide range of topics, including the history of historiography; British, French, and German history; the history of Christianity; diplomatic history; the history of science; general European history; theological reflection; and biography. His book *Christianity and History* (1949) reached a wide public with his reading of a Christian view of history shaped by his Methodist convictions. In *Origins of Modern Science, 1300–1800* (1949) he helped define the history of science as a field of study while showing the significance of Protestant and Catholic beliefs about God and the world for the new science that emerged in the early modern period.

See also Anglicanism; Nonconformity; Orthodoxy

References and Further Reading

Cowling, Maurice. *Religion and Public Doctrine in Modern England,* vol. I, 191–250. Cambridge, UK: Cambridge University Press, 1980.

McIntire, C. T. *Dissenting Religion, Dissenting History: the Unsettling Thought of Herbert Butterfield.* 2003.

C. T. MCINTIRE

BUXTEHUDE, DIETRICH
(c. 1637–1707)

Lutheran musician. The specifics of Buxtehude's birth are unknown; apparently he considered himself a native of DENMARK. Probably trained musically by his father Johannes (c. 1601–1674), Buxtehude became organist at his father's former post in Helsingborg's St. Maria Kyrka in 1657–1658, and then in 1660 took a position with the German-speaking Marienkirche in Helsingør (both cities were under Danish control). In April 1668 he succeeded Franz Tunder as organist for the Marienkirche at Lübeck in northern GERMANY, a position, along with that of Werkmeister, he held until his death. While at Lübeck Buxtehude was visited by other musicians, most notably GEORGE FRIDERIC HANDEL and JOHANN SEBASTIAN BACH. Buxtehude died May 9, 1707.

As required for Lübeck's Lutheran LITURGY, Buxtehude accompanied the choir and provided preludes, solo verses, and interludes for congregational hymn singing at Saturday and Sunday Vespers and at the principal morning service (Haupt-Predigt) on Sundays and festal days. Among his surviving keyboard works are numerous settings of Lutheran chorales that show his distinct employment of rhetorical device and counterpoint. Buxtehude set music for other parts of the service using liturgical and nonliturgical texts in Latin or German, and engaging musical instruments in addition to or in lieu of the organ. Other compositions exist for weddings and funerals and for extraliturgical occasions. Among the latter are the Abendmusiken (evening concerts), dramatic sacred "oratorios" performed on the last two Sundays of Trinity and the last three Sundays of Advent.

With his innovative use of soloists, ensembles, and instrumentalists, Buxtehude redefined the prose-text concerto and poetry-text aria. He occasionally combined the two in a new composite form later labeled the "cantata." Besides the Vulgate and MARTIN LUTHER's Bible, Buxtehude drew for texts upon Latin mystical prose and German strophic poetry. Although he borrowed substantially from the devotional poetry of Lutheran PIETISM, his Italianate style and settings of Latin texts placed him at odds with Pietism's liturgical reform.

References and Further Reading

Snyder, Kerala J. *Dieterich Buxtehude: Organist in Lübeck.* New York: Schirmer, 1987.

Webber, Geoffrey. *North German Church Music in the Age of Buxtehude.* Oxford, UK: Clarendon, 1996.

KAREN B. WESTERFIELD TUCKER

C

CADBURY, GEORGE (1839–1922)

English businessman. George Cadbury was born on September 19, 1839, to a family whose ancestors had belonged to the SOCIETY OF FRIENDS for several generations. These Friends, or Quakers, prized hard work, self-discipline, social egalitarianism, and CHARITY, and Cadbury assiduously applied these values to his business.

In 1861, George and his brother Richard inherited a struggling family coffee and tea business that they would, by the turn of the century, transform into a paragon of Christian welfare capitalism. First, they abandoned coffee and tea for cocoa and chocolate, products considered socially useful because they could be partaken in lieu of alcohol. Then, in 1878, they decided to move their factory from the family's hometown of Birmingham, ENGLAND, to a bucolic site four miles outside the city. These decisions enabled the company and its workers to thrive, despite a depressed business climate, and reflected the Cadbury family's religious values.

The company offered generous pay and benefits. Cadbury promoted clean living by building an idyllic town around the factory, complete with cottages, gardens, and parks—but no pub. He extended decision-making power to his employees through a series of committees. When a female employee married, he sent her off with a BIBLE, a flower, and a small sum. (He did not believe that married women should work.) In his spare time, Cadbury taught reading and religion in the slums of Birmingham.

Cadbury received occasional criticism for his PACIFISM, his paternalistic treatment of employees, and for buying cocoa from countries where workers suffered abuse. Overall, though, he enjoyed great respect. After his death on October 24, 1922, more than 16,000 people attended his memorial service.

References and Further Reading

Dellheim, Charles. "The Creation of a Company Culture: Cadburys, 1861–1931." *The American Historical Review* 92 no. 1 (1987): 13–44.
Gardiner, A. G. *The Life of George Cadbury*. London: Cassell and Company, 1923.

ELESHA COFFMAN

CALIXT, GEORG (ORIGINAL SURNAME CALLISEN) (1587–1656)

German theologian. This embattled scholar of controversial THEOLOGY was born on December 14, 1587, in Medelby, GERMANY, near Flensburg, and died on March 19, 1656, in Helmstedt. His initial schooling came from his father, who had been a student of PHILIPP MELANCHTHON. Calixt's further studies in Helmstedt (after 1603), the center of late German Humanism, as well as his travels to the NETHERLANDS, ENGLAND, and Paris, profoundly influenced his moderate Lutheran humanism.

In 1614 Calixt became professor of controversial theology in Helmstedt. He emphasized the notion in no way new at the time, that the proclamation of DOCTRINE during the first five centuries of the Christian church could serve as the measure for the church of his time and could be turned polemically against Roman Catholicism. However, the horrors of the Thirty Years War, with its psychological devastation and physical destruction, prompted Calixt to reinterpret this notion with irony. He came to believe that despite many theological differences, all Christian churches recognized some essential truths, and that these were expressed in the first five centuries of Christianity in interpretations to which all Christians are bound. In this way of thinking (*consensus quinquesaecularis*), a concept not coined by Calixt, but one he adopted in 1648 from Johann Georg Dorsche, his opponent in Strasbourg, both reason and love were to compel a consensus within the CHURCH.

Catholics did not react when Calixt vigorously advocated this position, which did, however, provoke growing distrust from the strict Lutheran ORTHODOXY. He was attacked as a "rationalist," because he emphasized reason by downplaying the verbal inspiration of the BIBLE and by rejecting both the Lutheran doctrine of ubiquity and the distinction between theology and FAITH. In addition, Orthodox Lutherans objected that limiting oneself to the teachings of the apostles dismissed the central importance of the doctrine of JUSTIFICATION and with it Martin Luther's confessional writings.

Attacks against Calixt became even more severe with the efforts of Elector Friedrich Wilhelm of Brandenburg, the most powerful of the German electoral princes, who wanted Lutherans and Reformed within his territory to reconcile on the basis of the distinction between fundamental and nonfundamental articles of faith. At the colloquy of Turin in 1645, Lutherans distanced themselves from Calixt. When Calixt offered counsel to the Reformed a full controversy broke out. Calixt was considered a "syncretist" and "adulterator of religion." During the syncretist dispute that erupted in 1648, all German Lutherans opposed Calixt and Helmstedt theology. What resulted was a narrow, particularist understanding of the Lutheran church.

See also Lutheranism; Catholicism, Protestant Reactions

References and Further Reading

Calixt, Georg. *Werke in Auswahl.*, 4 vols. Göttingen, Germany: Ethische Schriften, 1970–1978.

MARTIN GRESCHAT

CALVERT FAMILY

The Calvert Family was a prominent Catholic household of seventeenth- and eighteenth-century ENGLAND and Maryland. George Calvert (1580–1632), the first baron of Baltimore, served as a knight in the court of King James I until he converted from ANGLICANISM to Roman Catholicism in 1625. James I, amid controversy over the CONVERSION, continued to support George by granting him a charter to start a colony in North America. When George died in 1632, the charter transferred to his son Cecil Calvert (1605–1675), the second Lord Baltimore. Cecil stayed in England to secure the prosperity of colonization, whereas his younger brother Leonard Calvert (1606–1647) led the Protestant and Catholic colonists to Maryland in 1634.

Maryland was the first English colony founded by Catholics in the New World. However, because the number of Protestant colonists outnumbered Catholics, Governor Leonard Calvert signed into law the "Act Concerning Religion" (1649) to guarantee the religious TOLERATION of all Christian churches subscribing to a belief in the Trinity.

Leonard ruled under the "Maryland Model" of religious toleration until a group of Protestant Virginians invaded the capital St. Mary's City in 1645. Charles Calvert (1637–1715), the third Lord Baltimore, tried to prevent the ascendancy of Protestant politicians, only to be overthrown by supporters of the GLORIOUS REVOLUTION in 1689. Afterward the Crown withdrew the proprietorship from the Calvert Family until Benedict Leonard Calvert (1679–1715) converted to the CHURCH OF ENGLAND in 1713. Charles Calvert (1699–1751) and Frederick Calvert (1731–1771), the last two lords of Baltimore, saw their proprietary influence gradually diminish in the face of a strengthening Protestant legislature.

See also Roman Catholicism, Protestant Reactions

References and Further Reading

Bossy, John. *The English Catholic Community 1570–1850.* New York: Oxford University Press, 1976.
Dolan, Jay. *The American Catholic Experience: A History From Colonial Times to the Present.* Garden City, NY: Doubleday, 1985.

MICHAEL PASQUIER

CALVIN, JOHN (1509–1564)

Protestant reformer and theologian. John Calvin was the most prominent spokesperson for the Reformed variety of sixteenth-century Protestantism, as distinguished from the variety led by MARTIN LUTHER (1483–1546).

Background

Calvin was born in Noyon, France, July 10, 1509, the son of a notary who worked for the local bishop. As a boy he was awarded a benefice to make possible his education for the priesthood. He went to Paris in 1523, where he studied first at the Collège de la Marche and then at the Collège Montaigu, famous for the rigor of its training in the classical humanities. When he finished that relatively elementary course, however, his father directed him to go on to study law, and he dutifully moved on to Orleans, where he completed requirements for a degree in law, with a brief period of legal study in Bourges as well. He then returned to Paris and began advanced study in the classical humanities, primarily with French scholar Guillaume Budé (1467–1540; an adviser and librarian to King Francis I; 1494–1547), who was a great authority on the Greek versions of Roman law. Calvin soon published a commentary on Seneca's *De clementia,* which was a typical exercise in Renaissance humanistic scholarship, closely examining the text of this classical essay, lingering over details in Seneca's use of rhetoric and pointing out details in its composition that had been overlooked by the great Erasmus.

During these years Calvin became interested in Protestantism and became active in a circle of Frenchmen who shared this interest, including Nicolas Cop, rector of the University of Paris, who created a sensation with his inaugural address in 1533 endorsing a Protestant approach to Christianity. That was followed in 1534 by the "affair of the placards," in which posters attacking the Roman Catholic Mass, with considerable virulence, were distributed all over France, provoking a major crackdown by the government on all Protestants. This led Calvin to abandon his benefice and leave the country, moving to the Protestant city of Basel and plunging into the systematic study of theology, apparently for the first time. There he voraciously read the writings of Protestant Reformers, most notably Luther, and the writings of the church fathers, most notably Augustine. The end result was the publication, in 1536, of a first Latin edition of the INSTITUTES OF THE CHRISTIAN RELIGION, a general summary of the entire Protestant theological position, basically an expansion of Luther's catechisms. Calvin spent much of the rest of his career enlarging and revising this book, translating it back and forth into French and Latin. It became one of the most important single summaries of Protestant theology.

Calvin then made quick trips to Italy, where he visited the court of the Duchess of Ferrara, Renée de France (daughter of a former king of France), who had a great interest in Protestantism, and to France, where he helped settle his parents' estate. On his way back toward GERMANY, Calvin stopped in Geneva, a city that had just revolted against the rule of its prince-bishop and his ally, the Duke of Savoy, and had declared its independence and its adoption of the Reformation. Geneva had been assisted in this revolution by the Swiss Protestant republic of Bern, then committed to Zwinglian Protestantism. Bern had sent William Farel to Geneva to lead the campaign to make that city Protestant. Farel visited Calvin in his lodgings and insisted that Calvin remain help in the work of reforming the local church. Calvin hesitated but finally agreed and was appointed a public lecturer in religion September 5, 1536. For the next two years Calvin assisted Farel in the work of creating a truly Reformed Church. Their efforts irritated the bourgeois ruling the city, however, and both were thrown out on short notice in 1538. Farel moved to Neuchatel, where he spent the rest of his life superintending its Re-

formed Church. Calvin moved to Strasbourg, where he became minister of the Church of French Protestant refugees. There he became well acquainted with MARTIN BUCER (1491–1551) and other local religious leaders. He had a chance to see how Strasbourg had organized its Reformed Church and to experiment in ways of organizing the community of Frenchmen there. He also attended a number of interconfessional conferences in various parts of Germany and met other Protestant leaders, most notably PHILIPE MELANCHTHON (1497–1560).

Geneva

Meanwhile Geneva had been drifting without well-qualified clerical leadership, subjected to pressures to return to Catholicism. Most notably Jacopo Sadoleto, the reforming Catholic bishop of Carpentras, had written a public letter to the Genevans begging them to return to the bosom of the Holy Mother Church. Genevan political leaders asked Calvin to publish a considered reply to Sadoleto's letter, and it became one of the best early summaries of his entire doctrinal position. These leaders then asked Calvin, alone, to return to Geneva and take over responsibility for creation of a truly Reformed Church in their city. In 1541 Calvin did return to Geneva, now accompanied by a new wife (who soon died), and remained in that city for the rest of his life.

One of Calvin's first responsibilities was to write sets of laws for the new republic. He first drafted the Ecclesiastical Ordinances, which created a kind of constitution for the Reformed Church. These were adopted by the city government, with only a few minor amendments, late in 1541. Calvin also helped draft, as a member of a small committee, a set of ordinances on offices and officers, which created a kind of constitution for the state. They were also adopted by the city government, with some more substantial amendments, in 1543. Both "constitutions" committed Geneva to collective leadership, resisting the notion common at that time that the most efficient government was the type that vested supreme power in one individual.

Calvin's Ecclesiastical Ordinances created four orders of ministry for the Reformed Church. The first order was of pastors, whose job it was to proclaim the Word of God by preaching and to administer the two remaining sacraments of communion and baptism. The second order was of doctors, who studied the Holy Scriptures and who instructed others in their content and meaning. Both pastors and doctors were full-time employees of the city of Geneva. The third order was of elders, who helped the pastors in maintaining Christian discipline. The fourth order was of deacons, who administered charity. Most of the elders and deacons were laymen who worked in these capacities on only a part-time basis. One deacon, however, did become a full-time city employee. He became the director of the General Hospital, the main center for charitable activity in Geneva, and lived with his wife in its building. In later years, when the city became flooded with refugees with their own special needs, additional deacons were selected from among refugees of wealth and prominence, who then helped take care of their less fortunate fellows.

The pastors and doctors met once a week in a body called the Company. Calvin became its moderator, presiding over its meetings and presenting its recommendations to the councils that actually ruled the city. The elders and pastors met once a week in a body called the Consistory, charged with examining local residents suspected of misbelief or misbehavior. Its presiding officer was one of the four syndics chosen every year as supreme magistrates of the republic. Calvin attended its meetings regularly, and was often called to administer the "remonstrances" or public scoldings that ended most of its cases.

The deacons also met once a week to act on requests for assistance and to regulate the General Hospital. Calvin did not take an active role in their activities, but he did take an active role later in the group of deacons created from among French refugees to supervise the granting of welfare to their indigent countrymen.

Calvin served as both a pastor and a doctor. He gave formal talks almost every day on the Holy Scriptures, either sermons in French intended for the general population or lectures in Latin intended primarily for students. He used the method of *lectio continuo* in his speaking, choosing one book of the Bible and going through it verse by verse, pericope by pericope, often taking the better part of a year to complete the analysis of it. He spoke on books of the New Testament and the Psalms on Sundays, interrupting his *lectio continuo* method on special feast days such as Christmas and Easter, with sermons based on biblical texts of relevance to the events in the life of Christ those days commemorate. He spoke on books of the Old Testament on weekdays and delivered his talks from memory without prepared texts. The city soon hired secretaries to copy them down verbatim; many of these copies survive, although a few of them have disappeared. Some of them were prepared for publication during Calvin's own lifetime, but others were never published and were not edited until the twentieth and twenty-first centuries. Over the course of his career, Calvin prepared commentaries on almost every book of the Bible. The one most obvious omission was the book of Revelations in the New Testament.

Calvin found it obscure and deliberately decided not to comment on it.

Calvin also helped institute and regularly attended public "congregations," or adult Bible classes. One or another of the pastors would present a commentary on a pericope drawn from Holy Scripture, and laymen would be invited to ask questions and present their own views of the passage. It was at one of these congregations in 1551 that Jerome Bolsec attacked Calvin's view of predestination, provoking an enormous uproar and a trial ending in Bolsec's expulsion from the city.

Through much of his career, Calvin was the only public lecturer charged with instructing Genevans (and a growing number of religious refugees) on the meaning of their faith. From the beginning, however, he had hoped that an institution of higher education could be created to take on this task on a more concerted basis. Finally in 1559, the College of Geneva was duly created, with THEODORE BEZA as its rector, and chairs of Hebrew and Greek as well as other relevant disciplines added. Calvin's lectures then became a part of its curriculum. This college eventually evolved into the present University of Geneva.

Calvin's success in Geneva was made possible by great numbers of religious refugees who came flooding into the city, most whom were from France, Italy, and other countries. Some of the local residents resented the influence and the power of these refugees and tried to restrict them. They were led by a sometime captian-general of Geneva's armed forces named Ami Perrin (?–1561). The issue between the followers of Calvin and Perrin centered around the powers of the Consistory and its right to excommunicate unrepentant sinners. The Perrinists wanted this right limited and subject to reversal on appeal by the city government. The Calvinists insisted that only the Consistory had the power to levy and to lift sentences of excommunication. A showdown occurred in 1555 and the Perrinists were decisively defeated; some of them were put to death, but most escaped into exile. From then on, Calvin's power in Geneva was without any effective challenge.

This made it possible for Geneva to provide international leadership to a new branch of Protestantism. Men trained to be Protestant ministers fanned out from Geneva into many other countries in Europe to spread the message of the new faith. Most of them went to France, but significant numbers went to Britain, including JOHN KNOX, the reformer of Scotland; to Germany, including Caspar Olevianus, the reformer of the palatinate; and the Marnix brothers, lay leaders of the Reformation in the Netherlands. In all of these countries, Calvin's followers adopted, often in consultation with Calvin himself, confessions of faith and books of discipline designed to replicate those used in Reformed Churches of the type favored by Calvin.

Geneva also became a major center of printing during Calvin's ministry, attracting a couple dozen printers, including Robert Estienne, who had been royal printer to the king of France. Calvin became the best-selling author of the works these printers published, including further editions of Calvin's *Institutes*, Bible editions and commentaries in which he had a role, liturgical guides and catechisms he had drafted, and a significant number of religious polemics aimed at Catholics, religious radicals, and, increasingly, Lutheran extremists.

Calvin also served during these triumphant years as an adviser to political leaders, particularly those representing the Protestant party in France. In these diplomatic initiatives he coordinated his activities closely with those of Henri Bullinger, Swiss religious reformer Huldrych Zwingli's (1484–1531) successor as leader of the Reformed Church in Zurich. Indeed a Geneva-Zurich understanding became crucial to the survival and spread of Calvinist Protestantism. It made it possible for Geneva to maintain the formal alliance with Zwinglian Bern that was necessary to guarantee its survival against Savoy. It also made it possible for the ideas and examples of Calvin and Bullinger to spread throughout Europe, creating the new form of Protestantism called Reformed Protestantism.

When Calvin died on May 27, 1564, his form of Protestantism was on the ascendant throughout Europe. Ironically, it was not to be very successful in the long run in his French homeland. It rather won its greatest success in other areas like Britain, including the British colonies of North America, in the NETHERLANDS, in parts of GERMANY, and in HUNGARY. In all of these areas, Calvinist movements survive to the present.

References and Further Reading

Primary Sources:

Barth, Petrus, and Guilielmus Niesel, eds. *Opera Selecta.* Munich: 1962–1952.
Baum, Guilielmus, Eduardus Cunita, and Eduardus Reuss, eds. *Ioannis Calvini Opera quae supersunt omnia.* Brunswick: 1863–1900.
International Congress on Calvin Research. *Ioannis Calvini Opera Omnia.* Geneva: Droz, 1992. Updated version of Baum, et al., *Ioannis Calvini Opera quae sipersunt omnia.*

Secondary Sources:

Bergier, Jean-François, and Robert M. Kingdon, eds. *Registres de la Compagnie des Pasteurs de Genève au temps de Calvin.* Geneva: Droz, 1962, 1964.
Bouwsma, William J. *John Calvin: A Sixteenth-Century Portrait.* New York and Oxford: Oxford University Press, 1988.
Doumergue, Emile. *Jean Calvin: Les Hommes et les choses de son temps.* Lausanne: Bridel and Neuilly-sur-Seine: Editions de "La Cause," 1899–1927.
Ganoczy, Alexandre. *Le jeune Calvin: Genèse et évolution de sa vocation reformatrice.* Wiesbaden: Steiner, 1966.
Lambert, Thomas A., and Isabella W. Watt, eds., under the supervision of Robert M. Kingdon. *Registres du Consistoire de Genève au temps de Calvin.* Geneva: Droz, 1996.
Rückert, Hanns, et al., eds. *Supplementa Calviniana: Sermons inédits.* Neukirchen Vluyn: Neukirchener Verlag, 1936– .
Wendel, François. *Calvin: Sources et évolution de sa pensée religieuse.* Paris: Presses universitaires de France, 1950.

ROBERT M. KINGDON

CALVINISM

The historical and theological movement associated with the teachings of JOHN CALVIN (1509–1564). Calvinism spread through Europe in the sixteenth century and into the new world. It became international in scope, exerting many influences on a variety of life-forms, both theological and cultural. Its importance as a social force as well as a theological understanding for Christian belief and living continues in many places through a multiplicity of churches, theologians, institutions, publishers, and activists. Calvinism as a living tradition still takes shape in communities whose realities are shaped by the ways their forebears in the Calvinistic stream have understood and appropriated the Christian faith in lives of dedicated service to the God they worship and know in Jesus Christ by the power of the Holy Spirit.

Historical Developments

Calvinism derives its name from John Calvin, and its spread can be traced historically through Europe from Geneva, where Calvin spent most of his career. Calvinism is often also designated as the "Reformed tradition." This term indicates the broad stream of theological thought that emerged from the reform movement associated with HULDRYCH ZWINGLI (1484–1531) in Zurich, which Calvin appropriated and shaped in his work in Geneva and, for a brief period, in Strasbourg. The "Reformed tradition" was a reformation movement in contrast to the Lutheran tradition (LUTHERANISM) and the Anabaptist tradition (ANABAPTISM), and with them in common opposition against ROMAN CATHOLICISM. Calvin was the major systematizer and leading theologian of the Reformed tradition and thus the equivalence with the term "Calvinism" is often made.

Yet other important theologians were also part of the Reformed tradition and were both influential on Calvin and influenced by him. These include JOHANNES OECOLAMPADIUS (1482–1531), MARTIN BUCER

(1491–1551), Peter Martyr Vermigli (1500–1562), JOHN KNOX (c. 1513–1572), JOHANN HEINRICH BULLINGER (1504–1575), Girolamo Zanchi (1516–1590), and Calvin's immediate successor as leader of the Genevan reformation, THEODORE BEZA (1519–1605). These reformers shaped the theology of the movement and contributed to its organizational life in churches and by their impact on their surrounding cultures.

Switzerland

Zwingli's reforms of the Zurich church helped spark reforms in Basel and Bern. He emphasized reform according to the word of God in Scripture, and began the practice of PREACHING on successive texts through a biblical book (LECTIO CONTINUA). Theologically, he came into conflict with MARTIN LUTHER (1483–1546), particularly on the issue of the presence of Christ in the Lord's Supper. The two split at the MARBURG COLLOQUY (1529). Zwingli argued that sacraments "represent" Christ rather than "present" Christ through any mode of special presence. Jesus's words at the Lord's Supper: "This is my body" (Matthew 26:26) were interpreted by Zwingli as "This signifies my body." Zwingli initiated WORSHIP reforms, destroying images in churches, and declared that the mass was not a sacrifice but a remembrance of the sacrifice of Jesus Christ. Zwingli's successor Bullinger, and Oecolampadius in Basel, continued his reforming tradition.

Calvin came to Geneva as a young humanist scholar who published the first edition of his *Institutes of the Christian Religion* in 1536. The French reformer Guillaume Farel (1489–1565), who introduced Reformation thought to the city, persuaded Calvin to join him in the work of reform. In the next two years they sought such thorough reforms of the church—both in belief and practice—that they were asked to leave. In 1538 Calvin journeyed to Strasbourg, where for the next two years he was pastor of a French refugee congregation and imbibed much from Bucer, whose influence can be detected in Calvin's later writings, especially on the DOCTRINES of election and the sacraments.

When Cardinal Sadoleto tried to persuade Geneva to return to Roman Catholicism, the city council asked Calvin to respond to the cardinal and also to return to give leadership to the church and the city. Calvin did so in 1541 and remained there until his death. His activities and writing output were prodigious as he lectured on the Bible, preached, wrote theological treatises, met with the Consistory and the Company of Pastors, wrote numerous letters, and was active in virtually every aspect of the city's life. In addition, he revised the *Institutes* until its final Latin edition

(1559). Calvin's active life, including his way of understanding Scripture, theological perceptions, and leadership in church organization and educational establishments, notably the Genevan Academy (1559), made him, along with Luther, the most significant church reformer of the Protestant movement.

Geneva was described by Calvin's disciple, John Knox, as "the most perfect school of Christ on earth since the days of the apostles." It had become a center of refugee traffic and sought diligently to integrate these new residents into city life. The establishment of DEACONS as an office in the church brought with it a commitment to the social welfare and care of the poor. Calvin's reform of the church meant reform in society as well. He emphasized CHURCH DISCIPLINE and an ordered church life that was "presbyterian" in focus, establishing authority in the church through pastors and elected lay leaders from a number of local churches, which constituted a "presbytery" (or "colloquy"). Decision making was thus corporate rather than individual. These aspects of Calvin's work were also features of later "Calvinism."

Calvin's substantial influence meant that the growing number of Swiss Reformed churches looked more to Geneva than to Zurich for leadership. When Calvin died (1564) he was succeeded by his colleague Beza, who was also influential on Reformed churches throughout Europe. Areas of theological conflict had arisen, such as predestination and the Lord's Supper, with variations of thought found among leading Reformed theologians.

Those who looked to Calvin as the seminal influence for their theologies also went on to build methods and ways of understanding that developed Calvin's thought in more systematic and detailed ways. This seventeenth-century movement is sometimes called "Calvinist scholasticism" or "Reformed orthodoxy." Contemporary scholars have argued the legitimacy of these developments and whether later Calvinist theologians made shifts that would not have been approved by Calvin himself. Yet these later theologians wrote in their own historical contexts—warding off particularly the attacks of Roman Catholic theologians—and that new forms of Calvin's views were needed to provide viable theological positions.

A prominent example of a scholastic Calvinist theologian was FRANCIS TURRETINI (1623–1687), who became professor of theology at the Geneva Academy in 1648. His three-volume *Institutio theologiae elencticae* (1679–1685) became the most important work of systematic theology produced in Geneva in the seventeenth century. The Helvetic Consensus Formula (1675), adopted by four Swiss cantons and some individual cities, also reflected the developed, scholasticizing tendency and is most notable for its view that the words of Scripture (including the Hebrew vowel points) were directly inspired by God.

Turretin's son, Jean-Alphonse Turretin (1671–1737), succeeded his father but did not continue strict Calvinism. Later theological developments in Geneva and throughout Switzerland moved toward the rationalistic tendencies of the ENLIGHTENMENT. Yet as the birthplace of Calvinism and for its many contributions to developments of Calvinism, Switzerland holds a prime place in the story of Calvinism's historical and theological emergence.

France

Calvin's works became known in FRANCE from the early 1540s. Calvin continually produced French editions of the successive volumes of his *Institutes*, and nine of Calvin's writings appeared on the first comprehensive Index of Forbidden Books issued by the Roman Catholic Church. Geneva was tagged as a center of heresy by King Henry II's Edict of Châteaubriand (1551) and all contact with the city was forbidden.

In the following decade, however, groups of French evangelicals that emerged as Christians nourished by Calvin's writings became more formalized through the planting of Calvinist churches. By 1559 the French Calvinist church developed a basic organization with its first national synod meeting in Paris, where eleven churches were represented. This synod adopted a church discipline and common Confession of Faith (French confession) that laid the foundation for the national church to increase its strength. This national polity featured a local church consistory (session), a colloquy (presbytery), provisional synod, and a national synod. Here was a Presbyterian form of government enacted on a national level (see PRESBYTERIANISM). In 1571 the French Confession was revised in minor ways and adopted by the synod of La Rochelle. It became one of the premier expressions of the Reformed faith.

The Wars of Religion in France (from 1562) hampered the spread and growth of Calvinism. French Reformed Christians, called Huguenots, were persecuted. Most notorious was the massacre of St. Bartholomew's Day (August 24, 1572) in which Roman Catholics killed some 3,000 Huguenots in Paris and thousands more in the provinces. This violence was initiated through an assassination attempt on Gaspard II de Collgny (1519–1572), a Huguenot leader and admiral who was the political leader of the Reformed churches. Catherine de Médicis, mother of the French King Charles IX, had secretly ordered the assassination at a time when many leaders were in Paris for the marriage of Henry of Navarre (Henry IV); during the

reign of Louis XIV (1643–1715), some 250,000 Huguenots fled to Holland, England, Germany, Switzerland, and North America. Through their efforts the Calvinist faith was spread throughout Europe and into the new world.

In 1594 Henry of Navarre (Henry IV) was crowned king. Henry was a Protestant who gave up his religion with the famous expression, "Paris is worth a Mass!" to become ruler. However, Calvinist communities under his reign gained freedoms—with restrictions—through the EDICT OF NANTES (1598). This edict granted them the status of a "state within a state" with civil rights and freedom of worship. It was later revoked (1687) and persecutions of Calvinist believers resumed until the French Revolution (1789) brought religious toleration to the nation. In the following century, French Calvinism began to erode.

Netherlands and the Low Countries

The penetration of Calvinism into the Netherlands has been more pervasive than in any other country. Dutch Calvinism has been a leading force in contributing to the society in a wide variety of ways. In the struggle for independence from Spain, Dutch Calvinists were exemplary models of courage and faithful conviction. The SYNOD of Dort (1618–1619) was a significant turning point, providing a definitive theological statement of Calvinist belief over the ARMINIANISM of James Arminius (1560–1609) and his followers. Later, important Calvinist leaders such as ABRAHAM KUYPER (1837–1920), Herman Bavinck (1854–1921), and G. C. Berkouwer (1903–1996) provided significant theological and cultural contributions that permeated Dutch society.

European refugees brought Calvinism to the Netherlands. In Geneva, Calvin met a number of leaders of the Dutch reform. He sent his successor as pastor of the French refugee church at Strassbourg, Pierre Brully, to preach in the Netherlands. After three months, Brully was burned to death for expressing his faith, but his work led to a steady growth of Reformed churches into the southern Netherlands and the Low Countries.

Calvin's writings became known and his 1559 *Institutes* was translated into Dutch (1560). This work and Bullinger's *Decades* were the key theological texts for Dutch Reformed Christians. Calvin also wrote treatises for his followers there. Three of them (1543; 1544; 1562) indicated how they should live in the midst of papists and persecutions. Two others analyzed the threats to the Reformed movement posed by Anabaptism and spiritualism.

This spreading Calvinism was marked by steadfastness in the face of persecution as well as by variations within theology. Some believed Calvin's injunctions to practice faith openly were too rigorous. Others sought a more Erasmian theology, while still others preferred the high Augustinianism Calvin represented. The church's first national synod met in Emden in East Friesland (1571). This synod endorsed the BELGIAN CONFESSION (1559; revised 1561), which was modeled after the French Confession (1559), and sought to instruct the faithful within the church while summarizing the Reformed faith for those outside. The HEIDELBERG CATECHISM (1563), written in the palatinate, was also important in providing a strong, personalized appropriation of Calvinist perspectives. Preaching and teaching from the catechism on a regular basis, especially to the young, were important ingredients in strengthening the Reformed faith in the Netherlands.

Calvinist communities joined in the long fight against Spain. By 1608 the United Provinces gained independence and the Reformed church came to dominate the nation's life, though for a long period Calvinist Christians did not constitute a majority of the population. The Synod of Dort established Calvinist doctrine with the famous "Five Points of Calvinism": Total Depravity, Unconditional Election, Limited Atonement, Irresistible Grace, and the Perseverance of the Saints (TULIP). It clarified the church's POLITY and provided for a new translation of the Scriptures into Dutch. After Dort, the Reformed church became the privileged church of the Dutch republic.

The "Further Reformation" (*Nadere Reformatie*) of the seventeenth century emerged through a mixture of Reformed scholasticism and PIETISM. Prominent Dutch theologians such as Willem Teellinck (1579–1629) and William Brakel (1635–1711), influenced by English PURITANISM, sought a revival of piety within the church and a stronger emphasis on experiential religion in the face of precise doctrinalism. The theologian Gisbert Voetius (1589–1676) became a champion of Calvinist orthodoxy while also being deeply influenced by the pietist movement.

The Enlightenment and its movement toward a "rational faith" affected the Netherlands in the eighteenth century. Yet the Dutch emphasis on missions and piety continued, and the nineteenth-century revival (*Réveil*) in Europe strongly affected the Dutch church in its reaction against the French Revolution and Enlightenment tendencies. Many Dutch Calvinists emphasized repentance, conversion, and practical Christian living as well as faithfulness to theological standards of the church. A secession from the established church of those affected by the revival occurred (1834), followed by another (1886) led by theologian and statesman Abraham Kuyper. The two seceder groups formed the Reformed Churches of the Netherlands (1892). This group emphasized confessional fidelity and church discipline as well as mission outreach. Church leaders founded the Free University of Amsterdam.

Germany

Reformed congregations in the Rhineland in Germany were active beginning in the time of John Laski (à Lasco; 1499–1560), who became pastor in Emden (1543) and introduced worship that was structured like that of Strasbourg and Geneva. Reformed churches expanded in Lower Saxony after Elector Frederick III of the palatinate was converted to Reformed Protestantism (1563), and later, congregations were begun in the Rhineland. These congregations endured through the Thirty Years War (1618–1648) and were influenced by theologians such as Zacharias Ursinus (1534–1583) and Caspar Olevianus (1536–1587) and nourished by the Heidelberg Catechism (1563), which became the backbone of German Calvinism. This catechism, commissioned by Frederick III and written by Ursinus and Olevianus, was to be a standard of doctrine to bring peace and unite the regional churches.

Calvinist theologians who were active in the University of Heidelberg included Ursinus, Girolamo Zanchi (1516–1590), and THOMAS ERASTUS (1524–1583). Zanchi was a key figure in the development of Reformed scholasticism. Erastus, a theologian and physician, was influenced by Zwingli, and advocated the view that the civil state has final earthly authority over the expression and practice of religious beliefs as well as over ecclesiastical organizations.

Lutheranism became the primary faith of Protestant Christians in Germany, where the Formula of Concord (1577; see BOOK OF CONCORD) forced all theologians to choose sides between Luther and Calvin. It was not until the nineteenth century that "Union churches," which blended Reformed and Lutheran congregations, were established in the Prussian territories. The Reformed theologian Friedrich Schleiermacher (1768–1834) taught at the University of Berlin and was co-pastor of Trinity Church with a Lutheran colleague, Philipp Marheinecke, for twenty-six years. Schleiermacher's *The Christian Faith* (1821–1822; 2nd ed. 1831–1832) earned him the title "the father of modern theology."

Hungary

Calvinism in HUNGARY has been a powerful force. The Reformed interpretation of the Reformation spread rapidly among the agricultural towns in the eastern and southern parts of Hungary from the 1550s. The primary theological influence was from Bullinger in Zurich, who sent the *Consensus Tigurinus* ("Agreement of Zurich" [1551]), composed jointly with Calvin, to Hungary for approval. Hungarian churches accepted Bullinger's Second Helvetic Confession (1566; see HELVETIC CONFESSION[s]) and the Confession at Debrecen (1567) as doctrinal standards. A Reformed theological academy was established at Debrecen and the first Hungarian Bible was published (1590). During the "dark decade" (1671–1681), Hungarian churches were severely repressed and occupied under the Hapsburgs. The Edict of Toleration (1781) led to more normal activity, but persecution followed again in the mid-1800s. The United Synod (1881) established a presbyterian system of church government and helped to revive spiritual life.

England

The English Reformation, ignited by King HENRY VIII's (1491–1547) renunciation of papal authority and his establishment of the Church of England (1534), led to a process of church reform. The BOOK OF COMMON PRAYER (1549) reformed worship, and the Forty-Two Articles (1553; later the THIRTY-NINE ARTICLES, 1571) reformed doctrine. The established Anglican Church maintains elements of both Catholicism and Protestantism.

ELIZABETH I (1533–1603; queen from 1558) instituted a "middle way" called the "Elizabethan Settlement" (1559) as a means of reestablishing the Protestant directions provided under the reign of Edward VI (1547–1553). A "Puritan party" emerged that wanted fuller church reforms along Calvinistic lines. Many "Puritans" later became Presbyterians or Congregationalists (see CONGREGATIONALISM). They were influenced by Calvinist theology, with Calvin's authority as primary. During the period of Mary Tudor's Catholic rule (1553–1555), a number of "Marian Exiles" had fled to the European continent and imbibed theology in such places of Reformed influence as Geneva and were influenced by the teachings of Calvin. When they returned under Elizabeth, they came to places of power within the established church, bringing with them to various degrees a "Calvinism" that permeated both their theological and ecclesiastical outlooks.

Those Puritans who wished to "purify" the church along lines of Presbyterianism were unsuccessful in establishing this polity as the national norm. During the 1640s, however, in the midst of the English Civil War, they controlled the English Parliament and participated in the WESTMINSTER ASSEMBLY (1643–1649), which adopted the WESTMINSTER CONFESSION of Faith and Catechisms. When Oliver Cromwell (1599–1658) became the "Lord Protector," Presbyterian members of Parliament were purged and Congregationalists were favored. But the reign of Charles II (1660–1685)

led to a return to an episcopal form of church government where "nonconformists" (Presbyterians and Congregationalists) were deprived of legal status. The Toleration Act (1689) legalized the position of dissenters to the established church. Both the Presbyterians and Congregationalists were Calvinist in theology, with differing amounts of influence from later Calvinist scholastics also being apparent.

Scotland

The Scottish Reformation was led by John Knox, who studied in Geneva under Calvin and was the primary author of the Scots Confession (1560). Knox returned to Scotland to establish Calvin's theology and a system of church reform based on the pattern of Calvin's Geneva. A Book of Common Order and Book of Discipline were enacted. In the act of 1592 the king and Parliament recognized the Scottish church system. In 1689 Presbyterianism was permanently established.

Calvinism in Scotland remained vital as a theological and cultural force through the following centuries. Notable theologians reflected Calvinism in various shades. These include Donald (1887–1954) and JOHN (1886–1960) BAILLIE, JOHN MCLEOD CAMPBELL (1800–1872), P. T. FORSYTH (1848–1921), James McCosh (1811–1894), Hugh R. Mackintosh (1870–1936), and James Orr (1844–1913).

North America

Calvinism spread to North America through a variety of influences, most prominently the Puritans of England and the Netherlands who emigrated to the new world and the Scotch-Irish settlers. These forms of Calvinism were expressed in Baptist, Congregational, and Presbyterian churches and polities. One estimate indicates that by the time of the American Revolution (1776), three fourths of the people in the future United States were directly influenced by the Reformed tradition. Other eighteenth-century immigrant groups to America, such as the Dutch and German Reformed, were also important in establishing churches.

The Reformed tradition of Calvinism was brought to CANADA by Presbyterians who had come from the British Isles and the American colonies, Congregationalists who emigrated from New England, and by Congregationalist "independents" who arrived from Great Britain. Each continued to maintain the Calvinist traditions of their homelands until gradually, Calvinist churches that are distinctively Canadian emerged.

The theological heritage of North American Calvinism owes much to Calvin and the other continental Calvinists who followed him. The confessional tradition that includes the Westminster Confession and Catechisms, the Scots Confession, the Second Helvetic Confession, and the Heidelberg Catechism has also been significant. Later followers of Calvin whose theological works convey a more fully developed Calvinism also played key roles in the development of North American Calvinism. These include theologians such as WILLIAM PERKINS (1558–1602), WILLIAM AMES (1576–1633), John Owen (1616–1683), and Francis Turretin.

Calvinism in the United States also became a leading cultural force in the colonial period. Emphases on learning and the importance of higher education led to the establishment of numerous colleges. Cultural transformation has been sought through a variety of means including evangelical, social, political action. Calvinists have been particularly involved in POLITICS with the American JOHN WITHERSPOON (1723–1794; born in Scotland), President of the College of New Jersey (later Princeton University), being the only clergyperson to sign the Declaration of Independence.

The first permanent Calvinist settlements in the United States were by separatist Puritans in Plymouth (1620) and conforming Puritans in what became Massachusetts (1628). New England PURITANISM with its Calvinistic expressions was guided by the Cambridge Synod and CAMBRIDGE PLATFORM (1646–1648). A congregational church polity was adopted and modifications made in the Westminster Confession. Thus the prevailing ethos of New England Calvinism has been Congregationalist.

Significant New England Puritans include JOHN COTTON (1585–1652), INCREASE MATHER (1639–1723), COTTON MATHER (1663–1728), TIMOTHY DWIGHT (1752–1817), HORACE BUSHNELL (1802–1876), and JONATHAN EDWARDS (1703–1758), whom many consider America's greatest theologian. Edward's modifications to New England Calvinism laid the groundwork for the "New England Theology" and its exponents Joseph Bellamy (1719–1790) and SAMUEL HOPKINS (1721–1803).

American Presbyterianism in the United States was dominated by the "Princeton Theology," associated with three dominant professors of Princeton Theological Seminary (1812). Archibald Alexander (1772–1851), CHARLES HODGE (1797–1878), and Benjamin B. Warfield (1851–1921) taught a scholastic Calvinism that was the dominant tradition in the United States throughout the nineteenth and early twentieth centuries. Hodge taught more theological students than any other professor in the period, while his three-volume Systematic Theology (1872–1873) became the major theological textbook for generations of Calvinist adherents.

The MERCERSBURG THEOLOGY from the Theological Seminary of the German Reformed Church in Mercersburg (later Lancaster), Pennsylvania was a more moderate form of Calvinism. Its leaders were John W. Nevin (1803–1886) and PHILIP SCHAFF (1819–1893). This movement stressed the centrality of Christ, his presence in the Lord's Supper, and an irenic stance toward non-Reformed Christians.

International Calvinism

During its first 300 years, Calvinism was primarily centered in Europe and North America. The missionary movements of the nineteenth and twentieth centuries, however, and especially post-World War II efforts, have led to the establishment of new churches in AFRICA and Asia. The fastest current growth of churches with Calvinist roots are in areas such as KOREA, South America, and Africa. The World Alliance of Reformed Churches (WARC), a worldwide organization of churches that claim a Reformed or Calvinist heritage, now embraces 215 member churches in 106 countries, representing over 75 million Christians. The largest numbers of member churches are in Asia and Africa.

Theological Understandings

The theology of Calvinism has been defined and explicated in many ways. First-generation theologians of the Reformed tradition each made significant contributions and promulgated certain theological understandings and emphases. The development of Calvinism through the centuries has meant a further proliferation of theological systems, themes, and particular doctrines to be stressed. Calvinism has produced a number of highly important theologians who have attempted to practice theology in obedience to God's revelation in Scripture and in a way that is intelligible to their contemporaries in many cultural settings.

In addition to the numerous systematic theologies and theological books, there are also many Reformed confessions and creedal statements from churches throughout the world from the sixteenth century until the present day. Each of these was written to expound an understanding of what Scripture teaches and to witness or confess Christian faith at a particular time and place in history. It has been a particular Calvinistic conviction that Christian faith needs to be confessed anew in the cultural contexts in which Christians find themselves.

Calvinism has produced theologies that have held firmly to the orthodoxies of the early Christian centuries on such key Christian doctrines as the Trinity and CHRISTOLOGY. Early Reformed theologians in the sixteenth century and their followers constantly stressed their allegiance to the views of God and Jesus Christ expressed in the ancient church councils.

The distinctive marks of Calvinist theology come with the ways in which the implications of the Trinity and Christology are expressed under the authority of the Holy Scriptures, which Calvinism has continually affirmed as God's divine revelation and the place where the Word of God is written and heard. Some Calvinist theologians have held to a view of the verbal inspiration of Scripture. Because "all Scripture is inspired by God" (2 Timothy 3:16) it must also share in God's attributes of perfection and truthfulness. This has led some to support a view of "biblical inerrancy" in which the original autographs of Scripture are held to be without error in what they teach and affirm. Other Calvinist theologians have spoken of the "infallibility" of Scripture in that the Bible is infallible in its theological purpose—to be God's revelation of how SALVATION may be found. Yet for these theologians, the infallibility of Scripture does not necessarily imply its inerrancy or factual accuracy at every point because Scripture's purpose is primarily theological. Still other theologians of the Reformed tradition, notably KARL BARTH (1886–1968), spoke of Scripture as the "witness" to the Word of God—who is ultimately Jesus Christ. Scripture becomes "Word of God" when, by the Holy Spirit, it points beyond itself to God's divine revelation in Jesus Christ. Thus the Bible itself does not need to be infallible or inerrant to accomplish this purpose.

One of Calvinism's central convictions is that God is the initiator of all things and that humans respond. Calvinism's impulse through all Christian doctrines is God's gracious initiative and humanity's grateful response. This is seen, for example, in the doctrine of election or predestination with which Calvinism has been strongly associated. Calvinism affirms that in salvation, it is God who does for humanity what humans cannot do for themselves: saves them. Humans are captive to the power of sin, which has been with us since the origins of the human race (thus "origin-al sin"). Sin is so pervasive that the totality of life—thought and will—are affected ("total depravity"). Sinful humans themselves are not capable of responding to God's love and gracious desire to live in a relationship of trust and obedience. Without this response, life has no ultimate meaning and death and judgment follow. Yet God takes a gracious initiative and saves those whom God has "elected" to receive salvation. Through the work of the Holy Spirit, the gift of faith is given and humans become a "new creation" with a new will and desire to love and serve God. This is possible through the death of Jesus Christ on the cross, who achieved reconciliation between God and sinful humanity. Calvinism has understood the Scriptures to teach that this election has taken place "before the foundation of the world" (Eph. 1:4) and is thus a totally free gift of God's grace with no human achievement involved at all. Humans receive the gift of faith through the Holy Spirit and respond in gratitude, trust, and love to God's gracious initiative. Thus, election or predestination means that salvation occurs purely by God's grace ("Unconditional Election").

Calvinism's understandings of other doctrines also emphasize this divine priority. The church is the body or fellowship of all those who have realized their election and is drawn together by the power of God's Spirit, not by human volition. The sacraments—BAPTISM and the Lord's Supper—are God's gracious ways of strengthening and nourishing faith, given as gifts to the church. Christians are sustained in their lives of faith and discipleship by the power of the Holy Spirit at work within them and among them in the church. They persevere to ultimate salvation by God's power constantly exercised in their lives ("Perseverance of the Saints"). Thus, the instinct of Calvinism through all doctrines is to move in the direction of stressing God's prior initiative and our grateful response. God is sovereign; God is the Lord; humans receive God's gifts gratefully and live in joyful obedience to God in Jesus Christ. Thus, Calvinism affirms Paul's injunction: "Do everything for the glory of God" (1 Corinthians 10:31).

See also Calvin, John; *Book of Concord*; Congregationalism; Helvetic Confession; Presbyterianism.

References and Further Reading

Benedetto, Robert, Darrell L. Guder, and Donald K. McKim. *Historical Dictionary of Reformed Churches.* Lanham, MD: Scarecrow Press, 1999.

Duke, Alastair, Gillian Lewis, and Andrew Pettegree, eds. *Calvinism in Europe 1540–1610: A Collection of Documents.* Manchester: Manchester University Press, 1992.

Graham, W. Fred, ed. *Later Calvinism: International Perspectives.* Kirksville, MO: Sixteenth Century Journal Publishers, 1994.

Heppe, Heinrich. *Reformed Dogmatics.* Reviewed and edited by Ernst Bizer, translated by G.T. Thomson. Grand Rapids, MI: Baker Book House, 1978.

Hillerbrand, Hans J., ed. *The Oxford Encyclopedia of the Reformation.* New York: Oxford University Press, 1996.

Leith, John H. *Introduction to the Reformed Tradition.* Atlanta: John Knox Press, 1977.

McKim, Donald K., ed. *Encyclopedia of the Reformed Faith.* Louisville, KY: Westminster John Knox Press, 1992.

McKim, Donald K., ed. *Major Themes in the Reformed Tradition.* Eugene, OR: Wipf and Stock, 1998.

McNeill, John T. *The History and Character of Calvinism.* New York: Oxford University Press, 1954.

Naphy, William G. *Calvin and the Consolidation of the Genevan Reformation.* Manchester: Manchester University Press, 1994.

Pettegree, Andrew, Alastair Duke, and Gillian Lewis, eds. *Calvinism in Europe 1540–1620.* Cambridge: Cambridge University Press, 1994.

Prestwich, Menna, ed. *International Calvinism 1541–1715.* London: Oxford University Press, 1985.

Reid, W. Stanford, ed. *John Calvin: His Influence in the Western World.* Grand Rapids, MI: The Zondervan Corporation, 1982.

DONALD K. McKIM

CAMBRIDGE PLATFORM

In 1648 Puritan leaders from Connecticut and Massachusetts set forth their understanding of the CHURCH and its faith in the document called the Cambridge Platform. It remained the basis of New England church order until about 1760, by which time religious pluralism and political rumblings clearly had changed the social context. Drafted at the time of the Puritan Commonwealth in ENGLAND, the document aligned the beliefs and practices of New England Puritans with those of Reformed churches across the Atlantic.

Adopting the WESTMINSTER CONFESSION, the Platform placed primary AUTHORITY in the local church, but allowed for oversight on matters of faith by representative synods. Encouraged by the General Court of Massachusetts, the Platform also encouraged an integration of CHURCH AND STATE in New England. Ecclesiastical and civil authorities were to occupy their own, separate spheres of influence. No theocracy was intended; however, the work of both state and church was to be grounded in biblical law, and each was expected to honor the authority of the other in its sphere.

In particular the Platform envisioned that magistrates would uphold biblical precedent in administering civil law. Thus, "Idolatry, Blasphemy, Heresie, venting corruption and pernicious Opinions, that destroy the Foundation, open contempt of the Word preached, Profanation of the Lords Day, disturbing the peaceable Administration and the Exercise of the Worship and holy things of God, and the like, are to be restrained and punished by Civil Authority."

See also Pilgrim Fathers; Puritanism

References and Further Reading

Handy, Robert T. *A Christian America.* Oxford: Oxford University Press, 1984.

McNeill, John T. *The History and Character of Calvinism.* Oxford: Oxford University Press, 1967.

Smith, H. Shelton, Robert T. Handy, and Lefferts Loetscher, eds. *American Christianity: An Historical Interpretation With Representative Documents.* New York: Scribner, 1960–1963.

WILLIAM SACHS

CAMBRIDGE PLATONISTS

The seventeenth century was a time of strident theological controversy, but in England a group of men called the Cambridge Platonists attempted to take a moderate view. They were linked by friendship and residence at the same university in the middle of the seventeenth century. They were a part of the English Platonic movement and were rational supranaturalists. Their foundational biblical text was Proverbs 20:27, "The spirit of man is the candle of the Lord." Among the Cambridge Platonists were Benjamin Whichcote, John Smith, HENRY MORE, Ralph Cudworth, Nathaneal Culverwel, John Norris, Joseph Glanvill, Peter Sterry, Richard Cumberland, George Rust, Theophilus Gale, and John Worthington.

All the Cambridge Platonists were university teachers and placed a heavy emphasis on classical antiquity and learning. They continued the humanism that came from the Renaissance and Erasmus and that permeated the English Reformation. They were all faculty at Emmanuel College, the most Puritan (see PURITANISM) and Calvinistic of the Cambridge colleges. Although critical of the CALVINISM that dominated the CHURCH OF ENGLAND before the Restoration in 1660, they were opposed to the ARMINIANISM that triumphed with the Restoration and also critical of the High Church ANGLICANISM of the Caroline divines.

Although they were called Cambridge Platonists, they were really more influenced by Plotinus and were more accurately "Neo-Platonists." They inherited from this tradition the immutable principles of morality, a sincere trust in man and human reason, the spiritual interpretation of reality, and the role of reason and ideas in human life.

The spirit of man is reason. Human reason is what it means to be made in the image of God. Reason is the voice of God and the presence of God in humanity. To go against reason is to go against God. Jesus Christ is the Logos of God or God's reason become incarnate. This incarnate Logos enlightens human reason. Scripture confirms the natural truth that is discerned by reason. Scripture gives certainty to ideas anticipated in philosophy, such as the immortality of the soul, and HEAVEN AND HELL.

The Cambridge Platonists stressed that natural theology and revealed theology did not differ. They rejected the exclusive claims of revealed theology and Scripture and believed that human beings have a natural knowledge of God. Plato and Moses were inspired by the same God. This natural knowledge of God they called "the truths of first inscription." In this regard the Cambridge Platonists were in the tradition of Clement, Origen, and the Greek Apologists. They granted theological primacy to the Greek fathers led by Origen, and they also were in the Johannine tradition of the New Testament.

The moral element in Scripture was supreme for the Cambridge Platonists. The heart of the gospel is its ethical content (see ETHICS). The most important element in Christianity is moral. Thus they stressed ethics, conduct, and morality. Conduct is more important than creeds. There is a moral law and humans can know it by reason. Humans can know the right and do it.

The Cambridge Platonists taught that faith and reason worked together. Christianity does not repudiate reason but uses it. True religious faith never contradicts reason, that is, faith and reason are consistent. The seat of AUTHORITY in religion is the individual conscience governed by reason and illuminated by revelation.

They rejected Calvinism and could not "swallow down that hard doctrine concerning fate." They opposed that "Black doctrine of absolute reprobation," that is, that God condemns some people to hell. They believed that Calvinism had too rigid a separation of the human and the divine, that it distrusted all human affections and faculties, and that it played down reason. They opposed the doctrine of the depravity of human beings and believed that Calvinistic dogmatism promoted contention and bitterness.

At the same time, the Cambridge Platonists accepted the established Church of England and its episcopacy. They accepted episcopacy, that is, the historic episcopate on rational and aesthetic grounds. For them church POLITY was secondary. They were against the Laudians (followers of archbishop of Canterbury WILLIAM LAUD) who seemed to make polity more important than morality. They also accepted the BOOK OF COMMON PRAYER. They were comfortable with a middle way in thought as well as in ritual and church order.

The Cambridge Platonists were reasonable but not rationalistic. They were opposed to the controversies of their age and had what could be called a "sweetness of temper." They were convinced that argument does not promote the Christian life. As advocates for religious freedom and liberty of conscience, they stressed TOLERATION and had an influence on philosopher JOHN LOCKE contributing to the passing of the Toleration Act of 1689.

References and Further Reading

Campagnac, E. T., ed. *The Cambridge Platonists. Being Selections from the Writings of Benjamin Whichcote, John Smith and Nathanael Culverwel.* Oxford, UK: Clarendon Press, 1901.

Cassirer, Ernst. *The Platonic Renaissance in England.* Translated by James P. Pettigrove. Austin: University of Texas Press, 1953.

Cragg, Gerald R., ed. *The Cambridge Platonists.* New York: Oxford University Press, 1968.

DePauley, William Cecil. *The Candle of the Lord: Studies in the Cambridge Platonists.* Freeport, NY: Books for Libraries Press, 1970.

Pawson, Geoffrey Philip Henry. *The Cambridge Platonists and Their Place in Religious Thought.* New York: B. Franklin Reprints, 1974.

Powicke, Frederick J. *The Cambridge Platonists, A Study.* London: J. M. Dent, 1926.

Tulloch, John. *Rational Theology and Christian Philosophy in England in the Seventeenth Century.* Edinburgh: W. Blackwood, 1872.

Wood, Doreen Anderson. "The Spirit and the Candle: A Study of the Cambridge Platonists." *Historical Magazine of the Protestant Episcopal Church* 36 (March 1967): 63–79.

DONALD S. ARMENTROUT

CAMBRIDGE UNIVERSITY

For more than three hundred years, the University of Cambridge dominated English-speaking Protestant thought.

The English Reformation began in a Cambridge tavern in the 1520s known to insiders as "Little Germany." Thomas Bilney, HUGH LATIMER, WILLIAM TYNDALE, and MILES COVERDALE were all members of the University during the reign of HENRY VIII. THOMAS CRANMER, first Protestant archbishop of Canterbury, was a Fellow of Jesus College and University Examiner in Divinity. The German reformer MARTIN BUCER was Regius professor of divinity from 1549 to his death in 1551. All but one of the thirteen compilers of the BOOK OF COMMON PRAYER (1549) were Cambridge divines. During the reign of Mary (1554–1559) twenty-five Cambridge reformers were burned at the stake, including Latimer, Ridley, and Cranmer at Oxford.

After the final breach with Rome in 1570, the University was home to an ultra-Protestant "Puritan" movement in the CHURCH OF ENGLAND that espoused strict CALVINISM and hatred of liturgical ornaments ("rags of popery"). Led by the Lady Margaret professor THOMAS CARTWRIGHT, the movement fomented in Christ's College where JOHN MILTON later studied, and in the two new foundations: Emmanuel and Sidney Sussex. Missionaries from these colleges to Virginia and New England exported PURITANISM to the New World. One of thirty-three from Emmanuel alone, John Harvard endowed a new Cambridge in Massachusetts, Harvard University.

The Puritan attempt to control the Church of England during the Great Rebellion (1642–1659) finally collapsed at the Restoration (1660). Puritans abandoned the Church and formed "Nonconformist" congregations (see NONCONFORMITY), many migrating to the American colonies. Meanwhile, Cambridge divinity continued to exert a powerful, but now quite different influence on Protestant thought. HENRY MORE (1614–1687), Ralph Cudworth (1617–1689), and the other CAMBRIDGE PLATONISTS developed an anti-Calvinist, philosophical theology important for Shaftesbury, JOHN LOCKE, Reid and GOTTFRIED LEIBNIZ among others. In the eighteenth century the modernizing, rationalist circle of Edmund Law (1703–1787) fostered works by Richard Watson (1737–1816), John Hey (1734–1815), and WILLIAM PALEY (1743–1805) that remained standard throughout the English-speaking world until the 1860s.

References and Further Reading

Brooks, Christopher, ed. *A History of the University of Cambridge*. Several vols. Cambridge, UK: Cambridge University Press, 1988–.

Knappen, M. M. *Tudor Puritanism: A Chapter in the History of Idealism*. Chicago: University of Chicago Press, 1939.

Porter, H. C. *Reformation and Reaction in Tudor Cambridge*. Cambridge, UK: Cambridge University Press, 1959.

Waterman, A. M. C. "A Cambridge 'Via Media' in Late Georgian Anglicanism." *Journal of Ecclesiastical History* 42 no. 3 (1991): 419–436.

M. C. WATERMAN

CAMP MEETING

A camp meeting is an outdoor WORSHIP meeting held over several days to evangelize the unconverted and to renew existing church members. The hallmark is camping on the grounds of the meetings. Camp meetings were the product of American EVANGELICALISM at the beginning of the nineteenth century, being one of the main ways in which the Second Great Awakening spread (see AWAKENINGS). Beyond this revival they became a staple of American church life in the nineteenth century, continually evolving throughout this period. Today the meetings no longer hold the same prominence in Evangelicalism generally, although some evangelical groups still hold camp meetings, sometimes in a much-adapted form.

Origins

The phenomenon of extended—"protracted" would have been the original term—evangelistic meetings antedates the name itself. By the late 1800s several churches were holding various kinds of protracted meetings that featured outdoor settings for some or all of the worship. All such meetings had gained some level of standardization with respect to ritual routine and timing. Often they were heavily attended and were the highlight for Christians in an area. Two of these kinds of meetings, the Presbyterian and the Methodist versions, were especially important in the genesis of camp meetings (see PRESBYTERIANISM and METHODISM, NORTH AMERICA). The same was also probably true about large Baptist meetings (see BAPTISTS, UNITED STATES). The Presbyterian antecedents to camp meetings were the yearly sacramental occasions for a congregation, a gathering for celebration of the LORD'S SUPPER. Such occasions had been the setting for revival among Presbyterians since the seventeenth century in SCOTLAND. The Methodist version was the quarterly meeting. Since the American Revolution quarterly meetings had lasted several days, attracting large crowds to their multiple worship services, and were often the occasion for revival within any locale. Both Presbyterian and Methodist versions shared similar dynamics in that people purposely traveled to attend a meeting lasting several days and involving a variety of kinds of PREACHING, PRAYER, and sacramental services, often in an outdoor setting. Originally those traveling to the protracted meeting relied on the hospitality of host families.

At the dawn of the nineteenth century, as the first hints came of a widespread revival across the nation, another dimension began to be added to these meetings: widespread camping in wagons or tents. Because the first camp meetings were simply other kinds of protracted meetings to which widespread camping had been added, it is impossible to say precisely when the first camp meeting was held despite several claimants for the title. Indeed, camp meetings occurred for several years before the precise term began to be used. These first camp meetings—including famous ones like the 1801 Cane Ridge Presbyterian sacramental occasion in Kentucky—were simply the older forms of protracted meetings with the innovation of widespread camping. Contemporaneous reports call these meetings by their older names, noting the new feature by referring to an "encampment" or to "camping." Camping allowed the meetings to last longer and for more people to attend. Often ministers of multiple denominations participated in a single meeting.

The term "camp meeting" itself seems to have been a secondary development. At first the camping was spontaneous and unplanned. Then denominational officials began to invite people to camp at the next round of protracted meetings. Seeing great numerical success in these meetings, officials began to schedule specially designated "camp meetings" to intentionally replicate this phenomenon. The term appears to have first been used in North Carolina, South Carolina, and Georgia in 1802, and the promotion of this kind of protracted meeting spread rapidly along the Eastern seaboard. By 1805 camp meetings by that name were held from CANADA to Mississippi. They occurred both in rural and near urban settings. In 1807 camp meetings were introduced to ENGLAND. By 1811 Methodist bishop FRANCIS ASBURY, a zealous promoter of camp meetings, estimated that Methodists alone were holding 400 to 500 camp meetings annually.

Many of the first prominent camp meetings were held in Kentucky and Tennessee. This fact has led some to closely identify camp meetings with a western frontier region. Such a connection can be overemphasized. Neither the meetings themselves nor their characteristic worship practices were distinct to the American West or to newly settled regions. The manner of worshiping, including the exuberance, had been part of evangelical protracted meetings before camp meetings in the West, but the establishment of camp meetings by that name did create a greater degree of public ritualizing of these practices. Similarly, the music used in the earliest camp meetings was soon gathered and published as special collections of camp meeting hymns and spiritual songs.

The first decade of camp meetings saw several stages in their development: spontaneous emergence, naming, zealous promotion, and standardization. Naming was the critical stage in that it distinguished the particular phenomenon, thus allowing active promotion by that name. Beyond this initial decade, camp meetings entered an established phase, all the time undergoing further change, often as some practitioners became more genteel as the nineteenth century progressed. By this progression through stages, camp meetings are an excellent guide to the life cycle of other kinds of worship innovations in free-church Evangelicalism. They represent a threshold for a growing pragmatic approach in how American evangelicals view worship's purpose.

Early camp meetings usually lasted between four and seven days. Worshipers spent each day in a round of multiple worship services including family or "private" prayers in the tents, group prayer meetings, and preaching services. The large-scale services were held in a prepared space with preachers and exhorters occupying a stand. The goal was to acquire CONVERSION of the "unsaved" or, in the case of Methodist camp meetings, to lead Christians to a SANCTIFICATION experience. Preaching services often ended with a call for those responding to the preaching and exhorting to come to an area before the stand. The services could become quite loud and exuberant. Crying, weeping, and shouting were common, as were different kinds of stupors or bodily movements. The blowing of trumpets often marked the start of a new activity. From the earliest camp meetings, planners created sets of rules for regulating the camp because in effect they were creating a small community. Making tallies of each day's conversions and sanctifications was common. Communion or baptismal services often climaxed meetings, and some meetings ended with an elaborate ritual of parting.

Although primarily an American phenomenon, camp meetings have not been exclusively so. England's PRIMITIVE METHODIST CHURCH, for instance, partly grew out of the introduction of camp meetings to that nation (see METHODISM, ENGLAND). Into the twentieth century this church's membership tickets gladly bore notice of its first camp meeting in 1807. Camp meetings have been held also in Canada, INDIA, and AFRICA.

Late Nineteenth-Century Developments

In the nineteenth century, some camp meetings declined as denominations or parts of denominations rejected them. Other Christians worked hard at preserving camp meetings, hoping to maintain their original revivalistic purpose as an important part of church life. An example of this tactic was the instructional handbook written by Barlow Weed Gorham, a Methodist minister, entitled *Camp Meeting Manual, A Practical Book for the Camp Ground* (1854). Not only a practical guide for holding the most effective camp meeting, Gorham's book was an appeal for the camp meeting's ongoing usefulness. In addition, churches splintering from denominations that began the camp meetings sometimes emphasized them.

Even strongly committed devotees of camp meetings continued to adapt them, however. One important example was the increased building of permanent shelters or "tabernacles" over the worship space, supplanting the use of constructed arbors or natural groves. Similarly, the mid-nineteenth century onward saw an increasing number of permanent cabins built to house the participants and tents were eliminated in many locales. After the American CIVIL WAR, the incorporation of scores of camp meeting associations whose purposes were to establish and maintain permanent outdoor meeting grounds facilitated this development.

The second half of the nineteenth century also saw even more radical adaptation of the basic camp meeting idea. One such adaptation was the creation of the camp meeting as resort or vacation. In effect, camp meeting became not only a type of extended worship setting but also a kind of planned community ideally situated in a restful, natural location. Indeed, many of these communities developed into incorporated cities. Martha's Vineyard, Massachusetts, is perhaps one of the most famous. In these "resort" camp meetings, the set, multiple-day schedule of worship services was only part of the summer agenda. Some participants lived at the camp meeting site for the entire summer. Their cottages grew increasingly complex, often including interesting use of Victorian architecture.

Such camp grounds were begun to offer an alternative resort site for Christians. The idea was to offer an escape from the city by retreating into a natural, wholesome setting. As camp grounds became sites of summer-long residence, there was less concern for conversion of the lost and a greater emphasis on nurturing the already converted in the faith. Ministers introduced educational elements into the camp ministry, including some aimed at children. The typical day incorporated several kinds of meetings such as family devotion, plenary sessions in the tabernacle, and various instructional groups. The growing success of the Chautauqua movement in the late nineteenth century helped spark this educational interest. Starting on New York's Chautauqua Lake, this parallel movement operated religious educational institutes in a rural retreat setting.

Often the tone for these meetings reflected the increased gentility of some branches of the churches that had originated camp meetings. The intense emotional exuberance and physical responses that had characterized these churches' meetings in the early part of the century were gone.

Another adaptation of camp meetings in the latter half of the nineteenth century was the development of the purpose-oriented camp meeting. One example was the use of camp meetings for the specific goal of promoting TEMPERANCE. Another, more widespread example was the linking of camp meetings to promotion of particular doctrinal concerns like sanctification or holiness (see HOLINESS MOVEMENT). Camp meetings became occasions to preach these doctrines and, more important, lead people into experiencing their reality. For example, the National Association for the Promotion of Holiness, also known as the National Camp Meeting Association, began holding camp meetings immediately after the Civil War at Vineland, New Jersey in 1867. The organization's influence grew. By 1900 it had conducted more than one hundred holiness camp meetings with several million estimated in attendance. This association intentionally held such camp meetings as "national," interdenominational meetings. Eventually this association ceased sponsoring camp meetings. However, some denominations, birthed in the late nineteenth century and early twentieth centuries as "Holiness" churches and often tracing their roots to the National Association for the Promotion of Holiness, included camp meetings as a regular part of their life. The Christian Holiness Partnership, the organization descended from the National Camp Meeting Association, claims there are still two thousand holiness camp meetings in America.

There is some degree of overlap between those who developed the resort camps and those who promoted holiness camps. The founders of the Ocean Grove camp meeting, located on the Atlantic Ocean in New Jersey, for example, had interest in both concerns.

Twentieth-Century Developments

The history of camp meetings in the twentieth century has seen similar trends. In some circles the growth of theological liberalism caused a depreciation of camp meetings (see LIBERAL PROTESTANTISM AND LIBERALISM). Such liberalism could see urban life not as a thing to be escaped but as a locus for finding the KINGDOM OF GOD. In addition, the loss of emphasis on crisis experiences in a typical liberal doctrine of SALVATION undercut the nature of classic camp meeting evangelism.

In other recent circles, specific nineteenth-century camp meeting formats have declined but not the basic idea that underlay them. In these circles the notion of meeting for religious purposes away from one's normal setting for an extended time has spawned new versions of religious camping, although without the term "camp meeting." Special summer youth camps, outdoor Christian music festivals, and denominational retreat centers are examples.

A more traditional approach to camp meetings has been preserved in some respect by the rise of PENTECOSTALISM in the twentieth century. That some Pentecostal groups would keep camp meetings as a regular fixture for evangelism and renewal is not surprising, given Pentecostal roots in the Holiness Movement and given the emphasis on crisis experiences in Pentecostal understandings of salvation. Sometimes the term seems used in a way only remotely connected to its origins. In such a case, camp meeting seems to refer to a multiple-day series of worship services regardless of actual camping or connection with an outdoor setting.

Some long-term camp meetings, often with roots in the early nineteenth century, continue to exist. Many are Methodist, and attendance at times can be quite large. The aim may be as much the renewal of church members as large-scale outward-oriented evangelism. If so, such meetings have shifted one of camp meetings' original purposes.

References and Further Reading

Brown, Kenneth O. *Holy Ground, Too: The Camp Meeting Family Tree.* Hazleton, PA: Holiness Archives, 1997.

Cooley, Steven D. "Manna and the Manual: Sacramental and Instrumental Constructions of the Victorian Methodist Camp Meeting during the Mid-Nineteenth Century." *Religion and American Culture* 6 (1996): 131–159.

Eslinger, Ellen. *Citizens of Zion: The Social Origins of Camp Meeting Revivalism.* Knoxville: University of Tennessee Press, 1991.

Johnson, Charles A. *The Frontier Camp Meeting: Religion's Harvest Time.* Dallas: Southern Methodist University Press, 1955.

Lippy, Charles H. "The Camp Meeting in Transition: The Character and Legacy of the Late Nineteenth Century." *Methodist History* 34 (1995): 3–17.

Messenger, Troy. *Holy Leisure: Recreation and Religion in God's Square Mile.* Minneapolis: University of Minnesota Press, 1999.

Parker, Charles A. "The Camp Meeting on the Frontier and the Methodist Religious Resort in the East—Before 1900." *Methodist History* 18 (1980): 179–192.

Richey, Russell E. "From Quarterly to Camp Meeting." In *Early American Methodism*. Bloomington: Indiana University Press, 1991.

Robins, Roger. "Vernacular American Landscape: Methodists, Camp Meetings, and Social Respectability." *Religion and American Culture* 4 (1994): 165–191.

Ruth, Lester. "Reconsidering the Emergence of the Second Great Awakening and Camp Meetings Among Early Methodists." *Worship* 75 (2001): 334–355.

Schmidt, Leigh Eric. *Holy Fairs: Scottish Communions and American Revivals in the Early Modern Period.* Princeton: Princeton University Press, 1989.

Weiss, Ellen. *City in the Woods: The Life and Design of an American Camp Meeting on Martha's Vineyard.* New York: Oxford University Press, 1987.

LESTER RUTH

CAMPBELL FAMILY

Thomas and Alexander Campbell, father and son, were key leaders in an indigenous America religious movement to restore original Christianity, with three major wings in the twenty-first century: DISCIPLES OF CHRIST, Churches of Christ, and CHRISTIAN CHURCHES, CHURCHES OF CHRIST. The Campbells heralded the AUTHORITY of Scripture, promoted independent elder-ruled congregations, noncreedalism, immersion of believers, weekly observation of the LORD'S SUPPER, and ministers appointed by local congregations.

Thomas Campbell was born in County Down, Ireland, February 1, 1763, and died in Bethany, West Virginia, January 4, 1854. He united with the Anti-Burger branch of the Seceder Presbyterian Church (see PRESBYTERIANISM), attended the University of Glasgow, then completed a seminary course at Whitburn. He taught school as well as serving the Ahorey Seceder Church from 1798 to 1807. With others he helped form the ecumenical Evangelical Society of Ulster. In 1807, because of ill health, he visited America and decided to stay. He preached among Seceder Presbyterian Churches near Pittsburgh, but invited all to participate at the Lord's Table. He was soon accused of HERESY, brought to trial, and found guilty, resulting in his withdrawal. With other Presbyterians he formed the Christian Association of Washington so as to promote Christian unity, forbearance, and the preaching of the pure gospel. He authored a major statement in 1809, "The Declaration and Address," on behalf of the Society. The Society formed a church at Brush Run, Pennsylvania in 1811. With his family he lived in Pennsylvania, Ohio, Kentucky, and West Virginia. Both Thomas and Alexander, having decided for BAPTISM by immersion, entered the Redstone Baptist Association, then the Mahoning. By 1830 they departed from the BAPTISTS and started merging with Christian Churches throughout the Ohio Valley.

Alexander Campbell was born in County Antrim, Ireland, September 12, 1788, and died in Bethany, West Virginia, March 4, 1866. He attended the University of Glasgow for a year. Arriving in America in 1809 with his mother and siblings, Alexander Campbell preached among the churches, taught in schools, married, and was given a farm in West Virginia by his father-in-law. There he remained the rest of his life, and by 1830 became the leading proponent of the expanding movement. He founded *The Christian Baptist* in 1823. Upon realizing that relationships with the Baptists were coming to an end, he launched *The Millennial Harbinger* in 1830 and served as editor until his death in 1866. Campbell achieved notoriety through debating far and wide, holding six major debates, four with Presbyterian ministers, and more important, with Robert Owen and Roman Catholic Bishop John B. Purcell. He founded Bethany College in 1840 and continued as president until his death, by which time there were approximately 200,000 persons in the movement.

See also Stone, Barton W.

References and Further Reading

Thomas Campbell:

Primary Source:

Campbell, Alexander. *Memoirs of Elder Thomas Campbell.* Cincinnati: H. S. Bosworth, 1861.

Secondary Source:

Olbricht, Thomas H., and Hans Rollmann, eds. *The Quest for Christian Unity, Peace, and Purity in Thomas Campbell's Declaration and Address: Text and Studies.* Lanham, MD: Scarecrow Press, 2000.

Alexander Campbell:

Primary Source:

Richardson, Robert. *Memoirs of Alexander Campbell.* 2 vols. Philadelphia: J. P. Lippincott & Co., 1868, 1870.

Secondary Source

Seale, James M., ed. *Lectures in Honor of the Alexander Campbell Bicentennial, 1788–1988.* Nashville, TN: Disciples of Christ Historical Society, 1988.

THOMAS H. OLBRICHT

CAMPBELL, JOHN MCLEOD (1800–1872)

Scottish theologian. Campbell was born May 4, 1800 in Argyll, Scotland, where his father served as minister. He was educated at the universities of Glasgow and Edinburgh, and entered the ministry at Row in Dunbartonshire in 1825. Campbell was especially interested in the spirituality of his parishioners and by 1826 concluded that they needed to be first taught the assurance of divine love in Christ. He further decided that corollary with such love is universal ATONEMENT, that is, that Christ died for all. Both DOCTRINES as set forth by Campbell were perceived to be contradictory to the WESTMINSTER CONFESSION of faith. Opposition arose within his congregation and eventually the General Assembly of the CHURCH OF SCOTLAND deposed him from ministry in 1831. A group of friends encouraged him to form an independent congregation at Blackfriars Street in Glasgow for which he ministered from 1833 to1859, at which time he resigned because of poor health. His views later came to be widely accepted in the Church of Scotland and in 1868 the University of Glasgow conferred upon him the D.D.

Campbell was influenced by Thomas Erskine, EDWARD IRVING, and FREDERICK D. MAURICE and he in turn influenced them. His style was more directed to interior biblical truth and consciousness than to explicit conventional doctrines. The manner in which he expressed himself sometimes made it seem that Campbell was farther from classical THEOLOGY than was the case. He argued that Christ died for all people, not that all would eventually be saved. The atonement was not an appeasement of the wrath of God, but a genuine addressing of that wrath from the context of the love of God and the Son. He argued that those unsettled should "Believe in the forgiveness of- . . . sins because they are forgiven." He died at Dunbartonshire, Scotland, February 27, 1872.

References and Further Reading

Primary Sources:

Campbell, John McLeod. *The Nature of the Atonement*, Fourth edition. London: 1873.
———. *Reminiscences and Reflections, Referring to his Early Ministry in the Parish of Row, 1825–31*. Edited with an Introductory Narrative by his son, Donald Campbell. London: 1873.
———. *Memorials of John McLeod Campbell, D. D. Being a Selection from his Correspondence*. Edited by the Rev. Donald Campbell. 2 vols. London: 1877.

Secondary Sources:

Jinkins, Michael. *Love is of the Essence. An Introduction To The Theology of John McLeod Campbell*. Edinburgh: 1993.
Tuttle, G. M. *So Rich a Soul: John McLeod Campbell on Christian Atonement*. Edinburgh: 1986.

THOMAS H. OLBRICHT

CANADA

The history of Protestantism in Canada is largely the history of but four traditions: the Anglican, Presbyterian, Baptist, and Methodist. Whether the future of Canadian Protestantism rests on these traditions is, however, quite a different matter.

The Colonial Period to Confederation: 1610 to 1867

Protestant Christianity first came to Canada on the Atlantic coast between 1610 and 1630 under the sponsorship of private adventurers in Newfoundland and Nova Scotia. A few clergy also accompanied explorers of Canada's northwest—the first Protestant communion in Canada might well have been that celebrated by the chaplain of explorer Martin Frobisher on Baffin Island in 1577. A continuous, rooted Protestant presence, however, would await the substantial settlement of immigrants from Britain and the future United States.

In the second half of the eighteenth century, Newfoundland and Nova Scotia became year-round homes for significant numbers of immigrants. The expulsion of Francophone Roman Catholic Acadians in 1755 invited migration from the American colonies. Soon the Maritimes were populated by Ulster Presbyterians, Highland Scots (both Catholic and Presbyterian), Yorkshire Methodists, and Irish Catholics, as well as Anglicans and Congregationalists (see PRESBYTERIANISM, METHODISM, ANGLICANISM, CONGREGATIONALISM). After the American Revolution in the 1770s and 1780s, Loyalists fled north and substantially increased the colonial populations—New Brunswick became a separate colony as a result in 1784.

This region experienced perhaps its most dramatic Protestant development during this period. New England expatriate HENRY ALLINE led a New Light revival that brought vital religion to many colonists (see REVIVALS). As this revival stabilized and merged with the growing numbers of BAPTISTS in the region, it joined with the smaller Methodist initiatives to stamp Nova Scotia and New Brunswick with evangelical contours (see EVANGELICALISM).

American immigration after the Revolution made an even greater difference in Upper Canada (present-day Ontario): as many as eight out of ten settlers came from America between 1750 and 1812. By the time of the War of 1812, Upper Canada included Anglicans, Methodists, Lutherans (see LUTHERANISM), Presbyterians, Baptists, Congregationalists, MENNONITES, Tunkers (see BRETHREN, CHURCH OF THE), Moravians (see MORAVIAN CHURCH), and Quakers (see FRIENDS, SOCIETY OF), as well as Roman Catholics, making it by far the most religiously diverse region in British North America.

The war shaped not only Canadian culture in general, but its religious makeup as well. This conflict with the United States stemmed immigration from the south. With increased British immigration at the end of the Napoleonic Wars, Anglophone Canadian loyalties tilted decisively back toward Britain. Canadian Protestant churches reflected this alignment in different ways. The continued predominance of the CHURCH OF ENGLAND in Canada (later, the Anglican Church of Canada) was the most obvious sign, but the British dominance of Methodism (in the case of Upper Canada, Methodism had been primarily an import largely from the south) and Baptist traditions showed it as well.

The precarious existence of the colonies encouraged cooperation among various Protestant groups and even occasionally between Protestants and Catholics—in the latter case, cooperation that would largely disappear in the second half of the century. Church buildings were erected and clergy recruited from Britain as the churches sought to enfold colonial populations indifferent to or remote from organized religion. By mid-century, this central task had been completed: the sketchy records available indicate that at least half of the population regularly attended services. The churches also had devoted themselves to an increasing program of civilizing the colonies: TEMPERANCE societies began in the 1820s, assistance for orphans and prostitutes (see PROSTITUTION) was available in some centers, and SUNDAY SCHOOLS were established to spread literacy, Christianity, and virtue in equal measure.

The bone of contention among Protestants during this period was the question of establishment. The Anglicans and, less successfully, the Presbyterians claimed certain privileges by right of being established churches in Britain, particularly in the crucial areas of clergy salaries and education. The young Methodist activist Egerton Ryerson, however, led a campaign against such privileges, and by 1854 all official supports had been removed in Upper Canada. The Maritimes also officially disestablished the Church of England by mid-century and experienced the rise of denominationalism (see DENOMINATION) as the characteristic Canadian pattern.

The Evangelical Century: 1867 to 1967

By the time of Confederation and new nationhood, Christianity deeply informed the culture of Canada's four founding provinces (Ontario, Quebec, Nova Scotia, and New Brunswick) and those that would soon join (Prince Edward Island, British Columbia, and the

prairie provinces of Manitoba, Saskatchewan, and Alberta). Quebec, as the great Francophone Roman Catholic exception, was marked by a profound ultramontanism (support for a traditional Rome-centered church). Anglophone Canada, for its part, increasingly fell under the sway of a broad, moderate evangelical Protestantism that was more nationalistic in the second half of the nineteenth century.

Churches were built with considerable civic enthusiasm across the country, many of them large and impressive in Gothic or Romanesque architectures that proclaimed God's sovereignty over the "Dominion of Canada." Temperance societies, especially the Women's Christian Temperance Union, helped not only to stem the tide of alcohol abuse (various provinces supported Prohibition from 1910 into the 1930s), but also supported women's suffrage, literacy, care for unwed mothers, and many other causes (see WOMEN). Sabbatarian Legislation (see SABBATARIANISM) that limited business and entertainment on the Sabbath was in force for almost a century. The federal Lord's Day Act was instituted in 1906, and some jurisdictions finally lifted their own "blue laws" only in the 1980s and 1990s. Missionary work both to India and the Far East and, to a lesser extent, in Canada's own west and north, was undertaken with such enthusiasm that Canada became, per capita, the largest missionary-sending country in the world (see MISSIONS-MISSIONARY ORGANIZATIONS).

Evangelicalism in Canada had its fiery episodes and institutions, its branches of the HOLINESS MOVEMENT and Pentecostal (see PENTECOSTALISM), and its own Fundamentalist (see FUNDAMENTALISM) schisms among the Baptists in Ontario and British Columbia in the first quarter of the twentieth century. However, evangelicalism formed the dominant culture of the major churches as well. Methodism, Presbyterianism (particularly influenced by the FREE CHURCH movement in Scotland), and Anglicanism were joined by the smaller Baptist groups to constitute a cultural hegemony of religious fervor, moral seriousness, and increasing missionary interest.

The period from 1867 to 1967 saw the erection of most of Canada's universities by Catholic and Protestant churches. Only a few (such as the University of Toronto) were secular in origin, although almost all became secularized under financial pressures by the centennial year of 1967. Bible schools (see BIBLE COLLEGES AND INSTITUTES) sprang up across the country, and especially in the prairie provinces in the 1930s through 1950s, primarily to offer cheap Christian education to laypeople and to the clergy of smaller denominations unimpressed by university credentials. Elementary and secondary education was administered by each province but—even outside the separate schools enjoyed by Roman Catholics in some jurisdictions, notably Ontario—with distinct Christian elements. The Lord's Prayer was recited in opening exercises throughout this period, for example, and the Ten Commandments hung on many school walls.

Not all Protestants, to be sure, shared equally in this evangelical alliance. The OXFORD MOVEMENT gained converts among Anglicans, and Anglo-Catholicism became an influential tradition by the turn of the century. Some leaders of the SOCIAL GOSPEL movement arising out of World War I, originally a branch of the general evangelical social crusade, eventually despaired of the conservatism of their fellow church members and promoted causes that were more radical both politically and theologically. At the other end of the spectrum, sectarian movements arose, many of them ministering to the working classes outside the largely middle-class evangelical mainstream. Some of these only later joined in the national evangelical network, whether the PLYMOUTH BRETHREN (influential out of all proportion to their small size through their distinctive theology of DISPENSATIONALISM and their participation in transdenominational organizations, such as student groups and foreign missions), the SALVATION ARMY (which became a fixture among Canadian benevolent agencies from coast to coast), or the Pentecostals (vilified by many evangelicals themselves as personifying the "hot gospel" past they had left behind).

The most notable centripetal event in this era, however, was the founding of the UNITED CHURCH OF CANADA in 1925. The world's first interconfessional union, it joined most of Canada's Methodists and Congregationalists and a majority of its Presbyterians—groups that had already experienced considerable denominational consolidation in the late 1800s in Canada. It thus became the country's largest Protestant denomination, and took up alongside the Anglican Church a role of chaplain to the nation.

After the Second World War, Canada experienced a general increase in cultural confidence and immigration and an economic boom. The churches shared in this expansion as their numbers grew, church building increased substantially, and a wide range of special interest groups proliferated. Weekly church attendance was over half the Protestant population, and it seemed by 1960 that a new era had dawned. Indeed it had, but it was not a new day of Protestant renewal.

From the Centennial to the New Millennium

Quebec underwent its Quiet Revolution in the 1960s, during which time it threw off the "ancien régime" of church and state (see CHURCH AND STATE OVERVIEW) and secularized with breathtaking swiftness. Outside Quebec, the changes were not so dramatic, but they were nonetheless quite similar.

Legislatures and courts increasingly articulated a vision of Canada that was no longer predominantly Christian, but multicultural, pluralistic, and liberal. The new Constitution of 1982 might have included the word "God" in its preamble, and the national anthem a similar reference, but theism had no privileged place in Canadian public life, much less the evangelical or Roman Catholic Christianity that had dominated the previous century.

Weekly church attendance declined sharply (to perhaps two or three out of ten by the 1990s), membership rolls and church finances followed suit, and by the 1980s it was clear that Canada was no longer a Christian country in any important sense of the word—even as Canadians continued to tell census-takers and pollsters that they were indeed mostly Christian. (More than eighty percent said so in 1991.) Sexual scandals involving clergy of all stripes brought general opprobrium on Christianity, with lawsuits over mistreatment of native peoples in residential schools threatening to bankrupt United, Anglican, Catholic, and Presbyterian churches at the turn of the millennium. Despite the checkered history of encounters with white Christians, however, native peoples identified with Christianity in the same proportion as the national population: over eighty percent in 1991.

Controversy was hardly new to the churches. The mainline denominations began to ordain women (see WOMEN CLERGY) in this period (the United Church had done so as early as the 1920s), and the United Church began to ordain homosexuals in 1992. In both cases, fierce acrimony weakened the communions. Liberal theology became the norm in most of their seminaries, sending hundreds of other theological students each year to join students from smaller evangelical denominations at transdenominational schools such as Tyndale Theological Seminary in Toronto and Regent College in Vancouver—the largest seminaries in the country by the 1980s. Conservative "ginger groups," or agitators, formed within the United, Anglican, and Presbyterian churches tried to stem the leftward drift on theological and moral issues, but were increasingly frustrated as they failed.

Evangelicalism thus became the label for smaller, uniformly evangelical denominations (such as the CHRISTIAN AND MISSIONARY ALLIANCE) and for those of similar sympathies in the mainline denominations. By the 1980s, however, more active churchgoers were identified with this evangelical network than with any single Protestant denomination, including the United and Anglican. The Evangelical Fellowship of Canada, founded in 1964, brought some cohesion and cooperation to this loose affiliation of churches and individuals as various as the Mennonite Brethren, Christian Reformed (see DUTCH PROTESTANTS IN AMERICA), Pentecostal (by 1991 a group almost as big as the Presbyterians or Baptists), and low-church Anglicans. The continued expansion of independent special purpose groups, however, was at least as important a phenomenon among Protestant Christians. These included fellowships of Christian athletes, lawyers, or businesspeople; the wide range of youth ministries; groups concerned with political and social activism (such as Citizens for Public Justice and Focus on the Family); radio, television, and especially print media; and so on.

Education continued to be a contested zone as Canadian public schools shed the last vestiges of their Protestant past. Parents began to agitate for public funding of confessional Protestant schools, citing the support for Catholic schools in some regions originally mandated in Canada's Constitution. Others educated their children themselves as the leading edge of the society-wide increase in home-schooling. Still others founded independent Christian universities, with at least three earning full public recognition by the close of the century (Trinity Western, King's, and Redeemer).

By the beginning of the new millennium, then, the growing edge of Canadian Protestantism was no longer among the denominations that had dominated it for two centuries. It was now the smaller evangelical groups who ran the most popular schools, supported the most missionaries, attracted the most youth, spent the most money, and built the largest churches. Increasingly, too, it was their spokespersons who received media attention on public issues, and not only the representatives of the mainline denominations.

The general cultural picture, though, was simply one of increasing marginalization of Canadian Protestantism and of Christianity in general. At the turn of the millennium, the 2001 census was expected to show an increase in Canadians citing "no religious affiliation" from the thirteen percent of 1991 to over twenty percent, with a corresponding drop in Christian affiliation from eighty-three to about seventy percent—with about half of that being Protestants. The decline in national and regional church attendance figures showed no sign of bottoming out. Over ninety percent of Canadian congregations claimed less than 200 members. Even the relative success story of the evangelicals was tempered by the realization that they were barely holding their own as a proportion of the population. They might, that is, have been the immediate future of Canadian Protestantism, but it was a future as a minority in a thoroughly pluralistic culture.

References and Further Reading

Bibby, Reginald W. *Fragmented Gods: The Poverty and Potential of Religion in Canada.* Toronto: Irwin, 1987.
———. *Unknown Gods: The Ongoing Story of Religion in Canada.* Toronto: Stoddart, 1993.
Gauvreau, Michael. *The Evangelical Century: College and Creed in English Canada from the Great Revival to the Great Depression.* Montreal and Kingston, ON: McGill-Queen's University Press, 1991.
Grant, John Webster. *The Church in the Canadian Era.* Rev. ed. Vancouver: Regent College Publishing, 1998 [1988].
———. *Moon of Wintertime: Missionaries and the Indians of Canada in Encounter since 1534.* Toronto: University of Toronto Press, 1984.
Moir, John S. *The Church in the British Era.* Toronto: McGraw-Hill Ryerson, 1972.
Murphy, Terrence, and Roberto Perin, eds. *A Concise History of Christianity in Canada.* Toronto: Oxford University Press, 1996.
Rawlyk, G. A., ed. *Aspects of the Canadian Evangelical Experience.* Montreal and Kingston, ON: McGill-Queen's University Press, 1997.
———. *The Canada Fire: Radical Evangelicalism in British North America 1775–1812.* Montreal and Kingston, ON: McGill-Queen's University Press, 1994.
———, ed. *The Canadian Protestant Experience.* Montreal and Kingston, ON: McGill-Queen's University Press, 1990.
Stackhouse, John G., Jr. *Canadian Evangelicalism in the Twentieth Century: An Introduction to Its Character.* Toronto: University of Toronto Press, 1993.

JOHN G. STACKHOUSE JR.

CANTERBURY

Ancient capital city of Kent in southeast England, Canterbury is the primal see of *all* England. In 597 Augustine arrived in England as a missionary, established a church at Canterbury, and became its first bishop. From 1070 to 1089, Lanfranc was bishop of Canterbury. He oversaw a dramatic administrative reform of the church in England and asserted Canterbury's primacy over the English church, an attempt resisted by the bishop of York. Finally, the Archbishop of York was deemed the Primate of England, whereas the Archbishop of Canterbury was deemed the Primate of All England. Canterbury remains the primal see in Great Britain and the titular head of the worldwide Anglican Communion. St. Anselm (author of *Cur Deus Homo*) was bishop from 1093 to 1109.

Canterbury's most famous bishop was Thomas Becket (1162–1170), assassinated by aides to King Henry II. Becket's martyrdom, Henry II's penance for the murder, and the shrine built to Becket would continue to play an important role in the conflict between the church and the state in England for centuries (see CHURCH AND STATE, OVERVIEW). Because of Becket, Canterbury also became a very important pilgrimage site (thus the *Canterbury Tales* by poet Geoffrey Chaucer [c. 1342–1400]). For example, in 1420 nearly 100,000 people visited Becket's shrine.

In the late fifteenth and early sixteenth century, this level of visitation and adoration began to wane. Then, in the 1530s, Becket's antagonism to the crown became fodder in the battle over the church in England; to Roman Catholics Becket was a hero and model (for example, on July 5, 1535, statesman and author Thomas More [1478–1535] wrote his daughter Margaret a letter in which he wished to be executed the next day for it is "St. Thomas' eve"); to Protestants Becket was a traitor to crown and country.

In 1533 THOMAS CRANMER (1489–1556), a proponent of HENRY VIII's divorce from Catherine of Aragon and hostile to the heroic interpretation of Becket, became archbishop. In May of 1533 he declared Henry's marriage to Catherine invalid, and proclaimed the secret marriage of Henry to Anne Boleyn valid. This act was in itself a usurpation of papal authority and over time, Cranmer took to himself more and more roles usually identified with the pope. In 1535 he oversaw the reform of the liturgy in England. In 1538 he oversaw the dismantlement and destruction of Becket's shrine, and the chapel house that supported it was dissolved. In 1547, with Henry VIII's death, Cranmer was able to continue his reformation agenda.

With Edward VI's death, Canterbury again became a battleground in the fight for the church in England. Mary Tudor reinstituted many of the abandoned rites of the church, reestablished the chapel house, and persecuted many of the Protestant leaders in Canterbury. During her reign, forty-one Protestants were executed in Canterbury (second only to London). With Mary's death and the ascension of ELIZABETH I, the city and the cathedral returned to Protestantism. In 1570 Canterbury became a haven for Protestants fleeing religious persecution on the Continent. Most of the refugees earned a living by weaving wool, and by 1580 there were nearly 1,000 looms in operation. By 1620 there were more French-speaking inhabitants in Canterbury than English. At first, the refugees worshiped at St. Alphege's Church. Eventually they moved into a chapel in the cathedral. A French service continues to be held in that chapel to the present day.

In the 1630s Archbishop WILLIAM LAUD (1633–1645) led a reaction to the increasingly Calvinist bent to English Protestantism from Canterbury (see CALVINISM). In large measure, he resacramentalized the church by focusing on prayer, the SACRAMENTS, an increased reverence for sacred space, and the reinstitution of VESTMENTS. He also attempted to reinvigorate the authority of the church's hierarchy. In 1642 these attempts came to a stunning halt as forces loyal to Parliament occupied Canterbury as part of the Puritan Revolution (see PURITANISM CIVIL WAR). The cathedral was sacked and many of the altars and images installed or refurbished under Laud were destroyed.

After a 1643 act of Parliament that declared that images were to be destroyed, the stained-glass windows of the cathedral were smashed. However, the Puritan cause did not completely dominate Canterbury during this time. In fact, in 1647 a violent riot against the recently passed prohibition of Christmas was so large that Parliamentary forces were required to suppress the insurrection. Like much of England, Canterbury seemed to welcome the restoration of the monarchy in 1660. Upon his return to the throne, Charles II spent his first night in Canterbury and worshipped the next morning in the cathedral. In 1662 the 1552 *Prayer Book* was republished.

From the beginning of the eighteenth century to the middle of the nineteenth Canterbury was embroiled in a series of controversies that struck the whole church. First, JOHN WESLEY and the "Evangelical Movement" challenged the church's staid conservatism (see EVANGELICALISM); later the Oxford "Tractarians" called for a restoration of High Church standards of the seventeenth century (see OXFORD MOVEMENT). Over time, a cohort of the Tractarians began to argue for a much closer (even subordinate) relationship with Rome. The archbishops of Canterbury were hostile to both movements.

Since 1867 the bishops and prelates of the Anglican Communion have met every ten years in a conference chaired by the Archbishop of Canterbury. Since the middle of the twentieth century, the Archbishops of Canterbury have been firmly committed to a wider ecumenical vision that has included dialogues with Orthodox, Roman Catholic, and Protestant denominations. In 1982 Pope John Paul II visited Canterbury Cathedral and knelt together in prayer with Archbishop Robert Runcie.

References and Further Reading

Collinson, Patrick, et al., eds. *A History of Canterbury Cathedral: 598–1982*. New York: Oxford University Press, 1995.
Moorman, J. R. H. *A History of the Church in England*, 3rd ed. Harrisburg, PA: Morehouse, 1980.

DAVID M. WHITFORD

CANTERBURY AND YORK, CONVOCATIONS OF

These provincial synods dated in some form back to the establishment of the church in England. Originally only bishops participated, but in the thirteenth century, abbots, deans, archdeacons, and proctors (or representatives) of the CLERGY were also added. Eventually, the convocations divided into Upper (bishops and abbots) and Lower (all the rest) Houses. Until the REFORMATION the Convocations enacted canon laws, taxed the clergy on behalf of the state, and served as an ecclesiastical court of last resort. During this time, the Convocations had relative independence from the crown and could be called either at the behest of the king (when taxes were to be raised) or by the arch-bishop alone. All of this changed under King HENRY VIII.

In 1532 Henry secured from the Convocations the submission of the clergy to the crown. Formalized by Parliament in the Act of the Submission of the Clergy, (25 Henry VIII c. 19), the clergy were forbidden to assemble unless they had the "king's most royal assent and licence." Further, the Convocations could not enact canons that were contrary to Acts of Parliament or the king's prerogative. Having achieved their sub-mission, Henry used the Convocations to enact his ecclesiastical reforms. Under Edward the Convoca-tions endorsed clerical marriage and communion in both kinds (both bread and wine). Under Henry's Catholic daughter Mary, the Convocations revoked many of the earlier reforms and reasserted papal su-premacy. Contrary to the wishes of ELIZABETH I, the Convocations continued to take a pro-Rome stance early in her reign. In 1563 a new Convocation sup-portive of Elizabeth oversaw the revision of the Arti-cles of Religion and continued to serve as an integral part of the Elizabethan Settlement from that point forward.

The Convocations continued to meet each year at the same time as Parliament until 1640. Because of civil war and the Commonwealth, the Convocations did not meet from 1640 to 1661. In 1717 the king prorogued the Convocations over a controversy sur-rounding the bishop of Bangor. The Convocations did not again sit formally until the early twentieth century. In 1969 the Synodical Government Measure largely replaced the Convocations with a General Synod.

See also Clergy, Marriage of; Synod

References and Further Reading

Riley, H., ed. *Acts of the Convocations of Canterbury and York.* London: S.P.C.K., 1961.

Spalding, James, ed. *The Reformation of the Ecclesiastical Laws of England, 1552.* Kirksville, MO: Sixteenth Century Journal Publishers, 1992.

DAVID WHITFORD

CAPITAL PUNISHMENT

Capital punishment, the practice of imposing death as the penalty for serious lawbreaking, has been sanc-tioned in many cultures on religious grounds. Autho-rized in the law codes of the Hebrew Scriptures and reinforced by numerous prescriptions of Roman law, it was well known in the world of early Christians. Christians' most common involvement, however, was

as its victims, condemned for witnessing to their faith in the unjustly executed Jesus as their Lord.

The basic Christian preference for life was ex-pressed in the insistence that "the church abhors bloodshed," while the church, at the same time, rec-ognized that the state as created by God to maintain social order had the right to use necessary force. The clergy were prohibited from taking any part in the administration of the death penalty, and the church provided sanctuary for persons fleeing from arrest, acting on the belief that "God desires not the death of the sinner but that he be converted and live." How-ever, this ideal became more and more problematic once Emperor Constantine I in the fourth century made Christianity the preferred religion of the Roman Empire. The execution of Priscillian of Avila in 385 provided a troubling illustration of what was to come.

Medieval Church Acceptance of Lethal Coercion

With the emergence of the papal monarchy in the eleventh-century Gregorian reform, use of violence in the direct service of the church gradually became the uncontested norm. Christians were knighted in reli-gious ceremonies and their swords were consecrated. The launching of Crusades against infidels and wars against heretics overwhelmed the earlier reservations about shedding blood. In 1177 Emperor Frederick Barbarossa promised the pope the full force of the secular arm to suppress heretics, and by 1231 Pope Gregory IX formally endorsed burning at the stake as the appropriate mode of dealing with any who refused to recant. The church courts conducted the "inquisi-tion" and condemnation phase, but then handed the convicted over to the secular arm for execution. This convenient system reached its apex in 1252 when Pope Innocent IV declared such extirpation of heresy to be "the chief duty of the state." Thereafter, capital punishment was so completely entrenched as the in-dispensable instrument of divine justice in European Christendom that the practice was exempted from serious moral criticism for centuries.

Two Aspects of the Protestant Reformation

The major Protestant reformers were trained in this ethos of religiously sanctioned violence, and the heightened hostility between factions led to even firmer conviction of the necessity of the death penalty on all sides. As MARTIN LUTHER put it, "Let no one imagine that the world can be governed without the shedding of blood. . . . The world is wicked and bound to be so. Therefore, the sword is God's rod and ven-geance for it." JOHN CALVIN's action in having Michael

Servetus executed (1553) was approved by PHILIPP MELANCHTHON with much the same reasoning, although he ranked Servetus as a blasphemer rather than a heretic and thus considered his death as fully warranted by Roman law.

During these centuries in which the institutional churches consistently affirmed the practice of capital punishment as God's will, an important undercurrent of religious dissent periodically emerged. Some pre-Reformation groups, especially the Waldensians in the thirteenth century, the Wycliffites in the fourteenth, and the Hussites in the fifteenth, questioned and even rejected capital punishment. Many lay people, upon hearing the nonviolent words and deeds of Jesus in the vernacular, had doubts about the use of capital punishment without absolutely rejecting it. A more powerful undercurrent appeared in the sixteenth-century REFORMATION, especially in Anabaptist (see ANABAPTISM) pockets of PACIFISM associated with the names of CONRAD GREBEL, MICHAEL SATTLER, JAKOB HUTTER, and MENNO SIMONS. By the end of the seventeenth century British Quaker John Bellers—who seems to have been the first who actually went so far—called for the "utter abolition of the death penalty" (see FRIENDS, SOCIETY OF).

This radical break with the entrenched tradition—building opposition to capital punishment on religious grounds despite Old Testament acceptance of it—preceded and prepared the ground for the secular utilitarian criticism of the ENLIGHTENMENT, begun by Cesare Beccaria (1764), and the anticlerical assault on the gallows by Voltaire (1766). This combined attack dislodged the death penalty from the privileged place it had enjoyed in European culture for over five centuries, but two factors soon stalled the movement toward abolition: (1) the excesses of the French Revolution, and (2) the staunch moral retributivism of IMMANUEL KANT.

Modern Protestant Disagreement

The impact of Kant on prominent nineteenth-century Protestant theologians like Richard Rothe was substantial. Kant's philosophy was viewed as a providential reinforcement of "traditional" Christian support for capital punishment, although a very real change had nonetheless occurred. From this point forward, repudiation of capital punishment was a live option, not just a peripheral minority phenomenon. FRIEDRICH SCHLEIERMACHER, before his death (1834), concluded in defiance of Kant that "the death penalty has absolutely no place in a Christian state," and that "all Christians must constantly work for its abolition."

In the nineteenth and twentieth centuries, widespread disagreement over capital punishment pre-vailed within Protestantism in both Europe and America. In 1947 West Germany provoked an unprecedented public debate, involving major Protestant theologians (including Paul Althaus, KARL BARTH, Werner Elert, and Walter Kuenneth) when it adopted Article 102 of its Basic Law, declaring that "the death penalty is abolished." This disagreement, along with the United Nations' adoption of the *Universal Declaration of Human Rights* (1948), opened an era of growing abolitionism.

In the UNITED STATES the loss of church support for the death penalty in the 1960s was attributed in part to the CIVIL RIGHTS MOVEMENT, which focused attention on the unfairness and racism of the penal system, especially in the South. In 1968 the NATIONAL COUNCIL OF CHURCHES of Christ endorsed (103–0) a statement offering ten reasons why member churches should favor abolition of the death penalty. The first reason was "belief in the worth of human life and the dignity of human personality as gifts of God," and the last one was "our Christian commitment to seek the redemption and reconciliation of the wrong-doer, which are frustrated by his execution."

This trend, however, was significantly countered in the 1970s with the rise of a newly politicized conservative EVANGELICALISM, which supported capital punishment on the basis of its reading of the BIBLE. After ten years without executions, the U.S. Supreme Court decision in *Gregg v. Georgia* (1976) cleared the way for the resumption of state killings. The impact of this reversal was to some degree offset by the surprising turnaround of the Roman Catholic Church after Vatican II. Pope John Paul II not only spoke out against the death penalty but undertook an unprecedented campaign calling on modern states to stop using it. Many American Catholic bishops rejected it even more absolutely. This provided the basis for an unusual level of agreement and cooperation between many progressive Protestants and Roman Catholics.

Divided We Stand

As a result, evaluating capital punishment continues to be an area of disagreement. The European countries in which the Protestant Reformation began and flourished have all reversed their enthusiastic support of the death penalty and abolished it as incompatible with basic human rights. In contrast, American Protestantism is far more divided: those in favor of the death penalty usually appeal to a literal reading of the Bible and its affirmation of the death penalty. In contrast many who read the Bible more critically contend that "our use of the death penalty cannot be justified by the use of the Hebrew Scriptures" and is actually in conflict with "the basic tenet of Christianity—forgiveness is stronger than sin; love is stronger than death" (Hanks, 137; 233). Old Testament passages that specifically impose the death penalty for various offenses are seen as vestiges of the culture and morals of their own time rather than as expressions of God's will and purpose. The impasse between these two approaches is virtually intractable, given the divergent premises and the highly politicized atmosphere in which the controversy continues.

References and Further Reading

Bedau, Hugo Adam, ed. *The Death Penalty in America: Current Controversies.* New York: Oxford University Press, 1997.

Evans, Richard J. *Rituals of Retribution: Capital Punishment in Germany 1600–1987.* New York: Oxford University Press, 1996.

Gloege, Gerhard. *Die Todesstrafe als theologisches Problem.* Cologne: Westdeutscher Verlag, 1966.

Hanks, Gardner C. *Capital Punishment and the Bible.* Scottdale, PA: Herald Press, 2002.

Megivern, James J. *The Death Penalty: An Historical and Theological Survey.* New York: Paulist Press, 1997.

JAMES J. MEGIVERN

CAPITO, WOLFGANG (c. 1487–1521)

German theologian and reformer. Born Wolfgang Köpfel in the free imperial city of Hagenau in about 1487, Capito was educated at the universities of Freiburg in Breisgau and Basel. He received his doctorate in THEOLOGY in Freiburg and took a call as professor and cathedral preacher in Basel in 1515. He became a close acquaintance of the humanist Desiderius Erasmus after the publication of his own Hebrew grammars in Basel. With other young humanists, Capito joined the cause of the Wittenberg reformers at an early date.

While serving as cathedral preacher and ecclesiastical advisor to the archbishop of Mainz, Capito visited Wittenberg. As a result of his meetings with PHILIPP MELANCHTHON and MARTIN LUTHER, he came to disagree with Erasmus on the issues of the clarity of scripture and the freedom of the will.

Taking a post in Strasbourg in 1523 Capito openly joined the reform movement. His Strasbourg career shows both the REFORMATION'S connection to humanism and the way Luther's theology and reforms were implemented. His work in Strasbourg began with a lecture series, to which the city's leaders and clergy were invited (and because of which most were converted to the Reformation's cause). Capito's Strasbourg reforms included not only changes in teaching, ecclesiastical structures, and LITURGY, but also a renewal of public life with educational changes, public oversight over MARRIAGE and morality, and public welfare.

Capito was probably the author of the TETRAPOLITAN CONFESSION, submitted at the 1530 Diet of Augsburg. He worked with MARTIN BUCER and others to produce the Wittenberg Concord, under which cities subscribed to the AUGSBURG CONFESSION.

See also Lutheranism, Germany

References and Further Reading

Kittelson, James M. *Wolfgang Capito: From Humanist to Reformer.* Leiden: Brill, 1975.

———. *Toward an Established Church: Strasbourg from 1500 to the Dawn of the Seventeenth Century.* Mainz: P. von Zabern, 2000.

Millet, Olivier. *Correspondance de Wolfgang Capiton, 1478–1541: Analyse et index.* Publications de la bibliothèque Nationale et Universitaire de Strasbourg, no. 8. Strasbourg: National Library/University of Strasbourg, 1982.

Stierle, Beate. *Capito als Humanist.* Quellen und Forschungen zur Reformationsgeschichte. no. l, 42. Gütersloh: Gütersloher Verlagshaus G. Mohn, 1974.

KEN SUNDET JONES

CAPPEL, LOUIS (1585–1658)

French Huguenot philologist, Bible exegete, and divine. Born in Saint Élier near Sedan in northeast FRANCE, Cappel was famous for contending that the vowel markings in the Hebrew Bible were subsequent to the earliest transcriptions of the BIBLE, inventions of the Masorete Jews of Tiberias, dating from the fifth century A.D. Modern scholars now date their invention from the seventh century.

Appointed at age twenty-eight to a chair of Hebrew at Saumur, he taught for twenty years before proceeding to teach THEOLOGY. He was not the first to suspect Masoretic markings, but by virtue of his knowledge of Aramaic, Chaldean, and Arabic, learned during two years at Oxford University, and also his understanding of noncanonical Jewish writings, Cappel concluded that the Hebrew Bible had been altered over time.

His discovery that the square characters (Aramaic) had replaced the earlier Hebrew ones was anathema to critics, especially to Johannes Buxtorf, Jr., whose father, Johannes Sr., learned rabbinic scholar at the University of Basle, had maintained otherwise. Cappel's insistence that clarity was more important than textual tradition shocked Protestant contemporaries. They believed his conclusions threw doubt on the verbal inspiration of Scripture.

His great work, *Critica Sacra* (1634), could not be published by any Protestant press in the Low Countries or at Geneva, but had to await the help of Catholic scholars (Petau, Morin, and Mersenne) who obtained the necessary permission to publish at Paris (1650). Cappel's view of Scripture as having been altered over time gradually gained acceptance and is now acknowledged by all reputable experts.

See also Biblical Inerrancy; Bible Translation

References and Further Reading

Primary Source:

Cappel, Louis. *Critica Sacra.* Paris: 1634.

Secondary Sources:

Laplanche, François. *La Bible en France Entre Mythe et Critique (XVIe–XIXe siècle).* Paris: Éditions Albin Michel, S.A., 1994.
Van Stam, F. P. T*he Controversy Over the Theology of Saumur, 1635–1650.* Amsterdam and Maarssen: APA Holland University Press, 1988.

BARBARA SHER TINSLEY

CAREY, WILLIAM (1761–1834)

English baptist missionary. Born in a humble setting on August 17, 1761, at Paulerspury, Northamptonshire, England, William Carey was destined for greatness as a Baptist missionary in INDIA and Serampore though baptized as an infant in the Anglican Church. His father, Edmund, directed a small free school, and so from the start William became sensitive to the values of education.

In his mid-teens he became a shoemaker's apprentice in Hackleton and was introduced to NONCONFORMITY by John Warr, a fellow apprentice. Converted to nonconformist beliefs around 1779, Carey became convinced of Baptist doctrine and was baptized by immersion on October 5, 1783 by Dr. John Ryland, Baptist pastor of Northampton (see BAPTISTS).

For many years he continued shoemaking but also began to preach as a layperson. In 1786 he became pastor of the Baptist church at Moulton and was formally ordained in 1787 with the dually famous Ryland and Andrew Fuller being members of the ordaining council. Cobbling, running a day school, and serving as a pastor, Carey also commenced his long history as an excellent linguist by teaching himself Hebrew, Greek, Latin, French, and Dutch.

Soon, breaking the strict antimissions stance of Calvinistic Particular Baptists, Carey became convinced that the great commission to evangelize the nations should be specifically implemented. In 1791 at the Northampton Association he presented his missions beliefs and a bit later completed his amazing-for-its-time *An Enquiry into the Obligations of Christians to Use Means for the Conversion of the Heathens* with its program of "pray, plan, pay." In 1792 at the Baptist Association meeting in Nottingham, this

"hare-brained enthusiast" presented his position again and actually gave the motto to the modern MISSIONS movement: "Expect great things from God; attempt great things for God." Because of the strong support of Andrew Fuller, on October 2, 1792, at a Baptist ministers' meeting in Kettering, the Particular Baptist Society for the Propagation of the Gospel Amongst the Heathen came into being. This "first of its kind" missionary society would become a model for hundreds of other future societies.

In 1793 Carey and John Thomas, a physician, were sent as missionaries to India by the society. Late in 1793 they arrived in Bengal but for economic reasons soon moved to Malda where Carey became the superintendent of an indigo factory. Carey was committed from the start to being self-supporting in his missionary endeavors. By 1795 he had founded a Baptist church there and preached in the vernacular language. During his years in Malda he traveled widely to several hundred villages and also translated the New Testament into Bengali. The factory closed in 1799 and Carey moved to Serampore, a Danish colony friendlier to missionaries. Carey joined other missionaries there and the "Serampore Trio" (Carey, William Ward, and Joshua Marshman) evolved into a genuine missionary team, stressing through the years the spread of the Christian gospel by means of PREACHING, teaching, and BIBLE TRANSLATION.

In 1801 Carey was appointed as Professor of Sanskrit, Bengali, and Marathi at Fort William College. He retained the appointment for some thirty years. Beginning with a mission chapel in Calcutta, by 1814 there were at least twenty-nine other mission stations in surrounding areas. The mission eventually also founded primary schools as well as Serampore College and a very productive printing press.

Carey made major contributions to numerous Bible translations as well as language grammars and dictionaries. He published grammars of Mahratta, Sanskrit, Punjabi, Telinga, and Bhotanta, and dictionaries of Mahratta, Bengali, and Bhotanta. Carey and Marshman translated three volumes of the *Ramayana* into English and Carey edited Roxbugh's *Flora Medica.* Carey himself was an excellent botanist, having developed a five-acre botanical collection, presented scholarly papers in agriculture, and been involved in founding the Horticultural and Agricultural Society in Calcutta. At one time he was even elected president of the Agricultural Society of India.

Sometimes referred to as the "Wyclif of the East," Carey made mammoth contributions to Bible translation. In addition to his early Bengali translation, Carey taught himself numerous other languages and dialects and then completed a variety of biblical translations, including Sanskrit, Marathi, Hindi, and Oriya. He supervised numerous other translations such as Kashmiri and Teluga. It is estimated that because of his work, the entire Bible or parts of it were translated into thirty-four languages. He was truly a linguistic genius and used this unusual ability in Bible translations over many years in India. However flawed were his translations as judged by contemporary standards, "in the first three decades of the modern missionary movement forty-nine percent of the first translations into new languages anywhere in the world were published at Serampore, most of them translated by Carey or under his supervision" (Smalley 1991:47).

Although not the first foreign missionary, Carey was the first to be sent out by a missionary society. All of his income was funneled back into his mission projects; he was virtually self-supporting. He also believed that Indians could best be converted to Christianity by Indians. His teaching program and the founding of Serampore College was geared toward this end. Following his own early advice in his *Enquiry* of 1792, he mingled with the people and communicated in their own language. To his credit, he successfully agitated on behalf of the legal prohibition of suttee (the custom of putting widows to death at the husband's funeral) in 1829.

At the time of his death on June 9, 1834, in Serampore, India, he was truly an internationally known man and destined to be named as one of the fathers of the modern missionary movement.

See also Baptist Bible Union; Bible Translation; Missionary Organizations

References and Further Reading

Primary Source:

Carey, William. *An Enquiry into the Obligation of Christians.* London: Carey Kingsgate Press, reprinted 1961.

Secondary Sources:

Carey, Eustace. *Memoir of William Carey.* Boston: Gould, Kendall and Lincoln, 1836.

Carey, S. Pearce. *William Carey.* London: Hodder and Stroughton, 1923.

George, Timothy. *Faithful Witness: The Life and Mission of William Carey.* Birmingham, AL: New Hope, 1991.

Oussoren, A. H. *William Carey, Especially His Missionary Principles.* Leiden, Netherlands: A.W. Sijthoff, 1945.

Smalley, William A. *Translation As Mission.* Macon, GA: Mercer University Press, 1991.

Smith, George. *The Life of William Carey.* London: J. M. Dent and Sons, 1909.

Stanley, B. *The History of the Baptist Missionary Society.* Edinburgh: T. and T. Clark, 1992.

GEORGE H. SHRIVER

CARIBBEAN

The spread of Protestantism to the Caribbean coincided with the settlement of territories in this region by European Protestants in the early decades of the seventeenth century. Although the Dutch had been in what would later become Guiana in 1611, the first settlement of Protestants in the Caribbean occurred in the 1620s with the English occupation of St. Christopher. The CHURCH OF ENGLAND had modest success converting African slaves in the rest of the seventeenth century but, in the eighteenth, the Evangelicals—the Moravians, Methodists, and Baptists—flourished. Other Protestant groups arrived in the nineteenth and twentieth centuries mainly from the UNITED STATES and a strong Protestant presence remains there today.

Definitions

Protestants and Protestantism, as used herein, refer primarily to the earliest groups of dissenters from the AUTHORITY of the Church of Rome and the belief systems they developed in the sixteenth and seventeenth centuries. The Protestant REFORMATION and its impact in GERMANY, ENGLAND, FRANCE, Scandinavia, and the NETHERLANDS is primarily in view. The Caribbean is a modern designation for a group of islands and countries between North and South America, situated mostly within the Caribbean Sea, including some areas that technically could be grouped in other ways. Bermuda, though in the middle of the Atlantic ocean, is sometimes included in discussions of the Caribbean, as are Belize, Guyana, and Surinam though each of these is in Central/South America. The American (formerly Danish) Virgin islands have long been connected with the English-speaking Caribbean, as have the Bahama islands. Different names have been used for clusters of these islands over the centuries—the Greater and Lesser Antilles, the Leeward and Windward islands, the Cayman Islands, the Turks and Caicos Islands, the Netherlands Antilles, and so on. The whole area was referred to as the West Indies for centuries, but in the postcolonial era, Caribbean, referring back to the precolonial inhabitants of the region, is preferred. In much of what follows, the British Caribbean is the primary focus.

Seventeenth-Century Developments

The story of Protestantism in the Caribbean begins with the occupation of this region by foreigners: first by Europeans—Spanish, English, Dutch, and French; later by Africans imported against their will, and later still, Asians brought as indentured servants after the abolition of SLAVERY in the nineteenth century. German religious leader MARTIN LUTHER (1483–1546) flourished a mere quarter century after Columbus landed on a Bahama island in 1492, renaming it San Salvador (Holy Savior) and claiming it for the Spanish crown. In the years thereafter, Spain held a virtual monopoly in the region with respect to resources, people, and religion; the Caribbean Sea was considered the Spanish lake. The story of Spanish contacts with indigenous peoples and the exploitation and extirpation of them is well known. Much of the sixteenth century in the Caribbean was dominated by conflicts between Spanish Catholics and other European nations that increasingly were represented by Protestants wishing to wrest some power from Spain. By the middle of the century, French Protestant corsairs, called Huguenots after 1559, challenged the monopoly of Spain, raiding Spanish ships for gold and even capturing cities in Cuba. Likewise, a strong Protestant faith was represented among English sailors to the region; Dutch seamen included many Calvinist Protestants. Indeed, the defeat of the Spanish Armada in 1588 prepared the way for Protestant colonization of the region in the following century.

Given Spain's control over the larger territories—Jamaica, Cuba, Hispaniola, Puerto Rico, and Trinidad—in this early period, English and other Protestant settlers confined their exploratory efforts to the smaller islands and the Guyana coastlands. In the 1620s, the English occupied St. Christopher (later with the French), Barbados, and Nevis. In the 1630s Antigua and Montserrat were occupied by the English and Irish; Martinique, Guadeloupe, and Tortuga by the French; and St. Martin, St. Eustatius, Saba, Curaçao, Aruba, and Bonaire by the Dutch in the 1640s. The Danish were in the Virgin Islands as early as 1666, establishing the first Lutheran congregation in the Western world there. It was on one of these small islands, St. Christopher (later St. Kitts), that we hear of the first Protestant clergyman in any permanent English colony in the Caribbean, Master John Featley, a Calvinist Episcopalian who accompanied Thomas Warner to the island, occupied by the English in 1622. In 1625 Barbados was occupied by opposing English settlers whose early memoirs include a reference to a certain Kentlane, a pious clergyman functioning as an intermediary between them. Yet another clergyman is mentioned as a passenger on a ship bound for Nevis from Barbados in 1629. By 1630, after the appointment of the first governor of Barbados, six parishes had been defined there, following the pattern of ecclesiastical organization of the English, and churches built shortly thereafter. A similar pattern was followed in many of the smaller islands in the following two decades. Parishes were demarcated in St. Kitts by 1655, in Nevis and Montserrat in the 1670s, and in Antigua by 1681.

In addition to the official English Church, other radical Protestant groups were present in the colonies at this time. HUGUENOTS are mentioned in St. Kitts, Puritans in the Bahamas, and Anabaptists, Quakers, and other dissenters are mentioned in official correspondence. English Quakers made a significant mark in the seventeenth century. As early as 1655 they arrived in Barbados to proclaim the new faith. Others followed and were initially quite successful so that later missionaries were sent to Nevis, Jamaica, Antigua, and Bermuda. Despite ill treatment by the planters, Quakers flourished for some time in the latter islands, but ceased to exist in the region by the next century.

Protestantism in the colonies was developed initially and practiced among English settlers and indentured white servants; everyone was nominally Christian whether Welsh, English, Scottish, or Irish. Its character changed with the introduction of African slaves in the middle of the seventeenth century. Planters exhibited little regard for, and a universal refusal to address, the spiritual needs of the slaves in the earliest years. The morality of slavery was unchallenged by the churches; accounts by visitors relate the particularly brutal treatment meted out to slaves in the Caribbean by Christian planters. However, the last two decades of the seventeenth century witnessed a shift in the attitude of the Church of England, a preoccupation with saving the souls of slaves, culminating with the formation in London of the SOCIETY FOR THE PROPAGATION OF THE GOSPEL IN FOREIGN PARTS (SPG) in 1701 whose declared purpose was to Christianize slaves and Indians in the colonies.

Eighteenth-Century Developments

Soon thereafter, SPG missionaries spread to the colonies but, with the notable exception of Christopher Codrington's bequest to them of an estate in Barbados, their efforts in the Caribbean failed for a number of related reasons. Planters were generally uncooperative, believing that Christianity would make slaves proud and entertain notions of freedom; the missionaries themselves acted condescendingly toward potential converts, using terms like pagans, heathens, and barbarians to describe them. Refusing to believe that slaves could find them and their version of Christianity objectionable, missionaries maintained a consistent approach in the face of initial failure. It is not clear whether BAPTISM initially altered the status of slaves; slaves who were attracted to Christianity required a period of education before they could be baptized and, once admitted, were seated in separate sections of the meeting places. Traditional African religion was more appealing than Protestantism of the SPG variety; however, Protestantism's greatest strides among the masses of people in the Caribbean in the days of slavery were made by lay preachers and missionaries from the Evangelical Movement—Moravians, Methodists, BAPTISTS, and Congregationalists—to whose story we now turn.

In general, three features common to evangelical Protestants contributed to their success in the Caribbean—emphasis on spiritual equality, emphasis on direct oral communication with the supernatural, and dramatic forms of worship and ritual. The first Protestant effort at evangelizing slaves in the Caribbean came about as a result of the fusion in HERRNHUT in Saxony of two streams of faith—the (Moravian) United Brethren and German Lutheranism (see LUTHERANISM, GERMANY)—into the MORAVIAN CHURCH. A female slave on the Danish Caribbean island of St. Thomas initiated a request, relayed through her brother, also a slave, to Count NIKOLAUS LUDWIG VON ZINZENDORF, that missionaries be sent to the island's slave population. Two single Moravian missionaries, Johann Dober and David Nitschmann (1696–1772), having volunteered, left Herrnhut and arrived in St. Thomas in 1732. Moravian success in this region among slaves was remarkable, due in no small measure to their employment of novel techniques that were emulated by subsequent evangelical groups, especially the Methodists. Unlike SPG missionaries, Moravians welcomed slaves into multiracial communities, practiced early Christian forms of WORSHIP including the kiss of peace, the laying on of hands and foot washing, visited slaves in their cabins, shared food and clothing, offered warm handshakes, and used locals both as interpreters and helpers. Above all, Moravians taught reading skills to slaves. Such approaches led to expansion to other Virgin Islands—St. Croix and St. John—by the middle of the century; in the first fifty years, Moravians had baptized nearly 12,000 persons in the Danish territories.

Moravian missionary work in the British Caribbean began first in Jamaica in 1754, but unlike the situation in the Danish islands, fewer than 1,000 blacks were baptized after fifty years. Moravians were most effective in Antigua, where they had established a mission in 1756, and showed the largest pattern of growth, aided in part by the presence on that island of the first Methodist Society of the West Indies. The combined activities of these two evangelical groups produced remarkable results for Protestantism in Antigua and surrounding islands, so that by the last quarter of the eighteenth century, black evangelical communities had been established in Jamaica, Barbados, St. Kitts, and the Danish Virgin Islands.

The final decades of the eighteenth century witnessed the expansion of METHODISM and the establishment of the Baptist faith in the Caribbean. The story of Methodism begins, as mentioned above, in Antigua, where since the middle of the century, there had been a thriving Methodist Society comprised mostly of slaves originally organized by a planter, Nathaniel Gilbert, a convert to this new way of thinking as early as 1760. Gilbert, a lawyer and member of the Antigua legislature, became persuaded by reading some of the writings of evangelical preacher JOHN WESLEY (1703–1791) sent to him from England by his brother. He visited England in 1758 to hear Wesley for himself; two of his slaves, most probably women, were the first blacks ever to be baptized by Wesley during this visit. On Gilbert's death in 1773, the work was carried on by two women of color until the arrival from England of a local Methodist preacher, John Baxter, in 1778. Under his leadership, and with the support of these and other women, the society began to grow again; a chapel capable of holding 2,000 people was built in St. Johns by 1783. But on Christmas day 1786, the Reverend THOMAS COKE (1747–1814), who had earlier been instrumental in establishing the Methodist Episcopal Church in the United States, having been diverted because of bad weather from his original plan to sail from England to Nova Scotia, arrived instead in Antigua together with three other ministers. Coke's coming led to the rapid spread of Methodism in Antigua and throughout the region. In only a few years, Methodists had been established not only in St. Kitts, Barbados, and Jamaica, where they worked alongside the Moravians, but also in the ceded (from France) islands of St. Vincent, Dominica, and Grenada. In these latter three islands, Methodists were first to establish an evangelical presence. Work was also initiated on a variety of smaller islands—Nevis, Tortola, Montserrat, St. Bartholomew—by the beginning of the next century. In 1793, Methodists in the Caribbean numbered 6,570, more than three times what Coke had met in 1786; by 1804 there were 14,376 in the Caribbean, only 112 of whom were white.

Religious fervor in America prior to the revolution spread in time to the south, where evangelists preached both to slaves and to whites. This led to the conversion of many slaves and free blacks to the Baptist and Methodist faiths and, in time, to the formation of entirely black congregations. An early and famous Baptist church of this kind was founded between 1773 and 1775 at Silver Bluff, South Carolina, with whose congregation was associated a gifted slave named George Liele (1750–1820). Ordained in 1775, Liele was given his freedom by his master because of his religious work and, due to his sympathies with the British during the revolution, emigrated from the

United States to Kingston, Jamaica, in 1782 where he, with four other émigrés from America, established the Baptist mission in 1784. Another black preacher and friend of Liele's, "Brother Amos," went to New Providence in the Bahamas in 1788. In time, these two men expanded the Baptist faith in each of these regions by organizing and nurturing individual congregations. Both were so successful that, by the end of the century, Baptist churches were flourishing in many parishes of Jamaica and also in the Bahamas, much to the alarm of planters.

Nineteenth- and Twentieth-Century Developments

By the first decade of the new century, the Jamaican Assembly attempted to silence the Methodist and Baptist missionaries, especially black ministers like Liele and his colleagues, who were considered "ill-disposed," "illiterate," or "ignorant enthusiasts." When, after a decade of repression, the Jamaican Assembly relaxed the legal restrictions on preaching by white missionaries in 1816, it explicitly retained those restrictions for black preachers. Although no black preacher was licensed in Jamaica before emancipation in 1833, a greater number of black Jamaicans heard of Protestant evangelical Christianity through self-proclaimed black preachers and exhorters than through missionaries. Alongside Liele's version of the Baptist faith there also emerged in Jamaica Native Baptists fusing elements of African traditional religions with Baptist beliefs.

The spread of Methodists and Baptists to the southern Caribbean—Trinidad and Guyana—took place in the early decades of the nineteenth century. Middle decades were marked by several events involving Protestants, only a few of which can be summarized here. Evangelical Protestant churches supported the push for abolition of slavery (see SLAVERY, ABOLITION OF), which occurred in 1834 and 1838 and, as a result, enjoyed a period of further growth. The Church of England joined the evangelical churches in supporting education for former slaves, with the result that its membership increased considerably. Presbyterians arrived in Jamaica as early as 1813 and later in other territories, conducting successful missions to Indian immigrants in Guyana and Trinidad, and the DISCIPLES OF CHRIST church was established. In the final decades of the nineteenth century a large number of Protestant denominations of various kinds made their way to the Caribbean. Among these were separatist groups from established traditions. The AFRICAN METHODIST EPISCOPAL CHURCH, the first independent black denomination in America, had very early set as its priority the evangelization of the Caribbean and AFRICA so that

missionaries of that denomination along with its related organizations—the British Methodist Episcopal Church (from CANADA) and the AFRICAN METHODIST EPISCOPAL ZION (AMEZ) church, an early splinter group—arrived from the United States. Joining these was another divergent group from Methodism, the SALVATION ARMY, which, established in 1887 in Jamaica, spread thereafter to other islands. In addition, other newer denominations, mostly from the United States, took hold in the colonies. Notable among these were the Seventh-day Adventists, who were particularly successful in Jamaica and Trinidad, and holiness churches of various kinds including the CHURCH OF GOD, Pilgrim Holiness, CHURCH OF THE NAZARENE, and Wesleyans (see WESLEYAN CHURCH, WESLEYANISM). Protestant missionaries spread to formerly French and Spanish Catholic territories like Puerto Rico, Cuba, and the Dominican Republic in this period.

PENTECOSTALISM, developed in the United States in the early twentieth century, spread to the Caribbean region soon thereafter, augmenting the numbers and influence of holiness churches in several ways. Finally, in this period a number of indigenous religious movements fused various elements of Protestant beliefs with elements of African religion to constitute new belief systems. The patterns of the spread of Protestantism in the Caribbean in the rest of the twentieth century are too complex to summarize briefly, but a few general assertions are in order. Protestant bodies grew at a rapid rate in the first half of the century, while in the second half the most extensive growth was among Pentecostal-type groups. A Caribbean Conference of Churches, consisting mainly of mainline Protestants, was formed in 1973, and there have also been church unions consisting of smaller discrete groups. A United Theological College of the West Indies in Jamaica trains ministers for some eleven denominations. Studies of the history of particular Protestant groups are in the reference list and may be consulted further, but it should suffice to indicate that religion for most current residents of the Caribbean region consists of some form of Protestant belief.

See also Holiness Movement; Presbyterianism; Methodist Episcopal Church Conference; Evangelicalism

References and Further Reading

Bisnauth, Dale. *History of Religions in the Caribbean.* Trenton, NJ: Africa World Press, 1996.

Drayfoot, Arthur Charles. *The Shaping of the West Indian Church.* Gainesville, FL: University Press of Florida, 1999.

Frey, Sylvia R., and Betty Wood. *Come Shouting to Zion: African American Protestantism in the American South and British Caribbean to 1830.* Chapel Hill, NC: The University of North Carolina Press, 1998.

Gates, Brian, ed. *Afro-Caribbean Religions.* London: Ward Lock Educational, 1980.

Simpson, George Eaton. *Black Religions in the New World.* New York: Columbia University Press, 1978.

Titus, Noel F. *The Development of Methodism in Barbados 1823–1883.* Paris: Peter Lang, 1993.

MELVIN K. H. PETERS

CARNELL, EDWARD JOHN (1919–1967)

American theologian. Carnell was born in Antigo, Wisconsin on June 28, 1919. He earned degrees from Wheaton College and Westminster Theological Seminary; a Th.D. on REINHOLD NIEBUHR (Harvard, 1948), and a Ph.D. on SÖREN KIERKEGAARD (Boston University, 1949).

After teaching briefly at Gordon College and Divinity School (1945–1948), Carnell moved to Fuller Theological Seminary, where he became professor of ETHICS and philosophy of religion. He was also Fuller's president from 1954 to 1959. Carnell died suddenly on April 25, 1967 at age 47.

Carnell distanced himself from FUNDAMENTALISM and identified himself as Evangelical (see EVANGELICALISM). However, he regularly wrote for the theologically liberal *Christian Century* magazine (see LIBERAL PROTESTANTISM AND LIBERALISM), and was the only evangelical theologian invited to pose questions to KARL BARTH during his 1962 University of Chicago lectures.

Carnell was a Christian apologist. Although he considered himself a "Christian rationalist," scholars have characterized his apologetic method as "presuppositionalism" (Nash), "combinationalism" (Geisler), and the "verificational approach" (Lewis). However, these characterizations do not readily account for Carnell's interest in Kierkegaard. Whereas many evangelical apologists of Carnell's day sought to defend the reliability of Scripture (a concern he shared), Carnell also analyzed the existential situation of the human self. Thus, the apologetic defense of conservative orthodox Christianity, as a belief system, is proven both by its epistemological and existential consistency. As Carnell noted, "Systems are verified by the degree to which their major elements are consistent with one another and with the broad facts of history and nature. In short, a consistent system is a true system." But ultimately, the truth of a theological hypothesis is verified "when it smoothly interprets life."

References and Further Reading

Primary Source:

Carnell, Edward J. *An Introduction to Christian Apologetics.* Grand Rapids, MI: Eerdmans, 1948.

Secondary Source:

Sims, John A. *Edward John Carnell: Defender of the Faith.* Washington DC: University Press of America, 1979.

DAVID GURETZKI

CARTWRIGHT, PETER (1785–1872)

American Methodist. The most famous of the Methodist itinerants to emerge from the Second Great Awakening in the Ohio River Valley during the early 1800s, Peter Cartwright lived an active life that embraced not only the ministry, but also politics. Born in 1785 in Amherst County, Virginia, Cartwright experienced CONVERSION in 1801 and joined the Methodists. Within a year he received a license to exhort and soon organized a Methodist circuit in Livingston County, Kentucky. From 1803 until 1824, he served as a CIRCUIT RIDER, emphasizing "experimental" religion at CAMP MEETINGS and protracted meetings and setting himself against not only "sinners," but also those preachers whose inspirations came from "book learning" rather than unmediated contact with the Holy Spirit.

Cartwright was a strong supporter of METHODISM and helped organize that Protestant denomination in Kentucky, Indiana, and Illinois, where he settled in 1824. An ardent abolitionist, Cartwright entered secular politics and became part of what was known as the "Methodist Militia" in the Illinois legislature, where he served for 16 years. He engaged in two political campaigns involving ABRAHAM LINCOLN, defeating the future president for a seat in the state legislature in 1832, but losing a place in the U.S. Congress to him in 1846.

Cartwright also had literary leanings. He founded the *Central Christian Advocate*, a newspaper edited by his son-in-law. His most important written work was *Autobiography of Peter Cartwright, the Backwoods Preacher*, published in 1856. This volume dramatically recounts many of the events in his early circuit-riding ministry that represented his emphasis on personal religious experience. He also compiled *Fifty Years as a Presiding Elder* in 1871 in celebration of his ministerial jubilee.

Cartwright died in 1872 in Pleasant Plains, Illinois, where a United Methodist Church bears his name.

See also Itinerancy; Slavery, Abolition of; Awakenings

References and Further Reading

Chrisman, Richard. "Peter Cartwright as a Presiding Elder." *Methodist History* 27 (1988–1989): 151–162.

Dvorak, Katharine L. "Peter Cartwright and Charisma." *Methodist History* 26 (1987–1988): 113–126.

WILLIAM M. CLEMENTS

CARTWRIGHT, THOMAS (1535–1603)

English Puritan. Thomas Cartwright was born in Hertfordshire and began his education in 1547 at Clare Hall, Cambridge. In 1550 he was elected a scholar of St. John's College, which was known for its strong attachment to REFORMATION ideals. During the reign of the Catholic Mary, Cambridge was an inhospitable place for progressives, and Cartwright left the university to work for a time as a clerk to a lawyer. After the accession of ELIZABETH I, he returned to Cambridge, where he distinguished himself as a preacher and scholar. During the early 1560s he was a fellow at St. John's and later at Trinity College, and in 1564 he participated in a theological disputation staged for the queen's visit. A brief stint in IRELAND (1565–1567) as chaplain to Archbishop Loftus of Armagh allowed him to escape some of the disputes then raging in the university over the religious settlement of Elizabeth. However, shortly after his appointment as Lady Margaret Professor of Divinity in November 1569, controversy arose over a series of lectures Cartwright gave on the Book of Acts wherein he compared English church POLITY unfavorably with that of the apostolic church, which he understood as essentially Presbyterian in its organization. He was severely criticized and lost his chair. In 1571 Cartwright left ENGLAND for the safe haven of Geneva, SWITZERLAND, where he was welcomed warmly by JOHN CALVIN'S successor THEODORE BEZA. At the entreaty of his friends, Cartwright returned to Cambridge in 1572, only to become immediately embroiled in further controversy due to his defense of the *Admonition to the Parliament*, an anonymously published tract that forcefully advocated Presbyterian discipline. He was obliged to leave England once again at the end of 1573 to avoid arrest. During the next twelve years, Cartwright moved regularly, living and ministering in Heidelberg, Basel, Antwerp, and Middelburg. He returned to England in 1585 and was briefly imprisoned, but found a patron in Robert Dudley, the Earl of Leicester, and soon became master of the Earl's hospital in Warwick. Cartwright maintained his support for Presbyterian reform during the latter 1580s, and in 1590 he was arrested, tried before the High Commission, and imprisoned. Through the intercession of William Cecil, Lord Burghley, he gained his freedom in 1592. From 1595 to 1601 he ministered in the Channel Islands, where he helped revise the Presbyterian discipline already in use there. Cartwright spent the last two years of his life in Warwick, where he died December 27, 1603.

In his promotion of Presbyterian polity, Cartwright's chief opponent was JOHN WHITGIFT, master of Trinity College (1567), vice-chancellor of Cambridge (1570), and archbishop of Canterbury (1583). Following the appearance of the *Admonition*, the two engaged in a written debate wherein Cartwright laid out the key Presbyterian arguments in three treatises: *Reply to an Answer Made of M. Doctor Whitgift* (1573), *Second Replie* (1575), and *The Rest of the Second Replie* (1577). Claiming that scripture allowed only for Presbyterian polity, Cartwright emphasized equality among ministers, the right of congregations to call ministers, a separation of the spiritual and temporal realms, and the familiar Puritan theme of the need to purge the church of all "popish" remnants in its worship practices and the BOOK OF COMMON PRAYER. In his defense of the established church, Whitgift argued that no one form of church government was prescribed by scripture, and that a Christian prince had authority to direct the external form of the church and set policy on such indifferent matters.

Despite the intensity of their polemic, Cartwright and Whitgift did share some fundamental positions. Significantly, Cartwright held that the CHURCH OF ENGLAND was a true CHURCH, albeit in need of serious reform. In this, he may be distinguished from the separatists, who believed the church to be so riddled with errors that it was necessary to withdraw entirely. An extant letter records Cartwright's begrudging defense of the Church of England as he attempts to win his sister-in-law, Anne Stubbe, back from the separatist camp. Presbyterians and separatists shared many of the same complaints about the English church's ministry and worship, yet the threat of separatism backed Cartwright into the uncomfortable role of defending the very church he would reform. Cartwright also agreed with Whitgift and all English Protestants in holding the Roman Catholic Church to be a false church. In this context, the Puritans frequently cooperated with the established church by turning their pens to antipapal polemic. So it was that friends and patrons encouraged Cartwright to write against the translation of the New Testament completed by English Catholics living abroad. The result was his massive *Confutation of the Rhemists Translation* (1618), completed in the 1580s but not published until long after his death, apparently as a result of Whitgift's continuing displeasure and unwillingness to provide tacit endorsement to Cartwright's opinions.

A gifted scholar and rhetorician, Cartwright remained an influential leader of Elizabethan Puritans throughout his life. At the time of his death, he was scheduled to plead the Puritan cause to the newly enthroned James I at the Hampton Court Conference (January 1604).

See also Presbyterianism; Puritanism; Catholicism, Protestant Reactions; Church Discipline

References and Further Reading

Lake, Peter. *Moderate Puritans and the Elizabethan Church.* Cambridge, UK: Cambridge University Press, 1982.

———. *Anglicans and Puritans? Presbyterian and English Conformist Thought from Whitgift to Hooker.* London: Unwin Hyman, 1988.

McGinn, Donald Joseph. *The Admonition Controversy.* New Brunswick, NJ: Rutgers University Press, 1949.

Pearson, A. F. Scott. *Thomas Cartwright and Elizabethan Puritanism.* Cambridge, UK: Cambridge University Press, 1925.

Peel, Albert, and Leland H. Carlson, eds. *Cartwrightiana.* Elizabethan Nonconformist Texts, I. London: George Allen and Unwin, 1951.

SCOTT MCGINNIS

CARY, LOTT (c. 1780–1828)

Slave, freedman, preacher, and leader of African American settlers in Liberia in the 1820s. Born in rural Virginia, Cary was hired out in Richmond tobacco warehouses. After a conversion experience in 1807 inspired by John 3, Cary became a lay exhorter to blacks. Freed in 1815, he was ordained and accepted for missionary service by the Baptist General Convention. He emigrated in 1821 to the colony governed by the AMERICAN COLONIZATION SOCIETY (ACS). He emerged as leader of the black settlers, becoming peer and confidant of the white ACS agent, Jehudi Ashmun (1794–1828). Cary undertook little missionary work. He committed his energies to commerce and the subjugation of indigenous Liberians, and died in an explosion as he was preparing munitions for use against them. He left little writing.

Cary's importance in Protestantism derives not from his writings or his missionary activity, which has sometimes been mistakenly praised, but from his partnership with Ashmun. With Cary as his exemplar, Ashmun announced that in Africa energetic, forceful Protestant men could rule and "civilize" native peoples as well as prosper through trade in African raw materials and American finished goods. Resisting his Calvinist background, Ashmun was drawn to Cary's free-will Christianity, which seemingly encouraged the drive and agency exercised in governing natives and trading. The Baptist Cary helped Ashmun overcome Calvinism. Cary's life and death elucidate the influence on missions of "civilizationist" and commercial tendencies and hostility toward native peoples. Cary's heirs were the black Protestant "civilizationists" MARTIN DELANY (1812–1885), ALEXANDER CRUMMELL (1819–1898), and Henry McNeal Turner (1834–1915).

See also American Colonization Society; Liberia.

References and Further Reading

Gurley, Ralph Randolph. *Life of Jehudi Ashmun.* New York: 1835.

Saillant, John, ed. "'Circular Addressed to the Colored Brethren . . .': An Unpublished Essay by Lott Cary," *The Virginia Magazine of History and Biography* 104: (1996): 481–504.

Taylor, J. B. *Biography of Elder Lott Cary.* Baltimore, 1837.

JOHN SAILLANT

CASTELLIO, SEBASTIAN (CASTELLION, CASTALIO, CHATILLON, OR CHATEILLON) (1515–1563)

French Protestant theologian and humanist. Castellio was born in 1515 in Saint-Martin-du-Fresne in Savoyen and died in Basel in 1563. The son of a peasant, Castellio's scholarly aptitude brought him first to Lyon where he encountered JOHN CALVIN'S INSTITUTES OF THE CHRISTIAN RELIGION, and in 1540 to Strasbourg where he lived briefly with Calvin. After becoming rector of a Latin school in Geneva in 1541, Castellio published his *Dialogi sacri,* a widely circulated manual of Bible stories in dialogue form that was praised by Calvin. However, Castellio developed differences with Calvin on PREDESTINATION, the canonicity of the Old Testament book Song of Solomon, and the literality of Christ's descent into hell. As a result he resigned his position in 1544.

He moved in 1545, with his wife and eight children, to Basel where he worked as a proofreader, and completed two BIBLE TRANSLATIONS, a classical Latin one in 1551 containing a controversial excursus on the freedom of the will, and a popular French one published in 1555. He and his family lived in great poverty until his appointment as professor of Greek at the University of Basel in 1553. The burning of MICHAEL SERVETUS in Geneva later that year occasioned the publication of *De haereticis, an sint persequendi* (If Heretics Are to Be Persecuted?) in which Castellio, using the pseudonym of Martin Bellius, called for religious TOLERATION and freedom of conscience. The tract brought sharp replies from Geneva, particularly from the pens of Calvin and THEODORE BEZA. Castellio remained in Basel until his death, working in his final year on his unfinished *De arte dubitandi* (On the Art of Doubting). Because of Castellio's advocacy of religious tolerance and his criticisms of predestination and the bondage of the will, many Unitarians regard him as a spiritual ancestor (see UNITARIAN UNIVERSALIST ASSOCIATION).

References and Further Reading

Primary Sources:

Castellion, Sebastian. *Concerning Heretics.* Translated by Roland Bainton. New York: Octagon Books, 1935.

———. "*Dialogi quatuor.*" In *Sebastiano Castellion, il riformato umanista contro il riformatore Calvino.* Edited and translated by Carla Gallicet Calvetti. Milan: Vita e pensiero, 1989.

Secondary Sources:

Buisson, Ferdinand. *Sebastien Castellion, sa vie et son ouvre, 1515–1563.* 2 vols. Paris: Librairie Hachette, 1892.

Guggisberg, Hans Rudolf. *Sebastian Castellio 1515–1563: Humanist und Verteidiger der religiösen Toleranz im konfessionellen Zeitalter.* Göttingen, Germany: Vandenhoeck & Ruprecht, 1997.

DENNIS BIELFELDT

CATECHISM(S)

Catechism, a summary of religious doctrine, and catechetical instruction were hardly new, much less unique, to the Protestant REFORMATION of the sixteenth century. From its earliest history, the Christian church had provided oral instruction in the basics of the faith for those entering the church through baptism. This catechetical instruction eventually developed a specific syllabus that included the Decalogue (Ten Commandments), Apostle's Creed, and Lord's Prayer. Additional instruction was provided on BAPTISM and the LORD'S SUPPER. Under the influence of MARTIN LUTHER and the power of the printing press, explanations of that catechetical syllabus became fixed in the form of a booklet—a catechism—and taken to a wide audience that extended beyond the clergy to the laity, adults, and children alike. As a result, catechisms emerged as some of the most powerful and popular vehicles for spreading the message of the Protestant Reformation.

Catechism in the Early Church and Middle Ages

Of the five components constituting catechetical instruction, the Creed and Lord's Prayer had been used since the third and fourth centuries for the prebaptismal instruction of adult converts. The Creed, which unfolded the baptismal formula, was part of the formal consignment of the Creed on Palm Sunday and its subsequent recitation by the baptismal candidate on Easter eve. The imparting of the Creed in Rome was accompanied with the Lord's Prayer, which provided access to common participation in the liturgical service. As the church moved into the Middle Ages and infant baptism became the norm, sponsors and parents acted in the infant's stead for the imparting and recitation of the Creed and Lord's Prayer. More in-depth instruction was later given to children as part of their examination in preparation for CONFESSION and communion, which had been mandated by the Fourth Lateran Council (1215).

The Decalogue emerged later within the church's tradition as the third component of the catechism. In the early church, the twofold command of love for God and for neighbor was the most common basis for ethical instruction. This gave way to an exposition of vices (e.g., seven deadly sins) and virtues (e.g., seven principal virtues) as catechetical teaching became linked with confession. Instruction often included lengthy catalogues of sins. It is also in connection with the confessional that the Decalogue is first introduced and consistently used after the Synod of Trier in 1227. The Ten Commandments did not, however, become widespread as a replacement for the lists of vices and virtues until the fifteenth century, by which time nearly every confessional manual required the priest to examine the penitent on the Ten Commandments as well as the Creed and the Lord's Prayer.

Early on in the church's history, the prebaptismal instruction was supplemented with a postbaptismal instruction on a fourth topic, that is, the SACRAMENTS, as was the case with the catechetical lectures of Cyril in Jerusalem, Ambrose, and Theodore of Mopsuestia. During the Middle Ages, however, instruction on the sacraments was not a featured part of catechetical instruction. In the manuals for priests, instruction might be given on how to perform the sacraments properly. In other manuals the sacraments would simply be listed for the people. It was enough to know which rites were sacraments. The topic of confession received the greatest amount of attention in connection with the sacrament of penance. As a whole, though, expositions of the nature and benefits of the sacraments were not common, as they would become in the Protestant reformation.

Before the invention of the printing press, oral instruction on the basic texts of the faith was conveyed in the form of sermons, some of which were subsequently written down to provide sermon resources for other priests (see PREACHING). Such was the case with Cyril's thirty-eight lectures as well as Augustine's. The best known catechetical sermons from the high Middle Ages were a series of short instructions preached by Thomas Aquinas in the vernacular in Naples during Lent of 1273. When the practice of oral confession was used as an opportunity for catechetical instruction, manuals called "mirrors" were written as aids for the self-examination required in confession, for example, *The Mirror of a Christian Man* (1470) by Dietrich Kolde. One of the first books of instruction to which the term "catechism" is applied was *The Lay Folks Catechism* in 1357, written at the direction of Archbishop John Thoresby of York.

Catechisms of the Protestant Reformation

With the dawn of the sixteenth century, catechisms emerged as important tools for spreading the message of Reformation when the printing press made them affordable and numerous. The term "catechism" begins to be used extensively for these instructional booklets in the mid- to late-1520s, when a flood of catechisms appeared on the market. In Germany alone there were over 170 produced by the end of the decade. In these booklets, the Reformers adopted the traditional catechetical syllabus but provided explanations of it that highlighted the Reformation teaching on JUSTIFICATION. Several of the more important catechisms include those of Luther, JOHN CALVIN, and the HEIDELBERG CATECHISM OF 1563.

Luther's catechisms trace their origins to three events. In 1523 Nicholas Hausmann, a pastor in Zwickau, requested the elector to assign someone the task of preparing a catechism for children. Eventually, *A Booklet for the Laity and Children* appeared in Wittenberg in 1525. Although not written by Luther, it included excerpts from several of his writings. Second, the collapse of the old church structures in the wake of the Reformation raised the need for a formal visitation of the churches to assess their condition. Luther's participation in the visitations during the fall of 1528 profoundly affected him as he discovered that the peasants had learned nothing, rarely prayed, and did not go to confession or communion. Third, in connection with the visitations, a theological conflict erupted in Electoral Saxony over the place of the law in the Christian life. Johann Agricola argued that repentance was a consequence of the preaching of the Gospel and not the law, views that he expressed in the catechism, *One Hundred and Thirty Common Questions for the Girls School at Eisleben.*

Luther's catechism first appeared beginning in January 1529 on large sheets of paper, sold like newspapers and hung up in churches, schools, and homes. On May 16, 1529, the Wittenberg book edition appeared in the book stalls under the title, *The Small Catechism for Ordinary Pastors and Preachers.* It is characterized by its simplicity and elegance in the presentation of the faith. In a society where oral communication still predominated, Luther used a wide variety of rhetorical devices (alliteration, assonance, rhythm, etc.) to render it pleasing to the ear and easily imprinted upon the mind. *The Large [German] Catechism of Martin Luther* also appeared in May 1529. It is characterized by a theological depth and an earthiness of expression that remain remarkably relevant and true to the human experience.

Both catechisms are best known for their arrangement of the traditional catechetical syllabus. Rather than beginning with the Creed and proceeding to the Lord's Prayer and the Ten Commandments, Luther began with the Ten Commandments and proceeded to the Creed and Lord's Prayer. This reflected Luther's own Law–Gospel dialectic for preaching the Word of God. In addition, this pattern for Luther was rooted in

human experience. As sin-sick people, human beings must first receive the diagnosis (Law) before they are given the cure (Gospel/Creed), and learn how to receive it (Prayer).

In 1536 John Calvin was given the task of reforming the church in Geneva. As part of that responsibility, he composed a catechism in the conviction that faith must be nourished by understanding or it will wither and die. Written in French for the youth of Geneva, it was translated into Latin a year later to reach a wider audience "in order that the sincerity of the faith may be manifest to other churches everywhere" (preface, Latin edition). "In this way other churches can become more certain of our union with them." The first catechism was published between the first and second editions of his INSTITUTES OF THE CHRISTIAN RELIGION (1536, 1539). It is a clear and concise introduction to his thought and a good condensation of his *Institutes.* Following a brief exile in Strasbourg, Calvin produced another catechism in French in 1540 and in Latin in 1545. He noted that his first catechism was a bit too difficult for children with its topical and paragraph format, and so he adopted the question and answer approach of other catechisms.

The structure of Calvin's first catechism follows the basic plan of Luther's in that it begins with the Law, and proceeds to the Creed, Lord's Prayer, and a discussion of two sacraments. It differs in that it begins with a treatment of the knowledge of God and concludes with a section on civil magistrates. It also discusses ELECTION and PREDESTINATION, topics not found in later Geneva catechisms. The catechism expresses the warm, personal faith of Calvin, who contends in the catechism that the chief concern and care of life ought to be "to seek God, to aspire to him with our whole heart, to rest nowhere else but in him."

The *Heidelberg Catechism* (1562) stands out as an attempt to bridge the gap between Luther and Calvin. Within a year of becoming Protestant, the city of Heidelberg experienced the harsh measures of the Holy Roman Emperor Charles V as he reimposed Catholic practices upon recently conquered German territories in 1548. After the Religious Peace of Augsburg in 1555, Heidelberg experienced further turmoil brought about by the struggle between Calvinists and Lutherans (see CALVINISM, LUTHERANISM). In frustration, elector Frederick III of the Palatinate commissioned his theologians in 1562 to prepare a catechism with the idea of providing an instrument that would establish the new Church of the Palatinate and put an end to the snarling partisanship of the various parties.

Although it is difficult to identify a single author of the catechism, Zacharias Ursinus (1534–1583) can be cited as the major contributor. He had written a *Small Catechism* a few years earlier with 108 questions, 90 of which were carried over into the *Heidelberg Catechism.* Whereas Ursinus provided much of the content for the catechism, Caspar Olevianus (1536–1587) gave the catechism a warm and devotional form. Although the catechism attempted to straddle the divide between Lutherans and Calvinists, it found acceptance primarily in Reformed-leaning territories within Germany, Switzerland, Hungary, and the Netherlands.

In terms of structure the Heidelberg Catechism introduces the syllabus of Creed, Lord's Prayer, and Ten Commandments, along with two questions that set the tone for the entire catechism: "What is your only comfort in life and death?" and "How many things must you know that you may live and die in the blessedness of this comfort?" The answer to the first question affirms the transcendent goodness of God's providence to comfort a persecuted people. The answer to the second question introduces the three parts of the catechism under the rubrics of human misery, deliverance of human beings, and gratitude of human beings for deliverance. In this way it attempted to hold together the distinctive emphases of Luther and Calvin.

Catechisms of the Roman Catholic Counter-Reformation

Although slow to address the need for instruction in the rudiments of the faith being met by Protestant catechisms, the Roman Catholic church launched an effort in connection with the Council of Trent and produced several popular catechisms of its own. Some of these catechisms had a more polemical tone than that of their Protestant counterparts; others sought to present the Catholic faith in as winsome a manner as possible. Several of the more notable include those by Peter Canisius and the Roman Catechism.

Peter Canisius (1521–1597) wrote a catechism in three versions (Summa, Minor, and Minima). Just as Luther's catechism became one of the most potent instruments by which the Reformation took root, so Canisius's catechisms became the great documents of the COUNTER-REFORMATION. In fact, it would eventually become the most widely used catechism in the Catholic world. Like Luther's catechism, it was characterized by succinctness, clarity, and serenity. Unlike Luther's, however, it was more polemical in tone to the point that it was less a presentation of Catholic doctrine and more a refutation of Protestant teachings.

Canisius organized his catechism into two sections. Under the heading "Wisdom," he placed the traditional components of Creed, Prayer, Decalogue, and Sacraments. Under the heading "Justice," he placed a number of medieval formularies such as the capital sins, the cardinal virtues, the gifts of the Holy Spirit, the Beatitudes, and the works of mercy. As to its theme, Canisius recognized that the doctrine of justification was the taproot of the Reformation and had to be disproved and dislodged. To that end he emphasized grace as an aid to the Christian life and the necessity of good works.

The origins of the Roman Catechism reach back to the earliest stages of the Council of Trent, when on January 22, 1546, the council set up a commission to assess the state of catechetical instruction. On April 5 it made its report and recommended that the council "should authorize the publication of a catechism by men noted for learning and piety, written in both Latin and the vernacular, and based on the Sacred Scriptures and the Fathers of the Church." It should serve the instruction of children and uneducated adults, "for whom milk and not solid food is in order." The matter resurfaced during the final and decisive period of the council. In March 1563 two theologians were appointed to collaborate with Cardinal Seripando to produce a catechism that appeared on January 7, 1566, under the title "Catechism for Parish Priests as decreed by the Council of Trent and published by order of Pontiff Pius V."

Like other catechisms, it contains four parts: Creed, Sacraments, Decalogue, and the Lord's Prayer. It follows a sequence of knowledge of God's past deeds (Creed), proceeds to a focus on the gift of grace-assisted love (Sacraments and Decalogue), and concludes with future hope (Lord's Prayer). The preface explains that whatever needs to be known about God is found within the Creed. The sacraments are signs whereby divine grace is given and thus function as a center of gravity for the catechism in terms of the active presence of Christ. Whatever laws lead us to love are given in the Ten Commandments. The object of human hope is found in the Lord's Prayer.

The catechisms produced as a result of the Protestant Reformation found widespread acceptance and use in the centuries that followed, and, in some cases, down to the present day. Although often supplemented with additional explanations, these catechisms served not only to instruct the baptized in the basics of the Christian faith, but also to instill a confessional identity in the laity with regard to the particular tradition into which they were being accepted.

References and Further Reading

Primary Source:

Jansz, Denis. *Three Reformation Catechisms: Catholic, Anabaptist, Lutheran.* New York: Edwin Mellen Press, 1982.

Secondary Sources:

Arand, Charles P. *That I May Be His Own: An Overview of Luther's Catechism.* St. Louis: Concordia Academic Press, 2000.

Bradley, Robert I. *The Roman Catechism in the Catechetical Tradition of the Church: The Structure of the Roman Catechism as Illustrative of the "Classic Catechesis."* New York: University Press of America, 1990.

Hesselink, I. John. *Calvin's First Catechism: A Commentary.* Louisville, KY: Westminster John Knox Press, 1997.

Jürgen-Fraas, Hans, Wolfgang Grünberg, Gerhard Bellinger, and Peter Hauptmann. "Katechismus." In *Theologische Realenzykopädie,* vol. I, 710ff. Edited by Gerhard Krause and Gerhard Müller. Berlin: de Gruyter, 1988.

Marthaler, Bernard. *The Catechism Yesterday & Today: The Evolution of a Genre.* Collegeville, MN: Liturgical Press, 1995.

McGatch, Milton. "Basic Christian Education from the Decline of Catechesis to the Rise of the Catechisms." In *A Faithful Church: Issues in the History of Catechesis.* Edited by John H. Westerhoff III. Wilton, CT: Morehouse-Barlow, 1981.

CHARLES P. ARAND

CATHOLIC REACTIONS TO PROTESTANTISM

The 1996 address of Pope John Paul II to German Protestants affirms: "Luther's call for church reform in its original meaning was an appeal for repentance and renewal, which must begin in the life of every individual. Nevertheless, there are many reasons why division arose from the beginning. Among these is that failure in the Catholic Church for which Pope Adrian VI [1459–1523] had already grieved in moving words; the interference of political and economic interests; and also Luther's own passion, which led him well beyond his initial intention to a radical criticism of the Catholic Church, her structure and her doctrine. We are all guilty. . . ." This reassessment of the Protestant REFORMATION is a dramatic shift from the sixteenth-century reactions.

Here we will assess (1) the sixteenth-century reactions to the Reformation, (2) developments through the intervening centuries, (3) the reevaluation at the second Vatican Council, subsequent Dialogue (see DIALOGUE, INTERCONFESSIONAL), and (4) debates since the Council.

The Reformation

The Reformation is generally dated from MARTIN LUTHER'S posting the ninety-five theses on indulgences in 1517. However, "Protestant" came into usage only in 1529 with the protest of the evangelical princes at the DIET OF SPEYER against the curtailment of evangelical preaching. Dialogue between the protesting theologians and those representing Catholic authorities ceased only after the colloquy at Regens-burg in 1541. Catholic positions were formalized at the Council of Trent (1546–1563). Although specific reformers or the emerging churches were not mentioned by name, many of their positions were implicitly condemned by this Council.

During this and subsequent centuries the Catholic Church evaluated the Reformation as a tragedy that separated many of her members into what were understood to be heretical communities (see HERESY). However, the Catholic Church never denied the validity of Protestant BAPTISM, and recognized elements of the Christian tradition continuing in these communities, including the scriptures, the core elements of the apostolic faith, and various elements of the sacramental life of the church.

Subsequent Developments

There were always voices within the Catholic Church that resonated with the reformer's calls for doctrinal and disciplinary renewal of the Church. Leaders like French Bishop Jacques-Benigne Bossuet (1627–1704) sought bridges in the faith of Protestants and Catholics. Johann Michael Sailer (1751–1832) encouraged Protestant and Catholic resistance to the ENLIGHTENMENT in Germany. However, much of Catholic theology, religious education, and preaching were devoted to resisting the theological positions and the development of the Protestant churches.

In the nineteenth century genuine seriousness was given to the study and evaluation of Protestant scholarship. JOHANN ADAM MÖHLER (1796–1838) contributed to both an irenic approach to Protestant thinkers and a reassessment of Catholic formulations of its own self-understanding as a church. With the emergence of the biblical, liturgical, and historical movements of this same century, a more positive appreciation emerged, opening the way to the first stirrings of dialogue.

Dom Lambert Beauduin (1873–1960) in Belgium launched several important initiatives, both toward Eastern Christianity and toward ANGLICANISM. The rise of the modern Ecumenical movement (see ECUMENISM) after 1910, and the approach to the Catholic Church for participation in the Faith and Order movement, led Pope Pius XI to criticize the ecumenical movement in the 1928 encyclical *Mortalium animos.*

During this first half of the twentieth century, voices began to emerge calling for a theological and historical reassessment of Protestantism. Figures like Josef Lortz (1887–1985) and Yves Congar (1904–1995), by the depth of their scholarship and their reorientation of interpretive perspectives, created a new context for Catholic relations to Protestantism. The Second World War also created a situation in Europe where collaboration and common witness became imperative for Christians together. Already by the 1950s the Holy See was opening the possibilities of more Catholic ecumenical participation.

Second Vatican Council (1962–1965)

One of the express purposes of the Catholic ecumenical council was to open the way for ecumenical rapprochement among Christians. Protestants and others were invited to observe the council. During the course of the council, Catholics were authorized to participate as observers in WORLD COUNCIL OF CHURCHES' gatherings.

The 1965 *Decree on Ecumenism* and the *Dogmatic Constitution on the Church* moved away, definitively, from considering Protestants heretical Christians, to recognizing them as "separated brethren," and acknowledging their communities as having ecclesial status: "There are many who honor sacred Scripture, taking it as a norm of belief and of action, and who show a true religious zeal. They lovingly believe in God the Father Almighty and in Christ, the Son of God and Savior. They are consecrated by baptism, through which they are united with Christ. They also recognize and receive other sacraments within their own churches or ecclesial communities" (Constitution on the Church no. 15).

A reformulation of the relationship between Scripture and TRADITION, an affirmation of religious liberty, support of the biblical and lay renewal, and dramatic liturgical reforms all rested on common Protestant and Catholic scholarship. These developments also brought Catholicism more in line with some of the reforms advocated in the sixteenth century. In addition to these decisions, the Catholic Church also began to enter into dialogue with all of the historic Protestant traditions of the sixteenth century and several of the later Protestant communities. Since that time, Catholics have also moved into dialogue with Pentecostals and Evangelical churches (see PENTECOSTALISM, EVANGELICALISM).

These dialogues have produced remarkable results leading to resolution of issues intractable in the sixteenth century. The most dramatic of these is the 1999 signing of the *Joint Declaration on the Doctrine of Justification,* between the Catholic Church and the LUTHERAN WORLD FEDERATION. By 1995 Pope John Paul II was able to say, in his encyclical *Ut Unum Sint,* that Catholics no longer look upon Protestants as "separated brethren," but rather as fellow Christians. Although the Catholic Church recognizes that not all of the differences between Catholics and the Reformation churches have been resolved, the official position of the Church is openness to dialogue, to internal renewal, and to the hope that, under the guidance of the Holy Spirit, issues standing in the way of full communion might someday be resolved.

Continuing Debates

The official Catholic position toward Protestantism is an openness to dialogue, a recognition of elements of the one true church in these communities, while still claiming that the fullness of the church "subsists in" the Catholic Church. However, there is considerable debate about the expression "subsists in." Those who drafted the language of the Vatican Council hold that this language was used in place of "is" to make clear that ecclesial reality is not exhausted by the Catholic Church as an institution.

Others will hold that "subsists in" is virtually equivalent to "is." Although the fullness of the means of grace may be available in the Catholic Church, some of these means may be more effectively realized in one or another of the churches separated from the Catholic Church. The Catholic Church recognizes that it is itself "wounded" because of the lack of communion with other Christian communities.

A second debate, over the evaluation of Protestant communities, takes place over the appropriate language to use in their regard. Those who drafted the language of the council, speaking of "churches and ecclesial communities," would hold that this is inductive language, not definitional in nature. That is, "ecclesial communities" was used of communities that do not use "church" of themselves. No definitive closure was given to whether any particular community was to be considered "church." Such a determination was to be left to the process of dialogue and mutual understanding.

On the other hand, there are those who take the distinction "churches and ecclesial communities" to be definitive. "Churches" would refer to the Orthodox (see ORTHODOXY, EASTERN) and those churches of the West, like the Old Catholic Church, which have the full range of sacramental reality, including priests ordained in the apostolic succession, and therefore the full Eucharist mystery, short only of full communion with the Bishop of Rome. "Ecclesial communities," then, is taken to refer to the Reformation churches, whose ecclesial status cannot be spoken of as "church in the proper sense."

These debates over how the various Protestant churches are evaluated theologically by the Catholic Church, and the fact that Protestants would be even interested in this evaluation, demonstrates the dramatic history through which Protestant and Catholic relations have passed in the 500 years since the Reformation. The over thirty years since the second Vatican Council traverse as dramatic a history of reconciliation as a similar period of time after Luther's posting of the ninety-five theses and the alienation it entailed.

References and Further Reading

Hotchkin, John. "The Ecumenical Movement's Third Stage." *Origins* 25 no. 21 (1995): 353–361.

John Paul. *Ut Unum Sint: On Commitment to Ecumenism.* Washington, D.C.: U.S. Catholic Conference, 1995. http://www.vatican.va/holy_father/john_paul_ii/encyclicals/documents/hf_jp-ii_enc_25051995_ut-unum-sint_en.html

Lehmann, Karl, and Wolfhart Pannenberg, eds. *The Condemnations of the Reformation Era, Do they Still Divide?* Minneapolis: Fortress Press, 1990.

Minus, Paul. *Catholic Rediscovery of Protestantism.* New York: Paulist Press, 1976.

O'Connell, M. R., P. Soergel, and S. Barron. "Reformation, Protestant." In *The New Catholic Encyclopedia,* vol. 12, 5–22. Washington, D.C.: The Catholic University of America Press, 2003.

Pontifical Council for Promoting Christian Unity. *Directory for the Application of Principles and Norms on Ecumenism.* Washington, D.C.: US Catholic Conference, 1993. http://www.vatican.va/roman_curia/pontifical_councils/chrstuni/documents/rc_pc_chrstuni_doc_25031993_principles-and-norms-on-ecumenism_en.html

Riggs, Ann, Eamon McManus, and Jeffrey Gros. *Introduction to Ecumenism,* chapters 9, 10, 11. New York: Paulist Press, 1998.

Sobolewski, Gregory. *Martin Luther: Roman Catholic Prophet.* Milwaukee: Marquette University Press, 2001.

JEFFREY GROS

CATHOLICISM, PROTESTANT REACTIONS

When the Catholic Church and the LUTHERAN WORLD FEDERATION signed the *Joint Declaration on the Doctrine of Justification* in 1999, some Catholics asked whether it was appropriate to use "Protestant" of these churches any longer. Likewise, some conservative Protestant groups wondered whether these Lutheran churches had not betrayed the Reformation. Because the designation "Protestant" was used to characterize the evangelical princes at the DIET OF SPEYER in 1529, the very identity of this movement and later churches has depended on their reaction to the Catholicism from which they emerged.

We will survey here (1) the variety of confessional Protestant positions on the Catholic Church, (2) developments toward an Ecumenical reassessment, (3) the progress of Protestant and Catholic Dialogue, and (4) the basis for continued rejection of Catholicism by some Protestants.

Reformation Reactions

Both MARTIN LUTHER and JOHN CALVIN considered themselves reformers within the Catholic Church.

They were very slow to allow their followers to set up alternate structures parallel to, and eventually outside of, the Catholic Church of their own era. The AUGSBURG CONFESSION (1530) affirmed the episcopal structure of the church as a possibility and carried no criticism of the papacy. It was only after the REGENSBURG COLLOQUY (1541) that the new continental Reformation churches and the Catholic Church of the COUNTER-REFORMATION definitely went their separate ways.

Although the critiques of Catholicism were harsh in the Lutheran and Reformed movements, the ecclesial reality of Roman Catholicism was never wholly excluded. Catholic BAPTISM was recognized and ministers joining the REFORMATION were not reordained. The Scriptures, elements of the sacramental life, and the holiness of some members continued to be recognized. The traditional "ANTICHRIST" epithet of the Middle Ages was used of the papacy and institutions of Catholicism, recognizing that the perversion of what claims to be most holy is the most diabolical element in Christendom.

For the Anabaptists (see ANABAPTISM) and later gathered churches, like the eighteenth-century BAPTISTS, both magisterial Reformation churches and the Catholic Church were not seen as churches in the proper sense. They were not a gathered community of born-again believers, committed to a common discipline of life, incorporating adult believers through baptism.

The CHURCH OF ENGLAND emerged through struggles in the sixteenth and seventeenth centuries between its Puritan (see PURITANISM) and more Catholic elements. The Elizabethan Settlement of 1559, and the theological and canonical formulation of RICHARD HOOKER (1554–1600) charted a middle way, in which the claim was made that ANGLICANISM continued the Catholic Church of previous centuries as a branch of Christendom with its episcopal, canonical, and sacramental structures. This view was reinforced by the nineteenth-century OXFORD MOVEMENT. From the beginning of the modern ecumenical movement, Anglicans have been among the strongest advocates of rapprochement with the Roman Catholic "branch" of the church universal.

Reassessment

The nineteenth century brought not only the Anglican reassessment of the Oxford Movement, and attempts to find bridges between the THIRTY-NINE ARTICLES and the Catholic Council of Trent (1546–1563). There was also a historical revival and liturgical renewal that embraced both Protestant and Catholic scholars. Characteristic of this reassessment on the Protestant side was the work of PHILIP SCHAFF (1819–1893) and the Mercersburg Movement (see MERCERSBURG THEOLOGY).

By the Edinburgh Missionary Conference of 1910 (see WORLD MISSIONARY CONFERENCE), the Protestant churches were ready to recognize that Latin America was not to be considered a "mission field" because of the presence of the Gospel brought there by the Catholic Church. American missionaries from the historical Protestant churches took a different, less positive view, and organized the 1916 Panama Congress. Pentecostal and evangelicals also saw the Catholic faithful, as well as members of the mainstream Protestant churches, as a fertile mission field (see PENTECOSTALISM, EVANGELICALISM).

However, by 1914 an approach was made to the Vatican on behalf of the proposed World Conference on Faith and Order. It would be a full half century before the Catholic Church would fully commit itself to this ecumenical initiative, although the bridge had been erected that was to create a new context for Protestant evaluations of Catholicism and its ecclesiological reality.

Ecumenical Dialogues

Well before the second Vatican Council (1962–1965), Protestants had begun to engage in dialogue with Catholic theology, collaborate in social ministry, and pursue the common liturgical tradition together. The council raised these relationships to an institutional, ecclesiastical level.

The WORLD COUNCIL OF CHURCHES facilitated Catholic invitations to representatives of the Christian World Communions to be observers at the council. During and after the council, the Anglican Communion, Lutheran World Federation, WORLD METHODIST COUNCIL, and the WORLD ALLIANCE OF REFORMED CHURCHES initiated dialogues, all with the goal of full communion. These dialogues have gone through the phase of clarifying differences and proposing agreements, to suggesting stages toward visible unity, and, with some, making concrete decisions along this path.

The BAPTIST WORLD ALLIANCE, World Evangelical Alliance, Mennonite World Conference, and some Pentecostal churches and leaders have also sponsored dialogues. These dialogues have been devoted to mutual understanding, with no goal of visible unity.

Continued Negative Evaluations

These ecumenical dialogues have not resolved all the outstanding controversial issues, even with the ecumenically minded Protestant churches. Nineteenth-century NATIVISM in the United States, and the theological positions of DISPENSATIONALIST and FUNDAMENTALIST Christians have also provided a more negative view of Catholicism than even the sixteenth-century reformers (see DISPENSATIONALISM, FUNDAMENTALISM). For some evangelicals and Pentecostals, Catholicism, like the ecumenical movement, fits into Eschatological schemes (see ESCHATOLOGY) that make them the harbinger of Christ's second coming at the end of time.

Common concerns over issues like abortion, euthanasia, and family values have given some evangelicals and Catholics a new appreciation of one another's commitments and core elements of the Christian faith. In some parts of the world, cultural divides between Protestants and Catholics are as deep a source of division as are the theological differences.

Given the diversity of views of Catholicism and the hopes of reconciliation by many, "Protestant" becomes a rather fragile designation. Many heirs of the Reformation are as much in "protest" with one another as with the Catholicism from which they emerged.

References and Further Reading

Armstrong, John, ed. *Roman Catholicism: Evangelical Protestants Analyze What Divides and Unites Us.* Chicago: Moody Press, 1994.

Braaten, Carl, and Robert Jenson. *The Catholicity of the Reformation.* Grand Rapids, MI: Wm. B. Eerdmans, 1996.

Gros, Jeffrey. "Reception and Roman Catholicism for the 1990's." *One in Christ* 31 (1995): 295–328.

The Joint Declaration on Justification by Faith. Grand Rapids, MI: Wm. B. Eerdmans, 2000.

Lehmann, Karl, and Wolfhart Pannenberg, eds. *The Condemnations of the Reformation Era, Do they Still Divide?* Minneapolis: Fortress Press, 1990.

Rausch, Thomas, ed. *Catholics and Evangelicals: Do They Share a Common Future?* Downers Grove, IL: InterVarsity Press, 2000.

Rouse, Ruth, and Stephen Neill, eds. *A History of the Ecumenical Movement 1517–1948.* Geneva: World Council of Churches, 1986.

Rusch, William Harding Meyer, and Jeffrey Gros, eds. *Growth in Agreement II.* Geneva/Grand Rapids: World Council of Churches/Wm. B. Eerdmans, 2000.

Sproul, R. C. *Faith Alone: The Evangelical Doctrine of Justification.* Grand Rapids, MI: Baker, 1995.

Vischer, Lukas, and Harding Meyer, eds. *Growth in Agreement. Reports and Agreed Statements of Ecumenical Conversations on a World Level.* New York: Paulist Press, 1984.

JEFFREY GROS

CELIBACY

Celibacy is the temporary or lifelong abstinence from sex, usually out of religious devotion, and many religions have practiced it. Christian celibacy derives from the New Testament in which the Apostle Paul urged celibacy upon all Christians who were able to practice it. Despite this, celibacy was initially not required of the clergy, although it was demanded of women who served the church. Monks and nuns were the first and most committed celibates from the third century. Popes required celibacy from priests and bishops from the fourth century, whereas the Orthodox Churches have continued to allow priests to be married (see ORTHODOXY, EASTERN). Celibacy allowed monks, nuns, and the clergy to devote themselves exclusively to the service of God. It helped to achieve a well-ordered soul. Celibacy also prevented what was thought to be the "pollution" caused by sexual intercourse. Celibacy was considered a necessary qualification for sanctity in the Middle Ages. Lapses, especially for priests, were not rare, and the church undertook repeated reforms to enforce the requirement.

MARTIN LUTHER and the other Protestant reformers rejected clerical celibacy as both unbiblical and impossible. Protestants were always deeply suspicious of celibate clerics. In effect Protestants replaced the requirement of celibacy with a requirement of MARRIAGE for the clergy. Differing attitudes toward celibacy clearly demarcated the Protestant and Catholic Churches. Although celibacy is still required by the Catholic Church, the secularization of the modern world has robbed it of its cachet among many Catholics in the West and made it increasingly difficult to recruit men to the priesthood.

Celibacy is a common phenomenon among world-denying religions, for example, Christianity, Hinduism, Taoism, and Buddhism. In the ancient world the Vestal Virgins and Priests of the Great Mother were held to strict celibacy. Greek philosophy provided a rationale for celibacy. Most philosophical schools (e.g., Platonism, Stoicism, Aristotelianism) emphasized the need for the mind to control the body, the passions, and the emotions. As the strongest of desires, sex was viewed as especially problematic. The Pythagoreans favored celibacy, as did some Stoics. The philosophers were chary of matrimony because of the distractions that it involved. Xanthippe, the harridan wife of Socrates, became a symbol of what was to be avoided.

The New Testament

Although Greek philosophy would later inform the Christian celibate ideal, its origins are to be found in the Bible. Most influential was Paul's advice that Christians abstain from marriage and sex, given the imminent second coming of Christ (I Corinthians 7:25–38). Paul was concerned about the many distractions that married life brings and was celibate (I Corinthians 7:7), although other apostles were not (I Corinthians 9:5).

Jesus instructed his disciples to give up family to follow him (Matthew 19:29). Although Jesus insisted on the inviolability of the marriage bond (Matthew 5:31,32; 18:3–9; Mark 10:2–12), Jesus also treated the family as an obstacle to discipleship (see Mark 3:21, 31–35; Matthew 8:21,22; Luke 8:19–21). The angels have no marriages, nor will the resurrected (Matthew 22:30; Mark 12:25; Luke 20:35). Jesus also seems to have favored celibacy in this life for those capable of it (Matthew 19:10–12). The patriarchal family of antiquity limited the freedom of its members to join new movements such as Jesus inspired. Because the families of the first generation of followers were Jewish or pagan, freeing individuals from the grip of the family was crucial. Only when families themselves became Christian could they be viewed as pillars of the church.

In both Paul and Jesus there was no disapproval of sex as such, no sense that it was sinful or degrading in itself, but merely that it was a distraction from the commandment to love "God with all your heart, and with all your soul, and with all your mind, and with all your strength" (Mark 12:30; Matthew 22:37; Luke 10:27).

The Deutero-Pauline letters reversed that stance as the Christian community made accommodations to Greco-Roman society (I Timothy 2:2; 3:7; 6:1; Titus 2:9,10). Timothy requires that bishops and deacons be the husbands of one wife (I Timothy 3:1–13), and models the church on the patriarchal household (I Timothy 3:4,5; Titus 1:6–11). Women were to be subordinated to their husbands and would be saved by bearing children. I Timothy 2:11–15 may be directed against Paul's advice to Corinthians, which assumes that the celibate, and presumably childless, were better prepared to meet the returning Christ. Moreover, if I Corinthians 14:33–35 is in fact not from Paul but rather from the author of Timothy, women were dependent on their husbands for religious guidance. The role of the Greco-Roman Pater Familias as priest in his own household was thus transferred to the new Christian community. Timothy did, however, make provision for older widows. These women, who had passed their childbearing years, were to serve the community in their celibate widowhood (I Timothy 5:9–16).

Early Christianity

Some early ascetic Christians (Encratites) did adhere to celibacy as part of their world-denying form of life. Montanism also combined an emphasis on celibacy with prophecy and an uncommon prominence of women, a combination that one sees in Paul. The association of celibacy and the possession of special spiritual powers is found in early MONASTICISM. Although St. Anthony is traditionally viewed as the first monk, the monastic drive embraced many in the third century. When Anthony left for the desert he could entrust his sister to an already existent community of virgins. Individual "virgins" also chose to remain in their family homes.

For those who chose celibacy, it was not a sacrifice, but a liberation. Society's need to maintain its population and to combat the demographic decline experienced in Late Antiquity and the early Middle Ages created relentless pressure on each of its members, but particularly women, to reproduce. Sexual desire in the young was the instrument with which society drew them into matrimony and the familial responsibilities that resulted. Wives were expected to bear as many children as possible, while husbands struggled to provide for the family. Social expectations thus became a prison for many, escape from which was made possible by a celibate life. Because women's lives were very severely constrained to fully exploit their reproductive capacity, celibacy allowed women to exercise some self-determination and to pursue activities that were denied to the married.

In the first three centuries there was no requirement or tradition of clerical celibacy, although some CLERGY assumed a celibate life after raising families and reaching what was considered an advanced age (CLERGY, MARRIAGE OF). At the end of the second century, Tertullian (c. 155 to after 220) praised the many clerics who had embraced a continent life. However, his contemporary, Clement of Alexandria (150 to between 211 and 215) made clear that "All the same, the Church fully receives the husband of one wife whether he be priest or deacon or layman, supposing always that he uses his marriage blamelessly, and such a one shall be saved in the begetting of children" (Stromateis, III, xiii). From at least the second century, the church sought to exclude men from the clergy who had married twice (digamus). The Spanish Church Council of Elvira issued the first legislation on celibacy (between 295 and 302). The council ordered the deposition of any bishop, priest, or deacon who had children with his wife after ordination. An attempt at the first Council of Nicaea (325), however, to extend that requirement to the whole church was rejected. Nonetheless, in 384–386 Popes Damasus and Siricus imposed on all clergy in major orders (Bishop, Presbyter/Priest, Deacon) a vow of celibacy that forbade sex between clergy and their wives on pain of deposition. This papal requirement applied only to Western Christendom. The Orthodox Churches of the East wavered on the extent and rigor of clerical celibacy. The Council in Trullo (692) resolved the matter. It forbade any of the higher orders (bishop, priest, deacon, and subdeacon) to marry after ordination. Bishops were to separate from their wives, but the other orders were enjoined to continue their conjugal duties to their wives. This remains the practice today. Bishops are, in fact, normally chosen from the ranks of the celibate, that is, monks.

There have been many explanations of this requirement, for which the papacy did not claim scriptural warrant. An important consideration concerned the sacral purity of the clergy. In the Old Testament, sexual intercourse made one "impure" in the sense that one was forbidden to enter the Temple precincts. Sexual intercourse was not sinful. It was in fact enjoined elsewhere in the Old Testament. Like the restrictions on foods, these prescriptions arbitrarily established ritual boundaries. Temple priests, who were all married, were required to refrain from sex with their wives during the time that they served the altar. The priesthood was divided in two and each half took turns at the altar for weeklong periods. Christians would argue that because the New Testament and its sacrifice far outshone the Old Testament and its sacrifices, the Christian priesthood was held to a higher standard.

On a more mundane level, some have seen celibacy as a way to protect the property of the increasingly wealthy church from the desire of fathers to bequeath something to their children. Others have seen it as a way to separate and elevate the clergy above the laity. Of course, this would assume already a higher valuation of celibacy over marriage.

Leading figures in both the East (e.g., Chrysostom) and the West (e.g., Jerome, Augustine) had begun to impugn sex and to devalue marriage in comparison to celibacy at precisely this time under the growing influence of Platonism in the church. This had already led Origen (c. 185–c. 254) to take all too literally Christ's claim that some "have made themselves eunuchs for the sake of the kingdom of heaven" (Matthew 19:12) and to emasculate himself. Augustine (354–430), also a Platonist, argued that original sin was passed on to each human by the sexual act, which since the Fall was always in some way sinful. For Augustine the intensity of sexual pleasure robbed humans of reason and precluded both love of God and love of one's partner. Only marriage could exonerate this sin, but sin it was nonetheless. Augustine's combination of the biblical exhortation to exclusive love of God and the Platonic distaste for the carnal would remain powerfully attractive to Christians for more than a millennium.

The ascetic trajectory of the church in late antiquity was not unopposed. St. Jerome (c. 347–419/420), himself a priest and monk, wrote intemperate rejoinders to Helvetius and Jovinianus, both of whom denied virginity's superiority to marriage. Jerome, however, went much further than even his supporters approved. He disparaged marriage rather than merely ranking it below celibacy as a good, but not the highest good. His work also betrays a disturbing misogyny. When these attitudes were combined with a moral interpretation of ritual impurity as sin, the result was a visceral distaste for all things sexual that ill-accorded with God's creation of the two sexes. Jerome's writings were very popular, especially among monks, throughout the Middle Ages.

Helvetius and Jovinianus had also denied the perpetual virginity of the VIRGIN MARY. The virginity of the Mother of God was used to validate the superior status of the celibate and to provide a model of purity for both men and women. As a result, despite at times considerable clerical resistance to the requirement, few questioned the assumption concerning sex. Most heresies, in fact, criticized the church's laxity in both theory and practice. Sexual abstinence and voluntary poverty were the hallmarks of sanctity.

The Middle Ages

Celibacy found its most enduring institutional setting in monasticism. Of the traditional three monastic vows—poverty, chastity, and obedience—celibacy/chastity was the most constant. The Rule of St. Benedict of Nursia, the model for all later Western monastic rules, maintained the twin goals of self-abnegation and freedom from societal constraints. Benedict was especially concerned to break all the monk's family ties because more monasteries fell victim to the destructive effects of familial loyalty than to sexual impropriety. Both threats were particularly pressing at the end of the Middle Ages, given that the involuntary professions of those placed in monasteries as part of familial strategies produced a weak commitment to the monastic ideals, including celibacy. The resulting abuses contributed to the widespread anticlericalism that fueled the early Reformation.

Despite clear papal and conciliar legislation, clerical celibacy was unevenly practiced in the early Middle Ages. There were many practical difficulties, especially in the countryside. Clerics, and men generally, were not trained to run the household, a task that demanded many skills and ceaseless activity. In the disorders of the age, supervision of the clergy often lapsed, and the power of lay nobles to appoint priests and even bishops did not always produce the most committed incumbents. In the ninth and tenth centuries the collapse of the Carolingian Empire and invasions by Arabs, Magyars, and Norsemen brought a new low in the quality of the clergy. The Gregorian Reform of the eleventh and twelfth centuries targeted

clerical marriage. The pervasiveness and widespread acceptance of clerical marriage initially forced the reformers to allow priests who were already married to retain their wives while forbidding any new priests from marrying. Despite clerical resistance, some of it from the learned elite, the papacy and its lay allies made celibacy once again the recognized standard, even if one that was often not met. The First Lateran Council (1123) marks their triumph. It made clerical marriage simply impossible. Clerics could not contract a marriage under any circumstances. Whereas the earlier tradition had punished married clergy with deposition, the new legislation refused to recognize these unions as marriages at all. They were reduced to "concubinage" and the children branded as illegitimate. Furthermore, "concubines" and their children were declared to be the slaves or serfs of the Church, although there is little or no evidence that this was ever enforced. Despite these draconian measures, clerical celibacy was never universal. The rigor of its application varied from region to region. In England celibacy seems to have been the norm, but in some parts of Germany in the fourteenth century approximately half of the parish priests seem to have been "married." Interestingly, an association of South German priests called for the abolition of mandatory celibacy in the early nineteenth century, before being suppressed by the Papacy. Such resistance was exceedingly rare after the reformation, given that rejection of clerical celibacy was considered a peculiarly Protestant "error."

The Protestant Reformation

The first real challenge to the ideal of celibacy, as opposed to the practice, came from Martin Luther and other Protestant Reformers. Luther began by impugning the power of the papacy, a human institution, to impose the burden of celibacy on the clergy when God had not done so. The Catholic Church admitted that there was no biblical injunction demanding clerical celibacy, but argued that the Church did have the power to impose on the clergy disciplinary regulations that reflected biblical norms and values. Thus, the real disagreement concerned the value and viability of celibacy itself. For Luther, celibacy constituted a rare exception, not the norm. Given the fallen state of humanity, the ability to restrain one's sexual desires could result only from a special gift of God, something that Luther did not expect to be frequent. Catholic theology was more optimistic about human nature, especially after BAPTISM, and claimed that such self-control was not altogether rare. Furthermore, Catholics thought God more profligate with his grace. Both through ordination and the ongoing bestowal of grace, God gave each cleric the resources to bear his celibate state, if he so chose.

However, disagreement was even more fundamental since Luther and other Protestants established and praised marriage as the new norm. They appealed to the Deutero-Pauline epistles against Paul himself. Combining Timothy/Titus and Peter with the Old Testament, the Protestant reformers promoted a triumphant patriarchalism. They lent a new dignity and importance to the married woman and mother, but they also abolished any alternative to marriage and motherhood for respectable women. The usually Augustinian Luther even disagreed with Augustine by rehabilitating conjugal sex as a gift of God and a weapon against the DEVIL. Martin Luther's openly expressed joy in family life and in marital sex was unprecedented and found few imitators. English Puritans (see PURITANISM), however, also warmly praised conjugal intercourse, something that may seem surprising considering their otherwise dour reputation. In any event, the Catholic requirement of clerical celibacy was replaced by a Protestant insistence on clerical marriage. Monastic houses, nonetheless, continued in some Protestant German regions to house supernumerary daughters of the upper classes. Protestant theologians also preached the virtues of virginity for the many women of all classes who through no fault of their own remained unmarried.

England remained an anomaly for much of the sixteenth century. Despite his break with Rome, HENRY VIII (1509–1547) remained Catholic in many ways, including the insistence of a celibate clergy. In the Six Articles (1539), he reaffirmed clerical celibacy and vows of chastity. The Forty-Two Articles (1552) under his Protestant successor Edward VI (1547–1553) specifically allowed priests and bishops to marry. However, popular resistance was such that the government felt it necessary to pass a bill that declared clerical marriage superior to celibacy and not just a necessary concession. After the Catholic Queen Mary (1553–1558), the triumph of Protestant Elizabeth I (1558–1603) reaffirmed the legality of clerical marriages. However, Elizabeth herself disapproved of it and forbade clerical wives at court.

The Catholic Council of Trent pointedly reaffirmed the value and superiority of celibacy. An explosion of new religious orders shows that popular veneration for sexual renunciation had by no means diminished in large parts of Europe. Official models for sanctity were most often clergy, monks, friars, or nuns vowed to celibacy. Attitudes toward celibacy thus became some of the most important markers distinguishing Catholicism and Protestantism.

An interesting measure of the differences separating them concerned the virginity of Mary, the mother of Jesus. For the Catholic Church, Mary was "ever virgin," physically intact both before and after the birth of Jesus. Increasingly, Protestant theologians contested that and argued that biblical references to the brothers and sisters of Jesus told another story. At the very least, Scripture never ascribed perpetual virginity to Mary.

Protestant antagonism toward Catholicism often took the form of scandalous "exposés" of the sexual abuse of women by supposedly celibate confessors, or of debauched nuns whose nunneries served as brothels for their monastic and clerical "brothers." Catholics, in turn, retold stories of Protestant mockery of the Virgin Mary and the sexual abuse of defenseless nuns. Such Protestant and Catholic topoi survived well into the twentieth century.

The Modern World

Attitudes toward sex, marriage, and celibacy were not unchanging, however. Catholic theology and pastoral practice came to place greater weight on mutuality of love and pleasure that husband and wife owed to each other. This evolution seems to have begun with the Jesuit Order and may have contributed to their reputation as lax confessors, a charge often made by the Augustinian rigorist and ascetic Jansenists in the seventeenth century. In the eighteenth century St. Alfonsus Liguori, the most influential of Catholic pastoral theologians of the modern era, also laid great emphasis on love and mutuality in marriage and in marital sexual relations. Whether consciously or not, the Jesuit and Liguorian initiatives served as part of the Catholic Church's campaign, after being robbed of its societal and legal hegemony by secularism and revolution in much of Europe, to reestablish its influence on society on the basis of the Catholic family. This shift is reflected in the prominence given Joseph and Mary as models for mothers and fathers.

Catholic developments dovetailed nicely with the romanticization of domestic life in Protestant societies in the nineteenth century. Interestingly, in the eighteenth and early nineteenth centuries Protestant sects like the SHAKERS and the Ephrata community embraced celibacy, often together with a strong emphasis on the workings of the spirit, a combination that was common in the ancient Church, as we have seen. Monastic orders also reappeared in England in the middle of the nineteenth century.

The twentieth century, however, saw further erosion of celibacy. More conservative Protestant denominations maintained their traditional devotion to the patriarchal family, the role of woman as wife and mother, and the glorification of what has come to be called "family values" toward the end of the century.

Interestingly, in this they closely agreed with conservative Catholics and the papacy. More liberal Protestant denominations have accepted a more permissive attitude toward sex, allowing more easily for divorce, and often according legitimacy to homosexuality and homosexual intercourse.

The Catholic retention of celibacy as an honored option suffered in the West from the pervasive secularism. Self-denial in any form, but especially sexual self-denial, seemed perverse, or at least anachronistic. The deliberations and decrees of the Second Vatican Council designed to open the Catholic Church to the modern world unintentionally undermined the prestige and appeal of the celibate life. Priests, monks, and nuns left the celibate life in great numbers to marry. Love and service to the neighbor took clear priority over love for God, or simply subsumed it. Catholic moral theology glorified the affective and sexual union of marriage as profoundly sacramental, that is, as a source of grace and as a "sign" of God's love for human beings. In such a theological climate, it is not surprising that fewer in the West are willing to embrace the celibate life. Celibacy continues, however, to be reverenced in the Catholic Church outside the West, where most Catholics now live, although it does encounter some resistance in some cultures (e.g., in Africa). Not surprisingly, the number of vocations to the priesthood in the non-Western Church has not suffered the catastrophic decline that plagues the Western Church.

The Second Vatican Council (1962–1965) made provision for married deacons and some hoped to see the requirement of clerical celibacy abolished. However, Pope Paul VI (1963–1978) reaffirmed clerical celibacy in 1967 and his successor John Paul II (1978–) is a fervent defender of the institution. It remains an important pillar of a Catholicism that also retains the traditional reverence for the priesthood, the sacraments, and the Virgin Mary.

References and Further Reading

Abbott, Elizabeth. *A History of Celibacy.* New York: Scribner, 2000.

Atkinson, Clarissa. " 'Precious Balsam in a Fragile Glass': The Ideology of Virginity in the Later Middle Ages." *Journal of Family History* 8 (1983): 131–143.

Baldwin, John. "A campaign to reduce clerical celibacy at the turn of the twelfth and thirteenth centuries." In *Etudes d'histoire du droit canonique dediee a Gabriel le Bras,* vol. 2, 1041–1053. Paris, 1965.

Brown, Peter Robert Lamont. *The Body and Society: Men, Women, and Sexual Renunciation in Early Christianity.* New York: Columbia University Press, 1988.

Burrus, Virginia. *Chastity as Autonomy: Women in the Stories of the Apocryphal Acts.* Lewiston, NY: E. Mellen Press, 1987.

Callam, D. "Clerical Continence in the Fourth Century: Three Papal Decretals." *Theological Studies* 41 (1980): 3–50.

Cochini, Christian. *Apostolic Origins of Priestly Celibacy.* San Francisco: Ignatius Press, 1990.

Deming, Will. *Paul on Marriage and Celibacy: The Hellenistic Background of 1 Corinthians 7.* Cambridge/New York: Cambridge University Press, 1995.

Foster, Lawrence. *Women, Family, and Utopia: Communal Experiments of the Shakers, the Oneida Community, and the Mormons.* Syracuse, NY: Syracuse University Press, 1991.

Frassetto, Michael, ed. *Medieval Purity and Piety: Essays on Medieval Clerical Celibacy and Religious Reform.* New York: Garland, 1998.

Kitch, Sally. *Chaste Liberation: Celibacy and Female Cultural Status.* Urbana: University of Illinois Press, 1989.

Lea, Henry C. *The History of Sacerdotal Celibacy in the Christian Church.* New York: Russell & Russell, 1957.

Robson, John M. *Marriage or Celibacy?: The Daily Telegraph on a Victorian Dilemma.* Toronto: University of Toronto Press, 1995.

Schillebeeckx, Edward. *Celibacy.* New York: Sheed and Ward, 1968.

Vogels, Heinz-Jürgen. *Celibacy: Gift or Law?: A Critical Investigation.* Kansas City, MO: Sheed & Ward, 1993.

R. EMMET MCLAUGHLIN

CHALMERS, THOMAS (1780–1847)

Scottish presbyterian minister, theologian, and political economist. Thomas Chalmers is best known for his pioneering efforts to revive the parish ministry in industrial society, and for his leading role in the Disruption of the CHURCH OF SCOTLAND in 1843. He was born on March 17, 1780, in the small coastal burgh of Anstruther, in Fife, where his father was a merchant and his mother was active in charitable work. Here young Chalmers grew up amid the close communal culture of preindustrial SCOTLAND, in which a sense of mutual responsibility united the social orders. Educated at St. Andrews and Edinburgh Universities, he was ordained to the ministry of the Church of Scotland in 1803. His early ministry of the rural parish of Kilmany in Fife was not a success. Influenced by the ethos of the ENLIGHTENMENT, he neglected his pastoral duties while he pursued, unsuccessfully, a university appointment in mathematics or natural science. Then in 1810–1811, after a prolonged illness, he experienced a conversion to an intense Evangelical piety (see EVANGELICALISM). He soon established a reputation as a fiery preacher, proclaiming the vanity of worldly ambition when set against the prospect of eternal life.

In 1815 Chalmers was appointed to the Tron parish in the industrializing city of Glasgow. Distressed by the poverty he encountered in Glasgow, he became convinced that the main cause of urban deprivation was the breakdown of community in the overcrowded urban parishes. His response was to work to revive the traditional parish system in the urban environment.

His urban parish work included two main principles: first, what he termed "aggression," or regular house-to-house visiting among the parishioners; and second, "territoriality," or the subdivision of crowded urban parishes, many of which had populations of 10,000 or more, into small neighborhood districts of about 400 inhabitants, in which pastoral supervision would be more feasible. His aim was to re-create in the new industrial environment the communal culture that he had known in his youth in Anstruther. In 1819 he became minister of a newly formed working-class Glasgow parish, St. John's, where the civic authorities gave him a free hand to pursue his parish plans. Subdividing the large parish into twenty-five districts, he recruited an activist parish agency of elders and deacons, and assigned an elder and deacon to visit regularly in each district. The elders were to promote moral and religious values, and encourage regular church and school attendance. The deacons were to oversee social welfare. In particular, deacons were to reduce dependency on legal poor relief among the laboring orders by promoting thrift, delayed marriage, and communal sharing. Chalmers also established a system of Sunday and weekday schools (see SECONDARY SCHOOLS), for the education of the parish youth, and held Sunday evening services, which laboring people were encouraged to attend in their work clothes. His St. John's "experiment" in urban ministry had considerable success in promoting social responsibility, and it attracted widespread interest.

In 1823 Chalmers left the parish ministry for an academic career, becoming first professor of moral philosophy at St. Andrews University and then, after 1828, professor of divinity at Edinburgh University. In his lectures and voluminous writings in social theology, he sought to demonstrate the workings of providence in social and economic organization. From about 1831 he was the acknowledged leader of the Evangelical party, and under his leadership the Evangelicals in 1834 gained the ascendancy in the Church of Scotland. Chalmers now worked to revive the parish system on a national level, seeking to transform Scotland into a "godly commonwealth" of close-knit parish communities modeled on his St. John's experiment. Between 1834 and 1841 he led a national church extension campaign, which collected voluntary donations and erected over 220 new churches in Scotland, mainly in the new towns and cities. Chalmers combined this church-building campaign with petitions to Parliament to provide endowments to the new churches. Endowments, he insisted, would be necessary to enable the new churches to pursue a pastoral mission among the poorest inhabitants of the industrializing districts. However, in 1838 Parliament re-fused to provide the endowments, and his church extension campaign waned.

In the later 1830s his efforts to revive the established church were also overshadowed by a bitter dispute between church and state over lay patronage in the appointment of parish ministers (see CHURCH AND STATE, OVERVIEW). According to the civil law of Scotland, patrons, mainly the monarch or large landowners, had the right to appoint ministers to vacant parish churches. In 1834 the Evangelical-dominated General Assembly had acted to give parishioners a voice in ministerial appointments, by permitting a majority of male heads of family in a parish to veto a patron's candidate, if they conscientiously believed that the candidate would not be acceptable as their minister. The civil courts, however, proclaimed this "veto" to be an illegal encroachment on the civil rights of patrons. The courts threatened the clergy of the Church of Scotland with fines and imprisonment unless they ignored the wishes of parishioners and participated in the ordination of patrons' candidates, whereas Parliament gave its support to the courts. Chalmers and the Evangelicals refused to back down, insisting that a Christian people must have a voice in the selection of their ministers.

The struggle of church and state culminated at the Disruption of 1843, when Chalmers led over a third of the clergy and perhaps half the lay membership out of the Church of Scotland to form the FREE CHURCH. They gave up the endowed incomes, churches, manses, and parish schools of the established church, and undertook to build a free national church through voluntary contributions. Chalmers played a leading role in the financial organization of the Free Church, which within five years of the Disruption had erected over 730 churches, 500 schools, and 400 manses. He also served as the principal and professor of divinity of New College, the Free Church seminary for the training of ministers, and continued his urban mission work in a deprived district of Edinburgh. Chalmers died on May 30, 1847. His Christian social vision, and above all his conscientious stand in 1843 for the independence of the church from state control, have continued to influence Protestantism in the North Atlantic world.

References and Further Reading

Primary Sources:

Chalmers, Thomas. *Collected Works.* 25 vols. Glasgow: Collins, 1835–1842.
———. *Posthumous Works.* 10 vols. Edinburgh: Sutherland and Knox, 1849.
Hanna, William. *Memoirs of Dr. Chalmers.* 4 vols. Edinburgh: Thomas Constable, 1849–1852.

Secondary Sources:

Brown, Stewart J. *Thomas Chalmers and the Godly Commonwealth in Scotland.* Oxford: Oxford University Press, 1982.

Cheyne, A. C., ed. *The Practical and the Pious: Essays on Thomas Chalmers.* Edinburgh: Saint Andrew Press, 1985.

Roxborogh, W. John. *Thomas Chalmers: Enthusiast for Mission.* Carlisle, Cumbria: Paternoster Press, 1999.

Voges, Friedhelm. *Das Denken von Thomas Chalmers im Kirchen- und Soczialgeschichtlichen Kontext.* Frankfurt am Main: Peter Lang, 1985.

Watt, Hugh. *Thomas Chalmers and the Disruption.* Edinburgh: Thomas Nelson, 1943.

STEWART J. BROWN

CHANNING, WILLIAM ELLERY (1780–1842)

North American Unitarian. William Ellery Channing played an important role in developing New England Unitarianism during the early to mid-nineteenth century. He was born into a wealthy family in Newport, Rhode Island on April 7, 1780. After graduating from Harvard in 1798, he returned there in 1802 to prepare for the ministry. From his ordination in 1803 until his death on October 2, 1842, Channing held a pastorate at the Federal Street Church in Boston.

Channing's sermons and writings epitomized the controversial LIBERAL PROTESTANTISM of his era. In his 1819 ordination sermon, "Unitarian Christianity," Channing categorized human nature as essentially good; thus conflicting with orthodox Calvinists who saw humanity as helplessly flawed due to original sin. In "A Moral Argument against Calvinism" (1820), Channing argued against the traditional Trinitarian doctrine. He posited that Jesus was not God, but rather a spiritual and moral exemplar sent by God to those craving the Holy Spirit.

Channing's theological statements found support from many like-minded ministers. In 1820 he organized the Berry St. Conference of Ministers, which eventually gave birth to the AMERICAN UNITARIAN ASSOCIATION in 1825. Channing also assisted in developing the *Christian Register* (est. 1821), a Unitarian journal. Besides making some important theological contributions, Channing also addressed the arts. In "Remarks on National Literature" (1830), he declared that American writers needed to create a unique style. Channing's thoughts influenced the Transcendentalists, such as RALPH WALDO EMERSON and Henry Wadsworth Longfellow. "Self-Culture" (1838) typified Channing's later work, which focused keenly on social matters, such as abolition of slavery, labor reform, and public education.

See also Arminianism; Slavery, Abolition of; Calvinism; Orthodoxy; Sin

References and Further Reading

Primary Source:

Robinson, David, ed. *William Ellery Channing, Selected Writings.* New York: Paulist Press, 1985.

Secondary Source:

Mendelsohn, Jack. *Channing: The Reluctant Radical.* Boston: Little, Brown, 1971.

ARTHUR J. REMILLARD

CHAO, T. C. (CHAO TZU-CHEN, ZHAO ZICHEN) (1898–1979)

Chinese theologian. T. C. Chao was China's outstanding Protestant theologian of the first half of the twentieth century, as well as a leading educator and church leader. He was also a prominent ecumenical figure and was elected one of the first presidents of the WORLD COUNCIL OF CHURCHES (WCC) at Amsterdam in 1948. T. C. Chao resigned that position in protest over the WCC's stance on the Korean War. In the mid-1950s, he came under political attack in China, and fell into obscurity until after the end of the Cultural Revolution.

Born in Deqing, China, in 1898, Chao received a classical education and graduated from Soochow (Dongwu) University in 1910. He studied at Vanderbilt University from 1914 to 1917, where he received both a B.D. and an M.A. On his return to China, he taught first at Soochow University and then moved to Yenching (Yanjing) University in Beijing, where he served as professor of theology and dean of the School of Religion from 1928 to 1952. He was ordained an Anglican deacon and priest in Hong Kong in 1941.

Chao was a pioneer in the contextualization of Chinese theology, and he challenged the church by continuing to question the relevance of Christian faith to society and CULTURE. His work moved from the liberalism of his earlier writings, such as *Life of Jesus* (1935), to the influence of NEO-ORTHODOXY in *An Interpretation of Christianity* (1947), to the personal or even mystical reflections in *My Experience in Prison* (1948). Chao's theological writings—a dozen books and hundreds of essays, speeches and poems—reveal his classical education and Buddhist upbringing, as well as a hopeful response to the political and social movements of his time.

In his last years, Chao distanced himself from his earlier Christian beliefs and wrote that he had failed as a theologian. But by the twenty-first century, he was again being studied in China and the West, and a complete collection of his writings is being prepared in Beijing. Chao died in Beijing in 1979.

See also China; Theology, Twentieth Century Global; Anglicanism

References and Further Reading

Gluer, Winfried. *Christliche Thedologie in China: T. C. Chao, 1918–1956.* Gütersloh, Germany: Mohn, 1979.

Luo Zhenfang, "T. C. Chao's Last Letter to Me." *Chinese Theological Review* (1986): 75–78.

Ng Lee-Ming. "An Evaluation of T. C. Chao's Thought." *Ching Feng* 21 (1979).

Yamamoto, Sumiko. *History of Protestantism in China: The Indigenization of Christianity.* Tokyo, Japan: Toho Gakkai, 2000.

PHILIP L. WICKERI

CHAPLAINCY

Introduction

Chaplaincy has been variously defined, but for our present purpose it is Christian ministry that takes place primarily in or is related to an institution. It is a ministry therefore that does not take place within the normal parochial or congregational setting, but it is carried out largely, though not wholly, by ordained members of the church.

The word we use for CLERGY working in such settings, "chaplain," is derived from the Latin *capella* meaning cloak. Tradition holds that the fourth-century saint, Martin of Tours, divided his cloak to share with a beggar one cold night. After Martin's death his half of the cloak became a relic and the priests who guarded it became known as "capellani" or chaplains in English. What is especially interesting in this story for contemporary chaplains, is that etymologically the word comes from a situation of pastoral care, driven by religious devotion, directed toward one in need.

History of Chaplaincy

There is a long history of clergy working full-time, in a stipendiary capacity, outside the parochial or congregational systems. In the United States the parochial system owes much to the heritage of the church in ENGLAND and other European countries. The parochial system was first sketched out in England by Theodore, archbishop of Canterbury (died c. 690), drawing on patterns already established on the Continent. Theodore's plan was to establish that defined geographical areas should each have a parish church and a resident priest (*ibi ecclesia et presbyter*). Since the beginnings of the formation of the parish system, clergy have served outside parishes or regular congregations as cathedral staff, archdeacons, bishops' chaplains, domestic chaplains to families, and as chantry priests amongst others. None of these clergy, however, could easily be described as "chaplains" in the sense used above. Nevertheless, their existence does remind us that parochial or congregational clergy have not been the only expression of the church's ordained ministry.

In addition to these ordained ministers, other clergy for centuries have also ministered in three particular settings: the army and navy; hospitals; and prisons. The larger medieval households contained regular garrisons of soldiers and these often required the attention of a designated cleric to act as chaplain. Although there was a long history of bishops, priests, and other clergy engaging in wars as combatants, priests also accompanied armies into battle as noncombatant pastors as early as the Battle of Crecy (1346) and on ships of the English fleet at Cadiz (1597). Clergy, especially the monastic orders, were intimately involved in setting up medieval institutions that ministered to the sick and the dying. Many charitable foundations, such as almshouses or lazah houses (dedicated to caring for those with leprosy), had nonparochial clergy working in them. In all such places the boundaries between physical care and spiritual care were blurred. Chaplains were also appointed to the newly built British prisons of the late eighteenth and early nineteenth centuries where they ministered to the condemned, administered the sacraments, and organized welfare and education programs. They also exercised a statutory function where they were required to meet all prisoners on their entry to and exit from jail.

The range and numbers of clergy working outside the parochial system was not insignificant. Nevertheless, for the most part people in Europe, and later in other places in the world, were ministered to by a member of the parish clergy who lived among them and whose own life was thus closely linked to theirs. This was the pattern of pastoral care that most people experienced most of the time. The parish system lasted without much alteration, despite the REFORMATION, until the onset of the Industrial Revolution in the late eighteenth century. Until this time it was quite usual for a person to receive the occasional offices of the church: BAPTISM, MARRIAGE, and funeral (see FUNERARY RITES), in the church of the parish where they were born, lived, worked, and died. Although there was some degree of mobility, people lived fairly static lives. An examination of the marriage registers from the beginning of the nineteenth century, when the effects of INDUSTRIALIZATION began to be felt, shows that marriage partners were drawn from a much wider area than had hitherto been the case. The urbanization and mechanization that the Industrial Revolution brought had obvious consequences for the church. As a significant part of the population shifted from small, intimate villages to the new, impersonal cities and towns the attachment of the people to the local parish church weakened. Links with a particular church building and with a particular member of the clergy were damaged. As the century progressed attachment to the church diminished still further. By the beginning of the twentieth century large swathes of the population had little or no contact with the church or its ordained representatives.

The experience of the First World War (1914–1918), however, profoundly affected the religious mood of North America, Europe, and elsewhere. Few chaplains were recruited at the start of the war, as the expectation was that the conflict would soon be over. Although many of the men thought that the "God-botherers" had no place in the trenches, many others had fond affection for chaplains such as Philip "Tubby" Clayton and Geoffrey Studdart-Kennedy (known as "Woodbine Willie" because of his distribution of cigarettes to the troops). Because of such experiences many of the armed forces around the world came to feel that there was a need for greater, permanent provision of chaplains to meet the needs of the military community. By the conclusion of the Second World War (1939–1945) such provision was regarded as commonplace, and when peace was declared many former service personnel and church leaders thought that the experience of having chaplains involved in every aspect of the life of an institution might be replicated in a civilian environment.

Expressions of Chaplaincy

In the last sixty years, in addition to the historic spheres of chaplaincy (armed forces, hospitals, prisons), new expressions of Christian ministry in and to particular institutions have emerged both within Protestantism (including ANGLICANISM), Roman Catholicism, and to a lesser extent Orthodoxy (see ORTHODOXY, EASTERN). Chaplains are now established in a wide variety of institutions and in various sectors of society. Chaplains are to be found in such areas as schools, universities, industry (either generally or in specific parts of it), agriculture, airports, the emergency services, railways, SPORTS, and the legal profession. Although this is by no means an exhaustive list of the current areas of activity it does at least give a flavor of the range of spheres in which chaplains carry out their Christian ministry. However, just as it might be regarded as a mistake to talk of parochial or congregationally based ministry as if it were a single, homogeneous whole, talking of "chaplaincy" generically is even more complex given the wide range of provision. Nevertheless, as thumbnail sketches the following points do warrant particular mention.

One important consideration when looking at chaplaincy is the differences between the work of full-time and part-time chaplains. Full-time chaplains work solely outside the parochial or congregational ministry. Chaplains who work in an institution or in a particular sector of society see their ministry as being both to the institution and to the individuals who work within it. Some chaplains may feel that it is easier for them to understand the structures and more fully appreciate the life of the institution if they work in the institution full-time. They may feel that this increases their identification with those who work there and gives greater opportunity for chaplains to be accepted as part of the institution. Other chaplains, however, may feel that being part-time brings its own merits, such as allowing the chaplain to make significant links with the wider community or ensuring that the chaplain does not get institutionalized and fail to relate primarily to the church. Some ministers who work full-time as chaplains may work part-time in more than one institution or work in a sector (such as industry) where they visit more than one place each week. They may therefore see themselves as full-time chaplains but be perceived by others as part-time.

The naming of chaplaincy has caused some difficulties. Some chaplains feel that the title of nonparochial or noncongregational ministry means that their work is defined by what it is not rather than by what it is. Some such chaplains have chosen therefore to call themselves "sector ministers" because they minister to a sector or segment of society. Other chaplains feel that such adoption limits the scope of this ministry and that chaplains can fall into the trap of seeing their ministry as restricted to only one part of the people of God. Some chaplains and some church documents have called chaplaincy a "specialized" ministry; what is meant here is that chaplaincy often calls for a particular body of knowledge or skill if one is to minister adequately. It might be difficult, for instance, to be a good chaplain in a prison if one did not know enough of the workings of the penal system to be able to relate effectively to staff and inmates. Other clergy, who do not work as chaplains, naturally feel that the labeling "specialized" demeans their own work, given that it suggests that parish- or congregation-based ministry is not itself specialized or particular.

It is interesting to note that even chaplains' labeling within their sphere of work may sometimes reveal something about how the chaplains perceive their work or how they are regarded by others. A chaplain described as chaplain *to* an institution might indicate that the position is funded by the church and the chaplain may thus be seen as a guest within the institution. A chaplain described as chaplain *of* an institution may well be paid by the institution itself and may thus be seen in the institution as "one of us." Increasingly chaplains are choosing to adopt the more neutral term chaplain *at* an institution.

Such labeling is widely used by others in institutions. It is more likely, for instance, that nurses at a hospital would describe themselves as nurses *at* the hospital, than nurses *of* the hospital.

Some Issues Arising from Chaplaincy

One major issue that chaplains have to face (or at least should face) is that of identification with the institution. The question of who pays the chaplain, although giving some indication as to the value the chaplain's role is given, also raises the question of allegiance. Chaplains might, for instance, feel that "he who pays the piper calls the tune" and thus give primary allegiance to the institutions that pay them, be it the church or institution in which they work. Even if the acknowledgment is not as obvious as this, chaplains can succumb to what we might call creeping institutionalization. Here, over time chaplains may become so inculcated into the life and work of the institution that they fail to see its faults and become unable to offer an adequately Christian critique of the institution's working practices.

The fine balance between identification with and unquestioning acceptance of an institution is related to the possible tensions that chaplains can experience in this role. Chaplains might feel that they should be whistle-blowers against individuals or the institution in certain situations and this will obviously have implications for the position of neutrality that some chaplains feel they should have. Indeed, neutrality itself has been questioned and there are some who believe that chaplains should ask, "Whose side are we on?" If a chaplain in a mental health hospital sees abuse taking place, for instance, or a military chaplain witnesses a potential war crime, what should the chaplain do? Is remaining quiet really an option? Related to this, some have argued that the holding of rank in military situations compromises the work of chaplains because there is immediately a stronger identification with the officer class than other ranks. Indeed, even the presence of chaplains, paid by the state, confuses the separation of church and state where this is constitutionally required. Similarly, chaplains in educational settings may feel that a teaching role, although adding to full participation in the life of an institution, means that their pastoral effectiveness is compromised because they also are part of student assessment.

One certain benefit that many chaplains experience from their work is the greater intimacy ministers feel they have with those among whom they work. Because the numbers of people in many of the institutions are relatively small when compared to the numbers who live within areas that are defined in parochial or congregational settings, chaplains can become better known than

might otherwise be the case. Chaplaincy can offer the prospect of daily contact with the same group of people and this may well have pastoral benefits.

ECUMENISM and interfaith relations are often more easily established and built on within chaplaincy than in other areas of the church's ministry. Many institutions that have a chaplaincy provision draw the chaplains from a range of denominational backgrounds and, increasingly, from other faith backgrounds too. Daily work with such colleagues helps foster a greater understanding of the other's faith and its expression. Those in a parochial or congregational setting may not be so fortunate as this. Dialogue with those of another denomination or faith opens up exciting possibilities for the chaplain, the institution, and the wider church and society.

Conclusion

Clergy working outside the normative structures of parochial or congregational ministry have a long and distinguished history in the life of the church. Although there have been chaplains in some spheres for centuries, much of contemporary chaplaincy is in part a response to the changing circumstances and increased SECULARIZATION of the modern world. The fragmentation of modern living (we live in one place, work in another, and take our leisure in others) has meant that attachment to the local church has weakened. At its best, however, the work of chaplaincy helps the church to more easily engage with the challenges of the society the church seeks to serve. Chaplaincy represents the church to the world and the world to the church and thus it helps ensure that the church is fully enmeshed in the complexities and intimacies of the modern society.

References and Further Reading

Beckford, James A., and Sophie Gilliat. *Religion in Prison: Equal Rights in a Multi-Faith Society.* Cambridge, UK: Cambridge University Press, 1998.

Budd, Richard M. *Serving Two Masters: The Development of Military Chaplaincy, 1860–1920.* Lincoln: University of Nebraska Press, 2002.

De Revere, David W., Wilbert A. Cunningham, Tommy Moberley, and John A. Price. *Chaplaincy in Law Enforcement: What it is and How to do it.* Springfield, IL: Charles C. Thomas, 1989.

Gibson, William. *A Social History of the Domestic Chaplain: 1530–1840.* London: Leicester University Press, 1997.

Holst, Lawrence E. *Hospital Ministry: The Role of the Chaplain Today.* New York: Crossroad, 1985.

Legood, Giles. *Chaplaincy: The Church's Sector Ministries.* London: Cassell, 1999.

Rogerson, John W. *Industrial Mission in a Changing World.* Sheffield, UK: Sheffield Academic Press, 1996.

Shockley, Donald G. *Campus Ministry: The Church Beyond Itself.* Louisville, KY: Westminster/John Knox Press, 1989.

GILES LEGOOD

CHARITY

Terminology and Origin

Definitions of "charity" include (1) older synonym for Christian love, (2) specific act of kindness, (3) organization devoted to assistance of the needy and amelioration of society, (4) ethical criterion of behavior, (5) major aspect of Christian character/theological virtue/sanctification, (6) characteristic of the Church, and (7) the divine nature. "Charity" is the early modern English translation of New Testament *agape* (see the precepts of charity in Mark 12: 28-31, Matthew 22: 36–40, Luke 10: 25-28, I Corinthians 13), by way of the Latin Vulgate's *caritas*. As distinct from other Greek terms (*philia*, *eros*, *storge*), the New Testament term avoided overtones of lust, mere comradeliness, or familiarity, but in English the word "charity" came to have equally negative associations of institutional beneficence without humane personal respect; hence the proverbial expression, "as cold as charity," or "I don't want to depend on charity." Nineteenth-century and later Bible versions, and devotional literature since at least the eighteenth century, prefer the expression "love."

Works of Charity, Individual and Institutional

Even in English, "charity" has survived also in a more positive sense of works of individual kindness for the needy, and of organizations for the relief of need. The medieval Church's commitment to care of the poor and enslaved continued through the Reformation into all churches, Roman Catholic and Protestant. The nineteenth century in particular saw a vast growth in Christian charitable organizations in most churches, to meet the needs of increasingly industrialized and urbanized society in Europe and America. Among Protestant churches, these organizations often took the form of new religious orders (Sisters of the People, Sisters of the Children, in British Methodism, for instance), on lines comparable with the vowed communities of Roman Catholicism, but with a different understanding of vows, and no suggestion that the vowed life is necessary to evangelical perfection. Combined with these moves went the rediscovery of diaconal ministry, and of the Order of Deacon as a vocation in its own right and not merely as an obligatory career stage preparatory to the presbyterate—this rediscovery was pioneered in the German Evangelical Churches (for example, by the Lutheran Wilhelm Löhe at Neuendettelsau in Hessen).

Charity as a Divinely Commanded Criterion of Behavior

The Commandments of Charity have already been mentioned. They feature both in the Hebrew Bible (Leviticus 19: 18, 34), and next, as "the first and great commandment in the law, and the second . . . like to it," in the New Testament, (Romans 13: 9; Timothy 1: 5, as well as the cited Gospel verses). Paul's comment is that the second commandment covers all the prohibitions of wrong and hurtful behavior. Charity guides decisions by looking to the best results of our plans; by treating the neighbor as our equal or superior in need, and by pointing away from revenge or resentment to forgiveness.

Charity as a Hallmark of Christian Character, Theological Virtue, Essence of Sanctification

I Corinthians 13 describes charity not as a discrete act or series of acts, but as an enduring feature of personal character, together with faith and hope (some Protestant moral theology continues the medieval categorization of these as the three "theological" virtues, as distinct from the "cardinal" virtues of the Aristotelian-based scholastic theology). All Protestant moral teaching requires a vision of Christian maturation in which charity, springing from faith, is paramount (Luther's *quellende Liebe*, "love springing up like a fountain"): this charity, like faith itself, is a grateful response to redeeming love, and; also like faith, is itself a divine gift, not a human achievement. Charity is a reflection in the redeemed creature of the character of the Creator-and-Redeemer, and is therefore an aspect of the divine image, intended by the Creator from the beginning, lost in the Fall, and restored in redemption. Lutheran and Reformed (and Methodist) views differ in emphasis at this point: Lutherans are careful to insist that the believer never passes the need for justification, while Methodists and Reformed traditionally assert that God works an inherent sanctifying change in the believer. Methodist and other Holiness theologies see the essence of this change as a gift of transforming love, and that it is possible even in this life for God so to transform a personality that no motive other than love may become dominant in that person – although the gift may be forfeited by loss or relinquishment of faith, and require renewal.

Charity: The Vocation and Nature of the Church

From New Testament times, the Christian Church has known itself to be called to be a community of mutual charity, an instrument of charity for society in general, for unbelievers as well as believers. In all traditions, ministry and local structures have been defined by purposes of charity: Protestant examples are church-wardens and care of the poor, Methodist Poor Stewards, prison visitors, and grief support groups. Charity is, in Protestant understanding, the overriding purpose of CHURCH LAW and the sole basis of ecumenism.

Charity: The Divine Nature

In individual and corporate sanctification, in the Church, and in all creation, charity is the response to divine redemptive mercy, which response is itself possible only as the gift and self-bestowing act of the Trinity, whose very nature is the mutual indwelling of love.

References and Further Reading

Durnbaugh, Donald F., ed. *Every Need Supplied. Mutual Aid and Christian Community in the Free Churches 1525–1675.* Philadelphia, PA: Temple University Press, 1974.

Flew, Robert Newton. *The Idea of Perfection in Christian Theology,* Oxford, UK: Oxford University Press, 1937.

Gassmann, Günther. "The Church Is a Communion of Churches," in *The Catholicity of the Reformation,* edited by Carl F. Braaten and Robert W. Jensen, 93–105. Grand Rapids, MI: Eerdmans, 1996.

Hirst, Edward W. *Studies in Christian Love.* London: Religious Book Club, 1944.

Kreutziger, Sarah Sloan. "Going on to Perfection. The Contributions of the Wesleyan Theological Doctrine of Entire Sanctification to the Value Base of American Professional Social Work Through the Lives and Activities of Nineteenth Century Evangelical Women Reformers," PhD dissertation, Tulane University, 1991.

Nygren, Anders. *Agape and Eros.* Translated by Philip S. Watson. Philadelphia, PA: Muhlenberg Press, 1953.

Williams, Daniel Day. *The Spirit and the Forms of Love.* New York: Harper & Row, 1968.

Ziemke, Donald C. *Love for the Neighbor in Luther's Theology. The Development of his Thought 1512–1539.* Minneapolis, MN: Augsburg, 1969.

DAVID H. TRIPP

CHERBURY, EDWARD LORD HERBERT OF (c. 1582–1648)

English philosopher. Recognized as the father of English DEISM, Edward Lord Herbert of Cherbury (born March 3, ca. 1582, at Eyton-on-Severn, Shropshire and died August 1648 in London) was in his lifetime far more noted—as a politician, diplomat, and author—than his younger brother GEORGE HERBERT, the poet and country priest. Despite the latter's greater fame today, the influence of Edward's Deist thought has remained considerable on religion and politics of the subsequent centuries.

Educated at Oxford in classics and languages, Herbert began his maturity as parliamentarian, then soldier, traveler, frequent dueler, and lover on the Continent. In 1619 he became ambassador to FRANCE, a post that embroiled him in religious conflicts between Protestants and Catholics. Although loyal to the Protestant cause throughout, Herbert's motivations were political rather than religious. Nevertheless, his thought arose from his experience with these "wars of religion."

The main notions of Herbert's religious philosophy are stated in his *De Veritate* (*Concerning Truth*) of 1624, written with the inspiration of Hugo Grotius, who had just written a *De Veritate Religionis Christianae* (*Concerning the Truth of the Christian Religion*), and published partly at his instance, partly by divine sanction, as Herbert himself claimed. Although Hugo's work was a plea for peace and tolerance among Christians—and in its nonsectarian THEOLOGY a forerunner of C. S. Lewis's *Mere Christianity*—Edward's book extended the common denominator to all religions. Instead of arguing for a universal Christianity, he advocated natural religion not only as preparation for revealed religion, but the whole of truth indeed. Herbert's work draws from ancient skepticism revived in sixteenth-century religious debates, but in an opposite direction from fideism, which replaces reason with FAITH: What cannot be agreed upon as certain truth, he argued, cannot be affirmed DOCTRINE. Herbert makes "common notions" the basis of religion. These are the fruit of "natural instinct," which is much more reliable and universally valid than "discursive reasoning"—the source of much gratuitous error. Only what is common to all is easily believed and should be taken as essential truth for all. For Herbert this truth constitutes five elements: (1) the existence of God, (2) the rightful worship thereof, (3) consisting principally of virtuous living, (4) the default of which requires repentance, (5) and the success of which determines the afterlife. As for special revelation, Herbert views it under the category of TRADITION and history—separate from truth—in the realm of probability. Only revelation to oneself, like individual reason, holds as valid.

In his later writings Herbert expands these fundamental views. In *De Religione Laici,* he blames priests for propagating religious errors and counsels their correction by reasonable lay thinking. Then in *De Religione Gentilium* he salvages from the pagan religions the five essential points of religion from his first book, whereas in the *Dialogue* he explicitly attacks revealed religion. In sum Herbert's thought was a secular development on earlier discussions of Nikolaus Cusanus, Guardano Bruno, and Hugo Grotius, and became foundational, through his follower CHARLES BLOUNT, in EN-LIGHTENMENT Deism and beyond.

See also Collins, Anthony; Hobbes, Thomas; Kant, Immanuel; Jefferson, Thomas; Tindal, Matthew; Toland, John; Toleration

References and Further Reading

Primary Sources:

Herbert, Edward Lord of Cherbury. *De veritate.* 1624.
———. *De Religione Laici.* After 1630.
———. *De Causis Errorum.*
———. *The Life and Reign of King Henry the Eighth.*
———. *A Dialogue between a Tutor and His Pupil.*
———. *Autobiography.*

Secondary Sources:

Hill, Eugene D. *Edward, Lord Herbert of Cherbury.* Boston: Twayne Publishers, 1987.
Rossi, Mario. *La vita, le opere, i tempi* [*The life, works and times*] *di Edoardo Herbert di Cherbury.* 3 vols. Firenze: Sansoni, 1947.
Stroppel, Clemens. *Edward Herbert von Cherbury, Wahrheit-Religion-Freiheit.* Tübingen: Francke Verlag, 2000.

DAVID LIU

CHILDHOOD

The study of children and childhood is a growing area of inquiry in a number of academic disciplines. It has developed well beyond those fields that have typically devoted attention to children, such as education and child development, to include history, political science, law, sociology, anthropology, philosophy, religious studies, and theology. Rising interdisciplinary interest in children and childhood was prompted in part by the influential study by Philippe Ariès, originally published in French in 1960 and translated two years later as *Centuries of Childhood: A Social History of Family Life.* Ariès convincingly showed that conceptions of childhood and even the experience of being a child vary and change over time. Although historians have challenged many of his specific findings, his work has motivated scholars in several fields to reexamine the development and experiences of children and to explore conceptions of children and childhood in various periods of history and within diverse cultures.

Biblical Perspectives

Christian conceptions of childhood and attitudes and behaviors toward children are also complex and diverse, reflecting the particular historical, cultural, and theological contexts in which they develop. These varied attitudes and behaviors are also based in part on the diverse and sometimes paradoxical notions about children found in the Bible. Some biblical texts speak of children as gifts of God, signs of God's blessing, and sources of joy. Others depict children as ignorant and capricious and in need of instruction and discipline. Several biblical passages command parents to teach their children the faith. Other passages address obligations of the community to children, especially the poor and orphans. In New Testament epistles, children are commanded to obey their parents, and fathers are urged not to provoke their children to anger but to "bring them up in the discipline and instruction of the Lord" (Ephesians 6:1–4). In the Gospels, children are depicted in striking, even radical ways. At a time when children occupied a low position in society, Jesus receives children, blesses them, touches them, and heals them. He is indignant toward those who have contempt for them. He even equates welcoming a little child in his name to welcoming himself and the One who sent him. Furthermore, he depicts children as models for adults of entering the reign of God, as models of faith, and as vehicles of revelation. The ways in which Christians have wrestled with these diverse biblical texts and the particular texts that they eventually either incorporate into their theology or neglect determine in part their particular perspectives on childhood and their understanding of their obligations to children themselves.

Historical Perspectives

In the history of Protestantism, childhood has been viewed both as a stage in life before adulthood as well as a metaphor for spiritual maturity. In regard to the former, almost all Protestant theologians have emphasized that children are sinful and in need of instruction. However, their particular conceptions and treatment of children vary. The notion that children are sinful is deeply tied to Protestant understandings of the fall and original SIN. Some scholars have assumed that regarding children as sinful inevitably leads to the punishment and even abuse of children. Yet this is not the case. Although some Protestants in the past and even today emphasize that because children are sinful they should be physically punished and their "wills must be broken," and although there are dark chapters in the history of Christianity of the brutal treatment and abuse of children, other Protestants who have also viewed children as sinful have treated children with compassion and have created positive social and ecclesiastical reforms on their behalf. Thus, any view of children as sinful must be examined within the larger framework of any given theology and in relation to the actual treatment of children themselves.

For example, although the Protestant reformer JOHN CALVIN (1509–1564) viewed children as affected by original sin, and although his views have been used at times to justify the harsh treatment of children, he did not recommend physically punishing children. He did emphasize the depth of human depravity and claims the nature of infants is a "seed of sin." However, he did not dwell on evidences of corruption in children. Furthermore, building on biblical passages, he claimed that infants are gifts of God and can proclaim God's goodness. He also underscored the duties of parents to teach their children godliness and the obligations of society to provide for the educational and physical needs of children. He himself wrote two CATECHISMS and supported school reforms in Geneva.

August Hermann Francke (1663–1727), a German Lutheran Pietist (see PIETISM), also believed that children are born with a fallen nature and even claimed that their "self-will" must be "broken." However, his particular understanding of "breaking the self-will" within the context of his major theological convictions led him not only to treat children with respect and kindness but also to pay attention to the needs of poor children. In contrast to many contemporaries in his highly class-conscious period, Francke showed a concern for children that extended to orphans and children of the poor, and he built an extensive complex of charitable and educational institutions to address their needs. He even allowed gifted poor students and orphans to prepare for a university education alongside children of the upper and middle classes. His notion of original sin provided a kind of positive, egalitarian framework of thought that opened a door to responding to the needs of poor children, seeing them as individuals with gifts and talents to be cultivated, and positively influencing educational reforms in GERMANY.

Some Protestant theologians have devoted little attention to the sinful nature of children and have focused instead on elements within contemporary culture or family life that influence children. For example, HORACE BUSHNELL (1802–1876) and FRIEDRICH SCHLEIERMACHER (1768–1834) both stressed proper nurture for children in the home, the church, and the community. Bushnell claimed children "by nature" do not need to choose evil, but they often do because parental sins and unjust social structures negatively influence them. Thus, in his popular book, *Christian Nurture* (1861), he emphasized the importance of daily rituals and practices in the home for positively influencing children and nurturing their faith. Schleiermacher claimed that children are born with as much potential for salvation as for sin and that it is the duty of parents to nurture their children's "higher self-consciousness," which connects them to the tran-scendent and thereby opens their hearts to love of others. Influenced by Moravian Pietists (see MORAVIAN CHURCH), he understood the family to be the center of a child's religious formation. Nevertheless, he also recognized that efforts within the home must be supported by the church. He thereby worked to strengthen religious education and preached a series of "Sermons on the Christian Household." Finally, more than many other theologians, he emphasized the ways in which children are models for adults.

Throughout the history of Protestantism there has been an emphasis on the need to educate and to care for children. Protestants in the past and today have established schools, orphanages, and hospitals for children. They have also written catechisms and religious educational materials for the home and created educational programs in the church. In general, Protestants have provided education for their children not only to enable them to read the Bible but also to prepare them for service to church and society. They have also emphasized the role of parents in the religious formation of children, and they have outlined particular obligations of the church and state for education and child welfare.

For example, MARTIN LUTHER (1483–1546) wrote catechisms for use in the home and encouraged parents, especially fathers, to take responsibility for the moral and spiritual formation of their children. He also believed that well-educated citizens would serve both church and society. Thus, he urged both parents and civil authorities to provide children with a strong education so that they could read the BIBLE and gain the skills and knowledge necessary for them to use their gifts and talents to serve others. At a time when education was viewed as unnecessary for most children and educational opportunities were limited, Luther and his colleague PHILIPP MELANCHTHON stressed the significance of education and training in the liberal arts. They also proposed several reforms that influenced German schools and universities, including public education for all children.

JOHN WESLEY (1703–1791), the founder of METHODISM, supported several educational and charitable institutions for children and established his own schools. The goal of education, for Wesley, was to join knowledge with piety and to help children to know and to love God and to serve others. Wesley was concerned for all children, including the poor. In his schools he therefore mixed students from different socioeconomic backgrounds. He also offered food, clothing, and medical and financial support to poor families. His attention to the poor inspired Methodists from that time to today to care for the poor and to establish a number of institutions and initiatives to serve them.

Wesley's reforms follow a general trend in eighteenth century Europe and North America toward greater attention to children's emotional, physical, and intellectual welfare. Although childhood was certainly not "discovered" in the eighteenth century, as some have claimed, during this period several movements both inside and outside the church initiated social and educational reforms on behalf of children. Orphanages and schools were built. The Sunday School movement flourished. Publishers marketed a host of children's literature and Bibles. States adopted new child labor and welfare laws. More attention was given to the developmental importance of children's play, which was linked to a burgeoning toy industry. Aspects of this general shift in approaches to children were informed by the ideas of the French philosopher, Jean-Jacques Rousseau (1712–1778), who believed that children are naturally innocent and can learn through play and that negative social influences can spoil their natural goodness.

Despite many positive initiatives on behalf of children, the church throughout its history has not consistently cared for the needs of children or treated them with respect and dignity. For example, the history of boarding schools for NATIVE AMERICAN children in CANADA reveals disturbing accounts of child abuse and neglect by both Catholics and Protestants. In this case, the state also played a role in establishing the schools. Much more scholarly research needs to be pursued to provide an adequate account of conceptions of childhood and the treatment of children in the history of Christianity and in diverse communities of faith around the world today. This kind of research requires the exploration of a range of issues, including theological statements regarding children, the legal status of children, educational policies, family structures, literary and artistic representations of childhood, the material culture of childhood, and the treatment of children. Most difficult to uncover in any research regarding children are the experiences and ideas of children themselves.

Ethical and Theological Concerns

Children today continue to face numerous challenges in many countries, and Protestant communities of faith are working to address these concerns. Although one might argue about whether the overall situation of children is "better" or "worse" than in the past, most people agree that children today face real and serious problems that need to be addressed. Several studies and reports have outlined in detail the kinds of problems experienced by children and young people around the world, such as poverty, abuse, neglect, malnutrition, inadequate educational opportunities,

teenage pregnancy, drug and alcohol abuse, suicide, and depression. Protestant communities of faith today are responding to the needs of children in a variety of ways. Many have established day care centers and after-school programs. Most traditions offer religious education programs for children. Churches have also tried to incorporate children more fully into the worship service. Furthermore, a number of churches are serving poor children and families and are working to change economic and social policies that negatively affect the lives of children.

Although communities of faith offer these and other kinds of services to children and their families, there is little serious theological and ethical reflection by either contemporary Protestant or Catholic theologians on childhood, children, and obligations to children. Although theologians have highly developed teachings on other issues, such as ABORTION, women's ordination (see WOMEN CLERGY), biblical AUTHORITY, and economic justice, they have not offered well-developed and historically and biblically informed teachings about children. Certainly, issues regarding children have sometimes been addressed in theological reflection on the family. However, little is said beyond encouraging parents to teach children the faith and to help the poor. Contemporary systematic theologians and ethicists have generally viewed issues regarding children as "beneath" the serious theologian, and have left attention to children primarily to those in the areas of religious education and pastoral care. Perhaps as literature regarding children develops in a range of disciplines outside theology, children and childhood will play a more significant role in the way that systematic theologians and ethicists think about central theological themes, such as the human condition, the nature of faith, the task of the church, and the nature of religion. They will also perhaps devote more attention to a number of significant ethical issues affecting children, such as children's rights, the moral and spiritual development of children, the responsibilities of parents, and the obligations of church and state to children.

See also Baptism; Confirmation; Education Overview; Family

References and Further Reading

Anderson, Herbert, and Susan B. W. Johnson. *Regarding Children: A New Respect for Childhood and Families.* Louisville: Westminster John Knox, 1994.
Ariès, Philippe. *Centuries of Childhood: A Social History of Family Life.* Translated by Robert Baldick. New York: Vintage Books, 1962.
Bunge, Marcia J., ed. *The Child in Christian Thought.* Grand Rapids, MI: Eerdmans, 2001.

Cunningham, Hugh. *Children and Childhood in Western Society since 1500.* New York: Longman Publishing, 1995.

"Gottes Kinder." In *Jahrbuch für Biblische Theologie.* vol. 17 (Special issue: 2002).

Greven, Philip J., Jr. *The Protestant Temperament: Patterns of Child-Rearing, Religious Experience, and the Self in Early America.* New York: Alfred A. Knopf, 1977.

Hawes, Joseph M., and N. Ray Hiner, eds. *Children in Historical and Comparative Perspective: An International Handbook and Research Guide.* New York: Greenwood Press, 1991.

Ozment, Steven. *The Loving Family in Old Europe.* Cambridge: Harvard University Press, 2003.

Whitmore, Todd David, with Tobias Winright. "Children: An Undeveloped Theme in Catholic Teaching." In *The Challenge of Global Stewardship: Roman Catholic Responses,* edited by Maura A. Ryan and Todd David Whitmore, 161–185. Notre Dame: University of Notre Dame Press, 1997.

Wood, Diana. "The Church and Childhood." In *Studies in Church History,* vol. 31. Oxford: Blackwell Publishers, 1994.

MARCIA J. BUNGE

CHILIASM

Chiliasm refers to the belief in a literal one thousand–year rule of the saints at the close of history, particularly where it inspires an altered approach to the present age. Based on the Greek word for 1,000, chiliasm thus bears close resemblance to the movements known as millenarian or millennialist, based on the equivalent Latin word. The distinction between the usage of these terms is understood in different ways by different scholars, but loosely chiliasm is regarded as the belief in the millennium, widely held within general Christian opinion, whereas millennialism refers specifically to separatist sectarian movements.

That chiliast views were widely held in the early church is now generally acknowledged. Some scholars have suggested that first-century Christians expected Christ to return within their lifetime. Chiliast beliefs were suggested by the Book of Revelation, which implied that there would be a future period when Satan would be bound and the CHURCH would flourish. This led to the view that the initiation of the millennium would come only after the appearance of the ANTICHRIST. Augustine's *City of God* emphatically rejected this view. What was later called the postmillennial interpretation came to view the millennium as a description of the latter and triumphant part of church history, which would be followed by the return of Christ and the day of judgment.

Chiliast views seem to have been an important influence on early Protestant thought. Identifying the popes as the Antichrist, Protestant reformers expected a crisis before the appearance of the millennium. MARTIN LUTHER went partway along this path in his view that the Roman Catholic church was the harlot of the Book of Revelation and the pope of his day the Antichrist. JOHN FOXE's immensely influential *Book of Martyrs* (see ACTS AND MONUMENTS) subscribed to a chiliast interpretation of the Marian martyrs who died under the reign of Queen Mary, and as a result identified Elizabethan England as the "elect nation," localizing the millennium in a manner not dissimilar to the nineteenth-century Mormons. The best-known advocates of this position were some of the Anabaptists in South Germany in the sixteenth century. Hans Hut and his HUTTERITES were one key group; MELCHIOR HOFMANN's followers were another, making the "Melchiorites" an important chiliast strand within the German Reformation. Melchiorist views initially inspired the Anabaptists at Münster in the 1530s.

Such views reached their culmination with the appearance in ENGLAND during the Commonwealth period of the "Fifth Monarchy men" who proposed to launch a war against Rome to force the coming millennium. The Muggletonians and some of the early Quakers were some of those among the Fifth Monarchy men.

Yet the chiliast position never received widespread support. Calvinists in particular abominated chiliasm, dismissing it as a childish fantasy. Establishment Protestants in general were uneasy about the potential that such views would unsettle attitudes toward the state church. Yet the chiliast position was able to claim some scholarly support, notably in the writings of the Lutheran seventeenth-century scholar, J. H. Alsted in his *Diatribe de Mille Apocalypticis* (1627). This work staunchly advocated a future millennium in which the church will experience an unfamiliar epoch of blessing. This work, translated into English as *The Beloved City* in 1643, deeply influenced religious thinking during the Commonwealth. Joseph Mede was a reader of Alsted, and in his *Clavis Apocalyptica* (1642) he saw the Book of Revelation as explaining the crises of history up to the REFORMATION and beyond. He expected historical events that would complete the outpouring of the vials described in Revelation before the coming judgment. HENRY MORE, one of the CAMBRIDGE PLATONISTS, was profoundly influenced by his reading of the last book of the Bible. In a different way Sir ISAAC NEWTON defended such a view, according to recent scholarship. Chiliasm was maintained even in the untroubled circumstances of the eighteenth century by the English scholar, bishop Thomas Newton, in his *Dissertation on the Prophecies* (1754) and by the Pietist German expositor, JOHANN ALBRECHT BENGEL.

Such millennialism did not, of course, need to emphasize the preceding time of tribulation. Postmillennialists could be chiliasts too. Some of the early evangelicals, including JONATHAN EDWARDS, believed that revival would bring about the millennium. This was a key to the argument of his *Humble Attempt to promote Agreement . . . for Revival and the Advancement of the Kingdom of God* (1748). A similar approach was a factor in the development of the missionary movement in the late eighteenth century. WILLIAM CAREY interpreted scriptures of the Old and New Testaments to explain a great day of Christian domination coming to the world. Confident expectation of the blessings of the "latter days" inspired a fresh missionary vision.

A new form of chiliasm, known as premillennialism, developed in the nineteenth century through the advocacy of J. Hatley Frere, who in 1813 published his interpretation of Napoleon as the Antichrist who would shortly trigger the tribulation that preceded the millennium. Such views were taken up by a number of extremists, among them HENRY DRUMMOND, the Evangelical Anglican; EDWARD IRVING, the prominent Scottish minister in London and founder of the Catholic Apostolic Church; and JOHN NELSON DARBY who seceded from the Anglican Church of Ireland to form the PLYMOUTH BRETHREN. The premillennial position gained strong support within the conservative wings of the established churches. This was even more the case in North America, where the pre-millennial view was almost universaly embraced by fundamentalist Protestants from the late 19th century onward. Evangelical Anglicans, notably Henry Venn, J. C. Ryle, and Lord Ashley, for this reason supported the evangelization of the Jews and the Jerusalem bishopric, which was shared with the Prussian Lutheran Church.

Study of this topic has often been distorted with fascination with millenarian sects. For all its rich and fascinating dimensions, Norman Cohn's famous book, *The Pursuit of the Millennium,* explores chiliasm with an assumption that believers were necessarily psychologically disordered. Anthropologists and sociologists have used the concept in a loose sense to explain religious adaptations to changing social conditions. However, chiliasm needs to be seen first as a theological position, albeit one with powerful social and cultural appeal in troubled times.

See also Anabaptism; Devil; Friends, Society of; Millenarians and Millennialism; Mormonism

References and Further Reading

Capp, Bernard. *The Fifth Monarchy Men: a Study in Seventeenth-century English Millenarianism.* London: Faber, 1972.
Cohn, Norman. *The Pursuit of the Millennium.* 3d edition, London: Granada Publishing, 1970.
Firth, Katherine R. *The Apocalyptic Tradition in Reformation Britain 1530–1645.* London: Oxford University Press, 1979.
Haller, William. *Foxe's Book of Martyrs and the Elect Nation.* London: Jonathan Cape, 1963.
Hempton, D. N. "Evangelicalism and Eschatology." *Journal of Ecclesiastical History* 31 no. 3 (1980): 179–194.
Hillerbrand, Hans J., ed. *Radical Tendencies in the Reformation: Divergent Perspectives, Sixteenth Century Essays & Studies.* vol. IX. Kirksville, MO: Sixteenth Century Journal Publishers, 1988.
O'Leary, Stephen. *Arguing the Apocalypse: A Theory of Millennial Rhetoric.* New York: Oxford University Press, 1994.
Oliver, W. H. *Prophets and Millennialists: The Uses of Biblical Prophecy in England from the 1790s to the 1840s.* Oxford: Oxford University Press, 1978.
Toon, Peter, ed. *Puritans, the Millennium and the Future of Israel: Puritan Eschatology, 1600 to 1660: a Collection of Essays.* Cambridge, UK: James Clarke, 1970.
Wilson, Bryan R. *Magic and the Millennium.* London: Heinemann, 1973.

PETER LINEHAM

CHILLINGWORTH, WILLIAM (1602–1644)

English theologian. Chillingworth was the son of a mayor of Oxford, England and godson of WILLIAM LAUD (1573–1645), archbishop of Canterbury. In 1618 he became a scholar and in 1628 a fellow of Trinity College, Oxford, where he had earned a reputation as a learned and tenacious debater. In 1630 he made a celebrated conversion to Roman Catholicism and spent some months in Douai, France, the town that was the center of English Catholics; he then returned to Oxford and the CHURCH OF ENGLAND in 1631, eventually subscribing with reservations to the THIRTY-NINE ARTICLES and receiving a living in the church. During the 1630s he stayed at the country estate of Lucius Cary, Second Viscount Falkland, Great Tew near Oxford, where he became respected as the most important theologian of the Great Tew circle, and wrote his single major work, *The Religion of Protestants, A Safe Way to Salvation* (1638). A moderate royalist, he served as chaplain and military engineer during the early battles of the CIVIL WARS, was captured, and died at Chichester of disease contracted while a prisoner. He was badgered by his Presbyterian jailer/chaplain for his Arminian theology (see ARMINIANISM) and was accused of Socinianism. During the restoration, his works were reprinted and respected by those who led the latitudinarian church (see LATITUDINARIANISM), and by thinkers such as JOHN LOCKE.

The Religion of Protestants is a work of controversy in response to the Jesuit, Edward Knott, and in defense of an Oxford colleague, Christopher Potter. Chillingworth attempted to chart a path between the Roman Catholic claim to infallibility, Laudian authority based on administration of the SACRAMENTS, and the constricting of Reformed doctrine at Dordt. To do this he appealed to the BIBLE as the religion of Protestants, as the source of teaching for the way of life of Christians, and as the source for doctrine that must be believed for salvation. He was concerned with the breakup of Christendom into multiple contending churches and polities, with multiple interpretations of scripture and doctrines, and the potential violence of prophetic and millenarian teaching (see MILLENARIANS AND MILLENNIALISM). Scripture requires interpretation that must rely on reason, he argued; some of its difficult, if not contradictory passages, must be interpreted through those that are simpler and plainer. TRADITION only partly supplies a resource, given that the Church Fathers disagreed with each other, as did the Councils, and the reformers of the sixteenth century. He outlined only tentatively where those simple, clear statements of belief and a universal tradition might be found.

His conversion to the Roman Catholic church was in part motivated by a search for an infallible religious authority, although he was disappointed not to find within the intellectual circles of Catholicism tolerance and room for a reasoned and skeptical theology. He argued that desire for infallibility does not require that there exist such an AUTHORITY. The best one can hope for are probable arguments, and this requires tolerance and charity in religious belief and ongoing debate as the method of theological development. We might be required to believe in mysteries, in articles of faith beyond reason, but not against it. Religious commitments and assent must be freely given; this is a moral necessity that God allows for. To assume otherwise would be to believe in a God who is not good. There is no infallible authority, and when someone or an institution claims it, it becomes a tyranny that destroys a person's moral responsibility and sensibility. Sufficiency, not certainty, is provided by the Bible, our use of reason in interpreting it, and the witness of tradition and the church.

Chillingworth did not always reveal his sources, and he used them for his own purposes. He was in touch with the humanist tradition exemplified by Erasmus, though in the more Tacitean (skeptical and stoical) form of later Humanism, rather than the Ciceronian form of the earlier Renaissance. He quoted the theologian RICHARD HOOKER (1554–1600), although his argument does not have the breadth of Hooker's understanding of reason, scripture, and tradition. His use of reason was less constructive and more critical than that of Hooker, and than that of the Cambridge Platonists, who shared with him an appeal to reason and toleration. He was deeply influenced by skepticism and by Hugo Grotius, who was discussed at Great Tew, although there is debate about the extent of Grotian influence in Chillingworth's writings. He was part of the Arminian movement in the Church of England, with Falkland, LANCELOT ANDREWES, JEREMY TAYLOR, and Laud. In the seventeenth century, the accusation of Socinian sympathies might be directed at reliance on reason in religious understanding, or for an adoption of Arianism and Unitarianism. Regarding the former, the label is justified, although Chillingworth did not limit religion solely under the authority of reason. Regarding Arianism, he left the question open, which did not comfort his critics.

Chillingworth's writings were collected and reprinted during the restoration, and portraits of him and the Great Tew circle were written by Edward Hyde, Earl of Clarendon, in his *Life*. His work has been criticized for it repetitiveness, digressions, and organization, which follows the arguments of his opponents. However, the fullness of his quotation of them and his thoroughness in response provide a balanced and complete compendium of the issues he faced, and the method of controversy in his day. He reveals himself in these writings as a well-read, fair, and balanced controversialist. THOMAS HOBBES noted that sometimes he criticized his friends as well as his opponents. His theological construction was not, and could not be, final. It flowed from historical circumstances that were dangerous and eventually issued in bloodshed. He raised and formulated issues and responses that have remained with the Protestant tradition to the present. He is frequently discussed in histories and theologies of biblical interpretation and ecclesiology today, and is sometimes noted as an example of the plain style in preaching.

References and Further Reading

Primary Source:

Chillingworth, William. *The Works of William Chillingworth.* 10th ed. 1742; reissued in a three-volume English edition of 1838, and a single volume American editior. Brooklyn, NY: AMS Press, 1844.

Secondary Sources:

"Chillingworth, William." In J. A. Garraty et al., eds. *The Dictionary of National Biography.* Oxford: Oxford University Press, 1999.

Cragg, Gerald R. *Freedom and Authority: A Study of English Thought in the Early Seventeenth Century.* Philadelphia: Westminster, 1975.

Orr, Robert R. *Reason and Authority: The Thought of William Chillingworth.* Oxford: The Clarendon Press, 1967.

Trevor-Roper, Hugh. *Catholics, Anglicans and Puritans: Seventeenth Century Essays.* Chicago: University of Chicago Press, 1988.

Weber, Kurt. *Lucius Cary, Second Viscount Falkland.* New York: Columbia University Press, 1940.

STEPHEN VARVIS

CHILUBA, FREDERICK (1943–)

Protestant president of Zambia. Born 1943 in Kitwe, Chiluba became chairman of the Zambian Congress of Trades Unions, leading it into opposition to Kaunda's one-party state. He was imprisoned in 1981. With redemocratization, he became the opposition presidential candidate. His victory seemed to symbolize a new democratic era for AFRICA.

Soon, however, Chiluba was perceived as reintroducing authoritarianism (persecution of opposition leaders, HUMAN RIGHTS abuses, alteration of the constitution to guarantee reelection in 1996), and practicing corruption. The economy declined. In 2001 he attempted an unconstitutional third term, but foundered on resistance from inside and outside Zambia.

In politics Chiluba gave visibility to his FAITH. Raised in the United Church of Zambia, he had a "born-again" experience in prison. Close to charismatic groups, he received prophecies that he would be president. After victory he had the State House "cleansed" of evil spirits, organized an "anointing" modeled on that of King David, and then declared Zambia "a Christian nation." The declaration was included in the 1996 constitution, despite opposition from Catholic bishops and the Christian Council, and ambiguous reactions from evangelicals. Some pastors gained cabinet appointments, and churches that supported him received benefits, although some church leaders were disappointed that all government posts were not occupied by "born-agains" and that other religious measures were not taken. However, other evangelical leaders were critical of the "Christian nation" declaration, on principle or because scorn for government extended to them. Eventually Chiluba lost much church support with his third-term bid.

See also Evangelicalism; Catholic Reactions to Protestantism

References and Further Reading

Freston, Paul. *Evangelicals and Politics in Asia, Africa and Latin America*. Cambridge, UK: Cambridge University Press, 2001.
Gifford, Paul. *African Christianity: Its Public Role*. London: Hurst, 1998.
Phiri, Isabel. "Zambia: Christian Nation and Democracy." In a forthcoming book, edited by T. Ranger.

PAUL FRESTON

CHINA

Whereas Chinese Catholicism dates continuously back to the late 1500s, Protestantism came to China less than 200 years ago. On the surface, the first century and a half of the Protestant scene was dominated by the foreign missionary presence, but in fact a Chinese church was growing strong roots at the same time. Since 1950, Chinese Christians have survived restrictions and persecution under COMMUNISM, and since the late 1970s, the Protestant community has grown at an exponential rate. Protestantism is also well established in Taiwan and in overseas Chinese communities around the world.

Protestant Beginnings, 1807–1860

From the arrival in 1807 of the first Protestant missionary, Robert Morrison (1782–1834) of the London Missionary Society, the first generation of China missionaries labored under severe restrictions of residence and movement on the fringes of China, alternating their activities between Guangzhou (Canton), Macao, and the Chinese communities of Southeast Asia. Christianity was still prohibited in China, as it had been since the early 1700s, and Chinese converts to Protestantism were very few. The Manchu-ruled Chinese imperial state, as well as the native Chinese scholar-elite class, considered Christianity to be a dangerous and subversive sect.

The prospects for Protestant evangelism in China seemed to brighten considerably after China's defeat by Britain in the Opium War of 1839–1842 and the resulting "unequal treaties" between China and the Western nations, led by the British. This new framework of China's intercourse with the West, in addition to granting extraterritoriality and expanded residence in five coastal cities for foreigners, also lifted the prohibition on Christianity. At the same time it tied Christianity closely to the imperialist treaty system, establishing a linkage between Christianity and Western military and diplomatic rights in China that lasted until the mid-twentieth century. Through the 1840s and 1850s, Protestantism grew slowly in and around the five port cities permitted to foreign residence; the number of missionaries remained well under 100. In the meantime, after 1850, central China was convulsed by the throes of the Christian-inspired Taiping Rebellion (1851–1864), one of the largest and most destructive civil wars in world history. There were many reasons for the emergence of the Taipings and their quixotic leader Hong Xiuquan, who on the basis of spotty exposure to Protestantism believed himself to be the younger brother of Jesus, and it is highly debatable whether the movement was truly Christian (foreign missionaries for the most part considered it rank heresy). But the Chinese government and the nation's elite class certainly viewed it as Christian, considering it to be confirmation of their suspicions that Christianity meant subversion and rebellion. The efforts and image of Protestant as well as Catholic missions for decades in the late nineteenth century

CHINA

were hampered by Chinese memories of the Taipings, although the foreign missionaries were only dimly aware of this liability.

In the two decades before 1860, we can detect the seeds of an indigenous Chinese Protestantism. Because foreign missionaries could not go beyond the five authorized port cities, Bibles and other literature were carried into the interior by colporteurs and Chinese evangelists, who often worked quite autonomously. Karl Friedrich August Gutzlaff (1803–1851), a flamboyant and controversial independent Prussian missionary, organized the Chinese Union in the 1840s and sent many such Chinese agents into south China. The scheme collapsed with Gutlaff's death, but many decades later the independent agency of Chinese Christians was revived.

Expansion and Institution Building, 1860–1905

Another round of wars with the West and new sets of treaties in 1858–1860 created the final elements of the system defining China's relations with the West until the 1940s. As in 1842, diplomatic terms dictated by the victors defined the nature of the Protestant presence in China. For Christian missions, including Protestants and Catholics alike, the key element of these treaties was the provision that missionaries could now travel anywhere in China and could buy property and erect buildings outside the designated coastal and riverine "treaty port" cities. This opened the floodgates to the spread of Christian evangelism and institutions throughout the entire Chinese empire, although the increases in Chinese Protestant converts remained modest.

The four decades after 1860 witnessed a remarkable spurt of Protestant missionary activism and institutional development. Mission outposts spread to every province and even to distant hinterlands. The number of Protestant missionaries soared from barely more than 100 in 1860 to almost 3,500 in 1905. They were products of increasingly professionalized mission societies at home in Europe and North America, motivated by the high confidence of the Victorian era that the gospel to be preached in fulfillment of the Great Commission included not only Christianity, but also the basics of Western civilization. The number of Protestant mission societies represented in China grew to several dozen by 1900, and China became the major focus of many mission societies' endeavors, with extensive publicity and often romantic depictions of events and claimed successes. In 1905 the nondenominational CHINA INLAND MISSION (CIM), originally British but increasingly international, had more than 800 missionaries in China, almost three times the next

largest group, the British Church Missionary Society. The only American group with more than 200 missionaries was the Methodists (see METHODISM, GLOBAL; PRESBYTERIANISM); the Presbyterians were the next-largest denomination. Single women, not permitted on the field in the early 1800s, came to constitute a significant portion of the Protestant missionary force.

This was a generation of high achievers and strong personalities among Protestant missionaries in China. Several served well over a half-century, including Hudson Taylor of the CIM, Griffith John of the London Missionary Society, U.S. Presbyterian Hunter Corbett, Chauncey Goodrich of the American Board, and others. Many were indefatigable institution builders. Under their direction, coordinated from mission headquarters in the coastal cities, mission compounds arose in hundreds of locations, usually complete with residences, a hospital or dispensary, and a school. Preaching chapels manned by Chinese evangelists were established in thousands more towns and villages. Protestant missionaries also threw themselves into the translation and publication of Christian literature, as well as secular works on science, geography, and other subjects. An imposing edifice of institutions, constituting a substantial investment of human and financial resources, was in place by the early 1900s. The missionary school system is representative. In 1906 there were 57,000 students in more than 2,500 Protestant schools, with the larger denominations having a hierarchy culminating in secondary schools and with fledgling "colleges" that later in the twentieth century would become important institutions of modern higher education in China. By the early 1900s, more and more missionaries were coming to the China field as professionals, to serve as educators in the mission schools or elsewhere in the institutional structures of the mission, not as evangelists.

Despite the growing size and complexity of the Protestant establishment by 1900, and differences of opinion among individuals and groups, the essential unity of the missionary "force" was clearly visible in the large nationwide conferences of 1877, 1890, and 1907, the records of which still make useful reading today. No mission society in China failed to attend these conferences.

In Protestant missionary reports and literature of the late 1800s, the foreign missionary took center stage. For example, the nationwide Shanghai conference of 1907, with 1,100 delegates, included fewer than 10 Chinese. But Chinese collaboration and assistance in the Protestant mission effort was absolutely crucial, even in these decades when the Chinese did not figure prominently in the formal record. Protestantism was a joint Sino–foreign partnership from the earliest stage. Chinese colleagues played key roles in religious activities as preachers and translators, and they staffed the thousands of mission stations with no resident missionaries. Chinese personnel also staffed the schools, hospitals, and publishing houses supervised by Protestant missionaries, and in many cases they shared top decision-making roles; all in all, they did most of the real work of the mission. This emergence of a cadre of Chinese institutional personnel points to the fact that by the turn of the century, a number of Chinese, especially in the coastal cities, had found in Protestantism not only a religious faith, but also an avenue of upward mobility, from an education in the mission schools to careers in mission institutions. This group of educated urban converts would become even more important later in the twentieth century. Other groups of converts, typically in more rural areas, originally entered the church for reasons of social solidarity within an ethnic or clan community in a context of competition for local resources. Still other converts were attracted by clearly religious factors, finding a faith that to some resonated with traditional Chinese popular religion.

Protestant foundations were thus firmly laid by 1900, although the number of Chinese converts was still small; in 1905 there were about 250,000 Protestants. This indicates the continued resistance of Chinese society, especially the elite class, to Christianity in the last part of the nineteenth century. Indeed, the same years that saw the steady expansion of mission operations were consistently punctuated with acts of violent resistance to missionaries' arrival and continued presence in many communities. This resistance was often led by the local elite (or "gentry class"), to whose local cultural, social, and political hegemony the missionaries posed a profound threat by their privileged status and access to officialdom under the treaty system. Although some segments of the rural population were attracted to Protestantism, as noted earlier, the elite class and the most conservative elements of the imperial court in Beijing remained basically anti-Christian and more broadly anti-foreign. These sentiments erupted in the dramatic events of 1900 known as the Boxer Uprising, in which hundreds of foreigners, almost all of them missionaries, and perhaps 30,000 Chinese Christians were killed. This was a discouraging time for the Christian movement in China.

The Golden Age of Missions and the Sino–Foreign Protestant Establishment, 1905–1925

Ironically, the tragic events of the Boxer violence and the national humiliation that China suffered in the foreign military retribution that followed ushered in an age of rapid growth and respectability for Protestants. Obscurantist resistance to reform having proven disastrous, the Qing dynastic government embarked on an ambitious reform program during the decade after 1900. This included abolition of the old examination system and promotion of modern education, which put the mission schools temporarily in the vanguard of the quest for modernity and vastly increased their popularity. In education and other areas of institutional reform, including political constitutionalism, foreign missionaries and Chinese Protestants alike had a new status and reputation, which carried well into the 1920s.

On the surface, the Protestant movement went from one success to another during these two decades. When revolution toppled the Qing dynasty in 1911–1912, a Christian, Sun Yat-sen (1866–1925), became the first president of the new Republic of China. The number of Protestant missionaries increased rapidly, reaching 8,000 in 1925, and the number of Protestant converts reached a half million by then as well. In North America, the Student Volunteer Movement directed a stream of idealistic college graduates to Protestant work in China, where they staffed the rapidly expanding network of YMCAs and YWCAs (see YMCA/YWCA) and taught in the growing number of Christian colleges strategically placed in major cities. There were 13 such colleges, most of them union efforts of several Protestant denominations, with 3,500 students in 1925. They crowned a Protestant educational system, which by the mid-1920s had 250,000 students. During these decades, the Protestant school system and other church-related institutions remained the foremost area in Chinese society where Chinese girls and women could receive a modern education, including college-level work, and also develop their own careers (in, e.g., teaching, medicine, and social work) and personal autonomy. Protestantism seemed for a time both modern and progressive. Just before World War I, JOHN MOTT and Sherwood Eddy made remarkably successful evangelistic tours of China, speaking to packed houses of mainly young urban middle-class Chinese, many of whom responded favorably.

The worlds of both the missionaries and Chinese Protestants were changing early in the twentieth century. The impressive increase in foreign missionaries came largely from the proliferation of new, small, often nondenominational faith missions and many independents who differed from the established missionary pattern. Theologically, many of these were at the fringes of the traditional evangelical consensus that had characterized Protestants until the early 1900s. SEVENTH DAY ADVENTISTS, Holiness groups (see HOLINESS MOVEMENT), and Pentecostals all stretched the Protestant spectrum, and fast-growing established conservative missions, such as the CHRISTIAN AND MISSIONARY ALLIANCE and of course the CIM, weighted that spectrum much more toward the conservative/fundamentalist pole. Seemingly inevitably, in retrospect, the Chinese Protestant missionary community was sorely riven in the 1920s by the acrimonious fundamentalist–modernist controversy; indeed, protest against the perception of "MODERNISM" on the China mission field was one of the opening salvos of the great controversy.

These two decades were of crucial importance for the Chinese Protestant community, as it developed its own leaders and began to mark out its priorities more independently of (yet for the most part in continued cooperation with) foreign missionaries. The term "Sino–foreign Protestant establishment" is meant to convey this much more visible collaboration between missions and Chinese Protestant leaders. Its socioeconomic foundation was in the continued development of well-educated and moderately prosperous Chinese Protestant communities in several coastal cities. In Fuzhou on the southeast coast, for example, Chinese Protestant leaders not only emerged more as partners and less as subordinates of foreign missionaries in church affairs, but also responded to the national issues of the day by becoming active in politics and social reform issues quite independently of the church.

The new Sino–foreign partnership seemed apparent in the big 1922 National Christian Conference, the first since the Centennial Conference of 1907, which had had such a paltry representation of Chinese. In contrast, the 1922 conference had a majority of Chinese members, as did its institutional follow-up, the National Christian Council, which was formed in 1924 as an ecumenical coordinating body among Protestants. These representatives, and the ordained and lay Chinese leaders of many of the individual denominations, constituted a new generation of Chinese Protestant leaders. These leaders included pastors and theologians like Cheng Jingyi (1881–1939) and Zhao Zichen (1888–1979), professors at Christian colleges such as Liu Tingfang (1890–1947), respected YMCA leaders such as Yu Rizhang (David Yui, 1882–1936), and Protestant doctors, lawyers, and businessmen. They were highly respected and were in many ways almost equal partners with the foreign missionaries. The latter, however, tended to retain practical control, mainly through their continuing control of the finances necessary for the large institutional operations of the Protestant world in China. In retrospect, this period from the early 1900s to the mid-1920s was a missed opportunity for foreign missions to devolve real power to their Chinese colleagues within the established Protestant structures.

An unprecedented new development in these years, one that pointed to important trends for the rest of the century, was the emergence of several Chinese Christian movements that were wholly independent of foreign missions. One of these movements was the formation after 1910 of two federations of economically self-sufficient former missionary-led denominational congregations, many of them Presbyterian, in the Shanghai and Beijing areas. Others were products of the radical sectarian currents new to the twentieth century, with talented and dynamic Chinese evangelists as leaders. These included the True Jesus Church and the Jesus Family, both shaped by PENTECOSTALISM as well as by native Chinese elements, and the "Little Flock" of WATCHMAN NEE (Ni Tuosheng, 1903–1972), with Brethren (see BRETHREN, CHURCH OF THE) and Holiness inputs. These movements were all still quite small in the 1920s.

The Multiple Crises of Chinese Protestantism, 1925–1950

If the first quarter of the twentieth century was basically an optimistic time for Protestantism in China, the second quarter was a time of trauma and uncertainty. As powerful new nationalistic political forces began to target Christianity as part of the imperialist presence in China that needed to be demolished, a beleaguered mood settled on Protestants, one which in many ways was not lifted until the late 1970s.

This reversal occurred with striking rapidity. After the patriotic May Fourth Movement of 1919, and the ensuing rise of the Guomindang (Nationalist) Party and the Chinese Communist Party, by the mid-1920s Christianity was on the defensive. The continuing foreign missionary domination of many aspects of the Protestant movement made it hard for Chinese participants in the Sino–foreign Protestant establishment to rebut the charge of cultural imperialism brought against Christianity. Indeed, it put Chinese Protestant leaders in an untenable position, caught between loyalty to their foreign colleagues and their own patriotic instincts. Much of the self-confidence of the missionaries was eroded by the violence of the nationalistic forces in the civil warfare of 1926–1927, when almost all of the foreign missionaries fled interior China to the coast, or left China altogether. Never again would foreign missionary numbers ever approach the level of the mid-1920s. This did result in greater responsibility for Chinese Christians to take over local work, but it put the Sino–foreign sector of Protestantism even more on the defensive.

By the early 1930s, most missionaries had returned to their posts; the most virulently anti-Christian political element, the Communists, had been suppressed;

and Chiang Kai-shek, paramount leader of the Guo-mindang and of the new Nationalist government at Nanjing, had married into a prominent Chinese Protestant family (the Sung family) and had been baptized. But these positive trends were swamped by the double blow of the decimation of China mission budgets by the Great Depression and the issuance in 1933 of the *Laymen's Report on Foreign Missions* under William Ernest Hocking, which, by questioning many of the traditional assumptions of the whole foreign missions enterprise, further sapped the morale of many missionaries. To add further liabilities to the Protestant movement, civil war between Nationalists and Communists resumed in the early 1930s, and then rising tension between China and JAPAN overrode that civil conflict with full-scale war as Japan launched its devastating invasion of China in 1937, plunging China into eight years of desperate warfare that ended only with the conclusion of the Pacific War in 1945. The Chinese pillars of the denominational and Sino–foreign Protestant sectors tended to be liberal and pacifist in their stance, and, although quite patriotic, they were not in the forefront of any national political movement, including the movement to fight back against Japan, in the 1930s and wartime years.

Thus Protestants in effect retreated yet further from leadership on the central national issues that China seemed to be facing after the 1920s. Communists had the social revolution issue, the Nationalists had (until 1945) the card of patriotic resistance to Japan, and Chinese Protestants were figuratively out in the cold, with their ally, the foreign missionary establishment, both materially weakened and a political liability in the sense that a continuing large foreign role in the Chinese church was offensive to Chinese nationalism. This was true despite the fact that many foreign missionaries stood bravely with the Chinese people in the first stages of the war with Japan from 1937 to 1941, and some continued to make great sacrifices to serve in unoccupied areas throughout the wartime years, whereas others were interned by the Japanese under harsh conditions in civilian concentration camps from 1942 to 1945. Despite the foreign contribution, however, the age of foreign leadership, or even partnership, was gone.

Of course, some Chinese Protestant groups did not have the liability of foreign connections. Thus, those Protestant movements whose beginnings were barely noted earlier in this article grew steadily in these decades of national turmoil. These movements now included not only the organized networks of congregations in the True Jesus Church, the Jesus Family, and the "Little Flock," but also followers of several dynamic independent evangelists. All of their leaders were theological conservatives and effective revival speakers; examples include Wang Mingdao (1900–1991) and Song Shangjie (John Sung, 1901–1944). These groups avoided the burden of foreign connections, and they likewise were not bedeviled by the issue of patriotism because they avoided it, stressing repentence, personal SALVATION, miracles, and a millenarian doomsday conviction in the imminent end of this world. They attracted tens of thousands who were beset by war, political turmoil, and impossible conditions of daily life.

The story of Protestantism in the wartime years, 1937–1945, is not well known. It awaits its chronicler. What we do know is that the partial exodus of foreign missionaries after the war began in 1937, and then the total elimination of missionaries of the Allied nations after December 1941 in those parts of China occupied by the Japanese, resulted in an extended period of Chinese Christians being in charge of their own affairs in the difficult circumstances of wartime. After Japan's defeat, foreign missionaries began to return to China in 1946, but there were far fewer of them than in the prewar era. As Protestant missions and denominational Chinese leaders grappled with the task of rehabilitating and rebuilding Christian institutions, China beginning in 1946 was engulfed in civil war between the Communists and Chiang Kai-shek's Nationalists. Although some Chinese Protestant leaders such as Wu Yaozong (Y. T. WU, 1893–1979) and Jiang Wenhan (1908–1984) were inclined favorably toward the radical social programs of the Communists, most Protestants with political opinions, including almost all missionaries, were pro-Nationalist. Many of the indigenous Pentecostal or sectarian evangelical groups avoided politics altogether and occupied themselves with the repentence and salvation of the lost. As the civil war ended in 1949 with a Communist victory, Protestants, amidst uncertainty, hoped for the best: that the new government would finally bring stability and basic social equity, and that perhaps national unity and peace might even facilitate Christian growth.

Protestants Controlled and Suppressed, 1950–1978

Chinese Protestantism in 1950 was very different from what it had been in 1900. It was much more diverse, with a whole range of independent churches and evangelical sects having joined the traditional denominational churches derived from the missionary movement. It was also much more under Chinese leadership and much more dependent on its own resources. It was still not very large, however, with about 800,000 or at most 1 million adherents, and its staying power was uncertain.

In the successes and failures of the previous half-century, one factor that had not influenced the course of the Protestant movement was the existence of a strong Chinese central government in control of all of society. No such government existed in those decades. Such a government—a thoroughly secular, avowed Marxist one with a pronounced antireligious bias—came into existence after 1950, of course, and heavily impacted the churches. The status of the remaining foreign missionaries, already precarious because of the Communist Party's perception of them as anti-Communist and as imperialists, was determined decisively by the Korean War in late 1950. In the anti-Western mood that then prevailed, they were all expelled, except for a handful jailed as spies. Likewise, the Korean War brought heightened suspicion of Chinese Protestants, many of whom naturally had close foreign connections. There were no moves to abolish religion or the churches; however, the impetus of the new state apparatus and the organizational network of Communist Party control created pressure to unify the Protestant movement and put it under state supervision. Humiliating orchestrated public mass denunciations of a few Chinese Protestant leaders were examples of the fate that awaited any who failed to cooperate with the new regime.

Between 1950 and 1954, a series of government-directed measures, implemented through a group of Protestant leaders trusted by the Party (foremost among whom was Y. T. Wu), created the structures officially defining the arena within which Protestantism would be permitted to exist. First, all Protestants were urged to sign the "Christian Manifesto," which denounced foreign imperialism and capitalism, and pledged loyalty to the new regime; about 400,000 did so. Then, all nonreligious Protestant institutions, such as schools and medical/social service facilities, were taken over by the state. Finally, parallel to what occurred with other religions, a more politically dependable Protestant organization, the Three-Self Patriotic Movement (TSPM; i.e., self-supporting, self-governing, self-propagating) was created for the purpose of interfacing between the political regime, in particular, the newly created state Religious Affairs Bureau (RAB), and all of the Protestant entities. The TSPM was "ratified" by delegates at the first National Christian Conference in 1954, at which the old National Christian Council and all of the individual denominational structures were abolished. It should be said that the abolition of old denominational distinctions was not a wholly unpopular policy. As early as 1927, the Church of Christ in China had been formed out of elements from the major mainline denominations, indicating a desire on the part of many Protestants to

erase foreign-derived denominational lines. This was accomplished in the 1950s by coercion, however.

During the remainder of the 1950s, the TSPM attempted to bring all of the disparate elements of the Protestant scene under its aegis, with partial success. Some stubbornly uncooperative evangelical leaders, such as Wang Mingdao, resisted and were jailed. Other strong-willed small Protestant groups withdrew to private religious life. Remaining public churches were drastically amalgamated and reduced in number, as were SEMINARIES, and most pastors and religious personnel were put into the work force. Sermons were politicized, and church attendance steadily declined. By the 1960s, very few churches were open, and the only remaining seminary was in Nanjing, under Bishop K. H. TING (Ding Guangxun, 1915–). With the Cultural Revolution in 1966, all Protestant churches, along with all other places of religious worship or activity, were closed, and they would remain closed to Chinese believers until 1979. It was during this long period that the resilience of Chinese Protestants and the extent to which the Christian faith had become rooted in their hearts and spirits was tested. The faith survived surprisingly well in the small groups or "house churches," where it was lodged during these years. Their decentralized pattern of local leadership served Protestants well in this situation, and actual growth occurred in some areas where the Cultural Revolution had paralyzed or destroyed the local authority structures that normally would have suppressed Christian activities.

Protestantism in Recent and Contemporary China

Protestantism returned to public visibility beginning in 1979, as part of the overall liberalization and regularization of many policy areas under the post-Mao national leadership group around Deng Xiaoping. Since then, it has achieved perhaps the most remarkable growth within the general pattern of resurgence of all religious groups and the establishment of several new ones in the past twenty years. In doing so, it has seemingly finally overcome the negative historical legacy of association with the Western presence in China and has become contextualized in Chinese society and culture.

In 1979 and 1980, the old TSPM structure was re-established to link Protestants to the RAB and the government as before, and it was complemented by a new organization, the China Christian Council (CCC), designed to deal with the internal religious affairs of the churches. Thus in many ways the system of the 1950s was rebuilt, with several of the same individuals from that era, including Bishop K. H. Ting, in the

TSPM/CCC leadership. This, and continued wariness toward the authorities on the part of the autonomous Protestant groups (house churches) that were already well established by 1980, has resulted in two different tracks of Protestantism today, both growing rapidly. There are more than 13,000 churches, tens of thousands of smaller "meeting points," more than twenty seminaries and Bible schools, and at least 15 million believers in the government-sanctioned TSPM sector, which enjoys a certain amount of security from harassment. There are many more gatherings in the autonomous non-TSPM sector, especially in the countryside, and probably more believers as well, even though Protestants in this sector can have no formal public institutions and are vulnerable to persecution. Thus a good estimate of total Protestants in 2001 is 30–35 million, although some foreign observers think the figure is much higher. Although in some localities the lines between the two sectors are blurry, in many others they are very distinct and even antagonistic. Clearly, the government's hope to be able to monitor all Protestant activity through the TSPM has not materialized, and it is uncertain how much longer the TSPM will retain its monopoly of officially representing the Protestant community.

Although the church is supposedly "post-denominational," there is an immense variety of currents on the Protestant scene today. Vestiges of the old Western denominations are visible in many urban churches, and pre-1950 Chinese churches, such as the True Jesus Church and the Little Flock, still command followings. In the countryside, quasi-Christian sects that have incorporated elements of folk religion exist alongside orthodox Protestant groups. Several ethnic minority groups have undergone widespread conversion to Christianity, and a certain number of Chinese academics and intellectuals have been attracted to Protestant ideas of ETHICS and public morality, as well as (for some of them) to personal faith. All in all, although there is no organized public voice for Protestants, they constitute a dynamic force in society. Protestantism is malleable and adaptable, in localized forms appealing to many in the urban educated business-related classes as well as to the peasantry. Indeed, the size, resources, and virtually nationwide presence of the Protestant movement make it one of the most important nongovernmental entities in China today. It seems a permanent feature of the Chinese scene.

Protestantism in Greater China

There are active and firmly established Protestant movements in Hong Kong, Taiwan, and Singapore, and also in the minority Chinese communities of Ma-laysia, INDONESIA, the PHILIPPINES, and North America. In fact, Chinese churches exist anywhere that communities of "overseas Chinese" can be found. Protestant congregational associations have proven important as a focus of Chinese identity and social networks in places where Chinese are a minority. Many college-educated businesspeople, entrepreneurs, and professionals in these Chinese communities, including places with a majority of Chinese (e.g., Singapore), are evangelical Protestants or Pentecostals. Chinese Protestantism, both inside and outside of China, thus seems to be taking the pattern of wider worldwide trends, stressing both salvation and pragmatic results, manifesting sectarian diversity within a context of disintegrating old denominational affiliations, showing indigenous cultural traits, and adapting well to a market economy. Insofar as it is part of that newly emerged majority of Protestants in the non-Western world, Chinese Protestantism in the twenty-first century and beyond will probably best be analyzed as part of this new center of gravity outside Europe and North America, as well as a part of the legacy of Western missions.

See also Asian Theology; Evangelicalism; Evangelism; Fundamentalism; Millenarians and Millennialism; Missions; Missionary Organizations Bible Translation; Bible Colleges and Institutions Communism

References and Further Reading

Barnett, Suzanne Wilson, and John King Fairbank, eds. *Christianity in China: Early Protestant Missionary Writings.* Cambridge, MA: Harvard University Press, 1985.

Bays, Daniel H., ed. *Christianity in China, From the Eighteenth Century to the Present.* Palo Alto, CA: Stanford University Press, 1996.

Brown, G. Thompson. *Earthen Vessels and Transcendent Power: American Presbyterians in China, 1837–1952.* Maryknoll, NY: Orbis, 1997.

Dunch, Ryan. *Fuzhou Protestants and the Making of a Modern China, 1857–1927.* New Haven, CT: Yale University Press, 2001.

Hersey, John. *The Call: An American Missionary in China.* New York: Knopf, 1985.

Hunter, Alan, and Kim-Kwong Chan. *Protestantism in Contemporary China.* Cambridge: Cambridge University Press, 1993.

Whyte, Bob. *Unfinished Encounter: China and Christianity.* London: Collins, 1988.

Wickeri, Philip L. *Seeking the Common Ground: Protestant Christianity, the Three-Self Movement, and China's United Front.* Maryknoll, NY: Orbis, 1988.

DANIEL H. BAYS

CHINA INLAND MISSION

The China Inland Mission (CIM) was founded in 1865 by J. HUDSON TAYLOR (1832–1905). It rapidly became the largest of the Protestant missions in China, and was a prototype for later faith missions around the world. In the early twentieth century, the CIM became a multinational voluntary association. It continues today as one of the world's largest evangelical missions agencies under the name Overseas Missionary Fellowship (OMF).

The Early CIM

Born in Yorkshire, ENGLAND, Taylor was raised a Methodist, but as a young man he joined the BRETHREN Movement (see BRETHREN, CHURCH OF THE), which stressed lay leadership. He had an early fascination with CHINA and served a term as a missionary in southeast China from 1853 to 1860. Taylor was also married in China in 1858, to Maria Dyer (1837–1870), who had been born in Penang, Malaya, of London Missionary Society parents.

Taylor had to return to England in 1860 because of poor health, but he continued to plan for the evangelization of the vast interior of China beyond the coastal cities. His sense of urgency was acute, fuelled by a premillennialist focus on rapidly evangelizing the world. He also believed that the best missionary method was the mobilization of laymen and women from various Protestant denominations as workers. In 1865 he articulated his ideas in *China's Spiritual Need and Claims*, and also founded the CIM. The first group of twenty-two CIM missionaries, including Hudson and Maria Taylor, went to China in 1866. From the first they were unique on the China field. Not only were they laypersons, but also they were guaranteed no salary. Thus the faith mission model was laid down.

Maria Taylor died in 1870, after bearing eight children in twelve years of marriage (all four who survived childhood became CIM missionaries). In 1871 Hudson Taylor married Jenny Faulding (1843–1904), a member of the first CIM group of 1866, who bore him three more children and played an important role in the organization both in China and back in England, including editorial work on the CIM's magazine, *China's Millions*.

Expansion of the CIM

Besides the use of laypersons and the faith principle in finances, the CIM was also innovative in its extensive use of single WOMEN and in requiring its members to wear Chinese dress (while at the same time after the late 1870s insulating mission children from Chinese society at its own boarding school). In the 1880s, as the CIM expanded rapidly and extended its recruitment to North America and AUSTRALIA as well as to continental European evangelical groups, an impor-

tant strategic decision moved the administrative headquarters of the mission from London to China itself. The CIM was then operated for decades by its China Committee in Shanghai. The China Committee in turn was dominated by a strong leader; Taylor himself was general director of the CIM until 1901, when Dixon E. Hoste (1861–1946) succeeded him and served until the 1930s.

Hoste was one of the famed "Cambridge Seven" of 1885, emblematic of the extension of the recruiting attraction of the CIM beyond the British lower-middle class to higher levels of society. Much of the success in building an attractive public image for the CIM derived not only from Hudson Taylor's own charisma, but also from the organizational genius and extensive personal networking of Benjamin Broomhall (1829–1911), who directed CIM operations in London. Broomhall married Amelia Taylor, Hudson's sister, in 1859; of their ten children, five became CIM missionaries. He became general secretary of the CIM in 1878 and served until 1895. He also edited *China's Millions* and overall did much to make the CIM a respected and leading component of the British evangelical establishment. Broomhall's son Marshall (1866–1937) in turn edited *China's Millions,* and directed the very effective CIM editorial and publishing efforts for most of the first four decades of the twentieth century.

The Twentieth Century

At the time of Taylor's death in 1905, the CIM was by far the largest Protestant mission in China, with 825 missionaries in more than 300 mission stations. Meanwhile, from the 1880s onward, the CIM exploded in growth in CANADA and the UNITED STATES. In 1889 Taylor appointed Henry W. Frost (1858–1945) as secretary-general (later home director) of the CIM for North America. Frost established a branch council in Toronto on equal footing with the London council, and in 1901 he moved the North American headquarters to Philadelphia. Frost built a sophisticated support network all through Canada and the United States and in effect engineered much of the internationalization of the CIM during the first three decades of the twentieth century. By the 1930s, North America provided one-third of the CIM missionary force of well over 1,000, as well as one-half of the total budget.

Despite its large size, however, the CIM had only a thin institutional apparatus. It had no colleges and only a few middle schools for Chinese, and only a small number of hospitals and clinics. It remained true to its primary calling of EVANGELISM. Accordingly, it attracted the great majority of its members from among conservative evangelicals and fundamentalists (see EVANGELICALISM, FUNDAMENTALISM). Thus many

CIM missionaries were suspicious of social reform as a substitute for the Gospel, though some distinguished themselves in local humanitarian endeavors when faced with crises of famine or war.

The CIM still had several hundred missionaries in China in the late 1940s, despite the upheavals of the Pacific War after 1937 and the Chinese Civil War after 1945. But after the new Communist government was established in 1949, CIM missionaries, like others, were forced to leave China, and all were gone by 1953 (see COMMUNISM). In the early 1950s, the CIM adapted quickly and became the OMF, sending both its China veterans and new recruits to several other Asian countries. Today the OMF remains a leading international evangelical missions enterprise, organized in national offices in more than ten countries around the world.

See also Millenarians and Millennialists; Publishing, Media

References and Further Reading

Austin, Alvyn J. "Blessed Adversity: Henry W. Frost and the China Inland Mission." In *Earthen Vessels: American Evangelicals and Foreign Missions, 1880–1980*, edited by Joel A. Carpenter and Wilbert R. Shenk. Grand Rapids, MI: Eerdmans, 1990. 47–70.
—— "Pilgrims and Strangers: The China Inland Mission in Britain, Canada, the United States and China, 1865–1900." Ph.D. dissertation, York University, 1996.
Broomhall, A. J. *Hudson Taylor and China's Open Century*. 7 vols. Sevenoaks, UK: Hodder and Stoughton, 1981–1989.
Taylor, Howard, and Mary Geraldine Taylor. *Hudson Taylor and the China Inland Mission: The Growth of a Work of God*. London: Morgan & Scott, 1919.

DANIEL H. BAYS

CHRISTADELPHIANS

The Christadelphians emerged in the mid-nineteenth century from the wing of the Restorationist movement associated with Alexander Campbell (see RESTORATIONISM). John Thomas (1782–1871), an English physician, immigrated to the UNITED STATES in 1832 and quickly became associated with Campbellite Adventism, serving for a time as editor of Campbell's early paper, the *Apostolic Advocate*. Moving to Richmond, Virginia, in 1835, Thomas broke from Campbell two years later because Thomas argued that persons who were members of another Christian body before accepting Restorationist belief needed to be rebaptized. Thomas began to preach his own Adventist message to a small group of followers, and in 1846 he relocated to the New York City area, then a center of Adventist expectation. Except for several preaching tours among American followers and some lengthy stays in Britain, where he successfully planted his version of the Adventist gospel, Thomas remained based in the New York area until his death.

Basic to Christadelphian belief is a lively expectation that the Second Coming of Christ is imminent. Hence, Christadelphians evidence a keen interest in biblical prophecy and a conviction that current events, correctly interpreted, correlate with biblical prophecy to signal the nearness of the end. Christadelphians thus place great emphasis on having correct knowledge of biblical prophecy, simply called "the Truth," and baptize by immersion in running water only mature persons who testify to their knowledge of this Truth (see BAPTISM).

Because much of biblical apocalyptic prophecy is grounded in the Hebrew scriptures, and because they believe that those who possess biblical truth are adopted into Israel, Christadelphians identify strongly with the nation of Israel and the Jewish tradition (see JUDAISM; PHILO-SEMITISM), looking especially to events in the Middle East for clues indicating Christ's impending return. At the same time, Christadelphians link Roman Catholicism with the false teaching of the ANTICHRIST (see CATHOLICISM, PROTESTANT REACTIONS).

Despite reading the import of current events as indicators of Christ's imminent return, Christadelphians have remained aloof from engagement in public affairs. Refusal to bear arms has long marked Christadelphian teaching; John Thomas actually adopted the name Christadelphian ("brothers of Christ") at the time of the U.S. CIVIL WAR to secure exemption from military service for his followers. Most Christadelphians do not vote, although they acknowledge the legitimacy of civil authority.

The Christadelphians have defied the expected pattern of gradually developing denominational structures, remaining more of a stable sect. There are no CLERGY or headquarters. Local fellowships that own their own buildings refer to them by the Greek term "ecclesia" rather than "church," to signal a rejection of institutionalization. Like some other Restorationist groups, the Christadelphians have nurtured bonds among believers through an array of periodicals, locally sponsored BIBLE conferences, and weekend gatherings where men regarded as adept at communicating biblical teaching lecture to those attending. Such occasions also offer opportunities for the faithful to reinforce a common identity and to meet potential spouses. Women do not lecture at such gatherings, because Christadelphians insist that the New Testament mandates the subordinate status of women. Baptized Christadelphians are strongly encouraged to marry fellow believers.

In their sense of continuity with the Jewish tradition, keen APOCALYPTICISM, eschewing of clergy and formal structures, and desire to remain separate from a corrupt society, Christadelphians believe that they have captured the essence of New Testament Christianity of the apostolic era and replicated it in their own belief and practice.

Never attracting large numbers of Americans, Thomas had somewhat greater success gaining a following in his native ENGLAND, where the area around Birmingham has been the center of Christadelphian activity. Robert Roberts (1839–1898), an early convert to the Christadelphian message, became the unofficial leader of the movement there and also served as editor of the *Christadelphian*, a periodical that remains vital to the movement in Britain. In turn, Roberts also visited believers in the United States after Thomas's death. Roberts himself died in San Francisco while on a preaching tour of AUSTRALIA, NEW ZEALAND, and then North America.

Concern for the purity of the truth, however, has led to dissension in the Christadelphian ranks, with the most serious rifts emerging while Roberts was still alive. Debates arose over the nature of the resurrection and last judgment that would come after Christ's return, what Christadelphians called "resurrectional responsibility." Whereas virtually all believed that persons who died simply remained "asleep" rather than entering some eternal state at death, some argued that only those baptized into the Christadelphian truth would be resurrected for judgment, with not all being found worthy of everlasting life. Others insisted that all would be resurrected for judgment. So divisive were these debates that many local ecclesias refused to remain in fellowship with those whose perspective was different; consequently two historic statements of faith developed to reflect the differences. Over the years, additional differences have caused some ecclesias to sever fellowship with others, but none has caused as much ongoing controversy and sparked so many fruitless efforts at reunion as the debate over resurrectional responsibility.

Most American Christadelphians adhere to what is called the "Unamended Statement of Faith," which insists that only believers will be resurrected for judgment. Most British Christadelphians—and those in other English-speaking areas like Australia—accept an Amended Statement of Faith that proclaims that all humanity will face final judgment after a general resurrection.

In North America, ties among Christadelphians adhering to the Unamended Statement of Faith were cemented by Thomas Williams (1847–1913), a Welsh immigrant who traveled widely among the various local communities as an itinerant teacher and preacher (see ITINERANCY), wrote several treatises explaining Christadelphian belief and edited the *Christadelphian*

Advocate, the primary periodical serving the Unamended community.

The lack of formal structure to the Christadelphian movement makes an accurate count of members impossible. Estimates suggest that at the beginning of the twenty-first century, probably not more than 6,000 identified with either the Amended or Unamended fellowships in North America, whereas the number in Britain was likely about three times as large. A few international missions have planted small clusters of Christadelphians in other countries, but the numbers are very small. In addition, a handful of other Adventist-oriented groups reflect the influence of Christadelphian teaching; among these are the Church of God of the Abrahamic Faith and the Megiddo Mission Church.

See also Campbell Family; Eschatology

References and Further Reading

Lippy, Charles H. *The Christadelphians in North America.* Lewiston, NY: Edwin Mellen, 1989.
Roberts, Robert. *Dr. Thomas: His Life and Work.* 3rd ed. Revised by C. C. Walker and W. H. Boulton. Birmingham, UK: The Christadelphian, 1954.
Thomas, John. *The Faith in the Last Days.* Edited by John Carter. Birmingham, UK: The Christadelphian, 1965.
Wilson, Bryan R. *Sects and Society.* Berkeley and Los Angeles: University of California Press, 1961.
——. *Religious Sects: A Sociological Study.* New York: McGraw Hill, 1970.

C. H. LIPPY

CHRISTIAN AND MISSIONARY ALLIANCE

The Christian and Missionary Alliance (C&MA) is a North American–based evangelical denomination, one of the few turn-of-the-century Holiness groups that did not follow Wesleyan thought. Initially two late-nineteenth-century parachurch organizations that merged in 1897 to create a DENOMINATION emphasizing personal SANCTIFICATION and world EVANGELISM, the Christian and Missionary Alliance reflected a number of intellectual streams within the larger evangelical movement. This "evangelical ecumenism" was largely the result of its founder, Albert Benjamin Simpson (1843–1919), a Presbyterian minister who was deeply affected by KESWICK MOVEMENT doctrines of holiness that accompanied his beliefs in divine healing, Christocentric THEOLOGY, premillennialism, and global evangelism.

This ability to synthesize different aspects of evangelical Christianity and cooperate with disparate groups made the Christian and Missionary Alliance far more influential in twentieth-century EVANGELICALISM than its numbers might indicate. Although hardly a major player on the American scene, with under 200,000 members and 400,000 total adherents in 2001, the missionary spirit it has maintained has produced nearly ten times that many members globally. Working with a variety of denominations and para-church groups, the Christian and Missionary Alliance has established a reputation for commitment to its influential "fourfold gospel" (Christ as savior, sanctifier, healer, and coming king) and dedication to the task of world evangelism.

The spiritual journey and personality of A. B. Simpson shaped the denomination's beliefs, practices, and organization. The product of a strict Presbyterian upbringing on Prince Edward Island, CANADA, Simpson prepared for the ministry at Knox College in Toronto. Renowned for his oratory, he landed the prestigious pulpit at Knox Church in Hamilton, Ontario immediately after graduation. During his eight years there the membership rolls doubled. In 1874 he took the challenging pulpit at the Chestnut Street Presbyterian Church in Louisville, Kentucky, whose divided congregation had undergone lawsuits for control of the church soon after the American CIVIL WAR. Simpson's liberal spirit helped heal many of the wounds left by the conflict. Despite five flourishing years there, Simpson felt called to a greater ministry, one that corresponded to what had been happening within.

Over the preceding decade Simpson had developed a growing interest in and dedication to many of the principles of the Evangelical Alliance, an English organization that sought to create a worldwide fellowship of evangelicals for cooperation. Having participated in the revivalist campaign of D. W. Whittle and PHILIP BLISS in Louisville (see REVIVALS), he saw firsthand how conversions could be affected through cooperative efforts at evangelism. Moreover Simpson had been influenced by the Reformed wing of the HOLINESS MOVEMENT, particularly its emphasis on the "deeper life" or the "higher life," as compared to the more Wesleyan ideas of perfect sanctification. Simpson sought a place of ministry where he could live out these two inner drives—evangelism and a deeper spiritual life—and found it in New York City.

As the pastor of the prestigious Thirteenth Street Church, Simpson had the attention and support of New York City's elite Presbyterians. He launched an illustrated missionary periodical, *The Gospel in All Lands,* soon after his arrival in 1880, editing the publication and writing all the major articles. He also began holding meetings for the unchurched in less-desirable areas of the city. On top of that he continued the strenuous pace of his duties to his parishioners. After only one year in New York, his health collapsed. Various treatments and sabbaticals from work failed

to strengthen his weak heart, and soon he suffered from deep depression.

Simpson found relief in the message of Charles Cullis, a Boston physician who preached that the BIBLE promised physical healing to believers. Hearing Cullis at the convention grounds at Old Orchard Beach, Maine, Simpson studied the issue for himself and concluded that Cullis was correct. Tied to the idea of healing, in Simpson's mind, was the promise of a deeper Christian life that came with the empowering of the Holy Spirit, virtually a second (although ongoing) religious experience available to Christians after their initial CONVERSION experience. Simpson claimed the newfound truth for himself and set off again on his busy schedule, only now convinced that the Holy Spirit empowered him not only for great preaching but also for physical exertion far beyond what doctors suggested.

This strand of the Holiness Movement differed from Wesleyan notions and came to characterize the Christian and Missionary Alliance, the organization that grew from Simpson's activities over the next four decades. Rather than teaching a sanctification distinguished by the eradication of SIN, the Keswick Movement—the Reformed, non-Arminian brand of Holiness—taught the suppression of sinful desires and the empowerment for service that came from the indwelling of the Holy Spirit (see ARMINIANISM). Although Simpson cooperated generously with those of the Wesleyan persuasion, and even welcomed speaking in TONGUES in Christian and Missionary Alliance congregations when it occurred in the early-twentieth century, he remained committed to the "deeper life" wing of the larger Holiness Movement.

Feeling called and empowered by God to renew his efforts in New York, Simpson sensed his support slipping within the well-heeled congregation. His new emphasis on healing brought derision from the press, and his attempts to move beyond pew rents so outsiders might be brought into the church occasioned ill-feelings among influential congregants. A crisis of conscience over the issue of infant BAPTISM, which concluded in Simpson's immersion baptism in an Italian Baptist church, proved to be the last straw. Clearly open to sanctions by the presbytery, Simpson chose to resign the prominent pulpit to begin a new work. His final sermon there in 1881 was based on Luke 4:18: "The Spirit of the Lord is upon me because he has anointed me to preach the gospel to the poor."

He started the Gospel Tabernacle, which he hoped would replicate the London churches of Newman Hall and CHARLES SPURGEON, "comprising thousands of members of no particular class, but of the rich and poor side by side." Holding meetings every night and three on Sunday, Simpson and his band of workers built a dedicated congregation that kept moving to ever larger facilities. Armed with a constitution of only eight articles and five hundred words, the congregation purposefully eschewed doctrinal debates for the simple gospel of SALVATION they felt nonchurchgoers most needed.

The following decade saw an impressive array of activities as Simpson aligned himself with those who appreciated his "radical and aggressive measures." In 1882 he started the Missionary Training Institute (now Nyack College) to prepare people for overseas evangelism. He started a new missionary magazine, *The Work, The Word, and the World* (later *The Alliance Witness,* now *The Alliance Life*), having sold the previous one. He created a "healing house" ministry called Berachah (Hebrew for "blessing"), where those in need of physical or spiritual healing could come for counseling during extended stays. The congregation created its own Missionary Union for the Evangelization of the World, which effectively combined into one concern the education, publication, and healing emphases of Simpson. The Union supported missionaries trained at the Tabernacle's Institute as well as other faith missionaries who sought their support.

All of Simpson's far-flung efforts came to a head in 1887, when directing a deeper life and missionary convention at the Old Orchard Beach campgrounds. Having made so many strides outside the usual strictures of denominational polity, Simpson and his closest colleagues determined to create two parachurch organizations that could more effectively push American Christians of all denominational stripes toward a deeper Christian life and greater interest in global evangelism. There they constituted both the Christian Alliance (which emphasized holiness and evangelism, much like the English Evangelical Alliance) and the International Missionary Alliance (which emphasized greater understanding and support for missionary activity). Both of these organizations encouraged believers to remain in their own congregations, but to attend the respective Alliance branches to learn more about the deeper Christian life or world missions and then carry those messages back to their home churches.

By 1897 it was apparent that the two organizations needed to merge. Virtually the same individuals sat on both boards and both were presided over by Simpson. The newly constituted "Christian and Missionary Alliance" did not roll off the tongue easily, but it did reflect the cooperative efforts of many toward a higher Christian life and world evangelism. Its purpose remained to educate and inspire Christians in North America in matters of spirituality and missions through a system of "branches" in urban centers of population—some 300 by 1897—to help support over 200 missionaries in a dozen countries.

Disagreements with the fledgling Pentecostal movement in the early twentieth century moved the Christian and Missionary Alliance toward a denominational structure. Because of Simpson's emphasis on the indwelling presence of the Holy Spirit, many seeking sanctification trained in his Missionary Training Institute. When glossolalia (tongues speaking) came to characterize this second experience for many, Simpson and many of his colleagues were open to the possibility. Many leaders of Alliance branches throughout the country spoke in tongues and taught, alongside other Pentecostal founders, that the experience was the sign of the baptism of the Holy Spirit. Simpson, unable to experience the gift despite years of seeking it through PRAYER, concluded that, although glossolalia was of God in many instances, it did not constitute the sign Pentecostals claimed. Rather Simpson emphasized selections in the Pauline epistles that enumerate many "gifts of the Spirit," tongues being but one of them.

This rift between Simpson and the New York leadership and many of the branches throughout the country resulted in the loss of many Alliance branches, many of which became leading Pentecostal congregations. Consequences of this episode were significant for both sides. Pentecostals borrowed many of the Christian and Missionary Alliance's ideas and means, including the fourfold gospel, the three-year Bible institute as the primary tool for education, many of Simpson's hymns, and the use of the title "Gospel Tabernacle" for local congregations. The Christian and Missionary Alliance, on the other hand, sought protection from further loss of branches by reorganizing itself beginning in 1912 to place more AUTHORITY in the annual Councils. By 1930 most local branches of the Christian and Missionary Alliance operated like churches—with pastors, boards, and bylaws—but they still rejected the term.

Not until 1974 did the Christian and Missionary Alliance officially vote itself as a Protestant DENOMINATION, after years of discussion between the home and foreign departments of the organization, each of which had operated rather freely until that time. This was preceded by an attempt to write an official statement of faith. Having for eighty years eschewed doctrinal debates that might divide Christians' attention from the purpose of world evangelism, this was no easy task. They studied a Christian and Missionary Alliance 1928 doctrinal statement written at the height of the fundamentalist–modernist battles, but this document merely attached the fourfold gospel to the nine articles of the Christian Fundamentals Association. The 1965 statement, however, attempted to go beyond that by affirming beliefs long held by the organization. The product, hammered out by leaders and LAITY, adheres closely to the historic fundamentalist doctrines (divinity of Jesus, virgin birth, ATONEMENT through Christ's death, inerrancy of scriptures) as well as Christian and Missionary Alliance distinctives, including sanctification as "both a crisis and progressive experience" marked by the indwelling Holy Spirit "for holy living and effective service," "the healing of the mortal body . . . in this present age," the Great Commission of the Church to "preach the gospel to all nations," and the "imminent, . . . personal, visible, and premillennial" return of Christ.

Trendsetters in the area of world missions among evangelicals, the Christian and Missionary Alliance has held tightly since its founding to the "indigenous church" ideal. In 1927 the annual Council adopted a policy of self-support, self-government, and self-propagation. The expectation was that Christian and Missionary Alliance missionaries would enter a country to build the initial foundation for a self-sustaining national church. At times this caused difficulties for missionaries who believed they needed to keep tighter control on the developing churches; but tough sanctions against missionaries, beginning in the mid-1950s, kept the Christian and Missionary Alliance from the charge of COLONIALISM that other evangelical missions have suffered. The goal is always to found a series of churches and schools to train pastors so that, in time, the local converts would control their own national church. The Alliance World Fellowship, created in 1975, meets every four years to renew and sustain the bonds among the various national churches around the globe—with the UNITED STATES and Canada as but two of many.

By the beginning of the twenty-first century the Christian and Missionary Alliance was enjoying two decades of record growth. During the 1990s missionaries and national workers in AFRICA reported over 400,000 conversions. Christian and Missionary Alliance national churches could be found in seventy-five countries, fifty-two of which employed nearly 1,100 North American missionaries in hospitals, seminaries, and church-planting ministries. However, most of the work being done was by the nearly 20,000 national workers (5,000 ordained), clearly marking the success of the "indigenous church" movement the Alliance propounded. Missionaries and national workers worldwide cooperated in numerous ventures of evangelization and Christian education, including 365 weekly radio broadcasts in forty languages and dialects, and 110 full-term theological schools with nearly 10,000 students. In 2001 the Christian and Missionary Alliance reported 2.73 million inclusive members worldwide. Proof of the Christian and Missionary Alliance's commitment to MISSIONS, the denomination's membership in the United States virtually tied for third worldwide: both Vietnam (540,000 bap-

tized members) and Côte d'Ivoire (256,500 baptized members) surpassed the United States (191,318), with INDONESIA (188,072 baptized members) set to overtake the States.

That is not to say that the Christian and Missionary Alliance has seen slow growth in North America. Cutting against the grain of other historic Holiness denominations in the late twentieth century, which have seen precipitous declines in membership, the Alliance has continued nearly to double each decade since 1980. Some observers believe that this growth has not come without a price. Clearly today's congregations, dominated by those new to the movement, are less familiar with the traditional beliefs and practices of the denomination. In many respects, local congregations appear no different from those of other evangelical denominations. Whether the Alliance's distinctive Christocentric theology and emphases on personal sanctification, divine healing, and worldwide evangelism will be the casualty of such growth remains to be seen.

Clearly, though, one reason for the denomination's recent success in North America is its familiarity with global cultures, many of which have made their way to the United States and Canada in recent decades. By concentrating on immigrant populations, even to the degree that national districts dedicated to ethnic groups were created to sit alongside the traditional regional districts, the denomination put to use its international experience at home in the United States. New districts include: Cambodian; Haitian North and South; Hmong; Korean; Laotian; Native American; Spanish Central, Eastern, and Western; and, of course, Vietnamese. Together these churches constituted more than one-fifth of the U.S. congregations by 2001.

The Christian and Missionary Alliance in the United States is served by its four historic colleges: Nyack College (New York), Toccoa Falls College (Georgia), Crown College (Minnesota), and Simpson College (California), with graduate programs at the New York, Minnesota, and California campuses (see HIGHER EDUCATION). The Alliance Theological Seminary is also in Nyack, New York, which was the Alliance's headquarters for nearly 100 years (see SEMINARIES). The Christian and Missionary Alliance is presently headquartered in Colorado Springs, Colorado. The autonomous Canadian Christian and Missionary Alliance is centered in Toronto and is served by Canadian Bible College and Canadian Theological Seminary in Regina.

See also Bible Colleges and Institutes; Faith Healing; Fundamentalism; Pentecostalism; Tongues, Speaking in; Biblical Inerrancy

References and Further Reading

Niklaus, Robert L., John S. Sawin, and Samuel J. Stoesz. *All For Jesus: God at Work in The Christian and Missionary Alliance Over One Hundred Years.* Camp Hill, PA: Christian Publications, Inc., 1986.

Pardington, George P. *Twenty-five Wonderful Years.* New York: Christian Alliance Publishing Co., 1914.

Thompson, A. E. *The Life of A. B. Simpson.* New York: The Christian Alliance Publishing Co., 1920.

Tozer, A. W. *Wingspread.* Harrisburg, PA: Christian Publishing, Inc. 1943.

PHILIP GOFF

CHRISTIAN CHURCH (DISCIPLES OF CHRIST)

See Disciples of Christ

CHRISTIAN CHURCHES, CHURCHES OF CHRIST

Rooted historically in the Stone-Campbell reformation movement on the trans-Appalachian frontier in nineteenth-century America, the Christian Churches (Churches of Christ) gradually emerged as a distinctive body of congregations protesting the perceived liberal drift of the mainline DISCIPLES OF CHRIST in the early and mid-twentieth century. That separation was consummated amid the restructure of the Christian Church (Disciples of Christ) in the 1960s and 1970s. Christian Churches (Churches of Christ) committed, by and large, to the pursuit of Christian unity through restoration of the "ordinances" of apostolic Christianity enshrined in the New Testament (baptism of believers by immersion; weekly observance of the Lord's Supper; congregational polity; etc.), though there has arisen significant diversity among the churches over the interpretation and applicability of the restoration agenda. The churches remain networked by support of international missionary and educational endeavors, and participation in a national (non-delegate) convention, but not by any permanent denominational infrastructure.

Overview

The reform movements of Barton Stone and Thomas and Alexander Campbell on the trans-Appalachian frontier merged in 1832, and the conglomerate Disciples of Christ rapidly expanded through the middle and latter decades of the nineteenth century, principally in North America, Britain, Australia, and New Zealand. Subsequent division among the Disciples resulted from divergent appropriations of the first-generation Stone-Campbell appeal for Christian unity, conservatives embracing a strict restoration of the ancient apostolic order, and liberals embracing a more ecumenical and accommodationist agenda. Long-standing hermeneutical and organizational differences induced the departure of the (acappella) Churches of Christ, a division that was virtually effective long before its formal recognition in the 1906 religious census. The second major division within the Disciples of Christ, with the emergence of the so-called independent Christian Churches (some of which have opted for the title Churches of Christ), was a long process of ideological alienation and institutional realignment beginning in the 1920s and consummated by the denominational restructure of the Christian Church (Disciples of Christ) in the late 1960s.

Historical Perspective

Early on, a cluster of interrelated ecclesiological issues helped consolidate the conservative resistance that birthed the Christian Churches (Churches of Christ). Posturing toward the Ecumenical Movement was an early test. When certain Disciples progressives began actively participating in church federation endeavors as early as 1902, conservative leadership disputed the compatibility of cooperative or "federal" unity with restorationist principles. After the Federal Council of Churches was established in 1908, a gradually increasing number of Disciples congregations began practicing open membership, admitting persons who had been sprinkled as infants but not immersed as conscientious believers—clearly an overture toward mutual denominational recognition. Once the practice achieved approval of the Disciples's premier agency, the United Christian Missionary Society, as well as their international convention, reaction was swift from conservatives insistent that believers' immersion had been a nonnegotiable principle of apostolic Christianity and, for the founders of the Stone-Campbell movement, an indispensable rallying point for Christian unity. Institutional reconfiguration and consolidation of the Disciples, mainly the merger of six separate agencies to form the United Christian Missionary Society (est. 1919), further sparked the fears of conservatives that too much power was being concentrated in the hands of denominational executives of questionable loyalty to restoration principles, and that such a massive agency would enforce its theological positions and missiological policies in a way that violated the free networking of individual local congregations. The transformation of the Disciples' General Convention into a delegate convention in 1914 had likewise provoked conservative suspicions of an increasing politicization and denominationalization of the Disciples of Christ.

Ideologically, conservatives decried the perceived modernist drift of the Disciples of Christ as manifested in the emergence of the Disciples Divinity House (est. 1894) at the University of Chicago, the liberal tilt of new journals like *The Christian Century,* and the commitment to biblical higher criticism in Disciples academic institutions such as the College of the Bible in Kentucky (now Lexington Theological Seminary). Yet it would be an oversimplification to identify the conservative dissent within the Disciples of Christ in this period purely as a "Fundamentalist" reaction. To be sure, there is evidence in the 1920s that various conservative Disciples leaders and journals, when faced with modernist enthusiasm for the monumental paradigm shift in the natural sciences and in biblical studies, sympathized with the Fundamentalist defense of biblical inerrancy and creationism. Numerous spokesmen defended the Virgin Birth, divinity of Christ, and verbal inspiration of the Scriptures as "restoration" principles. But Disciples conservatives at this time were theologically insulated from the Reformed theological tradition underlying FUNDAMENTALISM, and, even among themselves, admitted some significant diversity of perspective. For example, Frederick Kershner (1875–1953), for many years the dean of the Butler University School of Religion in Indianapolis and a key moderate conservative, repudiated the doctrine of plenary verbal inspiration of Scripture (as had American cleric Alexander Campbell [1788–1866]), and articulated an ecclesiology upholding the sacramental character of the church and repudiating "mechanical" restorationism as a means to Christian unity. Another moderate, Edwin Errett, editor of the conservative journal the *Christian Standard* from 1929 to 1944, opposed compromises of the restoration ideal of unity, yet, like Kershner, remained open to ecumenical involvements and even participated actively in the early Faith and Order Movement.

Institutional Realignment

The more strident conservatives, however, were largely responsible for the institutional realignment that paved the way for a separate body of independent Christian Churches. Two crucial activists were James DeForest Murch (1892–1973), first president of the Christian Restoration Association (est. 1925), and Robert Elmore (1878–1968), long-time editor of its journal *The Restoration Herald.* The Christian Restoration Association was both a conservative brain trust and a clearinghouse for mission agencies and other ministries operating independently of the United Christian Missionary Society. Elmore was the single most vocal critic of that society. Murch, meanwhile, became the architect of the free church ecclesiology,

devoted to congregational integrity and the prerogatives of local congregations to work in voluntary cooperation to sponsor direct support missions and educational initiatives, which largely shaped a sense of corporate identity among disaffected churches in the period leading to the denominational reorganization of the Disciples of Christ. Murch championed the view that authentic "New Testament Christianity" was historically carried on through a lineage of steadfast restoration movements that had survived the rise of Catholicism and centuries of ecclesiastical strife and persecution. Accordingly, faithful Disciples of Christ stood in that heritage. Murch fervently criticized mainline Protestant liberalism and encouraged conservative Disciples to find common cause with other evangelical bodies; he was himself a cofounder of the National Association of Evangelicals and one-time managing editor of *Christianity Today.*

Three other important developments in the institutional consolidation of independent Christian Churches stand out. One was the ever-increasing editorial reorientation of the *Christian Standard,* an influential journal originally founded in 1866 and published by the Standard Publishing Company in Cincinnati, as a mouthpiece of conservative Disciples causes. In 1919 the journal, obviously countering the inclinations of progressive Disciples publications like the *Christian-Evangelist* and *The Christian Century,* editorially committed itself to "The Rescue of the Restoration Movement," and by 1943 had conscientiously postured itself as an advocate for conservative churches opposing the leftward, denominationalizing drift of the Disciples of Christ. This policy would continue well into the 1950s. A second development was the burgeoning of conservative Bible colleges from the 1920s on. Though not the first of such schools, Cincinnati Bible Seminary, founded in 1924, led the way of restorationist fundamentalism and worked out a Bible-centered curriculum thoroughly resistant to modernist influences and biblical higher criticism. In subsequent decades, more than thirty such Bible colleges were founded in North America, some of which were financially burdened out of existence; these schools have been pivotal in the training of ministers and missionaries for the emerging independent Christian Churches (Churches of Christ). A third significant development was the organization of the North American Christian Convention in 1926 and 1927 by a committee of individuals frustrated by the policies of the Disciples's International Convention in concert with the United Christian Missionary Society. This new open (nondelegate) convention first met in Indianapolis in 1927, but only became a regular national assembly from 1950 on. Apologists for this convention argued that its purpose was principally to foster evangelism and promote fellowship among Disciples at a time of increasing institutional strife. Frederick Kershner, who had served as a president the Disciples's International Convention while still supporting the North American Christian Convention, insisted that the latter was not schismatic. Once the convention began gathering annually, however, Disciples critics viewed it as clear evidence of a developing separatist coalition.

Perhaps the last best hope for averting a second schism in the Disciples of Christ was the Commission on Restudy appointed by the Disciples's International Convention in 1934 to evaluate polarization in the denomination's ranks. In its fifteen-year duration, the commission ultimately boasted a broad ideological representation, including such committed liberals as Edward Scribner Ames (1870–1958; premier liberal theologian of the Disciples of Christ) and C. C. Morrison (first editor of *The Christian Century*), and such committed conservatives as P. H. Welshimer (minister of the Disciples's largest congregation in Canton, Ohio) and James DeForest Murch. Frederick Kershner served as chair of the commission for most of its duration. In its final report to the Disciples's International Convention in 1948, the Commission on Restudy, having identified the major differences alienating conservative and liberal Disciples, nevertheless by its own consensus recommended a course of action to maintain solidarity within the ranks. The report was subsequently ignored by the convention and had little impact on the churches. The commission's failure to avert division foreshadowed further estrangement. By 1955 a national "Directory of the Ministry" for independent churches, Bible colleges, mission organizations, and other ministries, was published. Further impetus for separation appeared in the wake of the Disciples's inauguration of a plan for denominational restructuring in the 1960s. Efforts at reconciliation were few and far between. A Consultation on Internal Unity met from 1959 to 1966 and exchanged papers of concerned Disciples and "Independents," but to no ultimate avail. Most independent Christian Churches (Churches of Christ) had already declared independence, at least from supporting Disciples denominational agencies, by the time the restructuring was consummated, at which time as many as 3,000 congregations officially requested to be removed from the register of the Disciples of Christ *Yearbook*.

1970 to the Present

From 1970 to the present, the Christian Churches (Churches of Christ) have experienced continued institutional expansion and moderate growth in membership. Their heaviest geographical concentration is in the American Midwest, west coast, southwest, and southeast, and primarily in suburban and rural settings. Ethnic diversity within the United States is minimal (the vast majority of adherents are Caucasian and middle class); yet Christian Churches have made significant inroads of late among Hispanic, Filipino, and Portuguese communities on the east coast, and among Asians on the west coast. The increasing number of overseas mission-based churches in AFRICA and Asia has also broadened the ethnic base internationally. Statistics from the early 1990s suggest a total of around 5,200 Christian Churches (Churches of Christ) with upwards of 677,000 actual members and 1,200,000 adherents, making this body approximately the thirteenth largest religious communion in the United States. It has no centralized structure and continues in principle to repudiate a "denominational" status in favor of what some insiders have called a fraternal relationship or brotherhood, and others a "free church catholicism." The annual North American Christian Convention remains a nondelegate assembly aimed primarily at encouraging evangelism, missionary outreach, and congregational ministry. No formal intercongregational accountability structures exist among the Christian Churches (Churches of Christ) such as are found in the regional ministry system of the Christian Church (Disciples of Christ). Individual congregations are self-ruling bodies normally under the pastoral supervision of a group of elected elders who do not report to synods or other structures beyond the local congregation. Ordination to pastoral ministry is itself congregationally based, and the screening process rests on institutions of ministerial education and on the congregations themselves.

International Activities

Christian Churches have continued to sponsor substantial international mission work, usually through minimally bureaucratic mission organizations supported by, and accountable to, congregational networks that often have a wide geographical distribution. The largest mission agency of the Christian Churches, the Christian Missionary Fellowship (established in 1949 and headquartered in Indianapolis), operates extensive missions in Europe, Africa, and Asia, yet disclaims any political representation of the Christian Churches (Churches of Christ) as a whole. As of 1999 the Christian Churches (Churches of Christ) operated some thirty-one Bible colleges in North America, some of which developed liberal arts curricula either internally or in association with adjacent state universities. Milligan College in Tennessee remains the only fully accredited liberal arts college.

The churches also support three major graduate seminaries within the United States. Overall, evangelistic, missionary, and educational initiatives of the independent Christian Churches have not been matched by commitment to ecumenical activities. There is no membership in the World Council of Churches, and no formal representative participation in Faith and Order. Concern for reconciliation with (acappella) Churches of Christ helped inaugurate annual restoration forums in 1984, and in 1989 a group of Christian Church leaders and scholars began cooperating in a bilateral open forum with representatives of the Church of God (Anderson, Indiana), resulting in the publication of substantial studies of the ecclesiological and soteriological compatibilities and incompatibilities between the two traditions. The result was a nonbinding Consensus Statement of Faith, published in 1996. One other important initiative of late is the trilateral Stone-Campbell Dialogue, bringing together representatives of Churches of Christ, Christian Churches (Churches of Christ), and the Christian Church (Disciples of Christ). Like the Commission on Restudy of the 1940s, this working group devotes itself to rethinking differences and common concerns of the Stone-Campbell churches with a view to more irenic relations.

Confessional Theology

Historically, the Christian Churches (Churches of Christ) have resisted developing a well-defined confessional theology. The ecumenical creeds are not, in most cases, used in worship or in catechesis, though in some limited quarters there is a renewed interest in using the creeds doxologically but not as tests of communion. The classic Stone-Campbell resistance to Reformed (Calvinist) orthodoxy has strongly shaped these churches. Divine grace is understood not as the actualization of eternal decrees but as a free personal and ecclesial relationship of believers to Christ enacted through faith, repentance, and baptism (Acts 2:38). Christian Churches hold up the Petrine Confession (Matthew 16:16) as the basic declaration of faith and expect penitent believers to submit to immersion for the remission of sins and for membership in the church. The highly sacramental view of baptism has typically not been paralleled by a sense of the LORD'S SUPPER as sacrament. Alexander Campbell himself resisted theories of the Real Presence and claims that the supper bestowed a unique grace. Christian Churches (Churches of Christ) have dwelt more on the "ordinance" of weekly observance of the Lord's Supper and on its memorialistic character, though again, in some quarters, there has been a marked renewal of emphasis on the sacramental dimension of the eucha-

rist, in sympathy with classic Lutheran, Reformed, and Anglican views. On the whole, the worship of the Christian Churches has been nonliturgical, centered on preaching and the Lord's Supper, with differences of complexion between the poles of traditional Disciples worship and newer contemporary modes directed toward evangelistic outreach.

Diversification

Recent studies have demonstrated an increasing diversification of theological and ecclesiological orientation among Christian Churches (Churches of Christ). Three broad categories are observable: (1) quasi-evangelical churches tending to minimize indebtedness to the Stone-Campbell tradition and drawn toward the mainstream of American Evangelicalism or toward identification as "Bible churches" or independent fellowships; (2) restoration fundamentalists, strongly resistant to affiliations with other denominations and devoted wholeheartedly to the original Stone-Campbell plea to restore the ordinances of the apostolic church; and (3) moderates or progressives, sometimes calling themselves "classic Disciples," who seek a reinterpretation and reappropriation of the restoration agenda through constructive engagement with the church at large, and most immediately with the two other major branches of the Stone-Campbell tradition.

References and Further Reading

DeGroot, A. T. *Church of Christ Number Two.* Birmingham, UK: privately published, 1956.

———. *New Possibilities for Disciples and Independents.* St. Louis: Bethany Press, 1963.

Garrison, W. E., and A. T. DeGroot. *The Disciples of Christ: A History.* St. Louis: Christian Board of Publication, 1948.

Johnson, H. Eugene. *The Christian Church Plea.* Cincinnati, OH: Standard Publishing, 1975.

Kragenbrink, Kevin. "The Modernist/Fundamentalist Controversy and the Emergence of the Independent Christian Churches/Churches of Christ." *Restoration Quarterly* 42 (2000): 1–17.

Murch, James DeForest. *Christians Only: A History of the Restoration Movement.* Cincinnati, OH: Standard Publishing, 1962.

———. *The Free Church.* Louisville, KY: Restoration Press, 1966.

North, James. *Union in Truth: An Interpretive History of the Restoration Movement.* Cincinnati, OH: Standard Publishing, 1994.

Phillips, G. Richard. "From Modern Theology to a Post-Modern World: Christian Churches and Churches of Christ." *Discipliana* 54 (1994): 83–95.

Richardson, William, ed. *Christian Doctrine: "The Faith Once Delivered . . . ".* Cincinnati, OH: Standard Publishing, 1983.

Smith, Rondal. "The Independent Christian Churches Face a Multicultural Twenty-First Century," *Discipliana* 57 (1997): 35–46.

Toulouse, Mark. "Practical Concern and Theological Neglect: The UCMS and the Open Membership Controversy." In *A Case Study of Mainstream Protestantism: The Disciples' Relation to American Culture, 1880–1989.* Edited by D. Newell Williams. Grand Rapids, MI: Eerdmans, 1991, 194–235.

Watkins, Keith. "Shifting Left/Shifting Right: Changing Eucharistic Practices in Churches of the Stone-Campbell Tradition," *Discipliana* 56 (1996): 35–48.

Webb, Henry. *In Search of Christian Unity: A History of the Restoration Movement.* Cincinnati, OH: Standard Publishing, 1990.

Yeakley, Flavil. "Recent Patterns of Growth and Decline Among Heirs of the Restoration Movement," *Restoration Quarterly* 37 (1995): 45–50.

PAUL M. BLOWERS

CHRISTIAN REFORMED CHURCH IN NORTH AMERICA

The Christian Reformed Church in North America (CRCNA) is a DENOMINATION in the Reformed tradition consisting of approximately 280,000 members in 1,000 congregations spread throughout the UNITED STATES and CANADA, with concentrations in Michigan, California, Iowa, and Ontario. Denominational headquarters are located in Grand Rapids, Michigan. The CRCNA began in 1857 when it separated from the REFORMED CHURCH OF AMERICA. However, the roots of the CRCNA lie in two nineteenth-century secession movements from the State Church of the NETHERLANDS. In the twentieth century, the CRCNA's identity has been shaped by three periods of struggle over the denomination's identity and its theology of GRACE, Scripture, and ecclesiastical office.

Early History

In 1834, a number of groups of Reformed Christians seceded from the State Church of the Netherlands. These groups sought to be free of government control; they returned to the Church Order of the Synod of Dort (1618–1619), to the singing of Psalms only (not hymns), and to the Word of God as interpreted by the three Reformed CONFESSIONS (the BELGIC CONFESSION, the HEIDELBERG CATECHISM, and the CANONS OF DORT). One of the secessionist pastors, Albertus Van Raalte, led his family and a few dozen followers to the United States in 1846. This group settled in and around what is now Holland, Michigan, and in 1850 it joined the DUTCH REFORMED CHURCH, later known as the Reformed Church of America. In 1857, four congregations seceded from this union and formed the CRCNA. Among the reasons cited for this move were a perceived lack of sound doctrinal teaching and piety among American pastors, the use of hymns by the Americans, and the perceived lack of solidarity on the part of the Americans with the secessionist cause in the Netherlands.

Between 1880 and 1915, the CRCNA's membership swelled dramatically due to immigration. The views of these new members were shaped largely by the Dutch statesman and theologian ABRAHAM KUYPER and his Doleantie movement, which separated from the State Church of the Netherlands in 1886. Kuyper's vision was to claim Christ's lordship over all of life. Believers were called to use Christian schools, institutions, and organizations to extend God's kingdom into all parts of society. Carrying this vision to America, Dutch immigrants spurred the infant CRCNA to engage its CULTURE. Thus, at the turn of the century, the CRCNA slowly began the transition from the Dutch language to English, and its members became increasingly Americanized.

Theological Struggles

After World War I, the CRCNA had difficulty defining itself. It wanted to become American but also clung tenaciously to its Reformed beliefs and Dutch heritage. In the 1920s, this identity crisis was the background for theological disagreements about Scripture and grace. Ralph Janssen was deposed as Professor of Old Testament at Calvin Seminary in 1922 after undergoing numerous investigations for his alleged "history of religions" approach to Scripture. Janssen's supporters charged pastors Herman Hoeksema and Henry Danhof with misconstruing Janssen's views because they denied common grace and therefore violated the Reformed confessions. Hoeksema and Danhof were deposed from the CRCNA and, in 1926, were leaders in forming the Protestant Reformed Churches in America.

During the next two decades, the CRCNA was a fortress of Reformed distinctiveness. World War II further Americanized the CRCNA and caused its membership to swell as Dutch Calvinists emigrated from the Netherlands to Canada. By the 1960s, the denomination's identity and relationship to its culture again formed the context of theological debates related to Scripture and grace. Missions-minded theologians sparked debates on limited ATONEMENT and double PREDESTINATION, two doctrines articulated in the Reformed confessions. After decades of conservative dominance, power in the CRCNA shifted to the progressives in the 1960s. This shift is clearly seen in a 1974 denominational report on biblical AUTHORITY, which argued that Scripture's truthfulness lay in its redemptive message not in the accuracy of its statements in domains such as geology, biology, and history.

From the early 1970s to the mid-1990s, the CRCNA struggled over the role of WOMEN in ecclesiastical office. In the end, women's ordination was permitted, but more than 40,000 members had left the denomination (see WOMEN CLERGY).

Denominational Characteristics

The CRCNA still holds to the three historic Reformed confessions, but it is no longer as distinctively Dutch as it has been through much of its history. Twelve different languages are used in worship. The CRCNA's POLITY recognizes the offices of minister, elder, deacon, and evangelist (see CLERGY). Each congregation is governed by a council. Classes (36 in the United States, 11 in Canada) are composed of congregations in geographical proximity to each other, and they meet two or three times each year. A general SYNOD, made up of two ministers and two elders from each classis, meets annually.

The denomination has many agencies, including Calvin Theological Seminary, Calvin College, three MISSIONS agencies, a television and worldwide radio ministry ("The Back to God Hour"), a publishing house, and denominational offices related to abuse prevention, chaplaincy ministries, disability concerns, pastor church relations, social justice, and race relations. Six other colleges or universities are affiliated with the CRCNA.

See also Christian Colleges; Seminaries; Higher Education; Publishing Media

References and Further Reading

Bratt, James D. *Dutch Calvinism in Modern America: A History of a Conservative Subculture.* Grand Rapids, MI: Eerdmans, 1984.
———. "Wars of Words, Wars of Grace: A Brief History of the Battles That Have Shaped the CRC." *Banner* (Dec 20, 1999): 14–17.
DeKlerk, Peter, and Richard De Ridder, eds. *Perspectives on the Christian Reformed Church: Studies in Its History, Theology, and Ecumenicity.* Grand Rapids, MI: Baker, 1983.
Kromminga, Dietrich H. *The Christian Reformed Tradition: From the Reformation to the Present.* Grand Rapids, MI: Eerdmans, 1943.
Schaap, James C. *Our Family Album: The Unfinished Story of the Christian Reformed Church.* Grand Rapids, MI: CRC Publications, 1998.
Van Dyk, Wilbert M. *Belonging: An Introduction to the Faith and Life of the Christian Reformed Church.* Grand Rapids, MI: CRC Publications, 1982.
Zwaanstra, Henry. *Reformed Thought and Experience in a New World: A Study of the Christian Reformed Church and Its American Environment, 1890–1918.* Kampen, Netherlands: J.H. Kok, 1973.
———. *Catholicity and Secession: A Study of Ecumenicity in the Christian Reformed Church.* Grand Rapids, MI: Eerdmans, 1991.

DAVID RYLAARSDAM

CHRISTIAN RIGHT

Also referred to as the "Religious Right" or the "New Christian Right," the Christian Right is a conglomeration of organizations and individuals that emerged in U.S. politics in the latter half of the 1970s. Drawing on the well-developed subculture of fundamentalist and evangelical churches, Christian academies and home-schooling organizations, BIBLE COLLEGES, and TELEVANGELISM media networks, the Christian Right overcame denominational divisions to ally with Pentecostals and charismatics, conservative Catholics, and some conservative Jews. Common to these groups was the argument that the U.S. in the 1960s had forsaken its roots in the BIBLE, losing its Christian identity and therefore its strength. These concerns often crystallized around children, whom many on the Christian Right believed to be the target of a secular humanist onslaught (enacted through multicultural education, sex education programs, and the MASS MEDIA) seeking to control the nation by reprogramming its children, particularly regarding SEXUALITY, MARRIAGE, and the FAMILY (see CHILDHOOD). Issues around which the Christian Right mobilized include opposition to ABORTION, feminism, HOMOSEXUALITY, pornography, affirmative action, and welfare. The Christian Right campaigned for mandatory school PRAYER, school-supported Bible clubs, the teaching of CREATION SCIENCE, and school vouchers. As these issues indicate, the Christian Right is often analyzed as protesting MODERNISM or modernity, not in the sense of eschewing modern technologies (its leaders have pioneered TV, video, and internet ministries), but rather in the sense of protesting concomitant cultural changes. Seen by the Christian Right as "permissiveness," these changes are analyzed by sociologists under the term "SECULARIZATION." In addition to cutting across denominational lines, the Christian Right cuts within religious identifications. Not all fundamentalists, evangelicals, or conservative Christians would identify with the Christian Right, either its politics or beliefs. Indeed, the main controversy surrounding the Christian Right concerns the degree to which its elites represent a grass-roots constituency.

History

Although evangelical religion has long been an important force in U.S. political life, the Christian Right's emergence into politics in the mid-1970s reversed decades of withdrawal by conservative Protestants (who in the 1920s felt forced out of public life by Liberal Protestants). Yet unlike nineteenth-century EVANGELICALISM, which sought such progressive reforms as the abolition of SLAVERY and WOMEN's suffrage, this "return" was marked by a more defensive and reactionary agenda, as evidenced by its catalyst (see SLAVERY, ABOLITION OF).

In 1976, Jimmy Carter, a Southern Baptist who proclaimed himself "born again," was elected President. Many Bible-believing Protestants (particularly in the South) were at first encouraged by his leadership, only to feel betrayed later by Carter's liberal Democratic party politics. For some, the turning point occurred when Carter's administration announced plans to revoke the tax exemptions of private schools that practiced racial segregation. Although continuing practices begun before his presidency (particularly regarding Bob Jones University, a fundamentalist school in South Carolina), Carter was perceived as attacking fundamentalist values. In response, and aided by political conservatives like Paul Weyrich (a founder of the Heritage Foundation), JERRY FALWELL formed the "Moral Majority" in 1979, just in time for the 1980 presidential election. Falwell took credit for registering millions of new voters who helped elect President Ronald Reagan.

For others, the turning point was the White House Conference on the Family held by Carter's administration in 1980. Conservatives like Connie Marshner and Beverly LaHaye saw the Conference as an attempt to broaden the accepted definition of the family beyond the white middle class heterosexual norm. Although the Moral Majority is the most well known, other Christian Right organizations include Concerned Women for America (founded by Beverly LaHaye in 1979), the Traditional Values Coalition (founded by Louis Sheldon in 1980), Focus on the Family (founded by James Dobson in 1977 and which developed a large international division), the Council for National Policy (founded by Tim LaHaye in 1981 as an invitation-only forum to network Christian Right leaders with funders like Richard DeVos of Amway and the Coors family), and the Christian Coalition.

The Christian Coalition was founded by PAT ROBERTSON in 1989, one year after Robertson's run in the Republican presidential primaries. With Ralph Reed as executive director, the Coalition became an influential force in Republican politics, thanks in part to its "voter guides." In 1992, both Robertson and Pat Buchanan spoke at the Republican National Convention. Throughout the decade, Christian Right issues influenced the Republican Party agenda, dismaying some Republican regulars, as well as, ultimately, some Christian Right activists (such as James Dobson), who accused Republicans of using the Christian Right to get elected only to neglect their issues afterward.

Reception

The increasingly high profile of the Christian Right did not go unchallenged. In the religious realm, in 1996 politically liberal evangelicals (including Jim Wallis and Tony Campolo) formed Call to Renewal to contest the Christian Right's claim to speak for all evangelicals. Politically, the Christian Right was opposed by organizations like AMERICANS UNITED FOR THE SEPARATION OF CHURCH AND STATE, as well as the Fight the Right Initiative of the National Gay and Lesbian Task Force.

Controversy

Analysts seeking to understand the Christian Right are divided concerning the degree to which it represents a grass-roots constituency. Sociologist Christian Smith, for example, argues for a gap between the political agenda of Christian Right leaders and the actual (more tolerant) views of ordinary evangelicals. Although evangelicals seek to be engaged with the public sphere, their preferred method of engagement is not politics, but rather personal relationships. In contrast, it may be argued that the narratives disseminated by the media ministries of the Christian Right shape individuals at a level more profound than individual consciousness or will, because the conservative narrative evokes and builds on mainstream cultural memories.

See also Abortion; Darwinism; Fundamentalism; Liberal Protestantism & Liberalism; Pentecostalism; Publishing Media; Televangelism

References and Further Readings

Burlein, Ann. *Lift High the Cross: Where White Supremacy and the Religious Right Converge*. Durham, NC: Duke University Press, 2002.

Martin, William. *With God on Our Side: The Rise of the Religious Right in America*. New York: Broadway Books, 1996.

Smith, Christian. *Christian America?: What Evangelicals Really Want*. Berkeley, CA: University of California Press, 2000.

ANN BURLEIN

CHRISTIAN SCIENCE

Toward the end of the nineteenth century, Protestants were deeply divided over the relationship of religion and SCIENCE. Although fundamentalists were adamant that science is factual only insofar as it accommodates the BIBLE, modernists accepted scientific developments—such as evolutionary theory—and interpreted the Bible to accommodate their findings (see DARWINISM). In 1875 MARY BAKER EDDY (1821–1910) introduced a new variety of Protestantism with a radical rendition of the modernist position: not only can Christianity accommodate science, it *is* science.

The Early Years

In 1875 Eddy published the first edition of her principal work, *Science and Health,* in which she explained "Moral Science," her metaphysical understanding of the Bible's teachings as scientific—coherent, objective, verifiable, and containing the methodology for eradicating disease. Eddy had developed this understanding over a period of years, perhaps beginning with her poor health as a child in a Calvinist household (see CALVINISM). Eddy, whose ill health followed her into adulthood, experimented with many of the healing treatments in vogue in the midnineteenth century, but found the most relief when she visited Phineas Parkhurst Quimby (1802–1866) in 1862.

Quimby based his treatment on Anton Mesmer's (1734–1815) work, which, building on EMANUEL SWEDENBORG's (1688–1772) theory that an invisible substance connects all NATURE and spirit, demonstrated a way for one person to affect another by manipulating that substance. Quimby used Mesmer's technique, mesmerism, to heal, but believed that it changed a person's mind, not body: people are sick because they believe they are sick; correct their beliefs and the maladies disappear. Eddy became one of Quimby's students after he treated her illness, and they remained correspondents until his death in 1866.

Shortly after Quimby's death, Eddy took a serious fall on an icy sidewalk. Still bed-bound three days later, she read New Testament stories of Jesus's healing and, particularly, of his raising Lazarus from the dead. She observed that he did not treat symptoms but demonstrated the unreality of sickness and death, and, at this discovery, rose from bed fully cured. She believed that the change in her thought and the accompanying healing demonstrated the science of Jesus's teachings and began to study the rest of the Bible in this light.

By the end of 1868 Eddy had taken a small cadre of students under her wing, teaching them Moral Science through *The Science of Man,* a textbook she fashioned by adapting Quimby's technique to her revelation. Practitioners of her Science corrected patients' false beliefs in illness, but Eddy taught them that this health was restored through the power of the Divine Mind, as she called God, not the human mind as Quimby had

believed. Eddy fleshed out her understanding of Moral Science over the next few years, incorporating it into an expanded treatment, *Science and Health,* in 1875. Beginning in 1883 Eddy included biblical exegesis according to Moral Science, republishing the text as *Science and Health with Key to the Scriptures.* This work was Eddy's explanation of her revelation, and she continually fine-tuned it to ensure its clarity, producing over 200 editions by her death in 1910, while writing other books and numerous hymns, prayers, sermons, newspaper articles, and letters.

Eddy also continued to promote her Moral Science on several other fronts. In 1879 she founded a church based on its principles, the Church of Christ, Scientist. With this name, she depicted her religion as distinctly Christian and proclaimed Jesus as *the* Scientist—the one who fully understood Moral Science. Two years later, in 1881, she opened the Massachusetts Metaphysical College, where students could take courses and earn a degree, either Bachelor of Christian Science or Doctor of Christian Science. By the time Eddy closed the college in 1889 nearly 1,000 students had crossed its threshold. Eddy's students, at her behest, also formed the National Christian Science Association in 1886, which she disbanded in 1892. Eddy began the Christian Science Publishing Society in 1898, and the Publishing Society's trademark periodical, the *Christian Science Monitor,* in 1908.

Beliefs

Christian Science THEOLOGY derives from Mary Baker Eddy's conviction that God is good and, as such, would not have created anything that is not good. Hence, disease is not God's creation but human fallacy. As she explained in *Miscellaneous Writings, 1883–1896,* "good being real, evil, good's opposite, is unreal" (63). From this premise, Eddy derived what she called the "Triune Principle of all pure theology": Life, Truth, and Love. Recognition of this triad's reality brings about realization of the unreality of its opposite—sickness, sin, and death—and remedies the latter's ills. Sin is error, creating the illusion of matter, and belief in this false world furthers that error.

Christian Science is more than a healing system, but disease provided Eddy with the most concrete examples of error—and of error compounding error—while its cure provided her with the most powerful demonstrations of her Truth. For instance, many might reject Eddy's contention that disease is illusion caused by false beliefs, but even her critics had to concede that there are times when one's belief in the immanence of disease, such as after forgetting to wear a hat in a snowstorm, produces the very symptoms one expects. Similarly, Eddy recognized the fashionableness that accompanied new diseases, blaming the press for providing information on illnesses because, as she wrote in *Science and Health*, "A new name for an ailment affects people like a Parisian name for a novel garment. Every one hastens to get it" (197). Likewise, medical students often see symptoms in themselves or those around them that resemble diseases about which they are studying; for Eddy this process is exactly how illness spreads, whether one reads about diseases in a medical journal or the daily newspaper, or hears about them in a medical consultation. Accordingly, not only do non–Christian Science practitioners treat patients incorrectly, but they produce the illness in the first place by examining symptoms, diagnosing illnesses, and treating patients accordingly. Better that the patient, practitioner, and family members not think about the illness, much less talk about it.

Eddy explained relapses as former patients falling back into SIN, and slow recoveries as patients needing time to "overcome" their faith in illness and medication. Eddy recommended the use of surgeons when cases were clearly organic, as with broken bones. Such cases, and illnesses in seemingly good Christian Scientists, proved that no one in this lifetime has sufficiently advanced in Science to transcend mortal mind completely, an advance that remains for a future millennium, when Christian Science is realized universally and, therefore, illness, pain, and death are no more.

Stopping short of a doctrinal creed, Eddy encapsulated Christian Science into six tenets, listed in *Science and Health*:

1. As adherents of Truth, we take the inspired Word of the Bible as our sufficient guide to eternal Life.
2. We acknowledge and adore one supreme and infinite God. We acknowledge His Son, one Christ; the Holy Ghost or divine Comforter; and man in God's image and likeness.
3. We acknowledge God's forgiveness of sin in the destruction of sin and the spiritual understanding that casts out evil as unreal. But the belief in sin is punished so long as the belief lasts.
4. We acknowledge Jesus' atonements as the evidence of divine, efficacious Love, unfolding man's unity with God through Christ Jesus the Way-shower; and we acknowledge that man is saved through Christ, through Truth, Life, and Love as demonstrated by the Galilean Prophet in healing the sick and overcoming sin and death.
5. We acknowledge that the crucifixion of Jesus and his resurrection served to uplift faith to understand eternal Life, even the allness of Soul, Spirit, and the nothingness of matter.
6. And we solemnly promise to watch, and pray for that Mind to be in us which was also in Christ Jesus; to do unto others as we would have them do unto us; and to be merciful, just, and pure. (497)

Although some of these tenets resemble those of other Protestant religions, their phrasings demonstrate distinctive beliefs. For instance, the first tenet positions the Bible as a *guide* to "Eternal Life," whereas the second emphasizes humanity's shared image and likeness with God. According to Eddy, God is a spiritual rather than a physical being who created humans in the divine image; therefore, they must be spiritual beings as well. Human error, or sin, creates the material world and its attending maladies, and therein lies the third tenet: this sin creates its own punishment, the illnesses and death humans believe exist; yet, God forgives this sin and provides the remedy—understanding of the unreality of sickness, sin, and death. The fourth and fifth tenets emphasize Jesus's role as Scientist, depicting human unity with God—the oneness of all that is real—as well as demonstrating the way out of the sin that creates matter, sickness, and death. In addition to affirming the Golden Rule, the sixth tenet vows effort to emulate Jesus, to destroy the sin that keeps people invested in the material world they create.

Controversies I: Animal Magnetism

Once she developed Christian Science, Mary Baker Eddy fought to distance herself from Phineas Quimby's mesmerism. He was her most influential teacher and her theology is clearly indebted to his system. This led some critics to claim that Christian Science is Quimby's work repackaged, overlooking the new direction in which she had taken his ideas. Her critics likely missed this because, although she believed that it was dangerously misguided, Eddy also believed that mesmerism worked.

Mesmerism, or animal magnetism as Eddy called it after discovering Christian Science, is human manipulation of another's mind. Used as a medical treatment it could change a person's belief of sickness into a belief of health; used another way it could change a person's belief of health into one of sickness. A practitioner of animal magnetism could even make a devout Christian Scientist sick by introducing doubts or thoughts of sickness into that person's mind. Eddy reviled even the well-intentioned, healthful uses of animal magnetism as invasions into another's mind, but she saved her greatest condemnations for mal-intended, or "malicious," animal magnetism. The line between mesmeric and Christian Science treatments was thin, but for Eddy and her followers it was vitally important. Once a practitioner began to correct beliefs of illness by manipulating the patient's mind rather than appealing to Divine Mind, that practitioner had violated the patient, and stepped on the slippery slope to malicious animal magnetism.

Eddy accused many former students of practicing animal magnetism, or "mental malpractice," and increased their ranks by accusing other students of stepping onto that slippery slope. When students exhibited doubts—whether vocally or through botched healings—Eddy was just as likely to attribute the doubts to a former student's malicious animal magnetism, working to undermine her in their minds, as she was to attribute them to the current students' false belief. She also blamed malicious animal magnetism for her continuing illnesses and the 1882 death of her third husband, Asa Gilbert Eddy.

Eddy believed that animal magnetism posed a public threat and fought to expose it. In 1878 her lawyer, a student named Edward Arens, filed suit against one of Eddy's former students, Daniel Spofford, for maliciously injuring another student, Lucretia Brown, through animal magnetism. Brown refused to appear in court, but gave Eddy power of attorney to appear on her behalf. Although the judge dismissed the suit, it made a sensation in the press, particularly because Arens had filed it in Salem, Massachusetts, historic site of the infamous witch trials. Eddy quickly revised *Science and Health* with an expanded section warning of animal magnetism's dangers.

Controversies II: Leadership

Questions of leadership arose in the church's early years and continued for a decade after Mary Baker Eddy's death. Students often chafed under Eddy's critical eye, particularly when Eddy blamed their failures on their wrong beliefs. A number of practitioners treated patients according to *Science and Health* without training—or sanction—from Eddy. Yet, of those who did study with her, many left, often becoming her most vocal critics, and others tried to undermine her AUTHORITY from within.

Most apostates maintained—or modified—what Eddy had taught them, either practicing on their own or creating new organizations. Perhaps the most notable of these apostates was Emma Curtis Hopkins (1849–1925), whom Eddy excommunicated in 1885. With the assistance of Mary Plunkett, another former student, Hopkins founded the Emma Curtis Hopkins College of Christian Science in 1885 and the Hopkins Metaphysical Association in 1886. Through these organizations, and an allied publication called *Christian Science,* founded by former student Ida Nichols, Hopkins expanded New Thought from a lay healing movement based on Quimby's work to a religious congregation with ordained clergy. Hopkins's background in Christian Science and her use of similar terminology led many to confuse New Thought and Christian Science, and with regard to both movements' indebtedness to Quimby. Yet, there are key differences between them: New Thought emphasizes the power of human mind, whereas Christian Science emphasizes the power of Divine Mind; New Thought advocates mind over matter, whereas Christian Science professes that there is *only* mind, no matter.

Hopkins's defection may have been the most influential with its resulting development of New Thought, but significant strife among Eddy's adherents first threatened her leadership in 1888, after Massachusetts authorities charged one of her students, Abby Corner, with manslaughter. Corner, who had taken classes with Eddy, attended to her daughter's premature labor with a non–Christian Science nurse-midwife's assistance. After several hours, at her daughter's request, Corner sent for a medical doctor. Mother and infant died before he arrived, however, and, believing that not having called for him sooner was criminal, the doctor alerted the authorities. The state agreed and charged Corner with her daughter's death. Local newspapers printed the story and the public was outraged. Eddy wrote an open letter to the *Boston Globe* and the *Boston Herald* denouncing Corner, and Christian Scientists were outraged. Eddy had blamed practitioners for failed healings before, but this public disavowal crossed the line for many who thought it disloyal. Enough Christian Scientists agreed with Eddy and blamed Corner—her use of a nonbelieving assistant posing an inherent danger to her daughter even if Corner's own beliefs were correct—that Eddy maintained control. Those Christian Scientists who could not accept Eddy's leadership left, including a group of thirty-six who took the church's records, holding them hostage until Eddy agreed to let the students leave without excommunication.

Eddy held onto her leadership, but made several changes. In 1889 she closed the Massachusetts Metaphysical College, although the church continued to award degrees under the college's charter. That year she also resigned as pastor of the Boston congregation—while dissolving it as a legal entity—and as president of the National Christian Scientist Association; the association's local Christian Scientist Association disbanded on her recommendation, and the national one followed in 1892, again on her recommendation. These changes led to more defections, but they also allowed Eddy to centralize the church, reorganizing it around the Mother Church in Boston, with a five-person board of directors she appointed to oversee church affairs.

Eddy further solidified her leadership in a series of bylaws she published in 1895's *Manual of the Mother Church.* Through this and succeeding editions of the *Manual,* Eddy standardized the Church of Christ, Scientist and its services. For instance, Eddy abolished the ordained CLERGY and named the BIBLE (KING JAMES VERSION) and *Science and Health* the pastor, limiting the clerical position to that of lay "reader." Each congregation has two of these readers, usually a woman and a man, who, instead of a sermon during Sunday services, read passages from the pastor—the Bible and *Science and Health.* The church administration in Boston chooses the passages, listing them in the *Christian Science Quarterly* since its publication in 1890. As per the bylaws, readers cannot comment on the passages, nor answer questions, allowing congregants to concentrate on the pastor's words. The bylaws allow some interpretation outside of these services, however, particularly in a SUNDAY SCHOOL for the under-twenty crowd and in practitioner training. Traveling lecturers, appointed by Eddy until her death, then by the directors, visit each congregation and speak to its members, often in a public hall. Their lectures reinforce the link among local, or "branch," churches and between them and the Mother Church, and allow a representative of the Mother Church to address local concerns and, perhaps, attract converts. Eddy also continued the popular practice of Wednesday evening testimonial meetings, at which Christian Scientists, particularly those who have been healed, share their stories.

This meticulous centralization and standardization successfully staved off another leadership crisis until after Eddy's death. Christian Scientists minimize the importance of death, including Eddy's, stressing its unreality, but her passing in 1910 caused substantial problems for church administration. Eddy had vested the board of directors with administrative powers, but according to the *Manual,* the board needed her consent for any significant action it might take. In the years after her death the board substituted its judgment for hers in proxy, greatly increasing its powers.

Many Christian Scientists were displeased, but the board easily quashed each challenge until the "Great Litigation." When Eddy had established the Christian Science Publishing Society in 1898, she had done so under her own aegis. Yet, after her death, the board of directors tried to stand in for her there as well, replacing trustees and making policy decisions. The Publishing Society rebelled. From 1918 to 1921 the trustees and directors brought their differences to court. The long legal battles took their toll, and the membership split between the factions. The largest group, backing the directors, boycotted the Publishing Society and stopped enough subscriptions to endanger it. The trustees won the first battles, but the directors held out and eventually won in a Supreme Judicial Court of Massachusetts decision. Accepting this, the majority of Christian Scientists buried their differences, and the board's expanded powers—reaching across all church interests—minimized further power struggles. Dissension reemerged among the ranks in the 1990s when the church found itself in financial trouble, and when rumors circulated about financial mismanagement, but the controversies that have caused the most trouble for the church have been those surrounding failed healings of children.

Controversies III: Treatment of Children

There have been critics of Christian Science since its beginnings, but they are never as vocal as when a child dies in a Christian Science practitioner's care. Just as the 1880s public was outraged after Abby Corner's daughter and her infant died during childbirth, the 1980s public was outraged after Robyn Twitchell died of a bowel obstruction and Amy Hermanson died of juvenile diabetes. Rennie Schoepflin has identified thirty-two cases between 1887 and 1990 in which Christian Science practitioners were charged with crimes for their treatment of children, ranging from practicing medicine without a license to second-degree murder, yet among recent cases the Twitchell and Hermanson cases received the most media attention, and roused the most vocal backlash against the church (see MASS MEDIA).

Boston authorities arrested David and Ginger Twitchell for manslaughter after Robyn, aged two and a half, died in 1986; Sarasota County, Florida authorities arrested William and Christine Hermanson for felony child abuse and third-degree murder when Amy, aged seven, died the same year. Opponents such as Children's Healthcare is a Legal Duty, Inc. (CHILD) had long fought Christian Science parents' right to choose religious practitioners for their children's care, but the Twitchell and Hermanson cases visibly boosted their campaigns against the church. Although the parents lost their original cases, both state supreme courts overruled the verdicts—three years later for the Twitchells, in 1993, and five years later for the Hermansons, in 1992. The sensational media attention the cases received and the original guilty verdicts, however, revived old criticisms.

Christian Scientists' critics often accuse them of child abuse for their refusal to allow medical doctors to treat their children, but for many Christian Scientists the opposite is true: *submitting* their children to medical treatment would be abuse. Sickness is error, illusion—whether created by the child or a parent—and acknowledging it exacerbates that illusion, making the child worse, even to the point of death. To heal, patients must be surrounded by those who believe and can help them realize the disease's unreality. Doubts and thoughts about the symptoms affect patients and worsen their conditions. Yet, although most Christian Scientists uphold this position, others have interpreted their theology to allow medical treatment, at least for children, or have left the church.

Membership

The Mother Church, built to hold 1,000 in 1894, quickly became too small for its purposes, causing Mary Baker Eddy to order a 3,000-capacity annex built alongside it, allowing the use of both facilities after its completion in 1906. By 1907 there were 652 Christian Science branch churches in the United States and another fifty-eight abroad; today there are over 2,000 worldwide. Although Eddy prohibited publication of church statistics in 1908, some numbers are available. According to the 1890 U.S. Census, 8,724 Americans identified themselves as Christian Scientists, followed in 1906 with the U.S. Census of Religious Bodies' count of 40,011, although this number is somewhat exaggerated because of Christian Scientists' practice of joining both their local branch church and the Mother Church, as is required for those in leadership positions. Church authorities reported a membership of 268,915 in 1936, the last year for which they publicized the report. This number likely reached 500,000 by the 1950s, but has been on the decline since then.

The Church of Christ, Scientist controls its membership as well as its membership figures. Those over twelve years old who are interested in joining the church must apply for membership, attesting to belief in Christian Science as laid out in *Science and Health* and denying membership in another denomination. Applicants must submit a completed application to a Christian Scientist willing to sponsor them. Sponsors send the applications to a teacher for a signature, then to the clerk of the Mother Church for consideration. The church admits new members twice yearly, in early June and November.

Although Eddy's earliest students were primarily working-class, by 1910 the majority of her followers were middle-class, a trend that continues today. Her earliest students also included a balance of men and WOMEN but, although Eddy tended to appoint men to positions of power, women quickly dominated the

ranks of Christian Scientists, as they do today. Christian Science caught on most quickly in urban areas in the Northeast, Midwest, and California, with important centers in Boston, New York, and Chicago by the end of the nineteenth century, although it progressed more slowly in the South, taking root there only in the later years of the twentieth century.

Christian Science Today

Despite the controversies that have plagued the church, Christian Science remains a vital religion for many, and the Church of Christ, Scientist continues to reach out to non–Christian Scientists as well. The *Christian Science Monitor* has won a number of journalism awards, including seven Pulitzer prizes, and the church's reading rooms, where one can read the *Monitor* and other Christian Science Publishing Society materials, are regular fixtures in downtowns across the United States. The church also has a growing international population, and offers all of its publications in a number of languages. The Christian Science Plaza in Boston—Mother Church, Mother Church Sunday School, Christian Science Publishing Society, Church Administration Building, Mary Baker Eddy Library for the Betterment of Humanity, and a reflecting pool—remains a popular site for visitors touring downtown Boston, and many visitors take advantage of free tours of the Mother Church. Since its public opening on September 28, 2002, many also have explored the Mary Baker Eddy Library's exhibits and research room. The church's population is aging, but such outreach may well rejuvenate the Church of Christ, Scientist as it approaches the centennial of its founder's death. Christian Science has captured many imaginations over the years, and promises to continue that tradition for the foreseeable future.

See also Faith Healing

References and Further Reading

Primary Sources:

Eddy, M. B. *Manual of the Mother Church; The First Church of Christ, Scientist, in Boston, Massachusetts*. Boston: The Christian Science Publishing Society, 1889.
———. *Mary Baker Eddy: Speaking for Herself*. Boston: Writings of Mary Baker Eddy, 2002.
———. *Miscellaneous Writings, 1883–1896*. Boston: Trustees under the Will of Mary Baker G. Eddy, 1896.
———. *Prose Works Other Than Science and Health*. Boston: Trustees under the Will of Mary Baker G. Eddy, 1925.
———. *Science and Health with Key to the Scriptures*. Reprint. Boston: The First Church of Christ, Scientist, 1994.

Secondary Sources:

Anonymous. *A Century of Christian Science Healing*. Boston: The Christian Science Publishing Society, 1966.

Conkin, P. K. *American Originals: Homemade Varieties of Christianity*. Chapel Hill: The University of North Carolina Press, 1997.

DesAutels, P., M. P. Battin, and L. May. *Praying For a Cure: When Medical and Religious Practices Conflict*. Lanham, MD: Rowman & Littlefield, 1999.

Fuller, R. C. *Alternative Medicine and American Religious Life*. New York: Oxford University Press, 1989.

———. *Mesmerism and the American Cure of Souls*. Philadelphia: University of Pennsylvania Press, 1982.

Gill, G. *Mary Baker Eddy*. Radcliff Biography Series. Cambridge MA: Perseus Books, 1998.

Gottschalk, S. *The Emergence of Christian Science in American Religious Life*. Berkeley: University of California Press, 1973.

Knee, S. E. *Christian Science in the Age of Mary Baker Eddy*. Westport, CT: Greenwood Press, 1994.

Meyer, D. B. *The Positive Thinkers: A Study of the American Quest for Health, Wealth and Personal Power from Mary Baker Eddy to Norman Vincent Peale*. Garden City, NY: Doubleday, 1965.

New York City Christian Science Institute. *Vital Issues in Christian Science: A Record of Unsettled Questions which Arose in the Year 1909, Between the Directors of the Mother Church, the First Church of Christ, Scientist, Boston, Massachusetts, and First Church of Christ, Scientist, New York City, Eight of its Nine Trustees and Sixteen of its Practitioners*. New York: G. P. Putnam's Sons, 1914.

Peel, R. *Christian Science: Its Encounter with American Culture*. New York: Henry Holt & Company, 1958.

———. *Mary Baker Eddy: The Years of Authority*. New York: Holt, Rinehart & Winston, 1977.

———. *Mary Baker Eddy: The Years of Discovery*. New York: Holt, Rinehart & Winston, 1966.

———. *Mary Baker Eddy: The Years of Trial*. New York: Holt, Rinehart & Winston, 1971.

Satter, B. *Each Mind a Kingdom: American Women, Sexual Purity, and the New Thought Movement*. Berkeley: University of California Press, 1999.

Schoepflin, R. B. *Christian Science on Trial: Religious Healing in America*. Baltimore MD: The Johns Hopkins University Press, 2003.

Smith, C. P. *Historical Sketches, from the Life of Mary Baker Eddy and the History of Christian Science*. Boston: The Christian Science Publishing Society, 1941.

Thomas, R. D. *"With Bleeding Footsteps": Mary Baker Eddy's Path to Religious Leadership*. New York: Alfred A. Knopf, 1994.

Ward, G. L., ed. *Christian Science: Controversial and Polemical Pamphlets*. New York and London: Garland Publishing, 1990.

AMY E. LORION

CHRISTOLOGY

Christology is the doctrine of the person of Christ: of who and what kind of being he is. Its basis is in the New Testament's attributing to Jesus of Nazareth both human and divine characteristics and actions, and as a central discipline of Christian theology it is concerned with elaborating and explaining the meaning of those claims. In all of its main streams, early Protestant christology adopted the teaching of the orthodox Christian tradition, and Catholic accusations of heresy did not, for the most part, touch on this aspect of its teaching. The tradition taught that Jesus Christ is the eternal Son of God made flesh for human salvation—the doctrine of the incarnation—and that his historic person was a unity—"one Christ" made known in two natures. By "natures" was meant not separate entities but ways in which Christ was at once one in being (*homoousios*) with God the Father—as truly God as he—and one in being with human beings—as truly human, sin apart, as they. The Chalcedonian Definition of 451 set its face against two distortions of this, the "Nestorian," which divided the person by separating the human and the divine, and the "monophysite," which tended to submerge Christ's humanity within the "one nature" of his divinity. All christology tends to one of those distortions, and it is said to be characteristic of Lutheran christology to tend to the monophysite, and of Reformed theology to tend to the Nestorian. This article will both illustrate and qualify that scholarly commonplace.

The Legacy of the Reformers

Differences between the leading Reformers took shape not in controversies about christology itself so much as about its bearing on the doctrine of the Lord's Supper. Luther's concern was to maintain the real presence of Christ in the bread and wine and his views were developed particularly in controversy with HULDRYCH ZWINGLI (1484–1531), whom he believed to deny it. His position involved a strong doctrine both of the divinity of Christ and of the communication of attributes, a doctrine holding that anything predicated of Christ's divinity must also be predicable of his humanity, although the reverse was not at first taught. We shall see that this teaching has had an immense long-term effect. It enabled MARTIN LUTHER (1483–1546) to argue that because divinity implies omnipresence, the human body of Christ could be present in the eucharistic elements by virtue of its participation in the divine nature. The Formula of Concord (1577) attributed to Christ's manhood the power of being present simultaneously in many places. Thereafter, Lutheran christology, while not denying the full humanity of Christ, has tended to experience some of the problems consequent in a monophysite position.

The view of JOHN CALVIN (1509–1564) and the Reformed, in contrast, was that humanity implied spatial location and this was denied by Lutheran omnipresence. Christ's body was therefore, by virtue of his ascension, in heaven, and worshippers were enabled to participate in his benefits by the work of the

Spirit who brought them into union with him. Calvin also directed criticism against the christology of An-dreas Osiander (1496?–1552) with its tendency to imply the transfusion of divine substance into the human being. Calvin's christology was not Nestorian, and has recently been shown to owe much to that of Cyril of Alexandria, a primary influence on the Chalcedonian Definition. Reformed christology has, however, sometimes tended in a Nestorian direction because of lingering suggestions that the two natures should be treated almost as entities to be balanced rather than as principles of Christ's being. Another aspect of Calvin's christology, which has proved crucial for later developments, is his return to another patristic theme, that the Son remains outside the universe while also becoming incarnate, the so-called Calvinist "extra." This enabled later Reformed thought to maintain a distinction between God and the world, which is sometimes endangered in recent Lutheran thought. A further influential development was Calvin's exposition of the relevance of christology by appeal to the three "offices" of Christ as prophet, priest, and king. The ascended Christ exercises his continuing saving activity in the present from the right hand of the Father in the three ways suggested by the offices.

It would be no exaggeration to say that all Protestant christology has thereafter been decisively shaped by the difference between Luther and Calvin. Much of the work of succeeding Protestant theologians, especially on the Reformed side, was dominated by the elaboration and defense of the dogmatic implications of this fundamental divide. The so-called Protestant scholastics were not, however, as that sometimes pejoratively intended description suggests, concerned with abstract elaborations of theological topics, for many of their central concerns arose from a need to respond to objections raised by early modern criticism. At the heart of christological controversy was a renewed concern for the humanity of Christ, supposedly neglected by earlier theology. Faustus Socinus (1539–1604) who could perhaps be called the first modernist Protestant, began the assault by questioning the doctrine of the Trinity and conceiving Jesus as a man endowed with divine powers who was, after his resurrection, endowed with a power equal to God's (see Socinianism). Later and more radical versions of this approach were to stress Jesus's humanity at the expense of his divinity, moving toward an assertion of the incompatibility of the divine and human, so that to claim that someone was both divine and human amounted to a logical contradiction. Charges of the inconsistency were reiterated by the philosophers of the Enlightenment, building on Benedict Spinoza's (1632–1677) assault on the credibility of the historical narratives of scripture and the Deists' denial of the credibility of divine interaction with a mechanistic universe (see Deism).

Lutheran and Reformed Christology

The supposed failure of Lutheran christology to give space for a truly human Christ attracted criticism in two main forms. According to Johannes Brenz (1499–1570), the incarnate Christ fully exercised divine powers, albeit in a hidden manner, so that his humanity is fully ubiquitous. The position of Martin Chemnitz (1522–1586) was that while Christ had the power to be present in many places at once, he suspended its exercise during his incarnation. To opponents this appeared to be so total an identification of the Word with the human flesh of Jesus that effectively he had no existence outside the flesh. This involved a strong doctrine of the communication of attributes, which was in this case taken to imply that the divine qualities of the Word were transferred to the man Jesus. This came into conflict with modern streams of thought that stressed the humanity of Jesus. Suggestions that qualities such as omnipotence and omniscience were to be attributed to the incarnate Word appeared to contradict the picture presented in the Gospels. This led, in the nineteenth century, to forms of kenotic theory (still largely within the Lutheran tradition) justified by appeal to "he emptied himself" of Philippians 2:7. Kenotic christology represents the development of a distinction sketched by Philipp Melanchthon (1497–1560), the first to attempt to provide a handbook of Lutheran teaching, between Christ's being and his state of humiliation, and especially suffering and death, when "his power is not in this moment manifested" (Melanchthon 1982:35).

In later development, the idea that Christ suspended the use of the attributes was radicalized to teach that he renounced them at the incarnation. It was taught that in order to be truly human the eternal Son of God divested himself of those divine attributes that appeared to be inconsistent with humanity. It was sometimes held that God's immanent attributes, love for example, could not be altered (note here the line of Charles Wesley's well-known hymn: "emptied himself of all but love") while the relative attributes, those consequent upon God's relation to the world, could. Christian Thomasius spoke of the finitization rather than alienation of deity, in an act of will according to which the divine consciousness in Jesus became "latent." Notice that the reference to "consciousness" shifts the discussion into characteristically modern terms, for ancient conceptuality was concerned with ontological status rather than some internal characteristic. While Thomasius taught a divesting of the relative divine attributes in order that the immanent attributes—power, truth, holiness, love—might be revealed, more radical exponents rejected the distinction between different forms of attributes, and taught the complete depotentiation of the Word.

The mythological overtones of the teaching of the depotentiation of deity and the criticism that salvation requires the presence and action of one who is truly God, effectively ended the movement in GERMANY. In the twentieth century, the Scottish Congregationalist PETER TAYLOR FORSYTH (1848–1921) so revised the theory that it was scarcely kenosis at all. According to him, the attributes were not renounced but exercised in a new mode of their being. Christ is the Godhead, self-reduced but real, an expression rather than retraction of the infinite God whose infinity contains a capacity for the finite, and whose kenosis leads to a plerosis, a fulfillment. While versions of kenotic theory lingered into the twentieth century, they have suffered damaging criticism, particularly for their mythological form and for appearing to suggest that Christ can only become incarnate by being in some way less than fully divine.

The approach of some of the Reformed to the challenge of Socinianism was rather different. Rather than using kenosis as a theory to bring the human and divine into logical consistency, John Owen (1616–1683) sought a solution in a strong doctrine of the humanity of Christ understood with the help of the doctrine of the Holy Spirit. His Son was indeed self-emptied into the flesh, but remained fully the Word. After the incarnation, however, which is indeed the act of the divine Word (that is to say, in the hypostatic union of divine and human in Jesus) it is the Spirit rather than the Word who is the motive force of Jesus' actions. We have Christ as God incarnate, and so fully both human and divine, but maintained in his human integrity by his relation to the Father through the Spirit. Similarly, mainstream Reformed christology on the continent of Europe, as summarized in Heinrich Heppe's compendium of 1861, was classically patristic in form. The divinity of Christ is not that of the divine nature, but of the Word, who did not take to himself a ready-made human being, but added human nature to his eternal and infinite being, a human nature subject in its servant form to all its attendant weaknesses, although in a sinless way. Like Owen, the Reformed dogmaticians taught that the Holy Spirit was the agent of Christ's human formation and sanctification.

Enlightenment and Liberalism

In sum: at the center of the difference between the Lutheran and Reformed christology lay the treatment of the communication of attributes, according to which divine and human attributes are, so to speak, transferable. For Lutherans, what is at stake is the relation between the two natures, so that their monophysite tendency derives from a Nestorian question. The Reformed position, by contrast, takes the doctrine, after Cyril of Alexandria, to mean that both divine and human predicates are attributable to the *person* of Christ by virtue of the union of divine and human in the incarnation. Both christologies, however, were subjected to radical critique in the Enlightenment. Different aspects of the critique can be found in the work of HERMANN S. REIMARUS (1694–1768), GOTTHOLD E. LESSING (1729–1781), and IMMANUEL KANT (1724–1804). In a work published posthumously by Lessing, Reimarus contended that the resurrection of Jesus and the subsequent dogmatic teaching of his divinity was a deliberate invention to mask the failure of his ministry. Rejecting such a simplistic thesis on the grounds of the moral integrity of the writers and the conflicts to be expected in eyewitness accounts, Lessing's challenge was essentially hermeneutic. For him, between the present and the past lay an "broad ugly ditch" separating modernity from the Jesus of history and epistemologically denying the capacity of historical events, even the Resurrection, to found the certainties of religious belief. Kant's rationalist and more radical refusal to base christology on anything traditional or historical led him to an essentially moralistic interpretation. The significance Jesus had was as the teacher of a pure rational ethic, of which he accordingly served as an example of what might be discovered by reason, but no more.

Conceding Kant's case against an objective christology derived from transcendent revelation, FRIEDRICH SCHLEIERMACHER (1768–1834), influenced as he was also by both Moravian piety and Romantic reaction against rationalism (see MORAVIAN CHURCH, ROMANTICISM) sought to expand beyond Kant's restrictive limits. His was a historical Jesus whose uniquely real experience of God represented the virtual existence of God within him, and so was constitutive and not merely exemplary for succeeding generations. This involved the rejection of two polar considerations that had been definitive for orthodox Protestant theology until that time. On the one hand, the concept of a transcendent redeemer who became incarnate is displaced by an immanent divine force welling up from within history; Jesus' significance derives from his supreme and unclouded God-consciousness. On the other, the rejection of the Resurrection and ascension as definitive for christology meant the loss of a present Christ—"at the right hand of the Father"—mediated by the Spirit (Calvin's position), in favor of a form of redemptive experience mediated historically from the past Jesus through the experience of the Christian community transmitted through time. Schleiermacher is one of the first to attempt to base his christology on a historical quest for Jesus, in an attempt to subvert the criticism of Reimarus, Lessing, and Kant. In the appeal to consciousness and to history he is definitive for Protestant christology thereafter. In his hesitancy to accept the full reality of Jesus' temptation in favor of a concept of "unclouded blessedness," there is evidence that his historical quest in practice subverted the full humanity of Christ. This is also represented by his marginalizing of the Jewishness of Jesus, something being increasingly corrected in christology after the Second World War.

The other main founder of nineteenth-century Protestant christology, G. W. F. HEGEL (1770–1831), sought to break free from the limits of Kantian rationalism, not by an appeal to experience but by an altered conception of rationality. At the root of his christology is an attempt to mediate between *Vorstellung* (representation), which referred to the historical and imaginative form in which biblical truth was expounded, and *Begriff* (concept), which he took to be its inner rational meaning. The essential modernity of Hegel's christology is shown in its tendency to theological immanence, conceiving christology as the realization of divine realities *within* general history and consequently giving an essentially subjective account of the unique incarnation of the Son of God at a particular time. Christianity is an absolute revelation as the realization of the consciousness of God-manhood rather than its unique historical instantiation. Here the Lutheran communication of attributes is radicalized. Before this, despite the occasional rhetorical reference to God's death on the cross, the conception had not been reversed because the doctrine of the immutability of God prevented the attribution of human characteristics to God. Hegel, however, not only promotes a strong version of the identity of the divine and human (for him the divine nature is the human), but also develops a christology of the death of God that is of both cultural and theological significance. Earlier theologians had said that God was crucified but construed that in terms of the death of the incarnate Word. Hegel moves a step further, at least suggesting that God *simpliciter* so dies. Culturally this was later used to argue—for example in Nietzsche—that God has died in our history and is no longer significant for human life. Theologically, it suggests a revised christology according to which the locus of divine action is immanent rather than transcendent. Ultimately, in combination with the cultural trend, it founded an irreversible movement from *Vorstellung* to *Begriff* such that it is the human race that is now the only divine Christ. The Lutheran tendency to suggest that

what can be attributed to one nature must also be attributable to the other thus leads inexorably to modern secular and "death of God" theologies.

That was not, however, Hegel's position, which was, rather, ambiguous: it remains unclear whether the historical Christ remains "elevated" to a higher philosophical level, or is "abolished" (the two meanings of Hegel's *Aufhebung*) in favor of a merely immanent cultural process. After Hegel there was a division between the "right" and "left" Hegelians, the former concentrating on the historical, the latter on the conceptual aspects, and this led ultimately to the atheism of Karl Marx (1818–1883) and others. An important transitional figure is DAVID F. STRAUSS (1808–1874), whose radical Hegelianism involved the rejection of all theological interpretation of Jesus on the grounds that it was myth, by which was meant the projection of primitive minds untutored in modern philosophical sophistication. This is another way in which an atheist "christology" became a paradoxical development of the monophysite Lutheran strain in Hegel, according to which the divinity of Jesus becomes the divinity of all.

SÖREN KIERKEGAARD (1813–1855) believed that such general divinizing of the human was but the logical development of Hegel's theory of *Begriff*, which transmuted the unique divinity of Jesus of Nazareth into something quite different. According to him, Christianity teaches that one man only is divine, while to transmute that into a general human divinity is to revert to paganism. In reaction against it, he returned to the orthodox tradition and proclaimed its essential paradox: the infinite and the finite being contraries, the intellectual and moral offense of christology could not be thought away but only solved practically by living the faith. Only for those who appropriate the truth does its logic become intelligible. Kierkegaard actively welcomed Lessing's challenge because it demonstrated that the logic of christology is equally difficult for any age, including Christ's contemporaries who thus have no advantage over those facing the challenge of belief in the modern age. This was a relatively lone voice, but was to bear fruit in the twentieth century.

Christological immanence tended to rule the day in the nineteenth century, though there are exceptions, which we shall meet. Within a wide range of variations, the following tendencies were prominent. (1) A basis was sought in a more or less modified Hegelianism, according to which history is seen as the locus for divine action, centrally in Jesus. Notable here was the work of I. A. Dorner, who combined elements of Hegel, Schleiermacher, and the classical christological tradition. (2) A basis for christology was sought in historical research, oriented either to a (Kantian) moralism, as in ALBRECHT RITSCHL (1822–1889), or a more experimental approach deriving from Schleiermacher (Rudolf Herrmann). Using a method now characterized as "christology from below," an attempt was made to ground Jesus' divinity in features of his historical career. As with Schleiermacher, however, this method often failed to produce the human Jesus that was so desperately sought, tending to a christology of a divinized man by so elevating the religious or moral qualities of the human being that a Hegelian divinization of the human was reproduced. Paradoxically, an attempt to emphasize the humanity of the savior led to its etherialization.

A Return to Transcendence

At the end of the century, the quest for the historical Jesus came under two-pronged attack. Biblical scholars, prominently Johannes Weiss and Albert Schweitzer, indicated the bourgeois character of the figure presented, and argued that Jesus was a (failed) eschatological preacher rather than a moralist or conveyor of religious experience. Hermeneutical and dogmatic criticism was supplied by Martin Kähler (1835–1912), whose importance lies also in the fact that he influenced KARL BARTH (1886–1968), PAUL TILLICH (1886–1965), and RUDOLF BULTMANN (1884–1976). For him, the gospel writers portrayed the Christ of the gospel proclamation and were wrongly quarried for merely historical information. Unlike Bultmann, however, Kähler was not a historical sceptic, for he believed that the gospel portrayals presented an essentially credible picture. He rather sought a properly theological interpretation of the texts. In America, christology followed a similar course, but under rather different impulses. Defenses of the faith against Arianism and Socinianism in the generations after Jonathan Edwards's strongly trinitarian christology gave way before the influence of unitarianism. During the nineteenth century a rational defense of orthodox Calvinist christology was attempted by Charles Hodge (1797–1878), J. W. Nevin developed a christology with central orientation to the church and the eucharist, while HORACE BUSHNELL (1802–1876) based one on symbol and an appeal to feeling rather than to objective dogmatic truth.

Theological immanentism was not, however, the only direction of nineteenth-century christology, and the example of the Scottish Presbyterian, EDWARD IRVING (1792–1834), is significant for his seeking another route than historical research to establish an adequate doctrine of the humanity of Christ. Apparently, for he does not reveal his sources, building upon Puritan theologians like Owen, Irving argued that the incarnation represented a complete self-emptying of

the eternal Son into the human being, Jesus, not at the expense of but as the expression of his divinity. This identification involved his sharing what Irving rashly, for he was convicted of heresy by a church court, called his sinful humanity. His point was not that Christ was sinful, but that the Holy Spirit subdued the sinful tendencies of the flesh to enable the eternal Son to redeem it as truly man through the course of his life and the offering of his death. Like Owen, Irving builds upon Calvin's appeal to the importance for the believer of the human priesthood of Christ as it was expressed in the Letter to the Hebrews.

Another exception to the liberalizing tendency was provided late in the century by P.T. Forsyth, a Scottish pupil of Ritschl teaching in London, who experienced an evangelical conversion on the basis of which he returned to a dogmatic christology. Still influenced by Ritschl, however, he sought a "moralized" dogma from which metaphysics was excluded. Forsyth's Anglican contemporaries—and if some of them were more Catholic than Protestant in orientation, they were affected by and, in turn, helped to shape liberal Protestantism—were mostly exercised with another problem, that of evolution. Following Charles Darwin's (1809–1882) challenge to Christian belief (see DARWINISM), they (particularly J. R. Illingworth) sought to show that the incarnation represented a qualitatively new development of a universal immanence of the Logos in the world. More conservative Anglicans saw in this too much of an accommodation to the intellectual currents of the day, and much twentieth-century English christology did indeed move away from Illingworth's strong hold on the patristic tradition, via the kenoticism of Gore, into scepticism about the orthodox position.

The early Karl Barth changed the direction of much Protestant christology by (1) rejecting as inconsistent his teacher Rudolf Herrmann's combination of experience and historical christology; (2) accepting the eschatological christology of recent New Testament interpretation, which he took to be a virtue rather than a problem; and (3) adding a liberal dose of Kierkegaardian paradox. This was not, however, a dogmatic christology as much as one of event, according to which in Jesus Christ the unknown God breaks "vertically," and so, according to this conception, eschatologically, on to the horizontal plane of history. Dogma was held at bay by what Barth later believed was an excessive appeal to existentialist—and so subjectivist—conceptuality. Although he replaced this with a trinitarian theology of revelation to which God the Son's revelatory incarnation in space and time was central, his later dogmatic christology remains one of event, according to which Jesus Christ is God taking place in time in order to bring about his purposes of universal reconciliation. This was, however, by no means a straightforward return to classical christology, for Barth sought to transcend the static conceptuality of the tradition by weaving together, in a single multivolume development, both what dogmatics had distinguished as the person and work of Christ and the Reformed notion of Christ's three offices as priest, king, and prophet (notice the change of order). Jesus Christ is at once God's priestly condescension to the human condition, the "Royal Man" brought by God to authentic human action and the "Victor," the prophet who overturns evil by the revelation of divine reconciliation achieved in him. In its tendency to identify Jesus as God's self-giving in time, Barth's christology is, in many respects, more Lutheran than Calvinist in shape, with a heavy stress on the incarnation as God's self-humiliation to the human condition. This was a successful way of overcoming the kenotic approach, for God's very divinity is not renounced but revealed and expressed in his capacity to become human. However, there is a price to pay in the fact that Barth is more successful in characterizing the humanity of God (as he later summed up his approach) than the humanity of Jesus, which tends to fade into the background.

Barth and Beyond

Widespread influence was also exercised by two of Barth's contemporaries, who maintained a more positive orientation to existentialism. Rudolf Bultmann eschewed all historical and dogmatic basis for christology, centering on the rise of the Resurrection faith in the church and the appeal of the proclaimed Christ. Where Kähler had said that the real Christ is the proclaimed Christ, Bultmann made it *only* the preached Christ. Tillich is more difficult to characterize. His christology in his *Systematic Theology* 2 was widely greeted as a modern version of orthodox christology, but both rejected patristic conceptuality and marginalized the historical Jesus in an inverted kenotic christology according to which Jesus is conceived to empty himself of his particular humanity in order that the New Being might be realized through him.

Of Barth's pupils, the first to make a major impact was DIETRICH BONHOEFFER (1906–1945), to whose legacy there are two sides. His early lectures, published in English as *Christology*, focused on the question of who, rather than what, is Jesus, and were strongly oriented to the Chalcedonian tradition. Under the impact of his later criticism of Barth, his christology took on a more Lutheran character, strongly identifying God with the one who died on the cross in a suggestion that on the cross God allows himself to be driven out of the world for the sake of a "religionless" Chris-

tianity. Though clearly not intended by Bonhoeffer, this later helped to give rise, especially in America, to death of God christologies, with their Hegelian suggestion that God immolates himself in the death of Jesus on the cross.

More directly in line with Barth in the later twentieth century is T. F. Torrance (1913–) who, however, injected a more directly patristic note. For Torrance, Athanasius's concept of the *homoousios*—God the Son as "one in being" with God the Father—serves several purposes. It establishes a positive relation between God and the created realms of time and space and enables parallels to be drawn between patristic theology and the epistemology of modern science. At the same time, it provides the basis for a strong reassertion of the classical teaching of the divinity of God the Son and his unique, revelatory, and saving historical incarnation. While Torrance's strong objectivism and appeal to rationality represent developments beyond Barth, albeit within a similar framework, two of his German successors have proved more critical. Wolfhart Pannenberg (1928–) critical of Barth's subjectivism (his irrational appeal to revelation) sought to base christology not in credal assertions from above, but from below in the findings of historical research, where he sought also to undermine Bultmann's historical scepticism. Combining an argument for the historicity of the resurrection with a conception of history adapted from Hegel, he argued that Jesus is, by virtue of the Resurrection, retroactively confirmed in oneness with God. In his *Systematic Theology*, Pannenberg bases this on the trinitarian notion of the Son's self-distinction from the Father, a self-distinction taking form in the incarnation and confirmed by the Resurrection to be such. In some contrast, while sharing an eschatological orientation, JÜRGEN MOLTMANN (1926–) developed a christology whose orientation was political and apologetic. Taking his starting point from the problem of Auschwitz, he developed a concept of Jesus as the "crucified God" redeeming the suffering of the world by sharing it. This was expanded into a "messianic" christology whose political implications are prominent.

The latter half of the twentieth century opened with the reassertion in the English-speaking world of christologies, some of them atheist, owing much to Bultmann and Strauss. More recently it has become common to encounter theologies of the incarnation that are undefensively articulated as intrinsic to any Christian theology. Most striking is the christology of the Lutheran Robert Jenson, who makes appeal to the christology of Brenz in developing a doctrine strongly oriented to church and Eucharist, and teaching that Jesus is raised from the dead into, almost as, the church. Jenson is relatively uninterested in the lineaments of the human life and sinlessness of Jesus, and thus his work is in marked contrast with recent developments in Reformed christology, which take up the appeal to the Spirit in Owen and Irving, and to the notion of recapitulation in Irenaeus of Lyons. According to this, Jesus of Nazareth is the eternal Son of God who does the work of God as one who is fully human, recapitulating the human story and offering to God the Father, through the Spirit, a truthful, free, and obedient gift of his whole life on behalf of others.

References

Heppe, Heinrich. *Reformed Dogmatics.* Translated by G. T. Thomson. Grand Rapids, MI: Baker, 1978, 371–509.

Mackintosh, H. R. *The Doctrine of the Person of Jesus Christ.* Edinburgh: T & T Clark, 2000.

McCormack, Bruce. *For Us and Our Salvation. Incarnation and Atonement in the Reformed Tradition.* Princeton: Princeton Theological Seminary, 1993.

Pannenberg, Wolfhart. *Jesus—God and Man.* Translated by L. Wilkins and D. Priebe. London: SCM Press, 1968.

Schweitzer, Albert. *The Quest of the Historical Jesus.* Translated by W. Montgomery. London: Adam and Charles Black, 1954.

Stevens, B. M. *The Prism of Time and Eternity. Images of Christ in American Protestant Thought from Jonathan Edwards to Horace Bushnell.* Lanham and London: Scarecrow Press, 1997.

Thompson, John. *Christ in Perspective in the Theology of Karl Barth.* Edinburgh: St. Andrew Press, 1978.

Welch, Claude, ed., *God and Incarnation in Mid-Nineteenth Century German Theology.* London: Oxford University Press, 1965.

COLIN GUNTON

CHUBB, THOMAS (1679–1747)

Radical Deist. Chubb was born September 29, 1679 in Salisbury, ENGLAND. He was self-taught, working as a glover and then a tallow-chandler. His reading of WILLIAM WHISTON's *Primitive Christianity Revived* inspired his own writing, in an Arian frame, of the *Supremacy of the Father Asserted* (1711), the first of a long line of books, which appeared in the 1730s and 1740s, discussing the relationship of reason and revelation and the personhood of God. In this he had the financial support of Sir Joseph Jekyll, Master of the Rolls, and others. Chubb claimed to be a Christian and a believer.

His works were noted by Alexander Pope (who described him as "a wonderful phenomenon of Wiltshire") and other admirers for the radical way in which they popularized Edward's Deist views and challenged older theological and philosophical assumptions. He merited a direct challenge from JONATHAN EDWARDS in treatise "On the Freedom of the Will" (1754). Chubb proclaimed the supremacy of reason over scripture. The New Testament was called the "fountain of confusion and contradiction" that required verification and restoration to its primitive simplicity. In his book *The True Gospel of Jesus Christ Asserted. . . morality alone can make men acceptable to God* (1738), Chubb maintained that following the teaching of Jesus Christ, exemplified in Jesus's life-words, was sufficient for SALVATION. He considered Jesus a unique person, fully human but subordinate to the Father.

He remained single and went regularly to his parish church in Salisbury. After his death on February 8, 1747 several of his writings appeared as *Posthumous Works.* His work continued to be read widely in the UNITED STATES.

See also Deism

References and Further Reading

Hillerbrand, Hans J. *A Fellowship of Discontent.* New York: Harper and Row, 1967.

TIM MACQUIBAN

CHURCH

According to the Christian understanding the church is found in the Old Testament as well as in the New. In both Testaments, the church means the "gathered people of God" (literally, "the assembly"). A common thread—the verb "to call"—links the Hebrew and the Greek meanings. The church is the community called by the covenant-making and covenant-keeping God from among the nations to worship God and to be the instrument of God's purpose in the world. In the New Testament, *ekklesia* (assembly = church) is used in three senses: of the local congregation, the community where spiritual gifts are exercised; of the church generically, wherever it is found; and of the mystical church, the body that has Christ as its head. The Latin equivalent *ecclesia* gives us the English words "ecclesiastical" and "ecclesiology." (The word "church" for a building comes from a different word, related to the Scots "kirk" and meaning "belonging to the Lord.")

Forms of the Church

All Christian traditions acknowledge at least two fundamental expressions or instantiations of church: the church in a parish or neighborhood and the universal church. The REFORMATION emphasized the idea of "particular" churches, which were coterminous with nations, countries, or cities (e.g., the CHURCH OF ENGLAND, the Church of Geneva), while also acknowledging the universal visible church, made up of particular churches. The reformers claimed that these churches had the AUTHORITY and duty to reform themselves, even when the universal church could not act as one. The notion of particular churches is important for the Reformation principle of diversity of traditions and practices (as opposed to centrally enforced global uniformity). In modern terms, it promotes the inculturation of the Gospel in diverse contexts.

The Roman Catholic Church is a globally organized church, with its symbolic and administrative center in Rome, made up of dioceses led by their bishops and referred to as "local churches." Episcopally ordered churches understand the diocese ecclesiologically, not merely functionally or administratively, and see it as an authentic expression of church. There is an unresolved disagreement in Roman Catholic thought over the question of whether the local church or the universal church is primary. Does the diocese exist because there is already a universal church, or is the universal church possible because it is made up of dioceses? The question can be translated into congregational–universal terms for non-Episcopal churches.

In today's culture, the ecclesial center of gravity rests with the local church, and it is not easy to persuade Christians to invest ecclesial value in more remote structures. The notion of the "gathered church," which belongs to the Congregationalist strand of ecclesiology and is found among BAPTISTS and Pentecostalists, is the image of church that is most congenial to postmodern CULTURE, which looks for an eclectic convergence of the like-minded. Christians today find it hard to see that they could be part of something on a regional, national, or global scale, or that they could be accountable to a "higher" level of oversight for what is done locally. The territorial understanding of church, based on the parochial and diocesan structure that remains important to the historic churches of Europe, is an opaque concept to many modern Christians. Its mission potential, involving the offer of pastoral ministry to all in the community, is seldom appreciated.

One, Holy, Catholic, and Apostolic Church

In the Nicean-Constantinopolitan Creed, Christians confess that they believe in "one, holy, catholic and apostolic Church." In its creedal context, this statement is clearly an affirmation of faith. Its reference is eschatological, looking to the fulfilment of the purposes of God, rather than empirical, looking at the church as we know it. Churches shaped substantially by the Reformation (the Protestant churches) or touched significantly by it (the Church of England and the other churches of the Anglican Communion) are careful not to identify their institutions with the "one

church" of the creed, though they believe their churches to be expressions of the one church or to participate in it. The Roman Catholic Church articulates an ambiguous relation to the "one church", holding that the latter "subsists in" the former, but not identifying the two without remainder. It is the Orthodox churches, however, that come closest to identifying themselves with the church of the creed in an exclusive sense. They do not recognize any other church—not even the Roman Catholic Church—as "the church."

The four dimensions or attributes of the church that are affirmed in the creed are widely interpreted along the following lines. They are to be seen as both gift and task; they belong to the realm of GRACE, yet they entail a human responsibility to actualize them. Ordained ministers and especially bishops (in churches that have them) are particularly entrusted with this responsibility.

The *unity* of the church is grounded confessionally in the apostolic faith, to which the Scriptures testify and that the creeds articulate. It is grounded sacramentally in BAPTISM and comes to fuller expression in the Eucharist (see LORD's SUPPER). The unity of ministry and oversight also belongs to the oneness of the church. Whereas Christian history contains a sorry tale of division and fragmentation, doctrinal disagreement, and formal schism, the ecumenical movement has begun to reverse this inveterate trend, and relations between churches have been transformed during the twentieth century. Church unity is not an all-or-nothing matter and should not be identified with some hypothetical future "crunch point." It is inherent in the existence of the church and comes to expression in a graduated and progressive way.

The *holiness* of the church does not refer primarily to the actual purity of its members, for they remain imperfect and do not entirely avoid sin; rather, it refers to the sanctifying purpose of God. It is God who chooses, calls, justifies and sanctifies the church and will in the end glorify her and make her perfect in Christ. However, the church is progressively made holy in each generation by the ministry of the Word and of the SACRAMENTS, combined with pastoral care and oversight.

The *catholicity* of the church refers to its universal scope. (MARTIN LUTHER substituted "universal" for "catholic" in the Creed: he brought out the meaning but sacrificed a precious Christian term.) The church catholic is intended to meet the needs and embrace the aspirations of all humankind. As the mother of Christians, the church catholic embraces all God's children. As with the other creedal attributes of the church, catholicity is often impaired and lacks credibility, especially when particular marginalized groups feel themselves excluded.

The *apostolicity* of the church refers to its foundation in the teaching and witness of the apostles as we find it in the New Testament, and to the imperative of continuing their mission. The marks of apostolicity consist of all of the permanent characteristics of the church of the apostles as these have been perpetuated in the church in visible continuity, especially the ministry of the Word, of the sacraments and of oversight. The reformers stressed that apostolicity resided in faithfulness to the apostles' DOCTRINE, not in a chain of ordinations. However, ecumenical dialogue has tended to recognize that episcopal succession can be a sign, though not a guarantee of the continuing apostolicity of the church, because bishops have a particular (but not exclusive) responsibility for teaching and defending the apostolic faith. As with unity, holiness, and catholicity, the church often fails to be completely faithful to its apostolic foundation and falters in its mission. This makes it all the more important that she should confess the one, holy, catholic, and apostolic church as an act of faith and commitment.

The Reformation and the Church

The reformers may be said to have concentrated single-mindedly on the christological center of the church—on what makes the church the church—and to have been fairly unconcerned with the circumference of the visible church and with patrolling the boundary. Sixteenth-century Christians agonized over the question of the true church, the assumption being that one was true and others were false; in one, SALVATION was to be found; in the other, it was not. Luther and JOHN CALVIN found the marks of the true church in word and sacrament truly taught and practiced according to Christ's institution. But John Calvin, a second generation reformer added the mark of discipline (effective pastoral oversight that required the cooperation of the magistrate) to the word and sacrament. The Anabaptists insisted on forming the true church, composed of conscious beliefs, a church "without spots or wrinkles." Some on the radical wing of the Reformation took an intense interest in the doctrinal and liturgical (or rather nonliturgical) purity of the congregation and reveled in the power of excommunication.

The popular rhetoric of the Reformation condemned the Roman Catholic Church, in its incorrigibly unreformed state, as ANTICHRIST, but Luther, PHILIPP MELANCHTHON, and Calvin were more judicious. The papacy was one thing—it persecuted the reform—but the community of the baptized faithful, with all its ignorance, was another. True Christians were to be found in every time and place. The Roman Church contained vestiges of the Church of Christ. Certain reforms that were resisted by the Roman Catholic Church in the sixteenth century, such as the vernacular liturgy, communion in both kinds (the wine as well as the bread), and promoting the study of Scriptures throughout the church, were implemented four centuries later by the Second Vatican Council. Other issues were partly resolved or at least clarified by ecumenical dialogue, notably the doctrine of JUSTIFICATION and the ministry of the Bishop of Rome. Relations between the Protestant (and Anglican) churches on the one hand and the Roman Catholic Church on the other hand have been transformed by the ecumenical movement.

Anglican Developments

In Anglican ecclesiology at the turn of the sixteenth century, RICHARD HOOKER and Richard Field placed more emphasis than the continental reformers did on the universal visible church and on the profession of baptismal faith taken at face value. Hooker affirmed that pre-Reformation Christians had been saved. He rejected the term "the invisible church" and spoke instead of "the church mystical." Field saw the Council of Trent as the watershed when the Roman Catholic Church decisively rejected the reform and canonised false doctrine.

For two centuries after the Reformation, the Church of England saw itself as a sister church of the Lutheran and Reformed churches. Anglican divines, however High Church, recognized non-Episcopal Protestant ministries on the Continent, though they condemned nonconformists in England for schism (see NONCONFORMITY). After 1662, the Church of England required Episcopal ordination for all her clergy. The influence of the Nonjurors (from 1688) and then of the OXFORD MOVEMENT (from 1833) soured the Anglican view of non-Episcopal churches until Anglican ecclesiology came back into balance in the late twentieth century. Agreements such as MEISSEN, PORVOO, and Called to Common Mission made possible various degrees of communion between Anglican and Lutheran churches in Europe and North America.

Visible and Invisible

For Luther, the empirical church, even when reformed, was deceptive; it could never be revelatory of the real church, which was a mystery that was hidden and could be glimpsed only by the eyes of FAITH. Calvin also stressed the mystical dimension of the church and located it in the union of believers with Christ through the Holy Spirit, by means of the instrumentality of faith, BAPTISM, the Lord's Supper, and the local fellowship. Calvin's emphasis on the means of grace indicates that he had a stronger doctrine of the institutional fabric of the church than Luther did.

The relationship between the visible and the invisible (mystical) dimensions of the church is an index of Catholic and Protestant emphases (albeit dealing in simplifications and stereotypes). Precisely in this area, the Leuenberg Fellowship document *The Church of Jesus Christ* reveals both development and tension in modern Protestant ecclesiology. For all the gains of the ecumenical movement, including basic agreement on a range of disputed doctrines (not least justification), Roman Catholics, Orthodox, Protestants, and Anglicans have not succeeded in reaching solid agreement about the nature or being of the church.

See also Anglicanism; Bishop and Episcopacy; Ecclesiology; Ecumenism; Dialogue, Interconfessional; Lutheranism; Pentecostalism; Orthodox, Eastern

References and Further Reading

Avis, P. *The Anglican Understanding of the Church*, London: SPCK, 2000.
———. *Anglicanism and the Christian Church: Theological Resources in Historical Perspective*, revised and expanded ed. London and New York: Continuum/T. & T. Clark, 2002.
———. *The Church in the Theology of the Reformers*, Eugene OR: Wipf and Stock Publishers, 2002b.
———, ed. *The Christian Church: An Introduction to the Major Traditions.* London: SPCK, 2002.
Carter, D. *Love Bade Me Welcome: A British Methodist Perspective on the Church*, Peterborough, UK: Epworth Press, 2002.
Küng, H. *The Church*, London: Search Press, 1971.
Leuenberg Church Fellowship Main. *The Church of Jesus Christ: The Contribution of the Reformation Towards Ecumenical Dialogue on Church Unity.* Frankfurt, Germany: Otto Lembeck, 1996.
Preston, G. *Faces of the Church: Meditations on a Mystery and Its Images.* Edinburgh, UK: T. & T. Clark, 1997.
Schwöbel, C. The Creature of the Word: Recovering the Ecclesiology of the Reformers, in *On Being the Church: Essays on the Christian Community*, edited by C. E. Gunton and D. W. Hardy. Edinburgh, UK: T. & T. Clark, 1989, pp 110–155.

PAUL AVIS

CHURCH AND STATE, OVERVIEW

Protestants have adopted varying understandings on church–state issues, ranging from an advocacy of theocracy (the church controlling the state) to Erastianism (the state controlling the church). Many Protestants have favored an established church, where the church receives governmental support, but many Protestants have also advocated the separation of church and state. The disparity in Protestant church–state views arises from the multitude of theological, cul-

tural, and historical factors that have influenced the development of differing church traditions.

Martin Luther and Lutheranism

Early in its history the Western church sought to delineate the roles played by church and state. In *The City of God* Augustine of Hippo argued that the City of God (roughly, the church) and the City of Man (roughly, the state) were two separate kingdoms with different loves and different organizing principles. MARTIN LUTHER sought to preserve the Augustinian distinction of the two kingdoms, but over time, he granted the state greater control over the life of the church. He eventually went so far as to declare that it was incumbent on the magistrate to root out HERESY and ensure proper church order. In 1528 Luther was instrumental in giving legitimacy to the visitations, a program in which the rulers sent out visitors to inquire and correct errors in the Protestant churches. Luther also abandoned his early opposition to persecution of heretics, and by 1530 he consented to the imposition of the death penalty for Anabaptists.

The determinative role played by the state in Lutheran church affairs was codified in law as LUTHERANISM spread. The Danish Church Ordinance of 1539 declared that the Christian monarch should supervise the PREACHING of the word, the administration of the SACRAMENTS, and the Christian care and upbringing of children and the poor (see CHILDHOOD; CHARITY). Other Scandinavian countries that embraced the Lutheran REFORMATION passed similar ordinances. The Peace of Augsburg of 1555, a settlement between the territorial rulers of GERMANY and the emperor, stipulated that princes were to determine whether their territory would embrace Lutheranism or Catholicism, giving the ruler the supreme right to determine religious affairs within its borders.

John Calvin and the Reformed Churches

JOHN CALVIN's social vision was of a holy commonwealth united under God wherein state and church remained institutionally separate but worked together to transform society. As with Luther, Calvin declared that only spiritual tools were available to the church's ministry. The state, on the other hand, was charged with maintaining order and enforcing outward conformity to the Ten Commandments and other biblical precepts. Calvin appealed to the biblical example of Old Testament kings who were "much praised in Scripture for restoring the worship of God when it had been corrupted and overturned."

Some commentators have labeled Calvin's church-state program a theocracy, but this term is misleading.

A theocracy is literally a governmental system in which God rules the nation, but the word is used loosely to describe a government in which clergy hold the reins of power. Calvin never advocated such a system and insisted that the church was not to be a territorial power. Calvin even declared that Jesus Christ himself "intended to debar the ministers of his word from civil domination and worldly powers."

An important church-state idea that emerged in Calvin's writing was the doctrine of interposition. Lesser magistrates had the right and Christian duty to restrain the wickedness of a tyrannical king, even to the point of deposing him. JOHN KNOX, a disciple of Calvin and a leader of early Scottish PRESBYTERIANISM, went beyond Calvin regarding the right to revolution. Whereas Calvin limited the right of interposition to lesser magistrates, Knox declared it the duty of all Christians to overthrow a tyrant. For Knox silence in the face of tyranny implied complicity with injustice.

Anglicanism and the English Reformation

The English Reformation of HENRY VIII was marked by the Erastian tendency in most forms of religious establishment, that is, the priority of the state over the church. Henry VIII severed his nation's ties to the papacy when the pope refused to annul Henry's marriage to Catherine of Aragon. Henry made himself the head of the English church, and Parliament issued the Supremacy Act of 1534, which declared the monarch to be "the supreme head in earth of the CHURCH OF ENGLAND," with "full power and authority from time to time to visit, repress, redress, reform, order, correct, restrain, and amend all such errors, heresies, abuses, offences, contempts, and enormitie," within the church. He and his successors sought to establish a single, uniform religious policy for all of ENGLAND. Every aspect of church life—DOCTRINE, sacraments, vestments, education, and charity work—came under the purview of the crown. When Queen ELIZABETH I came to the throne, the Supremacy Act was reaffirmed in 1559 with only slight alteration, and all church officials were required to swear that the monarch was "the only supreme governor of this realm."

English Puritanism

In doctrine and temperament Henry and most of his heirs were not truly interested in reforming their church along Protestant lines, but their break from Rome opened the door for more thoroughgoing Protestants to push for greater ecclesiastical reform. Calvinistic Puritans, the largest group of Protestant dissenters, wanted to do away with the trappings of Roman Catholicism that remained in the Anglican church (see CALVINISM; PURITANISM; ANGLICANISM). Their agitation for a more thoroughly Protestantized church threatened to undo the complex *via media,* or middle way, established by Queen Elizabeth to placate moderate Catholics and Protestants. When James I came to the English throne, he sought to stamp out the Puritan challenge and forced many of them to flee to relative safety in the New World. Later King Charles I appointed WILLIAM LAUD as archbishop of Canterbury, and Laud's zealous pursuit of Puritan dissenters caused growing popular unrest. By 1642 Puritans in Parliament presented the king with their "Grand Remonstration," a statement of grievances and suggested solutions, but it was then too late. Puritan militants and other opponents of the crown rebelled, and in the wake of this CIVIL WAR, the king was executed and a Puritan commonwealth formed in 1649. Under the leadership of OLIVER CROMWELL, the commonwealth sought to advance Protestant interests, and Protestants of all stripes were given a fair degree of toleration. Cromwell urged Anglicans, Presbyterians, and Independents to learn how to coexist. When Cromwell died in 1658, however, the monarchy granted TOLERATION to both Puritans and Catholics, but such toleration came at the price of periodic persecution and the removal of certain rights. The Test Act of 1673, for example, excluded all nonconformists (i.e., non-Anglicans) from holding civil, ecclesiastical, or military posts.

Anabaptists and the Radical Reformation

Perhaps the most important Protestant reinterpretation of church-state relations was promoted by the Anabaptists. Unlike other Protestants, these "Radical Reformers" rejected any state-established church and sought to create a pure church made up of only sincere believers. Most Anabaptists embraced a dualistic theology that highlighted the disjunction between the church and the world. The SCHLEITHEIM CONFESSION, an early Anabaptist statement of faith, declared that all people are "in but two classes, good and bad, believing and unbelieving, darkness and light, the world and those who have departed the world, God's temple and idols, Christ and Belial; and none can have part with the other." This dualism, when combined with a principle of nonresistance, led most Anabaptists to withdraw from all association with the government. Anabaptists neither sought nor accepted aid from the state. Whereas Luther and Calvin saw the two spheres of temporal and spiritual power as harmonious in the plan of God, the Anabaptists tended to see them at war with each other. MENNO SIMONS, a leader of Dutch ANABAPTISM, declared: "No, no, Christ Jesus and His powerful Word and the Spirit of God are the caretakers and defenders of the church, and not, forever not, the emperor, king, or any worldly power!"

Menno Simons became the spokesperson for the movement after Protestant and Catholic magistrates had martyred most of the early Anabaptist leaders. Menno recognized the state as an institution established by God, but he insisted that it lay outside the perfection of Christ. Most Anabaptists therefore disavowed that a Christian could serve in civil government and refused to pass judgment in civil disputes with unbelievers.

Contemporary Protestant Developments

Each of the church–state positions that developed during the Reformation continues to provide the foundation for current Protestant ideas on this subject. Most Protestants, especially in the UNITED STATES, have moved away from the exclusivist forms of religious establishment that emerged in the Reformation, although a few Protestant communities continue to advocate a closer union between church and state.

In the seventeenth and eighteen centuries the Lutheran establishment continued relatively unchanged in most countries. Although church and state were separated in Germany in 1919, many Protestants supported the "German Christian" movement, which favored a close alliance between the church and Hitler's Third Reich (see GERMAN CHRISTIANS). Those who opposed this attempt to establish a Nazified church formed the CONFESSING CHURCH movement, whose BARMEN DECLARATION proclaimed Jesus Christ alone as Lord of his church. After World War II most Lutheran nations in Europe retained some form of church establishment, although SWEDEN officially disestablished the Lutheran church in 2000. In America Lutherans have embraced the separation of church and state inherent in America's constitutional system.

The Anglican church–state model has also remained relatively unchanged, although this may change in the early years of the twenty-first century. The British state takes a less active role in church affairs, but Parliament must still give approval to important clerical decisions and appointments. At the end of the twentieth century, there have been repeated calls for full disestablishment of the Church of England. Already, the English government funds schools across religious lines, including Anglican, Jewish, Muslim, Catholic, Sikh, and Adventist schools. Prince Charles, the presumptive heir to the throne at the turn of the twenty-first century, indicated that he would prefer to be called the Defender of the Faiths, rather than the Defender of the Faith.

A diversity of views marks the contemporary state of Reformed Protestant understandings of church and state. Mainline Presbyterians and Congregationalists in the United States have been among the strongest supporters of church–state separation. Barry Lynn, the executive director of AMERICANS UNITED FOR SEPARATION OF CHURCH AND STATE, is an ordained minister in the UNITED CHURCH OF CHRIST, a progressive denomination with Calvinistic roots. On the other hand, some conservative Presbyterians have become strong proponents of greater cooperation of church and state (see PRESBYTERIANISM). In the late nineteenth and early twentieth centuries, the Calvinistic Dutch theologian and prime minister ABRAHAM KUYPER helped formulate the doctrine of sphere sovereignty, which declared that society was made up of various institutions like church, state, and FAMILY that exercised authority in clearly defined social spheres. Because such structural pluralism is normative, each social sphere is able to safeguard society from lapsing into some form of authoritarianism. According to this doctrine, church and state support each other in an attempt to promote wholesome community life. KARL BARTH, a Reformed theologian and important advocate of NEO-ORTHODOXY in the middle part of the twentieth century, stressed that the state was not outside of Christ's dominion and that the church had an obligation to oversee and, when necessary, criticize the state whenever government sought to establish itself as an absolute power.

In America the Christian Reconstructionist movement has taken the emphasis on God's moral law found in the thought of John Calvin and turned it into a theological system advocating the reconstruction of civil society according to the dictates of Old Testament civil and moral law. Reconstructionists have gone so far as to advocate the reestablishment of the death penalty for such infractions as blasphemy or HOMOSEXUALITY. Christian Reconstructionism has had an impact outside of traditional Reformed circles, and a number of charismatic churches have adopted part of the Christian Reconstructionist theology under the rubric of "Dominion Theology."

Modern Anabaptists have remained true to their view of the disjuncture between church and state. Many conservative Anabaptists such as the AMISH in North America have adopted a "come-outer" mentality of withdrawing from all aspects of society, including participation in government. Other MENNONITES have sought to walk a finer line concerning the amount of participation they should have in the state. Anabaptist theologian John Howard Yoder argued quite persuasively in his book, *The Politics of Jesus,* that Anabaptist principles should play an important role in modern society. Although not confusing the kingdoms of this world with the KINGDOM OF GOD, Yoder and similar Anabaptists like Ronald Sider of Evangelicals for Social Action have sought to bring the ETHICS of the Sermon of the Mount into play in the political arena.

Although the churches of the Radical Reformation are relatively small today, Anabaptists' church–state views have had a great impact on the large and growing Baptist church movement. Most contemporary Baptist groups are not directly related to the Anabaptist movement of the Reformation, but they have historically embraced the Anabaptist emphasis on the separation of church and state. BAPTISTS of the eighteenth century like ISAAC BACKUS and John Leland were at the forefront for disestablishment in colonial America. Today, such organizations as the Baptist Joint Committee on Public Affairs and the BAPTIST WORLD ALLIANCE remain strong advocates of religious liberty worldwide. Nevertheless, with the rise of the CHRISTIAN RIGHT in the United States in the last quarter of the twentieth century, many conservative Baptists have moved to a more accommodationist perspective in church-state matters. Although still wishing to promote religious liberty for all, groups like the SOUTHERN BAPTIST CONVENTION have sought to counter a perceived trend toward secularism in public life. Conservatives like Richard Land, the head of the Southern Baptist Ethics and Religious Liberty Commission, see themselves as moderate separationists who remain vigorously opposed to religious coercion but are unwilling to accept perceived government hostility toward religion. Some independent, fundamentalist Baptists have gone beyond accommodation and embraced parts of the Christian Reconstructionist agenda developed by conservative Calvinist theologians (see FUNDAMENTALISM).

Liberal Protestantism, a term that covers the "Mainline" Protestant churches represented in the NATIONAL COUNCIL OF CHURCHES and WORLD COUNCIL OF CHURCHES, has adopted a position that embraces a transformational role for the church in society (see LIBERAL PROTESTANTISM & LIBERALISM). Emphasizing the prophetic need for social justice, the World Council of Churches has stated that the church must make common cause with oppressed people around the globe, even to the point of supporting mass political movements and revolution.

References and Further Reading

Baylor, Michael G., ed. *The Radical Reformation.* Cambridge: Cambridge University Press, 1991.

Cromartie, Michael, ed. *Caesar's Coin Revisited: Christians and the Limits of Government.* Grand Rapids, MI: Wm. B. Eerdmans, 1996.

Feldman, Stephen M. *Law and Religion: A Critical Anthology.* New York: New York University Press, 2000.

Hankins, Barry. "Principle, Perception, and Position: Why Southern Baptist Conservatives Differ from Moderates on Church-State Issues." *Journal of Church and State* 40 (1998): 343–370.

Holloway, James Y., ed. *Barth, Barmen, and the Confessing Church Today.* Lewiston, NY: Edwin Mellen Press, 1995.

Hopfl, Harro. *Luther and Calvin on Secular Authority.* Cambridge: Cambridge University Press, 1991.

Kelly, Douglas F. *The Emergence of Liberty in the Modern World.* Phillipsburg, NJ: P & R Publishing, 1992.

Maclear, J. F., ed. *Church and State in the Modern Age: A Documentary History.* New York: Oxford University Press, 1995.

Sanders, Thomas G. *Protestant Concepts of Church and State: Historical Backgrounds and Approaches for the Future.* New York: Holt, Rinehart & Winston, 1964.

Smith, Gary Scott, ed. *God and Politics: Four Views on the Reformation of Civil Government.* Phillipsburg, NJ: Presbyterian and Reformed, 1989.

Villa-Vicencio, Charles. *Between Christ and Caesar: Classical and Contemporary Texts on Church and State.* Grand Rapids, MI: Wm. B. Eerdmans, 1986.

Yoder, John Howard. *The Politics of Jesus.* Grand Rapids, MI: Wm. B. Eerdmans, 1972.

ALBERT BECK

CHURCH DISCIPLINE

The term "church discipline" was used among sixteenth-century Protestants in a variety of interlocking ways. Its principal meanings include proper polity and moral and social control exercised by the CHURCH.

In one usage, church discipline denotes proper polity. This was particularly common in francophone areas, where *discipline* and *police* were used nearly interchangeably to convey the notion of proper ordering of church government. "Discipline" in this sense is listed as the third mark of the true church (along with proper preaching and administration of the sacraments) in THEODORE BEZA's *Confession*, where the Latin *disciplina* translates the French *police*; it also appears in this sense in the *Discipline ecclésiastique* (the church order for the French Reformed Churches), the *Police de l'Eglise Réformée de Bayeux* (1563), and the *Police et Discipline de l'Eglise de Saint-Lô* (1563), both local church orders, as well as in the Presbyterian Church's *Book of Discipline.*

The primary and better known meaning of church discipline, however, involves enforcement of Christian morality and behavior. Although church discipline in this sense is frequently considered a characteristic of Reformed Protestantism, communities across all the confessional divides in early modern Europe shared a concern about improving public and, in many areas, private morality. The late fifteenth and sixteenth centuries saw an increase in legislation intended to raise the moral standards of society. This could take a variety of forms, ranging from prohibitions of begging, to restrictions on WOMEN's participation in public life, to shutting down brothels. Many scholars associate this development with the beginnings of ABSOLUTISM, noting that it coincides with the growing centralization of the state and its increasing reach into people's lives. In this context church discipline has been seen as the tool used by the state to claim moral authority and exert social control over their communities, particularly in Protestant regions where the church was itself a branch of the state. Yet some of the most extreme views of church discipline came not from state churches but from sectarian groups that self-consciously separated themselves from the state. A complete explanation of the rise of church discipline must therefore take into account elements unrelated to incipient absolutism; one particularly significant influence seems to have been economic uncertainty caused by the Price Revolution, which led to a growing anxiety about moral standards in society similar to the call to return to traditional values that arises in times of economic uncertainty in American history.

Church discipline has been part of Christianity from its earliest days. The early church insisted on its right to oversee and enforce standards of faith and practice within the community. Over time this developed into the penitential system of the medieval church. There were two basic approaches to discipline in this period, one for the LAITY and secular clergy, and the other for the regular CLERGY. The laity and secular clergy were subject to discipline by the episcopal hierarchy, administered by parish priests through the sacrament of penance, episcopal courts, and the papal court; bishops also ordered visitations to oversee the morals of the laity and clergy in their diocese. Sanctions included prohibition from participating in the SACRAMENTS (minor excommunication), complete exclusion from the Christian community (major excommunication), and eventually cutting off all sacraments from a region whose ruler was in rebellion against papal authority (interdict). For the regular clergy the rule of life under which they lived was ideally at the heart of their discipline: it both governed their external behavior and ordered their inward life, creating an interior discipline that was far different from what was expected of secular clergy and the laity.

Both secular and regular forms of discipline carried through in different ways into Protestantism. MARTIN LUTHER repudiated much of the monastic concept of discipline, arguing that one's inner life should be shaped by PREACHING and teaching, whereas external discipline was a matter of rules and regulations rather than the Spirit. Luther himself tended to leave institutional matters to laymen and the civil government. Although some of his followers attempted to introduce disciplinary institutions, these were generally unsuccessful: ecclesiastical involvement in social control

was seen as a return to "papal tyranny," and thus regulation of morals was typically left in the hands of the government with limited involvement of pastors. For HULDRYCH ZWINGLI and the Reformed tradition, on the other hand, internal and external discipline were connected. The church had a responsibility to enforce Christian standards of behavior both for the sake of the sanctity of the community and for shaping the internal life of the believer. Thus Zwingli and the Zurich city council established a marriage court whose provenance included not simply betrothals, marriages, and the regulation of SEXUALITY, but other moral issues such as gambling, profligacy, drunkenness, gluttony, and sumptuary laws. The involvement of the civil government tended to overshadow the church's role in discipline in Zurich and most other Zwinglian areas, however. Nonetheless, one particularly important contribution to the development of Reformed concepts of discipline came from JOHANNES OECOLAMPADIUS in Basel. He attempted to establish courts in each parish composed of a group of lay elders plus the pastor to enforce Christian standards of behavior. Although he met with only limited success, these courts would become the prototype for disciplinary institutions in much of the Reformed world in the coming decades.

Neither the Lutheran nor the Reformed approaches to social discipline were strict enough for some, notably many of the Anabaptists and other sectarian groups (see ANABAPTISM). These groups typically rejected the idea of a state church and condemned the lax moral and spiritual standards of the churches of their day. Instead, they saw themselves as an elite minority, the pure and spotless Bride of Christ, living in a sinful world. They insisted that the church be a voluntaristic organization, one in which the members chose to become a part. This led directly to their rejection of pedobaptism as an initiation rite into the church in favor of adult BAPTISM. Standards for entry into the community were strict, as were standards of conduct for the members. Discipline was maintained by severe sanctions against those who failed to live up to the group's expectations. One Anabaptist practice that was particularly controversial was the ban, also called shunning. This was akin to the medieval concept of major excommunication and involved complete social exclusion from the community, including prohibiting family members from speaking to the banned individual.

Largely in response to Anabaptist criticisms of the church, MARTIN BUCER developed a view of church discipline drawn from the monastic union of internal and external discipline. Although Bucer agreed with the Anabaptists regarding the problem of laxity within the church, he and the other mainstream reformers viewed the Anabaptists' use of the ban and other disciplinary practices as excessively harsh. Thus Bucer's approach to discipline not only emphasized enforcement of proper behavior, but also included a comprehensive program of Christian formation as well: as in the monasteries, discipline was connected to discipleship. Because Christ commanded the church to make disciples, Bucer saw discipline as an essential mark of the true church (along with proper preaching and administration of the sacraments), and identified it with the power of the keys (Matthew 18:19–20). At its most basic level Bucer's view of discipline involved religious education, both through teaching CATECHISM and in private confession, which Bucer viewed as a form of counseling. In each of these there was a twofold emphasis on doctrinal formation and on learning how the believer should live in response to the Gospel.

The second aspect of discipline was a "public profession of faith and obedience to the church and its ministers" on the part of the catechized; he saw this as a reformed CONFIRMATION ceremony stripped of medieval Catholic superstitions and restored to the purity of the practice of the early church. The emphasis on the promise of obedience to the church leads into the third element of discipline: mutual, fraternal admonition on the part of all church members, together with oversight on the part of the pastors and elders of the church—the "ministers" to whom obedience was particularly promised. Only at this point did discipline in the sense of enforcement of morality enter the picture. The goal of mutual admonition, and indeed discipline in general, was to get sinners to repent. Whenever possible, admonition was to be done privately, then with a few supporting witnesses, and finally with the leadership of the church, following the outline in Matthew 18:15–18. Only if the sinner refused to repent were ecclesiastical penalties, up to and including excommunication, to be invoked. Even if the sinner did repent, it might be necessary to demand proof of that repentance by having the penitent perform some act of public penance, such as abstaining from the LORD'S SUPPER for a time, fasting, and so forth. If this was refused it was to be taken as a sign that the repentance was not genuine, and the process outlined in Matthew 18 was to continue. These ideas led Bucer to propose a number of disciplinary institutions in Strasbourg, although opposition from the magistrate prevented them from being implemented for the most part.

Despite the failure to fully implement them in Strasbourg, Bucer's ideas on polity and the responsibilities of church officers had a profound effect on JOHN CALVIN's ecclesiology. Although Calvin never listed discipline as a mark of the church, he clearly saw it as an essential element of the church's ministry: his insistence on the church's right to excommunicate the unrepentant resulted in his exile from Geneva in 1538. On his return to the city, he devoted quite a bit of time and attention to the CONSISTORY, the moral and religious court of Geneva. This was the most important institution Calvin created and became a model for disciplinary institutions wherever Calvinist churches were established. The Genevan consistory was headed by First Syndic of the city and was composed of the pastors plus a group of lay elders chosen from the city councils. Initially its work focused on religious belief and practice and was primarily aimed at teaching the people how to act as Protestants. This included not only the elimination of prayers for the dead, the *Ave Maria,* and other Catholic practices, but also condemned the use of magic and charms, failure to attend or participation in amusements during Sunday services, and other religious crimes and misdemeanors. The consistory also handled other sorts of cases that generally did not involve criminal charges. Particularly common were quarrels that had become public enough to cause a scandal, including wives nagging husbands (and occasionally vice versa), husbands beating their wives excessively (and occasionally vice versa), elder abuse, brawling, loud arguments among neighbors, and the like. Next came various types of marital or sexual irregularities. The most common of these cases involved determining whether a promise of marriage had been made and enforcement of such promises; the category also included less frequently fornication, adultery, and the like. The consistory also dealt with other moral issues, such as public drunkenness and gambling.

The principal goal of church discipline in Geneva as in the rest of the Reformed world was to encourage the sinner to repent and to sin no more. Because most problems of mistaken belief or religious practice could be solved by better religious education, the most common "sanction" in these cases was an admonition to hear more sermons. For moral and social lapses, penalties were aimed more at the person's ego: a severe scolding in most cases, followed in more serious cases by a public confession of sin at the main church service on Sunday. Such public confessions not only shamed the sinner, thereby discouraging the person from repeating the behavior, but also provided a warning against those who might be tempted to similar sins. Particularly serious issues could be sent to the civil magistrate for further action. Finally those who refused to acknowledge their faults (or to recognize the authority of the consistory) could be excommunicated, that is, banned from participating in the sacraments, both the Lord's Supper and baptism. This could have serious social consequences, given the importance of godparentage in establishing ties between families in the period.

The Genevan consistory was the first successful attempt to establish church discipline in the Protestant REFORMATION. It changed in profound ways the moral climate in Geneva, as evidenced by the vast reduction in the rate of illegitimacy as well as by the testimony of visitors to the city. Because of these results, the consistory had many imitators: wherever CALVINISM spread, the consistory generally followed. These consistories proved remarkably effective in promoting an austere lifestyle characterized by strict morality, rejection of superstition, and obedience to the civil magistrate within the boundaries of God's Law and of conscience, all of which were typical elements of Calvinist piety. They were thus instrumental in promoting "puritanical" approaches to morality and social life and were critical to the propagation of Calvinist ideologies (see PURITANISM). At the same time, their success also made them very attractive to Protestant governments as an effective tool of social control. Consistories and governments worked closely together, and frequently the consistory would include local magistrates and members of town councils. In Roman Catholic territories with Calvinist minorities, however, consistories functioned independently of the government to whatever extent was necessary or possible. Where the magistrate supported the church, church discipline supported the magistrate; where the magistrate opposed the church, church discipline reinforced the boundaries of the elect community in opposition to the magistrate. Calvinist churches typically called for obedience to the powers that be whenever possible, but they insisted on obedience to God above all—even if this should mean civil disobedience or outright rebellion. In Calvinist churches ecclesiastical discipline thus not only served the religious functions of helping believers grow in godliness and restraining the wicked, but also had important political implications by defining the elect community and its relationship to the civil powers.

See also Church and State, Overview

References and Further Reading

Burnett, Amy Nelson. *The Yoke of Christ: Martin Bucer and Christian Discipline*. Kirksville, MO: Sixteenth Century Publishers, 1994.
Hsia, Ronnie Po-chia. *Social Discipline in the Reformation: Central Europe, 1550–1750*. Reprint, London and New York: Routledge, 1992.
Kingdon, Robert M. "Calvin and the Establishment of the Consistory Discipline in Geneva: The Institution and the Men who Directed It." *Nederlands Archief voor Kerkgeschiedenis* 70 (1990): 158–172.
Mentzer, Raymond A., ed. *Sin and the Calvinists: Morals Control and the Consistory in the Reformed Tradition*. Kirksville, MO: Sixteenth Century Publishers, 1994.
Schilling, Heinz. "Between the Territorial State and Urban Liberty: Lutheranism and Calvinism in the County of Lippe." In *The German People and the Reformation*, edited by R. Po-chia Hsia, 263–283. Ithaca, NY: Cornell University Press, 1988.
Sunshine, Glenn S. "Discipline as the Third Mark of the Church: Three Views." *Calvin Theological Journal* 33 (1998): 469–480.

GLENN S. SUNSHINE

CHURCHES OF CHRIST, NONINSTRUMENTAL

The Churches of Christ, Noninstrumental are a group of churches within the Stone-Campbell Movement (CHURCHES OF CHRIST and DISCIPLES OF CHRIST). These churches emphasize a reliance on the New Testament for POLITY and practice. This effort to focus on the New Testament is often understood as a return to the original form of practice in the earliest church and thus implicitly is a rejection of practices that developed in the medieval and REFORMATION periods. Thus the churches embrace a "restorationist" ideology, and the movement is often called the "Restoration Movement." There is no central denominational structure for this fellowship; a strong emphasis on congregational autonomy is dominant, although certain standards of faith and practice are maintained through informal mechanisms.

History

The nineteenth-century movement for restoring the New Testament church, which had significant leadership from Alexander Campbell (see CAMPBELL FAMILY) and BARTON W. STONE, originated primarily as a reformation movement within Presbyterian churches (see PRESBYTERIANISM). This movement, often called the Disciples of Christ, generally named individual churches either a "church of Christ" or a "Christian church." These churches emphasized a rejection of creeds, a reliance on the New Testament alone for matters of faith and practice, and a call for Christian unity around a return to the original practices of the church.

After the American CIVIL WAR, the movement began to fracture over ecclesiologic and sociologic issues. The specific ecclesiologic issues involved cooperative societies (primarily missionary societies) and instrumental music in WORSHIP. Missionary societies, in which multiple congregations banded together to support missionary efforts, were viewed by some as an innovation that could not be supported by the New Testament practice and furthermore that violated the priority of congregational autonomy. Instrumental music was seen as an innovation not supported by New Testament practice.

The concern about the introduction of "innovations" in the life of the church culminated in the Sand Creek Declaration in 1889, which stated that nothing be introduced into the practice of the church that was not based on a clear "thus saith the Lord" statement from Scripture. Thus the conservative wing of the movement increasingly adopted a restrictive hermeneutical approach to silence of the Scripture; silence on a matter is taken to be a ban on such practices.

In addition to the ecclesiologic concerns, sociologic differences resulting from the Civil War aggravated a deepening schism in the movement. The churches in the South were often poor and developed a simple perspective to church life, one that viewed the introduction of organs and missionary societies as evidence of a departure from the original emphasis of the movement. The concerns of the conservative wing of the Disciples were originally voiced by Benjamin Franklin in his popular journal the *American Christian Review*, and by David Lipscomb in his journal the *Gospel Advocate*, which continues to this day. These views were countered by the *Christian Standard*, founded by Isaac Errett, which took a decidedly progressive stand. Thus these competing journals tended to develop significantly different perspectives on a number of theological and practical issues. By the end of the nineteenth century, the tensions between various factions in the movement had led to a *de facto* split. In 1906, those churches that rejected organs and missionary societies consented to be listed separately in the U.S. census, thus explicitly recognizing the split. Those churches that rejected instruments in worship and societies called themselves simply "Churches of Christ," often with a small "c" in "churches" to indicate their rejection of denominational status.

The Churches of Christ (a cappella) grew rapidly during the first part of the twentieth century and rapidly established congregations not only in the South, but also in the West and Midwest. (The body tends to be weakly represented in the Northeast.) The Churches of Christ established a number of colleges, which have become centers of support for the movement. The Churches of Christ also began to develop strong African-American congregations, especially as a result of the evangelistic efforts of Marshall Keeble and G. P. Bowser. These black churches have developed their own strong subculture, often noted for their powerful evangelists.

The Churches of Christ have suffered internal divisions over certain issues that create tension within the body of churches. A minor division occurred in the early twentieth century over the issue of premillenni-

alism. A popular preacher named Foy Wallace, Jr. actively opposed premillennial interpretations of the Scripture, and "mainstream" Churches of Christ today oppose such interpretations; however, a rather distinct subgroup of Churches of Christ were and remain "premillennial" Churches of Christ. There are other subgroups within the movement; some churches resist SUNDAY SCHOOLS, others resist any cooperation, others believe in single cups for communion. These subgroups tend to communicate among themselves and resist the main tendencies in the Churches of Christ.

The latter part of the twentieth century saw a new emphasis within the Churches of Christ that came to be called the "Crossroads movement." This new group emphasized formal "discipleship" of members by elders, with strong control of individuals by the elders, and a very intrusive pattern of EVANGELISM. This unique group of churches was dubbed the "Boston Church of Christ" because of the dominant role the church in Boston played, a controlling role that violated the central ethos of congregational autonomy of the movement. This new group, which now calls itself the "International Churches of Christ," is shunned by the mainstream Churches of Christ and is not now considered part of the main movement.

Polity

Churches of Christ emphasize a strict pattern of congregational autonomy. There is no denominational structure, and there are no official conventions or formal conferences to coordinate activities. The local church's leadership ideally rests with lay elders, of whom there is always a plurality, and deacons, who are also a plurality. Most churches have elders appointed permanently, although some have regular elections. Most congregations have paid ministers who are selected by the local congregations and are always subject to the oversight of the local eldership. In most cases the elders are responsible for the hiring of ministers and key financial matters, although some congregations delegate these issues to the deacons or to a vote of the entire congregation. The paid ministry is increasingly well-educated, many at graduate SEMINARIES, although formal ordination is not widely practiced and carries no special status. Increasingly, congregations have a variety of paid ministries; youth, education, and worship ministers are commonly found in addition to the senior or preaching minister. Churches of Christ never use the title "Reverend" and rarely call their ministers "Pastor," reserving that title for their elders. Most paid ministers are called "Minister" or "Evangelist." In most Churches of Christ, WOMEN cannot serve as ministers, elders, or deacons, although a few churches allow women to serve as deacons or on committees with significant ministerial responsibility.

The strict congregational polity generally means that missionary activity and other parachurch activities (such as retirement homes and sometimes preaching schools) are sponsored under the leadership of a single congregation and subject to oversight by elders of that congregation. Under that sponsorship, financial support might be solicited from members of other congregations, although rarely from other congregations as such.

Practices

Several distinctive practices are consistently found in Churches of Christ. All Churches of Christ practice adult immersion BAPTISM and do not accept sprinkling or infant baptism as valid. Baptism is available to anyone on a simple statement of repentance and a declaration of faith in Jesus. Rebaptism by immersion of those baptized as infants is common. Local membership in churches is open to all immersed believers, and membership is automatically accorded to a person who is immersed. Most churches have baptisteries in their church buildings, and frequently baptisms are done at the close of worship services following an open invitation to respond to the Gospel.

All Churches of Christ celebrate the LORD'S SUPPER each Sunday. The Lord's Supper is usually open to any who want to participate without proof of membership or even baptism, although baptism is usually expected of participants. The Lord's Supper is usually administered by elders and deacons, although often any baptized believer can officiate. Most congregations use individual cups and wafers, although a few believe that only a single cup is authorized by Scripture.

Worship services in the Churches of Christ are a cappella, without any musical instruments. Congregational singing is usually a significant part of the worship services. The a cappella emphasis has resulted in extensive use of musical parts and harmonies in hymns and songs. Many congregations follow a fairly fixed pattern of worship, although this is not universal. In the vast majority of Churches of Christ, women do not participate in leadership or speaking roles, although this is changing in a few congregations.

Beliefs

In general, the Churches of Christ are organized around issues of practice, not THEOLOGY. The overriding concern is to replicate within the life of the church the worship, structure, and community as believed to have been practiced in the early church. As a result,

the New Testament serves as a blueprint for practice and beliefs; in particular, the Book of Acts serves as an important model for church patterns and behavior. No creeds or confessions are accorded any value within the individual churches, these being seen as later developments of the church. Moreover, creeds and confessions are viewed as potentially divisive. Theoretically at least, members of the Churches of Christ are free to develop theological beliefs as long as these beliefs are supported by Scripture. Thus one can find persons within the individual churches who hold to significantly divergent beliefs, as long as these are opinions or conclusions derived from Scripture and do not violate an express statement found in Scripture. Historically, for instance, the Churches of Christ have used orthodox language to speak of the Trinity, but a minority has held reservations about this concept because it is not expressly addressed in the New Testament. Barton Stone, one of the earliest leaders of the movement, was skeptical of the concept of the Trinity because it was not used in Scripture. There is a strong undercurrent of rationalism within the belief structure of the churches and little interest in the effects of emotion on CONVERSION or practice.

One can say that the prevailing approach within the Churches of Christ is Arminian. In general, the churches believe that all people can respond to the Gospel by belief and baptism. There is broad skepticism about PREDESTINATION and of the role of the Holy Spirit in leading individuals to accept the Gospel. SALVATION in the Churches of Christ is inextricably tied to baptism, which is linked directly to the confession of Jesus as the Christ. The act of CONVERSION is thus defined as a process that includes belief in Jesus Christ, public confession of this belief, repentance, and baptism. All of these aspects are considered parts of a single act of conversion, and efforts to distinguish the point at which salvation occurs in this process are rejected. Few accept any idea of the impossibility of apostasy; just as an individual can come to believe, he or she can fall away from belief or from salvation. The role of the local church in sustaining an individual's belief is important. The importance of baptism and church involvement could be seen as emphasizing a form of "works" righteousness, but this is firmly rejected by the churches. Instead, salvation is viewed as a gift of GRACE, but it is received when one believes and demonstrates that by confession, repentance, baptism, and subsequent involvement in the local church.

There is no official recognition of CLERGY in the Churches of Christ. In concept, every believer is a "priest" and has equal access to God through prayer and communion. This rejection of clergy as having a special status means that local churches often have significant involvement by members in the worship services. Members often lead singing, lead prayers, officiate and serve at the Lord's Supper, and even preach and conduct baptisms. This broad participation in the congregational worship is usually restricted to male members, however; women generally do not have leadership roles in the worship service based on the passages in the New Testament stating that women should keep silent in the assembly. But there is usually a distinction between the formal worship assembly and other meetings of the church, where women are allowed significant, albeit informal, roles.

Connective Ties in the Fellowship

While the Churches of Christ have no formal denominational structure, a fairly well-established system of connections ties the local congregations together and provides a remarkable consistency across the movement. The formative mechanisms for these linkages were magazines and journals, and these still remain influential. However, the role of colleges supported by members of the Churches of Christ has superseded the importance of the journals and now provides the primary mechanism for connectivity.

In the early stages of the movement, journals such as the *Gospel Advocate* helped develop and accentuate the Churches of Christ's attitudes and beliefs, often in distinction from other segments of the Stone-Campbell Movement. In fact, the late nineteenth and early twentieth centuries could probably be seen as a period of competing journals that shaped emerging groups within the Restoration Movement. Other journals and magazines, including *The Firm Foundation*, were also very influential, especially in the early part of the twentieth century. Various smaller journals, often espousing divergent editorial stances within the movement, continue to be published, but these have less significance than previously. *The Christian Chronicle*, a newspaper published by Oklahoma Christian University, has a wide distribution and presents news about the Churches of Christ.

A number of directories of the Churches of Christ have been published, most notably *Churches of Christ in the United States*, compiled by Mac Lynn. These listings are often a way of determining whether a church is considered part of the Churches of Christ (a cappella) or lies outside this circle of churches (e.g., an instrumental Church of Christ). Many of these listings provide information about subgroupings within the churches (e.g., one cup or premillenial).

Colleges and universities in the Churches of Christ undoubtedly provide the major source of linkages between congregations today, both through their education of members and ministers and through lectureships. A high percentage of members of the Churches

of Christ send their college students to colleges affiliated with the body. Most of these colleges strongly emphasize the practices and beliefs of the movement; many require that all faculty members belong to the Churches of Christ. The primary colleges serving the movement are Abilene Christian University, David Lipscomb University, Freed Hardeman University, Harding University, and Pepperdine University. There are, however, a number of additional colleges that are clearly affiliated with the Churches of Christ. Some of the colleges, such as Abilene Christian University and Pepperdine University, host lectureships wherein members from churches across the country come to listen to preachers, attend workshops, and worship, thus providing a strong sense of cohesiveness to the churches.

See also Arminianism; Higher Education; Restorationism; Music; Millenarians & Millenialists; Publishing, Media; Christian Colleges

References and Further Reading

Allen, C. Leonard, and Richard T. Hughes. *Discovering Our Roots: The Ancestry of the Churches of Christ.* Abilene, TX: ACU Press, 1988.

Casey, Michael, and Douglas Foster, eds. *The Stone-Campbell Movement: An International Religious Tradition.* Knoxville, TN: University of Tennessee Press, 2002.

Childers, Jeff W., Douglas A. Foster, and Jack R. Reese. *The Crux of the Matter: Crisis, Tradition, and the Future of Churches of Christ.* Abilene, TX: ACU Press, 2002.

Garrett, Leroy. *The Stone-Campbell Movement: The Story of the American Restoration Movement.* Joplin, MO: College Press, 1994.

Hughes, Richard T. *Reviving the Ancient Faith: The Story of Churches of Christ in America.* Grand Rapids, MI: Eerdmans, 1994.

Lynn, Mac. *Churches of Christ in the United States: Inclusive of Her Commonwealth and Territories.* Nashville, TN: 21st Century Christian Publishing, 2003.

North, James B. *Union in Truth.* Cincinnati, OH: Standard Publishing, 1994.

Webb, Henry. *In Search of Christian Unity.* Cincinnati, OH: Standard Publishing, 1990.

West, Earl. *The Search for the Ancient Order.* 4 vols. Indianapolis, IN: Religious Book Service, 1950.

MARK A. MATSON

CHURCH LAW

Church law comprises the constitution, discipline, requirements, legislative, administrative and judicial structure and procedures, governing membership and officers, acquisition and administration of finance and property in, and the external as well as internal relationships of any Christian community. It varies in scope, form, and style according to each community's understanding of God and of human relations with God, and each community's size and self-definition.

Protestant church law generally differs from Roman Catholic Church law in the degree and character of AUTHORITY claimed for the church as an institution. The statutory style also differs from ancient Eastern and Latin legislation in most Protestant churches, although the form of canons survives in the Anglican Communion, which also traditionally appeals to patristic precedent in its legal thought. However, all churches are obliged by the realities of experience to legislate on the same issues, however much the respective laws may vary. These issues also overlap; for example, questions about membership are distinct from, but inevitably overlap with, rules about church officials, and ecumenical policy affects and is affected by both of those areas.

The basic issue in all church law is the definition of DOCTRINE: What do we teach, and on what authority? (The second part of the question is also inherent in the first). At one extreme are the few communities that insist that they have no stated doctrine at all. Some Protestant churches (Lutheran, Anglican, some Reformed, some Methodist) agree that the creedal decisions of the early councils (Nicaea, Constantinople, Chalcedon) are still binding on the modern church, and that REFORMATION decisions (confessions, catechisms, articles) are similarly normative, whereas other Protestant denominations claim that only the BIBLE has claim to allegiance. (The confessional churches may observe that the definition of the Biblical canon is itself a tacit acceptance of the early church's informal process of decision, or an acceptance of Reformation decisions, or of a late Reformation reversion to the rabbinic decisions of 70 A.D.). Also diverse are the effective statuses given to the admitted standards: binding on all teaching programs and their contents, or normative of the character of those programs, or "articles of peace" (i.e., not to be disowned or opposed), or "landmark documents"; the last may mean that the past decrees mark vital and lasting decisions (like the admission of the Gentiles) or fascinating and venerable irrelevancies. Equally variable, among churches and in all churches through time, is the important legal distinction between what must be policed and enforced and ADIAPHORA, the things that can be tacitly tolerated.

Church law reflects differing Protestant ecclesiologies, that is, differing understandings of the church: if the church is the Body of Christ, and essentially one, may or must it have a single governmental system, or are the different gatherings of Christians to be autonomous (not, that, literally self-governing, but discerning and applying the will of Christ through more local instruments? In the Reformation period Protestant churches were national churches or separatist congregations, whose interdependency, even if adjudged to be divinely mandated, was voluntary and nonbinding. This range of ecclesiologies and structures survives to the present day (see ECCLESIOLOGY). Each church has its appropriate constitution, from the national establishment to the COVENANT of a Congregational or Baptist congregation. Protestant churches have developed international jurisdictions, although in most cases "third world" provinces, dioceses, presbyteries, or conferences have been granted autonomy. International denominational bodies have become consultative and not legislative. Ecumenical bodies, international, national, or regional, are likewise consultative—but the growth of ECUMENISM has obliged churches to examine their membership and ministerial criteria. If BAPTISM and ordination are valid in one church, on what terms may or must those baptisms and ordinations be acceptable in another?

Who is a member of a particular church, or of the Church Catholic (the Christian body as a whole)? Nearly every Protestant church prescribes BAPTISM (and its matter and form), its ministers, and its conditions: for children of families professing (practicing?) Christianity, or on personal profession. Most churches forbid rebaptism. Confirmation is more disputed, as to its necessity, ministers (bishops? episcopally ordained clergy?), its terms, and its nature and content (imposition of hands? public affirmation?), and repeatability. Churches also legislate on transfer of membership, on continuing duties of members and the resultant criteria for continued good standing, on discipline of members, on the offenses and penalties, on excommunication or the ban (or the Amish *Meidung*, or shunning), and the conditions and procedures for restoration.

Churches legislate on WORSHIP, whether or not they admit it. Legislation may be informal (local preference, custom, historic tradition, recorded or remembered—these concepts are logically distinct, but in application readily confused), or by statute (especially in reference to SACRAMENTS), or by recommendation, especially through approved service books and hymnals. Hans Dombois has argued that the essence of worship (PREACHING, sacraments) creates a distinctively Christian concept of law as an instrument of the outworking of grace, so that the church grows as image of the Trinity.

Each church law system, in growing, must seek its priorities of purpose: the glory of God by means of the purity of the church, its apostolic effectiveness, the stewardship of the Gospel, the restraint of power, healing, and the CHARITY that may make the Church a means of SANCTIFICATION.

References and Further Reading

Bayne, Stephen F. Jr., ed. *Mutual Responsibility and Interdependence in the Body of Christ, with Related Background*

Documents. London: SPCK; New York: Seabury Press; Toronto: Anglican Book Centre, 1967.

Brouwer, Arie. "Some Reformed—and Reforming—Perspectives on Church Order," *Reformed Review*, 38 (Spring 1985): 196–203.

Dombois, Hans. *Das Recht der Gnade: Ökumenisches Kirchenrecht* (The Law of Grace: Ecumenical Church Law), vols. 1–3. Witten, Germany: Luther-Verlag 1961/1969, 1974, 1983.

Long, Edward LeRoy Jr. *Patterns of Polity: Varieties of Church Governance.* Cleveland, OH: Pilgrim Press, 2001.

Noll, Mark A., ed. *Confessions and Catechisms of the Reformation.* Grand Rapids, MI: Baker Book House, 1991.

Reuver, Marc. *Faith and Law: Juridical Perspectives for the Ecumenical Movement.* Geneva, Switzerland: WCC Publications, 2000.

Roberts, Tom Aerwyn. "Law, Morality and Religion in a Christian Society." *Religious Studies,* 20 (March 1984): 79–98.

Sehling, Emil et al., eds. *Die Evangelischen Kirchenordungen des XVI.* (The Evangelical Church Orders). Tübingen, Germany: J.C.B. Mohr, vols. I–XV. 1970–1977.

Völker, Alexander. "Hans Dombois," unpublished manuscript.

DAVID TRIPP

CHURCH MISSION SOCIETY; CHURCH MISSIONARY SOCIETY

The Church Mission Society, or Church Missionary Society (CMS), is a voluntary mission movement within the worldwide Anglican Communion. It consists of loosely networked sister organizations in ENGLAND, AUSTRALIA, NEW ZEALAND, IRELAND, the Czech Republic, and the UNITED STATES. Other mission agencies closely affiliated with CMS, and whose origins are tied to the work of CMS missionaries, include the Mid-Africa Ministry, the Mar Thoma Evangelistic Association, and the Church of Nigeria Missionary Society.

CMS was founded in Britain in 1799 during the Evangelical revival that had arisen under the influence of early English PURITANISM and the Methodist movement of JOHN and CHARLES WESLEY. Among the key figures who started The Society for Missions to Africa and the East (the original name) were John Venn, WILLIAM WILBERFORCE, CHARLES SIMEON, and other members of an Evangelical group loyal to the CHURCH OF ENGLAND known as the CLAPHAM SECT. Societies outside England were founded as the missionary movement expanded: Australia (1825); New Zealand (1892); Ireland (1976); United States (1998); Czech Republic (2001).

The ministry of CMS missionaries contributed to the rapid expansion of the Anglican Communion into many parts of AFRICA and Asia, mostly in tandem with the growth of the British Empire throughout the 1800s. The first missionaries of CMS-Britain were German Lutherans sent to SIERRA LEONE in 1804. Henry and William Williams, CMS missionaries to New Zealand, were pioneers in bringing the gospel to the Maoris. Under the leadership of Henry Venn (clerical secretary, 1841–1872) CMS adopted the Three-Self Principle for church planting whereby missionaries sought to raise up self-promoting, self-governing, and self-supporting indigenous churches. The application of this principle resulted in the consecration of SAMUEL AJAYI CROWTHER as Africa's first Anglican bishop in 1864. The work of CMS greatly increased as a result of the East African Revival of the 1930s. CMS missionaries also played a supporting role alongside Bishop V. S. AZARIAH in the foundation of the united CHURCH OF SOUTH INDIA in 1947.

In the modern era CMS affiliate organizations support more than 500 mission personnel in Africa, Asia, LATIN AMERICA, the Middle East, and Eastern Europe, as well as scores of non-Western missionaries located in Britain and North America.

References and Further Reading

Martin, John, ed. *200 Years of the Church Mission Society.* London: CMS, 1999.

Murray, Jocelyn. *Proclaim the Good News: A Short History of the Church Missionary Society.* London: Hodder and Stoughton Ltd., 1985.

Taylor, John V. "The Church Missionary Society." In *Concise Dictionary of the Christian World Mission,* edited by Stephen Neill, Gerald H. Anderson, and John Goodwin. Nashville, TN: Abingdon Press, 1971.

GEOFFREY A. LITTLE

CHURCH OF CHRIST, SCIENTIST

See Christian Science

CHURCH OF ENGLAND

Roots

The roots of the Church of England go back to the time of the first Christian presence during the Roman Empire. Reestablishment took place from 597 onward under Augustine, first archbishop of Canterbury, which gradually brought about an English Church under papal authority but often independent in mind. The break with Rome under HENRY VIII in 1534 and consolidated under his successors resulted in a church that kept much of the old diocesan structure and liturgical features but whose THEOLOGY combined elements of European Reformed thinking. By the following century it could no longer contain all Protestants within its wide bounds, but it remained "established" with the monarch as "Supreme Governor" (i.e., leading lay figure). Subsequent centuries brought the break with METHODISM, the Evangelical, and High Church movements. The twentieth century saw it gaining almost total self-government, with new liturgical texts and benefiting from ecumenical convergence, while at the same time retaining a position to challenge prime ministers on social issues in an age of increasing secularism.

British bishops attended the Synod of Arles, which the Emperor Constantine summoned in 314, and archaeological evidence points to the survival of a native British (Celtic) Christian presence as the pagan Anglo-Saxon invaders pressed westward in the following centuries. Knowledge of this situation prompted Pope Gregory the Great's mission in 596 to rebuild the English Church, with an archiepiscopal seat at London, a task that he entrusted to Augustine, who was the prior of St. Andrew's Abbey in Rome. On arrival a year later he could get no further than CANTERBURY, capital of the East Saxons, whose pagan King Ethelbert was married to a Frankish Christian princess, Bertha. The success of his mission can be shown in Ethelbert's conversion to Christianity, and the way he established other episcopal sees, including at York, as well as slowly gaining the confidence of the bishops and leaders of the British Church, spread through the various kingdoms. However, there were significant differences that persisted, notably over how to calculate Easter, the cause of considerable confusion. A SYNOD was called at Whitby in 664 that, although not as immediately definitive as it has been represented by the Venerable Bede (ca. 673–735) in his *History of the English Church,* judged in favor of the Roman method, which eventually won the day. York was made into a separate archbishopric in 735, with Canterbury remaining the senior.

By the time Duke William of Normandy ("The Conqueror") defeated King Harold at the Battle of Hastings in 1066, ENGLAND was a kingdom that had been united against the Viking invasions of the preceding centuries; and the archbishop of Canterbury William brought with him, Lanfranc, a learned Benedictine monk, had to take care with the native saints in the liturgical calendars. Church and state came into direct conflict when Henry II had his chancellor, Thomas à Becket, made archbishop of Canterbury, hoping to control a church that was showing marked signs of independence; Henry had him murdered in his cathedral on December 29, 1170. Bishops were taking on governmental roles in advising the monarch; this found expression in their presence in the House of Lords as "Lords Spiritual," which continues to this day. Liturgical practice which although loyal to Rome included its own traditions, gave rise to the Sarum Use, which from the thirteenth century onward gradually made the Salisbury LITURGY more or less standard throughout England. However, the impressive edifice of the medieval church could not conceal real tensions under the surface. John Wycliffe, who died in 1384, is often seen as a harbinger of the REFORMATION. He wanted the BIBLE available in the English tongue; he questioned the theology of eucharistic transubstantiation proclaimed in Rome by the Fourth Lateran Council in 1215; and his writings influenced the Bohemian reformer Jan Hus. Perhaps the greatest reforming teacher on the eve of the Reformation was John Colet, who studied in Paris and Italy, and who gave a series of lectures on the Pauline Epistles about 1497 onward back in Oxford. He inveighed against the worldliness of the church, calling it back to the simplicity and discipline of the primitive church.

Reformation

When Henry VIII came to the English throne in 1509 he was already married by papal dispensation to Catherine of Aragon because she had previously been married to Henry's older brother, who had died. Henry's initial response to the ideas of the European Reformation coming to England was a show of loyalty to Rome, asserting the verity of the seven SACRAMENTS in a theological treatise drafted by others for which Pope Leo X gave him the title "Defender of the Faith." Henry soon realized, however, that to ensure a male heir he would need to find another wife, and he was already in love with Anne Boleyn. There was little enthusiasm on the part of Pope Clement VII to grant a DIVORCE. Henry's hand was strengthened when he was able to secure the appointment of THOMAS CRANMER as archbishop of Canterbury in 1533, and the following year he married Anne in secret. During this time Henry had been passing measures in Parliament undermining papal authority, so that when the Act of Supremacy was passed in 1534, declaring him head of the Church of England, the break was finally made with Rome, with the concurrence of the Convocations of Canterbury and York, representative bodies of the BISHOPS and CLERGY of the two Provinces that had met for synodical purposes since the thirteenth century.

Henry had considerable support for reforming the church beyond the administrative and financial. Convocation was now under the control of the king and the monasteries and religious houses had been dissolved, amply filling the coffers of the king, and his courtiers. He walked a careful tightrope, allowing the avowedly Protestant THOMAS CROMWELL, adviser in ecclesiastical affairs and main link with Parliament, to advance the cause by issuing injunctions in 1536 and 1538 that in every parish church there should be a copy of the Great Bible, the translation by MILES COVERDALE. We have to wait, however, until the reign of Edward VI, Henry's only surviving son by Jane Seymour, his third wife, before the Church of England took a decisive theological and liturgical move away from the Catholicism in which Henry had left it. Edward, whose mother had died giving birth to him, came to the throne at the age of ten in 1547. He was surrounded by Protestant advisers, including a cooperative archbishop, Thomas Cranmer, who was well-read in European Reformed theology.

The first move came in 1548 with a form of corporate confession and distribution of communion—in both kinds—that was to be inserted into the Latin mass. This proved a preliminary to the *Book of Common Prayer* that appeared in the following year. A literary masterpiece reputed to be largely the work of Cranmer himself, it was by Reformed standards a conservative service-book. The eucharist (see LORD'S SUPPER) is still celebrated with the priest facing east at the ALTAR and many liturgical VESTMENTS are retained; the shape of the liturgy remains that of the mass, although much of the language of sacrifice has been abolished, and the departed are commemorated but no longer explicitly prayed for; and where the priest once elaborately offered the bread and wine at the altar, the people are now expected to make their offering of money. MARTIN BUCER, the Strasbourg reformer who at Cranmer's invitation took refuge in England and became a professor at Cambridge, made a detailed critique of the 1549 Prayer Book, much of which was incorporated into the Second Prayer Book, in 1552. Where the 1549 texts are altered, they are simplified; only the surplice is to be worn, the table is to be set lengthwise in the chancel when it is required for Holy Communion, and the eucharistic prayer is now split up into different parts, the people receiving the elements immediately after the institution narrative, which, however, is still part of a prayer, unlike the liturgies of JOHN CALVIN and MARTIN LUTHER. Morning and Evening Prayer begin with a lengthy penitential rite, and the few remaining signings with the cross were reduced to one at BAPTISM. To accompany this still elaborate (by Reformation standards) liturgical project, forty-two "Articles of Religion," largely the work of Cranmer, were issued in the following year, which contain distinct signs of circumspection; for example, Article 28 on the eucharist condemns TRANSUBSTANTIATION but manages to come up with a formula that could embrace both a doctrine of the real presence and of a spiritual/memorial presence.

Cranmer's work in the short term was not to last. Edward died and Mary Tudor, Catherine of Aragon's daughter and a Catholic, came to the throne in 1553 and reigned until her death in 1558. During that time, England officially returned to the Catholic fold and the leading reformers were either burned (like Cranmer) or they fled (like JOHN JEWEL to Frankfurt, Strasbourg, and finally Zurich). On the accession of ELIZABETH I,

Anne Boleyn's daughter, in 1558, the Reformation position was reasserted, but with slight nuances. No longer "Head" of the church, Elizabeth was "Supreme Governor," and although 1552 was the basis of the Elizabethan Prayer Book, there were small significant changes that indicated a less Reformed position, including the words of distribution of communion. The (now) THIRTY-NINE ARTICLES, a moderate revision of the "Forty-Two," were issued in 1563. Theologians such as Jewel, bishop of Salisbury and author of the *Apology of the Church of England* (1562), and RICHARD HOOKER, parish priest and author of the *Laws of Ecclesiastical Polity* (in eight books, published in 1593, 1597, and the last three posthumously in 1648 and 1661) defended the Church of England against her critics. Jewel countered the claims of Roman Catholics, a continuing political threat for much of the reign, whereas Hooker answered the rising tide of PURITANISM, which wanted a Genevan form of service and Presbyterian form of church government, although there were Puritans, like the popular preacher and writer, WILLIAM PERKINS, who found ways of staying within the national church.

When Elizabeth died in 1603 she was succeeded by James VI of Scotland. Anxious to promote further the notion of the divine right of kings, episcopacy and monarchy were for him closely tied together, although his efforts to secure an episcopally ordered Scottish Church were unsuccessful. However, in the face of pressure from all sides, Presbyterian and Puritan included, he instigated a new translation of the Bible, which would replace both those of Coverdale and WILLIAM TYNDALE, as well as the versions of the GENEVA BIBLE in common use through Elizabeth's reign. Begun in 1607 it was completed in 1611; once again, careful nuancing can be detected, for example in the use of "Church" instead of "Congregation" and "Baptism" instead of "Washing." Among those who worked on the Old Testament was LANCELOT ANDREWES, who as dean of Westminster prepared James for his coronation, and who as bishop successively of Chichester, Ely, and Winchester was one of the foremost preachers and theologians of the reign. Among the other luminaries of this time were JOHN DONNE, dean of St. Paul's Cathedral, and GEORGE HERBERT, country parish priest, both of them famous poets.

James, once referred to as "the wisest fool in Christendom," was succeeded in 1626 by his son, Charles I. He tried to impose a Prayer Book on the Scottish Church in 1637, which led to riots and—aided and abetted by his dishonest handling of the English Parliament—CIVIL WAR; he was executed in 1649. Unlike his father, whose theological position was moderate Calvinist, Charles held a more Arminian position (see ARMINIANISM), not unlike that of Andrewes, but aggressively expressed, and imposed on the church by his archbishop of Canterbury, WILLIAM LAUD, who was executed as a result of calls from Parliament in 1645. That year saw the abolition of episcopacy in England, the imposition of the Westminster Directory (forms of worship) and Confession of Faith, with OLIVER CROMWELL eventually made "Lord Protector" in 1653. The Church of England was now officially an amalgam of PRESBYTERIANISM and CONGREGATIONALISM; clerics associated with the monarchy and the Prayer Book (e.g., John Cosin) lived in exile, mainly in FRANCE, or else they remained at home, in an internal exile (e.g., JEREMY TAYLOR) or survived in relative quiet (e.g., Simon Patrick).

Restoration

Charles II's return in 1660 heralded a new era. Many popular aspects of community life that had been outlawed under the Commonwealth were back, like HOLIDAYS and SPORTS, as well as joyful MUSIC in church. The Prayer Book of 1662 included the introduction of such terms as "the prayer of consecration" in the eucharist and a stronger indication that episcopacy was a separate order from the presbyterate. There were attempts to make the Restoration Church inclusive; some were successful, such as the appointment of the Presbyterian John Reynolds as bishop of Norwich, others less so; the Puritan leader RICHARD BAXTER was offered the bishopric of Worcester but instead refused to "conform" and spent the rest of his years as a freelance preacher and writer.

The Restoration brought with it a renewed enthusiasm for Prayer Book services. Cathedrals and collegiate churches started having choirs again and liturgical vesture returned. Taylor and Patrick wrote devotional manuals, with a strong theological and moral bent, on the importance of regular Communion. Samuel Crossman wrote poems among which numbered "My song is love unknown," which was to become a popular hymn in the twentieth century. Among those who captured the mood of the era was JOHN TILLOTSON, like Reynolds an ex-Presbyterian, whose PREACHING combined the biblical basis of the Puritans with a practical application that took the heat out of recent unhappy religious controversies. Returning exiles from France such as John Cosin had to face the question of mutual eucharistic hospitality with the French Reformed Church; he brought with him two Channel Islanders, Jean Durel who as dean of Windsor translated the Prayer Book into French, and Daniel Brevint whose treatise on eucharistic theology (1673) was to have a profound effect on JOHN and CHARLES WESLEY when they produced their eucharistic hymns in 1745.

Charles II died in 1685 and was succeeded by his brother, James II, who was a Roman Catholic. His short reign ended in a confrontation with Parliament and the church in 1689, when William of Orange invaded the country in an almost bloodless revolution. The new joint monarchy of William and Mary pricked the consciences of many traditional monarchists, resulting in the resignation of a number of bishops, including Archbishop Sancroft, who refused to crown them. Although many of these "Non-Jurors" kept in touch with the Establishment it was nonetheless a loss, and they were joined by others in 1714, when George of Hanover became king rather than one of the Stuarts. King William was frostily received by the Scottish bishops, whose rejection of him ensured that the episcopalians in Scotland would long be identified with the Stuart cause and become a small minority in consequence; they made contact with the Non-Jurors in England. The overall effect of the Restoration and its aftermath was that the Church of England was no longer a "national" church; it could no longer contain within its confines every single Christian community, although it was still "established"; those who did not conform joined one or other of the Nonconformist churches, the Presbyterian, Congregationalist, or Baptist (see NONCONFORMITY). Roman Catholics were only slowly tolerated because of the stigma of being antipatriotic, which went back to the threat of invasion by Spain under Elizabeth I, and the "Gunpowder Plot" on November 5, 1605, when a group of Roman Catholics attempted to blow up the Houses of Parliament.

As part of overseas English interests and for the benefit of foreign merchants residing in London the Prayer Book was translated into several other languages including Spanish (1707) for use at Gibraltar, Portuguese (1695) for the East Indies, Dutch (1710) for New York City, as well as German (1704), this latter partly as an ecumenical gesture to Lutherans and Reformed in Prussia and also for the six German-speaking congregations in London during the early Hanoverians. Translations such as these formed the very first step in a development that was to see a worldwide Anglican Communion of independent provinces in communion with Canterbury. This era also saw a small number of WOMEN writers, who had to publish their work anonymously: Mary Astell published her *Christian Religion as Profess'd by a Daughter of the Church of England* (1705).

Enlightenment

The eighteenth and nineteenth centuries were once seen as contrasting eras, with the first holding the Church of England in the spell of staid dullness, in which a God of order and beauty was preached, waiting to be awakened by the Evangelical and Catholic Revivals that were to come. That view has been shifted considerably. The eighteenth century began with signs of real hope, with a scholarly archbishop of Canterbury, William Wake, in correspondence with the French Roman Catholic Church about prospects of reunion. On the other hand, theological controversy surrounding the liberal views of Benjamin Hoadly in 1717 led to the suspension by the bishops of the Convocations of Canterbury and York, which were dominated by High Church clergy. There was indeed an understandable reaction to the conflicts of the preceding century, but the spirit of the Restoration theologians lived on in writers like WILLIAM LAW, a layman whose *Serious Call to a Devout and Holy Life* (1728) was aimed at those whose religion was outwardly dry because it seemed to many to have no heart, no prayerful background.

By mid-century, however, the Evangelical Revival was coming to life. John Wesley, whose "heart was strangely warmed" on May, 24, 1738, when attending a MORAVIAN CHURCH service in London, set out to preach the gospel to those many people who had no opportunity to hear it. Wesley himself was a mixture of a strong sacramentalist (he believed in constant communion, several times a week, if possible) and a strong Puritan (he was ready to preach in the open air, and he did). Although his followers, soon nicknamed "Methodists" because of the methodical strictness of their way of life, were exhorted not to leave the Church of England, they became so great in number, both in England and in America, that a break became inevitable. His brother Charles, also a priest of the Church of England and collaborator with him in writing those many hymns that bear the Wesley name, was opposed to any such move (see HYMNS & HYMNALS). However, it finally took place in 1784 when John ordained THOMAS COKE as the first bishop or superintendent for the Methodists in North America, and in the same year, he compiled a simplified version of the Prayer Book for his American followers that was soon taken up in England as well; in that year also SAMUEL SEABURY, the first American bishop, was consecrated in Aberdeen by Scottish Bishops, England not being allowed to do so after American Independence. If blame is to be laid for the Wesleyan schism, however, part must be placed before the Church of England, which was unable to respond to the growing need for more churches, more social and educational work, as the Industrial Revolution gathered pace. There were those in the Established Church who tried to cooperate with Wesley, like Bishop George Horne of Norwich who allowed him to function as an itinerant preacher in his diocese, unlike some other of his episcopal colleagues. Moreover there were evangelicals in the Church of England, like Samuel Walker, a country parish priest in Cornwall, who corresponded with him, although they found Wesley's inclusive preaching insufficiently demanding and his increasingly antichurch stance unacceptable. Walker and others like William Cowper and John Newton remained firmly in the Church of England, where their fervor and preaching helped to bring new life. They understood—like the Methodists—the potential of hymn-singing as a vehicle of EVANGELISM and popular piety, of which Augustus Toplady's "Rock of Ages, cleft for me," written in 1775, is an example. Nonetheless the gospel had to be applied as well as preached, and WILLIAM WILBERFORCE, a prominent evangelical and Member of Parliament, tirelessly campaigned against SLAVERY, persuading Parliament to outlaw the slave trade in 1807 and the practice of slavery altogether in 1833 (see SLAVERY, ABOLITION OF).

The nineteenth century in many ways opened with the continuation of the trends of the eighteenth. High Church bishops like Robert Horsley taught what could now be seen as a traditional ANGLICANISM that was open to new discoveries, and evangelicals like CHARLES SIMEON influenced generations of students at Cambridge with his biblical preaching. Questions about the identity of the Church of England, however, came to a head in the OXFORD MOVEMENT, which began in 1833 with a sermon by JOHN KEBLE, an Oxford theologian, on "National Apostasy." For Keble and his colleagues, who included EDWARD PUSEY and JOHN HENRY NEWMAN, the Established Church was in danger of becoming no more than a vehicle of the government, which was at the time planning to suppress a number of Irish bishoprics, and which had recently abolished religious tests for state office. They set about writing a number of "Tracts for the Times," hence their nickname "Tractarian," holding a firmer line on TRADITION than many of the older High Churchmen of the previous centuries. A different generation of CLERGY who were suspicious of church–state relations took this renewal of Catholic heritage into the parishes, which resulted in a higher standard of liturgical setting, ARCHITECTURE, and music, and placing a renewed stress on baptismal regeneration and the real presence of Christ in the Eucharist. Some of the Tractarians, including Newman, eventually joined the Roman Catholic Church, whose hierarchy was restored in 1850.

One of the many challenges of the time was the need for better education, and to that end the National Society for Promoting the Education of the Poor in the Principles of the Established Church had been formed in 1811, which ensured that the Church of England was in the forefront of building schools in the new centers of population. This is a legacy that has persisted down to the present time. Another issue was the need for more churches and in this quest the church soon had to learn that the government was not going to provide the money; the nineteenth century saw an immense amount of church building, many by private patronage, together with the founding of new dioceses. Theological tensions, too, continued; "Essays and Reviews" (1860) brought together a number of liberal scholars who were keen to interpret such questions as biblical inspiration in the light of scientific knowledge, and another collection, "Lux Mundi" (1889), represented a more modest but trenchant attempt by a later generation of Tractarians in what came to be called the Liberal Catholic strand of ANGLICANISM. Indeed, the very word Anglicanism is a nineteenth-century term, first used in England by Newman in 1838 and since then projected back into the preceding centuries as a way of expressing what the Church of England's theological tradition embodied. The first LAMBETH CONFERENCE of bishops in communion with Canterbury, which by now included SCOTLAND, the UNITED STATES, CANADA, and INDIA, was called together in 1867 and has met regularly since that time, usually every ten years. The Church of England had responded—not always with great speed—to the demands of a changing world.

Ferment

In 1906 the Royal Commission on Ecclesiastical Discipline reported the need for Prayer Book revision. It was certainly overdue because many clergy working in the new parishes were finding that the 1662 Book needed adaptation or enrichment (or both). The response of the Church of England to World War I was of a Christian community unable to cope with the questions of the men in the trenches who witnessed needless suffering on a scale hitherto unknown and who went back home to an economically wounded nation. To deal with this new situation the church needed to travel lighter, and part of that process involved a measure of self-government. Parliament had neither the time nor the interest to govern the church in detail, and the Church Assembly was set up in 1919, modeled on the old Convocations, but with lay representation. Unfortunately, when a new Prayer Book was proposed, Parliament threw it out twice—in 1927 and 1928. This action left a legacy of resentment that was only met by the formation of the General Synod in 1970, a legislative development of the Church Assembly, and the passing of the Worship and Doctrine Measure in 1974, which gave the church the power to authorize alternative forms of service, but without altering the *Book of Common Prayer* of 1662.

Secularization proceeded throughout the twentieth century, with the numerical decline of most of the Christian Churches. This produced a theological ferment, in which the Church of England continued to feed not only on its own tradition but on other churches as well. Strangely, however, whereas European Protestantism was strongly influenced by the radical dialectical theology of KARL BARTH before and after World War II, in England the 1930s represented the apogee of the liberal "Modern Churchman's Union" under an Oxford theologian, Henry Major, along with the Anglo-Catholic Movement, under the leadership of theologians such as Kenneth Kirk and the liturgical scholar, the Anglican Benedictine monk, Dom Gregory Dix, whose *Shape of the Liturgy* (1945) had an influence on postwar liturgical renewal and reconstruction far outside the confines of the Church of England. Indeed old controversies about eucharistic faith and practice were beginning to diminish in the wake of new discoveries about antiquity, ecumenical dialogue, and the growth of a single, mid-morning Sunday Holy Communion, which many saw as what the reformers had intended anyway. Influential women writers like EVELYN UNDERHILL, a convert from agnosticism, and Dorothy L. Sayers, a daughter of the vicarage, began to make their mark. Before and during World War II, however, the dominant figure was WILLIAM TEMPLE, archbishop of Canterbury, whose blend of philosophical idealism and social concern helped to give the Church of England a wider acceptability and prophetic edge. Bishop GEORGE BELL of Chichester, however, proved one of the most controversial leaders, making a speech in the House of Lords during the war condemning area bombing on GERMANY in a manner that was said to have made Prime Minister Winston Churchill refuse to have his name mentioned again in his presence. Archbishop MICHAEL RAMSEY, like Temple a keen ecumenist and a weighty theologian (see ECUMENISM), visited Pope Paul VI in 1966 and laid the groundwork for the first Anglican–Roman Catholic International Commission; but he also took an unpopular stand against apartheid in SOUTH AFRICA. The archiepiscopate of Robert Runcie coincided with the prime ministership of Margaret Thatcher, resulting in a number of controversies, including the "Faith in the City" Report of 1985, commissioned by Runcie himself, which unearthed a maze of issues about urban life. After its hostile reception, the report soon proved its worth and helped to pave the way for urban regeneration.

Many of the old theological tensions regarding the limits of ORTHODOXY began to shift in new directions. The revival of EVANGELICALISM brought a renewed stress on biblical preaching, together with a mixture of conservatism in DOCTRINE and a radical openness about ways of being the church, which walked uneasily with that part of mainstream Anglicanism that is more comprehensive in theology but at the same time more traditional on questions of liturgy and ECCLESIOLOGY. The *Alternative Service Book* (1980), the Church of England's late twentieth-century response to liturgical revision, in company with many new service-books, placed considerable emphasis on font and altar. It was in turn superseded by *Common Worship* (2000), with its richer language and greater attention to structure. After some heartache, women were ordained priests in 1994 but not yet as bishops, in spite of pressure from elsewhere in the Anglican Communion. Ecumenical progress brought about the "Porvoo Common Declaration" of 1994 whereby the Anglican Churches of the British Isles entered into communion with Nordic and Baltic Lutherans. All in all the Church of England lives with the creative tensions of being both Catholic and Reformed; of being English in a multicultural nation (its first black bishop, Wilfrid Wood, was consecrated in 1985) yet part of the Anglican Communion; of being a responsible ecumenical partner with Roman Catholics as well as Methodists; and of responding to the spiritual paradoxes of a postmodern society. The death of the princess of Wales in 1997 demonstrated the durability of folk religion; a Royal Commission on the Reform of the House of Lords in 1999 recommended the retention of bishops in the nation's Second Chamber of Parliament; and the Labour Government in 2001 produced an education policy that envisaged a substantial increase in the number of church schools. The journey that started with Augustine at the capital of the East Saxons has been long, rich, and at times tortuous. How the Church of England responds to these new opportunities, and the work of theological reconstruction involved, remains to be seen.

References and Further Reading

The Book of Common Prayer. 1662.

Carpenter, Edward. *Cantuar: The Archbishops and their Office.* London: Mowbrays, 1971, 1988, 1997.

Chadwick, Owen. *The Victorian Church.* Pts I and II. London: A. and C. Black, 1970.

Common Worship: Services and Prayers for the Church of England. London: Church House Publishing, 2000.

Cuming, G. J. *A History of Anglican Liturgy.* London: Macmillan, 1969, 1982.

Hastings, Adrian. *A History of English Christianity, 1920–1985.* London: Collins, 1986.

MacCulloch, Diarmaid. *Thomas Cranmer.* New Haven and London: Yale University Press, 1996.

Rowell, Geoffrey, Kenneth Stevenson, and Rowan Williams, eds. *Love's Redeeming Work: The Anglican Quest for Holiness.* Oxford: Oxford University Press, 2001.

Spurr, John. *The Restoration Church of England, 1646–1689.* New Haven and London: Yale University Press, 1991.

Wilkinson, Alan. *The Church of England and the First World War.* London: S.P.C.K. 1978, S.C.M., 1996.

KENNETH W. STEVENSON

CHURCH OF GOD (CLEVELAND, TN)

The Church of God (COG) is a Holiness-Pentecostal denomination that traces its roots to the formation of the Christian Union on August 19, 1886. Founded by Baptist ministers Richard and R. G. Spurling, who rejected the exclusivity of the Landmark Baptist movement, the DENOMINATION became part of the WESLEYAN HOLINESS movement in 1896 and a participant in the PENTECOSTALISM movement by 1908. Early pastor and general overseer A. J. Tomlinson transformed the denomination to an Episcopal form of polity. In 2002, the COG had a total of 6.5 million members, with about 1 million of those in the UNITED STATES.

Call for Reformation

Richard Spurling (1810–1891) and his son Richard Green Spurling (1857–1935) were missionary Baptist clergymen in eastern Tennessee. After two years of prayer and study of the BIBLE and the history of Christianity, they came to believe that Protestant churches needed further reformation. The church had fallen after the Council of Nicea in 325 A.D. because it relied on creeds rather than the New Testament. According to the Spurlings, creeds were fallible human statements used to divide Christians and often used to justify violence against other Christians.

The Spurlings taught that a further reformation was needed to eliminate creeds and the divisions creeds caused. For R. G. Spurling, the Baptist churches in east Tennessee were an ongoing example of the need for reformation as their Landmark exclusive ecclesiology prohibited him from ministering in other denominations and eventually led to his being excluded from the Baptist Church. Thus, on August 19, 1886, the Spurlings arranged a meeting near their grist mill on Barney Creek in Monroe County, Tennessee, to further the reformation. R. G. Spurling called for the forsaking of creeds, taking the New Testament as the "only rule of faith and practice," giving one another the right to interpret scripture according to individual conscience, and covenanting together as the church of God. The Spurlings named their movement the "Christian Union" because they believed that an emphasis on Christ's command to love God and neighbor would bring about the union of all Christians.

A Holiness Revival

Over the next 10 years R. G. Spurling organized several congregations. But his greatest success came as pastor of a holiness congregation in nearby Camp Creek, North Carolina. Previously, in 1896, four holiness preachers had held a revival at the Shearer Schoolhouse in Camp Creek. They preached that after JUSTIFICATION, one should experience a second work of GRACE that sanctified the believer. This doctrine infuriated the BAPTISTS of the area, and many of the holiness converts were excluded from the Baptist churches. Meeting in homes and temporary structures for SUNDAY SCHOOL and WORSHIP, the persecuted holiness band also experienced an extraordinary outpouring of the Holy Spirit. According to the earliest history, many people spoke in TONGUES and experienced divine healing (see FAITH HEALING). William F. Bryant, Jr. emerged as the leader of this holiness group and held an organizational meeting in his home on May 15, 1902. The organizing presbyters were R. G. Spurling and R. Frank Porter, who had previously been a ruling elder in the Fire-Baptized Holiness Association. The newly formed congregation named themselves the Holiness Church and called R. G. Spurling as their pastor.

The next year, Ambrose Jessup Tomlinson joined and was selected as pastor. Tomlinson was from the Quaker community of Westfield, Indiana (see FRIENDS, SOCIETY OF). After his conversion, he began visiting the mountains of western North Carolina as a "missionary evangelist." In 1899 he settled in Culberson, North Carolina, where he established a school and clothing distribution center. Following his call as pastor of the Holiness Church, he established congregations in Georgia and Tennessee. In 1904 Tomlinson moved to Cleveland, Tennessee, which became the home of the movement.

A Developing Movement

In 1906 the Holiness Churches held an Assembly to discuss developing practical and theological issues. The General Assembly became the primary means of government at the international level. The name "Church of God" was selected at the second Assembly in 1907 based on Paul's letters to the "church of God" in Corinth.

Under Tomlinson's leadership, the movement developed an Episcopal polity (see BISHOPS AND EPISCOPACY). Tomlinson became general overseer in 1909; he appointed state overseers in 1911; and the Assembly approved an Elders Council in 1916 and an Executive Council (now Committee) in 1922. The denomination quickly developed a variety of ministries,

including world MISSIONS (1909), publication of a periodical called the *Church of God Evangel* (1910), and the founding of a Bible school, now known as Lee University (1918).

Although perhaps 130 people experienced a Spirit-baptism, including speaking in tongues, in 1896, early members apparently had no doctrine of the Holy Spirit that could be considered Pentecostal until about 1907, when Tomlinson began to preach that the sanctified Christian should seek a baptism of the Holy Spirit with the "Bible evidence" of speaking in tongues (see PENTECOSTALISM).

Differences between Tomlinson and some members of the Elders Council, questions about financial irregularities, and a growing diversity within the movement led to the exclusion of Tomlinson from office in 1923. Flavius J. Lee then served as the second general overseer until his death in 1928.

In 2002 the COG was in 163 countries worldwide. The general overseer is the presiding bishop; administrative bishops serve at state and national levels. The International General Assembly meets biennially; the International Executive Council meets between Assemblies. The COG is a participant in the Pentecostal/Charismatic Church of North America, the Pentecostal World Fellowship, and the NATIONAL ASSOCIATION OF EVANGELICALS.

References and Further Reading

Conn, Charles W. *Like a Mighty Army*, definitive edition. Cleveland, TN: Pathway Press, 1996.

Crews, Mickey. *The Church of God: A Social History*. Knoxville, TN: The University of Tennessee Press, 1990.

Roebuck, David G. "Restorationism and a Vision for World Harvest: A Brief History of the Church of God (Cleveland, Tennessee)." *Cyberjournal for Pentecostal-Charismatic Research* 5 (April 14, 2003): http://www.pctii.org/cyberj/index.html .

Tomlinson, A. J. *The Last Great Conflict*. Cleveland, TN: Press of Walter E. Rogers, 1913; reprint Cleveland, TN: White Wing Publishing House and Press, 1984.

DAVID G. ROEBUCK

CHURCH OF GOD, ANDERSON, INDIANA

Like most bodies bearing this name, The Church of God with headquarters in Anderson, Indiana, understands itself to be a reformation movement rather than a DENOMINATION. The church dates its existence to 1881, when its founder, Daniel S. Warner, was expelled from the Churches of God (General Eldership), a German pietist group, for teaching the Wesleyan doctrine of "entire sanctification" as a second definite work of GRACE in the life of a Christian believer. Through a weekly journal, *The Gospel Trumpet*, and his work as an independent evangelist, Warner quickly gathered a growing number of local congregations together in a loose association that was initially known as "The Evening Light Saints."

Warner taught that the experience of entire SANCTIFICATION in the Christian believer led to an identification with the visible CHURCH, the concrete embodiment of the spiritual body of Christ. This body of believers should be known only as The Church of God. Because he believed that God alone knew who had truly been sanctified, no membership roll was taken. Indeed, in the early years, membership to a denomination was considered sinful. Rejecting any formal creed, Warner taught that the Holy Spirit was the sole overseer of the church and that the BIBLE was its only statement of FAITH. He envisioned that the mission of the movement was to restore unity and holiness to the church universal. Promoting primary allegiance to Jesus Christ, he felt, was the way to transcend sectarian divisions created by denominationalism.

Although having no formal creed, adherents held to a theological consensus of the broader HOLINESS MOVEMENT that dominated North America in the nineteenth century. The leadership taught that the Bible was the inspired word of God; the orthodox view of the Trinity; the divinity of Christ; the indwelling of the Holy Spirit in the regenerate believer; the universal fall of human kind through the SIN of the first parents, Adam and Eve; and the vicarious ATONEMENT in Christ through his death and resurrection. Breaking with the Holiness consensus, the leadership taught an amillennial view of ESCHATOLOGY. Equating the millennium with the church age, adherents believed that Christ would return to earth once the Church's divisions had been transcended and its DOCTRINE fully reformed. Adherents practiced three ordinances: BAPTISM by immersion, the LORD'S SUPPER, and foot washing. Although emphases have changed through the years, the early theology and practice have remained largely intact.

The church uses a congregation form of government, teaching that this is the only model that enables the AUTHORITY of God to function. As noted earlier, no membership is held in a formal way; there is no formal initiation rite for members, and membership lists are not kept. Local churches are organized in state and regional associations. Each year the representatives of the entire body meet in a General Assembly in connection with an International Convention.

In the absence of a governing body, The Gospel Trumpet Company and its editor assumed the body's leadership function during the early years of the church. The company issued ministerial credentials, functioned as the teaching magisterium, created a mis-

sion sending board, and established a Christian education agency to produce church school curricula. Publication offices of *The Gospel Trumpet,* which had moved several times during Warner's lifetime, permanently settled in Anderson, Indiana, in 1906 under the leadership of the second editor, Enoch E. Byrum. The third editor, F. G. Smith, established a Bible training school in 1917 that eventually became Anderson University. In that same year he created the General Ministerial Assembly mentioned earlier. Under the leadership of the fourth editor, Charles E. Brown, in the 1920s, the church instituted structures that are still largely intact. In response to growing criticism over the charismatic leadership of a single person, Brown sought to democratize the church, shifting much of the governance to the general, regional, and state assemblies.

With its origins rooted among the socially marginalized, the church moved quickly to reach out to several immigrant groups, including Germans, Greeks, Hispanics, Scandinavians, and Slovaks. Adherents were especially active within the African American community. As in other holiness churches, WOMEN were free to preach and exercise leadership; more than one-third of the ordained ministers were women until well into the twentieth century. Overseas MISSIONS were also an emphasis from the outset. By the end of the twentieth century, congregations were found in eighty-nine countries, including CHINA, DENMARK, ENGLAND, Egypt, GERMANY, Greece, INDIA, IRELAND, JAPAN, Kenya, KOREA, Lebanon, MEXICO, SWITZERLAND, and nations throughout the CARIBBEAN and all of Central and South America. Although formal membership rolls are still not allowed, the church can make a fairly accurate estimate of its adherents. According to figures available for 1999, the membership was 234,311 in 2,353 congregations in North America, and 385,000 in 4,310 congregations throughout the rest of the world.

In addition to Anderson University and School of Theology, the church operates five other institutions of higher learning in North America: Bay Ridge Christian College (Kendleton, TX), Gardner College (Camrose, Alberta, Canada), Mid-America Bible College (Oklahoma City, OK), Warner Pacific College (Portland, OR), and Warner Southern College (Lake Wales, FL). Countless training centers are operating throughout the world.

Like other denominations that began as movements promoting the unity of the church, both exclusive and inclusive tendencies have been readily apparent in the membership over the years and have been the source of some divisions within the body. Overall, the inclusive tendency has prevailed, resulting in the church working closely with the WORLD COUNCIL OF

CHURCHES and the NATIONAL COUNCIL OF CHURCHES. It is also a long-time member of the Christian Holiness Partnership, the association of WESLEYAN HOLINESS denominations.

See also Bible Colleges and Institutes; Christian Colleges; Feet, Washing of; Millenarians and Millennialism; Pietism

References and Further Reading

Callen, Barry L. *It's God's Church: The Life and Legacy of Daniel Sidney Warner.* Anderson, IN: Warner Press, 1995.

Crose, Lester A. *Passport for a Reformation: A History of the Church of God's Reformation Movement's Missionary Endeavors Outside North America.* Anderson, IN: Warner Press, 1981.

Smith, John W. V. *Quest for Holiness and Unity: A Centennial History of the Church of God.* Anderson, IN: Warner Press, 1980.

D. WILLIAM FAUPEL

CHURCH OF GOD IN CHRIST

The largest African American Pentecostal denomination in the world and the second largest Pentecostal denomination in North America, the Church of God in Christ (COGIC) is rooted in the lines of a humble preacher and his fellow Holiness preachers in the mid-southern United States.

Founder and Origins

The name "Church of God in Christ," as the story goes, was revealed to the young Holiness preacher Charles Harrison Mason (1866–1961) while he walked the streets of Little Rock, Arkansas, in 1897, the official incorporation year of COGIC. The son of Missionary Baptist parents, who also were former slaves, Mason was born just outside Memphis on September 8, 1866. Said to have an attraction to religion early in his life, Mason's desire was to preserve the vibrant "slave religion" he saw in his community. From this passion Mason came to believe that God gave him unique spiritual characteristics, particularly dreams and visions. Soon after an experience of divine healing in 1880, in which he claimed to have been spontaneously cured of a severe illness, the charismatic Mason began to travel southern Arkansas as a lay preacher, planning to be ordained into the Missionary Baptist Church.

In November 1893 after a short, unsuccessful marriage, Mason entered Arkansas Baptist College, only to withdraw after three months. He found that the promotion of HIGHER CRITICISM in the college did little to preserve the slave religion he longed to safeguard. It is during this time that Mason came under the influence of the WESLEYAN HOLINESS MOVEMENT, particularly the tenet that a believer can be completely sanctified through an act of divine GRACE, which he soon claimed to have experienced. It is also during this time that he came to befriend another Arkansas Baptist College alumnus, Charles Prince Jones, a Missionary Baptist minister in Selma, Alabama, who had also experienced entire SANCTIFICATION. The holiness preaching of these two ministers created church divisions and their eventual expulsion. After this expulsion Jones began an annual convention for fellow Holiness ministers in 1896, which led to the incorporation of the Church of God in Christ in 1897.

This new DENOMINATION, one of the first American-born African American denominations, expanded quickly. Mason nevertheless believed that his inability to heal the sick and exorcise demons hindered his ministry. Consequently, in early 1907 after Mason heard reports of the AZUSA STREET REVIVAL, the revival that sparked the American Pentecostal movement (see PENTECOSTALISM), he and two other COGIC ministers traveled to California, where they claimed to have experienced the Pentecostal teaching of Baptism in the Holy Spirit evidenced by speaking in TONGUES.

After their five-week visit Mason and his companions returned eager to testify to this new teaching and found that another Azusa Street graduate, Glen A. Cook, had been laying the groundwork in their own church. With Cook's help Mason began to transform COGIC into a Wesleyan-Holiness Pentecostal church. C. P. Jones, Mason's cofounder, disagreed with this new teaching, and in the summer of 1907 left the denomination with the faction of ministers and congregations that supported him. [They later reorganized as the Churches of Christ (Holiness) U.S.A.] Mason regrouped what remained in 1907, keeping the name "Church of God in Christ," and included a Pentecostal clause in the denomination's statement of beliefs.

Mason led the denomination until his death in 1961, and under his leadership the denomination grew phenomenally. So influential was Mason that the FBI created a file on him, tracking his pacifist (see PACIFISM) and interracial activities. In 1945 Mason dedicated Mason Temple, the denomination's new headquarters in Memphis, and the largest African American–owned auditorium at the time. Its pulpit has supported historic speeches by preachers and leaders, such as MARTIN LUTHER KING JR.'s final "Mountain Top" speech and President Bill Clinton's "Memphis Speech." COGIC has been, without debate, a dominant force in AFRICAN AMERICAN PROTESTANTISM. This influence can be seen in its pioneering work in Gospel music and its leadership in African American ECUMENISM. C. H. Mason Seminary is one of the seven-member consortium of African American seminaries that constitute the International Theological Center of Atlanta, Georgia.

Doctrine and Ordinances

Doctrine

The Church of God in Christ holds to a conservative evangelical Trinitarian DOCTRINE that includes belief in the inerrancy of Scripture, the original sin of humanity, the existence of angels and demons, the need for EVANGELISM, the need for a personal CONVERSION experience, and the second coming of Jesus. COGIC is also found within the Pentecostal family, particularly the Wesleyan-Holiness branch of this family. This meant that the church maintained, and somewhat still maintains, a number of distinct doctrines.

Historically the Church of God in Christ has promoted a holy life, maintaining conservative social values and modest dress. As a Wesleyan-Holiness church, however, COGIC has emphasized the doctrine of sanctification, where the Holy Spirit delivers the believer from the pollution of SIN. During Mason's tenure the denomination officially affirmed the Wesleyan-holiness doctrine of entire sanctification. Here, based on a doctrine established by JOHN WESLEY, the believer experiences an additional work of divine grace, besides JUSTIFICATION, where they are entirely and instantaneously delivered from the pollution of sin. Wesley taught that, although divine justification forgave the sinner of sins of commission, the stain of Adam's original sin remained. God thus provided as a second gift of grace that cleaned the person of sin. A believer then had some physical manifestation that testified to this experience. After Mason the denomination officially moved away from the doctrine of entire sanctification, although it is still widely held. Officially COGIC maintains that the Spirit's deliverance from sin is a continuous process.

As a Pentecostal denomination COGIC maintains that God is dynamically active in the world and within the believer's life. This can be seen, first, in the doctrine of the Baptism of the Holy Spirit, understood as a third distinct crisis experience of divine grace in which the believer is given spiritual power for the purpose of doing supernatural service for the church. This gift is believed to be "evidenced" by speaking in unknown tongues (Acts 2), which is a consequence of Spirit baptism and a manifestation of the "fruit of the Spirit" (Galatians 5). Second, the Pentecostal aspect of COGIC is seen in the affirmations of spiritual warfare against Satan, divine healing (see FAITH HEALING), and miracles. According to official and popular teaching, Satan and demons (see DEVIL) can be subdued and conquered by believers, through the power given to believers by Jesus (Mark 16:17). The acts of divine healing and miracles are believed to be visible acts of divine power that prove the authority of God's word and support the mission of the church.

Ordinances

For COGIC members, the only ordinances that are valid are those they believe originate in Christ himself. They are believed to be signs of divine grace that represent, seal, and apply the COVENANT made between God and believer biblically. The Church of God in Christ exercises three ordinances: water BAPTISM, the LORD'S SUPPER, and foot washing (see FEET, WASHING OF). Water baptism, for COGIC, is a full-immersion believer's baptism. In other words, although water baptism alone does not provide SALVATION, it is a step within a process where a person outwardly demonstrates his or her inward conversion. Because baptism symbolizes the death and resurrection of Jesus Christ, COGIC asserts that water baptism must involve the full immersion of the believer in water. The Lord's Supper, or Holy Communion, symbolizes Christ's death and suffering as seen in the last meal Jesus had before crucifixion. Furthermore it symbolizes the believer's identification and participation with the death of Christ and provides spiritual union with Christ and fellow believers. Foot washing, an ordinance not exclusive to COGIC, is believed to have been ordained by Jesus when he washed his disciples' feet (John 13:1–20). It is an act that characterizes the humility of service expected by those who are members of the Kingdom of God.

Early Racial Controversy

The Church of God in Christ held a unique position in 1907, being the only incorporated denomination to have become officially Pentecostal. Many of the early Pentecostal ministers, both black and white, were ordained into ministry under elder Charles H. Mason. The value in obtaining ordination for Pentecostal preachers was discounted railroad fees and the ability to perform marriages. For the period, then, between 1907 and 1914 COGIC was largely interracial. This position echoed the interracial characteristic of early Pentecostalism and the Azusa Street Revival, a value that ran counter to the culture of the southern United States where Pentecostalism was born. This did not mean that racial issues were absent, or that COGIC somehow transcended its time and culture. A number of white ministers who attended the Azusa Street Revival were appalled by the racial mixing in Christian worship. Additionally the Church of God in Christ did have a racial divide, in which white and black congregations and ministers largely operated independently, having denomination name alone in common.

The issue of entire sanctification, however, became a dividing line among the largely northern and white Pentecostals, who denied this Wesleyan-holiness doctrine and felt the need to organize with like-minded independent Pentecostal churches for the purpose of missions and ministerial education. Furthermore the southern white Pentecostals were feeling the pressure of cultural norms that expected segregation. In December 1913, therefore, William Durham and COGIC ministers E. N. Bell and H. A. Goss issued calls and invitations for a general assembly of "all Pentecostal saints and the Churches of God in Christ," to be held the following April in Hot Springs, Arkansas. The invitations went out to white Pentecostals only. During this General Assembly a new denomination was formed, called the ASSEMBLIES OF GOD, and E. N. Bell was elected its first chairman. Elders William Seymour and Charles Mason were the only African Americans invited, Mason preaching a sermon on the Thursday evening to bless the new denomination. It is believed that Mason understood this move as something white Pentecostals needed in order to work in a racially segregated culture, and never spoke ill of the split. In October 1994, however, in an event know as the "Memphis Miracle," a number of Pentecostal denominations gathered in Memphis to publicly reconcile the racial rift created between COGIC and other groups in 1914.

Expansion and Organization

Expansion

After the 1914 divide the Church of God in Christ reverted to its African American roots. Initially held together by Mason's leadership, the annual General Convention, and a periodical (the *Whole Truth*), it rapidly grew to become one of the largest denominations in the world. In 1934 COGIC claimed 345 churches in twenty-one states, consisting of 25,000 members. By 1962, a year after Mason's death, the denomination numbered 382,679 members. In 1991 the COGIC global membership was reported to be five and a half million members, with more than 15,000 churches and 30,000 clergy. Published statistics after the year 2000 have placed the global membership to be approximately eight million members.

Although still largely African American in the United States, the modern COGIC stands as a multi-national and multicultural denomination, largely as a result of its missionary endeavors. During the 1920s COGIC moved out from the UNITED STATES into MEXICO, Panama, the CARIBBEAN (Jamaica, Turk Islands,

Trinidad, Haiti), and CANADA. The denomination had its largest success within the Caribbean, particularly Haiti, where it has established more than 150 churches, schools, and an orphanage. Moreover, in the 1930s COGIC began its work in AFRICA through a former Assemblies of God missionary to LIBERIA, Elizabeth White, who remained in the country as a COGIC missionary. Liberia became COGIC's main African mission until it entered SOUTH AFRICA in 1952 and then Ghana and Nigeria in the 1960s. COGIC is now found in eighteen African countries, with churches led primarily by African nationals. After World War II, COGIC moved into Europe and Asia, initially through establishing churches to serve American military personnel in JAPAN, the PHILIPPINES, GERMANY, and ITALY. Then, with freer movement of British Commonwealth citizens, the denomination established congregations in ENGLAND and INDIA. The large success of COGIC in African and Latino/a communities is attributed to the perception that this denomination does not spread the "white man's religion," but a Christianity that is free from past European imperialism.

Organization

Church governance and POLITY are important ongoing issues for the Church of God in Christ. Conflicts have arisen between the denominational leadership, local elders, bishops, and local congregations that have led, at times, to secular courts cases. Initially the organization and governance of the denomination were guided by Mason's charisma. During this time COGIC's ECCLESIOLOGY followed a congregational model of church governance, with independent congregations and state overseers who worked with Mason and the national government. Additionally a gender-separated leadership created particular offices for men and women, following a more traditional African American spirituality. (It is important to note that each male leadership office has a female counterpart.) Mason's death led to a difficult transitional time for the denomination concerning issues of leadership. During the 1960s, however, COGIC adopted a hybrid of congregational and Episcopal governing models, which has served the denomination better.

Ministry within the denomination follows a specific chain of leadership. The local congregation is the foundational element of the denomination. The ordained minister, or "elder," governs the local congregation. Although a trustee board is established, which primarily monitors finances, the church's power is entrusted to the largely autonomous elder. A group of churches, normally no less than three and no more than fifteen, constitute a "district." Each district is presided over by a district superintendent (male) and a district missionary (female). The district leaders are responsible for serving the needs of their ministers and churches in general. From there, a group of districts constitute a "jurisdiction," which historically encompassed one state, although jurisdictions now may overlap states or countries. Each jurisdiction, which also has gender-specific leadership, formally deals with the affairs of its districts, provides annual meetings, develops ministerial education opportunities, and ordains its CLERGY.

Policy decisions for the international body are made through a governing structure similar to that of the United States government. First, the "General Assembly," which represents the entire denomination, constitutes the legislative branch and has the ultimate political authority in the denomination. Meeting twice as year—most importantly during the annual "Holy Convocation" meeting in November—clergy and LAITY representatives from each jurisdiction monitor denominational affairs. Second, when not in session, the General Assembly is represented by an elected twelve-person executive branch, known as the "presidium." The presidium is headed by the "presiding bishop," the formal representative head of the denomination, although meetings of the General Assembly are managed by a chair and vice chair. Decisions made by the presidium are ratified by the legislative branch at its meetings. Third, the judiciary branch, which consists of members elected from the General Assembly for seven-year terms, is responsible for settling disputes between churches, members, and clergy.

References and Further Reading

Anderson, Robert Mapes. *Vision of the Disinherited: The Making of American Pentecostalism.* Oxford: Oxford University Press, 1985.

Clemmons, Ithiel C. *Bishop C. H. Mason and the Roots of the Church of God in Christ.* Bakersfield, CA: Pneuma Life, 1996.

Daniels, David. "Church of God in Christ." In *Religions of the World,* edited by J. Gordon Melton and Martin Baumann, vol. 1, 318–320. Santa Barbara, CA: ABC-CLIO, 2002.

Jones, C. E. "Church of God in Christ." In *Dictionary of Pentecostal and Charismatic Movements,* edited by Stanley M. Burgess and Gary B. McGee, 203–204. Grand Rapids, MI: Zondervan, 1988.

MacRoberts, Iain. *The Black Roots and White Racism of Early Pentecostalism.* New York: Palgrave Macmillan, 1988.

Paris, Arthur E. *Black Pentecostalism: Southern Religion in an Urban World.* Amherst: University of Massachusetts Press, 1982.

Shannon, David T., and Gayraud S. Wilmore, eds. *Black Witness to the Apostolic Faith.* Grand Rapids, MI: Wm. B. Eerdmans, 1988.

Synan, Vinson. *The Holiness-Pentecostal Movement in the United States.* Grand Rapids, MI: Wm. B. Eerdmans, 1971.

Wacker, Grant. *Heaven Below. Early Pentecostalism and American Culture,* Cambridge, MA: Harvard University Press, 2001.

H. CHAD HILLIER

CHURCH OF GOD OF PROPHECY

The faith community that came to be known (in 1952) as the Church of God of Prophecy (CGP) has been captive to the spiritual journey of founder A. J. Tomlinson, an Indiana Quaker. Nowhere is this more evident than in the distinction that CGP is the only Pentecostal denomination in the United States that has always been racially integrated. This stands in stark contrast to the axiom that most Pentecostal groups failed at interracialism within a decade of the fabled 1906 AZUSA STREET REVIVAL.

The CGP often claims to share the history of the early years of the CHURCH OF GOD (Cleveland, Tennessee). As a result of sociological, theological, historical, and personal factors, the Church of God of Prophecy came into existence in 1923. The CGP has laid considerable emphasis on several CG events before 1923 when A. J. Tomlinson was general overseer. In fact the CGP counts among its binding polities those decisions of the general assemblies from 1906 onward, unless later clarified or reversed by the CGP. Also, the home that hosted the first general assembly of 1906 is owned by the CGP. An annual service is held by the CGP in this house to commemorate the first assembly and to honor its participants, activities, and resolutions.

A. J. Tomlinson served as general overseer of the CGP until his death (1943), at which time his youngest son, Milton A. Tomlinson, was chosen for the position. M. A. Tomlinson oversaw international departments that directed prayer groups, organized MISSIONS, worked with young people, utilized modern media, sought out military personnel, and encouraged BIBLE study and EVANGELISM. CGP still maintains the multi-million-dollar, 216-acre biblical theme park in western North Carolina known as the Fields of the Wood.

Under the Tomlinsons the term "theocracy" was employed to describe a POLITY that proclaimed the annual general assembly to be the highest tribunal, whereas the entire ecclesiastical structure collapsed on the office of the general overseer. All of the general assembly resolutions, which were projected to be unanimous decisions of all male members of the 20,000 attendees, were predicated on Holiness Pentecostal thought (see HOLINESS MOVEMENT, PENTECOSTALISM). Various ministries of evangelism, missions, and Christian education were prompted at these assemblies by the international departments, accompanied by much fervent PREACHING (some delivered in

Spanish and everything translated into Spanish and French) and praying, whereas the doctrinal and business concerns were held to a minimum. The greatest attendance at each assembly was during the annual address by the general overseer. Much time was devoted to state and national marches (started in 1925), which were swept along by the Bahamas Brass Band until discontinued in 1988.

In terms of officially determined doctrinal propositions, at the center stands an Arminian version of the *ordo salutis* with an emphasis on SANCTIFICATION (see ARMINIANISM). It culminates with a doctrine of Spirit baptism that regards TONGUES-speaking as the initial evidence. Other prominent teachings from the once-fixed list of twenty-nine include an imminence-oriented ESCHATOLOGY that involves a premillennial return of the risen Jesus; a call for the sanctity of the nuclear family, which includes denial of a multiple marriage of an adulterous person and fornication (as related to a person who can remarry) is defined as a single person marrying a person who has a living married companion; the practice of water BAPTISM by immersion and rebaptism after "reconversion"; the LORD'S SUPPER (with grape juice) and the washing of the saints' feet (see FEET, WASHING OF); total abstinence from intoxicating beverages and tobacco; a concern for modesty in all dimensions of life; and an emphasis on nine Holy Spirit charisms with special attention given to divine healing (see FAITH HEALING). For the most part the formulas have positively influenced adherents' lives, but there have been some aberrant results as well. Included in the failure column has been the refusal to purchase life insurance, opposition to formal education, opposition to medicine to the extent that pain and death were accepted rather than seek medical treatment, and dissolution of existing marriages.

The restorationist impulse was manifested, until recent years, in an exclusive body ECCLESIOLOGY (see RESTORATIONISM). The latter influenced the fact that the CGP has had a high percentage of female pastors and may be the Pentecostal church most consistent in working toward racial reconciliation. African Caribbeans, African Americans, and Latin Americans are charged with the leadership of states whose composition includes European Americans as the majority. Bible Training Camp opened in 1941 with an integrated student body. In some states the CGP may have been the first church to defy Jim Crow laws in their worship services and they have long opposed the KU KLUX KLAN. WOMEN ministers may administer SACRAMENTS but are excluded from the elevated rank of presbyter (see WOMEN CLERGY). Yet the international headquarters has a long tradition of female executives.

Billy D. Murray was chosen to fill the position of general overseer when M. A. Tomlinson resigned in 1990. The church experienced rapid changes such as the closing of Tomlinson College, financial restructuring with an emphasis on local churches, plurality of office of general overseer, and relaxing of some previous taboos. Fred S. Fisher followed Murray in 2000 and quickly embraced sister pentecostal bodies. CGP is active in the PENTECOSTAL CHARISMATIC CHURCHES OF NORTH AMERICA (PCCNA), the PENTECOSTAL WORLD CONFERENCE, and the International Charismatic Consultation on World Evangelization (ICCOWE). Starting with the Third Quinquennium (1985–1989) of the International Pentecostal–Roman Catholic Dialogue, CGP was among the first Pentecostal denominations to send an official representative. Various ministers attend functions organized by the NATIONAL ASSOCIATION OF EVANGELICALS (NAE), whereas a few have engaged with the NATIONAL COUNCIL OF CHURCHES and the WORLD COUNCIL OF CHURCHES (WCC).

The official mouthpiece remains the monthly periodical *White Wing Messenger*. The magazine is published in eight languages and has 6,500 subscribers. The CGP reported in 2002 a membership of 77,609 in the UNITED STATES with 1,876 churches, whereas 125 countries outside the United States had an aggregate membership of 514,000 with 5,590 churches. In the earlier decades the membership was almost exclusively from a low socioeconomic stratum. Yet the working poor have been increasingly replaced by the middle class in the industrialized West. Accompanying the social upward mobility of the membership has been a moderation of many of the sectarian idiosyncrasies and a concomitant lack of membership gains in the United States. The organization at large continues its anti-intellectual tradition, while the official doctrinal formulas fade in significance for the emerging middle-class constituency.

References and Further Reading

Cyclopedic Index of Assembly Minutes and Important Business Acts of the Church of God of Prophecy: 1906 to 1974. Cleveland, TN: White Wing Publishing House, 1975.

Davidson, C. T. *Upon This Rock*. 3 vols. Cleveland, TN: White Wing House & Press, 1974–1976.

HAROLD D. HUNTER

CHURCH OF JESUS CHRIST OF LATTER DAY SAINTS

See Mormonism

CHURCH OF SCOTLAND

"The Kirk," as it is known in SCOTLAND, is the national church of Scotland, but not a state church. It is Presbyterian in government and Reformed in doctrine. In 2001 the church had 590,824 communicant members organized in forty-nine presbyteries and 1,543 congregations served by 1,090 ministers and 43,499 elders. In the 2001 national census, more than two million adults identified themselves with the Church of Scotland, suggesting that almost half the population would regard the Kirk as "their church." It has exercised significant international influence.

History

Tracing its roots to the missionary work of Ninian and Columba in the fifth and sixth centuries, the Kirk adopted a Protestant and Reformed identity with the sixteenth-century Scottish REFORMATION. Through the leadership of JOHN KNOX the movement for reform in Scotland took the distinctively Calvinist form that is evident in the Scots Confession and the First Book of Discipline, both completed in 1560. Building on Knox's work, ANDREW MELVILLE developed the presbyterian form of church government and the broad social vision that have been at the core of the Kirk's identity. During the seventeenth century the Stuart kings attempted to impose an episcopal polity on the Kirk. Resistance found expression in the National Covenant of 1638 and in armed struggle against the Stuarts. In 1647 the WESTMINSTER CONFESSION of Faith was completed and became the principal subordinate standard of the church. Under the Revolution Settlement of 1690, the Kirk was established by law as presbyterian. When the Scottish and English Parliaments united in 1707 the Treaty of Union secured the presbyterian government of the Church of Scotland.

From the struggles of the seventeenth century there emerged in Scotland a passion to uphold the spiritual independence of the Kirk. The restoration of patronage, whereby the initiative in the appointment of ministers lay with civil rather than ecclesiastical authority, was seen by many as a breach of the Treaty of Union. This led to several secessions during the eighteenth century, most of the seceding bodies entering the United Presbyterian Church that was formed in 1847. Meanwhile the early nineteenth century had seen growing tension between the Evangelical Party that was determined to uphold the spiritual independence of the Kirk, and the civil courts, which asserted the rights of the patrons in ministerial appointments. This led to the Disruption of 1843 and the formation of the Free Church of Scotland. Almost half of the ministers and members of the Kirk, "came out" of the Estab-

lished Church to form what they understood to be the true—that is, Free—Church of Scotland. Compelled to choose between state connection and spiritual independence they opted for the latter.

The Church of Scotland was therefore split into three streams for the remainder of the nineteenth century and a feature of many Scottish towns is three church buildings in close proximity. The Free Church and United Presbyterian Church united in 1900 to form the United Free Church. A conservative minority of the Free Church declined to enter the union and remained separate, seeking to be loyal to the doctrines and principles on which the church was founded in 1843. In 1929 the "Auld Kirk" and the United Free Church united as the Church of Scotland. A minority of the United Free Church declined to enter the union, fearing that it brought the church too close to the state without securing its spiritual independence. However, the great majority of Presbyterians were once again united in the national church.

An important part of the preparation for the 1929 union was the composition of the Articles Declaratory of the Constitution of the Church of Scotland in Matters Spiritual. These were recognized by Parliament in 1921 and made clear that church government in spiritual matters is derived from the Lord Jesus Christ and is not subject to civil authority. Thus the Kirk resolved its long struggle to secure the spiritual independence of the church while maintaining its character as a national church. At its annual General Assembly a throne gallery is provided for the monarch (usually represented by a Lord High Commissioner) who is invited to address the Assembly but not entitled to intervene in its business. This symbolizes the mutual recognition of church and state while making clear the independence of the church in its own government. The General Assembly consists of ministers and elders in equal numbers, commissioned by presbyteries. In the absence of the Scottish Parliament between 1707 and 1999, the Assembly often functioned as a national debating chamber and a means of giving voice to concerns of the Scottish people.

Leading Features

Throughout its history the Church of Scotland has been inspired by the ideal of the "Godly Commonwealth"—the Calvinist vision that not only spirituality and personal morality but the whole life of society ought to be subject to the Lordship of Christ. It played a major role in the provision of education and social welfare until the state took over this responsibility in the late nineteenth century. Whereas the Kirk had once represented the faith of the people of Scotland, in the twentieth century it came to recognize that it was one voice in a pluralist society. Nevertheless it continued to engage prophetically with all aspects of national life, as well as offering a range of social services in partnership with the state. Eschewing the privileges of Establishment, the Kirk sees its national role in terms of service and witness to every part of Scottish life. Human and material resources are channeled to particularly needy and strategic areas.

Its national character finds expression in a commitment to bring the ordinances of religion to the people in every part of Scotland through a territorial ministry. An aspiration since the REFORMATION has been to place a church building and the services of an ordained minister within easy reach of every community in the country. The nineteenth century saw the realization of this ideal but twentieth century decline has led to many church buildings being closed and a sharp reduction in the number of ministers. This unprecedented slump presents a major challenge to the Kirk and, at the turn of the millennium, it was endeavoring to find ways to reconnect with the community.

Since the abolition of patronage in 1874 the appointment of ministers to parishes is by the free election by all the members and registered adherents of the vacant charge, subject to the call being sustained by Presbytery. Although elders play a prominent role, it is the minister who has been the face of the Kirk in Scottish society, leading public worship and often being a guiding influence in many aspects of community life. More team ministries and lay leadership suggest that a different pattern of church life may emerge in the twenty-first century.

The Kirk has aimed to maintain an educated ministry and an informed LAITY; in practice theological education has concentrated on the former. Ministers receive their theological training at one of the four ancient universities: Aberdeen, Edinburgh, Glasgow, and St. Andrews. In terms of theological persuasion the church is characterized by diversity. From those who adhere strictly to Westminster CALVINISM the spectrum stretches across to those with very liberal views, with most ministers and members somewhere in the middle. The Declaratory Acts of 1879 (United Presbyterian) and 1892 (Free Church) allow liberty of opinion on such points of DOCTRINE as do not enter into "the substance of the faith." What constitutes the substance and how great is the liberty permitted have never been defined. The Articles Declaratory, which were recognized as constitutive by the Church of Scotland Act of 1921, contain a brief statement of doctrine in the First Article, which is declared to be "essential to the continuity and corporate life" of the church and which may never be altered.

The Kirk's theological tradition is predominantly Evangelical and Reformed, with a succession of thinkers who were prepared to work creatively within that tradition to meet the challenges of their times. John Knox and Andrew Melville laid foundations in the Reformation era. Samuel Rutherford, George Gillespie, and David Dickson were exponents of the high Calvinism of the Westminster Confession (see COVENANT THEOLOGY). Resisting any descent into legalism in the early eighteenth century, Thomas Boston and Ebenezer Erskine championed the priority of God's GRACE. A century later JOHN MCLEOD CAMPBELL controversially challenged the doctrine of limited ATONEMENT in favor of an emphasis on God's universal fatherhood and grace, which has come to be widely accepted. The nineteenth century witnessed a galaxy of outstanding scholars, many associated with the Free Church, such as THOMAS CHALMERS, John "Rabbi" Duncan, William Cunningham, A. B. Davidson, HENRY DRUMMOND, James Denney, James Orr, George Adam Smith, and H. R. Mackintosh. None was more brilliant than WILLIAM ROBERTSON SMITH, who introduced HIGHER CRITICISM to the Free Church at the cost of his own chair. In the twentieth century JOHN BAILLIE and T. F. Torrance expounded the apostolic and Reformed faith in relation to the post-ENLIGHTENMENT world of thought, whereas the biblical commentaries of William Barclay enjoyed wide influence.

Worship in the Kirk has been distinguished by the central place accorded to the PREACHING of the Word. Typically erudite, evangelical, and delivered with quiet intensity, the sermon has had a unique place in shaping Scottish life and character. Traditionally Holy Communion, or LORD'S SUPPER, is celebrated infrequently but solemnly. The twentieth century saw greater frequency and less formality in the celebration of Communion. With the Reformation came metrical psalms, which were sung for centuries until, from the later nineteenth century, increasingly supplemented by hymns (see HYMNS AND HYMNALS). The simple, biblical worship of the Reformers precluded observance of the Christian Year but it has found increasing acceptance in modern times.

After the Scottish Reformation the national church was maintained by a system of tax. Landowners were required to construct and maintain a church and manse and to provide a stipend for a minister. The eighteenth-century Secession Churches introduced a "voluntary" system, the expenses of each congregation being met by the freewill offerings of its members. The nineteenth-century Free Church operated by the same method, although with a more centralized system. The work of the Kirk since the 1929 union has been financed almost entirely by the freely given offerings of its members. The demands of an affluent society and the realities of a declining membership put pressure on the Kirk budget.

Commitment to a territorial ministry within a parish system has ensured that the presence and witness of the Kirk is spread fairly evenly across the country. Historically, Reformed worship began in urban and lowland areas of the south and east and it was not until the eighteenth century that it took root in the Gaelic-speaking communities of the Highlands to the north and west. Revival movements (see REVIVALS) brought a deep piety and Highland Christianity took on a distinctive character, perhaps drawing on the mystical tradition of its people. Highland churches have mostly remained conservative in doctrine and WORSHIP and, as a result, several Presbyterian denominations maintain separation from the Kirk.

Architecturally the Kirk is a major feature of Scottish life, with its church buildings among the most prominent and beautiful in both urban and rural areas. After the Reformation transepts were often added to the nave and chancel of medieval times, making the T-shape with pulpit and communion table at the center a common church design. The nineteenth century was a great period of church building with the Classical Revival creating churches of restrained elegance and the Gothic Revival producing more elaborate buildings, often with impressive spires.

Movements of renewal in modern times have drawn on a variety of sources. The Church Service Society has contributed to liturgical renewal within a broadly Reformed tradition, whereas the Scottish Church Society has aimed to influence worship from a "high church" perspective. The IONA COMMUNITY, founded by GEORGE MACLEOD in 1938, restored Iona Abbey as its base and promoted urban mission, which integrated innovative spirituality and radical social commitment. Meanwhile a Conservative Evangelical movement, drawing inspiration from the Aberdeen ministry of William Still after World War II, promoted systematic expository preaching and a return to the essentials of Christian FAITH. The membership of the Woman's Guild, founded in 1887, peaked at over 160,000 in the 1950s. Its nationwide network provided a fellowship for WOMEN to deepen and extend their Christian commitment.

The immigration of Irish Roman Catholics in the nineteenth and early twentieth century was greeted initially by suspicion and hostility from the Church of Scotland, a reaction that contributed to the formation of a sectarian environment in the west of Scotland. In the late twentieth century the Church of Scotland took the initiative in cultivating good relations with the Roman Catholic Church and played a leading role in the creation of Action of Churches Together in Scotland, an ecumenical instrument including the Catholic Church, in 1990 (see CATHOLICISM, PROTESTANT REACTIONS).

Scots migrants founded Presbyterian Churches in IRELAND, the UNITED STATES, CANADA, SOUTH AFRICA, AUSTRALIA, and NEW ZEALAND. In the nineteenth century the Church of Scotland played a leading role in the missionary movement (see MISSIONS). JOHN R. MOTT declared that Scotland sent more missionaries overseas per head of population than any other country in the world. Alexander Duff of Calcutta, William Chalmers Burns of China, Robert Laws of Livingstonia, David Clement Scott of Blantyre, John Ross of Manchuria, MARY SLESSOR of Calabar, David Torrance of Tiberias, and J. E. LESSLIE NEWBIGIN of south India are among those who exercised great influence. Through the work of such missionaries many new churches were planted, notably in Jamaica, INDIA, Pakistan, CHINA, NIGERIA, Ghana, MALAWI, Zambia, Kenya, and South Africa. Scots such as J. H. Oldham played a leading role in the development of mission theory, as seen at the epochal WORLD MISSIONARY CONFERENCE OF 1910, held in Edinburgh. Thus a national church became part of a movement of faith that spans the continents. Through partnership links with churches overseas and its membership in the WORLD COUNCIL OF CHURCHES and WORLD ALLIANCE OF REFORMED CHURCHES, this international dimension remains integral to the life of the Church of Scotland at the beginning of the twenty-first century.

References and Further Reading

Blakey, Ronald S., ed. *The Church of Scotland Year Book 2002/2003.* Edinburgh: St. Andrews Press, 2002.

Burleigh, J. H. S. *A Church History of Scotland.* London: Oxford University Press, 1960.

Cameron, Nigel M. de S., ed. *Dictionary of Scottish Church History and Theology.* Edinburgh: T. & T. Clark, 1993.

Cheyne, A. C. *The Transforming of the Kirk.* Edinburgh: St. Andrews Press, 1983.

Hewat, Elizabeth G. K. *Vision and Achievement 1796–1956: A History of the Foreign Missions of the Churches United in the Church of Scotland.* London: Thomas Nelson, 1960.

Kirk, James. *Patterns of Reform: Continuity and Change in the Reformation Kirk.* Edinburgh: T. & T. Clark, 1989.

———, ed. *The Second Book of Discipline.* Edinburgh: St. Andrews Press, 1980.

Murray, Douglas. *Rebuilding the Kirk: Presbyterian Reunion in Scotland 1909–1929.* Edinburgh: Scottish Academic Press, 2000.

Records of the Scottish Church History Society. Edinburgh, 1923ff.

Weatherhead, James L. *The Constitution and Laws of the Church of Scotland.* Edinburgh: Board of Practice and Procedure, 1997.

KENNETH R. ROSS

CHURCH OF THE NAZARENE

General Description

The Church of the Nazarene is a Wesleyan/Holiness denomination with a total constituency of 3.7 million and a membership of 1.35 million in about 13,000 congregations in 120 nations (see WESLEYAN HOLINESS MOVEMENT). Just under half of the constituency live in the United States and CANADA. It is served by about 13,000 ordained elders, 400 ordained deacons, and 5,500 licensed ministers. From its beginnings, the denomination has received and ordained women into its ministry (see WOMEN CLERGY). Its headquarters are in Kansas City, Missouri.

From its earliest days the denomination has maintained both liberal arts colleges and schools for clergy preparation. Currently it operates fifty-one postsecondary educational institutions in thirty-two countries (see COLLEGES, PROTESTANT). These include two post-baccalaureate theological seminaries, nine liberal arts institutions offering baccalaureate degrees (eight offer graduate degrees as well), and baccalaureate-level theological colleges in a dozen countries. It operates a number of Bible institutes at the primary and secondary levels (see BIBLE COLLEGES AND INSTITUTIONS).

It also runs two schools of nursing, a hospital, and a number of medical clinics. Its independently incorporated international relief agency may take its own initiatives and also works with a variety of humanitarian agencies.

The denomination also maintains Nazarene Publishing House (publishing under its own and Beacon Hill Press of Kansas City imprints) and a music publishing subsidiary (Lillenas Publishing Company imprint). Both of these institutions service all of the major language groups in the denomination and in the holiness movement at large (see PUBLISHING, MEDIA).

The Nazarenes are attempting to remain one international denomination rather than to develop a federation or association or alliance.

Polity

The polity of the Church of the Nazarene mixes Episcopal, Presbyterian, and Congregational forms.

Strictly speaking, the local congregation is the church. Congregations of twenty-five or more members have the right to make their own pastoral arrangements and to control the disbursement of their own funds. Each congregation annually elects an official board that oversees the finances, properties, personnel, and programs of the congregation. Most congregations also elect councils and principal officers for the major auxiliaries, such as religious education and youth work.

Each local congregation is incorporated into one of 350 districts. Most districts are geographically defined. Formally, the district's work is administrative and promotional, aimed at helping congregational growth and development, and at the establishment of new congregations. In addition, many districts hold annual camp meetings and youth camps, which are primarily evangelistic in purpose. The policy-making body of a district is the annual district assembly, to which each congregation elects delegates in proportion to its membership. This assembly elects the district's principal executive officer, the district superintendent, who may be reelected indefinitely. It also elects standing committees, other district officers, and trustees to the board of regents or trustees that serves that district's region. Local congregations are not legally bound by a district assembly's decisions, but generally understand themselves to be honor bound to meet them. Generally, title to all local church property is held by the district to which it belongs.

In addition to carrying out assembly directives and initiatives, the district superintendent works with congregations to maintain appropriate pastoral arrangements.

A still-developing level of organization is that of "region," each region consisting of a varying number of districts. Its principal executive officer is the regional director. This officer is appointed by and reports directly to the denominational Director of World Mission and is responsible for all phases of the denomination's work in all of the districts in a given geographical area. Current "regions" with directors are AFRICA, Asia-Pacific, Canada, CARIBBEAN, Eurasia, MEXICO and Central America, and South America. The USA–Canada is an anomaly. It is divided into nine regions, each with its liberal arts college or university, but these regions do not have regional directors.

The supreme governing body of the Church of the Nazarene is the General Assembly, eighty percent of which is a district-elected, delegated body, half lay and half clergy. The additional twenty percent are ex officio: district superintendents, and regional- and general-level administrators. Between meetings of the General Assembly, the denomination's governing body is the General Board, a half lay–half clergy body elected by the entire assembly and answerable to it. This board meets annually.

General Assembly decisions concerning policy, polity, and doctrine are binding on the entire denomination. However, those that involve the basic Articles of Faith of the denomination and the denomination's Constitution require ratification by two-thirds of the 350 annual district assemblies before they are binding.

The principal executive officers of the General Assembly are the general superintendents (currently six), who are clergy individually elected to four-year, renewable terms by the General Assembly. The general superintendents constitute themselves as a board. Their principal tasks are to execute the decisions of the General Assembly, to oversee all denominational policies and programs, to ensure denominational fidelity to its written polity and doctrinal statements (contained in the Manual, the denomination's official written constitution and collection of rituals), to preside over district assemblies and to preside over the ordination of ministers at district assemblies (or to delegate persons to do so in their absence), and to approve or disapprove nominations from the appropriate entities for various denominational offices and institutions. They are also the ultimate interpreters of the Manual.

Doctrinal Description

The basic requirement for church membership is confession of faith in Jesus Christ as personal Lord and Savior, agreement with the sixteen "Articles of Faith," consent to abide by the "General Rules," and a vow to seek grace of entire SANCTIFICATION if one is not already in the experience. Confession of faith in Jesus Christ and entire sanctification are understood in terms developed by WESLEYANISM and revivalism (see REVIVALS). The sixteen articles of faith are directly related to the "Twenty-five Articles of Religion" of the United Methodist Church (USA) and the "THIRTY-NINE ARTICLES of Religion" of the Anglican tradition. The "General Rules" also clearly relate to historic METHODISM: avoidance of the appearance of evil; doing good to all; and not inveighing against the polity and practices of the denomination.

In its "Historical Statement," the Church of the Nazarene

> confesses as its own the history of the people of God recorded in the Old and New Testaments, and that same history as it has extended from the days of the apostles to our own. It embraces as its own the people of God through the ages, those redeemed through Jesus Christ in whatever expression of the one church they may be found. It receives the ecumenical creeds of the first five centuries as expressions of its own faith.

Recent rulings have allowed that the Nicene Creed may be said with or without the "filioque" in traditionally Orthodox areas, and that in those areas Easter may be celebrated according to the Orthodox calendar (see ORTHODOXY, EASTERN). Some congregations omit the "descensus." The "Articles of Faith" are clearly Protestant, upholding the doctrines of SALVATION by grace alone through FAITH alone, Scripture (the sixty-six-book canon) as the sole rule for faith and practice, and the priesthood of all believers.

A significant minority of Nazarenes are fundamentalists regarding the Scripture. The Articles of Faith themselves speak of "plenary inspiration" and focus on the soteriological function of biblical inspiration and "inerrancy." This allows for both Fundamentalist and non-Fundamentalist approaches to the Bible.

The Nazarenes retain two sacraments: Baptism and the Lord's Supper. They celebrate them in compliance with the basic traditional requirements as to material used (in the Lord's Supper, unfermented wine), the form of words, and sacramental intention. They practice both paedo-baptism and believer's baptism by any of the traditional modes. The rather common practice of rebaptism of those coming to them from paedo-baptist traditions is increasingly discouraged. The Lord's Supper is open to all who confess Christ as Savior, regardless of denominational affiliation, but must be presided over by a duly (but not necessarily Nazarene-) ordained clergyperson. Congregations must celebrate quarterly. Many celebrate more frequently.

Anointing of the sick for healing is commonly practiced, and modern medical care is also fully encouraged.

Distinguishing Tenet

Theologically the Church of the Nazarene is rooted in JOHN WESLEY's doctrine of Christian perfection; ideologically, it is rooted in nineteenth-century North American revivalism. Wesley (1703–1791) believed that Christ's atoning work makes available to believers a grace-given unconditional love for God and neighbor in this life, which begins in the cleansing of the heart from all that is not love, hence the term "Christian perfection," a perfection in love. In a strict sense, this experience is a second basic work of grace, justification being the first. Wesley insisted that although both works are receivable only by faith, both come sola gratia. The atonement provides for both and is continually necessary for maintaining both. Both are entire or complete or full in themselves and are instantaneously received, but these characteristics do not foreclose on spiritual growth or "growth in grace." Rather, growth in grace is one of their most marked concomitants. In fact, refusal to grow in grace may ultimately frustrate the gifts of grace and in their loss. Assurance that either experience has been granted comes from the Holy Spirit in the Spirit's own good time.

The distinguishing tenet of the Church of the Nazarene is almost precisely this Wesleyan doctrine of Christian perfection—also referred to as "entire sanctification," "holiness," "full salvation," "the baptism of the Spirit," "the second blessing," "heart purity," and "perfect love," among other terms. Nazarenes diverge from Wesley at only one basic point. They tend to believe that assurance comes with the gift of entire sanctification itself. Many also diverge at two ancillary points: Wesley was not so sure as they that the gift should be equated with "the baptism of the Holy Spirit," and they place much greater emphasis on its instantaneousness than he did.

History

In nineteenth-century Methodist revivalism, emphasis fell on the instantaneousness of both justification and entire sanctification. (The terms "holiness" and "entire sanctification" had come to more prominent use than the term "Christian perfection." Formally, nuances were recognized; practically, the terms were synonymous.) By the 1830s Methodists were debating the relationship between the instantaneousness of entire sanctification and the gift of assurance. All agreed that assurance was a gift of divine grace and had no specific or universally recognizable marks. All agreed that it was simply a matter of the Holy Spirit witnessing to the seeker's spirit. However, did assurance, the "witness of the Spirit," come with the work of entire sanctification, or might it come later?

Also in the 1830s perfectionist Methodists began to debate whether there was any necessary prerequisite to receiving the grace of entire sanctification aside from already having been justified and regenerated by grace through faith. Some argued that entire consecration must precede entire sanctification. It seemed to others that this put the doctrine of sola gratia, sola fide at risk, making consecration and faith over into good works.

By the 1860s most revivalist perfectionists, which now included many who were not Methodists, held that complete consecration must precede entire sanctification and that assurance comes with the work of entire sanctification, for assurance depends on one's personal appropriation of the biblical promises concerning the work.

The principal figure in propagating this understanding throughout this period was PHOEBE WORRALL PALMER (1807–1874). She and her husband Walter Palmer, a physician, through publishing, writing, and speaking, led a large number of persons within and outside both British and American Methodism into the experience of entire sanctification and encouraged yet many others in "the way of holiness," as she called it. These included a significant number of American bishops and bishops-to-be.

In 1867 a handful of prominent Methodist Episcopal (ME) pastors in the Middle Atlantic states (see METHODIST EPISCOPAL CHURCH CONFERENCE), all of them deeply influenced by Phoebe Palmer, sponsored an ecumenical, but Methodist-run campmeeting for the "promotion of holiness" in Vineland, New Jersey. It was to respond to three issues: the coarsening of moral and ethical standards produced by the CIVIL WAR, the growing neglect of "holiness" in Methodist faith and practice, and the surrender of the campmeeting to emotionalism. The ME bishops unofficially approved it and at least one participated in it. So successful was the Vineland meeting that the sponsors formed themselves into the National Campmeeting Association for the Promotion of Holiness.

The "National," as it was called, then held "holiness" camp meetings across the country for about two decades. It encouraged an ecumenical spirit but was itself punctiliously episcopal Methodist. It always carefully secured bona fide invitations and permissions from bishops in jurisdiction, presiding elders, and local Methodist pastors, and local support. The success of these campmeetings led to the formation of large numbers of regional, state, and county holiness associations in the 1870s to 1890s, each with its (annual) campmeeting. The majority of their members were ME, but they also attracted and accepted significant numbers of Wesleyan and Free Methodists, a significant number of persons affected by CHARLES FINNEY's preaching and Oberlin perfectionism (developed by Finney and Asa Mahan), a smaller proportion of Restorationists (see RESTORATIONISM), and scatterings of Anabaptists (see ANABAPTISM) and others. This more ecumenical base placed an ever-increasing proportion of the holiness movement beyond the reach of episcopal Methodist polity, policy, etiquette, and discipline. By the mid-1870s, deep tensions between the "National" (still mostly ME, but now including some Methodist Episcopal, South [MES], ministers) and several of the more regional associations became obvious, and intra-Methodist tensions in and between the ME and MES, in large part over "holiness," were also becoming obvious.

The aggressiveness of the holiness evangelists, Methodist and otherwise; their disregard for the "National's" model of etiquette and sensitivity to hierarchical concerns; and the revivalist enthusiasm and apparent behavioral phariseeism of the holiness advocates made for often chilly receptions in their own local congregations. Moreover, it created a sort of homelessness for those who now sought congregational affiliation in consequence of having been converted or sanctified wholly in a holiness meeting. The "National" itself faced accusations of temporizing. It seemed to many holiness people, Methodist and otherwise, that episcopal Methodism had given itself over to the quest for social status and acceptability. Such were the makings of the "church question."

By the late 1870s the "church question" had taken firm root: should the holiness people create their own denomination(s)? Sociological factors, such as social location, did and do play some role in the way in which holiness people have formed responses to the "church question," although it may be argued that doctrine and piety have been a more basic element.

The Church of the Nazarene arose as one of several responses, a later one, to that question, and it was a more pervasively urban, middle-class response than some others. Its original leadership generally retained closer relationships to the "National," and to Methodism, than did the leadership of the various regional holiness associations. Some hoped (a few feared), in fact, that the Church of the Nazarene would serve to gather most of the holiness "forces" in the United States and become the principal expression of Wesleyan revivalist perfectionism.

Phineas F. Bresee (1838–1915), a distinguished ME pastor and presiding elder in Iowa and Southern California, and a member of the "National," along with Joseph P. Widney (1841–1938), prominent educator, ME lay preacher, and first president of the University of Southern California, established the First Church of the Nazarene, Los Angeles, California, in mid-October, 1895. Widney gave the congregation its name. (In 1898 he returned to Methodism and then moved into theosophy.)

From its beginnings this congregation sought to propagate holiness doctrine and experience and to relieve the socially distressed in central Los Angeles, but Bresee clearly envisioned a denomination from the very first. By 1905 there were twenty-six Nazarene congregations, among them ten in southern California, five in Washington and Idaho, and five in Illinois.

The denomination that emerged even by 1915 is the product of a long series of mergers and aggressive evangelism, with some of the merging partners having longer histories than that of Bresee's congregation, but it was Bresee's active commitment to his vision and his unique capacity for attracting and uniting people that were the principal forces facilitating those mergers. The retention of the name of the Los Angeles organization as the denominational name reflects the depth of Bresee's influence and the long-held prominence of that first Nazarene congregation.

The first merger occurred in 1907, creating the Pentecostal Church of the Nazarene. The Nazarenes' partner in this union was the Association of Pentecostal Churches of America, itself the project of mergers in New York state and New England (see PENTICOSTALISM). Its oldest congregation had formed in 1894,

in Providence, Rhode Island. The Association's principal leader was H. F. Reynolds (1854–1938), an ME pastor; however, a number of others—predominantly, but not at all exclusively, disaffected Methodists, clerical and lay—played significant roles in the Association and in the merger.

In 1908, at Pilot Point, Texas, the Holiness Church of Christ, the product of earlier mergers in Oklahoma, Texas, and the old South, and influenced by restorationism and the holiness movements in both the ME and MES churches, united with the Pentecostal Church of the Nazarene. This group had no central or galvanizing figure such as Bresee or Reynolds; and at the time of the merger, it still had not completely resolved some of its own major internal issues. Nonetheless, many consider the date of this merger, October 12, 1908, to be the founding date for the denomination. The occasion was actually the Second General Assembly of the Pentecostal Church of the Nazarene.

With this merger the denomination became nationwide, with more than 10,000 members in 228 congregations. Several of the west coast congregations were predominantly Oriental; at least one on the east coast was Portuguese-speaking; as many as two dozen had African-American members.

J. O. McClurkan (1861–1914), a Cumberland Presbyterian clergyman, had founded the Pentecostal Alliance in Nashville, Tennessee, in 1898. By 1901 it had become the Pentecostal Mission. By 1915, when it merged with the Pentecostal Church of the Nazarene, it had congregations in all of the larger cities of Tennessee, in Columbia, South Carolina, and in Atlanta, Georgia. This group brought with it strong Cumberland Presbyterian, Christian and Missionary Alliance, and MES influences. Perhaps more important, it brought to the merger strong social-work institutions and missionaries working abroad. Also in 1915 the Pentecostal Church of Scotland, formed in 1909 by four holiness congregations, merged with the Nazarenes. Its principal leader was George Sharpe (1865–1948), former pastor of the Parkhead (Congregational) Church in Glasgow. This body, too, carried on a strong program of social service and had sent missionaries to Africa before merger with the Nazarenes.

Each of the groups in this string of mergers brought to the union at least a school for the education of the ministry, if not a nascent liberal arts institution. Each merging group also brought missions enterprises. As early as 1908 the Nazarenes had congregations in Mexico, the Cape Verde Islands, INDIA, JAPAN, and southern Africa. They only slowly accepted the notion of indigenized administrative leadership, but from their earliest days, they had developed indigenous preachers and teachers. "National workers (or preachers)," as they were called, outnumbered missionaries five to one by the early 1930s.

Modern American Pentecostalism made an exponential leap into public awareness with the well-publicized Azuza Street (Los Angeles) Revival in 1901. Its roots lay in much the same soil that had produced the Holiness Movement three decades earlier. In fact, on into the 1910s, many thought the two movements to be but two styles of the Holiness Movement. Adherents of one freely mingled in revival services, if not in congregations, with adherents of the other. Their primary contention had to do with whether glossalalia (usually called "tongues") was the necessary evidence of entire sanctification. By the mid-1910s, however, non- and anti-Wesleyan factions had arisen in Pentecostalism, and a strong antiglossalalic faction had arisen among the holiness people. In 1919 the Pentecostal Church of the Nazarene dropped the adjective "Pentecostal" from its name and the names of a number of its academic institutions. It was now, simply, the Church of the Nazarene, and it generally opposed the idea that "tongues" was a contemporary gift of the Spirit.

Still, the process of merging continued. The Laymen's Holiness Association in the Dakotas and Minnesota, led by J. G. Morrison (1871–1939), an ME clergyman, joined the Church of the Nazarene in 1922. The Association was predominantly ME, but it included significant numbers of adherents to the Evangelical Association, a group tracing its origins to the work of Jacob Albright (1759–1808), a Lutheran-become-Methodist in Pennsylvania.

The 1950s brought both gain and loss by way of merger and secession. Four small holiness denominations joined the Church of the Nazarene. In the early 1950s the Hepzibah Faith Missionary Association, founded in 1893 and centered in Tabor, Iowa, joined the Nazarenes, bringing with it missionary work in six countries. In 1952 the International Holiness Mission, founded as the Holiness Mission, in the Clapham area in London, in 1907, brought into the Church of the Nazarene a strong commitment to social work and a very active missionary presence in sub-Saharan Africa, and about two dozen congregations across England. Three years later, the Calvary Holiness Church, formed in 1934 by itinerant evangelists in the International Holiness Mission, joined the Nazarenes as well, nearly doubling the Nazarene constituency in ENGLAND and WALES. In 1958 the five congregations of the Gospel Workers Church of Canada, a denomination founded in 1918, with its work concentrated in Ontario, merged with the Nazarenes.

Other mergers have occurred since the 1950s, the largest being that of 1988, with a Wesleyan/Holiness group in NIGERIA already calling itself the Church of

the Nazarene. This merger brought thirty-nine congregations and 6,500 members with it.

A secession in the mid-1910s, rooted in both doctrine and polity but also entangled in personalities, almost destroyed the denomination. The doctrine in question was premillennialism; the political issue was the authority of the district superintendency over a local congregation. Many of the dissidents eventually joined another holiness body. The Nazarenes continued to refuse official endorsement to any particular form of millennialism and to uphold a strong superintendency (see MILLENARIANS AND MILLENNIALISM).

The secessions of the 1950s and 1960s generally arose from the conviction that the denomination had lost much of its evangelistic fervor and was surrendering to American popular culture. The specific points of critique, which were akin to HOLINESS MOVEMENT critiques of episcopal Methodism eighty years earlier, were the failure of the Nazarene General Assemblies of 1952 and 1956 to condemn television and the critics' perceptions that Nazarenes had become too ready to accept contemporary styles of dress, cosmetics, and jewelry; and had developed a tendency to rely on administrative structures and programs at the cost of spiritual dependency on God. None of the dissident groups departed with more than 500 members, although their exodus removed certain concerns for piety at a time when the denomination was indeed concerned with gaining social acceptability. Perhaps most significant was the formation of the Bible Missionary Union in 1956, which in 1957 became the Bible Missionary Church. The most recent of significant secessions was that of the Church of the Bible Covenant in 1967. Its rationale for secession paralleled that of the Bible Missionary Church.

From its beginning, whether 1908, 1907, or 1895, the Church of the Nazarene has understood its principal mission to be the propagation of the doctrine and experience of entire sanctification, or holiness, or Christian perfection. To engage in this mission, Nazarenes have generally developed a strong set of common mores and pieties, such as commitment to regular attendance at worship, tithing, teetotalism, and to their regional educational institutions; and heavy giving to world mission and compassionate causes. They have also usually avoided debates over the nature of biblical inspiration, baptism, millennialism, divine healing, and forms of worship, among other things. However, since the late 1970s, emphasis on following the sociological principles developed by the Church Growth Movement, coupled with a decreasing emphasis on the mores and pieties noted earlier, has tended to dull the sharp edge of holiness evangelism in favor of a socially more acceptable, less doctrinaire evangelicalism.

See also Evangelicalism; Wesley, Charles

References and Further Reading

Jones, Charles Edwin. *Perfectionist Persuasion: The Holiness Movement and American Methodism, 1867–1936.* ATLR Monograph Series, no. 5. Methuen, NJ: Scarecrow Press, 1974.

Purkiser, W. T. *Called Unto Holiness. Volume 2: The Second Twenty-Five Years, 1933–1958.* Kansas City, MO: Nazarene Publishing House, 1983.

Smith, Timothy L. *Called Unto Holiness. The Story of the Nazarenes: The Formative Years.* Kansas City, MO: Nazarene Publishing House, 1962.

PAUL MERRITT BASSETT

CHURCH WORLD SERVICE

The Protestant, Orthodox, and Anglican traditions that compose the NATIONAL COUNCIL OF CHURCHES support ecumenical humanitarian relief through the Church World Service (CWS). In 1946 the Federal Council of Churches, Foreign Missions Conference, and American Committee of the WORLD COUNCIL OF CHURCHES established CWS in response to the proliferation of church relief endeavors during the Second World War. The new organization represented ecumenical Protestant efforts to address issues of hunger, reconstruction, and displacement in postwar Europe and Asia.

In its early years CWS worked in the areas of food relief and refugee resettlement. A network of Christians from across the United States formed the Christian Rural Overseas Program (CROP) to donate food and funds for CWS programs. CWS grew into a global organization, creating partnerships with local Christians in Southeast Asia, Latin America, and AFRICA to sponsor development projects. Throughout the 1960s CWS expanded its assistance to refugees through its work in Vietnam, Palestine, and Cuba. In the 1970s CWS created offices to respond to international and domestic disasters.

CWS's work with relief and development reflects a theology of compassionate response to all human need. In the 1970s its leaders added the emphases of global education and public advocacy to the agency's original goals of providing for physical necessity, assisting refugees, and supporting development projects. CWS has also added a focus on the root causes of poverty and powerlessness.

CWS includes thirty-six member denominations. Headquartered in New York City, CWS works with local partners in more than eighty countries. Two thousand local CROP events raise funds for CWS programs each year. In 2002 CWS operated on a budget of $69,000,000.

References and Further Reading

Fey, Harold E. *Cooperation in Compassion: The Story of Church World Service.* New York: Friendship Press, 1966.

Stenning, Ronald E. *Church World Service: Fifty Years of Help and Hope.* New York: Friendship Press, 1996.

JENNIFER GRABER

CIRCUIT RIDER

Circuit riders were itinerant ministers who advanced the rapid growth of Wesleyan METHODISM in the UNITED STATES during the late eighteenth and early nineteenth centuries (see ITINERANCY). A system of traveling Methodist preachers was first envisioned by JOHN WESLEY as a means of propagating and servicing Methodist Society class meetings in rural ENGLAND. After the founding of the American Methodist Episcopal Church at the BALTIMORE CONFERENCE, in 1784, FRANCIS ASBURY organized American Methodist societies or churches into circuits. Pastoral circuit riders were appointed to travel the circuits on horseback: their responsibilities included visiting each church at least once a year and reporting back to the conference, as well as preaching extemporaneously, holding CAMP MEETINGS, and organizing new Methodist churches along the way. This efficient and effective organizational system contributed to the populist appeal of Methodism and enabled the church to grow with the westward territorial expansion of the United States. Especially in the American South and West and among African Americans, circuit riders were instrumental in building Methodism from fewer than 1,000 adherents in 1770 to more than 250,000 by 1820. Despite the hardships of wilderness travel and occasional anti-Methodist violence, Asbury himself was a devoted itinerant who traveled more than 270,000 miles during his career. Other well-known circuit riders include PETER CARTWRIGHT (1785–1872), Freeborn Garrettson (1752–1827), and the African American Harry Hosier (1750?–1806).

See also Evangelicalism; Methodism, North America; Methodist Episcopal Church Conference.

References and Further Reading

Andrews, Dee. *The Methodists and Revolutionary America, 1760–1800: The Shaping of an Evangelical Culture.* Princeton, NJ: Princeton University Press, 2000.

Wigger, John. *Taking Heaven by Storm: Methodism and the Rise of Popular Christianity in America.* New York: Oxford University Press, 1998.

JOANNA BROOKS

CIVIL RIGHTS MOVEMENT

The modern civil rights movement, usually placed in the middle of the twentieth century from the mid-

1950s to the late 1960s, was a coalition of organizations and leaders with the primary goal of eradicating racial injustice from American society. This movement, however, had its roots in nineteenth-century slave rebellions, abolitionists, and a post-CIVIL WAR proactive congress that passed destiny-determining (for African Americans) amendments to our Constitution: the 13th Amendment (1865), which freed the slaves; the 14th Amendment (1868), which guaranteed equal protection, due process, and full citizenship for freed slaves; and the 15th Amendment (1870), which gave them the right to vote.

This modern movement also had significant twentieth-century roots with the pre-World War I founding of the National Association for the Advancement of Colored People (NAACP) and The National Urban League; the Marcus Garvey "Back to Africa Movement" in the 1920s; President Franklin Roosevelt's 1941 executive order to prohibit discrimination in federal employment (as a result of pressure by A. Philip Randolph of the Brotherhood of Sleeping Car Porters—the largest black labor union); the formation of CORE (Congress of Racial Equality) by James Farmer in 1943; President Harry Truman's executive order to desegregate the armed services in 1948; and Thurgood Marshall's successful argument of the *Brown v. Board of Education of Topeka, Kansas* case (1954) before the U.S. Supreme Court to integrate public schools. This landmark case overturned *Plessy v. Ferguson* (1896), which had declared that separate facilities were equal, a judicial endorsement of Jim Crow laws. In reversing Plessy, Brown stated that "separate was not equal" and made a full circle back to the 14th Amendment on which Marshall's argument heavily depended.

Combine this rich historical context with the immediate sense of horror in the black community over the murder of teenager Emmett Till in the summer of 1955 in Mississippi and one can see how Rosa Parks, often called the Mother of the Civil Rights Movement, was ready and willing to deny her seat to a white man on December 1, 1955, in Montgomery, Alabama. The courageous act of this black seamstress from Montgomery gave birth to the Montgomery Improvement Association that, in turn, sponsored the year-long Montgomery Bus Boycott (December 1955 to December 1956), which saw, as well, the emergence of a new black leader, Dr. MARTIN LUTHER KING JR. For all intents and purposes, that year ignited the new civil rights movement and became a turning point in American history.

Soon after the success of this boycott, in 1957, several civil rights leaders including King, Ralph Abernathy, Bayard Rustin, Ella Baker, Harris and Clare Wofford, and Stanley Levison formed the Southern Negro Conference on Transportation and Nonviolent Integration with the primary purpose of integrating buses. The name was soon changed to Southern Negro Leaders Conference and, to be as clear as possible about its source and expanding mission, it received its final designation as Southern Christian Leadership Conference—the SCLC became the virtual center of the movement, and its first president, Dr. King, was the heart of that center. Upon King's death, the mantle of leadership was passed to Abernathy, King's close friend and associate. After a decade with Abernathy at the head, SCLC became a weaker organization and lost its effective voice. In 1977 Joseph Lowery, a Methodist, took the reins and for the next twenty years returned the SCLC to it original vibrant witness for civil rights. Nonetheless, every preceding civil rights group would join with SCLC in all the major campaigns (from Birmingham to Selma to Memphis to the Poor Peoples Campaign). Other groups and leaders spawned by SCLC would, in one form or another, take their cue from SCLC.

The modern civil rights movement, in its several manifestations, wanted social justice and equality for America—that is, political, social, and economic freedom. Each organization would contribute its unique emphasis to achieve these goals and each director would share his or her own gifts of leadership. Their protests were directed mainly at the deep South, but the consequences reverberated throughout the country.

One way to view the accomplishments of the civil rights movement is to survey the work done by the various organizations and their leaders and suggest how their specific gifts contributed to the overall success of what the movement achieved. These goals were achieved by different methods, but always nonviolently.

1. The *National Association for the Advancement of Colored People* (NAACP) was founded in 1909 by an interracial group, which included W. E. B. Dubois, to advance the struggle for civil and political liberty. It is the oldest, most enduring civil rights organization and is always there, directly or indirectly, when an advance is made for minorities. Its Legal Defense and Education Fund with lawyers trained in civil and constitutional law has served the African-American constituency well for almost a century. The high water mark of their history of litigation on behalf of minorities was the Brown decision in 1954. The NAACP supported every campaign for social justice before, during, and after the 1950s and 1960s, with Roy Wilkins as president. Their members

were critical to the success of the African-American cause, including for example, Rosa Parks, Medgar Evers, and the college students who sat in at the Woolworth lunch counter in Greensboro, North Carolina, in 1960. It is active today under the leadership of Kweisi Mfume (who became president in 1996), with many branches in small communities throughout the United States.

2. The *Congress of Racial Equality* (CORE) was founded in 1942 by James Farmer in Chicago. It was a nonviolent direct action group that organized demonstrations and educated volunteers in various forms of civil disobedience. This activist stance found them in the famous Freedom Rides that tested interstate commerce public transportation in the early 1960s, the March on Washington in 1963, in all the major campaigns, especially the one in Birmingham in 1963. When Farmer left the directorship in 1966, Floyd McKissick replaced him and turned CORE into a more segregated, militant advocacy group for black people with his championing of Black Power. When Roy Innis became head in 1988 he further moved CORE toward a conservative path, becoming critical of traditional civil rights groups and affirmative action.

3. *The National Urban League* was formed in 1911, dedicated to caring for the increasing number of blacks migrating to northern cities. The League was instrumental in helping new, often low-income city dwellers find employment in an industrial setting, rent and buy houses, and understand real estate terminology. The League provided financial aid and assistance with child care, and interpreted the rights and responsibilities of home ownership—in short, prepared the urban poor to live self-confidently and with as much economic well-being as possible in cities. Edmund Haynes was the first director of this necessary community service agency; Whitney Young was its successful director during the civil rights era and worked closely with Martin King and SCLC campaigns.

4. *The Student Nonviolent Coordinating Committee* (SNCC) grew out of the student sit-ins in Greensboro, North Carolina, and Nashville, Tennessee, in February of 1960. Ella Baker, a Shaw University graduate, community organizer, trusted advisor, and a progressive in social and political affairs, was a key figure in initiating this student-operated arm of the movement. She wanted to create a network of communication for all students throughout the South to avoid duplication of their effort and to keep the students' esprit de corps alive.

By the end of February 1960 it was an active group with a membership from which would come some of the most well-known leaders the movement was to produce. They were "the children" made famous by David Halberstram in a well-known book by that name. The early leaders were James Lawson, a Vanderbilt seminary student and Gandhian pacifist (see PACIFISM), Diane Nash, a Fisk University student from Chicago who became a civil rights activist and educator; and John Lewis, an American Baptist seminary student who was involved in the Selma campaign and became a Georgia congressman. Membership in the early years of SNCC also included Bernard LaFayette, Marion Barry, Stokely Carmichael, Julian Bond, and Robert Moses, among others—all of whom have become national figures. SNCC saw itself as a second generation, a more impatient and aggressive organization than the traditional civil rights groups. It was difficult for them to wait for the Urban League's social service, SCLC's well-thought-out campaign strategy, and the NAACP's lengthy court battles. SNCC's voter registration drives (the trio of Schwerner, Chaney, and Goodman were killed in Mississippi in 1964 working for SNCC), their continual sit-ins and other acts of civil disobedience kept the fire of the movement burning in between the major and nationally televised campaigns. Nevertheless, SNCC supported those more publicized crusades as well.

In the mid-1960s, noticing that young black men were disproportionately drafted and subject to a higher percentage of casualties from the Vietnam war, SNCC issued an articulate and passionate antiwar position paper, asking, "Where is the draft for freedom fighters in the USA?" They combined the civil rights movement and the antiwar movement with much the same rationale King used later in his infamous 1967 antiwar sermon: "I've been around segregation too long now to segregate my moral concerns."

The impact of SNCC is largely overlooked, but the civil rights movement would never have been as successful without the energy and vision of the many youth who made their distinctive contribution to help blacks achieve self-determination.

5. The *Council of Federated Organizations* (COFO) was founded in 1962 as a coordinating agency for the several civil rights groups working in Mississippi. Its most significant leader, Robert Moses, had come to Mississippi soon after receiving a master's degree in philosophy to work with SNCC's voter registration drives. Its main contribution was the formation of the Freedom Summer of 1964 in Mississippi. That summer's achievements were many, despite overwhelming local odds. Some of the results were black voter registration drives, the organization of the Mississippi Freedom Democratic Party with Fannie Lou Hamer as its delegate to the 1964 convention, and the providing of places ("freedom schools") for black children to learn basic educational skills and to aid adult blacks with legal, medical, and work needs.

The most disturbing fissure in the movement came as a result of the growing impatience of young blacks with the civil rights' establishment and the perceived undue influence and co-opting of the movement by "privileged" black leaders and affluent white liberals. The turning point came in Greenwood, Mississippi, on June 16, 1966, when SNCC member Stokely Carmichael, standing on a flatbed truck, began to shout "We want black power!" This cry for dignity and respect in the name of black people's humanity and for black political and economic power made an indelible imprint on the movement, so much so that Martin King devoted a whole chapter to "black power" in his book *Where Do We Go From Here: Chaos or Community?* King's dialectical understanding of this new tone was instrumental in the eventual incorporation of its more positive aspects into the larger movement.

Jesse Jackson, one of the many young black clergy supporters of King, became the most nationally famous alumnus of the movement. He ran for president of the UNITED STATES in 1984 and 1988 and is the founder and president of Rainbow/Push, a Chicago-based organization currently active in advocating for minority contractors and business people.

The civil rights movement was an extension of the black, mostly Baptist, church. It could not have been sustained without its energy and leadership. The introduction of "Christian" in the final name of SCLC was an intentional reminder that it was anchored in the tradition of the black church. Oppressed people tend to see religion, as indeed Israel's prophets did, as a praxis—the unity of faith and action, prayer and politics. So it was natural for Martin King to call the work for justice of the civil rights coalition "a spiritual movement," or for Joseph Lowery to say "if the earth is the Lord's, it includes economic and political aspects as well as spiritual aspects." The roll call of movement leaders consists primarily of young black clergy or those whose primary influence was from the church, for example, James Lawson, Bernard LaFayette, Fred Shuttlesworth, Wyatt Tee Walker, John Lewis, Ralph Abernathy, Julian Bond, Floyd McKissick, and others.

The black church also produced a large and significant band of women who played a central, indispensable role in the movement. We have mentioned Rosa Parks, Diane Nash, Ella Baker, and Fannie Lou Hamer. There were many others. Dorothy Cotton was cofounder of SCLC and its education director for twelve years; Septima Clark was very involved in the network of Citizenship Schools and an activist who exposed the rather pervasive sexism in the movement. SNCC was heavily dependent on women's leadership, especially in the aforementioned Citizenship Schools and voter registration drives. The most famous are Gloria Richardson Dandridge, Ruby Smith, Colia LaFayette, Ruth Howard Chambers, Eleanor Holmes Norton, Ruth Harris, Bernice Johnson Reagon, and Ethel Minor. Two SNCC workers, Casey Hayden and Mary King, following the lead of Septima Clark, wrote a revealing statement about gender discrimination in the movement that has been considered one of the founding documents of the feminist movement.

These leaders represent the best of what PAUL TILLICH called an essential religious impulse—the Protestant (Prophetic) Principle. This is the necessity to call into question, to say a Divine "no," to all attempts at absolutizing historical, finite, relative authorities, for example, race, patriarchy, class, war, wealth, and other forms of entrenched power and privilege. Although the movement included Jewish, Roman Catholic, and other ecumenical support, those young clergy were embodying "pro-testare," their unmediated Protestant vocation to speak truth to power on behalf of God, to testify for, to witness to justice and peace.

All these extraordinary and often very ordinary people succeeded in achieving the original goals of the movement and advancing the cause of minority populations. Their work in the movement helped realize a more politically just and economically equitable society. Some concrete examples include: federal legislation and Supreme Court decisions on behalf of civil rights, the large number of current elected black officials, a much larger black middle class, universal suffrage, and a more fully integrated society. However, in the interest of full intellectual disclosure and honesty, Martin Luther King Jr., the unifying, if not mythical, center of the movement would say, "We still have a long way to go."

See also Ecumenism; Slavery; Slavery, Abolition of; Womanist Theology

References and Further Reading

Branch, Taylor. *Parting the Waters: America in the King Years, 1954–63.* New York: Simon and Schuster, 1988.
———. *Pillar of Fire: America in the King Years, 1963–65.* New York: Simon and Schuster, 1998.
Carson, Clayborne. *Martin Luther King, Jr., Papers Project.* www.stanford.edu/group/king.
Fairclough, Adam. *To Redeem the Soul of America: The Southern Leadership Conference and Martin Luther King, Jr.* Athens: The University of Georgia Press, 1987.
Garrow, David. *Bearing the Cross: Martin Luther King, Jr., and the Southern Christian Leadership Conference.* New York: William Morrow and Co., 1986.
———. *Martin Luther King, Jr., and the Civil Rights Movement.* 18 vols. New York: Carlson Publishing, 1989.
Halberstam, David. *The Children.* New York: Random House, 1998.

IRA G. ZEPP JR.

CIVIL WAR, ENGLAND

During the 1640s ENGLAND was wracked by Civil War. The conflict had a number of causes, of which religion was one of the most important. Many Puritans (see PURITANISM) believed that the church, led by King Charles I and WILLIAM LAUD, the archbishop of Canterbury, had adopted objectionable popish and superstitious practices and beliefs, and they were willing to fight to preserve Protestantism as they understood it. After six years of fighting, with large armies on both sides, the royalist Anglicans were defeated by the parliamentary Puritans, who insisted on the execution of the king and archbishop. During the Interregnum (1649–1660) England was governed without a king, first by parliament and then by the Lord Protector OLIVER CROMWELL. After Cromwell's death the monarchy and state church were restored in 1660, much as they had been before the conflict.

The hostilities can be separated into the First Civil War (1642–1646), the Second Civil War (1647–1648) and the Third Civil War (1649–1651). Some writers have used other terms to refer to these disruptions. Edward Hyde, earl of Clarendon, called it the Great Rebellion in his history written during the seventeenth century itself, whereas the twentieth-century historian Christopher Hill preferred to term it the Puritan Revolution.

Causes and Historiography

Historians have argued about the causes of the English Civil War ever since its outbreak and are not likely

ever to reach agreement. Their views are to some extent a reflection of their own times—it is often said that each age rewrites the past according to its own interests, and the generalization is particularly apt with reference to the great conflict of the seventeenth century.

During the period itself the war was widely viewed as a religious conflict led by those who opposed the increasingly high-church policies of King Charles and Archbishop Laud. These included greater emphasis on the Eucharist, more elaborate ceremonial, VESTMENTS, and music, and railed altars. The movement is often referred to as ARMINIANISM, although the belief in free will, which characterized the views of Dutch theologian Jacobus Arminius himself, was not an important aspect of it. Both the Independents or Congregationalists (see CONGREGATIONALISM), who opposed a state church altogether, and the Presbyterians (see PRESBYTERIANISM), who favored a state church but one without bishops, joined in opposing the established CHURCH OF ENGLAND. Oliver Cromwell once said that although he did not originally regard religion as the principal issue in the war, he was driven to that opinion as the hostilities progressed.

During the eighteenth and nineteenth centuries the war was generally regarded as a protest against Charles I's arbitrary Personal Rule without parliament (1629–1640). The popular Whig interpretation of history looked on earlier events in England as leading inevitably to the ideal form of representative government and liberal democracy that reached its peak during the reign of Queen Victoria. The Civil War, then, was a necessary stage in reducing the power of the monarch, enhancing the role of parliament, and making the case for broader representation of the people in government. The brief account of the war that prefaces Thomas Babington Macaulay's famous *History of England* (1848) is one example of such an interpretation. Another can be found, as late as 1904, in *England under the Stuarts* by his great-nephew George Macaulay Trevelyan.

Trevelyan himself helped initiate the study of social history, and a number of twentieth-century writers have attempted to analyze the war as an example of social conflict. Because seventeenth-century England was not yet divided into social classes, at least in the sense that the Marxists used the terminology, the war could not satisfactorily be viewed as a class conflict, although more than one Russian historian attempted to do so and such an explanation could still be encountered in CHINA in the 1980s. However, more acute historians, among them Christopher Hill, were able to discern more subtle social divisions, with the "godly" and "industrious sort" asserting their rights in opposition to the entrenched privilege of monarchy and nobility. Lawrence Stone, approaching the matter from a different angle, chronicled a "crisis of confidence" in the aristocracy and a loss of faith in their leadership.

A number of mid–twentieth-century writers saw the war in terms of regional divisions, sometimes arising from local conflicts between leading families. John Morrill held this view when he published his study of Cheshire in 1974 and his more general *Revolt of the Provinces* in 1976, but his more recent work emphasizes religious considerations and can be thought of as completing a circular development by reverting to opinions like those of Cromwell and the Puritans or, on the other hand, those Anglicans who supported king and church. Stanford Lehmberg's study of *Cathedrals under Siege* (1996) emphasizes the fact that those who cherished the established church, with its beautiful buildings and liturgies, fought to preserve the monarchy as well.

The most important recent discussions of the issue have come from the pen of Conrad Russell. Both his brief account *The Causes of the English Civil War* and his massive narrative *The Fall of the British Monarchies* stress the fact that the Civil War was not a single event and thus had no single cause. At one point Russell separates the complex into seven specific problems: the Bishops' Wars between England and SCOTLAND; England's defeat in that conflict; Charles' inability to secure a settlement with Scotland; his failure to dissolve or prorogue the Long Parliament; his subjects' choice of sides; the failure to negotiate; and the matter of "the king's diminished majesty." Russell shows the ways in which Charles's own personality contributed to the conflict. More important, he concludes that there were three long-term causes. The first, the problem of multiple kingdoms, arose from the fact, hitherto insufficiently appreciated, that Charles was king of Scotland and IRELAND as well as England; he faced different difficulties in each of these realms and had insufficient understanding of the convictions of his Scottish and Irish subjects. The second cause, the problem of religious division, affected the several realms in differing ways. The Scots Covenanters rebelled against the king's attempt to make the church in Scotland more like the Church of England and to increase the power of bishops. The Irish inevitably clung to Catholicism, whereas in England the gulf between Puritans and Arminians deepened during the years of Personal Rule. Finally, old financial and political systems broke down in the face of inflation and the rising costs of warfare. The conjunction of these problems in all three realms was no doubt partly fortuitous, but the long-term causes were sufficiently persistent that they were bound to result in an eventual conflict.

A variety of further views have been expressed. The distinguished narrative historian C. V. Wedgwood renounced any attempt to tease out general causes, believing that only particular events and personalities can explain the flow of history. Sir Geoffrey Elton used to argue that the war should not have occurred because none of the causes propounded by others was an adequate explanation. If pressed to account for the fact that it did take place he sometimes took refuge in blaming the personal ineptness of the king and his advisors.

If a general explanation or synthesis is ever achieved it is likely to admit the partial validity of all the causes identified in the past. A theory of multiple, rather than unitary, causation would acknowledge that the English Civil Wars were a series of conflicts involving three realms and motivated by differences of opinion about religion, political and constitutional issues, and social and economic conditions, with due allowance for the role of regional divisions and personalities. Religious disagreements, however, may emerge as the irreconcilable underlying issue.

Events

The outbreak of Civil War in England was prefaced by the Bishops' Wars in Scotland, a protest against Charles I's desire to make the Scottish kirk more like the Church of England. The necessity of raising money for a Scottish war led to the summoning of the Long Parliament, which was not officially dissolved until 1660. Charles's attempt to arrest the five members of the House of Commons whom he blamed for opposition to his policies (January 1642) probably spelled the end of any possibility of compromise between the king and parliament. Throughout the spring both sides raised armies. Charles's order to hoist the battle standard at Nottingham on August 22 was the sign that hostilities had commenced.

The royalists, often called Cavaliers, enjoyed initial advantages and might have won the war had it lasted only a year or two. They had a single army, already well organized and disciplined, and an experienced cavalry force; the role of the king as commander-in-chief ensured a unified chain of command. Charles's nephew Prince Rupert, who had come to England after growing up in the midst of the Thirty Years' War on the Continent, also proved himself an excellent military leader. The king's opponents suffered from divisions. Leadership was theoretically provided by a committee of parliament. After parliament and the Scots joined in the Solemn League and Covenant (1643) a Committee of Both Kingdoms was placed in charge; it was an inherently inefficient arrangement. In addition, several separate armies fought for parliament, and their leaders often failed to communicate or cooperate with each other. Robert Devereux, third earl of Essex, was initially appointed the parliamentary general and instructed to raise a force of 20,000 foot soldiers and 5,000 horse soldiers. The most important of the other parliamentary armies was the so-called Ironsides of the Eastern Association, commanded by the earl of Manchester with Oliver Cromwell as his aide. More than the other contingents, this army was dominated by those who supported Independency in religion and the abolition of the state church. Parliament's chances of victory were enhanced by the Solemn League and Covenant, which brought the Scottish army into the field alongside the English "Roundheads" and by the creation of a single New Model Army in 1645. Parliament eventually fielded a larger army than that of the king, and as its leaders, especially Sir Thomas Fairfax and Oliver Cromwell, acquired experience they proved themselves equal or superior to Charles's officers. The religious zeal of many of the fighting men finally tipped the scales in favor of the king's opponents.

The chief engagements of the First Civil War were the battle of Edgehill (October 1642), a draw or perhaps a royalist victory presenting opportunities that Charles failed to seize; parliament's success in turning back the king's soldiers marching on London at Turnham Green (November 1642); battles at Newbury in Berkshire (September 1643 and October 1644), both indecisive but favoring the parliamentarians; Marston Moor, near York, where the royalists were routed and lost control of northern England (July 1644); Lostwithiel in Cornwall, where the parliamentary infantry led by the earl of Essex into an untenable position were forced to surrender to the king's men (September 1644); and Naseby, near Northampton, a great triumph for the New Model Army and the determining disaster for the royalists (June 14, 1645). In June 1646 the king's headquarters at Oxford surrendered. Charles had already slipped away incognito; he gave himself up to the Scottish forces at Newcastle, thinking that they would treat him better than his English foes.

The First Civil War was thus won by a coalition including parliament, the army (theoretically under the control of parliament but now often acting independently), and the Scots. Each of these groups attempted to negotiate a settlement that would end the hostilities. Parliament's Propositions of Newcastle were not accepted by the king, nor were the army's Heads of the Proposals, although in December 1647 Charles and a group of Scottish leaders did enter into an agreement called the Engagement. In it the Scots committed themselves to reopen the war, now fighting for the king rather than against him, on condition that he establish the Presbyterian church in both Scotland and England, at least for a trial period, and extirpate Independency in religion.

The only significant battle of the Second Civil War was fought at Preston in Lancashire in August 1648. Here Oliver Cromwell, with only 9,000 men, triumphed over a Scottish army more than twice as large. Cromwell regarded this victory as a sign of God's providence and favor toward his cause.

After the king's second defeat the army demanded his execution. When parliament was reluctant to take action against him a group of soldiers led by Colonel Pride blocked the doors of the parliament house, excluding those who opposed the army's demands. This came to be known as Pride's Purge of the Commons (December 1648). The House of Lords had already been abolished on the grounds that it was not elected and thus unrepresentative. The so-called Rump Parliament that remained in session established an irregular commission to try the king, the charge being that he had committed treason by making war on his subjects. A small group of men, known as the Regicides because they were responsible for killing the king, found him guilty and signed his death warrant. He was beheaded outside the Banqueting House in Whitehall on January 30, 1649. The date is still commemorated by those who regard Charles as a martyr for the sake of the state church.

The Scots soon proclaimed his son Charles II as their new king. Parliament then resolved to force Scotland into compliance with its orders. In what is sometimes known as the Third Civil War an English army was sent to Scotland. Commanded by Cromwell, this force crossed the border in July 1650 and routed the Scottish army at Dunbar on September 3. The young Charles, who had gone to Scotland and had been crowned by the Scots, was able to make his way across the border into northeastern England, where he thought he had many friends, although he too was defeated at Worcester on September 2, 1651, a year to the day after Dunbar. When he succeeded in fleeing to FRANCE the Civil Wars were finally at an end.

After the execution of Charles I England embarked on the eleven-year Interregnum, the only period in its history when there was no monarch. Parliament attempted to run the government as a Commonwealth from 1649 to 1653. When it became evident that a single leader was needed, Oliver Cromwell became Lord Protector. The Protectorate lasted from 1653 until Cromwell's death in 1658. His son Richard Cromwell succeeded him but soon resigned, leaving the country in a state of virtual anarchy during 1659. Finally the Long Parliament was reassembled and offered the throne to Charles II. His return to England in 1660 brought about the Restoration of both the monarchy and the state church.

References and Further Reading

Ashton, Robert. *Counter Revolution: The Second Civil War and its Origins.* New Haven and London: Yale University Press, 1994.

Burne, Alfred H., and Peter Young. *The Great Civil War.* London: Eyre & Spottiswoode, 1959.

Fissel, Mark Charles. *The Bishops' Wars: Charles I's Campaign against Scotland, 1638–1640.* Cambridge: Cambridge University Press, 1994.

Hibbert, Christopher. *Cavaliers and Roundheads.* London: HarperCollins, 1993.

Morrill, John. *The Nature of the English Revolution.* London and New York: Longman, 1993.

Russell, Conrad. *The Causes of the English Civil War.* Oxford: Clarendon Press, 1990.

———. *The Fall of the British Monarchies.* Oxford: Clarendon Press, 1991.

Stone, Lawrence. *The Causes of the English Revolution.* London: Routledge & Kegan Paul, 1993.

Wedgwood, C. V. *The King's War.* London: Collins, 1958.

STANFORD LEHMBERG

CIVIL WAR, UNITED STATES

By virtually any historical account, the Civil War is *the* defining event in American history. Statistics often seem cold and abstract, but numbers count and the Civil War brings some impressive statistics that were sufficiently horrendous to have involved virtually every living American, North and South.

Although Civil War enlistments and casualties cannot be known exactly, there are several reliable approximations. In compiling his indispensable chronology of the Civil War, E. B. Long estimates that total enlistments in the Federal forces numbered 2,778,304, including about 189,000 African Americans, in a population of 18,810,123. Confederate forces numbered 1,400,000 in a white population of 6,500,000. In addition there were slightly less than four million slaves. Of these soldiers 623,026 died and 471,427 were wounded, for a total casualty count of 1,094,453. In breaking the numbers down by each "nation," Federal army deaths totaled 360,222 of which 110,100 were killed in battle and 224,580 of disease in camp. Confederate deaths totaled 94,000 killed in battle and 164,000 from disease for a total of 258,000 dead. These casualty totals combined, in a total population of only thirty million, almost equal losses from all other American wars (see WAR). If translated into an equal proportion of the current U.S. population, the casualty rate would total ten million American soldiers and countless civilians. From another perspective, there were more killed in three days at Gettysburg (60,000) than in all eight years of the Revolution or War in Vietnam. Without exaggeration one can say that in terms of the kill ratios the Civil War was America's most appalling act of human destruction.

For later professional historians and popular history writers alike, the Civil War is a cottage industry that probably rivals all other American history combined in output, sales, and general interest. There have been over 100,000 books, articles, and dissertations written by professional scholars together with easily that number in the popular fiction and nonfiction markets. There are Civil War Roundtables and reenactments that draw thousands. America's best-selling novel and movie remains *Gone With the Wind,* and television documentaries abound.

Yet in all of this ferment and unending fascination there are some remarkable gaps and silences. Most notably there is no comprehensive history of Protestantism's role in the Civil War. A moment's reflection suggests that the unwritten religious history of the Civil War is not because religion was unimportant. To the contrary, Christianity was the most powerful cultural system in the antebellum North and South, and the great majority of these Christians were evangelical Protestants. On the eve of the Civil War the country had one church for every 580 people and could seat three-fifths of the population at one time. As C. C. Goen observed, "no other organization in the country was in closer direct touch with more people." Of these, the vast majority were evangelical Protestants, in particular BAPTISTS and Methodists and, as Goen shows, the bitter divisions of Presbyterian, Methodist, and Baptist churches over SLAVERY and secession prefigured the political divisions to follow. To a significant extent then, we can say that the Civil War represented a Protestant bloodletting.

The reason there is such silence on Protestantism's role in the Civil War is largely because of the almost complete co-option of the churches by politicians on both sides of the conflict. Instead of offering a prophetic voice independent of their "nations"—one that could be framed in a compelling narrative—Protestant churchmen were awash in a sea of patriotism and, if anything, accelerated the blood lust by proclaiming God's blessing on the respective "cause" of North and South.

When news of the firing on Fort Sumter reached Northern and Southern audiences, all quibbles disappeared and in both nations, patriotism displaced religious and partisan loyalties. As flags flew everywhere and even became the subject of sermons, the center of Northern and Southern religiosity shifted decisively toward their nations. Individual sectarian life continued alongside an undoubted personal piety, but now it was a *Union* piety or a *Confederate* piety that transcended any common personal faith the two nations might share. The cultural captivity of churchmen and churches explains why the greatest sermon produced in the Civil War was delivered by a politician, not a minister, and in far fewer words than most ministers then preferred. President ABRAHAM LINCOLN was not only America's greatest politician, he was its greatest preacher, and in the Gettysburg Address and Second Inaugural, he offered a gospel for the republic that has proved enduring.

Of course Protestants continued to preach sermons and commented on the war (see PREACHING). The favored time for religious commentary was the "Thanksgiving" and "Fast" Days proclaimed by Congress and the executive in both North and South. In all Lincoln would proclaim three national fasts throughout the war while, in the same period, Jefferson Davis would proclaim ten. In addition there were multiple state and local fasts in the Confederacy, and even more important, ongoing fasts and REVIVALS in the Confederate army.

In looking at the content of the political sermons preached on these occasions (and expanded on in the religious press), what is most striking is the extent to which both present their cause as a "sacred cause" and a "just war." Both would employ interchangeable language to invoke the Puritan categories of "COVENANT," "divine protection," and "New Israel," and both would portray themselves as a "redeemer nation."

At the outset of war leaders in the Union and Confederacy assumed a quick and bloodless victory filled with heroism and martial valor. One writer for the *Richmond Daily Dispatch* casually observed that, "The nations most favored by God have been baptized in the crimson lever of battle, and the holiest of saints have not worn the crown until they have borne the cross."

By September 1862, however, it became apparent on both sides that this would be no ordinary baptism in blood. The battlefield at Sharpsburg (Antietam Creek) would put to permanent rest all notions of approving smiles and splendid little wars. On the evening of that warm autumn day, after the fifth Federal drive was repulsed, 26,193 soldiers lay dead, wounded, or missing. The scale was unprecedented, impelled, James McPherson observes, by "a sort of fighting madness . . . a superadrenalized fury that turned [men] into mindless killing machines heedless of the normal instinct of self-preservation." For the press no less than the pulpit, nothing but religion could justify so demonic a fury. In the following week's letters to the editor, the *Richmond Enquirer* printed an address to the shell-shocked "soldiers of the Confederate Army" under the pseudonym "Peter the Hermit":

What are we fighting for? You will answer my question by saying, "we fight for the liberties and independence of our country—for the safety of our wives and children—for the inheritance our fathers left us, and the graves where their bones are buried." Noble objects are these. . . . But, fellow soldiers, I am impressed by the belief that we are battling for a higher and nobler cause than any and all of these combined, and one that can and ought and will bring out the highest energies of our natures. I mean *the cross of Christ* and the purity of Christianity. (*Richmond Enquirer*, September 22, 1862)

The notions of "separate spheres" or "the spirituality of the church," which insisted that ministers not "preach politics," were reduced to empty rhetoric during the course of the war. In fact the CLERGY followed the politicians' lead at almost every juncture, leaving transcendent morality at the footstool of a sacralized patriotism. It is true that even more than the politicians, and certainly more than the secular Northern press, the Northern clergy trumpeted the virtues of universal emancipation and the sin of slavery, and on this count deserve praise. Some even went so far as to protest racism in the North as Moses Smith did in a Thanksgiving sermon to his Plainville, Connecticut, Congregational church:

[A]s to the black man, he is as really, and I have sometimes believed more terribly enslaved at the North than at the South. He knows that he is a slave there, and expects a slave's reward. But here he is tantalized with the name of freedom, but denied its privileges. . . . Do what he will and be what he will, he is hated everywhere at the North, banished from society, denied often so much as a seat in the cars. . . . We talk of liberty? Of all galling bondage, this bondage to social feelings, this servitude to caste, this being a "nigger" in society, and "a nigger" at the communion table is probably the most heartless and unrelenting slavery beneath the skies. It may not shackle the body, but it crushes the mind and kills the heart. (*Our Nation Not Forsaken*, Hartford 1863:10–13)

As heroic as these rare voices were, however, they were not saying anything that the relatively small number of abolitionists were not also saying inside and outside of the church; and they met the same deaf ear (see SLAVERY, ABOLITION OF). As for the conduct of the war and protection of innocents, silence prevailed.

The crusading spirit was not limited to the North. One Confederate chaplain, caught up in his own country's civil religion, wrote in *The* [*Richmond*] *Central Presbyterian* in December 1862: "we should add to the prayer for peace, let this war continue, if we are not yet so humbled and disciplined by its trials, as to be prepared for those glorious moral and spiritual gifts, which Thou designest it should confer upon us as a people, and upon the Church of Christ in the Confederacy, and upon mankind."

In Northern churches and denominational publications, patriotism and morbid fascination with destruction often eclipsed serious moral inquiry. In an unprecedented reach, children were not exempted from the blood lust of war. Children were co-opted early on in the war effort and encouraged to wear uniforms and play war games. Parents would have photographs taken of their children with guns and swords. Patriotic songs and "panoramas" brought home the nobility of war to children on a dramatic scale. Awed children learned to revere the war and the warriors of Christ who prosecuted it. There was nothing to learn of right conduct or just cause, let alone acceptable scales of suffering or the protection of innocents. Only a romanticized glory endured. In a column entitled "The children at home," the New York *Evangelist* provided a "Chapter about Heroes," which began with a conversation between two brothers:

> "Is it not grand to hear about all these brave men? I am so glad that I live in these war times!" said George. "So am I," said his brother William. "We did not think that the men who live now-a-days could be such heroes. It seems like reading the histories of old times." "Don't you wish, Will," said George, after a pause, "that we were men and could do such things?" (June 26, 1862, April 3, 1862, Presbyterian Historical Society)

Northern clergy and denominational publications were hardly alone in fueling the blood lust. Stonewall Jackson's aide-de-camp and chaplain, Robert Dabney, took the occasion of a funeral sermon for a fallen soldier to urge his young hearers to be Christlike in fighting to the end:

> Let me exhort the young men of this community to be "followers of him as he also was of Jesus Christ." And especially would I now commend by his example, the sacred and religious duty of defending the cause for which he died. . . . Surely [his] very blood should cry out again from the ground, if we permitted the soil which drank the precious libation, to be polluted with the despot's foot! Before God, I take you to witness this day, that its blood seals upon you the obligation to fill their places in your country's host, and "play the men for your people and the cities of your God," to complete the vindication of their rights. (*Central Presbyterian*, March 12, 1863)

James M. McPherson suggests that the religious intensity for war and unquestioning patriotism may well have succeeded in extending the war for the last—and bloodiest—year.

With war's end churchmen on both sides of the conflict struggled to find meaning. Divided Protestant churches would not reunite until the twentieth century. "Union" and "Confederate" continued to define their identity more than a common faith. In the South,

Protestant churchmen played the lead role in enobling the memory of fallen soldiers and the Confederate cause. The Confederacy would live on in defeat, as Charles Regan Wilson has shown in his book *Baptized in Blood*, through the "Religion of the Lost Cause." The vanquished Confederate nation, Wilson observes, "never resurrected, but it survived as a sacred presence, a holy ghost haunting the spirits and actions of post–Civil War Southerners." Jim Crow segregation and the politics of white supremacy would encapsulate the innermost meaning of that Southern way.

In the North some noble Protestant ministers and educators strove nobly to uplift the freed slaves and the SOCIAL GOSPEL may have been their greatest legacy. For many others, however, war's victory meant a return to business as usual, that is, the business of a "gospel of wealth."

All was not gloom though. There was a great Protestant success story coming out of the Civil War and that was to be found in the black church. Here there were no divided denominations, as Protestant African Americans from all regions came together and led the struggle for spiritual and civil equality. All of the major African American denominations (AFRICAN METHODIST EPISCOPAL, AFRICAN METHODIST EPISCOPAL ZION, National Baptist Convention, Colored Methodist Episcopal Church) evidenced growth rates between 40 and 70 percent in the decades between 1865 and 1900. Among Protestants the biggest gainer was the National Baptist Convention, which displaced the Methodists as the largest African American denomination, claiming over 2.2 million communicants in 1900. In monetary terms the African American church was the dominant "industry" in the black community, with combined assets of over $26 million by 1890. The National Baptist Convention was the single largest black organization in the world.

Clearly these are prodigious figures and do not begin to plumb the full measure of African American Protestant achievements. Besides organizing the spiritual life of the community and sustaining material needs through mutual aid societies, the black church would pave the way for African American education and literacy. They would succeed to an astounding degree, lifting literacy rates from at most 5 percent during slavery, to rates as high as 70 percent in some states.

Whether through worship, aid, or education, the African American church proclaimed a message of solidarity and pride that would sustain freedom in their arduous journey from freedom to equality. It is a journey that is still incomplete, and a journey that continues to look to the church and the clergy for leadership and inspiration. Here we see the greatest prophetic legacy of Protestant churches in the Civil War era.

References and Further Reading

Blight, David W. *Frederick Douglass' Civil War: Keeping Faith in Jubilee.* Baton Rouge: Louisiana State University, 1989.

Chesebrough, David B., ed. *God Ordained This War: Sermons on the Sectional Crisis, 1830–1865.* Columbia: University of South Carolina Press, 1991.

Faust, Drew Gilpin. *The Creation of Confederate Nationalism: Ideology and Identity in the Civil War South.* Baton Rouge: Louisiana State University, 1988.

Goen, C. C. *Broken Churches, Broken Nation: Denominational Schisms and the Coming of the Civil War.* Macon, GA: Mercer University Press, 1985.

Marten, James. *The Children's Civil War.* Chapel Hill: University of North Carolina Press, 1998.

McPherson, James M. *For Cause and Comrades: Why Men Fought in the Civil War.* Oxford: Oxford University Press, 1997.

Miller, Randall M., Harry S. Stout, and Charles Reagan Wilson, eds. *Religion and the American Civil War.* Oxford: Oxford University Press, 1998.

Moorhead, James H. *American Apocalypse: Yankee Protestants and the Civil War, 1860–1869.* New Haven, CT: Yale University Press, 1978.

Noll, Mark A. *America's God, from Jonathan Edwards to Abraham Lincoln.* Oxford: Oxford University Press, 2002.

Shattuck, Gardomer J. *A Shield and Hiding Place: The Religious Life of the Civil War Armies.* Macon, GA: Mercer University Press, 1987.

White Ronald C. Jr. *Lincoln's Greatest Speech: The Second Inaugural.* New York: Simon & Shuster, 2002.

Wills, Garry. *Lincoln at Gettysburg.* New York: Simon and Schuster, 1992.

Wilson, Charles Reagan. *Baptized in Blood: The Religion of the Lost Cause, 1865–1920.* Athens: University of Georgia Press, 1980.

HARRY S. STOUT

CLAPHAM SECT

The Clapham Sect was a loose association of parliamentarians and others concerned with religious, moral, and humanitarian issues in British public life, especially active from about 1790 to 1820. The name was first given pejoratively by the essayist Sydney Smith, who accused them of "patent Christianity." It was not a sect in any ecclesiastical sense; its members were generally loyal adherents of the established church, of a strongly evangelical persuasion [although one, William Smith (1756–1835), had Unitarian leanings]. The link with Clapham (then a quiet suburb of London) came from several of the group having houses there, or regularly visiting. There was no fixed membership; the group functioned through shared outlook and personal friendship, strengthened in some cases by kinship or marriage relations. It included WILLIAM WILBERFORCE, the best-known evangelical layman of his day and an outstanding parliamentary figure; Henry Thornton (1760–1815), a wealthy philanthropist who financed many of their concerns; Smith, Member of Parliament for Norwich; Thomas Gisborne (1758–1846), moralist and writer; Thomas Babington (1758–1837), Member of Parliament for Leicester; James Stephen (1758–1832); and Zachary Macaulay (1768–1838).

The two last, who had seen Caribbean SLAVERY first hand, were the chief researchers and publicists, and Macaulay edited the *Christian Observer,* a periodical that normally reflected the Clapham outlook and views. Associated with them in Indian affairs were Charles Grant (1746–1822), a high official of the East India Company, and Lord Teignmouth (1751–1834), who as Sir John Shore had been governor-general in INDIA. GRANVILLE SHARP, a generation older and somewhat different in outlook and churchmanship, shared their concerns about slavery and AFRICA, whereas John Venn (1759–1813), rector of Clapham and secretary of the CHURCH MISSIONARY SOCIETY, was a friend.

The principal Clapham cause was opposition to slavery (see SLAVERY, ABOLITION OF). From 1791 Wilberforce and his colleagues made almost annual attempts to outlaw the British slave trade by parliamentary legislation, eventually succeeding in 1807. The cruelties of the trade were carefully documented and economic and strategic arguments against slavery used to bolster the moral and theological arguments. The group appealed beyond Parliament to public opinion and in particular mobilized Christian opinion, with skillful use of literature, the press, and public meetings. Evangelicals in particular rallied to the antislavery cause. After the act abolishing the trade, the Clapham group worked to enforce and extend the ban and to seek the end of slavery itself. Wilberforce handed over leadership of this campaign to Thomas Fowell Buxton in 1821; slave emancipation in the British dominions was declared in 1833. Long before this their desire for economic answers to slavery led the Clapham group into projects to develop African agriculture and trade, to participation in the African Institution, and above all to the establishment and early oversight of the colony of SIERRA LEONE. Of all the antislavery forces in Britain, Clapham was probably the most effective.

Their second major concern was India. The goal of the reformers was to end the East India Company's ban on missionaries in the territories it controlled and its obtaining tax revenue from Hindu temple worship; to legislate against cruel and oppressive customs (increasingly documented by missionaries); and to secure explicit acknowledgment of Christianity by the Company, which represented the British administration in India. The renewal of the Company's charter in 1813 gave opportunity for parliamentary debate on these issues, with partial success for the reformers.

Clapham domestic concerns included the provision of schools for the poor, reform of prisons, relief of urban hunger, and action against dueling, the national lottery, and manifestations of vice in general, with vigorous support for Bible, tract, and missionary societies (see BIBLE SOCIETIES, MISSIONARY ORGANIZATIONS). "The Saints," as they were often called, were moral rather than political radicals, contrasting, in Wilberforce's words, "the prevailing religious system of the upper and middle classes of this country with real Christianity." They brought EVANGELICALISM in a disciplined, morally earnest, and socially engaged form into the mainstream of British political, social, and intellectual life, deeply influencing the accepted values of the early Victorian period.

Several of the children of the Clapham group continued the same concerns into the next generation. Other descendants are more noted for their literary activity: Lord Macaulay, Leslie Stephen, Virginia Woolf, and E. M. Forster all came from Clapham families.

References and Further Reading

Anstey, Roger. *The Atlantic Slave Trade and British Abolition, 1760–1810.* London and Atlantic Heights, NJ: Macmillan, 1975.

Bradley, Ian. *The Call to Seriousness.* London: Jonathan Cape, 1976.

Embree, A. T. *Charles Grant and British Rule in India.* London: Allen and Unwin, 1962.

Hennell, M. M. *John Venn and the Clapham Sect.* London: Lutterworth Press, 1958.

Howse, E. M. *Saints in Politics.* Toronto, Canada: Toronto University Press, 1952.

Ingham, Kenneth. *Reformers in India.* Cambridge: Cambridge University Press, 1956.

ANDREW F. WALLS

CLERGY

Although charismatic prophets and apostles initially dominated the Christian clergy, by the second century three offices had developed: bishop, presbyter, and deacon. During the third century, the growth of the church and the extent of its charitable activities required the additional offices of the minor clergy. Bishops and presbyters also took on the character of priests and the liturgy became ever more elaborate. The conversion of the Roman emperor Constantine and the adoption of Christianity as the official religion of the Roman Empire by later emperors raised the power and status of the clergy, but also subsumed the church and the clergy into the imperial government. The church developed the complete hierarchical structure that the Catholic Church retains today. The early Middle Ages saw the conversion of most of Europe, but also a decline in the quality of the clergy. The Gregorian Reform beginning in the eleventh century raised the standards, but also claimed for the clergy an elevated status and power. The rise of the universities in the twelfth and thirteenth centuries helped raise the educational level of the clergy during the later Middle Ages. The Protestant Reformers were usually the products of the universities.

The REFORMATION redefined the character and activity of the clergy. Emphasis switched from the sacraments to the preached word, and ministers, preachers, and pastors were deprived of the privileges of the medieval clergy. Despite the "priesthood of all believers," the clerical position of AUTHORITY was revived, but was based on education, not on sacramental status. More open to the world, the Protestant clergy has contributed significantly to Western culture, but it has also been more vulnerable to changing historical developments.

The First Two Centuries

The first clergy predate the death of Jesus. Jesus personally chose the Twelve (the early church would add "Apostles" after that office developed) as his closest disciples, and as eschatological judges over the twelve tribes of Israel. The need to maintain that number explains the replacement for Judas (Acts 1:20–25). However, no successors were chosen for the Twelve in later less eschatological times. Jesus sent the Twelve to preach and heal the sick during his lifetime, but they had no "apostolic" role immediately after the Resurrection. Instead they remained in Jerusalem, awaiting the return of the Lord. In the 50s, Paul mentions only Peter as the "Apostle" to the Jews, while claiming the apostleship to the Gentiles (Galatians 2:7,8). The Twelve governed the Jerusalem church initially, but Paul later lists only two, Peter and John, along with James, the brother of Jesus, as "pillars" of the church (Galatians 2:9). James played the leading role. Apostles (from Greek *apostolos,* meaning messenger) were sent by local churches as messengers to carry the Gospel. It was one of Paul's distinctive claims that he that had been commissioned directly by the risen Lord. However chosen, there were a number of other Apostles, some mentioned by Paul, and the office continued to be exercised at least until the early second century.

In addition to peripatetic apostles, prophets and deacons provided continuous stationary leadership in the earliest decades. Prophets were charismatic figures, and we do not know whether there was any process for recognizing and acknowledging them.

DEACONS (servants, ministers), on the other hand, are traditionally associated with the Seven (Acts 6:3–6), although the Seven seem to have had apostolic and prophetic functions as well. The Apostles chose the Seven from a list proposed by the community. They were charged with the daily administrative tasks of the community, especially CHARITY. The Apostles ordained the Seven by the laying on of hands, a rite that remained central to ordination for all clerics throughout the early church. Despite Paul's preference of CELIBACY for all (I Corinthians 7:25–39), there is no evidence that it was usual for the clergy.

Paul's letters describe a less structured church with a rich diversity of gifts and offices. Reliance on the direct guidance of the Spirit made a clerical order unnecessary. This allowed for a more egalitarian church order in which women and those of lower social station took prominent roles. Worship was nonhierarchical. Paul mentions no leader for either the LORD'S SUPPER (I Corinthians 11:17–34) or the worship service (I Corinthians 14:26–33). He also mentions no sermon or homily. Presumably, prophetic utterances from the congregation sufficed. However, Paul also reveals an interest in a more ritualized Lord's Supper, a development that would lead to formal liturgical leadership.

We do not know how this early group of apostle–prophet–deacon was replaced with a new one, bishop–presbyter–deacon, by the second century. Presbyters (elders) usually formed a "college" that presided over the community but did not administrate. Their relationship to the episcopacy in the earliest period is still debated. In the New Testament there are combinations of bishop and deacon (Philippians 1:1) or presbyter and deacon (I Timothy 3:8, 4:14, 5:17) or bishop and presbyter (Titus 1:5–7). The office of bishop (overseer) may have developed out of the presbytery as individual presbyters were given administrative responsibility and authority; or the episcopacy and presbyteries may have initially been alternative forms of organization that were combined. In any event, by the second half of the second century the monarchical episcopate presided over the presbytery, supervised the deacons, and ruled over the community. To the present, this remains the clerical structure of the Roman Catholic, Anglican (see ANGLICANISM), and Orthodox Churches (see ORTHODOXY, EASTERN).

The bishop, assisted by his presbyters, assumed liturgical leadership, including preaching. Presbyters taught neophytes and prepared candidates for BAPTISM. In the Letter of James (James 5:14–16), the presbyters anoint and pray over the sick. The primary role of deacons was the administration of church wealth and charity, both of which took on enormous proportions with the passage of time. The clergy were usually married. Some individuals may have assumed a celibate life as had Paul, but it was by no means required or even expected. Election of clergy by the community was the norm. With time clerics were increasingly drawn from the economically and socially prominent in the community.

These developments were not unopposed. Some continued the more egalitarian pneumatic practices of the Pauline churches. For them prophecy remained crucial, and women had a public prominence. Celibacy may also have been more common in such groups. The struggle is apparent in the deutero-Pauline letters, which sought to suppress the earlier practices and replace them with the hierarchical and patriarchal bishop or presbyter and deacon model (Titus 1:6–9; I Timothy 3:1–13, 5:17–22). Opposition was marginalized and then hereticized (see HERESY).

Third to Fifth Centuries

The third to fifth centuries were pivotal for the formation of the Christian clergy. The number of Christians grew dramatically despite spasmodic brutal persecutions. Charitable activities and the administration of cemeteries burdened the clergy with greater economic responsibilities. As a result, the clerical hierarchy expanded to include "minor orders," lesser ministries (e.g., *cemetarius,* gravedigger) that were finally fixed at four: subdeacon, acolyte, exorcist, and doorkeeper. The "major orders" were increasingly absorbed in church service. In the larger cities and communities their offices became their sole profession and the church provided for their support. The liturgy, increasingly formal and elaborate, achieved written form for the first time. However, throughout the period some clerics remained illiterate. No schools similar to the modern seminaries and divinity schools existed, but learned bishops and presbyters provided training and some measure of education. The catechetical school in Alexandria and Origen's school in Antioch achieved scholarly distinction, but whether they taught the clergy is not clear. They may have been similar to the pagan philosophical "schools" in which upper-class disciples gathered around famous thinkers. If clergy participated, their education would have been limited to biblical exegesis and theological speculation. There was no "practical" component to train clerics in the LITURGY or PREACHING.

In the liturgy the bishop assumed a sacerdotal role. The originally separate services of the Word (Paul's worship service) and Lord's Supper had been combined in the second century and the unified liturgy, the Mass, assumed the character of a sacrifice. Bishops resisted the title of "priest" until the third century because of its association with pagan practice. The

Old Testament priesthood, however, provided precedent, and the belief that Christ's death replaced the Temple sacrifices made the priestly title more acceptable. This was an important step in the sacralization of the clergy, a process that continued in the Middle Ages. The detailed and elaborate instructions for the ordination of clergy in the early liturgies reflect this development well. The creation of a sacred clerical estate, however, took place only after the conversion of the Emperor Constantine and the Christianization of the Roman Empire.

Constantine's (280–337) Edict of Milan (313) granted toleration only to the church, but Theodosius the Great (347–395) outlawed paganism. JUDAISM was allowed an uncertain toleration. For the rest of the population, Christianity was the sole legal religion. The emperors lavished privilege, wealth, and status on the church and its clergy. Imperial facilities, for example, the imperial post system, were made available. Taxes were reduced or eliminated. The clergy were exempted from the many military and civic duties that burdened the rest of the population. In a rigidly hierarchical society, bishops were accorded the status of high government officials, a fact that was reflected in their official garb. Until this point clergy had had no distinctive clothing. Now, during the liturgy and on important occasions, bishops adopted forms of imperial court costume. Some elements of liturgical VESTMENTS derived from this source remain in use in the modern world. Daily attire would remain indistinguishable, however, from that of the upper classes until the late Middle Ages.

The social promotion of the clergy was part of a larger process that turned the clergy into a body separate from and superior to the LAITY. In imitation of the Roman cursus honorum by which one rose through the ranks to ever higher government office, there were efforts, never completely successful, to require clerics to climb the rungs of the clerical hierarchy. This promoted better-trained clerics, but it reinforced the sense of a closed corporation with its own interests and *esprit de corps*. The papal decision to impose celibacy upon bishops, presbyters, and deacons had the same effect. Celibacy heightened clerical sacrality required by the priestly character of the bishops and presbyters, but also demanded a visibly higher level of commitment than that found among the laity. Realizing the worldly advantages of Church membership, and the disadvantages of loyalty to the old gods, many converted for worldly reasons. These new Christians lacked the fervor and commitment of their persecuted predecessors. A similar concern with lowered standards led to the development of monasticism.

The learned elite had steadfastly resisted Christianity as a pernicious superstition that threatened the stability and moral character of society. In the fourth century, however, some of the leading intellects were Christian, and often they belonged to the clergy, for example, Basil the Great (329–379), Gregory of Nyssa (335–394), Jerome (347–420), and Augustine (354–430). They produced a sophisticated theology that defined fundamental Christian doctrine: the Trinity and the nature of Christ (see CHRISTOLOGY). In ecumenical (universal) Councils called by the emperors, the bishops and learned clergy argued and promulgated dogma for the whole church. Battles over Christ's divine and human natures were particularly violent, spilling over out of the council chambers into the streets.

Because the wealth of the church, the influence of the clergy upon the urban masses, and the ability to call on imperial support often made the bishops the most powerful officials in their cities, there was intense competition whenever a bishop died. In Rome and elsewhere this led to division, disputed elections, and even street fighting between adherents of competing candidates. This would remain a problem during the entire Middle Ages.

By the fourth and fifth centuries there had developed not only an impressive Eucharistic service, but also an elaborate baptism. A third major SACRAMENT, Penance, involved public penitential exercises (e.g., fasting, special clothing, exclusion from services) and, perhaps, public confession of major sins (murder, adultery). Such penance could be undergone only once, however.

All three sacraments, and most other rituals and liturgies, were performed by the bishop, often assisted by presbyters and deacons. As the church grew, it became impossible for bishops to retain sole competence. Presbyters were delegated to say Mass, perform baptisms, and, more rarely, administer Penance. As a result, some theologians (e.g., Jerome) developed a "presbyterian" ecclesiology that argued for the sacramental equality of presbyters and bishops, although conceding a primacy of institutional authority to the bishops. This ecclesiology remained an option in the theological tradition, although social conditions in the centuries after Jerome elevated the authority of the bishops far above that of the presbyters.

Early Middle Ages

The imperial church created the basic clerical organization of the Catholic and Orthodox Churches that continues to this day. After the collapse of the Western Roman Empire in the fifth century, that structure ensured the church's survival. Germanic kings exercised much effective power over the church. Under Charlemagne (742–814), the reestablishment of the

Roman Empire in the West brought renewed imperial control. The church was feudalized. Bishops became great magnates and servitors of the crown. Local churches came to be "owned" by secular landlords. The expansion of the church north of the Alps created a network of parishes even in the rural areas, leaving some parish clergy at the mercy of the powerful. Lay nobles also founded on their estates churches that they considered to be their property. The bishops lost the authority to appoint, or even discipline, the clergy of such churches.

The quality of the lower clergy plummeted. Many took wives and engaged in secular business. Indistinguishable from their lay parishioners they provided baptism, the Eucharist, Christian burial, and other liturgical services. Preaching was not expected, not only because the clergy often lacked education, but also because the bishop had a monopoly on preaching. Presbyters could be delegated, but few were, because the laity did not expect or particularly desire preaching.

The Gregorian Reform

The Gregorian Reform (so named for Pope Gregory VII [1020–1085]) and the Investiture Crisis marked a turning point. (Investiture was the ceremony by which a secular ruler "invested" a bishop with his bishopric.) Clerical and lay reformers sought to elevate the quality and status of the clergy, and they targeted clerical marriage (concubinage) and the buying and selling of church offices (simony). Although the emperors helped initiate the reform, they eventually came to oppose it because a thoroughgoing abolition of simony would strip the emperors of their control of the bishops. The emperors had given great wealth and power to the bishops in an effort to counterbalance the often unruly secular magnates. The resulting Investiture Crisis affected all of Europe, not just the empire. Although never completely successful, the Gregorian Reform did limit lay "ownership" of churches and made clerical celibacy an often ignored, but universally recognized, requirement for deacons, presbyters, and bishops.

High and Later Middle Ages

From the twelfth to fifteenth centuries, the functions of the clergy achieved the form that Roman Catholic priests still retain. The common practice of calling presbyters "priests" reflects the exaltation of the sacrifice of the Mass (Eucharist). The traditional belief in a real presence of Christ in the bread and wine received precise theological definition and authoritative promulgation at the Fourth Lateran Council (1215) (see Transubstantiation). The council required that all Christians receive the eucharist and confess to a priest at least once a year. Public penance had evolved into private repeatable confession, absolution by the priest, and an often nominal penance (e.g., prayers, fasts, charity). University-trained clerics produced a flood of increasingly sophisticated manuals for confessors. The ability of the priest to transubstantiate the bread and wine in the Eucharist and to absolve sins was ascribed to ordination. This sacrament of Holy Orders impressed a supernatural indelible "character" on the soul of the priest that endowed him with sacramental power. Its irremovability reinforced the difference separating and elevating the clergy above the laity. Tax exemption and immunity from secular courts for clergy found widespread, if not uniform and universal, acceptance.

The expectation that priests and bishops preach on a regular basis comes from this period. During the Gregorian era, clergy and laity demanded frequent preaching in imitation of the Apostles. Religious orders such as Franciscans and Dominicans made it central to their mission. Competition from the friars encouraged parish clergy to preach as well. Although preaching would be required of Catholic clergy thereafter, the focus of their activity and function remained the sacraments.

The enhanced power and prestige of the clergy raised expectations concerning their education, sanctity, and zeal that were not, and probably could not be, met. A rising lay anticlericalism resulted, but the most biting critiques of the clergy came from within the clerical ranks. Paradoxically, the clergy on the eve of the Reformation was better educated than any previous generation, and it would be from its most committed members that the Protestant reformers would be drawn. In some ways, the medieval church was the victim of its own success.

Martin Luther

With the posting of the ninety-five theses, Martin Luther (1483–1546) began a process that ultimately redefined the clergy. Catholic clergy who sought to reform the church by rethinking their own function as clerics began the reformation. Anticlericalism provided popular support, but it was the theological agenda of the reformers that allowed this reform to transcend the limits of medieval reform and rebellion. The reformers joined the anticlerical populace in criticizing the abuses of the Catholic clergy. They went on to reject the theology on which the Catholic clergy was based. The reformers did not just condemn the failure of the clergy to live up to the high standards placed on them by both hierarchy and laity; they also attacked the very standards by which the anticlerical populace had judged the clergy to be wanting.

Martin Luther's critique of the Catholic understanding of the clergy became normative for Protestantism. Luther rejected Catholic teaching on (1) the "character" or definition of the clergy as a separate estate, (2) clerical celibacy, and (3) the sacrificial function of the "priest." Under the slogan "priesthood of all believers," Luther abandoned the Catholic clergy's claim to be supernaturally distinct from the Christian laity. He repudiated the "indelible character" that Catholic theology taught was impressed on the priest's soul during ordination. The value of ordination was hotly debated in the early Reformation, but Luther was content merely to deny its status as a sacrament and its ability to empower the priest to celebrate the Eucharist/Lord's Supper and to absolve sins in confession.

Luther argued that all Christians were made "priests" by their baptism. The clergy differed from the laity solely by their office. Once chosen, the clergy had the right and the responsibility to preach, administer the sacraments, and exercise pastoral care. However, neither before, during, or after their tenure of that office were they supernaturally different from the laity. The lack of such a distinction allowed Luther to reject clerical celibacy, which had been intended to protect the inherent sacrality of Catholic priests by preventing the so-called pollution contracted by sexual intercourse.

Luther also challenged Catholic doctrine concerning the sacrament most crucial to the Catholic priesthood—the Eucharist. Luther rejected opus operatum, which taught that Christ's saving presence in the bread and wine unfailingly occurs when the priest intoned the correct form of words with the correct intention to confect the Eucharist. Instead Luther argued that the recipient's FAITH made the objectively present Christ effectually present as grace and forgiveness. Luther's denial of a sacrifice in the Eucharist had the greatest impact on the clergy. Luther made unnecessary a "priestly" character for the clergy because it was the sacrificial function of the mass that required an officiating priest. The denial of the sacrifice also reduced the numbers of clergy dramatically by eliminating the many priests solely employed in offering the mass for the dead. In Geneva it took only nine Protestant ministers to replace hundreds of Catholic priests. The disappearance of the minor orders, for which there was no biblical warrant, further reduced the clerical estate. Clerical nomenclature made clear the difference between Catholic and Protestant clergy. Whereas Catholic clergy remained "priests," most Protestant clerics became "ministers," "pastors," and "preachers."

Luther's theology represented a fundamental shift not only in the character of the clergy, but in their function and in the religiosity of the churches they served. The Catholic clergy was, and is, primarily a sacramental entity both in form and office. Protestant clergy are constituted by their relationship to the Word, preaching foremost. Luther's reduction of the number of sacraments to two, his emphasis on faith in the sacraments, and his teaching of JUSTIFICATION by faith alone had achieved this shift. The primary goal of the Protestant cleric was to help evoke faith, not to convey grace. Public worship would center on the sermon, not on the Lord's Supper. The Protestant preacher primarily proclaimed God's Word; the Catholic priest primarily mediated the grace of God and the real presence of Jesus Christ.

The fundamental changes in the clergy had social and political consequences. The clergy assimilated to the other learned professions as part of secular society. Urban and princely governments absorbed the clergy into the body politic as citizens and subjects, no longer enjoying the canon law tax exemption and judicial immunity. Instead, in most states the government absorbed the church and made the clergy civil servants. The prince or urban magistracy usually appointed, oversaw, and disciplined them. Luther's Saxony was the model. Luther initially accorded the Elector of Saxony only the role of "emergency Bishop." However, Luther recognized that the prince, by virtue of the "priesthood" he had in common with all other Christians, and the position of leadership that he occupied within Saxon society, had the responsibility to govern and protect the inchoate Lutheran state church as a "Godly Prince."

Calvin and the Reformed Tradition

Disagreements concerning the Lord's Supper caused the acrimonious division of Protestantism into Lutheran and Reformed (primarily Calvinist) Churches (see CALVINISM; LUTHERANISM). However, the two traditions also had differing visions of the clergy. Unlike Luther, the Reformed tradition rejected the real presence of Christ in the bread and wine of the Lord's Supper. This further desacramentalized their clergy, although the structure of the clergy, their role in discipline, and the relationship of church and clergy to secular authority were also distinctive. JOHN CALVIN proposed three offices alongside the pastor: deacon, presbyter, and teacher. The diaconate administered charity; the teacher educated both clergy and laity. The presbyters, unlike the Catholic presbyter-priests, were lay elders (Greek presbyteros, elder) who, along with the pastor, ran the church by administering, overseeing, and representing it. Consistories composed of pastors and presbyters governed the community in faith, morals, and social welfare. The resulting discipline (see CHURCH DISCIPLINE) often enforced by excommunication, public chastisement, and, where possible, civil penalty, is common to most of the Reformed tradition. Collective leadership and incipient ecclesiastical self-sufficiency often made for tensions with the secular government, even in lands where the Reformed was the official church, such as SCOTLAND, Geneva, and the NETHERLANDS. In Protestant England and Catholic FRANCE, Calvinist resistance to government dictates and even open warfare resulted.

The Free Church Tradition

Beginning with the Anabaptists of the sixteenth century, the understanding of the ministerial office among the Anabaptists, Socinians, and (in the seventeenth century) the various English separatists was to see the minister first as expositor, that is, teacher, of Scripture. Since these traditions eschewed the notion of sacraments and saw baptism and the Lord's Supper not as vehicles of divine grace but as memorial and confessional acts, the role of the Anabaptist clergy was that of a presider at baptisms and the Lord's Supper. While the Polish Socinians, formally structured in the Minor Reformed Church of Poland were able to establish training institutions for clergy, the Anabaptists as an underground movement had to wait for a measure of formal tolerance in the Netherlands in the seventeenth century before they were able to offer training for future clergy. Also, Anabaptists chose their clergy from their own ranks, frequently by lot, a practice which among the Amish has survived into the twenty-first century. The disposition among the churches of the Free Church tradition to see little theological significance between clergy and laity allowed such churches as the Baptists to make substantial gains in nineteenth century North America, since they were not as dependent on a trained and ordained clergy.

England and Anglicanism

Unlike almost all Continental Protestant churches, the CHURCH OF ENGLAND kept the full episcopal hierarchy with the exception of the pope. Retention of the bishops was thought to give the monarch practical control over the church and to lend religious legitimization to the social hierarchy that supported the monarchy itself. As James I (1566–1625) argued: "No bishop, no king." The episcopacy became the flashpoint for more rigorous Protestants of dissatisfaction with the degree of church reform. By the end of the seventeenth century two visions of the church and the clergy competed, that of "church" and "chapel." The state

"church" remained staunchly episcopal. "Chapel" referred to a non-Episcopal ecclesiology and a less liturgically rich religiosity (Low Church) than that of the dominant episcopal party (High Church). The unbroken apostolic tradition of episcopal consecration made easier an eventual rapprochement with the Catholic Church, both for individual clerics and the Anglican Church itself. The High Church tradition (see ANGLO-CATHOLICISM) favored a priestly understanding of the clergy and the use of the term "priest." Celibacy remained an option, though not a requirement.

Early Modern and Modern Clergy

The centrality of preaching and the exclusive authority of Scripture brought to completion the late medieval movement toward an educated clergy. University training was required of most aspiring ministers, and governments often provided financial support for those studying for the ministry. The Protestant clergy was distinguished from the laity by education as once the Catholic clergy had been by their indelible character. The authority of the preacher in the pulpit replaced that of the priest at the altar. The clergy were seen and saw themselves as agents of "civilization" in the rural parishes, where the differences of class and education isolated the cleric in a way usually not seen in the Middle Ages. The medieval parish priest was often indistinguishable from his parishioners and may have felt more solidarity with his local community than with the international church. Both Protestant and Catholic reformers sought to give the clergy a new position of power and respect from which they could more effectively rule and instruct their congregations. The high educational standards of the Jesuits and the Council of Trent's (1545–1563) mandate that every diocese have a seminary to train priests served this purpose. The Catholic seminary proved to be a more effective instrument than the Protestant university, given that the seminary drew aspirants to the priesthood out of the larger lay intellectual community. While ensuring theological conformity and moral rectitude, however, the seminaries also limited the intellectual growth of the seminarians. By contrast, the university-trained Protestant clergy was a crucial part of the intelligentsia and provided philosophers, scientists, writers, and other thinkers to the larger society. The Protestant parsonage became an important seedbed of intellectuals and culture.

The Protestant clergy was more exposed to the winds of change in the early Modern and Modern eras. Their Christianity often reflected the latest and the best that Western culture had to offer. The result was a form of Christianity (often called Liberal Protestantism) that was well adapted to modern culture, but which had little in common with the concerns of Luther and the other Reformers.

In Europe, despite revolution and secularization, the Protestant state churches and the Catholic Church determined the form of the clergy. The United States, with its separation of church and state (see CHURCH AND STATE, OVERVIEW), experienced a proliferation of churches that re-created all the earlier clerical types. Prophets, priests, presbyters, and preachers peopled the religious landscape. Without government backing, the clergy had to cater to the laity, even in the mainline denominations. The clergy sometimes transmuted into a social welfare service as love of neighbor appeared to eclipse love of God. Tradition and theological systems gave ground to the concerns and values of a secularized society, and clergy assumed roles as psychologists, social workers, philosophers, or inspirational speakers. The ordination of women constitutes undoubtedly the most significant development in mid-twentieth century; virtually all Protestant denomination—the major exception in the United States is the Southern Baptist Convention—have endorsed the ordination of women. Unresolved in the early twenty-first century is the ordination of openly homosexual individuals.

Conservative churches do not face this challenge, but their dissonance with modern culture marginalizes their clergy. The Catholic Church faces the additional hurdle of attracting men to the priesthood in an age when celibacy is viewed as aberrant. Paradoxically, however, it is precisely those churches that maintain a higher clerical profile that many laity seem to favor. The forces that created the Christian clergy in the first centuries of the church continue to operate.

References and Further Reading

Benson, Robert Louis. *The Bishop-Elect; a Study in Medieval Ecclesiastical Office.* Princeton, NJ: Princeton University Press, 1968.

Campenhausen, Hans Freiherr von. *Ecclesiastical Authority and Spiritual Power in the Church of the First Three Centuries.* Translated by J. A. Baker. Stanford, CA: Stanford University Press, 1969.

Collins, John N. *Diakonia: Re-interpreting the Ancient Sources.* New York: Oxford University Press, 1990.

Ferguson, Everett, ed. *Church, Ministry, and Organization in the Early Church Era.* New York: Garland, 1993.

Harnack, Adolf von. *Sources of the Apostolic Canons, with a Treatise on the Origin of the Readership and Other Lower Orders.* London: A. and C. Black, 1895.

Lécuyer, Joseph. *What is a Priest?* New York: Hawthorn Books, 1959.

Nichol, Todd, and Marc Kolden, eds. *Called and Ordained: Lutheran Perspectives on the Office of the Ministry.* Minneapolis: Fortress Press, 1990.

Osborne, Kenan B. *Priesthood: A History of Ordained Ministry in the Roman Catholic Church.* New York: Paulist Press, 1988.

Pettegree, Andrew, ed. *The Reformation of the Parishes: The Ministry and the Reformation in Town and Country.* New York: Manchester University Press, 1993.

Sheils, W. J., and Wood, Diana, eds. *The Ministry: Clerical and Lay.* [Papers read at the 1988 Summer Meeting and the 1989 Winter Meeting of the Ecclesiastical History Society.] Oxford, UK: B. Blackwell, 1989.

Smith, Ralph F. *Luther, Ministry, and Ordination Rites in the Early Reformation Church.* New York: P. Lang, 1996.

Spijker, W. van 't. *The Ecclesiastical Offices in the Thought of Martin Bucer.* New York: E. J. Brill, 1996.

R. EMMET MCLAUGHLIN

CLERGY, MARRIAGE OF

The prohibition of marriage for Catholic deacons, priests, and bishops is one of the differences separating Protestant and Catholic Churches. St. Paul advocated CELIBACY for all who could maintain it, but he recognized the right of other Apostles to have wives. Deutero-Pauline letters show marriage to be expected or perhaps required. Clerical marriage was the norm in the first centuries of the church, although some individuals followed Paul's advice. In the fourth century the papacy began to require an oath of celibacy from the upper clergy. Those who married before their ordination were to practice abstinence, but were not separated from their wives. The Eastern Orthodox Church (see ORTHODOXY, EASTERN) allowed marriage to priests, but not to bishops. In the early Middle Ages priests in the West were often married. Attempts in the eleventh and twelfth centuries to reinforce the requirement and to make it more stringent faced opposition. In practice, many clerics were husbands and fathers. Protestant reformers condemned clerical celibacy. Ministers were encouraged to marry. The minister's family was a model for the rest of society and a source for new clerics.

The Bible

The Old Testament and the later rabbinic tradition hold MARRIAGE in high esteem. The command to be fruitful and multiply (Genesis 1:28), the definition of Israel as descendants of the patriarchs, and the fundamental importance of the patriarchal FAMILY to society and religion made marriage central. Even more than later Protestant Christianity, JUDAISM remains a family-centered religion both in the definition of its membership and its most fundamental rites. The Old Testament expected the temple priesthood to be married because the priesthood was hereditary in the families of Levi and Aaron. Because sexual intercourse made one ritually impure, however, priests served the altar in alternate weeks during which they abstained. Some prophets and their disciples may have practiced a temporary celibacy. This may have been the case for John the Baptist and Jesus.

Jesus's attitude toward marriage was equivocal. Some of his sayings emphasize an antagonism between discipleship and the bonds of marriage and family (see Mark 3:21, 31–35; Matthew 8:21–22, 19: 29; Luke 8:19–21). This reflected the eschatological expectation of the Gospels. However, Jesus nowhere forbids marriage, not even for the Twelve Apostles.

Because the Apostle Paul also expected the imminent end of the world and return of Christ, he urged celibacy for all able to maintain it (I Corinthians 7:25–38). However, he conceded marriage to the weak. He also recognized that other apostles had married and traveled with their wives (I Corinthians 9:5). The house-churches of the early period were often the homes of married Christians who exercised leadership. It is against this background that Titus's and Timothy's injunctions should be understood. Eager to achieve respectability in Greco-Roman society, the church embraced the patriarchal family in private life and the church (I Timothy 2:2, 3:7, 6:1; Titus 2:9,10). Those who accepted Paul's preference for celibacy were accused of forbidding marriage (I Timothy 4:3). Bishops and deacons were expected to be husbands and fathers because the qualities needed to rule the church were the same as those of a successful *pater familias* (I Timothy 3:1–13; Titus 1:6–11). Patriarchy demanded subordination of wives, children, and slaves to the authority of the father. This model for marriage and family remained even after clerical celibacy was introduced. The patriarchal model created a paternalistic relationship of the clergy to the laity. The use of the honorific "Father" for Catholic priests continues that tradition. Movements that challenged the authority of the clerical hierarchy often accorded women unusual authority and placed the family under pressure.

The Ancient Church

The church's attitude toward clerical marriage began to change in the third century. At the beginning of the century Tertullian (c. 155 to after 220), a presbyter, was not self-conscious about his marriage, although he praised the many clerics who were celibate. Cyprian (d. 258), the bishop of Carthage, remained unmarried, perhaps because of the threat of persecution. Origen (c. 185–c. 254) went so far as to emasculate himself. The Spanish Council of Elvira (between 295 and 302) forbade married clerics to have sexual relations with their wives. In the fourth century, the papacy imposed celibacy on deacons, priests, and bishops. Married men who were ordained need not separate from their wives, although sexual abstinence

was more difficult if the couple remained together. Many clerics were older men who had raised families and no longer suffered the sexual desires of the young. Wives welcomed their husband's promotion because it raised their social status. Some wives were referred to as "priestess" and "bishopess." But there is also evidence that some were "priests" in their own right. Nonetheless, the social pretensions of the wives caused complaint wherever clerical marriage was allowed.

The Middle Ages

The fall of the Roman Empire prevented the effective enforcement of celibacy. Many early medieval clerics were married, especially in the rural parishes where supervision was absent. Aside from sexual desire, practicality also played an important role. It was simply impossible for a man to maintain a premodern household alone. The skills required and the tasks involved were traditionally woman's work.

Clerical marriage was the source of new clerics because, as in other trades, sons followed fathers. In the later Middle Ages there is evidence that many priests were themselves the sons of priests. This relationship explains how many new priests learned their craft. When clerical celibacy was reestablished new methods would be required.

Clerical families posed a problem. Clerics often provided for their offspring out of the church's wealth. In the Middle Ages, that wealth was usually land that could be sold, given, or bestowed as dowry. Even when celibacy was successfully enforced, the extended family of a cleric were often the beneficiaries. Families put members in clerical positions to exploit the church's power and wealth to the family's advantage. Emperors and kings placed sons, nephews, and other relatives on the episcopal throne. They were imitated on every level of society.

Clerical marriage anchored the cleric in the community that he served. The concerns of the local community came to outweigh those of the universal Church. Caught up in local feuds and rivalries, clerics were often unable to minister to the entire congregation. They lacked the distance from the laity that celibacy provided the Catholic priest and that education gave the Protestant minister. The clergy assimilated to their surroundings. In the early Middle Ages, when paganism was still a recent memory, Christian–pagan hybrids resulted. At the very least, clerical marriage hindered the *esprit de corps* that professions need to maintain their identity and standards.

In an effort to reform the church, clergy and laity attacked clerical marriage during the eleventh and twelfth centuries. Severe laws were passed to prevent such unions and to break up the ones that already existed. The Second Lateran Council (1123) went further than earlier legislation by arguing that marriage and clerical office were simply incompatible. As a result, no marriage contracted by a cleric could be recognized. Despite vocal resistance on the part of many clergy, clerical marriage became a contradiction in terms; it became "concubinage." In certain areas (e.g., Spain and Scandinavia) clerical marriages continued. Some laity preferred a married clergy because unmarried priests were perceived as threats to the honor of wives and daughters, although the mass of the population valued celibacy as a mark of holiness. Although many clerics maintained relationships that were marriages to all intents and purposes, it was clearly considered to be a failing, if an understandable one. Even the most radical heresies (see HERESY) accepted the value of celibacy as they targeted clerical misbehavior in their condemnation of the church.

Nonetheless, the hierarchy had to recognize the reality of clerical marriage under whatever name. Whereas in many dioceses (e.g., in ENGLAND) the rules were rigorously enforced, in some dioceses (e.g., Constance) priests paid a yearly fine in order not to separate from their wives. In effect the bishop levied a tax on married clergy. The papacy also profited. It did not dispense from celibacy, but it did sell dispensations allowing the sons of priests to become clerics, despite canon law, which refused ordination to the illegitimate.

The fifteenth century saw the beginning of a change, however. Some reform proposals, for example, the Reformatio Sigismundi, advocated clerical marriage and, to avoid scandal, Pope Pius II may have favored it and predicted its eventual acceptance. On the eve of the REFORMATION, Erasmus of Rotterdam also supported clerical marriage.

The Reformation

Nonetheless, it required the theological innovations of the Protestant Reformation to overturn a millennium of tradition and to undermine the religious assumptions that lay at its base.

One of HULDRYCH ZWINGLI's earliest reform efforts was a petition in 1522 to the bishop of Constance requesting permission for priests to marry. Zwingli married in 1524. MARTIN LUTHER initially did not focus on the question and resisted marriage until 1525. Having discovered the joys of sex and married life, he went beyond mere opposition to celibacy to praise and recommend marriage. Few Protestant writers would be as openly positive about sex, but the promotion of marriage became central to Protestant social teaching.

The Protestant rejection of celibacy implied a major revaluation of what constituted the sacred. For Catholics, sexual purity was an important element in the sacral status of the clergy. This objective physical sacrality went beyond mere morality. It contributed to the supernatural aura that also accompanied the SACRAMENTS, church buildings, and saints' relics. Like the Old Testament Temple or Ark of the Covenant, such people and objects were viewed as extensions of the sacred or the divine into the profane world. Protestant theology all but eliminated it. Although God was spiritually present *to* believers everywhere, God was not present *in* the world anywhere. God's power and knowledge simply extended to everything and everyone. For Luther the one exception was the Eucharist, but most other Protestants denied the real presence. The denial of the sacral status of the clergy secularized them. They might achieve a moral holiness, but so could the laity.

The arguments for clerical marriage drew upon core Protestant teachings to question the feasibility of celibacy. Given humanity's fallen condition, few could aspire to it. Only the grace of God could make it possible, and Protestant theologians did not think such grace was widely shed. The Catholic Church was more sanguine about both human ability and the extent of God's grace in this regard.

Protestants and Catholics also interpreted Titus 1:6 and I Timothy 3:2,12 differently. The Catholic Church understood Titus/Timothy to specify that if a bishop or a priest or a deacon were to be married, he be married only once. It did not require or even urge marriage; it limited it. Luther agreed that Titus/Timothy did not require marriage of the clergy, but it did establish marriage as the normal condition for the clergy. Luther and the Protestant tradition praised marriage as the preferred sexual arrangement for all Christians. Where once celibacy was required of the clergy, now the unmarried cleric was the object of grave suspicion. Marriage became, in effect, obligatory. Protestant theologians rejected the Catholic claim that marriage was a sacrament, but they anchored marriage in the order of creation. Although divorce was now possible in theory, in practice it was as difficult to divorce in Wittenberg or Geneva as it was in Rome.

The patriarchal family became both the center of religious instruction—a little church as it were—and the basic building block of secular society. The effects of these changes on women were mixed. On the one hand, the Protestant position elevated the status of marriage and the roles of wife and mother. On the other, it eliminated any legitimate alternative to marriage, family, and subordination. Feminist historians have seen it as a setback for women.

Having advocated clerical marriage, Protestant clergy required guidance. The marriage and family life of Luther and Katherine von Bora was held up as a model for clergy and for all Christians. An innovative literature detailing the responsibilities of husbands and wives, parents and children, flowed from the printing presses. The medieval church had dealt with marriage primarily in a penitential setting in which limits and failings were emphasized. Protestant literature retained those concerns, but placed a greater emphasis on positive injunctions for behavior and attitudes. Protestant authors also put more weight on the companionate nature of marriage. The mutual support and consolation of spouses, more than sexual satisfaction, were the greatest loss for the celibate clergy. Of course, with marriage and family came business and cares. St. Paul had warned of this and the entire philosophical tradition had made the harridan wife of Socrates, Xanthippe, a standing warning against marriage.

The Modern World

Clerical marriage remains one of the most visible markers distinguishing Protestantism and Catholicism. However, modern Catholic theology has promoted a deeper appreciation for the married state that is at odds with traditional understanding of clerical celibacy. After the Second Vatican Council (1962–1965), many priests were "laicized" (i.e., ceased to function as priests) and allowed to marry. Despite hopes for an end to the requirement, Pope Paul VI (1963–1978) and Pope John Paul II (1978–) forcefully reaffirmed it. However, unlike the ordination of women (see WOMEN CLERGY), which the hierarchy holds to be divinely prohibited, clerical celibacy is a purely disciplinary matter that lies within the competence of the church. As the shortage of Catholic priests in the Western world becomes ever more pressing, the Catholic Church has been urged to rethink the ban on clerical marriage. The Second Vatican Council's re-institution of married deacons may serve as precedent.

See also Celibacy; Judaism; Luther, Martin; Orthodoxy, Eastern; Zwingli, Huldrych

References and Further Reading

Barstow, Anne Llewellyn. *Married Priests and the Reforming Papacy: The Eleventh-Century Debates.* New York: E. Mellen Press, 1982.
Brennan, Brian. " 'Episcopae': Bishops' Wives Viewed in Sixth-Century Gaul Church." *History* 54 (1985): 311–323.
Brooke, Christopher. "Gregorian Reform in Action: Clerical Marriage in England, 1050–1200." In *Medieval Church and Society. Collected Essays,* 69–99. New York: New York University Press, 1972.
Cocke, Emmitt W., Jr. "Luther's View of Marriage and Family." *Religion in Life* (1973): 103–116.
Hardwick, Julie. *The Practice of Patriarchy: Gender and the Politics of Household Authority in Early Modern France.* University Park: Pennsylvania State University Press, 1998.
Kokkinakis, Athenagoras T. *Parents and Priests as Servants of Redemption; an Interpretation of the Doctrines of the Eastern Orthodox Church on the Sacraments of Matrimony and Priesthood.* New York: Morehouse-Gorham, 1958.
Ozment, Steven E. *When Fathers Ruled: Family Life in Reformation Europe.* Cambridge, MA: Harvard University Press, 1983.
Parish, Helen L. *Clerical Marriage and the English Reformation: Precedent, Policy, and Practice.* Burlington, VT: Aldershot/Ashgate, 2000.
Prior, Mary. "Reviled and Crucified Marriages: The Position of Tudor Bishops' Wives." In *Women in English Society,* 118–148. London/New York: Methuen, 1985.
Sipe, A. W. Richard. *Sex, Priests, and Power: Anatomy of a Crisis.* New York: Brunner/Mazel, 1995.
Yost, John, "The Reformation Defense of Clerical Marriage in the reigns of Henry VIII and Edward VI." *Church History* 50 (1981): 152–165.

R. EMMET MCLAUGHLIN

COCCEJUS, JOHANNES (1603–1669)

Reformed theologian. A seminal figure in COVENANT THEOLOGY, particularly as subsequently developed by the English Puritans, and a significant contributor to the development of historically and linguistically based biblical theology, Coccejus was born Johannes Koch, in Bremen, in 1603. Federal both in theology and politics, the republican city was a significant influence on Coccejus's thought. At Bremen's *gymnasium* he studied Latin, Greek, Hebrew, Chaldee, Syriac, and Arabic with Matthias Martini, who had been a leading moderate against the High Calvinists in the controversy over the Articles of Remonstrance at the Synod of Dort. After completing his studies with Martini, Coccejus undertook rabbinical studies at Hamburg, and then went to Franeker to study under the Orientalist Sixtinus Amama and with Maccovius and WILLIAM AMES. Between 1630 and 1636, Coccejus taught sacred philology at Bremen. He then returned to Franeker, teaching biblical languages and exegesis. In 1643 he was appointed professor of both Hebrew and THEOLOGY, and the focus of his work shifted from exegesis to DOCTRINE, although his theology always remained strongly biblical. In 1650 he was appointed professor of theology at Leiden, where he remained until his death in 1669. His major works include an exposition of his federal theology, *Summa Doctrinae de Foedere et Testamento Dei,* and the exegetical *Summa Theologiae ex Sacris Scripturis Repetita.*

Coccejus's exegesis was shaped by his linguistic studies. Locking horns with Reformed scholasticism, he vehemently opposed proof-texting and extrascriptural philosophizing in exegetical method (although he was not fully immune from either in his own work). Instead, he advocated applying the best available linguistic, archeological, and historical evidence to gain the most accurate possible reading of a biblical text. Each text was to be understood by grasping its author's intention, and by understanding it through both its textual and historical context. Truth was found not by amassing individual passages, but rather in the whole biblical witness.

At the same time, faithful reading meant not being limited by the written word. Although scripture preceded TRADITION and provided the yardstick for doctrine, Coccejus derided narrow literalism that "put Scripture in place of the Pope." To Coccejus, the biblical text was written with the inspiration of the Holy Spirit and must be read with the same inspiration. The words are accessible to "carnal man," but only a reader of faith can encounter the transforming "spiritual truth" of the Word, Jesus Christ. Nor is any one interpretation or system exhaustive. God speaks to different people and different parts of the church in different ways, through the same scripture. Plural interpretations may point to different aspects of the divine will.

Coccejus stood in the tradition of federal theology and political thought stemming from such figures as HEINRICH BULLINGER and Kaspar Olevianus. COVENANT formed the key to Coccejus's understanding of the relationships between human beings, between individuals and their communities, between humans and God, and between God and the world.

In keeping with his evolutionary view of salvation history, the idea of successive covenants allowed Coccejus to draw a sharp distinction between the First and Second Testaments. This structured his entire theology. For Coccejus, covenant precedes creation: the Father and Son freely enter a pretemporal covenant binding the Son to become sponsor of the covenant between God and human beings, realized at creation. The ensuing "covenant of works" (or "covenant of nature") between God and humans has three aspects: law (setting out the way for people to learn God's love), promise (pertaining to God's love and mercy), and threat (ruling out all other paths and showing the inevitability of punishment for sin). The covenant of works is abrogated in five stages. First, it is broken by human disobedience. Second, it is replaced through the inauguration of the "covenant of grace," which itself has two stages, of the Old Testament (anticipating Christ) and New Testament (fulfillment). Thus, the third abrogation of the covenant of works is the incarnation of Christ as Testator, fulfilling the covenant of GRACE. Fourth, the death of the body marks the end of the struggle against sin. In the resurrection of the body, the consequences of the covenant of works are swept away—its fifth abrogation—by the consummation of the covenant of grace.

Coccejus's stages retain the Reformed emphasis on divine sovereignty and PREDESTINATION. The covenant is entirely a divine initiative, which humans receive as an unmerited gift and to which they respond in FAITH. At the same time, his schema importantly returns significance to history and to human response to divine grace, avoiding High Calvinism's tendency to mechanistic determinism.

The covenant theme permeates Coccejus's thought, issuing in a political as well as theological vision. Scripture is to be read in the community of faith; individuals are to perceive themselves as the products of, and participants in, communities of all levels, from family to the entire Christian community. Theology is done in conversation with others and under the inspiration of the Holy Spirit. Magistrates are to enact the will of Christ (collaboratively understood) and, if they fail, may be resisted. One may find the roots of American political federalism and an anti-individualist republicanism in Coccejus's federalism (McCoy and Baker 1991).

References and Further Reading

Primary Sources:

Coccejus, Johannes. *Summa Doctrinae de Foedere et Testamento Dei*. 1st ed. 1648 (subsequent editions 1653, 1660).

Secondary Sources:

Faulenbach, Heiner. *Weg und Ziel der Erkenntnis Christi: Eine Untersuchung zur Theologie des Johannes Coccejus*. Neukirchen-Vluyn, Germany: Neukirchener Verlag, 1973.
McCoy, Charles S. "Johannes Cocceius: Federal Theologian." *Scottish Journal of Theology* 16 (1963): 352–370.
McCoy, Charles S., and J. Wayne Baker. *Fountainhead of Federalism: Heinrich Bullinger and the Covenantal Tradition*. Louisville, KY: Westminster/John Knox Press, 1991.
Schrenk, Gottlob. *Gottesreich und Bund im Älteren Protestantismus Vornehmlich bei Johannes Coccejus*. Giessen: Brunnen Verlag, 1985 (1923).

MARION MADDOX

COFFIN, HENRY SLOANE (1877–1954)

American theologian. Coffin was a Presbyterian minister, liberal theologian, advocate for the SOCIAL GOSPEL, promoter of foreign MISSIONS and ECUMENISM, and educator. He was one of the most important Protestant leaders in the UNITED STATES in the first half of the twentieth century and a shaper of the Protestant establishment in his generation.

Coffin was born January 5, 1877, and he was educated at Yale. After a call to ministry he attended New

College, Edinburgh, in SCOTLAND and the University of Marburg in GERMANY. He returned to the United States and earned his B.D. at Union Theological Seminary in New York.

Ordained to the ministry of the Presbyterian Church in the U.S.A. by the New York Presbytery in 1900, he accepted a call to the Bedford Park Presbyterian Church in the Bronx. Five years later he became the minister of Madison Avenue Presbyterian Church in New York City and led that church into a period of expansion of its ministry and influence.

Coffin began to teach part time at Union Seminary in 1904. Soon his teaching and PREACHING attracted widespread attention. The periodical *The Christian Century* conducted a poll in 1924 to identify the twenty-five most respected and influential clergymen in America, and Coffin made the list. In 1926 Union Seminary elected him president. He led the seminary into a rich period of expansion and leadership. Both REINHOLD NIEBUHR and PAUL TILLICH joined the faculty. WOMEN were admitted as students, and he helped create the School of Sacred Music.

From the beginning of his ministry he was a leader in the informal movement for theological liberalism and MODERNISM. He became involved in the fundamentalist–modernist controversy at the national Presbyterian level between 1924 and 1927, and he hailed the decision of the General Assembly of 1927 when it decided to tolerate a diversity of theological positions. He served the Presbyterian Church as its representative at a number of ecumenical meetings in the 1930s and 1940s, and he was elected moderator in 1943.

Henry Sloane Coffin died November 25, 1954. His papers are in the Burke Library of Union Theological Seminary in New York City.

See also Fundamentalism; Liberal Protestantism and Liberalism; Presbyterianism

References and Further Reading

Handy, Robert T. *A History of Union Theological Seminary in the City of New York.* New York: Columbia University Press, 1987.

Longfield, Bradley J. *The Presbyterian Controversy: Fundamentalists, Modernists, and Moderates.* New York: Oxford University Press, 1991.

Niebuhr, Reinhold, ed. *This Ministry: The Contribution of Henry Sloane Coffin.* New York: Charles Scribner's Sons, 1946.

Noyes, Morgan Phelps. *Henry Sloane Coffin: The Man and His Ministry.* New York: Charles Scribner's Sons, 1964.

JOHN PIPER

COKE, THOMAS (1747–1814)

Methodist bishop. One of the first two Methodist bishops in America, Thomas Coke was the most important early proponent of Methodist MISSIONS outside of ENGLAND and UNITED STATES. Born in WALES in 1747, Coke earned a doctorate in law from Oxford before becoming an Anglican priest. After six years of parish ministry, Coke was dismissed from his parish in 1777 due to his Methodist sympathies, and began serving as the primary assistant to JOHN WESLEY. In 1784, Wesley appointed Coke the first superintendent of the Methodist Episcopal Church and sent him to America to appoint FRANCIS ASBURY as his co-superintendent. The Christmas Conference in Baltimore elected Coke and Asbury joint superintendents of the Methodist Episcopal Church. (To Wesley's dismay, each later assumed the title of "bishop.")

Coke's frequent travels between America and Britain (18 crossings of the Atlantic) maintained ties between the Methodists in America and Britain despite the hostilities created by the American Revolution. Although Coke spent only three years in America and never renounced his British citizenship, he significantly expanded Methodism's geographical reach by appointing missionaries to the Channel Islands, SCOTLAND, IRELAND, the West Indies, north Wales, AFRICA, Ceylon, and INDIA. Coke assumed almost single-handed financial responsibility for these missionaries, exhausting his personal fortune and those of his two wives. He died and was buried at sea while traveling to India in 1814.

A prolific author, Coke penned a BIBLE commentary, tracts, and sermons. He was instrumental in establishing Methodism's POLITY with bishops and superintendents.

See also Baltimore Conference; Methodism, England; Methodism, North America; Methodism

References and Further Reading

Primary Sources:

Coke, Thomas. *A Commentary on the Holy Bible.* London: George Whitfield, 1801.

———. *Extracts of the Journals of the Late Rev. Thomas Coke, L.L.D.* Dublin, Ireland: R. Napper, 1816.

Lloyd, Gareth. *Catalogue of the Thomas Coke Papers.* Manchester, UK: The Centre, 1991.

Secondary Source:

Vickers, John A. *Thomas Coke: Apostle to Methodism.* Sussex, UK: World Methodist Historical Society, 1969.

THOMAS E. PHILLIPS

COLENSO, JOHN WILLIAM (1814–1883)

Anglican bishop of Natal. Colenso was born at St. Austell, Cornwall, ENGLAND on January 24, 1814. He studied at Cambridge, becoming a Fellow of St. John's. In 1846 he became vicar of Forncett St. Mary, Norfolk. Theologically he was a liberal and a disciple of his friend, FREDERICK DENISON MAURICE.

Colenso was appointed to the new bishopric of Natal in SOUTH AFRICA in 1853, a task that was essentially a missionary one. In 1861 he published a controversial commentary on Romans in which he argued for UNIVERSALISM. Many Broad Churchmen at that time pursued Pauline studies as a way of asserting their Protestantism. Their forthright Protestantism, in turn, was a way of being anti-Tractarian and, as Colenso described his own work, of fighting "for a great principle—no less than the essential principle of Protestantism—free enquiry." In 1862 Colenso published the first volume of his *The Pentateuch and Book of Joshua Critically Examined* in which he baldly asserted that the events narrated in these books were unhistorical. A public sensation ensued. His High Church metropolitan, Bishop Gray of Capetown, held a somewhat dubious ecclesiastical trial in 1863, found Colenso guilt of erroneous teaching, went on to pronounce him deposed, and ultimately excommunicated him (1866). Colenso won an appeal on technical grounds and thus he retained the legal right to be the bishop of Natal, although most of his fellow bishops, and the archbishop of Canterbury himself, considered him spiritually deposed.

As a missionary Colenso contributed to the study of the Zulu language and is remembered for denouncing unjust treatment of Zulus by the colonists. He died in Natal on June 20, 1883.

See also Broad Church; Colonialism Oxford Movement; Liberal Protestantism and Liberalism

References and Further Reading

Guy, Jeff. *The Heretic: A Study of the Life of John William Colenso 1814–1883.* Pietermaritzburg, South Africa: University of Natal, 1983.
Hinchliff, Peter. *John William Colenso: Bishop of Natal.* London: Nelson, 1964.
Larsen, Timothy. "Bishop Colenso and His Critics: The Strange Emergence of Biblical Criticism in Victorian Britain." *Scottish Journal of Theology* 50 no. 4 (1997): 433–458.

TIMOTHY LARSEN

COLERIDGE, SAMUEL TAYLOR (1772–1834)

English poet. Although Coleridge's reputation as a poet has rarely been in question, the problem of his status as philosopher and theologian has always been equivocal. For contemporaries like Carlyle and De Quincey, or twentieth-century philosophers like Rene

Wellek and Mary Warnock, or critics like Norman Fruman, his religious thinking could either be "explained," *ad hominem,* in terms of his own psychological problems, or seen as an extension of his unphilosophical rehash of contemporary German philosophy, mostly plagiarized, and assembled without any insight into the "essential incompatibility of different trends of thought" (Wellek 1931:67). Thus even by the time H. D. Traill came to write Coleridge's biography in 1884 he could safely be dismissed as a "legend which has only slowly died out."

> The actual truth I believe to be that Coleridge's position from 1818 or 1820 until his death . . . was in no sense one of the highest, or even of any considerable influence. . . . A few mystics of the type of Maurice, a few eager seekers after truth like Sterling, may have gathered, or fancied they gathered, distinct dogmatic instruction from the Highgate oracles; and, no doubt to the extent of his influence over the former of these disciples, we may justly credit Coleridge's discourses with having exercised a real if only a transitory directive effect upon nineteenth century thought. But the terms in which his influence is sometimes spoken of appear, as far as one can judge the matter at this distance of time, to be greatly exaggerated. (Traill 1884:205,207)

Yet, in the century since, Coleridge's reputation has consistently grown—and it is the Protestant theologian who has come, retrospectively, to dominate the Coleridgean "legend."

As early as 1856, F. J. A. Hort, the Anglican theologian, saw that Coleridge's attempt to find a unity between philosophy, theology, and aesthetics was not merely unique for his time, but had made him that much more difficult to appreciate as a whole.

> Classification is our pride and pleasure; and woe be to that which refuses to be classified. An author whose opinions will not range with those of any recognised party, or whose works never seem quite rightly lodged in any one division of a well-regulated library, occupies in general estimation what was once the place of a zoophyte or platypus—an uncanny creature, possibly of demonical origin. Such a divine monster was Coleridge. (Hort vol. II:292)

Granted that much of what his detractors said was true about his opium addiction, his propensity to plagiarism, and the exaggeration of his claims, it is remarkable that many of his greatest admirers were themselves philosophers of opposing schools, like John Stuart Mill, or theologians and historians like Hort and Julius Hare, who had studied his German sources. "I rejoice to think," wrote FREDERICK DENISON MAURICE, "that those who have most profited by what he has taught them, do not and cannot form a school"

[Maurice 1838 (4th ed. 1891):xi]. The originality most valued by his successors was, rather, a unity and width of vision perhaps historically unique—and certainly approached only by such later theologian-poets as JOHN HENRY NEWMAN and T. S. ELIOT. Although he first gained a reputation as a poet with the copublication with WILLIAM WORDSWORTH of the *Lyrical Ballads* (1798), and it was only later that he developed a career as political journalist, literary critic, philosopher, social commentator, and theologian, such a rough chronological list fails to reveal how much all these activities ran in parallel throughout his relatively long life. The myriad-mindedness, only fully revealed to the late twentieth century with the full publication of his massive correspondence and notebooks, had already been shown in the mid-1790s by lectures on politics and religion in relation to the Revolution then in progress in FRANCE, and by his aptly named, but then unique, hybrid form of "lay sermons."

The importance of Coleridge's theology lies not in particular doctrines, but in its *development*. The son of an Anglican priest, educated at Christ's Hospital, he was attracted to the rationality of Unitarianism as a student at Cambridge, under the influence of his tutor. Essential to this stage of his thought was *Observations on Man* (1749) by David Hartley—after whom Coleridge named his eldest son. Although not explicitly Deist (see DEISM) or Unitarian, Hartley's so-called philosophy seemed to many the logical epitome of both. It was, in effect, a theory of developmental psychology that allowed for the growth of the mind in seven stages from simple sensation to what Hartley called "theopathy" and finally "moral sense." An essentially physical system, working by means of "vibrations" in the nervous system, Hartley's psychology had little room for SIN and none for evil. Occasionally the normal progression from one level to another was interrupted or blocked, so that some individuals failed to fulfill their potential, and, not having reached moral sense, behaved in antisocial ways, although such problems for Hartley were no more than "shadows" in the light of God's beneficence.

The first blow to this eighteenth-century "optimism" came with the failure of the French Revolution to produce peace and universal brotherhood. If it was only with the discovery of IMMANUEL KANT and the German idealists while in GERMANY from 1798 to 1800 that Coleridge began to formulate a new THEOLOGY philosophically, such works as *The Ancient Mariner* already show as early as 1797 a sense of original sin and mysterious evil unaccounted for by Hartley. As the name of his second son, Berkeley, indicated, Coleridge remained rooted in English as well as German thought at this period, but, with the progressive development of his opium addiction and the failure of his marriage in the early years of the new century, it was clear that no theology that did not give due weight to human frailty and depravity would serve. A journey to Malta and ITALY from 1805 to 1807 gave Coleridge firsthand experience, and a deep dislike, of contemporary Catholicism that was to last throughout his life.

Despite some important publications, including the first version of a philosophical periodical entitled *The Friend,* and his *Lectures on Shakespeare,* other personal disappointments, including, most seriously, a quarrel with Wordsworth and his wife (mostly over his drug addiction) gave his middle years, from 1807 to 1817, a growing sense of a life and opportunities wasted. In 1816–1817 came the two *Lay Sermons,* together with his greatest critical work, *Biographia Literaria.* Although few could detect the binding theological thread joining this mixture of literary and political work, it was to become clearer in the next decade.

In 1817, too, Coleridge's personal life was dramatically altered by his move to the house of Dr. Gilman of Highgate, where he was freed from his previous financial worries, and deprived of the drugs that had so hampered his creativity in the past. In the 1820s there followed the *Philosophical Lectures, Aids to Reflection,* and *Church and State*—works of sometimes confusing originality. Thus, whereas the former show little that is new philosophically, they convey with peculiar clarity the *development* of ideas—in particular the process of "desynonymy," by which new ideas claim new terms in separating from their linguistic matrix. Similarly *Aids,* purportedly a manual on meditation, also reveals a radical theological and psychological agenda—insisting that it is *need,* rather than argument, that draws the individual toward God. *Church and State,* apparently an eccentric sociological or political work on the balance of forces within society, occasioned by Coleridge's obstinate and futile opposition to the Catholic Emancipation Bill of 1828, was to prove seminal in later nineteenth-century politics—inspiring such unlikely Coleridgeans as Prime Minister Benjamin Disraeli and the Conservative welfare reforms of his Home Secretary Richard Cross.

Only in retrospect can be seen behind this succession of apparently occasional pieces an overall unifying theological theme, in which the possibilities of incremental change are explored in areas as seemingly diverse as history of ideas, devotional meditation, and social organization. Critics describing this later thought as "conservatism" or "orthodoxy" miss its radicalism in the prevalent context of Romantic Spinozistic thought, where the closing of the gap between God and NATURE implied the ultimate perfectability of mankind—an idea taken up by GEORG W. F. HEGEL, and through him LUDWIG FEUERBACH, and Karl Marx.

Coleridge's insistence on traditional Trinitarian notions of fallen Nature, redeemable only by divine action, prevented him from ever embracing the facile optimism that in the twentieth century inspired such tyrannies as fascism, COMMUNISM, and various terrorist "liberation" movements such as the Irish Republican Army, the Red Brigades, or ETA.

Coleridge's unpublished notebooks of the period reveal a similar radicalism in biblical criticism and hermeneutics, and it is here, if anywhere, that the common charge of uncompleted work is most justified. Few thinkers, let alone theologians, up to this time had seriously engaged with the idea of human consciousness as in a process of continual growth and development, or had considered the implications of such growth to AESTHETICS, politics, or religious experience without losing a corresponding sense of human fallibility. The question of Coleridge's theology, therefore, has to be considered less in terms of his treatment of specific doctrines (important as these are) than in the way he relates all parts of human experience to a single fluid and developmental unity—a process as much aesthetic as philosophic.

Although little noticed at the time, the influence of these late works was to prove enormous and lasting—for a time even eclipsing his poetic achievement. Two of Hare's Cambridge students, Maurice and James Sterling, introduced to Coleridge's ideas (by a process described by Disraeli in one of his novels in terms of the spreading of arcane secrets) founded the "Apostles" (or Cambridge Conversatzione Society) whose avowed aim was "Coleridgean." In addition to Hort and Maurice himself, Coleridge was read by ALFRED LORD TENNYSON (a later Apostle), F. C. Robertson, and, with obligatory reservations, by the Arnolds—THOMAS, Matthew, and Mary Augusta (Mrs. Humphry Ward). Perhaps even more surprisingly there is evidence that Coleridge influenced his German contemporaries—astonishingly, even Schelling, from whom Coleridge had himself plagiarized key passages for his *Biographia Literaria*. Through Charles Kingsley, who was taught at Helston Grammar School by Coleridge's third son, the Reverend Derwent Coleridge, much of his political thought was channeled into the Christian Socialist movement, and thence into the modern British Labour Party (see SOCIALISM, CHRISTIAN). Through RALPH WALDO EMERSON, whose meeting with Coleridge is described in *English Traits,* a different tradition of Coleridgean ideas passed through the New England Transcendentalists in American thought. Even while he was dismissed as practicing "a liberty of speculation no Christian could tolerate"—other aspects were taken up by the OXFORD MOVEMENT from EDWARD B. PUSEY and JOHN KEBLE to Newman, and by novelists from George MacDonald to GEORGE ELIOT,

G. K. Chesterton, and even Disraeli. In the twentieth century he was no less influential on T. S. Eliot, the Oxford "Inklings" like C. S. LEWIS and J. R. R. Tolkein, Dorothy Sayers, and Owen Barfield.

Few, if any, Romantic thinkers have done more to change the way in which not merely the nineteenth but even the twentieth century was to discover and understand itself. If this was initially based on an essentially Protestant sense of individuality, those ideas were to become through Newman no less characteristic of later Catholic thought.

See also Romanticiam; Catholicism, Prostestant Reactions; Individualism

References and Further Reading

Primary Sources:

Coleridge, Samuel Taylor. *Aids to Reflection* London 1839.
———. *Biographia Literaria.* 1817.
———. On the Constitution of Church and State. *Church and State,* 1830.
———. *Lay Sermons,* edited by R. J. White. Routledge, 1972.
———. *Philosophical Lectures.* London: Routledge, 1950.
———. *Shakespeare Criticism.* London: Athlone, 1989.

Secondary Sources:

Ashton, Rosemary. *The German Idea.* Cambridge: Cambridge University Press, 1980.
Fruman, Norman. *Coleridge: the Damaged Archangel.* London: G. Allen and Unwin, 1972.
Hedley, Douglas. *Coleridge, Philosophy and Religion: Aids to Reflection and the Mirror of the Spirit.* Cambridge: Cambridge University Press, 2000.
Hort, F. J. A. "Coleridge." In *Cambridge Essays,* 2 vols. London: John W. Parker and Son, 1856.
Maurice, F. D. *The Kingdom of Christ.* London: Macmillan, 1838.
Prickett, Stephen. *Coleridge and Wordsworth: the Poetry of Growth.* Cambridge: Cambridge University Press, 1970.
———. *Romanticism and Religion: the Tradition of Coleridge and Wordsworth in the Victorian Church.* Cambridge: Cambridge University Press, 1976.
———. *Words and the Word: Language, Poetics, and Biblical Interpretation.* Cambridge: Cambridge University Press, 1986.
Traill, H. D. "Coleridge." In *English Men of Letters Series.* London: Macmillan, 1884.
Warnock, Mary. *Imagination.* Berkeley: University of California Press, 1976.
Wellek, Rene. *Immanuel Kant in England.* Princeton, NJ: Princeton University Press, 1931.

STEPHEN PRICKETT

COLIGNY, GASPARD DE (1519–1572)

French Protestant political figure. Gaspard de Coligny was a key Protestant military and political leader during the first decade of the religious wars in sixteenth-century FRANCE. Born to a powerful noble family, he initially pursued a military career. In 1552 he was named admiral of France, a post that conferred prestige but—despite the name—was not associated with naval command. Captured by the Spanish in 1557, he spent two years in prison. Observers have long regarded this confinement as critical to Coligny's CONVERSION to Protestantism. After his release, he endeavored in vain to mediate the mounting tension between the crown and emerging Protestants.

With the eruption of outright hostilities in 1562, Coligny became a principal commander of the Protestant army. He fought in defense of the HUGUENOTS, as French Protestants were known, even as he counseled them to pursue political negotiation. By the early 1570s, Coligny urged King Charles IX and Queen Mother Catherine de Médicis to instigate war against the Spanish as a means to deflect bellicose energies and reconcile their subjects. Coligny's association with the project further angered staunch Catholic opponents, who regarded Spain as a confessional ally. When he and other Huguenot leaders gathered in Paris for the marriage of the Protestant Henry of Navarre and the king's sister, Coligny's enemies attempted unsuccessfully to assassinate him on August 22, 1572. Two days later, the king ordered the slaughter of the Huguenot nobles lodged in the Louvre Palace and nearby private residences. Soldiers loyal to the extreme Catholic Duke of Guise murdered Coligny in the opening act of the infamous Saint Bartholomew's Day Massacre.

References and Further Reading

Crété, Liliane. *Coligny*. Paris: Fayard, 1985.
Hotman, François. *La vie de Messire Gaspar de Colligny admiral de France (c. 1577)*. Geneva, Switzerland: Droz, 1987.
Shimizu, J. *Conflict of Loyalties: Politics and Religion in the Career of Gaspard de Coligny, Admiral of France, 1519–1572*. Geneva, Switzerland: Droz, 1972.

RAYMOND A. MENTZER

COLLEGES

See Colleges, Protestant; Higher Education

COLLEGES, PROTESTANT

The American Protestant institutions of higher education developed from three types of institutions: (1) the medieval European monastic and cathedral schools; (2) the late medieval European societies of masters and students that, beginning in the thirteenth century, evolved into universities; and (3) more specifically, the models provided by the early modern British universities at Oxford, Cambridge, and Edinburgh and the fledgling dissenting academies in England and Scotland.

During the Colonial era, very few young men and essentially no women attended the largely Christian-oriented colleges in British North America. These institutions graduated fewer than 10,000 baccalaureate students before 1800. Of the "Colonial nine" institutions, only Benjamin Franklin's University of Pennsylvania professed largely secular purposes. For most of the seventeenth century the Puritans/Congregationalists operated the only college, Harvard (founded 1636). Reluctantly, the oldest colony, Virginia, finally established William and Mary (Anglican) in 1693. Conservative Congregationalists opened Yale (founded 1701) in reaction to non-Calvinist and even Unitarian tendencies at Harvard. Five denominations began colleges when inspired by the First Great Awakening (see AWAKENINGS): Princeton (1746, New Light Presbyterian), Kings/Columbia (1754, Anglican), Brown (1765, Baptist), Queens/Rutgers (1766, Dutch Reformed), and Dartmouth (1769, New Light Congregationalist).

Although ministers and other religious leaders were the primary founders of the colonial schools, established primarily to educate a native supply of future ministers, these early colleges never operated exclusively for that purpose. The institutions also sought to provide breadth of thought for other societal leaders including lawyers, doctors, teachers, and even country gentlemen. The percentage of ministerial graduates at seventeenth century Harvard was approximately fifty percent, but the percentage of ministerial graduates from Harvard, Yale, and Dartmouth combined before 1850 and at Princeton in the late eighteenth century was about twenty-five percent.

The first two generations of the newly independent United States witnessed arguably the most significant period of college growth in the history of the country. Between the Revolution and 1800, the number of new permanent colleges to appear was twice the colonial nine, and the total number of permanent colleges reached 180 by the CIVIL WAR. Meanwhile in the 1800 to 1860 era, the college student population grew four times faster (to 30,000) than did the general population (which increased from 5,300,000 to 31,400,000).

The major factors that contributed to this pre–Civil War growth included: (1) the spirit of the Second Great Awakening, especially as it affected two rapidly growing denominations, the Methodists (see METHODISM, NORTH AMERICA) and the Baptists; (2) the westward expansion; (3) the growing spirit of democratization and the resultant movement toward popular education; and (4) the growing tendency for local communities to want to have their own colleges for the general cultural advantages for all their people as well as the readily accessible educational opportunities (on the secondary as well as the higher level) for their youth.

The typical college to appear in the early nineteenth century was founded less often by a denomination than by individual preachers working with community leaders. It then operated less as a denominational institution than as a Christian community college that gained support from the members of a variety of denominations as well as the primarily affiliated one. Most often the large majority of the enrollees studied on the secondary level. The colleges welcomed this arrangement, as it generated enough income to warrant supplying college-level instruction for a limited number of students, and it helped to ensure a supply of college-ready students in this period when few communities operated secondary institutions.

After the Revolutionary War, individual states, beginning with Georgia in 1785, founded public colleges and universities; there were 22 major state universities in existence by the Civil War. With very few exceptions (most notably THOMAS JEFFERSON's Virginia), these universities operated as primarily Protestant Christian institutions through much of the nineteenth century. Similarly, one could not sharply distinguish the private and public institutions of this period on the basis of the amount of public financing they received or how they were controlled. The contrasting features between the public and private institutions in the twentieth century appeared only gradually.

The curriculum of the old-time college emphasized the Greek and Latin languages and classics, mathematics, and, after the colonial period, some science. Typically the most popular courses throughout most of the nineteenth century were the senior-level set of classes, usually taught by the president, in what we now would call philosophy, religion, and the social sciences. The courses assumed such labels as mental philosophy, moral philosophy, intellectual philosophy, natural philosophy, evidences of Christianity, logic, and ethics. Surprisingly, a college almost never offered a course in biblical literature; the assumption was that the students learned the Scriptures on their own in study and worship groups. Essentially the curriculum was prescribed, and all students who matriculated together studied in the same set of classes for four years.

By far the most influential extracurricular activity in the antebellum period was the literary society. From its origins in the eighteenth century until its demise in the early twentieth century, the literary society provided the one major campus activity that the students controlled and operated. Most colleges had at least two societies that competed in a host of activities,

intellectual no less than social. They vigorously recruited members, decorated their sometimes elegant halls, collected libraries that sometimes excelled over the college library, enforced their own set of rules and regulations, provided student services, and above all, competed with the rival society or societies in a set of public performance literary contests that included debate, oral declamation, and oral criticism. The emphasis on developing public persuasion skills served a practical purpose when such a high percentage of the students were preparing for careers in politics, law, the ministry, and teaching. Many of the students prepared for the contests with more intellectual rigor than they did for their classroom activities. The popularity of the literary societies declined when their social and competitive functions were replaced by intercollegiate athletics and fraternities and sororities, and when new generations of students began to prepare for a broader range of careers including those that relied less on the development of oral persuasion skills.

The post–Civil War period witnessed the founding of new schools to serve constituencies that previously had rarely attended college, that is, women, African Americans, and immigrant groups. Pre–twentieth century colleges begun for women and blacks operated almost without exception as strongly committed Christian colleges.

Noteworthy of the few colleges to admit African Americans before the Civil War were Wilberforce in Ohio and Berea in Kentucky. Most of the original students at Wilberforce were mulatto children of southern planters. After the war, the AFRICAN METHODIST EPISCOPAL CHURCH acquired the institution, thus making it the first black-controlled college in America. Berea became the first college in a slave state to admit both blacks and whites. After the war, Northern American missionary societies opened more black Protestant colleges in the South than have been founded in all other periods (see MISSIONS, NORTH AMERICA; MISSIONARY ORGANIZATIONS). The most effective of these church groups was the AMERICAN MISSIONARY ASSOCIATION of the Congregational Church, which opened, for example, Atlanta, Fisk, Hampton, Howard, Talladega, and Tougaloo. Before 1900 almost all African-American colleges were private Protestant institutions.

The eastern elite "Seven Sisters" colleges included Vassar (founded 1865), Wellesley (1870), Smith (1871), Radcliffe (1879), Bryn Mawr (1885), Barnard (1889), and Mount Holyoke (1893). Meanwhile in the South, Spelman opened in 1881 as the first college for black women. In contrast to the East and South, higher education for women in the more egalitarian West was coeducational, beginning in the early to middle part of the century. By 1873 the majority of coeducational colleges were in the western states. Most of the African-American colleges also operated as coeducational institutions.

Ethnic groups outside of the mainstream culture who founded colleges after the mid-nineteenth century included the Dutch Reformed groups (see DUTCH REFORMED CHURCH)—Reformed and Christian Reformed, especially in western Michigan; the Swedes and Norwegians, largely in the northern prairie and Plains states; and the German Brethren and the MENNONITES in the mid-Atlantic and midwestern states. The Dutch and the Scandinavians recognized the need for higher education, especially for their preachers and teachers, but the Brethren and Mennonites, although having been longer in the country, were very slow to accept the idea of higher education for any reason.

By the late nineteenth and early twentieth centuries, the United States had become the leading industrial producer in the world. Some of the nouveaux riches used their wealth to found new or greatly enhanced institutions that had been founded by churches. These included Vanderbilt, Duke, and Emory with Methodist connections; Chicago by the Northern Baptist oil magnate, John D. Rockefeller; and Stetson, Baylor, and Wake Forest by the Southern Baptists.

Between approximately 1880 and 1960 American higher education in general changed its religious orientation to the point that by the late twentieth century it exerted primarily a negative effect on the spiritual orientation of its students. Whereas during the late nineteenth century nearly all institutions of higher education included religious goals among their aims for their students, by the early twentieth century perhaps only half did, and by mid-century, studies showed that the commitment to religious values by the average college student actually declined during the undergraduate years. The process of secularization followed this course: (1) the major state universities and some of the elite private institutions began the secularization process in the late nineteenth century; (2) the second-line state universities and more of the elite private schools followed in the early twentieth century; and (3) after 1920 most of the colleges of the mainline denominations began to follow the trend. During this intellectual revolution, American higher education changed from being a force that was much more Christian in nature than society in general, to the place where it is now—more secular than is the overall population.

Christian students, denominations, and parachurch organizations sought to counter the secular revolution in higher education through a variety of organizations, including the student-led Young Men's Christian Association (YMCA) and Young Women's Christian Association (YWCA) chapters, the denominational foundation houses, and the Bible institutes and colleges. Between 1875 and 1940 the student Y's served as the single most significant religious presence in the lives of students in the majority of colleges and universities of all types. Originally a social and spiritual agency to serve the needs of city youth in an era of rapid industrialization and urbanization, the movement began funding chapters on college campuses on the eve of the Civil War and then grew rapidly to 40 chapters in 1877, 181 in 1884, 345 in 1891, 628 in 1900, and 731 with nearly 100,000 members in 1920. The campus chapters provided a variety of services for the students in a period before the development of the modern student activities offices; these included freshman orientation, book-exchange services, student employment and financial aid programs, and tutorial assistance.

The best known "Y" activities, however, included Bible study, mission promotion (especially through the Student Volunteer movement), and both on- and off-campus evangelistic activity.

The "university pastorate" or denominational student centers brought the major denominations to the campus where they provided a variety of services (e.g., worship, counseling, and fellowship) especially to help the students of their specific faiths to grow spiritually while the professors helped them to grow intellectually. Originating at the turn of the century, these denominational houses by 1930 operated on over 100 state and independent private campuses, and the movement continues to the present.

Since World War II, the most prominent intercollegiate and interdenominational student religious organizations have been INTERVARSITY CHRISTIAN FELLOWSHIP, Campus Crusade, and the Navigators. They continue the spirit of the Y movement even if they attract a much smaller percentage of the students.

Arising in the late nineteenth and early twentieth centuries, the Bible college movement for Christ began after the Y's but before the denominational student centers. This development was less a reaction to secularization in higher education than a result of three factors: (1) a response to the late nineteenth century revivalism of DWIGHT LYMAN MOODY and others (the Third Great Awakening); (2) an element in the movement toward popular education; and (3) a reaction against liberalism in American Protestantism. The Bible colleges primarily served a constituency that had not attended the secularizing schools. As undergraduate, theological institutions that have varied greatly in quality, Bible colleges sought to train Christian workers from the working classes to serve the underserved in Christian ministry—the lower classes in the American cities and remote areas and the neglected peoples on the mission field. By 1950 the Bible colleges provided a majority, and by 1980 the large majority of Protestant missionaries from this country. These twentieth-century American missionaries have inspired the founding of hundreds if not thousands of Bible colleges in Third World countries, thus making the Bible college one of the primary educational exports from America.

Meanwhile the small, denominational liberal arts colleges reached their low point of morale between the world wars, especially in the 1930s. Added to the secularizing effect in many of them were the travails of the nation's worst economic depression. Recovery began in the late 1940s as the GI Bill brought record numbers of students to colleges of all types. Also, by 1960 most of the church colleges that were going to secularize had already begun to do so; however, the secularizing church colleges tended to be the more affluent ones. Steadily the recovery process continued through the second half of the twentieth century to the point where the Christian colleges today are as strong economically and academically as they have been at any time since the secular revolution. The reasons for the recovery include factors that have aided higher education in general (e.g., a strong economy, the mounting popularity of attending college, increasing financial aid packages). In addition, since the 1950s the evangelical/conservative groups of the church-attending public (the segment that would be most likely to send its youth to the continuing Christian colleges) have grown faster than have the mainline churches. At the beginning of the twenty-first century, continuing Christian colleges numbered approximately 200 liberal arts institutions plus the Bible colleges.

References and Further Reading

Brereton, Virginia L. *Training God's Army: The American Bible Schools, 1880–1940.* Bloomington: Indiana University Press, 1990.

Holmes, Arthur F. *The Idea of a Christian College.* Grand Rapids, MI: Wm. B. Eerdmans, 1975.

Marsden, George. *The Soul of the American University.* New York: Oxford University Press, 1994.

Ringenberg, William C. *The Christian College: A History of Protestant Higher Education in America.* Grand Rapids, MI: Wm. B. Eerdmans, 1984.

Rudolph, Frederick. *The American College and University.* Athens: University of Georgia Press, 1990.

Shedd, Clarence P. *Two Centuries of Student Christian Movements.* New York: Association Press, 1934.

WILLIAM C. RINGENBERG

COLLINS, ANTHONY (1676–1729)

English Deist. A freethinker and philosopher, Collins was born at Hounslow in Middlesex on June 21, 1676 of well-to-do parents, and was educated at Eton and at King's College, Cambridge before training in law at the Temple. In addition to serving for many years as

justice of the peace and deputy lieutenant in Middlesex and in Essex, Collins was a man of letters and wrote extensively on theological and philosophical issues of the day, an interest that was nurtured in part through his friendship with JOHN LOCKE for two years until Locke's death in 1704. Collins accepted Locke's arguments for the reasonableness of Christianity and added the right and necessity to inquire into all subjects, including religion, freely and without fear, which he argued was the genius of the Protestant REFORMATION.

In his *Essay Concerning the Use of Reason* (1707), he argued that reason is "that faculty of the Mind whereby it perceives the Truth, Falsehood, Probability or Improbability of Propositions." Consistent with most Deists of the eighteenth century, Collins, in his *Priesthood in Perfection* (1710), attacked religious dogmas that were contrary to reason and argued that an appeal to mystery or AUTHORITY would not suffice. In *A Discourse of Free-Thinking* (1713) he championed the right to think freely and pointed out how the new science, the new philosophy, and the Reformation had exposed superstitions and pretenders to divine revelation. Collins advocated the application of historical-critical methods to the BIBLE as in any text in *The Discourse of the Grounds and Reasons of the Christian Religion* (1724) and *The Scheme of Literal Prophecy Considered* (1725). Collins' argument was that since Jesus was understood as messiah, miracles were inadequate to sustain his messianic claim. Prophecy, the other traditional ground for proving the claims of Jesus, was also problematic since the notion of a literal fulfillment in Jesus could not be sustained. Despite a lifetime of controversy and attacks on his writings Collins died in 1729 as one of high personal repute and was buried in Oxford chapel.

See also Deism; Locke, John

References and Further Reading

Stephen, Leslie. *History of English Thought in the Eighteenth Century.* London: Smith, Elder & Co., 1902.

Torrey, Norman. *Voltaire and the English Deists.* New Haven, CT: Yale University Press, 1930.

TIMOTHY E. FULOP

COLONIALISM

Colonialism, often a loosely used term of abuse, is properly applied to a system of social, economic, political, and intellectual relationships in which one or several nations, states, or peoples are ruled by and their interests subordinated to another. Colonial systems, or empires, have been important features of the early modern and modern worlds. They have embodied various forms of institutional and cultural control, associated with Protestantism in four much-debated ways. Protestantism has influenced the establishment and consolidation of colonialism; it has played a part in colonialism's development, as forms of colonial administration and control have changed; and it has often shaped the conditions of life under colonialism as experienced by colonized people. Protestantism has also contributed to the progressive subversion and termination of colonialism since the eighteenth century, beginning with the American Revolution and War of Independence.

Protestant THEOLOGY and beliefs initially offered no obvious encouragement or sanction for either a general state-sponsored colonial enterprise or popular involvement in colonization. It was rather the fragmentation of Protestantism, religious conflict at home, and instincts of self-preservation that prompted the first Puritans in 1620 (see PURITANISM) and many others later to emigrate from ENGLAND to form their new, religiously disciplined and tight-knit communities in what became New England. But North American colonial settlement, like settlement in many other parts of the world, brought encounters with local peoples. Temporary alliances could not disguise the general pattern of misunderstandings, hostility, conflict, and dispossession that spawned an aggressive settler-driven colonialism. Finding itself spurned by local inhabitants, Protestant Christianity was readily identified with white settler notions of civilization, as against the "savagery," "barbarism," and probable inconvertibility of indigenous people. Settlers, including the Germans and Dutch from continental Europe no less than the British, endorsed this intertwining of colonialism and Protestantism, which was also a potent source of solidarity in the face of Catholic FRANCE and Spain.

Early settlers were largely obliged to fend for themselves in matters of religion. However, formation of the SOCIETY FOR THE PROMOTION OF CHRISTIAN KNOWLEDGE (1699) and the SOCIETY FOR PROPAGATION OF THE GOSPEL (1701) illustrated the Anglican wish within Britain's governing circles to provide ecclesiastical support for colonial societies. At first, this entailed providing libraries, schools, and colonial CLERGY; after the 1780s, it involved the establishment of colonial bishoprics. Other denominations in the eighteenth century also steadily developed trans-Atlantic networks in which preachers, funds, and literature moved to and fro. With its growing denominational rivalries, its powerful Protestant institutional and cultural cement, its varying degrees of religious indifference, and its authoritarian and exclusive attitudes towards indigenous peoples, this pattern of European settler colonialism was replicated elsewhere throughout the nineteenth century—in CANADA, SOUTH AFRICA, the Australian Colonies (see AUSTRALIA), and NEW ZEALAND.

From the mid-eighteenth century, there also developed a clear Protestant missionary commitment to the CONVERSION of the extra-European world. It was pushed on at first by the pietist revivalism of the Moravian Brethren and Wesleyan evangelicals (see MORAVIAN CHURCH; EVANGELICALISM METHODISM). It was informed by a fresh sense of obligation and providential direction, evident in the expansion of knowledge, communication, and trade symbolized in Captain James Cook's Pacific voyages of the 1770s. It was taken up by the principal denominations—BAPTISTS, Congregationalists, Anglicans, Presbyterians, and Methodists—and from the 1790s was systematically organized chiefly by voluntary lay societies, not only in Britain, but also from Boston to Basel and Berlin (see CONGREGATIONALISM ANGLICANISM; PRESBYTERIANISM). Still lacking any specific colonial commitment, Protestant MISSIONS were also kept at arm's length by colonial authorities. Often with good reason, West Indian planters, Cape colonists, and East India Company officials in INDIA all saw Protestant EVANGELISM and church or chapel building as seriously disruptive of colonial control, hierarchy, and the good order essential to commerce.

Protestant expansion nevertheless carried with it not only religious ideas, but also aspects of Western culture—the printing press, books, schools, GENDER relations, technology, and medicine. Indigenous peoples, both governments and individuals, and gradually colonial rulers as well learned to appreciate the value of missionary activity for its secular attributes. Missions in turn saw the advantages of negotiating a place for themselves with local rulers and colonial officials. Protestant influence thus spread widely, not only in formal colonies (especially those belonging to Britain), but also beyond their borders. Converts were always fewer in number than those who had been affected in other ways by Protestant teaching or example, but already by the mid-nineteenth century, local "native" evangelists and pastors rather than Western missionaries were the mainstay of Protestant expansion and the developing churches.

Explicit support from Protestants for colonialism has nevertheless varied greatly in time and place. It has fluctuated with the shifting balance between belief in the fundamental equality of humankind (strong in the late eighteenth and mid-twentieth centuries) and fears (especially between 1850 and 1914) that racial character and cultural attainment were biological constants. The former led Protestants to question both the necessity for colonialism and its likely duration; the latter, pessimistic in its assessment of the possibilities for "progress," encouraged the view that colonialism was indispensable. Support has perhaps been strongest in those territories—for example, many parts of late nineteenth-century AFRICA or CHINA—where missions and converts felt in sore need of security and protection, and where Western governments looked to the presence of their own nationals in asserting colonial claims against rivals.

The extent to which the impact of a Protestant presence and following can be equated with colonialism has long been hotly debated. From the mid-nineteenth century onward, Protestant missionaries themselves were often anxious to separate Christianity from Western civilization and CULTURE. Some came to see in Christianity the fulfillment of local religious belief and custom, or avoided altogether operating within the formal structures of colonialism. Others emphasized the role of Protestants as intermediaries between colonial rulers and the ruled, as defenders of indigenous rights at law and to land or labor, and as moderating influences on otherwise secular societies. Equally contested, especially by anthropologists and historians, has been the degree to which Protestant Christianity has either undermined indigenous cultures or has subverted colonial domination. Have they weakened the traditional bonds of local communities by questioning customary ways, and so opened the door to an intensified colonialism? Or have they facilitated the adaptation of local societies—through literacy, education, and new forms of social organization—to the point where Protestantism and resistance to colonialism have become not synonymous but often inseparable? In China from the late 1890s to the 1930s, the enormous growth of American Protestant interests provoked powerful expressions of Chinese religious independence and DISSENT. From John Chilembwe to Julius Nyerere, indigenous Protestants have certainly been prominent, above all in colonial Africa, both as political leaders and as vocal minority communities in the twentieth-century political struggle for independence. In part as a consequence of this involvement, especially since the 1920s and 1930s, Protestantism has flourished where colonialism in any formal political sense has long since disappeared.

References and Further Reading

Comaroff, Jean, and Comaroff, John. *Of Revelation and Revolution: I, Christianity, Colonialism and Consciousness in South Africa; II, The Dialectics of Modernity on a South African Frontier.* 2 vols. Chicago, IL: University of Chicago Press, 1991, 1997.
Fieldhouse, D. K. *The Colonial Empires: A Comparative Survey From the Eighteenth Century.* London: Macmillan, 1966; reprint 1982.
Hastings, Adrian. *The Church in Africa, 1450–1950.* Oxford: Oxford University Press, 1994.
Louis, William Roger, ed. *The Oxford History of the British Empire.* 5 vols. Oxford: Oxford University Press, 1998–1999.
Neill, S. C. *Colonialism and Christian Missions.* London: Lutterworth, 1966.
Osterhammel, Jürgen. *Colonialism: A Theoretical Overview.* English translation. Princeton, NJ: Markus Wiener; Kingston, Jamaica: Ian Randle, 1997.
Stanly, Brian. *The Bible and the Flag: Protestant Missions and British Imperialism in the Nineteenth and Twentieth Centuries.* Leicester, UK: Apollos, 1990.

ANDREW PORTER

COMENIUS, JOHN (KOMENSKY, JAN AMOS) (1592–1670)

Czech pedagogue and theologian. Comenius is best known for his innovations in methods of pedagogy. Comenius served as the pastor and last bishop of the Unity of Brethren (*Unitas Fratrum*), a small Czech Protestant group inspired by the Hussite movement of the fifteenth century and later revived as the MORAVIAN CHURCH under Count NIKOLAUS VON ZINZENDORF (1700–1760).

Life

Born in the Moravian village of Nivnice on March 28, 1592, Comenius lost both parents to the plague at the age of twelve. He began his formal education at the age of sixteen at the Latin school of Přerov. His scholarly abilities won him the recognition of the Moravian noble Charles the Elder of Žerotin, who had himself studied with Theodore Beza (1519–1605) in Geneva and was eager to send capable Czech students abroad to study in Calvinist centers of learning. With Žerotin's patronage, Comenius matriculated at the Reformed gymnasium of Herborn in 1611, where he studied with several leading continental scholars, most notably Johann Heinrich Alsted (1588–1638). Alsted's anti-Aristotelian approach to learning, his chiliasm, and his work as an encyclopedist significantly influenced Comenius's own thought and future endeavors. Continuing his studies at Heidelberg, Comenius benefited from the irenic and ecumenical spirit of the Reformed scholar David Pareus (1548–1622).

He returned to Moravia in 1614, taught for two years at P_erov, and in 1616 was ordained a minister in his church. With the outbreak of the Thirty Years War in 1618 and the Hapsburg victory at the Battle of White Mountain in 1620, Protestant leaders were forced to flee. Comenius himself went into hiding, and under trying circumstances began writing *The Labyrinth of the World and the Paradise of the Heart* (1623), a masterpiece of Czech literature and Protestant spirituality. In 1628 Comenius led a band of the Bohemian Brethren into exile in Leszno, POLAND, where he served as pastor of this refugee community and director of the local gymnasium. As Protestants had been officially expelled from Bohemia and Moravia, he never returned to his homeland but spent the remainder of his life as a wandering scholar in several European countries. Comenius died on November 15, 1670.

Educational and Pansophic Endeavors

Comenius was a polymath who worked in many different fields, but he is best known as a pedagogical reformer. He criticized the educational methods of his day, especially the emphasis on rote memorization and recitation, and proposed instead a system that drew analogies from the natural world and favored the concrete over the abstract. Many of his pedagogical principles were presented in his treatise *The Great Didactic* (). His *Janua linguarum reserata* (1631) attempted to implement some of his innovations in teaching and his *Orbis sensualium pictus* (1658) was one of the first illustrated schoolbooks for children. Both these textbooks were soon translated into many European languages, and the *Orbis* was popular for the next two centuries.

These pedagogical works were expressions of a broader vision to reform all of human society through education. Comenius was a leading representative of the late Renaissance movement known as pansophism, which sought the underlying harmony of the universe and attempted to unite all science, philosophy, and religion on that basis. He spelled out his program for the unification of knowledge and a universal system of education in a seven-volume work entitled *A General Consultation Concerning the Improvement of Human Affairs* (). Emphasizing both human rationality and divine revelation, Comenius sought truth on both an empirical and mystical level. This approach to knowledge brought him into conflict with the French philosopher Rene Descartes (1596–1650), whose strict division between mind and matter Comenius found unacceptable. His pedagogical and pansophic proposals drew the attention of many other leading intellectuals and rulers of his era. He accepted an invitation from ENGLAND to establish a pansophic college there, but his plans were thwarted by the outbreak of the English civil war. The American Puritan John Winthrop, Jr. (1606–1676) seems to have hoped that the noted Czech educator-theologian would accept a position as the first president of Harvard College. Comenius was also involved in educational initiatives in SWEDEN and in Sárospatak, HUNGARY.

Theology and Religious Leadership

Comenius's untiring dedication to pedagogical reform stemmed partly from his conviction that education would pave the way for an ecumenical religious settlement in a confessionally fractured Europe. He perceived all his educational and pansophic endeavors as part of his broader calling as a theologian. Central to his theology and spirituality and bracketing his long career are the *Labyrinth* (1623) and *Unum necessarium* (1668). While these works reveal a Christocentric spirituality akin to that of the early Pietists and a biblicism indebted to the German Reformed tradition in which Comenius was educated, they also reflect the theology of the *Unitas Fratrum*. In keeping with elements of his own tradition, Comenius stressed the importance of a personal relationship with Christ, the need for an ecumenical reformation, and a theology of hope. The development of this last theme was most problematic for Comenius's reception because it was intertwined with his chiliastic views. These have led some interpreters to dismiss Comenius as a fanatic.

As a religious leader Comenius helped maintain the faith and vision of his church through its final days. The 1648 Peace of Westphalia, which marked the end of the Thirty Years War, was a bitter disappointment for the Bohemian Brethren, for it dashed their hopes of religious liberty in their homeland. In the same year Comenius was consecrated as the last bishop of the *Unitas Fratrum*, but his church would soon fall prey to the political intrigues of the day. Comenius foresaw and reflected on its imminent demise as a unified body in *The Bequest of the Unity of Brethren*, a short treatise reflecting many of the beliefs of the Brethren as well as his own theological and ecumenical vision. War between Poland and Sweden led to Comenius's final exile at age sixty-four. He ended his prolific career as a refugee in the NETHERLANDS, where he continued to promote educational reforms as well as political and confessional peace, until his death November 15, 1670.

References and Further Reading

Primary Sources:

Comenius, John. *The Labyrinth of the World and the Paradise of the Heart.* Translated and introduced by Howard Louthan and Andrea Sterk. New York: Paulist Press, 1998.
————. *The Bequest of the Unity of Czech Brethren.* Translated and edited by M. Spinka, Chicago: National Union of Czechoslovak Protestants, 1940.

Secondary Sources:

Blekestad, Milada. *Comenius. Versuch eines Umrisses von Leben, Werk und Schicksal des Jan Amos Komensky.* Oslo: 1969.
Spinka, Matthew. *John Amos Comenius: That Incomparable Moravian.* Chicago: University of Chicago Press, 1943.

ANDREA STERK

COMMUNICATION

See Best Sellers in America, Religious; Mass Media; Publishing, Media; Televangelism

COMMUNION

See Lord's Supper

COMMUNION TABLES

In Protestant tradition, this is the table at which the Communion meal (Lord's Supper) or sacrament is served. The use of COMMUNION tables developed early in the REFORMATION period as Protestant reformers lambasted the doctrine of TRANSUBSTANTIATION and notions of the sacrament as a reenactment of Christ's sacrifice, views closely associated with the use of a consecrated ALTAR. Among the first of the Protestant reformers to substitute a table for the altar was HULDRYCH ZWINGLI, who in 1525 served a Communion meal at a table placed between the nave and the choir during the Maundy Thursday service in the Great Minster, Zurich. This table was intended to approximate the original Passover meal at which Christ initiated the Communion ritual and to demonstrate the understanding of the sacrament as symbolic of Christ's gift of GRACE and the gathering of the spiritual community of the CHURCH.

Protestants widely adopted the COMMUNION table in the late sixteenth century, and placed it as near the congregation as possible, abandoning the chancel as the location for the sacrament. In ENGLAND, Archbishop WILLIAM LAUD reversed this process by stipulating that COMMUNION tables be located in the chancel and enclosed by rails, a directive that stirred significant controversy, as Puritans (see PURTANISM) argued that the sacrament of community affirmation required that participants sit as equals around a table (rather than kneel at an altar rail), breaking the bread themselves and passing it on.

Communion tables emulate domestic tables, are typically made of wood, and feature no overt religious symbols. Easily moved and stored when not in use, wooden tables suited the Reformed Christian reduction in the frequency of the sacrament, which was celebrated between four and twelve times each year. Scottish Presbyterians set up tables outdoors during sacramental festivals or placed several down the center aisle of churches. Congregationalists in New England devised hinged tables attached to pews and pulpits that could be lowered when not in use. Telescoping tables were used in England during the Commonwealth. Tables with drawers were used in the UNITED STATES during the Federal period. Presbyterian and Puritan sacramental services included a rhetorical segment called "fencing of the table," in which the minister warned the unworthy to abstain from Communion. A variety of cloths have been used to cover Communion tables.

In Reformed denominations, the permanent placement of the table beneath the elevated pulpit became popular in the eighteenth century. But with the development of the raised pulpit platform in the nineteenth century, the table again became peripatetic, appearing sometimes in front of the platform and, in the case of platforms with moveable pulpits, sometimes centered on the platform.

With the rise of ECUMENISM in the twentieth century and renewed emphasis on Christian community, the table gained wider use as the center of liturgical space. Many Catholics, following suggestions made by the Vatican II Council, and some Lutherans and Episcopalians substituted tables for their altars. Reformed groups joined them in rearranging WORSHIP space, often placing a large table in the center of the room and arranging the seats around it in a ring.

See also Architecture, Church; Liturgy; Sacraments; Presbyterianism; Congregationalism; Lutheranism; Anglicanism

References and Further Reading

Benes, Peter, and Phillip D. Zimmerman. *New England Meeting House and Church: 1630–1850.* Boston: Boston University and The Currier Gallery of Art for the Dublin Seminar for New England Folklife, 1979.

Cox, J. Charles, and Alfred Harvey. *English Church Furniture.* London: Methuen, 1907.

Potter, G. R. *Zwingli.* Cambridge, UK: Cambridge University Press, 1976.

Schmidt, Leigh Eric. *Holy Fairs: Scottish Communions and American Revivals in the Early Modern Period.* Princeton, NJ: Princeton University Press, 1989.

White, James F. *Protestant Worship and Church Architecture: Theological and Historical Considerations.* New York: Oxford University Press, 1964.

Zimmerman, Philip D. "The Lord's Supper in Early New England: The Setting and the Service." In *New England Meeting House and Church: 1630-1850,* edited by Peter Benes for the Dublin Seminar for New England, 124–134. Boston, MA: Boston University Press, 1979.

JEANNE HALGREN KILDE

COMMUNISM

Communism is the communal ownership of goods with the concomitant abrogation of private property. Two forms of communism may be distinguished: religious communism and political communism. In Protestantism, religious communism made its appearance among the adherents of the "Radical Reformation" such as Thomas Münster or the Münster Anabaptists. The HUTTERITES made the abrogation of private property one of their principal tenets. Subsequent representatives of Protestant groupings disavowing personal property can be found in 17th century England and later (Moravian Brethren, Shakers, etc.). In all instances, the argumentation rests on the precedent of the earliest Christian community as described in the Book of Acts and on Jesus's strictures against money and wealth. Political communism, likewise of long history, is expressed in modernity primarily in terms of the thought of Karl Marx (1818–1883). Marx and his successor Friedrich Engels advocated economic reforms to liberate workers from capitalist exploitation by abolishing private property and redistributing resources according to need. According to Marxism, religion justified the exploitation of the masses; the oppressed turned to religion to explain their tragic situation and to anticipate future rewards. Marxist economic reform, therefore, eliminates the need for religion.

Marxist religious and economic principles were translated into the first Communist party in RUSSIA in 1917. Vladimir Lenin was the first to implement a program of religious persecution. Church-owned property was seized, religious teaching ceased, the authority of the Orthodox Church was limited, and religious leaders (Orthodox, Catholic, and Baptist) were harassed, imprisoned, and killed.

Other Communist states replicated Russia's religious persecution. Christians in these countries responded variously to atheistic state policies; some complied with compulsory registration, whereas others formed "underground" churches and resistance movements (notably the Baptist *Initsiativniki*). Western visitors were shown only registered churches, and thus misinformation regarding the extent of persecution spread. Many ecumenical groups and mainline denominations remained silent, while parachurch organizations (mostly Protestant) and research institutes (e.g., Keston College) revealed and boldly criticized persecution and aided underground Christians.

With the Communist reform policy of *glasnost,* and eventually the fall of Communism in Russia and Eastern Europe in the 1980s and 1990s, religious groups saw more freedom, and the degree of persecution was globally exposed.

See also China; Socialism, Christian; Orthodoxy, Eastern; Baptists

References and Further Reading

Boase, Paul H. *The Rhetoric of Christian Socialism.* New York: Random House, 1969.
Bourdeaux, Michael. *The Gospel's Triumph Over Communism.* Minneapolis, MN: Bethany House, 1991.
Christensen, Torben. *Origin and History of Christian Socialism, 1848–1854.* Aarhus: Universitetsforlaget, 1962
Dombrowski, James. *The Early Days of Christian Socialism in America.* New York: Octagon Books, 1966.
Elliott, Mark, ed. *Christianity and Marxism Worldwide: An Annotated Bibliography.* Wheaton, IL: Institute for the Study of Christianity and Marxism, 1989.
Friedmann, Robert. *The Christian Communism of the Hutterian Brethren.* Espanola, WA: Paul S. Gross, 1971.
Murchland, Bernard. *The Dream of Christian Socialism: An Essay on Its European Origins.* Washington, DC: American Enterprise Institute for Public Policy Research, 1982.
Ramet, Sabrina Petra, ed. *Protestantism and Politics in Eastern Europe and Russia.* Durham, NC: Duke University Press, 1992.

KRISTI UPSON-SAIA

CONCORD, BOOK OF

See Book of Concord

CONE, JAMES HAL (1938–)

Theologian. James Hal Cone was born in Fordyce, Arkansas, on August 5, 1938 to Charles M. and Lucille Cone. In 1958 he received a B.A. from Philander Smith College, in Arkansas. He then attended Garrett Theological Seminary in Evanston, Illinois, where he received a B.D. degree in 1961. Four years later Cone was awarded a Ph.D. from Garrett- and Northwestern jointly. His dissertation focused on the doctrine of man in the theology of Karl Barth.

Cone married Rose Hampton and they had four children. His teaching career began at Philander Smith College as assistant professor in 1964. He also served as assistant minister at the Woodlawn African Methodist Episcopal Church. He became assistant professor at Adrian College in Michigan in 1966, and in 1969 went to Union Theological Seminary in New York, where he became assistant professor of systematic theology.

In the summer after Martin Luther King, Jr.'s death, Cone wrote his landmark volume, *Black Theology and Black Power* (1969). This book marked his radical break with white European theology. He introduced the term "black theology" into religious discourse. This book was quickly followed by a more systematic statement of theology in the spirit of the Black Power Movement and the pronouncement of black church leaders (The National Committee of Black Churchmen). The latter volume was entitled *A Black Theology of Liberation* (1986).

Cone stressed the "liberation from oppression" theme religiously and culturally. Jesus and the Bible were called as witnesses to his liberation motif theology. God, in Jesus, a Jew, was identified in history with the oppressed. God, through Christ, demonstrated a willingness to suffer for liberation of oppressed humanity. Blackness became the ultimate symbol of this suffering God who would liberate the oppressed.

Cone's theology was readily received by black religious leaders. It was the proper articulation of the Gospel of freedom in the black church and community. It set off a serious dialogue within and without black religious and academic circles, stimulating much discussion by other black religious thinkers.

Cone's book, *Martin and Malcolm and America: A Dream on a Nightmare* (1991) is representative of his mature theology. From the outset, the influence of Malcolm X and Martin Luther King, Jr. on Cone was evident. However, the volume is helpful in revealing these influences on his decades of reflection. Cone's *Risks of Faith* (1999) sums up his witness as a theologian.

References and Further Reading

Primary Sources:

Cone, James Hal. *My Soul Looks Back.* Nashville, TN: Abingdon Press, 1982.
———. *Speaking the Truth: Ecumenism, Liberation and Black Theology.* Grand Rapids, MI: Eerdmans, 1986.
———. *A Black Theology of Liberation.* 2nd Edition, Maryknoll, NY: Orbis, 1987.
———. *God of the Oppressed.* Rev. ed. Maryknoll, NY: Orbis, 1987.
———. *For the People: Black Theology and the Black Church.* Maryknoll, NY: Orbis, 1994.

J. DEOTIS ROBERTS

CONFERENCE

Conference is a POLITY concept that has been effectively used by Methodists since their beginning in the eighteenth century. Many Methodist denominations are structured as connectional systems of conferences. For example, in the UNITED METHODIST CHURCH, the largest Methodist denomination, every congregation is affiliated with a local charge conference. Charge conferences send at least one delegate to a regional annual conference. Annual conferences send delegates to a Jurisdictional or Central conference and to the denomination's General Conference.

The conference concept is rooted in the thought of Methodism's founder, JOHN WESLEY (1703–1791). Wesley identified "Christian conference" as one of the principal means by which God's GRACE is conveyed to Christian people. He was convinced that Christians need to associate with other Christians to become and remain mature in their faith. Fellowship and conversation are gifts made possible by divine grace to assist them. The early Methodist societies and their small groups (bands and classes) were designed to provide Christian conference.

As a structural feature of METHODISM, "conference" usually refers to the manner in which the various Methodist denominations have organized to consider mission, determine policy, and set strategy. Wesley initiated this type of conference structure in June 1744 when he gathered a few sympathetic Anglican clergymen and his lay preachers in London to consult on fundamental theological and ministerial issues. They considered, "1. What to teach; 2. How to teach; and 3. What to do. . . . " (Davies 1988:IV,67). Wesley met annually thereafter with most of his preachers, and this conference became the predominant means of managing the Methodist movement. Among its most important functions were the selection, training, and appointment of preachers to their ministries. After Wesley's death, the conference became more powerful and remains the principal governing body in British Methodism. In the nineteenth century, lay people were given voice and vote in the British conference.

Shortly after his arrival in America, Thomas Rankin (1738–1810), one of the lay preachers Wesley dispatched to the colonies, convened the first annual conference of Methodist preachers in June 1773 in Philadelphia. Like its British counterpart, this was a spiritual brotherhood that managed the fledgling movement. American Methodists have held annual conferences ever since.

With Wesley's blessing, the American Methodist preachers held a "Christmas Conference" in Baltimore, Maryland, in December 1784, (see BALTIMORE CONFERENCE) at which they formally organized the Methodist Episcopal Church (MEC). As the new church grew, geographical considerations prompted the MEC to organize regional annual conferences of its preachers, each presided over by a bishop (see BISHOPS AND EPISCOPACY). In 1792 the MEC held its first General Conference, to which all of its ordained preachers in full connection with annual conferences were invited. Among its other actions, the General Conference claimed authority to legislate for the church, to revise its official book of DOCTRINE and discipline (see CHURCH DISCIPLINE), and to meet every four years thereafter.

At the 1796 General Conference, the boundaries of six geographical annual conferences (New England, Philadelphia, Baltimore, Virginia, South Carolina, and Western) were fixed. As the church continued to grow, the 1808 General Conference adopted a plan for a delegated General Conference to which the various annual conferences sent elected representatives. As the supreme legislative body of the MEC, the General Conference was often the scene of bitter and divisive debate. For instance, the 1844 MEC General Conference debate over SLAVERY resulted in a denominational schism and the formation of the Methodist Episcopal Church, South (see SLAVERY, ABOLITION OF).

The quadrennial General Conference remains the preeminent legislative body of the larger Methodist denominations, that is, United Methodist, AFRICAN METHODIST EPISCOPAL, AFRICAN METHODIST EPISCOPAL ZION, and Christian Methodist Episcopal churches. The General Conference authorizes revisions to the denominations' official Books of Discipline. With the exception of The United Methodist Church, the General Conference of these churches also elects bishops who serve as their chief executive officers. United Methodists elect bishops at their quadrennial Jurisdictional (U.S.) or Central (outside the U.S.) conferences. All four denominations are also organized into regional annual conferences. After considerable discussion and negotiation, mostly in the late nineteenth and early twentieth century, each of these churches granted lay people (see LAITY) the right to serve as delegates at General Conference in equal numbers with the CLERGY. They have also sought lay/clergy voting parity in their annual conferences.

Many Methodist or Methodist-related denominations in nations other than the UNITED STATES also utilize a conference structure. British Methodism holds an annual delegated conference that serves as its supreme legislative body (see METHODISM, ENGLAND). The Korean Methodist Church is organized with a General Conference and annual conferences. Other denominations may have a General Conference and annual conferences or their equivalent that may bear a different name, for example, archdiocese and diocese (Methodist Church Nigeria) or regions (Methodist Church in Brazil).

Conferences, whether local, annual, or denominational, usually produce reports of their ministries. Most annual conferences publish annual journals of their work that include reports, a record of proceedings, and a list of the names and addresses of their churches, clergy, and representative lay people. Thorough records of General Conferences are also published. These records and publications serve as primary historical documents of the denomination's ministry.

References and Further Reading

Baker, Frank. "The People Called Methodists: 3. Polity." In *A History of the Methodist Church in Great Britain,* vol. 1. Edited by Rupert Davies and Gordon Rupp. London: Epworth Press, 1965.

Davies, Rupert, A. Raymond George, and Gordon Rupp. *A History of the Methodist Church in Great Britain*, vol. 4. London: Epworth Press, 1988.

Frank, Thomas E. *Polity, Practice, and the Mission of The United Methodist Church.* Nashville, TN: Abingdon Press, 1997.

Kirby, James E., Russell E. Richey, and Kenneth E. Rowe. *The Methodists.* Westport, CT: Greenwood Press, 1996.

Richey, Russell E. *The Methodist Conference in America.* Nashville, TN: Kingswood Books, 1996.

CHARLES YRIGOYEN

CONFESSING CHURCH

Confessing Church (Bekennende Kirche) was the name adopted in the spring of 1934 by one section of the German Evangelical Church. The group mobilized support from both pastors and laity in opposition to the rival section that called itself the "Faith Movement of German Christians" and insisted on a Christianity purged of all semitic influences. The feud between these contenders for the allegiance of German Protestants lasted through the Nazi era.

Origins and Establishment

The "GERMAN CHRISTIANS" welcomed Adolf Hitler's advent to power in January 1933 and supported the Nazi political platform, including the purging from German society of all Jewish elements. They wanted to adopt similar goals in the life and structures of the German Evangelical Church. In the church elections of July 1933 they gained control of most of the administrative positions in a majority of the provincial branches of the church. Under the leadership of Hitler's appointee as Reich Bishop, Ludwig Müller, they planned to remove pastors of Jewish origin from their offices, at the national synod to be held in September 1933.

However, such a challenge to the church's autonomy, especially when drawn from an outside political source, prompted a vigorous response. The beginnings of what became the Confessing Church occurred when a group of Berlin pastors, under the leadership of MARTIN NIEMÖLLER, formed the Pastors Emergency League, whose aim was to defend ORTHODOXY in doctrine and the autonomy of the church structures, and to prevent the adoption of measures drawn from ideological movements, such as National Socialism.

During the winter months of 1933–1934 opponents of the Nazification of the church recognized the need for a theologically defensible manifesto. At the Synod of Barmen in May 1934, under KARL BARTH's leadership, they produced the Barmen Confession (see BARMEN DECLARATION), which was to become the main platform of the Confessing Church for the remainder of the Nazi period. The six articles of the Barmen Confession affirmed both the independence of the Church from any politically influenced interference, and the need to uphold the supremacy of Christian witness over against alternative ideologies. They specifically rejected the totalitarian claims of the state both over the church (see CHURCH AND STATE, OVERVIEW) and in the political field.

The significance of the Barmen Confession lay in its successful definition of Christian involvement in politics and the limits of Christian loyalty to the state. By rejecting the heretical ideas and practices of the "German Christians," the Confessing Church steadfastly maintained the view that it alone constituted the "true Church."

The result was a complex and often confusing situation. In the majority of provinces, particularly the largest, Prussia, the Confessing Church formed a minority, refusing to acknowledge the authority of the now "German Christian"–controlled bureaucracy. Instead, a rival structure, claiming to be the true inheritor of past traditions, gained support from those parishes willing to pay the price of defiance. Only in three provinces, Hannover, Bavaria, and Württemberg, was the Confessing Church in a majority, and so retained control of the church administration. *De facto*, if not *de jure*, there were now two German Evangelical Churches, which led to incessant conflicts within parishes at the local level. Personal, local, and political differences frequently reinforced the basic theological disagreements. The strength of the Confessing Church lay in its refusal to compromise. Its pastors, for example, rescinded their loyalty to "German Christian" bishops, refused to accept communications from diocesan offices, and resolutely defended their own congregations from unwanted interference. They formed local, provincial, and national Councils of Brethren *(Brüderräte)*, which exercised doctrinal and practical authority and which were organized on a presbyterian model, drawn from the Reformed tradition.

Political Implications

In the eyes of the Confessing Church leadership, their stance was adopted solely for theological reasons. At no time did the Confessing Church seek to play the role of leading opposition to the secular goals of the Nazi Party, nor to organize resistance to the increasing tyranny that was to engulf the whole country. Their more limited ambition was to defend the autonomy and doctrine of the church against evident distortion and heresy by the "German Christians." Later criticized as short-sighted, it was principally attributed to three factors. First, these men were theologians, not politicians, and they often sought to draw a strict line between theological definitions and political controversy. Throughout the Confessing Church, loyalty to Hitler was professed by both CLERGY and LAITY. The vast majority did not recognize, nor were they prepared to admit, that these political loyalties were incompatible with their church professions.

The second factor was the Lutheran tradition of respect for the ruling power (see LUTHERANISM). There was no history of organized DISSENT. The third factor was the no less inhibiting condition that most of the Evangelical clergy refused to be committed to any political involvement, either with the "German Christians" or with the Confessing Church. The ingrained tradition of PIETISM maintained the belief that "politics do not concern the church," whose goal was the search for personal, not political, salvation. As a result, the Confessing Church leaders were unsuccessful in mobilizing the majority of church members to a critical opposition to the Nazis' authority except on matters directly affecting church life and doctrine. Basically, no part of the German Evangelical Church, including the Confessing Church, had a theology adequate to mount any sustained attack on the actions of its political rulers, and for that reason, even at the end of the Nazi era, there was no more than what has been called a "reluctant resistance."

This position was easily and often deliberately misunderstood. The political authorities, from Hitler downward, interpreted the Confessing Church's stance as a political act of disobedience. The fulsome declarations of national loyalty made by Confessing Church leaders and supporters were regarded as hypocritical dissimulation. So, too, the "German Christians" regarded the Confessing Church pastors' and parishes' defiance as insubordination, motivated for church-political reasons. They sought to bring these dissenters to heel, using the highly political argument that the church must show its dedication to and unity with the National Socialist state and its leaders. Refusal to endorse such a platform was regarded as political treachery rather than theological obduracy.

The Nazis' expectation that the German Evangelical Church would willingly allow itself to be "coordinated" into the new regime's totalitarian plans was shattered by the determined opposition of the Confessing Church. In 1934 it became clear that this recalcitrance would not be overcome by the hamhanded activities of the "German Christian" authorities. In 1935 Hitler ordered the creation of a new Ministry of Church Affairs under a Nazi stalwart, Hanns Kerrl, although his plans for a more positive relationship seemed to presage yet another breach of the church's autonomy. Furthermore, Kerrl's policies were known to be continually under attack from his own more radical colleagues, who successfully undermined his authority. By 1938 the dominant Nazi policy toward the Confessing Church was one of confrontation and suppression. At the outbreak of the war in 1939 Hitler ordered the cessation of all antichurch moves, although this did not stop the Gestapo from continuing its campaign to destroy the influence of the clergy, and especially of the Confessing Church. Had the war ended with a Nazi victory, there can be little doubt that the staunch defiance of the Confessing Church would have been ruthlessly eliminated.

For their part, the members of the Confessing Church were to become increasingly divided in their opinions about the moral and political legitimacy of the Nazi state and its policies. Already in 1935 this division could be observed between the "moderates," particularly in the so-called intact provinces of Bavaria, Hannover, and Württemberg, and the more "radical" wing, especially in the "destroyed" province of Prussia, under the leadership of the "Dahlemites," so called from the name of Niemöller's parish in Berlin. The former continued to uphold their traditional obedience to the existing political authorities, refused to encourage open acts of defiance, and instead sought accommodation by working within the limits of the Nazi system. The latter, or "Dahlemite" group, even though maintaining their patriotic loyalty to the German nation, came to see the Nazi policies in the church sphere as unacceptable, and were, if necessary, prepared to accept the consequences of dissent. However, only a handful of these Confessing Church supporters were ready to recognize that the regime they served was determined to implement criminal policies of military aggression and racial persecution and genocide without regard to established law or ethics. Hence only a few far-sighted opponents of the regime, such as Pastor DIETRICH BONHOEFFER, were to become actively involved in the Resistance Movement, and eventually to pay the price of its failure.

Conflicting Dilemmas and Witness in the Face of Persecution

The Confessing Church's ambivalence toward the Nazi regime was well illustrated in 1935 when 700 pastors, mainly in Prussia, were arrested for defying Nazi regulations. In 1936 the radical wing prepared, and sent privately to Hitler, a strong protest against the regime's policies, such as the extension of the concentration camp system and the increasing persecution of the Jews. By some error, this document was publicized in a Swiss newspaper. The authors were at once accused of national treachery and forced to retreat. Such actions reinforced the Gestapo's repressive intentions. In July 1937 Martin Niemöller was arrested together with some fifty other leading Confessing Church figures. Despite worldwide intercessions for his release, he was held without bail for nine months until a show trial was held, heavily orchestrated by Joseph Goebbels's Propaganda Ministry. The judges, however, returned a verdict of not guilty on the major charges, and declared that Niemöller's minor infractions of the law had been fully expiated

by his months in prison. Hitler was not to be defied, however. Niemöller was immediately rearrested and remained incarcerated until the end of the war.

The subsequent wave of intimidation by the Gestapo saw numerous pastors arrested for various alleged breaches of Nazi ordinances. Most sentences were short, designed to compel submission in the future, although a few pastors paid a stiffer price, such as Paul Schneider, who was sent to Buchenwald concentration camp in November 1937 and put to death there eighteen months later, the first pastor of the Confessing Church to lose his life as a result of Nazi persecution.

With the loss of its most pugnacious leader, Niemöller, and the enforced exile of its most distinguished theologian, Karl Barth, the Confessing Church inevitably suffered grave doubts about its future. Both the desire to maintain political loyalty and the pragmatic pressures to conform counseled an opportunistic compromise with the official church authorities. Others, however, remained staunch in their witness to the Gospel. In September 1938, on the occasion of the Sudetenland crisis and with the threat of imminent war, the Confessing Church leaders wrote a special Peace Liturgy, calling on the church members to repent, and asking for God's forgiveness of the personal and corporate sins of all nations, including their own. The Munich Conference was then announced and this liturgy was never circulated. However, a copy fell into Nazi hands and was seen as final and irrefutable proof of the Confessing Church's political treachery against Hitler's leadership. Cowed and intimidated by such virulent attacks, the Confessing Church made no response two months later to the outrageous and very public crimes of the anti-Jewish Crystal Night pogrom.

The constant threat of Gestapo surveillance and interrogation, or even of imprisonment in a concentration camp, and the unpredictability of such repressive attacks, lay heavily upon all Confessing Church members. To be sure, gestures of solidarity were made, such as the intercessory reading out during the Sunday services of the names of those members arrested, banished, or forbidden by the Gestapo to preach, although even these "Fürbittenlisten" were problematic in that it was virtually impossible to distinguish between those punished for purely theological protests and those accused of political agitation. This menacing repression created almost irreconcilable and paralyzing dilemmas for the pastors affected. Their desire to serve their congregations without conflict with the authorities, and their continuing national ties, were in reality incompatible with their theological insights and obligations, although only a small handful were prepared to recognize this fact.

In this atmosphere of doubt and uncertainty, the Confessing Church took no action as the clouds of war gathered in 1939. The same conflict of loyalties increased when the outbreak of war led to the escalation of violence and the perpetration of atrocities. The Nazi campaign during 1939–1940 for the so-called euthanasia of the mentally ill met with the same ambivalent response from the Confessing Church as had been the case earlier. Their refusal to challenge the Nazi state publicly, and their preference for private remonstrances, even if ignored, was a truly frustrating situation for the few who called for more decisive action based on Christian moral imperatives.

This crisis of conscience only increased as the news began to percolate about the atrocities committed on the eastern front and against the Jews. At a time of unprecedented challenge to their moral courage and conscience, all save a handful of Confessing Church members continued to turn a blind eye on events, or retreated into apathetic indifference as bystanders. Not until 1943 did Bishop Theophilus Wurm of Württemberg protest privately to the Nazi authorities against the ongoing breaches of God's moral commandments. In October 1943 the Confessing Church's Prussian Synod, more publicly, wrote to all its congregations to say: "Terms like 'eradication,' 'liquidation,' or 'unfit to live' are not known in the laws of God. The murdering of men solely because they are members of a foreign race, or because they are old, or mentally ill, or the relatives of a criminal, cannot be considered as carrying out the authority entrusted to the State by God."

Such an appeal to the ethical standards of earlier years was doomed to fail; but so too, in the circumstances of total war, were efforts to mobilize public opinion in protest against the crimes of their leaders. The abortive July 20, 1944, attempt on Hitler's life was greeted with shock and dismay by the majority of Confessing Church members.

The military defeat of the National Socialist regime in May 1945 forced a reevaluation of the Confessing Church's stance. Only a few months later, the surviving leaders met in Stuttgart to consider their past failings and their future opportunities. Largely inspired by the newly released Martin Niemöller, the Declaration of Guilt issued on this occasion aptly summarized the Confessing Church's experience of the previous twelve years: "We know ourselves, with our people, to be not only in a community of suffering, but also in a solidarity of guilt. With great anguish we state: through us inestimable suffering was inflicted on many peoples and lands. . . . We have struggled for many years in the name of Jesus Christ against the spirit which found its terrible expression in the National Socialist regime of tyranny, but we accuse ourselves for not witnessing more courageously, for not praying more faithfully, for not believing more joyously, and for not loving more ardently."

It was a fitting epitaph.

References and Further Reading

Bergen, Doris. *The Twisted Cross: The German Christian Movement in the Third Reich.* Chapel Hill: University of North Carolina Press, 1996.
Besier, Gerhard. *Die Kirchen und das Dritte Reich. Spaltungen und Abwehrkämpfe 1934–1937.* Berlin: Propyläen Verlag, 2001.
Bethge, Eberhard. *Dietrich Bonhoeffer: A Biography:* Revision by V. J. Barnett. Minneapolis: Fortress Press, 2000.
Bonhoeffer, Dietrich. *Letters and Papers from Prison.* London: Collins, 1959.
Cochrane, Arthur C. *The Church's Confession under Hitler.* Philadelphia: Westminster, 1962.
Conway, John S. *The Nazi Persecution of the Churches, 1939–1945.* London: Weidenfeld and Nicolson, 1968.
Ericksen, Robert P. *Theologians under Hitler.* New Haven: Yale University Press, 1985.
Gerlach, Wolfgang. *And the Witnesses Were Silent: The Confessing Church and the Persecution of the Jews.* Lincoln: University of Nebraska Press, 2000.
Helmreich, Ernst C. *The German Churches under Hitler: Background, Struggle and Epilogue.* Detroit: Wayne State University Press, 1979.
Kershaw, Ian. *Hitler: A Biography.* 2 vols. New York: W. W. Norton, 1999.
Schmidt, Dietmar. *Pastor Niemöller.* London: Odham Press, 1959.
Scholder, Klaus. *The Churches and the Third Reich,* vol. 1: 1918–1934; vol. 2: 1934. London: SCM Press, 1987.

JOHN S. CONWAY

CONFESSION

The term "confession" had two distinct meanings in the REFORMATION period: the confession of SIN and the confession of FAITH. One might say that the controversy generated over the nature of the confession of sin led in large part to the development of confessions of faith that expressed the nature of true faith over against the teaching of the Roman Church.

I. Confession of Sin

The confession of sin was directly related to the practice of private penance because that had first developed in the Celtic monasteries of the Carolingian period. The canonical penance of the patristic period had consisted of contrition for sin, public confession of sin before the bishop and the congregation, satisfaction to manifest the sincerity of contrition, and finally public absolution by the bishop. Private penance reversed the last two parts, so that satisfaction followed absolution. Thus when Peter the Lombard defined penance as one of the seven SACRAMENTS in his

Sentences of 1150, he defined penance as contrition, confession, and satisfaction. In this understanding of penance confession to the priest both manifests the sincerity of contrition and reveals the circumstances of each sin, so that the priest can both "loose" the sinner by absolution and "bind" the sinner with the appropriate remedy and punishment for sin by satisfaction.

The Fourth Lateran Council in 1215 mandated private confession for all Christians and made clear the close connection between the confession of sin and the willingness to perform the satisfactions imposed by the priest. "All believers of both sexes shall after coming to the age of discretion faithfully confess all their sins at least once a year in private to their own priest, and strive to fulfill to the best of their ability the penance imposed upon them." The only sins that had to be confessed were those that elicited the consent of the will against the love of God, even when no external deed resulted from such consent. However, when the consent of the will was lacking, and the root of love was left intact, then the sin was venial, or forgivable, because the love that remained was thought to cover a multitude of sins (I Peter 4:8). Any thought or desire that did not elicit the consent of the will was seen to be the remnant of original sin in the form of concupiscence, and such concupiscence was not thought to be sin, but rather the "tinder" or "occasion" of sin, which only became sin by the consent of the will.

The practice of private confession was closely associated with another mandate of the Fourth Lateran Council, that of the yearly reception of Communion, usually at Easter. To prepare for their annual confession penitents were encouraged to use the season of Lent as a period of penitential introspection, to bring to mind all the mortal sins that had been committed in the past year, so that all such sins could be fully confessed to the priest, usually during Holy Week, and ideally on Holy Saturday. The priest, on the other hand, was seen to be like a physician "diligently inquiring into the circumstances both of the sinner and of the sin, so that he may wisely understand what advice he should give him and what remedy he should apply, trying different tests to heal the patient." The failure to confess a sin of which the penitent was aware, or to confess all the circumstances of the sin, resulted in the lack of forgiveness for the penitent. On the other hand, the disclosure of sin confessed in private to the priest resulted in the priest being "dispatched to a monastery of strict discipline to do penance for the rest of his life."

Upon hearing the full confession of sin, the priest made two judgments regarding the sinner. On the one hand, the priest judged that the contrition of the penitent was sincere; and because it was contrition that removed sin, the priest could pronounce a judgment of absolution. On the other hand, given that satisfaction now followed absolution, the priest also determined the requisite punishments, remedies, and satisfactions for sin, after the traditional penitential remedies of PRAYER, fasting, and alms. However, for what would one be making satisfaction after one had been absolved of sin? To answer this question the church developed a distinction between the eternal guilt and penalty of sin, which was fully satisfied by Christ, and the temporal guilt and punishment that remained, that the penitent must satisfy by his or her own efforts, in cooperation with Christ. Unlike BAPTISM, which was a full participation in the satisfaction of Christ needing nothing to complete it, the commission of mortal sin grieved the Holy Spirit and forfeited the GRACE received at baptism, so that penance was seen to be a "laborious baptism" that required the efforts of the penitent. The church, by the authority vested in priests, bishops, and the pope, had the ability both to discern and to assign the temporal punishments and satisfactions remaining after absolution; and were the penitent to die before the completion of these satisfactions, then they would have to be completed after death in purgatory before eternal life could be fully enjoyed.

In their desire to lighten the burden of satisfactions as much as possible, lay people turned to two major spiritual resources to help them make appropriate satisfaction: the monks and the sacrifice of the mass. Because monks were seen voluntarily to obey the "counsels of perfection" taught by Jesus, especially poverty, chastity, the renunciation of self-defense, and obedience, they were thought to perform works over and above those required by the law, which could therefore be applied to the satisfactions of others. Moreover, beginning in the Carolingian period, it became increasingly common for monks to be ordained as priests, so that they might say private masses on behalf of others. Because the mass was seen to be both a sacrifice offered by the priest to God and a sacrament offered by Christ to his people, the priest could offer the sacrifice of Christ in the mass for the benefit of those on whose behalf it was being offered, including not only those present during the mass in a spirit of devotion, but also those not present, and possibly even deceased and thought to be in purgatory. The endowment of monasteries by LAITY, both for the benefit of their works of supererogation and for the saying of masses on behalf of the patrons, became an increasingly common way for those patrons with means to make satisfaction for their sin.

MARTIN LUTHER was a lifelong devotee of private confession, and his understanding of the gospel could be said to emerge as a reform of private confession in particular, a reform that soon extended to all aspects of the Roman Church (see CATHOLICISM PROTESTANT REACTIONS; CATHOLIC REACTIONS TO PROTESTANTISM). By 1507 Luther was both an Augustinian monk following the counsels of perfection and a priest offering the sacrifice of the mass. Luther initially agreed with the Roman Church that it was contrition that removed sin, a contrition made perfect by the infusion of love for God by the Holy Spirit, and that only those sins that accused the conscience needed to be confessed. Luther also sought to strengthen his conscience after confession and absolution by zealously performing the satisfaction and penance imposed on him, especially by the strict observance of his monastic vows and life. However, the more Luther strove to confess and make satisfaction for his sin, the more his conscience accused him of sin, not only for those things that had the consent of will, but also for those thoughts and desires that he fought against with all his will. Indeed, by 1515 Luther was overwhelmed by experiences of tribulation that he called *Anfechtung,* in which the awareness of his own sin and the wrath of God against sin overwhelmed his conscience. Luther concluded from this experience that sin can never be eradicated by contrition, confession, and satisfaction; rather, the infusion of love reveals sin and wrath in the conscience, so that we might confess that we are sinners deserving of wrath, and consign ourselves to suffer the punishments of hell with Christ, out of love for God. Such confession justifies God in God's Word, for God tells us that we all have sinned and have fallen short of the glory of God, and we acknowledge this to be true when our own consciences experience the terror of sin and wrath.

However, Luther was to be led in yet another direction because of the influence of his own confessor, Johann von Staupitz. In private confession Staupitz told Luther not to look to his own contrition and terror, but rather to Jesus Christ crucified, for he has taken our sins on himself and has given us his righteousness in a "royal marriage." In light of this growing understanding of Christ as the one who takes on himself the sin that we acknowledge to be our own, Luther came to see that it is not the grace of God, but the law of God, that reveals sin in the conscience and terrifies it with the sense of the wrath of God. The terrified conscience despairs of removing sin by its own efforts, including its own contrition, confession, and satisfaction. Once the conscience has been terrified by the knowledge of its sin, the word of absolution needs to be proclaimed to it by the priest. However, this word is not a judgment about the sincerity of the penitent's contrition, but is rather the promise of forgiveness won by Christ on our behalf by his death on the cross. Sin is removed not by our contrition and

satisfaction, but by faith in the promise of forgiveness spoken to us individually by the person of the priest. By faith the penitent no longer sees his or her sin in the conscience, but in the flesh of Christ, where it is taken away and put to death; and the penitent believes that the righteousness of Christ is now his or her own. Such faith in the promise of absolution brings genuine peace to terrified consciences, especially in the context of private confession.

On the basis of this new understanding and experience of confession, inspired in large part by the spiritual counsel of Johann von Staupitz in private confession, Luther came to see the whole ministry of the church in terms of the word of absolution. Instead of limiting absolution to private confession itself, Luther claimed that Christ left us with many promises of absolution, to strengthen and comfort the terrified consciences of the faithful. The word of absolution should be proclaimed in the sermon, and is also contained in the Lord's Prayer, when we pray that we may be forgiven as we forgive others. However, Luther especially prized those forms of absolution that were addressed by Christ to the individual directly. Thus in baptism the promise of absolution is applied individually to me with the accompanying sign of the water applied to my body. In private confession the priest or pastor speaks the word of absolution directly to me individually, after having heard my own terrified conscience in confession, thereby returning me to the promise of absolution spoken to me in my baptism. In the LORD'S SUPPER the promise of absolution is spoken to me individually, confirmed by the sign of the body and blood of Christ that died for my forgiveness, which I eat and drink as I hear the word of absolution, "Shed for you and for many for the forgiveness of sin." Luther also extended the power to proclaim absolution to every faithful Christian, in light of "the priesthood of all believers." However, Luther himself tended to focus on those forms of absolution proclaimed by ordained ministers to the faithful, especially baptism, private confession, the sermon, and the Supper. Indeed the worship life of the Christian could be seen to cycle through all four forms of absolution on a routine basis. In preparation for receiving the sacrament, the faithful would go to private confession, in which the word of absolution would return them to faith in the promise made to them in baptism. They would then hear the same word proclaimed in the sermon and prayed in the Lord's Prayer, culminating in Communion, in which the promise of absolution was once again applied to them individually, to console and strength their consciences in their lifelong struggle with sin.

Luther was ambivalent about the status of private confession as a sacrament. He was never in doubt about its essential character in the life of the church, defending it vigorously in 1522 after ANDREAS RUDOLF BODENSTEIN CARLSTADT had suggested that the only absolution needed by the faithful is found in the Supper. However, it lacked an accompanying sign, and hence could not really fit the definition of a sacrament as a promise of absolution with a confirming sign attached to it by Christ. By 1531 PHILIPP MELANCHTHON, who himself was decisively impacted by Luther's teaching on confession and absolution, defined both absolution and ordination as sacraments, and included this teaching in his magisterial *Loci communes* of 1543. Like Luther, Melanchthon especially treasured the way the promise of absolution is spoken directly to the individual by the pastor in private confession, making it the best form of absolution offered in the church, together with the Supper. Hence it is not surprising that private confession was always required by the Wittenberg Reformation before one could receive Communion, even though the requirement of yearly confession by the Fourth Lateran Council was also rejected as "tyranny."

JOHN CALVIN, on the other hand, was very suspicious of the practice of private confession to a priest. Although he always allowed that rightly understood it could be an edifying practice, he was always concerned about the lack of accountability created by the practice in the Roman Church. The priest, in conjunction with his bishop and possibly the pope (in reserved cases), was the only person who heard and judged sin, and was the only person with the AUTHORITY to excommunicate. Calvin appreciated the concern to maintain the holiness of the Supper as much as possible, but was very concerned that the priest and bishop could act tyrannically, excommunicating people over financial matters or personal grudges, as had been the case with Calvin's own father. Moreover, by the time Calvin emerged as an evangelical teacher, the study of the patristic period had uncovered the fact, unmentioned by Luther or Melanchthon, that private confession was unknown in that period, and only emerged later, in conjunction, so Calvin thought, with the emergence of the "papal tyranny." To preserve the goal of protecting the holiness of the Supper, while also avoiding the abuses possible in private confession, Calvin created an ecclesiastical senate of pastors and elders that he called the CONSISTORY. Although the Consistory made its investigations into the sins of the congregation in private, it did not allow an individual to make such inquiries, but rather pastors and elected laity together inquired into the sins and prescribed the remedies, and also kept minutes of the proceedings for the record, again to establish mutual accountability. Calvin thus moved the church away from private confession, favored so highly by Luther and Melanchthon, toward something approximating the canonical penance of the patristic period. Calvin agreed with Melanchthon that ordination could be considered a sacrament, but did not accept the idea that confession should also be a sacrament, and pointed out this disagreement in his preface to the French translation of Melanchthon's 1543 *Loci*, which Calvin himself sponsored.

One practice on which all evangelical reformers could agree was the establishment of prayers of general confession in worship services. Such general confession could never take the place of private confession for the Lutherans, or of the Consistory for the Reformed, but it did remind the faithful right in the heart of their worship life that the gospel is offered only to those who have first been humbled by the awareness of their own sin, and who make a genuine confession of that sin together with others in the congregation. Once private confession was no longer obligatory in the Lutheran churches, and Consistories were no longer a prominent part of Reformed communities, the only confession of sin left was the prayer of general confession in Protestant worship services.

The Council of Trent responded to the teaching of Luther and Melanchthon by reasserting the teaching of the Fourth Lateran Council concerning the necessity of confessing one's sins at least once a year to one's priest. Trent denied that the word of absolution should be sought anywhere other than in the sacrament of penance, and asserted again that it was contrition that removed sin, not faith in the word of absolution. Trent denied Luther's and Melanchthon's definition of penance as the terrified conscience and faith, and reasserted the traditional definition of penance as contrition, confession, and satisfaction. Trent also asserted that only priests and bishops had the authority to bind and loose sins, and that penitents had to be simultaneously loosed from sin by the word of absolution, and bound to satisfactions for the punishment, correction, and satisfaction of sin. Trent denied that one could know with certainty that one's sins had been absolved in the sacrament of penance. Finally Trent denied the validity of general, public confessions of sin, as lacking in the efficacy of the sacrament of penance.

II. Confession of Faith

The confession of faith was a direct outgrowth of the criticism of the Roman Church begun by Martin Luther, centering on his objections to the Roman understanding of the confession of sin. At the Leipzig Debate of 1519 Luther had claimed that both popes and councils have erred, and that only the Word of God in Scripture is without error. In *The Babylonian*

Captivity of 1520, Luther claimed that nothing could be made into an article of faith that was not clearly taught in Scripture. Both claims had the result of casting radical doubt not only on the more recent councils such as Constance (1415) and Fourth Lateran (1215), but also on the whole of the dogmatic tradition of the church, from the Council of Nicea (325) onward. Given the need to judge all previous conciliar pronouncements on the basis of the Word of God in Scripture, it is not surprising that the various reforming movements of the sixteenth century came to develop their own public statements of authoritative teaching in the form of confessions of faith, both to distinguish the movements from what they considered to be the errors of Rome, and to bring about a public consensus about what the true teaching of Scripture really is.

The first confession of faith to emerge in the sixteenth century came from a community of reformers who rejected both Rome and the reforming agendas of Luther and Melanchthon in Wittenberg and HULDRYCH ZWINGLI and JOHANNES OECOLAMPADIUS in Zurich and Basel. The SCHLEITHEIM CONFESSION of 1527 was drafted by MICHAEL SATTLER the same year he was to be executed, and represented the consensus reached by members of the Swiss Brethren. The Confession makes a sharp distinction between membership in the civil world of the magistrate and the sword, and the kingdom of Christ that is governed by the gospel. The confession rejects the practice of infant baptism, insisting on faith and obedience prior to baptism. The Supper is only for those baptized upon their confession of faith, and is eaten and drunk in remembrance of Christ's death by those who are one body with Christ. The confession also rejects the use of civil authority in the church, insisting that the only disciplinary authority in the church is the ban—that is, excommunication. The baptized cannot take part in the bearing of the sword and oath taking, for Christ has forbidden his followers from so doing. The Schleitheim Confession became a very effective way by which this community spread its teaching, and Zwingli and Calvin both devoted entire treatises to refuting its teaching from their interpretation of the Word of God in Scripture.

The AUGSBURG CONFESSION of 1530 was submitted to Charles V by the German rulers who had allowed evangelical teaching to take place in their territories and had allowed the reform of abuses in the churches in their lands. Drafted by Melanchthon, the Augsburg Confession defended evangelical teaching on the basis of its catholicity, using the Apostles' Creed, the Creed of Constantinople, and the Definition of Chalcedon as the basis of catholic doctrine. The changes allowed by the rulers in their territories were said to be the elimination of recent abuses introduced into the church under the papacy, and hence represented a return to genuine catholic practice. Augsburg defines an abuse as any teaching or practice that is said to be a sacrifice or satisfaction for sin, or to merit anything from God, or that is made binding on conscience without the express command of God in Christ. The Roman theologians responded to the Augsburg Confession with the Pontifical Confutation, which was read aloud to the Emperor, but which was not provided in writing to the evangelicals. Although the Confutation agreed that many of the teachings of the Augsburg Confession were in fact catholic (although with some qualifications in each instance), it rejected the definition of abuses in the Confession, and asserted the catholicity of penitential satisfactions, the sacrifice of the Mass, the meriting of eternal life, and the authority of bishops to teach laws binding on conscience even when those laws cannot be found in Scripture. Melanchthon defended the Augsburg Confession in light of these criticisms, and published his defense as the *Apology for the Augsburg Confession* (see AUGSBURG CONFESSION, APOLOGY OF) in 1531. In the *Apology* Melanchthon for the first time teaches that both ordination and confession are sacraments, along with baptism and the Supper. Although these texts were both addressed to the Emperor in light of the Diet of Augsburg in 1530, they quickly became the foundational confessional texts of the Wittenberg reform movement.

The Augsburg Confession was submitted at the height of the disagreement between Luther and Zwingli concerning the presence of the body and blood of Christ in the bread and wine of the Eucharist. Zwingli taught that the bread and wine were the signs of the body and blood of Christ that referred us to his death out of gratitude for our redemption. Zwingli denied that the body and blood of Christ could be offered in or with the bread and wine, because his true human body is in heaven. Luther responded by claiming that the body and blood of Christ in the bread and wine are the sign that the promise of forgiveness applies to us personally. Because Christ is both divine and human in one person, his humanity is present wherever his divinity is present, especially where he offers his flesh and blood to us in his Word. The MARBURG COLLOQUY of 1539, at which Luther, Melanchthon, MARTIN BUCER, Zwingli, and Oecolampadius were all present, failed to overcome the different understandings of the Supper in Wittenberg and Zurich. As a consequence, the leaders of Zurich were not signatories of the Augsburg Confession, but were instead represented by Zwingli's *Account of Faith* at Augsburg, which never attained the status of a confessional document. Subsequent to Augsburg, Oecolampadius drafted his own confession that was edited by Myconius after his death in 1531, which was adopted by the city of Basel as the First Basel Confession of 1534. This confession set the tone for subsequent confessions of the Reformed tradition until the latter part of the sixteenth century: they were developed by emerging Reformed churches in various cities or territories, and represented their first public teaching of the major doctrines of faith upon their emergence as organized churches. Thus, two years after the First Basel Confession, both the Geneva Confession and the First HELVETIC CONFESSION emerged, representing the teaching of the pastors of Geneva and Zurich, respectively. The emergence of Reformed churches in France, Scotland, and the Netherlands led to the publication of the French Confession of 1559, the Scots Confession written by JOHN KNOX in 1560, and the BELGIC CONFESSION of 1561.

John Calvin had a hand in helping to draft the French Confession, and liked the fact that the Reformed allowed for a wide variety of local confessions, unlike the Lutherans, who insisted that no one could be in fellowship with them unless they had signed the Augsburg Confession. Calvin had in fact signed the Augsburg Confession in 1541, although it was the *Variata* of 1540 drafted by Melanchthon to incorporate the Wittenberg Concord of 1536 between Strasbourg and Wittenberg. The Concord taught that the body and blood are both represented and presented by the bread and wine. Calvin strove for the following decades to overcome the division between Zurich and Wittenberg by adopting the language of the Wittenberg Concord, and did in fact arrive at an agreement between the churches of Geneva and Zurich, the *Zurich Consensus* published in 1551. However, far from leading to a reconciliation between Zurich and Wittenberg, the *Zurich Consensus* was itself attacked by the Lutheran theologians Westphal and Heshusius as a betrayal of the Augsburg Confession, which even Melanchthon was suspected of betraying in his 1540 *Variata*. The Lutherans subsequently sought to purge the "Crypto-Calvinists" from their midst, leading to the adoption of the Formula of Concord of 1577, in which Luther's writings against Zwingli in 1527 were used to interpret Melanchthon's Augsburg Confession of 1530, along with the 1531 *Apology,* Luther's Small and Large Catechisms, Melanchthon's treatise on the power and primacy of the pope, and Luther's SMALKALDIC ARTICLES of 1537.

The controversy between the Lutherans and the Reformed over the Supper led to the adoption of Reformed theology by Frederick III of the Palatinate. Frederick obtained from HEINRICH BULLINGER his last will and testament for the church at Zurich, which became in Frederick's hands the Second Helvetic Confession of 1566. Like the Augsburg Confession, the Second Helvetic Confession makes the claim to teach catholic doctrine, over and against the more recent innovations of the Roman Church. This confession also reflects the *Zurich Consensus,* by teaching that we commune spiritually with the flesh and blood of Christ at the same time we eat and drink the bread and wine of the Supper. The Second Helvetic Confession is the closest thing the Reformed tradition has to the Augsburg Confession, as it rapidly became adopted by Reformed communities throughout eastern and western Europe, as well as in England and Scotland.

As this historical survey shows, the development of confessions of faith in the sixteenth century was necessitated by several factors all converging at once. First, there was the need to set forth truly catholic doctrine and practice, over against the more recent abuses of the Roman Church. Such an agenda is clearly reflected in both the Augsburg Confession and the Second Helvetic Confession. Both confessions establish their continuity not only with the prophets and apostles, but also with the fathers and the councils of the patristic period. The claim for catholicity was made even more urgent by the Council of Trent, which claimed to be a true ecumenical Council under the guidance of the Holy Spirit, thereby attempting to make the various reformation confessions appear to be schismatic and sectarian in nature. Second, there was the need to give an account of faith taught in various territories and cities when they first emerged as organized churches. This was the trajectory taken by all the Reformed confessions up until the Second Helvetic Confession: they were all seen to be the confession of faith of a particular church—French, Belgic, or Scots—in a particular place and time—Basel, Geneva, Zurich—that was nonetheless in communion with other churches in which the gospel was preached and the sacraments rightly administered. The Reformed explicitly resisted the attempt by the Lutherans to have the Augsburg Confession become the only confession of the reforming movement, and also resisted having any one of the locally generated confessions become binding on all churches in all times and places, although eventually this kind of role was assumed de facto by the Second Helvetic Confession. However, the emergence of two distinct evangelical confessional traditions was resisted all along the line by Melanchthon, Bucer, and Calvin, who ultimately failed in their attempts to unite the increasingly separated confessional camps. Finally there was the need to come to agreement regarding the essential heads of doctrine taught by a specific reforming community. This was the primary reason for the development of the Schleitheim Confession, and is one of the major impulses behind the Augsburg Confession and the many confessions of the Reformed tradition, culminating in the Second Helvetic Confession. The development of such confessions was often accompanied by the creation of catechisms as well, as in the case Luther's catechisms of 1529, the GENEVA CATECHISM of 1541, and the HEIDELBERG CATECHISM of 1561, making them important means for the propagation of evangelical faith in still other cities and territories.

In post-sixteenth century Protestantism, a number of confessions of faith were formulated to posit one's own belief over against that of competing churches. The driving force, in each instance, was the absence of an authoritative confession speaking to the controversial issues or the conviction that an existing confession needed to be modified.

In England, Calvinist sentiment is relfected in the WESTMINSTER CONFESSION OF 1647, and its accompanying catechism, which grew out of the Anglican-Puritan controversies of the late sixteenth and early seventeenth centuries. The Helvetic Consensus (Consensus Helveticus), of 1675, written by Johann Heinrich Heidegger and in use in Swiss Reformed churches until the middle of the eighteenth century, focused on several specific topics, such as the inspiration of the Bible (with the point that the Hebrew vowel marks were divinely inspired) and the various ramifications of the teaching of universal grace.

The Anabaptist-Mennonite tradition has, alongside the SCHLEITHEIM CONFESSION, the Dordrecht confession of 1632 as a major confessional document. The confession grew out of the attempt to unite the two divided branches of Dutch Mennonites, the Frisian and the Flemish

In the Baptist tradition, confessions have played a considerably more modest role in view of the insistence that the Bible itself should be the proper confession of faith.

Protestant confessions of the modern period are akin to the earlier Protestant confessions by their focus on specific issues. This holds true for the *The Fundamentals* articles, which were written in the late 19th and early 20th centuries in response to modernism and liberal theology. While never seen as a confession in the strict sense of the word, these articles summarized conservative (now beginning to be called "fundamentalist") faith. The BARMEN CONFESSION 1934 likewise spoke to the specific German situation created by the Nazi government support of the GERMAN CHRISTIANS. Church mergers also called for restatements of the faith in terms of both the theological background of the merging churches and the effort to state the Christian faith in contemporary terms. This holds true for the statement of faith of the UNITED CHURCH OF CHRIST, of 1959, which in turn was preceded by the Basis for Union of 1943. The independence movement of Protestant churches in former European colonies also challenged these churches to write confessions.

References and Further Reading

Primary Sources

Book of Confessions: Study Edition. Louisville, KY: Geneva Press, 1999.

Calvin, John. *Institutes of the Christian Religion, 1559.* Edited by John T. McNeill and translated by Ford Lewis Battles. vol. 1, book III, chapters iii–v, 592–684. Philadelphia: Westminster Press, 1960.

Canons and Decrees of the Council of Trent. Translated by H. J. Schroeder. Rockford, IL: Tan Books and Publishing, 1994.

Cochrane, Arthur. *Reformed Confessions on the Sixteenth Century.* Philadelphia: Westminster Press, 1966.

Kolb, Robert, and Timothy J. Wengert, eds. *The Book of Concord: the Confessions of the Evangelical Lutheran Church.* Minneapolis, MN: Fortress Press, 2000.

Lambert, Thomas A., and Isabella M. Watt, eds. *Registers of the Consistory of Geneva in the Time of Calvin.* Grand Rapids, MI: Wm. B. Eerdmans, 2000.

Leith, John H., ed. "Fourth Lateran Council (1215)." In *Creeds of the Churches*, 3d edition, 56–59. Atlanta, GA: John Knox Press, 1982.

Luther, Martin. "The Babylonian Captivity of the Christian Church, 1520." In *Three Treatises*, translated by A. T. W. Steinhauser. Philadelphia, PA: Fortress Press, 1970.

Melanchthon, Philip. *Loci communes, 1543.* Translated by J. A. O. Preus. St. Louis, MO: Concordia Publishing, 1992.

Noll, Mark A., ed. *Confessions and Catechisms of the Reformation.* Grand Rapids, MI: Baker Books, 1991.

The Schleitheim Confession. Translated and edited by John Howard Yoder. Scottdale, PA: Herald Press, 1977.

Secondary Sources

Kolb, Robert, and James A. Nestingen, eds. *Sources and Contexts for the Book of Concord.* Minneapolis, MN: Fortress Press, 2001.

Lualdi, Katherine Jackson, and Anne T. Thayer, eds. *Penitence in the Age of Reformations.* Aldershot, UK: Ashgate, 2000.

Rohls, Jan. *Reformed Confessions: Theology from Zurich to Barmen*, translated by John Hoffmeyer. Louisville, KY: Westminster John Knox Press, 1998.

Tentler, Thomas. *Sin and Confession on the Eve of the Reformation.* Princeton, NJ: Princeton University Press, 1977.

RANDALL C. ZACHMAN

CONFESSIONALIZATION

"Confessionalization" is a concept that was developed in German historiography in the late 1970s and early 1980s. This concept aims to provide a confessionally neutral perspective on the period between ca. 1550 and ca. 1650 by describing the development of the Lutheran, Calvinist, and Catholic churches within one interpretive framework. The concept has mostly been applied to the history of the Holy Roman Empire but attempts to interpret European history in the sixteenth and seventeenth centuries. The concept of confessionalization has been a fruitful research tool, but has also led to lively historiographical controversies.

The Historiographical Concept of Confessionalization

Traditionally historiography divided the sixteenth century in two halves, with the Protestant REFORMATION in the first half and the Catholic COUNTER-REFORMATION in the second half of the century. For the Protestant churches in the Holy Roman Empire, the terms "Lutheran orthodoxy" and "Second Reformation" (denoting the Calvinist Reformation after the first, or Lutheran Reformation) were also used. In the 1950s the German historian Ernst Walter Zeeden first suggested that all the major creeds developing out of medieval Christianity—that is, LUTHERANISM, CALVINISM, and Catholicism—started to build modern, clearly defined confessional churches during the second half of the sixteenth century. He called this process "confession-building."

Two scholars of the next generation, Heinz Schilling, who focused on Protestantism, and Wolfgang Reinhard, who focused on Catholicism, developed the concept of "confession-building" into the concept of "confessionalization."

This concept proceeds from the general observation that in the Middle Ages and in the early modern period, the religious and the secular, church and state, were closely intertwined. When medieval Christianity was broken up by the Reformation, this close connection between CHURCH AND STATE resulted in an equally close linkage between the process of confession-building and the process of state formation. According to Schilling and Reinhard, the principle *cuius regio, eius religio* ("whose territory, whose religion"), which was established in the Holy Roman Empire by the Peace of Augsburg in 1555, was afterward successfully enforced by the German princes in their territories, resulting in the establishment of unified confessional states.

All in all Schilling and Reinhard see confessionalization as a fundamental process in society and as a process of modernization with the following results: first, confessional homogenization of the population; second, the intensification of state formation (i.e., confessionalization as the first phase of ABSOLUTISM because the state gained control over the church); third, a general process of social disciplining resulting from the disciplining measures of church and state; fourth, the development of cultural and political identities in which the confessional factor played a key role. The concept of confessionalization thus sees the three confessional churches not from the point of view of their doctrinal differences but from a comparative perspective that stresses the "functional similarities" of the confessions, for instance, their contributions to the development of social control. The terms "Lutheran orthodoxy," "Second Reformation," and "Counter-Reformation" have therefore been replaced by "Lutheran/Calvinist/Catholic confessionalization."

Periodization of the Process of Confessionalization in the Holy Roman Empire

Schilling has developed a periodization of the process of confessionalization in the Holy Roman Empire between the Peace of Augsburg in 1555 and the Thirty Years' War. He defines the following phases:

- First, the "preparatory phase" of confessionalization from the late 1540s until the early 1570s. In this phase the Augsburg peace system was fully functioning, but Tridentine Catholicism and Calvinism entered the Empire and began to make the confessional situation more precarious. The first territorial princes, notably Frederick III of the Palatinate, converted to Calvinism.
- Second, the 1570s brought the "transition to confessional confrontation." After the conflicts within Lutheranism after MARTIN LUTHER's death in 1546, the Lutheran concord movement once again defined Lutheranism unambiguously through the BOOK OF CONCORD and the Formula of Concord. Lutheran ORTHODOXY was thus defined in clear contrast to Calvinism. Consequently Protestant princes were increasingly forced to chose between Lutheranism and Calvinism. In this phase Catholicism also became more dynamic because princes and prince bishops embraced the Tridentine decrees and introduced the Jesuits to their lands.
- Third, the "apogee of confessionalization" occurred between the 1580s and the 1620s. Several German princes became Calvinist during this phase and the concord movement was vibrant in Lutheran GERMANY. In Catholic territories Tridentine Catholicism was actively stopping Protestant inroads or fighting Protestant remains. All this took place against a political background that was increasingly characterized by conflicts on all levels of Imperial politics and a lacking will for compromise by a new generation of politicians. Even time became confessionalized in this period: When Pope Gregory introduced his calendar reform in 1582, Protestants in the Empire did not accept the new calendar until

1699 or 1700. (In ENGLAND the Gregorian calendar was introduced only in 1752.)

- Fourth, "the end of confessionalization under the conditions of war and on the basis of the Peace of Westphalia" began in the 1620s when people realized that confessional conflict led to destruction and devastation. As a result irenisms and new religious movements such as PIETISM were on the rise.

Methods of Confessionalization

Reinhard has identified seven methods or mechanisms of confessionalization that were used by church and state to establish confessional homogeneity.

1. *The establishment of "pure DOCTRINE" and its formulation in a CONFESSION of faith.* This meant distinguishing one confessional church from other churches and eliminating possible sources of confusion.
2. *The distribution and enforcement of these new norms* (for example, through confessional oaths and subscription). In this way, the religious orthodoxy of personnel in key positions—for instance, theologians, CLERGY, teachers, and secular officials—was to be ensured and "dissidents" were to be removed.
3. *Propaganda and censure.* This meant making use of the printing press for propaganda purposes on the one hand and preventing rival churches from using the printing press on the other hand. Although the propaganda weapon of scholars was controversial, THEOLOGY, CATECHISMS, and sermons were used to influence the masses.
4. *Internalization of the new norms through education.* By founding new educational institutions, especially universities, all confessional churches hoped to keep their flock from attending their rivals' institutions and to "indoctrinate" future generations.
5. *Disciplining the population.* Visitations and CHURCH DISCIPLINE were used to create a confessionally homogeneous population. The expulsion of confessional minorities also served as a means to this end.
6. *Rites and the control of participation in rites.* In view of the importance of rites for the coherence of the confessional group, participation in rites like BAPTISM and MARRIAGE was ensured through the keeping of registers. Rites that served as markers of confessional difference were cultivated in particular.
7. *Confessional regulation of language,* to which Reinhard refers, a field in which little research has been done so far. As an example he mentions the fact that Calvinists preferred names from the Old Testament, whereas saints' names were particularly appealing to Catholics, these in turn being forbidden in Geneva.

Controversies about the Concept of Confessionalization

From the beginning the concept of confessionalization has met with positive reception as well as strong criticism in historiography. The critique falls broadly within five different categories: (1) the discussion about the periodization of the confessionalization process; (2) the controversy about the neglect of the theological characteristics of the confessional churches; (3) macro-historical criticism of the concept of confessionalization as a fundamental process of society; (4) the critique of confessionalization as a modernization process; and (5) the debate about the "top-to-bottom approach" of the concept of confessionalization.

With regard to periodization, even Reinhard and Schilling are not in agreement. Whereas Schilling has proposed the periodization of confessionalization in Germany between 1555 and the Thirty Years' War explained above, Reinhard has extended the confessionalization process much further, starting with the AUGSBURG CONFESSION in 1530 and ending with the expulsion of the Salzburg Protestants in 1731–1732. As a consequence there have been discussions about an early or late periodization of the confessionalization process with Harm Klueting, for example, arguing for 1525 as the end of the Reformation as a popular movement and thus the beginning of confessionalization as a state-sponsored process. Other authors like Thomas Kaufmann have completely rejected the idea of a parallel development of the confessional churches, arguing that the importance of the Protestant Reformation as an upheaval in early modern society will be underestimated if the development of the three confessional churches is regarded as parallel.

Second, both Protestant and Catholic scholars, for example, Thomas Kaufmann and Walter Ziegler, have criticized the concept of confessionalization for ignoring the specific characteristics—the so-called *propria*—of the confessional churches in theology, piety, and spirituality as well as the question of theological truth. The treatment of religion in the concept of confessionalization has been described as "functional-reductionist": "functional" because the concept looks only at the function of religion within state and society and "reductionist" because the *propria* of the confessional churches are thus leveled.

Third, from the very beginning historians have doubted Schilling's and Reinhard's thesis that confessionalization was a fundamental process of society and have described phenomena and processes of the sixteenth and seventeenth centuries that existed independent of and uninfluenced by the process of confessionalization. Although acknowledging that religion was an important factor, historians like Winfried Schulze and Anton Schindling have identified more and more elements and developments in the age of confessionalization that were unconfessional or could not be confessionalized: Roman law and many aspects of matrimonial law, the Humanist republic of letters, the mystic-spiritual tradition, alchemy, and astrology.

Fourth, younger historians have criticized Reinhard's and Schilling's view of confessionalization as a modernization process. They see this particular aspect of the concept as an expression of the historiographical background of the 1970s, when German historiography proceeded on the assumption that there was a teleological process of social change, moving toward improved social and political structures. Luise Schorn-Schütte has stressed that, because this notion of modernization has been replaced in historiography by the idea of different potentials and aims of development coexisting simultaneously in history, the modernization aspect of the concept of confessionalization can no longer be maintained.

Fifth, younger historians have also expressed doubts about the close connection between confessionalization and state formation postulated by Reinhard and Schilling. This point of criticism impinges on the general debate about the relationship between macro- and micro-history, between societal history (German *Gesellschaftsgeschichte*) and cultural history (see CULTURE). From a micro-historical viewpoint as well as from the perspective of his research into the workings of church discipline in early modern Berne, Heinrich Richard Schmidt has severely criticized the etatistic focus of the concept of confessionalization. According to Schmidt, Reinhard and Schilling have overemphasized the role of the state in the process of confessionalization, thus interpreting it as a top-to-bottom process in which the common people appear as subjects who were controlled and disciplined by church and state. Although Schmidt does not deny that there were pressures toward confessionalization "from above," he argues that the process of confessionalization could be successful only if it fit in with the need for regulation within society. He does not see the state but the communities and groups in society as "actors" in the process of confessionalization and therefore postulates a view "from below." Similarly Marc For-

ster has drawn attention to the bishopric of Speyer, where the Catholic communities developed a Catholic identity "from below" without being influenced by Tridentine reform or confessionalization measures by the state.

The critique of the concept of confessionalization has thus shed a clear light on its more problematic aspects and "blind spots": first, the thesis of confessionalization being a fundamental process of society and a process of modernization has been falsified by historiography. Second, it seems clear that confessionalization can no longer be regarded as a successful process "from above," but that the concept has to be modified to allow for various attempts at confessionalization "from above" and "from below" within one political and geographical entity. Thus, conflict and resistance as major factors in the process of confessionalization have been brought into the forefront: conflicts between competing confessional churches on the one hand and forms of resistance "from below" against confessionalization, social disciplining, and early modern state-building "from above" on the other hand.

One of the fundamental questions connected with the critique of the concept of confessionalization is whether falsification in one or some points leads to a complete dismissal of the concept or whether it can still function as a useful research tool, in which modifications are discussed and accepted according to the case study to which the concept is applied. It is striking that, in spite of the criticism, the concept of confessionalization continues to inspire research and is no longer applied only to Germany, but has been discussed in relation to the confessional histories of the NETHERLANDS, ENGLAND, IRELAND, Bohemia, FRANCE, and Spain among others. It is to be expected that the historiographical interest in micro-history, the history of everyday life, and the new cultural history will lead to more research on the meaning of confessionalization for the lives and identities of the common people. Whatever the outcome of the discussion, it can already be said that the concept of confessionalization has given important impulses to historiography.

See also Catholic Reactions to Protestantism; Catholicism, Protestant Reactions

References and Further Reading

Bahlcke, Joachim, and Arno Strohmeyer, eds. *Konfessionalisierung in Ostmitteleuropa. Wirkungen des religiösen Wandels im 16. und 17. Jahrhundert in Staat, Gesellschaft und Kultur.* Stuttgart: Steiner, 1999.
Farr, James R., Wietse de Boer, and Allyson M. Poska. "Focal Point. Confessionalization and Social Discipline in France,

Italy, and Spain." *Archiv für Reformationsgeschichte/Archive for Reformation History* 94 (2003).

Forster, Marc R. *The Counter-Reformation in the Villages. Religion and Reform in the Bishopric of Speyer, 1560–1720.* Ithaca, NY/London: Cornell University Press, 1992.

Frieß, Peer, and Rolf Kießling, eds. *Konfessionalisierung und Region.* Konstanz: Universitätsverlag Konstanz, 1999.

Kaufmann, Thomas. "Die Konfessionalisierung von Kirche und Gesellschaft. Sammelbericht über eine Forschungsdebatte." *Theologische Literaturzeitung* 121 (1996): cols. 1008–1025 (part 1), cols. 1112–1121 (part 2).

Lotz-Heumann, Ute. *Die doppelte Konfessionalisierung in Irland. Konflikt und Koexistenz im 16. und in der ersten Hälfte des 17. Jahrhunderts.* Tübingen: Mohr Siebeck, 2000.

———. "The Concept of 'Confessionalization'. A Historiographical Paradigm in Dispute." *Memoria y Civilización. Anuario de Historia* 4 (2001): 93–114.

Reinhard, Wolfgang. "Reformation, Counter-Reformation, and the Early Modern State. A Reassessment." *Catholic Historical Review* 75 (1989): 383–404.

———, and Heinz Schilling, eds. *Die katholische Konfessionalisierung. Wissenschaftliches Symposion der Gesellschaft zur Herausgabe des Corpus Catholicorum und des Vereins für Reformationsgeschichte.* Gütersloh: Gütersloher Verlagshaus, 1995.

Rublack, Hans-Christoph, ed. *Die lutherische Konfessionalisierung in Deutschland. Wissenschaftliches Symposion des Vereins für Reformationsgeschichte 1988.* Gütersloh: Gütersloher Verlagshaus, 1992.

Schilling, Heinz, ed. *Die reformierte Konfessionalisierung in Deutschland—Das Problem der "Zweiten Reformation." Wissenschaftliches Symposion des Vereins für Reformationsgeschichte 1985.* Gütersloh: Gütersloher Verlagshaus, 1986.

———. "Confessionalization in the Empire. Religious and Societal Change in Germany between 1555 and 1620." In Schilling, Heinz. *Religion, Political Culture and the Emergence of Early Modern Society. Essays in German and Dutch History.* Leiden/New York/Cologne: Brill, 1992.

———. "Confessional Europe." In *Handbook of European History, 1400–1600. Late Middle Ages, Renaissance and Reformation,* edited by T. A. Brady Jr., H. A. Oberman, and J. D. Tracy, vol. 2, Visions, Programs and Outcomes. Leiden/New York/Cologne: Brill, 1995.

UTE LOTZ-HEUMANN

CONFIRMATION

Although the sixteenth-century Protestant reformers rejected confirmation as a sacrament, certain churches developed a rite called confirmation that retained some continuity with medieval Catholic sacramental practice. The CHURCH OF ENGLAND was the most conservative of the reforming groups in this regard. It is the one Protestant tradition that has had a rite called "confirmation" universally practiced from the sixteenth century to the twenty-first century. The rite of confirmation in the BOOK OF COMMON PRAYER of 1549 and 1552 included the imposition of hands and, like the Catholic sacrament, was administered only by the bishop (see BISHOPS AND EPISCOPACY). For all the sixteenth-century reformers, the need to provide cat-

echetical instruction to everyone, particularly children, was of much greater importance than the need for a liturgical rite of dubious origin and purpose (see CHILDHOOD). The pattern of catechetical instruction, examination of candidates in the basic tenets of the Christian faith by the CLERGY and/or LAITY, and a profession of faith and vows by the candidate became the prerequisites for admission to the LORD'S SUPPER in many Reformation traditions. Among the sixteenth-century reformers, MARTIN BUCER was the strongest proponent of an "evangelical" rite of confirmation, influencing its practice in ANGLICANISM and LUTHERANISM. His THEOLOGY and extensive writings on the topic grew out of his attempts to reconcile certain Anabaptists (see ANABAPTISM) with other Protestants and out of his deep concern for a proper and effective form of CHURCH DISCIPLINE. Due to Bucer's influence in some Lutheran regions of GERMANY, a public rite of confirmation that included the imposition of hands by the pastor served as the culmination of catechetical instruction for young adolescents and as the gateway that admitted them to the Lord's Supper.

Throughout the centuries since the REFORMATION, Protestant denominations that practice infant BAPTISM have developed rites that either marked the end of catechetical instruction or admitted one to the Lord's Supper or both. By the twentieth century in most Protestant denominations, these rites also included the imposition of hands by the pastor, were commonly (although not uniformly) called "confirmation," and had become important rituals in the lives of individual Christians and congregations. Theologically, the rite of confirmation has been understood in different and sometimes contradictory ways. PIETISM stressed the need for heartfelt CONVERSION and conviction in the CONFESSION of faith on the part of the confirmand. The ENLIGHTENMENT heightened the emphasis on the vows of the confirmands as the conscious decision of the autonomous individual. In the UNITED STATES, confirmation was often associated with membership in a particular denomination in contrast to baptism, through which one became a member of the universal church. In many parts of Europe and the United States in the eighteenth and nineteenth century, confirmation coincided with end of formal education and marked the youth's coming of age.

Most commonly, confirmation has been viewed by both lay Christians and theologians as the young person's affirmation or public declaration of faith and an opportunity to renew, ratify, or affirm promises made by godparents on behalf of the child at baptism. Until the latter decades of the twentieth century, the rite of confirmation had been linked to both baptism and the Lord's Supper. The connection to baptism came through the confession of faith that is part of the rite.

Confirmation and the Lord's Supper were linked, because confirmation traditionally served as the gateway to the Lord's Supper. Liturgical and patristic studies along with ecumenical dialogue and liturgical renewal in the latter half of the twentieth century affirmed the sacrament of baptism as *the* rite of initiation into full eucharistic fellowship in the church. This consensus called into question some aspects of the theology and practice of confirmation and, in some instances, has effected change in the practice of confirmation.

Origin, Development, Practice, and Theology of Confirmation up to the Reformation

Modern liturgical scholarship views the development of a separate rite of confirmation in the West as a disintegration of what was once a unified ritual of initiation that included baptism and anointing and the imposition of hands of the candidate by the bishop, and that then culminated in the newly baptized person's participation in the Lord's Supper. A number of factors contributed to the disintegration of this unified ritual into three independent rites, each of which would attain the status of sacrament in medieval theology. Most important among these factors were three developments: (1) the shift from adult to infant baptism, which was becoming the common practice by the end of the fifth century, and in which the priest rather than the bishop became the regular minister of baptism; (2) the continuation of the bishop as the proper minister for the postbaptismal ritual of anointing and imposition of hands, which developed into the sacrament of confirmation in the Western Christian tradition; and (3) the geographically large dioceses in most of Europe that prevented bishops from regularly participating in the baptismal rites of parishes.

By the twelfth century, the number of SACRAMENTS in the West had been fixed at seven: baptism, penance, confirmation, eucharist (Lord's Supper), MARRIAGE, ordination, and extreme unction. Because confirmation was administered by the bishop, there was no set age at which a person was confirmed. Rather, when a bishop visited a given locale, parents brought their children of all ages to be confirmed. Within the medieval Roman Catholic sacramental system, confirmation did not hold an important place in the lives of laity, and it was not associated with catechetical instruction or a person's first communion. The sacrament serving this latter function was penance. The unimportance of confirmation during the medieval period is illustrated through an account that extols one bishop for dismounting from his horse to confirm people. It seems that this practice placed him among a minority of bishops during this period.

According to medieval theologians, confirmation marked the person with an indelible character and therefore was unrepeatable; it completed baptism and conferred the Holy Spirit on the confirmand to strengthen the person for battle in the Christian life. The matter of the sacrament was the chrism, or perfumed oil, used in the anointing or signing, and the form of the sacrament was the words spoken by the bishop, "I sign you with the sign of the cross and I confirm you with the chrism of salvation, in the name of the Father, and of the Son, and of the Holy Spirit." The rite included prayers invoking the Holy Spirit, the signing on the forehead of the candidate with chrism by the bishop, and exhortations to the godparents to instruct their godchildren in good manners and works and to teach them the Apostles' Creed, the Lord's Prayer, and the Hail Mary. The imposition of hands that had been part of the unified initiation rite of the early CHURCH had evolved into a light blow on the candidate's cheek by the bishop and was interpreted as a ritual expression of the strife the person would face in living the Christian life.

This ritual and its theology were resoundingly rejected by all of the sixteenth-century Protestant reformers. First, the reformers limited the number of sacraments to those rites that clearly involved a New Testament witness of institution by Jesus Christ. Hence they concluded that only baptism and the Lord's Supper met this criterion and rejected Roman Catholic appeals to New Testament evidence for a separate rite of confirmation that used examples from the Acts of the Apostles involving the imposition of hands. Second, the reformers rejected it on the basis of Roman Catholic theology that described confirmation as the completion of baptism. The reformers viewed this claim as a denigration of baptism, which they sought to highlight and exalt in reaction against a medieval social structure that had elevated monastic life above that of the lay Christian. Third, the reformers rejected the use of chrism because of the magical quality with which it was invested by the laity. In place of superstition, the reformers sought to strengthen the faith of the laity through education in the basic doctrinal teachings of the Christian church.

Development of Evangelical Confirmation in the Sixteenth Century

MARTIN LUTHER and JOHN CALVIN both wrote disparagingly about the Roman Catholic sacrament of confirmation, with Luther calling it "mumbo jumbo" and "monkey business" and Calvin describing it as "a deceptive promise of the devil." While Luther and Calvin rejected the Roman Catholic sacrament and its ritual with chrism, they both found a basis for the custom of the imposition of hands in Scripture and in the practice of the ancient church. In his INSTITUTES OF THE CHRISTIAN RELIGION, Calvin suggested reviving the ancient practice in which the bishop examined the candidates in the catechism, their faith was approved, and they then received the imposition of hands. Luther proposed a similar process, carried out by the pastor, in a sermon in 1523. Yet the primary concern of most reformers was not the revision of a rite with this ritual gesture, but rather the instruction of the laity in the teachings of the church. After participating in the visitations of parishes in Saxony in 1528, Luther was so appalled by the ignorance of the faithful in the basics of Christian teaching that he wrote both his *Small Catechism* and *Large Catechism* in 1529. The former quickly became the standard for catechetical instruction of young Lutherans and is still used by Lutherans throughout the world. A host of other CAT-ECHISMS were produced by many reformers in their mother tongues, expressing each reformer's particular interpretation of the Christian FAITH. But it was Martin Bucer who not only wrote a catechism and advocated strongly for catechetical instruction, but also wrote extensively about and promoted a so-called "evangelical confirmation." His views on a rite of confirmation can be found in the following documents: *What We Should Believe About Infant Baptism According to God's Scripture* (1533); *Ziegenhainer Zuchtordnung* (Ziegenhain Discipline) and *Kasseler Kirchenordnung* (Kassel Church Order) (1539), church orders written after his successful compromise with Anabaptists in Hesse; *Hermann's Consultation* (1543), a document prepared by Bucer and PHILIPP MELANCHTHON for Archbishop Hermann of Cologne as part of a thwarted attempt to introduce Lutheran reforms there; *A Brief Summary of Christian Doctrine* (1548), written in opposition to the AUGSBURG INTERIM; *De Regno Christi* (1550), a proposed means of introducing the Reformation in ENGLAND; and *Censura* (1551), his critique of the 1549 English *Book of Common Prayer*.

Bucer's zeal on the subject stemmed from his defense of the practice of infant baptism along with his certainty that infants could not have faith. In 1538, Bucer was called to the territory of Hesse in Germany by the local ruler, Landgrave Philip (see PHILIP OF HESSE), to negotiate with a group of Anabaptists who had been arrested for their religious beliefs. In his theological debates with the Anabaptists, Bucer acknowledged the need for both formal religious education and a public rite of confirmation, in which persons baptized in infancy would make a public confession of faith and a vow of obedience to the church. His efforts at mediation between the ruling Lutherans and minority Anabaptists bore fruit, for about 200 Anabaptists joined the state church. In some

of his writings, Bucer also stressed that the profession of faith in the rite of confirmation involved more than just rote memorization of a catechism. To ensure the genuine nature of the confession of faith, Bucer insisted that those to be confirmed exhibit signs of the fruits of faith in their lives.

The basic components of the rite of confirmation advocated and outlined by Bucer in the two church orders of 1539 used in Hesse (*Ziegenhainer Zuchtordnung* and *Kasseler Kirchenordnung*) would become standard among Protestant denominations for youth who had been baptized as infants. The rite was preceded by instruction in the catechism and was administered when children had gained the Christian knowledge necessary to be admitted to the Lord's Supper. The children were examined in the basic tenets of the Christian faith by the pastor in the presence of the elders. The rite itself included a series of questions addressed to the candidate that were understood as the profession or confession of faith and included promises or vows to remain faithful and to be obedient to the church. These questions began with a recitation of the Apostles' Creed. The profession of faith by the candidates was followed by the imposition of hands by the pastor with a blessing invoking the Holy Spirit, and the rite concluded with prayers on behalf of the congregation for the newly confirmed. Thus this early form of the rite was linked to both baptism and the Lord's Supper. In many respects, it bore little resemblance to the Roman Catholic sacrament, which was not preceded by instruction in the faith, included no profession of faith, and was not the gateway to the Lord's Supper. The primary ritual action in the Roman Catholic sacrament—anointing the forehead with chrism—was replaced in the Protestant rite with the imposition of hands. However, theologically, the Roman Catholic sacrament was said to complete baptism and to confer the Holy Spirit. Although Protestant theology did not use the language of completion, it was understood that through the rite the candidates renewed or ratified their baptismal vows. In most rites, the words spoken with the imposition of hands invoked the Holy Spirit. Thus the Protestant rite of confirmation maintained continuity with the Roman Catholic sacrament through the association with baptism and with the giving of or strengthening by the Holy Spirit through the imposition of hands.

Rites of Confirmation or Affirmation of Baptism in Anglicanism, Lutheranism, Presbyterianism, and Methodism

As has already been noted, the Anglican communion is the one Protestant tradition that retained the bishop as the minister of confirmation. In other respects, the rite of confirmation in the revised *Book of Common Prayer* of 1552 was similar to that proposed by Bucer. It presumed instruction in the catechism before the rite; the 1549 *Book of Common Prayer* had placed the catechism before the rite to emphasize this connection, and subsequent revisions maintained this order and included directives for the days and times of catechetical instruction. Instruction and confirmation were required before one could receive the Lord's Supper, based on a rubric added at the end of the rite in the 1552 edition. The words spoken by the bishop with the imposition of hands asked God for the daily increase of the Holy Spirit in the candidate. Preceding the imposition of hands was a prayer for strengthening by the Holy Spirit and an increase in the sevenfold gifts of the Holy Spirit. In the 1662 *Book of Common Prayer*, confirmation was described as the ratification of the promises made by the godparents at baptism. In 1662, the rubric that required confirmation before receiving the Lord's Supper was amended to allow those who had received instruction and desired to be confirmed to come to the table. This change reflected the reality of situations in which the bishop served a large diocese and could not manage the required triennial visitation to all parishes. The rite of confirmation in the 1662 *Book of Common Prayer* and rubrics governing its administration were the standard throughout the worldwide Anglican community until the latter half of the twentieth century, when widespread liturgical experimentation began, followed by the adoption of distinct prayer books in individual provinces. The LAMBETH CONFERENCE of 1948 endorsed a set of proposals that in the case of adult baptism called for baptism and confirmation to be combined in a single service. This innovation was an attempt to show the unitive nature of baptism, confirmation, and the Lord's Supper as the complete and threefold process of initiation. The Lambeth Conference of 1968 directed each province to study baptism and confirmation and to consider one of two revisions in practice: (1) the separation of confirmation from admission to the Lord's Supper or (2) infant baptism and confirmation administered together. In the first model, younger children would be allowed to commune and confirmation would be deferred to young adulthood; in the second model, after instruction regarding the sacrament, young children would be admitted to the Lord's Supper. Since 1968, many provinces in the Anglican community have adopted a variety of practices based on the first of these two models, which breaks the long tradition of confirmation as the gateway to the Lord's Supper.

In the Lutheran tradition, through the influence of Martin Bucer, Philip Melanchthon, and Martin Chemnitz, some Lutheran regions introduced a rite of confirmation in the sixteenth century. However, in those areas where Lutherans objected strongly to the Leipzig Interim, an attempt to blend essential Lutheran doctrine with some Roman Catholic practices after the political and military defeat of Lutherans by Emperor Charles V, a different practice developed. This practice included instruction in the catechism and an examination of candidates in the basic teachings of the Christian faith before admittance to the Lord's Supper, but there was no public liturgical rite and the term "confirmation" was not used. Instead, this process was called "catechetical instruction" (*catechismus*), "confessional examination" (*beichtverhör*), or "communion of children" (*communiciren der kinder*). Throughout the sixteenth century and most of the seventeenth century, this practice was the norm in areas of Germany influenced by GNESIO-LUTHERANS and in all of the Scandinavian countries.

A public rite of confirmation among Lutherans was only gradually accepted through the influence of PHILIPP JAKOB SPENER and the spread of German Pietism in the seventeenth and eighteenth centuries. Spener also revised the goal of catechetical instruction. No longer was its aim the worthy reception of the Lord's Supper; rather, instruction in the catechism became an opportunity for conversion of the individual. This new focus for the instruction also influenced the liturgical rite so that the confession of faith and vows or promises to remain faithful were viewed in this light as a sign of one's personal conversion rather than as a confession of the faith of the church. Lutheran rites of confirmation maintained the connection to both baptism and the Lord's Supper until the latter decades of the twentieth century and generally included the components of Bucer's rite: instruction in the catechism before the rite, some form of examination of the candidate, the confession of faith and vows, and the imposition of hands by the pastor with an invocation of the Holy Spirit. Later rites also included vows or promises that bound the candidate to the teachings of the Lutheran Church and statements indicating that the confirmand was thereby a member of the Lutheran Church. Since the 1970s, some Lutheran denominations have, like Anglicans, separated first communion from confirmation.

The development of a rite of confirmation among English-speaking Presbyterians and Methodists, both with roots in ANGLICANISM, illustrates the power of Bucer's argument for a public rite of confirmation to ratify the baptismal promises made by godparents for infants (see PRESBYTERANISM; METHODISM). Presbyterians in the UNITED STATES, with roots in English PURITANISM, accepted the WESTMINSTER CONFESSION OF FAITH, the Larger and Shorter Catechisms, and a seventeenth-century Directory for Worship. In reaction against the Anglican practice, the word "confirmation" was not part of these documents, but the 1789 Directory for Worship for American Presbyterians included detailed instructions regarding instruction for children in the catechism and their examination by the session, or governing body of elders, before receiving the Lord's Supper. Because of Presbyterian suspicion toward set liturgical forms, there was no prescribed rite to mark this event. It was not until 1905 that the Presbyterian hymnal included rites corresponding to the prescriptions in the Directory for Worship and introduced the nomenclature "confirmation" with a rite titled "Order for the Confirmation of Baptismal Vows." In addition to questions about ratification of one's baptismal vows and the Lord's Supper, the rite included the imposition of hands with the same PRAYER for the increase of the Holy Spirit in the 1662 Anglican *Book of Common Prayer*. Throughout the twentieth century, subsequent hymnals alternately omitted and then reinstated the word "confirmation" from the title of the rite, indicating continued ambivalence regarding the use of the term while at the same time recognizing that the rite served an important purpose (see HYMNS AND HYMNALS). Like Anglicans and Lutherans, American Presbyterians since the 1970s have begun to admit younger children to the Lord's Supper before the rite of confirmation.

Methodism also began without a rite of confirmation. To regulate those who were permitted at the Lord's Supper, JOHN WESLEY instituted "communion tickets" issued to those who were genuinely seeking faith and the GRACE of God; instruction in the basic teachings of the Christian faith, a prerequisite for others before confirmation and admittance to the Lord's Supper, is absent from Methodism at this point. As American Methodism evolved from a movement into a denomination, rites for membership were introduced in the middle of the nineteenth century (see METHODISM, ENGLAND; METHODISM, NORTH AMERICA). By the twentieth century, the rite for membership, although not called "confirmation," bore a marked resemblance to a rite of confirmation. The rite for membership was preceded by instruction in the faith, the questions addressed to the candidates in the rite included a confession of faith and renewal of vows, and candidates received the imposition of hands by the pastor. Not until 1964 did the Methodist church introduce the word "confirmation" into the title of the rite. At that time and later, in *The United Methodist Hymnal* of 1989, the rite was not explicitly tied to admission to the Lord's Supper. Nevertheless, the tradition of confirmation preceding first communion has been the practice among Methodists in some areas. The hymnals from 1964 and 1989 both interpret the rite of

confirmation as a public profession of faith by those baptized in infancy.

Theological Debates and Unresolved Issues

Ecumenical dialogue (see ECUMENISM) and advances in liturgical studies in the twentieth century have sparked reflection on the meaning of confirmation within many denominations and have reshaped the theology and practice of confirmation throughout the Protestant world (see DIALOGUE, INTERCONFESSIONAL). Liturgical studies have made two important and related contributions. First, the early church pattern of instruction in the Christian faith of adults, followed by a unified complex of rituals that included baptism, anointment with chrism, imposition of hands along with the invocation of the Holy Spirit, and then immediate sharing with the faithful in the Lord's Supper, is viewed as exemplary. The Roman Catholic Church, with the adoption of the Rite of Christian Initiation for Adults (RCIA) following the Second Vatican Council (1962–1965), restored this model, and Protestant traditions have drawn on this pattern in their liturgical revisions. Second, increased knowledge and understanding of this early church pattern of initiation have led to an ecumenical consensus that baptism is *the* sacrament that joins a person to the church and the Body of Christ, and is all that is needed for participation in the Lord's Supper.

In the middle of the twentieth century, the Anglican theologian and liturgist Gregory Dix sparked debate over the meaning of confirmation in general and of the imposition of hands in the rite in particular. He argued that the New Testament showed evidence of a two-stage process of initiation—baptism into the death and resurrection of Christ and the pentecostal baptism of the Holy Spirit—both of which are necessary. On the basis of this interpretation of initiation in the New Testament, Dix further argued that the then-current practice of the Anglican Church was consistent with the New Testament, and that confirmation was the rite that conferred the Holy Spirit on the individual and completed baptism. While Dix convinced some with his argument, G. W. H. Lampe challenged Dix with his own study of New Testament and patristic evidence. Lampe concluded that New Testament evidence showed that the Holy Spirit was received in the single event of baptism. He also suggested that a ritual of anointing, which has pneumatic imagery, was better as part of the baptismal liturgy than in the rite of confirmation. His conclusions were supported by the work of J. D. C. Fisher, who traced the disintegration of the unified rite of initiation in the West. It was the work of Lampe and Fisher that first influenced Anglican liturgical revisions of the rite of baptism, which in turn impacted liturgical renewal in other Protestant denominations. By the beginning of the twenty-first century, nearly all main-line Protestant denominations had revised their baptismal rites to include a postbaptismal anointing with oil and/or imposition of hands with a prayer for the Holy Spirit. This change in baptismal rites raises the as-yet unanswered question: Why, then, should the church have another rite with the imposition of hands and prayer asking for the strengthening of Holy Spirit?

Ecumenical consensus in the late twentieth century that baptism was all that was necessary for the admission to the Lord's Supper called into question the connection between Protestant confirmation and first communion, an aspect of the rite that dates to the sixteenth century. In the latter decades of the twentieth century, Anglicans and Lutherans, denominations in which confirmation and first communion had been linked for centuries, separated first communion from confirmation and lowered the age for first communion. This change can also be traced to the influence of liturgical studies and ecumenical dialogue, as well as psychosocial studies of faith development. Liturgical studies had shown that in the West, the practice of communing infants immediately after baptism continued into the eleventh century. Ecumenical dialogue brought greater awareness of the practice of infant baptism in Orthodox communities (see ORTHODOXY, EASTERN). Finally, educators and pastoral theologians made the case that the faith of a Christian cannot be reduced to cognitive knowledge about Christian teaching. They argued that participation in the Lord's Supper, too often linked in the minds of laity as a reward for completion of an educational program, is itself a means through which a person's—even a young child's—faith can be strengthened. The severing of the connection between confirmation and first communion begs the question: Why, then, continue to practice the rite of confirmation?

The answer seems to lie in the rite's connection to baptism, especially in the confession of faith and promises or vows made by the person being confirmed. In the sixteenth century, the necessity for those baptized in infancy to make a public confession of their faith was at the core of Martin Bucer's arguments for a rite of confirmation. For Bucer, the confession of faith had to be more than recitation of knowledge learned in catechetical instruction. Spener emphasized the personal nature of the confession of faith as a sign of one's true conversion. In the twentieth century, for some Christians living under Communist rule, the rite of confirmation was countercultural, a personal and public pledge that stood in contrast to the atheistic youth dedication rites of the government. Since the Great Awakening (see AWAKENINGS), evangelical piety in American has resonated with language of confessing Jesus as one's personal Savior. The same language permeates the worldwide evangelical movement (see EVANGELICALISM). Such arguments, while illuminating the resilience of the rite of confirmation and its popular appeal among the laity, also pose new questions.

One serious objection that the sixteenth-century reformers had of Roman Catholic confirmation was that the bishop's action completed baptism. The reformers insisted that such language denigrated the dignity of baptism. How can Protestants of the twenty-first century avoid the notion that infant baptism is complete only by the action not of the bishop or any other minister of confirmation, but of the person's confession of faith at a later time? The ecumenical document *Baptism, Eucharist, and Ministry*, prepared by the WORLD COUNCIL OF CHURCHES in 1982, defined baptism as both a gift of God and humanity's response to that gift. Clearly, confirmation relates to the latter part of the meaning. Given its importance in terms of the rite of baptism in the lives of the laity within many denominations, does the rite of confirmation tip the balance too far toward the latter meaning and obscure the priority of the former? These issues are addressed in part through the current language of the rites, which commonly refer to the rite as an affirmation or reaffirmation of baptism rather than a renewal or ratification of baptism, and through rubrics that allow for and encourage multiple uses for the rite. These rubrics indicate that the rite should not be limited to one-time use by adolescents completing a course of Christian education. Rather, the twenty-first century rites affirming baptism can be used throughout a person's life, whenever one recognizes the grace of God active in his or her life.

References and Further Reading

Book of Common Prayer, 1662. http://www.eskimo.com/~lhowell/bcp1662 (May 12, 2003).

Browning, Robert L., and Roy A. Reed. *Models of Confirmation and Baptismal Affirmation*. Birmingham, AL: Religious Education Press, 1995.

Burnett, Amy Nelson. "Martin Bucer and the Anabaptist Context of Evangelical Confirmation." *Mennonite Quarterly Review* 68 no.1 (January 1994): 95–122.

Dix, Gregory. *The Theology of Confirmation in Relation to Baptism*. London: Dacre Press, 1950.

Fisher, J. D. C. *Christian Initiation: Baptism in the Medieval West*. London: SPCK, 1965.

———. *Christian Initiation: The Reformation Period*. London: SPCK, 1970.

Kavanagh, Aidan. *Confirmation: Origins and Reform*. New York: Pueblo, 1988.

Lamp, G. W. H. *The Seal of the Spirit*. London: SPCK, 1967.

Pauck, Wilhelm, ed. *Melanchthon and Bucer.* Library of Christian Classics 19. Philadelphia, PA: Westminster Press, 1969.

Repp, Arthur C. *Confirmation in the Lutheran Church.* St. Louis, MO: Concordia, 1964.

Sehling, Emil, ed. *Die Evangelischen Kirchenordnungen des XVI. Jahrhunderts.* Vol 3. Tübingen, Germany: J. C. B. Mohr, 1965.

Turner, Paul. *Sources of Confirmation From the Fathers Through the Reformers.* Collegeville, MN: The Liturgical Press, 1993.

World Council of Churches. *Baptism, Eucharist, and Ministry.* Geneva, Switzerland: World Council of Churches, 1982.

Wright, David F., ed. *Common Places of Martin Bucer.* The Courtenay Library of Reformation Classics 4. Appleford, UK: The Sutton Courtenay Press, 1972.

RHODA SCHULER

CONGREGATIONAL CHURCH OF ENGLAND

See Congregationalism

CONGREGATIONALISM

"Congregationalism" is an ECCLESIOLOGY and POLITY with roots in the earliest Christian Churches that found its initial denominational expression in Puritan and Separatist gatherings in sixteenth-century ENGLAND. Congregational churches are marked by the autonomy of the local congregation as an expression of Christ's immediate, not mediate, headship of that gathered fellowship of believers. For churches of this orientation, the polity takes precedence over confessional concerns, each church being formed through its own Church COVENANT. The churches do, however, understand the responsibility to and for other churches of the same polity. This mutual care found early expression in local associations in counties and colonies (referred to in Congregational polity as the "vicinage"), only much later finding a national expression that began to resemble a DENOMINATION.

Origin and Development

The churches of the Apostolic era, in practice if not principle, were local gatherings composed exclusively of people who believed in Jesus as the Christ. The Book of Acts and the Pauline epistles tell us something about the concern and care expressed by one church for another. Those bases remain the underpinnings of the Congregational churches.

Later with the practical necessity for clarifying the tenets of the Christian faith in the face of heretical deviation, the church became an organization composed of all the congregations and individuals who received the SACRAMENTS from properly vested CLERGY. Nonetheless the practice of believers gath-ered locally and with the full authority under Christ to determine their own affairs remained alive within the church through many of the religious orders and through free spiritual associations.

The REFORMATION brought renewed opportunity for this polity to find expression and permanence. Even before MARTIN LUTHER and JOHN CALVIN, John Wycliffe (1330–1384) had argued that it was both the duty and the right of the LAITY themselves to listen to the voice of God. The early Reformation polemic focused much on the AUTHORITY of the local congregation to order its own affairs. It was, however, in the milieu of the English Reformation that Congregationalism began to take shape in its modern sense.

Theologically ambivalent about the Protestant cause, King HENRY VIII began to initiate a period of religious change. Queen ELIZABETH I's settlement of religion (1559) did not satisfy, because of its moderate character, those who wanted more comprehensive reform and a "pure" church. The Puritans included those who sought both to change the CHURCH OF ENGLAND into a church based on congregational principles that was presbyterian in orientation, and those who came to believe that separation from the established church was the only viable path. Later, some Puritans argued that the church as an instrument and organ of the state—embracing all who resided within the parish, and served by incompetent and often immoral clergy—was a condition not to be tolerated (see PRESBYTERIANISM; PURITANISM).

Countless nonconforming Christians were imprisoned during Elizabeth's reign (see NONCONFORMITY). By at least 1567 a "separated Church" organized on congregational principles had been established in London under Richard Fitz. A few years later the first Congregational theorists, ROBERT BROWNE, began to write. Although he would eventually find himself back in the established church, he emerged from Cambridge University and became pastor at Norwich and an articulate voice for the developing Congregationalism. His most famous publication was the *Treatise of Reformation without tarrying for Anie* (1582).

John Robinson (1576–1625), also a Cambridge graduate with Norwich connections, was the critical connector between English Congregationalism and North America. In 1608, under severe pressure, Robinson's congregation from the village of Scrooby emigrated to Leyden, in Holland. Threatened by cultural absorption and pressed by economic need, many members of this church, but not Robinson, arranged to relocate in the New World and became the Pilgrims at Plymouth, Massachusetts (see PILGRIM FATHERS). Robinson also led in the development of Congregational theory, enhancing the concept of inter-church relatedness and opening the door to a view of accepting all faithful Christians in communion, regardless of denominational affiliation.

The Separatist settlement at Plymouth (1620), followed quickly by the Puritan settlements at Salem (1628) and Massachusetts Bay (1630), provided all that was required for a Congregational establishment in New England. The industry, commitment, and competence of these New England settlers and their progeny ensured that Congregational principles would not be ignored in an emerging and diverse nation.

Other early sources of Congregational growth, especially in the eighteenth century, were the English colonies throughout the world. This was particularly true of the English settlements in CANADA and AUSTRALIA, where the rugged frontier and the distance from the seat of the church necessitated a more independent way of thinking and doing. Early outreach to foreign areas was generated by the London Missionary Society (est. 1795) whose earliest efforts were indifferent as to whether the churches being founded would be Congregational, Episcopal, or Presbyterian but which soon became essentially Congregational. The American Church joined the missionary effort in 1810 with the founding of the AMERICAN BOARD OF COMMISSIONERS FOR FOREIGN MISSIONS with Asia as its initial field of service.

Congregationalists have been reluctant to embrace statements of faith that could be construed as confessional requirements imposed on autonomous churches and have remained suspicious of overarching ecclesiastical structure, although the historic creeds of the Christian Church have consistently been commended for whatever value is found in them. Congregationalists formally embraced the WESTMINSTER CONFESSION, apart from its Presbyterian polity, in the CAMBRIDGE PLATFORM in America, and the Savoy Declaration in ENGLAND. Theological openness has limited major departures on theological grounds to the formation of the Separate Baptist Churches in the mid-eighteenth century and the more substantive Unitarian departure in the nineteenth century (see UNITARIAN UNIVERSALIST ASSOCIATION).

Theological Contributions

Congregationalism stands in the Reformed theological tradition, along with the Presbyterians and BAPTISTS, among others. During the nineteenth century the theological position of Congregationalism became far less reliant on its Calvinist roots and increasingly liberal in theological orientation (see LIBERAL PROTESTANTISM AND LIBERALISM). From 1850 to 1950 Congregationalism, in both the UNITED STATES and Britain, produced a number of important thinkers such as HORACE BUSHNELL, NATHANIEL TAYLOR, WASHINGTON GLADDEN, PETER TAYLOR FORSYTH, R. W. DALE, C. H. DODD, and Albert Peel. The movement was also involved in the Liturgical Movement, especially through the work of Nathaniel Micklem and others in Britain. Because of its essentially nonsectarian stance, Congregationalism has been able to embrace a broad range of theological positions and provide a platform for creative dialogue.

Congregationalism's distinctive feature is its ecclesiology, which emphasizes the completeness of the local church under the "headship" of Christ. The local church is seen as the only true, or visible, representation of the church. The Cambridge Platform makes clear that while the "Catholick Church" exists it cannot, by its very nature, have officers or exercise the true function of a church. Only in the visible church is one able to discover the classical "marks" of the church: the Word rightly preached, the sacraments rightly administered, and discipline rightly applied (see CHURCH DISCIPLINE).

For Congregationalists the church is a gathered body of believers joined in COVENANT relationship. It has been fundamental to the Congregational Way that only those who could profess a belief in the Lordship of Christ could become members of a church. The emphasis on a "gathered" fellowship stems from early Continental Anabaptist influences (see ANABAPTISM). The Church Covenant idea, likewise, comes as a result of exposure to the Federal (Covenant) Theology of HEINRICH BULLINGER, JOHANNES COCCEJUS, and others. COVENANT THEOLOGY serves as the foundational approach for the Congregational way of church life. The church, as a body of believers gathered by a Church Covenant, is central to the Puritan/Federal theologies of WILLIAM AMES, John Owen, THOMAS HOOKER, and JOHN COTTON, for example. The covenantal nature of the church carries with it a certain voluntaristic emphasis in that a level of intentionality is required of the believer. This stress on the covenant relationship had an effect on the development of the political system, particularly in the United States.

The twin foci of Congregationalism have traditionally been described as the autonomy (or independence) of the local church and the fellowship of those churches with one another. The fellowship of the churches was envisioned as a means for mutual encouragement, counsel, and, to some extent, correction. The vehicles of interchurch fellowship have been, principally, the Ecclesiastical Council of the Vicinage and the various associations entered into by the churches.

The Vicinage Council appears to be unique to the Congregational tradition and flows out of the tradition of the gathered church in broader fellowship. The same direct headship of Christ that draws believers into a church binds churches of a like mind into relationship. Through the Vicinage Council the local church calls on its "sister" churches to send ministers and delegates to meet in council, to consider the matters at hand, and to offer advice. The matter under consideration can be church business, a dispute between a minister or other member and the church, or the ordination or installation of a candidate for the ministry. The Vicinage Council recognizes and honors the autonomy of the church that calls it into existence, and carries only the authority granted to it by the call. The inviting church may ask for advice, counsel, or judgment. In cases of ordination the Vicinage Council does not itself ordain because only the covenanted community can ordain "officers." Rather, it reviews the candidate and the process and "proceeds with" the church to the ordination. The Council's concurrence grants recognition to the ministry of the individual within the context of the broader fellowship. By conferring the "right hand of fellowship" (Galatians 2:9) it confirms and legitimates the action of the calling church. The Vicinage Council also serves as the primary means for granting recognition to a church seeking to become "Congregational."

The second vehicle of interchurch fellowship is the Association (although the Saybrook Articles in eighteenth-century Connecticut promoted the development of a quasi-Presbyterian system called the "consociation"). The Association provides, in some ways, a means for covenant communities to share in a broader covenant relationship. The earliest Association, formed in Massachusetts in 1633, was not of churches, but ministers. Various forms of Association developed over time, all designed to provide means for achieving the goal of interchurch relationships for mutual benefit. The nineteenth century, which saw so many advances for the Congregational movement, witnessed the first state association, begun in Maine in 1820, and the development of various national fellowships in Britain and the United States.

National Bodies

It is not until 1832 that a highly limited national expression is found in England in the Union of Congregational Churches and Ministers in England and Wales; and in America in the 1871 formation of the National Council of Congregational Churches. The essential ECUMENISM of Congregationalism has led, especially in the twentieth century, toward efforts for merger with other Protestant bodies. Successful mergers in the American experience include the merger with the Evangelical Protestant Churches (ca. 1925) and the General Convention of the Christian Church (1931). The major portion of Congregational Churches joined the UNITED CHURCH OF CHRIST that

was formed by merger of the General Synod of the EVANGELICAL AND REFORMED CHURCH and the General Council of Congregational Christian Churches (1957).

Congregational Churches for whom classical Congregational polity took precedence over desire for organic union joined with other continuing Congregationalists in the National Association of Congregational Christian Churches or the Conservative Congregational Christian Conference or became independent. The UNITED CHURCH OF CANADA embraces the Congregationalists, Presbyterians, and Methodists. Like their American counterparts, the churches in the United Kingdom are located in The United Reformed Church, whereas continuing churches find fellowship in the Congregational Federation in England, Union of Welsh Independents, and the Congregational Federation in Wales.

The International Congregational Fellowship was begun at a meeting in Chiselhurst, United Kingdom, in 1974. The International Congregational Fellowship is a nonrepresentative body consisting of Congregationalists from a broad range of nations, including Argentina, AUSTRALIA, BRAZIL, Bulgaria, Greece, Guyana, INDIA, INDONESIA, JAPAN, Kenya, KOREA, the Marshall Islands, Micronesia, PHILIPPINES, Rwanda, Samoa, SOUTH AFRICA, the United Kingdom, and the United States. The Fellowship meets every four years. Through its Theological Commission it produces a twice-yearly scholarly journal, *The International Congregational Journal*. The International Congregational Fellowship also has a youth movement, C-Way, which meets simultaneously with the Fellowship.

References and Further Reading

Atkins, Gaius Glenn, and Frederick L. Fagley. *History of American Congregationalism*. Boston: The Pilgrim Press, 1942.

Blake, S. L. *The Separates or Strict Congregationalists of New England*. Boston: The Pilgrim Press, 1902.

Dale, R. W. *History of English Congregationalism*. London: Hodder and Stoughton, 1907.

Dexter, Henry Martyn. *The Congregationalism of the Last Three Hundred Years As Seen in its Literature*. New York: Harper & Brothers, 1880.

Horton, Douglas. *Congregationalism, A Study in Church Polity*. London: Independent Press Ltd., 1952.

Kohl, Manfred Waldemar. *Congregationalism in America*. Oak Creek, WI: The Congregational Press, 1977.

Payne, Ernest A. *The Free Church Tradition in the Life of England*. London: SCM Press, 1951.

Peay, Steven A., and Lloyd M. Hall Jr., eds. *Congregationalism: The Church, Local and Universal*. Oak Creek, WI: The Congregational Press, 2001 (1954).

Rohr, John von. *The Shaping of American Congregationalism*. Cleveland, OH: The Pilgrim Press, 1992.

Routley, Erik. *The Story of Congregationalism*. London: Independent Press Ltd., 1961.

Walker, Williston. "A History of the Congregational Churches in the United States." In *The American Church History Series*. New York: The Christian Literature Co., 1894.

———. *The Creeds and Platforms of Congregationalism*. Cleveland, OH: United Church Press, 1991 (1893).

LLOYD M. HALL JR. AND STEVEN A. PEAY

CONSCIENTIOUS OBJECTION

Conscientious objection is the principled repudiation of war by individuals or groups. This position has been consistently represented in a small portion of Protestant tradition. The medieval church incorporated three strands of thought regarding war, which survived in one form or another at the beginning of the Protestant REFORMATION: the crusade, the just war, and nonresistance. Although the concept of crusade, or holy war, showed signs of reemergence during the wars of religious domination in the sixteenth and seventeenth centuries, for the most part Protestant theology leaned heavily toward a just war theory. Nonresistance resided in the radical sects of the time, from which emerged the triad of the historic peace churches, ANABAPTISTS, QUAKERS, and BRETHREN. From the two main traditions, nonresistance and just war, evolved the foundations for conscientious objection in modern time.

Nonresistance

Radical reformers in the sixteenth century primarily wanted a more pronounced break with the old church hierarchy than did the followers of MARTIN LUTHER or JOHN CALVIN. Some of these disparate groups gathered under Menno Simons and gave rise to the first historic peace church, Anabaptists (see ANABAPTISM). Nonresistance was but one of their agreed principles; others included BAPTISM of adults, separation of CHURCH AND STATE, separation from unbelievers, and refusal to swear an oath. Strict dispensationalists, they argued that the New Testament was a radical departure from the Old. Therefore, they found a new, overriding commandment in Jesus's command that they "turn the other cheek." However, the circumstances of their time also influenced other beliefs. Eschewing infant baptism and demanding rebaptism on joining their church, the Anabaptists became a threat to the established churches of the time. Under a realized threat of death from governments controlled by both Catholics and other Protestant groups, Anabaptists pulled away. Although Anabaptists affirmed that God created government and its police powers to control the ungodly, they firmly believed that as children of God they had no need for the government's police powers. Integrating this concept of a necessary and God-ordained division between church and state with their pacifist interpretations of the New Testament, the Anabaptists developed an innovative concept of nonresistance. Over time, Anabaptists split over issues of property and church discipline into MENNONITES, HUTTERITES, and AMISH, all of which have retained the basic precepts.

The next group, the Quakers (see FRIENDS, SOCIETY OF), emerged in England in the seventeenth century. Early Friends were followers of OLIVER CROMWELL; some even participated in his army. During the years of the Cromwell protectorate some radical reformers objected both to the refined theological arguments of the Puritans (see PURITANISM) and to the rituals of Catholics and Anglicans (see ANGLICANISM). They formed a new group, renouncing theologically trained preachers and relying on an inner light of the Holy Spirit to first convict and then give joy. When PACIFISM became a part of this mix is open to dispute. Certainly by the late seventeenth century it was a fundamental part of Quaker beliefs. Early Friends may not have relished doctrinal debates like the Puritans, but they did have biblical bases for their beliefs. Their pacifism, however, appears to have been founded on the concept of inner light, equality of humankind, and a realization that killing meant permanently extinguishing another person's inner light. Unlike Anabaptists, Quakers did not despair of the world, and so were more willing to participate in politics and to assume some "inner light" within others. Therefore, their view tended more to pacifism than nonresistance. Within short decades they moved to the New World and later onto continental Europe.

The Brethren (see BRETHREN, CHURCH OF), the last of the historic peace churches, appeared in the lower Germanic states at the beginning of the eighteenth century. Their roots in the Reformation can be traced to Radical Pietists (see PIETISM) and an established Anabaptist tradition. The source of their nonviolent stance is uncertain, although most would argue that Brethren base this on scripture. Few written records of early Brethren exist and much present analysis depends on contemporary Anabaptist accounts. Most argue that church leaders were heavily influenced by local Anabaptists, but that does not explain why they chose nonresistance.

All three of the peace churches migrated to the New World, so much so that by 1770 there were no Brethren left in Europe. Most found a welcome home in Pennsylvania by invitation of WILLIAM PENN, an English Quaker of influence. Penn's new land, founded on Quaker principles of forthright and egalitarian treatment of NATIVE AMERICANS, proved hospitable, although the immigration of settlers was open to all and eventually these plain people were outnumbered. Quakers withdrew from active participation in the government. By the time of the Revolution, Pennsylvania threw itself into the war, leaving these gentle people in an untenable position. Not only was the bearing of arms a problem, but so was the payment of taxes to a state at war. Nonresistant Brethren in particular came under suspicion by their neighbors as loyalists, which to some extent was true.

Some Mennonites and other smaller pacifist churches, such as the Molokans and Doukhobors, remained in Eastern Europe, although as conscription became reality in some of these countries the issue of conscientious objection surfaced. Many fled to other nations where they hoped to find a more friendly environment. Those coming to the United States were able to avoid the issue of conscientious objection until the southern states seceded. The CIVIL WAR produced particular problems for Quakers, whose creed forbade slave ownership (see SLAVERY; SLAVERY, ABOLITION OF). Over the preceding decades some Friends had become more actively involved in reform issues; to ignore the largest reform issue of the century was difficult. Some Quakers did join the Union army; others, however, along with Mennonites and Brethren, used the substitution provisions to avoid military service. Most of the peace churches merely felt relieved to have the option of substitution and did not worry about the issue of morality in buying one's way out of service.

Shortly thereafter a new millennialist church arose in the United States under CHARLES TAZE RUSSELL (see MILLENIALIST AND MILLENNIALISM). This new church, The Watchtower Bible and Tract Society or JEHOVAH'S WITNESSES, was neither pacifist nor nonresistant, for they fully planned and expected to fight at Armageddon, which they anticipated imminently. However, because of their belief in the innately corrupt nature of this world, they refused to cooperate with any government no matter how important or righteous the cause; they preferred to hasten the return of Jesus Christ by allowing events to take their course. Determining their position in a peace tradition became problematic for themselves and for outsiders, especially at the start of WORLD WAR I.

Not until the reinstitution of a draft in World War I did the peace churches have to confront the difficulty of adhering to nonresistance in conflict with a strong national government. The intervening period had been so peaceful that many of the church districts found that the new generation needed instruction as to why the churches chose nonresistance. Indeed, they also found that they needed to explain to the government and their neighbors the sincerity and reality of their beliefs. As patriotism hit a fever pitch in the United States, those not supporting the war effort found themselves called slackers, and at times painted yellow, or

tarred and feathered. Those not purchasing war bonds were ostracized at best, assaulted at worst. Nonresistance men, drafted into the army and promised alternative service, found an uncertain world with no rules or regulations for either the army, the government, or the nonresistant draftee. Treatment at camps varied, ranging from gentle persuasion to outright, unapologetic abuse. Accounts differ as to how many eventually took up arms, but the number was high. Others made some accommodation. Still others, absolutists, refused all participation, and many of these, especially Jehovah's Witnesses, ended up incarcerated at Fort Leavenworth .

Two decades later storm clouds rumbled over Europe; the historic peace churches took note and decided to actively seek change in federal policy. In 1940, in an unprecedented move, representatives of the historic peace churches and their offshoots met with President Franklin Roosevelt and then with representatives from the Selective Service Board in Washington, D.C., to present a plan for an alternative service. With the full support of the churches, the government, and the military, Civilian Public Service became a reality. By the end of the war these conscientious objectors were doing important work, often taking the place of drafted orderlies and nurses in mental hospitals, volunteering as guinea pigs for medical testing, and jumping forest fires. Many of the men began to question their roles, their lack of pay, and their hidden presence in the system, although groups like the Old Order Amish and the Hutterites liked the system. Jehovah's Witnesses, for the most part, simply refused even to participate in Civilian Public Service and went to prison.

Just War Adherents

The pre-Reformation originators of the just war theory—St. Ambrose and St. Augustine of Hippo—based their understanding of moral theology on the circumstances of their world. In simplest terms these theologians felt that a just war was one fought for a just cause, justly conducted by a Christian ruler, and aimed for a just peace. During the Reformation, Martin Luther, wrestling with similar circumstances, came to a similar conclusion. John Calvin took the theory a step further when he closely identified the church with a godly state. Within the next decades most Protestants adhered to the concept of just wars, leaving nonresistance to the radical wings.

As the nations of Europe shifted from wars of religion to wars of national conquest, few Protestants worried about the morality of war, only the immediate effects. With the start of the ENLIGHTENMENT in the eighteenth century, however, others began to question the wisdom of using war to solve disputes. In his advocacy of the supremacy of human reason, Voltaire noted with interest the Quakers in England as rational, peaceful individuals. Like many Enlightenment philosophers, Voltaire was a deist, and not Christian, and certainly not Protestant, although these arguments for reliance on reason and science to produce an improving world and belief in progressively improving civilization for human kind engendered calls for civil reform. These reform movements inevitably merged with Protestant churches in Europe and America. Reform issues actively supported by Protestant churches in this period included abolition, woman suffrage, social welfare, child labor, and pacifism. Utopian societies sprouted within secular and religious communities.

Emphasis on the perfectability of humankind, or at least improvement, created a fundamental change in the nature of Protestant denominations, moving away from salvation by FAITH to an emphasis on social responsibility; this shift culminated in the SOCIAL GOSPEL of the late nineteenth century. Protestant churches, however, did not limit themselves to their own nations, but moved outward across the world in missionary movements to save souls and improve social and cultural standards, according to their own views (see MISSIONS, MISSIONARY ORGANIZATIONS).

Reality made perfectability ephemeral. In the United States, secular and religious pacifists faced a moral dilemma in the Civil War because most who chose pacifism were also abolitionists. A similar dilemma in World War I frustrated not only pacifists in the United States, but also those in Europe. The British struggled with the intransigence of local pacifists; GERMANY resorted to putting them in mental hospitals. Caught up in war fever on both sides of the Atlantic, ministers blessed the war effort from their pulpits. After the war, in a general revulsion against the horrific events of a war to end all wars, a revival of the repugnance against all things military emerged in areas of Europe as well as the United States. WOODROW WILSON's vision of a League of Nations may have been a well-worn joke among diplomats in Paris, but the concept caught the imagination of intellectuals and ecclesiastica. Diplomats amended their views and signed a series of arms-reduction treaties in the 1920s, capped by an effort to outlaw war at the end of the decade. Protestant churches backed this new antiwar sensitivity, but the backing tended to be superficial only, espoused by elites with advanced university degrees and college students with a rosy view of their own generation. The Fellowship of Reconciliation, the Federal Council of Churches, and the Peace Pledge Union found a constituency in the 1920s and 1930s among ecumenical Protestant churches at the time on

both sides of the Atlantic. How much all of this fed into a growing isolationism in the United States is unclear, but isolationism appears to have been more prevalent at all levels of society than a nascent pacifism.

Events in Germany undermined this widely held Protestant belief in the progressively improving lot of humankind. Mainland European Protestant pacifists faced the issue faster than those in the United Kingdom, the dominion, or in the United States, but the realization came hard to many. REINHOLD NIEBUHR, originally a mainline Protestant pacifist, found the realism of Nazi Germany difficult to reconcile with a pacifism based on the assumption of the goodness of humankind. His shift toward a reinterpretation of the Augustinian position of the just war illustrates the intellectual evolution of many at the time.

Although there was initial reaction on both sides of the Atlantic to the war, and some participation in alternative military service by Protestant members of nonhistoric peace churches during the war, the relative numbers were surprisingly small, given the expressed support of a Christian or secular peace stance in the preceding decades. The war enjoyed wide support, but the events in Hiroshima shifted the dynamics once again. Although the start of the Cold War went largely unquestioned in the United States, the fervent Cold War mentality and actions created a backlash, unleashing the quiescent undercurrents of pacifism, although the foundations of this new pacifism had shifted. No longer did it depend on the assumption of the perfectability of humankind, but rather on the objection to certain wars, types of wars, and types of weaponry. The definition of a just war no longer centered on the leadership of church or state, but on the consciences of individuals.

In addition, this new pacifism among Protestants emerged not only along the traditional north Atlantic nexus, but in AFRICA and in the south Pacific. As colonies broke with their mother countries, Protestant churches established by colonial missionaries created their own identities. The definition of "just" reflected their unique circumstances. For instance, South African Protestant, non-Afrikaner churches, black and white, questioned a draft to support a government founded on the dishonorable structure of apartheid (see SOUTH AFRICA).

Throughout the world, the 1960s produced cultural and social changes within many societies. For the United States, the Vietnam War and civil rights efforts in the South engendered a cultural revolution reflected in a notable segment of society that was antiwar and pro–social justice. A typical slogan was "If you want peace, work for justice." This amalgam of social reform spilled into unexpected areas of the country. The historic peace churches that had always maintained the need for a separation from society began to debate among themselves involvement in wider social issues, if not outright participation in government. Mennonites and Brethren found antinuclear weaponry, antiwar, antidraft, and civil rights activism based on civil disobedience easy to support. Moreover, young church members found the alternative to military service disturbingly easy because it did not involve suffering or personal witness. Growing momentum within these churches toward a proactive stance threatened to split the conservative from progressive branches, although points of doctrine were also at issue—separation from the fundamentalist movements of the earlier part of the century. Yet the movement of the historic peace churches from nonresistance toward the newer forms of pacifism exhibited in mainline Protestant churches worldwide is noteworthy. Reevaluation of church/state relations remains problematic and is certainly premature. Passive acceptance of the state with firm traditions of noninvolvement appears to have mutated into a proactive self-view of witness in an evil world. The primary exception to this shift, however, remains the Jehovah's Witness groups worldwide, who maintain their old separation from other denominations and the state. They will not fight on behalf of any earthly, corrupt government, but wait expectantly for the imminent return of Christ, where they plan to fight at Armageddon. Not surprisingly, small numbers of the Jehovah's Witness were found in prisons as conscientious objectors in most of the old Soviet Union satellites at the collapse of communism.

References and Further Reading

Bainton, Roland H. *Christian Attitudes Toward War and Peace: A Historical Survey and Critical Re-evaluation.* New York: Abingdon Press, 1960.
Brock, Peter, and Nigel Young. *Pacifism in the Twentieth Century.* Toronto: University of Toronto Press, 1999.
Bush, Perry. *Two Kingdoms, Two Loyalties: Mennonite Pacifism in Modern America.* Baltimore: The Johns Hopkins University Press, 1998.
Duffy, Michael K. *Peacemaking Christians: the Future of Just Wars, Pacifism, and Nonviolent Resistance.* Kansas City, KS: Sheed & Ward, 1995.
Dyck, Harvey L., ed. *The Pacifist Impulse in Historical Perspective.* Toronto: University of Toronto Press, 1996.
Moskos, Charles C., and John Whiteclay Chambers II, eds. *The New Conscientious Objection: From Sacred to Secular Resistance.* New York: Oxford University Press, 1993.
Stoffer, Dale R. *Background and Development of Brethren Doctrines, 1650–1987.* Philadelphia: Brethren Encyclopedia, Inc., 1989.
Yoder, John Howard. *Christian Attitudes to War, Peace, and Revolution: A Companion to Bainton.* Elkhart, IN: Goshen Biblical Seminary, 1983.

DOROTHY O. PRATT

CONSERVATIVE BAPTIST ASSOCIATION

The association of about 1,200 congregations and 225,000 members was founded in Atlantic City, New Jersey, in 1947, mainly as a result of the fundamentalist–modernist controversy in the old Northern Baptist Convention (NBC, now the AMERICAN BAPTIST CHURCHES/USA).

In 1920, conservatives in the NBC founded the Fundamentalist Fellowship to stop the spread of theological liberalism throughout the denomination and to resist the growth of the NBC's centralized denominational bureaucracy (see FUNDAMENTALISM, LIBERAL PROTESTANTISM AND LIBERALISM). The fundamentalists focused their attention on the American Baptist Foreign Mission Society (ABFMS), whose "inclusive policy" of appointing both conservatives and liberals as missionaries they found especially worrisome. Conservatives objected to the society's using their contributions to support unorthodox missionaries and accused the ABFMS of being unresponsive to their complaints. To overturn this policy, the fundamentalists proposed that the NBC adopt a binding statement of faith that would necessarily drive liberals from the DENOMINATION. But they soon divided over the best way to achieve their goals. In 1923, militant fundamentalists withdrew from the Fundamentalist Fellowship to form the BAPTIST BIBLE UNION; but even its more aggressive approach failed to achieve success. In 1933, most of the militants withdrew from the NBC to establish a denomination of their own, the GENERAL ASSOCIATION OF REGULAR BAPTISTS.

The moderate fundamentalists remained in the NBC but were no more successful than the militants at influencing denominational direction. In the early 1940s, conservatives again mounted a campaign against the theological inclusiveness of the ABFMS, which continued to resist the conservatives' demands for tighter theological controls over missionary appointments. After decades of trying, the conservatives finally despaired of ever reforming the ABFMS and took steps to found the Conservative Baptist Foreign Mission Society (CBFMS) in 1943. Denominational leaders, fearing adverse financial consequences, resisted the conservatives' attempt to get the CBFMS recognized as one of the approved agencies of the NBC. In retaliation, conservatives withheld funds from the NBC, which in response changed denominational bylaws in 1946 to give voting rights in the annual convention only to contributing churches to the NBC. Thus outmaneuvered and excluded from denominational influence, about 200 congregations withdrew from the NBC and founded the Conservative Baptist Association of America (CBA) in 1947.

Over the next few years, hundreds of additional congregations joined the new CBA. In Arizona and Minnesota, Conservative Baptists gained control of the NBC-affiliated state Baptist conventions. Over the next few years, Conservative Baptists founded a number of other institutions. In 1950, they established the Conservative Baptist Home Missions Society and the Conservative Baptist Theological Seminary in Denver, Colorado. The seminary was founded after both the Northern Baptist Theological Seminary in Chicago and the Eastern Baptist Theological Seminary in Philadelphia, the NBC's most conservative SEMINARIES, refused to break ties with the Convention and join the new Conservative Baptist movement. A couple of years later, Conservative Baptists also recognized Western Baptist Theological Seminary, which was founded as an NBC seminary in 1927 in Portland, Oregon. In addition, over the years Conservative Baptists founded or approved a number of other educational institutions: Southwestern Bible College in Phoenix, International College in Hawaii, Northeastern Bible College in New Jersey, and the Seminary of the East in Pennsylvania.

Despite this proliferation of institutions, Conservative Baptists insisted on remaining organizationally decentralized. From the NBC's formation in 1908, many Baptists had opposed denominational centralization because it undercut the autonomy of the local churches and their freedom to pick and choose which Baptist agency or society that they wanted to support. Thus Conservative Baptists took care to keep their various societies and schools structurally and financially independent of one another. Each entity had its own board of directors, statement of faith, and fundraising strategies. Local congregations contributed to them as they saw fit. In this way, Conservative Baptists preferred independence over efficiency.

During the 1950s and 1960s, Conservative Baptists struggled over THEOLOGY and the issue of affiliations with groups outside their movement. Many Conservative Baptists were troubled that the doctrine of premillennialism was not affirmed in all of the statements of faith adopted by Conservative Baptist organizations. The Conservative Baptist Home Mission Society included premillennialism in its founding statement of faith, but the Foreign Missionary Society did not. The Conservative Baptist Theological Seminary's doctrinal statement contained premillennialism, but some Conservative Baptists complained that the statement was not explicitly *dispensational* premillenialism, a distinction that many Conservative Baptists thought should be required (see DISPENSATIONALISM). In addition to this theological dispute, Conservative Baptists argued over the propriety of Conservative Baptist churches affiliating with non-Conservative Baptist or-

ganizations. Some congregations in the movement maintained an official, but low-key relationship with the NBC, while others joined the new multidenominational NATIONAL ASSOCIATION OF EVANGELICALS. Many Conservative Baptists insisted on a more separatistic line that prohibited any association with those with whom there was not complete theological and denominational agreement. By the mid-1960s, several hundred separatistic Conservative Baptist congregations, mainly in the Midwest and Rocky Mountain region, withdrew to form the Fundamentalist Baptist Fellowship and other groups.

By 2000, the Conservative Baptist movement had undergone considerable change, though its overall number of churches and members had remained more or less static for decades. The CBFMS and the CBHMS changed their names to CBInternational and Mission to the Americas, respectively. In 1999 Conservative Baptist headquarters, which contained offices for the CBA and the two mission agencies, moved from Wheaton, Illinois, to Littleton, Colorado. The CBA is now organized into nine regions, whose leaders (directors) make up the CBA board. Despite early fears over centralized denominational structures, the CBA is now working to establish a sense of "denominational" loyalty and identity, and has developed the beginnings of mutual financial relationships by which the Conservative Baptist regions donate a percentage of their collections to the CBA and the CBA donates back a percentage of its collections to the regions. As with many other church organizations in the twenty-first century, the growing edge of the Conservative Baptist movement comes from new ethnic congregations as a result of recent immigration patterns in the United States.

See also Bible Colleges and Institutions

References and Further Reading

Finzel, Hans W., ed. *Partners Together: 50 Years of Global Impact, The CBFMS Story.* Wheaton, IL: CBFMS, 1993.
Shelley, Bruce L. *A History of Conservative Baptists.* Wheaton, IL: CB Press, 1971.

TIMOTHY P. WEBER

CONSISTORY

In Catholic usage, the word "consistory" refers to an assembly of cardinals presided over by the Pope called to ratify decisions of particular importance for the entire CHURCH, such as the selection of new cardinals. In Protestant usage, it came to mean a court called to make important decisions within a particular area controlled by a Protestant government. These decisions often dealt with problems of marriage, and in that respect Protestant consistories can be regarded as successors not to the Consistory in Rome but rather to the courts of Catholic bishops, which also spent much of their time handling problems of MARRIAGE, especially cases alleging breach of promise. The earliest consistories established in Saxony by MARTIN LUTHER and his associates had this as a primary function. In many Lutheran states, however, the Consistory developed into an administrative body appointed by the sovereign to supervise the church within his state. It inherited many of the powers exercised by bishops in areas that were Catholic.

A different model of the consistory developed in areas that adopted the Calvinist version of Protestantism. JOHN CALVIN emphasized the importance of discipline, on the responsibility of a Protestant church not only to establish correct belief, but also to require correct behavior (see CHURCH DISCIPLINE). To this end, when he was invited to take over supervision of the Reformed Church in Geneva, he insisted on the creation there of a new disciplinary institution called the Consistory, and actually drafted himself the ECCLESIASTICAL ORDINANCES that created it. The Consistory of Geneva was technically a committee of the local city government, made up of all the pastors on the city's payroll plus a dozen lay commissioners or "elders" selected for one-year terms in the elections in which that government was reconstituted every year. It summoned before it a high percentage (about one-fifteenth) of the entire adult population of the republic every year for questioning.

People were questioned not only on marriage and related morals problems, but also on survivals of Catholic practices, on displays of disrespect for government and church officials, and on quarrels within families or among business associates. In the area of marriage cases, the Consistory exercised the right to recommend DIVORCE with permission to remarry, a right not allowed in Catholic courts. The Consistory resolved many of these problems by itself, acting as a kind of compulsory counseling service. But it could refer behavior involving suspected violations of law to the city government for further examination and punishment. And it also claimed the right to levy sentences of excommunication, without any right of appeal to the councils governing the city, for people judged to be guilty of serious offenses who seemed unwilling to change. This claim was hotly challenged, but after an extended controversy, the Consistory won the uncontested right to use excommunication, and repeatedly did, asking for further penalties, including banishment, for people who did not display repentance sufficient to win back from the Consistory the right to receive Communion.

In every area into which CALVINISM spread, consistorial discipline went with it, and bodies modeled on the Geneva Consistory were created. In FRANCE they were called "consistories." In SCOTLAND they were called "kirk sessions." In the German community of Emden, the mother church for Dutch Calvinism, it was called the "presbyterium." Local circumstances, to be sure, led to considerable changes in the operations of these bodies. In France, where Protestants were at best tolerated but distrusted minorities, a consistory was created entirely within the Reformed community, often included deacons as well as pastors and elders within its membership, and usually spent more time in resolving quarrels than in administering discipline. In the NETHERLANDS, where Calvinist Protestants were a privileged minority, consistories were again voluntary associations depending on the consent of members without assured support from local governments to enforce decisions, and thus were hesitant to use excommunication. Only in Scotland, where the entire country adopted Calvinist Protestantism, did institutions fully resembling the Geneva Consistory take root. In almost every state in which Calvinism became important, however, discipline came to be highly valued, and some sort of institution was created to help maintain it.

References and Further Reading

Mentzer, Raymond A., ed. *Sin and the Calvinists: Morals Control and the Consistory in the Reformed Tradition.* Kirksville, MO: Sixteenth Century Publishers, 1994.

Lambert, Thomas A., and Isabella M. Watt, eds. *Registres du Consistoire de Geneve au Temps de Calvin.* Translated by Wallace McDonald. Geneva, Switzerland: Droz, 2000.

Die Kirchenratsprotokolle der Reformierten Gemeinde Emden (1557), edited by Heinz Schilling and Klaus-Dieter Schreiber, 2 vols. (1989, 1992), and the works there cited, a number of which, by Schilling, have been translated into English under the title *Calvinism* (1991).

Graham, Michael F. *The Uses of Reform: 'Godly Discipline' and Popular Behavior in Scotland and Beyond, 1560.* Leiden, Netherlands: E. J. Brill, 1996. ch. 9.

ROBERT M. KINGDON

CONSULTATION ON CHURCH UNION

The Consultation on Church Union (and also, for a time within that context, the Church of Christ Uniting) was known in the UNITED STATES by the acronym COCU. The project stemmed from a sermon preached in 1960 in Grace Cathedral, San Francisco, by EUGENE CARSON BLAKE, then stated clerk of the Presbyterian Church and later general secretary of the WORLD COUNCIL OF CHURCHES. The goal was "a church truly catholic, truly evangelical, and truly reformed." Participating denominations have included the AFRICAN METHODIST EPISCOPAL CHURCH, the AFRICAN METHODIST EPISCOPAL ZION CHURCH, the Christian Church (DISCIPLES OF CHRIST), the Christian Methodist Episcopal Church, the EPISCOPAL CHURCH, the International Council of Community Churches, the PRESBYTERIAN CHURCH (USA), the UNITED CHURCH OF CHRIST, and the UNITED METHODIST CHURCH.

COCU's first "plan of union," published in 1970, envisaged full institutional merger, but failed to win approval from the sponsoring bodies. Continuing discussions developed and refined a "theological consensus" (1984) that by 1989 had been accepted by the churches as an "expression in the matters with which it deals, of the apostolic faith, order, worship, and witness of the church." Meanwhile, the form of unity envisaged had shifted to a "covenant communion" that still claimed "organic" character while stopping short of the "organizational."

Difficulties remained, however, over questions of ministerial order, especially at the level of "oversight" or "episcopé." Presbyterians retained a historic suspicion of bishops, whereas Episcopalians were concerned to preserve a historic succession of them (see BISHOP AND EPISCOPACY).

COCU stagnated for much of the 1990s, but at the turn of the century seemed to perk up again. At its plenary meeting in 1999 (the first for ten years), a recommendation was issued that called on the denominations to declare by 2002 a mutual recognition as churches that would cover the apostolic faith (as "expressed in the Apostles' and Nicene Creeds"), BAPTISM (mutually recognized since 1978), ordained ministries (as "given by God as instruments of God's grace"), "celebration of the Eucharist together with intentional regularity," shared engagement in mission, and development of "structures of accountability, consultation, and decision making." The churches would work at finding by 2007 the means for a full reconciliation of ordained ministries such as would allow complete interchangeability of service between the denominations (see CLERGY). Integral to the entire process would be a pledge to "erase racism," particularly to "combat systematic white skin color privilege." More broadly, there would be a commitment to "oppose all marginalization and exclusion in church and society based on race, age, gender, forms of disability, sexual orientation, and class." The new relationship among the denominations would operate under the title of Churches Uniting in Christ.

References and Further Reading

Consultation on Church Union. *Churches in Covenant Communion: The Church of Christ Uniting.* Princeton, NJ: Consultation on Church Union, 1989.
Consultation on Church Union. *In Quest of a Church of Christ Uniting: An Emerging Theological Consensus,* rev. ed. Princeton, NJ: Consultation on Church Union, 1980.

"Consultation on Church Union," *Mid-Stream* 39 (January/April 2000).

GEOFFREY WAINWRIGHT

CONVENTICLES

The term "conventicles" refers to groups of Christians meeting privately to pray together and study the BIBLE. Conventicles are characterized by two basic criteria. First, they are attended by people with common religious practices, whose piety and the resulting *praxis pietatis* is significantly different from the way of religion usually practiced. Second, conventicles distance themselves in a critical, usually separatist manner from the official CHURCH recognized by the authorities.

Although the term did not yet exist in the sixteenth century, conventicles are initially linked in Protestantism with the radical wings of the REFORMATION. From the early BAPTISTS (CONRAD GREBEL in Zurich, from 1523), through the foundations of Christian core communities (JAKOB HUTTER in Mähren, from 1533) to the ecclesiologically new approaches of MENNO SIMONS, conventicles form the nuclei of new religious entities. In terms of theological history, the conventicles of English PURITANISM had a particularly significant impact. Although the early separatism of the Elizabethan period had become insignificant by the beginning of the seventeenth century, the need for a closer, voluntary community of like-minded believers continued to exist. Starting in 1616, Henry Jacob developed the model of a semiseparatist church in England, taking his example from the I Corinthians 14, which met with great popularity. The members of this church made a COVENANT with God and with each other characterized by particular religious convictions and a pointedly dedicated *praxis pietatis*.

English refugees in the NETHERLANDS introduced the body of Puritanic thought to the Reformed ORTHODOXY. With his reform movement *Nadere Reformatie*, the Dutchman Gisbert Voetius took up the Puritans demand for pious gatherings, which were termed "conventicles" in the Netherlands, for mutual strengthening and edification in FAITH. However, Voetius's reform movement continually stressed that these gatherings should always remain within the framework of the recognized state church. But Jean de Labadie, from Middelburg, the Netherlands, opposed this demand, and in 1669 made an exodus from "Babel," the state church, with his conventicle. This tension between the conventicles and the official church shaped the development of PIETISM and the revivalist movement in Europe (see REVIVALS). Whereas the recognized authorities of Pietism (PHILIPP JAKOB SPENER, AUGUST HERMANN FRANKE, and JOHANN ALBRECHT BENGEL) pleaded for the continued existence of the conventicles, by then mostly called *Collegia pietatis,* radical Pietists set up their conventicles as new communities of true believers. Of those who detached themselves from the recognized church, only NIKOLAUS LUDWIG VON ZINSENDORF's *Herrnhuter Brüdergemeine* (MORAVIAN CHURCH) gained recognition from the authorities in some territories. The exodus from the European Babel became a leitmotif of a large number of pietistic conventicles. In this context, and on the basis of the personal contacts of WILLIAM PENN to European conventicles, Pennsylvania became a preferred exile land and mission area.

References and Further Reading

Bellardi, Werner. *Die Vorstufen der Collegia pietatis bei Philipp Jakob Spener.* Breslau: 1930; reprint Gießen 1994.

Brecht, Martin, ed. *Geschichte des Pietismus: Der Pietismus vom siebzehnten bis zum frühen achtzehnten Jahrhundert.* vol. 1. Göttingen: Vanderhoeck & Ruprecht, 1993.

Gäbler, Ulrich, *Auferstehungszeit. Erweckungsprediger des 19. Jahrhunderts.* Munich: C. H. Beck, 1991.

Goertz, Hans-Jürgen, ed. *Radikale Reformatoren.* Munich: C. H. Beck, 1978.

ANDREAS MÜHLING

CONVERSION

The word *conversion* appears infrequently in the BIBLE, yet it is integrally related to such biblical concepts as repentance, regeneration, JUSTIFICATION, and being born anew. Conversion refers to the human turning to God that is the result of and response to divine GRACE. It is a radical turning in that it changes the very root and core of a person's life, marking a wholesale reversal of beliefs, values, and behavior, as well as a realignment of allegiances. In the Bible, conversion is a turning from SIN to the obedience God desires, from idolatry to the one true God, from darkness to light, from evil to the goodness of God. It means dying to self and rising again in Christ. Throughout church history, the nature and substance of this turning have often been debated, sparked by the question of where FAITH begins. Does faith originate within human beings as they experience a capacity for good works and then turn to God for help in attaining them? Or does it originate solely within the freedom and grace of the sovereign God to love the human family despite the fact that "all have sinned and fall short of the glory of God" (Romans 3:23)? Similarly, is conversion a one-time, unrepeatable, life-changing event that grows out of a soul-shaking crisis? Or is it a gradual, lifelong process that involves many turnings in the course of one's life? To address these questions, we turn first to the Bible and then to some of the major voices in the history of the church: Saint Augustine in the fourth century, JOHN CALVIN and MARTIN LUTHER in the sixteenth, and KARL BARTH in the twentieth.

Conversion in the Bible

The Hebrew word *shub,* meaning "to turn back" or "to return," is used in the Old Testament to denote the change of direction by which human beings turn away from sin and radically reorient their lives in the service of God. In the New Testament *epistrophe, metanoia,* and their cognates denote repentance and conversion, both of which involve the total "turning around" of human life. These words signify both a physical turning and a radical reorientation of one's inner self, emphasizing the totality of a person's life. The English word "conversion" comes from the Latin *conversio,* meaning "to turn around." Being converted is rather like making a U-turn.

In the Old Testament the turning involved in conversion is sometimes applied to God, who turns divine anger toward the Israelites in some instances and away from them in others (cf. Numbers 25:4; Joshua 7:26, 24:20). The predominant use of this idea, however, is its application to the nation of Israel. The prophets never tired of calling the Israelites to turn around—to repent and begin anew—in their relationship with God and neighbor. They were to turn away from their self-destructive fascination with foreign gods to the WORSHIP and service of the sovereign Lord who had freed them from the bonds of slavery and given them the promised land. The prophet Joel trumpets an oft-repeated prophetic theme: "Yet even now, says the Lord, return to me with all your heart, with fasting, with weeping, and with mourning; rend your hearts and not your clothing. Return to the Lord, your God, for he is gracious and merciful, slow to anger, and abounding in steadfast love, and relents from punishing" (Joel 2:12–13). Thus, turning to God is an act of human volition firmly rooted in the nature of God to be gracious and loving and merciful. So thoroughly committed was God to the Israelites' return that God promised through Ezekiel, "A new heart I will give you, and a new spirit I will put within you; and I will remove from your body the heart of stone and give you a heart of flesh. I will put my spirit within you, and make you follow my statutes and be careful to observe my ordinances" (Ezekiel 36:26–27). The picture that emerges is (1) conversion is the work of God; (2) it involves a total inner change born of the Spirit of God; and (3) not only the inner life is changed, but also one's behavior as God's statutes and ordinances are carefully followed (cf. Jeremiah 32:39–40).

Turning to the New Testament, Paul's Damascus road experience (Acts 9:1–27; cf. Acts 22:1–21, 26:9–23; Galatians 1:11–17; Philippians 3:2–11) is often regarded as the prime example of conversion in the Bible. Yet it has been effectively argued by Krister Stendahl that Paul was called rather than converted, and that Paul certainly did not undergo a change of religion commonly associated with the word "conversion." Indeed, Paul continued to serve the same God, but with a new mission—that of proclaiming the gospel to the Gentiles. The moment of divine call on the Damascus road, therefore, stood in clear continuity with his religious past, a religious past that was itself prologue to the Damascus road experience. To be sure, what happened en route to Damascus was a radical turning point in Paul's relationship with God, a relationship now centered in the person and work of Jesus Christ.

Jesus himself introduces the theme of conversion in the New Testament by announcing that the KINGDOM OF GOD has come near and, on this basis, all are called to turn to God. Jesus is likewise clear that turning to God involves the confession of sin and the conviction that God has acted decisively for the SALVATION of the world (cf. Mark 1:14–15; Matthew 3:2, 6, 8). Indeed, for Jesus such turning to God is the very fruit of God's benevolence.

The New Testament is replete with images of this fruit of God's dawning kingdom. At times it is the direct result of healing (cf. Acts 9:35), and at other times is descriptive of a person's radical reorientation to the attachments of this world (cf. Acts 14:15) signified in the death of the old self and rebirth in Jesus Christ (cf. Ephesians 4:22–24; Romans 6:6–8; Colossians 3:9–10). Conversion is also seen as turning "from darkness to light and from the power of Satan to God" (Acts 26:18; cf. Acts 26:20; II Timothy 2:25), and sometimes as God's universal purpose for all creation (cf. Acts 15:19—even the Gentiles are turning to God—Acts 17:30, 26:19–20; Matthew 28:19–20; Luke 24:47; II Peter 3:9). Throughout the New Testament, God's mercy in Jesus Christ is the decisive element in conversion. In fact, the wide and generous mercy of God is the only reason that human beings have the ability to make a U-turn with their lives (cf. Matthew 20:15; Romans 2:4; Luke 5:31–32), a U-turn that leads to nothing less than joy within God's own being (Luke 15:7, 10).

Yet the stab of conscience is also a crucial part of turning to God—remorse for sin, and the deep desire to pick up the pieces of one's life and begin again, confident that one is not forever held captive to past sins. Reminiscent of Joel 2, Jesus describes repentance in foreboding terms as personal sorrow for sin (cf. Matthew 11:20–21) and sounds a solemn warning of the inevitable judgment of God (cf. Matthew 3:10; Luke 13:3–5).

One of the most remarkable references, however, is Paul's claim that "when one turns to the Lord, the veil is removed" (II Corinthians 3:16), suggesting that human turning and the very self-revelation of God are bound up together. In fact, Paul goes so far as to say that only through the revelation of Jesus Christ was he able on that Damascus road to turn to God (cf. Galatians 12b).

The prophetic voice calling human beings to turn from idolatry is also present in the New Testament. Conversion is not just intellectual assent, but also loving and serving the one true God to the exclusion of all others. Nothing less than the total transformation of human life is what conversion means, and for a new creature in Christ there will be a new outlook on God and neighbor, and new ethical standards to uphold (cf. I Thessalonians 1:9; Hebrews 6:1).

Saint Augustine

The Protestant Reformers were greatly influenced by the writings of Augustine of Hippo (354–430 A.D.). Like Paul, Augustine experienced a dramatic turning point, yet it was neither sudden nor abrupt. In fact, Augustine had long struggled with the realities of faith over against a wantonly sensual life. One day, in the midst of this struggle, he overheard a child's voice across a garden wall saying, *tolle, lege; tolle lege*, meaning *take up and read; take up and read*; and he opened the Bible to Romans 13:13–14 and heard the Word of God address the demons within. Augustine understood this as a moment of divine grace flooding into his life. There was no merit on his part to pave the way, only grace; no accomplishment to his credit, only grace; no innate capacity for goodness, only grace. His turning to God was not the object of his will or desire. Instead, it came quite from outside himself and was supremely the gift of God's love in Jesus Christ.

Augustine insisted that original sin renders the human will incapable of turning to God, so conversion is totally a work of divine grace. In Adam and Eve all have sinned and are prisoners of rebellion, totally helpless to free themselves. The human will is not free of its own volition to choose God, so God breaks down the dividing wall of hostility by divine grace. To be sure, the human will is not obliterated but is completely dependent on the grace of God (cf. I Corinthians 15:10). For Augustine, however, the hinge of the whole affair is ELECTION. The debt of sin is forgiven by grace, but the giving of grace is determined by election. Furthermore, only by grace do human beings persevere in their turning to God.

One of the more significant debates in the history of the church took place between Augustine and Pelagius over these very issues. Pelagius believed that humans have the innate ability to choose what is good and then to act on their good choice. The human creature knows what God desires because of the commandments God has given. But more than that, God has also bestowed on human beings the freedom to choose whether to obey or disobey them. In other words, inherent within human beings is the free will to do good, the free will to turn to God on their own. Augustine believed that Pelagius's teaching was HERESY and accused him of elevating sinners to the position of coauthor of their own salvation. Although Augustine won the argument, some form of Pelagianism always has been alive and well within the CHURCH.

From Martin Luther to John Calvin to Later Evangelicalism

At the time of the Protestant REFORMATION, conversion often referred to the vocational calling to monastic life as distinct from the secular world. Martin Luther (1483–1546), believing that this erroneously established two classes of Christians, refused to accept any distinction between "secular" and "religious" Christians. He insisted that the total self-commitment expected of monks and nuns should also be expected of every believer. Conversion, therefore, denoted for Luther the lifelong pilgrimage to complete self-commitment to God. He spoke of conversion as an unrepeatable entrance into the Christian life through BAPTISM, but also as a repeatable event occasioned by penitence and the confession of sin. Being a lifelong pilgrimage conversion functioned for Luther as a continual participation in the divine grace given in Jesus Christ, so that each time a sinner confesses and is forgiven, he is said to be converted anew.

John Calvin (1509–1564) also believed conversion to be a lifelong process of regeneration begun in baptism, although like Augustine, Calvin emphatically insisted that everything depends on the grace of God given to the elect. Divine grace is indeed the origin of all human goodness—the unceasing theme of gratitude and joy that holds the Christian life together. Furthermore, the only hope of persevering in grace is that God personally bends, forms, and directs the human heart to righteousness, although the work of grace is begun only in the elect. If a right will, an inclination toward goodness, exists in a person, it is because of that person's election by God before the foundation of the world. Those who turn to God and are converted were chosen to do so by divine will. Notably, Calvin also uses the word *conversion* to describe repentance, suggesting that turning to God requires not just inner remorse but also putting off the old nature to become new creatures in Jesus Christ.

Like Luther, the turning of conversion requires the total transformation of human life both in outward works and in the soul itself.

Although Luther and Calvin were of one mind concerning the lifelong process of regeneration begun in baptism, later evangelical movements soon began to speak of conversion as a single watershed event after years of discretion are reached. PHILIPP JAKOB SPENER (1635–1705), often considered the father of PIETISM, believed—true to his Lutheran heritage—that regeneration occurs at baptism in infancy. Yet he also insisted that Christians must undergo a second regeneration, and the pietists came to speak of this second regeneration as conversion. On this basis, a double standard was established whereby true Christians were distinguished from ordinary church members. Spener further believed that people may often lapse from the state of grace, requiring additional conversions, a position much in contrast with Calvin's understanding of the perseverance of the saints.

The Wesleyan Movement (see WESLEYANISM) in England, largely influenced by German Pietists, was responsible for yet another significant departure from Luther and Calvin by dissociating regeneration from baptism. JOHN WESLEY (1703–1791) practiced the baptism of infants, yet insisted that infants could not be regenerated because regeneration must be a conscious, subjective experience. Over time the evangelical movements (see EVANGELICALISM) emphasized more and more the subjective consciousness until, for many, this became the central goal of religion. These movements understood that people cannot be said to be converted to the Christian faith until they have passed through such a subjective experience. The Calvinists believed that the certain knowledge of one's election and regeneration, although highly desirable, does not necessarily follow. However, the Wesleyans came to believe that one's subjective awareness of regeneration is essential to regeneration itself. If a person has not experienced and felt it, then it has not happened. These evangelical movements thus paved the way for FRIEDRICH SCHLEIERMACHER (1768–1834) to define THEOLOGY as a systematizing of the religious self-consciousness, which opened wide the door to a theological emphasis on having a conversion experience.

Karl Barth

The NEO-ORTHODOXY of Karl Barth (1886–1968) was a strong reaction against Schleiermacher and the emphasis on religious experience, and thereby returned to many of the central themes of Protestant theology espoused by Luther and Calvin. For example, Barth speaks of the total transformation of a person's life and will that is involved in turning to God, and he emphatically states that the revelation of God's love in Jesus Christ is the center of conversion, not what human beings feel through subjective experience. Barth insists that the real subject of Paul's turning is not Paul, but the living Christ who encounters Paul on the Damascus road. God reveals not a truth or a philosophical concept that gives meaning to life, but Jesus Christ. Divine revelation therefore is the only thing that makes it possible for a human being to turn to God and be reconciled (Galatians 1:12). The crux of the matter is this: Jesus personally met Paul on the road to Damascus; Jesus made him both a witness to and a servant of the living God. Did Paul make a decision? Of course he did. However, Barth says that Paul's was "a decision which can only follow that already made concerning him by Jesus. He knows only as one who is known by Him. This is why his knowledge has the power . . . radically to transform his life" (Barth 1961:198).

Open-ended Discussion

The church will always struggle with discordant views of what turning to God means. There remains a distinct tension between the Reformed view that places God at the center of conversion as an objective, redeeming presence, and the evangelical emphasis on a subjective conversion experience particularly after years of discretion are reached. Yet the voices that remain in the mainstream of the Protestant tradition are those that sustain the melodies of divine grace in ceaseless doxology for the love of God poured out on the cross.

References and Further Reading

Saint Augustine. *Confessions.* Translated by Henry Chadwick. Oxford: Oxford University Press, 1991.
"Saint Augustine: Four Anti-Pelgaian Writings." In *The Fathers of the Church, Volume 86.* Translated by John A. Mourant and William J. Collinge. Washington, D.C.: The Catholic University of America Press, 1992.
Baillie, John. *Baptism and Conversion.* New York: Charles Scribner's Sons, 1963.
Barth, Karl. *Church Dogmatics IV.3.* Edited by G. W. Bromiley and T. F. Torrance. Edinburgh: T. & T. Clark, 1961.
Calvin, John. *Institutes of the Christian Religion, II.3.6–14., II.5.9., III.3.5–6.* Edited by John T. McNeill. Translated by Ford Lewis Battles. Philadelphia: The Westminster Press, 1960.
James, William. *The Varieties of Religious Experience.* Garden City, NY: Image Books, 1978.
Kerr, Hugh T., and John M. Mulder, eds. *Famous Conversions.* Grand Rapids, MI: Wm. B. Eerdmans, 1983.
Stendahl, Krister. *Paul Among Jews and Gentiles and Other Essays.* Philadelphia, PA: Fortress Press, 1976.

STEPHEN W. PLUNKETT

COOK, THOMAS (1859–1912)

Methodist evangelist. Cook was born August 20, 1859 in Middlesborough, ENGLAND. Converted at 16 during a mission at the South Bank WM Chapel, he became a member of its mission band, leading cottage and open-air meetings. He conducted his first mission in Cumbria in 1879. Shortly after he received the blessing of entire SANCTIFICATION and offered himself for the Methodist ministry. This offer was declined but his talents were recognized by the secretary of the Home Mission Committee who appointed him to the post of lay evangelist in the Halifax and Bradford District. There his efforts were rewarded with tremendous successes. In 1882 he became a Methodist minister and was immediately appointed Connexional Evangelist, as Methodists responded to the opportunities demonstrated by James Caughey (1810–1891), Methodist revival preachers. In his first year over 5,000 adults and children were led to SALVATION through his missions.

Cook conducted many of these missions all over Britain and the world, to NORWAY (1886), SOUTH AFRICA (1892), AUSTRALIA, and Ceylon (1894–1895). He was particularly effective as an evangelist to young people, at schools and colleges, publishing *Full Salvation: A Talk to Undergraduates. A Book on Soul Saving Preaching* that stressed repentance to God and the offer of full and free salvation from SIN. Cook was associated with the Southport Convention (est. 1885), the Wesleyan Methodist expression of a renewed emphasis on holiness springing from a rediscovery of JOHN WESLEY's doctrine of Christian Perfection (see HOLINESS MOVEMENT). His book *New Testament Holiness* (1920) was a classic of its time.

His involvement in the Gospel Mission Care movement, with rural and seaside campaigns, made him a natural successor to Thomas Champness as superintendent of the *Joyful News Mission* in 1903. The establishment of Cliff College as a training center for lay evangelists in Derbyshire with Cook as first principal was the apex of a career cut short by his death on September 21, 1912.

See also Evangelism, Overview; Methodism, England; Wesleyan Methodism

References and Further Reading

Wood, A. S. *On Fire for God : Thomas Cook.* Ilkeston, UK: Moorleys, 1983.

TIM MACQUIBAN

COOKE, HENRY (1788–1868)

Irish Presbyterian church leader and political activist. Cooke was born on May 11, 1788, the son of a county

Londonderry tenant farmer. Educated for the Presbyterian ministry at Glasgow University, he emerged in the 1820s as the eloquent and relentless leader of a campaign against the theological and political liberalism that had characterized mainstream eighteenth-century Irish Presbyterianism.

The liberals, some of whom had become Anti-Trinitarian (see ANTI-TRINITARIANISM), rejected the theology of the Westminster formularies, statements that had been required for ordinands (candidates for ordination to the ministry). Politically, some liberals had been leaders in a movement to unite Irish people of all denominations to achieve radical political reform and Irish independence.

Cooke succeeded in persuading the Synod of Ulster, the governing body of mainstream Irish Presbyterianism, to reaffirm its trinitarian theology and establish a committee to test the ORTHODOXY of future ordinands. Seventeen ministers and their congregations withdrew to form a nonsubscribing synod, whereas the orthodox victory led to a union of the Synod of Ulster with the conservative Secession Synod to inaugurate the Presbyterian Church in Ireland, embracing 650,000 souls and characterized by Cooke's EVANGELICALISM and anti-Catholicism (see CATHOLICISM, PROTESTANT REACTIONS).

He was less successful politically. Most Irish Presbyterians remained Liberals in politics until Home Rule in 1886, and rejected his efforts to draw them closer to the episcopal Church of Ireland in a united Protestant front against resurgent Roman Catholicism, including his death-bed appeal in 1868 to Protestant electors to vote Tory and save the Church of Ireland from disestablishment. They did support him, however, in his unionism and his opposition to Daniel O'Connell's campaign to repeal Ireland's 1801 parliamentary union with Britain.

He published nothing of substance, although some of his sermons and speeches were printed.

References and Further Reading

Holmes, Finlay. *Henry Cooke.* Belfast: Christian Journals, 1981.
Porter, J. L. *Life and Times of Henry Cooke.* Belfast: William Mullan, 1875.

R. FINLAY HOLMES

COTTON, JOHN (1585–1652)

Puritan theologian. Cotton was an influential Puritan preacher-theologian in ENGLAND and, after 1633, in New England's Massachusetts Bay Colony. Born in Derby, England, he embraced PURITANISM during his studies (B.A. [1602]; M.A. [1606]; B.D. [1613]) at Cambridge University. He was a Lincolnshire vicar from 1612 until 1632, when he fled to the Bay Colony to avoid arrest for NONCONFORMITY. As Teacher of Boston's First Church, he played a prominent role in church and civic affairs. Practical considerations alone prevented his participation in the WESTMINISTER ASSEMBLY.

Commonplaces of CALVINISM after JOHN CALVIN and particularities of Puritan reform combine in his thought. He espoused COVENANT THEOLOGY, Predestinarianism, Ramist logic, and "plain style" PREACHING. The inward experience of the Holy Spirit was his signature theme. This emphasis led him to urge limiting church membership to those giving testimony of their CONVERSION experience. It sometimes sparked disputes with colleagues over DOCTRINE, including—in the proceedings against ANNE HUTCHINSON, his devoted follower—Cotton's apparent softness on ANTINOMIANISM.

Milk for Babes (1646), his children's CATECHISM, was widely used until 1700. His ecclesiology distinguished CONGREGATIONALISM (a term he popularized and perhaps coined) from separatist independency, which he considered anarchy. Its principles shaped the CAMBRIDGE PLATFORM (1648). Against ROGER WILLIAMS, he defended Puritan legislation restricting "religious liberty."

No "Cottonian school of theology" arose; no critical edition of his collected works exists. Yet his life and works have long been recognized as indispensable resources for studies of trans-Atlantic Puritanism.

References and Further Reading

Bush, Sargent, Jr. "John Cotton's Correspondence: A Census." *Early American Literature* 24 no. 2 (1989): 91–111.
Emerson, Everett. *John Cotton,* rev. ed. Boston: Twayne Publishers, G. K. Hall & Co., 1990.
Hall, David D., ed. *The Antinomian Controversy, 1636–1638: A Documentary History,* 2nd ed. Durham, NC: Duke University Press, 1990.
Ziff, Larzer. *The Career of John Cotton: Puritanism and the American Experience.* Princeton, NJ: Princeton University Press, 1962.
———, ed. *John Cotton on the Churches of New England.* Cambridge, MA: Harvard University Press, 1968.

JAMES O. DUKE

COUNTER-REFORMATION

The terms "Counter-Reformation" and its counterpart "Catholic Reform" or "Catholic Reformation" have long been employed to characterize Roman Catholicism during the early modern era. The terms represent divergent interpretations of early modern Catholicism, and define it largely in terms of its relationship to Protestantism (see CATHOLIC REACTIONS TO PROTESTANTISM). Recent scholarship has questioned their adequacy and suggested alternatives, without denying their usefulness.

"Counter-Reformation" was first used by the German Lutheran historian Johann Stephan Pütter in a publication of 1776. Generally it came to connote the view that the Catholic Church was progressively declining during the late Middle Ages until something had to happen, that is, the Protestant REFORMATION. Measures subsequently taken by the Catholic Church were seen as essentially responses to the challenge of MARTIN LUTHER and the Reformers, most of them defensive and intended to counter or suppress the Protestant movements. Without the Reformation, there would have been no Catholic reforms, it was argued. "Counter-Reformation" points especially to the repressive measures taken against Protestants, such as the foundation of the Roman Inquisition (1542) and the first papal Index of Prohibited Books (1554). It constitutes the attempt of the Council of Trent (1545–1563) to clarify the Catholic position on doctrines called into question by the Protestants, and thus its decrees, for example, on the relationship between Scripture and TRADITION, JUSTIFICATION, and the SACRAMENTS. Emphasized by "Counter-Reformation" are the political and military efforts of Catholic princes and ecclesiastics to hold off Protestantism or to restore Catholicism, such as the Spanish Armada launched against England by Philip II of Spain in 1588, and the campaigns of Catholic emperors forcibly to recatholicize large areas in the Austrian lands and Bohemia in the seventeenth century. The confessional militance of the Counter-Reformation appeared prominently in the religious wars in FRANCE (1562–1598) and in the Thirty Years War (1618–1648).

Catholic Reformation

The term "Catholic Reformation," although coined earlier, was introduced into general usage by the Protestant historian Wilhelm Maurenbecher in a publication of 1880. Along with "Catholic Reform," it was developed in response to "Counter-Reformation." It located the origins of the Catholic Reform in measures undertaken or attempted in the late Middle Ages, such as the Observant movement in many religious orders that called them back to a stricter observance of their rules, or the reform decrees issued for Spain by the National Council of Seville in 1478. It thus indicated a continuity between these and the more effective measures that followed the shock of the Protestant Reformation. Indeed, for some the term "Catholic Reform" implied the extreme position that the Catholic Church would have reformed itself from within even had there been no Protestant Reformation. The Catholic Reform included the reform decrees of the Council of Trent. These laid down norms for bishops and pastors of parishes, especially regarding their obligations of residence and of preaching, and they established the parish as the center of Catholic life. They outlined a program for the education and formation of parish priests, which required each diocese to establish its own seminary, and they dealt with many abuses regarding, for example, the veneration of images, indulgences, and other practices. Implementation was another matter, and it took place only gradually and to varying degrees in different areas. The foundation of new active religious orders of men and women, usually by charismatic individuals, was a major part of the Catholic Reform. Most significant was the Society of Jesus or Jesuits, founded by the Spaniard Ignatius Loyola and approved by the papacy in 1540. Among the foundations of women, who often faced considerable ecclesiastical opposition, the Ursulines stood out. Their founder was the Italian lay woman Angela Merici, and they received initial papal approbation in 1544. The Catholic Reform also resulted in a revived papacy, which peaked in the pontificate of Clement VIII (1592–1605) and, in the long run, in a greater centralization of the church.

Recent Developments

Most scholars today agree that both "Counter-Reformation" and "Catholic Reform" characterized early modern Catholicism while disagreeing about the precise weight to be accorded to each. For some the two terms taken together do not exhaust the reality. For example, one cannot easily include under either of these terms the far-reaching missionary activity in Asia, the Americas, and to a lesser degree AFRICA of the early modern Catholic Church, nor the flowering of mysticism in Saints Teresa of Avila or John of the Cross, nor the efflorescence of Baroque art. For this reason they prefer the bland but more comprehensive term "Early Modern Catholicism," while recognizing that the two traditional terms will continue to be used, and legitimately so, provided that one realizes that a part is being used to designate the whole.

Some recent scholarship has tended to evaluate more positively the state of the Catholic Church on the eve of the Reformation and so to make it more difficult to attribute the success of the Reformation to abuses within the church. This view would tend to see in the Reformation movements and in Early Modern Catholicism competing attempts to update Christianity to the changing world and religious aspirations of the sixteenth century. Similar to this is the approach that, although not denying the differences between Protestant and Catholic, emphasizes the parallels between the Protestant movements and developments within

Catholicism, such as frequent close association with the state, concern for education at all levels, a more individualist piety, and attempts to elaborate spiritualities for Christians living in the world.

References and Further Reading

Bireley, Robert. *The Refashioning of Catholicism, 1450–1700: A Reassessment of the Counter Reformation.* London: Macmillan and Washington, DC: Catholic University of America Press, 1999.

DeMolen, Richard L., ed. *Religious Orders of the Catholic Reformation.* New York: Fordham University Press, 1994.

Duffy, Eamon. *The Stripping of the Altars: Traditional Religion in England, c.1400–c.1580.* New Haven: Yale University Press, 1992.

Hsia, R. Po-Chia. *Social Discipline in the Reformation: Central Europe, 1550–1750.* London and New York: Routledge, 1989.

O'Malley, John W. *The First Jesuits.* Cambridge, MA: Harvard University Press, 1993.

———. *Trent and All That: Renaming Catholicism in the Early Modern Era.* Cambridge, MA: Harvard University Press, 2000.

Peters, Edward. *Inquisition*: Berkeley: University of California Press, 1989.

ROBERT BIRELEY

COVENANT

In Christian (and Jewish) theology, *covenant* refers to the special relationship between God and the elect. This relationship was voluntarily engaged in by God, first in Paradise and renewed (Genesis 3:15) after Adam and Eve had disobeyed God's commandment not to eat from the tree of knowledge. This renewal was couched in the form of a promise to Adam and Eve that from their seed would be born the one who would destroy Satan. Christians understand this as referring to Jesus, the promised redeemer whose death of atonement releases the descendants of Adam and Eve from the consequences of the sin of disobedience. Because God had given Adam and Eve the commandment not to eat from the tree of knowledge, the contractual aspect of covenant with its obligations by both parties—God giving the creation and Adam and Eve obeying the commandment—was stressed by the term *double covenant,* which was used in Reformed theology in the seventeenth century.

Covenant historians hold that Protestant covenantal theology derives from the works of MARTIN BUCER (1491–1551), JOHN CALVIN (1509–1564), and in particular from those of HEINRICH BULLINGER (1504–1575). Primarily because of the great Reformation debate concerning the place of good works—or obedience to God's law—in the process of salvation, the contractual as well as the promissory nature of God's covenant continued to be stressed. Because Protes-

tants emphasized the gratuitous (free) character of the covenant and the inability of humans to fulfill the requirement of obedience without the work of the Holy Spirit, they preferred to speak of the *covenant of grace:* God not only established the contract but also enabled a person to fulfill its terms. PHILIPP MELANCHTHON (1497–1560), MARTIN LUTHER's (1483–1546) collaborator, used the promise of the covenantal relationship in his *Loci communes* and in his expositions on the gospel of Matthew in the early 1520s, but HEINRICH BULLINGER composed the first Protestant elaboration of the doctrine of the covenant (Baker, "Heinrich Bullinger"). Covenant historians have treated the development of that doctrine as almost exclusively the work of theologians in the REFORMED CHURCHES and in PURITANISM (Weir 1983). These Reformed Churches are generally referred to as Calvinist. The development of covenantal theology from the beginning of the Christian Church to its Reformed definitions ending with KARL BARTH (1886–1968) is treated here with summaries of the ideas of the major theologians and a critical evaluation of seventeenth-century convenantal theories by Bertus Loonstra. Loonstra also refers to Jacob Arminius's alleged introduction of a covenant between God the Father and Jesus, the Son, but like other ideas of sixteenth- and seventeenth-century theologians taken from late medieval mystics, that pact was the subject of fifteenth-century mystery plays.

The denominational correctness that marks Protestant polemics of the sixteenth and seventeenth centuries still plagues modern church historians, who often underline differences in covenantal theology by insisting on the primacy of a favorite Reformer and his independent development, or trace most subsequent development back to Bullinger, its sixteenth-century fountain (cf. Visser, "Ursinus"). The historical studies listed in the references demonstrate that covenant was (and is) a flexible concept that occasioned frequent disagreements. For example Bullinger, Melanchthon, and his student, Zacharias Ursinus, apparently saw no difficulty in integrating God's covenant with the doctrine of God's ELECTION (Coenen 1963: 128–134). But the covenantal condition of obedience to God's law led to questions such as those raised by Arminians that God's PREDESTINATION (election) was also conditional and thus not, as proposed by Calvin and stressed by his followers, absolute and eternal. Some interpreters of Calvin have even argued that the doctrine of the covenant is absent from his theology, but these are in a minority (Lillback, "Conundrum"). In the sixteenth century, disagreements among Protestants had already led to increasingly precise definitions of doctrine. These generally were summed up in CONFESSIONS of territorial and national churches. These confessions often occasioned elaborate explanations in defense of a territorial Church's right to exist. An important example of this is afforded by the HEIDELBERG CATECHISM (HC), which began its life in 1563 as a confessional document establishing a purer reformation in the German palatinate. It was later adopted as an official document of the Reformed Churches at the SYNOD of Dordt in 1618. Its explanation was written by Zacharias Ursinus. He was a student and lifelong admirer of Philipp Melanchthon, a fact that is usually overlooked by Reformed scholars. Covenant historians see Ursinus as an important link between Bullinger and seventeenth-century covenant developments. Ursinus treated covenant in his explanation of Question 18 of the Heidelberg Catechism, which follows on the questions concerning Sin, God's wrath, and the believer's inability to achieve salvation. The covenant is integrated into the theology of redemption: "Covenant is so called because it is the promise of reconciliation and while we speak of the Old and New Testament, there is but one eternal covenant." This he repeats in his treatment of Gospel under Question 19, where he reproduces a play on the two Greek words *Eppangelia* and *evangelia*. These have different meanings that are often glossed over: *eppangelia* means the promise of a future redeemer, and *evangelia* (gospel) the teaching of the redeemer who is already there (Visser, "Ursinus"). Ursinus repeats the well-known usages for covenant and also discusses the chronological sequence of the covenant of creation (at the beginning of the world), the Mosaic covenant (the establishment of the Ten Commandments that replaced the moral law of nature), and the fulfilment of the law by Christ and the subsuming of the Ten Commandments in the two commandments of the Sermon on the Mount.

Antecedents

The covenantal relationship was always implicit in the writings of the fathers of the church, and occasionally received special attention in polemics against heretics. Those of the third-century Irenaeus of Lyon were edited by Erasmus and thus available to the sixteenth-century reformers. In the exegetical writings of medieval scholars, the covenantal idea was often presented by the metaphor of marriage, namely the marriage between God and the Church, for which such texts as John 3:29 and Ephesians 5:30 served as evidence. The marriage ring or wedding band (in French *alliance*, which is also French for covenant) was described by medieval mystics as the symbol of the indissoluble link between God and the believer. It reinforced the meaning of religion, which is derived from the Latin for "binding together." The idea came naturally to speakers of German, which translates "covenant" with the word "*bund.*" This marriage metaphor dominated the writings of mystics such as Wessel Gansfort (1419–1489) and can also be found in those of Erasmus and Protestant reformers. Martin Luther clearly drew on Wessel Gansfort in 1520 in his *On the Freedom of the Christian,* and Melanchthon often spoke of marriage as an image of Christ's relationship to the church. The metaphor was still important in Samuel Willard's lectures on the *Shorter [Westminster] Catechism* (Boston, 1725). The believer is reminded of this bond by the two sacraments of baptism and communion as signs of the covenant at work, namely the washing away of sin and atonement through the death of Christ.

The Covenant and Salvation History

The covenantal relationship also became a vehicle for interpreting salvation history (e.g., Melanchthon and Bullinger) by focusing on God's repeated restoration of the covenant in spite of the people's frequent disobedience. The Reformers often prefaced their discussions of the covenant with an exposition of synonyms used in the Bible and by the church fathers such as treaty, contract, testament, and promise. Melanchthon stressed the consolation implicit in God's voluntary covenant and preferred the word promise. *Foedus,* the Latin word for covenant, became the term of choice. It gave rise to *federal theology,* which received its fullest treatment in the work of JOHANNES COCCEIUS, a professor of theology at the University of Leiden. He had received his preparatory education in Bremen, Germany, where the Reformed doctrine of communion had been introduced by Albert Hardenberg (1510–1574), a friend of Melanchthon's, and further defined by Christopher Pezel (1539–1564), who had set himself the task of gathering and publishing Melanchthon's works and correspondence. It is not surprising, therefore, that Cocceius based his systematic covenantal theology not only on scriptural evidence of God's love acting in salvation history, but also on events in the life of the Christian Church. This too was an elaboration of existing ideas, for example of the theory of the ages of the church and the program of Lutheran historians to write a history of the church that focused on the witnesses to faith who represented the visible church of past centuries. This project is known as the *Magdeburg Centuries,* the history of the church published by MATTHIAS FLACIUS.

Later Developments

In the development of covenantal theology, the debate on obedience reflects the polemics against the antinomians, who proposed that because of the salvation through Christ, the works of Mosaic law were suspended. The Reformers stressed the need for obedience to the law, not because it helped one obtain salvation, but as an act of gratitude for that salvation and as a sign by which Christians were known (cf. Büsser, in Coenen 1963: 159–170). In covenantal theology, the requirements of the law, also referred to as works of gratitude (e.g., in the HC), were discussed as the *covenant of works,* that is, the human counterpart to God's *covenant of grace.* In English PURITANISM, in the desire of the strict Calvinists for a further (or second) Reformation, and especially in later PIETISM, the covenant of works led to a large volume of manuals for the Christian life (Von Rohr) or what LUTHERANISM had defined as *vocation* according to Matthew 20:16. The emphasis placed on obedience through works also gave rise to more polemics, for example those concerning the observance of the sabbath and what type of work was permitted on the Lord's day. Some authors referred to the Fourth Commandment as the fourth covenant (Visser). The covenantal dimension of the Ten Commandments also comes to the fore in the utopian *Christianopolis* (1619) by the strict Lutheran superintendent of Wurtemberg, Johann Valentin Andreae (1586–1654), who made them into the constitution of his ideal city. Once incorporated into the systematic theology of the leading Protestant churches, the covenant retained its importance in the explanation of God's special relationship to the believer. The subsequent commentaries on the Heidelberg Catechism with the *Handbuch* edited by Lothar Coenen at the quarcentenary (1963) of the HC may serve as examples. The ethical dimension of covenant theology that dominated Puritan writings also remains important, for example in the writings of Paul Ramsey, which he admitted he derived from Karl Barth (Werpehowski, "Christian Love"). Barth wrote that the gracious election to the covenantal community with Jesus Christ was the purpose of God's creation, thereby recalling the socioethical consequences of covenantal theology (Barth 1958: Vol. III, pt. 1, 96, 231). In the latter part of the twentieth century, the covenant was also seen as an ecumenical tool by the various denominations interested in opposing the spread of secular ideologies in the Southern Hemisphere and for dealing with cultural pluralism in general (Mount, "The Currency of Covenant"). The ecumenical development is rather a departure, for the biblical concept of the covenant for a chosen people was exclusive, even superior (Jospe, "Chosen People"). This view also became prevalent in Reformed circles (Gerstner, "The Thousand Generation Covenant") and is based on the covenant with Abraham (Genesis 17) and the New Testamental 1 Peter 2:9. It

played a role in the opposition of Scottish Presbyterians or Covenanters to King Charles I (1600–1649), who was an Anglican. They, in common with other reformed countries, saw the nation as a new Israel. The concept of a chosen people is also one of the roots of South Africa's system of apartheid (Smith, "Covenant and Ethics"). The ecumenical movement's use of a universal or inclusive covenant is the focus of a series of articles in the *Journal of Ecumenical Studies.* Eric Mount's review of covenant studies further reveals a continued debate on the role of covenant in political developments, in particular that of federalism including the American Revolution (Bullinger). Among these studies, that of Daniel Elazar has met with approval. He recognizes the distinction between God's covenant and covenants engaged in between communities of equals to obtain and/or preserve their liberties, but he stresses Reformed covenantal thought as the source for a revival of ancient federalist traditions. In the second half of the sixteenth century, when rulers engaged in war to restore Roman Catholicism, numerous writings were produced to justify resistance based on the duty to obey God before a ruler who imposes erroneous (i.e., Roman) forms of worship. The arguments of these writings are summed up in the *Vindiciae contra tyrannos* (1579), in which the right to resist is derived from Roman and medieval contract theory. Its anonymous author wrote of a "double contract" requiring the individual to obey his contract with God before obeying that between the individual and the ruler when that ruler demands actions contrary to God's commandments. Feudal law, notwithstanding the practice of subinfeudation, recognized the primacy of a vassal's obligations to his liege lord, who to the believer is God. The *Vindiciae* addresses political exigencies created by the Reformation that might place a Protestant citizen or group of citizens under a Catholic (heretical) ruler (Visser, "Junius").

References and Further Reading

Baker, J. Wayne. "Heinrich Bullinger, the Covenant and the Reformed Tradition in Retrospect." *Sixteenth Century Journal* 29 (1998): 359–376.

Barth, Karl. *Church Dogmatics.* Translated by G. W. Bromiley. Edinburgh: Clark, 1958.

Bullinger, Heinrich. "A Brief Exposition of the One and Eternal Testament or Covenant of God." Translated and edited by J. Wayne Baker. In *Fountainhead of Federalism. Heinrich Bullinger and the Covenantal Tradition.* J. Wayne Baker and Charles McCoy. Louisville, KY: John Knox Press, 1991.

Coenen, Lothar, ed. *Handbuch zum Heidelberger Catechismus* [Manual of the HC]. Neukirchen-Vluyn: Neukirchner Verlag, 1963.

Elazar, Daniel J. *Covenant and Commonwealth: From Christian Separation Through the Protestant Reformation.* (The

Covenant Tradition in Politics, Vol. II). New Brunswick, NJ: Publisher's Transactions. 1996.

Gerstner, Jonathan N. *The Thousand Generation Covenant: Dutch Reformed Theology and Group Identity in Colonial South Africa. 1652–1814.* Leiden: Brill, 1991.

Jospe, Raphael. "The Concept of a Chosen People: An Interpretation." *Judaism: A Quarterly Journal of Jewish Life and Thought* 43 (1994): 127–148.

Lillback, Peter A. "The Continuing Conundrum: Calvin and the Conditionality of the Covenant." *Calvin Theological Journal* 29 (1994): 22–74.

Loonstra, Bertus. *Verkiezing—Verzoening—Verbond. Beschrijving en beoordeling van de leer van het* pactum salutis *in de gereformeerde theologie.* [Election—Reconciliation—Covenant. A Description and Critique of the Doctrine of the *Pactum salutis* in the Theology of the Reformed Churches]. The Hague: Boekencentrum, 1990.

Mount, Eric Jr. "The Currency of Covenant." *The Annual of the Society of Christian Ethics* (1996): 295–310.

Rohr, John von. *The Covenant of Grace in Puritan Thought.* Atlanta: Scholars Press, 1986.

Smith, David J. "Covenant and Ethics—Comments from a South-African Perspective. The Utilization of Calvinist Metaphors in the Growth of Apartheid Mythology." *Annual of the Society of Christian Ethics* (1996): 265–282.

Visser, Derk. "Zacharias Ursinus. Melanchthons Geist im Heidelberg Katechismus" [Melanchthons Spirit in the HC]. In *Melanchthon in seinen Schülern* [Melanchthon in his Students]. Edited by Heinz Scheible. Wiesbaden: Harrasowitz, 1997. 373–390.

Visser, Derk. "Junius, the Author of the Vindiciae contra tyrannos?" *Tijdschrift voor Geschiedenis* 84 (1971): 510–521.

Visser, Hugo B. *De Geschiedenis van den Sabbatstrijd onder de Gereformeerden in de zeventiende eeuw* [The History of Sabbatarian Polemics Among the Reformed in the Seventeenth Century]. Utrecht: Kemink, 1939.

Weir, David A. *Foedus Naturale: The Origins of Federal Theology in Sixteenth-Century Reformed Thought.* Ph.D. dissertation, University of St. Andrews, 1983.

Werpehowski, William. "Christian Love and Covenant Faithfulness." *The Journal of Religious Ethics* 19 (1991): 103–131.

DERK VISSER

COVENANT THEOLOGY

This term normally designates a mode of THEOLOGY that emerged in the second half of the sixteenth century and flourished primarily among theologians of the Reformed, or Calvinist (see CALVINISM), tradition in GERMANY, SWITZERLAND, ENGLAND, and the New England colonies of North America. Its characteristic feature was the organization of a theological system around the idea of dual covenants between God and humanity. By the mid-seventeenth century, the covenant, or "federal," theology shaped a considerable body of Reformed thought about GRACE, ETHICS, SACRAMENTS, the CHURCH, and the state.

Covenant thought represented the Protestant attempt to construct theology from scripture alone, and its adherents took their cues especially from the Old Testament narratives of God's COVENANT with Abraham (Genesis 15) and David (2 Samuel 7), which accentuated God's unconditional grant of favor; the Sinai Covenant (Exodus 19–24), which promised favor on condition of obedience; Jeremiah's vision of a "new covenant" with Israel, inscribed in the heart; and the New Testament's linkage of the new covenant with the sacrificial death of Jesus. By 1561, proponents of covenant thought began to join these ideas to a notion that God covenanted with Adam before the fall, that Adam (as humanity's representative) failed to meet the covenant conditions, and that God graciously responded through a second covenant with Abraham. One aim of the covenant theology was to hold in tension an affirmation of both divine sovereignty and human responsibility.

The Dual Covenants

JOHN CALVIN (1509–1564) in Geneva and HULDRYCH ZWINGLI (1484–1531) in Zurich both used the idea of covenant to emphasize the continuity between the Old and New Testaments and to defend infant BAPTISM by virtue of its analogy with the circumcision that sealed the Abrahamic covenant. Zwingli's successor, JOHANN HEINRICH BULLINGER (1504–1575), also represented the covenant as the foundation of a Christian republic. But the typical features of the covenant theology found expression only when Zacharias Ursinus (1534–1583), a professor of dogmatic theology at the University of Heidelberg, emphasized in his *Catechesis, summa theologiae* (c. 1561) a distinction between a "covenant of nature" (*foedus naturale*) made with Adam before the fall on behalf of all humankind and a "covenant of grace" providing SALVATION for the elect. The covenant of nature required perfect moral obedience as the condition of eternal happiness, a condition that Adam failed to meet. The subsequent covenant of grace required only FAITH, which Ursinus viewed as a gift of divine grace. The distinction helped explain why humanity bore the guilt of Adam's sin, why men and women remained subject to the moral demands of the natural covenant even after Adam's fall, and why they could no longer attain salvation by obedience to it.

The classic European exposition was the *Summa doctrinae de foedere et testamento Dei* (1648) of the German theologian JOHANNES COCCEJUS (1603–1669), who taught at the universities of Franeker and Leyden in the NETHERLANDS. The covenantal idea reached England especially through the *Sacra Theologia* (1585) of the English Calvinist Dudley Fenner (1558?–1587), who sharpened the concept by defining the natural covenant as a covenant of works (*foedus operum*). The covenant of works still obligated Adam's heirs to moral obedience, but salvation came only through the covenant of grace. Through the influence of Fenner and the Puritan preacher WILLIAM PERKINS (1558–1602), the covenant theology guided English Puritan reform, and by the end of the sixteenth century some Puritan separatists envisioned the church as a local congregation that required an explicit covenant among its members (see PURITANISM).

Some historians restrict the meaning of "covenant theology" to theological systems organized by the dual covenants of works and grace. Others extend the meaning to include any early modern theological system that made extensive use of the covenant metaphor. Some interpret the language of conditionality in covenantal thought as a softening of the Calvinist doctrine of PREDESTINATION or ELECTION. Others point out, more accurately, that covenant theologians incorporated subtle distinctions that preserved the Reformed insistence that salvation was entirely a gift of sovereign grace to God's elect, chosen from eternity. They observe that the covenant between God and humanity was both conditional and absolute, imposing conditions for salvation and pledging God's fidelity to the faithful, but also making absolute promises of saving grace to the elect, who alone would have true faith.

Political Thought

Covenantal thought had political implications that became evident as early as 1534, when Heinrich Bullinger argued that civil laws were founded in the covenant. The HUGUENOTS who resisted the Catholic monarch in France, especially the author of the *Vindiciae contra tyrannos* (1579), sometimes argued that the covenant with God governed the covenant between king and people. The German jurist JOHANNES ALTHUSIUS (1557?–1638) contended in his *Politics* (1603) that political life rested on implicit covenants, grounded in the covenant with God and logically prior to civil law, that enhanced human flourishing in families, voluntary associations, ascending levels of political governance, and a sovereign commonwealth administered by princes. Covenantal ideas inspired the Scottish Presbyterians who signed a National Covenant (1638) to resist the Prayer Book imposed by King Charles I in England and a "Solemn League and Covenant" (1648) with the English Parliament during the CIVIL WAR. A few historians have contended that covenant thought flowed into eighteenth-century political federalism.

As early as the mid-seventeenth century, Protestants outside the Calvinist tradition made use of covenantal images, continuing to use them into the nineteenth century, especially in the widely accepted definition of sacraments as seals of the covenant of

grace. The twentieth century saw a recovery of covenantal thinking, evident in sources as diverse as the theology of KARL BARTH and the religious sociology of the American Robert Bellah, but the label "covenant theology" is best reserved for the early modern Reformed thinkers, who defined the covenants of works and grace as the organizing principle for theology and biblical interpretation.

See also Church and State, Overview; Congregationalism; Presbyterianism

References and Further Reading

Holifield, E. Brooks. *The Covenant Sealed: The Development of Puritan Sacramental Thought in Old and New England, 1570–1720*. New Haven, CT: Yale University Press, 1974.
McCoy, Charles S., and Wayne J. Baker. *Fountainhead of Federalism: Heinrich Bullinger and the Covenantal Tradition.* Louisville, KY: Westminster/John Knox, 1991.
Von Rohr, John. *The Covenant of Grace in Puritan Thought.* Atlanta, GA: Scholars Press, 1986.
Weir, David A. *The Origins of the Federal Theology in Sixteenth-Century Reformation Thought.* Oxford, UK: Clarendon Press, 1990.

E. BROOKS HOLIFIELD

COVERDALE, MILES (1488–1568)

English Bible translator and reformer. Born in 1488 in the north of ENGLAND, Coverdale died in London in 1568. Known primarily as the first translator of the entire BIBLE into English, Coverdale was ordained into the Roman Catholic priesthood in 1514, but by the early 1520s had embraced Lutheran precepts (see LUTHERANISM), attending meetings at the famous White Horse Tavern. When fellow White Horse frequenter ROBERT BARNES was charged with HERESY, Coverdale helped him mount a defense, and then fled to the continent to avoid arrest. While abroad he drew on German translations of the Bible and Apocrypha, the Zurich Bible, and WILLIAM TYNDALE's New Testament to produce the first complete English Bible. After the Bible was introduced in England in 1535 Coverdale put forth several subsequent editions, and also provided English translations for a number of MARTIN LUTHER's writings.

Named bishop of Exeter during Edward VI's reign, he was deprived of his title when the Catholic Queen Mary assumed power. Although never officially reinstated, Coverdale assisted at archbishop MATTHEW PARKER's consecration in 1559. Coverdale's growing support of PURITANISM came to light when he attended this ceremony without cope and miter. After Coverdale earned a Doctor of Divinity from Cambridge, Edmund Grindal assigned him a living in a London church. Further evidence of Coverdale's Puritan leanings emerged when he resigned that living in 1563 rather than conform to a strict observance of the LITURGY. He died five years later and was buried in St. Bartholomew's Church in London.

References and Further Reading

Primary Sources:

Coverdale, Miles. *Remains of Myles Coverdale.* Edited by Rev. George Pearson, The Parker Society, vol. 14. Cambridge: Cambridge University Press, 1844.
———. *Writings and Translations of Myles Coverdale.* Edited by Rev. George Pearson, The Parker Society, vol. 13. Cambridge: Cambridge University Press, 1846.

Secondary Source:

Mozley, J. F. *Coverdale and His Bible.* London: Lutterworth Press, 1953.

KAREN BRUHN

CRANMER, THOMAS (1489–1556)

Archbishop of Canterbury and compiler of the ANGLICAN BOOK OF COMMON PRAYER. The future archbishop of Canterbury was born in July 1489 into a family of minor Nottinghamshire gentry, the son of Thomas Cranmer of Aslocton and his wife Agnes Hatfield. An uninspiring elementary education either at the hands of the parish priest or of a private tutor was followed by a period at grammar school, of which he later had dire memories. His father died in 1501, when he was twelve, and his elder brother John inherited the modest estate. Agnes decided to seek a career for her younger son and, perhaps detecting an ability that no one else had noticed, entered him at Jesus College, Cambridge, in 1503. A century later this would have been a normal rite of passage for a young gentleman, but that was not so when Cranmer was young, and it clearly signaled ecclesiastical ambitions. However, there was nothing brilliant about young Thomas, who plugged away at the arts curriculum for eight years before taking an undistinguished degree in 1511.

In 1514, at the age of twenty-five, Cranmer had received an M.A. degree. Dull as he may have found the formal curriculum, his intellectual curiosity was aroused by humanists such as Erasmus and Faber, whose influence was growing in the university during those years. Cranmer became a good classical Latinist, and began to study Greek and Hebrew. At about the time of his second graduation, Jesus College elected him to a fellowship, which was not a mark of distinction, but indicated a recognized commitment to academic life. However, shortly afterward he did something highly unconventional—he got married. This offended against no law, given that he was not in orders, but because college fellowships were designed for those intending to be ordained, he resigned in 1516. This episode later loomed large in the folklore of the English REFORMATION, but in fact it was brief and tragic. His wife's name was Joan, and they lived together at the Dolphin Inn, a circumstance that caused his enemies to claim that she was a barmaid. In fact she seems to have been of suitable status for a man in his position, and during their brief marriage he supported himself as reader at Buckingham College, which had no rule of celibacy. A year later Joan died in childbirth, taking their child with her.

We do not know how he took this blow, but his reaction was to return to his original career rather than to seek another wife. Very exceptionally, Jesus College then reelected him to his fellowship, indicating that he had become a valuable member of the college community. In about 1520 he was ordained a priest, and in 1521 received his bachelor of divinity degree. By this time he was over thirty, several heads of colleges were younger, and he showed no particular ambition. In 1525 he became reader in divinity, having rejected an invitation to move to Oxford as a founding fellow of Cardinal College, and in 1526 achieved the doctor of divinity degree. By this time he was noted in the university as a follower of the "new learning," and as an examiner was very strict in his insistence on biblical knowledge. This made him unpopular with some of his more conservative colleagues, but there was no suggestion that he was considered unorthodox.

By 1527 this relatively obscure don was beginning to get involved in high politics. Probably the initiative came from Cardinal Wolsey (1475–1530), who had recognized his abilities two years earlier. He did not leave Cambridge but began to travel to London for consultations about KING HENRY VIII'S matrimonial problems (which required experts in both theology and canon law) and even undertook some minor diplomatic missions. Clergy of his background were often used in this way, but Cranmer was unusual in that he held no benefice, and his only administrative experience was as proctor's auditor. However, these developments help to explain why he left the university in 1529 to work full time on the king's problem.

What had happened was that Henry was getting nowhere with his canon law case and was switching to scripture-based theology, on which Cranmer was an expert. In October 1529 he was summoned to see the king and left with instructions to prepare a treatise on the matter. He entered the service of the Earl of Wiltshire (Anne Boleyn's father) and took up residence at Durham House. The work that he wrote in response to this order does not survive, but we know that the king was pleased with it. In January 1530 he sent his new specialist advisor to Rome in a futile attempt to persuade Pope Clement VII to allow a public discussion of his "Great Matter."

What Cranmer did achieve during the months that he stayed in Rome was, however, almost as useful and a remarkable feat for so inexperienced an envoy. He obtained favorable judgments, or *censurae,* from several Italian universities and papal permission for these judgments to be published. This course was not his idea, but he was the most successful of the many who were trying to follow it. In 1531 Cranmer entered the king's direct service as a chaplain, and received his first benefice, the archdeaconry of Taunton.

The following year he was sent to chase the Emperor Charles V around his vast dominions, in another futile bid to persuade Charles to relax his hostility to an annulment. This mission was a steep learning curve. It was Cranmer's first experience of purely secular diplomacy, and his first encounter with the reformed, or Lutheran churches that were springing up all over Germany. There is no evidence that he was in any sense converted to the theology of the CONFESSION OF AUGSBURG, but he was impressed by the vernacular liturgies and vernacular scriptures these churches were using. Almost incredibly, he also married again, his bride being Margaret, niece to the wife of the Lutheran divine ANDREAS OSIANDER. They did not speak each other's languages, and can have known each other only a few weeks, but it was to be an enduring and fruitful union. It was also an appalling risk. Cranmer was now a beneficed priest in the king's service, and his marriage was a serious offense in canon law. He was to keep this union secret for over fifteen years, but it was a hostage to fortune, particularly as Henry found out, and connived at the deception. Worse was to follow.

In August 1532 the aged and obstructive archbishop of Canterbury, William Warham, died, and the king needed an archbishop who would do his bidding over the most important issue in his life. The archdeacon of Taunton may not have been an obvious successor, but he had two enormous advantages: he genuinely believed in the king's cause, and he was a man of recognized learning and integrity. The summons to office was certainly a shock, and in the circumstances may well have been as unwelcome as Cranmer claimed. By January 1533 he was back in London, and his appointment was made public.

The new archbishop was not a party to Henry's secret marriage to Anne Boleyn in the same month, a move enforced by the fact that she was pregnant, but he knew from the first what he would be expected to do. On May 28, after a show of due process, he declared that Catherine was not, and never had been, Henry's wife. Like the king's, Cranmer's conscience at this point was very important. His consecration (to

which Clement VII rather surprisingly raised no objection) involved an oath to the pope, which he knew he would have to break. He therefore entered a *caveat,* declaring that the said oath could not bind him against the laws of God, or of England. Not surprisingly he was later accused of hypocrisy, but it seems that he genuinely believed that the pope should have no jurisdiction in England, and went through the motions because Henry had not quite got to that point. Obviously, he also rejected clerical CELIBACY, but could hardly say so openly. His great strength was not only personal loyalty to the king, but a like-mindedness that did not have to be constrained. He honestly believed that God had given Henry (and indeed all kings) the authority to rule the church in his dominions, and for that reason he accepted the king's judgment in matters of jurisdiction and worship. He actively promoted the English translation of the BIBLE, finally authorized in 1539, but apart from that he supported initiatives that came from THOMAS CROMWELL or the king himself. This involved not only the formal declaration of the Royal Supremacy, which through parliamentary statute had declared the king "head of the Church of England," but also the dissolution of the monasteries. Like many orthodox Catholics by this time, he had no particular use for the *Opus Dei,* preferring other expressions of piety, but when he pressed for the resources to be redistributed within the church, he was ignored. When he dissolved the Boleyn marriage in 1536, in one of the more discreditable examples of his flexibility, he was obeying the king's direct orders; when he wormed the truth out of a distraught Catherine Howard, the Queen, in 1541 he was discharging a pastoral duty. Although there is no evidence that at this time he held any specifically Protestant doctrines, he was bitterly unpopular with conservatives, both clerical and lay. The rebels in 1536 denounced him as a heretic, and when Cromwell fell in 1540 many hoped that the archbishop would go as well, but Henry consistently supported him. In 1537 he became godfather to Prince Edward, and in 1539 the king excused him the painful duty of voting for the Act of Six Articles with its staunchly Catholic line. In 1543, when he was denounced by the clergy of his own cathedral, Henry gave him the commission to investigate, with the words ". . . now I know who is the greatest heretic in Kent."

When the old king died in January 1547, Cranmer in a sense emerged from cover. He had been experimenting with vernacular liturgy for some time, and had even used an English litany on occasion, but it is impossible to trace accurately the development of his theological thinking. He was immensely well read, not only in the Scriptures but also in the Greek and Latin fathers and the medieval schoolmen. His aim seems to have been to restore the purity of the early church, and it was not difficult to convince himself that papal authority and clerical celibacy were both comparatively late developments. By 1547 he seems to have come to the same conclusion about TRANSUBSTANTIATION, and that tipped him over into the Protestant camp. He had certainly read MARTIN LUTHER, HULDRYCH ZWINGLI, PHILIPP MELANCHTHON, and many other contemporary reformers, but his conclusions were not specifically based on any of them. Although not dramatically distinctive, his theology was *sui generis*. Until January 1547 Cranmer had paced himself by the king; now he became the pacesetter himself, aided and abetted by the sympathetic regime of the Lord Protector, the duke of Somerset.

In the summer he issued a set of homilies on the Eucharist and on justification that were clearly Protestant; in December the Act of Six Articles was repealed. In 1548 he wrote and issued an English order of Communion. Early in 1549 the First Act of Uniformity abolished the mass and many other traditional rites, and authorized instead the first Book of Common Prayer, Cranmer's slightly modified translation of the *Sarum Use,* the Roman rite for England, Wales, and Ireland. At the same time clerical marriage was legalized, and Margaret Cranmer was able to emerge from her long obscurity. Outside London these measures were not popular, and in the summer of 1549 there were widespread disorders to which the religious changes contributed. The protesters were pacified or suppressed, but in October the Regency Council decided that the Lord Protector had overreached himself; he was overthrown and imprisoned. Cranmer was caught in the middle of this, and as a close ally of the Protector, it was thought that he would be the next to go. This was particularly the case because many of those involved in the *coup* were religious conservatives who wanted to return to the Henrician settlement.

The archbishop survived, partly because of a close personal relationship with the young king, and partly by allying with the pragmatic Earl of Warwick, the most powerful of the councillors. After a tense struggle, Warwick became president of the Council, and the program of religious reform continued. In 1550 a reformed Ordinal (book of rites for ordination) was introduced, reflecting the Protestant view of orders, and in 1552 (after much consultation) a revised Prayer Book. Cranmer had been trying since 1548 to attract prominent continental reformers to England, and because of the uncomfortable circumstances at home, several had come. The most important were MARTIN BUCER and Peter Martyr Vermigli, and both these played an important part in reforming the liturgy, which was much more unequivocally Protestant than

its predecessor (which some conservatives had been willing to use). This was enforced by a second Act of Uniformity, but by that time Cranmer was at odds with Warwick, partly over the distribution of the property from the last of the religious foundations, the chantries. Warwick began to favor more radical reformers, such as JOHN KNOX and John Hooper, and Cranmer largely withdrew from the Council. In late 1552 he tried to introduce a reformed canon law, but Warwick killed it in the parliament, on the grounds that it would give the clergy too much power. At the same time the Council pressed the archbishop to prepare a reformed CONFESSION, which he did, but nothing was done with it until the summer of 1553, when it was promulgated as the 42 Articles.

By then King Edward VI (1537–1553), whose personal convictions had allowed this whole reformation to happen, was at the point of death. His lawful heir, Mary, was Catholic and a famous conservative, and Edward did his best to set up a scheme promoting his Protestant cousin, Jane Grey, in her place. This scheme, enthusiastically promoted by Warwick (now duke of Northumberland) and reluctantly supported by Cranmer, failed within days. Northumberland was swiftly tried and executed for treason, and Cranmer was one of those similarly tried and convicted during the autumn. He had already taken the precaution of putting his affairs in order, and sending Margaret and their children to Germany. He was executed not only because Mary believed that he was entirely responsible for what had happened to her mother, Catherine, and herself, but also because HERESY was a far worse crime than treason. However, until the papal jurisdiction was restored, there was no court in England competent to try him. Along with Nicholas Ridley and HUGH LATIMER, he was paraded in Oxford in April 1554 in what was officially termed an academic disputation but was in fact a show trial. He made no concessions, and remained in prison until the autumn of 1555.

The papal jurisdiction had been restored in January, but Cranmer's archiepiscopal status meant that a special commission had to be issued to try him. This took time, and it was not until September 1555 that James Brookes, bishop of Gloucester, presided at his trial in Oxford. Brookes wisely concentrated not on THEOLOGY, where Cranmer was robust, but on jurisdiction, where his enthusiasm for the Royal Supremacy made him vulnerable. "If you believe that the Queen has authority," Brookes asked him in effect, "why do you not obey her in what she is now telling you to do?" Cranmer was inevitably convicted, and relaxed to the secular arm, but his confidence had been undermined. Under intense pressure, he signed a recantation, and then another, more explicit. Neither Mary nor Cardinal Pole was pleased. In spite of the propaganda triumph that such a submission would have represented, Mary wanted him dead, without any moral complications. She chose to regard his recantation as insincere and pressed on with the plans for his burning. Perhaps conscience smitten, or perhaps realizing he had nothing to gain, Cranmer decided that Protestantism meant more to him than the Royal Supremacy, and spectacularly withdrew his recantation at the stake. He was burned in Oxford March 21, 1556, and thus became a MARTYR. But none of this would have mattered, and his career might have languished in academic obscurity if the Edwardian church had not been restored by ELIZABETH I and taken root. Cranmer thus became a founding father of an enduring ecclesiastical tradition, which has now spread all over the world.

Thomas Cranmer was not a saint, and not even a great theologian; he was, however, an incomparable liturgist who became one of the great creators of the English language. He was also a first-class ecclesiastical statesman who made a plausible church out of the jurisdictional and doctrinal mess created by Henry VIII's conscience and its attendant needs. When he got the chance, in Edward VI's reign, Cranmer became a religious leader of stature and accomplishment. When put to the test, he managed (just) to emerge as a Protestant hero and an example for later generations. How far this last was attributable to his own performance and how far to the evocative recreation of his life by author JOHN FOXE in *The Actes and Monuments of these latter and perillous days* (1563) is a subject still under discussion.

See also Calvinism; Lord's Supper; Lutheranism; Presbyterianism; Reformation; Theology; Transubstantiation; Bible Translation

References and Further Reading

Primary Sources:

Cranmer, T., *A Prologue or Preface (to the Great Bible) Made by the Reverende Father in God, Thomas Archbyshop of Cantorbury, Metropolytan Prymate of Englande.* 1540.

Cox, J. E., ed. *The Works of Thomas Cranmer.* 2 vols. Cambridge, UK: Parker Society, 1844, 1846.

Foxe, John. *The Actes and Monuments of these latter and perillous days.* 1563, 1570.

Ketley, J., ed. *The Two Liturgies, A. D. 1549, and A. D. 1552: with other Documents set forth by authority in the reign of King Edward VI.* Cambridge, UK: Parker Society, 1844.

Nicholas, J. G., ed. *Narratives of the Days of the Reformation.* Camden Society, 1859.

Robinson, H., ed. *Original Letters Relative to the English Reformation.* 2 vols. Cambridge, UK: Parker Society, 1846, 1847.

Selwyn, D. G. *The Library of Thomas Cranmer.* Oxford, UK: Oxford Bibliographical Society, 1996.

Surtz, E., and V. Murphy, eds. *The Divorce Tracts of Henry VIII.* 1987.

Secondary Sources:

Ayris, P., and D. G. Selwyn, eds. *Thomas Cranmer, Churchman and Scholar.* New York: Boydell, 1998.

Brooks, P. *Cranmer in Context; Documents of the English Reformation.* Minneapolis, MN: Fortress 1989.

Bromiley, G. W. *Thomas Cranmer; Archbishop and Martyr.* 1955.

———. *Thomas Cranmer, Theologian.* New York: Oxford U. Press 1956.

Loades, D. *The Oxford Martyrs.* New York: Stein 1970.

———. *Thomas Cranmer and the English Reformation.* 1991.

MacCulloch, D., *Thomas Cranmer.* New Haven, CT: Yale U. Press 1996.

Nicholson, G. "The Act of Appeals and the English Reformation." In *Law and Government in Tudor England*, edited by C. Cross, D. Loades, and J. Scarisbrick. New York, NY: Cambridge U. Press 1988.

DAVID LOADES

CREATION SCIENCE

"Creation Science" is a term adopted by American biblical literalists in the 1970s. It is part of the broader Creationist movement—that group committed to the accuracy of the account of creation as given in the first three chapters of the Book of Genesis. It is an outgrowth of American evangelical Protestantism of the nineteenth century, and continues to flourish today. The term of "Creation Science" is now subsumed under the category of "Intelligent Design."

Background History

With the enactment of Prohibition in the United States after World War One, anti-evolution religious groups were emboldened by their success in the fight against alcohol and pushed for the passage of laws forbidding the teaching of natural origins as argued by Charles Darwin. One of the states where the biblical literalists or fundamentalists were successful was Tennessee. This led, in 1925, to the notorious Scopes Trial, when a young teacher (John Thomas Scopes) was brought to task for teaching evolution. Prosecuted by three-time presidential candidate WILLIAM JENNINGS BRYAN and defended by the noted agnostic Clarence Darrow, Scopes was eventually found guilty, although the very light fine of $100 was overturned on appeal. The true drama of the story, however, was the defense of the BIBLE given by Bryan and the mocking of its literal interpretation by Darrow. The evolutionists lost the case but they won the battle as—thanks particularly to the savage reporting of *Baltimore Sun* reporter H. L. Mencken—much of America laughed at the arguments of the critics of modern science. Bryan boasted, for example, that he took his stand on the Rock of Ages rather than the age of rocks (Ginger 1958; Larson 1997).

Evolution triumphed in Tennessee, and the 1930s and 1940s were to see progress in the understanding of the evolutionary process. Paradoxically, however, in the classrooms of the UNITED STATES, teaching of evolution withered and died. Concerned about sales, publishers pressured their authors, textbooks, suppressed references to evolution, and Darwin's place as a seminal figure to Western thought was denied or ignored. This state of affairs lasted through the 1950s, when the Russian success with Sputnik spurred a push to revitalize American science education. Finally a whole new generation of evolution-friendly biology textbooks began to appear (Nelkin 1977).

Creation Science

With the textbooks however, came a revitalized opposition to evolution. The "Bible" of the anti-evolutionist movement, *Genesis Flood* by John C. Whitcomb and Henry M. Morris, appeared in 1961. Here was the definitive case for what now came to be called "Creationism," a literal reading of Genesis that assumed six days of creation, six thousand years ago, with the appearance of plants and animals followed by humankind. This account also assumed a worldwide flood at some point later. By then the politics of the situation had changed from Tennessee in 1925. The U.S. Supreme Court had ruled that evolution could be taught in state-supported schools and that religion (as opposed to "Religious Studies") could not have a place in such schools. Much therefore was made of the supposedly scientific case for Creationism, especially under the favored alternative name of "Creation Science." Gaps in the fossil record were given prominent treatment.

In major respects *Genesis Flood* had its roots in the past as much as in the present because it drew heavily on the ideas of a turn-of-the-century Canadian, Seventh-day Adventist George McCready Price. A literal six days of creation (with the days of durations as experienced by us) was a crucial part of Adventists theology, given the high place Adventists gave to the final day of rest. Price had long been advocating a literal reading of the Bible, and had given much time and effort to fitting the empirical facts into the biblical account. As with many dispensationalists (those who believe in epochs ended with major upheavals), Armageddon figured highly in Adventist theology, and one finds a corresponding (and complementing) fascination with the earlier time of worldwide destruction, Noah's Flood. For Price, as for later Creationists including Whitcomb and Morris, the progressivist fossil record is confirmation of the Flood, being not a record of life through long eons of time but an artifact of the rising waters.

The new Creationism gained an increasingly high profile. Sympathetic legislators introduced bills to mandate the teaching of Creation Science along with evolution. Arkansas in 1981 was the place and time of the ultimate showdown, when the American Civil Liberties Union—brought suit against a law that insisted on the teaching of Creationism alongside evolution. Once again the nation's eyes were fixed on a southern United States courtroom, although this time the judge found against Creationism, ruling its aspirations to become part of biology curricula were unconstitutional (Ruse 1988; Gilkey 1985).

Intelligent Design

A new generation of supporters has attacked evolution and argued that origins, including human origins, stand outside the normal course of NATURE. Initially, today's Creationists contented themselves with attacking evolution. They brought forward versions of the arguments that appeared in *Genesis Flood,* in Price and indeed in the writings of anti-evolutionists in the days of Darwin. If evolution be true, why does no one ever see it in action? How did life start? Could the inorganic really turn into flourishing life, without the intervention of a divine artificer? Why are there so many gaps in the fossil record, and where are the necessary intermediates? How could chance make the sophisticated functioning of the hand and the eye?

Perhaps spurred by the objections of the evolutionists, the new Creationists formulated and promoted an alternative notion of origins, that meshes with a literal reading of the early chapters of Genesis. In the eyes of anti-evolutionists, the adaptive complexity of the living world is too subtle to be the product of blind law. In its intricate functioning, it apparently exhibits "irreducible complexity." If blind law is inadequate, what alternative is there? The answer given is some form of "intelligent design." An intervention—or interventions—in the normal course of nature brought on the true marks of the living. The world shows the results of the direct intervention of a conscious intelligence.

The Intelligent Design theorists have been criticized by conventional scientists, no less severely than were the earlier generations of Creationists (Miller 1999). It is argued that the notion of irreducible complexity is conceptually confused and empirically unwarranted. The very idea of design itself, out of step with modern science, is not needed and raises as many problems as it supposedly solves. Is design something that happened in the distant past, held in check until needed? How could this holding operation have operated in any organisms, let alone those more primitive than today's forms? Is design something that was inserted in the recent past, or even in the present, in which case why do we not have direct evidence of its occurrence?

Criticisms have also been made of the theoretical defense of Intelligent Design by William Dembski (Ruse 2003). He argues that chance processes could never produce the complex functioning of organisms. Richard Dawkins (1985) has offered more sophisticated computer models to suggest how the kinds of objections by Dembski and those before him fade away as soon as one takes into consideration the real nature of evolution.

Science and Religion

One consequence of the Creationist movement has been increased efforts by theologians and concerned scientists and others (particularly philosophers and historians) to think hard about the science/religion relationship. They are challenged to formulate an adequate account of the true connections between science and religion in general, and between DARWINISM and Christianity in particular. One thing has become very clear: the conflict model of science and religion—that the two are natural enemies—is as much a phenomenon of the nineteenth century as is Creationism. For most of the Christian era, whether in Catholic or Protestant manifestations and the greatest friend of science has been religion—Copernicus was in minor orders and Darwin trained for the Anglican priesthood, and in both cases it shows.

There is still much work to be done in articulating the various options of the science/religion relationship. Some argue that the two are essentially things apart and hence truly cannot clash. This was the position of the late Stephen Jay Gould (1999) who talked of non-overlapping "Magisteria." Others do not see science and religion as apart and indeed argue for integration. Most famous in the twentieth century in the context of evolution was the French Jesuit paleontologist, Pierre Teilhard de Chardin (1955). Although few today accept his vision outright—a vision that moves progressively from the beginning of life to humans and thence beyond to the so-called Omega Point that Teilhard identified with Christ—there are many who still find his thinking stimulating and fertile.

There are also those who think that science and religion, although different, can at least impinge, one on the other, and that some kind of mutual respect must be achieved for them to exist in harmony (Barbour 1988). A key issue, obviously, is the understanding of "mutual respect." Some who work on the science/religion interface think that only if evolutionists are willing to temper the harshness of pure Darwinism—to soften the depiction of nature red in tooth and claw—can science and religion be harmonized. Others take the attitude that it is not for the religious to question exactly how God created the universe, but rather to reinterpret and understand faith in the light of the most modern (and prima facie uncomfortable) scientific advances.

These are intellectual matters. One must recognize, however, that these do not exhaust the issue. There is a significant political dimension. Although the arguments are scientific (or more accurately, claimed to be scientific)—what drives the anti-evolutionists of today, as the Creationists of yesterday, is as much issues of morality and culture as of anything empirical.

Underlying this kind of argument is a sense that evolution is committed to something that Creationists call "metaphysical naturalism." In the words of Phillip Johnson

"what is ultimately real is nature, which consists of the fundamental particles that make up what we call matter and energy, together with the natural laws that govern how those particles behave. Nature itself is ultimately all there is, at least as far as we are concerned. To put it another way, nature is a permanently closed system of material causes and effects that can never be influenced by anything outside of itself—by God, for example. To speak of something as 'supernatural' is therefore to imply that it is imaginary, and belief in powerful imaginary entities is known as superstition" (1995:37–38).

The creationists insist on being true "theistic realists," assuming "that the universe and all its creatures were brought into existence for a purpose by God" (p. 209). Given the ongoing social and political triumphs of the religious right (see CHRISTIAN RIGHT) in the United States, it is likely that, for all of the scientists' refutations, we shall see the continued existence—perhaps even flourishing—of the Creationist movement for many years yet to come. It is also likely this flourishing will continue to merge the scientific and religious with the political and social (Ruse 2000).

See also Biblical Inerrancy; Darwinism; Fundamentalism; Science

References and Further Reading

Barbour, I. "Ways of Relating Science and Theology." In *Physics, Philosophy, and Theology: A Common Quest for Understanding*, 21–48. Vatican City: Vatican Observatory, 1988.

Behe, M. *Darwin's Black Box: The Biochemical Challenge to Evolution*. New York: Free Press, 1996.

Darwin, C. *On the Origin of Species*. London: John Murray, 1859.

Dawkins, R. *The Blind Watchmaker*. New York: Norton, 1986.

Dembski, W. *The Design Inference: Eliminating Chance through Small Probabilities*. Cambridge: Cambridge University Press, 1998.

Denton, Michael. *Evolution. A Theory in Crisis*. Bethesda, MD: Adler and Adler, 1985.

Dobzhansky, T. *Genetics and the Origin of Species*. New York: Columbia University Press, 1937.

Gilkey, L. B. *Creationism on Trial: Evolution and God at Little Rock*. Minneapolis, MN: Winston Press, 1985.

Ginger, R. *Six Days or Forever? Tennesse v. John Thomas Scopes*. Boston: Beacon, 1958.

Gould, S. J. *Rocks of Ages: Science and Religion in the Fullness of Life*. New York: Ballantine, 1999.

Johnson, P. E. *Darwin on Trial*. Washington, DC: Regnery Gateway, 1991.

———. *Reason in the Balance*. Downers Grove, IL: InterVarsity Press, 1995.

Larson, E. J. *Summer for the Gods: The Scopes Trial and America's Continuing Debate over Science and Religion*. New York: Basic Books, 1997.

McMullin, E., ed. *Evolution and Creation*. Notre Dame: University of Notre Dame Press, 1985.

Miller, K. *Finding Darwin's God*. New York: Harper and Row, 1999.

Moore, J. *The Post-Darwinian Controversies: A Study of the Protestant Struggle to Come to Terms with Darwin in Great Britain and America, 1870–1900*. Cambridge: Cambridge University Press, 1979.

Morris, Henry M. *Scientific Creationism*. San Diego, CA: Creation-Life Publishers, 1985.

Nelkin, D. *Science Textbook Controversies and the Politics of Equal Time*. Cambridge, MA: MIT Press, 1977.

Numbers, R. L. *The Creationists: The Evolution of Scientific Creationism*. New York: Knopf, 1992.

Ruse, M., ed. *But is it Science? The Philosophical Question in the Creation/Evolution Controversy*. Buffalo, NY: Prometheus, 1988.

———. *The Evolution Wars: A Guide to the Controversies*. Santa Barbara, CA: ABC-CLIO, 2000.

———. *Can a Darwinian be a Christian? The Relationship between Science and Religion*. Cambridge: Cambridge University Press, 2001.

———. *Darwin and Design: Science, Philosophy, Religion*. Cambridge, MA: Harvard University Press, 2003.

Teilhard de Chardin, P. *Le Phénomème Humaine*. Paris: Editions de Seuil, 1955.

Whitcomb, John C., and Henry M. Morris. *The Genesis Flood: The Biblical Record and its Scientific Implications*. Philadelphia: Presbyterian and Reformed Publishing Company, 1961.

MICHAEL RUSE

CROMWELL, OLIVER (1599–1658)

English protestant statesman.

Early Life

Born in Huntingdon in East Anglia ENGLAND, on April 25, 1599, Oliver Cromwell was the only surviving son of Robert Cromwell and Elizabeth Steward. He became a statesman and military hero during the English CIVIL WARS and was named Lord Protector in 1653. Cromwell followed strict Puritan ideas in his early life, but propagated more radical religious views, including limited liberty of conscience, during his later years. He died in 1658.

Robert and Elizabeth Cromwell originally had ten children, but only seven survived to adulthood. Robert Cromwell was politically active at the national level, where he sat in one of Queen ELIZABETH I's parliaments, and at the local level, where he was a justice of the peace and a landlord. Both of Cromwell's parents were from gentry families and had gained influence by acquiring former monastic lands during the reign of HENRY VIII. The Cromwells came from a poor yet well-connected branch of the family. There was a tenuous blood connection to THOMAS CROMWELL, the earl of Essex, Henry VIII's lord chancellor and the mastermind of the dissolution of the monasteries.

Cromwell's education began at the local grammar school. He came under the influence of the Puritan schoolmaster Thomas Beard (d.1632). Beard's ideas closely parallel those of the mature Cromwell, though it is difficult to tell how much Beard's ideas affected him. Beard's most famous work, *The Theatre of God's Judgments*, acts as an important case study for strict Puritan beliefs of the period. It emphasizes God's interest in the grim aspects of human experience. Abbott notes that Beard's God was "less the loving Father than a strong avenging Deity much absorbed in the discovery and punishment of sin. . . intending to teach morality by fear" (Abbott 1937: 4.25).

Cromwell matriculated at Sidney Sussex College, Cambridge University, but left after a year due to his father's death and the need to assume family responsibilities. WILLIAM LAUD, the future archbishop of Canterbury, once referred to the school as a "hotbed of Puritanism." Abbott suggests that one can see Cromwell's educational and family experiences mirrored in his later career, such as his "remarkable command" of the BIBLE, his perception of God's intervention in his English history and in his own life, and his belief in the role of the "godly" in the community (Abbott 1937: 4.26).

Historians disagree over the extent of Cromwell's formal education and his military background. Some believe that he studied law at Lincoln's Inn in London and lived there for a time. In 1620 he married Elizabeth Bourchier, the daughter of a London fur merchant, after a courtship that took place in London. It is also difficult to determine where and how he obtained his military training. He possibly adapted his military style from the Dutch. However, he believed that men motivated by a cause would form a better army than regular, professional soldiers if provided with discipline and strong leadership. Such concepts affected his success at the battle of Marston Moor in June 1644 and influenced the creation of the New Model Army in 1645.

The Cromwells lived in Huntingdon after they were married; they had nine children. Though they owned land, the Cromwells frequently experienced financial difficulties. The English government made many demands for taxation throughout the 1620s, and there were some bad harvests. In 1638 Cromwell inherited property in Ely from his maternal uncle, and his financial worries ended.

Political and Military Career

Cromwell was elected to the House of Commons from Huntingdon in 1628. There he became a noted opponent of Caroline religious policy. This Parliament promoted the Petition of Right and a Remonstrance against corrupt government. The Petition of Right guaranteed civil liberties and established parliamentarian AUTHORITY. It maintained the concept of due process, in particular arguing that no one could be arrested and jailed without given cause, and limited military presence by forbidding martial law and requiring a subject's approval before quartering troops on his private property.

After Charles I dissolved Parliament in 1629, it would not be called again for eleven years. During this time, Cromwell became a force in local politics. Throughout his early career, Cromwell made a name for himself by supporting the popular cause. Two notable incidents included opposition to the central government, in one case to obstruct the purging of corporations and in another to prevent the draining of the fens. He also supported several lectureships in Huntingdon.

For both the Short and Long Parliaments, Cromwell served as a MP for Cambridge. In the Long Parliament, Cromwell at first supported the reform group led by John Pym and participated in the Committee on Religion. When war broke out in 1642, Cromwell raised troops in Cambridge and became an officer in the army of the Eastern Association under the earl of Manchester. He soon distinguished himself in combat, but became critical of the military leadership, including Manchester, who wanted to force the king to settle but not defeat him completely.

In 1644, Cromwell began to separate himself from the moderate reformers in favor of more radical notions. The signing of the Solemn League and Covenant and propagation of the covenant oath undoubtedly influenced him. The Solemn League and Covenant formed the foundation for a 1643 military alliance between the opponents of Charles I in SCOT-

LAND and England. The major point in the treaty was England's promise to establish a Reformed church in exchange for Scottish military assistance. It also required its supporters to take an oath of allegiance to the Covenant. In 1643 and early in 1644, Scottish armies proved their worth by helping to defeat royalist forces at the battle of Tippermuir; the king agreed to treaty talks at Uxbridge.

After failing to settle with the king in 1645, Parliament renewed military opposition. Passing the New Model Ordinance to reorganize the parliamentary army, it created the Self-Denying Ordinance to separate WAR from politics. This latter ordinance, which appealed to many pious parliamentary supporters because it encouraged self-denial to curry God's favor, prohibited members of Parliament from serving as military officers. In June 1645, the battle of Naseby resulted in spectacular success for the New Model Army, which comprised large numbers of Independents and sectaries.

Believing Charles I intended to establish an absolute monarchy of the continental type, Cromwell maintained that the king was responsible for the nation's ills and committed himself to the king's military defeat. Cromwell proved willing to use the social and religious radicals shunned by the moderate reformers and considered dangerous by most parliamentarians. He believed that the state should ignore opinions when it needed men to serve. Cromwell represented a new revolutionary spirit dedicated to both religious and political reform. In addition, he had a passionate commitment to his goals. Christopher Hill has attributed this view to a "strong strand of Christian pragmatism"(Hill 1970: 56–60, 77).

These ideas caused a permanent division between two groups of parliamentarians in 1647. One group, frequently termed the "political Presbyterians," saw the army as a threat to the authority of both Parliament and king; the other group, sometimes called the "political Independents," envisioned the soldiers as the true revolutionaries, those men wanting real reform. In 1649, Cromwell solidly supported the execution of Charles I. He had, in fact, encouraged the campaign to have him tried and convicted for treason, punishable by death.

The abolition of the monarchy ushered in a period of English history known as the Interregnum, which in turn was divided into the Commonwealth era, from 1649 to 1653, and the Protectorate era from, 1653 to 1660. In February 1649, setting up an alternative government became the most urgent concern for Cromwell and his associates. Power rested chiefly in two bodies, the Rump Parliament, which welcomed the return of close to 100 purged members, and the Council of State. The latter was an eclectic body consisting of army officers, peers, and members of Parliament nominated by the Rump. Though it excluded radicals such as Thomas Harrison and Henry Ireton, Cromwell and Thomas Fairfax were two of the most active members. In April 1653 the Rump Parliament was dissolved in favor of a Nominated Assembly, the so-called "Barebones Parliament" that continued to work with the Council of State as the executive body.

Through the work of the Commonwealth government, Cromwell began to implement some of his religious policies. Committees were created to supervise missionary movements abroad, and bills were passed to propagate the gospel in WALES, IRELAND, the northern counties, and New England. Other legislation enforced morality, made Sabbath observance stricter, considered adultery a capital offense, and prohibited swearing and blasphemy. The most contentious issues involved tithes and the right of lay patrons to control livings, and these concerns were bound up with interests of property and the necessity of maintaining a professional, university-educated, ordained ministry.

The ineffectiveness of the Nominated Assembly and the disillusion of its moderate members with radical proposals prompted its dissolution in 1653. Cromwell replaced it with a Protectorate grounded on the Instrument of Government; he himself was named Lord Protector. This regime succeeded where the previous two regimes had failed by providing a religious settlement, although it did not satisfy everyone. In religion, the Instrument patterned itself after the Agreement of the People, mandating public profession of Christianity and the protection of dissenting congregations as long as they remained orderly. Such toleration did not extend to Catholics or those Anglicans who still refused to accept the Directory of Worship, used by the new national Presbyterian Church established in 1645. Cromwell's ascension to Lord Protector earned him heavy criticism, both from his contemporaries and from historians, because he seemed to assume monarchical powers without the title of king.

Cromwell died in 1658, leaving the position of Lord Protector to his son, Richard. Richard's inability to continue his father's leadership contributed to the fall of the Protectorate and the restoration of the monarchy, but did not precipitate it. Weaknesses in the political system and divisions over contentious issues, including religion and the reform of law, meant that the English Republic was probably doomed to failure.

Religious Impact

Examining the themes of Cromwell's life, one is struck by its dichotomy. Cromwell was both a fearless soldier and a committed champion of Christ. Studying how he reconciled these two main aspects of his personality can be both confusing and enlightening. John Morrill has commented on the many interpretations of Oliver Cromwell, as a supporter of civil liberties and religious TOLERATION, as an "iconoclast" in both the literal and figurative senses of the term, as a murderer of the Irish people, and as a military hero (Morrill 1990:1). Examining Cromwell from any of these angles can give the student a clear understanding of Cromwell's actions and words; what is difficult is reconciling all of these different personas into one.

On one hand, Cromwell's religious beliefs reflected the Puritan influences on his education. He opposed the hierarchy of the CHURCH OF ENGLAND, in particular the role of the bishops (see BISHOPS AND EPISCOPACY). Cromwell held that the individual believer could have a personal relationship with God through PRAYER and WORSHIP, and despised the Episcopal teachings that emphasized the role of the priest as mediator. He wanted to abolish the BOOK OF COMMON PRAYER and believed that PREACHING should be emphasized. Like many other members of the "godly" party, Cromwell saw himself as a member of the elect chosen both for eternal SALVATION and to be the vessel for God's will on earth.

On the other hand, Cromwell's religion reveals some new spiritual aspects. He referred to himself as a "seeker" who desired to know the will of God and act on it. Morrill believes that Cromwell was motivated by "a fierce commitment to a cause he believed in," and one can see that the cause had political and spiritual implications (Morrill 1990:14). He called himself the "chief of sinners" whom God had completely saved. In a 1638 letter, Cromwell exclaims: "The Lord accept me in His Son, and give me to walk in the light. . . as He is the light! He it is that enlighteneth our blackness, our darkness" (Abbott 1937:101). Cromwell believed that his actions, military and otherwise, were part of God's great purpose, and that he was an agent in the fulfillment of God's will.

Cromwell's influence on Protestantism cannot be overestimated. Of particular note is his position on religious toleration. Cromwell believed that no one should be constrained in religion, that there should be "no compulsion" of religion. Barry Coward nicely asserted that Cromwell's "main aim was to erect a loose framework of state control within which individuals could find God for themselves" (Coward 1991:110). Yet there were limits to this religious toleration. Cromwell distrusted Catholics as well as radical sectarians. Although he could personally understand the spiritual perspective of some dissidents, his policy could not find a way to include them (see DISSENT). He sympathized with Quakers, yet purged them from the army and persecuted the radical Quaker

James Naylor. As Coward has pointed out, Cromwell wanted not religious plurality, but rather religious unity, a way to incorporate everyone who believed in Christ and accepted the GRACE resulting from his death and resurrection. Even his readmission of the Jews into England in 1655 had a greater purpose, because he considered acknowledgment of the Jews a prerequisite to complete reformation (Coward 1991: 110–112). Unfortunately, Cromwell's most enduring legacy might be his intolerance, not his tolerance. The treatment of Irish Catholics under Cromwell's rule exacerbated existing tensions between England and Ireland, and provided cause for long-term religious strife in the British Isles.

See also Anglicanism; Catholism, Protestant Reactions; Friends, Society of; Judaism; Philo-Semitism Presbyterianism; Preaching; Puritanism

References and Further Reading

Primary Sources:

Abbott, W. C., ed. *The Writings and Speeches of Oliver Cromwell.* 4 vols. Cambridge, MA: Harvard University Press, 1937.
Gardiner, S. R., ed. *Constitutional Documents of the English Revolution.* Oxford, UK: Clarendon Press, 1906.

Secondary Sources:

Ashley, Maurice, ed. *Cromwell.* Englewood Cliffs, NJ: Prentice-Hall, 1969.
Coward, Barry. *Oliver Cromwell.* New York: Longman Press, 1991.
Hill, Christopher. *God's Englishman: Oliver Cromwell and the English Revolution.* New York: Dial Press, 1970.
Morrill, John, ed. *Oliver Cromwell and the English Revolution.* New York: Longman Press, 1990.
Wheeler, James Scott. *Cromwell in Ireland.* New York: St. Martin's Press, 1999.

ALANA CAIN SCOTT

CROMWELL, THOMAS (1485–1540)

English statesman. Thomas Cromwell, earl of Essex was a key advisor to King HENRY VIII of ENGLAND in the early years of the Protestant REFORMATION. His most significant contribution was an effort to cement England's identity as a Protestant country by encouraging Henry's fourth marriage to Anne of Cleves, a daughter of Protestant royalty from Flanders. The failure of this marriage, which ended in DIVORCE, fueled Henry's suspicion of Cromwell's motives and galvanized the energies of Cromwell's opponents at court. Charged with treason in June 1540, he was beheaded nearly seven weeks later, on July 28, 1540.

Cromwell's significance has been obscured. Although Foxe's *Book of Martyrs* (see ACTS AND MON-

UMENTS) depicted him as a hero of Protestantism, Cromwell's obvious political adroitness seems more characteristic of one whose motives were self-serving. Cromwell's success in his ambitious pursuits was undeniable, but his commitment to political and religious reform offers the true key to his character and his achievement.

Born sometime in 1485 at Putney, Cromwell grew up in modest circumstances. His father struggled to earn a living from a variety of occupations, including blacksmith and brewer. As a young man he was known as unruly and, apparently after a quarrel with his father in 1503, went to ITALY to serve in the French army of Louis XII. Control of Naples was contested at that time, and in this case the French forces were defeated and Cromwell went to Florence where he entered the service of a noble family, the Frescobaldi, who were bankers. Apparently Cromwell traveled widely and learned quickly to represent influential interests in complex social situations. He also became familiar with European financial and political currents and gained administrative skills. After a few years of this service he moved to Flanders where he represented English economic interests with the merchants of Antwerp. In 1510 he also successfully negotiated the renewal of a papal charter for an English religious guild, meeting Pope Julius II in the process. By 1514 he had returned to England and married Elizabeth Wykes. It appears that his wife's family had important political connections, but it was also apparent that Cromwell had begun to attract the notice of influential circles by his work on the continent. As a result Cardinal Wolsey appointed him collector of his revenues in 1514.

Cromwell attracted a variety of influential clients as he built a law career, but Wolsey became his chief benefactor. Henry VIII's principal advisor at the time, Wolsey controlled considerable patronage and bestowed it on Cromwell as he proved his mettle. In 1523 Cromwell gained a seat in Parliament, for Taunton, and in 1524 he was admitted as a member of Gray's Inn. In the same year Wolsey enlisted Cromwell's services in launching one of Henry's main reform initiatives: the suppression of the monasteries and the redirection of monastic funds for such purposes as enhancing the church's diocesan structure and education. Cromwell became immersed in auditing monastic possessions, and demonstrated both his administrative ability and his political acumen in the process. As Wolsey gave his attention to foreign affairs and the law courts, Cromwell saw an opportunity to address issues of national finance and the state of the church. He approached the suppression of the monasteries with the passion of a reformer, as intent on promoting education as he was in undercutting the fabric of medieval monasticism in England.

By 1524 the influence of several reform currents was apparent in England. In part reform of the church arose as an assertion of government and the role of lay advisors in them. Cromwell represented a new kind of policy maker whose career was built not on royal blood nor on the church, but on his own motivation and innate ability. The measure of his accomplishment was a rapid advance, eventually taking him beyond Wolsey, whose star faded. As one historian notes, Cromwell caught "the attention of a king grappling with seemingly intractable problems" by bringing to them new imagination. For a time Cromwell remained loyal to Wolsey, although he gained the king's approval and, in 1531, was made a privy counselor. He gained further responsibilities in 1533 and 1534, when he became chancellor of the Exchequer and the king's secretary. As he gained ascendancy he also established close ties with Protestants determined to create a Lutheran Church in England.

Intent on encouraging England's break with Rome, Cromwell's supreme moment came in 1534 when the king authorized him to direct the implementation of the Act of Supremacy. By this Act Henry excluded papal AUTHORITY from England and made the sovereign head of the church. In the execution of Thomas More, and other leading figures who dissented, and in the king's divorce from Catherine of Aragon and marriage to Anne Boleyn, Cromwell proved to be the loyal servant. His loyalty proved steadfast when Anne was executed on a charge of adultery and Henry married Jane Seymour who died in childbirth.

Meanwhile Cromwell set about to establish a reformed Christian nation under a well-administered government. For his loyalty to Henry, however, the power and ability he possessed, and his hopes for religious reform, Cromwell attracted powerful opponents, notably Bishop Stephen Gardiner and the Duke of Norfolk. King Henry's disenchantment with Anne of Cleves ignited a general dislike of Protestant reformers and those who befriended them. Henry's capacity for disenchantment with those he once revered sealed Cromwell's fate. His reform program faltered with his death, but the Reformation took hold in England and his example encouraged the trend toward powerful, lay advisors at court.

References and Further Reading

Beckingsale, B. W. *Thomas Cromwell, Tudor Minister.* New York/London: Macmillan, 1978.
Dickens, A. G. *Thomas Cromwell and the English Reformation.* London: English University Press, 1959.
Elton, G. R. *Reform and Renewal: Thomas Cromwell and the Commonweal.* Cambridge: Cambridge University Press, 1973.
———. *Thomas Cromwell.* Bangor: Headstart History, 1991.
The Dictionary of National Biography. Oxford: Oxford University Press, 1960.
Wilson, Derek A. *In The Lion's Court: Power, Ambition, and Sudden Death in the Court of Henry VIII.* London: Hutchinson, 2001.

WILLIAM SACHS

CROSBY, FRANCES JANE (FANNY) (1820–1915)

American evangelical composer. Crosby was born March 24, 1820, in Southeast, New York, and died February 12, 1915, in Bridgeport, Connecticut. The daughter of John and Mercy Crosby, Frances (known as Fanny) came of old Puritan stock. The Crosby family traced its American roots to 1634, when Simon Crosby arrived from England to settle in the Massachusetts Bay Colony. Blinded in infancy as the result of unfortunate medical treatment, Crosby manifested an alert mind, and committed long passages of the BIBLE and English poetry to memory. At fifteen years of age she entered the New York Institution for the Blind in Manhattan. There she completed her education and cultivated her musical and poetic ability. She spoke frequently on behalf of the Institution, urging state and federal support for education for the blind. She published three small volumes of poetry and collaborated with one of her teachers, George F. Root, to produce cantatas and other popular music before she left the Institution in 1858 to marry blind musician Alexander van Alstyne. Eleven years her junior, van Alstyne was a music teacher and church organist who encouraged his wife to pursue her interests and to retain her maiden name.

Crosby wrote her first hymn in 1864, and over the next 50 years she produced thousands more. Her collaboration in New York City with others interested in SUNDAY SCHOOLS, EVANGELISM, and REVIVALS resulted in the creation of the popular religious songs known as gospel hymns, and brought her to prominence at an auspicious moment. Evangelist Dwight Lyman MOODY's songster, IRA DAVID SANKEY, popularized her music by including many of her texts in his influential *Gospel Hymns.* These were promptly translated and used around the world. Among her most enduring texts are "Blessed Assurance," "Rescue the Perishing," "To God be the Glory," and "Safe in the Arms of Jesus."

For most of her adult life, Crosby identified herself primarily with the METHODIST EPISCOPAL CHURCH. However, she attended with regularity many Protestant churches in Manhattan and Brooklyn and maintained an active interest in rescue mission work. A popular participant at such gatherings as Northfield Conferences, Chautauquas, and Christian Endeavor conventions, Crosby's winsome personality endeared her to young and old. Her enduring hymns remain popular among nonliturgical Protestants.

See also Hymns and Hymnals; Music; Music, American; Music, Popular

References and Further Reading

Primary Source:

Crosby, Fanny J. *Memories of Eighty Years*. Boston: James H. Earle & Co., 1906.

Secondary Source:

Ruffin, Bernard. *Fanny Crosby*. Cleveland: United Church Press, 1976.

EDITH BLUMHOFER

CROWTHER, DANDESON COATES (1844–1938)

Anglican missionary. Born in SIERRA LEONE in 1844 and raised in NIGERIA, Dandeson Crowther was the youngest son of Bishop Adjai Crowther. Destined for the ordained ministry in the Anglican Church, his extensive education included a period of study at the Church Missionary Society's (now the CHURCH MISSION SOCIETY) college at Islington in North London. He was ordained by his father in 1870 and subsequently took up superintendence of the all-African Niger Mission, which formed part of his father's wide-ranging jurisdiction under the auspices of the Church Missionary Society (CMS). His accomplishments as a pastor-missionary led to his appointment as archdeacon of the Niger Delta in 1874.

By the mid-nineteenth century, CMS's African policy was guided by a vision of creating a well-trained African ministry that would take the initiative in mission expansion and form the mainstay of autonomous African churches. Highly educated Africans like Archdeacon Crowther were vital to the realization of this vision. Zealous, pioneering, and by all accounts a resolute leader, he spearheaded one of the most successful evangelistic campaigns in modern African Christian history, guiding the flourishing mission through periods of mass conversions and violent persecution alike.

Revitalized European colonial expansion and the systematic introduction of Europeans into the hitherto all-African Mission were only two elements in the cocktail of events that precipitated the "Niger Crisis" of the early 1890s. This crisis marked a major turning point in Archdeacon Crowther's career. In 1892 he launched the Niger Delta Pastorate in revolt against European control. Partly as a result of his own abiding sense of loyalty to the Anglican church, the revolt lasted for only six years, although it marked one of the first significant, wholly African, attempts to establish a self-supporting, self-governing church in Western Africa. Ultimately Dandeson Crowther remains one of the most notable figures of the early Protestant encounter with AFRICA. He is perhaps best remembered for his determined, if inchoate, efforts to give substance to an African vision that inspired his generation and survived well into the twentieth century.

See also African Theology; Anglicanism; Colonialism

References and Further Reading

Primary Source:

Crowther, D. C. *The Establishment of the Niger Delta Pastorate Church*. Liverpool: J. A. Thompson and Co., 1907.

Secondary Sources:

Ajayi, J. F. A. *Christian Missions in Nigeria 1841–1891: The Making of a New Elite*. London: Longmans, Green and Co., 1965.
Ayandele, E. A. *The Missionary Impact on Modern Nigeria 1842–1914: A Political and Social Analysis*. London: Longmans, Green and Co., 1966.
Epelle, E. M. T. *The Church in the Niger Delta*. Niger Delta: Niger Delta Diocese, 1955.
Fashole-Luke, E. "Archdeacon Dandeson Coates Crowther on the Niger Delta Pastorate Church: 1892–1897." *Sierra Leone Bulletin of Religion* 2 (November 1981): 3–32.
Tasie, G. O. M. *Christian Missionary Enterprise in the Niger Delta 1864–1918*. Leiden: E.J. Brill, 1978.

JEHU J. HANCILES

CROWTHER, SAMUEL ADJAI (AJAYI) (c. 1806–1891)

West African missionary and bishop. Ajayi (the modern spelling, although Crowther used Adjai) was born in Oshogun, Western Nigeria, in about 1806 and grew up while the Yoruba empire of Oyo was collapsing. Ajayi was not dedicated in infancy to any of the Yoruba divinities because of a diviner's prophecy that he would serve the supreme God. In 1821, when he was thirteen or perhaps a little older, his town was sacked by Fulani and Oyo Muslims. He was taken as a slave and sold several times before being bought by European traders for the transatlantic market. His slave ship was intercepted by the British Navy and brought to SIERRA LEONE. At a CHURCH MISSIONARY SOCIETY (CMS) school, Ajayi became a Christian and was baptized with the name of Samuel Crowther, after an eminent English clergyman.

A promising student, Crowther was sent briefly to ENGLAND for education, and then became one of the first students of the Fourah Bay Institution, the premier CMS educational facility. He served as a CMS schoolmaster and catechist before returning to the Fourah Bay Institution as tutor in 1834. In 1841 he was appointed with the CMS missionary JAMES FREDERICK SCHÖN to accompany the expedition planned by Thomas Fowell Buxton to explore the potential for "Christianity, Commerce and Civilization" in the Niger basin. Although the expedition was generally deemed a failure, Crowther and Schoën saw great potential for missionary work by African Christians.

After studying at Islington College, London, Crowther was ordained in 1843, and in 1845 he returned to his homeland as part of the newly founded CMS Yoruba mission at Abeokuta. There he found the mother and sister from whom he had been separated by SLAVERY; they were among the earliest converts. In 1854 Crowther took part in another exploratory mission up the Niger, and in 1857 he took charge of a new CMS Niger mission covering the Delta, Igboland (Onitsha) and parts of what is now Northern Nigeria. In 1864 he became the first African Anglican bishop, with a diocese not territorially defined, and with a CLERGY entirely African. The arrival of European missionaries on the Niger from 1887 onward brought complaints about Crowther's clergy and lay assistants. As the European presence increased, Crowther was sidelined, his authority as bishop bypassed, and his staff displaced. He died in Lagos on December 31, 1891, a broken old man, and was replaced by an Englishman. His son ARCHDEACON DANDESON CROWTHER was able to retain oversight of the mission in the Niger Delta area, which was self-supporting, but mission policy avoided placing Africans in the highest positions of leadership for several decades.

The best-known African Christian of the nineteenth century, Crowther is significant for several reasons. He helped demonstrate the importance of African languages for the future of Christianity. He was PREACHING in Yoruba in Sierra Leone at a time when services here were invariably in English. He took a major part in the Yoruba Bible translation, the first time an African mother-tongue speaker had played such a role. As a mission leader he demonstrated application to African languages, including their accumulated proverbial wisdom, and also encouraged it in others. He also developed (after some searing early experiences in Sierra Leone) a courteous and irenic dialogue with Muslims in the Upper Niger area, at a time when a deliberately confrontational style was in use elsewhere. Above all, Crowther represents African responsibility for the spread of the Christian faith in Africa and for direction of the African CHURCH. This

was always the stated aim of Protestant MISSIONS, and by the middle of the nineteenth century it seemed in reach, with Henry Venn (a secretary of CMS from 1843 to 1872) articulating the principle that the object of mission was to produce self-governing, self-supporting, self-propagating churches. Crowther's unhappy last years saw the movement away from implementation of this policy in the colonial era. The next century brought a movement back again, as sub-Saharan AFRICA became Protestant Christianity's principal area of growth.

See also African Theology; Bible Translation; Colonialism; Nigeria

References and Further Reading

Primary Sources:

Journals of the Rev. J. F. Schoën and Mr. Samuel Crowther, Who Accompanied the Expedition up the Niger in 1841. London: 1843; reprint, London: Cass, 1970.
Crowther, Samuel. *Journal of an Expedition up the Niger and Tschadda in 1854.* London: 1855; reprint, London: Cass, 1970.
———. *Experiences With Heathens and Mohammedans in West Africa.* London: SPCK, 1892.
Crowther, Samuel, and J. C. Taylor. *The Gospel on the Banks of the Niger.* London: 1859; reprint, London: Dawsons, 1968.

Secondary Sources:

Ade Ajayi, J. F. *Christian Missions in Nigeria 1841–1891.* London: Longmans, 1965.
———. *A Patriot to the Core: Bishop Ajayi Crowther.* Ibadan, Nigeria: Spectrum, 2001.
Hair, P. E. H. *The Early Study of Nigerian Languages,* Cambridge: Cambridge University Press, 1967.
Walls, A. F. "Samuel Ajayi Crowther." In *Mission Legacies,* edited by G. H. Anderson, et al. Maryknoll, NY: Orbis, 1994.

ANDREW F. WALLS

CRUMMELL, ALEXANDER (1819–1898)

African American church leader. Crummell was born March 3, 1819, in New York City, the child of "free Africans," Crummell always insisted that he was of unadulterated African ancestry. The family of his mother, Charity (Hicks) Crummell, had been Long Islanders for several generations and "associated" with the Hicks family of Quakers, (see FRIENDS, SOCIETY OF). Her husband, Boston Crummell, was descended from the Temne people in West AFRICA, and was said to have converted to Christianity before he was enslaved at around fourteen and transported to New York. On reaching maturity he refused to serve his master any longer, and established himself as an oyster vendor. The Crummells became affiliated with "the Afro-American group of the Protestant Episcopal Church," as it was later called, and were able to provide Alexander a grammar school education, including mathematics and Latin, at New York's African Free School.

Crummell studied briefly in the Noyes Academy, at Canaan, New Hampshire, until the school was destroyed by an anti-integrationist mob. He resumed studies at Beriah Greene's Oneida Institute, in upstate New York, where the curriculum included biblical languages and some mechanical trades. For a short time he studied informally at Yale University, while ministering to a congregation in New Haven, Connecticut. Among his vestry men was Alexander Du Bois, the grandfather of W. E. B. Du Bois, who later wrote a short essay on Crummell's life.

During the early years of his marriage to Sarah Crummell he served small congregations in Providence, Philadelphia, and New York. Although his candidacy for admission to the General Theological Seminary in New York was denied on racial grounds, he was ordained an Episcopal priest after a course of private studies. He then conceived the idea of studying abroad, and during five years that he spent in ENGLAND, lecturing as an abolitionist and raising funds for his church in New York, he earned the bachelor's degree from Queens' College Cambridge, graduating in 1853.

Crummell's knowledge of biblical languages was not extraordinary, but he passed Cambridge examinations on Greek literature and was able to instruct students in the Greek testament. He was apparently influenced by the revival of Cambridge Platonism that occurred under the direction of William Whewell during the 1850s. In later years he wrote disparagingly of the tendency of black leaders toward "dogmatizing theories of sense and matter as the salvable hope of the race." Contemporaries spoke of his predilection for Platonic idealism and his ability to quote extemporaneously and at length from Greek authors.

On graduating from Cambridge, Crummell sailed, almost immediately, for LIBERIA, West Africa, and from 1853 to 1872 he spent sixteen years working as a farmer, educator, small businessman, and Episcopal missionary. During two trips to the UNITED STATES during that time he maintained his commitments to abolitionism and to the cause of the newly emancipated "freedmen." From 1861 to 1863 he worked with Edward Wilmot Blyden, an ordained Presbyterian clergyman, representing the Liberian government's colonization plans to the Lincoln administration. Crummell returned to the United States for good in 1872, and after some initial uncertainties, settled in Washington, D.C., where he established St. Luke's Episcopal Church in 1879, serving as its pastor until

1894 and holding a professorship at Howard University. He spent his final years writing and lecturing widely, and in 1897 he founded the American Negro Academy as a challenge to the Machiavellian schemes and pragmatic materialism of Booker T. Washington. Crummel died September 10, 1898.

Crummell had elitist notions of black power, evidenced in his allusion to JOHN MILTON's phrase "to be weak is miserable." His pronouncements were frequently ironic in tone and attempted to reconcile cultural assimilationism with black separatism in writings that revealed his erudition and his colorful travels and adventures on three continents. His essays and addresses, written in a style described by John Greenleaf Whittier as "clear, classic, and chaste," provide a unique, if somewhat sardonic perspective on nineteenth-century intellectual life. Although Crummell contributed substantially to the African American protest tradition, it would diminish the importance of his legacy to view him primarily as a racial protest writer. His writings, for the most part addressed to black audiences, are most often concerned with the relationship of human nature to the concept of AUTHORITY, the importance of traditions and institutions to human existence (see TRADITION), and the defense of literate CULTURE. His blend of Eurocentric and Afrocentric ideology influenced W. E. B. Du Bois and other younger persons, including Anna J. Cooper, John W. Cromwell, and the Rev. Francis J. Grimké. Two of his protégés, the autodidact John E. Bruce and the Yale graduate William H. Ferris, became senior officials in the black power movement led by Marcus Garvey in the 1920s. Ferris published an early biography of Crummell in the American Negro Academy Occasional Papers (1920).

Crummell argued vigorously for purging black Christianity and culture of the emotionalism of slave religion, which he considered vulgar, materialistic, and antinomian. A strict Episcopalian, exceedingly hostile to enthusiastic conversions, he wrote: "Sentiment, feeling, emotion . . . come from an *inferior* side of our nature. They are more allied to the physical than they are to the rational or spiritual of our being. . . . Easily excited, they as easily depart. And, at the best the feelings come and go, oftentimes independent of the will; dependent, not seldom upon health, or some peculiar physical condition; and hence evidently they are not the soil in which the Holy Spirit plants the seed of God's wonderful grace."

Crummell published numerous tracts and pamphlets, some of which were reprinted in the three published collections of his writings: *Africa and America: Addresses and Discourses* (1891); *The Future of Africa: Being Addresses, Sermons, Etc., Delivered in the Republic of Liberia* (1862); and *The*

Greatness of Christ and other Sermons (1882). The quotation above is taken from "Piety, Morality, and Enthusiasm," originally published in Wilson J. Moses, ed., *Destiny and Race: Sermons and Addresses by Alexander Crummell* (1992). W. E. B. Du Bois published a well-known rhapsody on Crummell's life and character in *The Souls of Black Folk* (1903). Most of Crummell's surviving manuscripts are in the Schomburg Collection of the New York Public Library, which holds over 400 of his sermons and some of his correspondence. Additional letters are in the Library of Congress, the Archives of the Protestant Episcopal Church, the Maryland Historical Society, and Columbia University.

See also Cambridge Platonists; Colonialism; Slavery, Abolition of

References and Further Reading

Ejofodomi, Luckson. "The Missionary Career of Alexander Crummell in Liberia, 1853–1872." Ph.D. dissertation, Boston University, 1974.

Moses, Wilson J. *Alexander Crummell, A Study of Civilization and Discontent.* New York: Oxford University Press, 1989.

WILSON J. MOSES

CULTURAL PROTESTANTISM

A cognate of the German compound noun *Kulturprotestantismus* (culture Protestantism), the term "cultural Protestantism" is of uncertain coinage. H. RICHARD NIEBUHR wrongly suggests that KARL BARTH "invented" it (Niebuhr 1951:84n.1); in fact, it had entered linguistic currency during the late nineteenth century. Often, but not always, applied pejoratively, the term has become a political-theological "cipher" (Müller 1992:21), suffering from the "ambiguities" of being used both descriptively and polemically (Rupp 1977: 9); some scholars dismiss it as an "anachronistic" and "misleading" category (Chapman 2002:1). In general, it connotes a theological tendency to accommodate Christian faith to the currently prevailing CULTURE, and thus to deemphasize or negate discontinuities between the mundane and the divine. Cultural Protestantism is commonly identified with LIBERAL PROTESTANTISM/LIBERALISM and associated with both INDIVIDUALISM and CHRISTIAN SOCIALISM. Niebuhr, construing the phenomenon within his ethical-Christological typology, equates it with the "Christ of Culture" type, or those Christians who seek to acculturate Christ and who themselves feel at home in their culture.

Antecedents

The acculturational orientation of Cultural Protestantism is adumbrated in the BIBLE. A linkage between divinity and Israelite culture is established at Sinai by the divine appointment of craftsmen and the filling of craftsmanship with the Spirit of God (Exodus 31:1–11). Jesus, despite his dictum about rendering to Caesar what is Caesar's and to God what is God's, hardly disdains everything about his own surrounding culture. A carpenter's son (Matthew 13:55) and a carpenter himself (Mark 6:3), Jesus teaches in parables that evoke sympathetically his listeners' rustic, agrarian lifestyle. Cultural Protestants have looked back on Jesus as the consummate moral philosopher and reformer whose legacy was the preparation of human beings in their current social circumstances for the future KINGDOM OF GOD.

In Niebuhr's typological scope, the tendency that Cultural Protestantism crystallizes finds anticipators from the Apostolic era on. Paul and those among his Jewish Christian antagonists who sought to "compel the Gentiles to Judaize" (Galatians 2:14) had in common a desire to accommodate the Gospel to a specific culture or TRADITION. But whereas the Judaizers espoused allegiance to Jesus Christ without forsaking the legal obligations of Jewish tradition, Paul's program for "grafting" the Gentile faithful onto the "tree" of faithless Israel (Romans 11:17–24) entailed a relaxation of some of those requirements, most notably circumcision, that were alien to Greco-Roman culture. In the Hellenistic world, Gnostic Christians, such as Basilides and Valentinus, construed Christ culturally and downplayed any sense of discrepancy between him and folkways by seeking to harmonize the gospel with contemporary philosophy and science. At the time of the Constantinian settlement, Lactantius aimed his culturally attuned Christian apologetics at demonstrating the sensibleness of the new faith in a Roman context. During the Middle Ages, however, as a pronounced tension prevailed between church and world, Peter Abelard proved somewhat exceptional in expounding Christian faith as a philosophy and ethics of cultural meliorism.

From the Reformation to the Present

The defining inclination of Cultural Protestantism to remain in harmony with the mores of the culture at large emerges in MARTIN LUTHER's doctrine that it is the duty of Christians to obey their political ruler and to carry out their divine calling (*Beruf*) in secular society. During and after the REFORMATION, Christian acculturation was promoted *Ipso Facto* through the proliferating translations of the BIBLE into the European vernaculars (see BIBLE TRANSLATION), a development encouraged by Luther's emphasis on *sola scriptura*. The basic impulse underlying Cultural Protestantism was also fostered by certain aspects of the "inner-worldly asceticism" (innerweltliche Askese) that MAX WEBER ascribes especially to the more Puritanical Protestant branches: their teaching the principle of dedicated fulfillment of worldly obligations as the sole means of proving religious merit, and their tendency to sanction, and adapt their ethic to, bourgeois capitalist pursuits.

During the ENLIGHTENMENT, efforts to accommodate the Christian religion to the current climate of hyperrationalism and scientism were made by such thinkers as JOHN LOCKE, who posited "the reasonableness of Christianity" on empirical, noncreedal grounds (which led to him to be accused of SOCINIANISM); IMMANUEL KANT, who construed religion itself "within the limits of reason"; and THOMAS JEFFERSON, who produced his own redaction of the Gospels, retaining only what he deemed Jesus's essential moral sayings and deleting all scenes that smack of the supernatural. Nonetheless, religion had been left threatened with oblivion by the harsh criticism to which eighteenth-century thinkers had subjected it, and in that predicament it was FRIEDRICH SCHLEIERMACHER's extremely influential *Speeches on Religion* (1799) that restored the religious dimension of life to intellectual respectability. Defending religion "to the educated classes (*die Gebildeten*) among its despisers," Schleiermacher distinguished it from theoretical science, abstract philosophy or metaphysics, moral behavior, and theological dogma, and reinterpreted it as a type of feeling (*Gefühl*), that of absolute dependence. This conceptualization, which accorded with the antirationalist views of the nascent German Romantic movement, had the effect of ensuring for religion a place of primary importance in subsequent discussions of modern culture. Far from being of peripheral interest or even obsolete, as they had been for skeptics in the Age of Reason, religion and piety were for Schleiermacher—and for the countless readers he influenced—indispensable to and inseparable from scientific knowledge, moral action, and the loftiest culture.

If the whole nineteenth century became "the time of cultural Protestantism" (Niebuhr 1951:94), Schleiermacher had also set the tone for this development through his advocacy of Evangelical Protestantism over Roman Catholicism as the correct way of propounding the true CHURCH (see CATHOLICISM, PROTESTANT REACTIONS). A similarly antihierarchical, anti-Roman conviction was shared by the prominent Lutheran and Reformed clerics and political leaders from the different states of GERMANY, who in 1863 founded the liberal *Protestantenverein* (Union of Protestants). Serving in effect as a Cultural Protestant agency, this association aimed at fostering the unity and advancement of the diverse *Landeskirchen* (established churches) of the nation in accord with the progress of culture, all in a Protestant spirit.

Among the theologians who carried the greatest sway after Schleiermacher in shaping Cultural Protestantism, ALBRECHT BENJAMIN RITSCHL stood preeminent. Interpreting Christian doctrine through the modern lenses of historical-critical BIBLE scholarship, Kantian ethics, and Hegelian idealism, Ritschl envisioned the Kingdom of God on earth, to which Jesus had beckoned humankind, as a goal realizable through the moral ordering of civilization in the manner of the modern West. The same belief in progress typified the leading perpetuators of Cultural Protestantism after him: the Germans ADOLF VON HARNACK, FRIEDRICH NAUMANN, and ERNST TROELTSCH; the Swiss LEONHARD RAGAZ; and the Americans SHAILER MATTHEWS and WALTER RAUSCHENBUSCH, whose conceptualization of the SOCIAL GOSPEL heeded Ritschl's construal of the Kingdom of God.

Assessments

Foreshadowed and considerably inspired by SØREN KIERKEGAARD's polemics against the worldly conformism of "Christendom," the harshest criticisms of Cultural Protestantism were those made by Barth, to whose DIALECTICAL THEOLOGY it served as a foil. Reaffirming Kierkegaard's insistence on the infinite "qualitative distinction" between God and humankind, Barth denied that religion is the firm basis on which human culture securely rests; on the contrary, he contended, religion constitutes the *Krisis* of culture and of barbarism alike, belying all efforts to enlist it for any social, political, humanistic, or other worldly ends. In his view, the "Declaration of German Professors" favoring the militaristic stance of Kaiser Wilhelm II at the outbreak of the First World War had effectually delegitimized the liberal accommodation of Christianity to culture.

As opposed to its disparagement by Barth and his Neo-Orthodox followers, some scholars reassess more neutrally or favorably the role of Cultural Protestantism not only in Wilhelmine Germany, but also in the Weimar Rupublic, when Cultural Protestants defended the place of Jewish citizens in German society (Nowak 1991:35).

As imagined in a later context far removed from the traumas of German history, Cultural Protestantism can seem quaint. The American radio-show host Garrison Keiller has been called "an elegiac poet of Culture Protestantism," as his remembrances of life in the (fictive) Calvinist community of Lake Wobegon, Minnesota, "appeal to a certain complacency in our faith, a nostalgia for the days when religion and culture went hand in hand and did not need to be too closely distinguished" (Heim 1987:517).

References and Further Reading

Chapman, Mark D. *Ernst Troeltsch and Liberal Theology: Religion and Cultural Synthesis in Wilhelmine Germany.* Oxford: Oxford University Press, 2002.

Heim, David. "Garrison Keillor and Culture Protestantism." *Christian Century* (3–10 June 1987): 517.

Hübinger, Gangolf. *Kulturprotestantismus und Politik: zum Verhältnis von Liberalismus und Protestantismus im wilhelminischen Deutschland* (Culture Protestantism and Politics: On the Relation of Liberalism and Protestantism in Wilhelmine Germany). Tübingen: J. C. B. Mohr (P. Siebeck), 1994.

Müller, Hans Martin, ed. *Kulturprotestantismus: Beiträge zu einer Gestalt des modernen Christentums* (Culture Protestantism: Contributions on a Form of Modern Christianity). Gütersloh: Gütersloher Verlagshaus Mohn, 1992.

Niebuhr, H. Richard. *Christ and Culture.* New York: Harper, 1951. Chap. 3.

Nowak, Kurt. *Kulturprotestantismus und Judentum in der Weimarer Republik* (Culture Protestantism and Judaism in the Weimar Republic). Wolfenbüttel: Lessing-Akademie, 1991.

Rupp, George. *Culture-Protestantism: German Liberal Theology at the Turn of the Twentieth Century.* Missoula, MT: Scholars Press, 1977.

ERIC ZIOLKOWSKI

CULTURE

Introduction

When we speak of culture in the context of Protestantism, faith, and religion, we are dealing with an evolving field of research and study. In terms of contemporary academic disciplines, the study of culture and religion and their relationship is a product of the ENLIGHTENMENT and MODERNISM. It involves the academic disciplines of sociology, cultural anthropology, religious studies, THEOLOGY, and MISSIOLOGY. The awareness of culture and its objectification for the purpose of description and analysis grows out of the Enlightenment ideal of understanding something by defining, describing, and analyzing it. Even though people have always been aware that different groups have different ways of life, practice, dress, music, and religion, the definition and description of this as culture are a modern phenomenon. Culture, as we understand it today, has always played a very important role in relationship to the Christian church. From its inception, the CHURCH struggled with the migration of its message and its self-expression from an Aramaic-Hebrew cultural context to a Greek and later a Latin cultural context. With the expansion of Christianity all over the world, new challenges of culture arose. It could be argued that the study of historical theology is an exercise in the study of the relationship between Christian faith and culture. Christian theology has always struggled with the unique problems represented in the translation of the Hebrew and Christian Scriptures from one language to another. Language makes up a core part of what can be considered culture.

The word "culture" in the English language has become associated with two different ideas. One idea describes culture as the products of human society. This can be called the anthropological definition of culture. The other understanding of culture could be called "high" or "high-brow" culture, which has to do with those things that are valued in Western society as products of academia and the arts. In this discussion we focus on culture in the sense of cultural anthropology in relation to Christian faith and Protestantism. In this regard, we focus particularly on issues associated with the translation of texts and the understanding and role of symbols across cultures.

Definitions

E. A. Hoebel (1972:6) described culture as "the integrated system of learned behavior patterns which are characteristic of the members of a society and which are not the result of biological inheritance." Evaluating this as a working definition of culture, it becomes clear that this is a value-neutral definition. That means that one culture is considered no better than another, simply different. This principle is known as cultural relativity. The assumption of the relativity of all cultures is largely a phenomenon of the twentieth century. Before this time, ideas of moral superiority or evolutionary superiority played an important role in thinking about cultures. Such ideas, particularly of the moral or evolutionary superiority of Western culture, were an uncritical part of the self-perception of Protestantism and its expansion all over the world during the colonial era (see COLONIALISM). Missionaries were often associated with colonial authorities and assumed their role was to indoctrinate what they perceived to be people of "primitive cultures" into "superior" Western culture and religion (see MISSIONS). Out of this idea of the superiority of Western culture developed the concept of syncretism. The idea behind syncretism is that there is somehow a culturally pure form of Christian faith. Where this "pure form" is mixed with outside cultural elements, including religious elements, faith becomes "syncretistic" or "impure." It was the practical experience of missionaries as well as the observations of cultural anthropologists together with the rise of secularism (see SECULARIZATION) that challenged the assumptions of cultural superiority and easy judgments of syncretism.

If religion is expressed in forms of WORSHIP and cultic practice, Hoebel's working definition of culture also implies that religion is part of culture. Whereas some within Protestantism, such as ERNST TROELTSCH (1865–1923), shifted their view from an idea of Christianity as a superior religion to the relativity of all religions, the idea of relativity among faiths has not enjoyed easy acceptance within Protestantism. Thus the question of the relativity of culture in relation to religion has become one of ongoing debate within Protestantism.

In the study and practice of mission, definitions of culture such as Hoebel's have provided a basis for the development of approaches for communicating the Christian message among cultures. In the process of doing so, many difficult questions are being raised. Among these are questions about the assumption of relativity and value neutrality. Are cultures that support systems perceived in Western culture as oppressive to WOMEN and the poor to be considered value neutral? Do assumptions of cultural relativity encourage uncritical acceptance of injustice and exploitation within one's own culture, including Western culture? How does the biblical prophetic call for justice fit with a blanket acceptance of cultural relativity? Does the Christian faith have an absolute claim to truth, or is it one way among many religions? Another result of the assumption of cultural relativity has been the growing awareness of how all people are influenced and even determined by their culture and context. This awareness of cultural bias and the recognition of the role of bias have confronted Protestant theology with the development of what is called "postmodern" thought (see POSTMODERNITY). Definitions such as Hoebel's have also been challenged in that they are not perceived as dynamic enough. More and more, it is recognized that culture is something dynamic, ever changing, and evolving. Within the global community, cultures are constantly interrelating in a process of ongoing change. The result of the recognition of this dynamism has been an increasing trend within Protestant thought to speak in terms of context and contextual theology rather than culture and cultural theology.

Culture and Faith

Paul's sermon to the Greek city leaders in Athens (Acts 17) represents one of the earliest examples of a Christian attempt to relate faith, culture, and a non-Christian religion. The early Christian apologists also struggled with making Christian faith intelligible within Greek philosophy and culture. One classic example from church history in which cultural issues were addressed in the context of faith is represented in a letter written by Pope Gregory the Great (540–604) and sent to Augustine of Canterbury. In this letter Gregory urges Augustine to destroy idols but to bless pagan temples with holy water for Christian use. He also instructs Augustine to maintain pagan feasts but to fill them with new Christian meaning. Within Western Protestantism, one of the key texts on the relationship between faith and culture is H. RICHARD NIEBUHR's book *Christ and Culture*. Niebuhr describes the relationship between Christ and culture in terms of five possible models: Christ against culture, Christ of culture, Christ above culture, Christ and culture in a paradoxical relationship, and Christ the transformer of culture. In traditional Protestant theology, MARTIN LUTHER can be seen as a proponent of the paradoxical relationship model and JOHN CALVIN as a proponent of the Christ the transformer of culture model.

Charles Kraft (1979) has developed the Christ the transformer of culture model in relation to cultural anthropology into a model for communicating the Christian message among cultures. In his argument he also draws on the developing field of translation theory and the idea of dynamic equivalent translation as developed by Eugene Nida (see BIBLE TRANSLATION). The dynamic equivalent approach to translation seeks to translate ideas from one language to another by seeking words and symbols that will evoke the same meaning in the hearer in the new language and culture as it would have evoked in the source language and culture. According to this principle, the translator's task is to find words, stories, and symbols in the new language that do not necessarily literally represent what was stated in the source language. Even though this principle is very conservatively applied in Bible translations, such highly popular modern English translations as the *Good News Bible* were based on it. Basic to these approaches is the assumption that the Christian message consists of a husk and a kernel. The husk is the culture in which the kernel of the message is encased. The husk must be removed from the kernel to allow one to translate this universal kernel into a new cultural husk. Missionary translators of the Christian Scriptures have found this approach helpful, particularly when faced with translating images or symbols that are totally unfamiliar in a new language and culture. One of the main problems of models such as those offered by Niebuhr and Kraft is their tendency to approach culture from a static and Western analytical perspective. Protestant thinkers in the Third World have argued that culture and faith are not that easily separated. Such models, as developed by Kraft, also seem to leave little space for the prophetic call of the Christian faith to challenge culture in areas of oppression.

The Japanese theologian Kosuke Koyama offered a very different perspective on culture and faith in his book *Mount Fuji and Mount Sinai: A Critique of Idols*. In his approach, Koyama wrestles with his Japanese history, religious heritage, and philosophical assumptions in a critical interplay with Western theology and TRADITION. Through the difficult task of self-critique and in a dialogue with Western religious tradition, Koyama places his own culture, Western culture, Christian faith, Buddhism, Shintoism, and history in a paradoxical conversation. This process does not offer neat answers and clear categories, but renders a constant challenge for action and reflection as culture meets culture and faith meets faith. Lamin Sanneh (1989) has wrestled with similar issues from an African perspective. He traced the history of the cross-cultural expansion of Christian faith and translation throughout church history and compared this with the expansion of the Muslim faith. The results of his study are surprising in that although the cultural impact of Christian missionaries has often been destructive to local cultures, the effect of Bible translation and missionary attempts at developing vernacular literacy tended to preserve and transform culture by codifying, sometimes even creating, language and cultural forms. Such reflections from within non-Western contexts of Protestantism have contributed to a growing awareness of the complexity of the relationship between faith and culture. It has also underlined the surprising shape of interactions between Western Christianity and cultures and faiths that are different. Most of all, however, it has pointed out that viewing faith in relation to culture from the standpoint of cultural anthropology is inadequate due to the absence of sociological and economic critique that may identify injustice, exploitation, and cultural imperialism.

Faith, Culture, and Context

In 1972, a report of the WORLD COUNCIL OF CHURCHES (WCC) Theological Education Fund first used the term "contextualization" to describe the complex process of theological education in the changing cultural and sociopolitical situation of the world (Ukpong 1987:150). A Taiwanese theologian, Shoki Coe (1976), argued that contextualization is a term that better reflects the complex dynamic and interplay of theological and ethical factors that involves the process of communicating the Christian message in a particular situation. It is also argued that contextualization better reflects the Christian theological tradition of seeing the incarnation of Christ as a model for understanding how the Christian message relates to a particular situation. The term contextualization quickly gained ground within both Protestant and Roman Catholic circles and gave rise to an increasing number of Third World theologies (see LIBERATION THEOLOGY). These are attempts to engage the Christian tradition and Scriptures from within a particular context rather than to try to translate an essential idea from a dominantly Western perspective into a new culture. Such contextual theologies share a common commitment to do theology from the viewpoint of the marginalized in society, are suspicious of the influence of Western theology and philosophy, assume that culture and context are part of a dynamic system, emphasize commitment to the poor and community as essential to the task, and begin with experience (praxis).

Conclusion

Culture has always played a critical role in relation to the Christian faith. Since the close of the nineteenth century, culture as a phenomenon has become an object of study and has been viewed as value neutral. The Christian church and Protestantism draw on a rich history of interaction between culture and faith. Particularly in the twentieth century, as the Protestant church became a global church, issues of faith and culture have become critical. Today Christians of many cultures express and understand their faith in a rich tapestry of multifaceted perspectives. Christians in the non-Western world practice and speak of their faith in terms of their context and culture. As these many perspectives interact in the world church, there is a growing understanding of the complexity as well as the beauty of the relationship between faith and culture. The Western cultural expression of the Christian faith can no longer dictate what the Christian faith would look like in another culture and context. Non-Western perspectives have also made it impossible to practice Christian faith without recognizing the plight of the poor and marginalized and without understanding the deep complexity of the relationship between Christian faith, culture, and religions.

See also African Theology; Asian Theology; Bosch, David Jacobus; Theology; Theology, Twentieth Century, Global; Feminist Theology; Black Theology; Womanist Theology

References and Further Reading

Bosch, D. J. *Transforming Mission: Paradigm Shifts in Theology of Mission*. New York: Orbis Books, 1991.
Coe, Shoki. "Contextualizing Theology," in *Mission Trends No. 3*. Edited by G. H. Anderson and T. F. Stransky, 19–24. Grand Rapids, MI: Eerdmans, 1976.
Good News Bible: Today's English Version. New York: American Bible Society, 1992.

Hoebel, E. A. *Anthropology: The Study of Man,* 4th ed. New York: McGraw-Hill, 1972.

Koyama, Kosuke. *Mount Fuji and Mount Sinai: A Critique of Idols.* New York: Orbis Books, 1984.

Kraft, C. H. *Christianity in Culture: A Study in Dynamic Biblical Theologizing in Cross-Cultural Perspective.* New York: Orbis Books, 1979.

Morse, Merrill. *Kosuke Koyama: A Model for Intercultural Theology.* Frankfurt, Germany: Peter Lang, 1991.

Nida, E. A. *Message and Mission: The Communication of the Christian Faith.* Pasadena, CA: William Carey Library, 1960.

Niebuhr, H. R. *Christ and Culture.* New York: Harper & Row, 1951.

Sanneh, Lamin. *Translating the Message: The Missionary Impact on Culture.* New York: Orbis Books, 1989.

Ukpong, J. "Contextualization: Concept and History." *Revue Africaine de Théologie* 11, no.22 (October 1987):149–163.

Yamamori, T., and C. R.Taber, eds. *Christopaganism or Indigenous Christianity?* South Pasadena, CA: William Carey Library, 1975.

CHARLES FENSHAM

CUMBERLAND PRESBYTERIAN CHURCH

The Cumberland Presbyterian Church was founded by Finis Ewing, Samuel King, and Samuel McAdow in the aftermath of the Cane Ridge Revival. The Cumberland Presbytery of the PRESBYTERIAN CHURCH IN THE U.S.A. was accused of ordaining illiterate ministers with beliefs contrary to the WESTMINSTER CONFESSION. These ministers were suspended in 1805, and the Presbytery itself was dissolved in 1806. They then formed a new Cumberland Presbytery in 1810, hoping to be readmitted. In 1813, the Cumberland Presbytery became the Cumberland Synod, comprising three presbyteries. The first General Assembly was held in 1829.

The accusation of illiteracy was false, though the men in question had not received a classical education in Eastern colleges. There were doctrinal irregularities, however. The ARMINIAN tendencies of the church were formalized in 1814 (see ARMINIANISM), when the Westminster Confession was revised to soften its Calvinistic doctrines of PREDESTINATION and ATONEMENT. A further revised Confession of Faith was adopted in 1883. In 1906, after the Presbyterian Church in the U.S.A. had also modified the Westminster Confession, two-thirds of the Cumberland Presbyterian Church merged with that body. The remaining Cumberland Presbyterian Church continues in a harmonious relationship with the Cumberland Presbyterian Church in America, which was founded as the Colored Cumberland Presbyterian Church in 1869 and was known as the Second Cumberland Presbyterian Church from 1960 to 1992. In 1984, they jointly adopted a new Confession of Faith shaped primarily by the doctrine of the Covenant of Grace.

See also Calvinism; Presbyterianism

References and Further Reading

Barrus, Ben M., Milton L. Baughn, and Thomas H. Campbell. *A People Called Cumberland Presbyterians.* Memphis, TN: Frontier Press, 1972.

Hudson, Mary Lin. "'Shall Woman Preach?': Louisa Woosley and the Cumberland Presbyterian Church." *American Presbyterians* 68 (1990): 221–230.

Morrow, Hubert W. "The Confession of Faith in Cumberland Presbyterian History." *Journal of Presbyterian History* 76 no. 3 (1998): 187–197.

NEAL HANSEN

CUMMINS, GEORGE DAVID (1811–1876)

American Episcopal churchman. Assistant bishop of the Protestant Episcopal Church and founder of the Reformed Episcopal Church, Cummins was born December 11, 1811, into an affluent Delaware family near Smyrna. His Methodist mother was a significant influence, and Cummins eventually graduated from Dickinson College in 1841. He was appointed a Methodist CIRCUIT RIDER by the BALTIMORE CONFERENCE, yet came to prefer Anglican worship and was drawn to the Protestant Episcopal Church. In 1847, Cummins married Alexandrine Macomb Balch and was ordained as a priest of the EPISCOPAL CHURCH. Cummins served parishes in Norfolk, Richmond, Washington, D.C., Baltimore, and Chicago before being elected assistant bishop of the Diocese of Kentucky in 1866. He died on June 26, 1876.

By the time of his elevation to the episcopate, Cummins had become identified with the low-church Evangelical party within the Episcopal Church and was one of its most outspoken leaders. Cummins grew increasingly alarmed by the inroads made by followers of the OXFORD MOVEMENT within the Episcopal Church. Cummins argued that the teaching of the Tractarians and the worship of their Ritualist successors undermined the Reformation formularies of classical ANGLICANISM.

Initially, Cummins believed that evangelicals should stay and fight this threat to evangelical truth, but his views changed (see EVANGELICALISM). A controversy erupted over Cummins's participation in an ecumenical communion service at a meeting of the Evangelical Alliance in New York in the fall of 1873. Cummins was harshly criticized for joining non-Episcopal ordained clergy in the sacrament, and responded by organizing a new denomination, the Reformed Episcopal Church, at a special meeting in New York on December 2, 1873. The new body sought to preserve the Protestant face of Anglicanism in their forthright "Declaration of Principles" and subsequent revision of the American BOOK of COMMON PRAYER. The split proved to be a small secession, however, because many prominent evangelical clergy (including several bishops) declined to throw in their lot with Cummins. While the evangelical party soon withered in the Episcopal Church in the United States, the Reformed Episcopal Church preserved a distinctive, though tiny, evangelical Anglican witness within American Protestantism for more than a century.

References and Further Reading

Aycrigg, B. A. *Memoirs of the Reformed Episcopal Church.* New York: Edward O. Jenkins, 1880.

Cummins, A. M. *Memoir of George David Cummins, D.D.* New York: Dodd, Mead & Co., 1878.

Guelzo, Allen C. *For the Union of Evangelical Christendom: The Irony of the Reformed Episcopalians.* University Park, PA: Pennsylvania State University Press, 1994.

GILLIS J. HARP